WESTERN
CIVILIZATIONS
BRIEF EDITION

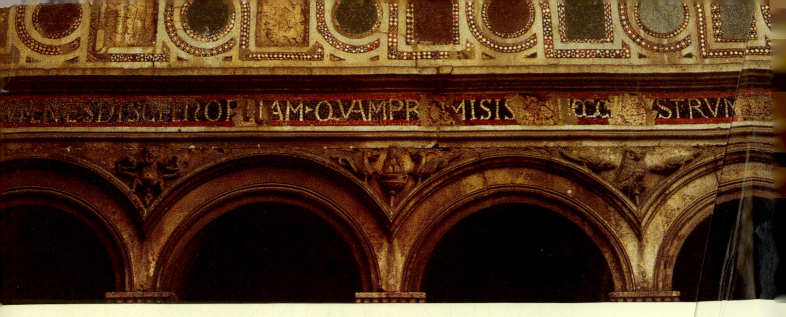

BRIEF EDITION

JUDITH G. COFFIN

ROBERT C. STACEY

BASED ON *WESTERN CIVILIZATIONS*
BY EDWARD MCNALL BURNS

ROBERT E. LERNER

STANDISH MEACHAM

W · W · NORTON & COMPANY · NEW YORK · LONDON

WESTERN
CIVILIZATIONS
BRIEF EDITION

THEIR HISTORY
& THEIR CULTURE

W. W. Norton & Company has been independent since its founding in 1923, when William Warder Norton and Mary D. Herter Norton first published lectures delivered at the People's Institute, the adult education division of New York City's Cooper Union. The Nortons soon expanded their program beyond the Institute, publishing books by celebrated academics from America and abroad. By mid-century, the two major pillars of Norton's publishing program—trade books and college texts— were firmly established. In the 1950s, the Norton family transferred control of the company to its employees, and today—with a staff of four hundred and a comparable number of trade, college, and professional titles published each year—W. W. Norton & Company stands as the largest and oldest publishing house owned wholly by its employees.

Copyright © 2005 by W. W. Norton & Company, Inc.

Printed in the United States of America

Composition: TSI Graphics
Manufacturing by Courier Corporation
Book design by Antonina Krass
Director of Manufacturing/College: Roy Tedoff
Editor: Karl Bakeman
Associate Director, Electronic Media: Steven S. Hoge
Copy Editor: Barbara Gerr
Production Editor: Chris Granville
Editorial Assistants: Sarah England, Sarah Mann

Library of Congress Cataloging-in-Publication Data

Coffin, Judith G., 1952–
    Western civilizations: their history & their culture / Judith G. Coffin, Robert C. Stacey.—Brief ed.
        p. cm.
    "Based on Western civilizations by Robert E. Lerner, Standish Meacham,
Edward McNall Burns."
    Includes bibliographical references and index.
    ISBN 0-393-92558-7
    1. Civilization, Western—Textbooks. 2. Europe—Civilization—Textbooks. I. Stacey,
Robert C. II. Lerner, Robert E. Western civilizations, their history and their culture. III Title.

CB245.C56 2005
909'.09821—dc22   2004063645

W. W. Norton & Company, Inc., 500 Fifth Avenue, New York, NY 10110
www.wwnorton.com

W. W. Norton & Company Ltd., Castle House, 75/76 Wells Street, London W1T 3QT
2 3 4 5 6 7 8 9 0

To our families—Robin, Will, and Anna Stacey, and Willy, Zoe, and Aaron Forbath—for their patience and support. They reminded us that books such as this are worth the work, and also that there are other things in life.

To Robert Lerner, Standish Meacham, Edward McNall Burns, and Marie Burns, our predecessors who successfully guided *Western Civilizations* for thirteen editions, spanning six decades.

About the Book

Used by over 1,000,000 students *Western Civilizations* is renowned for its balanced presentation, clear prose, and exceptional treatment of cultural history. Originally published in 1942, the book began as an outgrowth of Edward McNall Burns's western civilizations course at Rutgers University. Robert Lerner (Northwestern University) and Standish Meacham (University of Texas at Austin) took over authorship in the ninth edition and extended the book's traditional strengths to include the new social history. Beginning with the fourteenth edition, Judith Coffin (University of Texas at Austin) and Robert Stacey (University of Washington) debuted as the third generation of authors to lead this book. While Coffin and Stacey maintain the balanced presentation of *Western Civilizations*, they have enlarged the conception of "Western Civilization" to take in the diversity of the European world.

About the Authors

JUDITH G. COFFIN received her Ph.D. in modern French history from Yale University. She has taught at Harvard University and the University of California, Riverside, and is currently associate professor of history at the University of Texas at Austin, where she won a 1999 University of Texas President's Associates' Award for Teaching Excellence. Her research interests focus on the social and cultural history of gender, mass culture, slavery, race relations, and colonialism. She is the author of *The Politics of Women's Work: The Paris Garment Trades, 1750-1915.*

ROBERT C. STACEY is Dean of Social Sciences and Professor of History and Jewish Studies at the University of Washington in Seattle. A long-time teacher of western civilization and medieval European history, he has received Distinguished Teaching Awards from both the University of Washington and Yale University, where he taught from 1984 to 1988. The author or coauthor of four books, he is a Fellow of the Royal Historical Society and has held awards from the American Council of Learned Societies and from the Guggenheim Foundation. His current research deals with the history of Jews in medieval England.

ROBERT E. LERNER is professor of medieval history at Northwestern University, where he has served as director of the Humanities Program. He has won awards from the National Endowment for Humanities, the American Council of Learned Studies, the Guggenheim Foundation, and the Rockefeller Foundation. His books include *The Feast of Saint Abraham: Medieval Millenarians and the Jews; The Age of Adversity: The Fourteenth Century; The Heresy of Free Spirit in the Middle Ages;* and *The Powers of Prophecy.*

STANDISH MEACHAM is professor emeritus at the University of Texas at Austin. He has received grants from the Guggenheim Foundation, the American Council of Learned Studies, and the American Philosophical Society. His books include *Regaining Paradise: Englishness and the Early Garden City Movement; Henry Thornton of Clapman, 1760–1815; Lord Bishop: The Life of Samuel Wilberforce; A Life Apart: The English Working Class, 1890–1914;* and *Toynbee Hall and Social Reform, 1880–1914.*

CONTENTS

PART I THE ANCIENT NEAR EAST

DIGITAL HISTORY: Water: The Primary Element

PART II THE GREEK AND ROMAN WORLDS

DIGITAL HISTORY: Mystery Cults

DIGITAL HISTORY: Wine

PART III   THE MIDDLE AGES

DIGITAL HISTORY: The Marketplace

DIGITAL HISTORY: After the Black Death

DIGITAL HISTORY: Spices

CHAPTER 13   REFORMATIONS OF RELIGION   368

CHAPTER 14   RELIGIOUS WARS AND STATE BUILDING,
        1540–1660   392

PART V   EARLY MODERN EUROPE

CHAPTER 15   ABSOLUTISM AND EMPIRE, 1660–1789   422

DIGITAL HISTORY: Astrology, Astronomy, and Galileo

PART VI THE FRENCH AND INDUSTRIAL REVOLUTIONS AND THEIR CONSEQUENCES

DIGITAL HISTORY: Revolutionary Paris

CHAPTER 20   FROM RESTORATION TO REVOLUTION, 1815–1848   556

 DIGITAL HISTORY: Nationalism and Music

CHAPTER 21   WHAT IS A NATION? TERRITORIES, STATES, AND CITIZENS, 1848–1871   584

PART VII   THE WEST AT THE WORLD'S CENTER

CHAPTER 22   IMPERIALISM AND COLONIALISM, 1870–1914   614

DIGITAL HISTORY: The Olympics Past and Present

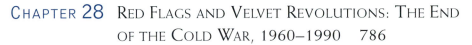
DIGITAL HISTORY: Cold War

PART VIII   THE WEST AND THE WORLD

DIGITAL HISTORY: War and Technology

CONTENTS

MAPS

CHRONOLOGIES

DOCUMENTS

PREFACE

Since the 1920s, the western civilization survey course has held a central place in the curricula of American universities and high schools. Yet the concept of "western civilization" remains both elusive and controversial. It seems appropriate, therefore, that we begin by defining our terms. How do we, as authors, conceive of our subject?

During much of the twentieth century, "western" civilization meant "the civilization of western Europe," to which the earlier history of the Ancient Near East was somewhat arbitrarily attached. Western civilization was therefore presented as beginning at Sumer, developing in Egypt, and then flowering in Greece. From Greece it passed to Rome, which transmitted it to France, Germany, England, Italy, and Spain, whose emigrating colonists then transferred it to the Americas after 1492. Rather like a train passing through stations, western civilization was thus conceived as picking up "cargo" at each of its stops, but always retaining the same engine and the same baggage cars.

This vision of western civilization was not only selective, it was often tied to a series of contentious assumptions. It cast the worldwide dominance of the European imperial powers between roughly 1800 and 1950 as the culmination of several thousand years of historical development, which it was the obligation of historians to explain. It also tended to presume that European global dominance in the nineteenth and twentieth centuries reflected and demonstrated the superiority of western European civilization over the African, Asian, and Native American civilizations the Europeans conquered during the heyday of their imperial expansion.

Historians today are keenly aware of how much such an account leaves out. It slights the use of force and fraud in European expansion. It ignores the sophistication, dynamism, and humanity of the many cultures it sidelines. By neglecting the crucial importance of Byzantium and Islam, it gives a misleadingly narrow account even of the development of European civilization. And it also misleads us about the western civilizations created in North and South America after 1492, which were creole, or hybrid, cultures, not simply European cultures transplanted to other shores. This is not to argue that a study of western civilization must give way to a study of world civilization. It is merely to insist that understanding the historical development of the West requires us to place this subject in a much wider geographical and cultural context; and that, shorn of its triumphalism, the history of western civilization becomes vastly more interesting.

In this textbook, we will argue that the West cannot be understood as a single, continuous historical culture. Rather, there have been a number of western civilizations, whose fundamental characteristics have changed markedly over time. We mean, therefore, for our title, *Western Civilizations*, to be taken seriously. We will treat "western" as a geographical designator referring to the major civilizations that developed in and around the Mediterranean Sea between 3500 B.C.E. ("Before the Common Era," equivalent to the Christian dating system B.C., "Before Christ") and 500 C.E. ("Common Era," equivalent to the Christian dating system A.D., "Anno Domini," "the Year of the Lord"). We will also treat as "western" the civilizations that emerged out of the Mediterranean world in the centuries after 500 C.E., as the Greco-Roman world of antiquity divided into Islamic, Byzantine, and Latin Christian realms. The interdependence and mutual influences of these three western civilizations upon each other will be a recurring theme of this book.

This Brief Edition is based on the new Fifteenth Edition of our best-selling *Western Civilizations* text. In preparing it, we have sought to meet the needs of instructors and students who have asked for a text that would fit better into the compressed time frame that many academic schedules now require. We have reduced the overall length of the book by about one-third. In making these cuts, we've reduced narrative detail without suggesting that developments were simple or predictable. Despite these abridgments, we have sought to preserve the strengths that have carried *Western Civilizations* into its seventh decade of life: a vigorous, connected historical narrative; clear and accessible prose that does not compromise on accuracy or ignore complexity; balanced coverage of politics, economics, religion, and culture; and a vision of the past that presents these elements as part of a shared world of historical experience common to both "elites" and "masses."

The strengths of this book owe much to the efforts and learning of Robert Lerner and Standish Meacham, the authorial team that carried the book forward and transformed it from the 1960s into the 1990s. Since taking over from them in 1999, we have continued to make changes to reflect the shifting historical interests of teachers, students, and scholars. We devote much more attention to the world outside western Europe

than once was customary. Although we have continued to integrate new scholarly work in social and cultural history and the history of gender into our narrative, we have also substantially increased the attention we pay to economic, religious, and military history. In this edition, we also pay special attention to the varying ways in which these very different western civilizations have sought to govern themselves and the territories they conquered. "Empire" has been a consistent theme in the history of the west for more than four thousand years. We have tried here to do justice to its importance.

INNOVATIVE PEDAGOGICAL PROGRAM

Western Civilizations, Brief Edition, is designed for maximum readability. The crisp, clear, and concise narrative is accompanied by a highly useful pedagogical program to help students study while engaging them in the subject matter. Highlights of this innovative program include:

- **NEW End-of-Chapter Key Terms.** In response to requests from professors, each chapter includes a list of ten to fifteen key terms to help students focus on the key ideas, events, or people in the chapter.

- **NEW Digital History Features.** Twelve Digital History Feature essays distributed throughout the text direct students to the Western Civilizations Digital History Center (www.wwnorton.com/wciv), where they can explore collections of primary sources on topics that include:
  The Primary Element—Water (Chapter 1)
  Women and Mystery Cults (Chapter 4)
  Grapes and Civilization (Chapter 6)
  The Market (Chapter 8)
  After the Black Death (Chapter 10)
  Spices (Chapter 12)
  Astrology, Astronomy, and Galileo (Chapter 15)
  Revolutionary Paris (Chapter 18)
  Nationalism and Music (Chapter 20)
  Olympics (Chapter 23)
  Cold War and Popular Culture (Chapter 26)
  Military Strategy and New Technology (Chapter 28)

- **In-Text Documents.** Designed to add depth to the more focused narrative of *Western Civilizations*.

- **Map Program with Enhanced Captions.** Approximately one hundred beautiful maps appear throughout the text, each accompanied by an enhanced caption designed to engage the reader analytically while conveying the key role that geography plays in the development of history and the societies of the world.

- **In-Chapter Chronologies.** Several brief chronologies built around particular events, topics, or periods appear in each chapter and are designed to provide road maps through the narrative detail.

- **Focus Question System.** To ensure that students remain alert to key concepts and questions on every page of the text, focus questions guide their reading in three ways: (1) a focus question box appears at the beginning of each chapter to preview the chapter's contents; (2) relevant questions reappear at the start of the section in which they are discussed; and (3) running heads on the righthand pages keep these questions in view throughout the chapter.

- **Pull Quotes.** Lifted directly from the narrative, pull quotes appear throughout each chapter to highlight key thoughts and keen insights while keeping students focused on larger concepts and ideas.

RESOURCES FOR STUDENTS

NEW Western Civilizations Digital History Center
www.wwnorton.com/wciv
by Steven Kreis, Wake Technical College
This online resource for students—designed specifically for use with *Western Civilizations*—provides access to online review and research materials. Its contents include:

Review Materials, consisting of chapter objectives and outlines, interactive chapter chronologies, focus questions and answers, interactive map exercises, and flash cards.

Online Primary Sources
Multimedia elements for each chapter are categorized by type—documents, images, maps, audio, and video.

Digital History Features
These twelve online explorations deal with topics that arc over several chapters in *Western Civilizations*. Each exploration is integrated with the text through a Digital History Feature essay that summarizes the topic and poses several critical thinking questions.

Media Analysis Worksheets
Each media element in the Digital History Features is accompanied by a Media Analysis Worksheet, which guides students through a three-part approach to the resources:

  Observation: prompts students to articulate what they see, hear, or read
  Expression: prompts students to write about or "voice" their observations
  Connection: prompts students to place their responses within a historical context

NEW Study Guide
by Margaret Minor and Paul Wilson, both of Nicholls State University
The Study Guide gives students a comprehensive means for review and self-assessment. Each chapter contains a chapter outline, identifications, multiple-choice questions, matching and true/false questions, chronologies, and short-answer and essay questions.

RESOURCES FOR INSTRUCTORS

NEW Instructor's Manual
by Steven Kreis, Wake Technical College
This valuable resource follows the chapter organization of the text and provides a wide array of teaching tools, including lecture outlines, lecture launchers, key lecture topis, various classroom/recitation activities, and lists of suggested films and readings. New to this edition are suggestions for integrating electronic media into the classroom.

NEW Test-Item File
By Michael Halvorson, Pacific Lutheran University, and Michael Prahl, University of Northern Iowa
Available in both print and electronic formats, this test bank contains over one thousand multiple-choice questions, approximately thirty to forty per chapter, ranging from factual to conceptual. In addition, there are twelve basic identifications and four to six essay/short-answer questions per chapter.

Norton Media Library
These PowerPoint slides are optimized for lecture use and contain audio and visual files as well as many of the images and maps from the text.

Map Transparencies

ACKNOWLEDGMENTS

The final version of the manuscript was greatly influenced by the thoughts and ideas of a select group of instructors to whom we are greatly indebted and wish to express our sincere thanks:

- Michael Bailey, St. Louis University
- Cindy Blackburn, Trident Technical College
- Jonathan Bone, William Paterson University
- Stephen A. Bourque, California State University, Northridge
- James Brophy, University of Delaware
- Pierre Cagniart, Texas State University—San Marcos
- Kevin K. Carroll, Arizona State University
- Mary Kay Carter, University of Michigan, Dearborn
- Christine Caldwell, St. Louis University
- Susan Carrafiello, Wright State University
- Katherine Crawford, Vanderbilt University
- Dora Dumont, State University of New York College at Oneonta
- Chiarella Esposito, University of Mississippi
- Mari Firkatian, University of Hartford
- Gerritdina (Ineke) Justitz, North Dakota State University
- Corbett Gottfried, Portland Community College
- Sylvia Gray, Portland Community College
- Michael Halvorson, Pacific Lutheran University
- Carla Hay, Marquette University
- Steven Kreis, Wake Technical College
- Michael Kulikowski, University of Tennessee, Knoxville
- Eileen Lyon, SUNY Fredonia
- Michael Meyer, California State University, Northridge
- John Montano, University of Delaware
- Fred Murphy, Western Kentucky University
- Heather O'Grady-Evans, Elmira College
- Michael Prahl, University of Northern Iowa
- George Robb, William Paterson University
- Shawn Ross, William Paterson University
- Geraldine Ryder, Ocean County College
- George Lawrence Simpson, High Point University
- Carol Taylor, SUNY Albany
- Stephen Wessley, York College
- Clayton Whisnant, Wofford College
- Linda York, Wallace Community College
- Margarita Youngo, Pima Community College
- Ina Zweiniger-Bargielowska, University of Illinois, Chicago

We want to thank Steve Forman and Jon Durbin at W. W. Norton & Company for their faith in this project; Karl Bakeman for his intelligent editing and remarkable good cheer; and Sarah England, Chris Granville, and Sarah Mann for their help with all aspects of the production process.

Robert Stacey is principally responsible for Chapters 1–15. He owes special thanks to Jason Hawke of Northern Illinois University for his extraordinary help in drafting Chapters 1–5. He would also like to acknowledge the assistance of a large number of friends and colleagues around the country who have taken the time to answer queries and offer suggestions: Jon Crump, Gerald Eck, Sandra Joshel, Mary O'Neil, Ben Schmidt, Julie Stein, Joel Walker, and Dan Waugh of the University of Washington; Michael Halvorson, University of Puget Sound; Shaun Ross, William Paterson University; Michelle Ferry, University of California, Santa Barbara; Byron Nakamura, Southern Connecticut State University; and Sylvia Gray, Portland Community College. He owes special thanks to Robert Stiefel, University of New Hampshire, whose criticisms of the Fourteenth Edition's treatment of monasticism have greatly improved the new account offered here.

Judith Coffin is principally responsible for the revisions to Chapter 16–29. Many colleagues have supplied expertise and references, but she is especially grateful to Caroline Castiglione, David Crew, Paul Hagenloh, Standish Meacham, John Merriman, Gail Minault, Joan Neuberger, Paula Sanders, Daniel Sherman, James Sidbury, Robert Stephens, Michael Stoff, and Charters Wynn. Special thanks to Tony Hopkins for consulting on imperialism, to James Brophy for his consistently excellent advice on many matters, and to Justin Glasson for all his writing and editing. Patrick Timmons, Marion Barber, April Smith, and, especially, Cori Crider were terrific research assistants. Geoffrey Clayton, Auburn University, drafted Chapters 16 and 29 and sections of 24, 26, and 28 and took on the abridgment. His gifts as a writer, historian, and teacher have made him an invaluable contributor to this project.

WESTERN CIVILIZATIONS

BRIEF EDITION

PART I

THE ANCIENT NEAR EAST

THE STORY OF Western civilizations begins in the Near East about thirteen thousand years ago. As the glaciers slowly receded, a new ecological world of marshes, grasslands, and domesticable animals emerged at the eastern end of the Mediterranean Sea. In this new world, humans made a momentous transformation from small hunting-gathering bands to larger, agriculturally based communities. A second "great leap forward" occurred around five thousand years ago when the first true cities appeared, first between the Tigris and the Euphrates rivers, and then throughout the Near East.

Traditions of urban independence and autonomy soon gave way to larger political configurations. In Old Kingdom Egypt, the pharaohs ruled an integrated realm that stretched for hundreds of miles along the Nile river. In Mesopotamia, Sargon of Akkad created an empire that would inspire imitators for fifteen hundred years. By 1500 B.C.E. ("Before the Common Era," equivalent to the Christian dating system B.C., "Before Christ"), an "international system" of trade and diplomacy encompassed the entire eastern Mediterranean world.

Around 1200 B.C.E., however, this international system collapsed in cataclysm, taking with it most of the established empires of the era. The resulting power vacuum made space for new states to emerge, particularly in the Middle East. But the imperial hiatus proved temporary. As iron slowly replaced bronze as the essential raw material for tools and weapons, new, more powerful Near Eastern empires emerged: larger, better armed and organized, and more aggressively expansionist than the Bronze Age empires that preceded them. By 500 B.C.E., the largest of these empires, Persia, was the undisputed master of the Near Eastern world.

Equally dramatic developments were occurring in religious and cultural life. The pyramids of Egypt, the *Epic of Gilgamesh,* the works of Homer, and the religious traditions of Zoroastrianism and Judaism had all taken shape by the time the period closed around 500 B.C.E. On these foundations, all the subsequent civilizations of the Western (i.e., the Mediterranean) world have continued to rest.

	POLITICS	SOCIETY AND CULTURE	ECONOMY	INTERNATIONAL RELATIONS
B.C.E. 40,000		Paleolithic Era (40,000–11,000 B.C.E.)		
10,000	The Predynastic Period in Egypt (c. 10,000–3100 B.C.E.)	End of the Ice Age, beginning of the Neolithic Era (11,000 B.C.E.) Settled agriculture in Fertile Crescent (8500 B.C.E.)	Grain storage begins (9500 B.C.E.)	
8000		Stone walls and tower of Jericho (8000 B.C.E.)	Emergence of pottery in Jericho (8000–7000 B.C.E.) Domestication of animals, raising of crops (7000 B.C.E.)	
6000	Ubaid culture governed by priestly class (5900 B.C.E.)		Copper tools appear (6000 B.C.E.) Ubaid culture builds irrigation channels of stone (5900 B.C.E.)	Ubaid culture (Mesopotamia) (5900 B.C.E.)
		Agriculture established in Egypt and the Balkans (5000 B.C.E.) Increased trade engenders social stratification (5000 B.C.E.) First known settlement in Egypt (4750 B.C.E.)	Long-distance trade emerges (5000 B.C.E.)	
4000		Uruk Period (4300–2900 B.C.E.) End of the Stone Age (4000 B.C.E.) Cities form in fertile Mesopotamia (3500–3000 B.C.E.)	Building of the White Temple at Uruk (3500–3300 B.C.E.) Pottery-throwing wheels (3500 B.C.E.) Ubaid/Sumerians begin inscribing symbols on tablets (3300 B.C.E.) Wheeled chariots (3200 B.C.E.) Egyptians build fortifications, temples, settlements (3200 B.C.E.) Appearance of cuneiform script (3100 B.C.E.)	Sumerian civilization (3100 B.C.E.)
3000	The Archaic Period in Egypt (3100–c. 2686 B.C.E.) Emergence of *lugal* leadership in Mesopotamia (2900–2500 B.C.E.) Early Dynastic Period (I & II) (2900–2500 B.C.E.) The Old Kingdom in Egypt (c. 2686–2160 B.C.E.) Early Dynastic (III) (2500–2350 B.C.E.) The Akkadian Period (2350–2160 B.C.E.) Sargon organizes Mesopotamia (2350 B.C.E.) First Intermediate Period (2160–2055 B.C.E.) Unity of Egypt dissolves (2150 B.C.E.) Ur Dynasty III (2100–2000 B.C.E.)	Beginning of the Bronze Age (3000 B.C.E.) Egyptians develop hieroglyphs and hieratic script (3000 B.C.E.) Great Pyramids of Giza (2640–2510 B.C.E.) Royal Tombs of Ur (2550–2450 B.C.E.) Epic of Gilgamesh (2500 B.C.E.)	Discovery of bronze (3000 B.C.E.)	Elamite (present-day Iran) culture (2500 B.C.E.) Sargon of Akkad conquers Mesopotamia (2360 B.C.E.) Gutians conquer Sumer and Akkad (2160 B.C.E.)

POLITICS	SOCIETY AND CULTURE	ECONOMY	INTERNATIONAL RELATIONS	
				B.C.E. 2000
he Middle Kingdom in Egypt (2055–c. 1650 B.C.E.)	Indo-European linguistic forms appear (2000 B.C.E.)	Horses introduced to Near East (2000–1700 B.C.E.)		
he "Palace Age" in Minoan culture (1900–1700 B.C.E.)		Major expansion of trade (1900–1700 B.C.E.)	Minoan civilization flourishes in Crete (1900–1500 B.C.E.)	
ammurabi unifies Sumero-Akkadian rea (1792–1750 B.C.E.)	Code of Hammurabi (1750 B.C.E.)			
		Minoan trade with Egypt, Anatolia, and Cyprus (1700 B.C.E.)		
cond Intermediate Period c. 1650–1550 B.C.E.)			The Hyksos overrun Egypt (1650–1550 B.C.E.)	
			Hittites capture Babylon (1595 B.C.E.)	
he New Kingdom in Egypt 1550–1075 B.C.E.)	Appearance of Linear B in Mycenaean Greece (1500 B.C.E.)	Trade surges with new international-ism (1500 B.C.E.)	The Mitannians adopt cavalry and chariot technology (1500 B.C.E.)	1500
			Mycenaean civilization established (1500 B.C.E.)	
utmosis III and Hatshepsut take he throne (1479 B.C.E.)			Age of internationalism begins (1500 B.C.E.)	
			Hittite empire (1450 B.C.E.)	
			Mycenaeans subjugate Crete (1400 B.C.E.)	
ign of Amenhotep III, the Magnifi-ent (1387–1350 B.C.E.)			Complex societies developed at Mycenae, Thebes, Athens, etc. (1400–1200 B.C.E.)	
ddle Assyrian Period 362–859 B.C.E.)				
enhotep IV, later Akhenaten, takes he throne (1350 B.C.E.)	Rise of Amon as Egyptian national god (1350 B.C.E.)			
			Treaty between Egypt and Hittite Empire (1286 B.C.E.)	
			Rise of Phoenicians (Canaanites) (1200 B.C.E.)	
			Mycenaean civilization implodes (1200 B.C.E.)	
			Sea Peoples ravage Near East (1200–1179 B.C.E.)	
			Ramses III defeats Sea Peoples (1179 B.C.E.)	
		Philistines introduce vine and olive tree to the Levant (1050 B.C.E.)	Philistine preeminence in the Levant (1050 B.C.E.)	
l becomes first Hebrew king 025 B.C.E.)			Egypt collapses (1000 B.C.E.)	1000
gn of King David 000–973 B.C.E.)				
brew kingdom splits upon death of ng Solomon (c. 933 B.C.E.)			Phoenicians establish Carthage (800 B.C.E.)	
o-Assyrian Empire 83–859 B.C.E.)			Assyrian Empire expands (800–700 B.C.E.)	
gn of Sargon II (722–705 B.C.E.)		Assyrians master iron-smelting (700 B.C.E.)		700
	Zoroaster, founder of Zoroastrianism (600 B.C.E.)		Hebrew captivity in Babylon begins (587 B.C.E.)	
gn of Darius I of Persia 21–486 B.C.E.)			Athens defeats Darius I at Battle of Marathon (490 B.C.E.)	
			Alexander the Great invades Persia (334 B.C.E.)	

Chapter ONE

The Origins of Western Civilizations

The human history of the Mediterranean world begins only about forty thousand years ago with the completed evolution of *Homo sapiens sapiens*, the modern human species to which we all belong. Civilization is an even more recent development. To the peoples of the ancient world, the characteristic manifestations of civilization—government, literature, science, and art—were necessarily products of city life. Cities, however, only became possible as a result of the agricultural and technological discoveries that emerged between the end of the last Ice Age, about thirteen thousand years ago, and the appearance, in Mesopotamia, of the first true cities approximately five thousand years ago. The story of Western civilizations is thus a short one. In geological time, it is merely a blip on a radar screen.

Why the world's first cities should have developed in the inhospitable region between the Tigris and the Euphrates rivers in modern-day Iraq is a question for which historians do not have a convincing answer. Once developed, however, the basic patterns of urban life quickly spread to other parts of the Near Eastern world. A steadily widening network of trading connections developed among these early cities; but so too did an intense competition for control over people and resources. Attempts during the third millennium B.C.E. to forge lasting empires out of these fiercely independent city-states did not succeed. By the middle of the second millennium B.C.E., however, it was becoming clear that the future of the ancient Near Eastern world would be determined not by the internecine struggles of the Mesopotamian cities, but by the competition between the emerging imperial powers of Anatolia (modern-day Turkey) and Egypt.

FOCUS QUESTIONS

• Why did human societies in the Paleolithic era change so slowly?

• What changes allowed the transition from hunter-gatherer to sedentary societies?

• What were the principal influences behind the early emergence of urban life in Mesopotamia?

• Why did a common religion not create peace among the Sumerians?

• How did Hammurabi bind his empire together?

• In what ways did patterns of development in early Egypt differ from those in Sumer?

THE STONE AGE BACKGROUND

Why did human societies in the Paleolithic era change so slowly?

"Prehistory," the era before the appearance of written records around 3000 B.C.E., is a period of much greater duration than human history. Humanlike ancestors first appeared in eastern Africa roughly 4 million years ago, and tool-making hominids (species belonging to the genus *Homo*, to which we as *Homo sapiens sapiens* belong) approximately 2 million years ago. Because early hominids made most of their tools out of stone, all human cultures down to around 5000 B.C.E. are referred to as belonging to the "Stone Age."

THE PALEOLITHIC (OLD STONE) AGE

Virtually all human societies before 11,000 B.C.E. consisted of small bands of hunter-gatherers, probably never exceeding more than a few dozen individuals, that moved incessantly in search of food. Because early humans had no domestic animals to transport their goods, they could have no significant material possessions—wealth—aside from basic tools they could carry with them. And because humans could not accumulate goods over time, disparities in individual wealth, with their attendant distinctions of rank and status, were unlikely to develop. These societies may well have been highly organized—it is a gross error to presume that early societies were necessarily primitive—but hierarchical structures of leadership were uncommon, and possibly unknown.

We do not know how labor was divided among the members of these Paleolithic bands. Although scholars once assumed that men did the hunting and women the gathering, such gendered presumptions do not reflect the complex realities of modern hunter-gatherer societies, and they are probably not applicable to the Paleolithic period either. It is more likely that all members of a Paleolithic band (except for the very young and the very old) engaged to some extent in all the basic activities of the group. Acquiring food and tools must have been the first concern of nearly everyone. Specialization—the process by which some members of the group are freed up to engage in activities other than food acquisition—was nearly impossible. Special-

ization requires the accumulation of storable surpluses, and this was something Paleolithic people lacked the technology to accomplish.

THE NEOLITHIC REVOLUTION

What changes allowed the transition from hunter-gatherer to sedentary societies?

Fundamental changes in human life began to take shape around 11,000 B.C.E., the dawn of the Neolithic or "New Stone" Age. These breakthroughs included the development of managed food production, the beginnings of semipermanent and permanent settlements, and the rapid intensification of trade, both local and long distance. For the first time, it now became possible for individuals and communities to accumulate and store wealth on a large scale. The results were far reaching. Communities became more stable, and human societies more complex. Specialization developed, along with distinctions of status and rank. This "revolution" was a necessary step before cities in the truest sense could appear toward the end of the fourth millennium B.C.E.

THE ORIGINS OF FOOD PRODUCTION IN THE ANCIENT NEAR EAST

During the last "Ice Age" (c. 40,000–11,000 B.C.E.), daytime temperatures in Mediterranean Europe and Asia averaged about 60° F (16° C) in the summer and about 30° F (–1° C) in the winter. Reindeer, elk, wild boar, bison, and mountain goats roamed the hills and valleys. But as the last glaciers receded northward such species retreated with them. Some humans moved north with the game, but others stayed behind to confront and create an extremely different sort of world.

Specifically, within about three thousand to four thousand years after the end of the Ice Age, the peoples living at the eastern end of the Mediterranean Sea accomplished one of the most momentous transformations in human history: a switch from food-gathering for subsistence to producing food for themselves. Substantial numbers of humans now

WHAT CHANGES ALLOWED THE TRANSITION FROM HUNTER-GATHERER TO SEDENTARY SOCIETIES?

THE NEOLITHIC REVOLUTION   9

Bison Carved from a Reindeer Horn. Perhaps the most graceful of all known European prehistoric carvings, this bison was carved from a piece of antler between fifteen thousand and twelve thousand years ago. Whatever its use might have been no one quite knows.

began to domesticate animals and raise crops, thereby making possible greater permanence and stability in their settlement patterns. Stable settlements in turn paved the way for further developments we associate specifically with civilization: the emergence of cities, the invention of writing, and the evolution of specialized social roles. A process that takes several thousand years may not seem "revolutionary" to our current sensibilities, but in fact it was. In a relatively short time, people living in a small area of southwestern Asia fundamentally altered patterns of existence that were millions of years old.

The story of this momentous transformation is roughly as follows. By around 11,000 B.C.E. most of the larger game herds had left the ancient Near East. Yet people living in the territories that today comprise Turkey, Syria, Israel, and western Iran were prospering because the warmer, wetter climate created an ideal environment for wild grains to flourish. Throughout this region (known as the Fertile Crescent because of its abundant natural food supply and high agricultural productivity), humans now enjoyed plant resources plentiful enough to sustain seasonal, and sometimes even permanent, settlements. This fact made the shift to a sedentary existence possible.

The emergence of semipermanent and permanent settlements, permitted by a larger and more dependable food supply, had profound effects on human life. Most important was a rapid increase in human numbers. By around 8000 B.C.E., the human population was already beginning to exceed the available supplies of wild food.

To support their growing numbers, humans had to increase the food-growing capacity of the land. This marked the beginnings of deliberately managed agriculture.

For a grain-dependent community to live permanently at a single site, however, residents had first to devise ways of preserving and storing grain between harvests. By around 9500 B.C.E., the peoples living along the eastern coast of the Mediterranean had learned how to preserve their grain in storage pits. Storage guaranteed food supplies in times of natural shortage. But it also allowed early Neolithic peoples to store seed they could use to produce even more grain the following year. Once humans began deliberately to sow seed, they could plant crops in a more concentrated fashion, thus producing the higher yields needed to support a higher population (with the effect of growing the population even faster). Intensified seeding and storage also provided humans with the stable and predictable surpluses they needed to support domestic animals, which they could now afford to feed year-round.

The earliest archaeological evidence for fully sedentary agriculture comes from several areas in the Fertile Crescent between roughly 8500 and 7000 B.C.E. By 6000 B.C.E., much of the Near East had adopted agriculture as its primary mode of survival, supplemented by the domestication of cattle, pigs, sheep, and goats. Domestic animals not only provided a more reliable supply of meat, milk, leather, wool, bone, and horn, but also provided animal power to pull carts and plows and to grind grain into flour.

THE GREAT VILLAGES OF THE NEAR EAST

Villages constituted the most advanced form of human organization in western Asia from about 6500 to about 3500/3000 B.C.E., when some villages began to evolve into cities. A typical Near Eastern village at this time might number around one thousand inhabitants, but numbers could vary greatly. At first almost all able-bodied men and women must have engaged in field work, with women also involved in cloth production and child rearing. But gradually there came to be full-time specialists in handicrafts, as well as a few full-time traders.

One of the first examples of the transition from preagricultural communities to fully agricultural, permanent settlements comes from Jericho in the disputed West Bank region that lies between modern Israel and Jordan. Jericho emerged as a seasonal settlement around 9000 B.C.E., probably due to its abundant freshwater springs. Around 8000 B.C.E., however, the inhabitants of Jericho undertook a spectacular building program. Many new dwellings were built on stone foundations, and a massive stone wall was constructed around the western edge of the settlement. Built into this perimeter wall was a circular tower whose excavated remains still reach to a height of thirty feet.

We do not know why this wall was built; nor do we know the purpose of the tower. But whatever their intended functions, the wall and its tower served an impressive population: the early site of Jericho covered at least eight acres and supported a population of three thousand people. This population was sustained by the intensive cultivation of recently domesticated strains of wheat and barley, irrigated with water from the nearby springs.

Jericho's inhabitants also produced some of the earliest known pottery. Pottery allowed the inhabitants of

Early Village Pottery. A shallow bowl from a western Asian village site dating from about 5000 B.C.E.

Jericho to store grain more effectively than ever before. It also enabled them, for the first time, to store and trade liquids such as beer, wine, and oils. Pottery production soon became an important Near Eastern industry.

Another early agricultural settlement, Çatal Hüyük, has been discovered in modern-day Turkey. At the peak of their prosperity, between about 6500 and 5500 B.C.E., the residents of Çatal Hüyük produced a wide range of agricultural foodstuffs, including peas, lentils, fruits, nuts, and cereal crops. Meat and dairy products were also an important part of their diet. But although their diets were relatively healthy, the people's life expectancies were still short. Men died on average around the age of thirty-four, and women around the age of thirty.

Çatal Hüyük also illustrates the impact storable agricultural surpluses could have on human social relations. For the first time, significant differences began to arise in the amount of wealth individuals could acquire and stockpile for themselves and their heirs. At the same time, dependence on agriculture made it more difficult for individuals to split off from the community when the consequences of social and economic differentiation became oppressive. The result was the emergence of a much more stratified human society, with more specialization of social roles than ever before.

The Jericho Tower. The remains of a stone tower built into the walls of Jericho c. 8500 B.C.E. Even in its present, ruined state, the tower stands thirty feet tall.

WHAT WERE THE PRINCIPAL INFLUENCES BEHIND EMERGENCE OF URBAN LIFE IN MESOPOTAMIA?

THE DEVELOPMENT OF CIVILIZATION IN MESOPOTAMIA   11

CHRONOLOGY

FROM PREHISTORY TO HISTORY

Appearance of figurative artwork	40,000 B.C.E.
End of the Ice Age	11,000 B.C.E.
Beginnings of sedentary agricultural societies	8500 B.C.E.
Emergence of villages	6500–3000 B.C.E.
Development of writing	3300–2500 B.C.E.
Emergence of cities	3100 B.C.E.

THE DEVELOPMENT OF CIVILIZATION IN MESOPOTAMIA

What were the principal influences behind the early emergence of urban life in Mesopotamia?

Surprisingly, the initial shift from village to city and from prehistory to history took place in one of the most inhospitable environments imaginable—the southern desert of Mesopotamia, known to the Greeks as the "Land Between the Rivers," but to modern historians as Sumer. Now part of Iraq, Sumer gets only about eight inches (20 cm) of rainfall per year, and summer temperatures there routinely exceed 110° F (44° C). The soils of the region are sandy and infertile unless irrigated. And the two rivers that supply this flat and largely featureless plain with water—the Tigris and Euphrates—are famous for their flooding and unpredictable course changes. Nevertheless, it was in this uninviting environment that the first true cities emerged.

UBAID CULTURE

The founders of Ubaid culture (so called from its best-known site at al-Ubaid in modern Iraq) appear to have moved into the Sumerian desert around 5900 B.C.E. What attracted them to the unfriendly confines of the Tigris and Euphrates is unclear. But whatever it was that compelled the Ubaid peoples to move into Sumer, it appears they brought their village culture with them. They were not hunter-gatherers who unluckily stumbled into difficult circumstances.

The most consistent features of Ubaid life were irrigation systems and temple building. Almost as soon as we find farming settlements in Sumer, we discover evidence for fairly sophisticated systems of irrigation. Ubaid farmers also constructed dikes and levies to control the seasonal flooding of the rivers and to direct the flow of water into irrigation canals. Despite the hostility of the environment, Ubaid agricultural communities were soon producing surpluses sufficient to support specialists in weaving, pottery making, metalwork, trade, and construction—the typical attributes of a Neolithic village.

There is also early evidence of central structures that served religious functions. Starting out as simple and

Trade was another important development in these early Neolithic villages. By 5000 B.C.E. long-distance trade networks were operating across the Near East. Trade accelerated the exchange of commodities and ideas throughout the Fertile Crescent. But it also contributed to the increasing social stratification evident within these village communities. Because elite social status was enhanced by special access to high-prestige luxury goods, local elites often sought to monopolize long-distance trade by organizing and controlling the production of marketable goods within their own communities. Control over specialist artisans thus emerged as an important feature of elite social status in these Neolithic village communities.

What underlay all these social and economic changes was the increasing degree of specialization that agricultural surpluses made possible. In hunter-gatherer societies, every member of the community participated in the basic business of food acquisition. In a well-organized agricultural community, however, certain people could devote at least a portion of their labor to pursuits other than agriculture: making pottery or cloth, manufacturing weapons or tools, building houses and fortifications, or facilitating trade. Surpluses and specialization also led to the emergence of social elites who, by organizing and exploiting the labor and production of others, were able to turn ruling itself into another specialist occupation. As villages grew larger and more sophisticated, the amount of specialization increased, until a significant fraction of the population could become full-time nonagriculturalists. This was an essential step in the development of true urban-based civilizations.

THE FERTILE CRESCENT

Notice the proximity of Sumerian cities to rivers; consider the vital role played by the Tigris and Euphrates in shaping the Mesopotamian civilizations. Also, note how close to each other the Sumerian city-states were. What challenges and opportunities did this phenomenon present? In what directions might Sumerian influence expand most quickly? Why?

fairly humble shrines, these buildings soon evolved into impressive temples built of dried mud brick (the scarcity of stone in the region compelled Ubaid builders to reserve that material for tools). Each larger settlement had such a building, which became progressively larger with successive rebuildings. From these temples, a priestly class acted as both the officiants of religious life and managers of the economic resources of the community, organizing the construction of ever-larger temples and maintaining the complex irrigation systems that made village life possible in the Mesopotamian desert.

URBANISM IN THE URUK PERIOD (4300–2900 B.C.E.)

By the beginning of the fourth millennium B.C.E., Ubaid settlements were coalescing into larger and more prosperous communities with more elaborate temples, buildings, and village planning. This period, named after its most impressive site, the great Sumerian city-state of Uruk (modern Warka), witnessed the transition from the Neolithic Ubaid village to the Sumerian city. It marks, therefore, the true beginning of civilization in the Mediterranean world.

WHAT WERE THE PRINCIPAL INFLUENCES BEHIND EMERGENCE OF URBAN LIFE IN MESOPOTAMIA?

THE DEVELOPMENT OF CIVILIZATION IN MESOPOTAMIA   13

Among the principal developments of this period is the further elaboration of temple architecture. This trend reflects not only the centrality of religion in Sumerian culture, but also the increasing wealth and control of the priestly class over economic life. The White Temple at Uruk provides a stunning example of this general trend. Sometime between 3500 and 3300 B.C.E., builders constructed a massive sloping platform that towered nearly forty feet above the surrounding flatlands. Atop the platform stood another structure, the shrine or temple proper, also dressed in brick but painted a brilliant white.

Such temples grew up across Sumer, reflecting the central role played by these shrines in civic life. Uruk in particular seems to have owed its rapid urban growth to its importance as a religious center. The larger villages of Sumer were also growing rapidly, however, their teeming economic activity attracting immigrants just as the great cities were doing. By 3400 B.C.E., Uruk and at least a half dozen other urban sites could boast densely packed dwellings accessed by winding streets. By the end of the Uruk Period, these cities also shared a common language, a fact made clear thanks to the invention that moves the Sumerians fully into the light of history: writing.

> By 3100 B.C.E. Sumerian scribes had largely abandoned writing with pointed sticks in favor of a more durable reed stylus. Because this stylus left an impression shaped like a wedge (the Latin word for which cuneus), we refer to this script as cuneiform.

THE DEVELOPMENT OF WRITING

Like many of the breakthroughs we have considered in this chapter, the invention of writing did not occur overnight. By 4000 B.C.E., villagers in the Near East had begun using clay tokens to keep track of inventories and to facilitate the burgeoning trade of the region. Ultimately, the practice developed of placing all the tokens from a single transaction inside a hollow clay ball, and inscribing, on the outside of the ball, the shapes of all the tokens it contained. By 3300 B.C.E., the priestly class (or those working for them) realized that they could dispense with the clumsy token-and-ball system altogether, and replace it with flat clay tablets on which they could note the desired information by inscribing the appropriate symbols.

In its earliest phases, writing thus evolved as a means of record keeping in connection with economic pursuits—another reflection of the growing wealth of the Uruk Period. For some time, writing remained purely pictographic: each symbol marked into the clay resembled the physical object it represented. Over the course of time, however, as the uses of writing evolved, a symbol might come to be used not only to evoke the physical object it represented, but also an idea associated with that object. The symbol for a bowl of food, *ninda* (a noun), might thus be used to express a more abstract notion such as bread or sustenance—an idea not otherwise easily represented by a quick sketch into soft clay. In time, such symbols might also come to be associated with a particular phonetic sound. Thus any time a Sumerian scribe needed to employ the sound *ninda*, even as part of another word or name, he would use the symbol for a bowl of food. Later, special marks were added to the script so that the reader could discern whether the writer intended the symbol to represent the object itself or the *phonogram* (the sound represented by the symbol).

By 3100 B.C.E. Sumerian scribes had largely abandoned writing with pointed sticks in favor of a more durable reed stylus. Because this stylus left an impression shaped like a wedge (the Latin word for which is *cuneus*), we refer to this script as *cuneiform*. The new stylus did make it more difficult, however, to draw pictograms that accurately reflected the original shape (such as a bowl of food) of the object they were meant to represent. As a result, cuneiform symbols became more and more abstract, until they barely resembled the original pictograms at all.

Symbols ultimately were invented for every possible vowel-consonant combination in the Sumerian language. As a result, the number of symbols ran into the several hundreds. Understandably, it took many years to learn to read and write cuneiform, and only a small minority of the population ever did so. Those who did, however, became important and influential people in Sumerian society. For the entirety of the third millennium, it was largely the sons of the elite who attended the scribal schools. But

CHRONOLOGY

ORIGINS OF MESOPOTAMIAN SOCIETY

Ubaid Period	5900–4300 B.C.E.
Uruk Period	4300–2900 B.C.E.
Early Dynastic Period	2900–2500 B.C.E.
Akkadian Period	2350–2160 B.C.E.
Ur Dynasty	2100–2000 B.C.E.

Cuneiform Writing. Above, a Sumerian clay tablet from about 3000 B.C.E. Here standardized pictures are beginning to represent abstractions. On the right, carvings on limestone from about 2600 B.C.E. The evolution of standardized cuneiform writing is now complete: the inscription proclaims that a king of Ur has built a temple.

despite the wide variety of symbols and the complicated nature of the script, cuneiform proved remarkably durable. For over two thousand years it remained the principal writing system of the ancient Near East, even for societies that no longer spoke the Sumerian language.

THE SUMERIANS ENTER HISTORY

Why did a common religion not create peace among the Sumerians?

After about 2500 B.C.E., the Sumerians used writing for a wide variety of economic, political, and religious purposes. These records make it possible for us to know a great deal more about the Sumerians than we do about any other human society of the time. We can begin to understand their political relationships, their feelings about their gods, and the social and economic structure of their society. The Sumerians are, in this sense, the first historical—as opposed to prehistorical—society.

The great centers of Sumerian culture—Uruk, Ur, Lagash, Eridu, Kish, and others—shared a common culture, language, and religion. This common religion did

not produce peace among the Sumerian cities, however. Although each Sumerian community recognized all the gods of the Sumerian pantheon (some fifteen hundred gods), the residents of each individual city-state viewed their city as the property of one particular god, whom they sought to glorify by exalting their city. The result was intense competition between cities, which frequently escalated into open warfare. For any city-state to surrender its independence to another city would have been an intolerable offense against the conquered city's god. The Sumerians shared a common culture and a common pantheon; but common government was impossible.

A significant proportion of the cultivable land of each city belonged outright to the temple of the patron god. During the third millennium, these great temples also began to control the production of textiles, creating protofactories that employed thousands of servile women and children. Temples also played a key role in long-distance trade, both as buyers and sellers of goods.

Each Sumerian city had a ruling aristocracy, from which the priests and important officials of the temples came; but it was the priests who stood at the top of these highly theocratic societies. In this early period of Sumerian civilization perhaps as much as half the population consisted of commoners, free persons who held a small parcel of land sufficient to sustain themselves and make required payments to the temple complex. The temples also had large numbers of legally free de-

THE FLOOD: TWO ACCOUNTS

The Epic of Gilgamesh preserves a traditional account of a destructive flood sent by the gods to punish humanity. This story probably dates from the first half of the third millennium B.C.E., making it at least fifteen hundred years older than the similar account in the Hebrew Bible. The striking similarities between these two accounts is evidence of the strong cultural influence exerted by older Near Eastern civilizations on the early Hebrews.

THE EPIC OF GILGAMESH

Utnapishtim spoke to Gilgamesh, saying: "I will reveal to you, Gilgamesh . . . a secret of the gods. . . . The hearts of the Great Gods moved them to inflict the Flood. Their Father Anu uttered the oath (of secrecy). . . . [But the god] Ea . . . repeated their talk [to me, saying]: 'O man of Shuruppak, son of Ubartutu: Tear down the house and build a boat! . . . Spurn possessions and keep alive living beings! Make all living beings go up into the boat. The boat which you are to build, its dimensions must measure equal to each other: its length must correspond to its width. Roof it over like the Apsu.' I understood and spoke to my lord, Ea: 'My lord, thus is the command which you have uttered. I will heed and will do it.' . . . On the fifth day I laid out her exterior. It was a field in area, its walls were each 10 times 12 cubits in height. . . . I provided it with six decks, thus dividing it into seven (levels). . . . Whatever I had loaded on it. . . . All the living beings that I had loaded on it. I had all my kith and kin go up into the boat, all the beasts and animals of the field and the draftsmen I had go up.

I watched the appearance of the weather—the weather was frightful to behold! I went into the boat and sealed the entry. . . . All day long the South Wind blew . . . , submerging the mountain in water, overwhelming the people like an attack. . . . Six days and seven nights came the wind and flood, the storm flattening the land. When the seventh day arrived . . . [t]he sea calmed, fell still, the whirlwind and flood stopped up. . . . When a seventh day arrived, I sent forth a dove and released it. The dove went off, but came back to me; no perch was visible so it circled back to me. I sent forth a swallow and released it. The swallow went off, but came back to me; no perch was visible so it circled back to me. I sent forth a raven and released it. The raven went off, and saw the waters slither back. It eats, it scratches, it bobs, but does not cirlce back to me. Then I sent out everything in all directions and sacrificed (a sheep). I offered incense in front of the mountain-ziggurat. . . .

The gods smelled the savor . . . and collected like flies over a sacrifice. . . . Just then Enlil arrived. He saw the boat and became furious. . . . 'Where did a living being escape? No man was to survive the annihilation!' Ea spoke to Valiant Enlil, saying . . . How, how could you bring about a Flood without consideration? Charge the violation to the violator, charge the offense to the offender, but be compassionate lest (mankind) be cut off, be patient lest they be killed.' Enlil went up inside the boat and, grasping my hand, made me go up. He had my wife go up and kneel by my side. He touched our forehead and, standing between us, he blessed us. . . ."

Maureen Gallery Kovacs, trans. *The Epic of Gilgamesh*, Tablet XI (Stanford, 1985, 1989), pp. 97–103.

BOOK OF GENESIS

The Lord saw that the wickedness of humankind was great in the earth and . . . said "I will blot out from the earth the human beings I have created . . . for I am sorry I have made them." But Noah found favor in the sight of the Lord. . . . God saw that the earth was corrupt and . . . said to Noah, "I have determined to make an end to all flesh. . . . Make yourself an ark of cypress wood; make rooms in the ark, and cover it inside and out with pitch. . . . Make a roof for the ark, and put the door of the ark in its side. . . . For my part I am going to bring a flood on the earth, to destroy from under heaven all flesh. . . . But I will establish a covenant with you; and you shall come into the ark, you, your sons, your wife, and your sons' wives with you. And of every living thing you shall bring two of every kind into the ark, to keep them alive with you. . . . Also take with you every kind of food that is eaten." . . . All the fountains of the great deep burst forth, and the windows of the heavens were opened. . . . The waters gradually receded from the earth. . . . At the end of forty days,

Noah opened a window of the ark . . . and sent out the raven, and it went to and fro until the waters were dried up from the earth. Then he sent out the dove from him, to see if the waters had subsided from the face of the ground, but the dove found no place to set its foot, and it returned. . . . He waited another seven days, and again sent out the dove [which] came back to him . . . and there in its beak was a freshly plucked olive leaf; so Noah knew the waters had subsided from the earth. Then he . . . sent out the dove, and it did not return to him anymore. . . . Noah built an altar to the Lord . . . and offered burnt offerings. And when the Lord smelled the pleasing odor, the Lord said in his heart, "I will never again curse the ground because of humankind . . . nor will I ever again destroy every living creature as I have done.". . . God blessed Noah and his sons.

Genesis 6:5–9:1, *The New Oxford Annotated Bible.* (Oxford: Oxford University Press, 1994).

---

pendents who worked as artisans or as agricultural laborers on temple lands.

There were also many slaves in Sumerian society. In Sumer, as elsewhere in the ancient world, slaves were often prisoners of war. If the slave came originally from another Sumerian city, the master's power over him was strictly limited, and he (or she—many slaves were women) had to be released after three years. Non-Sumerians could be held indefinitely, although slaves could sometimes buy their freedom. Despite these safeguards, slaves in Sumer were still the property of their owners. They could be beaten, punished, branded like animals, bought and sold on their owner's whim. Ancient slavery may not have been quite so horrible as more modern examples (such as that practiced in the New World), but it was still highly undesirable to be a slave.

THE EARLY DYNASTIC PERIOD BEGINS (2900–2500 B.C.E.)

Starting around 2900 B.C.E., the intense competition between the Sumerian city-states led to the emergence of a new type of war leadership that would eventually become a kind of kingship. As the city-states grew

larger (each now holding anywhere from ten thousand to fifty thousand inhabitants), competition for scarce resources intensified. Warfare became a regular feature of Sumerian life, and successful war leaders, known as lugals, began to acquire great prestige and power.

The most striking indication of the impression this new office made upon Sumerian society is the Epic of Gilgamesh, the first great literary work in world history, which recounts the legendary exploits of a historical king of Uruk named Gilgamesh. As he appears in the epic, Gilgamesh was a powerful *lugal* who had won his reputation through military conquest and general heroism, particularly against nonurbanized "barbarians." Through the fame and prestige he acquired, he became so powerful that he could ignore the constraints that bound lesser men. We hear at the start of the epic how the people complained about their king, even though they still revered him: he kept their sons away at war for too long; he showed no respect for the nobles, carousing with their wives and daughters as he pleased; he disappointed them by his sacrilegious conduct. His people prayed to the gods for relief, and ultimately the gods fashioned a wild man named Enkidu to challenge Gilgamesh.

The confrontation between Gilgamesh and Enkidu reflects the dichotomy the Sumerians perceived between city and wilderness, between what was "civilized" and what was not. We recognize in Enkidu the hunter-gatherer who was doubtless far more intimate with nature than were the Sumerians after centuries of civic life; but such "naturalness" was not a quality the Sumerians admired. Instead, the friendship that eventually forms between Gilgamesh and Enkidu illustrates the hostility and fear Sumerians felt toward the wilderness. Given the harsh climate and unpredictable environment in which the Sumerians lived, their adversarial relationship with the natural world is understandable. As they battled uncooperative rivers, searing heat, salinization of the soil, and the raids of less civilized folk, the Sumerians' pessimistic attitude toward their natural environment is mirrored not only in their general view of life, but also in their view of the gods.

SUMERIAN RELIGION

The Sumerians believed that humanity itself had been wrested from the inhospitable earth and created for one purpose, to serve the gods. The Sumerians therefore imbued every aspect of their life and culture with religiosity, reflecting their pervasive obligations to the gods. A powerful *lugal* might distance himself from the temple priesthood, but nonetheless, he owed his authority to the gods who had bestowed it on him.

Relations between the Sumerians and their gods were not warm. The gods wished to be exalted, and so massive temples called ziggurats evolved out of the increasingly elaborate shrines of the Uruk Period. The Sumerians also went to great pains to honor their gods with temples, festivals, and sacrifices. But the gods inspired no affection, nor did they offer any affection to human beings. Instead, they were objects of fear and suspicion: cruel, mean spirited, and capricious, with little concern for the effect their actions might have on humanity. The wide-eyed, apprehensive-looking human figures sculpted by Sumerian artists were offered to the gods by people hoping to ensure the gods' benign detachment toward humanity. To ask the gods for more positive help was a last resort in desperate circumstances, and was likely to backfire, as the residents of Uruk discovered when they asked the gods to rein in the tyrant Gilgamesh.

Sumerian views of the afterlife were equally pessimistic. They expected neither eternal punishment nor eternal reward from the gods after death. Instead, the dead simply crossed a man-eating river into the "Land of No Return," a gloomy place which enjoyed no light. Relatives buried the dead with basic articles such as food and clothing and diversions such as musical instruments and games, hoping to make the glum,

Sumerian Ziggurat. This edifice, built in Ur around 2100 B.C.E., is the best-preserved surviving ziggurat. As can be seen from the diagram of its original form at left, a shrine, reached by climbing four stories and passing through a massive portal, was the goal of the worshiper's ascent and the most sacred part of the temple.

unhappy underworld a bit more bearable for the departed. But the improvement, if any, would have been modest. The afterlife was essentially just a continuation of the anxious, grim existence the Sumerians led in this world, only worse.

Such negativism was accompanied by a kind of quiet resignation toward the unpleasantness and ultimate futility of life. When his friend Enkidu is killed by the goddess Inanna (whom both Gilgamesh and Enkidu had mocked), Gilgamesh's horror at Enkidu's death propels him to seek immortality for himself. Against the advice of other characters, he continues his quest until he learns of a plant of eternal life at the bottom of a deep pool. Gilgamesh swims to the bottom and retrieves it, only to have it stolen from him as he surfaces by a serpent, who then disappears below with Gilgamesh's only chance for immortality. In the end, Gilgamesh, the great king of Uruk, is left to ponder the futility of all human endeavor. Reflecting on the impermanence of his own deeds and even of Uruk's mighty walls, he asks, "Why do I bother working for nothing? Who even notices what I do?"

SCIENCE, TECHNOLOGY, AND TRADE

Sumerian pessimism was deeply rooted, but it was not paralyzing. Their distrust of the gods and their adversarial relationship with their environment instead inculcated in the Sumerians a high degree of self-reliance and ingenuity. These qualities helped make them the most technologically inventive people of the ancient world.

The Sumerians became first-rate metallurgists despite the fact that their land had no natural mineral resources. By 6000 B.C.E., a number of cultures throughout the Near East and Europe had learned how to produce copper weapons and tools. Mesopotamia itself had no copper; but by the Uruk period (4300–2900 B.C.E.), trade routes were bringing raw copper into Sumer, where the Sumerians processed it into weapons and tools. Shortly before 3000 B.C.E., perhaps starting in eastern Anatolia, people discovered that copper could be alloyed with arsenic (or later, tin) to produce bronze. Bronze is almost as malleable as copper, but pours more easily into molds and, when cooled, maintains its rigidity and shape better than copper. Because the Sumerians and neighboring cultures engaged in such widespread use of bronze, we refer to a Bronze Age beginning around 3000 B.C.E.

Alongside writing, the invention of the wheel stands at the top of any list of fundamental advances in human technology. The Sumerians were using potter's wheels by the middle of the fourth millennium B.C.E., allowing them to produce high-quality clay vessels in greater quantity than ever before. By around 3200 B.C.E., the Sumerians were also using two-wheeled chariots and four-wheeled carts drawn by donkeys (horses were unknown in western Asia until they were introduced by eastern invaders sometime between 2000 and 1700 B.C.E.). Wheeled chariots were used mainly in warfare; illustrations from about 2600 B.C.E. depict them trampling the enemy. Wheeled carts were an even more important advance, however, because they dramatically increased the productivity of the Sumerian work force. The Sumerians did not invent the wheel; they probably acquired it from nomadic peoples living on the steppes of southern Russia. But by adapting it to so many different uses, they vastly increased its technological possibilities.

The Sumerians also pioneered the study of mathematics. To construct their elaborate systems of irrigation canals, dikes, and reservoirs, they also developed sophisticated measuring and surveying techniques. Agricultural

Sumerian War Chariots. The earliest known representation of the wheel, dating from about 2600 B.C.E., shows how wheels were carpentered together from slabs of wood. (For a later Mesopotamian wheel with spokes, see the illustration on p. 45.)

WHY DID A COMMON RELIGION NOT CREATE PEACE AMONG THE SUMERIANS?

THE SUMERIANS ENTER HISTORY   19

concerns probably also lay behind the lunar calendar they invented, which consisted of twelve months, six lasting thirty days, and six lasting twenty-nine days. Since this produced a year of only 354 days, the Sumerians eventually discovered that they had to add a month to their calendars every few years in order to predict the recurrence of the seasons with sufficient accuracy. But the Sumerian practice of dividing time into multiples of sixty has lasted to the present day, not only in our notions of the thirty-day month (which corresponds approximately with the phases of the moon), but also in our division of the hour into sixty minutes, and the minute into sixty seconds. Mathematics also contributed to Sumerian architecture, allowing the Sumerians to build domes and arches thousands of years before the Romans would adopt and spread these architectural forms throughout the Mediterranean world.

The Sumerians' ability to engage in these activities depended on the acquisition of raw materials through trade, for their homeland was almost completely devoid of natural resources. The Sumerians therefore pioneered trade routes up and down the Tigris and Euphrates and into the hilly flanks of Mesopotamia, following the tributaries of these great rivers. They blazed trails across the deserts toward the west, where they interacted with and influenced the Egyptians. By sea, they traded with the peoples of the Persian Gulf and, directly or indirectly, with the civilizations of the Indus Valley. Like the Neolithic traders who conveyed goods from village to village, the Sumerians carried their ideas with them along with their merchandise, their literature, their art, their use of writing, and the whole cultural complex that arose from their urban way of life. From its Sumerians roots, the idea of civilization thus spread throughout the ancient Near Eastern world.

THE END OF THE EARLY DYNASTIC PERIOD (2500–2350 B.C.E.)

During this period, competition among the Sumerian city-states for prestige, power, and resources reached a fever pitch. Tensions between temple aristocracy and royal power were lessening, however, leading to the emergence of a more unified ruling elite, but leaving commoners with even less of a voice than they had had before.

The Royal Tombs of Ur, dating from 2550 B.C.E. to 2450 B.C.E., provide a breathtaking demonstration of the wealth of this newly unified Sumerian elite, and of the divide that had now opened up between leaders and followers in Sumerian society. The rich documentary evidence from this period deals mainly with the military exploits of these powerful kings. It tells of a cycle of brutal warfare among the leading city-states, as the *lugal* of each sought to establish his supremacy over the others by defeating their armies in battle and then forcing the defeated cities to pay him tribute. Inevitably, however, such supremacy was fleeting: conquered cities revolted, and the cycle of warfare began again. No Sumerian *lugal* ever attempted to create a true and lasting empire by imposing centralized rule over the cities he conquered. As a result, Sumer remained a collection of independent city-states, compelled periodically to acknowledge the supremacy of a particular *lugal*, but unable to forge any lasting structures of authority larger than an individual city and its patron god. This fact would prove its undoing when Sumer confronted a new style of imperial rulership in the figure of Sargon of Akkad.

As an outsider to Sumerian society, Sargon, the leader of the Akkadians, was not bound by the traditional assumptions and conventions of Sumerian warfare. Instead, he launched a systematic program of conquest, designed to subject all the areas around Sumer to his authority.

THE AKKADIAN EMPIRE (2350–2160 B.C.E.)

The Akkadians were the predominant people of central Mesopotamia, to the north of Sumer. The Sumerians had greatly influenced them. But although they adopted cuneiform script along with much of Sumerian culture, the Akkadians did not adopt the Sumerian language. Instead, they preserved their own Semitic language, a member of the linguistic family that includes Assyrian, Aramaic, Hebrew, Arabic, and Ethiopic. Sumerians tended to regard the Akkadians as barbarians, but in fact, the two peoples were culturally very similar.

As an outsider to Sumerian society, Sargon, the leader of the Akkadians, was not bound by the traditional assumptions and conventions of Sumerian warfare. Instead, he launched a systematic program of conquest, designed to subject all the areas around Sumer to his authority. Only when it was too late did the Sumerians realize that Sargon now had their land by the throat. Around 2350 B.C.E., he conquered Sumer, and then moved swiftly to establish direct control over all of Mesopotamia.

Objects from the Royal Tombs at Ur. On the right, a queen's headdress, made of gold leaf, lapis lazuli, and carnelian. Above, a helmet made of an alloy of gold and silver. Its cloth lining would have been attached through the holes visible around the edges of the helmet.

From his new capital at Akkad, Sargon installed Akkadian-speaking governors to rule the cities of Sumer, ordering them to pull down fortifications, collect taxes, and do his will. By so doing, Sargon transformed the independent city-states of Sumer and Akkad into a much larger political unit: a kingdom or empire. Sargon supported his empire (arguably the first true empire in human history) by managing and exploiting the network of trade routes crisscrossing the Near East. His economic influence stretched from Ethiopia to the Indus Valley in India, and his capital became the most splendid city in the world.

Sargon was eventually succeeded by his talented grandson Naram-Sin, who reigned, like his grandfather, for over a half century. Naram-Sin extended the Akkadian conquests and consolidated long-distance trade routes. An energetic promoter of culture and a patron of the arts, Naram-Sin encouraged literary and artistic endeavors. Through conquest and the quickened pace of commerce, he also helped to stimulate the growth of cities throughout the Near East.

Although the Akkadians' emphasis on political centralization and imperial organization represented a clear break with the Sumerian past, culturally the Sumerians and Akkadians differed little from one another. By 2200 B.C.E. most people in central and southern Mesopotamia would have been able to converse in either language. Although the Akkadians worshiped their own Akkadian deities, they were also careful to respect and revere the gods and practices of the Sumerians. Much of Akkadian literature and art was at its root Sumerian, translated and slightly transformed to appeal to Akkadian tastes. Scholars speak of a Sumero-Akkadian cultural synthesis, and indeed after the reign of Sargon the two civilizations were virtually indistinguishable except for their different languages. Despite its new imperial trappings, the urban civilization Sargon and Naram-Sin helped to promote across the Near East was still essentially the urban model of the Sumerians.

THE DYNASTY OF UR
(2100–2000 B.C.E.)

Court intrigue and a series of weak successors followed the long reign of Naram-Sin. After a brief period in which invading hill people from the Iranian Plateau ruled over Sumer and Akkad (2160–2100 B.C.E.), Sumer once again dissolved into a collection of rival, independent city-states. Around 2100 B.C.E., however, a new dynasty from Ur, the so-called Ur Dynasty III, established itself under the rule of its first king, Ur-Nammu, and his son Shulgi. Ur-Nammu and Shulgi modeled their kingship on that of Sargon and Naram-Sin, pursuing military conquests, the centralization of Sumerian government, commercial expansion, the patronage of art and literature, and an exalted ideology of charismatic imperial rulership. Together, the Akkadian rulers and Ur Dynasty III thus established a pattern of rule that would influence the region for centuries to come.

When Shulgi died, around 2047 B.C.E., he was succeeded by two competent sons who both died young. As a result the throne fell to Shulgi's grandson Ibbi-Sin, a hapless individual most charitably described as in over his head. Ibbi-Sin gradually lost control of his empire, until finally an enemy army sacked Ur itself and carried Ibbi-Sin off into captivity. For the inhabitants of Mesopotamia, his name would resonate for centuries as the epitome of criminal stupidity and hopeless incompetence.

For the next two centuries, Mesopotamian history would be characterized by incessant warfare among a group of small kingdoms based upon the great urban centers of the Sumero-Akkadian past. Not until the eighteenth century B.C.E. would one of these kings, the remarkable Hammurabi of Babylon, create a new imperial unity in the region.

THE "SUMERIAN RENAISSANCE" AND THE RISE OF THE AMORITES

The rulers of Ur issued their official documents in Sumerian, and consciously reasserted Sumerian culture against the influence of the Semitic-speaking Akkadians. But this backward-looking "Sumerian Renaissance" had little effect on the culture of Mesopotamia, which was by now thoroughly suffused by the influence of the Semitic-speaking peoples who would dominate the region for the next fifteen hundred years. Three such groups in particular deserve our attention now: the Akkadians, the Amorites, and the Assyrians. We will meet others, including the Phoenicians, the Canaanites, and the Hebrews, in Chapter Two.

The Akkadians were the first Semitic-speaking people to establish themselves in Mesopotamia, and became the most thoroughly assimilated into Sumerian civilization. They rapidly adapted to urban life, and became impor-

tant founders of cities elsewhere in the Near Eastern world. The Amorites, by contrast, were nomads, whose military skills made them valuable allies (and eventually masters) of the Sumerian and Akkadian cities. Like the Akkadians, the Amorites eventually urbanized, but culturally they retained much that reflected their rough-and-tumble roots. Northern Mesopotamia was home to the Assyrians, caravan merchants who pioneered trade routes into Anatolia (modern-day Turkey) soon after 2000 B.C.E. Deeply influenced by Sumero-Akkadian culture, the Assyrians would go on to found an important and long-lasting civilization in their own right. For the time being, however, they had their hands full fending off the advances of their Amorite cousins to the south.

THE OLD BABYLONIAN EMPIRE

How did Hammurabi bind his empire together?

In 1792 B.C.E. a young Amorite ruler named Hammurabi ascended the throne of Babylon, a weak kingdom in central Mesopotamia based in an insignificant city of the same name. When Hammurabi came to power, Babylon was both fragile and precariously wedged between a number of other, more powerful Amorite kingdoms. Babylon's site on the Tigris and Euphrates had great potential economic and military significance; but it was also dangerous, because Babylon sat perilously amid mighty antagonists who were often tempted to "play through" the city on their way to other conquests.

Hammurabi may have been the first sovereign in world history to understand that power need not be based on brute force. He recognized that the application of intellect, political strategy, and ruthless cunning might accomplish what his army could not. Hammurabi did not try to confront his mightier neighbors directly. Rather, through letters and embassies, double-dealing diplomacy, and general deceit, he induced his stronger counterparts to embroil themselves ever deeper in armed conflict with each other. While the other Amorite kingdoms exhausted themselves in costly and pointless wars, Hammurabi fanned their hatred for one another, skillfully and privately portraying himself as a friend to all sides. His value as a potential ally caused neighboring rulers to send him resources, in hopes that he might help them. Meanwhile, Hammurabi quietly

Mesopotamian Royal Head. A diorite head of a Mesopotamian king, conventionally identified as Hammurabi. Such headdresses were worn by the rulers of Mesopotamian cities between roughly 2100 and 1700 B.C.E. Hammurabi is shown wearing such a headdress on p. 23, but there is nothing else to identify this bust with Hammurabi.

consolidated his kingdom, augmenting his own strength, and when the time was right fell on his depleted and weary neighbors. By such policies, he transformed his small Amorite state into what historians describe as the Old Babylonian Empire.

Mesopotamia under Hammurabi's rule achieved an unprecedented degree of political integration. His realm ultimately stretched from the Persian Gulf into Assyria. The southern half of the region, formerly known as Sumer and Akkad, would for the rest of antiquity be known as Babylonia. To help unify these territories, Hammurabi introduced an important innovation by elevating the little-known patron deity of Babylon, Marduk, to be the ruler-god of his entire empire. Although the king was also careful to pay homage to the ancient gods of Sumer and Akkad, Marduk now

sat atop the official pantheon. People could continue to worship the ancient patron deities of their cities if they wished; but all now owed allegiance to Marduk.

RELIGION AND LAW

The notion that political rule rested on divine approval was nothing new, of course. Its foundations lay in the practices and beliefs of the Sumerians, and the notion was fully developed by Sargon, Narum-Sin, Ur-Nammu, and Shulgi. Hammurabi's innovation was to use Marduk's supremacy over all other gods to legitimate his own claim to rule, in Marduk's name, over all Mesopotamia because he was king of Marduk's home city of Babylon. Hammurabi thus became the first Near Eastern ruler to launch wars of aggression that he justified specifically by saying he undertook them in the name of his primary god. This precedent would become a characteristic feature of Near Eastern politics thereafter, as we will see in Chapter Two.

In Hammurabi's Babylon, political power and religious practice were thus completely interwoven with each other. At their annual new year celebration, the Babylonians would reenact the victory of Marduk over the Sumerian god of chaos, which had secured for Marduk his place as the chief god of both heaven and earth. Marduk's triumph over chaos in turn made it possible to predict and control the natural environment, the Babylonians believed, and so was intimately connected with the fertility of the land. To guarantee this continuing fertility, during the same new year festivities the king would retire with a sacred prostitute inside the temple, and the two would have ritual sexual intercourse. Like the pharaohs of Egypt and the emperors of ancient China, the Old Babylonian king was thus an essential link in the chain of relationships that bound human beings to the earth and the heavens.

Hammurabi did not rely solely on religion to bind his empire together. Building on the precedents of centuries and rulers past, he also issued a collection of laws valid throughout his empire. Preserved on an impressive eight-foot stele discovered in southwestern Iran and now in the Louvre, the so-called Code of Hammurabi addressed a wide range of legal concerns. Unlike a modern criminal code, Hammurabi's code did not prescribe remedies for all conceivable infractions that might occur in Babylonian society. Rather, it contained actual rulings handed down by the king in particular legal cases. Hammurabi's innovation was to publish his decisions throughout his empire, so that they could guide future judicial decisions by his local governors and judges.

Code of Hammurabi. The entire code of Hammurabi survives on an eight-foot column made of basalt. The top quarter of the column depicts the Babylonian king paying homage to the seated god of justice. Directly below one can make out the cuneiform inscriptions that are the law code's text.

OLD BABYLONIAN SOCIETY

Hammurabi's code also reveals much about the structure of Amorite Babylonian society. Overall, the more complicated social arrangements of Sumerian civilization had given way to a simpler but even more oppressive system. An upper class of nobles—palace officials, temple priests, high-ranking military officers, and rich merchants—controlled large estates and staggering wealth. Beneath this small stratum was an enormous class of legally free individuals who were nonetheless "dependents" of the palace or the temple, or who leased land from the estates of the powerful. These dependents included laborers and artisans, small-scale merchants and farmers, and the minor political and religious officials of the state.

At the bottom of Babylonian society were the slaves. Far more numerous in the Old Babylonian Empire than

they had been in the Sumerian period, slaves were also treated much more harshly. They were also more readily identifiable as a separate group within society. In Babylonia, free men, whether nobles or dependents, wore long hair and beards; male slaves, however, were shaven and branded. Some Babylonian slaves were acquired through trade, another departure from Sumerian practice. Others were captured in war, or were free people who had fallen into slavery through debt or as punishment for certain offenses. Slaves could accumulate property and borrow as a means of gaining their freedom, but this was probably not a frequent occurrence.

Old Babylonian society was also highly stratified by class. An offense committed against nobles carried a far more severe penalty than did the same crime committed against a dependent or slave (although nobles were also punished more severely than were commoners for crimes they committed against other nobles). Marriage arrangements and customs also reflected class differences, with bride-price and dowry depending on the status of the parties involved.

Hammurabi's code also provides evidence as to the status and treatment of women in Babylonian society. Women did enjoy certain protections under the law, including the right to divorce abusive, neglectful, or indigent husbands. If a husband divorced a wife "without cause," he was obliged to provide financial support for her and their children. Despite such protections, however, Babylonian law regarded wives as the property of their husbands. A wife who went around her city defaming her spouse was subject to drowning; she would suffer the same fate, along with her lover, if she were caught in adultery. Husbands, by contrast, had a legal right to have sexual relations not only with temple prostitutes, but also with slaves and concubines.

HAMMURABI'S LEGACY

Hammurabi died around 1750 B.C.E. Although some contraction of the Old Babylonian Empire followed under his successors, Hammurabi's achievements endured. His administrative reforms, combined with his innovations in religious imperialism, created a durable and important state in Mesopotamia. For another two centuries the Old Babylonian Empire played a significant role in the Near East, until invaders from the north sacked the capital and occupied it. Babylon itself remained the region's most famous city for another thousand years.

Hammurabi's legacy extended well beyond the borders of his own kingdom. His success, and the flair and

THE CODE OF HAMMURABI

The laws of Hammurabi, published on the authority of the king and set up throughout the Babylonian empire, exhibit the influences both of the urban society on which they were imposed and the rough justice of Amorite tradition. Although Hammurabi built on older, urban legal traditions, he sought to extend the authority of his law into more realms of life and provide sterner punishments for its violation. This sampling of his provisions illustrates the severity of his system for criminals, while providing protections in unusual circumstances.

If a man accuses a man, and charges him with murder, but cannot convict him, the accuser shall be put to death.

If a man steals an ox or sheep, ass or pig, or boat—if it belonged to the god or palace, he shall pay thirty fold; if it belonged to a common man, he shall restore ten fold. If the thief has nothing wherewith to pay, he shall be put to death.

If a fire breaks out in a man's house and a man who goes to extinguish it . . . takes the household property of the owner of the house, that man shall be thrown into the fire.

If a man aids a male or a female slave of the palace, or a male or female slave of a common man, to escape from the city, he shall be put to death.

If a man who is a tenant has paid the full amount of money for his rent for the year to the owner of the house, and he (the owner) says to him before "his days are full," "Vacate," the owner of the house, because he made the tenant move out of the house before "his days were full" shall lose the money which the tenant paid him.

If an agent should be careless and not take a receipt for the money which he has given to the merchant, the money not receipted for shall not be placed to his account.

If the wife of a man be taken in lying with another man, they shall bind them and throw them into the water.

If a woman hates her husband and says, "Thou shalt not have me," her past shall be inquired into for any deficiency of hers; and if she has been careful and without past sin and her husband has been going out and greatly belittling her, that woman has no blame. She shall take her dowry and go to her father's house.

If a man destroys the eye of another man, they shall destroy his eye. If a man knocks out the tooth of a man of his own rank, they shall knock out his tooth . . . if the tooth of a common man, he shall pay one-third mana of silver.

Sara Robbins, ed. *Law: A Treasury of Art and Literature.* (New York: Beaux Arts Editions), 1990, pp. 20–22 (slightly revised).

IN WHAT WAYS DID PATTERNS OF DEVELOPMENT IN EARLY EGYPT DIFFER FROM THOSE IN SUMER?

THE DEVELOPMENT OF CIVILIZATION IN EGYPT   25

aplomb with which he achieved it, was instrumental in shaping conceptions of kingship in the ancient Near East. After Hammurabi, unifying state religions would play an increasingly important role in the policies of Near Eastern kings. Hammurabi had also demonstrated the effectiveness of writing as a political tool. Diplomacy, the keeping of extensive archives, international relations—all would characterize subsequent Near Eastern empires. So too would the claim that kings should be the protectors of the weak and the arbiters of justice within their realms. Hammurabi's law code built on the traditions of previous Mesopotamian kings, but it was his greatness that transformed law giving into an imperative for any ambitious ruler of a future Near Eastern kingdom or empire.

THE DEVELOPMENT OF CIVILIZATION IN EGYPT

In what ways did patterns of development in early Egypt differ from those in Sumer?

The other primary civilization of the Mediterranean world arose in Egypt, roughly contemporaneous with Sumer. Unlike the Sumerians, however, the Egyptians did not have to wrest their survival from a hostile and unpredictable environment. Instead, their land was renewed every year by the regular summer flooding of the Nile River. The rich black soil the river left behind made the Nile Valley the richest agricultural region in the entire Mediterranean world. Much of the distinctiveness of Egyptian civilization rests on this fundamental ecological fact.

Ancient Egypt was a narrow, elongated land, snaking along both banks of the Nile for a distance of more than six hundred miles (1100 km). Outside this narrow band of territory—which ranged in breadth from a few hundred yards to no more than fourteen miles (23 km)—lay an uninhabitable desert, where rain almost never falls. This contrast, between the fertile "Black Land" along the Nile and the dessicated "Red Land" beyond, deeply influenced the way the Egyptians viewed their world. Egypt itself they saw as the center of the cosmos. The lands beyond Egypt, however, they regarded as lying utterly beyond the boundaries of civilized life.

As a land, a nation, and a civilization, Egypt has enjoyed remarkable continuity. The roots of Egyptian cul-

ture date back to at least 5000 B.C.E., and Egypt would continue to thrive as an independent and distinct culture until its assimilation into the Roman empire after 30 B.C.E. From about 3000 B.C.E. on, the defining element in ancient Egyptian culture would be the pervasive influence of a powerful, centralized, bureaucratic state headed by pharaohs whom their people regarded as living gods. No other ancient civilization was ever governed so tightly for so long as was Egypt.

For convenience, historians divide ancient Egyptian history into "kingdoms" and "periods," as shown in the accompanying chronology. As did ancient Egyptian writers, modern historians generally portray the Old, Middle, and New Kingdoms as times of strength, prosperity, and unity, separated by chaotic interludes when central authority broke down (the First, Second, and Third Intermediate Periods). Although we will follow these traditional divisions, we should note that they do reflect the centralizing (and perhaps therefore distorting) perspective of the ancient Egyptian state itself. As we will see, the First Intermediate Period in particular looks much less chaotic and dismal if viewed from the perspective of local society rather than from the pharaohs' court.

PREDYNASTIC EGYPT (C. 10,000–3100 B.C.E.)

Prehistoric or Predynastic Egypt is the period prior to the emergence of the pharaohs and their dynasties. In the Fertile Crescent, population growth forced the Mesopotamians to adopt settled agricultural life during the eighth millennium B.C.E. In Egypt, by contrast, a growing population was able to sustain itself through hunting and gathering until the fifth millennium B.C.E.

CHRONOLOGY

EGYPTIAN KINGDOMS AND PERIODS

Predynastic Period	c. 10,000–3100 B.C.E.
Archaic Period	3100–c. 2686 B.C.E.
Old Kingdom	c. 2686–2160 B.C.E.
First Intermediate Period	2160–2055 B.C.E.
Middle Kingdom	2055–c. 1650 B.C.E.
Second Intermediate Period	c. 1650–1550 B.C.E.
New Kingdom	1550–1075 B.C.E.

ANCIENT EGYPT AND THE NEAR EAST

Notice the peculiar geography of Egypt and the role played by the Nile. How did the lands on either side of the Nile help to isolate Egyptian culture from outside influences? Consider how the Nile helped to forge Egypt into a unitary state under a powerful centralized government. How was Egypt's relationship to the Nile as potentially hazardous as it was beneficial?

The first known permanent settlement in Egypt dates to approximately 4750 B.C.E., and was situated at the southwestern edge of the Nile Delta. Thereafter, the Egyptian economy rapidly became more sophisticated. By around 3500 B.C.E. this region already had extensive commercial contacts with the Sinai Peninsula, the Near East, and with the upper reaches of the Nile, several hundred miles to the south. Copper was a particularly important import, which allowed the residents to replace stone tools with metal ones. Many other Neolithic farming centers have also been discovered in or near the Nile Delta, where a degree of cultural unity was already developing. In later centuries, this area would be known as Lower Egypt (so called

IN WHAT WAYS DID PATTERNS OF DEVELOPMENT IN EARLY EGYPT DIFFER FROM THOSE IN SUMER?

THE DEVELOPMENT OF CIVILIZATION IN EGYPT   27

because it was downstream). Comparable developments were also occurring outside the delta. By the end of the Predynastic Period, Egyptian material culture and burial practices were more or less uniform from the southern edge of the delta all the way south to the First Cataract, a vast length of the Nile known as Upper Egypt.

Although towns in Lower Egypt were more numerous, it was in Upper Egypt that the first true Egyptian cities developed. By 3200 B.C.E., important communities such as Nekhen, Naqada, This, and Abydos had all developed high degrees of occupational and social specialization. They had encircled themselves with sophisticated fortifications and had begun to build elaborate temple and shrine complexes to honor the local gods.

This last fact may be key to explaining the growth of these towns into cities. As with Uruk in Mesopotamia, their role as regional cult centers attracted travelers and encouraged the growth of industries. But unlike in Mesopotamia, travel in Upper Egypt was relatively easy. Almost all Egyptians lived within sight of the Nile, enabling the great river to serve as a highway binding the nation together. It was due to the Nile,

therefore, that the region south of the delta, despite its enormous geographical length, was able to forge a cultural, and eventually political, unity.

The Nile fed Egypt and united it. The river was a conduit for people, goods, and ideas. Centralizing rulers could project their power quickly and effectively up and down its course. By the close of the Predynastic Period the cities of Upper Egypt had banded together in a confederacy under the leadership of This. The pressure exerted by this confederacy in turn forced the towns of Lower Egypt to adopt their own form of loose political organization. By 3100 B.C.E., the rivalry between these competing regions had given rise to the two nascent kingdoms of Upper and Lower Egypt.

THE UNIFICATION OF EGYPT: THE ARCHAIC PERIOD (3100–C. 2686 B.C.E.)

With the rise of powerful rulers who sought to unify these two Egyptian kingdoms, we enter the dynastic phase of Egyptian history. Among their number was an Upper Egyptian strongman known as "King Scorpion" from a mace head that details—in pictures—his assertion of authority over most of Egypt. Another, King Narmer, appears to have ruled both Upper and Lower Egypt, and may be identical with the legendary king Menes or Min whom later Egyptians credited with this feat. These kings probably orginated at Abydos in Upper Egypt, where they were also buried. Their administrative capital, however, was at Memphis, the capital city of Lower Egypt and an important center for trade with the Sinai Peninsula and the Near East.

Following the political unification of Upper and Lower Egypt, the basic features of pharaonic rule took shape along lines that would persist for the next three thousand years. From a very early date, the pharaoh was identified closely with divinity. By the first and second dynasties, he was already regarded as the earthly manifestation of the falcon god Horus. These early

Narmer Palette, c. 3000 B.C.E. One side shows King Narmer, wearing the white crown of Upper Egypt, striking an enemy with a mace, while Horus, the falcon god, looks on approvingly. The other side shows the king, wearing the red crown of Lower Egypt, viewing the decapitated corpses of his enemies. The long-necked beasts with intertwined necks represent the two kingdoms of Upper and Lower Egypt, united under Narmer.

Egyptian rulers thus laid claim to a sacred nature quite different from the early Sumerian *lugal*, a mortal who merely enjoyed divine favor.

How these early pharaohs established their claims to divinity is a mystery. We do know, however, that legitimating their rule over all Egypt was a difficult task. Local civic and religious loyalties remained strong, and for centuries Lower Egyptians would continue to see themselves as distinct from their cousins to the south. It seems probable that the pharaohs' claim to divinity was one approach to solving this problem of political unity. But however precisely the sacralization of Egyptian kingship occurred, it was an astonishing success. By the end of Dynasty 2 the pharaoh was not just the ruler of Egypt; in a sense he *was* Egypt, a personification of the land, the people, and their connection to the divine.

LANGUAGE AND WRITING

The development of hieroglyphic writing in Egypt dates to around 3200 B.C.E. As in Sumer, writing quickly became an important tool for Egyptian government and administration. Unlike Sumerian cuneiform, however, Egyptian hieroglyphics never evolved very far toward a system of phonograms. Instead, the Egyptians developed a simpler, faster, cursive script for representing hieroglyphics called *hieratic*, which they employed for the everyday business of government and commerce. They also developed a shorthand version of hieratic that scribes could use for rapid note taking.

Little early hieratic writing remains, due largely to the perishable nature of the medium on which it was usually written: papyrus. Produced by hammering, drying, and processing river reeds, papyrus was lighter, easier to write on, and more transportable than the clay tablets used by the Sumerians. When sewn together into scrolls, papyrus also made it possible to record and store large quantities of information in a very small space. Production of this versatile writing material remained one of Egypt's most important industries throughout ancient times, and papyrus became a valuable export item.

THE OLD KINGDOM (C. 2686–2160 B.C.E.)

Because so few of the routine business documents of the Old Kingdom survive, writing a history of this period is a difficult venture. Funerary texts from the tombs of the

The Rosetta Stone. This famous stone, carved in 196 B.C.E., preserves the text of a single decree in three different forms of writing: hieroglyphs (top), demotic (middle), and classical Greek (bottom). Nineteenth-century scholars were able to use the classical Greek text (which they could read) to decipher the hieroglyphic and demotic scripts (which had previously been undecipherable).

elite allow us to say something about the achievements of particular individuals and to gain an impression of everyday life, but we know little about the lives of ordinary Egyptians. Further complicating our problem is the attitude of the Old Kingdom Egyptians themselves. Because of their belief in the unchanging, cyclical nature of the universe, history and historical events as we think of them were of little interest to them. It is unlikely, therefore, that we will ever be able to reconstruct their history in any detailed way.

One feature that emerges clearly, however, is the degree to which the pharaohs of the Third Dynasty (c. 2686–2613 B.C.E.) had already built a powerful, centralized administration devoted to the self-glorification of pharaoh himself. Because pharaoh *was* Egypt, all the resources of Egypt belonged to him. Long-distance trade was entirely controlled by the pharaoh, and sys-

IN WHAT WAYS DID PATTERNS OF DEVELOPMENT IN EARLY EGYPT DIFFER FROM THOSE IN SUMER?

THE DEVELOPMENT OF CIVILIZATION IN EGYPT   29

tems for imposing taxation and conscripting labor were already well developed. To administer their kingdom, the pharaohs installed centrally appointed local governors (known to the Greeks as *nomarchs*), many of whom were members of the pharaohs' own family. Old Kingdom pharaohs kept tight control over the nomarchs and their armies of lesser officials, in order to prevent them from establishing local roots in the territories they administered.

Scribal literacy was widespread in Old Kingdom Egypt, because writing was critical to the management and exploitation of Egypt's vast wealth. And because literate bureaucrats were absolutely essential to Egyptian government at both the national and local level, scribal administrators enjoyed power, influence, and status. Even a child just beginning his scribal education was considered worthy of great respect. Training was difficult, but a Middle Kingdom document called "The Satire of the Trades" reminded the scribe in training how much his education would benefit him in the end, and how much better off he would be than the practitioners of other trades.

IMHOTEMP AND THE "STEP PYRAMID"

At the dawn of the Old Kingdom, we meet one of the greatest administrative officials in the history of Egypt. Imhotep rose through the ranks of the pharaoh's administration to become the right-hand man to Djoser, an early pharaoh of the Third Dynasty. Earlier pharaohs had already devoted enormous resources to their burial arrangements at Abydos. It was Imhotep, however, who designed the "Step Pyramid," the first great monument in world history built entirely of

Top: **Step pyramid of King Djoser,** C. 2650 B.C.E.
Bottom: **Pyramids at Giza,** with the Great Pyramid of Khufu (Cheops) in the center, C. 2560 B.C.E.

dressed stone. It was not only to be the final resting place of Djoser, but a symbol and expression of his transcendent power as pharaoh.

Imhotep may have intended his pyramidal design to evoke the descending rays of the life-giving sun; or perhaps the pyramid was meant as the means for the pharaoh's *ka* (his spirit after death, see below) to ascend into the sky and incorporate itself with the sun on its journey west after death. But no one could miss the pharaonic power that lay behind its construction. Imhotep had set a precedent to which pharaohs throughout the Old Kingdom would aspire. Ultimately, the competition to build ever larger and more elaborate pyramids would ruin them.

Old Kingdom Egypt reached its height in the Fourth Dynasty (2613–2494 B.C.E.), the period during which the great pyramids of Giza were built. These were true pyramids, which have become timeless symbols of Egyptian civilization. The Great Pyramid, built for the pharaoh Khufu, was originally 481 feet high and 756 feet along each side of its base, constructed from more than 2.3 million limestone blocks and enclosing a volume of about 91 million cubic feet. With the exception of a few airways, passages, and burial chambers, the structure is completely solid. In ancient times, the entire pyramid was encased in gleaming white limestone and topped by a massive capstone gilded in gold, as were the two massive but slightly smaller pyramids at the site built for Khufu's successors Khafre (Chephren) and Menkaure (Mycerinus). During the Middle Ages, the builders and rulers of the great Muslim capital of Cairo stripped the casing stones from these pyramids and used them to construct and fortify their new city. The gold capstones had probably disappeared already. But in antiquity these pyramids, with their gleaming limestone facing, would have glistened brilliantly in the bright Egyptian sunshine, making them visible for miles in all directions.

Once thought to have been the work of slaves, the pyramids were in fact raised by tens of thousands of peasant workers, who labored most intensively upon the pyramids while their fields were under water. Some workers may have been conscripts, but most probably participated willingly in the building projects, which glorified the living god who ruled them and served as their link to the cosmic order. There can be little doubt, however, that the massive investment of labor and wealth required to build the great pyramids put grave strains on

> Once thought to have been the work of slaves, the pyramids were in fact raised by tens of thousands of peasant workers, who labored most intensively upon the pyramids while their fields were under water.

Egyptian society. Natural resources were exploited more intensively than ever before; governmental control over the lives of individual Egyptians increased; and the number of administrative officials employed by the state grew ever larger. At the same time, however, a gap was opening between the centralizing religious pretensions of the pharaoh and the continuing loyalties of Egyptians to their local gods and their local leaders. These tensions would ultimately spell the end of the Old Kingdom and usher in the important changes of the First Intermediate Period.

SOCIETY IN OLD KINGDOM EGYPT

The social pyramid of Old Kingdom Egypt was extremely steep. At its apex stood the pharaoh and his family. During the Third and Fourth Dynasties their status, prestige, and power were so great as to set them entirely apart from all other Egyptians. There was a class of nobles, but until the Fifth Dynasty, their primary role was to serve as priests and officials of pharaoh's government. Despite their subordination to pharaoh, however, Egyptian elites lived in considerable luxury. They owned extensive estates with exotic goods and fine furniture. They kept dogs and cats and monkeys as pets and hunted and fished for sport.

Beneath the tiny minority represented by royalty and nobility was everyone else. Most Egyptians were poor, living in crowded conditions in simple mud-brick dwellings. During the period of prosperity, however, skilled artisans—jewelers, goldsmiths, and the like—could elevate themselves and enjoy nicer surroundings, though we should not think of them as anything like a "middle class." Potters, weavers, masons, bricklayers, brewers, merchants, and schoolteachers also enjoyed some measure of respect and prestige, as well as a higher standard of living than most other Egyptians. The vast majority of Egyptians, however, were peasants: unskilled laborers who provided the brute force necessary for agriculture and construction. Beneath them were slaves, typically captives from foreign wars rather than native Egyptians. But despite the theocratic nature of pharaonic rule and the enormous demands the pharaohs placed on Egypt's wealth, Egyptian society does not appear to have been particularly oppressive. Even slaves had certain legal rights, including the ability to own, dispose of, and bequeath personal property.

IN WHAT WAYS DID PATTERNS OF DEVELOPMENT IN EARLY EGYPT DIFFER FROM THOSE IN SUMER?

THE DEVELOPMENT OF CIVILIZATION IN EGYPT   31

WOMEN IN THE OLD KINGDOM

Egyptian women also enjoyed an unusually high degree of legal status and protection by the standards of the ancient world. They were not allowed to undergo scribal training or serve as important officials, but short personal notes between women of social standing suggest at least some degree of female literacy. In times of crisis, a woman of the royal family might assume pharaonic authority, although usually she would represent herself in rather mannish fashion. Egyptian women had standing before the courts as their own persons; they could initiate complaints (including suing for divorce), defend themselves, bear witness, and possess property on their own, without the male guardian or representative who was typically required of women in other ancient societies.

None of this should obscure the fact that Egypt was, at its heart, a rigidly patriarchal society. Aside from the role of priestess, women were barred from state office. While most Egyptians practiced monogamy, important and powerful men could and did keep harems of lesser wives, concubines, and female slaves. Furthermore, any Egyptian man could practice sexual freedom, married or not, with legal impunity; a wife who did so was subject to severe legal punishments. Gender divisions may have been less clearly defined among the peasantry than they were among the elites. Peasant women often worked in the fields during the harvest, and carried out a number of menial but vital tasks. As usual in the ancient world, however, we can only glimpse the lives of Egyptian peasants through the eyes of their social superiors.

> The Egyptians did devise effective irrigation and water-control systems, but they did not adopt such labor-saving devices as the wheel until much later than the Sumerians, perhaps because the available pool of peasant manpower seemed inexhaustible in densely populated Egypt.

SCIENCE AND TECHNOLOGY

Their monumental architecture notwithstanding, the Egyptians lagged behind the Sumerians and Akkadians in science and mathematics, as they did in technology generally. Only in the calculation of time did the Egyptians make notable advances. The solar calendar they developed was far more accurate than the Mesopotamian lunar calendar; adopted for Rome by Julius Caesar, it is the direct ancestor of our modern western calendar. The Egyptians did devise effective irrigation and water-control systems, but they did not adopt such labor-saving devices as the wheel until much later than the Sumerians, perhaps because the available pool of peasant manpower seemed inexhaustible in densely populated Egypt. Nor did the laws and other "civil" documents produced by the lugals of Mesopotamia have any Old Kingdom parallels. The Egyptians of the Old Kingdom apparently had no need for written law: the law was whatever their pharaoh, a living god, proclaimed it to be.

EGYPTIAN RELIGION AND WORLD VIEW

Old Kingdom Egyptians saw themselves as utterly set apart from all other civilizations. Egyptians' confidence in their own superiority stemmed from their self-conscious awareness of the uniqueness of their country, nurtured by the Nile and guarded by the brutal deserts and vast seas that surrounded it. For Egyptians, it was simply self-evident that their country was the center of the world.

Although the Egyptians constructed a variety of creation myths about the world, they did not concern themselves greatly with how humanity came to exist. Rather, what mattered to the Egyptians was the means by which life itself was created and re-created in an endless cycle of renewal. This cyclical conception gave a certain repetitive, predictable, and ultimately static cast to the way Egyptians perceived the cosmos. They viewed many phenomena as cyclical events, not surprising given the dependence of these people on the annual cycles of the Nile.

At the heart of Egyptian religion lay the myth of the gods Osiris and Isis, brother and sister, husband and wife, and two of the "original" nine gods in Egyptian belief. Osiris was the first to hold kingship on earth, but his brother Seth wanted the throne for himself. Seth betrayed and killed Osiris, sealing him in a coffin. Through great effort, Isis retrieved the corpse, but Seth seized it once again, hacked his brother into pieces, and spread his remains throughout Egypt (all Egypt could thus claim Osiris, and shrines to him were prevalent throughout the land). Still undeterred, Isis sought the help of Anubis, the god of mummification, and together they managed to reassemble Osiris. Isis then revived Osiris long enough to conceive a child by

Funerary Papyrus. The scene shows the heart of a princess of the Twenty-first Dynasty being weighed in a balance before the god Osiris. On the other side of the balance are the symbols for life and truth.

him, who became the god Horus. With the help of his mother's magic, Horus withstood the assaults of Seth and his henchmen; Horus and Seth then competed over the vacant throne of Osiris until finally Horus prevailed and avenged his father.

This mythology was extremely important to the Egyptians. The tale of Osiris is a myth about life arising out of death, but it is not a resurrection story: Osiris was revivified only temporarily. The notion the tale embodies, of new life arising from the dead, may have arisen in the earliest farming settlements of Egypt, where already bodies were being interred with extensive grave goods and special care. The promise of the continuation of life—rhythmic, cyclical, inevitable—as embodied by Osiris made him an important agricultural deity to the Egyptians.

THE EGYPTIAN DEATH CULT

Osiris was also a central deity in the death cult of the Egyptians. Unlike the Sumerians, the Egyptians did not have a bleak view of death and the underworld. Death was an unpleasant rite of passage, a necessity to be endured on the way to an afterlife that was more or less like one's earthly existence, only better. But the passage

was not automatic and was full of dangers. After death, the deceased's *ka*, or otherworldly existence, would have to roam the underworld, searching for the House of Judgment. Demons and evil spirits might try to frustrate the *ka*'s quest to reach the House of Judgment, and the journey might take some time. If successful and judged worthy, however, the deceased would then enjoy immortality as an aspect of Osiris.

Because of their beliefs about death, the Egyptians developed elaborate rituals for dealing with it. It was first of all crucial that the corpse be preserved: this is why the Egyptians developed their sophisticated techniques of embalming and mummification. The body was desiccated, all its vital organs removed (except for the heart, which played a key role in the final judgment), then the body was treated with chemicals to preserve it. A funerary portrait mask was also placed on the mummy before burial, so that the corpse would still be recognizable in death despite being wrapped in hundreds of yards of linen. To sustain the deceased on his or her journey through the underworld, food, clothing, utensils, and other items of vital importance would be placed in the grave along with the body. In the third millennium this privilege was reserved for the royal family alone, but by the Middle Kingdom participation in these death rituals had become accessible to many Egyptians.

IN WHAT WAYS DID PATTERNS OF DEVELOPMENT IN EARLY EGYPT DIFFER FROM THOSE IN SUMER?

THE DEVELOPMENT OF CIVILIZATION IN EGYPT   33

The careful detail with which Egyptians confronted death has often led to the erroneous assumption that theirs was a "death culture," completely obsessed with the problem of death. In fact, Egyptian practices and beliefs were mostly life affirming, and the role of Osiris (also, remember, a god of returning life) and the underworld were viewed not with horror, but with hope. The Egyptians' confidence in the cyclical nature of the cosmos meant that life always triumphed.

Binding together this endless cycle of life, death, and the return of life was *ma'at*. Like many words in the Egyptian language, it has no exact English equivalent. Our concepts of harmony, order, justice, and truth would all fit comfortably within *ma'at*, though none of these words captures its entire sense. Both the abstract notion and its personification as a female deity named Ma'at were what kept the universe running in its serene, repetitive, predictable fashion. Thus, unlike the Sumerians, the Egyptians of the Archaic Period and the Old Kingdom were a supremely confident and optimistic people. They believed that they lived at the center of the created universe, a paradise where stability and peace were guaranteed by *ma'at* and their connection to it through their pharaoh, who was the earthly manifestation of the gods who ruled them. For most of the third millennium, thanks to a long period of successful Nile floods and Egypt's geographic isolation from the outside world, the Egyptians were able to maintain their belief in this perfectly ordered paradise, in which they perceived that little if anything ever changed.

THE END OF THE OLD KINGDOM

For reasons that are not entirely clear, the Fifth and Sixth Dynasties (2494–2181 B.C.E.) witnessed the slow erosion of pharaonic power. Although pyramid construction continued, the monuments of this period were less impressive in architecture, craftsmanship, and size, mirroring the diminishing prestige of the pharaohs who constructed them. Most tellingly, however, the nomarchs began to evolve into precisely the type of hereditary local nobility that the vigorous Third and Fourth Dynasty kings had refused to permit.

Scholars are uncertain how these local officials and priests wrested power away from the pharaonic center. It may be that the extraordinarily costly building efforts of the Fourth Dynasty had overstrained the economy, leading to resentments and shortages outside the

capital city of Memphis. Other evidence points to changing climatic conditions that may have disrupted the regular inundations of the Nile, leading to famine and even starvation in the countryside. To make matters worse, small states were also beginning to form in Nubia to the south, perhaps in response to Egyptian aggression. With better organization and equipment, the Nubians may have restricted Egyptian access to precious-metal deposits in and around the First Cataract, further crippling the Egyptian economy.

With Egypt suffering these woes, pharaoh's claim to be a link to *ma'at* diminished accordingly. Instead, local governors and religious authorities began to emerge as the only effective guarantors of stability and order in the countryside. By 2160 B.C.E., when the First Intermediate Period begins, Egypt had effectively ceased to exist as a united country. The central authority of Memphis collapsed, and an ancient pattern of Egyptian history reemerged: a northern center of power, based at Nekhen, opposed by a southern regime headquartered at Thebes, with each dynasty claiming to be the legitimate pharaohs of all Egypt.

> By 2160 B.C.E., when the First Intermediate Period begins, Egypt had effectively ceased to exist as a united country.

Beneath the political chaos, however, the First Intermediate Period witnessed some important developments in Egyptian society. Wealth became much more widely and evenly distributed than had been the case during the Old Kingdom. So too did culture, and especially art. Resources that the pharaoh's court had once monopolized now remained in the localities, enabling local elites to emerge as both protectors of local society and as patrons for local artists. The result was a rapid diffusion of cultural forms throughout Egyptian society.

Warfare between the two competing pharaonic dynasties would continue until 2055 B.C.E., when the Theban Mentuhotep II conquered the northerners at Nekhen and declared himself the ruler of a united Egypt. His reign marks the beginning of the Middle Kingdom period of Egyptian history.

MIDDLE KINGDOM EGYPT (2055–C.1650 B.C.E.)

With the reestablishment of unified government, now centered in the south on Thebes, Egypt entered the period of the Middle Kingdom. Soon after Mentuhotep II's death, a usurper, the vizier Amenemhet, established himself and his descendants as Egypt's brilliant Twelfth

THE INSTRUCTION OF PTAH-HOTEP

Egyptian literature often took the form of "instructions" to important personages, meant to inculcate behaviors and ideals that would lead to success. This document, authored around 2450 B.C.E. by the vizier of a Fifth Dynasty pharaoh, sought to instruct the vizier's son and eventual successor as to the proper conduct of a high-born Egyptian official. Note the emphasis placed on ma'at *in this Old Kingdom document.*

Be not arrogant because of your knowledge, and be not puffed up because you are a learned man. Take counsel with the ignorant as with the learned, for the limits of art cannot be reached, and no artist is perfect in his skills. Good speech is more hidden than the precious greenstone, and yet it is found among slave girls at the millstones. . . . If you are a leader commanding the conduct of many seek out every good aim, so that your policy may be without error. A great thing is *ma'at*, enduring and surviving; it has not been upset since the time of Osiris. He who departs from its laws is punished. It is the right path for him who knows nothing. Wrongdoing has never brought its venture safe to port. Evil may win riches, but it is the strength of *ma'at* that endures long, and a man can say, "I learned it from my father.". . . If you wish to prolong friendship in a house which you enter as master, brother or friend, or any place that you enter, beware of approaching the women. No place in which that is done prospers. There is no wisdom in it. A thousand men are turned aside from their own good because of a little moment, like a dream, by tasting which death is reached. . . . He who lusts after women, no plan of his will succeed. . . . If you are a worthy man sitting in the council of his lord, confine your attention to excellence. Silence is more valuable than chatter. Speak only when you know you can resolve difficulties. He who gives good counsel is an artist, for speech is more difficult than any craft.

Nels M. Bailkey, ed. *Readings in Ancient History: Thought and Experience from Gilgamesh to St. Augustine*, 5th ed. (Boston: Houghton Mifflin, 1995), pp. 39–42.

Dynasty. Amenemhet retained Thebes as a center of power but also built a new capital just south of Memphis. Dynasty 12 remained in power for nearly two hundred years, producing a succession of remarkable pharaohs.

Under this dynasty, the Egyptians began to exploit more thoroughly the potential for trade to the south. They mounted expeditions to the land of Punt (probably the coast of Somalia), and secured their border with Nubia. By the middle of the nineteenth century B.C.E., Nubia was firmly under Egypt's control, and the small states and principalities of Palestine and Syria were under heavy Egyptian influence. But despite Egypt's renewed strength, the Egyptians did not incorporate the lands to the northeast into their realm. Instead, Amenemhet I constructed the "Walls of the Prince" in Sinai to guard against incursions from Egypt's Near Eastern neighbors.

The great fortifications built along Egypt's frontiers during Dynasty 12 demonstrate the great resourcefulness of these pharaohs, but they also betray a marked shift in the Egyptian outlook on the world. Long gone was the placid serenity epitomized by *ma'at*. Middle Kingdom Egyptians viewed the world beyond their borders with suspicion and fear. Egypt was not yet an imperial power, because Middle Kingdom pharaohs made no attempt to incorporate their conquests into their kingdom in any meaningful way. But unlike their Old Kingdom counterparts, the Egyptians of the Middle Kingdom were now taking a direct and active interest in events beyond Egypt's borders.

Pharaoh's position had also changed. None of the Middle Kingdom pharaohs portrayed themselves with the serene confidence of Old Kingdom depictions. Rather, in the Middle Kingdom pharaohs represented themselves as—and were expected to be—good shepherds, tenders of their Egyptian flock. *Ma'at* could not help them in these duties; only by diligently protecting Egypt from a hostile outside world could pharaohs provide the peace, prosperity, and security desired by

Sesostris III (1870–1831 B.C.E.). This powerful Twelfth Dynasty pharaoh led military campaigns into Nubia, constructed massive, garrisoned fortresses along the Nile, and dug new waterways near Aswan. More than one hundred portrait busts of Sesostris survive, all with similar features. The overhanging brow, deep-set eyes, and drawn-down mouth are all intended to communicate the enormous burden of responsibility the pharaoh bore as the ruler of all Egypt.

their subjects. Portraits of the great pharaohs of Dynasty 12 poignantly reflect the concern and anxiety with which they lived.

Egyptians had lost that vision of the Old Kingdom wherein the land was a perfect and inviolable paradise. The literature of the Middle Kingdom demonstrates the change in attitude. Among the most popular literary forms were "Instructions" to various kings, such as the *Instruction of King Merykare* or *the Instruction of Amenembet*. This literature is characterized by cynicism and resignation. A pharaoh must trust no one: not a brother, not a friend, not intimate companions. He must crush the ambitions of local nobles with ruthless ferocity, and he must always be on the lookout for potential trouble. In return for his exertions on behalf of his people, he should expect neither gratitude nor reward; he should expect only that each new year will bring new dangers and more pressing challenges both at home and abroad. Egyptian chauvinism continued; but their confident isolationism had been shattered.

Although the attitude of Middle Kingdom Egyptians may strike us as overwrought, their feelings of insecurity were justified. Egyptians recognized that they had been drawn, slowly and unwillingly, into a much wider world. But precisely because Egypt remained a highly distinct culture unto itself, this wider world beyond the frontiers of the Two Lands appeared all the more alien, frightening, and potentially dangerous to them. Middle Kingdom pharaohs were greatly alarmed by the growing power and imperial ambitions of Hammurabi of Babylon. They would soon discover, however, that even greater dangers lay much closer to home.

ONCLUSION

Starting around 11,000 B.C.E., human beings in the eastern Mediterranean world began to make a slow transition from hunter-gatherer societies into settled agricultural and pastoral communities. With the ability to produce and store surpluses, larger villages began to emerge, allowing both a greater degree of functional specialization and a wider differentiation in wealth and status among individuals and families. In Sumer, where the first cities emerged during the fourth millennium B.C.E., cities were also religious centers with elaborate temple complexes and shrines to the city's gods. By around 2500 B.C.E., a sophisticated form of writing, known as cuneiform, had emerged as an important tool in trade and in the management of these temple complexes.

The third millennium B.C.E. saw the emergence of larger city-states, with more intense warfare between them. The Mesopotamian city-states were now led by kings who claimed divine sanction for their rule and whose power and wealth set them farther and farther apart from their subjects. Around 2350 B.C.E., Sumerian political life was transformed by the emergence of a new, Semitic-speaking people, the Akkadians, whose conquests resulted in the creation of the first true empire in world history. This empire would become the model future rulers of Mesopotamia would aspire to emulate.

In Egypt, the other major center of Near Eastern civilization during these centuries, political consolidation occurred around 3000 B.C.E., a process assisted by the unique importance of the Nile River system. From that time on, Egypt would be ruled by a powerful, highly centralized bureaucracy, headed by pharaohs whom their people regarded as living gods. But despite the divisions between Upper and Lower Egypt, Egypt in the Old and Middle Kingdoms was never an empire maintained through conquest. It was a highly unified but deeply parochial society, capable of mobilizing resources on a massive scale, but almost always for internal purposes.

Behind these differences in outlook lay fundamental differences in the ecology of these two civilizations. Unlike the Sumerians, the Egyptians did not have to struggle to wrest a precarious living from a forbidding environment. So long as the annual flooding of the Nile occurred, Egyptians could feed themselves easily, with a relative minimum of social tension. This fact lent an air of confidence and ease to Egyptian art that is wholly lacking in Mesopotamia.

These two civilizations have many similarities. During the third millennium, both underwent a process of political consolidation, an elaboration of religious life, and a melding of religious and political leadership. Both engaged in massive building projects; and both mobilized resources on an enormous scale for temples, monuments, and irrigation projects. At the same time, however, each of these two civilizations developed an inward focus, verging on parochialism. Although they had some trade relations with each other, there were few signficant political or cultural interactions between them. For all intents and purposes, they inhabited separate worlds. This relative isolation was about to change, however. The next millennium would see the emergence of large-scale, land-based empires in the Near Eastern world that would transform life in Mesopotamia, Egypt, and the lands that lay between them. These are the developments we will examine in Chapter Two.

KEY TERMS

Sargon	Fertile Crescent	Ubaid
Sumerians	Gilgamesh	cuneiform
Neolithic	Imhotep	Hammurabi

SELECTED READINGS

Aldred, Cyril. *The Egyptians*. 3d ed. London, 1998. An indispensable, lively overview of Egyptian culture and history by one of the great masters of Egyptology.

Baines, J. and J. Málek. *Atlas of Ancient Egypt*. Rev. ed. New York, 2000. A reliable, well-illustrated survey, with excellent maps.

Bottéro, Jean. *Everyday Life in Ancient Mesopotamia*. Translated by Antonia Nevill. Baltimore, 2001. A wide-ranging, interdisciplinary account by an acknowledged master.

George, Andrew, trans. *The Epic of Gilgamesh: A New Translation. The Babylonian epic poem and other texts in Akkadian and Sumerian*. New York and London, 1999. The newest and most reliable translation, which carefully distinguishes the chronological "layers" of this famous text; also includes many related texts.

Hornung, Erik. *History of Ancient Egypt: An Introduction*. Ithaca, N.Y., 1999. Concise and authoritative.

Kemp, Barry J. *Ancient Egypt: Anatomy of a Civilization*. London, 1989. An imaginative examination of Egyptian social and intellectual history.

Leick, Gwendolyn. *The Babylonians: An Introduction*. London and New York, 2002. A wide-ranging survey of Babylonian civilization across the centuries.

Lichteim, Miriam. *Ancient Egyptian Literature: A Book of Readings*. 3 vols. Berkeley, 1973–1980. A compilation used by students and scholars alike.

McDowell, A.G. *Village Life in Ancient Egypt: Laundry Lists and Love Songs*. Oxford, 1999. A fascinating collection of translated texts recovered from an Egyptian peasant village, dating from 1539 to 1075 B.C.E.

Mertz, Barbara. *Red Land, Black Land: Daily Life in Ancient Egypt*. Rev. ed. New York, 1990. Emphasizes the role of the Nile and the forbidding natural environment of Egypt.

Pollock, Susan. *Ancient Mesopotamia*. Cambridge, 1999. An advanced textbook that draws on theoretical anthropology to interpret Mesopotamian civilization up to 2100 B.C.E.

Redford, Donald B., ed. *The Oxford Encyclopedia of Ancient Egypt*. 3 vols. New York, 2001. An indispensible reference work, intended for specialists and beginners.

Roaf, Michael. *Cultural Atlas of Mesopotamia and the Ancient Near East*. New York, 1990. An informative, authoritative, and lavishly illustrated guide, with excellent maps.

Robins, Gay. *The Art of Ancient Egypt*. London, 1997. An excellent survey, now the standard account.

Shafer, Byron E., ed. *Religion in Ancient Egypt: Gods, Myths, and Personal Practice*. London, 1991. A scholarly examination of Egyptian belief and ritual, with contributions from leading authorities. Excellent bibliographies.

Shaw, Ian, ed. *The Oxford History of Ancient Egypt*. Oxford, 2000. An outstanding collaborative survey of Egyptian history from the Stone Age to c. 300 C.E., with excellent bibliographical essays.

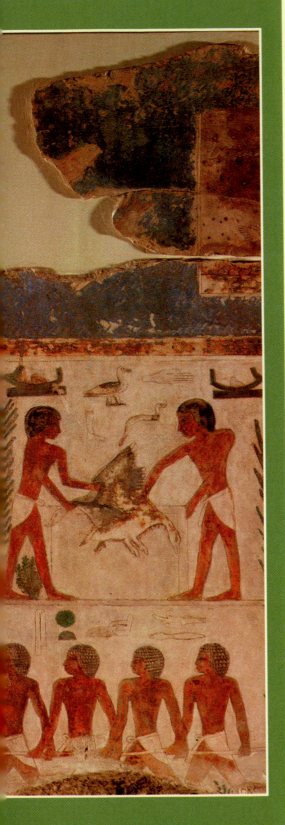

WATER: THE PRIMARY ELEMENT

Hail to thee, O Nile! Who manifests thyself over this land, and comes to give life to Egypt! Mysterious is thy issuing forth from the darkness, on this day whereon it is celebrated! Watering the orchards created by Re, to cause all the cattle to live, you give the earth to drink, inexhaustible one! Path that descends from the sky, loving the bread of Seb and the first-fruits of Nepera, You cause the workshops of Ptah to prosper!
—Egyptian Hymn to the Nile

ALTHOUGH WE ARE SEPARATED from the ancients by the vast expanse of time, we moderns also believe that water is truly the essence of life. Of course, we can quench our thirst more freely than they could. For the ancients, obtaining life-giving water often involved hardship. The first civilizations in the West were hydraulic civilizations, which means that they were expert in the management of water. These earliest civilizations began in the Ancient Near East in the delta region of the Tigris and Euphrates Rivers in Mesopotamia—the "land between the rivers"—and along the Nile River in Egypt.

Irrigation ditches and canals had to be built to carry water from the shores of these important rivers. Such construction involved the skilled management of men and material, and it eventually made some kind of bureaucratic control essential. Once these irrigation systems had been built, humankind could settle down into more permanent villages, and from these the villages empires of the Ancient Near East and Egypt arose.

While water is essential for maintaining life, the Ancients also believed that it possessed life-giving and regenerative powers. And, of course, the civilizations of the Ancient Near East and Egypt attributed these powers to their pantheon of gods and goddesses. On a more practical level, the Greeks mixed water with the fruit of their vines, and the Romans constructed aqueducts to carry water to their many cities. The management of water, then, was perhaps one of the most important challenges faced by humanity at its earliest stage of civilization.

The images and documents in the *Water* Digital History Feature at www.wwnorton.com/wciv reveal how the pursuit of water shaped the way early societies in the Near East lived and helped build the first permanent civilizations. As you explore the *Water* feature, consider the following:

• Why did the first civilizations in the West appear in the Fertile Crescent of the Ancient Near East and along the Nile in Egypt?

• How did the management of water lead to the development of vast empires in the ancient world?

• What difficulties did the management of water create?

• What does the building of massive aqueducts tell you about the ancient Romans?

CHAPTER TWO

GODS AND EMPIRES IN THE ANCIENT NEAR EAST, 1700–500 B.C.E.

IN THE SECOND MILLENNIUM B.C.E., the ancient Near East was transformed by the arrival of new population groups and by the emergence of extensive, land-based empires built up through systematic military conquest. These migrations and conquests left a great deal of destruction and upheaval in their wake. But they also led to widespread cultural assimilation, deepening economic integration, and the emergence of an international system encompassing most of the eastern Mediterranean world.

The Late Bronze Age (1500–1200 B.C.E.) in particular was a period of intensifying diplomacy, trade, and internationalism. The two great imperial powers of this age were New Kingdom Egypt and the Hittite empire of Anatolia (modern-day Turkey). Between these two empires, however, a constellation of smaller states emerged along the eastern Mediterranean coast, fully engaged in the burgeoning trade and cosmopolitan culture of the age. By the thirteenth century, nations from the southern Balkans to the western fringes of Iran had been drawn into a wide-ranging web of cultural and economic relationships. By 1250 B.C.E., these early states depended in great measure on one another for their prosperity.

This international system proved more fragile than its participants had imagined. Around 1200 B.C.E., a new wave of invasions emanating from the Aegean Sea led to the destruction of nearly every great empire of the Late Bronze Age. Centuries-old centers of political, economic, and military power—not to mention great cultural achievement—were wiped out. As a result, we enter a new world around the turn of the first millennium B.C.E., organized along profoundly different lines from the great empires of the Near Eastern past.

In the new age that was dawning, iron would slowly replace bronze as the primary component of tools and weapons. New, larger, and more brutal empires would

FOCUS QUESTIONS

• What impact did Indo-European-speaking peoples have on the patterns of Near Eastern life?

• In what ways did New Kingdom Egypt differ from the Old and Middle Kingdoms?

• What were the principal features of the Late Bronze Age international system?

• How similar was Mycenaean culture to Minoan culture?

• Why did Phoenician cities prosper during the Early Iron Age?

• What were the foundations of Assyrian imperial power?

• In what ways did the Persian empire differ from its Near East predecessors? How would you account for those differences?

• What developments marked the Hebrew transition from polytheism to monotheism?

emerge, and new ideas about gods and their relationship to humanity would begin to displace older ones. In the Iron Age Near East, two of the Western world's most enduring religious traditions—Judaism and Zoroastrianism—were born, fundamentally altering conceptions of religion, politics, ethics, and the relationship between humanity and the natural world. The Iron Age would prove a fateful historical crossroads for Western civilizations, as elements both old and new combined to reconfigure the ancient Near Eastern world.

THE INDO-EUROPEAN MIGRATIONS

What impact did Indo-European-speaking peoples have on the patterns of Near Eastern life?

In 1786 Sir William Jones, a British judge serving in India, made a discovery that transformed knowledge about prehistory and began the formal study of historical linguistics. Turning his spare time toward the study of Sanskrit, the ancient language from which the predominant languages of the South Asian subcontinent derive, Jones discovered that Sanskrit shares features of grammar and vocabulary with Latin and ancient Greek to an extent inexplicable by sheer coincidence. His interest piqued, he then examined the early Germanic tongue called Gothic, the ancient Celtic languages of Europe, and Old Persian, and found that they too exhibited marked similarities to Sanskrit. He concluded that all these languages must have evolved from a common but now-extinct linguistic source. Within another generation, the ancient language whose existence Jones had hypothesized, and the later languages derived from it, would be labeled Indo-European, reflecting their wide distribution from India to Ireland.

Indo-European linguistic forms began to appear in the Near East and eastern Mediterranean shortly after 2000 B.C.E., when speakers of early forms of Persian and Sanskrit made their way into and across the Iranian plateau, and the Hittites arrived in their historical homeland in central Anatolia. Around this same time, another group of Indo-European-speaking peoples began to move into the Aegean basin, combining with indigenous linguistic elements to produce an early form of Greek. Other groups of Indo-Europeans went east; some may even have reached western China.

The Indo-Europeans were not the only new peoples moving into the Near East during this period. Semitic-speaking peoples were also entering the region, beginning with the Akkadians and continuing with the Amorites, the Assyrians, the Phoenicians, and the Canaanites. The impact of these migrations was enormous. From the second millennium onward, Western civilizations would be dominated by cultures speaking Semitic or Indo-European languages. But however rude they may have been when they first came into contact with the older civilizations of the Near East, these newcomers generally accommodated themselves quickly, spreading and developing already established patterns of urban life and organization.

HITTITES AND KASSITES

The Hittites were one of a number of Indo-European-speaking peoples who settled in Anatolia around 2000 B.C.E. Over the course of several centuries, however, the Hittites imposed themselves and their language on the other peoples of the region as a ruling minority class.

Hittite rulers established themselves in the growing cities of central Anatolia. But they remained politically independent of one another until about 1700 B.C.E., when the ruler of one of these city-states integrated the Hittites into a larger kingdom. About fifty years later, a subsequent ruler of this larger kingdom organized his warrior nobility into a more efficient military machine, expanded the frontiers of the kingdom, and captured Hattusas, a strategic mountain stronghold that dominated the area. To reflect his new capital, the king changed his name to Hattusilis; he was the founder of the Hittite Old Kingdom.

Under Hattusilis I, the Hittites extended their power throughout the Anatolian plateau. Combining plunder with trade, Hattusilis transformed his Hittite kingdom into an economic and military power. Hattusilis's grandson and successor, Mursilis I (c. 1620–1590 B.C.E.) proved even more ambitious. He sought to control the upper Euphrates and to subjugate northern Syria. In a brilliant campaign he also drove southeastward into Mesopotamia, collecting booty and tribute until he found himself before the fabled gates of Babylon. Babylon was still the center of an Amorite kingdom, now ruled by a distant descendent of Hammurabi. Mursilis I captured and sacked Babylon in 1595 B.C.E. He then withdrew and abandoned the ruined city to its fate.

WHAT IMPACT DID INDO-EUROPEAN-SPEAKING PEOPLES HAVE ON THE PATTERNS OF NEAR EASTERN LIFE?

THE INDO-EUROPEAN MIGRATIONS   43

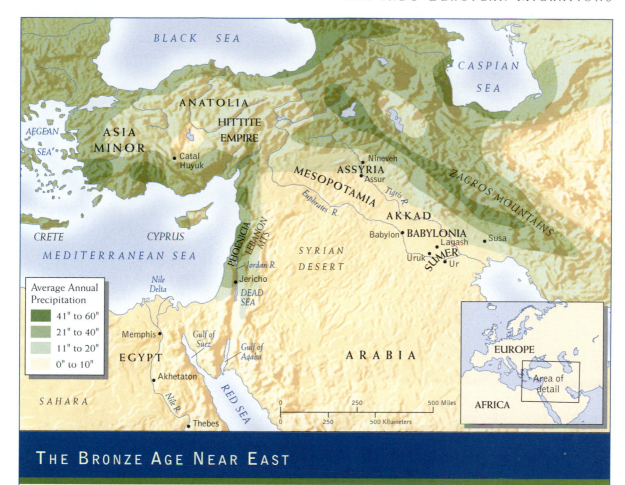

THE BRONZE AGE NEAR EAST

Notice the geographical relationship among the older centers of Sumer and Egypt, and among the newer civilizations such as Babylonia, Assyria, Phoenicia, and the Hittite empire of Anatolia. Which of the emerging cultures were most likely to show the strongest Sumerian influence, and why? Which cultures were more likely to become conduits for trade, and what was their role in spreading the Mesopotamian urban model? Also note where the major civilizations are located, and examine them in relation to the average rainfall displayed in the inset map. What does the comparison demonstrate regarding the relationship between urban activity and environmental factors such as climate?

A group known as the Kassites later moved into the devastated city and seized control of the Old Babylonian Kingdom. The origins and language of the Kassites are highly debatable; but like many previous invaders of Mesopotamia, the Kassites assimilated themselves speedily to the older civilization they found there. They presided over a largely peaceful and prosperous Babylonian realm for the next five hundred years.

The Hittites, by contrast, brought no stability to the region. Mursilis's growing strength alarmed the warrior nobility, who were not yet ready to cede so much prestige and authority to a centralized kingship. Shortly after his arrival back in his capital Hattusas, he fell victim to a palace conspiracy. After his assassination, Hittite power ebbed for the next century or so.

THE KINGDOM OF MITANNI

Like the Hittites, the Mitannians were an Indo-European minority who first imposed themselves on the native peoples of the upper Euphrates as a ruling class, and then penetrated northern Syria around 1550 B.C.E. Assuming control of territories that Mursilis had already undermined, they knitted the upper Euphrates and northern Syria into a single kingdom, the kingdom of Mitanni.

The Mitannians introduced a number of innovations into Near Eastern warfare, including a lighter,

THE NEAR EAST, C. 1400 B.C.E.

How has the spread of the urban model forced us to widen our geographical focus? Notice the proliferation of cities along the eastern shores of the Mediterranean; what does this tell us about the rise of the trade in this region of the Near East? Consider the centrality of this region in relation to the major empires of the time, as well as the emerging civilization of the Aegean basin. How crucial is trade becoming to the world of the Late Bronze Age?

horse-drawn chariot with spoked wheels, which they used to carry archers around the field and strike terror into their enemies. They were also masters of horse training and cavalry tactics. For a time, these innovations allowed them to keep the Hittites in check to their west, while to their east they reduced the powerful Assyrians to the status of a vassal kingdom. But when the opponents of the Mitannians began employing chariots themselves and using scale armor to protect both infantry and cavalry, the military balance of power quickly turned against Mittani.

Weakened by a dynastic dispute in the mid-fourteenth century, Mitanni finally collapsed in the face of renewed Hittite aggression. The Hittites allowed a rump kingdom of Mitanni to survive as a buffer state between themselves and Assyria. But the destruction of the Mitannian kingdom in northern Syria meant that the Egyptians and Hittites now embroiled themselves directly in military conflict with each other, with enormous consequences for both empires. To understand this conflict, however, and the emergence of New Kingdom Egypt as an imperial power, we need to return to Egypt at the end of the Middle Kingdom.

IN WHAT WAYS DID NEW KINGDOM EGYPT DIFFER FROM THE OLD AND MIDDLE KINGDOMS?

EGYPT IN THE SECOND MILLENNIUM B.C.E.   45

A Near Eastern War Chariot, here used for lion hunting by the Assyrian king Assurnasirpal II (883–859 B.C.E.).

EGYPT IN THE SECOND MILLENNIUM B.C.E.

> In what ways did New Kingdom Egypt differ from the Old and Middle Kingdoms?

Egypt too was transformed by the dynamic changes occurring in the early second millennium B.C.E. During the First Intermediate Period, foreigners from western Asia and Nubia penetrated the "center of the cosmos" in large numbers. Some came as immigrants; others were brought to Egypt as mercenaries. This strategy preserved Egypt from large-scale armed invasion. But when the pharaohs of the Middle Kingdom restored central government from Thebes soon after 2000 B.C.E., the confidence Old Kingdom Egyptians had once placed in *ma'at* had been irreparably shattered. Middle Kingdom Egypt was an anxious, uncertain place, uncomfortably aware that it could no longer safely ignore events beyond its borders, but not yet committed to being an actively interventionist imperial power in Nubia, Sinai, and the Middle East. Commercial contacts with all these regions were growing, as was Egyptian influence within them. But none of this made Middle Kingdom Egyptians feel secure behind their walls.

Their concerns only deepened after 1700 B.C.E., when Egypt was conquered by a foreign army called the Hyksos. These invaders—whose exact origins are unknown but who may have been Amorites from the Middle East—carved out a kingdom in the eastern delta and projected their authority over most of Lower Egypt. Hyksos domination lasted about a century, from 1650–1550 B.C.E., and came to be regarded as the great shame of Egyptian national history, despite the fact that the Hyksos established Egypt as the most significant power in the Near East. In the south, however, the Hyksos conquest did allow the Nubians to break free and found an independent kingdom called Kush. This Nubian kingdom was a much greater threat to the native dynasty at Thebes than to the Hyksos in the north; it therefore provided additional incentive to the southern pharaohs to play on nationalist sentiment by launching "wars of liberation" against the Hyksos in the north. Ultimately, this strategy succeeded. By the end of the sixteenth century B.C.E., the southern pharaoh Ahmose had driven out the invaders, establishing the Eighteenth Dynasty and a new era in Egyptian history.

THE NEW KINGDOM (1550–1075 B.C.E.)

During the New Kingdom, Egyptian civilization reached the height of its magnificence and power. Although established forms of religious, economic, cultural, and political life continued, the New Kingdom also marked a radical departure in Egyptian history and culture. The dynamism of the New

Kingdom—particularly its focus on imperialism and militarism—changed the very fabric of Egyptian life.

PHARAONIC RULE IN DYNASTY 18

Dynasty 18 ruled Egypt for more than two and a half centuries. Striking developments took place during this period. Most important, we witness the rise of a new type of nobility in Egyptian society, an aristocracy of military commanders and leaders whose wealth was acquired through war: not just plunder, but also crown lands (and the slaves to work them) received from pharaoh as rewards for their service.

The Eighteenth Dynasty was forged in battle. Ahmose himself won fame as the man who expelled the Hyksos and reunited Egypt. Soon thereafter, Ahmose and his heirs turned their attentions south, toward Nubia. By this time, gold had become the standard for Near Eastern commerce and finance. If Egypt was to prosper in this world, it needed to control the rich Nubian gold mines. Under Thutmosis I (c. 1504–1492 B.C.E.), the Egyptians also penetrated deep into Syria and Palestine. No previous pharaoh had ever held sway over so much territory.

New Kingdom pharaohs pursued an ambitious strategy of defense through offense. The embarrassment of Hyksos domination translated itself into a steely determination to prevent such an episode from occurring ever again, not by preparing for the day when more invaders might arrive, but by actively projecting Egyptian strength into regions from which danger might come. The Egyptians also learned something about battle tactics from the Hyksos, employing the horse-drawn battle chariots the Hyksos had used against them to devastating effect against their new enemies.

QUEEN HATSHEPSUT AND THUTMOSIS III

Military activity peaked during the fifteenth century, in the wake of what could have been a crisis for Dynasty 18. In 1479 B.C.E., Thutmosis II died young, leaving a youth as his heir, the future Thutmosis III. In the past, such incidents often led to instability and even changes of dynasty. On this occasion, however, family politics and a remarkable personality served as a force for cohesion and continuity. It was customary in the New Kingdom for pharaoh—himself a manifestation of a god—to marry as his official "queen," his own sister. Such brother-sister unions do not appear to have been the routine way to produce heirs: pharaohs also had a vast harem of subsidiary wives and concubines with whom to procreate. Such was the case with Thutmosis II, whose queen was his sister Hatshepsut, but whose son and heir had been borne to him by another wife.

On the death of Thutmosis II, Hatshepsut assumed pharaonic authority along with her stepson/nephew Thutmosis III. Hatshepsut was careful to mask her femininity from the majority of Egyptians. Her inscriptions typically utilize masculine pronouns, and many of her monumental statues portray her with the long, narrow beard of her male counterparts. But she was clearly the ruling force within the government. Egyptian women had always enjoyed a relatively high status compared with those in other Near Eastern cultures, and a few had even ruled as queens. Even so, however, Hatshepsut deemed it necessary, at the very least, not to flaunt the fact she was a woman to her subjects.

Hatshepsut's statecraft proved crucial to the continued vitality of the dynasty and of Egypt. For twenty-two years she reigned as co-ruler with Thutmosis III, and several military campaigns are recorded under her

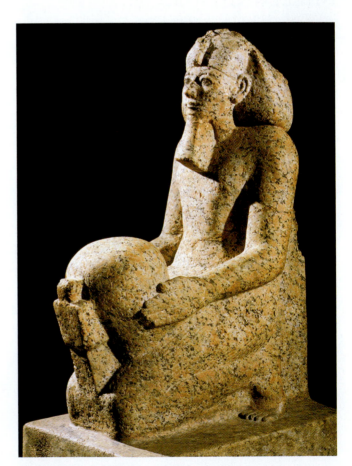

Hatshepsut as Pharaoh, c. 1460 B.C.E. Notice her masculine figure and ceremonial beard.

IN WHAT WAYS DID NEW KINGDOM EGYPT DIFFER FROM THE OLD AND MIDDLE KINGDOMS?

EGYPT IN THE SECOND MILLENNIUM B.C.E.   47

name. She is best remembered, however, for her spectacular mortuary temple, a turning point in the process by which the actual burial site and the mortuary temple to the pharaoh became separate. Cult rituals in honor of the deceased pharaoh continued to be performed at such elaborate temples. But during the New Kingdom, the famous "Valley of the Kings" near ancient Thebes was established as the pharaonic burial site: a remote location where—it was hoped—the pharaonic tombs would remain hidden and thus safe from robbers.

Thutmosis III accepted the tutelage and protection of his stepmother for many years. Eventually, however, he began to chafe at sharing rule with her. Around 1458 B.C.E., after a revolt in Palestine against Egyptian rule, she disappears from surviving records, and Thutmosis III began his thirty-two years of sole rule. He defaced Hatshepsut's monuments and removed her name from inscriptions, creating the impression that he had always ruled alone.

Despite his ingratitude, Thutmosis III was a great pharaoh. Launching a total of seventeen military campaigns, he penetrated deep into Palestine, capturing the strategic town of Megiddo (Armageddon) and seizing many of the vital port towns of the Syrian coast. Thutmosis's son Amenhotep II (c. 1428–1400 B.C.E.) continued his father's conquests, campaigning deep into Syria, crossing the Orontes River and capturing several important cities.

> By 1550 B.C.E., the Amon-Ra godhead had become something like an Egyption national god, around whom the Thebes-based Eighteenth Dynasty rallied Egypt against the Hyksos.

These campaigns were intended not only to augment Egyptian strength, but also to undermine the economic and military might of the kingdom of Mitanni. In this they were entirely successful, but to ironic effect. Mitanni was now so weakened that the Hittites were able to reassert themselves in Syria and Mesopotamia. The Assyrians also broke free of their vassalage to Mitanni, and would ultimately prove a far more aggressive foe to Egypt than Mitanni had ever been. At the time, however, the long-term consequences of Mitanni's demise were not apparent, and the Eighteenth Dynasty basked in the glow of its military accomplishments.

RELIGIOUS CHANGE AND RELIGIOUS CHALLENGE

The great conquests of Dynasty 18 brought mindboggling amounts of spoil to Egypt. Much of this wealth went to the personal glorification of the pharaoh

through grand temples, tombs, and other monuments. Another significant portion of the booty went to the military aristocracy that made such conquests possible. But vast quantities of wealth still remained, which went to propitiate the gods with thank offerings for Egypt's bountiful success. Temples throughout Egypt enjoyed the profits of conquest, and as the temples became wealthy and powerful, so too did their priests. But no temple complex made out quite so well as that dedicated to Amon in Thebes.

THE TEMPLE OF AMON

Thebes was the capital of the Eighteenth Dynasty; as the city's patron deity, Amon therefore played an important role in the dynasty's own self-image. But Amon was more than just a local god. He had grown in stature and popularity throughout Middle Kingdom Egypt. Increasingly he was identified or incorporated with the sun god Ra (thus the common New Kingdom formulation Amon-Ra). By 1550 B.C.E., the Amon-Ra godhead had become something like an Egyptian national god, around whom the Thebes-based Eighteenth Dynasty rallied Egypt against the Hyksos. The dynasty therefore had much reason for gratitude to Amon, whose support had been crucial in their efforts to reunite Egypt.

The favor shown to the priesthood of Amon at Thebes, coupled with the tremendous wealth deposited there, made the priests of Amon a formidable political and economic force. Indeed, by the end of Amenhotep III's reign (c. 1390–1352 B.C.E.), the priesthood of Amon enjoyed political clout surpassing even that of the officer class, and the priests themselves had become influential persons at the pharaoh's court. The dynasty's prestige was completely intertwined with that of Amon; but it was starting to be unclear whose was the controlling voice in this relationship.

THE REIGN OF AKHENATEN (1352–1336 B.C.E.)

All these factors came to a fateful intersection in one of history's most intriguing figures. On the death of Amenhotep III, his son succeeded him as Amenhotep IV. Amenhotep IV showed an early inclination toward

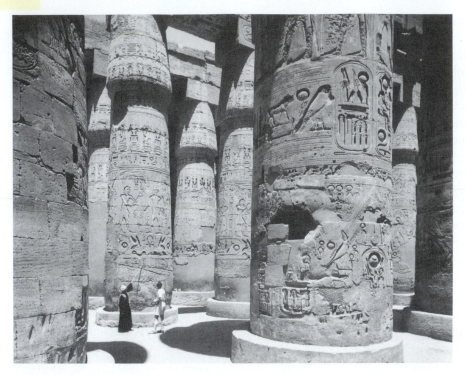

The Temple of Amon at Karnak. This massive temple, just outside Thebes, testifies to the Eighteenth Dynasty's support for the god Amon and his priests.

Great controversy still surrounds Akhenaten's motives for this religious and cultural revolution. Some see him as the world's first revolutionary intellectual, who applied imaginative force and exceptional insight to break the bonds of tradition. Others see him as a reactionary, troubled by the absorption of Ra into Amon and attempting to reassert the traditional worship of the sun. Others see him as a cagey politician, who sought to undermine the influence of Amon's priests by instituting a new religious regime.

These various explanations are not mutually exclusive. Politics and religion were inextricably intertwined in the ancient Near East, as they would be in Greece and Rome also. His own dynasty's particular identification with Amon guaranteed, however, that Akhenaten's religious revolution would also be politically revolutionary, because it would require that the legitimacy of his dynasty be re-established on new foundations.

sun-god worship, as distinct from worship of Amon: Amenhotep's earliest inscriptions exalt Ra, not as an aspect of Amon, but as a discrete divinity, visibly manifest in the light of the sun's rays. In his dedications to Ra, Amenhotep laid aside the traditional depiction of a falcon (or a falcon-headed man), replacing it with the *Aten*, the sun disc itself, its rays of light reaching toward earth. But soon the new pharaoh went much farther. He changed his name from Amenhotep ("Amon is pleased") to Akhenaten ("He is effective for the Aten"). As Akhenaten, he built a new capital halfway between Memphis in the north and Thebes in the south, calling it Akhetaten ("the place where the Aten becomes effective"), the modern site of el-Amarna. The short-lived but quite distinctive culture of Akhenaten's reign is therefore known as the Amarna Period.

Akhenaten introduced a variety of innovations into Egyptian religion and culture. Aten worship was more stringently monotheistic than the evolving view of Amon had been. Whereas Theban Amon theology recognized other gods as aspects of Amon, Akhenaten recognized only the life-giving power of light, embodied by the Aten. Unlike the ancient Egyptian deities, Aten could not be captured or represented in art. The image of the Aten, a dominant feature of Amarna-period art, is therefore an elaboration of the Egyptian hieroglyph for "light."

But despite the tremendous energy Akhenaten expended in trying to achieve this revolution, most Egyptians did not follow him. Traditional Egyptian religion may seem bewilderingly complex to us, but

Akhenaten, His Wife Nefertiti, and Their Children. The Aten is depicted here as a sun disk, raining down power on the royal family.

WHAT WERE THE PRINCIPAL FEATURES OF THE LATE BRONZE AGE INTERNATIONAL SYSTEM?

THE "INTERNATIONAL SYSTEM" OF THE LATE BRONZE AGE   49

Egyptians apparently preferred it to the remote, benevolent but impersonal god their pharaoh was offering them. The powerful priesthood of Amon also put up strenuous resistance to Akhenaten's religious innovations. To make matters worse, Akhenaten seems also to have been largely uninterested in military affairs. His exertions on behalf of his new god may even have encouraged him to neglect Egypt's interests abroad. The revolts that followed cost him the support of his military nobility. Akhenaten's revolution failed.

His failure was the harbinger of the Eighteenth Dynasty's decline. He was ultimately succeeded by Tutankhaten, who changed his name to Tutankhamon (the famous "King Tut") to reflect his rejection of Akhenaten's heresies and the restoration of the god Amon and his priesthood. The new capital city of Akhetaten was abandoned and its memory cursed; its neglect thereafter is largely responsible for its high state of preservation today. Akhenaten, meanwhile, was remembered only as "Akhetaten's heretic." His monuments were destroyed throughout the land. But the damage had been done. Egypt's position in the wider world had eroded at an astonishing rate since the outset of Akhenaten's reign, and his heir was a sickly teenager. After the early death of the boy king, confusion ensued until an important military commander named Horemheb assumed the throne in 1323 B.C.E. Horemheb maintained stability for nearly three decades but had no heir. He passed his position to another general, Rameses I, the founder of the Nineteenth Dynasty, which would restore Egypt to glory in the Near East.

THE "INTERNATIONAL SYSTEM" OF THE LATE BRONZE AGE

What were the principal features of the Late Bronze Age international system?

The fates of many nations after 1500 B.C.E., including Egypt, are only intelligible within the wider context of international relations. For the next three hundred years, the destinies of the various Near Eastern kingdoms became increasingly interwoven as an international system developed throughout the eastern and central Mediterranean.

The Late Bronze Age was an age of superpowers. As we have seen, the great pharaohs of the Eighteenth Dynasty had transformed Egypt into a conquering state, feared and respected throughout the Near East. But the pressure they applied to the kingdom of Mitanni allowed the emergence of a revived Hittite empire after 1450 B.C.E. The Assyrians also revived, and the Kassite kingdom of Babylonia remained a significant force in the economic and military relationships of the age. Between these imperial powers numerous smaller but important states emerged, concentrated along the coasts and river valleys of Syria, but extending westward to Cyprus and the Aegean Sea.

INTERNATIONAL DIPLOMACY

Though warfare remained a characteristic feature of international relations, the most powerful states of the Late Bronze Age evolved a balance of power that helped to stabilize trade and diplomacy as the period progressed. Internationalism had existed to some degree since the age of Hammurabi. In the fourteenth century, however, many nations and their leaders came to understand that security and stability helped trade to flourish, whereas war could prove disruptive and—in the long run—unprofitable for all concerned.

The archives discovered by modern archaeologists at Akhenaten's abandoned capital of el-Amarna provide us with a clear picture of this international diplomatic standard. Flurries of correspondence took place between the leaders of nations, sometimes over great matters, but often simply to "stay in touch" with one another. A language of diplomatic rank developed, in which the most powerful rulers would address one another as "brother," while the princes of lesser states showed their deference and respect to pharaoh, the Hittite king, or other powerful sovereigns by calling them "father." Rulers also exchanged lavish gifts and entered into marriage alliances with each other. Professional envoys journeyed back and forth between the centers of Near Eastern power, conveying valuable gifts and handling politically sensitive missions. In Egypt, such emissaries were often merchants, sent not only to handle matters of diplomacy but also to explore trade opportunities for pharaoh.

INTERNATIONAL TRADE

Trade became an increasingly important aspect of international relations during the Late Bronze Age. The great coastal cities of the eastern Mediterranean became

AKHENATEN, THE HEBREWS, AND MONOTHEISM

One of the great literary monuments of Akhenaten's religious revolution was his "Hymn to the Aten," extolling the life-affirming virtues of the god he sought to place atop the Egyptian religious system. Although Akhenaten's experiment failed in Egypt, it may have played a significant role in shaping the religious traditions of other societies throughout the Levant, including the ancient Hebrews.

HYMN TO THE ATEN

You appear beautifully on the horizon of the heavens, living Aten, the beginning of life! When you arise on the eastern horizon, you have filled every land with your beauty. You are gracious, great, glistening, and high over every land; your rays encompass the lands to the limit of all that you have made. . . . When you set in the western horizon, the land is in darkness, in the manner of death. They sleep in a room, with heads wrapped up, nor sees one eye the other. All their goods which are under their heads might be stolen, but they would not perceive it. . . .

Creator of seed in women, you who makes fluid into man, who maintains the son in the womb of his mother, who soothes him with that which stills his weeping, you nurse even in the womb, who gives breath to sustain all that he has made! . . . How manifold it is, that which you have made! They are hidden from the face of man. O sole god, like whom there is no other! You created the world according to your desire, while you were alone: all men, cattle, and wild beasts, whatever is on earth, going upon its feet, and what is on high, flying with its wings. . . .

The world came into being by your hand, according to how you have made them. When you have risen they live, when you set they die. You are lifetime itself, for one lives only through you.

Based on James B. Pritchard, ed. *Ancient Near Eastern Texts Relating to the Bible,* 3rd rev. ed. with supplement. (Princeton, N.J.: Princeton University Press, 1969), pp. 370–371.

PSALM 104

Bless the Lord, O my soul. . . . You are clothed with honor and majesty, wrapped in light as with a garment. You stretch out the heavens like a tent. . . . You set the earth on its foundations, so that it shall never be shaken. You cover it with the deep as with a garment; the waters stood above the mountains. At your rebuke they flee. . . . You cause the grass to grow for the cattle, and plants for people to use, to bring forth food from the earth, and wine to gladden the human heart. You make darkness, and it is night, when all the animals of the forest come creeping out. The young lions roar for their prey, seeking their food from God.

O Lord, how manifold are your works! In wisdom you have made them all; the earth is full of your creatures. . . . These all look to you to give them food in due season; when you give them to them, they gather it up; when you open your hand, they are filled with good things. When you hide your face, they are dismayed; when you take away your breath they die.

The New Oxford Annotated Bible. (Oxford: Oxford University Press, 1994).

WHAT WERE THE PRINCIPAL FEATURES OF THE LATE BRONZE AGE INTERNATIONAL SYSTEM?

THE "INTERNATIONAL SYSTEM" OF THE LATE BRONZE AGE   51

wealthy entrepôts for the exchange of a bewildering variety of goods. A single merchant vessel's cargo might contain scores of distinct items originating anywhere from the interior of Africa to the Baltic Sea. At the same time, the great states of the region continued to exploit their control of overland trade routes, relying more than ever on moving goods to an international market. Trade was rapidly becoming the lifeline of all these Late Bronze Age empires.

Busy and lucrative trade routes also served as a conduit for artistic motifs, literary and religious ideas, architectural forms, and ideas in tool making and weapon smithing. Whereas in the past such influences spread slowly and unevenly, the societies of the Late Bronze Age were now developing a very self-conscious cosmopolitanism. Egyptians delighted in Canaanite glass; Bronze Age Greeks prized Egyptian amulets; and the merchants of Ugarit admired and desired Greek pottery and wool.

This cosmopolitanism was particularly marked in large merchants towns. At Ugarit, the swirl of commerce and the multiplicity of languages may have been what impelled its citizens to develop a simpler form of writing than the cuneiform system still current throughout most of the Near East. An Ugaritic alphabet appears at the end of the Bronze Age, consisting of about thirty symbols representing consonants. Vowels had to be inferred, potentially sacrificing some clarity between reader and audience; but the alphabetic system was more easily mastered and more flexible than cuneiform for recording the heady pace of trade in the city's harbors.

The search for markets, resources, and trade routes heightened economic competition but also promoted greater understanding between cultures. After a fierce battle between Egypt and the Hittites near Kadesh (c. 1275 B.C.E.), the powerful Nineteenth Dynasty pharaoh Ramses II realized that more was to be gained through peaceful relations with his northern neighbors than through pointless warfare. The treaty he established with the Hittites served as a pillar of geopolitical stability in the region and allowed even further economic integration to develop during the thirteenth century B.C.E. But greater integration also meant greater mutual dependence. If one economy suffered in this international system, the effects of that decline were sure to be felt elsewhere.

The Temple of Ramses II at Abu-Simbel. Each of these colossal figures stands sixty-six feet high. The smaller figures at Ramses' feet represent his wives and relatives. Ramses II (1279–1213 B.C.E.) lived to be more than ninety years old and fathered at least one hundred children.

EXPANSION AND FRAGILITY

Over the course of several centuries, this integrated system of trade and diplomacy grew to encompass the entire eastern Mediterranean world. The farther this system spread, however, the more fragile it became. This fragility was heightened by the fact that many of these new markets involved societies whose own degree of "civilization" was modest at best. Their rough, warlike spirit made them unreliable partners but even more dangerous adversaries within this integrated, Late Bronze Age world. We turn now to their story.

AEGEAN CIVILIZATION: MINOANS AND MYCENAEANS

How similar was Mycenaean culture to Minoan culture?

The ancient Greeks treasured many legends about their heroic and distant past, when great men mingled with the gods, and powerful kingdoms—larger and stronger than any known to the later world of classical Greece—contended for power and glory. For a long time, however, scholars dismissed any suggestion that there might be a "prehistoric" component of Greek experience. Tales of the Trojan War, Theseus and the Minotaur, and the great adventures of Odysseus were regarded as myths—products of Greek imagination that reflected no historical truth whatsoever.

In the late nineteenth century, an amateur archaeologist named Heinrich Schliemann became convinced that these myths were in fact historical accounts. Using the epic poems of Homer as his guide, he found the site of the great city of Troy near the coast of northwest Anatolia. He also discovered a number of once-powerful citadels on the Greek mainland, including the home of the legendary king Agamemnon at Mycenae. Soon thereafter, Sir Arthur Evans found a large palace at Knossos on the island of Crete that predated any of the major citadel centers on the Greek mainland. Evans dubbed this wealthy and magnificent culture "Minoan," after King Minos, the powerful ruler who later Greeks believed had once dominated the Aegean Sea from Crete.

Although many of their initial conclusions were erroneous, the discoveries by Schliemann and Evans forced a reevaluation of Greek civilization and its roots. It is now clear that Bronze Age Greece (or, as it is more often termed, Mycenaean Greece, after the mighty kingdom of Greek myth based at Mycenae) was an important and well-integrated part of the Mediterranean world during the second millennium B.C.E., and that the foundations of classical Greek culture were established during this period. Much about these cultures remains mysterious. But their importance can no longer be denied.

THE MINOAN THALASSOCRACY

In the fifth century B.C.E. the Athenian historian Thucydides wrote that King Minos had ruled a "thalassocracy," that is to say, a sea empire. Until Evans's discoveries at Knossos, Thucydides' claim seemed fanciful. It now appears that he was substantially correct.

Minoan civilization flourished from about 1900 to 1500 B.C.E., making it contemporary with Middle Kingdom Egypt and the Hittite Old Kingdom. Minoan success depended on overseas trade. They exchanged a range of exotic goods with Egypt, southwest Anatolia, and Cyprus. Through Cyprus, the Minoans also had contacts with the Levantine coast of modern-day Lebanon and Syria. Artistic influences also traveled along these trade routes; among much else, Minoan-style paintings appear regularly from this period in the Nile delta and in the Levant.

One focus of Minoan commercial activity was clearly the mainland of Greece. The presence of a wide variety of Minoan objects there, including pottery, metalwork, and textiles, suggests the export of Minoan technologies, and perhaps even Minoan craftworkers, from Crete to the mainland. But the exact nature of the relationship between Minoan Crete and Mycenaean Greece remains

CHRONOLOGY

CIVILIZATIONS OF THE LATE BRONZE AGE

Minoan civilization	1900–1500 B.C.E.
Mycenaean civilization	1600–1200 B.C.E.
Near Eastern international "system"	1550–1200 B.C.E.
New Kingdom Egypt	1550–1075 B.C.E.

Cretan Labyrinth Coin. According to legend, King Minos of Crete built a labyrinth to pen in the Minotaur, part man, part bull. This coin from about 300 B.C.E. shows the labyrinth as the emblem of Knossos.

controversial. Before 1600 B.C.E., the Minoans were clearly much more sophisticated than the mainland Greeks. As a result, they may have been able to dominate the inhabitants of Greece's rocky landscape, at least commercially and perhaps politically. The myth of Theseus and the Labyrinth claims that the hero went to Crete as a hostage, intending to free Athens from the heavy tribute laid on the city by King Minos. Might this story preserve a memory of a time when Crete did so dominate the Greeks of the mainland?

Close contacts between the Minoans and the mainland led to a variety of developments in Mycenaean Greece. The quality of material culture increased, and the mainland was drawn more tightly into the network of international commercial and diplomatic relationships that characterized the Near East during these centuries. The inhabitants of the mainland learned how to build great fortified palaces, hybrids of the Minoan palaces and the imposing strongholds the Hittites favored. The mainland Greeks became famous throughout the Near East as mercenaries. The Greeks also learned to write from the Minoans, taking the Minoan script and modifying it to suit their own language better. The resulting script is the one Sir Arthur Evans called Linear B—the earliest written form of Greek.

THE MYCENAEANS

When Linear B was finally deciphered in the 1950s, it turned the world of Greek scholarship decisively toward a reckoning with the Bronze Age past. Until then, scholars could continue to wonder whether the impressive sites unearthed by Schliemann, Evans, and others had anything at all to do with the story of classical Greek civilization. That Linear B represented an ancient but unmistakably Greek dialect proved conclusively that Greek history stretched well back into the Bronze Age. But what role did the Mycenaean Greeks play in that story?

Greek-speaking Indo-Europeans entered Greece in several waves. But there was never a single, decisive moment at which Greece became "Greek." As the eminent Mycenaean scholar John Chadwick has suggested, during the Middle and Late Bronze Age the Greeks were always in the process of "becoming Greek."

Mycenaean civilization represents the culmination of this process. By 1500 B.C.E., powerful citadels dotted the Greek landscape, ruled by warriors who touted their martial prowess on their gravestones and had themselves buried with their implements of war. These early rulers based their authority on their ability to lead men successfully into battle and to reward their followers with plunder. The most successful of them managed to gain control of strategic sites from which they could exploit the major routes through Greece, while never straying too far from the sea, where they engaged in both trade and piracy. By the thirteenth century B.C.E., some rulers had carved out territorial kingdoms with as many as one hundred thousand inhabitants, dwarfing the typical Greek city-state of the Classical Period.

These palace centers were an adaptation of a Near Eastern model; but their massive size was not ideally suited to the Greek landscape. In war also, Mycenaean imitation of Near Eastern examples had its limits. Although Mycenaean kings cherished the war chariots used by their Near Eastern contemporaries, such chariots were highly impractical on Greece's rocky terrain.

Linear B Tablet from Knossos.

MYCENAEAN GREECE

Note the mountainous landscape of Greece and how the peculiar shape of the region creates thousands of miles of coastline; consider that Greece is almost devoid of major rivers but that few places are far from the sight of the open sea. Notice that a map of "Greece" in antiquity always includes the western coast of Asia Minor as well as the islands of the Aegean. How would this dry, mountainous country surrounded by the sea potentially affect the nature of Greek civilization and its economic interests? Would the Near Eastern model be a good "fit" for Greece?

Despite these and other differences from their neighbors, the Mycenaean Greeks played an important role in the closing stages of the Near Eastern Bronze Age. By about 1400 B.C.E., they had subjugated the island of Crete, taking over Knossos and using it as a Mycenaean center. In western Anatolia, at least one Mycenaean king exercised enough influence for a Hittite king to address him as "my brother." The Mycenaeans also enjoyed great prestige in the Near East as warriors and mercenaries. It was their combined activities as traders and raiders that made it possible for the Mycenaeans to support the huge populations of their citadels; by itself, the surrounding hinterland could not begin to sustain such numbers.

The political and commercial foundations of the Mycenaean world—a powerful palace, headed by a king who was also a war leader; a warrior aristocracy; a bureaucracy of local officials; state-regulated land holdings; a redistributive economy; large territorial kingdoms—were more typical of the contemporary Near Eastern world than they were of the Greek Classical Age. Nevertheless, we can trace important features of later Greek civilization back to the Mycenaeans, including of course the Greek language. The Linear B tablets speak of a social group with considerable economic and political rights, the *damos*; this may be precursor of the *demos*, a popular group that sought full political empowerment in many Greek cities later on. The tablets also preserve the names of several Greek gods familiar from the Classical Period, such as Zeus, Poseidon, Dionysos, and (possibly) Demeter; others, however, are absent, or their identities obscured behind completely different names. Perhaps most important, however, the Classical Greeks themselves believed that they were descended from these legendary Mycenaean forebears, whom they credited with superhuman achievements. In fact, later Greeks knew little about their Mycenaean ancestors; but the impact on the Greek imagination of what they thought they knew about them was considerable.

The Mycenaean world seems to have collapsed under its own weight around the end of the thirteenth century B.C.E. What triggered this collapse is impossible to say: natural disasters, drought, famine, disease, and social unrest have all been posited as causes. But because it was such an integrated part of this international network of commercial, political, and military relationships, the reverberations from the Mycenaean world's collapse were felt across the entire Near East.

> Depopulated by as much as 90 percent over the next century, Greece entered into a "dark age" of cultural and economic isolation that would last for the next two and a half centuries. The Greeks would have to reinvent urbanism, in forms better suited to their unique environment.

THE SEA PEOPLES AND THE END OF THE BRONZE AGE

As the Mycenaean world collapsed, a wave of destruction swept from north to south across the the Near East. The nature of this devastation is obscure, because it was the handiwork of a people so thorough that they obliterated everything in their path until they reached Egypt. Were it not for the narrow victory of Ramses III in about 1176 B.C.E., we might know nothing at all of the invaders who so suddenly unraveled the international system of the Late Bronze Age.

In an inscription and relief set up at Medinet Hebu to commemorate his victory, Ramses III referred to the invaders as the "Sea Peoples." Several of the groups he named as part of this coalition were familiar to the Egyptians, who had employed them as mercenaries or confronted them as mercenaries in the pay of other leaders. From Ramses' depiction of their battle gear and dress, it is also clear that many of the Sea Peoples were Aegean. Most notable of these were the Peleset, who, after their defeat by Egypt, withdrew to populate the coast of the region named after them, Palestine.

The arc of annihilation started in the north, and may have helped to trigger the final collapse of Mycenaean Greece. Disruption of the northern trade networks must have had a profound effect upon the Mycenaean kingdoms, which suddenly faced an apocalyptic combination of overpopulation, drastic food shortages, and incessant warfare. The undermining of commerce in the north also devastated the economy of the Hittites, whose kingdom collapsed with astonishing rapidity. We catch only a few glimpses in our sources of a desperate Hittite king fighting to save Hattusas against myriad enemies.

Along the Mediterranean coast we find other clues. The king of Ugarit wrote a letter to his "brother" the king of Alashiya on Cyprus, begging his counterpart for immediate help. Poignantly, however, we have his letter only because the clay tablet on which it was written was baked hard in the fire that destroyed his palace. The letter was never sent. Ugarit was destroyed, and the Sea Peoples moved on.

The eruption of the Sea Peoples destroyed much of civilization as the Mediterranean world had known it. The destruction was not total. Cities did not all disappear, and trade did not vanish. But the Hittite empire was gone, replaced by a bewildering variety of weak, short-lived principalities. The great cosmopolitan cities of the eastern Mediterranean coast lay in ruins, and new groups—sometimes contingents of the Sea Peoples—populated the seaboard. The citadels of Mycenaean Greece also collapsed. Depopulated by as much as 90 percent over the next century, Greece entered into a "dark age" of cultural and economic isolation that would last for the next two and a half centuries. The Greeks would have to reinvent urbanism, in forms better suited to their unique environment.

Egypt of course survived the invasions, but with its major trading partners destroyed, it too went into a long decline. Assyria likewise suffered from the effects of the invasions. The next few centuries would see the Assyrians fighting for their very survival, while to the south, the peaceful and prosperous rule of the Kassites also collapsed, along with Babylon's economy.

The centuries immediately after the Sea Peoples' invasion saw no great empires arise in the Near East. The international system of the Late Bronze Age, carefully elaborated over half a millennium, had disappeared. In the wake of its destruction, however, new traditions and new cultural experiments began to emerge. New political and religious configurations took shape, and a new metallurgical technology—based on iron—began to supplant the use of bronze. Out of the ashes of the Late Bronze Age, a more enduring, more vibrant cultural world arose, the culture of the Iron Age Near East.

THE SMALL-SCALE STATES OF THE EARLY IRON AGE

Why did Phoenician cities prosper during the Early Iron Age?

With the destruction of the superpower balance of the Late Bronze Age, the geopolitical map of the Near East changed significantly. In Anatolia, a patchwork of small, largely Indo-European realms emerged from the collapse of the Hittite empire. Similar developments took place in the Levant, the eastern Mediterranean coastal area that today comprises Israel, Lebanon, and parts of Syria. For centuries, this area had been controlled by either the Egyptians or the Hittites. With the collapse of both these empires, the resulting power vacuum in the region allowed new states to emerge. As political and military powers, the small-scale states of the Early Iron Age were at best second rate. However, they had a profound impact on the intellectual and religious development of Western civilizations.

THE PHOENICIANS

The Phoenicians were Canaanites who spoke a Semitic language closely related to Ugaritic, Hebrew, Amorite, and other West Semitic dialects. Their cultural and po-

litical roots lay firmly in the ancient Near East. Phoenician cities were all independent of one another; as in Sumer, a Phoenician's first loyalty was to his or her city, not to any abstract notion of being a Phoenician.

During the Late Bronze Age, most Phoenician cities had been controlled by Egypt. The erosion of Egyptian imperial power after 1200 B.C.E. gave them the opportunity to capitalize on commercial advantages they had already established. One Phoenician city, Gubla, had been a teeming center of trade under Egyptian rule, particularly as an entrepôt for papyrus, the highly prized Egyptian writing material. This connection with the papyrus trade continued during the Iron Age, so much so that the Greek name for the city, Byblos, became the basis for the Greek word *biblion*, meaning "book." The seabeds off the Phoenician coast yielded a valuable purple-reddish dye from the murex snail—hence the Greek term "Phoenician," which essentially means "purple people." Phoenician textiles commanded a high price everywhere their merchants went. So too did timber (especially cedar) and the famous Canaanite glass. The Phoenicians also became expert metalworkers, ivory carvers, and shipbuilders.

PHOENICIAN CITIES

Tucked along a mountainous coast riven by deep valleys, Phoenician cities oriented themselves toward the sea. Phoenicians became famous as merchants and seafarers. They were also aggressive colonists, planting trading colonies across the Mediterranean. At the end of the ninth century B.C.E., colonists from Tyre established Carthage in modern-day Tunisia. Carthage would ultimately become the preeminent power in the western Mediterranean, bringing it into conflict with Rome centuries later.

CULTURAL INFLUENCE

The widespread colonial and mercantile efforts of the Phoenicians meant that they influenced cultures across the Mediterranean. Among their early overseas trading partners were the Greeks. Here the Phoenicians may have played an important role in reintroducing urban life into the Greek world after the collapse of the Mycenaean citadels. They also brought with them a number of Near Eastern artistic and literary influences. Without question, however, the most important contribution the Phoenicians made to Greek life was their alphabet.

WHY DID PHOENICIAN CITIES PROSPER DURING THE EARLY IRON AGE?

THE SMALL-SCALE STATES OF THE EARLY IRON AGE   57

PHOENICIAN COLONIZATION

Examine the map and compare the more detailed one of Palestine on p. 59. Why would overseas colonization be of such crucial importance to Phoenician city-states? Consider in what ways the Phoenicians may have been partly driven by necessity. Notice that Phoenician colonization is concentrated in the western Mediterranean; then consider that the Phoenicians were the most active merchants of the eastern Mediterranean as well. What does their westward colonization imply about the Phoenicians' aims and the level of civilization in the West as compared with the East?

As we have seen, a thirty-character alphabet had evolved at Ugarit by the end of the Bronze Age. Around 1100 B.C.E., the Phoenicians refined this writing system to twenty-two characters, all representing consonants; vowel sounds had to be inferred from context, as is still the case today with modern Arabic and Hebrew. This simpler, more flexible writing system probably helped facilitate trade and accounting. Why they chose to share their invention with the previously illiterate Greeks is less certain; they may have sought to encourage among the Greeks the type of trading and record-keeping practices with which the Phoenicians were already familiar. But whatever the explanation, the Greeks remained very aware of their debt to the Phoenicians. Later Greek legends ascribed the invention of their alphabet to Cadmus, a

Phoenician who had settled in Greece. The debt is also clear from the close relationship between Greek (alpha, beta, gamma, delta...) and Phoenician letter names (aleph, bayt, gimel, dalet...) and from the obvious similarities in letter shapes evident in the accompanying table.

THE PHILISTINES

South along the Levantine coast from Phoenicia lay the land of the Philistines. Few cultures have enjoyed historical reputations as bad as theirs. The Philistines were among the great villains of the Hebrew scriptural tradition. *Philistine* continues today as an adjective to describe a boorish, uncultured, and ignorant person. Their infamy stems from their unique position in the

Phoenician	Hebrew	Classical Greek	Modern Alphabetic
ⲕ	א	A	A
�4	ב	B	B
^	ג	Γ	G
◿	ד	Δ	D
∃	ה	E	H
Y	ו	Y	W
I	ז	Z	Z
⊟	ח	H	H
⊗	ט	Θ	T
⅃	י	I	Y
ⲕ	כ ך	K	K
(	ל	Λ	L
ⵢ	מ ם	M	M
ל	נ	N	N
‡	ס	Ξ	S
O	ע	O	O
⏌	פ	Π	P
ⳁ	צ		S
φ	ק		Q
ⴷ	ר	P	R
W	ש	Σ	S
×	ת	T	T

The Evolution of the Alphabet. This table illustrates how letter shapes changed as the Phoenician alphabet was adapted by the Hebrews, the Greeks, and the Romans (from whom the modern English alphabet derives).

and they gradually adopted a Canaanite dialect—but their material culture, behavior, and organization all exhibit close affinities with the Mycenaean world. The Philistines introduced grapevines and olive trees to the Levant from the Aegean basin. With the profits from these industries, they created powerful armies that dominated the region in the twelfth and eleventh centuries B.C.E. They also established a monopoly over metalsmithing in the southern Levant, making it virtually impossible for their enemies to forge their own weapons.

Philistine power was based on five great strongholds: Gaza, Ashkelon, and Ashdod on the coast, Ekron and Gath inland. From these heavily fortified citadels, the Philistines sought to dominate the surrounding countryside by organizing agricultural production and controlling major trade routes. An independent lord ruled over each Philistine citadel, and no doubt tensions and rivalries existed among them. But much like the heroes of Greek epic, the Philistines could set aside their differences to confederate for the purpose of waging war.

The Hebrews had good reason to fear the Philistines. Philistine pressure on the central Hebrew hill country of Ephraim was constant, threatening the holy sanctuary at Shiloh, the original resting place of the sacred Ark of the Covenant, which contained the original tablets of the law given by the Hebrew god Yahweh to Moses on Mount Sinai. In Hebrew tradition, the desperate tribes of Israel carried the Ark before them against the Philistines, only to lose it in battle and witness the destruction of Shiloh. The Philistines then established garrisons throughout the land of the Hebrews and denied them access to metallurgical technology. Meanwhile, they exacted tribute and, according to the biblical account, engaged in the typical abuses of an occupying people.

Levant at the beginning of the Iron Age, where as descendants of the Peleset—one of the Sea Peoples defeated by Ramses III—they settled, urbanized, and quickly gained the upper hand over their pastoralist neighbors in the region. Among those peoples were the Hebrews, for whom the Philistines were the great national enemy.

The Philistines retained a separate identity from the other peoples of the region for several generations; each new archaeological discovery roots this identity more firmly in their Aegean past. We know little about the Philistine language—few written materials survive,

THE HEBREWS

We will have occasion at the end of this chapter to discuss the central feature of Hebrew cultural experience, the development of their monotheistic conception of divinity. In this section, we will focus our attention on the political development of Hebrew society within the Iron Age Levant. In any discussion of Hebrew society, however, religious conceptions and practices can never be far from the surface. Like all ancient cultures, the Hebrews initially made little distinction between politics and religion. What set them apart, however

WHY DID PHOENICIAN CITIES PROSPER DURING THE EARLY IRON AGE?

THE SMALL-SCALE STATES OF THE EARLY IRON AGE   59

THE HEBREW KINGDOM, c. 900 B.C.E.

Notice the scale of the map and consider the comparatively small orbit of this world. Why did the Philistines and Phoenicians present such a perceived cultural challenge to the Hebrews? What advantages did the Philistines and Phoenicians possess, geographically and otherwise? What political and religious consequences might have resulted from the division of the kingdom of Israel after the death of King Solomon, especially the position of Jerusalem and the Temple in the south?

ORIGINS

We are blessed as historians with one of the unique achievements of the Hebrews: the Hebrew Bible, known to Christians as the Old Testament. The Bible is an unparalleled historical resource, full of extraordinary detail about cultural practices and historical events, as well as being a guide to the intellectual unfolding of the most important religious tradition of the Western world. It is not, however, a history as modern people would conceive of it. Although it contains some ostensibly historical accounts, the Bible is essentially a story about the relationship between a transcendent, creator god and the Hebrews, whom he chose to be his special people; of the covenant that was forged between them; and of the trials by which that relationship was repeatedly tested and reaffirmed.

The historical accounts contained in the first five books of the Bible are particularly problematic. Aside from the chronological difficulties posed by a series of impossibly long-lived patriarchs (Methusaleh, for example, is said to have lived for more than nine hundred years), much of this material appears to have been borrowed from other Near Eastern cultures. The creation and flood stories have Sumerian parallels; the laws and practices of the patriarchs have clear Hurrian antecedents; and the tale of Moses' childhood is virtually a replica of Sargon's legend. Even the story of the exodus from Egypt is fraught with problems from a historical standpoint. Although the Book of Joshua claims that the Hebrews who returned from Egypt conquered and expelled the native Canaanites, archaeological and linguistic evidence suggests that the Hebrews were themselves essentially inland Canaanites, who may have merged with scattered Hebrew refugees from Egypt in the aftermath of the Sea Peoples' invasions, but who for the most part had been continuously resident in Canaan for centuries. Important religious and cultural developments clearly occurred among the Hebrews of the second millennium B.C.E., but the first five books of the Bible have the look and feel of retrospective extrapolation and justification, not secure historical record.

Once we move into the so-called historical books of the Bible, the information becomes more credible; but it remains extremely difficult to confirm any of it from archaeological sources. In the Book of Judges, for example, the Hebrews appear as wandering pastoralists who were just beginning to establish

was their unusual theology and the impact it had on their development as a people. Were it not for the resilience of their religious tradition and the fundamental impact it has had on the subsequent development of Western civilizations, we would have little reason to discuss the early Hebrews at length. As it is, however, the Hebrews were one of the most important cultures in world history.

permanent settlements. The Hebrews were organized into twelve "tribes"—extended clan units in which families owed mutual aid and protection to one another in times of war, cattle raiding, and judicial dispute. Each tribe was ruled over by a "judge," who exercised the typical functions of authority in a clan-based society: war leadership, high priesthood, and dispute settlement. By the middle of the twelfth century B.C.E., these tribes had established some kind of rough territorial "turf," those in the south calling themselves Judah, and those in the north Israel.

In practice, however, the Hebrew tribes had few effective mechanisms for concerted action, a fact made plain when the Philistines conquered the Levantine coastal region around 1050 B.C.E. To meet the Philistine threat, a tighter, "national" form of government was needed. Accordingly, around 1025 B.C.E., Samuel, a tribal judge and holy man, selected a king named Saul to lead Hebrew resistance against the Philistines.

Saul, however, quickly provoked the resentment of Samuel, who withdrew his support from the embattled king. Saul also proved an indifferent general. So Samuel threw his support behind a young warrior, David, a member of Saul's court who now schemed actively to draw popular support away from Saul. Waging his own independent military campaigns, David achieved one triumph after another over the Philistines. In contrast, the armies of Saul met frequent reverses, which the biblical authors portrayed as divine retribution for Saul's own inadequacies. David, however, was not exactly a national patriot. When Saul finally drove him from his court, David first became an outlaw on the fringes of Hebrew and Philistine society, then a mercenary in Philistine service. It was as a Philistine mercenary that David fought against Saul in the climactic battle in which Saul was killed. Soon thereafter, David himself became king, first over Judah, his home territory, and later over Saul's home kingdom of Israel also.

CONSOLIDATION OF THE HEBREW KINGDOM

With David's ascension to the throne around 1000 B.C.E., the most glorious period in the political history of the ancient Hebrew kingdom began. Through cunning, opportunism, and inspired leadership, David re-

duced the Philistines to an inconsequential strip of coastal land in the south. He also defeated the neighboring Moabites and Ammonites, extending his control east of the River Jordan and Dead Sea. By David's death in 973 B.C.E., his kingdom stretched from the middle Euphrates in the north to the Gulf of Aqaba in the south, and from the Mediterranean coast in the west into the Syrian deserts beyond the River Jordan. Israel was now a serious force in the politics of the Near East, its status increased by the temporary weakness of its imperial neighbors Egypt and Assyria.

As David's power and prestige grew, he was able to impose on his subjects a highly unpopular system of taxation and forced labor. His goal was to build a glorious political and religious capital at Jerusalem, a Canaanite settlement that he transformed into the central city of his kingdom. It was a shrewd choice. As a newly conquered city, Jerusalem had no previous affiliation with any of Israel's twelve tribes, and so stood outside the ancient rivalries between them. Geographically too, Jerusalem lay between the southern tribes of Judah (of which David was a member) and the northern tribes of Israel (from which Saul had come). David also took steps to exalt the city as a religious center by making Jerusalem the resting place of the sacred Ark of the Covenant and reorganizing the priesthood of Yahweh. By these measures, he sought to forge a new national identity, focused on the House of David and its connections to Yahweh, that would transcend the old divisions between Israel and Judah.

> By David's death in 973 B.C.E., his kingdom stretched from the middle Euphrates in the north to the Gulf of Aqaba in the south, and from the Mediterranean Coast in the west to the Syrian deserts beyond the River Jordan.

CHRONOLOGY

THE TRANSFORMATION OF HEBREW SOCIETY

Early efforts to form national government	1025 B.C.E.
David crowned king of Israel	1000 B.C.E.
Split between Israel and Judah	924 B.C.E.
Fall of Judah and start of Babylonian Captivity	586 B.C.E.

THE REIGN OF KING SOLOMON (973–937 B.C.E.)

Continuing his father's policies but on a much grander scale, King Solomon built a great temple complex at Jerusalem to house the sacred Ark of the Covenant. Such visible support of the Yahweh cult played particularly well with the writers of the Hebrew scripture, who portrayed Solomon's reign as a golden age for the Hebrews.

Despite his proverbial wisdom, however, Solomon was a ruthless and often brutal ruler whose promotion of the Yahweh cult coincided with a program of despotic rule and royal self-aggrandizement. His palace complex—of which the temple was a part—allowed him to rule in the grand style of ancient Near Eastern potentates. To finance his expensive tastes and programs, Solomon instituted a variety of oppressive taxation and administrative schemes. He imposed customs duties on the lucrative caravan trade that passed through his country. With the help of Hiram, the Phoenician king of Tyre, Solomon also constructed a commercial fleet based at the head of the Gulf of Aqaba. These ships plied the waters of the Red Sea and beyond, trading among other commodities the gold and copper mined by Solomon's slaves in the southern Negev. Wealth poured into Israel as never before.

But it was not enough. To undertake his ambitious building program, Solomon required many of his subjects, particularly from the agricultural north, to perform forced labor four months out of every year. This level of oppression was too much for many Israelites. The north seethed with rebellion against the royal capital, and after Solomon's death, his son and successor was faced with revolt. Before long the united monarchy had split in two, the House of David ruling the southern kingdom of Judah with its capital at Jerusalem, the ten northern tribes banding together into the kingdom of Israel with its capital at Shechem.

Although the two Hebrew kingdoms would maintain their independence for several centuries—the north until 722 B.C.E., the south until 586 B.C.E.—the changing political situation of the Near East made their divided state increasingly vulnerable. The united Hebrew monarchy created by David and Solomon arose at a time when the traditional imperial powers in the region were temporarily in eclipse. Within a few generations of Solomon's death, however, the Hebrews and the other small states of the Near and Middle East would find themselves menaced by the revived Mesopotamia-based empire of the Assyrians.

CHRONOLOGY

EVOLUTION OF ASSYRIA IN THE IRON AGE

Assyria begins to reestablish its influence	1362–883 B.C.E.
Assurnasirpal II founds neo-Assyrian empire	883–859 B.C.E.
Birth of the Sargonid dynasty	722 B.C.E.
Destruction of the Assyrian state	612–605 B.C.E.

THE ASSYRIAN EMPIRE

What were the foundations of Assyrian imperial power?

The Assyrians were a Semitic-speaking people whose homeland lay in northern Mesopotamia. As we saw in Chapter One, by 1900 B.C.E. the Assyrians were already taking advantage of their geographical position to establish trade routes between Mesopotamia and Anatolia. They also a played an important role in spreading urban society and organization across the Anatolian plateau. Thereafter, however, they struggled to protect themselves against a series of aggressive neighbors: first the Old Babylonian empire of Hammurabi, then the Egyptians, the Mittanians, the Hittites, and finally the Sea Peoples.

This centuries-long fight for existence had a profound effect on the Assyrian world view. Starting in the ninth century B.C.E., the Assyrians would in turn become the aggressors, extending their power and influence through brutal, systematic victimization of their neighbors. Its terrors notwithstanding, their aggression helped to shape the religious and political traditions of their neighbors, extending Near Eastern culture to the Aegean basin, synthesizing a new type of imperial organization, and imparting important lessons about what did and did not make for successful governance of a far-flung, international empire.

THE MIDDLE ASSYRIAN PERIOD (1362–859 B.C.E.)

The decline of the kingdom of Mitanni in the fourteenth century gave the Assyrians their first opportunity

THE ASSYRIAN EMPIRE, C. 700 B.C.E.

Compare this map with the one on p. 86. What do you find striking about the geography of the Assyrian empire? Why would the Assyrians concentrate their efforts in the river valleys and along the coast, leaving the Syrian interior largely alone? Notice the location of the Assyrian capitals of Nineveh and Assur; how was their situation in Mesopotamia likely to affect the Assyrians' sense of their own historical identity? Consider the position of Egypt. Why did the Assyrians find it difficult to subjugate Egypt permanently, despite the violence of their conquests?

to establish themselves as a great realm. As Hittite pressure wore down Mitanni from the west, local Assyrian potentates extended their control in the east. Finally one such ruler, the governor of the city of Assur (sometimes spelled Ashur), adopted the name of his city's patron deity and declared himself king of Assyria. Assur-uballit I (1362–1327 B.C.E.) and his successors extended their power over northern Mesopotamia and attacked the Kassite kings of Babylonia, whom they regarded as usurpers. But otherwise, they did little to upset the delicate balance of power in the region.

With the succession of Tukulti-Ninurta I in 1244 B.C.E., however, the restraint was dropped. Tukulti-Ninurta was a conqueror of the first order, remembered in the Hebrew Bible as Nimrud and in Greek tradition as Ninos. Tukulti-Ninurta sacked Babylon,

carrying its Kassite king and its patron deity, Marduk, into captivity and claiming the prestigious kingship of Babylon for himself. To maintain his tenuous grip over Babylonia, however, Tukulti-Ninurta had to engage in constant campaigning. This, plus his sacrilegious treatment of the Babylonian god, alienated his own subjects, who murdered him in about 1208 B.C.E.

A century of Assyrian decline followed as its neighbors sought both vengeance and control over the vital trade routes that crisscrossed Assyrian territory. This struggle for survival continued until the close of the Middle Assyrian period, when a brutal but brilliant ruler, Assurnasirpal II (883–859 B.C.E.) revived Assyrian strength and founded the neo-Assyrian empire. Under his ruthless leadership, the Assyrians conducted aggressive military campaigns on an annual basis. The targets of Assyrian might had to pay tribute or face the full onslaught of the Assyrian war machine, which under Assurnasirpal acquired a deserved reputation for savagery and viciousness. The great Near Eastern scholar A. H. Olmstead referred to Assurnasirpal's policy as one of "calculated frightfulness," a refined name for a strategy of military terror and the extraction of protection money through plunder.

THE NEO-ASSYRIAN EMPIRE (859–627 B.C.E.)

The conquests of Assurnasirpal and his son, Shalmeneser III, inspired stiff resistance to Assyrian expansion. The northern kingdom of Israel, along with several other states in the region of Syria-Palestine, formed an alliance to stop Shalmeneser III (853–827 B.C.E.). Ultimately this coalition fought him to a standstill, forcing him to settle

for smaller victories against the Armenians to his northwest and the Medes to his northeast, until a great revolt within Assyria ended his reign. But the respite proved brief. A usurper who took the name Tiglath-Pileser III seized the Assyrian throne in 744 B.C.E. and immediately prepared a great western campaign. In his first year he demanded tribute from various western kingdoms that had not paid up for generations. Those who refused fell victim to an immediate Assyrian onslaught.

When Tiglath-Pileser III died in 727 B.C.E., many of these recently conquered states rebelled, perhaps hoping that a famiiar pattern of Assyrian dynastic instability would reassert itself on the death of the usurping monarch. But Tiglath-Pileser's son, Shalmeneser V, energetically crushed the rebellions. When he died in battle, he was quickly replaced by one of his military commanders, who took the name Sargon II (722–705 B.C.E.). With typical Assyrian historical consciousness, Sargon II regarded Sargon of Akkad as the "first"

Assyrian Winged Human-Headed Bull. This relief was found in the palace of King Sargon II (722–705 B.C.E.). It measures sixteen feet wide by sixteen feet high and weighs approximately forty tons.

Sargon; he was thus claiming to be the direct successor to a Near Eatern empire nearly fifteen hundred years in the past. The dynasty that Sargon II founded is called the Sargonid; its century of rule proved the most magnificent in all of Assyrian history.

The Sargonids extended the frontiers of the Assyrian empire from western Iran to the shores of the Mediterranean. Briefly, they even subjugated parts of Egypt. Sargon himself put an end to the kingdom of Israel and scared the southern kingdom of Judah into remaining a loyal and quiet vassal. By the seventh century B.C.E. Assyria was the unrivaled power of the ancient Near East.

THE ASSYRIAN MILITARY-RELIGIOUS ETHOS

Assyrian religious, political, and military ideas took shape in the centuries during which Assyria fought for its survival. As the Assyrians gained the upper hand, however, this ethos became the foundation for their empire's relentless conquests.

The two fundamental characteristics of this Assyrian military-religious ethos were holy war and the exaction of tribute through terror. The Assyrians were convinced that their god Assur demanded that his worship be extended through military conquest. Even more than to the king, therefore, the Assyrian army belonged to Assur; and all who did not accept Assur's supremacy were, by that fact alone, enemies of Assur's people, the Assyrians. Ritual humiliation of a defeated city's gods was therefore a regular feature of Assyrian conquests.

Frequently the conquered gods would be carried off to the Assyrian capital, where they would "live" as hostages at the "court" of Assur. Meanwhile, an image of Assur himself (usually represented as a sun disk with the head and shoulders of an archer) would be installed in the defeated city, and the conquered people would now be required to worship him. Worship of Assur did not necessarily mean that conquered peoples abandoned their previous gods altogether. But in Assyrian eyes, there was no question that Assur should be the supreme deity for all the peoples of their empire.

Rather than defeat their foes once and impose formal tribute thereafter, the Assyrians raided even their vanquished foes each year, extracting tribute by force. This strategy succeeded in terrifying Assyria's subjects and keeping the Assyrian military machine primed for battle. But perpetual reconquests did little to inspire loyalty among subject peoples, who eventually reached a point of desperation at which they had little to lose through rebellion. Moreover, these annual Assyrian invasions not only sharpened the Assyrian army, but also the forces of subjects.

Assyrian warfare was also notoriously savage. Ancient warfare was always brutal: mutilations of prisoners, decapitations, rape, and the mass deportations and/or enslavement of civilian populations were commonplace. The Assyrians, however, relished and celebrated such barbarities as did no other ancient empire. Their artwork and inscriptions revel in the butchering and torture of their enemies. Smiling Assyrian archers are shown shooting fleeing enemies

Assurbanipal Feasting with His Wife in a Garden. The head of his defeated enemy, the king of Elam, can be seen hanging from the pine tree on the left.

THE SENJIRLI STELE OF KING ESARHADDON

Set up in northern Syria by the Assyrian king Esarhaddon, this inscribed stone monument is one of the most important records of his reign. Accompanying the text (which proclaims his victories over Egypt and the Phoenician coast of Syria) was a depiction of Esarhaddon holding a cup in his right hand and a mace in his left. His left hand also grasped reins fastened to shackles holding a captured prince of Egypt and a Syrian ruler, both of whom begged for mercy. The inscription demonstrates Assyrian kingship's bombastic propaganda, its conscious connection to the Sumero-Akkadian past, and the cruelty that characterized Assyrian conquests. (Assur, Anu, Ba'al, Ea, and Ishtar were all gods or goddesses.)

To Assur, father of the gods, lover of my priesthood, Anu mighty and pre-eminent, who called me by name, Ba'al, the exalted lord, establisher of my dynasty, Ea, the wise, all-knowing . . . Ishtar, lady of battle and combat, who goes at my side . . . all of them who determine my destiny, who grant to the king, their favorite, power and might . . . the king, the offering of whose sacrifices the great gods love . . . their unsparing weapons they have presented him as a royal gift . . . [he] who has brought all the lands in submission at his feet, who has imposed tribute and tax upon them; conqueror of his foes, destroyer of his enemies, the king, who as to his walk is a storm, and as to his deeds, a raging wolf; . . . the onset of his battle is powerful, he is a consuming flame, a fire that does not sink: son of Sennacherib, king of the universe, king of Assyria, grandson of Sargon, king of the universe, king of Assyria, viceroy of Babylon, king of Sumer and Akkad. . . . I am powerful, I am all powerful, I am a hero, I am gigantic, I am colossal, I am honored, I am magnified, I am without an equal among all kings, the chosen one of Assur . . . the great lord [who] in order to show to the peoples the immensity of my mighty deeds, made powerful my kingship over the four regions of the world and made my name great. . . . Of Tirhakah, king of Egypt and Kush, the accursed . . . without cessation I slew multitudes of his men, and him I smote five times with the point of my javelin, with wounds, no recovery. Memphis, his royal city, in half a day . . . I besieged, I captured, I destroyed, I devastated, I burned with fire. . . . The root of Kush I tore up out of Egypt and not one therein escaped to submit to me.

Daniel David Luckenbill, ed. *Ancient Records of Assyria and Babylonia*, Vol. 2. (Chicago: University of Chicago Press, 1926–1927), pp. 224–227.

in the back, while remorseless soldiers fling the citizens of a captured Judean town from the walls, impaling them on stakes below.

The army itself had developed by the ninth century into a devastating force. Like many ancient societies, the Assyrians had originally employed a seasonal peasant army of part-time soldiers. But from the reign of Assurnasirpal II onward, the Assyrians recruited a massive standing army of more than one hundred thousand soldiers. The Assyrians also mastered large-scale iron-smelting techniques, and by the ninth century could equip their fighting men with high-quality steel weapons that overwhelmed opponents still reliant on bronze.

THE END OF ASSYRIA AND ITS LEGACY

The successors of Sargon II continued Assyrian military policies while also devoting great energy to what we might broadly consider "culture." Sargon's immediate successor Sennacherib (704–681 B.C.E.) rebuilt the ancient Assyrian city of Nineveh, fortifying it with a double wall with a circuit of nine miles. He constructed an enormous palace there, raised on a giant platform decorated with marble, ivory, and exotic woods, and ordered the construction of a massive irrigation system, including an aqueduct that carried fresh water to the city from thirty miles away. His son Esarhaddon (681–669 B.C.E.) rebuilt the conquered city of Babylon and was a famous patron of the arts and sciences.

Esarhaddon's son Assurbanipal (669–627 B.C.E.) was perhaps the greatest of all the Assyrian kings. He maintained a strong military presence throughout the empire, and for a time ruled the entire delta region of Egypt. After the Assyrian adventure in Egypt ultimately ended in failure, he turned his attention to a series of internal reforms, seeking ways to govern his empire other than through the traditional weapons of military terror and religious imperialism. Like his father, Assurbanipal was something of an "enlightened" Assyrian king, who hoped to transform the empire into something more enduring than an armed camp in a perpetual state of warfare with its subjects and neighbors.

When Assurbanipal died in 627 B.C.E., the Assyrian empire appeared to be at its zenith. Its borders were secure, the realm was largely at peace with its neighbors, and its kings had adorned their capitals with magnificent artwork and hanging gardens. The end of Assyria is therefore all the more dramatic for its suddenness. Within fifteen years of the mighty Assurbanipal's reign, Nineveh lay in ruins; a few years later, the Assyrian state was no more, obliterated from the face of the earth with the same speed and violence by which it had established itself.

Despite the reform efforts of Esarhaddon and Assurbanipal, hatred of the Assyrians remained widespread. Centuries of savagery had not been forgotten. After the death of Assurbanipal, a coalition formed between the

Reconstruction of the Ishtar Gate. Visitors to the Near Eastern Museum in Berlin can see this impressive reconstruction of the gate built in Babylon by King Nebuchadnezzar around 575 B.C.E. rising to a height of fifty feet. About half of the reconstruction is original.

IN WHAT WAYS DID THE PERSIAN EMPIRE DIFFER FROM ITS NEAR EASTERN PREDECESSORS?

THE PERSIANS   67

Indo-European-speaking Medes of Iran and the Chaldeans, a Semitic-speaking people who once controlled the southern half of Babylonia. In 626 B.C.E., the allies launched a revolt in southern Babylonia. In 612 B.C.E., they captured and burned the Assyrian capital of Nineveh. By 605 B.C.E., the Chaldeans (also known as neo-Babylonians) had destroyed the last remnants of Assyrian power on the upper Euphrates. The Medes retired to the Iranian plateau to extend their suzerainty there. The Chaldeans succeeded to Assyria's position as the predominant imperial power in Mesopotamia and the Levant.

The Chaldeans proved little better than the hated Assyrians, exercising the same cruelty that had made the Assyrians infamous, including the mass deportation of conquered foes from their homelands. The most famous example of this policy came in 587/586 B.C.E., when the ruthless Chaldean king Nebuchadnezzar captured Jerusalem. He destroyed the temple and removed tens of thousands of Hebrews to Babylon, an exile known in Jewish history as the Babylonian Captivity.

THE PERSIANS

In what ways did the Persian empire differ from its Near Eastern predecessors? How would you account for those differences?

Built as it was on plunder and fear, the Chaldean empire (612–539 B.C.E.) had a very short life. The Indo-European-speaking Lydians had carved out a wealthy kingdom in western Anatolia, but they tended to orient themselves west toward the Aegean and the Greeks. The Medes, meanwhile, sought to secure dominance over the various, closely related peoples of the Iranian plateau, effectively keeping themselves out of Mesopotamian and Levantine politics. It was the Persians who would emerge to topple the Chaldeans and reunite the ancient Near East.

THE ORIGINS OF THE PERSIAN EMPIRE

The Persians emerged from obscurity suddenly, under an extraordinary prince named Cyrus, who succeeded to the rule of a single Persian tribe in 559 B.C.E. Shortly thereafter Cyrus made himself ruler of all the Persians.

Around 549 B.C.E. he threw off the lordship of the Medes, claiming dominion over lands stretching from the Persian Gulf to the Halys River in Asia Minor. Cyrus thus became a neighbor of the kingdom of Lydia. The Lydians had attained great prosperity as producers of gold and silver, and as intermediaries for overland commerce between Mesopotamia and the Aegean Sea. They dominated the wealthy Greek cities along the western Anatolian coast and were the first people in the ancient Near East to use a precious-metal coinage as a medium of exchange for goods and services.

When Cyrus reached their border, the reigning king of the Lydians was Croesus, a great admirer of the culture of the Greeks he ruled. Distrusting his new neighbor, Croesus decided in 546 B.C.E. to launch a preventive war against the Persians to preserve his own kingdom from conquest. According to Herodotus, Croesus asked the oracle at Delphi in Greece whether he should attack immediately. The oracle replied that if he crossed the Halys he would destroy a great nation. Croesus attacked, but the nation he destroyed was his own. Cyrus defeated his forces and annexed Lydia to the Persian empire.

Cyrus invaded Mesopotamia in 539 B.C.E., striking so quickly that he took Babylon without a fight. Once he was in Babylon, the entire Chaldean empire was his. Cyrus allowed the Hebrews captive in Babylon since the time of Nebuchadnezzar to return to Israel and set up a semi-independent vassal state. Cyrus allowed other conquered peoples considerable self-determination as well, especially in terms of cult practices, making Persian rule a welcome change from

An Early Lydian Coin. Probably struck during the reign of Croesus.

THE PERSIAN EMPIRE UNDER DARIUS I, 521–486 B.C.E.

What accounts for the enormous extent of the Persian empire in comparison to earlier imperial realms? Why is the "royal road" especially noted on this map? Consider the location of the Persian heartland and the four administrative centers of Persepolis, Susa, Ecbatana, and Sardis. What purpose did such multiple "capitals" serve? Examine the northwest frontiers of the empire. Why would the Persians have an interest in continuing to expand in this direction?

that of the Assyrians and Chaldeans. Cyrus fell in battle in 529 B.C.E. from wounds he suffered while campaigning against barbarian tribes near the Aral Sea. He left behind the largest empire the world had yet seen. Persian expansion continued, however, even after his death. In 525 B.C.E., his son and successor Cambyses would conquer Egypt.

THE CONSOLIDATION OF THE PERSIAN EMPIRE

Cambyses was a brilliant general, a worthy successor to his father's military greatness. Difficulties abounded during his reign, however, as both contemporaries and

historians have argued over whether the young king was insane. In any event, he died young and without a son, throwing open the question of succession and leaving the Persian empire a cumbersome and poorly organized collection of rapid conquests.

After a short period of civil war, the aristocratic inner circle that had served both Cyrus and his son settled on a collateral member of the royal family as the new king. Cambyses's successor, Darius I, ruled Persia from 521 to 486 B.C.E. and concentrated on consolidating his predecessors' military gains by improving the administration of the Persian state. Darius divided the empire into provinces called satrapies, each administered by a satrap. The satraps enjoyed extensive powers and considerable political latitude, but they owed

IN WHAT WAYS DID THE PERSIAN EMPIRE DIFFER FROM ITS NEAR EASTERN PREDECESSORS?

THE PERSIANS   69

fixed tributes and absolute loyalty to the central government, as did vassal states such as the technically autonomous Hebrew kingdom.

Adhering to the tolerant policy of Cyrus, Darius allowed the various peoples of the Persian empire to retain most of their local institutions while enforcing a standardized currency and system of weights and measures. Throughout their empire the Persians required modest tribute payments; but otherwise, they were little interested in imposing onerous taxes, martial law, or their own religious practices on subject peoples. After centuries of Assyrian and Chaldean tyranny, the light hand of Persian rule was welcomed throughout the Near East.

Darius was also a great builder. He erected a new royal residence and ceremonial capital, which the Greeks called Persepolis ("Persia City"). Darius also expanded the Assyrian road system to enhance trade and communications in his far-flung realms. The most famous was the "Royal Road" stretching sixteen hundred miles from Susa near the Persian Gulf to Sardis (the old Lydian capital) near the Aegean. Government couriers along this road were the first postal system, carrying messages and goods in relay stages from one "post" to another. An extensive imperial spy network also utilized this postal system to inform the crown of developments throughout the massive empire. The "intelligence service" founded by Darius was famed throughout Persian history as "the eyes and ears of the king."

Darius was an extraordinarily gifted administrator. As a military strategist, however, he made an enormous mistake when he attempted to extend Persian hegemony into Greece. Cyrus's conquest of Lydia had made Persia the ruler of the Greek-speaking cities on the western coast of Asia Minor, but these cities disdained Persian toleration and yearned for the idealized freedom of other Greek city-states. Consequently, between 499 and 494 B.C.E. the Greeks on the Asian mainland waged a war for independence and briefly gained the support of troops from Athens, who joined the Asian Greeks in burning the important Persian regional administrative center at Sardis. After quelling the uprising in Asia, Darius sent a force across the Aegean to punish Athens and serve notice of his dominion to all European Greeks. At the battle of Marathon in 490, the Athenians dealt Darius the only major setback of his reign. In 480 his son and successor, Xerxes, attempted to avenge this humiliation by crushing Greece with a tremendous army, but heroic resistance by Athens and Sparta forced him to retreat and abandon his plans a year later. At that point the Persians realized that they had reached the limits of their expansionism; they concentrated on their Asian possessions and settled for using money and diplomacy to meddle in Greek affairs.

Nevertheless, the cosmopolitan nature of Persian culture and the general toleration they exhibited served the Persians well in maintaining their enormous empire. Unlike the Assyrians or Chaldeans, the Persians could often count on the loyalty—sometimes even the affection—of their subjects. The Persians established an imperial model based on the accommodation of local institutions and practices, steady and consistent administration through a trained bureaucracy, and rapid communications between center and periphery. Both the Macedonians and the Romans would learn much from this model in later centuries.

ZOROASTRIANISM

Even more enduring than Persia's political legacy was its religious one, embodied in Zoroastrianism. This important world religion, along with Buddhism and Judaism, was one of the three major universal and personal religions known to the world before Christianity and Islam. The religion's founder was Zoroaster (the Greek form of the Persian name Zarathustra). Zoroaster was a Persian who probably lived shortly before 600 B.C.E., although some of the writings attributed to him may be as much as four hundred years older than this. Zoroaster sought to purify the traditional customs of the Persian tribes by eradicating polytheism, animal sacrifice, and magic, and to redefine worship in ethical rather than ritualistic terms. He was, arguably, the first true theologian in world history, insofar as he attempted to devise a fully developed system of religious belief.

Zoroaster taught that there was one supreme god in the universe, whom he called Ahura-Mazda, the "wise lord." Ahura-Mazda embodied the principles of light, truth, and righteousness; there was nothing wrathful or evil about him, and his light shone everywhere, not just on one tribe. Because evil and suffering were inexplicable by reference to Ahura-Mazda, Zoroaster posited the existence of a counterdeity, Ahriman, treacherous and malignant, who presided over the forces of darkness and evil. Zoroaster presented Ahura-Mazda as vastly

> Because evil and suffering were inexplicable by reference to Ahura-Mazda, Zoroaster posited the existence of a counterdeity, Ahriman, treacherous and malignant, who presided over the forces of darkness and evil.

stronger than Ahriman; but later, the priests of Zoroastrianism, the magi, emphasized the dualistic aspect of the founder's thought by insisting that Ahura-Mazda and Ahriman were evenly matched, engaged in a desperate struggle for supremacy. According to them, only on the last day would "light" decisively triumph over "darkness," when Ahura-Mazda would overpower Ahriman and cast him into the abyss.

Zoroastrianism was a personal religion, making private, spiritual demands as opposed to public, cultic, and ritual ones. Unlike earlier Near Eastern cults, it did not exalt the power of a godlike king. The devotion of the Persian dynasty to Zoroaster's teachings nevertheless made Zoroastrianism important to the conduct of Persian government, and helps to explain the general eclecticism and tolerance of Persian rule. Unlike the Assyrians, the Chaldeans, or even the Egyptians, all of whom tried to impose their own cultural practices on conquered peoples, the Persian kings saw themselves as presiding over an assemblage of different nations whose customs and religious beliefs they were prepared to tolerate. Whereas Mesopotamian potentates characteristically called themselves "true king," Persian rulers took the title "king of kings" or "great king," implying that they recognized the legitimacy of those other kings who ruled under the canopy of Persian overlordship.

Ahura-Mazda patronized neither tribes nor states but only individuals who served his cause of truth and justice. Humans possessed free will and could choose to sin or not to sin. Zoroastrianism urged people to be truthful, love and help one another, aid the poor, and practice generous hospitality. Those who did so would be rewarded in an afterlife, for the religion posited the resurrection of the dead on "judgment day" and their consignment to a realm either of bliss or flames. In the scriptures of the Zoroastrian faith, known as the Avesta, the rewards for righteousness are explicit.

Zoroastrianism has numerous similarities to Judaism and Christianity. Its ethical universalizing resembles the teachings of the Hebrew prophets; its heaven and hell resemble Christian ideas about the afterlife; and its concern with the day of judgment is paralleled in both these other traditions. We should not, however, think of these similarities as simple borrowings from one faith by another. The religious and intellectual traditions of the ancient Near East took shape in a world characterized by pervasive cross-cultural influences. Rarely if ever is it possible to trace an idea or a religious belief to a single, original source. Zoroastrianism, Judaism, and Christianity all emerged out of the rich cultural "soup" of the Iron Age Near Eastern world, as of course did the very idea of a universal religion itself.

Persian Gold Drinking Cup. Persian fondness for lions probably derived from the art of the Assyrians.

THE DEVELOPMENT OF HEBREW MONOTHEISM

What developments marked the Hebrew transition from polytheism to monotheism?

Of all the cultural developments that took place in the Iron Age Near East, none was of greater significance to the civilizations of the West than was monotheism—the belief, that is, in but a single god, the creator and ruler of all things. This development is traditionally, and rightly, associated with the Hebrews. But even the Hebrews were not always monotheists. Those who argued for the exclusive worship of Yahweh—a group whom we shall refer to as the Yahwists—were often a minority within Hebrew society, albeit a vocal and assertive one. That the Hebrews came ultimately to regard Yahweh as the only divine being in the universe, and to root their iden-

WHAT DEVELOPMENTS MARKED THE HEBREW TRANSITION FROM POLYTHEISM TO MONOTHEISM?

THE DEVELOPMENT OF HEBREW MONOTHEISM   71

tity as a people in such an exclusive religious outlook, is a development that can only be explained against the backdrop of the tumultuous and confusing world in which Hebrew society itself arose.

FROM MONOLATRY TO MONOTHEISM

Hebrew monotheism emerged in a world conditioned by polytheism. For those who later advocated the exclusive worship of Yahweh, the early history of the Hebrews was full of embarrassments. At every turn, the Hebrews of the twelfth through tenth centuries B.C.E. can be found worshiping gods other than Yahweh, and especially those of their Canaanite neighbors. Even Yahweh himself, in commanding that his people should "have no other gods before me," seemed implicitly to acknowledge that there were indeed other gods whom his people worshiped. Solomon included symbols of Ba'al and altars to Ashtart in the temple complex he built for Yahweh at Jerusalem. Later Hebrew kings also continued to tolerate non-Yahwist cult practices despite the protests of religious purists advocating the exclusive worship of Yahweh.

Despite lingering polytheism, however, by the beginning of the first millennium Hebrew religion had clearly moved into a new stage of national *monolatry*— the exclusive worship of one god, without denying utterly the existence of others. Although Moses is often credited with beginning the ascendancy of the cult of Yahweh, the promotion of the Yahweh cult probably took place later, under the auspices of the Levites, a tribe whose unique claims to priestly authority made them a religious elite within Hebrew society. The Levites sought to enhance their own power and prestige by exalting Yahweh above the other gods traditionally revered in Hebrew and Canaanite society.

The Levites also enjoyed a higher degree of literacy than most of their fellow Hebrews. In an age of constant threats to Hebrew religious and political sovereignty, the literacy of the Levites helped to preserve and promote Yahweh worship. So too did the House of David, which by promoting the Yahweh cult and centralizing it in Jerusalem helped to link the political and the religious identity of the Hebrews to the worship of Yahweh as the supreme (if not yet the only) god of the universe. Nevertheless, the worship of other gods persisted.

Religious figures as late as Jeremiah (c. 637–587 B.C.E.) continued to rail against "foreign" cults, and to warn of the disastrous consequences that would arise if Yahweh's people did not remain faithful to Yahweh alone.

Despite these polytheistic holdovers, some of the Hebrews' most important contributions to subsequent Western religious thought had emerged by the middle of the eighth century B.C.E. One was their unique *transcendent theology*. In the eyes of his priests and prophets, Yahweh was not part of nature but entirely outside of it. He could therefore be understood in purely intellectual or abstract terms, entirely apart from the operations of the natural world he had created. Complementing this principle of divine transcendence was the belief that Yahweh had appointed humans to be the rulers of nature by divine mandate. The famous line from Genesis in which Yahweh orders Adam and Eve to "be fruitful and multiply, and replenish the earth and subdue it, and have dominion over . . . every living thing," stands in striking contrast with Babylonian creation accounts, in which humans are created merely to serve the gods, "so that the gods might be at ease." Finally, while not fully developed, universalizing ethical considerations are also present in Hebrew religious thought during this period.

The Hebrews honored Yahweh during the period of monolatry by subscribing to moral precepts, rituals, and taboos. The exact form of the Ten Commandments may not have existed before the Babylonian Captivity. But the Hebrews certainly observed some commandments, including injunctions against murder, adultery, bearing false witness, and "coveting anything that is thy neighbor's." In addition they observed ritualistic demands, such as refraining from labor on the seventh day and not boiling a kid in its mother's milk. But the moral standards enjoined by Yahweh on the Hebrew community were not necessarily binding when the Hebrews dealt with outsiders. Lending at interest, for example, was not acceptable between Hebrews, but was quite acceptable between a Hebrew and a non-Hebrew. Such distinctions applied also to more serious issues, such as the killing of civilians in battle. When the Hebrews conquered territories in Canaan, they took "all the spoil of the cities, and every man they smote with the sword . . . until they had destroyed them, neither left they any to breathe." Rather than having any doubts about such a brutal policy, the Yahwists believed it had been ordered

> Although Moses is often credited with beginning the ascendancy of the cult of Yahweh, the promotion of the Yahweh cult probably took place later, under the auspices of the Levites, a tribe whose unique claims to priestly authority made them a religious elite within Hebrew society.

by their Lord himself—indeed, that Yahweh had inspired the Canaanites to resist so that there would be reason to slaughter them: "For it was of the Lord to harden their hearts, that they should come against Israel in battle, that He might destroy them utterly" (Joshua 11:20).

With the fragmentation of the united Hebrew kingdom after Solomon's death, important regional distinctions also arose within the Yahweh cult. The rulers of the northern kingdom discouraged their citizens from participating in cultic activities at Jerusalem, thereby earning the scorn of the Jerusalem-based Yahwists who shaped the biblical tradition. Disunity and the loss of Hebrew identity was accelerated by the Assyrians, who under Sargon II absorbed the northern kingdom as a province and deported nearly twenty-eight thousand Hebrews—the famous Ten Lost Tribes of Israel—to the interior of the Assyrian Empire. The southern kingdom of Judah survived, but found it expedient to become an Assyrian vassal state. As we have seen, however, political collaboration with the Assyrians also meant acceptance of the Assyrian god Assur.

This Assyrian threat was the whetstone on which the Yahwist prophets sharpened their demands for an exclusive monotheism. Prophets were political as much as religious figures, and most understood that military resistance to the Assyrians was futile. If the Hebrews were to survive as a people, then they had to exalt the one thing that separated them from everyone else in the region: the worship of Yahweh. The prophets' insistence, during the eighth and seventh centuries B.C.E., that Yahweh alone should be worshiped and that no other gods even existed, was thus an aggressive reaction to the equally aggressive promotion of Assur by the Assyrians. Nor could there be any room for compromise in the Yahwists' demand for a thoroughgoing and exclusive monotheism. Only by worshiping Yahweh alone could the Hebrews combat the insinuating effects of Assyrian religious imperialism.

Although the word *prophet* has come to mean someone who predicts the future, its original meaning is closer to "preacher"—more exactly someone who has an urgent message to proclaim, because he or she believes that the message derives from divine inspiration. The foremost Hebrew prophets were Amos and Hosea, who preached in the Kingdom of Israel before it fell to the Assyrians in 722 B.C.E.; Isaiah and Jeremiah, who prophesied in Judah before its fall in 586 B.C.E.; and Ezekiel and the second Isaiah (the Book of Isaiah was written by at least two, and possibly three

different authors), who prophesied "by the waters of Babylon" during the exile.

Despite some differences in emphasis, the prophets' messages were sufficiently similar to each other to warrant treating them as if they formed a single coherent body of religious thought. Three doctrines made up the core of the prophets' teachings: (1) absolute monotheism; Yahweh is the ruler of the universe; he even makes use of nations other than the Hebrews to accomplish his purposes; the gods of others are false gods; (2) Yahweh is exclusively a god of righteousness; he wills only the good, and evil in the world comes from humanity, not from him; (3) since Yahweh is righteous, he demands ethical behavior from his Hebrew people above all else; he cares less for ritual and sacrifice than that his followers should "seek justice, relieve the oppressed, protect the fatherless, and plead for the widow." The eighth-century-B.C.E. prophet Amos summed up "the prophetic revolution" and marked one of the epoch-making moments in human cultural development when he expressed Yahweh's resounding warning in words that have echoed down to our own day (Amos 5:21–24):

> I hate, I despise your feasts, and I take no delight in
>   your solemn assemblies.
> Even though you offer me your burnt offerings and
>   cereal offerings,
> I will not accept them, and the peace offerings of your
>   fatted beasts I will not look upon.
> Take away from me the noise of your songs; to the
>   melody of your harps I will not listen.
> But let justice roll down like waters, and righteousness
>   like an ever-flowing stream.

JUDAISM TAKES SHAPE

Through their insistence that Yahwist monotheism was the cornerstone of the Hebrews' identity as a people, the Yahwists made it possible for the Hebrews to survive under Assyrian domination. As the Assyrian threat receded in the late seventh century B.C.E., the Yahwists triumphed religiously and politically. The new king of Judah, Josiah (621–609 B.C.E.) was a committed monotheist who employed prominent prophets at his court, including Jeremiah.

To the dismay of the Yahwists, however, Josiah died in battle against the Egyptians. With his death, the monotheists fell hard from power. Jeremiah was placed under house arrest, denied the right to speak in public, and finally carried off into Egypt where he was murdered. All the while, he continued to denounce the corruption of the Hebrews, suggesting that they would fall before the Chaldeans just as they had before the Assyrians, in punishment for their disobedience to Yahweh.

Within a generation of King Josiah's death, Jeremiah's predictions were fulfilled. The Chaldeans under Nebuchadnezzar conquered Jerusalem, destroyed the Temple, and carried thousands of Hebrews off to Babylon. The Babylonian Captivity brought many challenges for the Hebrews living there, paramount among them being the maintenance of their religious and ethnic identity. The leading voices in defining that identity continued to be the patriotic Yahwists, the same people who would later spearhead the return to Palestine after Cyrus's capture of Babylon. Among the Yahwists, the prophetic tradition thus continued, even in a foreign land. The prophet Ezekiel stressed that salvation could only be found through religious purity, which meant ignoring all foreign gods and acknowledging only Yahweh. States and empires and thrones did not matter in the long run, Ezekiel said. What mattered for the Hebrews living in exile was the creature God had made in his image—man—and the relationship between that creator god, his chosen people, and his creation.

The disassociation of political identity from religious practice that triumphed during the Babylonian Captivity was decisive for the emergence of Judaism as a universalizing religion. In Babylon, Judaism became something more than simply the national cult of the Hebrews. No longer was Yahweh's worship tied to any particular political entity or dynasty, for after 586 B.C.E., neither a Hebrew state nor a Hebrew ruling dynasty existed. Nor was his worship tied to any specific place. In Babylon and in the Holy Land, Judaism survived the destruction of the Temple and the exile of the Hebrew people from their land. In the ancient world, this was an unparalleled achievement. No other ancient people is known to have survived so long an exile from its central holy place.

After 538 B.C.E., when Cyrus permitted the Hebrews of Babylon to return to the Holy Land and rebuild the temple, Jerusalem became once again the central holy place of Hebrew religious life. But the new developments that had arisen within Judaism during the captivity would prove lasting. Increasingly, Jewish religious teachings would be presented in ethical terms, as obligations owed by all human be-

ings toward their creator, independent of place or political identity. Ritual requirements and religious taboos, by contrast, would remain the exclusive obligation of Jews, for whom they symbolized the special covenant that bound Yahweh to his people; and these would be rigorously reinforced by the late fifth century B.C.E. ruler Nehemiah.

The notion of a creator god who existed outside time, nature, place, and kingship became ever more powerful in Second Temple Judaism, and would be taken up later by Christianity and Islam. So too would the Hebrew claim that Yahweh was a jealous god who would not permit his followers to worship any other divinity in any form. In the context of the ancient world, both remained peculiar ideas that would not be fully absorbed for a millennium. But despite their peculiarity, the transcendental monotheism developed by the Hebrews would ultimately become a fundamental feature of the religious outlook of all Western civilizations.

The Babylonian Captivity brought many challenges for the Hebrews living there, paramount among them being the maintenance of their religious and ethnic identity.

CONCLUSION

The centuries from 1700 to 500 B.C.E. were an age of empires. The two great powers of the second millennium B.C.E. were New Kingdom Egypt and the Hittite empire of Anatolia. But a host of lesser empires also emerged during this period, including Minoan Crete, Mycenaean Greece, the kingdom of Mitanni, and Middle Kingdom Assyria. All these empires were sustained by a sophisticated network of international trade and diplomacy; we can speak even of an international system binding them together by the Late Bronze Age. At the heart of all these Bronze Age empires, however, lay a very old model of social organization: the Mesopotamian city-state as it had developed in Sumer. With the arguable exception of New Kingdom Egypt, none of these empires came close to being an integrated, territorial state. Instead, they were collections of cities, ruled by kings who claimed some sort of divine sanction for their rule.

Between 1200 and 1000 B.C.E., the devastation wrought by the Sea Peoples cleared the way for a number of new, small groups to establish states in the Near and Middle East, including the Phoenicians, the Philistines, the Hebrews, and the Lydians. Many of the crucial cultural and economic developments of the early Iron Age began in these small states, including alphabetic writing, coinage, exclusive monotheism, and mercantile colonization. But the dominant states of the early Iron Age Mediterranean world continued to be the great land empires centered in western Asia: first the Assyrians, then the Chaldeans, and finally the Persians.

On the surface, it may appear therefore as if nothing very dramatic had changed since the middle of the second millennium B.C.E. But such geographical continuities can be deceiving. The empires of the early Iron Age were quite different from the collections of quasi-independent city-states that had dominated the Near East a thousand years before. These new empires were much more highly unified than earlier empires had been. They had capital cities, centrally managed systems of communication, sophisticated administrative structures, and ideologies that justified their aggressive imperialism as a religious obligation imposed on them by a single, all-powerful god. They commanded armies of unprecedented size, and they demanded from their subjects a degree of obedience impossible for any Bronze Age empire to imagine.

At the same time that these great land empires were declaring themselves to be the chosen instruments of their god's divine will, we also mark the emergence of more personalized monotheistic traditions in the early Iron Age. Zoroastrianism in particular proved fully compatible with an imperialist ideology and became the driving spiritual force behind the Persian empire. Judaism, by contrast, was forged in the struggle to resist the religious imperialism of Assyria and Chaldean Babylonia. But both Zoroastrianism and Judaism added an important new emphasis on personal ethical conduct as a fundamental element in religious life, and both pioneered the development of authoritative, written scriptures as a foundation for their religious teachings. These developments would exercise an enormous influence upon Western religious life, and would provide the models on which Christianity and Islam would ultimately erect their own imperial traditions.

KEY TERMS

Indo-European	Akhenaten	Cyrus
Assyrians	Nefertiti	Zoroastrians
Mycenaeans	Minoans	David
Semitic	Phoenicians	Hittites

SELECTED READINGS

On New Kingdom Egypt, see also the readings listed in Chapter One.

Aubet, Maria Eugenia. *Phoenicia and the West: Politics, Colonies, and Trade.* Translated by Mary Turton. Cambridge, 1993. An intelligent and thought-provoking examination of Phoenician civilization and its influence.

Boardman, John. *Assyrian and Babylonian Empires and Other States of the Near East from the Eighth to the Sixth Centuries B.C.* New York, 1991. Scholarly and authoritative.

———. *Persia and the West.* London, 2000. A great book by a distinguished classical scholar, with a particular focus on art and architecture as projections of Persian imperial ideologies.

Boyce, Mary. *Textual Sources for the Study of Zoroastrianism.* Totowa, N.J., 1984. An invaluable collection.

Bryce, Trevor. *The Kingdom of the Hittites.* Oxford, 1998. And *Life and Society in the Hittite World.* Oxford, 2002. An extraordinary new synthesis, now the standard account of Hittite political, military, and daily life.

Curtis, John. *Ancient Persia.* Cambridge, Mass., 1990. Concise, solid, reliable.

Dickinson, O. T. P. K. *The Aegean Bronze Age.* Cambridge, 1994. An excellent summary of archaeological evidence and scholarly argument concerning Minoan, Mycenaean, and other cultures of the Bronze Age Aegean basin.

Dothan, Trude, and Moshe Dothan. *People of the Sea: The Search for the Philistines.* New York, 1992. The essential starting point for Philistine culture and its links to the Aegean basin.

Drews, Robert. *The End of the Bronze Age: Changes in Warfare and the Catastrophe ca. 1200 B.C.* Princeton, 1993. A stimulating analysis and survey, with excellent bibliographies.

Finkelstein, Israel, and Nadav Na'aman, eds. *From Nomadism to Monarchy: Archaeological and Historical Aspects of Early Israel.* Jerusalem, 1994. Scholarly articles on the Hebrews' transformation from pastoralists to a sedentary society focused on Yahweh worship.

Fitton, J. Lesley. *Minoans: Peoples of the Past* (British Museum Publications). London, 2002. A careful, reliable debunking of myths about the Minoans, written for nonspecialists.

Kamm, Antony. *The Israelites: An Introduction*. New York, 1999. Concise, accessible introduction covering the period up to 70 C. E. that balances biblical, archaeological, and historical sources.

Kuhrt, Amélie. *The Ancient Near East, c. 3000–330 B. C.* 2 vols. London and New York, 1995. An outstanding survey, written for students, that includes Egypt and Israel as well as Mesopotamia, Babylonia, Assyria, and Persia. Excellent bibliographies.

Luckenbill, Daniel David, ed. and trans. *Ancient Records of Assyria and Babylonia*. 2 vols. Chicago, 1926–1927. Still one of the best and most readily accessible collections of primary sources on Assyrian attitudes and policies in war, religion, and politics.

Metzger, Bruce M., and Michael D. Coogan, eds. *The Oxford Companion to the Bible*. New York, 1993. An outstanding reference work, with contributions by leading authorities.

Niditch, Susan. *Ancient Israelite Religion*. New York, 1997. A short, suggestive introduction designed for students, emphasizing the diversity of Hebrew religious practice.

Redford, Donald B. *Egypt, Canaan, and Israel in Ancient Times*. Princeton, 1992. An up-to-date overview of the interactions between these peoples from about 1200 B. C. E. to the beginning of the Common Era.

Renfrew, Colin. *Archaeology and Language: The Puzzle of Indo-European Origins*. Cambridge, 1987. A masterful but controversial work by one of the most creative archaeologists of the twentieth century.

Saggs, H. W. F. *The Might That Was Assyria*. London, 1984. A lively narrative history of the Assyrian empire, with analysis of the institutions that underlay its strength.

Sandars, Nancy K. *The Sea Peoples: Warriors of the Ancient Mediterranean*. Rev. ed. London, 1985. The essential starting point for students and scholars.

Tubb, Jonathan N., and Rupert L. Chapman. *Archaeology and the Bible*. London, 1990. A good starting point for students that illustrates clearly the difficulties in linking archeological evidence to biblical accounts of early Hebrew history and society.

Wood, Michael. *In Search of the Trojan War*. New York, 1985. Aimed at a general audience, this carefully researched and engagingly written book is an excellent introduction to the late Bronze Age context of the Trojan War.

PART II
THE GREEK AND ROMAN WORLDS

THE CLASSICAL CIVILIZATIONS of Greece and Rome dominated the Mediterranean world from the sixth century B.C.E. until the sixth century C.E. Both drew heavily on the traditions and achievements of the ancient Near East, but each represented a distinct departure from this earlier world. Together, however, Greece and Rome constituted the seedbed out of which all subsequent Western civilizations would develop.

Beginning in the eighth century B.C.E., Greek civilization took shape in the warring, particularistic, and fiercely independent city-states that grew up around the Aegean and the Adriatic Seas. But it was not until the end of the fourth century B.C.E., when the conquests of Alexander the Great created an empire that stretched from Greece through Persia to India and Egypt, that Greek civilization became the common cultural currency of the Mediterranean and Near Eastern worlds.

In central Italy, the city of Rome was slowly extending its dominion over the Italian peninsula. In the last two centuries B.C.E., Rome expanded its rule throughout the entire Mediterranean world and into western Europe. By the end of the first century C.E., Rome had built an empire larger even than Alexander's. In an extraordinary triumph of organization, discipline, and cultural adaptability, the Romans maintained that empire, substantially intact, for the next four hundred years.

	POLITICS	SOCIETY AND CULTURE	ECONOMY	INTERNATIONAL RELATIONS
B.C.E. 1150		The Dark Age of Greece (1150–800 B.C.E.)	Greek trade increases in Aegean Sea (1000–800 B.C.E.)	
	Birth of the Greek polis (800 B.C.E.)	Introduction of Phoenician alphabet into Greece (900 B.C.E.)		Carthage founded (800 B.C.E.)
		Archaic Greece (800–480 B.C.E.)		
		Homer's *Iliad* and *Odyssey* are written down (800 B.C.E.)		
		First Greek colonies appear (800–600 B.C.E.)		
		First Olympic games (776 B.C.E.)		Rome founded (753 B.C.E.)
	Spartans enslave Messenians (700–680 B.C.E.)			
	Kylon sent into exile for tyranny (632 B.C.E.)			
600	Hoplite tactics become military standard (600 B.C.E.)		Solon encourages cash-crop farming and urban industries (600–550 B.C.E.)	Miletus becomes colonial power (600–400 B.C.E.)
	Tarquin the Proud gains kingship over Rome (543 B.C.E.)			
500	Roman Republic (500–527 B.C.E.)		Athens becomes principal exporter of olive oil, wine, and pottery (500 B.C.E.)	
	Xerxes succeeds Darius the Great (486 B.C.E.)	Sophocles, author of *Oedipus*, (496–406 B.C.E.)		The Ionian Revolution (499–494 B.C.E.)
	Plebian rebellion leads to Law of the Twelve Tables (480 B.C.E.)	Emergence of Greek sculpture (490–480 B.C.E.)		Persians sack Eritrea (490 B.C.E.)
		Golden age of Greek civilization (480–323 B.C.E.)		Hellenic League formed (480 B.C.E.)
		Socrates (469–399 B.C.E.)		Persian army defeated at battle of Salamis (480 B.C.E.)
	Pericles elected strategos of Athens (462–461 B.C.E.)	Thucydides (460–400 B.C.E.)		Athens gains control of Delian League (450s B.C.E.)
		Sophists emerge (450 B.C.E.)		
		Parthenon built in Athens (447–438 B.C.E.)		Peloponnesian War (431–404 B.C.E.)
		Plato, author of the *Republic* (429–349 B.C.E.)		
		Aristotle, author of *Nicomachean Ethics* (384–322 B.C.E.)		Corinthian War (394–387 B.C.E.)
	Reign of Philip II (359–336 B.C.E.)	Greek migrations into western Asia (325–225 B.C.E.)	Alexander's conquests open commercial routes between Greece and Asia (323 B.C.E.)	Philip II defeats Greek alliance and forms League of Corinth (338 B.C.E.)
	Reign of Alexander III, the Great (336–323 B.C.E.)	Euclid, *Elements of Geometry* (300 B.C.E.)		Reign of Alexander the Great (336–323 B.C.E.)
300				Ptolemy establishes dynasty in Egypt (332 B.C.E.)
				Alexander defeats the Persian army (331 B.C.E.)
			First standard coinage in Rome (269 B.C.E.)	Seleucus establishes dynasty in Persia (281 B.C.E.)
				Punic Wars (264–146 B.C.E.)
	Roman slave revolts (146–130 B.C.E.)			Carthage razed (146 B.C.E.)
100		Cicero (106–43 B.C.E.)	Roman commerce relies on one million slaves (100 B.C.E.)	
	Spartacus's revolt (73–71 B.C.E.)	Virgil, author of the *Aeneid* (70–19 B.C.E.)		
		Horace (65–8 B.C.E.)		
	Caesar defeats Pompey (48 B.C.E.)	Livy, author of *History of Rome* (59 B.C.E.–17 C.E.)		
	Octavian becomes emperor (27 B.C.E.)	Ovid, author of *Metamorphoses* (43 B.C.E.–17 C.E.)		
	The Principate of early Roman empire (27 B.C.E.–180 C.E.)			

POLITICS	SOCIETY AND CULTURE	ECONOMY	INTERNATIONAL RELATIONS	
				C.E. 10
	Jesus (c. 4 B.C.E.–c. 30 C.E.)			
	Saul of Tarsus, or Paul the Apostle (10–67 C.E.)			
	Christians begin arriving in Rome (40 C.E.)		Claudius enters Britain (48 C.E.)	
Pax Romana (96–180 C.E.)	Gospel of Mark is written (70 C.E.)	Romans excel in engineering aqueducts and roads and develop new tax system under Trajan (98–117 C.E.)	Romans destroy the Temple of Jerusalem (70 C.E.)	100
The Third-Century Crisis in Roman empire (180–284 C.E.)			Romans destroy the city of Jerusalem (135 C.E.)	
	Neoplatonism (200–300 C.E.)	One-third of population of Roman empire dies as a result of disease, low birthrate, and war (180–284 C.E.)		
	Growth of monasticism (300s C.E.)		Goths defeat Romans and cross the Danube (251 C.E.)	
The Dominate or later Roman empire (284–610 C.E.)		Currency is stabilized and new coinage introduced under Diocletian (284–305 C.E.)		
Diocletian, soldier-emperor (284–305 C.E.)				
	The Great Persecution of Christians (303–313 C.E.)			300
Reign of Constantine over Western Roman empire (312–324 C.E.)	Conversion of Constantine to Christianity (312 C.E.)		Council of Nicea condemns Arianism (325 C.E.)	
Reign of Constantine over Roman empire from Constantinople (324–337 C.E.)	Saint Jerome (c. 340–420)		Visigoths defeat Romans (378 C.E.)	
	Saint Ambrose (c. 340–397)			
	Saint Augustine, author of *Confessions* and *On the City of God* (354–430)		Visigoths sack Rome (410 C.E.)	400
	Christianity becomes official Roman religion (c. 392)			
	Saint Benedict (480–547)			
			Vandals sack Rome from the sea (455 C.E.)	
Justinian rules as emperor in East (r. 527–565 C.E.)			Justinian recaptures Italy from Ostrogoths (536 C.E.)	
Corpus Juris Civilus (534 C.E.)			The Lombards seize northern parts of Italy (568 C.E.)	
Tenure of Pope Gregory I (Saint Gregory the Great) (590–604 C.E.)	Papacy of Saint Gregory the Great (590–604)			

CHAPTER THREE

THE GREEK EXPERIMENT

THE image that comes most often to mind when Americans or Europeans think of the ancient world is the Acropolis of Athens, its gleaming temples and shrines still impressive despite their age and ruined condition. The rationality, harmony, and repose of this symbol of Greek culture seem to many to bespeak something quintessentially "Western": the triumph of reason and freedom over the "superstition" and "despotism" of "Eastern" cultures such as Assyria or Persia.

Such easy and self-congratulatory contrasts tell us more about ourselves than they do about the ancient Greeks. In fact, Greek civilization has been deeply influenced by its Near East neighbors from the Mycenaean period until the present day. The achievements of classical Greek civilization would have been impossible without the debt Greece owed to Phoenician, Assyrian, and Egyptian examples.

The flowering of Greek civilization during the first millennium B.C.E. is nonetheless a watershed in the development of Western civilizations. Building on their historical experiences after the Bronze Age collapse, the Greeks of the Iron Age came to cherish assumptions and values that differed greatly from those of their Near Eastern neighbors. Human dignity, individual liberty, participatory government, artistic innovation, scientific investigation, constitutional experimentation, confidence in the creative powers of the human mind—the Greeks espoused all of these values, although, as ever in human affairs, practice often fell short of their ideals.

What we mean by such terms as democracy, equality, justice, and freedom differs from what the Greeks meant by them. Nonetheless, the modern West can find an intelligibility in the institutions and beliefs of this tenacious, quarrelsome, and energetic people, whose small-scale societies started a cultural revolution and created a civilization distinctly different from any before it. The democracies of the modern Western world are not the only heirs of this Greek experiment, but they are unimaginable without it.

FOCUS QUESTIONS

- What cultural changes marked the end of the Dark Age of Greece?

- How did the emergence of hoplite tactics affect Greek political norms?

- How and why did the Athenian, Spartan, and Milesian poleis differ from each other?

- How were the Greek armies able to defeat the much larger Persian forces?

- To what extent was the culture of Athens in the golden age the product of Athenian democracy?

- How did the Peloponnesian War influence Greek philosophy?

THE DARK AGE OF GREECE (1150–800 B.C.E.)

What cultural changes marked the end of the Dark Age of Greece?

By the end of the twelfth century, the last remnants of Mycenaean civilization had vanished, and Greece entered an undocumented Dark Age. Mainland Greece witnessed depopulation of up to 90 percent in the century or so following 1200 B.C.E. Except at Athens, the great citadels were destroyed in the conflagrations at the end of the Bronze Age; and even at Athens, the population steadily declined.

Depopulation had severe effects on the social organization, economy, and material culture in Greece. Settlements shrank in size and moved inland, away from vulnerable locations near the sea. Pottery and burial remains suggest a world that remained static and backward, cut off from the centers of Near Eastern civ-

ilization. Even nearby Greek communities had little economic contact with each other. Some villages may have had chiefs, but a chief's home and material possessions differed little from those of his neighbors. This Dark Age background, with its presumptions of the political and economic equality of self-sufficient households, had a profound effect on the later political assumptions of the classical Greeks.

HOMER AND THE HEROIC TRADITION

By the year 1000 B.C.E., the complete isolation of Greece was ending, and Greek society was becoming gradually more complex. Pottery also became more sophisticated, reflecting an upswing in the material culture and prosperity of the Greek mainland, and providing Greek traders with a valuable commodity to exchange for luxury goods from abroad.

As trade became an increasingly important feature of the Dark Age Greek economy, wealth increased and social stratification became more pronounced. A small group of aristocrats began to emerge, who justified their preeminence as a reflection of their own superior

The Parthenon. The largest and most famous of Athenian temples, the Parthenon is considered the classic example of Doric architecture. Its columns were made more graceful by tapering them in a slight curve toward the top. Its friezes and pediments were decorated with lifelike sculptures of prancing horses, fighting giants, and confident deities.

WHAT CULTURAL CHANGES MARKED THE END OF THE DARK AGE OF GREECE?

THE DARK AGE OF GREECE (1150-800 B.C.E.)   83

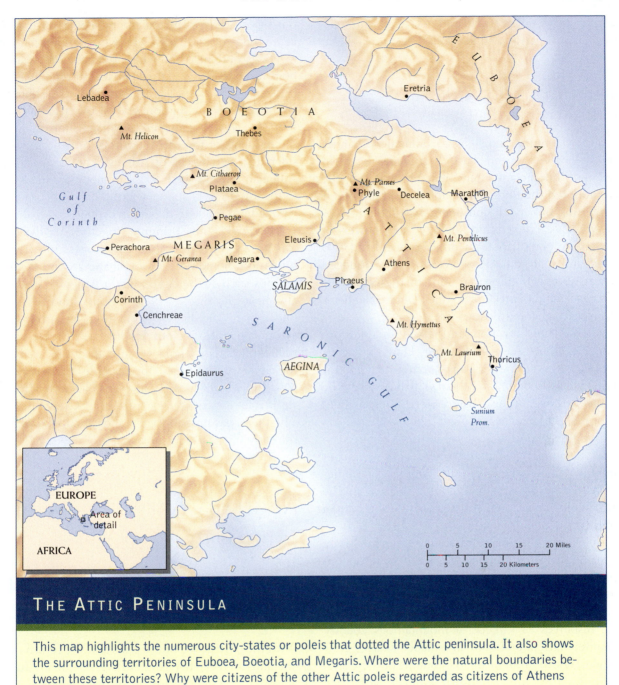

THE ATTIC PENINSULA

This map highlights the numerous city-states or poleis that dotted the Attic peninsula. It also shows the surrounding territories of Euboea, Boeotia, and Megaris. Where were the natural boundaries between these territories? Why were citizens of the other Attic poleis regarded as citizens of Athens also, even though they did not live in Athens?

qualities as the "best men." Wealth alone was not sufficient to establish aristocratic standing. A great man had also to be a singer of songs, a doer of deeds, a winner of battles, and above all favored by the gods. In short, he had to be a hero.

Most of what we know about the heroic ideal of late Dark Age Greece derives from the *Iliad* and the *Odyssey*, epic poems ascribed to the authorship of Homer, but not written down until after 800 B.C.E. Homer depicts a world in which competition and status are of paramount concern to the warrior elite. Competition among artistocratic households frequently led to violence, as it did during the Trojan War. But it could also take religious form in the creation of hero cults. The heroic ideal thus became a deeply ingrained feature of Greek society, which

Homer's epics would preserve and propagate through-out the classical period and beyond.

FOREIGN CONTACTS AND THE RISE OF THE POLIS

The ninth century B.C.E. saw dramatic changes through-out the Aegean basin. Contacts between Greeks and Phoenicians intensified. Most crucial, the Greeks adopted the Phoenician alphabet, improving it by converting unneeded consonantal symbols to represent vowels. The rolling melody and power of Homeric epic could now not only be heard but also recorded and read. The Phoenicians also introduced many artistic and literary traditions of the Near East into Greece, which the Greeks incorporated and reshaped to their own purposes.

The Phoenicians also pointed the way to a new activity among the Greeks—seafaring. Until the tenth century B.C.E., most Greeks traders waited at home for the Phoenicians to come to them. By the end of the Dark Age, however, Greeks had copied Phoenician designs for merchant vessels, allowing them to set out on trading ventures of their own and also to engage in piracy. As commercial activity increased, significant numbers of Greeks began to move among the homeland, the islands, and Anatolia, foreshadowing the colonial explosion that would issue from the Aegean in the eighth and seventh centuries B.C.E.

These economic and cultural developments were accompanied by dramatic growth in the Greek population. Around Athens, the population may have quadrupled during the ninth and early eighth centuries. Such rapid population growth placed heavy demands on the resources of Greece, a mountainous country with limited agricultural land. As smaller villages grew into towns, it also brought the inhabitants of these rival communities into more frequent contact with each other. Some degree of economic, political, and social cooperation among the inhabitants of these towns soon became necessary. But the heroic values of Dark Age Greek society did not make such cooperation easy. Each local community treasured its traditional autonomy and independence, celebrated its own religious cults, and honored its own aristocratic luminaries. On what basis, then, could such communities unite?

The Greek solution to this challenge was the *polis*. The Greek polis was a unique blend of institutional and informal structures of organization. Although poleis (the plural of polis) differed widely in size and organiza-tion. Most were organized around a political and social center known as the *asty*, where markets and important meetings were held and where the basic business of the polis was conducted in the open air. Surrounding the urbanized asty was the *khora*, the "land." The khora of a larger polis might support several other towns besides the asty, as well as numerous villages; for example, all the residents of the entire territory of Attica were considered to be citizens of Athens. The vast majority of Athenian citizens were thus farmers, who might come to the asty to participate in the affairs of their polis, but who did not reside in the urban center.

Synoikismos (the "bringing together of dwellings") was how Greeks described the process of early polis formation. Some poleis took shape around defensible hilltops such as the Acropolis in Athens. Greeks may also have borrowed a Near Eastern (and particularly Phoenician) practice of orienting an urban center around a temple precinct. In Greece, however, the central temple site of a polis was not always located within the city's walls; at Argos, for example, the massive temple to Hera was located several miles away from any sizable settlement. As was typical of Greek life generally, there was probably no standard pattern by which the early Greek poleis took shape.

ARCHAIC GREECE (800–480 B.C.E.)

How did the emergence of hoplite tactics affect Greek political norms?

With the emergence of the polis and the return of writing and literacy, the Archaic Age begins. After languishing in obscurity for nearly four centuries during the Dark Age, Greek civilization now burst forth with breathtaking dynamism and energy. Archaic Greece is remarkable not only for its achievements, but also for its willingness to explore new avenues in religion, society, and politics. Aptly, this period has also been called the "Age of Experiment."

COLONIZATION AND PANHELLENISM

In the eighth and seventh centuries, smaller-scale Greek trading ventures and migrations throughout the Aegean developed into a full-fledged colonization ef-

HOW DID THE EMERGENCE OF HOPLITE TACTICS AFFECT GREEK POLITICAL NORMS?

ARCHAIC GREECE (800–480 B.C.E.) 85

fort. Each colony was an independent foundation, with emotional and sentimental ties to its mother city, but no political obligations. By the end of the sixth century B.C.E., Greeks had founded several hundred new colonies from the Black Sea to the western Mediterranean, permanently altering the cultural geography of the Mediterranean world. The western shores of Anatolia would remain a stronghold of Greek culture until the end of the Middle Ages; so many Greeks settled in southern Italy and Sicily that the Romans called the region Magna Graecia, "Greater Greece." By the fourth century B.C.E., more Greeks lived in Magna Graecia than in Greece itself. Greek colonies could also be found farther westward, in North Africa and along the southern coast of France.

Colonial expansion intensified Greek contacts with other cultures, especially Egypt and Phoenicia. At the same time, however, intensified contact with other cultures sharpened Greeks' awareness of their own common identity and peculiarity as "Hellenes" (the Greeks' name for themselves). Such self-conscious "Hellenism" did not necessarily lead to greater political cooperation among the fiercely independent poleis. Like the Sumerians, the Greeks were particularists who had little use for permanent political associations larger than the individual polis. But it did encourage the growth of Panhellenic ("all-Greeks") cult sites such as the Oracle of Delphi, and of Panhellenic festivals such as the Olympic Games. Predictably, such competitions did little to stop contentiousness and rivalry between the poleis; but they did strengthen the Greeks' sense that they shared a common culture, despite their political and linguistic differences.

HOPLITE WARFARE

During the Dark Age, the military power of a Greek community rested with the elite, who had the time, resources, and training to become "Homeric" warrior heroes. Common foot soldiers played a secondary role as followers and supporters of the aristocratic warriors who dueled in single combat. This aristocratic monopoly on military prowess gave the aristocracy tremendous political and social leverage within the nascent poleis. As a result, aristocrats dominated political offices and priesthoods as well as economic life.

The introduction of hoplite tactics during the Archaic Period brought aristocratic military dominance to an end. Hoplites were foot soldiers, armed with spears or short swords, and protected by a large round shield (a *hopla*), a breastplate, a helmet, and sometimes wrist and leg guards. In battle, hoplites stood shoulder to shoulder in a close formation called a phalanx, several rows across and several lines deep, with each hoplite carrying his shield on the left arm to protect the unshielded right side of the man standing next to him. In

Hoplite Infantry Advancing into Combat. This Corinthian vase, dating to around 650 B.C.E., is the earliest known depiction of hoplites.

his right hand each hoplite carried a thrusting weapon such as a spear or short sword, so that an approaching phalanx presented a nearly impenetrable wall of armor and weaponry to its opponents. If a man in the front rank fell, the one behind him stepped up to take his place; indeed, the weight of the entire phalanx was literally behind the front line, each soldier aiding the assault by leaning with his shield into the man in front of him. The tight formation and heavy armor (as much as seventy pounds including the shield) required but one skill: the ability to stay together. As long as the phalanx remained intact, it was a nearly unbeatable formation. By the end of the seventh century B.C.E., hoplite tactics were a standard element in Greek warfare.

The result was a social and political revolution. Since every polis needed a hoplite force to protect its independence, farmers who could afford the requisite armor soon became a political and social force within the archaic polis—a "hoplite class." But the sacrifices demanded by hoplite warfare were great, and the men who had now become indispensable to the polis's survival quickly grew restless without a share in its decision making. Scholars once believed their disquiet was sufficient by itself to force concessions from the aristocrats, including access to political decision making and the writing down of laws to guarantee "equal" justice. But the real impetus toward political change may in fact have come from disgruntled aristocrats.

A bearded Greek male and his young lover. This illustration is from a red-figure cup, c. 480 B.C.E.

ARISTOCRATIC CULTURE AND THE RISE OF TYRANNY

The aristocrats of the Archaic Age pursued not only wealth, power, and glory, but also a distinct culture and defining lifestyle. Holding office and participating in politics was part of this lifestyle; but so too was the symposium, an intimate gathering at which elite men would enjoy wine (sometimes in prodigious quantities), poetry (ranging from epics to bawdy drinking songs), dancing competitions, and female courtesans who provided both musical and sexual services. Respectable women were excluded from such meetings, as they were from all other aspects of social and political life. So too were nonaristocratic men. The symposium was thus far more than a social occasion. It was an essential feature of aristocratic male life within the polis.

Homosexuality was another important aspect of aristocratic culture in the Archaic Period. Appropriate aristocratic homosexual behavior was regulated by social custom. Typically, a man in his late twenties to late thir-

ties and on the rise in political life would take as his lover and protégé an aristocratic youth in his early to mid-teens. The two would form a close and intimate bond of friendship, in which sexual intercourse played an important role. This intimate bond between man and boy was believed to benefit the younger partner, as he learned the workings of government and society, and through his older lover made important political and social connections that would benefit him later in life.

A whole complex of values, ideas, practices, and assumptions thus informed aristocratic identity in the Archaic Period. As a result, it was impossible for those outside this elite world to participate fully in the public life of the polis. By the middle of the Archaic Age, however, the circle of the aristocratic elite was narrowing even further. As a result, many aristocrats were left on the outside of their own culture, looking in.

As the circles of political power narrowed during the seventh century, violence between aristocratic groups increased, ultimately giving rise to the emergence of tyranny as an alternative form of government. The word *tyrannos* was not originally Greek, but borrowed from Lydia, signifying someone who seized power and ruled outside the traditional constitutional framework. A tyrant in Archaic Greece was thus not necessarily an abusive ruler. Often, he was an aristocrat who had tired of his exclusion from the elite or had become frustrated with the petty rows of aristocratic factions

HOW AND WHY DID THE ATHENIAN, SPARTAN, AND MILESIAN POLEIS DIFFER FROM EACH OTHER?

THE ARCHAIC POLIS IN ACTION   87

within the polis. To strengthen themselves, tyrants appealed instead to the hoplite class, whose armed might could propel them to a position of sole power. In return, tyrants would then extend rights of political participation to the hoplites, while striving to retain the reins of power in their own hands. This was an inherently unstable state of affairs, because after the original tyrant had fulfilled the wishes of the hoplites, the continuance of tyranny became an obstacle to even greater power for the people, the *demos*. For this reason, tyrannies rarely lasted for more than two generations. Tyranny more often served as a way station on the road from aristocracy to more broadly participatory forms of government, such as democracy.

THE ARCHAIC POLIS IN ACTION

How and why did the Athenian, Spartan, and Milesian poleis differ from each other?

The Archaic poleis developed in very different ways. To illustrate this diversity, we will examine three particularly well-documented examples: Athens, Sparta, and Miletus. None, however, is "typical" of the historical development of the Greek poleis as a whole. There were approximately one thousand such poleis in Greece. About most of them we know almost nothing. It seems unlikely, however, that amid such diversity we will ever be able to describe a "typical" polis.

ATHENS

Athens emerged from the Dark Age with a distinctly agricultural economy. The city's orientation toward the Aegean, together with the excellent harbors along the Attic coast, would eventually make Athens famous as a mercantile and seafaring polis. But until the sixth century B.C.E., the aristocracy of Athens remained firmly entrenched on the land.

Aristocratic dominance over Athens rested on the elected magistracies, which they monopolized, and the council of state, which was composed of former magistrates. By the early seventh century B.C.E., aristocratic officials called archons wielded executive power in Athens; ultimately nine archons in all presided over the civil, military, judicial, and religious functions of the polis. The archons served a term of one year, after which they became lifetime members of the Areopagus Council. The council was where the real power in Athens resided. The Areopagus elected the archons, thus controlling its own future membership. It also served as a kind of "high court," with tremendous influence over the judicial procedures of Athens.

Deep economic and social divisions developed in Athenian society during the seventh century, as a significant proportion of the population fell into debt slavery (the practice of securing a loan with one's person as collateral and, when unable to pay up, becoming indentured to the creditor). Rivalries between aristocratic political factions also destabilized the polis. In 621 B.C.E., an aristocrat named Drakon was charged with "setting the laws"; in particular, he sought to control homicide through harsh ("draconian") punishments. His attempt at stabilizing Athens failed, however, and the city soon found itself on the brink of civil war. Hoping to avoid this, in 594 B.C.E. aristocrats and hoplites alike agreed to make Solon the sole archon for one year, and to give him sweeping powers to reorganize Athenian government. Solon was an aristocrat who had made his name and fortune as a merchant; this led everyone in Athenian society to trust Solon, as he was not beholden to any single interest.

Solon's reforms laid the foundations for the later development of Athenian democracy. He forbade the practice of debt slavery, and set up a fund to buy back Athenian debt slaves sold abroad. He encouraged the Athenians to cultivate olives and grapes, thus spurring cash-crop farming and the urban industries (such as pottery, oil production, and shipbuilding) necessary to make Athens a commercial power. He also broadened rights of political participation. Solon set up courts in which a broader range of citizens served as jurors, and to which any Athenian might appeal if he disliked a decision of the Areopagus. He based eligibility for political office on property qualifications, thus making it possible for someone not born an aristocrat to gain access to power through the accumulation of wealth. He also gave the Athenian citizen assembly (known as the *ekklesia*) the right to elect the archons. This was a significant step, since all free-born Athenian men over the age of eighteen could participate in the assembly.

Solon's reforms did not succeed. The aristocracy thought them too radical, the demos (common people), not nearly radical enough. In the resulting turmoil, an aristocrat named Peisistratos finally succeeded in establishing himself as tyrant in 546 B.C.E. By enforcing

THRASYBOULOS ON HOW
TO BE A TYRANT

The fifth-century historian Herodotus relates how Periander, tyrant of Corinth from 627 to 587 B.C.E., sought advice from his older contemporary, Thrasyboulos of Miletus, on how best to secure tyrannical power. The excerpt below describes Thrasyboulos's response to Periander's emissary, and the Corinthian's response to his strange reply. Although Herodotus's negative attitude toward tyranny is typical of later classical thought, Periander and his father before him had in fact been instrumental in breaking a narrow aristocratic regime and increasing Corinth's commercial prosperity.

At the beginning Periander was gentler than his father [Cypselus] had been. But afterwards, when he had dealt with Thrasyboulos, prince of Miletus, he became yet bloodier than Cypselus. . . . Thrasyboulos had led out Periander's messenger, outside the city, and with him entered a sown field; then he walked through the corn, questioning, and again questioning the herald, about his coming from Corinth. And ever and again as he saw one of the ears growing above the rest he would strike it down, and what he struck down he threw away, until by this means he had destroyed all the fairest and strongest of the corn. So he passed through the whole place and, having added no suggestions, sent the herald away. When the herald came back to Corinth, Periander was anxious to know what suggestion Thrasyboulos had made. But the man said that Thrasyboulos had made no suggestion at all, and indeed he wondered what sort of man this was he had been sent to, a madman and a destroyer of his own property. . . . But Periander understood the act of Thrasyboulos and grasped in his mind that what he was telling him was that he should murder the most eminent of the citizens. And so from this time forth he displayed every form of wickedness toward his fellow countrymen. Whatever Cypselus had spared of death and banishment, Periander completed.

Herodotus, v. 92. Translated by David Grene (Chicago and London: University of Chicago Press, 1987), pp. 397–398 (somewhat revised).

Solon's reforms, Peisistratos strengthened the demos and encouraged the taste for self-government. He remained a popular ruler until his death. His sons, however, proved much less popular; and after one son was murdered in an aristocratic feud, the other was quickly overthrown with the help of the Spartans. However, two generations of increasing access to power left the Athenian demos with no interest in returning to an elite oligarchy. For the first time in history, the populace at large spontaneously rose up and overthrew the government. They rallied behind Cleisthenes, an aristocrat who had served the Peisistratid government ably and championed the cause of the demos. Once voted in as archon in 508/7 B.C.E., Cleisthenes quickly took steps to limit aristocratic power. He also introduced the practice of ostracism, whereby the Athenians could decide each year whether they wanted to banish someone for ten

HOW AND WHY DID THE ATHENIAN, SPARTAN, AND MILESIAN POLEIS DIFFER FROM EACH OTHER?

THE ARCHAIC POLIS IN ACTION   89

Ostracism. The system took its name from the potsherds (in Greek, *ostraka*) on which the names of unpopular citizens were scratched. Many of the "ballots" have survived.

years, and if so, whom. Cleisthenes believed that with this power, the demos could prevent the return of a tyrant and quell factional strife if civil war seemed imminent.

By 500 B.C.E., Athens had become the principal exporter of olive oils, wines, and pottery in the Greek world. The political struggles of the sixth century had also given it a far more democratic temper than any other Greek polis possessed, simultaneously strengthening its institutions of central government. Athens was poised to assume the role it would claim for itself during the fifth century, as the exemplar of Greek culture and the proponent of its own style of participatory democracy.

SPARTA

Located in the southern part of the Peloponnesus (the large peninsula that forms southern Greece), the Spartans represented everything that Athens was not. Athens was cultured, sophisticated, cosmopolitan; Sparta was basic, earthy, and traditional. Depending on one's point of view, either set of adjectives might serve as admiration or criticism.

Sparta took shape when four villages (and ultimately a fifth) combined to form the polis of Sparta. Perhaps as a relic of the unification process, Sparta retained a dual monarchy throughout its history, with two royal

families and two lines of succession. Although seniority or capacity usually determined which of the two ruling kings had more influence, neither was technically superior to the other, a situation that led to political intrigue within Sparta.

The Spartan system depended on its conquest of Messenia, an agriculturally wealthy region west of Sparta. Around 720 B.C.E., the Spartans subjugated the region and enslaved the population. These *helots* (as the enslaved Messenians were now called) remained to work the land, which was now parceled out among the Spartiates. Around 650 B.C.E., however, the helots revolted, gaining support from several neighboring cities and briefly threatening Sparta with annihilation. Eventually, Sparta triumphed; but the shock of this rebellion brought about a permanent transformation in Spartan society.

Determined to prevent another uprising, Sparta became the most militarized polis in Greece. By 600 B.C.E., everything in Sparta was oriented to the maintenance of its hoplite army, a force so superior that the Spartans confidently left their city unfortified. The Spartan system made every full citizen, called a Spartiate, a professional soldier of the phalanx. At a time when Athenian society was becoming more democratic, in Sparta the citizenry was "aristocratized," making every citizen-soldier into a warrior-champion of the hoplite phalanx.

Sparta became a society organized for war. At birth, every child was examined by Spartan officials who determined whether it was healthy enough to raise (if not, the infant was abandoned in the mountains). If deemed worthy of upbringing, a child was

CHRONOLOGY

THE CHANGING LANDSCAPE OF ARCHAIC GREECE

Panhellenic colonial expansion by Greek poleis	900–800 B.C.E.
Hoplite tactics become standard in Greek warfare	725–650 B.C.E.
Emergence of tyrannical governments	700–600 B.C.E.
Militarization of Sparta	600 B.C.E.
Solon's reforms	594 B.C.E.
Cleisthenes' reforms	508 B.C.E.

THE PELOPONNESUS

Located on the Peloponnesian peninsula, the highly militarized society of Sparta dominated the southern region known as Laconia. How might Sparta's geographical position have influenced its outlook on foreign affairs? Did geography make conflict between Athens and Sparta inevitable?

placed at age seven in the state-run Spartan educational system. Boys and girls trained together until age twelve, participating in exercise, gymnastics, and other physical drills and competitions. Boys then went to live in the barracks, where their military training would commence in earnest. Girls continued an education in letters until they married, usually around the age of eighteen.

Barracks training was rigorous, designed to accustom the young Spartan male to physical hardships. At age eighteen, the young man would try to gain membership into a *syssition*, a communal mess tent as well as

a kind of fighting brotherhood. Failure meant that the young man could not become a full Spartiate and would lose his rights as a citizen. If accepted into a syssition, however, men remained in the barracks until they were thirty years of age. Although they were required to marry between the ages of twenty and thirty, men living in the barracks were only permitted to meet their wives surreptitiously—a fact that may account in part for the notably low birthrate among Spartiate couples. After age thirty, a Spartiate male could live with his family. He remained on active military duty, however, until he was sixty, although he was unlikely

HOW AND WHY DID THE ATHENIAN, SPARTAN, AND MILESIAN POLEIS DIFFER FROM EACH OTHER?

THE ARCHAIC POLIS IN ACTION   91

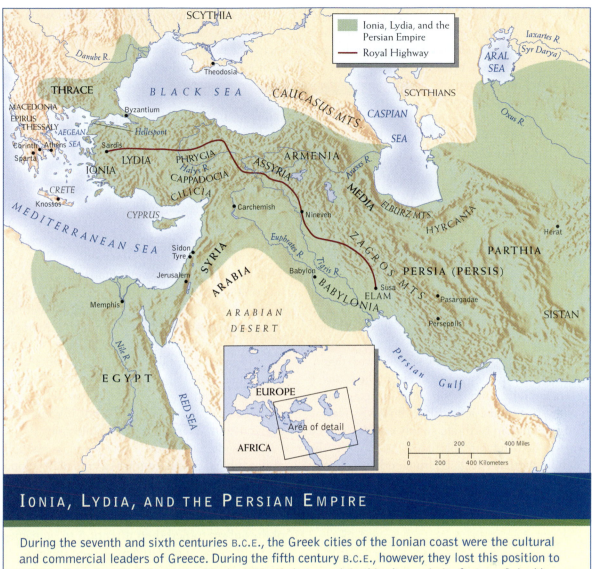

IONIA, LYDIA, AND THE PERSIAN EMPIRE

During the seventh and sixth centuries B.C.E., the Greek cities of the Ionian coast were the cultural and commercial leaders of Greece. During the fifth century B.C.E., however, they lost this position to Athens. How does Ionia's geographical position help to explain this change in its fortunes? And how might this change have influenced Ionian attitudes toward the Persian empire?

to participate in phalanx combat beyond the age of forty-five.

All Spartiate males aged thirty and over were members of the citizen assembly, the *apella*, which voted yes or no, without debate, on matters proposed to it by a council consisting of twenty-eight elders (the *gerousia*) plus the two kings. The gerousia was the main policy-making body of the polis and also its primary court. Its members were elected by the apella for life, but had to be over the age of sixty before they could stand for election. Five ephors, elected annually by the apella, supervised the educational system and acted as guardians of Spartan traditions. In the latter role, an ephor

could even depose an errant king from command of the army while on campaign. The ephors also supervised the Spartan secret service, the *krypteia*, recruiting agents from among the most promising young Spartiates. Agents spied on citizens, but their main job was to infiltrate the helot population, identify potential troublemakers, and kill them.

Spartan policy often hinged on the precarious relationship between the helots and the Spartiates. The helots outnumbered the Spartiates ten to one, and Messenia routinely seethed with revolt. Every year the Spartans ritually declared war on the helots, as a reminder that they would not tolerate attempts to break free. But the Spartiates never rested easy in their beds; Spartans were notoriously reluctant to commit their army abroad, in part because they feared its prolonged absence might encourage a helot uprising at home.

Spartiates were forbidden to engage in trades or commerce, because wealth might distract them from the pursuit of martial virtue. Nor did Spartiates farm their own lands. Economic activity in the Spartan state fell either to the helots or to the free residents of the other Peloponnesian cities (known as the *perioikoi*, "those dwelling round about"). The perioikoi enjoyed certain rights and protections within Spartan society, and some grew wealthy handling its business concerns. They exercised no political rights within the Spartan state, however, and Sparta conducted their foreign policy for them. Spartiates who lost their rights as citizens also became perioikoi.

The fatal flaw in the Spartan system was demographic. There were many ways to fall from the status of Spartiate, including criminal behavior and cowardice. The only way to become a Spartiate, however, was by birth—and the Spartan birthrate simply could not keep pace with the demand for Spartiates. As a result, the number of full Spartiates declined from perhaps as many as ten thousand in the Archaic Period to only about one thousand by the middle of the fourth century B.C.E.

MILETUS

Across the Aegean from the Greek mainland lay the Greek cities of Anatolia. During the Archaic Period, Miletus was the foremost commercial, cultural, and military power of Ionia, a narrow coastal strip dominating the central part of the western Anatolian coast. Miletus had long been a part of the Greek world, but Near Eastern influences also shaped Milesian culture in important ways. Ionia was the birthplace of Greek epic, and debate continues over the extent to which Near Eastern models might have influenced the Homeric epics.

Miletus also became a center for Greek speculative thinking and philosophy. Beginning in the sixth century B.C.E., a series of thinkers known as the "pre-Socratics" (because they came before the great philosopher Socrates) raised serious questions about the relationship between the natural world (the *kosmos*), the gods, and men. Oftentimes, their explanations moved divine agency to the margins or removed it altogether—and for

> By making the observations of men, not the will of the gods, the starting point for their thinking, the Milesian School began to formulate rational theories to explain the physical universe they observed.

that, everyday Greeks looked on them with suspicion. All built on older traditions of Near Eastern learning, such as Babylonian astronomy; but in typically Greek fashion, they turned those ideas on their heads. Calculating and observing the movements of the heavens, the thinkers of the Milesian School sought physical explanations for what they saw, refusing to presume that the heavenly bodies were gods. By making the observations of men, not the will of the gods, the starting point for their thinking, the Milesian School began to formulate rational theories to explain the physical universe they observed.

Stimulated by the cosmopolitanism of their city, Milesian philosophers also began to rethink their place in the human world, inaugurating what has sometimes been called "the Ionian revolution in thought." Xenophanes of Colophon concluded that human beings made gods in their own image, not the other way around. If oxen could speak and make objects, Xenophanes declared, they would pray and fashion idols to gods who looked like oxen. Such relativism was new, but it would become a distinctive strand in later Greek philosophy.

This widening fissure between religious belief and philosophical speculation was a crucial development in the history of Western thought. It was less complete, however, than is often imagined. Philosophy was a game for a few, not for the average Greek; and as philosophers turned their attention to humanity's relationship to the gods, citizens in even the most progressive of poleis were unnerved. The gods were too central a part of daily life for the average Greek not to feel threatened by such impious philosophizing.

THE PERSIAN WARS

How were the Greek armies able to defeat the much larger Persian forces?

The Archaic Period of Greek history closed with dramatic struggles against Persia. For two decades the threat of Persian conquest loomed on the Greek horizon. When finally the immediate danger to Greek freedom receded, the experience of war had changed the Greek world immeasurably.

HOW WERE THE GREEK ARMIES ABLE TO DEFEAT THE MUCH LARGER PERSIAN FORCES?

THE PERSIAN WARS 93

THE PERSIAN WARS WITH GREECE

Imagine you are Xerxes, planning the conquest of Greece in 480 B.C.E. To what extent would geographical considerations dictate your military strategy? Xerxes' attempt at conquest failed. What would you have done differently? Could any Persian expedition have succeeded in conquering Greece?

THE IONIAN REVOLT (499–494 B.C.E.)

Our main source for the Persian Wars is Herodotus, the "Father of History." His account reflects many of the intellectual currents of mid-fifth-century Athens, where he lived and worked. Reflecting a kind of geographical and cultural determinism, he ascribed the war between Persia and Greece to an ancient hatred between Europe and Asia. But his own narrative shows that the immediate cause of the war was a political conflict in Miletus.

By 501 B.C.E., Aristagoras—the Persians' puppet tyrant of Miletus—grew concerned that his days as a favorite of Darius the Great were numbered. Turning from puppet to patriot, he roused the Milesians and the rest of Ionia to revolt against Persian rule. He also sought military support from the Greek mainland. The Spartans refused to send their army abroad, but

CHRONOLOGY

THE PERSIAN WARS

Croesus, king of Lydia, conquers Greek cities of Anatolia	c. 560 B.C.E.
Cyrus, king of Persia, conquers Lydia and controls Greek cities	546 B.C.E.
Ionian Revolt	499–494 B.C.E.
Battle of Marathon	490 B.C.E.
Xerxes invades Greece	480 B.C.E.
Battles of Thermopylae and Salamis	480 B.C.E.
Battle of Plataea	479 B.C.E.
Formation of the Delian League, led by Athens	478–477 B.C.E.

Athens and the city of Eretria on Euboea sent a small force that captured and burned the Persian administrative center of Sardis. The Athenians and Eretrians then sailed home, leaving the Ionians to their own devices. After five years of brave struggle, the rebels were finally overwhelmed by the vastly superior might of Persia in 494 B.C.E.

Darius realized, however, that so long as his Greek subjects in Asia Minor could cast a hopeful eye to their cousins across the Aegean, they would long for freedom. Darius therefore set out on a punitive expedition to teach Athens and Eretria a lesson. Landing on Euboea in the summer of 490, Persian forces sacked and burned Eretria and sent its population into captivity in Persia. They then crossed the narrow strait to Attica, landing in the plain of Marathon.

MARATHON AND ITS AFTERMATH

Recognizing the danger they now faced, the Athenians sought help from the Spartans, who responded that they were unable to assist due to an ongoing religious festival. Only the small, nearby polis of Plataea offered the Athenians aid. The Athenian phalanx would have to engage the mighty Persians on its own.

Heavily outnumbered, the Athenian phalanx took a position between two hills blocking the main road to the asty. After a standoff of several days, the Athenian general Miltiades received word that the Persians were watering their horses, and that the Persian infantry (numerically superior but poorly equipped compared with the ten thousand Athenian hoplites) was vulnerable. Miltiades led a charge that smashed the Persian force and resulted in catastrophic losses for the Persians. Herodotus records that sixty-four hundred Persians fell, compared with only 192 Athenians. The Persians withdrew.

The Athenians had defeated the world's greatest empire, and they had done it without Spartan help. It was a tremendous boost to Athenian confidence, and many exulted in their victory, a victory of the demos. The Athenian politician Themistocles believed, however, that Greece had not seen the last of the Persians, who would inevitably return in much greater force. In 483 B.C.E., the Athenians discovered a rich silver vein in the Attic countryside. Themistocles persuaded them not to divide the windfall among themselves (the customary practice), but to use it to build a fleet of two hundred triremes, state-of-the-art warships. Athens thereby transformed itself into the preeminent naval power of the Greek world just in time to confront a new Persian onslaught.

XERXES' INVASION

Darius died in 486 B.C.E. and was succeeded by his son Xerxes, who began preparing a massive overland invasion of Greece designed to conquer the entire country. Supported by a fleet of six hundred ships, Xerxes' grand army (which numbered at least one hundred fifty thousand men, and may have been as large as three hundred fifty thousand) set out from Sardis in 480 B.C.E., crossing the narrow strait separating Europe from Asia on pontoon bridges. Unlike his father, who had dispatched talented generals against Athens, Xerxes led this campaign himself.

Many Greek cities capitulated immediately. Athens, Sparta, Corinth, and some thirty others refused to bow, however, and formed the Hellenic League to defeat the Persian menace. Under the military leadership of Sparta, the outnumbered Greek allies confronted Xerxes at the pass of Thermopylae in August of 480. For three days the Greeks held off the Persian multitude, while the Greek fleet engaged a Persian flotilla at nearby Artemisium. The defense at Thermopylae failed, but their sacrifice allowed the fleet, under Themistocles' guidance, to

> The defense at Thermopylae failed, but their sacrifice allowed the fleet, under Themistocles' guidance, to inflict heavy losses on the Persians and then withdraw safely to the south.

TO WHAT EXTENT WAS THE CULTURE OF ATHENS IN THE GOLDEN AGE THE PRODUCT OF DEMOCRACY?

THE "GOLDEN AGE" OF CLASSICAL GREECE   95

inflict heavy losses on the Persians and then withdraw safely to the south.

Realizing he could no longer defend the city, Themistocles abandoned Athens for the island of Salamis off the coast of Attica. In early September, the Athenians watched the Persians put Athens to the torch. Time, however, was on Themistocles' side. Xerxes' massive army depended on his fleet for supplies. Bad weather made sailing the Aegean in autumn a risky business; the Persians were now desperate to force a decisive battle before the season turned against them.

In late September, the numerically superior Persian fleet, believing the Greeks were about to flee Salamis, sailed into the Bay of Eleusis, only to find that Themistocles had the Greek fleet ready for combat. The Greeks smashed the Persian fleet while Xerxes watched the disaster from a throne above the bay. The following year, a Greek army prevailed on land at the battle of Plataea, driving the Persians completely from mainland Greece. Against all odds, the small, fractious, outnumbered Greek poleis had defeated the mightiest empire of the Mediterranean world. It was a turning point in the history of Greece, ushering in the Classical (or "golden") Age.

THE "GOLDEN AGE" OF CLASSICAL GREECE

To what extent was the culture of Athens in the golden age the product of Athenian democracy?

In the half century after the battle of Salamis, Athens enjoyed a meteoric rise in power and prestige, becoming the premier naval power of the eastern Mediterranean and a military rival even of Sparta. Athens also emerged as the leader of the Delian League, a group of poleis pledged to continue the war against Persia. As the leader of the league, Athens controlled its funds and resources. This fact allowed the Athenians to make their polis—in the words of their brilliant political leader Pericles—the "school of Hellas." The fifth century B.C.E. witnessed the greatest achievements of Greek culture and the flowering of Athenian democracy. Both were fueled, however, by the increasingly awkward relationship Athens enjoyed with its allies, who by the 430s had begun to look more like Athenian subjects than free poleis.

Bust of Pericles. A Roman copy, in marble, of a Greek original, made in bronze during Pericles' own lifetime. Like the tyrant Peisistratos, Pericles is said to have had a deformed head. Pericles wore a helmet to conceal this potentially provocative resemblance.

PERICLEAN ATHENS

The reforms of Cleisthenes encouraged further experiments in Greek democracy, including the selection of major officeholders by lot. Only one key position was now filled by traditional voting: the office of *strategos*, or general. Because a man could be elected strategos year after year, this office became the focus for Athens' most talented and ambitious public figures. Themistocles had been strategos, as was Cimon, who led the Delian League to stunning victories over Persia in the 470s and 460s. But Cimon also turned the league against members who tried to opt out, suppressing their "revolts" by force of arms, and turning the league more and more into an instrument of Athenian policy.

Cimon's military successes made him the most powerful politician in Athens. By the 460s, however, the political mood in Athens was changing. New voices were demanding a greater role in government, especially the *thetes*, the lowest of the four classes established by Solon. As rowers, these men were the backbone of the all-important Athenian fleet; as citizens, however, they played little role in the government of their polis.

A political rival of Cimon's, Pericles used a platform of greater enfranchisement of the thetes and an anti-Spartan foreign policy to defeat Cimon. Pericles was elected strategos for 462–461 and secured the ostracism of Cimon from Athens. He then pushed through reforms to make Athens more fully democratic. He gave every Athenian citizen the right to propose and amend legislation, not just to vote yes or no in the citizen assembly. He also made it easier for poorer citizens to participate in the assembly and the great appeals courts of Athens by paying an average day's wage for attendance. Through these and other measures, the thetes became a dominant force in politics, loyal to the man who had made that dominance possible.

Pericles glorified Athens' democracy with an ambitious scheme of public building and lavish festivals to the gods, especially Athena. He was also a generous patron of the arts, sciences, and literature, attracting the greatest minds of the day to Athens. His populist political stance, combined with his ability to inspire a sense of Athenian superiority, ensured his reelection as strategos for the next three decades. During these years, Athenian culture flourished as never before. Pericles would prove to be a disastrous political leader; but Periclean Athens represents a dramatic and brilliant moment in the history of Western civilizations.

LITERATURE AND DRAMA

Periclean Athens was not the only city to produce great works of literature during the golden age, but our knowledge of classical Greek literature is dominated by the poetry and drama (both tragic and comedic) produced there. Epic and lyric poetry were already well-established Greek literary forms when the fifth century began. Drama, however, appears to have been an innovation that developed in Athens out of the poetic odes chanted by choruses to the god Dionysius at the great spring festival devoted to him. Credit for transforming the Dionysian odes into a genuine drama with characters and a chorus belongs to the great

Greek Theater in Epidauros. Greek dramas were invariably presented in the open air. The construction of this theater, which takes advantage of the slope of the hill, and the arrangement of the stage are of particular interest. The plan for the theater is shown above.

TO WHAT EXTENT WAS THE CULTURE OF ATHENS IN THE GOLDEN AGE THE PRODUCT OF DEMOCRACY?

THE "GOLDEN AGE" OF CLASSICAL GREECE   97

tragedian Aeschylus (525–456 B.C.E.), who by introducing a second (and later a third) character into the performance, made it possible to present conversation, and hence human conflict, on the stage for the first time. Staging remained very simple, but the emotional impact of tragic drama could be overwhelming.

The themes of Greek tragedy—justice, law, and the conflicting demands of piety and obligation that drove a heroic man or woman to destruction—were derived from Homer. But tragedy could also have a decidedly contemporary aspect. Sophocles' (496–406 B.C.E.) great masterpiece, *Oedipus at Colonus*, was presented in the midst of Athens' disastrous war with Sparta. Euripides' (485–406 B.C.E.) *Trojan Women* was presented in 415, the year of the expedition to Syracuse and the turning point in the Athenians' march toward defeat in the Peloponnesian War (see below). Tragedy dealt in absolutes, most memorably perhaps in Sophocles' *Antigone*, the story of a clash between justice and law, and the competing obligations of familial piety and civic necessity; but its context was inevitably the history of Athens in the period of its own greatest achievements and failures.

Comedy was even more directly a genre of direct political commentary. Comedy was crude, parodic, and outspoken, full of slapstick, absurdity, and vulgarity. Its themes were (in the scholar Peter Levi's words) "sex, life on the farm, the good old days, the nightmare of politics, the oddities of religion, the strange manners of the town." Aristophanes (c. 448–382 B.C.E.), the greatest of the Athenian comedic playwrights, ridiculed everything that offended or amused him: the philosophy of Socrates, the tragedies of Euripides, and especially the imperialistic warmongering of contemporary politicians such as Cleon. But above all else, Aristophanes was a social critic, who routinely savaged the powerful political figures whom he believed (with justice) were leading Athens to its doom. He was repeatedly dragged into court to defend himself against the politicians whom he had attacked. But despite their anger, the politicians never dared to shut down the comedic theater for long. It was too much a part of the spirit of democratic Athens.

Periclean Athens was also fertile ground for the development of Greek prose. During the sixth century, Greeks typically expressed ideas through poetry. In the fifth century, however, the prose emerged as a distinct literary form. Herodotus found a ready market for his "inquiries" (*historiai*) in Athens. His younger contemporary Thucydides (c. 460–c. 400 B.C.E.) wrote a masterful history of the great war between Athens and Sparta. Between them, these two historians developed a new approach to history, emphasizing the reliability of their sources and looking for human explanations for historical events. The development of prose would make possible in the fourth century even further literary achievements, such as the great philosophical treatises of Plato and Aristotle and the stirring political and legal speeches of the great Attic orators we will meet in the next chapter.

ART AND ARCHITECTURE

The Greeks of the golden age revealed the same range of genius in the visual arts as they did in their drama. Their comic gift—exuberance, cheerful sensuality, and coarse wit—can be seen especially in their "black figure" vases and jugs, whose characters often look like glinting rascals up to some sort of mischief, usually sexual. More dignified were the marble statues and sculptured reliefs the Greeks made for temples and public places. Athenian sculptors in particular took human greatness as their theme, depicting the beauty of the human form in statuary that was simultaneously naturalistic and idealizing.

> Athenian sculptors in particular took human greatness as their theme, depicting the beauty of the human form in statuary that was simultaneously naturalistic and idealizing.

The Athenians also made exceptional contributions to architecture. All Greek temples sought to create an impression of harmony and repose, but the Parthenon of Athens, built between 447 and 438 B.C.E., is generally considered the finest example of its genre. Construction of this stunning, expensive, and difficult building was urged on the Athenians by Pericles, who saw it as a symbol of devotion to their patron goddess, Athena, and a triumphant celebration of their own power and confidence.

WOMEN AND MEN IN THE DAILY LIFE OF ATHENS

Toward the end of his famous Funeral Oration, Pericles urged the married women of Athens to do three things: rear more children for the sake of Athens; show no more weakness than was "natural to their sex"; and avoid gossip. His remarks reveal widely held

Apollo of Tenea; Apollo of Piombino; the "Critian Boy." These three statues, dating from about 560, 500, and 480 B.C.E. respectively, display the progressive "unfreezing" of Greek statuary art. The first stiff and symmetrical statue is imitative of Egyptian sculpture. Roughly half a century later it is succeeded by a figure that begins to display motion, as if awakening from a sleep of centuries in a fairy tale. The last figure introduces genuine naturalism in its delicate twists and depiction of the subject's weight resting on one leg.

male attitudes toward women in classical Greece, but especially in Athens.

Rather than leading to greater equality among the sexes, the growth of democracy had the opposite result. In the Dark Age, aristocratic women were sometimes portrayed as possessing extraordinary traits of beauty, wisdom, or courage. These women gave shrewd advice on political and military matters and played an active role in the world around them. But as aristocratic ideals gave way to more democratic ones, life in the shadows increasingly became women's lot. Public spaces were restricted to male activities such as athletics and political gatherings, while domestic, private spaces were reserved for female activities such as

child rearing and weaving. By the fifth century B.C.E., "respectable" women lived in seclusion, rarely if ever venturing forth from their houses.

In Athens, girls could be married at age fourteen—as soon as they were biologically capable of childbearing—to husbands more than twice their age. A girl's father arranged her marriage and provided a dowry that her husband could use for her support. Shortly after a wife entered her new home, a regular schedule of childbearing would usually begin. Typically the interval between births was between two and four years, meaning that the average young wife would bear between four and six children before she died, usually around the age of thirty-five.

Flute Player. An Athenian marble relief dating from about 470 B.C.E. The relaxed pose (reclining position, crossed legs) and naturalistic representation of the naked female form were unprecendented in human art before the classical age of the Greeks.

Women seldom went out of doors, as it was thought immodest for them to be seen by other men. Slaves did whatever shopping or marketing the household required. Even at home, women were expected to withdraw into private rooms if visitors arrived. Because the ideology of democratic Athens opposed excessive displays of wealth or leisure, women were not supposed to sit around idly; their main occupation was probably cloth weaving. But since "women's work" was basically menial, men looked down on women for engaging in it. Available evidence suggests that husbands customarily had little emotional attachment to their wives, regarding them as natural inferiors. In a revealing passage Herodotus says of a certain Lydian king, "[T]his Candaules fell in love with his own wife, a fancy that had strange consequences. . . ." An Athenian orator remarked, "[P]rostitutes we have for pleasure, concubines for daily physical attendance, wives to bear us legitimate children and be our faithful housekeepers."

Athenian society was as dependent on its slaves as the Spartans were on the helots. Without slavery, none of the extraordinary Athenian accomplishments in politics, thought, or art would have been possible. The Athenian ideal of dividing and rotating governmental duties among all free men depended on slaves who worked in fields, businesses, and homes while free men engaged in politics. Freedom and slavery were inescapably linked.

LEAGUE BUILDING AND THE PELOPONNESIAN WAR

How did the Peloponnesian War influence Greek philosophy?

Athenians saw themselves as the freest of men, but their freedom rested on the servitude of others. Slaves performed much of the labor at home, while Athens' allies in the Delian League provided the resources that underlay Athenian greatness. Without the surplus wealth flowing into Athens from the league, none of the projects Pericles undertook—pay for political participation, massive building projects (also, incidentally, an employment program for poorer citizens), the patronage of Athenian drama—would have been possible. These projects kept Athens powerful, her democracy vibrant, and Pericles popular and in power. But Athens' democratic achievements rested upon its control over an alliance it had transformed into an empire.

Since the 470s, Athens had faced attempts by its allies to break away, and it had crushed those efforts ruthlessly. Through the 450s, such revolts were rare. But in the early 440s, Pericles determined on a more aggressive policy toward Sparta, by then Athens' only real rival for supremacy in the Greek world. To give himself a freer hand, he concluded a formal peace with Persia. After this peace, the purpose of the Delian League evaporated, and Athens had no justification for compelling its allies to remain within it. Many remained loyal nonetheless, paying their contributions and enjoying the economic benefits of warm relations with Athens. Others, however, did not, and Athens found itself increasingly forcing its allies back into line, often installing Athenian garrisons and planting Athenian colonists—who retained their Athenian citizenship—to ensure future loyalty.

In the context of Greek culture, such behavior was disturbing. The Delian League had been established to

THE PELOPONNESIAN WAR

Consider the balance of power between Athens and Sparta at the outbreak of the Peloponnesian War. Which side had the geographical advantage? Which neutral powers might have been able to tip the balance by entering the war on one side or the other? What strategic and military choices did geography impose on the two combatants and their allies?

preserve Greek independence against the Persians. Now many Greeks accused Athens of having become a tyrannical empire itself. Foremost among the accusers were the Corinthians, whose own economic standing was seriously threatened by Athenian dominance of the Aegean. The Corinthians were close allies of the Spartans, the dominant power in what historians call the "Peloponnesian League." (The Greeks called it simply the "Spartans and their allies."). When war finally erupted

between Athens and Sparta, the great historian Thucydides ascribed it to the growing power of Athens, and the fear and envy this inspired in Sparta. No modern historian has improved on Thucydides' formulation. For the Athenian democracy and its leader, there could be no question of relinquishing the empire, the cornerstone of Athens' cultural and political ascendancy. By the 430s, however, Athens could not preserve that empire without threatening the interests of Sparta and its allies.

THE PELOPONNESIAN WAR ERUPTS

After a series of provocations, the Athenians and Spartans found themselves at war with one another in 431 B.C.E. Athens could not defeat Sparta on land; but neither Sparta nor its allies had a fleet capable of facing the Athenians on the seas. Pericles therefore developed a bold strategy: he would pull the entire population of Attica within the walls of Athens and its harbor, abandoning the countryside to Sparta, while the superior Athenian fleet supplied Athens from the sea and ravaged the coasts of Spartan territory. As in many of history's pivotal contests, both sides believed a conclusion would come quickly.

Time appeared to be on Athens' side, but in 429 B.C.E. the crowded conditions of the besieged city gave rise to an epidemic that killed over a third of the Athenian population, including Pericles. Pericles' death showed that he was the only man capable of managing the democratic political forces he had unleashed. His successors were mostly demagogues, ambitious men who played to the worst instincts of the demos to gain power for themselves. The most successful of these was a warmonger named Cleon, a particular target of Aristophanes' invective, who refused a Spartan offer of peace in 425 B.C.E. and continued the war until his own death in battle four years later.

A short-lived truce then ensued, authored by an able Athenian leader named Nicias. But the Athenian demos was in no mood for a long peace and soon fell under the spell of a charming, flamboyant, but unscrupulous aristocrat named Alcibiades, who convinced the Athenians in 415 B.C.E. to reopen hostilities with an ill-advised attack on the distant city of Syracuse in Sicily. The expedition failed, with thousands of Athenians killed or enslaved in Sicily.

News of the Syracusan disaster shattered the Athenian demos. Recriminations began immediately. Many political leaders were driven from the polis, and in 411 B.C.E. the demos suffered a momentary but monumental lack of self-confidence. While the rowers in the fleet were away from the city, the Athenians essentially voted the democracy out of existence, replacing it with an oligarchy of four hundred citizens. The Athenian fleet, stationed in Samos, responded by declaring a democratic government in exile under the leadership of none other than Alcibiades. The oligarchy proved to be brief, and democracy was restored to Athens by 409. But the fact that the war could force such desperation did not bode well for the future.

A Modern Replica of an Athenian Trireme. These versatile warships were powered by both oars and sail.

THE END OF THE WAR

The Spartans too despaired of bringing the war to an end. Despite Athens' problems, its fleet was still invincible. Finally, Sparta turned to the Persians, who agreed to supply the gold and the naval expertise necessary to create an effective Spartan fleet. By 407, a talented and ambitious Spartan commander, Lysander, was successfully harrying the Athenians throughout the eastern Aegean Sea.

The result should have been predictable. Lysander destroyed the poorly led Athenian fleet in 404 B.C.E. Without their fleet the Athenians could neither feed themselves nor defend their city. Lysander sailed around the Aegean unopposed, installing pro-Spartan oligarchies among the former allies of Athens. Finally, he besieged Athens itself. Facing the inevitable, the Athenians surrendered. Corinth and Thebes called for Athens' destruction. The Spartans refused to allow this, but imposed harsh terms: the dismantling of Athens' walls, the scrapping of its fleet, and the acceptance of an oligarchic government of thirty Athenians.

For the Greeks, the Peloponnesian War was a disaster. From the long perspective of historical distance, we may view it as demonstrating the limitations of the polis system. The competitive ethos that characterized the Greek poleis proved to be their tragic flaw. To the Greeks themselves, however, the war offered no such clear lessons. Instead, it brought demoralization and a questioning of all the old certainties. Democracies had collapsed, empires had crumbled, and oligarchies like Sparta had proven incapable of rising to the challenges they now confronted. Even the gods seemed to be in disarray. These were the circumstances in which the great Athenian philosopher Socrates (469–399 B.C.E.) attempted to refound ethical and political life on new

and more certain principles. To understand his accomplishments, however, we must trace briefly the history of philosophical speculation in the half century before his birth.

THE LIFE AND THOUGHT OF SOCRATES

Prior to Socrates, philosophy in Athens was dominated by a new group of professional teachers known as "Sophists," a term simply meaning "those who are wise." The Sophists were not a coherent philosophical school. Their work did display some common threads, however, that are best exemplified by Protagoras, who was active in Athens from about 445 to 420 B.C.E. His famous dictum, "man is the measure of all things," meant that goodness, truth, and justice are relative to the needs and interests of human beings. In religious matters Protagoras was agnostic, declaring that he did not know whether the gods existed or what they did. Since he knew nothing of the gods, he concluded that

Socrates. According to Plato, Socrates looked like a goat-man but spoke like a god.

CHRONOLOGY	
EVOLUTION OF GREEK PHILOSOPHY	
Emergence of the "Milesian School" (pre-Socratics)	600–500 B.C.E.
Pythagoreans emerge in southern Italy	530 B.C.E.
Rise of the Sophists	450 B.C.E.
Death of Socrates	399 B.C.E.

TWO VIEWS OF SOPHISM

SOCRATES AS A SOPHIST

The image of Socrates held by most people is of the sage thinker who challenged the prevailing prejudices of his day and opposed the Sophists. During his own time, however, he was not so universally admired. In his comedy The Clouds, *Aristophanes' protagonist Strepsiades—ruined by the wastefulness of his son—goes to Socrates and his "Thought Shop" so that Socrates can make him and his son Pheidippides orators capable of winning lawsuits and thus enriching himself. Aristophanes implies throughout that Socrates is essentially just another Sophist, a man who teaches word games and logic tricks for hire.*

STREPSIADES: See that he [Pheidippides] learns your two Arguments, whatever you call them—oh yes, Right and Wrong—the one that takes a bad case and defeats Right with it. If he can't manage both, then at least Wrong—that will do—but that he must have.

SOCRATES: Well, I'll go and send the Arguments here in person, and they'll teach him themselves.

STREPSIADES: Don't forget, he's got to be able to argue against any kind of justified claim at all.

RIGHT: This way, Let the audience see you. . . .

WRONG: Sure, go wherever you like. The more of an audience we have, the more soundly I'll trounce you.

RIGHT: What sort of trick will you use?

WRONG: Oh, just a few new ideas.

RIGHT: Yes, they're in fashion now, aren't they, [to the audience] thanks to you idiots. . . . [to Pheiddipides] You don't want to be the sort of chap who's always in the agora telling stories about other people's sex lives, or in the courts arguing about some petty, filthy, little dispute. . . .

WRONG: People here at the Thought Shop call me Wrong, because I was the one who invented ways of proving anything wrong, laws, prosecutors, anything. Isn't that worth millions—to have a really bad case and yet win? . . . Suppose you fall in love with a married woman—have a bit of fun—and get caught in the act. As you are now, without a tongue in your head, you're done for. But if you come and learn from me, then you can do whatever you like and get away with it . . . and supposing you do get caught with someone's wife, you can say to him. . . . "What have I done wrong? Look at Zeus; wasn't he always a slave of his sexual passions? And do you expect a mere mortal like me to do any better than a god?" . . .

STREPSIADES [to Socrates]: I wonder if you'd accept a token of my appreciation? But my son, has he learned that Argument we were listening to a moment ago?

SOCRATES: Yes, he has.

STREPSIADES: Holy Fraud, how wonderful!

SOCRATES: Yes, you'll now be able to win any case at all.

STREPSIADES: Even if the witnesses were actually there when I was borrowing the money?

SOCRATES: Even if there were a thousand of them.

Aristophanes, *The Clouds*, based on the translation by Alan H. Sommerstein. (New York: Penguin, 1973), pp. 148–150, 154, 159–160.

Sophistry in Action: The Melian Dialogue

During the truce authored by the Athenian statesman Nicias in 421 B.C.E., both Athens and Sparta continued to pursue a "dirty war," living by the letter of their agreement but not its spirit, while preparing for the inevitable reopening of the conflict. The Aegean island of Melos—originally a Spartan colony—had so far maintained a policy of neutrality between Athens and Sparta. In 416, however, the Athenians insisted on their submission, and the Athenian envoys justified their position with a chillingly logical argument that "might makes right."

ATHENIANS: For ourselves, we will not trouble you with specious pretenses—either of how we have a right to our empire because we overthrew the Mede, or are now attacking you because of wrong that you have done us—and make a long speech which would not be believed; and in return we hope that you, instead of thinking to influence us by saying that you did not join the Spartans, although their colonists, or that you have done us no wrong, will aim at what is feasible, holding in view the real sentiments of us both; since you know as well as we do that right, as the world goes, is only in question between equals in power, while the strong do what they can and the weak suffer what they must. . . . We would desire to exercise empire over you without trouble, and see you preserved for the good of us both.

MELIANS: And how, pray, could it turn out as good for us to serve as for you to rule?

ATHENIANS: Because you would have the advantage of submitting before suffering the worst, and we should gain by not destroying you.

MELIANS: So you would not consent to our being neutral, friends instead of enemies, but allies of neither side?

ATHENIANS: No; for your hostility cannot so much hurt us as your friendship will be an argument to our subjects of our weakness, and your enmity of our power.

MELIANS: Is that your subjects' idea of equity, to put those who have nothing to do with you in the same category with peoples that are most of them your own colonists, and some conquered rebels?

ATHENIANS: As far as right goes they think one has as much of it as the other, and that if they maintain their independence it is because they are strong, and that if we do not molest them it is because we are afraid; so that besides extending our empire we should gain in security by your subjection. . . .

MELIANS: What is this but to make greater the enemies that you have already, and to force others to become so who would otherwise have never thought of it? . . . we know that the fortune of war is sometimes more impartial than the disproportion of numbers might lead one to suppose; to submit is to give ourselves over to despair, while action still preserves for us a hope that we may stand. . . .

ATHENIANS: Hope . . . may be indulged in by those who have abundant resources, if not without loss, at all events without ruin; but its nature is to be extravagant, and those who go so far as to stake their all upon the venture see it in its true colors only when they are ruined. . . . Let not this be the case with you, who are weak and hang on a single turn of the scale; nor be like the vulgar, who, when abandoning such security as human means may still afford, when visible hopes fail them in extremity, turn to the invisible, to prophecies and oracles, and other such inventions that delude men with hopes to their destruction. . . . When we come to your notion about the Spartans, which leads you to believe that shame will make them help you, here we bless your simplicity but do not envy your folly. . . . You do not adopt the view that expediency goes with security, while justice and honor cannot be followed without danger; and danger the Spartans generally court as little as possible. . . . Is it likely that while we are masters of the sea they will cross over to an island?

MELIANS: Should the Spartans miscarry in this, they would fall upon your land, and upon those left of your allies . . . and instead of places which are not yours, you will have to fight for your own country and your own confederacy.

ATHENIANS: Some diversion of the kind you speak of you may one day experience, only to learn, as others have done, that the Athenians never once yet withdrew from a siege for fear of any. . . . Think over the matter, therefore, and reflect once and again that it is for your country that you are consulting, and that upon this one deliberation depends its prosperity or ruin.

Thucydides, Book 5. *The Landmark Thucydides*, edited by Robert Strassler. (New York: Landmark Press, 1995), pp. 352–356.

there could be no absolute truths or eternal standards of right and wrong. If sense perception was the only source of knowledge, there could be only particular truths valid for the individual knower.

Such teachings struck many Athenians as dangerous. By encouraging people to examine each new situation on its own terms and merits, Sophists for the first time made everyday life a subject for philosophical discussion. But the relativism of such Sophists as Protagoras could easily degenerate into the doctrine that the wise man is the one who knows best how to manipulate others and gratify his own desires, and so could be used to rationalize monstrous acts of brutality. To some critics, such ideas were antidemocratic; to others, they smacked of atheism and anarchy. If there was no final truth, and if goodness and justice were merely relative to the whims of the individual, then religion, morality, the state, and society itself could not be maintained. This conviction led to the growth of a new philosophical movement grounded on the theory that truth is real and that absolute standards do exist. The initiator of this new trend was Socrates. Socrates was an ardent patriot who believed Athens was being corrupted by the shameful doctrines of the Sophists. But he was not an unthinking patriot who cherished slogans. Rather, he wished to submit every presumed truth to rigorous examination, in order to reconstruct Athenian life on a firm foundation of ethical certainty. It is bitterly ironic that such a dedicated idealist should have been put to death by his own countrymen. Shortly after the end of the Peloponnesian War, in 399 B.C.E., when Athens was reeling from the shock of defeat and violent internal upheavals, a democratic faction decided that Socrates was a threat to the state. A democratic court agreed, condemning him to death for impiety and "corrupting the youth." Although his friends made arrangements for him to flee, Socrates decided to accept the popular judgment and abide by the laws of his polis. He died by calmly drinking a cup of poison.

Because Socrates wrote nothing himself, it is difficult to determine exactly what he taught. Contemporary reports, however, especially by his student Plato, make a few points clear. First, Socrates subjected all inherited assumptions to rigorous criticism. Styling himself a "gadfly," he continually engaged his contemporaries in "Socratic" questioning, seeking to show them that all their supposed certainties were merely unexamined prejudices resting on false assumptions. According to Plato, an oracle once said that Socrates was the wisest person in the world and Socrates agreed: everyone else thought he knew something, but he was wiser because he knew he knew nothing. Second, he sought to base his philosophical speculations on sound definitions of words. Third, he focused his attention on ethics rather than on studying the physical world. He shunned the traditional discussions of Milesian philosophers about why things exist, why they grow, and why they perish. Instead, Socrates urged people to reflect on principles of proper conduct, both for their own sake and for that of society. One should consider the meaning of one's life and actions at all times, for according to one of his most memorable sayings, "the unexamined life is not worth living."

All this might make Socrates sound rather like a Sophist; indeed, he felt compelled at his trial to insist that he was not. Like the Sophists, he was a "philosopher of the marketplace" who held tradition and cliché up to doubt in order to help people improve their lives. But the overwhelming difference between Socrates and the Sophists lay in his belief in certainties—even if he avoided saying what they were—and in the standard of absolute good rather than expediency he applied to all aspects of life. Socrates' death made clear, however, that in order to reestablish the polis, it would be necessary to go farther than Socrates himself had, by constructing a system that revealed a positive framework of truth and reality. This was the task Socrates' most brilliant student, Plato, would undertake in the wake of the disasters of the Peloponnesian War. In so doing, he would lay the groundwork for all subsequent Western philosophical thinking up to the present day.

CONCLUSION

Ever since the Renaissance, Europeans have liked to think of themselves as the heirs of the classical Greeks, and to imagine the Greeks as mirror images of themselves. Such uncritical admiration is misleading. Despite the religious skepticism of a few intellectuals, the Greeks were neither secularists nor rationalists. Although they invented the concept of democracy, only a small percentage of the population was ever permitted to play a role in political affairs. Greek statecraft was characterized by imperialism and aggressive war. The Greeks made no great advances in economic enterprise, and they scorned commerce. Finally, not even the Athenians could be described as tolerant. Socrates was not the only man put to death merely for expressing his opinions.

And yet the profound significance of the Greek experiment for the history of Western civilizations is undeniable. The typical political regime of the ancient Near Eastern world was that of an absolute monarch supported by a powerful priesthood. Culture was mainly as an instrument to enhance the prestige of rulers and priests, and economic life tended to be controlled by powerfully organized governmental and religious bodies. In contrast, the civilization of Greece, notably in its Athenian form, was founded on ideals of freedom, competition, individual achievement, and human glory. As Herodotus has a Greek (in this case a Spartan) say to a Persian, "You understand how to be a slave, but you know nothing of freedom. . . . If you had but tasted it you would counsel us to fight for it not only with spears but with axes."

Another way of appreciating the enduring importance of Greek civilization to the Western world is to recall some of the words that come to us from this civilization: politics, democracy, philosophy, metaphysics, history, tragedy. These are all ways of thinking and acting that have enriched human life immeasurably, but that had hardly been known before the Greeks invented them. To a startling degree the Western concept of "humanity" itself—the exalted role within nature of the human race in general and the individual human being in particular—comes to us from the Greeks. For the Greeks, the aim of existence was the fullest development of one's human potential: the work of becoming a person, called in Greek *paideia*, meant that every free man was supposed to be the sculptor of his own statue. When the Romans took up this ideal from the Greeks, they called it *humanitas*, from which we derive the English word "humanity." The Romans admitted their indebtedness when they remarked that "Greece was where humanity was invented." It is hard to doubt that they were right.

KEY TERMS

Polis

Hoplite

Solon

Spartiate

Pre-Socratics

Pericles

Peloponnesian War

Sophists

Socrates

SELECTED READINGS

Penguin Classics and the Loeb Classical Library both offer reliable translations of Greek literary, philosophical, and historical texts.

Boardman, John, Jaspar Griffin, and Oswyn Murray, eds. *Greece and the Hellenistic World*. Oxford, 1988. A reprint of the Greek and Hellenistic chapters from *The Oxford History of the Classical World*, originally published in 1986. Excellent, stimulating surveys, accessible to a general audience but provocative to specialists.

Brunschwig, Jacques, and Geoffrey E. R. Lloyd. *Greek Thought: A Guide to Classical Knowledge*. Translated by Catherine Porter. Cambridge, Mass., 2000. An outstanding, up-to-date work of reference.

Buckley, Terry, ed. *Aspects of Greek History, 750–323 B.C.: A Source-Based Approach*. London, 1999. An outstanding new collection of source materials.

Cartledge, Paul A. *Sparta and Laconia: A Regional History, 1300–362 B.C.* London, 1979. The standard survey of Spartan history by the leading English-speaking authority.

Dover, Kenneth J. *Greek Homosexuality*. Cambridge, Mass., 1978. The standard account of an important subject.

Fantham, Elaine, Helene Foley, Natalie Kampen, Sarah B. Pomeroy, and H. A. Shapiro. *Women in the Classical World: Image and Text*. Oxford, 1994. Wide-ranging analysis drawing on both visual and written sources, covering both the Greek and the Roman periods.

Fornara, Charles W., and Loren J. Samons II. *Athens from Cleisthenes to Pericles*. Berkeley, 1991. An excellent narrative history of Athenian politics during the first half of the fifth century B.C.E.

Freeman, Charles. *The Greek Achievement: The Foundation of the Western World*. New York, 1999. An admiring survey written for a general audience.

Garlan, Yvon. *Slavery in Ancient Greece*. Ithaca, N.Y., 1988. Now the standard account.

Hanson, Victor Davis. *The Other Greeks: The Family Farm and the Agrarian Roots of Western Civilization*. New York, 1995. Occasionally polemical and idiosyncratic, but convincing in its emphasis on small-holding farmers as the backbone of Greek urban society.

Jones, Nicholas F. *Ancient Greece: State and Society*. Upper Saddle River, N.J., 1997. A concise survey from the Minoans up to the end of the Classical Period that emphasizes the connections between the social order and politics.

Levi, Peter. *Atlas of the Greek World*. New York, 1984. Excellent maps and illustrations supplement an outstanding text.

Morris, Ian, and Barry Powell, eds. *A New Companion to Homer*. Leiden, 1997. A collection of thirty specialist but accessible scholarly articles, encompassing the most recent research on Homer and Dark Age Greece.

Pomeroy, Sarah B., Stanley M. Burstein, Walter Donlan, and Jennifer Tolbert Roberts. *Ancient Greece: A Political, Social, and Cultural History*. Oxford, 1999. An outstanding new textbook: clear, lively, and up to date, with good bibliographies.

Price, Simon. *Religions of the Ancient Greeks*. Cambridge, 1999. Concise and authoritative, this survey extends from the Archaic Period up to the fifth century C.E.

Rowlandson, Jane, R. S. Bagnall, Alan Bowman, and Willy Clarysse, eds. *Women and Society in Greek and Roman Egypt: A Sourcebook*. Cambridge, 1999. A wide-ranging collection of sources from an extraordinarily well-documented area of the ancient world.

Strassler, Robert B., ed. *The Landmark Thucydides*. New York, 1996. Reprints the classic Richard Crawley translation with maps, commentary, notes, and appendices by leading scholars.

Thomas, Carol G., and Craig Conant. *Citadel to City-State: The Transformation of Greece, 1200–700 B.C.E.* Bloomington, 1999. A lucid and accessible study that examines developments at a number of different Dark Age sites.

CHAPTER FOUR

THE EXPANSION OF GREECE

THE SUPREME TRAGEDY OF THE GREEKS was their failure to solve the problem of internecine political conflict. The fifth century in Greece had ended with a debilitating and destructive war of attrition between Athens and Sparta. The fourth century continued along much the same path, as the major poleis—Sparta, then Thebes, then Athens again—jockeyed for dominance within the Greek world. But the independent temper of Greek political life could not suffer such dominance for long; and so as each great polis appeared on the brink of realizing its goals, a coalition of age-old enemies would form to defeat it. Despite mounting calls for the Greeks to set aside their local differences and unite in a common cause, they could not escape their heritage of particularism.

Social and economic difficulties were also mounting, stemming from ideologically driven civil wars within the poleis as well as from the endemic warfare among them. Faith in the old ideals of equality decayed as a vast gulf opened up between the rich and the poor. Increasingly, the wealthy withdrew from politics altogether; meanwhile, the number of free citizens declined as poverty-stricken freemen and freewomen descended into slavery. The result was despair and cynicism.

The age did not lack for creative energy. Philosophy, science, and literature blossomed in the fourth century, as men of talent shunned public life, turning their attention instead to the life of the mind. As the polis system decayed, thinkers debated what the polis was, how and why it functioned, and how it might be improved. But even the greatest of these thinkers remained enclosed within the parochial world of the polis.

The unhappy equilibrium of the Greek world was shattered in the last half of the fourth century by the sudden emergence of the kingdom of Macedonia. The extraordinary conquests of Philip of Macedon unified Greece. Those of his son

FOCUS QUESTIONS

• What conditions led to the growing number of mercenaries in the fourth century B.C.E.?

• Why did Plato's ideal polis differ from Aristotle's?

• What accounts for the remarkable success of the Macedonian conquests?

• What characteristics defined and distinguished the three major Hellenistic kingdoms?

• Why was prosperity so unevenly distributed in the Hellenistic economy?

• What was the relationship between Epicureanism and Stoicism?

• What were the principal themes of Hellenistic architecture and sculpture?

• Why did science and medicine flourish in this period?

• What changes occurred during the Hellenistic period to the polis-based culture of classical Greece?

Alexander the Great extended Greek culture by force of arms from Egypt to Persia to the frontiers of India. Alexander's empire did not last. But the cosmopolitan, Greek-like (hence, *Hellenistic*, as opposed to *Hellenic*) culture to which it gave rise became the most powerful and pervasive cultural influence the Near Eastern world would know until the rise of Islam almost a thousand years later.

FAILURES OF THE FOURTH-CENTURY POLIS

What conditions led to the growing number of mercenaries in the fourth century B.C.E.?

The Peloponnesian War had left Sparta as the preeminent power in the Greek world, but the Spartans showed little talent for the position their unexpected victory had thrust upon them. In 395, a significant portion of Greece—including such traditional enemies as Athens, Argos, Corinth, and Thebes—aligned itself against Sparta in the Corinthian War (395–387 B.C.E.). The Spartans, for their part, could bring matters to a resolution only by forcing a peace on their fellow Greeks brokered from the outside—essentially composed and guaranteed by the Persians. This pattern was repeated time and again over the next fifty years, during which the advantage shifted steadily toward Persia.

SOCIAL AND ECONOMIC CRISES

The incessant warfare, combined with internal political struggles, profoundly affected society and economy throughout the Greek world. Even wealthy cities such as Athens and Sparta had exhausted their resources through war. Many personal fortunes had been lost, and many ordinary people had been driven from their homes or reduced to slavery. Country towns had been ravaged, some repeatedly, as had farmlands throughout Greece. The destruction of orchards and vineyards was particularly devastating, because of the long time it takes to nourish olive trees and grapevines to a productive state; but even arable land was now less productive than it had been earlier. As a result, standards of living declined significantly during the fourth century.

Unemployment was widespread, especially among the growing population of the cities. During wartime, men might find employment as rowers or soldiers in the service of their city. When their city was at peace, many turned instead to mercenary service. The Greek states of Sicily and Italy hired mercenaries from the mainland, as did Sparta to supplement her own campaigns in Asia Minor. A pretender to the Persian throne even hired a mostly Greek mercenary army in an attempt to overthrow his older brother, the reigning king. These Greeks fought their way into the heart of the Persian empire, and when the pretender fell in battle, the ten thousand Greek mercenaries fought their way back out. It was a stunning demonstration of what even a smallish Greek army might accomplish on Persian soil. But when mercenaries could not find work abroad, they were likely to terrorize the local Greek countryside. Such depredations only added to the disastrous cycle of destruction, inflation, and overpopulation caused by land failure.

THE CULTURAL AND INTELLECTUAL RESPONSE

Why did Plato's ideal polis differ from Aristotle's?

The breakdown of polis society during the fourth century had a profound impact on philosophy, the arts, and political thought. These developments laid the groundwork for the even more stunningly creative departures of the Hellenistic era. Scholars have sometimes presented fourth-century culture as if it represented a decline from the great artistic and intellectual achievements of the fifth century B.C.E. But such a sweeping verdict on fourth-century B.C.E. culture is unjustified. It underestimates not only the continuities between fifth- and fourth-century Greek culture, but also the originality and creativity of these new developments.

ART AND LITERATURE

Sculptors were already attempting to achieve a heightened sense of realism, especially in portraiture, when the fourth century B.C.E. began. Realism had been a hallmark of classical art as well, but in the fourth century artists tried increasingly to render objects as they actually looked, rather than portraying them in an idealized, dignified form. Fourth-century artists also paid more attention to life and movement, a trend that would culminate in the breathtaking works of the Hellenistic period.

Drama, by contrast, changed profoundly. No fourth-century authors emerged to match the great tragedians of the Athenian golden age. Nor did the comic genius of Aristophanes have any true fourth-century successors. Even in his own lifetime, however, Aristophanes' biting, satirical style was beginning to give way to a milder, less provocative drama that bears some resemblance to modern television comedies. It was this new style that laid the groundwork for the "New Comedy" of the fourth and third centuries B.C.E.

Perhaps the most striking development in fourth-century drama is the flight from social and political commentary. Fourth-century audiences looked to drama for diversion and escape; they no longer cared for the scathing indictments of society and of prominent individuals that Aristophanes had pioneered. Comedic humor was now based on mistaken identities, tangled familial relationships, comic misunderstandings, and breaches of etiquette. Similar trends are ap-

parent in novels, a new literary genre that emerged during the fourth century. Here, too, lovers face extraordinary obstacles, but their affairs almost always end happily, with the lovers reunited after perilous adventures and a long separation.

PHILOSOPHY AND POLITICAL THOUGHT IN THE AGE OF PLATO AND ARISTOTLE

The intellectual shift begun by Socrates was carried on brilliantly by his most talented student, Plato. Born in Athens to an aristocratic family around 429 B.C.E., Plato joined Socrates' circle as a young man and soon saw his mentor condemned to death. This experience made such an indelible impression on Plato that from then until his own death around 349 B.C.E. he shunned direct political involvement, seeking instead to vindicate Socrates by constructing a philosophical system based on Socratic precepts. Plato taught this system in Athens

Left: **Hellenistic Aphrodite.** This figure, dating from the fourth century B.C.E., displays the Hellenistic fascination with ungainly, "unnatural" postures.
Right: **French Bather.** This statuette done by Edgar Degas around 1890 shows some evident continuities between Hellenistic and modern art.

in an informal school (no buildings, tuition, or set curriculum) called the Academy, and also by writing a series of *dialogues* (treatises expressed in dramatic form) in which Socrates was the main speaker. The Platonic dialogues, including the *Phaedo*, the *Symposium*, and the *Republic*, are enduring works of literature as well as the earliest surviving complete works of philosophy.

Plato was influenced by the two worlds in which he lived. As a young man, he had watched his teacher engage the relativism of the Sophists; as an adult, he lived in a rapidly changing world that had lost confidence in absolute truths. Plato understood that in order to combat skepticism and refute the Sophists he needed to provide a secure foundation for ethics. This he did by means of his doctrine of Ideas. He conceded that relativity and change are characteristics of the world we perceive with our senses, but he denied that this world of appearances was an appropriate foundation for philosophy. A higher, spiritual realm exists, composed of eternal forms or Ideas that only the mind can grasp. These unchanging Ideas are not mere abstractions but have a real existence. The things we perceive through our senses are merely imperfect copies of the supreme realities, the Ideas, and relate to them as shadows relate to material objects. By understanding and contemplating the Idea of the Good, one might achieve the ultimate goal of fulfillment through virtue.

Plato addressed himself to politics in his most famous dialogue, the *Republic*, the first systematic treatment of political philosophy ever written. Because Plato sought social harmony and order rather than liberty or equality, he argued for an elitist state in which most of the people—the farmers, artisans, and traders—would be governed by an intellectually superior group of "guardians." Guardians would be chosen for their naturally superior attributes of intelligence and character. These enlightened rulers would see to it that every aspect of life was subordinated to the Idea of the Good, and would in turn choose only the wisest to succeed them. Later commentators have often found this ideal of rule by the wisest to be seductive, but they ask of Plato, "Who will guard the guardians?" Plato's system presumed that properly educated rulers would never be corrupted by power or wealth—a proposition that has yet to be sustained in practice.

> In contrast to Plato, who taught that everything we see and touch is but an untrustworthy reflection of some intangible truth, Aristotle believed in the objective reality of material objects and taught that systematic investigation of tangible things, combined with rational inquiry into how they function, could yield full comprehension of the natural order and of human beings' place within it.

ARISTOTELIAN THOUGHT

Such practical considerations were more typical of the thought of Plato's own greatest student, Aristotle (384–322 B.C.E.). Aristotle was the son of a physician, who learned from his father the importance of carefully observing natural phenomena. He accepted Plato's assumption that there are some things only the mind can grasp, but his own philosophical system was based on his confidence that the human mind could understand the universe through the rational ordering of sense experience. In contrast to Plato, who taught that everything we see and touch is but an untrustworthy reflection of some intangible truth, Aristotle believed in the objective reality of material objects and taught that systematic investigation of tangible things, combined with rational inquiry into how they function, could yield full comprehension of the natural order and of human beings' place within it.

Aristotle surveyed a wide variety of subjects in separate but interrelated treatises on logic, metaphysics, ethics, poetics, and politics. He was the first formal logician known to human history, and probably the greatest. He established rules for the syllogism, a form of reasoning in which certain premises inevitably lead to a valid conclusion, and he established precise categories underpinning all philosophical and scientific analysis. Aristotle's central belief was that all things in the universe consist of the imprint of form on matter. This was a compromise between Platonism, which tended to ignore matter, and the purest materialism, which saw no patterns in the universe other than the accidents of matter impinging on matter. For Aristotle, forms are the purposeful forces that shape the world of matter; thus the presence of the form of humanity molds and directs the human embryo until it ultimately becomes a human being. Since everything has a purposeful form, the universe for Aristotle is teleological—that is, every item and every class of items is inherently aiming toward its own particular end. Aristotle's universe is therefore in a constant state of motion, as everything within it moves toward its ultimate perfected form (known in Greek as its *telos*).

Aristotle's moral philosophy was expressed most fully in his *Nicomachean Ethics*, although important aspects of

WHAT ACCOUNTS FOR THE REMARKABLE SUCCESS OF THE MACEDONIAN CONQUESTS?

THE RISE OF MACEDON AND THE CONQUESTS OF ALEXANDER   113

his ideas are also contained in his *Politics*. Aristotle taught that the highest good consists in the harmonious functioning of the individual human mind and body. Humans differ from the animals by virtue of their rational capacities, and so they find happiness by exercising these appropriately. For most people this will mean exercising reason in practical affairs. Good conduct is virtuous conduct, and virtue resides in aiming for the golden mean: courage rather than rashness or cowardice, temperance rather than excessive indulgence or ascetic denial. Better than the practical life, however, is the contemplative life, for such a life allows those few men equipped for it by nature to exercise their rational capacities to the utmost. Aristotle believed therefore that philosophers were the happiest of men, but he understood that even they could not engage in contemplation without interruption. As a practical person, moreover, he deemed it necessary for them to intersperse their speculative activities with practical life in the real world.

Whereas Plato conceived of politics as a means to an end, the orderly pursuit of the supernatural Good, Aristotle thought of politics as an end in itself, the collective exercise of the good life. But Aristotle also took it for granted that some people—"barbarians"—were not fully human and so were meant by nature to be slaves. He also excluded women from the life of the polis, and so from a full measure of humanity, since they could not share in the life of the state in which human rational faculties enjoyed their fullest exercise. All male citizens, on the other hand, were meant to share in it, for, as Aristotle proposed, "man is by nature a political animal" (or, to be more faithful to the Greek, "a creature of the polis"). This view did not mean that the best form of government was democracy, however; like Plato, Aristotle saw that as a "debased" form of government. What he preferred was the polity, in which monarchical, aristocratic, and democratic elements were combined by means of checks and balances. Such a government would allow free men to realize their rational potential, showing themselves to be located in nature's hierarchy above the animals and right below the gods.

For all of their brilliance and originality, Plato and Aristotle could not "think outside the box" of their fourth-century world. Their answer to society's ills was not to restructure Greek political life, but to improve the life of the individual polis. Both imagined the perfect society as one made up of a few thousand households, largely engaged in agriculture and living in a face-to-face, participatory society. Although Greek civilization had begun in such a world, the realities of fourth-century political life were very different. The fact that Plato and Aristotle considered the problem at all is testament to their recognition that something was "wrong" with the polis; but for both men, the answer was a reorganization of the existing polity, not something new in its place.

THE RISE OF MACEDON AND THE CONQUESTS OF ALEXANDER

What accounts for the remarkable success of the Macedonian conquests?

By the middle of the fourth century, the Greeks had become so embroiled in turmoil that they at first barely noticed the growing power of Macedon, a kingdom on the northern fringes of the Greek world. They had little reason to do so; until the fourth century,

Philip II of Macedon. This tiny ivory head was discovered in the tomb of Philip of Macedon. The damaged right eye strongly suggests that it is a portrait of Philip himself, whose eye was damaged by a catapult bolt.

Macedon had been a weak kingdom, ruled by a royal house barely strong enough to control its own nobility, and beset by intrigue and murderous ambition from within. Most Greeks viewed the Macedonians themselves as barbarians, despite the efforts of a few Macedonian kings to add a bit of Hellenic culture to their court. When a young and energetic Macedonian king named Philip II consolidated the southern Balkans under his rule, many Greek patriots therefore saw it as a development no less troubling than the approach of the Persian "barbarians" in the fifth century.

THE REIGN OF PHILIP II
(359–336 B.C.E.)

Philip came to the throne of Macedon after his older brother died fighting a barbarian invasion, leaving as his heir a small boy. Philip had himself made regent for the boy, but soon dispensed with that fiction and took the throne himself. By 356, he certainly considered himself king. That same year a son was born to him; Philip named the child Alexander, and marked him out as his successor.

Philip's first problem was to stabilize his northern borders. Through a combination of warfare and diplomacy, he subdued the tribes of the southern Balkans and incorporated their territory into Macedonia. Philip's success had much to do with his reorganization of the Macedonian army. As a young boy, Philip had been a hostage at the court of Epaminondas; the observant youth may have learned something from watching the Theban general. In any event, Philip turned the Macedonian phalanx from an ill-organized peasant army into a highly drilled, well-armed fighting machine. The mineral resources Philip captured early in his reign made him wealthy enough to establish what was in essence a professional army—just one of his gold mines produced as much in one year as the Delian League collected annually at its height. Philip also organized an elite cavalry squad—the Companions—who fought with and beside the king. Philip recruited future Companions (and gained valuable hostages) by bringing the most promising sons of the nobility to his capital at Pella, where they trained as pages with the crown prince Alexander. Through a series of dynastic marriages, Philip also managed to gain the good will and alliance of many neighboring kingdoms.

The growing power of Macedon alarmed some in the Greek world, most notably an Athenian orator named Demosthenes. Whereas some Greeks, like Isocrates, saw in Philip a potential answer to Greece's woes, Demosthenes and others believed that Philip's ultimate aim was to subject Greece to his rule.

There is no doubt of the threat that Philip now posed; but Demosthenes and other Athenians misunderstood Philip's true goals. Philip's expansion in the north was not aimed at Athens; instead, it was designed to secure his frontiers and the resources necessary to support an invasion of Persia. From 348 on, he was keen to conciliate the major Greek poleis, especially Athens. At one point, he even asked for an alliance whereby the Athenians would provide the war fleet for his proposed invasion of the Persian empire; in return he would support their claim to hegemony over Greece. The Athenians took Demosthenes' advice, and refused to cooperate with Philip. This miscalculation would prove disastrous for Athens.

Philip's inability to reach any understanding with Athens, despite his strenuous diplomatic efforts, ultimately led to war between the Macedonians on one side and Athens, Thebes, and a number of smaller poleis on the other (Sparta remained aloof). At the battle of Chaeronea in 338 B.C.E., the Macedonians won a narrow victory over the Athenians and their allies. In the aftermath, Philip called delegates from around

Macedonian Phalanx. Philip of Macedon's infantry—and Alexander the Great's thereafter—was armed with two-handed pikes and massed in squares sixteen rows deep and wide. Members of the phalanx were trained to wheel in step in any direction or to double their front by filing off in rows of eight.

TWO VIEWS OF PHILIP

Philip II of Macedon provoked strong reactions among the Athenians, through whose eyes we must evaluate him due to the nature of our sources. As these passages illustrate, we could interpret his actions very differently, depending on whether we see in him a savior of Greece or a barbarian would-be conqueror.

ISOCRATES, TO PHILIP

As I kept going over these questions [of war and peace] in my own thoughts, I found that . . . the greatest states of Hellas should resolve to put an end to their mutual quarrels and carry the war beyond our borders into Asia. . . . I am going to advise you to champion the cause of concord among the Hellenes and of a campaign against the barbarian. . . . I affirm that, without neglecting any of your own interests you ought to reconcile Argos and Lacedaemon [Sparta] and Thebes and Athens; for if you can bring these cities together, you will not find it hard to unite the others as well. . . . If you can persuade four cities only to take a sane view of things, you will deliver the others also from many evils. . . . No quarrel should ever have arisen between you and any one of them. But unfortunately we are all prone by nature to do wrong more often than right. . . . For the future you must be on your guard to prevent a like occurrence, and must consider what service you can render them which will make it manifest that you have acted in a manner worthy both of yourself and what these cities have done. . . . It is a good thing to have the appearance of conferring benefits upon the greatest states of Hellas and at the same time to profit yourself no less than them. . . . You see how utterly wretched these states have become because of their warfare . . . and now perhaps someone will venture to object to what I have proposed, saying that I am trying to persuade you to set yourself to an impossible task. . . . While I grant that no one else in the world could reconcile these cities, yet nothing of the sort is difficult for you; for I see that you have carried through to a successful end many undertakings which the rest of the world looked upon as hopeless and unthinkable.

George Norlin, trans. *Isocrates.* Vol. 1. (Cambridge, Mass.: Harvard University Press, 1928), pp. 251, 255, 263–271.

DEMOSTHENES, SECOND AND THIRD OLYNTHIACS

I do not choose, Athenians, to enumerate the resources of Philip and by such arguments to call on you to rise to the occasion. Because it seems to me that any dissertation on that topic is a tribute to his enterprise, but a record of our failure. For the higher he has raised himself above his proper level, the more he wins the admiration of the world; but the more you have failed to improve your opportunities, the greater is the discredit you have incurred. . . . Now to call a man perjured and faithless, without drawing attention to his acts, might justly be termed mere abuse. . . . I have two reasons for thinking the whole story worth telling: Philip shall appear as worthless as he really is, and those who stand against his apparent invincibility shall see that he has exhausted all the acts of chicanery on which his greatness was founded at the first, and that his career has now reached the extreme limit. . . . He has hoodwinked everyone that has had any dealings with him; he has played upon the folly of each party in turn and exploited their ignorance of his own character. This is how he has gained his power. . . . Never was there a crisis that demanded more careful handling than the present. . . . Quite apart from the disgrace that we should incur if we shirk our responsibilities [to out threatened allies], I see not a little danger . . . if there is nothing to hinder Philip, when he has crushed his present foe, from turning his arms against Attica.

J. H. Vince, ed. and trans. *Demosthenes*, Vol. 1. (Cambridge, Mass.: Harvard University Press, 1930), pp. 23–27, 43,47.

mainland Greece to Corinth, where he established a new league. By and large, he left the independence of the major Greek poleis unaffected. The main purpose of the "League of Corinth" was to provide forces for the invasion of Asia Minor by electing Philip as their military commander. But the league also played some role in maintaining peace among the rival Greek poleis.

Philip never realized his dream of invading Persian territory. At a festival in Macedon in 336 B.C.E., a disgruntled lover charged into the arena and assassinated Philip. The kingship now fell to the twenty-year-old young man who had led his father's cavalry at Chaeronea, Alexander III. To the Greeks he would be known as Alexander Poliorcetes, the "Sacker of Cities." To the Romans, far more impressed by conquerors than were the Greeks, he was Alexander the Great.

THE CONQUESTS AND REIGN OF ALEXANDER (336–323 B.C.E.)

Alexander is a difficult figure for historians to understand, not least because in his own lifetime romantic legend had already built up around him and his achievements. Scholars have seen in Alexander a visionary, a genius, and a butcher; what he did was nothing less than transform the world, translating Greek culture from its parochial, small-scale homeland into a world culture, spreading it as far as the modern states of Afghanistan and Pakistan.

Alexander's military victories are well known. After first quelling revolts in Greece that erupted immediately on his father's death, by 334 he was ready to invade the Persian empire, then under the rule of Darius III. The Macedonian king won a series of startling victories, starting in northwest Asia Minor. Within three years of his initial invasion, Alexander had subdued Anatolia and the Syria-Palestine coast and had de-

tached Egypt from the Persian Empire. In 331 B.C.E., Darius mustered the remaining strength of his empire to face Alexander's Greco-Macedonian army in what is today northern Iraq. At the battle of Gaugamela, Alexander destroyed the Persian army. Darius himself fled to the hills, where he was captured and slain by a chieftain hoping to ingratiate himself to Alexander. The next spring, Alexander destroyed the Persian cap-

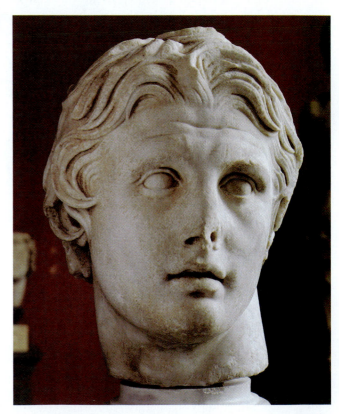

Marble Head of Alexander. Alexander the Great was reputed to have been very handsome, but all surviving representations doubtless make him more handsome still. This one dates from about 180 B.C.E. and is typical in showing Alexander with "lion's-mane hair."

WHAT ACCOUNTS FOR THE REMARKABLE SUCCESS OF THE MACEDONIAN CONQUESTS?

THE RISE OF MACEDON AND THE CONQUESTS OF ALEXANDER   117

THE CAMPAIGNS OF ALEXANDER

The conquests of Alexander the Great brought Greek culture to the vast area of the former Persian empire as far east as the Indus River. Notice the number of cities named after Alexander. Why did Alexander and his followers establish so many new cities, particularly in regions that were already highly urbanized?

ital of Persepolis, lest it serve as a rallying point for Persian resistance.

Over the next few years, Alexander campaigned in the mountains of Bactria (modern Afghanistan), the hardest fighting of the campaign. He ultimately succeeded in conquering much of the region, but his grasp there was tenuous. Among the Bactrians he found the woman he would take as his queen, Roxane. From there he moved down the Indus Valley, meeting stiff resistance. At the mouth of the Indus, his soldiers mutinied and refused to press on. Alexander reluctantly led them back toward Babylon, arriving there by the end of 324 B.C.E.

What Alexander planned to do with his new empire is difficult to say. Some scholars see him merely as a pirate, bent on conquest and plunder in a self-serving quest for glory worthy of the Homeric heroes from whom he claimed descent. Others counter by pointing to his systematic foundation of Greek-style poleis along his campaign route. These new cities served not only as garrisons to control the local populations but also as foci of Greek culture. There is also the bizarre mass marriage he forced on his officers, compelling them to put aside their wives and take Persian noblewomen as brides. Once seen as a reflection of Alexander's supposed visionary desire to eliminate ethnic distinctions within his empire, this act is now viewed as an attempt to breed a new nobility, loyal not to Macedonian or Persian concerns but to him and his successors alone. Alexander took no realistic steps to create an administration for his new realm, although he did move various officers and groups of veterans about in an attempt to reshuffle certain responsibilities. Our sources hint at plans for further conquests, perhaps Arabia, perhaps toward Italy and Sicily in the west. Given what we know about Alexander, it is hard to imagine him ever being satisfied with what he had.

We will never know for certain. In late May 323, Alexander fell ill with malarial symptoms and, ignoring the advice of his doctors, continued to play the part of the Homeric king, drinking mightily and exerting himself incautiously. His condition declined, until on June 10, 323 B.C.E., Alexander died, not yet thirty-three years old. His friends and officers had gathered around his deathbed, and asked to whom he wished to leave his empire. One source states that, just as he went unconscious, a wry smile adorned Alexander's face as he whispered "To the strongest." This might mean any of several talented and ambitious generals around him, who were second only to Alexander himself in prestige and martial skill.

THE HELLENISTIC KINGDOMS

> What characteristics defined and distinguished the three major Hellenistic kingdoms?

The wars and intrigues that took place in the two generations after Alexander's death are too involved to describe in detail. By 275 B.C.E., however, three separate axes of military and political power had emerged, each with a distinctive outlook despite their common background and their Greco-Macedonian ruling class.

PTOLEMAIC EGYPT

Following Alexander's death in Babylon, his inner circle met to decide the fate of his empire. The rest of Alexander's generals seem to have been glad to let Ptolemy have the hot, sweltering land of Egypt, but Ptolemy himself recognized the country's vast potential and its virtual invulnerability to attack. As soon as he arrived, Ptolemy set about making Egypt an independent kingdom under his rule. The dynasty he established would rule Egypt for the next three hundred years. The male heirs of the line all took the name Ptolemy, hence Ptolemaic Egypt.

Ruling from Alexandria, the great coastal city founded by Alexander, the Ptolemies acted as Macedonian kings toward their Greek and Macedonian subjects living in the thriving capital. Outside of Alexandria, however, they played the role of pharaohs, surrounding themselves with the trappings and symbols of Egypt's pharaonic heritage.

For the Ptolemies as for the ancient pharaohs, all of Egypt was basically crown land, to be exploited for the benefit of the royal house. The Ptolemies attempted to squeeze every last drop of wealth from the Egyptian countryside. Most of this wealth ended up in Alexandria. There was little interest in improving the lot of the Egyptian peasantry; in the ancient world it was often assumed that what kept the poor complacent and dutiful was their desperate poverty. The Ptolemies, however, overdid it, and from the end of the third century they faced regular and dangerous revolts from the native peasantry.

Nevertheless, Ptolemaic Egypt proved the most durable of the Hellenistic kingdoms. The dynasty used the wealth of the country to patronize science and the arts. Alexandria became a center of scholarship that attracted the greatest minds of the Hellenistic world. Many breakthroughs in astronomy, applied sciences, and physics took place in Alexandria, and the study of medicine advanced greatly under Ptolemaic rule. Freed from the taboos of their homeland, Greek medical researchers in Egypt were permitted to perform autopsies on the bodies of dead criminals, making it possible for anatomy to become a scientific discipline in its own right. The Ptolemies were not selfless patrons. They were largely interested in the glory and prestige their patronage brought them, rather than the practical benefits that might arise from the research they sponsored. But whatever its motives, Alexandrine scholarship left a permanent mark on the Mediterranean world.

SELEUCID ASIA

The vast Asian possessions of Alexander the Great eventually fell to another Macedonian, Seleucus, by 281 B.C.E. Unlike the Ptolemies, however, the Seleucid dynasty struggled with the problem of secession throughout its history. Their hold on the easternmost provinces was especially tenuous—even during Alexander's lifetime that had been the case—as Seleucus recognized. He therefore ceded much of the Indus Valley to the great Indian warrior-king Chandragupta in exchange for peace and a squad of war elephants. By the middle of the third century, the Seleucids had also lost control of Bactria, where a series of Indo-Greek states were emerging with a unique cultural complex of their own. By the 260s, they had also lost control of the

WHAT CHARACTERISTICS DEFINED AND DISTINGUISHED THE THREE MAJOR HELLENISTIC KINGDOMS?

THE HELLENISTIC KINGDOMS   119

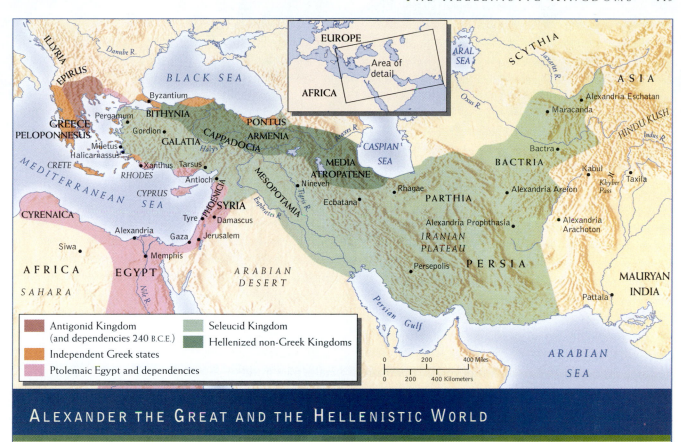

ALEXANDER THE GREAT AND THE HELLENISTIC WORLD

Note the position of the three successor kingdoms to Alexander's empire; notice how each was based on one of the three major axes of civilization we have studied so far: Egyptian, ancient Near Eastern, and Aegean. What might the division of Alexander's empire along such "traditional" lines suggest about the durability of his empire even if he had lived to rule it?

western half of Asia Minor. The Seleucid heartland now became Syria–Palestine, Mesopotamia, and the western half of Persia: still a great, wealthy kingdom, but far less than what Alexander had left.

Like the Ptolemies, the Seleucids offered two faces to their subjects, one rooted in ancient Near Eastern tradition for their Persian and Mesopotamian subjects, another decidedly more Greek for the heavily Hellenized populations of the coast. Seleucus' son, Antiochus I, proclaimed in terms reminiscent of a Sargon or a Hammurabi, "I am Antiochus, the Great King, the legitimate king . . . king of Babylon, king of all countries." Throughout their empire, shrines and temples were built for the cult of the living ruler.

Seleucid rulers continued the tradition of Alexander, planting new cities throughout their empire, cities that were fundamentally Greek in their assumptions but that grew to be thriving commercial and industrial centers. Although their bureaucracy was less organized than that

of the Ptolemies, in an empire of as many as 30 million inhabitants even haphazard tax collection could reap huge rewards. Like their Persian predecessors, however, the Seleucids did not reinvest their gains into what we would call capital improvements. Instead, they hoarded their wealth in great state treasuries. All the same, they had more than enough cash to provide for the smooth operation of their government and to defend their borders through the third century, a period of regular warfare with the Ptolemies. It was not until the second century, when Antiochus III lost a costly war with the Romans, that he had to plunder temples and private wealth in order to pay off his war indemnity.

ANTIGONID MACEDON AND GREECE

The Macedonian homeland remained highly unstable from the time of Alexander's death until 276 B.C.E., when a general named Antigonus was finally able to

THE GREEK INFLUENCE ON ISRAEL

Greek culture was a powerfully intoxicating force throughout the Hellenistic world, even in a comparative cultural backwater like Israel. In the second century B.C.E., the Hellenized ways of the Jewish upper classes in Jerusalem finally occasioned a revolt by a native Hebrew dynasty known as the Maccabees, who decried the "debaucheries" Greek culture had introduced into Jewish life. In the passage that follows, note that even the high priest of the Temple bears the Greek name Jason.

In those days [the reign of Antiochus IV Epiphanes, 175–164 B.C.E.] certain renegades came out from Israel and misled many, saying, "Let us go and make a covenant with the Gentiles [Greeks] around us, for since we separated from them many disasters have come upon us." . . . Some of the people went to the king, who authorized them to observe the ordinances of the Gentiles. So they built a gymnasium in Jerusalem, according to Gentile custom, and removed the marks of circumcision, and abandoned the holy covenant. They joined with the Gentiles and sold themselves to do evil. . . . When Antiochus succeeded to the kingdom, Jason the brother of Onias obtained the high priesthood by corruption. . . . He at once shifted his compatriots over to the Greek way of life. . . . Despising the sanctuary and neglecting the sacrifices, they hurried to take part in the unlawful proceedings in the wrestling arena after the signal for the discus-throwing, disdaining the honors prized by their ancestors and putting the highest value upon Greek forms of prestige. . . .

When the quadrennial games were being held at Tyre and the king was present, Jason sent envoys . . . to carry three hundred silver drachmas for the sacrifice to Heracles. . . . Harsh and utterly grievous was the onslaught of evil. For the Temple was filled with debauchery and reveling by the Gentiles, who dallied with prostitutes and had intercourse with women within the sacred precincts. . . . The altar was covered with abominable offerings that were forbidden by the laws.

1 Maccabees 2; 2 Maccabees 4–6. *The New Oxford Annotated Bible.* (Oxford: Oxford University Press, 1994).

establish his rule over the area. Macedon drew its strength from natural resources and Aegean trade, as well as its de facto overlordship of the Greek homeland. Furthermore, the Macedonians could still field the finest army of any of the successor states, and the Antigonid kings of Macedon held what many of the monarchs of the Hellenistic world desired, the kingship of the land once held by Philip and Alexander.

The Greeks, however, were restive under the Antigonids, and two emergent forces within the Greek world served as rallying points for cries of freedom and war against the "barbarian." These two forces, the Aetolian League and the Achaean League, were a departure in Greek political organization. Unlike the defensive alliances of the classical period, these two leagues represented a real political unification. So impressive was the degree of cooperation and unification that James Madison, John Jay, and Alexander Hamilton employed the Achaean League as one of their models in advocating federalism in the United States.

THE GROWTH OF TRADE AND URBANIZATION

Why was prosperity so unevenly distributed in the Hellenistic economy?

The Hellenistic world was generally prosperous, owing to the growth of long-distance trade, finance, and cities. Alexander's conquests opened up a vast trading area stretching from Egypt to the Persian Gulf, dominated by Greek-speaking rulers and newly established merchant communities. These conquests also stimulated the mercantile economy by putting into circulation hoards of Persian gold and silver coins, jewelry, and utensils acquired through plunder. Industries also benefited, because manufacturing was encouraged by autocratic rulers as a means of increasing their revenues through trade.

New trading ventures were particularly vigorous and lucrative in Ptolemaic Egypt and Seleucid Syria. Every facility was provided by the Ptolemies and the Seleucids for the encouragement of trade. Harbors were improved, warships were sent out to police the seas, and roads and canals were built. The Ptolemies even employed geographers to discover new routes to distant lands and thereby open up valuable markets. As a result of such methods Egypt developed a flourishing commerce in the widest variety of products. Into the port of Alexandria came spices from Arabia, gold from Ethiopia and India, tin from Britain, elephants and ivory from Nubia, silver from Spain, fine carpets from Asia Minor, and even silk from China. Profits for the government and for some of the merchants were often as high as 20 or 30 percent.

Cities grew enormously during the Hellenistic Age. Alexander the Great himself had founded some seventy cities as outposts of Greek domination, and in the next two centuries his successors founded about two hundred more. But urbanization also increased because of the expansion of commerce and industry and the proliferation of governmental bureaus. At Antioch in

Syria, the population quadrupled during a single century. Seleucia on the Tigris grew from nothing to a metropolis of several hundred thousand in less than two centuries. Alexandria in Egypt, the largest and most famous of all the Hellenistic cities, had half a million inhabitants. Before imperial Rome, no other city in ancient times surpassed it in size or in magnificence. Its streets were well paved and laid out in regular order. It had splendid public buildings and parks, a museum, and a library of half a million scrolls.

Despite the overall growth of the Hellenistic economy, by no means did everyone enjoy prosperity. Agriculture remained the major occupation and primary source of wealth in the Hellenistic world, and small farmers in particular suffered severely from the exploitative tax policies of Hellenistic monarchs. Although industrial production increased, industry continued to be based on manual labor by individual artisans, most of whom lived in poverty. Among the teeming populations of Hellenistic cities, unemployment was a constant concern. Those who could not find work were forced to beg, steal, or prostitute themselves in order to survive.

Even those who prospered in the new economy were often subject to drastic fluctuations in their fortunes. Merchants were particularly exposed to the "boom-and-bust" syndrome. A merchant, thinking he would make a fortune during an upward price spiral, might go into debt in order to take advantage of the upward trend, only to find that supply in the commodity he traded suddenly exceeded demand, leaving him nothing with which to pay back his creditors.

All told, therefore, it seems clear that the economic landscape of the Hellenistic world was one of contrasting extremes, an image worth remembering as we move to a consideration of Hellenistic thought and culture.

HELLENISTIC CULTURE: PHILOSOPHY AND RELIGION

What was the relationship between Epicureanism and Stoicism?

Hellenistic philosophy exhibited two trends that ran almost parallel throughout the civilization. The major trend, exemplified by Epicureanism and Stoicism, showed a fundamental regard for reason as the key to the solution of human problems. This trend was a manifestation of Greek influence, although philosophy and science, as combined by Aristotle, had now come to a parting of the ways. The minor trend, exemplified by the Skeptics and various cults, tended to reject reason, to deny the possibility of attaining truth, and in some cases to turn toward mysticism and reliance on faith. Despite the differences in their teachings, the philosophers and religious enthusiasts of the Hellenistic Age generally agreed on one thing: the necessity of finding some release from the trials of human existence, for with the decline of free civic life as a means for the expression of human idealism, alternatives needed to be found to make life seem meaningful, or at least endurable.

EPICUREANISM AND STOICISM

Epicureanism and Stoicism both originated about 300 B.C.E. The founders were, respectively, Epicurus (c. 342–270 B.C.E.) and Zeno (fl. after 300 B.C.E.), both residents of Athens. The two philosophies had several features in common. Both were individualistic, concerned not with the welfare of society but with the good of the individual. Both were materialistic, denying the existence of any spiritual substances; even divine beings and the soul were declared to be formed of matter. Stoicism and Epicureanism also contained elements of universalism. Both taught that people are the same the world over and recognized no distinctions between Greeks and non-Greeks.

But in most ways the two systems were quite different. The Stoics believed that the cosmos is an ordered whole in which all contradictions are resolved for ultimate good. Evil is, therefore, relative; the particular misfortunes that befall human beings are but necessary incidents to the final perfection of the universe. Everything that happens is rigidly determined in accordance with rational purpose. No individual is master of his or her fate; people are free only in the sense that they can accept their fate or rebel against it. But whether they accept or rebel, they cannot overcome it. Their supreme duty is to submit to the order of the universe in the knowledge that this order is good. Through such an act of resignation the highest happiness will be attained, which consists of tranquillity of mind. Those who are most truly happy are thus the ones who by the assertion of their rational natures have accomplished a perfect adjustment of their lives to the cosmic purpose and purged

their souls of all bitterness and protest against evil turns of fortune.

The Stoics' ethical and social theory grew from their general philosophy. Believing that the highest good is serenity of mind, they emphasized duty and self-discipline as cardinal virtues. Recognizing the prevalence of particular evils, they taught tolerance for and forgiveness of each other. They also urged participation in public affairs as a duty for those of rational mind. They condemned slavery and war, although they took no real actions against these evils since they believed that the results that might arise from violent measures of social change would be worse than the diseases they were meant to cure. With appropriate qualifications, the Stoic philosophy was one of the noblest products of the Hellenistic Age in teaching egalitarianism, pacifism, and humanitarianism.

The Epicureans based their philosophy on the materialistic "atomism" of an earlier Greek thinker named Democritus, who lived in the latter part of the fifth century B.C.E. According to this theory the ultimate constituents of the universe are atoms, infinite in number, indestructible, and indivisible. Every individual object or organism in the universe is the product of a fortuitous concourse of atoms. Taking this as given, Epicurus and his followers concluded that since there is no ultimate purpose in the universe, the highest good is pleasure—the moderate satisfaction of bodily appetites, the mental pleasure of contemplating excellence, and above all, serenity of soul. The last end can be best achieved through the elimination of fear, especially fear of the supernatural, since that is the greatest source of mental pain. The individual must understand that the soul is material and therefore cannot survive the body, that the universe operates of itself, and that no gods intervene in human affairs. The Epicureans thus came by a different route to the same general conclusion as the Stoics—nothing is better than tranquillity of mind.

> The Epicureans thus came by a different route to the same general conclusion as the Stoics—nothing is better than tranquility of mind.

The practical moral teachings and the politics of the Epicureans rested on utilitarianism. In contrast to the Stoics, they did not insist on virtue as an end in itself but taught that the only reason why one should be good is to increase one's own happiness. In like manner, they denied that there is any such thing as absolute justice: laws and institutions are just only insofar as they contribute to the welfare of the individual. Certain rules have been found necessary in every society for the maintenance of order. These rules should be obeyed

WHAT WERE THE PRINCIPAL THEMES OF HELLENISTIC ARCHITECTURE AND SCULPTURE?

HELLENISTIC CULTURE: LITERATURE AND ART 123

solely because it is to each individual's advantage to do so. Epicurus considered the state as a mere convenience and taught that the wise man should take no active part in politics. He did not propose that civilization should be abandoned; yet his conception of the happiest life was essentially passive and defeatist. Epicurus taught that the thinking person will recognize that evils in the world cannot be eradicated by human effort; the individual will therefore withdraw to study philosophy and enjoy the fellowship of a few congenial friends.

Skepticism

A more radically defeatist philosophy was that propounded by the Skeptics. Skepticism reached the zenith of its popularity about 200 B.C.E. under the influence of Carneades. The chief source of its inspiration was the teaching that all knowledge is derived from sense perception and therefore must be limited and relative. From this the Skeptics deduced that people cannot prove anything. Since the impressions of our senses deceive us, no truth can be certain. All we can say is that things appear to be such and such; we do not know what they really are. We have no definite knowledge of the supernatural, of the meaning of life, or even of right and wrong. It follows that the sensible course to pursue is suspension of judgment; this alone can lead to happiness. If we will abandon the fruitless quest for absolute truth and cease worrying about good and evil, we will attain peace of mind, which is the highest satisfaction that life affords. The Skeptics were even less concerned than the Epicureans with political and social problems. Their ideal was one of escape from a world neither reformable nor understandable.

Religion

Although Greek religion in the age of the city-states had emphasized the worship of gods associated with given cities to advance the fortunes of those cities, such civic-oriented worship was now losing its vitality. Its place was taken for many of society's leaders by the philosophies of Stoicism, Epicureanism, and Skepticism. Most ordinary people, on the other hand, tended to embrace emotional personal religions offering elaborate ritual in this world and salvation in the next. In Greek-speaking communities, cults that stressed extreme ascetic atonement for sin, ecstatic mystical union with divinity, and otherworldly salvation attracted ever more followers. Among these mystery cults, so called because their membership was secret and their rites held in private, one of the most popular was the Dionysiac cult, based on the myth of the death and resurrection of the god Dionysius. In Persian communities Zoroastrianism became ever more extreme in its dualism, with Zoroastrian magi insisting that everything material was evil and demanding that believers practice austerities in order to ready their immaterial souls for ethereal joy in the afterlife. Finally, among Greeks and non-Greeks alike, an offshoot of Zoroastrianism known as Mithraism gained ever more popularity.

Exactly when Mithraism became an independent religion is unknown, but it was certainly not later than the fourth century B.C.E. The cult gained its name from Mithras, at first a minor deity in Zoroastrianism. Gradually many recognized Mithras as the god most deserving of worship, probably because of his emotional appeal. He was believed to have lived an earthly existence involving great suffering and sacrifice. He performed miracles, giving bread and wine to humanity and ending a drought and also a disastrous flood. He proclaimed Sunday the most sacred day of the week, since the sun was the giver of light. He declared the twenty-fifth of December the most sacred day of the year because, as the approximate date of the winter solstice, it was the "birthday" of the sun, when its life-giving powers began to increase for the benefit of humankind. Drawing its converts mostly from the lower classes of Hellenistic society, Mithraism offered them an elaborate ritual, contempt for life in this world, and a clearly defined doctrine of redemption through Mithras, a personal savior. Not surprisingly it outlasted the Hellenistic period, becoming after about 100 C.E. one of the most popular religions in the Roman empire and exerting some influence on Christianity.

Hellenistic Culture: Literature and Art

What were the principal themes of Hellenistic architecture and sculpture?

Both the literature and the art of the Hellenistic Age were characterized by a tendency to take aspects of earlier Greek accomplishments to extremes. It is difficult to be certain of the reasons for this approach, but apparently writers and artists wished to demonstrate their purely formal skills in order to please their autocratic patrons. The greater uncertainties of existence in Hellenistic times may also have led consumers of art to seek gratification from more dramatic and less subtle forms of artistic expression. Whatever the case, rather than being an integral expression of civic activities, art during this period became more of a commodity. Artistic works became more numerous and more widely available: we know the names of at least eleven hundred Hellenistic authors. Many of these works are mediocre but some are enduring masterpieces of art and literature

PASTORAL LITERATURE

The most prominent Hellenistic verse form was the pastoral, a new genre depicting a make-believe world of shepherds and wood nymphs. The inventor of the genre was a Greek named Theocritus, who wrote around 270 B.C.E. in the big-city environment of Alexandria. Theocritus was a merchant of escapism. In the midst of urban bustle, faced with despotic rulers, and within sight of overcrowded, slumlike conditions, he celebrated the charms of hazy country values and idealized the "simple pleasures" of rustic folk. One of his pastorals might start like this: "Begin my country song, sweet muses, begin, I am Thrysis from Etna, this is Thrysis's lovely voice." To many the falseness of such verse is alienating; how could shepherds talk this way? But other readers enjoy its poetic lushness.

The Corinthian Order of Architecture. This characteristically Hellenistic style for constructing columns was much more ornate than its classical predecessors.

PROSE

Hellenistic prose literature was dominated by historians and biographers. By far the most profound of the writers of history was the mainland Greek Polybius, who lived during the second century B.C.E. From the standpoint of historical method, Polybius deserves to be ranked second only to Thucydides among all the historians of ancient times, and he even sur-passed Thucydides in his grasp of the importance of social and economic forces. Although most biographies of the time were light and gossipy, their popularity bears eloquent testimony to the literary tastes of the Hellenistic period.

ARCHITECTURE

Consonant with the despotic style of rule, the main traits of Hellenistic architecture were grandeur and ornamentation. In place of the balance and restraint that had distinguished Greek architecture of the fifth and early fourth centuries B.C.E., Hellenistic public building drew on Greek elements but moved toward standards set by Persian monarchs and Egyptian pharaohs. Two examples (neither of which survives) are the great lighthouse of Alexandria, which rose to a height of nearly

Old Market Woman, second century B.C.E. Sculptures of this period often showed ordinary people engaged in ordinary activities. This realistic marble sculpture is of an old, tired woman who is carrying a basket of fruits and vegetables and chickens to market.

WHAT WERE THE PRINCIPAL THEMES OF HELLENISTIC ARCHITECTURE AND SCULPTURE?

HELLENISTIC CULTURE: LITERATURE AND ART   125

four hundred feet, and the citadel of Alexandria, built of stone covered with blue-tinted plaster, and said by a contemporary to have "risen into mid-air." In Pergamon in Asia Minor an enormous altar to Zeus (transported in modern times to Berlin) and a huge open-air theater looked out over a high hill. In Ephesus, not far away, the streets were paved with marble. The "signature" of Hellenistic architecture of whatever dimension was the Corinthian column, a form of column more ornate than the simple and dignified Doric and Ionic alternatives that had predominated in earlier Greek building.

SCULPTURE

Whereas earlier Greek sculpture had sought to idealize humanity and to express Greek ideals of modesty by understated restraint, Hellenistic sculpture emphasized extreme naturalism and unashamed extravagance. In practice this meant that sculptors went to great lengths to recreate facial furrows, muscular

Laocoön. In sharp contrast to the serenity of the *Winged Victory* is this famous sculpture group from the first century B.C.E., depicting the death of Laocoön. According to legend, Laocoön warned the Trojans not to touch the wooden horse sent by the Greeks and was punished by Poseidon, who sent two serpents to kill him and his sons. The intense emotionalism of this work later had a great influence on western European art from Michelangelo onward.

The Winged Victory of Samothrace. In this figure, done around 200 B.C.E., a Hellenistic sculptor preserved some of the calmness and devotion to grace and proportion characteristic of Hellenic art in the golden age.

distensions, and complex folds of drapery. Awkward human postures were considered to offer the greatest challenges to the artist in stone, to the degree that sculptors might prefer to show people stretching themselves or balancing themselves on one leg in ways that hardly ever occur in real life. Since most Hellenistic sculpture was executed for wealthy private patrons, it is clear that the goal was to create something unique in terms of its conception and craftsmanship—something a collector could show off as the only one of its type. Not surprisingly, therefore, complexity came to be admired for its own sake, and extreme naturalism sometimes teetered on the brink of distorted stylization. Yet when moderns see such works they frequently experience a shock of recognition, for the bizarre and exaggerated postures of Hellenistic sculptures exerted an enormous influence on Michelangelo and his followers, and later inspired some of the most "modern" sculptors of the nineteenth and twentieth centuries. The *Dying Gaul*, done in Pergamon around 220 B.C.E., shows consummate skill in portraying a twisted human body; the *Winged Victory of Samothrace* of about 200 B.C.E. displays flowing drapery as if it were not stone but real cloth; and the *Laocoön* group, of the first century B.C.E., offers one of the most intensely emotional and complex compositions known in the entire history of sculptural art.

SCIENCE AND MEDICINE

Why did science and medicine flourish in this period?

The Hellenistic period was the most brilliant age in the history of science prior to the seventeenth century C.E. There are two major reasons for this. One was the enormous stimulus given to intellectual inquiry by the fusion of Mesopotamian and Egyptian science with the learning and the curiosity of the Greeks. The other was that many Hellenistic rulers were generous patrons of scientific research, subsidizing scientists who belonged to their retinues just as they subsidized sculptors.

Practical aims motivated the patronage of science in some areas, above all in medicine and anything that might relate to military technology. But the rulers who financed scientific endeavors did so primarily for motives of prestige: rulers could show off a scientific gadget to visitors just as they would show off their sculptures. Even purely theoretical achievements were so much admired among the Greek-speaking leisure classes that a Hellenistic prince who subsidized such a breakthrough would share the prestige for it in the way the mayor of an American city might bask in prestige today if his or her city's football team were to win the Super Bowl.

ASTRONOMY, MATHEMATICS, AND GEOGRAPHY

The major Hellenistic sciences were astronomy, mathematics, geography, medicine, and physics. The most renowned of the earlier Hellenistic astronomers was Aristarchus of Samos (310–230 B.C.E.), sometimes called the "Hellenistic Copernicus." His primary accomplishment was his deduction that the earth and the other planets revolve around the sun. This view was not accepted by his successors because it conflicted with the teachings of Aristotle and with the conviction of the Greeks that humanity, and therefore the earth, must be at the center of the universe. Later the fame of Aristarchus was overshadowed by that of Ptolemy of Alexandria (second century C.E.). Although Ptolemy made few original discoveries, he systematized the work of others. His principal writing, the *Almagest*, based on the view that all heavenly bodies revolve around the earth, was handed down to medieval Europe as the classic summary of ancient astronomy.

Closely allied with astronomy were mathematics and geography. The most influential Hellenistic mathematician was Euclid, the master of geometry. Until the middle of the nineteenth century his *Elements of Geometry* (written around 300 B.C.E. as a synthesis of the work of others) remained the accepted basis for the study of that branch of mathematics. Hellenistic geography owed most of its development to Eratosthenes (c. 276–c. 196 B.C.E.), an astronomer and librarian of Alexandria. By means of sundials placed some hundreds of miles apart, he calculated the circumference of the earth with an error of less than two hundred miles. Eratosthenes was also the first to suggest the possibility of reaching eastern Asia by sailing west. One of his successors divided the earth into the five climatic zones that are still recognized, and explained the ebb and flow of the tides as due to the influence of the moon.

MEDICINE

Other Hellenistic advances in science were in the field of medicine. Especially significant was the work of the Alexandrian scholar Herophilus of Chalcedon (c. 335–c. 280 B.C.E.). Herophilus was the greatest anatomist of antiquity and probably the first to practice human dissection. Among his achievements were a detailed description of the brain, with an insistence (against Aristotle) that the brain is the seat of human intelligence; the discovery of the significance of the pulse, and its use in diagnosing illness; and the discovery that the arteries contain blood alone (not a mixture of blood and air as Aristotle had taught), and that their function is to carry blood from the heart to all parts of the body. About the middle of the third century, Erasistratus of Alexandria discovered the valves of the heart and distinguished between motor and sensory nerves. In addition, he rejected Hippocrates' theory that the body consists of four "humors" and consequently criticized excessive bloodletting as a method of cure. Unfortunately the humoral theory and an emphasis on

WHAT CHANGES OCCURRED DURING THE HELLENISTIC PERIOD TO THE POLIS-BASED CULTURE OF GREECE?

THE TRANSFORMATION OF THE POLIS   127

CHRONOLOGY

SCIENTIFIC LUMINARIES OF THE HELLENISTIC WORLD

Herophilus of Chalcedon	c. 335–c. 280 B.C.E.
Euclid	330?–270? B.C.E.
Aristarchus of Samos	310–230 B.C.E.
Archimedes of Syracuse	c. 287–212 B.C.E.
Eratosthenes	c. 276–c. 196 B.C.E.

bloodletting were revived by Galen, the great encyclopedist of medicine who lived in the Roman Empire in the second century C.E. Galen's baleful influence lasted until the eighteenth century C.E.

PHYSICS

Prior to the third century B.C.E., physics had been a branch of philosophy. It was made a separate, experimental science by Archimedes of Syracuse (c. 287–212 B.C.E.), who discovered the law of floating bodies, or specific gravity, and formulated with scientific exactness the principles of the lever, the pulley, and the screw. Among his memorable inventions were the compound pulley and the screw propeller for ships. Although he has been considered the greatest technical genius of antiquity, he preferred to devote his time to pure scientific research. Tradition relates that he discovered "Archimedes' principle" (specific gravity) while pondering possible theories in his bath: when he reached his stunning insight he dashed out naked into the street crying "Eureka" ("I have found it").

THE TRANSFORMATION OF THE POLIS

What changes occurred during the Hellenistic period to the polis-based culture of classical Greece?

The Hellenistic period saw the creation of great kingdoms in Egypt and Asia Minor and the rise of new forms of political organization in the Greek world such as the Achaean League. What, however, became of the polis, the foundation of classical Greek culture?

The apparent eclipse of the poleis is to some extent misleading. Some poleis continued to thrive as centers of trade. It is also important to remember that the great Hellenistic kingdoms remained, in many respects, collections of cities; and that, for the most part, their Greco-Macedonian rulers continued to carry with them the cultural and political baggage of the polis world.

Nevertheless, the Hellenistic polis—even when it had not become a sprawling megalopolis such as Alexandria or Antioch—was in many ways a fundamentally different place from its classical precursor. As we have seen, changes in the fourth century were already disrupting the traditional bonds of Greek social and political life. Alexander's conquests had created a cosmopolitan world full of economic opportunity for a Greek-speaker; a common Greek-based culture that engulfed the eastern Mediterranean and western Asia; and a sense of "Greekness" that transcended political and geographical boundaries. Into this vast, exciting world, Greeks poured en masse, reducing the population of the Greek mainland by as much as one half in the century between 325 and 225 B.C.E. Hundreds of thousands of Greeks left Greece to seek their fortunes—financial and otherwise—in a Mediterranean world of massive empires and cosmopolitan cities whose scale dwarfed anything imaginable even in Periclean Athens.

Such a transformation had serious effects on Greek culture and the polis. The small-scale Dark Age communities and archaic poleis from which classical Greek culture grew were societies in which everybody knew virtually everyone else; innumerable social and political ties bound the citizens. Greek traditions of participation in government had led to a greater share in the franchise than any other culture had achieved in antiquity. Every citizen of the Greek world, to a lesser or greater extent, had some share, some stake in his society, its institutions, its gods, its army, and its cultural life.

If we transport this ingrained outlook into the swirling cosmopolitanism of the Hellenistic city, we can perhaps appreciate the magnitude of the change. All of those things that defined one's life as a person and a citizen were by and large gone. The intimate connection with the political life of the state had vanished. In place of the nexus of social and familial relationships prevalent in the Greek mainland, an average Greek in one of the Hellenistic kingdoms might have only his immediate family to rely on, if even that.

What resulted was a traumatic separation between the traditional values and assumptions of Greek life, and the social and political realities of the day.

CONCLUSION

Judged from the vantage of classical Greece, Hellenistic civilization may at first seem no more than a degenerate phase of Greek civilization. The autocratic governments of the Hellenistic Age appear repugnant in contrast to Athenian democracy, and the Hellenistic penchant for extravagance may appear debased in contrast to earlier Greek ideals. Even the best Hellenistic literary works lack the inspired majesty of the great Greek tragedies, and none of the Hellenistic philosophers matched the profundity of Plato and Aristotle. Yet Hellenistic civilization had its own achievements also, that the classical age could not match. Most Hellenistic cities offered a greater range of public facilities, such as museums and libraries, than earlier Greek cities did, and Hellenistic thinkers, writers, and artists left to posterity important new ideas, impressive new genres, and imaginative new styles. Scientific advances also demonstrate the intellectual creativity that marked the Hellenistic world.

Probably the most important contribution of the Hellenistic era to subsequent historical development was the role it played as intermediary between Greece and Rome. In some cases the Hellenistic contribution was simply that of preservation. Most of what the ancient Romans would know of classical Greek thought came to them through copies of Greek philosophical and literary texts preserved in Hellenistic libraries. In other areas, however, transfer involved transmutation.

Hellenistic art, for example, evolved from earlier Greek art into something related but quite different, and it was this "Greek-like" art that exerted the greatest influence on the tastes and artistic accomplishments of the Romans. A similar case might be made for drama.

Two aspects of Hellenistic culture deserve special comment—Hellenistic cosmopolitanism and Hellenistic "modernity." The word "cosmopolitan" itself comes from a Greek word meaning "universal city," and it was the Greeks of the Hellenistic period who came closest to turning this ideal of cosmopolitanism into reality. Around 250 B.C.E. a leisure-class Greek could have traveled from Sicily to the borders of India, always meeting people who "spoke his language," both literally and in terms of shared ideals. Nor would this same Greek have been a nationalist in the sense of professing any exclusive loyalty to a city-state or kingdom. He would more likely have considered himself a "citizen of the world."

Hellenistic cosmopolitanism was partly a product of the cosmopolitanism of Persia, and helped in turn to create the cosmopolitanism of Rome; but in contrast to both it was not imperial—that is, it was entirely divorced from constraints imposed by a supranational state—even though it was achieved by exploiting subject peoples. Other aspects of Hellenistic civilization will seem even more familiar to observers today. Authoritarian governments, ruler cults, economic instability, extreme skepticism existing side by side with intense religiosity, rational science existing side by side with irrational superstition, flamboyant art and ostentatious art collecting: all these aspects of the Hellenistic Age might make the thoughtful student of history regard it as one of the most relevant in the entire human record for comparison with our own.

KEY TERMS

Plato's Republic

Nicomachean Ethics

Philip II

Alexander

Ptolemy

Seleucus

Antigonus

Epicureanism

Stoicism

Euclid

SELECTED READINGS

Penguin Classics and the Loeb Classical Library both offer reliable translations of scores of literary and historical texts from this period. Particularly important are historical works by Arrian (*Anabasis of Alexander*) and Plutarch (*Lives*).

Adcock, F. E. *The Greek and Macedonian Art of War.* Berkeley, 1957. Still a valuable introduction to the guiding principles and assumptions of Greek and Macedonian warfare.

Austin, M. M. *The Hellenistic World from Alexander to the Roman Conquest: A Selection of Ancient Sources in Translation.* Cambridge, 1981.

Bagnall, R. S., and P. Derow. *Greek Historical Documents: The Hellenistic Period.* Chico, Calif., 1981.

Bosworth, A. B. *Conquest and Empire: The Reign of Alexander the Great.* Cambridge, 1988. A political and military analysis of Alexander's career that successfully strips away the romance, maintaining a clear vision of the ruthlessness and human cost of his conquests.

Borza, Eugene N. *In the Shadow of Olympus: The Emergence of Macedon.* Princeton, 1990. The standard account of the rise of Macedon up to the accession of Philip II.

Burstein, Stanley M., ed. and trans. *The Hellenistic Age from the Battle of Ipsos to the Death of Kleopatria VII.* Cambridge, 1985. An excellent collection, with sources not found elsewhere.

Cartledge, Paul A. *Agesilaus and the Crisis of Sparta.* Baltimore, 1987. A thorough but readable analysis of the social and political challenges besetting Sparta in the fourth century B.C.E.

Green, Peter. *Alexander to Actium: The Historical Evolution of the Hellenistic Age.* Berkeley, 1990. An outstanding, comprehensive, and wide-ranging history of the period; balanced and sensible.

———. *Alexander of Macedon, 356–323 B.C.* Berkeley, 1991. Revised edition of the author's 1972 biography; entertainingly written, and rich in detail and insight.

Hammond, Nicholas G. L. *The Genius of Alexander the Great.* Chapel Hill, 1998. A clear, authoritative, admiring account, distilling a lifetime of research on the subject.

Hansen, Mogens H. *The Athenian Democracy in the Age of Demosthenes.* Oxford, 1991. An intelligent examination of the political institutions of Athens in the fourth century B.C.E.

Lloyd, Geoffrey, and Nathan Sivin. *The Way and the Word: Science and Medicine in early China and Greece.* New Haven, 2002. An extraordinary comparative study of scientific thinking between 400 B.C.E. and 200 C.E. in the Hellenistic world and in China.

Ober, Josiah. *Mass and Elite in Democratic Athens: Rhetoric, Ideology, and the Power of the People.* Princeton, 1989. An excellent study of the ideology of democracy in Athens in the fourth century B.C.E. that borrows intelligently from modern social scientific insights.

Pollitt, Jerome J. *Art in the Hellenistic Age.* New York, 1986. The standard account, written from the perspective of cultural history as well as art history.

Sherwin-White, Susan, and Amélie Kuhrt. *From Samarkhand to Sardis: A New Approach to the Seleucid Empire.* London, 1993. A stimulating examination of the relationship between rulers and ruled in the vast expanses of the Seleucid empire.

Tritle, Lawrence A. ed. *The Greek World in the Fourth Century: From the Fall of the Athenian Empire to the Successors of Alexander.* New York, 1997. A wide-ranging collection of scholarly essays.

Worthington, Ian. *Alexander the Great: A Reader.* London and New York, 2002. A collection of influential interpretations of Alexander by modern historians.

MYSTERY CULTS

Greatly blessed of earth-bound men is he whom they propitiously love: to him they promptly send to the hearth of his great house Ploutos (wealth), who gives mortal men.

—Meyer, Marvin W., ed. *The Ancient Mysteries: A Source book of Sacred Texts* (Philadelphia: University of Pennsylvania Press, 1999) p. 30, lines 486–489.

MYSTERY RELIGIONS flourished in the Hellenistic Age as the Olympian gods of the fourth and fifth centuries fell from glory. Although many of these mystery religions began developing well before the Classical Age of Greece, it was only when the polis fell into decline and a more cosmopolitan worldview took its place that mystery religions became more prominent. With the decline of the polis and the confusion surrounding the appearance of the cosmopolis, Hellenistic men and women began to search for a more meaningful religious experience. The mystery cults—Demeter, Eleusis, Isis, Mithra, and Magna Mater—involved the worship of deities from Greece, Syria, Anatolia, Egypt, and Persia. Though diverse in geographic origin, these religions were somewhat similar in terms of historical development and theological orientation.

The mysteries themselves were secret religious groups of men and women who made a personal choice to be initiated into the profound reality of one deity or another. Whereas official religion required outward expression, the mystery religions stressed inward piety and devotion. Because initiates were required not to speak of their religious practices to anyone, our knowledge of the mystery religions is limited. Many of the mystery religions seem to have developed from various festivals celebrating the fertility of nature, and it is here that the Mother Goddess, or Magna Mater, makes her appearance, taking various shapes as Demeter, Kore, or Atargatis. Women played a large role in these religions. After all, the earth was nourished by the Magna Mater, who embodied the mysterious forces of life and death.

It has often been suggested that one of the reasons that Christianity spread so quickly in the Roman world was the existence of mystery religions and cults. Not surprisingly, many of the secret practices of these cults would find their way into Christian practice.

The images and documents in the *Mystery Cults* Digital History Feature at www.wwnorton.com/wciv uncover the similarities between the cults of Demeter, Eleusis, Isis, Mithra, and Magna Mater and show how these secret religions influenced early Christianity. As you explore the *Mystery Cults* feature, consider the following:

• What was the role of women in the formation of ancient mystery religions?

• In what ways did the image and idea of the Magna Mater influence the development of mystery cults?

• What effect did mystery cults have on the practice of early Christianity? Did belief in the Mother Goddess aid in the acceptance of Christianity by Roman women?

• How was paganism necessary to the development of Christianity?

Chapter FIVE

ROMAN CIVILIZATION

WHILE THE GREEKS STRUGGLED against the Persians and then each other, a new civilization was emerging on the banks of the Tiber River in central Italy. By the end of the fourth century B.C.E., Rome was already the dominant power on the Italian peninsula. For five centuries thereafter Rome's power steadily increased. By the first century C.E., it ruled most of the Hellenistic world as well as most of western Europe. Rome's conquests united the Mediterranean world for the first time, and made the Mediterranean itself a "Roman lake." Rome's empire brought Greek institutions and ideas not only to the western half of the Mediterranean world, but also to Britain, France, Spain, and Romania. Rome was thus the builder of a great historical bridge that connected Europe to the cultural and political heritage of the ancient Near East. Without Rome, European civilization as we know it would not exist.

Rome was deeply influenced by Greek culture, but it was also a distinctive civilization in its own right. The Romans were much more traditional minded than the Greeks. Rome revered its old agricultural traditions, its household gods, and its sternly military values. But as their empire grew, Romans also came to see themselves as having a divinely ordained mission to civilize the world by teaching it the arts of law and government that were Rome's own peculiar genius. Virgil (70–19 B.C.E.), the great epic poet of Rome, expressed this self-conscious sense of Rome's historical mission in the *Aeneid*, which tells one of the several competing legends Romans treasured about the founding of their city. Here, Anchises of Troy speaks prophetically to his son Aeneas, who (in Virgil's account) would go on to become one of the founders of the city of Rome. Speaking about the Romans, Anchises tells his son of his people's future:

FOCUS QUESTIONS

• How did the Etruscans and Greeks influence early Roman society?

• How democratic was the early Roman Republic?

• What were the consequences of Roman territorial expansion during the third and second centuries B.C.E.?

• What impact did Rome's expanding empire have on Roman society and culture?

• What issues caused the social struggles of the late republic?

 • Why did the "Augustan system" succeed?

• Why did so many critics of Roman life during the Principate focus their criticisms on the behavior of women?

• What factors brought the Roman empire to the brink of ruin?

• Did Rome fall? Why or why not?

"Others will cast more tenderly in bronze
Their breathing figures, I can well believe,
And bring more lifelike portraits out of marble;
Argue more eloquently, use the pointer
To trace the paths of heaven accurately
And accurately foretell the rising stars.
Roman, remember by your strength to rule
Earth's peoples—for your arts are to be these:
To pacify, to impose the rule of law,
To spare the conquered, battle down the proud."

Virgil, *Aeneid*, Book VI, lines 848–857, trans. Robert Fitzgerald (New York: Random House, 1982) p. 190.

Not all the peoples whom Rome conquered welcomed the experience. But all were transformed by it.

EARLY ITALY AND THE ROMAN MONARCHY

How did the Etruscans and Greeks influence early Roman society?

Ancient Italy had sizable forests and much fertile land. But it had few mineral resources, aside from excellent supplies of marble. Its extensive coastline had only a few good harbors, and most of these were on the western coast. Nor did it have any secure natural defenses. In short, Italy was rich enough to be attractive, but difficult to defend. The Romans were a sternly military society almost from the moment they settled on Italian soil, because they were continually forced to defend their own conquests against other invaders.

THE ETRUSCANS

The dominant early settlers on the Italian peninsula were a non-Indo-European-speaking people known as the Etruscans. By the sixth century B.C.E., the Etruscans had established a confederation of independent city-states in north-central Italy. They were skilled metalworkers, artists, and architects, from whom the later Romans took their knowledge of the arch and the vault, among much else. Not only the Roman arch and vault, but also the cruel sport of gladiatorial combat and the practice of foretelling the future by studying the entrails of animals or the flight of birds went back to Etruscan beginnings. The Roman practice of centering urban life around massive stone temples with their attendant cults

probably also derived from an Etruscan example. Even the two most famous myths the Romans told about the founding of Rome itself they probably drew from the Etruscans: that involving Aeneas of Troy (noted above in connection with Virgil's *Aeneid*), and that involving the infant twins Romulus and Remus, who were raised by a female wolf after being abandoned by their parents.

The Romans also borrowed heavily from the Greek settlers of Italy. Colonists from mainland Greece began to arrive in southern Italy and Sicily in large numbers during the eighth century B.C.E. Such famous Greeks as Pythagoras, Archimedes, and even Plato for a time lived in Greek Italy, which became a key battlefield in the Peloponnesian War between Athens and Sparta. From the Greeks, the Romans derived their alphabet, many of their religious concepts, and much of their art and mythology. The high culture of Rome thus became thoroughly and pervasively Greek in inspiration and imitation.

THE RISE OF ROME

The Romans were descended from a cluster of Indo-European-speaking peoples who crossed the Alps into Italy during the second millennium B.C.E. Rome's strategic location along the Tiber brought it many advantages. Trading ships—but not large war fleets—could navigate the Tiber as far as Rome, but no farther; the city could thus serve as a port without being threatened by attack from the sea. Rome's famous hills increased the defensibility of the site. Rome also sat astride the first good ford across the Tiber River, making it a major land and river crossroads. Its location on the frontier between Latium (the territory of the "Latins," i.e., the Romans) and Etruria (the Etruscan homeland) also contributed to its commercial and strategic importance.

At an early date, the Romans established with the other Latin communities a series of common "rights," including intermarriage and legal migration between cities. These privileges, known as the "Latin Right," stand in sharp contrast to the rigid particularism and jealous suspicion that divided the cities of Sumer or Greece. Roman willingness to extend the Latin Right even beyond Latium was a key factor in the success of their later expansion within Italy.

Roman government was initially a monarchy advised by a senate, or council of elders (*senex* is Latin for "old man"). The monarchy, however, did not last. Legend has it that in 534 B.C.E. an Etruscan tyrant, Tarquin the Proud, gained control of the kingship in Rome. Tarquin used Rome's strategic location to dominate Latium and the agriculturally wealthy district of

Campania to the south, but he ruled the Romans with extreme cruelty. The final indignity came in 510 B.C.E., when Tarquin's son raped a virtuous Roman wife, Lucretia. When Lucretia committed suicide rather than living on "in dishonor," the Romans rose up in revolt, overthrowing not only the Etruscan tyranny but the entire form of monarchical government itself.

The story of Lucretia is probably patriotic myth, but there was a change in government in Rome around 500 B.C.E. (whether gradual or sudden is unknown) that ended the kingship and replaced it with a republic. Thereafter, the Romans would hold kingship in the same fear and contempt with which Greeks ultimately held the name "tyrant." Whatever the truth of Lucretia's story, it does therefore tell us something important about early Roman attitudes toward government and the family.

Romulus and Remus. A sixth-century B.C.E. Etruscan bronze statue known as the "Capitoline Wolf." Although the present statues of the twins were added during the fifteenth century C.E., there were probably comparable figures of Romulus and Remus in the same basic posture in the original statue.

THE EARLY REPUBLIC

How democratic was the early Roman Republic?

The early Roman Republic was marked by almost constant warfare. The Romans were initially on the defensive; but as time went on they steadily gained ground, conquering first the other Latin territories, then Etruria and the Greek cities of southern Italy. The Romans did not usually impose heavy burdens on the cities they conquered. More often, they demanded that their defeated foes contribute soldiers to the Roman army. Rome also extended the Latin Right to many of the cities it conquered, giving them a further stake in Rome's continued political and military success.

This long series of conflicts confirmed among the Romans a steely military ideal. Many of the most familiar Roman legends of martial heroism date from the early republican period, including the story of Horatius, who held a key bridge against an entire army, and the retired soldier and statesman Cincinnatus (with whom George Washington would be frequently compared) who left his farm at a moment's notice to fight for Rome on the battlefield.

THE GOVERNMENT OF THE EARLY REPUBLIC

Meanwhile, Rome underwent a very gradual political evolution. Even the replacement of the monarchy was highly conservative: its chief effect was to substitute for the king two elected officials called *consuls*, and to exalt the position of the Senate by granting it control over the public funds. The consuls, who each served a one-year term, were inevitably senators who acted as the agents of aristocratic interests. Each consul exercised the full executive and judicial authority that the king had previously wielded, limited by the right each possessed to veto the action of the other. If a conflict arose between them, the Senate might be called on to decide; or in time of grave emergency, a dictator might be appointed for a term not greater than six months.

After the establishment of the republic the political dominance of the early aristocracy, known as the *patricians*, began to be challenged by the *plebeians*, who made up nearly 98 percent of the citizen population but who initially had no access to political power. The two-hundred-year struggle between them is sometimes known as the "Struggle of the Orders." The plebeians

ROMAN EXPANSION TO 265 B.C.E.
- Controlled by Rome in 485 B.C.E.
- To 387 B.C.E.
- To 334 B.C.E.
- To 300 B.C.E.
- To 290 B.C.E.
- To 265 B.C.E.

ROMAN EXPANSION IN ITALY, 485–265 B.C.E.

This map illustrates the pattern of early Roman expansion in central and southern Italy. What does this pattern of expansion suggest about the threats Rome faced? Why did the Romans wait so long to conquer Etruria, even though it was so close to Rome? By transforming itself into the dominant power on the Italian peninsula, whose interests would Rome now threaten after 265 B.C.E.?

were a diverse group. Some had grown wealthy through trade or agriculture, but most were small-holding farmers, merchants, or the urban poor. The grievances of the plebeians were numerous. Forced to serve in the army in time of war, they were nevertheless excluded from holding office. They frequently felt themselves the victims of discriminatory decisions in judicial trials. They did not even know what legal rights they were supposed to enjoy, for the laws were unwritten, and the patricians alone had the power to interpret them. Worst was the oppression that could stem from debt because a debtor could be sold into slavery outside Rome by his creditor.

These grievances prompted a plebeian rebellion in the early fifth century B.C.E. that forced the patricians to agree to the election of new officers known as *tribunes* who could protect the plebeians by vetoing unlawful patrician acts. This victory was followed by a successful demand for codification of the laws. Roughly a generation later the plebeians won eligibility to positions as lesser magistrates, and about 367 B.C.E. the first plebeian consul was elected. Gradually, plebians also gained access to the Senate. The final plebeian victory came in 287 B.C.E. with the passage of a law stipulating that measures enacted by the *concilium plebis* (an assembly composed only of plebeians) would be binding on the Roman government whether the Senate approved them or not. It is from the decisions of this citizen assembly that English derives its modern word *plebiscite*.

These reforms had several important consequences. Because successful plebeians could now work their way into the upper reaches of Roman society and government, the Roman aristocracy gradually shifted (at least to some degree) from one of birth to one of wealth. In an attempt to prevent wealth from becoming too much of a factor in Roman political life, laws were passed barring senators from engaging directly in commerce. But this restriction only fueled the rise of the "equestrian" order: men who had the wealth and influence of senators, but who chose a life of business rather than one in politics. Meanwhile, those few families who managed to win election generation after generation became increasingly prestigious and disproportionately influential. As a result, by the first century B.C.E. even powerful and aristocratic Romans were coming to feel excluded from real political influence within their city, tempting some to pursue their private political agendas by styling themselves the champions of a downtrodden public interest.

> In an attempt to prevent wealth from becoming too much of a factor in Roman political life, laws were passed barring senators from engaging directly in commerce.

CHRONOLOGY

THE RISE OF ROME, 750–FIRST CENTURY B.C.E.

Legendary founding of the city of Rome	753 B.C.E.
Establishment of the Latin Right	493 B.C.E.
Roman Republic established	c. 500 B.C.E.
Struggle of the Orders	c. 450–287 B.C.E.
Concilium plebis gains power	287 B.C.E.
Equestrian order established	Third century B.C.E.

CULTURE, RELIGION, AND MORALITY

Political changes in early republican Rome moved glacially. So too did intellectual and cultural ones. Although writing had been adopted as early as the sixth century B.C.E., the Romans made little use of it except for laws, treaties, and funerary inscriptions. Education was largely limited to instruction imparted by fathers to sons in manly sports, practical arts, and military virtues; as a result, literary culture long remained a minor part of Roman life, even among the aristocracy. War and agriculture continued to be the chief occupations for the bulk of the population. A few artisans could be found in the cities, and a minor development of trade had occurred. But the fact that the republic had no standard system of coinage until 289 B.C.E. reflects the comparative insignificance of Roman commerce at this time.

During the early republic, religion assumed the character it retained through the greater part of Roman history. In many ways Roman religion resembled that of the Greeks. But there were also significant differences between the two religions. One was that Romans literally revered their ancestors; their "household gods" included deceased members of a lineage who were worshiped in order to ensure a family's continued prosperity. Another difference was the extent to which Roman religion was tied up with political life. Religion and politics were always closely integrated in the ancient world. But the Roman state appointed committees of priests virtually as branches of government to tend to the worship of the city's gods, preside over public rites, and serve as guardians

A Roman noble of the first century B.C.E., shown here holding the busts of two of his ancestors. Honoring one's ancestors was an important part of Roman social and religious life, especially among the aristocracy.

of sacred traditions. These priests were not full-time professionals, but rather prominent aristocrats who rotated in and out of priestly offices while also serving as leaders of the Roman state. Their dual role as priests and politicians made Roman religion an even more integral part of the fabric of public and political life than it had been in Greece.

Roman morality emphasized patriotism, duty, masculine self-control, and respect for authority and tradition. Its chief virtues were bravery, honor, self-discipline, and loyalty to country and family. A Roman's primary duty was to honor his ancestors by his conduct, but the greatest honor attached to those who sacrificed themselves for Rome. For the good of the Republic, therefore, citizens had to be ready to sacrifice not only their own lives but, if necessary, those of their family and friends. The cold-bloodedness of certain consuls who put their own sons to death for breaches of military discipline was to the Romans a matter of deep admiration bordering on awe.

THE FATEFUL WARS WITH CARTHAGE

What were the consequences of Roman territorial expansion during the third and second centuries B.C.E.?

By 265 B.C.E. the Romans controlled most of the Italian peninsula, freeing them to engage in overseas ventures. Scholars disagree as to whether the Romans continually extended their rule as a matter of deliberate policy, or whether their conquests grew more accidentally, by a series of reactions to changes that seemed to threaten Rome's security. Probably the truth lies between these extremes. Whatever the case, beginning in 264 B.C.E., a year after its final victory over the Etruscans, Rome became embroiled in a series of wars with overseas nations that decidedly altered the course of its history.

THE PUNIC WARS

By far the most crucial was the struggle with Carthage, a great maritime empire that stretched along the northern coast of Africa from modern-day Tunisia to the Straits of Gibraltar and included parts of Spain, Sicily, Sardinia, and Corsica. Carthage had been founded about 800 B.C.E. as a Phoenician colony, but it developed into a

WHAT WERE THE CONSEQUENCES OF EXPANSION DURING THE THIRD AND SECOND CENTURIES B.C.E.?

THE FATEFUL WARS WITH CARTHAGE   139

rich and powerful independent state. In naval might, commercial prowess, and material resources, Carthage in the third century B.C.E. was far superior to Rome.

The protracted struggles between Rome and Carthage are known collectively as the Punic Wars because the Romans called the Carthaginians Poeni, that is, "Phoenicians." The First Punic War began in 264 B.C.E., apparently because of Rome's genuine fear that the Carthaginians might gain control of Messina, a Sicilian port directly across from the Italian mainland. Twenty-three years of bitter fighting ensued. Finally, by a peace agreement in 241, Carthage was forced to cede all of Sicily to Rome and to pay a large indemnity. Sicily thus became Rome's first overseas province.

Because the Romans had fought so hard to defeat Carthage, they were determined not to let their enemy extend its control to other Mediterranean areas. Accordingly, in 218 the Romans interpreted Carthage's attempt to expand its rule in Spain as a threat to Roman interests and responded with a declaration of war. The renewed struggle, known as the Second Punic War, raged for sixteen years. At first Rome was thrown off guard by the brilliant exploits of the famous Carthaginian commander Hannibal, who brought a Spanish army, including war elephants, through southern France and then over the Alps into Italy. With Carthaginian troops on Italian soil, Rome escaped defeat by the narrowest of margins.

Deep reserves of Roman manpower and the discipline of Rome and its closest allies ultimately overcame Hannibal's military genius. From 212 B.C.E. on, the Romans increasingly put the Carthaginians on the defensive in Italy, Sicily, and even Spain. The architect of the Spanish offensive, Publius Cornelius Scipio, then invaded North Africa and defeated Hannibal at Zama, near Carthage, in 201 B.C.E. His victory ended the Second Punic War, and Scipio was honored with the additional name "Africanus," the conqueror of Africa.

Carthage was now compelled to abandon all its possessions except the city of Carthage itself and its surrounding territory in Africa, and to pay an indemnity three times greater than that paid at the end of the First Punic War. Yet Roman suspicion of Carthage remained obsessive. By the mid-second century B.C.E. Carthage had recovered some of its former prosperity—and this was enough to provoke the displeasure of the Romans. Nothing short of the total demolition of the Carthaginian state would now satisfy influential Roman senators such as Cato the Censor, who ended every speech he made in the Senate with the same words: "Carthage must be destroyed." The Senate agreed, and in 149 B.C.E. seized on a minor pretext to demand that the

Hannibal. A coin from Carthage representing Hannibal as a victorious general, with an elephant on the reverse.

Carthaginians abandon their city and settle at least ten miles from the coast. Because this demand amounted to a death sentence for a nation dependent on commerce, it was refused—as the Romans probably realized it would be. The result was the Third Punic War, fought between 149 and 146 B.C.E. When the Romans finally breached the walls of Carthage, frightful butchery took place. Fifty-five thousand Carthaginians who survived

CHRONOLOGY

THE WARS WITH CARTHAGE

First Punic War	264–241 B.C.E.
Second Punic War	218–201 B.C.E.
Third Punic War	149–146 B.C.E.
City of Carthage destroyed	146 B.C.E.

THE EXPANSION OF ROME, 264–44 B.C.E.

By the death of Julius Caesar in 44 B.C.E., the Roman world had become an empire that united the eastern and the western Mediterranean regions. How did these two parts of the empire differ from one another? What impacts were these differences likely to have on the way Rome ruled its empire? What particular problems did Julius Caesar create by extending Roman rule into Gaul, well away from Rome's Mediterranean roots?

the massacre were sold into slavery, and their once magnificent city was razed to the ground.

TERRITORIAL EXPANSION

The wars with Carthage brought an enormous increase in Roman territory, leading to the creation of new overseas provinces in Sicily, North Africa, and Spain. This was the beginning of a policy of westward expansion that proved to be one of the great formative influences on the history of Europe.

Rome's expanding overseas commitments also brought it into conflict with eastern Mediterranean powers, paving the way for further conquests. During the Second Punic War, Philip V of Macedon entered into an alliance with Carthage; soon afterward, he moved aggressively into Greece and was rumored to have designs on Egypt. Rome sent an army to eject Philip from Greece; a decade or so later, another Roman army thwarted similar plans by the Seleucid monarch Antiochus III. In neither campaign did Rome set out to conquer Greece militarily; by 146 B.C.E.,

WHAT IMPACT DID ROME'S EXPANDING EMPIRE HAVE ON ROMAN SOCIETY AND CULTURE?

SOCIETY AND CULTURE IN THE LATE REPUBLIC   141

however, both Greece and Macedon had become Roman provinces, Seleucid Asia had been deprived of most of its territories, and Ptolemaic Egypt was largely a pawn of Roman commercial and naval interests.

SOCIETY AND CULTURE IN THE LATE REPUBLIC

What impact did Rome's expanding empire have on Roman society and culture?

Rome's "inadvertent" conquest of Greece and Asia Minor transformed the later republic. Vast new wealth poured into Rome, increasing the social and economic inequalities within Roman society and undermining traditional Roman values of austerity and self-sacrifice. Small farmers left the land for the cities, unable to compete with the huge agricultural estates (known as *latifundia*) owned by aristocrats and worked by gangs of slaves. Slaves also played an increasing role in Roman society as artisans, merchants, and household servants. Roman rule over the Hellenistic East also had a pervasive impact on the cultural life of the late republic; so much so, indeed, that by the end of the republican period, Romans were wondering openly whether they had conquered Greece, or whether it was Greece that had conquered Rome.

ECONOMIC AND SOCIAL CHANGE

Like nearly all the peoples of the ancient world, Romans took slavery for granted. Nothing in Rome's earlier experience prepared it, however, for the huge increase in slave numbers that resulted from its western and eastern conquests. By the end of the second century B.C.E., there were a million slaves in Italy alone, making Roman Italy one of the most slave-based economies known to history.

The majority of these slaves worked as agricultural laborers on the vast (and growing) estates of the Roman aristocracy. Some of these estates were the result of earlier Roman conquests within Italy itself. But others were constructed by aristocrats buying up the land holdings of thousands of small farmers who found themselves unable to compete with the great *latifundia* in producing grain for the market. Soldiers in particular—who might now be required to serve for years at a time on campaigns in Spain or the Greek East—often found it impossible to maintain their family farms. In-

stead, they moved to the city, selling their farms (often at a very good price) to aristocrats eager to invest in land the huge profits they had made from war and empire. In the cities, however, there was often little work to be had. Rome never made a transition to industrialism. With slaves to do all the hard work, a great disincentive existed for the technological initiative that might have led to industrialism; but without large-scale manufacturing, the urban population remained underemployed and politically volatile. By the first century B.C.E., almost a third of Rome's 1 million inhabitants were receiving free grain from the state, partly to keep them alive, and partly to keep them quiet.

As we have seen, the Roman economy remained fundamentally agrarian and noncommercialized until the mid-third century B.C.E. During the following century, however, Rome's eastern conquests brought it fully into the sophisticated commercial economy of the Hellenistic world. The principal beneficiaries of this economic transformation were the equestrians, the second of the four orders into which the society of republican Rome was divided (senatorial aristocrats, commoners, and slaves being the other three). As overseas merchants, the equestrians profited handsomely from Rome's voracious appetite for foreign luxury goods. As representatives of the Roman government in the provinces, they operated mines, built roads, and collected taxes, always with an eye toward their own profit. They were also the principal moneylenders to the Roman state and to distressed individuals. Interest rates were high, and when the state could not pay its bills, it would often allow the moneylenders to repay themselves by exploiting the defenseless population of the provinces.

Commoners who lost their lands certainly suffered from these economic changes; but the principal victims of Rome's transformation were its slaves. Roman slaves were scarcely considered people at all but instruments of production like cattle. Notwithstanding the fact that some were cultivated foreigners taken as prisoners of war, the standard policy of their owners was to get as much work out of them as possible until they died of exhaustion or were released in old age to fend for themselves. The ready availability and cheapness of slaves, a consequence of Rome's conquests, made slavery a far more impersonal and brutal institution in Rome than it had been in other ancient civilizations. Although domestic slaves were sometimes treated decently, and some slave artisans in the city of Rome were permitted to run their own businesses, the general lot of the slave was horrendous.

THE INFLUENCE OF GREEK LUXURY

Lucius Licinius Lucullus (106?–57 B.C.E.) was a partisan of the dictator Sulla and a member of Rome's highest aristocracy. He commanded Roman forces admirably in the East, but his demands for discipline from the army and his intolerance of corruption among the equestrians and senatorial governors made him powerful enemies. His conquests made him quite wealthy and, once he tired of trying to preserve his political career against his foes, he retired from public life. This passage from Plutarch's biography of him demonstrates the effects Eastern luxury could have on the Roman elite, the staggering wealth they could acquire, and their enjoyment of it especially once they abandoned the public career for one of private pleasure.

And indeed, Lucullus' life, like the Old Comedy, presents us at the commencement with acts of policy and of war, at the end offering nothing but good eating and drinking, feastings, and revelings, and mere play. For I give no higher name to his sumptuous buildings, porticos, and baths, still less to his paintings and sculptures, and all his industry about these curiosities, which he collected with vast expense, lavishly bestowing all the wealth and treasure he got in the war upon them, insomuch that even now, with all the advance of luxury, the Lucullean gardens are counted the noblest the emperor has. Tubero the Stoic, when he saw his buildings at Naples, where he suspended the hills upon vast tunnels, brought in the sea for moats and fish-ponds round his house, and built pleasure-houses in the waters, called him Xerxes in a toga. He had also fine seats in Tusculum, belvederes, and large open balconies for men's apartments, and porticos to walk in, where Pompey, coming to see him, blamed him for making a house which would be pleasant in summer, but uninhabitable in winter; whom Lucullus answered with a smile, "You think me, then, less provident than cranes and storks, not to change my home with the season." . . . Lucullus's daily entertainments were ostentatiously extravagant, not only with purple coverlets, and plate adorned with precious stones, and dancings, and interludes, but with the greatest diversity of dishes and the most elaborate cookery, for the vulgar to admire and envy. . . . Cato [the Younger] was his friend and connection, but, nevertheless, so hated his life and habits that when a young man made a long and tedious speech in praise of frugality and temperance, Cato got up and said, "How long do you mean to go on making money like Crassus, living like Lucullus, and talking like Cato?"

Plutarch, *Life of Lucullus*. Based on John Dryden, trans. *Plutarch's Lives.* (New York: Modern Library, 1992), pp. 621–622.

This extreme reliance on slave labor, combined with the relative cheapness of slaves, encouraged a mindset wherein the Romans had little use for labor-saving inventions. Water mills and a crude steam engine, among many potential industrial innovations, were known to the Romans during the course of their history, but they showed little interest in them. They had little need for such devices when cheap human labor seemed inexhaustible.

WHAT IMPACT DID ROME'S EXPANDING EMPIRE HAVE ON ROMAN SOCIETY AND CULTURE?

SOCIETY AND CULTURE IN THE LATE REPUBLIC   143

FAMILY LIFE AND THE STATUS OF WOMEN

Another change that accompanied the acquisition of new territories was a change in the nature of family life and the status of women. In earlier times the Roman family was based on the husband's nearly absolute powers over his household. During the second century B.C.E., however, changes in the laws governing divorce and property holding gave wives greater legal independence. The slave system also gave wealthy women greater practical independence, for slaves could now take over women's traditional tasks of child rearing and household maintenance. Upper-class Roman women now spent more time away from the home and began to engage in a range of social, intellectual, and artistic activities.

The conquest of the Hellenistic East also brought the wide-scale adoption of Greek ideas and customs into upper-class Roman life. In earlier centuries, Romans had taken pride in the simplicity of their cultural lives. Now, however, upper-class Romans began to see Greek culture as a mark of refinement which they had the wealth to pursue. The creature comforts that Hellenistic Greeks enjoyed in Syria and Egypt were also quickly adopted by the Roman conquerors of the Mediterranean world. Some Romans viewed such changes with repugnance. For them the "good old Roman ways" of paternal authority and stern military discipline were giving way to the debilitating allure of soft living. Their protests struck a chord, but they did little to stem the tide of change. Rome was being irreversibly transformed from a republic of farmers into a complex society with vast gaps between rich and poor and new habits of personal autonomy for both men and women.

EPICUREANISM AND STOICISM

The late republic was also deeply influenced by Greek philosophical ideas. The most renowned of the Roman exponents of Epicureanism was Lucretius (98–55 B.C.E.), the author of a book-length philosophical poem, *On the Nature of Things*. In writing this work Lucretius wished to explain the universe in such a way as to remove fear of the supernatural, which he regarded as the chief obstacle to peace of mind. Though he admitted the existence of the gods, he conceived of them as living in eternal peace, neither creating nor governing the universe. Everything is a product of mechanical evolution, including human beings and their habits and beliefs. Since mind is indissolubly linked with matter, death means utter extinction; consequently, no part of the human personality can survive to be rewarded or punished in an afterlife. Lucretius's conception of the good life was simple: "peace and a pure heart."

Stoicism was introduced into Rome about 140 B.C.E. and soon numbered among its converts many influential leaders of public life. The greatest of these was Cicero (106–43 B.C.E.), the "father of Roman eloquence." Cicero's ethical philosophy was based on the Stoic premises that virtue is sufficient for happiness, and tranquillity of mind is the highest good. He conceived of the ideal human being as one who has been guided by reason to an indifference toward sorrow and pain. But Cicero diverged from the Greek Stoics in his greater approval of the active, political life. To this degree he still spoke for the older Roman tradition of service to the state.

Cicero never claimed to be an original philosopher; his goal was to bring the best of Greek philosophy to the West. In this he was remarkably successful, for he wrote in a rich and elegant Latin prose style that has never been surpassed. Cicero's prose immediately became a standard for Latin composition and has remained so until the present century. Thus even though not a truly great thinker, Cicero was the most influential Latin transmitter of ancient thought to medieval and modern Europe.

RELIGION

The religious beliefs of the Romans also altered in various ways in the last two centuries of the republic—again mainly because of Rome's interaction with the Hellenistic world. Most pronounced was the spread of Eastern mystery cults, including the Persian cult of Mithraism, which offered awe-inspiring underground rites and a doctrine of the afterlife of the soul. But despite the attractions of these new cults, most Romans continued to honor the traditional gods of their household and their city. Roman polytheism was not an exclusive system. So long as the traditional gods were paid the reverence due them, newer gods could be added and honored also.

> Cicero's ethical philosophy was based on the Stoic premises that virtue is sufficient for happiness, and tranquility of mind is the highest good.

Roman Mystery Rites. The "Villa of the Mysteries" in Pompeii preserves an astonishing cycle of wall paintings done around 50 B.C.E. The exact meaning is debatable, but the most persuasive interpretation is that it shows a succession of cult rites. Here a young woman is being whipped, probably an initiation ceremony, while a cult member performs a solemn dance in the nude.

THE SOCIAL STRUGGLES OF THE LATE REPUBLIC

What issues caused the social struggles of the late republic?

The period from the end of the Third Punic War in 146 to about 30 B.C.E. was one of enormous turbulence. Social conflicts, assassinations, struggles between rival dictators, wars, and insurrections were common occurrences. Slave uprisings were also part of the general disorder. Some seventy thousand slaves defeated a Roman army in Sicily in 134 B.C.E. before this revolt was put down by Roman reinforcements. Slaves ravaged Sicily again in 104 B.C.E. But the most threatening slave revolt of all was led by a slave named Spartacus. Spartacus, who was being trained to become a gladiator (which meant certain death in the arena), escaped with a band of fugitives to Mount Vesuvius near Naples, there attracting a huge host of other fugitive slaves. From 73 to 71 B.C.E. the escapees under his leadership held off

Roman armies and overran much of southern Italy until they were finally defeated and Spartacus was slain in battle. Six thousand of those captured were left crucified along the length of a road from Capua to Rome (about one hundred fifty miles) to provide a terrible warning.

THE GRACCHI

Meanwhile, an extended conflict among elements of the Roman governing class began in 133 B.C.E. with the attempts at social and economic reform instituted by the two Gracchus brothers. Though of aristocratic lineage himself, Tiberius Gracchus proposed to alleviate social and economic stress by granting government lands to the landless. Conservative aristocrats bitterly opposed this proposal and engineered its veto by Octavius, Tiberius's fellow tribune. Tiberius then removed Octavius from office, a highly irregular action, and when his own term expired attempted to stand for re-election. These moves seemed to threaten a dictatorship and offered the conservative senators an excuse for resistance. Armed with clubs, they went on a rampage during the elections and murdered Tiberius and many of his followers.

WHAT ISSUES CAUSED THE SOCIAL STRUGGLES OF THE LATE REPUBLIC?

THE SOCIAL STRUGGLES OF THE LATE REPUBLIC   145

Nine years later, Tiberius's younger brother Gaius renewed the struggle. Though Tiberius's land law had finally been enacted by the Senate, Gaius believed that the campaign had to go further. Elected tribune in 123 B.C.E., and reelected in 122, he enacted several laws for the benefit of the less privileged. One stabilized the price of grain in Rome by building public granaries along the Tiber. Another imposed controls on governors suspected of exploiting the provinces for their own advantage. Gaius also proposed to extend full Roman citizenship to vast numbers of Italian allies. These measures provoked so much anger among the vested interests that they resolved to eliminate their enemy. The Roman Senate proclaimed Gaius Gracchus an outlaw and authorized the consuls to take all necessary steps for the defense of the republic. In the ensuing conflict Gaius was killed, and about three thousand of his followers lost their lives in vengeful purges.

CHRONOLOGY

STRUGGLES OF THE LATE REPUBLIC, 146–27 B.C.E.

Third Punic War	149–146 B.C.E.
Slave revolts in Sicily	134–104 B.C.E.
Gracchian reforms	133–122 B.C.E.
Rule of Marius	107–100, 86 B.C.E.
Sulla becomes dictator	82 B.C.E.
Spartacus leads slave revolt	73–71 B.C.E.
Pompey becomes sole consul	52 B.C.E.
Caesar becomes sole consul	48 B.C.E.
Caesar becomes dictator	46 B.C.E.
Caesar assassinated	44 B.C.E.
Rule of Octavian, Mark Antony, and Lepidus	42–31 B.C.E.
Octavian becomes sole consul	31 B.C.E.
Octavian becomes emperor	27 B.C.E.

ARISTOCRATIC REACTION

After the downfall of the Gracchi, two military leaders who had won fame in foreign wars successively made themselves rulers of the state. The first was Marius, who was elevated to the consulship by the plebeian party in 107 B.C.E. and reelected six times. Marius, however, was no statesman and accomplished little for his followers beyond demonstrating how easily a general with an army behind him could override opposition. Partly for political motives and partly to meet the shortfall in manpower, Marius scrapped the property qualification for the army altogether. Thereafter, Rome's soldiers would come increasingly from the ranks of the urban poor and the landless country dwellers. The result was that gradually, Roman armies became more loyal to the individual interests of their commanders than they were to the republic itself, because the political success of their generals could best guarantee rewards for the impoverished soldiers of the army.

Following Marius's death in 86 B.C.E., conservatives took a turn at governing through the army. Their champion was Sulla, another victorious commander. Appointed dictator in 82 B.C.E. for an unlimited term, Sulla ruthlessly exterminated his opponents. He extended the powers of the Senate (whose ranks, depleted by civil war, he packed with men loyal to himself), and curtailed the authority of the tribunes. After three years of rule Sulla decided his job was done and retired to a life of luxury on his country estate.

POMPEY AND JULIUS CAESAR

The effect of Sulla's decrees was to give control to a selfish aristocracy. Soon, however, new leaders emerged to espouse the cause of the people. The most prominent were Pompey (Gnaeus Pompeius Magnus, 106–48 B.C.E.) and Julius Caesar (100–44 B.C.E.). For a time they cooperated in a plot to gain control of the government, but later they became rivals and sought to outdo each other in bidding for popular support. Both were men who, despite their successes, failed to gain complete acceptance from the established elite. Pompey won fame as the conqueror of Syria and Palestine, while Caesar devoted his energies to a series of campaigns against the Gauls. These added to the Roman state the territory of modern Belgium, Germany west of the Rhine, and France, greatly increasing Caesar's reputation and cementing the loyalty of his army. They came at a high price to the Gauls, however: perhaps a million Gauls were killed in these campaigns, and another million were enslaved.

In 52 B.C.E., after protracted mob disorders in Rome, the Senate turned to Pompey and engineered his election as sole consul. Caesar, stationed in Gaul, was branded an enemy of the state, and Pompey conspired with the Senate to deprive him of political power. The result was a deadly war between the two men. In 49 B.C.E. Caesar marched on Rome. Pompey fled to the East in the hope of gathering an army large enough to

Julius Caesar.

regain control of Italy. In 48 B.C.E. the forces of the rivals met at Pharsalus in Greece. Pompey was defeated and soon afterward murdered by supporters of Caesar.

Caesar then intervened in Egyptian politics at the court of Cleopatra (whom he left pregnant). Then he conducted another military campaign in Asia Minor in which victory was so swift that he could report, "I came, I saw, I conquered" (*Veni, vidi, vici*). After that Caesar returned to Rome. No one now dared challenge his power. With the aid of his veterans he cowed the Senate into granting his every desire. In 46 B.C.E. he was named dictator for ten years, and two years later for life. In addition, he assumed nearly every other title that could augment his power. He obtained from the Senate full authority to make war and peace and to control the revenues of the state. For all practical purposes he was above the law, and rumors spread that he intended to make himself king. Such fears led to his assassination on the Ides of March (the 15th) in 44 B.C.E. by a group of conspirators under the leadership of Brutus and Cassius, who hoped to return Rome to republican government.

Although Caesar was once revered by historians as a superhuman hero, he is now often dismissed as insignificant. Both extremes of interpretation should be avoided. Certainly he did not "save Rome," nor was he the greatest statesman of all time. He treated the republic with contempt and made the problem of governing more difficult for those who came after him. Yet some of the measures he took as dictator did have lasting effects. With the aid of a Greek astronomer he revised the calendar so as to make a 365-day year (with an extra day added every fourth year). This "Julian" calendar—adjusted by Pope Gregory XIII in 1582—is still with us. Appropriately, the seventh month is named after Julius as "July." By conferring citizenship on thousands of Spaniards and Gauls, Caesar took an important step toward eliminating the distinction between Italians and provincials. He also helped relieve economic inequities by settling many of his veterans and some of the urban poor on unused lands. Vastly more important than these reforms, however, was Caesar's farsighted resolve, made before he seized power, to invest his efforts in the West. Whereas Pompey, and before him Alexander, went to the East to gain fame and fortune, Caesar was the first Roman leader to recognize the potential significance of northwestern Europe. By incorporating Gaul into the Roman world he brought Rome great agricultural wealth and helped bring urban life and culture to what was then the wild West. Western European civilization, later to be anchored in just those regions that Caesar conquered, might not have been the same without him.

THE PRINCIPATE OR EARLY EMPIRE (27 B.C.E.–180 C.E.)

Why did the "Augustan system" succeed?

In his will, Julius Caesar had adopted as his heir his grandnephew Octavian (63 B.C.E.–14 C.E.), then a young man of eighteen. On learning of Caesar's death, Octavian hastened to Rome to try to claim his inheritance. He soon found that he had to join forces with two of Caesar's powerful friends, Mark Antony and Lepidus. The following year the three formed an alliance to crush the political faction responsible for Caesar's murder. The methods employed were not to the new leaders' credit. Prominent members of the opposition were hunted down and slain and their property confiscated. The most notable of the victims was Cicero, brutally slain by Mark Antony's thugs; though he had taken no part in the conspiracy against Caesar's life, Cicero had actively sought to undermine Antony during his term as consul and have him branded a public enemy. Caesar's real murderers, Brutus and Cassius, escaped and organized an army, but they were defeated by Antony and Octavian near Philippi in 42 B.C.E.

With the "republican" opposition effectively crushed, tensions mounted between the members of the alliance, inspired primarily by Antony's jealousy of Octavian. The subsequent struggle became a contest between East and West. Antony went to the East and made an alliance with Cleopatra, hoping to use the resources of the Egyptian kingdom in the power struggle with Octavian. Octavian, as the junior partner, established himself in Italy and the West. It was a risky move: Octavian had to deal with the problems of resettling veterans while maintaining his position in the roiling political environment in Rome. But Italy provided him with manpower and the opportunity to style himself as the protector of Rome and its heritage against Antony, whom he skillfully portrayed as being in the clutches of a foreign, female potentate who intended to become queen over Rome. As in the earlier contest between Caesar and Pompey, the victory went to the West. In the naval battle of Actium (31 B.C.E.) Octavian's forces defeated those of Antony and Cleopatra, both of whom soon afterward committed suicide. Egypt's independent existence came to an end, and Rome reigned supreme throughout the Mediterranean world.

Octavian. When Octavian gained sole rule he became known as Augustus. Many statues of him survive, all of them idealized.

THE AUGUSTAN SYSTEM OF GOVERNMENT

The victory at Actium ushered in a new period in Roman history, the most glorious and the most prosperous that Rome ever experienced. When Octavian returned to Rome he announced the restoration of complete peace. This was a great relief to the people of Italy, who had suffered grievously from a decade of civil war. For four years he ruled as consul, until he accepted from the Senate the honorific titles of *imperator* (emperor) and *augustus*, a step that historians count as the beginning of the Roman empire. At the time, *imperator* meant only "victorious general"; *augustus* signified "venerable" or "worthy of honor." But gradually, after his successors took the title of emperor as well, it became the primary designation for the ruler of the Roman state. The title Octavian himself preferred was the more modest *princeps*, or "first citizen." For this reason the period of his rule and that of his successors is called the Principate (or, alternatively, the early empire), to distinguish it from the periods of the republic (c. 500–27 B.C.E.), the "Third-Century Crisis" (180 C.E.–284 C.E.), and the later empire or "Dominate" (284–610 C.E.).

Octavian, or Augustus as he was now called, was determined not to appear to be a dictator. He therefore left most republican institutions in place even though they now exercised little independent power. In theory the Senate and the citizens remained the supreme authorities; but in practice, Augustus himself controlled the army and determined governmental policy. Fortunately he was an able ruler. He instituted a new coinage system throughout the empire; he introduced a range of public services in the city of Rome; he reorganized the army; and he allowed cities and provinces more substantial rights of self-government than they had enjoyed before.

Augustus presented himself as a stern defender of traditional Roman morality. He rebuilt temples and prohibited Romans from worshiping foreign gods. In an attempt to increase the Roman birthrate, he penalized citizens who failed to marry and required widows to remarry within two years of their husbands' deaths. He also introduced laws punishing adultery and making divorces more difficult to obtain. To hammer the message home, Augustan propaganda portrayed the imperial family as a model of domestic virtue and sexual propriety. These portrayals were only moderately successful. The emperor's own extramarital affairs were well known; and the sexual promiscuity of his daughter Julia finally led Augustus to exile her to a distant island.

From the time of Augustus until that of Trajan (98–117 C.E.), the Roman empire continued to expand. Augustus gained more land for Rome than did any other Roman ruler. His generals advanced into central Europe, conquering the modern-day territories of Switzerland, Austria, and Bulgaria. Only in what is today central Germany did Roman troops meet defeat, a setback that convinced Augustus to hold the Roman borders at the Rhine and Danube. Subsequently, in 43 C.E., the emperor Claudius began the conquest of Britain, and at the beginning of the next century Trajan pushed beyond the Danube to add Dacia (now Romania) to the empire's realms. Trajan also conquered territories in Mesopotamia, but in so doing aroused the enmity of the Parthian rulers of Persia. His successor Hadrian halted the conquests and embarked on a defensive policy epitomized by the construction of Hadrian's Wall in northern Britain. The Roman empire had now reached its territorial limits; in the third century these limits would begin to recede.

When Augustus died in 14 C.E. after four decades of rule, his remarkable experiments in statesmanship might have died with him. His system was so ingenious, however, that Rome enjoyed nearly two centuries of peace, prosperity, and stability as a result of his reforms. Aside from one brief period of civil war in 68 C.E., the transition of power between emperors was generally peaceful, and the growing imperial bureaucracy managed affairs competently even when individual emperors proved to be vicious. Nevertheless, the fact that Rome had become an autocratic empire became harder and harder to conceal. Several talented men succeeded Augustus, but few of them had his panache for disguising the true power of the princeps.

> Aside from the brief period of civil war in 68 C.E., the transition of power between emperors was generally peaceful, and growing imperial bureaucracy managed affairs competently even when individual emperors proved to be vicious.

The height of the Augustan system came between 96 and 180 C.E., under the so-called Five Good Emperors: Nerva (96–98 C.E.), Trajan (98–117 C.E.), Hadrian (117–138 C.E.), Antoninus Pius (136–171 C.E.), and Marcus Aurelius (161–180 C.E.). All were capable administrators, and all proved worthy successors of Augustus, respecting the Senate and preserving republican forms while running an essentially autocratic government. Until 180, none had a son who survived him, and so each adopted a man worthy to succeed him. They thus avoided the difficulties of dynastic politics, one of the great horrors of first-century imperial life.

Rome's successful governance of such a vast empire from the time of Augustus to that of Marcus Aurelius was certainly one of its greatest accomplishments. During these two centuries, Rome had few external enemies. The Mediterranean was now under the control of a single military power; on land, Roman officials ruled from the borders of Scotland to those of Persia. A contemporary orator justly boasted that "the whole civilized world lays down the arms which were its ancient burden, as if on holiday . . . [A]ll places are full of gymnasia, fountains, monumental approaches, temples, workshops, schools; one can say that the civilized world, which had been sick from the beginning . . . has been brought by right knowledge to a state of health."

ROMANIZATION AND ASSIMILATION

This "Roman Peace" (*Pax Romana*) was not universal. In Britain, the Roman army massacred tens of thousands of Britons in the aftermath of Queen Boudicca's revolt. In Judea, perhaps the most restive of all the Roman provinces, a Roman army destroyed the Temple at Jerusalem in 70 C.E. in the wake of one rebellion, and in 135 C.E. destroyed the entire city of Jerusalem in the wake of another, massacring its inhabitants and scattering the survivors throughout the empire. Upwards of half a million people may have been killed in Judea during these years, and an equal number enslaved. Jerusalem, meanwhile, was refounded by the emperor Hadrian as a pagan capital named Aelia Capitolina. For the next five hundred years, Jews would be forbidden to live there.

THE ROMAN EMPIRE AT ITS GREATEST EXTENT, 97–117 C.E.

By the second century C.E., Roman expansion had pushed well beyond the Mediterranean basin and into northern and central Europe. This expansion largely followed the courses of the major European river systems. Why do you suppose this was so?

Such rebellions were not the norm, however, even in Judea. Although the Roman empire rested on the backs of its armies, the empire was not really a military occupation. Rome controlled its far-flung territories by assimilating their residents into the common cultural and political life of Rome itself. Local gods became Roman gods and were adopted into the Roman pantheon of divinities. Cities were constructed, and the amenities of urban life introduced: baths, temples, amphitheaters, aqueducts, and paved roads. Rights of citizenship were extended, and able provincials could rise far in Roman service. Some, like Trajan and Hadrian, even rose to become emperors.

Even the frontier areas of the empire need to be understood in this light. Although for convenience' sake historians speak of the empire's "borders," in fact these borders were highly fluid and permeable. We ought, more properly, to speak not of "borders" but of "frontiers," and to see these frontiers as zones of particularly intensive cultural interaction between provincial Romans and the non-Roman peoples who lived beyond them. Roman influence thus reached far beyond the frontier areas, across the Rhine and the Danube into the heartland of Germany and the Gothic lands to the east. When, in the third century, frontier garrisons were withdrawn in order to take part in civil wars within the empire itself, many of these Romanized Germans and Goths moved into the empire, sometimes as plunderers, but often as settlers and aspiring Romans.

CULTURE AND LIFE IN THE PERIOD OF THE PRINCIPATE

Why did so many critics of Roman life during the Principate focus their criticisms on the behavior of women?

The cultural and intellectual changes that began in Rome during the late republican period came to fruition during the Principate. Three eminent exponents of Stoicism lived in Rome during this period: Seneca (4 B.C.E.–65 C.E.), wealthy adviser for a time to Nero; the slave Epictetus (60?–120 C.E.); and the emperor Marcus Aurelius (121–180 C.E.). All of them agreed that inner serenity is the ultimate human goal and that true happiness can be found only in surrender to the benevolent order of the universe. They preached the ideal of virtue for virtue's sake, deplored the sinfulness of human nature, and urged obedience to conscience. Seneca and Epictetus both expressed deep mystical yearnings as part of their philosophy, making it almost a religion. They worshiped the cosmos as divine, governed by an all-powerful Providence that ordained all that happened for ultimate good. The last of the Roman Stoics, Marcus Aurelius, was more fatalistic and less hopeful. Although he did not reject the concept of an ordered and rational universe, he did not believe that immortality would balance suffering on earth and was inclined to think of humans as creatures buffeted by evil fortune for which no distant perfection of the whole could fully compensate. He urged, nevertheless, that people should continue to live nobly, that they should not abandon themselves to either gross indulgence or angry protest, but that they should derive what contentment they could from dignified resignation to suffering and tranquil submission to death.

LITERATURE OF THE GOLDEN AND SILVER AGES

Roman literature of the Principate is conventionally divided into two periods: works of the *Golden Age*, written during the reign of Augustus, and works of the *Silver Age*, written during the first and early second centuries C.E. Most of the literature of the Golden Age was vigorous, affirmative, and uplifting, and—it should be noted—much of it served the propagandistic purposes of Augustus's government. The poetry of the greatest

Marcus Aurelius. This equestrian statue is one of the few surviving from the ancient world: the Christians destroyed most Roman equestrian statues because they found them idolatrous, but they spared this one because they mistakenly believed that it represented Constantine, the first Christian Roman emperor. The statue stood outdoors in Rome from the second century until 1980, when it was taken into storage to protect it from air pollution.

WHY DID CRITICS OF ROMAN LIFE FOCUS THEIR CRITICISMS ON THE BEHAVIOR OF WOMEN?

CULTURE AND LIFE IN THE PERIOD OF THE PRINCIPATE   151

of all Roman poets, Virgil (70–19 B.C.E.), was proto-typic. In a set of pastoral poems, the *Eclogues*, Virgil expressed an idealized vision of human life led in harmony with nature, while implicitly extolling Augustus as the bringer of such peace and abundance. Virgil's masterpiece, the *Aeneid*, is an epic poem about a Trojan hero, Aeneas (whom the family of Caesar and Augustus claimed as an ancestor), who was reputed to have played a role in the formation of the Roman people (see p. 133). Written in elevated, yet sinewy and stirring metrical verse ("Arms and the man, I sing. . . ."), the *Aeneid* tells of the founding of a great state through warfare and toil and foretells Rome's glorious future.

Other major Golden Age writers were Horace (65–8 B.C.E.), Livy (59 B.C.E.–17 C.E.), and Ovid (43 B.C.E.–17 C.E.). Of these, Horace was the most philosophical. His *Odes* combined Epicurean justification of pleasure with Stoic fortitude in the face of suffering. Livy's *History of Rome* is often factually unreliable but is filled with dramatic stories designed to appeal to patriotic emotions. Ovid was the least typical of the Latin Golden Age writers insofar as his outlook tended to be more satiric than heroically affirmative. His main poetic accomplishment was a highly sophisticated retelling of Greek myths in a long poem of fifteen books, the *Metamorphoses*, full of wit and eroticism. Augustus delighted in the *Aeneid*, but found the mocking and dissolute tone of Ovid's verses so abhorrent that he banished Ovid from Rome. Augustus was trying to present himself as a stern moralist, whereas Ovid's verses treated such subjects as how to attract women at the race track and his adulterous (although perhaps imaginary) affair with the wife of a Roman senator.

The literature of the Silver Age was typically less calm and balanced than that of the Golden Age. Its effects derived more often from self-conscious artifice. The tales of Petronius and Apuleius describe the more exotic and sometimes sordid aspects of Roman life. The aim of the authors is less to instruct or uplift than to tell an entertaining story or turn a witty phrase. But an entirely different viewpoint is presented by two other important writers of this age. The satirist Juvenal (60?–140 C.E.) wrote with savage indignation about the moral degeneracy he saw in his contemporaries. A similar attitude toward Roman society characterized the writings of Tacitus (55?–117? C.E.). His *Annals* offer a subtle but devastating portrait of the political system constructed by Augustus and ruled by his heirs; his *Germania* contrasts the manly virtues of the German barbarians with the effeminate vices of the decadent Romans. Like Juvenal, Tacitus was a master of ironic wit and brilliant aphorism.

Referring to Roman conquests, he makes a barbarian chieftain say, "They create a wilderness and call it peace."

ART AND ARCHITECTURE

Roman art first assumed its distinctive character during the Principate. Before this time what passed for an art of Rome was really an importation from the Hellenistic East. Conquering armies brought back to Italy wagonloads of statues, reliefs, and marble columns as part of the plunder from Greece and Asia Minor. These became the property of the wealthy and were used to embellish their sumptuous mansions. As demand for such works increased, hundreds of copies were made

Diana. A Roman painting depicting the goddess of the hunt. Roman art was often gentle and impressionistic, far from the military grandeur most often associated today with the Romans.

A SCATHING CRITIQUE OF ROMAN SOCIETY

Roman society, even at its height under the "Five Good Emperors," was not without its critics. Among the most famous and resonant indictments were those of Juvenal, whose Satires attacked everything from the general erosion of public morality to the effete tastes of the elite. His language is often bitter, and he did not shy away from lacing his elegant verses with a vulgarity still shocking across the centuries. Like those of Aristophanes, many of his references are highly topical, and their exact meaning is lost to us. No doubt his audience understood the allusions, making his public excoriations all the more personal and pointed. Contrast this portrayal of contemporary women with the model of the virtuous Lucretia.

What conscience has Venus drunk? Our inebriated beauties can't tell head from tail at those midnight oyster suppers when the best wine's laced with perfume, and tossed down neat from a foaming conch-shell, while the dizzy ceiling spins round, and the tables dance, and each light shows double. Why, you may ask yourself, does the notorious Maura sniff at the air in that knowing, derisive way as she and her dear friend Tullia pass by the ancient altar of Chastity? And what is Tullia whispering to her? Here, at night, they stagger out of their litters and relieve themselves, pissing in long hard bursts all over the goddess's statue. Then, while the Moon looks down on their motions, they take turns to ride each other, and finally go home. So you, next morning, on your way to some great house, will splash through your wife's piddle. Notorious, too, are the ritual mysteries of the Good Goddess, when flute-music stirs the loins, and frenzied women, devotees of Priapus, sweep along in procession, howling, tossing their hair, wine-flown, horn-crazy, burning with the desire to get themselves laid. . . . So the ladies, with a display of talent to match their birth, win all the prizes. No make-believe here, no pretense, each act is performed in earnest, and guaranteed to warm the age-chilled balls of a Nestor or a Priam.

Juvenal, *Sixth Satire* 301–326. Based on Peter Green, trans. *Juvenal: The Sixteen Satires*. (New York: Penguin, 1974), pp. 138–139.

by Roman artisans. None, however, represent a truly indigenous Roman artistic style.

Encouraged by the patronage of Augustus himself, the Principate witnessed the development of a more distinctively Roman art. This art was more varied than is often assumed, running from the most magnificent public architecture to the most intimate wall paintings. Roman architecture was often grandiose, its massive proportions made possible by the expertise Roman engineers had developed in working with concrete. Among the largest such public buildings were the Pantheon, with its 142-foot-diameter dome, and the Colosseum, which could accommodate fifty thousand spectators at gladiatorial combats. Except on public monuments, Roman sculpture was less bombastic. Relief sculpture was particularly notable during this period for its delicacy and naturalism. Even on their coins, emperors were portrayed very much as they looked in real life;

WHY DID CRITICS OF ROMAN LIFE FOCUS THEIR CRITICISMS ON THE BEHAVIOR OF WOMEN?

CULTURE AND LIFE IN THE PERIOD OF THE PRINCIPATE   153

The Pantheon in Rome. Built by the emperor Hadrian, it boasted the largest dome without interior supports of the ancient world. The dome forms a perfect sphere, exactly as high as it is wide.

and since the images on coins were recut annually, we can trace on successive issues a ruler's receding hairline or his advancing double chin. Painting, however, was the Romans' most original and most intimate art. Romans loved intense colors; those who could afford to do so surrounded themselves with brilliant wall paintings and mosaics (pictures produced by fitting together small pieces of colored glass or stone). These created a gamut of effects from fantastic seascapes to dreamy landscapes to introspective portraiture.

Closely related to their achievements in architecture were Roman triumphs in engineering. The imperial Romans built marvelous roads and bridges, many of which still survive. Under Trajan, eleven aqueducts brought water into Rome from the nearby hills and provided the city with 300 million gallons daily for drinking and bathing and for flushing a well-designed sewage system. Water was cleverly funneled into the homes of the rich for their private gardens, fountains, and pools. The Emperor Nero built a famous "Golden House" in the center of Rome with pipes fitted for sprinkling his guests with perfume, baths supplied with medicinal waters, and a pond "like a sea." In addition, a spherical ceiling in the banquet hall revolved day and night like the heavens, all contributing to Nero's deserved reputation as a volup-

tuary. (Supposedly, when Nero moved in he was heard to say, "At last I can live like a human being.")

ARISTOCRATIC WOMEN UNDER THE PRINCIPATE

One of the most striking aspects of Roman society under the Principate was the important role played by upper-class women. As we have seen, the wealthy women of late-republican Rome were much less confined to domesticity than were their counterparts in Classical Athens. This trait became even more pronounced during the Principate. Despite laws that kept them formally under the legal supervision of a male guardian, in practice wealthy women could own property, invest in commercial ventures, and make public benefactions. They could not hold political office, but they could act as priestesses and civic patrons. Both roles gave them considerable influence in public affairs. With numerous slaves to take care of their households and wealth of their own on which to draw, upper-class Roman women were free to engage in intellectual and artistic pursuits. Some wrote poetry, others studied philosophy, and others presided over literary salons. They also exercised a degree of sexual freedom unknown elsewhere in the ancient world, and profoundly shocking to conservative male critics. Aristocratic Roman women often had their portraits painted or chiseled in stone. Several emperors' wives or daughters even appeared on Roman coinage.

The lives of lower-class women are far less well known. Most were probably married at some point in their lives, and the wives of shopkeepers in particular played an important role in the businesses that sustained their families. Married women who survived the dangers of childbirth could probably expect to give birth to three or four children, not all of whom would live to adulthood. But death rates were high, especially for women. In Rome, the median recorded age at death for women was 34; for men, between 40 and 46. If enslaved women were more fully represented in these figures, they would likely be even lower.

NEW RELIGIONS

The age of the Principate was characterized by an even deeper interest in salvationist religions than had prevailed under the late republic. Mithraism gained adherents by the thousands, and gradually became a favored religion of the Roman army. About 40 C.E. the first Christians appeared in Rome, following in the wake of the sizable Jewish communities that had already spread throughout the Hellenistic world. The new Christian sect grew steadily and eventually succeeded in displacing Mithraism as the most popular of the salvationist faiths, owing in part to its inclusion of women, at first on terms more or less equal to men. (These developments are considered more fully in Chapter Six.) But perhaps the most startling religious development of the early imperial period was the emergence and popularity of emperor worship. Although most emperors of the first and second centuries C.E. avoided claiming to be divine during their lifetimes, emperors from Julius Caesar on were routinely "deified" after their deaths. The widespread popularity of the cult reflected a deeply held and widely shared vision of the essential connections between human rulership and the divine order of the world.

ROMAN LAW

One of the most important legacies the Romans left to succeeding cultures was their system of law. This too was largely a product of the Principate. This was partly because, with the growth of the Roman empire, Roman law now extended over a much wider field of jurisdiction, embracing the far-flung provinces as well as the citizens of Italy. But the major reason for the rapid development of Roman legal thinking during these years was the fact that Augustus and his successors appointed a small number of eminent jurists to deliver opinions on the legal issues raised by cases under trial in the courts. Although most of them held high judicial office, they gained their reputations primarily as lawyers and writers on legal subjects. Their legal opinions came to embody a systematic philosophy of law unlike anything that had gone before, and became the foundation for all subsequent Roman jurisprudence.

Roman law as it was developed by the jurists comprised three great branches or divisions: the civil law, the law of peoples, and the natural law. The civil law was the law of Rome and its citizens. It included the statutes of the Senate, the decrees of the emperor, the edicts of magistrates, and also certain ancient customs operating with the force of law. The law of peoples was the law held to be common to all people regardless of nationality, a sort of rudimentary "international law." This law authorized slavery and private ownership of property and defined the principles of purchase and sale, partnership, and contract. It was not superior to the civil law but supplemented it, especially with respect to the alien inhabitants of the empire.

The most interesting and in many ways the most important branch of Roman law was the natural law, a product not of judicial practice but of philosophy. The Stoics had developed the idea of a rational order of nature that is the embodiment of justice and right. They had affirmed that all men are by nature equal, and that they are entitled to certain basic rights that governments have no authority to transgress. The father of the law of nature as a legal principle, however, was Cicero. "True law," he declared, "is right reason consonant with nature, diffused among all men, constant, eternal. To make enactments infringing this law, religion forbids, neither may it be repealed even in part, nor have we power through Senate or people to free ourselves from it." This law was prior to the state itself, and any ruler who defied it automatically became a tyrant. The practical law applied in local Roman courts often bore little resemblance to the laws of nature. Nonetheless, their development of the concept of abstract justice as a legal principle was one of the noblest achievements of Roman civilization.

> One of the most important legacies the Romans left to succeeding cultures was their system of law.

THE ECONOMY OF ITALY DURING THE PRINCIPATE

The establishment of stable government by Augustus ushered in a period of prosperity for Italy that lasted for more than two centuries. Trade was now extended to all parts of the known world, and manufacturing increased. Wealth poured into Rome, permitting the upper classes to live in spectacular luxury, and enabling even the urban poor to earn a dependable living.

But the prosperity was not evenly distributed. In the countryside, the diminishing number of slaves captured in war was beginning to result in labor shortages on the great aristocratic *latifundia*. These shortages were partially made up by the declining social and economic position of small farmers, many of whom wound up as semi-servile agricultural workers (known as *colonni*) tied to the great estates. In the cities also, production was bound to decline as the supply of slaves diminished, because slaves performed so much of the skilled labor in Roman society. Italy also had a decidedly unfavorable balance of trade; as a result, it was gradually drained of its supply of precious metals. By the third century the western Roman economy was beginning to collapse.

THE CRISIS OF THE THIRD CENTURY (180–284 C.E.)

> What factors brought the Roman empire to the brink of ruin?

With the death of Marcus Aurelius in 180 C.E. the period of beneficent imperial rule came to an end. One reason for the success of the "Five Good Emperors" was that the first four designated particularly promising young men, rather than sons or close relatives, for the succession. But Marcus Aurelius broke this pattern with unfortunate results. Although he was one of the most philosophic and thoughtful rulers who ever reigned, he was not wise enough to recognize that his son Commodus was a self-indulgent adolescent who lacked the discipline or the capacity to rule effectively. His erratic and frequently violent behavior resulted in a conspiracy originating inside his own palace: his wrestling coach finally strangled him in 192 C.E. Matters thereafter became worse. With no obvious successor to Commodus, the armies of the provinces raised their own candidates and civil war ensued. A provincial general, Septimius Severus (193–211 C.E.), emerged victorious, making it clear that provincial armies could now interfere in imperial politics at will.

THE SEVERAN DYNASTY

Severus and his successors aggravated the problem by eliminating even the theoretical rights of the Senate and ruling as military dictators. On his deathbed, Severus advised his two sons, "Enrich the soldiers, boys, and scorn the rest." His son Caracalla was little more than a thug who murdered his brother and co-emperor Geta. So desperate was Caracalla to raise revenues and pay bonuses to his increasingly covetous armies (especially to appease them after his assassination of his more popular brother), that he made everyone in the empire a Roman citizen. This was hardly an act of enlightenment, but rather was aimed at increasing the tax base of the Roman state. In the process, he cheapened Roman citizenship, once the prized glue that held the vast empire together. His successors in the Severan dynasty proved no better.

Commodus. The self-deluded ruler encouraged artists to portray him as the equal of the superhuman Hercules.

Elagabalus tried to introduce an eastern sun cult as the official religion of Rome, and he flouted sexual and moral convention on the very floor of the Senate.

If not for a series of remarkable imperial women fighting to keep the dynasty and empire together, the results might have been disastrous. First Julia Domna, the wife of Septimius Severus, helped to manage the empire for her son Caracalla, and seems to have acted as the one restraint on his vicious personality; she took her own life when he fell victim to an assassin in 217 C.E. Her sister Julia Maesa was the grandmother of both Elagabalus and his successor, Severus Alexander. Her political influence was considerable, and she proved instrumental in Elagabalus's downfall when his abuses endangered the state. Finally, her daughter Julia Mamaea, the mother of Severus Alexander, enjoyed unusual prominence and popularity during the reign of her young son (222–235 C.E.), and exercised an almost regentlike authority within his government. But they could not stem the tide started by the dynasty's founder, Septimius. The growing prominence of the army made it increasingly uncontrollable. Once the role of brute force was openly revealed, any aspiring general could try his luck at seizing power. Severus Alexander and Julia Mamaea were murdered in 235 C.E. when the army turned against them. Fifty years of endemic civil war followed. From 235 to 284 C.E. there were no fewer than twenty-six "barracks emperors," of whom only one managed to escape a violent death.

THE HEIGHT OF THE THIRD-CENTURY CRISIS

The half century between 235 and 284 C.E., was the height of the "Third-Century Crisis." Political chaos now combined with a number of other factors to bring the empire to the brink of ruin. Civil wars undermined the economy, not only by interfering with agriculture and trade, but also by encouraging aspiring emperors to enrich their soldiers by debasing the coinage and imposing exorbitant taxation on civilians in their provinces. Landlords, small farmers, and artisans thus had little motive to produce at a time when production was most necessary. In human terms the poorest, as is usual in times of economic contraction, suffered the most. Often they were driven to the most abject destitution. In the wake of war and hunger, disease also ran rampant. In the reign of Marcus Aurelius a terrible plague swept through the empire, decimating the army and the population at large. In the middle of the third

century the pestilence returned and struck at the population with its fearful scythe for fifteen years.

The resulting decline in population came at a time when Rome could least afford it, for still another threat to the empire in the middle of the third century was the advance of Rome's external enemies. With Roman ranks thinned by disease and Roman armies fighting each other, Germans in the West and Persians in the East broke through the old Roman defense lines. In 251 C.E. the Goths defeated and slew the emperor Decius, crossed the Danube, and marauded at will in the Balkans. An even more humiliating disaster came in 260 C.E. when the emperor Valerian was captured in battle by the Persians and made to kneel as a footstool for their ruler. When he died his body was stuffed and hung on exhibition. For a time, the western provinces broke free as an independent empire in their own right, despairing of Rome's ability to defend them. Clearly the days of Augustus were far in the past.

ROMAN RULE IN THE WEST: A BALANCE SHEET

Did Rome fall? Why or why not?

As Rome was not built in a day, so it was not lost in one. As we will see in the next chapter, strong rule returned in 284 C.E. Thereafter the Roman empire endured in the West for two hundred years more and in the East for a millennium. But the restored Roman state differed greatly from the old one—so much so that it is proper to end the story of characteristically Roman civilization here and to review the reasons for Rome's transformation into a distinctly different type of society, one that we will examine in detail in the next chapter.

EXPLAINING THE "DECLINE AND FALL" OF ROME

More has been written on the decline and fall of Rome than on the death of any other civilization. The theories offered to account for the decline have been many and varied. Perhaps the strangest recent one is that Rome fell from the effects of lead ingested from cooking utensils, but if this were true we would have to ask why Rome did so well for so long. Moralists have found the explanation for Rome's decline in the descriptions of lechery and gluttony presented by such authors as Juvenal and Petronius. Such an approach, however, overlooks the facts that much of this evidence is patently overdrawn, and that nearly all of it comes from the period of the early Principate: in later centuries, when the empire was more obviously collapsing, morality became more austere. One of the simplest explanations is that Rome fell because of the severity of German attacks. But German "barbarians" had always stood ready to attack Rome: German invasions succeeded only when Rome was already weakened internally. Indeed, from the fourth century C.E. onward, increasing numbers of Germanic tribes were less interested in destroying Rome than in becoming a part of it. Many of the Germanic tribes who would overrun the Western empire during the fifth century C.E. were in fact Roman allies, provoked to invade the empire by Roman bigotry, maladministration, and abuse.

POLITICAL FAILURES

It is best then to concentrate on Rome's most serious internal problems. Some of these were political. The most obvious failing of the Roman constitution under the Principate was the lack of a clear law of succession. Especially when a ruler died suddenly, there was no certainty about who was to follow him. For all of Augustus's achievements, this was his system's greatest failure. Indeed, because the reality of autocratic rule was disguised behind republican forms, there was little any emperor could do to provide for an orderly succession to an imperial position that did not officially exist. So long as prosperity and deference for the institutions of ancient Rome remained, transitions might be effected more or less smoothly. But from 235 to 284 C.E. warfare and instability fed on each other. Civil war was also nurtured by the lack of constitutional means for reform. If regimes became unpopular, as most did after 180 C.E., the only means to alter them was to overthrow them. But resorting to violence always bred more violence, especially as the soldiery became the arbiter of success or failure of an imperial regime.

ECONOMIC CRISIS

The Roman empire also had its share of economic problems. Rome's worst economic problems derived from its slave system and from labor shortages. Roman civilization was based on cities, and Roman cities existed largely by virtue of an agricultural surplus produced by slaves. Slaves were worked so hard that they did not normally reproduce to fill their own ranks. Until the time of Trajan (98–117 C.E.), Roman conquests provided fresh supplies of slaves to keep the system going, but thereafter the economy began to run out of human fuel. Landlords could no longer be so profligate with human life, barracks slavery came to an end, and the countryside produced less of a surplus to feed the towns.

Labor shortages also aggravated Rome's economic problems, especially in the West. With the end of foreign conquests and the decline of slavery there was a pressing need for people to stay on the farm, but barbarian pressures meant that there was also a steady need for men to serve in the army. The plagues of the second and third centuries sharply reduced the population just at the worst time. It has been estimated that between the reign of Marcus Aurelius and the restoration of strong rule in 284 C.E., disease, warfare, and a declining birthrate combined to reduce the population of the Roman empire by one third. The result was that there were neither sufficient farmers to work the land nor enough soldiers to fight Rome's enemies.

Despite all of this, it is important to remember that Rome was scarcely poverty stricken. Wealth still poured into Roman society from the East, but in the western provinces especially it tended to be concentrated in the hands of a very few families. These families gradually accrued to themselves such extensive privileges that they rarely contributed anything to the coffers of the Roman state. The burden for the upkeep of cities thus fell increasingly on a local elite that could not shoulder it, as these men were reduced to poverty or fled the cities altogether, the urban basis of classical Roman civilization and its commonly shared civic ideals were further undermined. Regional differences were also growing more pronounced, leading to a series of secessionist movements among the western provinces. Enormous dedication and exertion on the part of its citizenry might just possibly have saved the empire, but too few citizens were now willing to work hard for the public good. Ultimately, the decline of Rome was marked by a lack of interest among its citizens in preserving it. As a result, the Roman world

> The burden for the upkeep of cities thus fell increasingly on a local elite that could not shoulder it, as these men were reduced to poverty or fled the cities altogether, the urban basis of classical Roman civilization and its commonly shared civic ideals were further underminded.

came to an end not so much with a bang as with a whimper.

ROMAN ACHIEVEMENTS

Attention to the dynamics of Rome's decline in the West should not cause us to overlook the many ways in which Roman society was a towering success. No state has ever encompassed so much territory, with such a large percentage of the world's population under its dominion, for so long a span of time. Roman rule maintained its vitality in the West from the first century B.C.E. until the fifth century C.E. In the East, the Roman empire survived until 1453. Part of that success resulted from the Roman government's ability to create and maintain systems of communication, trade, and travel as no other state had done before, and as none would do again until modern times. Underlying these successes was the fundamental strength of the Roman economy. Although much is made of the collapse of the Roman economy in the third century C.E. and its runaway inflation, the Romans had maintained a relatively stable currency and a prosperous international trade for four previous centuries without any of the mechanisms or safeguards of a modern market economy. This too remains an unparalleled achievement.

Most fundamental, however, the Roman empire's survival was a political achievement. The Roman political system was inclusive to a degree no modern empire has ever matched. Through their willingness to extend the franchise to non-Romans, to allow even provincials to become senators and ultimately emperors, Rome gave a share of power to its population that no Near Eastern or Greek empire could have ever imagined. Although the Persians were tolerant of foreign cultic practice, and the Athenians generous with political rights among their own citizenry, extending real political power to "outsiders" was out of the question. For the Romans, extension of the franchise was key to their success, from the mechanism of the Latin Right in early Italy to the granting of citizenship to all the inhabitants of the empire under Caracalla. As a prominent historian of Rome once remarked, if the British empire had been as willing to extend its franchise as the Romans were to extend theirs, the American Revolution might never have occurred.

CONCLUSION

Resemblances between Roman history and the history of Great Britain or the United States in the nineteenth and twentieth centuries have often been noted. Like America's, the Roman economy evolved from a simple agrarianism to a complex urban system with problems of unemployment, gross disparities of wealth, and financial crises. Like the British empire, the Roman empire was founded on conquest. And like both the British and the American empires, the Roman empire justified itself by celebrating the peace its conquests allegedly brought to the world.

Ultimately, however, such parallels are superficial. Rome was an ancient, not a modern, society that differed profoundly from any of the societies of the modern Western world. The Romans disdained industrial activities. Neither did they have any idea of the modern national state; their empire was more like a collection of cities than an integrated territorial body politic. The Romans never developed an adequate representative government, and they never solved the problem of succession to imperial power. Nor were Roman social relations in any way comparable with those of more recent centuries. The Roman economy rested on slavery to a degree unmatched in any modern society. Technology was primitive; social stratification was extreme; and gender relations were profoundly unequal. Roman religion rested on the assumption that religious practice and political life were inseparable from one another, and Roman emperors were worshiped as living gods.

Nevertheless, the civilization of Rome exerted a great influence on later cultures. Roman architectural forms survive to this day in the design of many of our government buildings, and Roman styles of dress continue to be worn by the clergy of the various Christian churches. Through the sixth-century code of the emperor Justinian (see Chapter 6), Roman law was handed down to the Middle Ages and on into modern times. Roman sculpture provided the model on which virtually all modern sculpture rests, and Roman authors set the standards for prose composition in Europe and America until the twentieth century. Even the organization of the Catholic Church was adapted from the structure of the Roman state; today the pope bears the title of supreme pontiff (*pontifex maximus*), once borne by the emperor in his role as head of the Roman civic religion.

But perhaps the most important of all Rome's contributions to the future was its role in transmitting Greek civilization throughout the length and breadth of its empire. When, finally, the united Roman empire did collapse, three different successor civilizations would emerge to occupy Rome's former territories: Byzantium, Islam, and western Europe. Each of these civilizations would be characterized by a distinctive religious tradition, and each would adopt and adapt different aspects of its Roman inheritance. What these three Western civilizations shared, however, was a common cultural inheritance derived from Greece by way of Rome—an inheritance of urbanism, cosmopolitanism, imperialism, and learning that would forever mark the West as a unique experiment in human history.

This cultural inheritance would be Rome's epitaph; and in the mid-third century C.E., it must have seemed that an epitaph was the only thing needed to bring the Roman empire to an end. But in fact, the Roman empire did not collapse. It went on to enjoy another several centuries of life. Rome did not fall in the third century, or the fourth century, or even the fifth. But it was transformed, and in this transformed state the Roman inheritance would pass to the Western civilizations of the Middle Ages. It is to those transformations that we now turn.

KEY TERMS

Etruscans	Cicero	aqueducts
patricians	Augustus	Gaul
plebians	Virgil	Plotinus
Carthage		

SELECTED READINGS

Translations of Roman authors are available in the Penguin Classics series and in the Loeb Classical Library.

Beard, Mary, John North, and Simon Price. *Religions of Rome*, vol. 1: *A History*. Cambridge, 1998. An authoritative account, full of new ideas.

————. *Religions of Rome*, vol. 2: *A Sourcebook*. Cambridge, 1998. A definitive source collection that supplements vol. 1.

Boardman, John, Jasper Griffin, and Oswyn Murray. *The Oxford History of the Roman World*. Oxford, 1990. Reprint of relevant portions of the excellent *Oxford History of the Classical World* (1986). Stimulating, accessible topical chapters by British specialists.

Cornell, T. J. *The Beginnings of Rome: Italy and Rome from the Bronze Age to the Punic Wars* (c. 1000–264 B.C.). London, 1995. An expert, ambitious survey of the archaeological and historical evidence for early Rome.

Crawford, Michael. *The Roman Republic*. 2d ed. Cambridge, Mass., 1993. A lively, fast-paced survey of Republican Rome. An excellent place to start.

Fantham, Elaine, Helene Peet Foley, Natalie Boymel Kampen, Sarah B. Pomeroy, and H. Alan Shapiro. *Women in the Classical World*. Oxford, 1994. A lively, expert survey of both Greece and Rome.

Garnsey, Peter, and Richard Saller. *The Roman Empire: Economy, Society, and Culture*. Berkeley, 1987. A straightforward short survey.

Gruen, Erich S. *The Hellenistic World and the Coming of Rome*. 2 vols. Berkeley, 1984. A massive survey, focused on the unpredictable rise of Rome to a position of dominance within the Mediterranean world.

Harris, William V. *War and Imperialism in Republican Rome, 327–70 B.C.* Oxford, 1979. A challenging study arguing that Rome's need for military conquest and imperial expansion was deeply embedded in the political and social fabric of Roman life.

Lancel, Serge. *Carthage: A History*, trans. by Antonia Nevill. Oxford, 1995. An up-to-date account of Rome's great rival for control of the Mediterranean world.

Lewis, Naphtali, and M. Reinhold. *Roman Civilization: Selected Readings*. 2 vols. New York, 1951–1955. The standard collection, especially for political and economic subjects. Vol. 1 covers the republic; vol. 2, the empire.

Millar, Fergus G. B. *The Emperor in the Roman World, 31 B.C.–A.D. 337*. London, 1977. A classic work that showed (among much else) the importance of emperor worship to the religious outlook of the Roman empire.

————. *The Crowd in Rome in the Late Republic*. Ann Arbor, 1999. A revisionist account that emphasizes the reality of Roman democracy in the late republic, against those who would see the period's politics as entirely under the control of aristocratic families.

Ward, Allen M., Fritz Heichelheim, and Cedric A. Yeo. *A History of the Roman People*, 3d ed. Upper Saddle River, N.J., 1999. An informative, well-organized textbook covering Roman history from its beginnings to the end of the sixth century C.E.

Wells, Colin. *The Roman Empire*, 2d ed. Cambridge, Mass., 1992. An easily readable survey from the reign of Augustus to the mid-third century C.E., particularly useful for its treatment of the relationship between the Roman central government and its Italian provinces.

CHRISTIANITY AND THE TRANSFORMATION OF THE ROMAN WORLD

The Roman empire declined after 180 C.E., but it did not collapse. In 284 C.E. the soldier-emperor Diocletian began a reorganization of the empire that gave it a new lease on life. Throughout the fourth century the Roman state continued to encompass the entire Mediterranean world. During the fifth century the western half of the empire fell under the political control of German-speaking invaders; but many Roman institutions continued to function in these new Germanic kingdoms, and in the sixth century the emperor Justinian reconquered much of the western Mediterranean shoreline. Only in the seventh century did it become clear that the divisions between the eastern and western halves of the Roman empire would be permanent, and that the two regions would thereafter develop in fundamentally different ways. With this transition, the world of classical antiquity came to an end.

Historians used to begin their discussions of medieval history in the third, fourth, or fifth century C.E. But it is now more customary to conceive of ancient history as continuing after 284 C.E. and lasting until the Roman empire lost control over the Mediterranean in the seventh century. The period from 284 to about 610 C.E., although transitional (as, of course, all ages are), has certain themes of its own and is best described as neither Roman nor medieval but as the age of late antiquity.

Three major cultural trends characterized the world of late antiquity. The first was the spread and triumph of Christianity throughout the Roman world. At first Christianity was just one of many otherworldly religions that appealed to increasing numbers of people during the later empire. But in the fourth century it was adopted as the Roman state religion and thereafter became one of the greatest shaping forces in the development of Western civilizations.

The gradual extension of Christianity, first from city to city, and then from city to countryside, was one element in a larger process of cultural assimilation that characterized the entire late-antique world. New cultural developments were more widely

FOCUS QUESTIONS

• What were the principles by which Diocletian reformed the Roman empire?

• How did Christianity become the majority religion within the Roman empire?

• What major changes did Christianity undergo during the fourth century?

• Why did the Germanic invasions succeed?

• What distinctive themes of western Christian thought were emerging during the fourth and fifth centuries?

• How was classical culture Christianized?

• Why did Justinian's plan to reunite the Roman empire fail?

diffused than ever before, and a wider range of people participated in them. As Roman culture became more uniform and more widespread, however, it also became less sophisticated and distinctive. The result was a "watering down" of the high culture of the classical era—a process we shall call "vulgarization."

Cultural influences from outside the Mediterranean world were also having an increasing impact, especially on the western parts of the empire. The Romans called this process "barbarization," from the Greek word *barbaros*, meaning "foreigner." Barbarian culture was not necessarily primitive, but it was nonurban and non-Greek—and in the eyes of Mediterranean elites, these facts alone were enough to stigmatize it. But "barbarian" influence grew steadily nonetheless, first within the army, and then throughout society. None of these processes was cataclysmic; but by the end of the sixth century C.E., Christianization, vulgarization, and barbarization had combined to bring the ancient Mediterranean world to an end.

THE REORGANIZED EMPIRE

What were the principles by which Diocletian reformed the Roman empire?

The chaos of the mid-third century C.E. might well have destroyed the Roman empire. That it did not is largely due to the efforts of a remarkable soldier named Diocletian, who ruled as emperor from 284 to 305 C.E. Diocletian imposed a number of fundamental political and economic reforms on the empire. Most important, however, he restored the majesty and prestige of the emperorship itself. By so doing, Diocletian laid the foundations on which all subsequent Roman and Byzantine emperors would base their authority.

THE REIGN OF DIOCLETIAN

Like Augustus, Diocletian was acutely aware of the dignity of his imperial office, and of the importance of political symbolism in maintaining it. But unlike Augustus, who tried to cloak the reality of his power in the trappings of republicanism, Diocletian presented himself to his subjects as an undisguised autocrat. His title was not *princeps* ("first citizen"), but *dominus* ("lord"). Diocletian himself remained apart from the ordinary business of his court, physically removed behind a maze of door-

The Tetrarchy: Diocletian and His Colleagues in Rule. Every effort is made to make the two senior rulers and their two junior colleagues look identical. Note also the impassive, symmetrical faces and the emphasis on military strength.

ways, rooms, and curtains. Those lucky enough to gain an audience with him had to prostrate themselves before him; a privileged few would be allowed to kiss his robe. For the "barracks emperors" of the earlier third century, too much familiarity with their soldiers and courtiers had bred contempt. As a soldier-emperor himself, Diocletian was determined to avoid their mistake.

In another breach with Augustan tradition, Diocletian also took steps to define formal rules of imperial succession. Realizing that the empire had now become too large for a single, all-powerful ruler to control it effectively, Diocletian divided the empire in half, entrusting the western part to a reliable junior colleague named Maximian while retaining the wealthier, eastern half for himself. The two "augusti" (as Diocletian and Maximian called themselves) then each chose a lieutenant, called a caesar, to govern a subsection of their

WHAT WERE THE PRINCIPLES BY WHICH DIOCLETIAN REFORMED THE ROMAN EMPIRE?

THE REORGANIZED EMPIRE   163

DIOCLETIAN'S DIVISION OF THE EMPIRE, C. 304 C.E.

In a desperate bid to save the Roman Empire from collapse, Diocletian divided it in half. He would control the eastern portion while Maximian would have the west. Each emperor then chose a lieutenant, thus creating what was called the Tetrarchy ("the rule of four"). To what extent do the divisions shown on this map mirror those that would characterize the later history of Europe?

respective territories. When the two augusti retired, the caesars would step into their place, and appoint new caesars in turn to assist them. This system (known as the tetrarchy, the "rule of four") was intended to provide more effective governance over the empire by permitting a degree of decentralization. But it was also designed to end the succession disputes that had proven to be the fatal weakness of the Augustan political system and that had brought the third-century empire to its knees.

Diocletian was also an energetic administrative reformer. Although he retained close personal control over the army, he took steps to separate military from civilian chains of command. Never again would Roman armies make and unmake emperors as they had done in the third century. To control the devastatingly high rates of inflation that were undermining the economy of the empire, Diocletian stabilized the currency and attempted (without much success) to fix prices and wages by legislative fiat. He reformed the tax system, adjusting tax assessments and appointing a small army of new (and immensely unpopular) tax collectors. He also moved the administrative capital of the empire itself from Italy to Nicomedia in modern-day Turkey. Rome remained the spiritual and symbolic capital of the empire, not least because the Senate continued to meet there. But Diocletian had little need for the Senate's advice, and the growing disparities of wealth between the eastern and western regions made Nicomedia a more appropriate capital than Rome for an empire that now rested on the backs of its bureaucrats.

THE REIGN OF CONSTANTINE

In 305 C.E. Diocletian built a palace for himself at Split (Croatia) and retired there to raise cabbages—an unprecedented move for a late Roman ruler. At the same time he obliged his colleague Maximian to retire also, and their two caesars moved peacefully up the ladder of succession. But the concord did not last. Civil war broke out among Diocletian's successors and continued until Constantine, the son of one of the original caesars, emerged victorious. From 312 until 324 Constantine ruled as augustus over the western empire, while a junior augustus ruled in the east. In 324 Constantine did away with this arrangement, and ruled the reunited empire single-handedly until his death in 337.

Except for the fact that he favored Christianity (an epoch-making decision to be examined in the next section), Constantine's government followed the precedents laid down by Diocletian. Both men ruled by decree, and both relied on an extensive network of spies and informants to control their empire. In an attempt to ensure adequate numbers of troops, Diocletian had already declared army service hereditary. Constantine extended this policy, also binding farmers and craftsmen to their fathers' occupations. These restrictions cannot have been widely enforced, but they are powerful evidence of the social and political regimentation that both Diocletian and Constantine aspired to impose on the empire.

In keeping with Constantine's grandiose conception of himself, he built a new capital starting in 324 C.E. and named it Constantinople. Founded on the site of the ancient city of Byzantium, this new capital epitomized the continuing shift in the "weight" of Roman civilization toward the east. Situated at the mouth of the Black Sea on the border between Europe and Asia, Constantinople had commanding advantages as a center for communications, trade, and defense. Surrounded on three sides by water and protected on land by walls, it would remain the political and economic center of the Roman empire until

Colossal Head of Constantine. This enormous statue of the seated emperor was located just outside the Forum in Rome. It stood forty feet high; the head alone weighed nine tons. The enlarged eyes emphasize the emperor's spiritual vision.

1453, when the city was finally conquered by the Ottoman Turks.

In one crucial respect, however, Constantine abandoned the precedents established by Diocletian. By making succession to the imperial throne hereditary within his own family, Constantine brought Rome back to the principle of dynastic monarchy it had thrown off eight hundred years before. To make matters worse, Constantine divided the empire among his three sons on his death. Civil war was the predictable result, made worse by differences in the type of Christianity each son espoused.

Dynastic conflicts among Constantine's descendants would continue for most of the fourth century. But these conflicts were never so serious as the civil wars of the third century, and from time to time a contestant would still be able to reunite the empire. The last to do so was Theodosius I (379–395 C.E.). Before Theodosius died, however, he

> Situated at the mouth of the Black Sea on the border between Europe and Asia, Constantinople had commanding advantages as a center for communications, trade, and defense.

HOW DID CHRISTIANITY BECOME THE MAJORITY RELIGION WITHIN THE ROMAN EMPIRE?

THE EMERGENCE AND TRIUMPH OF CHRISTIANITY   165

followed his family's tradition by dividing the empire between his two sons: this time with disastrous results, as we shall see in a moment.

Behind these quarrels over the imperial throne we can also discern some larger developments in the history of the fourth-century empire. Most fundamental, divisions between the eastern and the western halves of the empire were becoming steadily more pronounced. As the Greek-speaking East grew more populous, more prosperous, and more central to imperial policy, the Latin-speaking West was becoming poorer and more peripheral to the political, economic, and cultural life of the empire. Many western cities now relied on transfers of funds from the East to keep them going; when these funds dried up, or military units were transferred away, these cities declined. Even Rome was becoming something of a backwater in its own empire. When emperors did reside in the west, they found it more convenient to live at Milan, or Ravenna, or on the Rhine frontier at Trier. After the early fourth century, no emperors lived in Rome, and only twice thereafter did an emperor even visit the city.

Nor were the divisions between East and West the only fault lines within an increasingly fractious empire. Secessionist movements cropped up repeatedly among the residents of Britain, Gaul, Spain, and Germany, who were beginning to think of themselves as citizens of a separate, Gaulish empire. Egyptians were particularly hard hit by high levels of taxation on their agricultural lands. North Africans felt ignored by emperors concerned primarily with defending their eastern frontiers against the Persians, the Goths, and the Huns. Beneath the surface of imperial autocracy, the fourth-century empire was slowly dissolving into its constituent parts.

THE EMERGENCE AND TRIUMPH OF CHRISTIANITY

How did Christianity become the majority religion within the Roman empire?

Between the first and fifth centuries C.E., Christianity grew from obscure beginnings in Judea to become the official state religion of the Roman world. Thereafter, it became a dominant (perhaps even the dominant) force in shaping the civilizations of the Western world

up to the present day. For Christians, their religion's extraordinary growth and impact is testimony to its truth. For historians, however, it poses an enormous interpretive problem: how can we explain the appeal of early Christianity without making its eventual success seem predictable or even inevitable?

In attempting to do this, it may be useful to recognize at the outset that Christianity appealed to differing groups of people at different stages in its early history, and that each of these groups understood its appeal in rather different ways. Christianity began with the teachings of Jesus, delivered to the Jews of Judea and Galilee around the year 30 C.E. It took firm root, however, largely among the Greek-speaking town dwellers of the eastern Mediterranean during the second and third centuries C.E. Then, starting with Constantine, it became the favored religion of the imperial family, and ultimately the official religion of the Roman empire. We will examine these stages in order, starting with the career of Jesus himself.

THE CAREER OF JESUS

There is no doubt that Jesus was a historical figure; but it is difficult to know very much about him. No strictly contemporary sources mention him, although we do have references to some of his opponents, including the Roman governor Pontius Pilate and the high priest Caiaphas. The earliest written sources that mention Jesus are the letters of one of his followers, the apostle Paul, written during the 50s and 60s C.E.; and the four "gospel" accounts of Jesus' life plus the Acts of the Apostles, all written between c. 70 and 100 C.E. All these works, together with a number of later sources, are contained in the New Testament, a collection of Christian writings added to the text of the Hebrew Bible during the first three centuries C.E. Other sources also circulated during these years, including a now-lost compilation of Jesus' sayings from which the gospel writers drew some material. It is possible, therefore, that even fairly late, nonbiblical sources such as the second-century "Gospel of Thomas" may preserve some authentic record of Jesus' teachings. Most historians, however, prefer to rely on the first-century sources in trying to interpret his career.

Jesus was born to a Galilean Jewish family sometime shortly before the beginning of the Common (or Christian) era. He was not born precisely in the "year one"— we owe this mistake in our dating system to a sixth-century monk. When Jesus was around thirty years of age, he was acclaimed by a preacher of moral reform,

John the Baptist, as one "mightier than I, whose shoes I am not worthy to untie." Thereafter, Jesus' career was a continuous course of preaching, healing, and teaching, mostly in the rural areas of Galilee and Judea. Around the year 30 C.E., however, he staged an openly messianic entry into Jerusalem during Passover, a religious holiday that brought large and excitable crowds of Jews into the city. The city's religious leaders quickly arrested him and turned him over to Pontius Pilate, the Roman governor, for sentencing. Pilate chose to make an example of Jesus by condemning him to death by crucifixion, a standard Roman criminal penalty for those judged guilty of sedition against Rome.

This might have been the end of the story. But soon after Jesus' execution, rumors began to spread that Jesus was alive and had been seen by some of his followers. He had risen from the dead, his followers now proclaimed, and after forty days had ascended into heaven, promising to return again at the end of time. In life Jesus had been a religious teacher and healer; in death, however, he had been revealed as something more. His entire career now had to be rethought and reinterpreted by his followers. The evidence of this reinterpretation has come down to us in the letters of Paul and in the gospel narratives of Matthew, Mark, Luke, and John.

In the centuries following the Jews' return from Babylon and the rebuilding of the Temple, Judaism became an uncompromisingly monotheistic religion, built on the covenantal relationship between Yahweh and his chosen people.

JESUS AND SECOND TEMPLE JUDAISM

In 1947, a Bedouin boy discovered an extraordinary cache of Jewish religious texts that had been hidden in a cave near Qumran at some point during the first century C.E. Only in the last decade, however, has the bulk of this material, known collectively as the "Dead Sea Scrolls," been made widely available to scholars. These scrolls have revolutionized our understanding of Jewish religious practice and belief around the time of Jesus. Most of all they emphasize its extraordinary diversity.

When Jesus was born, the Roman conquest of Judea was less than a generation old. Banditry, sometimes tinged with nationalism, was commonplace in the countryside; in the cities and villages, there was talk of rebellion, and hope for a messiah who would restore Jewish rule over the holy land of Israel. Most extreme of those who sought hope in politics were the Zealots, who sought to expel the Romans by force of arms. Their activities eventually led to two disastrous revolts. The first, between 66 and 70 C.E., brought about the destruction of the Jewish Temple at Jerusalem by the avenging Romans. The second, in 132–135 C.E., caused the destruction of the city of Jerusalem and the expulsion of its entire Jewish population.

This political context is important to understanding Pilate's decision to execute Jesus; but it tells us little about what Jesus actually taught, or how his teachings might have been understood by his fellow Jews. To this purpose, the religious divisions within contemporary Judaism are much more important.

In the centuries following the Jews' return from Babylon and the rebuilding of the Temple, Judaism became an uncompromisingly monotheistic religion, built on the covenantal relationship between Yahweh and his chosen people. By the first century B.C.E.,

Jesus. This depiction of Jesus with long hair and a beard from a third-century C.E. stone inlay is strikingly different from the Roman style.

HOW DID CHRISTIANITY BECOME THE MAJORITY RELIGION WITHIN THE ROMAN EMPIRE?

THE EMERGENCE AND TRIUMPH OF CHRISTIANITY 167

however, important differences had emerged in how Jews understood what that covenant required of them. Jesus' teachings need to be seen in the context of these debates.

The guardians of the written traditions enshrined in the Torah (the first five books of the Hebrew Bible) were the hereditary Temple priesthood and their aristocratic allies, a group known as the Sadducees. Before the Roman conquest, the high priest of the Temple at Jerusalem had been appointed by the Hasmonean Jewish monarchs. After the Roman conquest, however, the high priest was appointed by Rome. As a result, the Sadducees were inevitably tainted by suspicions of collaborationism, despite the central role they played in the religious observances of the Temple cult.

Their main rivals for the religious allegiance of the people were the Pharisees. In contrast to the Sadducees, who considered most of the requirements of religious law to pertain only to the priesthood, the Pharisees insisted that all 613 of Yahweh's commandments were binding on all Jews. The Pharisees urged rigorous devotion to religious law, but they were also quite flexible in applying it to daily life. They also believed in a life after death characterized by individual rewards and punishments. They actively sought out converts through preaching, and looked forward to the imminent arrival of the messiah whom God had promised to his people. In all these respects they differed from the more traditional Sadducees. Even more radical, however, were various splinter groups such as the Essenes, a quasi-monastic group that hoped for spiritual deliverance through asceticism, repentance, and strict sectarian separation from their fellow Jews.

Although some scholars see Essene influence behind the career of Jesus, his Jewish contemporaries probably saw Jesus as some sort of radical Pharisee. Jesus' emphasis on the ethical requirements of the law (love of God and neighbor; the obligation to do good even to those who harm you, and to forgive those who wrong you); his apparent belief in life after death, and in the imminent coming of "the kingdom of God"; and his exhortations to obey the spirit rather than the letter of religious law, all fitted well within a Pharisaic framework. Nevertheless, he seems to have carried these principles considerably further than did most Pharisees; when, for example, his followers broke the laws of the Sabbath by gathering grain to eat, Jesus justified

them by declaring, "The Sabbath was made for man, not man for the Sabbath." By extending Pharisaic reasoning to such a degree, Jesus' teachings threatened to undermine completely the obligatory nature of Jewish law as the Pharisees understood it.

None of these groups was monolithic; even the Essenes, the most sectarian of them all, included a variety of different beliefs and practices within their order. And the vast majority of Jews would not have identified themselves with any of these groups. Even the Sadducees are best regarded as a sect within the larger Temple priesthood. For most Jews at the time of Jesus, Judaism consisted of going up to the Temple at Jerusalem a few times a year on holy days; paying the annual Temple tax; reciting the morning and evening prayers; and observing certain fundamental religious laws, such as circumcision (for men), ritual purity.

While Jesus may have stretched such observances, there is no evidence he sought to abrogate them. Rather, what made him controversial within the larger Jewish community was his followers' claim that he was the messiah promised by God to deliver Israel from its enemies. After his death and alleged resurrection, such claims grew louder and more assertive; but they never persuaded more than a small minority of Jesus' fellow Jews. As his followers began to preach to non-Jewish audiences, however, they began to reinterpret Jesus' role as messiah in terms that drew on Greek theological ideas. Jesus, his followers now proclaimed, was not merely a messiah for the Jews. He was the "Christ" (from the Greek for "anointed one"), the divine Son of God sent to earth to suffer and die for the sins of all humanity, who had risen from the dead and ascended into heaven, and who would return to judge all the world's inhabitants at the end of time.

> In contrast to the Sadducees, who considered most of the requirements of religious law to pertain only to the priesthood, the Pharisees insisted that all 613 of Yahweh's commandments were binding on all Jews.

THE GROWTH OF CHRISTIANITY IN THE HELLENISTIC WORLD

The key figure in developing this new theological understanding of Jesus' messiahship was Saul of Tarsus (c. 10–c. 67 C.E.). Saul was a Jew born in southeast Asia Minor. A staunch Pharisee, Saul was initially a persecutor of Jesus' followers; but after a blinding conversion experience, he joined the "Jesus movement," changed his name to Paul, and devoted his limitless energy to

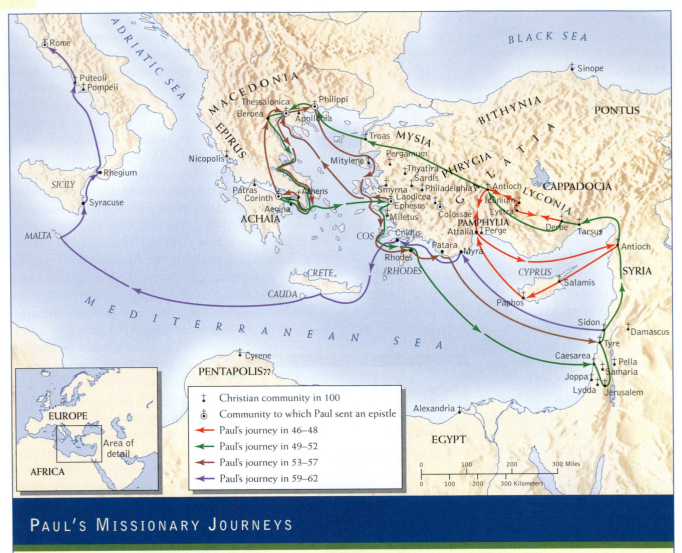

PAUL'S MISSIONARY JOURNEYS

Why did the message of Paul and the "Jesus movement" appeal to the non-Jews of the Mediterranean world? What was the main issue that divided Paul and the Christian Jews of Jerusalem? What were the consequences of Paul's travels throughout the Greek world?

interpreting and preaching the new faith to the Greek-speaking, mainly non-Jewish communities of Greece and Asia Minor. Declaring himself to be the apostle to the Gentiles (non-Jews), Paul rejected the binding nature of Jewish religious law, declaring it to be irrelevant to salvation for Jesus' followers. This stance initially caused offense among the Jewish Christians of Jerusalem, a group led by Jesus' brother, James; but after a wrenching debate, Paul's position triumphed. Some Christians would continue to obey Jewish religious law, but the movement's future now lay clearly with the non-Jewish converts it was making outside Judea and Galilee.

It is not entirely clear who the majority of these new converts were. By the first century C.E., sizable Jewish communities existed in most major cities of the eastern Mediterranean world, including Rome itself. These communities had already begun to reinterpret Jewish religious ideas within a Greek intellectual and cultural context. As Paul's own example suggests, to some of these Hellenized Jews the new Christian teachings must have been attractive. Even more so, however, Christianity probably appealed to the groups of non-Jews (known as "God-fearers") who tended to gather around these Greek-speaking Jewish communities.

HOW DID CHRISTIANITY BECOME THE MAJORITY RELIGION WITHIN THE ROMAN EMPIRE?

THE EMERGENCE AND TRIUMPH OF CHRISTIANITY   169

God-fearers did not follow all the precepts of Jewish law, but they admired Jews for their monotheism and for their uncompromising moral and ethical standards, and modeled their own lives after Jewish example. But Christianity must also have made inroads among ordinary Greeks, many of whom would already have been familiar with other, superficially similar cults (such as Mithraism) that also stressed elaborate initiation ceremonies (for Christians, baptism) and the importance of special religious knowledge for salvation.

Certain differences between Christianity and these other mystery religions do stand out. Organizational structures evolved very early; by the middle of the second century, the Christian church at Rome already had a bishop who presided over a small army of lesser officeholders, including priests, deacons, confessors, and exorcists. Women were also notably prominent in these early Christian communities, not only as patrons and benefactors (a role upper-class Roman women had

often played in new religious cults), but also as officeholders (although we know of no female bishops or priests, female deacons are well attested). This relatively high status of women was quite unusual and distinguished Christianity markedly from Mithraism, which excluded women even from membership in the cult, much less from holding any office within it. Christians were also well known for supporting their poorer members through charity. Christianity drew its adherents from a broad range of social classes, but it may have had a special appeal to people (such as urban artisans) whose livelihoods could disappear with a shift of the economic winds.

All these factors help to explain the appeal of the new religion, especially to the Greek-speaking urban dwellers who made up the vast majority of Christian converts during the second and third centuries C.E. Nevertheless, why people chose to become Christians remains an impossible question for historians to answer with certainty. It is often suggested that Christianity's promise of salvation was a powerful inducement to conversion, especially in the chaotic world of the third century C.E. This may be so; but the claim rests simply on the facts that Christianity was growing during the third century, and that Christians believed in life after death. We have no real way to prove that the second fact led to the first. All we can say for certain is that a growing number of people in the second- and third-century Mediterranean world believed Christian teachings to be true, and that they were prepared to accept these teachings despite the disapproval they generated within Greco-Roman and Jewish society.

CHRISTIANITY AND THE ROMAN EMPIRE

Throughout the second and third centuries C.E., Judaism remained a legally recognized religion within the Roman empire. Whatever their attitudes toward Jewish belief and practice, Romans respected the fact that Jews were at least maintaining the religious customs of their ancestors. Christianity, however, was an innovation; and in the eyes of traditional Romans, novelty in religion was not a good thing. Nevertheless, the official attitude of the Roman state toward Christianity was usually one of indifference. During the first and second centuries C.E., Christians were tolerated by Roman authorities except when local magistrates chose to prosecute them for refusing to worship the official state gods. During the third century there were

Saint Paul. This early Christian mosaic depicts the self-declared apostle to the Gentiles, formerly known as Saul of Tarsus, who was a key figure in developing the theological understanding of Jesus's messiahship.

PROSECUTING CHRISTIANS

THE LETTERS OF PLINY THE ELDER AND THE EMPEROR TRAJAN

Until the third century, the Roman imperial government rarely initiated the persecution of Christians. Local administrators, such as the younger Pliny, were anxious to follow proper legal procedures in dealing with the new sect, which they regarded as absurd but not particularly dangerous. But neither Pliny nor the emperor Trajan (98–117 C.E.) wanted to see the Roman state actively seek out Christians for punishment.

LETTER 97: PLINY TO TRAJAN

It is a rule, Sir, which I inviolably observe, to refer myself to you in all my doubts; for who is more capable of removing my scruples, or informing my ignorance? Having never been present at any trials concerning those who profess Christianity, I am unacquainted not only with the nature of their crimes, or the measure of their punishment, but how far it is proper to enter into an examination concerning them. . . .

The method I have observed towards those who have been brought before me as Christians, is this: I interrogated them whether they were Christians; if they confessed I repeated the question twice again, adding threats at the same time; when, if they still persevered, I ordered them to be immediately punished: for I was persuaded, whatever the nature of their opinions might be, a contumacious and inflexible obstinacy certainly deserved correction. . . .

But this crime spreading (as is usually the case) while it was actually under prosecution, several instances of the same nature occurred. An information was presented to me without any name subscribed, containing a charge against several persons, who upon examination denied they were Christians, or had ever been so.

They repeated after me an invocation to the gods, and offered religious rites with wine and frankincense before your statue (which for the purpose I had ordered to be brought together with those of the gods); and even reviled the name of Christ: whereas there is no forcing, it is said, those who are really Christians, into a compliance with any of these articles: I thought proper therefore to discharge them. . . .

I judged it . . . necessary to endeavor to extort the real truth [about Christian rites and beliefs] by putting two female slaves to the torture, who were said to administer in their religious functions: but I could discover nothing more than an absurd and excessive superstition. I thought proper therefore to adjourn all further proceedings in this affair, in order to consult with you. . . . For this contagious superstition is not confined to the cities only, but has spread its infection among the country villages. Nevertheless, it still seems possible to remedy this evil and restrain its progress. The temples, at least, which were once almost deserted, begin now to be frequented; and the sacred solemnities, after a long intermission, are again revived. . . . From hence it is easy to imagine, what numbers might be reclaimed from this error, if a pardon were granted to those who shall repent.

Letter 98: Trajan to Pliny

The method you have pursued, my dear Pliny, in the proceedings against those Christians which were brought before you, is extremely proper; as it is not possible to lay down any fixed plan by which to act in all cases of this nature. But I would not have you officiously enter into any enquiries concerning them. If indeed they should be brought before you, and the crime is proved, they must be punished; with the restriction, however, that where the party denies himself to be a Christian, and shall make it evident that he is not, by invoking our gods, let him (notwithstanding any former suspicion) be pardoned upon his repentence. Information without the accuser's name subscribed ought not to be received in prosecutions of any sort, as it is introducing a very dangerous precedent, and by no means agreeable to the equity of my government.

W. Melmoth, trans. *The Letters of Pliny the Consul, Vol.* 2 (London: J. Dodsley, 1770), pp. 671–677. Reprinted in *Western Societies: A Documentary History*, Vol. 1, edited by Brian Tierney and Joan Scott (New York: Knopf, 1984), pp. 166–168.

some concerted, centrally organized persecutions; the last of these took place toward the end of Diocletian's reign and the beginning of the reign of his successor Galerius. But these were too intermittent and short lived to do irreparable damage; and by the early fourth century, the religion had gained too many adherents to be wiped out by persecution, a fact Galerius finally recognized by issuing an edict of toleration just before his death in 311 C.E.

Still, however, the number of Christians was not large. No reliable statistics exist, but most scholars now believe that in the year 300 only 1 to 5 percent of the total population of the empire was Christian. Even in the relatively more Christianized eastern parts of the empire, no more than 10 percent of the population was Christian, and this estimate is probably generous. Christian numbers were growing, and might have continued to grow. But it seems unlikely Christianity would ever have become the majority religion in the empire without the help of the emperor Constantine.

Constantine's decision to become a Christian continues to puzzle historians. He must have had some contact with Christianity as a young man; he may even have been a nominal Christian at the time he launched his bid for the imperial throne. His real commitment to the faith came later, however, after he saw a Christian symbol in the sky while preparing for battle at the Milvian Bridge (312 C.E.) and heard a heavenly voice declaring, "In this sign, conquer." Constantine ordered his soldiers to paint the symbol on their shields; the victory they won that day propelled him to the imperial throne.

As emperor, Constantine showered favors on the Christian clergy and patronized the construction of churches throughout the empire. But Constantine did not make Christianity the official religion of the empire, nor did he prohibit pagan worship. He did, however, make Christianity the favored religion of the imperial family, transforming Christianity, almost overnight, into a prestigious religion for the ruling classes of the empire to adopt. Gradually, the rest of the citizens of the empire followed suit. By the end of the fourth century C.E., a clear majority of the empire was Christian, and bishops had emerged as dominating influences in the political life of their cities.

Constantine himself retained both pagan and Christian officials around his court, and was careful in his public pronouncements to speak in terms that would be acceptable to a non-Christian audience. His successors, however, became more and more uncompromisingly Christian in their orientation, and less and less inclined to tolerate competing faiths. A brief exception was the reign of Julian "the Apostate" (360–363 C.E.), who abandoned Christianity and attempted to revive traditional Roman paganism. But Julian was killed in battle with the Persians, his pro-pagan edicts were revoked, and the Christian officials around the imperial court became more insistent that imperial power be used to suppress competing cults. Finally, Theodosius the Great (379–395 C.E.) did so, prohibiting pagan

> As emperor, Constantine showered favors on the Christian clergy and patronized the construction of churches throughout the empire. But Constantine did not make Christianity the official religion of the empire, nor did he prohibit pagan worship.

worship of any sort within the empire, and removing the altar of the goddess Victory from the Senate house in Rome. Fifteen years later, Rome fell to the Visigoths. Pagan spokesmen noted the connection.

THE NEW CONTOURS OF FOURTH-CENTURY CHRISTIANITY

What major changes did Christianity undergo during the fourth century?

As Christianity became politically influential and socially prestigious, it underwent major changes in doctrine, organization, and outlook. As a result, Christianity at the end of the fourth century was in many respects a quite different religion from the one persecuted by Diocletian and Galerius only a century before.

DOCTRINAL QUARRELS

One consequence of Christianity's new prominence was the flaring up of bitter doctrinal disputes. Christians had of course disagreed about doctrinal matters before; but as long as Christianity remained the religion of an unimportant minority, these disagreements were of little political or social consequence. With Constantine's accession to the imperial throne, however, such disagreements now had the potential to ignite political quarrels (even rioting) between bishops and their opponents, and to undermine imperial support for the church itself. It was imperative, therefore, that such doctrinal disputes be resolved, if necessary through the active intervention of the Christian emperor himself.

The most fundamental doctrinal dispute to erupt was between the Arians and Athanasians over the nature of the Trinity. The Arians—not to be confused with Aryans (a racial term)—were followers of a priest named Arius who rejected the idea that Jesus, as the Christ, could be equal with God. Instead Arians maintained that Jesus as the Son of God, was created by the Father in time, and therefore was not coeternal with him or formed of the same substance. The followers of Saint Athanasius argued the opposite: even though Christ was the Son he was also fully God, and so Fa-

ther, Son, and Holy Ghost (the Trinity) were all absolutely equal and composed of an identical substance. After protracted struggles, the Athanasian doctrine became the orthodox Christian position, and Arianism was declared a heresy. But Arianism continued to attract followers for the next two hundred years.

Resolving such doctrinal disputes was intensely difficult. Often they involved not only doctrinal differences, but regional and political differences as well. As a result, the Roman state became increasingly enmeshed in the governance of the church, especially in the eastern half of the empire. Constantine himself began this process in 325 C.E., when he presided over the Council of Nicea, which condemned Arianism. His successors carried it much further. Gradually, these Christian emperors began to claim that in presiding over such councils, they were assuming a role as Christ's representative on earth that entitled them to decide what Christian doctrine was and should be. Some even dispatched troops to suppress Christian groups who refused to accept the emperor's decisions on orthodoxy. Those who rejected such decisions were labeled heretics, and could suffer both legal and ecclesiastical penalties.

GROWTH OF ECCLESIASTICAL ORGANIZATION

During the fourth century, the church became a much more clearly defined hierarchical organization, as urban-centered bishops (often from powerful local families) began to assert closer control over the priests and deacons of their surrounding areas. Distinctions of rank among the bishops themselves also began to emerge. Bishops who ruled from the larger cities came to be called metropolitans (today known in the West as archbishops), with authority over the clergy of an entire province. In the fourth century the still higher rank of patriarch was established to designate bishops who ruled over the oldest and largest Christian communities, such as Rome, Jerusalem, Constantinople, Antioch, and Alexandria. By 400 C.E., the Christian clergy thus comprised a definite hierarchy of patriarchs, metropolitans, bishops, priests, and deacons—from which women were now firmly excluded.

The climax of this development was the primacy of the bishop of Rome, or the rise of the papacy. The bishop of Rome's claim to preeminence over the other patriarchs of the church rested on several foundations. Rome itself was venerated by the faithful as the place

WHAT MAJOR CHANGES DID CHRISTIANITY UNDERGO DURING THE FOURTH CENTURY?

THE NEW CONTOURS OF FOURTH-CENTURY CHRISTIANITY   173

where the apostles Peter and Paul had been martyred. Peter was widely regarded as having been the first bishop of Rome; and the New Testament said (Matthew 16:18–19) that Jesus himself had commissioned Peter as his representative on earth, with the power to admit or deny the entrance of any Christian to the kingdom of heaven. As Peter's successors, subsequent bishops of Rome claimed to exercise the same powers Jesus had given to Peter.

The bishops of Rome also enjoyed some more prosaic advantages over the other bishops within the church. Unlike the eastern bishops, the Roman bishop after 330 C.E. rarely had an emperor on his doorstep. As a result, he could act with considerably more independence than could the patriarch of Constantinople. At the same time, however, it was often convenient for eastern emperors to support papal claims to authority over the western bishops as a way of maintaining some semblance of imperial control over the western empire. This was probably what lay behind the decree in 445 C.E. by the eastern emperor Valentinian III, commanding all western bishops to submit to the jurisdiction of the pope. Centuries later, this decree would be cited to justify the dominance the papacy had by then achieved over the western church. At the time, however, it was ignored by everyone except the pope himself. Most eastern bishops regarded the pope's claims to primacy over the entire church as brazen effrontery, and even many western bishops paid no attention to him. The prestige of the bishops of Rome was nonetheless growing during the fourth and fifth centuries; and although the popes were not yet the monarchical rulers they would eventually become, the roots of their primacy lie here.

The increasing effectiveness of ecclesiastical organization and administration during the fourth century helped the church both to conquer the Roman world and to minister to the needs of the faithful thereafter. The existence of an episcopal ("bishop-centered") administrative structure was particularly important in the West, as the Roman empire decayed and eventually collapsed during the fifth century. In the deepening chaos, western bishops took over many of the functions of urban government and preserved the vestiges of Roman rule. As a result, when barbarian armies arrived it was usually with the local bishop whom they negotiated.

THE SPREAD OF MONASTICISM

To most Christians, the increasing administrative responsibilities of the church seemed natural: religion and politics had always been closely connected throughout the history of the Roman empire. To some Christians, however, the new world seemed a far cry indeed from the simple faith of Jesus and his apostles. Monasticism was one outgrowth of such disillusionment. Today we tend to think of monks as groups of priests who live communally and dedicate themselves to contemplation and prayer. In their origins, however, monks were not priests but laymen, who almost always lived alone and who sought extremes of self-denial rather than ordered lives of corporate prayer and service.

Monasticism began to emerge in the third century, but it became a dominant movement within Christianity only in the fourth century. There were two main reasons for monasticism's appeal. As persecution of Christians ended, extreme asceticism sometimes functioned as a substitute for martyrdom. More obviously, however, the growth of monasticism was a response to the increasing worldliness of the fourth-century church. Christians seeking to avoid earthly temptations fled to the deserts and woods to practice an ascetic lifestyle altogether different from the lives led by the well-to-do men and women who were now flocking to join the religion of their emperor. In a church filled with such "social Christians," monasticism seemed to some purists the only certain road to salvation.

Monasticism did not initially spread so quickly in the West as it did in the East. Only in the sixth century, when Saint Benedict of Nursia (c. 480–c. 547) drafted his famous Rule, did monasticism begin to grow rapidly

CHRONOLOGY

THE GROWTH OF CHRISTIANITY, FIRST–FOURTH CENTURIES C.E.

Life of Jesus	c. 4 B.C.E.–c. 30 C.E.
Paul's missionary journeys	46–62 C.E.
Destruction of the Temple at Jerusalem	69–70 C.E.
Expulsion of the Jews from Jerusalem	132–135 C.E.
Constantine becomes the first Christian emperor	312 C.E.
Council of Nicea	325 C.E.
Christianity becomes official religion of the Roman empire	c. 392 C.E.
Era of doctrinal quarrels	fourth–fifth centuries C.E.

in western Europe. Benedict copied much of his Rule from an earlier and much harsher Latin text known as the "Rule of the Master." Benedict, however, produced a very different document: a "simple rule for beginners" as he called it, notable for its brevity, flexibility, and moderation. The Rule established a carefully defined cycle of daily prayers, lessons and communal worship. It laid down guidelines for how monks ought to live together; what they should eat; and how the work of the monastery should be performed. Physical labor was encouraged—idleness, Benedict declared, was "an enemy of the soul"—but he also reserved time for private study and contemplation. In all such matters, however, Benedict left much to the discretion of the abbot, the leader of the monastery, whom all the monks were expected to obey without hesitation.

THE GERMANIC INVASIONS AND THE FALL OF THE WESTERN ROMAN EMPIRE

Why did the Germanic invasions succeed?

The western Roman empire had already suffered a devastating series of attacks by Germanic tribes during the mid-third century C.E. Throughout the fourth century, however, relations between Romans and Germans were largely peaceful. But starting in the early fifth century, a series of German-led invasions overwhelmed the western half of the empire. Out of this collapse a group of new Germanic kingdoms emerged in western Europe that would permanently alter the region's history and culture.

GERMAN-ROMAN RELATIONS

The Germans were barbarians in Roman eyes because they did not live in cities and were illiterate; but in no sense were the Germans savages. They were settled agriculturalists and sophisticated metalworkers who had enjoyed trading relationships with the Roman world for centuries. In some frontier areas, entire tribes of Germans had been settled inside Roman borders as *foederati*, to reinforce depleted or withdrawn Roman garrisons. By the end of the fourth century, many German tribes had also adopted Christianity, albeit of the heretical, Arian variety. All these interactions made the "barbarians" very familiar with Roman civilization and substantially favorable to it.

It was actually Roman mistreatment rather than German aggression that began the sequence of events that led to the collapse of the western empire. During the 370s, a large group of Visigoths (the "West Goths") had been invited to settle on Roman lands along the Danube, in order to guard that frontier against incursions by other "barbarians." In 378, however, the Visigoths revolted when the Romans failed to supply the food and agricultural land they had been promised. A Roman army sent to suppress them was defeated at the battle of Adrianople, and the emperor Valens (who led the expedition) was killed. The new emperor, Theodosius the Great (379–395), quickly restored peace by accommodating the Visigoths' demands and enrolling them in the Roman army.

Before Theodosius died, however, he divided the empire between his two young sons, whose advisors quickly set about trying to undermine each other. In these promising circumstances, the Visigoths renewed and increased their demands on the empire. The eastern emperor bought them off, encouraging them instead to attack his imperial rival in the west. Under the brilliant military leadership of Alaric, the Visigoths did precisely that. After several years of wandering through the western empire in search of booty, food, and land, in 410 they arrived at the gates of Rome. Rome, however, had little to offer in the way of food or land. After sacking the city, the Visigoths moved on, eventually settling in southern Gaul and Spain where they established a kingdom.

Meanwhile, on New Year's Eve 406/7, a group of allied Germanic tribes led by the Vandals crossed the frozen Rhine. Capitalizing on the western emperor's preoccupation with the Visigoths, they streamed into Gaul and Spain. Ultimately the Vandals crossed the straits of Gibraltar and settled in the rich agricultural regions of Roman North Africa from which, in 455, they launched a seaborne attack upon Rome. Further Germanic tribes, including the Alans, the Franks, the Burgundians, and the Alemans, soon followed them across the Rhine into Gaul, where they busily set about erecting kingdoms.

In 476, the last Roman emperor in the west, an ineffectual usurper derisively known as Romulus Augustulus ("little Augustus"), was toppled by Odovacer, a Hun from Central Asia in charge of a mixed army of Germans, Huns, and disgruntled Romans. This event con-

THE BARBARIAN INVASIONS OF THE ROMAN EMPIRE

What do the invasion routes followed by these different barbarian-led armies suggest about the invaders' identity and motives? Why did so many different armies attack the city of Rome, even though the city was no longer the capital even of the western Roman empire?

ventionally marks the ending date of the western Roman empire. In the east, however, a Roman emperor continued to rule, and continued to claim authority over the western half of the empire. By 476, however, the eastern emperor could affect events in the west only by encouraging one barbarian king to depose another. To assert his own control over Italy, the emperor

Zeno therefore commissioned Theodoric to lead his Ostrogoth ("East Goths") army from the Balkans to Rome to get rid of Odovacer. In a decade of fierce fighting, the Goths completely eliminated the Huns from Italy. Theodoric thereupon established an Ostrogothic kingdom in Italy, which he ruled with imperial support until shortly before his death in 526.

THE SUCCESS AND IMPACT OF THE GERMANIC INVASIONS

Although textbooks sometimes paint these invasions as a kind of "human wave assault" on Roman lines, in fact the German armies were remarkably small. The Visigothic army at Adrianople numbered only about ten thousand men; the total number of the Vandal "hordes," including women and children, was about eighty thousand—the population of an average-sized American suburb. These armies probably grew "on the march," as they were joined by disgruntled Romans and Germanic *foederati* already settled within the empire. But the numbers involved were still very low. How then can we account for their success?

Roman armies along the western frontiers were already in a poor state. Some had been withdrawn to protect the eastern half of the empire, and those that remained were often severely undermanned. The population of the western empire had been declining for some time; soldiers, farmers, and craftspeople were all in short supply. Funding for the army was inadequate; to support themselves, many soldiers were married and some army units grew their own food, making them more and more indistinguishable from the civilian population around them. Morale was also low among civilians. The bureaucratic regime of the fourth-century empire inspired little loyalty, even among aristocrats; and the Germans were seldom regarded with horror, having become a familiar element in Roman society over several centuries. As a result, few pitched battles were fought (Adrianople was one of the few, and it took place in the East). More often, German armies triumphed by default, because the Romans simply did not care enough to defend themselves. And when battles were fought, they often featured mixed armies of Romans, Germans, and Huns on each side, each side fighting in the name of its own warlord.

Morale may have been higher in the eastern empire; but the primary reason that the eastern Roman empire survived while the western empire did not is that the east was simply richer. By the fifth century most western cities had shrunk to a small fraction of their former size; often they were little more than empty administrative shells or fortifications. In the east, by contrast, cities remained teeming centers of trade and industry. The east's borders were shorter, and its armies better supplied; it could also afford to buy off invaders willing to have their attentions redirected toward the west. For all these reasons, the eastern empire stayed afloat during the fifth century while the western empire floundered and sank.

The effects of the Germanic conquests in the west were not catastrophic. Western Roman cities were already in severe decline; the invasions only accelerated a well-advanced process of urban decay. On the land, Roman agricultural patterns continued unchanged under both German and Roman landlords. The invasions fractured the political unity of the western empire, but within the new Germanic kingdoms Roman administrative traditions usually continued, at least for a few generations. Most important, however, the invasions did not bring an end to Roman culture, or to the influence of Roman example on the new immigrants. As Theodoric, the Ostrogothic conqueror of Italy, was fond of remarking: "An able Goth wishes to be like a Roman; but only a poor Roman would want to be like a Goth."

THE SHAPING OF WESTERN CHRISTIAN THOUGHT

What distinctive themes of western Christian thought were emerging during the fourth and fifth centuries?

As the western Roman empire declined during the fourth and fifth centuries, a small group of western Christian thinkers formulated a theological outlook on the world that would guide western thought for the next eight hundred years. This concurrence of political decline and theological advance was not coincidental. As the western empire collapsed, it seemed clearer than ever to thinking Christians that the classical inheritance was passing away, and that God had not intended the world to be anything more than a transitory testing place. How, then, should Christians live? What did God require of them?

Answers to these questions were worked out by the four great "Fathers" of the western church: Saint Jerome (c. 340–420), Saint Ambrose (c. 340–397), Saint Augustine (354–430), and Pope Saint Gregory the Great (540–604). Jerome, Ambrose, and Augustine were contemporaries who knew and influenced one another. We will deal with their work here. Pope Gregory's contributions will be discussed in Chapter Seven.

ROMANIZED BARBARIANS AND BARBARIANIZED ROMANS

These two letters from Sidonius Apollinaris (c. 430–c. 480) illustrate the ways in which cultural assimilation in the late-fifth-century western empire was rapidly blurring the boundaries between "Roman" and "barbarian." Sidonius himself was the descendant of an illustrious Roman provincial family in Gaul. He was one of the admired Latin stylists of his day, in both poetry and prose. Although he eventually became a bishop and was regarded locally as a saint after his death, his letter collection (from which these extracts are taken) tells us much more about the late Roman literary culture of Visigothic southern Gaul than it does about his Christianity. Arbogastes was the Frankish governor of Treves; Syagrius was from an ancient Gaulish Roman family.

LETTER 4:17: SIDONIUS TO HIS FRIEND ARBOGASTES

My honored Lord, your friend Eminentius has handed me a letter written by your own hand, a really literary letter, replete with the grace of a three-fold charm. The first of its merits is certainly the affection which prompted such condescension to my lowly condition, for if not a stranger I am in these days a man who courts obscurity; the second virtue is your modesty. . . . In the third place comes your urbanity which leads you to make a most amusing profession of clumsiness when as a matter of fact you have drunk deep from the spring of Roman eloquence and, dwelling by the Moselle, you speak the true Latin of the Tiber: you are intimate with the barbarians but are innocent of barbarisms, and are equal in tongue, as also in strength of arm, to the leaders of old, I mean those who were wont to handle the pen no less than the sword.

Thus the splendor of the Roman speech, if it still exists anywhere, has survived in you, though it has long been wiped out from the Belgian and Rhenic lands: with you and your eloquence surviving, even though Roman law has ceased at our border, the Roman speech does not falter. For this reason . . . I rejoice greatly that at any rate in your illustrious breast there have remained traces of our vanishing culture. If you extend these by constant reading you will discover for yourself as each day passes that the educated are no less superior to the unlettered than men are to beasts.

LETTER 5:5 SIDONIUS TO HIS FRIEND SYAGRIUS

You are the great-grandson of a consul, and in the male line too—although that has little to do with the case before us; I say, then, you are descended from a poet, to whom his literary glory would have brought statues had not his magisterial glories done so . . . and the culture of his successors has not declined one whit from his standard, particularly in this respect. I am therefore inexpressibly amazed that you have quickly acquired a knowledge of the German tongue with such ease.

And yet I remember that your boyhood had a good schooling in liberal studies and I know for certain that you often declaimed with spirit and eloquence before your professor of oratory. This being so, I should like you to tell me how you managed to absorb so swiftly into your inner being the exact sounds of an alien race, so that now after reading Virgil under the schoolmaster's cane and toiling and working the rich fluency of [Cicero] . . . you burst forth before my eyes like a young falcon from an old nest.

You have no idea what amusement it gives me, and others too, when I hear that in your presence the barbarian is afraid to perpetrate a barbarism in his own language. The bent elders of the Germans are astounded at you when you translate letters, and they adopt you as umpire and aribitrator in their mutual dealings. . . . And although these people are stiff and uncouth in body and mind alike, they welcome in you, and learn from you, their native speech combined with Roman wisdom.

Only one thing remains, most clever of men: continue with undiminished zeal, even in your hours of ease, to devote some attention to reading; and, like the man of refinement that you are, observe a just balance between the two languages: retain your grasp of Latin, lest you be laughed at, and practice the other, in order to have the laugh of them. Farewell.

W. B. Anderson, ed. *Sidonius, Poems and Letters,* Vol. 2 (Cambridge, Mass.: Harvard University Press, 1980), pp. 127–129, 181–183.

SAINT JEROME AND SAINT AMBROSE

Jerome's greatest contribution was his translation of the Bible from Hebrew and Greek into Latin. His translation, known as the Vulgate (or "common" version), was not the first attempt to produce a Latin Bible; but it quickly became the standard one, and would remain so until the sixteenth century. Jerome's translation was vigorous, colloquial, and clear; its powerful prose and poetry would influence all subsequent Latin authors for a thousand years. Jerome was also important for arguing that classical learning could and should be studied by Christians, so long as it was thoroughly subordinated to Christian aims. Jerome himself was not certain, however, that he had succeeded in subordinating his love for the classics to his love for God. When, in a dream, he imagined himself arriving at the gates of heaven, God reproved him for being more of a follower of Cicero than of Christ.

Jerome was primarily a scholar. Saint Ambrose, in contrast, was principally a man of the world. As archbishop of Milan, the aristocratic Ambrose fearlessly rebuked even the Christian emperor Theodosius the Great for massacring innocent civilians at Thessalonica. Theodosius of course remained emperor; but until he did penance as a Christian for his sin, Ambrose refused to admit him into the church, declaring that on matters of faith, "The emperor is within the church, not above the church."

Like Jerome, Ambrose was an admirer of Cicero. Unlike Cicero, however, Ambrose argued that the beginning and end of human conduct should be reverence for God rather than social or political advancement. Ambrose also argued that although God assists all Christians by sharing with them the power of divine grace, God nonetheless gives more grace to some Christians than to others. Ambrose's emphasis on the necessity and mystery of grace (Why does God give more grace to some than to others?) would be refined and greatly amplified by his disciple, Saint Augustine of Hippo.

THE LIFE AND THOUGHT OF SAINT AUGUSTINE

Augustine was the greatest of all the Latin fathers; indeed he was one of the most powerful Christian thinkers of all time. Augustine's influence on medieval thought was incalculable, but his theology also had a profound influence on the development of Protestantism. Even in the twentieth century many leading Christian thinkers would describe themselves as neo-Augustinians.

Augustine's Christianity may have been so searching because he began his career by searching for it. Although his mother was a Christian, he hesitated until the age of thirty-three to be baptized, passing from one philosophical system to another without finding intellectual or spiritual satisfaction in any. Only his increasing doubts about all other alternatives, the appeals of Saint Ambrose's teachings on grace, and a mystical experience movingly described in his autobiographical *Confessions* led Augustine to embrace the faith wholeheartedly in 387. Thereafter he advanced rapidly in ecclesiastical positions, becoming bishop of the North African city of Hippo in

WHAT THEMES EMERGED IN CHRISTIAN THOUGHT DURING THE FOURTH AND FIFTH CENTURIES?

THE SHAPING OF WESTERN CHRISTIAN THOUGHT   179

395. Although he led an extremely active life as bishop (he died in 430 while defending Hippo against the Vandals), he still found time to write more than a hundred profound, complex, and powerful treatises analyzing the most fundamental problems of Christian belief.

Augustine's theology revolved around a single, fundamental question: how could humanity be so profoundly sinful, if human beings were created by an omnipotent God whose nature is entirely good? Augustine's answer to the question of evil went back to the Garden of Eden, where God had given Adam and Eve, the first human couple, the freedom either to follow his will or to follow their own. By eating the one fruit that God had forbidden them to eat, Adam and Eve chose to follow their own wills rather than God's will. Thereafter, says Augustine, God simply left Adam and Eve's descendants to their own devices, by withdrawing from human beings the divine power (grace) by which they might overcome their own wills in order to follow his. All the evils that plague the world are thus ultimately the result of the innate human propensity to place our own desires ahead of God's.

God would be justified if he condemned all human beings to hell; but since he is also merciful he chose instead to save some human beings through the sacrifice of his Son, Jesus. No one, however, has by nature the grace necessary to become a Christian, much less to deserve salvation. God alone makes this choice; by granting grace to some and not to others, he predestines a portion of the human race to salvation and sentences the rest to be damned. If this seems unfair, Augustine's answer is, first, that strict "fairness" would condemn everyone to hell; and second, that the basis for God's choice is a mystery shrouded in his omnipotence—far beyond the realm of human comprehension.

To respond to those who blamed Christianity for the fall of Rome in 410, Augustine wrote one of his most famous works, *On the City of God*. In this work, he developed his ideas about predestination into an interpretation of all human history. Augustine argued that the entire human race from the Creation until the Last Judgment was and will be composed of two opposing societies, those who "live according to man" and love themselves, and those who "live according to God." The former belong to the "City of Man"; their rewards are the riches, fame, and power they may garner on earth. The City of Man is not useless; earthly rulers bring peace and order, and therefore deserve the obedience of Christians. But only those predestined to salvation, and who are therefore members of the "City of God," will on Judgment Day put on the garment of immortality. Christians should therefore behave on earth as if they were travelers or "pilgrims," never forgetting that their true home lies in heaven.

Augustine was convinced that the Bible contained all the wisdom worth knowing. But he also believed that a certain amount of education was needed to understand it thoroughly. Augustine therefore approved of some Christians' acquiring an education in the liberal arts (as he himself had done), so long as they directed their education toward its proper end: the study of the Bible. Along with Jerome, Augustine thus laid the groundwork for western Christians to preserve the literary and educational traditions of the classical past. But Augustine intended liberal education only for an elite; most Christians simply needed to be taught the faith. He also thought it was far worse to study classical thought for its own sake than for someone to know nothing at all about classics. The true wisdom of mortals, he insisted, was piety.

> To respond to those who blamed Christianity for the fall of Rome in 410, Augustine wrote one of his most famous works, *On the City of God*.

BOETHIUS LINKS CLASSICAL AND MEDIEVAL THOUGHT

One of Augustine's most interesting and influential followers was Boethius, a Roman aristocrat who lived from about 480 to 524. Because Boethius was interested in ancient philosophy, wrote in a polished Latin style, and came from a noble Roman family, he has often been described as the "last of the Romans." But in fact he intended the classics to serve Christian purposes, just as Augustine had prescribed, and his own teachings were basically Augustinian.

Because Boethius lived a century after Augustine he could see far more clearly that the ancient world was coming to an end. His goal, therefore, was to preserve as much of the best ancient learning as possible by composing a series of handbooks, translations, and commentaries. He wrote handbooks on the liberal arts, summarizing what a Christian should know about each subject. He also translated from Greek into Latin several of Aristotle's logical treatises.

Boethius. This ivory diptych from the fifth century depicts the Roman aristocrat who was a follower of Augustine a century after his time.

cause it presented classical ideas within a clearly Christian framework, and most of all because it seemed to offer a real meaning to life. In times when earthly things seemed crude or fleeting, it was genuinely consoling to be told eloquently and philosophically that life has purpose if led for the sake of God.

Although Boethius was an exponent of Aristotle's logic, his world view was not Aristotelian but Augustinian. This can be seen both in his treatises on Christian theology and in his masterpiece, *The Consolation of Philosophy*. Boethius wrote the *Consolation* at the end of his life, after he had been condemned to death for treason by Theodoric the Ostrogoth, whom he had served as an official. (Historians are unsure about the justice of the charges.) In it Boethius asks the age-old question of what is human happiness and concludes that it is not found in earthly rewards such as riches or fame but only in the "highest good," which is God. Human life, then, should be spent in pursuit of God. Since Boethius speaks in the *Consolation* as a philosopher rather than a theologian, he does not refer to Christian revelation or to the role of divine grace in salvation. But his basically Augustinian message is unmistakable. *The Consolation of Philosophy* became one of the most popular books of the Middle Ages because it was extremely well written, be-

THE CHRISTIANIZATION OF CLASSICAL CULTURE IN THE WEST

How was classical culture Christianized?

None of the Christian intellectuals of late antiquity were prepared to throw out altogether the classical traditions of learning they had inherited. For all of them, however, this tradition posed severe challenges. It was, in the first place, thoroughly pagan, and paganism remained a significant threat to Christianity even after the empire became formally Christian. Classical learning was also associated with syncretism—that is to say, with the easy acceptance of both Christian and pagan beliefs simultaneously, which had been so marked a feature of aristocratic culture during the fourth century. Christian intellectuals—indeed, the Christian clergy generally—wanted desperately to replace the doctrines of pagan philosophy with the doctrine of Christ. To do this, however, they needed a way of Christianizing the classical inheritance and conveying it to the Christian masses in an intellectually satisfying way. It was, therefore, to the preservation and reinterpretation of classical Latin culture for a mixed audience of vulgar Romans and aspiring barbarians that the Christian intellectuals of the fourth, fifth, and sixth centuries devoted themselves.

Their challenge was to arrive at an understanding of the purposes of classical culture for a Christian audience. Tertullian had raised this question in the second century C.E. by asking, "What has Athens [the symbol of classical learning] to do with Jerusalem [the symbol of Christian salvation]?" Tertullian's answer had been "Nothing"; but this answer did not suit the changed circumstances of the Christian church from the fourth century on. Jerome and Augustine were more hopeful about Christianizing the classical tradition; but on the whole, the early monastic movement sided with Tertullian. Despite the role Benedictine monasteries would later play in copying and preserving Latin literary texts, Saint Benedict himself was no admirer of classical culture. Quite to the contrary, he wanted his monks to serve only Christ—not literature or philosophy. But unlike some of his monastic contemporaries, he did believe that monks should be able to read well enough to study the Bible. To guarantee this, some schooling within the monastery would be necessary, especially for boys given over from birth to the monastic profession. For Benedict, however, preserving classical learning was no part of a monastery's proper duties.

CASSIODORUS AND THE BENEDICTINE TRADITION OF LEARNING

The impetus behind the development of Benedictine monasticism's tradition of learning came not from Benedict himself, but from Cassiodorus (c. 490–c. 583), an official at Theodoric's Ostrogothic court. Early in his career, Cassiodorus wrote a *History of the Goths* for his barbarian overlord. He also composed (and eventually published) several volumes of his official correspondence, reflecting his training in the classical rhetorical tradition. During the last forty years of his life, however, Cassiodorus turned his attention toward religion, composing commentaries on the Psalms and founding an important monastery at Vivarium in southern Italy.

It was for his monks that Cassiodorus composed his most influential work, the *Institutes*. Inspired by Saint Augustine, Cassiodorus believed that study of classical literature was the essential preliminary to a proper understanding of the Bible and the Church Fathers. His *Institutes* were basically a reading list, comprising first the essential works of classical, pagan literature a monk should know before he moved on to the more difficult and demanding study of theology and the Bible. Through the *Institutes*, Cassiodorus thus defined a classical literary canon that would influence Christian educational practice until the end of the Middle Ages.

Cassiodorus. This frontispiece from a Bible, drawn in an English Benedictine monastery around 700 C.E., depicts Cassiodorus as a copyist and preserver of books. Because books were expensive and rare until the invention of printing in the fifteenth century, they customarily were stored in cupboards, lying flat, as we see them here.

Cassiodorus also encouraged his monks to copy manuscripts, arguing that such copying was in itself "manual labor" of the sort that Saint Benedict had demanded, and that it might even be more appropriate work for monks than laboring in the fields. As Benedictines began to subscribe to these ideas, Benedictine monasteries emerged as the most important centers for the preservation and study of classical literature in the Latin-speaking West. Hardly any works of classical Latin literature would survive today had they not been copied and preserved during the early Middle Ages by Benedictine monks following the example of Cassiodorus.

Boethius and Cassiodorus both worked at the court of Theodoric the Ostrogoth, the most thoroughly Romanized ruler in the sixth-century barbarian world. Yet all their efforts to extend, preserve, and Christianize the classical cultural tradition testify to their awareness that this world was passing away. Theodoric ruled Italy as the designated representative of the emperor at Constantinople. A great admirer of Roman civilization, he fostered agriculture and commerce, repaired public buildings and roads, patronized learning, and maintained a policy of religious toleration. In short, he provided Italy with a more enlightened government than it had known for several centuries. But none of this was sufficient to erase the corrosive distrust that in Theodoric's final years tore his kingdom apart. The problem was that for all their *romanitas* ("Romanness"), Theodoric and the Goths were Arian heretics, whereas the local bishops and landowners of Italy were orthodox Trinitarian Christians—and this fact made the Italian aristocrats the faithful subjects not of Theodoric, but of his imperial sponsor in Constantinople. When, in 523, the emperor pronounced an edict, valid also in Italy, forbidding Jews, pagans, and heretics (by whom he probably meant Arians) from holding public office, the storm broke. Although Cassiodorus remained loyal to Theodoric, Boethius was imprisoned, accused of conspiring to return Italy to direct imperial rule. Theodoric's last years were marked by his continuing persecution of Trinitarian Christians. When he died in 526, he left no son to succeed him, while religious tensions continued to tear his kingdom apart. Ten years later, Theodoric's fears would be confirmed when a new emperor, Justinian, attempted to reconstitute the Roman empire of Augustus by reconquering Italy from the Ostrogoths.

EASTERN ROME AND THE WESTERN EMPIRE

Why did Justinian's plan to reunite the Roman empire fail?

The conquest of the Ostrogoths was part of a larger plan to revive the Roman empire conceived and directed by the eastern emperor Justinian (527–565). The eastern empire, with its capital at Constantinople, had faced many external and internal pressures since the time of Theodosius (d. 395). But by the early sixth century it had recovered much of its strength. Although the eastern empire—which then encompassed the modern-day territories of Greece, Turkey, most of the Middle East, and Egypt—was largely Greek- and Syriac-speaking, Justinian himself came from a western province (modern-day Serbia) and spoke Latin. A student of history, he saw himself as the heir of imperial Rome, whose ancient power and western territories he aspired to restore. Although his efforts ultimately failed, they had a lasting impact on the entire Mediterranean world.

THE CODIFICATION OF ROMAN LAW

One of Justinian's most impressive and lasting accomplishments was his codification of Roman law. To carry out this work he appointed a commission of lawyers under the supervision of his minister Tribonian. Within two years the commission published the first result of its labors. This was the Code, a systematic compilation of all the imperial statutes that had been issued from the reign of Hadrian to Justinian's own. The Code was later supplemented by the Novels, which contained the legislation of Justinian and his immediate successors. By 532 the commission had also completed the Digest, a summary of the writings of the great jurists. The commission's final product was the Institutes, a textbook of the legal principles reflected in the Digest and the Code. All four volumes together constitute the *Corpus Juris Civilis*, or the "body of civil law."

Justinian's *Corpus* was a brilliant achievement: the Digest alone has been justly called "the most remarkable and important lawbook that the world has ever seen." In the East, the *Corpus* immediately became the foundation on which all subsequent legal developments would rest. In the West, by contrast, the *Corpus* was initially little

Justinian and Theodora. Sixth-century mosaics from the Church of San Vitale, Ravenna. The emperor and empress are presented here as holy figures (notice the halos around their heads) who exercise priestly responsibilities. As they advance toward the altar, they carry the communion dish and the chalice, symbols of the body and blood of Christ. On the hem of Theodora's gown, the "three wise kings from the East" who visited the infant Jesus are represented. Just as these "three magi" once had supernatural knowledge of Christ, so now do their counterparts, Justinian and Theodora.

THE MEDITERRANEAN WORLD UNDER JUSTINIAN, 527–565 C.E.

Compare this map with the one on p. 149. Which areas of the former Roman empire did Justinian not attempt to reconquer? Is there any strategic logic to Justinian's reconquests? What would have been necessary to hold this newly reconstituted Roman empire together after Justinian's death?

known; most early medieval law codes drew instead on the fifth-century compilation of the emperor Theodosius II (408–450). From the twelfth century on, however, Justinian's *Corpus* would be intensively studied in the West as well, influencing both the conduct of government and the developing legal systems of late medieval and early modern Europe.

JUSTINIAN'S MILITARY CONQUESTS

Justinian's initial attempts to reconquer the western Roman empire succeeded easily. In 533 his brilliant general Belisarius conquered the Vandal kingdom in Northwest Africa; by 536 Belisarius appeared to have conquered Italy, where he was welcomed by the Catholic subjects of the Ostrogoths. But the early victories of the Italian campaign were illusory; the war would drag on for decades until the exhausted imperial forces finally reduced the last Gothic outposts in 563. Because Justinian had already recaptured northwest Africa and the coastal parts of Spain, the Mediterranean was once again a "Roman" lake when he died in 565. But the costs of this endeavor had been enormous and would soon call into question the very existence of the eastern Roman empire.

Justinian's western campaigns were ill advised for two reasons. One was their enormous cost. Belisarius seldom had enough troops to do his job properly: he began his Italian campaign with only eight thousand men. To provide the troops his generals needed, Justinian imposed oppressive taxation which undermined support for the empire in such vitally important regions as Egypt and Syria. Even the Trinitarian Christians of Italy and North Africa resented the costs their liberation imposed on them. Justinian's Western campaigns also distracted attention from dangers closer to home: in particular, the developing strength of Persia. To respond to the Persian threat, Justinian's successors were forced to withdraw their troops from Italy and North Africa; this left both regions dangerously exposed to further barbarian invasions, but was still not sufficient to guarantee the safety of the eastern empire. Only a heroic reorganization of the eastern empire after 610 saved Constantinople from falling to the Persians; but this reorganization also marks the final end to Justinian's dream of reuniting the eastern and the western Mediterranean worlds.

THE IMPACT OF JUSTINIAN'S RECONQUEST ON THE WESTERN EMPIRE

Justinian's wars caused tremendous devastation throughout northern and central Italy. In 568, another, much more primitive Germanic tribe, the Lombards, took advantage of the chaos to conquer the northern third of the peninsula. Thereafter, Italy would be divided between Lombard territories in the north, east Roman territories in the south, and papal territories located precariously between them. This division among northern, central, and southern Italy would continue to characterize Italian political life until the nineteenth century.

Eastern Roman control over North Africa lasted only a few generations longer than it did in Italy. Weakened by religious dissension and heavy taxation, this area fell during the seventh century to the invading armies of Islam, along with Egypt and the rest of Roman Africa. When it did, Christianity in north Africa largely disappeared.

Further north, the Visigothic kingdom of Spain continued to control the interior portions of the country, despite Justinian's conquest of the Mediterranean coast. After the imperial armies departed, the Visigoths resumed such control as they had ever exercised over these coastal regions. But tensions between the Arian Visigoths and their Catholic subjects continued even after 582, when the Visigothic king finally converted to orthodox Christianity. Hostility among the Visigothic kings, their Catholic bishops, and the Romanized population of the Mediterranean coast would last

CHRONOLOGY	
THE ROMAN REVIVAL OF JUSTINIAN, 527–568 C.E.	
Reign of Justinian	527–565
Publication of the *Corpus Juris Civilis*	529–534
Justinian conquers the Vandal kingdom of northwest Africa	533
Justinian reconquers Italian peninsula	536
Justinian defeats last Gothic outposts	563
Justinian rules over Mediterranean world	563–565
Death of Justinian	565
Germanic Lombards conquer Italian peninsula	568

until the end of the Visigothic kingdom. Despite the Visigothic kings' efforts to pattern their rule on Byzantine example, their kingdom quickly collapsed in the early eighth century when Muslim armies crossed the Strait of Gibraltar. By the end of the century, Christian rulers controlled only the northern-most parts of the Iberian peninsula and the area around Barcelona. For the next three hundred years, Spain would be an important part of the Muslim world.

CONCLUSION

From its earliest days, Rome had been characterized by its remarkable capacity to assimilate the disparate cultures of the lands Rome conquered. In this process, both Rome and its empire were steadily transformed. The pace of these transformations accelerated markedly, however, from the mid-third century on—so much so that historians now commonly refer to the period from the mid-third century to the early seventh century as "late antiquity" to distinguish it from the classical Roman world that preceded it. During these centuries, larger numbers of immigrants entered the Roman empire than ever before, drawn by a combination of land hunger, opportunity, and the desire to participate in the material and cultural benefits of Roman life. In the western empire especially, the number of these new immigrants became so large during the late fourth and fifth centuries that the frontier areas of the empire ceased to be distinguishable from the more "Romanized" areas of the interior.

At the same time, two internal cultural processes were transforming what it meant to be Roman. The learned culture of the Greek and Roman world was being steadily extended to larger numbers of people; but in the process, learned culture itself was increasingly vulgarized. And finally, the empire itself became Christian, first by persuasion, as Constantine and his successors made it attractive for individuals to convert to the new religion, and later by coercion, as Christianity became the official religion of the entire Roman empire. As a result, a new fusion of Christian culture and late Roman governance began to evolve, not only around the imperial court at Constantinople, but also in the provinces.

What did not change, however, was the Mediterranean focus of this evolving late-antique world. Despite the emergence of new political units in the western Roman empire, Roman civilization in the fifth and sixth centuries remained firmly centered upon the Mediterranean Sea. That too, however, was soon to change. The seventh century would witness the final fracturing of this unified Mediterranean world and the emergence in its place of three quite different Western civilizations: Byzantium, Western Europe, and Islam. This development marks the end of the classical world and the beginning of the Middle Ages. It is to this development that we now turn.

KEY TERMS

tetrarchy

Constantinople

Pharisees

Paul

Arians

Saint Benedict of Nursia

Visigoths

Saint Augustine

Cassiodorus

Justinian

SELECTED READINGS

Saint Augustine. *The City of God.* Translated by Henry Bettenson. Baltimore, 1972.

_____. *Confessions.* Translated by Henry M. Chadwick. Oxford, 1991.

_____. *The Enchiridion on Faith, Hope and Love.* Translated by H. Paolucci. Chicago, 1961.

_____. *On Christian Doctrine.* Translated by D. W. Robertson, Jr. New York, 1958.

Boethius. *The Consolation of Philosophy.* Translated by R. Green. Indianapolis, 1962.

Bowersock, G. W., Peter Brown, and Oleg Grabar. *Late Antiquity: A Guide to the Postclassical World.* Cambridge, Mass., 1999. An authoritative compilation. The first half is devoted to essays on the cultural features of the period; the second half is organized as an encyclopedia.

Brown, Peter. *Augustine of Hippo.* Berkeley, 1967. A great biography, by the greatest living scholar of late antiquity.

_____. *The Body and Society: Men, Women and Sexual Renunciation in Early Christianity.* New York, 1988. A revealing study of one of the fundamental transformations Christianity brought to the late antique world.

_____. *Power and Persuasion in Late Antiquity: Toward a Christian Empire.* Madison, 1992. An important revisionist account of the impact of Christianization on the political culture of the later Roman empire.

_____. *The Rise of Western Christendom: Triumph and Diversity, 200–1000,* 2d ed. Oxford, 2002. Evocatively written picture of the diverse forms Christianity took as it spread east and north from the Mediterranean world.

_____. *The World of Late Antiquity.* New York, 1971. Still the best short survey of the period, with excellent illustrations.

Cameron, Averil. *The Later Roman Empire,* A.D. 284–430. London, 1993. Now the standard account of its period, with an emphasis on imperial politics.

_____. *The Mediterranean World in Late Antiquity,* A.D. 395–600. London, 1993. Masterful, with excellent, succinct bibliographical essays.

Cassiodorus. *An Introduction to Divine and Human Readings*. Translated by L. W. Jones. New York, 1946.

Chadwick, Henry M. *Augustine*. Oxford, 1986. The best short introduction to Augustine's thought.

———. *Boethius*. Oxford, 1981. The best intellectual biography of this important thinker.

Clark, Gillian. *Women in Late Antiquity*. Oxford, 1993. A clear, compact account of an important subject.

Coogan, Michael, ed. *The Oxford History of the Biblical World*. Oxford, 1998. A reliable, but rather traditional account of the historical events recounted in the Hebrew Bible and the New Testament.

Eusebius. *The History of the Church*. Translated by G. A. Williamson. Baltimore, 1965. An indispensible narrative account of Constantine's reign, written by one of his courtier-bishops.

———. *Eusebius' Life of Constantine*. Translated by Averil Cameron and Stuart Hall. Oxford, 1999. An admiring life that reflects Constantine's own vision of his religious authority.

Jones, A. H. M. *The Later Roman Empire, 284–602: A Social, Economic, and Administrative Survey*. 2 volumes. London, 1964. An immense, detailed analysis, difficult to read but packed with information.

Lane Fox, Robin. *Pagans and Christians*. New York, 1987. A subtle, perceptive, lengthy, but highly readable exploration of the pagan world within which Christianity grew up.

Lawrence, Clifford Hugh. *Medieval Monasticism*, 3d ed. London, 2000. Concise, intelligent, perceptive survey of monasticism from its beginnings to the end of the Middle Ages.

Markus, R. A. *The End of Ancient Christianity*. New York, 1990. An expert synthetic study of Christianity in the western Roman empire between 350 and 600 C.E.

Moorhead, John. *Justinian*. New York, 1994. An up-to-date survey of the emperor and his times.

Pelikan, Jaroslav. *The Christian Tradition, Volume I: The Emergence of the Catholic Tradition*. Chicago, 1971. A history of Christian doctrine that is one of the tours de force of twentieth-century scholarship. Synthetic, clear, and objective.

Procopius. *The Secret History*. Translated by G. A. Williamson. Baltimore, 1966. All the gossip from Justinian's court, much of it salacious.

Sanders, E. P. *The Historical Figure of Jesus*. London and New York, 1993. The best of the recent studies of Jesus in his first-century Jewish context.

Shanks, Hershel, ed. *Christianity and Rabbinic Judaism: A Parallel History of Their Origins and Early Development*. Washington, D.C., 1992. Accessible chapters written by top authorities, describing both Jewish and Christian developments from the first to the sixth centuries C.E.

Wallace-Hadrill, John Michael. *The Barbarian West*, 3d ed. London, 1966. Still the most interesting and suggestive analysis of the Romano-Germanic world created by the invasions of the fifth century C.E.

Whittaker, C. R. *Frontiers of the Roman Empire: A Social and Economic Study*. Baltimore, 1994. A convincing picture of the frontiers of the Roman empire as zones of intensive cultural interaction.

Williams, Stephen. *Diocletian and the Roman Recovery*. New York, 1997. A recent account that modifies, but does not replace, A. H. M. Jones (see above).

Wolfram, Herwig. *The Roman Empire and Its Germanic Peoples*. Berkeley, 1997. The best recent survey of its subject.

WINE

... let me drink bright wine, sitting in the shade, when my heart is satisfied with food, and so, turning my head to face the fresh Zephyr, from the everflowing spring which pours down unfouled thrice pour an offering of water, but make a fourth libation of wine.

—Hesiod's *Works and Days,* ll. 582–596, translated by Hugh G. Evelyn-White (1914)

It has become quite a common proverb that in wine there is truth.

—Pliny the Elder, *Natural History*

PLANTING VINEYARDS to grow grapes for making wine can be traced back almost eight thousand years to the mountainous regions of the Ancient Near East. Wine was used—along with beer—in many different ways in all ancient western civilizations. The Greeks used wine at their *symposia,* drinking parties that included philosophical debate. The Egyptians used wine to treat illnesses such as asthma. At Sparta, the strength of newborn children was tested by immersing the infant in a vat of wine. Wine was used in pagan religious ceremonies of all kinds. And wine became a central feature of the Christian celebration of the Eucharist. Ancient documents tell us that the Greeks developed more than 130 different types of wine, and the Roman scholar Pliny the Elder could talk about eighty different varieties found in Italy itself. As wine-making progressed, merchants began to use different containers to hold specific types of wine, and stoppers displayed marks containing information about the maker, vineyard, and age of the wine.

Wine was celebrated in various pagan festivals. Dionysus, the Greek god of vegetation and fruitfulness, was believed to have given wine to man, and a festival held in late December in his honor celebrated the new wine of the vintage. The Romans continued this practice with their god Bacchus. Wine also played a central role in religious cultures. According to Jewish rituals, each Sabbath began with a blessing over wine. For early Christians, wine played a key role in the miracle of Jesus at Cana, when he turned water into wine at a wedding ceremony.

The images and documents in the *Wine* Digital History Feature at www.wwnorton.com/wciv highlight the various roles of wine, ranging from its practical uses as a medicine to its sacred role in Greek and Roman religion. As you explore the *Wine* feature, consider the following:

• What does the history of winemaking in the ancient world tell us about the ancient economy itself?

• How central was the celebration of Dionysus for the ancient Greeks? Was there a major difference between the festival of Dionysus and the Bacchanalia at Rome?

• In what ways was the consumption and use of wine a point at which pagan religious practices and Christianity intersected? What might this connection tell us about the relationship between paganism and early Christianity?

PART III

THE MIDDLE AGES

THE TERM "MIDDLE AGES" was coined by Europeans in the seventeenth century to express their view that a long and dismal period of interruption extended between the glorious accomplishments of Greece and Rome and their own "modern age." Because the term became so widespread, it is now an ineradicable part of our historical vocabulary; but no serious scholar today uses it with the sense of contempt it once invoked. To the contrary, most scholars would now argue that it was during the Middle Ages—roughly the years between 600 and 1500—that the cultural, political, and religious foundations of all three Western civilizations were established. Whether we speak of Byzantium, the Islamic world, or Europe, the Middle Ages were a formative and creative period in the history of Western civilizations.

Only with respect to Europe, however, do the years between 600 and 1500 constitute a true "middle age." For the Islamic world, these centuries witnessed the birth, expansion, and maturation of a new civilization that drew heavily on its classical past, but fused that past with a sweeping new religious vision. For Byzantium, the so-called Middle Ages ended in 1453 with the conquest of the Byzantine empire by the Ottoman Turks. Even for Europe, the metaphor of a middle age is to some extent misleading. Like Islamic civilization, European civilization began to take shape from the seventh century on, but it was not until the twelfth century that a truly distinctive European tradition with respect to politics, religion, and art emerged.

	POLITICS	SOCIETY AND CULTURE	ECONOMY	INTERNATIONAL RELATIONS
570	Muhammad, founder of Islam, born (570) Pope Gregory I (Saint Gregory the Great) (590–604) Ascension of Byzantine emperor Heraclius (610) Shiite–Sunni schism (661) Umayyad family governs Islamic world (661–750)	Growth of monasteries (600–700) The Hijrah (622)	Economic unity of Mediterranean world ends (650)	Arabs, under Abu-Bakr, rout Byzantine army in Syria (636) Arabs take Antioch, Damascus, and Jerusalem (636) Attempts by Muslims to take Constantinople (677, 717)
700	The Carolingians share power with the Merovingian kings (717–751) Abbasid family governs Islamic world (750–1258) Pepin becomes king of the Franks (751)	Iconoclast Contoversy begins (717)	Agricultural revolution (700–1300)	Arabs take Visigothic Spain (717)
800	Charlemagne crowned Holy Roman emperor (800) Charlemagne dies (814)			
900	Capetian dynasty (987–1328)	Cluniac reform of monasteries (900–1050) Islamic civilization's "middle period" (900–1250) Rise of Romanesque architecture (900–1150) Avicenna, author of *Canon of Medicine* (980–1037)	Invention of iron horseshoe (900) Rus establish principality near Kiev (900s)	Rus sack Constantinople (860) Otto I defeats Hungarians at Lechfield (955)
1000	Split between Roman and Byzantine churches (1054) Saxon civil war begins (1073) Investiture Conflict (1075–1122)	European population triples (1000–1300) *Song of Roland* (1050) Number of monks increases tenfold (1066–1200) Peter Abelard (1079–1142) Cisterian order flourishes (1090–1153) Hildegard of Bingen (1098–1179)	Invention of tandem harness for plowing (1050) Water mill becomes widely used in Europe (1050)	Battle of Hastings, England falls to the Normans (1066) Norman Conquest (1066) Seljuk Turks overrun eastern Byzantine provinces (1071) Battle of Manzikert, Turks take Anatolia (1071) First Crusade (1095–1099)
1100	Concordat of Worms distinguishes temporal power of kings from spiritual power of clergy (1122) Reign of Frederick I, Barbarossa, as Holy Roman emperor (1152–1190)	Rise of Gothic architecture (1100–1300) Umar Hayyam, author of the Rubiyat (d. 1123) Averroës, Spanish philosopher, theologian, and physician (1126–1198) Catharism in southern France (1150–1300) Rise of chivalry (1150) Troubadour poets travel Europe (1150–1300) Chretien de Troyes, author of Arthurian legends (1165–1190) Saint Dominic (1170–1221) Rome decrees all cathedrals must support one schoolteacher (1179) Saint Francis of Assisi (1182–1226)	Manorial lords begin trading serfs' freedom for cash (1100s) Proliferation of windmills (1170s)	Muslim leader, Saladin, recaptures Jerusalem (1187)

POLITICS	SOCIETY AND CULTURE	ECONOMY	INTERNATIONAL RELATIONS
	Theater appears outside of church (1200)		Crusaders sack Constantinople (1204)
			England ousted from Normandy, Anjou, and Brittany (1204)
Magna Carta (1215)	*The Cid* and Norse sagas are written down (1200s)		Mongols conquer eastern Slavic region (1200s)
Fourth Lateran Council (1215)	Saint Thomas Aquinas, author of *Summa Theologica*, (1225–1274)		Mongols take Kiev (1240)
			Mongols dispose of Abbasid caliphate (1258)
Emergence of English Parliament (1272–1307)	Dante Alighieri, author of *The Divine Comedy*, (1265–1321)		
Formation of French Estates General (1285–1314)	Giotto of Florence, painter (1267–1337)		Jews expelled from southern Italy, England, and France (1288–1306)
French King Philip IV (1285–1314)	William of Ockham, founder of nominalism (1285–1349)		

ROME'S THREE HEIRS: THE BYZANTINE, ISLAMIC, AND EARLY MEDIEVAL WORLDS

A NEW PERIOD in the history of Western civilizations began in the seventh century. In the year 600, it was still possible for the rulers of the Roman empire living in Constantinople to imagine their empire as uniting the entire Mediterranean world. By the end of the seventh century, however, three different successor civilizations to the Greco-Roman world of antiquity had emerged: the Byzantine, the Islamic, and the western European, each with its own language and distinctive ways of life. The history of Western civilizations from the seventh to the eleventh centuries is largely a story of the rivalries and interactions among these three emerging worlds, each of which preserved and extended different aspects of the late-antique inheritance they shared.

Like the provinces of the eastern Roman empire over which it ruled, Byzantine civilization after 610 was Greek-speaking. It combined the bureaucratic and imperial traditions of late Roman governance with an intense pursuit of the Christian faith. This fusion had been pioneered in the fourth century by Constantine and his successors, and was continuously elaborated in the eastern Roman empire thereafter. Islamic civilization, in contrast, was Arabic-speaking. It was the most cosmopolitan and wide ranging (both geographically and culturally) of the three successor civilizations. The Islamic world was the heir both to the Roman ideal of an expansive empire itself, and to Roman ideals of cultural and religious assimilation as essential attributes of imperial rule. By combining the philosophical and scientific interests of the Hellenistic world with the literary and artistic culture of Persia, Islam created the most dynamic cultural amalgam of the early Middle Ages.

Western Christian civilization in the early Middle Ages was rooted in Latin, but with important cultural influences from Germanic, Celtic, and Latin-derived vernacular languages. In contrast to Byzantium and Islam, it owed relatively little to Roman ideals of empire, except briefly under the Carolingians. It was, however, profoundly influenced by Roman ideals of law and local government, which carried with them a continuing influence from the republican traditions of ancient Rome. For western Europe in the early Middle Ages, law and Latin Christianity were

FOCUS QUESTIONS

- How did the Byzantine state survive for nearly a millennium?

- How was Islam able to spread so rapidly?

- What forces combined to undermine the political unity of the Islamic empire?

- What caused economic and social change in seventh-century western Europe?

- How did Charlemagne redefine the relationship between Christianity and kingship?

the pinnacles of Roman cultural achievement. They were, indeed, the very essence of what it meant to be Roman; and to be Roman remained an almost universal aspiration in the early medieval West. If we measure civilizations by their highest philosophical and literary accomplishments, western Europe in the early Middle Ages was a laggard in comparison with Byzantium and Islam. It was also the least economically advanced of these three successor states, and faced the greatest organizational weaknesses in both government and religion. By the end of the eleventh century, however, Latin Christian civilization was no longer on the defensive against its rivals in military, economic, or religious terms. Rather, it stood on the verge of an extraordinary period of expansion and conquest that would bring it ultimately to a dominant position in world affairs during the early modern and modern eras.

THE BYZANTINE EMPIRE AND ITS CULTURE

How did the Byzantine state survive for nearly a millennium?

It is impossible to date the beginning of Byzantine history with any precision because the Byzantine empire was the uninterrupted successor of the Roman state. Justinian's reign was clearly an important turning point in the direction of Byzantine civilization because it saw the crystallization of new forms of thought and art that can be considered more "Byzantine" than "Roman." But only after 610 did a new dynasty emerge that came from the East, spoke Greek, and maintained a fully Eastern or "Byzantine" orientation. Hence, although good arguments can be made for beginning Byzantine history with Diocletian, Constantine, or Justinian, we will begin here with the accession in 610 of the Emperor Heraclius.

It is also convenient to begin in 610 because from then until 1071 the main lines of Byzantine military and political history were determined by resistance against successive waves of invasion from the East. When Heraclius came to the throne the very existence of the Byzantine empire was being challenged by the Persians, who had conquered almost all of the empire's Asian territories. By enormous effort Heraclius rallied Byzantine strength and turned the tide, routing the Persians and recapturing Jerusalem. But in his last years new armies began to invade Byzantine territory, swarming out of hitherto placid Arabia. Inspired by the new religion of Islam and profiting from Byzantine exhaustion after the struggle with Persia, the Arabs made astonishingly rapid gains. By 650 they had taken most of the Byzantine territories that the Persians had occupied briefly in the early seventh century, including Jerusalem, which became a holy site for Muslims no less than for Christians and Jews. Arab armies also conquered Persia itself, and rapidly made their way westward across North Africa, where Byzantine control had long been resented. Having become a Mediterranean power, the Arabs also took to the sea. In 677 they tried to conquer Constantinople with a fleet. They attempted to take the city again in 717 by means of a concerted land and sea operation.

The Arab threat to Constantinople in 717 marked a new low in Byzantine fortunes, but the threat was countered by the emperor Leo the Isaurian (717–741) with the same resolution Heraclius had shown against the Persians a century before. Leo's defense of Constantinople in 717 was one of the most significant battles in European history. Had the Islamic armies taken Constantinople there would have been little to stop them from sweeping through the rest of Europe. Over the next few decades, however, the Byzantines reconquered most of Asia Minor, which became the heartland of their empire for the next three hundred years. In the eleventh century, however, a new Islamic power, the Seljuk Turks, reversed the Byzantine gains. In 1071 the Seljuks annihilated a Byzantine army at Manzikert in Asia Minor, a stunning victory that allowed them to overrun Byzantium's eastern provinces. Constantinople was now thrown back on itself more or less as it had been in the days of Heraclius and Leo. By and large, it would remain on the defensive for the next four hundred years. The last remnants of the Byzantine empire fell to the Ottoman Turks in 1453. Turks continue to rule in Constantinople—which they renamed Istanbul—to the present day.

SOURCES OF STABILITY

Because Byzantine power was so completely focused on the imperial court at Constantinople, and because rulers followed their late Roman predecessors in claiming the powers of divinely appointed absolute monarchs, there was no way of opposing them other than by intrigue and violence. Hence Byzantine history was marked by repeated palace revolts involving mutilations, murders, and blindings. Fortunately for the empire, some very able rulers did emerge from time to time to wield their unrestrained powers effectively.

HOW DID THE BYZANTINE STATE SURVIVE FOR NEARLY A MILLENNIUM?

THE BYZANTINE EMPIRE AND ITS CULTURE   197

Byzantine Soldiers Clashing with Arab Soldiers. This illustration from the Scylitzes chronicle dates back to the eleventh century, when the Seljuk Turks started to reverse the Byzantine gains in Asia in an offensive that would ultimately end the Byzantine empire in the fifteenth century.

ported the state. But agriculture lay at the heart of the Byzantine economy. Byzantine agricultural history was marked by the struggles of independent peasant farmers to stay free of the encroachments of large estates owned by wealthy aristocrats and monasteries. Until the eleventh century the free peasantry managed to maintain its position with the help of state legislation. After 1025, however, the aristocracy gained power in the government and began to transform the peasants into impoverished tenants. This had many unfortunate results, not least that peasants became less interested in resisting the enemy. The defeat at Manzikert in 1071 was in part the result of the government's short-sighted acquiescence to aristocratic ambitions.

BYZANTINE RELIGION

So far we have spoken about military campaigns, government, and economics as if they were the keys to Byzantine survival. Seen from hindsight they were, but what the Byzantines themselves cared about most was the religious orthodoxy of their empire. Byzantines battled over abstruse religious questions as vehemently as we today

Even more fortunately, an efficient bureaucracy continued to function even during times of palace upheaval.

Efficient bureaucratic government was one of the major reasons for Byzantine success and longevity. Literate Byzantine bureaucrats supervised education and religion and presided over all forms of economic endeavor. Even chariot racing fell under strict governmental supervision, with the populace of Constantinople being assigned by governmental command to root for particular teams. Bureaucratic methods also regulated the army and navy, the courts, and the diplomatic service, endowing these agencies with organizational strengths incomparable for their time.

Another explanation for Byzantine endurance was the comparatively sound economic base of the state, at least until the eleventh century. Commerce and cities continued to flourish in the Byzantine East, as they had done in the late-antique period. Constantinople in the ninth and tenth centuries was a vital trade emporium for Far Eastern luxury goods and Western raw materials. The empire also nurtured and protected its own industries, most notably silk making, and it was renowned until the eleventh century for its stable gold and silver coinage.

Historians emphasize Byzantine trade and industry because these provided most of the surplus wealth that sup-

CHRONOLOGY	
THE BYZANTINE EMPIRE, 610–1100	
Ascension of the emperor Heraclius	610
Arabs seize most of Byzantine territory	c. 650
Constantinople nearly falls to the Arabs	717
Byzantines reconquer most of Asia Minor	717–750
Stalemate between Arabs and Byzantines	750–950
Byzantines reconquer most of Syria	c. 950–1000
Seljuk Turks overrun eastern Byzantine provinces	1071
First Crusade	1095–1099

might argue about politics and sports; they were often willing to fight and even die over words in a religious creed. This intense preoccupation with questions of doctrine could cause great harm during periods of religious dissension, but it also endowed the Byzantine state with a powerful sense of confidence and mission.

Byzantine doctrinal disputes were greatly complicated by the fact that the emperors took an active role in them. Emperors exercised great power in the life of the church. Nonetheless, rulers could never force all their subjects to believe the same doctrines they themselves did. Even Byzantine governmental authority did not stretch that far. Only after the loss of many eastern provinces and the refinement of doctrinal formulae did religious peace seem near in the eighth century. But then it was shattered for still another century by what is known as the Iconoclastic Controversy.

> The Iconoclasts wished to prohibit the worship of icons—that is, images of Christ and the saints. Honoring such images seemed to the Iconoclasts to smack of idolatry and paganism.

The Iconoclastic movement was initiated by Emperor Leo the Isaurian, and subsequently directed with even greater energy by his son Constantine V (740–775). The Iconoclasts wished to prohibit the worship of icons— that is, images of Christ and the saints. Honoring such images seemed to the Iconoclasts to smack of idolatry and paganism. Traditionalists responded that it was not the images themselves that worshipers honored, but the heavenly reality that lay beyond them. Like Byzantine art generally, icons were intended to act as windows through which a glimpse of heaven might be granted to human beings on earth.

The Iconoclastic Controversy was resolved in the ninth century by a return to the status quo, namely the worship of images, but the century of turmoil over the issue had some profound results. One was the destruction by imperial order of a large amount of religious art. Pre-eighth-century Byzantine religious art that survives today comes mostly from places such as Italy or Palestine, which were beyond the reach of the Iconoclastic emperors. A second consequence of the controversy was the opening of a serious religious breach between East and West. The pope, who until the eighth century had usually been a close ally of the Byzantines, strongly opposed Iconoclasm, not least because Iconoclasm tended to question the cult of saints, and the claims of papal primacy were based on the pope's role as Saint Peter's successor. Papal opposition to Iconoclasm during the eighth century led to worsening relations between East and West that culminated with the crowning of the Frankish leader Charlemagne as the new Roman emperor in the West on Christmas Day 800.

The ultimate defeat of Iconoclasm led to the reassertion of some major traits of Byzantine religiosity. One was a renewed emphasis on the traditional, Orthodox faith of the empire as the key to its political unity and military success. Religious tradition became the touchstone of doctrinal correctness and political legitimacy. This strengthened Byzantine religion by ending controversy and heresy, and helped the religion gain new adherents in the ninth and tenth centuries. But it also reinforced the hegemony of Constantinople's own religious traditions within the empire, thus marginalizing even further the differing religious traditions of Syrian and Armenian Christianity. The fear of heresy also tended to inhibit free speculation, not just in religion but also in related intellectual matters. Although the Byzantine emperors founded and supported a university in Constantinople, they never permitted it to exercise any significant degree of intellectual freedom, in marked contrast with the freewheeling intellectual atmosphere of the growing universities of twelfth- and thirteenth-century western Europe.

BYZANTINE CULTURE

Religion dominated Byzantine life; but commitment to Christianity by no means inhibited the Byzantines from revering and preserving their ancient Greek heritage. Byzantine schools based their instruction on classical Greek literature, and especially Homer, to an astonishing degree. Educated people around the Byzantine court could quote but a single line of Homer, and expect that their audience would know immediately the entire passage from which it came. Byzantine scholars studied intensively the philosophy of Plato and the historical prose of Thucydides. Aristotle's works were regarded with less interest. By and large, the Greek scientific and mathematical tradition was neglected by the Byzantines, and even philosophy was considerably restricted. Justinian, for example, shut down the Athenian philosophical academies that had existed since Plato's day, declaring that everything worth knowing was already known. Preservation rather than innovation was the hallmark of Byzantine classicism. Nevertheless, such dedicated classicism enriched Byzantine intellectual and literary life and helped preserve the Greek classics for later ages. The bulk of classical Greek literature that we have today survives only because it was copied by Byzantine scribes.

BYZANTINE CLASSICISM

This poem, by an eleventh-century Byzantine scholar, illustrates the sense of continuity learned Byzantines felt between their own Christian world and the world of the ancient Greek philosophers and authors.

May Christ Save Plato and Plutarch from Eternal Damnation

If perchance you wish to exempt certain pagans from punishment, my Christ,
May you spare for my sake Plato and Plutarch,
For both were very close to your laws in both teaching and way of life.
Even if they were unaware that you as God reign over all,
In this matter only your charity is needed,
Through which you are willing to save all men while asking nothing in return.

Deno John Geanokoplos, ed. and trans. *Byzantium: Church, Society, and Civilization Seen through Contemporary Eyes.* (Chicago: University of Chicago Press, 1984), p. 395.

Byzantine classicism was a product of an educational system for the laity that extended to women as well as to men. In the Byzantine world of the ninth, tenth, and eleventh centuries, learned women were praised for being able to discourse like Plato or Pythagoras. But in addition to such literary figures there were also female physicians in the Byzantine empire, a fact of note given their scarcity in Western European society until recent times.

Byzantine achievements in architecture and art are more familiar. The finest example of Byzantine architecture was the church of Santa Sophia (Holy Wisdom) in Constantinople, constructed at enormous cost by the emperor Justinian in the sixth century. Although designed by architects of Hellenic descent, it was vastly different from any Greek temple. Its purpose was not to express pride in human accomplishment, but rather to symbolize the inward and spiritual character of the Christian religion. For this reason the architects gave little attention to the external appearance of the building. Nothing but plain brick covered with plaster was used for the exterior walls; there were no marble facings, graceful columns, or sculptured friezes. The interior, however, was decorated with richly colored mosaics, gold leaf, colored marble columns, and bits of tinted glass set on edge to refract the rays of sunlight after the fashion of sparkling gems. To emphasize a sense of the miraculous, the building was constructed in such a way that light appeared not to come from the outside at all, but to be generated within. So many windows are placed around its rim that the dome appears to have no support at all but to be suspended in midair.

BYZANTIUM AND THE WESTERN CHRISTIAN WORLD

After the Iconoclastic period relations between eastern and western Christians remained tense, partly because Constantinople resented Western claims (initiated by Charlemagne in 800) to rule a rival Roman empire, but most of all because religious differences between the

Santa Sophia. The greatest monument of Byzantine architecture. The four minarets were added after the fall of the Byzantine empire, when the Turks turned the church into a mosque.

two continued to grow. In 1054, papal claims to primacy over the eastern church provoked a religious schism that has never healed. Thereafter the Crusades drove home the dividing wedge.

After the sack of Constantinople in 1204 by crusaders, Byzantine hatred of westerners became intense. "Between us and them," one Byzantine wrote, "there is now a deep chasm: we do not have a single thought in common." Westerners called easterners "the dregs of the dregs . . . unworthy of the sun's light." Easterners called westerners the children of darkness, alluding to the fact that the sun sets in the west. The beneficiaries of this hatred were the Turks, who conquered Constantinople in 1453, and soon thereafter conquered most of southeastern Europe.

In view of this long history of hostility (which we will discuss more fully in the next chapter), it is best to end our treatment of Byzantine civilization here by recalling how much the western European world owes to it. The Byzantine empire acted as a bulwark against Islam from the seventh to the eleventh centuries, thus helping to preserve an independent and Christian West. Western Europeans also owe an enormous cultural debt to Byzantine scholars, who preserved much of the classical Greek literary tradition during centuries when these texts were entirely unknown in western Europe. Byzantine art has also exerted a profound influence on the art of western Europe. Saint Mark's Basilica in Venice reflects this influence; so too does the art of such great Western painters as Giotto and El Greco. Modern travelers who view Byzantine mosaics

in such cities as Ravenna and Palermo are awestruck; those who make their way to Istanbul still find Santa Sophia breathtaking. In such jeweled beauty, the light from the Byzantine empire continues to glow.

THE GROWTH OF ISLAM

How was Islam able to spread so rapidly?

Believers in Islam, known as Muslims, currently comprise about one-seventh of the global population: in their greatest concentrations they extend from Africa through the Middle East and the states of the former Soviet Union to South Asia and Indonesia. All Muslims subscribe to both a common religion and a common way of life, for Islam has always demanded from its followers not just adherence to common forms of worship but also adherence to certain social and cultural norms. Indeed, more than Judaism or Christianity, Islam has been a great experiment in trying to build a worldwide society based on the fullest harmony between religious requirements and precepts for everyday existence. In this section we will trace the early history of the Islamic experiment, with primary emphasis on its westward expansion. Nonetheless we must remember that Islam expanded in many directions and that it ultimately had as much influence on the history of Africa and South Asia as it did on that of Europe or western Asia.

THE RISE OF ISLAM

Islam was born in Arabia, a desert land so backward before the founding of Islam that the two dominant neighboring empires, the Roman and the Persian, had not even bothered to conquer it. In the second half of the sixth century the protracted wars between the Byzantine and Persian empires made Arabia a safer transit route than other alternatives for caravans passing between Africa and Asia. Some towns grew to direct and take advantage of this trade. The most prominent of these was Mecca, which not only lay on the junction of major trade routes, but also had long been a local religious center. In Mecca was located the Kabah, a pilgrimage shrine that served as a central place of worship for many different Arabian clans and tribes. The men who controlled this shrine belonged to the tribe of Quraish, an aristocracy of traders and entrepreneurs who provided the area with what little government it knew.

Muhammad, the founder of Islam, was born in Mecca to a family of Quraish about 570. Orphaned early in life, he entered the service of a rich widow whom he later married, thereby attaining financial security. Until middle age he lived as a prosperous trader little different from his fellow townsmen, but around 610 he underwent a religious experience that changed the course of his life and ultimately that of a good part of the world. Although most Arabs until then had been polytheists who recognized at most the vague superiority of a more powerful god they called Allah, Muhammad in 610 heard a voice from heaven tell him that there was no god but Allah alone. Thereafter he received further messages that commanded him to accept the calling of "Prophet" to proclaim the monotheistic faith to the Quraish. At first he was not very successful in gaining converts beyond a limited circle, perhaps because the leading Quraish tribesmen believed that a new religion would deprive the Kabah, and therewith Mecca, of its central place in local worship. The town of Yathrib to the north, however, had no such concerns, and its representatives invited Muhammad to emigrate there so that he could serve as a neutral arbiter of local rivalries. In 622 Muhammad and his followers accepted the invitation. Because their migration—called in Arabic the Hijrah (or Hegira)—saw the beginning of an advance in Muhammad's fortunes, Muslims regard it as marking the beginning of their era: as Christians begin their era with the birth of Christ, so Muslims begin their dating system with the Hijrah of 622.

Muhammad changed the name of Yathrib to Medina ("city of the Prophet") and quickly established himself as ruler of the town. In the course of doing this he consciously began to organize his converts into a political as well as a religious community. But he still needed to find some means of support for his original Meccan followers, and he also desired to wreak vengeance on the Quraish for not heeding his calls for conversion. Accordingly, he started leading his followers in raids on Quraish caravans traveling beyond Mecca. The Quraish endeavored to defend themselves, but after a few years Muhammad's band, fired by religious enthusiasm, succeeded in defeating them. In 630, after several desert battles, Muhammad entered Mecca in triumph. The Quraish thereupon submitted to the new faith and the Kabah was not only preserved but made the main shrine of Islam, as it remains today. After the capture of Mecca other tribes throughout Arabia in turn accepted the new faith. Thus, although Muhammad died in 632, he lived long enough to see the religion he had founded become a success.

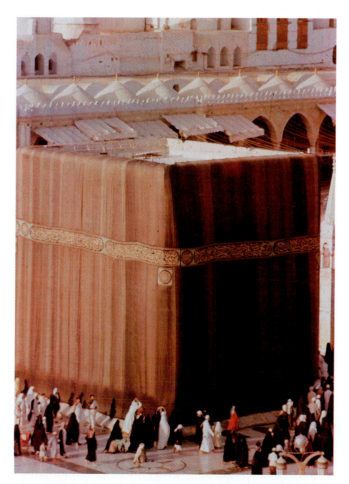

The Kabah. It contains the black stone which was supposed to have been miraculously sent down from heaven, and rests in the courtyard of the great mosque in Mecca.

Legend

- At the death of Muhammad, 632
- After the conquests of the first four caliphs, 661
- After the conquests of the Umayyad caliphs, 750
- - - Outer limits of the Byzantine Empire

THE EXPANSION OF ISLAM TO 750

This map shows the steady advance of Islam from the time of Muhammad to the middle of the eighth century. Note the rapid expansion in the generation after Muhammad's death. Which aspects of Islam's organization and fervor helped contribute to the spread of Muslim armies? What does the rapid advance suggest about the preparedness of their initial foes, such as Byzantium and Persia? Why were these foes not better able to resist? Why was the capture of Constantinople so crucial to successive Muslim rulers even after Islam had spread well beyond the eastern Mediterranean?

THE RELIGIOUS TEACHINGS OF ISLAM

The word *islam* means "submission," and the faith of Islam calls for absolute submission to Allah, the Creator, God Almighty—the same omnipotent deity worshiped by Christians and Jews. Instead of saying, then, that Muslims believe "there is no god but Allah," it is more correct to say they believe that "there is no divinity but God." In keeping with this strict monotheism, Muslims believe that Muhammad himself was God's last and greatest prophet, but not that he was God himself.

Men and women must surrender themselves entirely to God because divine judgment is imminent. Mortals must make a fundamental choice about whether to begin a new life of divine service: if they decide in favor of this, God will guide them to blessedness, but if they do not, God will turn away from them and they will become irredeemably wicked. The practical steps the believer can take are found in the Qur'ān, the compilation of the revelations sent by God to Muhammad, and hence the definitive Islamic scripture. These steps include thorough dedication to moral rectitude and compassion, and fidelity to set religious observances—a regimen of prayers and fasts, pilgrimage to Mecca, and frequent recitation of parts of the Qur'ān.

Islam resembles Judaism and Christianity in its strict monotheism, its emphasis on personal morality and compassion, and its reliance on written, revealed scripture. Although for Muslims the Qur'ān is the ultimate source of religious authority, Islam accepts both the Hebrew Bible and the Christian New Testament as divinely inspired. From Christianity Muhammad may also have derived his doctrines of the Last Judgment and the resurrection of the body with subsequent rewards and punishments, and his belief in angels. But although Muhammad regarded Jesus as one of the greatest of a long line of prophets, he did not believe in Christ's divinity. Nor did Muhammad claim to have performed any miracles himself other than the writing of the Qur'ān.

> Although for Muslims the Qur'ān is the ultimate source of religious authority, Islam accepts both the Hebrew Bible and the Christian New Testament as divinely inspired.

Islam is a religion without sacraments or priests. Instead of priests there are only religious scholars who comment on problems of Islamic faith and law, and who act as judges in disputes. Muslims are expected to pray together in mosques, but there is no such thing as a Muslim liturgy. The absence of clergy makes Islam more like Judaism, a similarity that is enhanced by Islamic stress on the inextricable connection between the religious, social, and political aspects of communal life. Unlike Judaism, however, Islam has historically aspired to unite the world into a single community of believers under the rule of Allah.

THE ISLAMIC CONQUESTS

Because the Arabs had no clear concept of political succession, it was unclear whether Muhammad's community would survive at all after his death. But his closest followers, led by his father-in-law, Abu-Bakr, and a zealous early convert named Umar, quickly took the initiative by naming Abu-Bakr *caliph*, meaning "deputy of the Prophet," and so the supreme religious and political leader of all Muslims. Immediately after becoming caliph Abu-Bakr began a military campaign to subdue various Arab tribes that had followed Muhammad but were not willing to accept his successor's authority. In the course of this successful military action Abu-Bakr's forces began to spill northward beyond the borders of Arabia, where they met only minimal resistance from Byzantine and Persian forces.

Abu-Bakr was succeeded as caliph by Umar, who continued to direct his armies against Byzantium and

Persia. In the following years Arab triumphs were virtually uninterrupted. In 636 the Arabs routed a Byzantine army in Syria and occupied Antioch, Damascus, and Jerusalem. In 637 they destroyed the main Persian army and marched into the Persian capital of Ctesiphon. By 651 the Arabian conquest of the entire Persian realm was complete. The Islamic forces now turned west toward North Africa, capturing Byzantine Egypt and extending their control throughout the rest of North Africa. Attempts in 677 and 717 to capture Constantinople failed; but in 711 the Arabs crossed from North Africa into Visigothic Spain and quickly took almost all of that area too. Thus within less than a century the forces of Islam had conquered all of ancient Persia and much of the late Roman world.

THE SHIITE-SUNNI SCHISM

While the Arabs were extending their conquests they ran into their first serious political divisions. In 644 the caliph Umar died; he was replaced by Uthman, a weak ruler who had the added drawback for many of belonging to the Umayyad family, a wealthy clan from Mecca that had not at first accepted Muhammad's call. Those dissatisfied with Uthman rallied around the Prophet's cousin and son-in-law Ali, whose blood, background, and warrior spirit made him seem a more appropriate leader of the cause. When Uthman was murdered in 656 by mutineers, Ali's partisans raised him up as caliph. But Uthman's powerful family and supporters were unwilling to accept Ali. In subsequent disturbances Ali was murdered and Uthman's party emerged triumphant. In 661 a member of the Umayyad family took over as caliph, and that house ruled the Islamic world until 750. Even then, however, Ali's followers did not accept defeat. As time went on they hardened into a minority religious party known as Shiites (*shi'a* is Arabic for "party" or "faction"); this group insisted that only descendants of Ali could be caliphs or have any authority over the Muslim community. Those who stood instead for the actual historical development of the caliphate and became committed to its customs were called Sunnis (*sunna* is Arabic for "religious custom"). The cleft between the two parties has been a lasting one in Islamic history. Often persecuted, Shiites developed great militancy and a

THE "PACT OF UMAR"

When the caliph Umar (d. 644) conquered the city of Jerusalem, he issued a charter of protection to the people of the city, defining the relationship that should exist in the future between the Muslim conquerors and their Christian subjects. In its surviving form, the "Pact of Umar" contains provisions that were probably not in Umar's original document. Nonetheless, the "Pact" does describe accurately the rules that governed Christians and Jews living under Muslin rule during the early middle ages.

This letter is addressed to Allah's servant Umar, the Commander of the Faithful, by the Christians of such-and-such city. When you advanced against us, we asked you for a guarantee of protection for our persons, our offspring, our property, and the people of our sect, and we have taken upon ourselves the following obligations toward you, namely:

We shall not build in our cities or in the vicinity any new monasteries, churches, hermitages, or monks' cells. We shall not restore . . . any of them that have fallen into ruin or which are located in the Muslims' quarters.

We shall keep our gates wide open for passersby and travelers. We shall provide three days' food and lodging to any Muslims who pass our way. . . .

We shall not teach our children the Koran.

We shall not hold public religious ceremonies. We shall not seek to proselytize anyone. We shall not prevent any of our kin from embracing Islam if they so desire.

We shall show deference to the Muslims and shall rise from our seats when they wish to sit down.

We shall not attempt to resemble the Muslims in any way. . . .

We shall not ride on saddles.

We shall not wear swords or bear weapons of any kind, or ever carry them with us. . . .

We shall not display our crosses or our books anywhere in the Muslims' thoroughfares or in their marketplaces. We shall only beat our clappers in our churches very quietly. We shall not raise our voices when reciting the service in our churches, nor when in the presence of Muslims. Neither shall we raise our voices in our funeral processions. . . .

We shall not build our homes higher than theirs. . . .

Norman A. Stillman, ed. and trans. *The Jews of Arab Lands: A History and Source Book.* (Philadelphia: Jewish Publication Society, 1979), pp. 157–58.

deep sense of being the only true preservers of the faith. From time to time they were able to seize power in one or another area, but they never succeeded in converting the majority of Muslims. Today they rule in Iran and are very numerous in Iraq but make up only about one tenth of the worldwide population of Islam.

UMAYYADS AND ABBASIDS

The triumph of the Umayyads in 661 began a more settled period in the history of the caliphate that would last until the tenth century. During these centuries there were two major governing orientations: the westward-looking one represented by the Umayyads, and the eastward-looking orientation of their successors, the Abbasids. The Umayyad capital was Damascus in the old Byzantine territory of Syria, and in many ways the Umayyad caliphate functioned as a Byzantine successor state, continuing even to employ formerly Byzantine bureaucrats. The Umayyads concentrated their energies on dominating the Mediterranean and conquering Constantinople. When their massive attack on the Byzantine capital failed in 717, Umayyad strength was seriously weakened.

A new perspective came with the takeover by a new family, the Abbasids, in 750. Their rule stressed Persian more than Byzantine elements. The Abbasid caliph built his new capital at Baghdad in Iraq, near the ruins of the old Persian city, and even appropriated stones from the ruins. The Abbasids developed their own Muslim administration and imitated Persian absolutism. Abbasid caliphs ruthlessly cut down their enemies, surrounded themselves with elaborate court ceremonies, and lavishly patronized sophisticated literature. This is the world described in the *Arabian Nights*, a collection of stories of dazzling splendor written in Baghdad under the Abbasids. The dominating presence in those stories, Harun al-Rashid, reigned as caliph from 786 to 809 and behaved as extravagantly as he was described, tossing coins in the streets, passing out sumptuous gifts to his favorites and severe punishments to his enemies.

The Umayyad rulers of Spain were equally lavish in their literary and cultural patronage. The caliph Al-Hakem II of Cordoba (961–976), for example, amassed a library of more than four hundred thousand volumes—the catalogue of titles alone ran to forty-four volumes—at a time when, in western Europe, a monastery with one hundred books qualified as a center of learning.

For the Christians of Byzantium and western Europe, the Abbasid caliphate was significant not only for its cultural achievements, but also because its eastern orientation took a certain amount of military pressure off the Mediterranean West. The Byzantine state, accordingly, was able to recover somewhat after a century of military pressure from the Umayyads. Farther

The Great Mosque of Córdoba, in Spain, was built in stages between 784 and 990. Its striped, horseshoe-shaped arches are characteristic features of Islamic architecture at this time. A Christian cathedral was later constructed within a small portion of this enormous building.

west, the Franks of Gaul also benefited from the advent of the Abbasids. Because an Umayyad dynasty continued to control Spain, the great Frankish ruler Charlemagne (768–814) maintained diplomatic and trade relations with the Abbasid caliphate of Harun al-Rashid against their common Umayyad enemy. The most famous symbol of this connection was the elephant that Harun al-Rashid sent to Charlemagne. More important, however, was the flow of silver that found its way from the Abbasid empire north through Russia and the Baltic and into the Rhineland in exchange for Frankish furs, slaves, wax, honey, and leather. Jewels, silks, spices, and other luxury goods from India and the Far East also flowed north and west into the Frankish world through the Abbasid empire. These trading links with the Abbasid world helped to fund the extraordinary cultural achievements of the Carolingian Renaissance which we will describe in the next section of this chapter.

THE CHANGING ISLAMIC WORLD

What forces combined to undermine the political unity of the Islamic empire?

During the ninth and tenth centuries, however, the power of the Abbasid dynasty rapidly declined. An extended period of decentralization followed that was mirrored during the eleventh century in Umayyad Spain. A major cause of the Abbasid collapse was the gradual impoverishment of their economic base—the agricultural wealth of the Tigris-Euphrates basin—resulting from ecological crises and a devastating revolt by the enslaved African work force that farmed the southern Iraqi marshlands. Tax revenues from the Abbasid empire were also declining, as provincial rulers in North Africa, Egypt, and Syria retained larger and larger portions of these revenues for themselves. As their revenues declined, the Abbasids found themselves unable to support either their large civil service or the new-style mercenary army they had built up. Massively expensive building projects, including the refoundation of the Abbasid capital of Baghdad, further exacerbated the fiscal, military, and political crisis.

Behind the Abbasid crisis lay two fundamental developments of great significance for the future of the Islamic world: the growth of regionalism and the in-

CHRONOLOGY

THE SPREAD OF ISLAM, 622–750

Expulsion of Muhammad from Mecca (Hijrah)	622
Muhammad returns to Mecca	630
Muhammad dies	632
Abu-Bakr becomes caliph	632
Umar becomes caliph	634
Arabs occupy Antioch, Damascus, Jerusalem	636
Arabs occupy Persian capital	637
Arabs invade Egypt	646
Arabs conquer Persian empire	651
Shiite-Sunni schism	661
Arabs conquer North Africa	646–711
Umayyad dynasty	661–750
Arabs invade Spain	711
Beginning of Abbasid dynasty	750

creasing religious divisions between Sunnis and Shiites and among the Shiites themselves. In 909 a local Shiite dynasty known as the Fatimids seized control of the Abbasid province of North Africa. In 969, the Fatimids succeeded in conquering Egypt also. Meanwhile, another Shiite group, rivals of both the Fatimids and the Abbasids, attacked Baghdad in 927 and Mecca in 930, seizing the Kabah. Thereafter, the effective power of the Abbasids over their empire collapsed entirely. In its place a new order began to emerge in the eastern Muslim world centered around an independent Egyptian kingdom and a new Muslim state based in Persia.

In Spain, Umayyad weakness was more directly a consequence of political failures and succession disputes than of economic collapse. Muslim Spain in the ninth and tenth centuries was an enormously wealthy agricultural and commercial region. But from the mid-ninth century on, renewed military pressure from the reviving Christian kingdoms of northern and eastern Spain exacerbated the internal political difficulties of the Umayyad caliphate. In the opening years of the eleventh century, the united Umayyad caliphate in Spain finally dissolved, to be replaced by a host of small-scale kingdoms, some of which were now paying tribute to the Christian rulers of the north. One by one, these local kingdoms gradually fell victim to the advancing forces of the Christian kings of Spain. Although the last Muslim kingdom, the

WHAT FORCES COMBINED TO UNDERMINE THE POLITICAL UNITY OF THE ISLAMIC EMPIRE?

THE CHANGING ISLAMIC WORLD   207

principality of Granada, would not fall to the Christians until 1492, the Christian reconquest of Spain was essentially complete by the middle of the thirteenth century.

Extravagance and incompetence by the Abbasid and Umayyad caliphs certainly played a role in their collapse. But there were larger factors at work in breaking up the unity of the Islamic world that transcended the failures of particular caliphs. Although Islamic society was religiously tolerant, at least with respect to Jews and Christians, ethnic tensions within the Islamic world were rampant and grew more divisive as the early idealism of the initial conquests faded with time. These ethnic tensions among Arabs, Turks, Berbers, sub-Saharan Africans, and Persians also complicated the deep regional divisions that had characterized this area of the world for centuries before the Islamic conquests began. Adding further to the political instability of the Muslim world was the uncompromising monotheism and religious egalitarianism of Islam itself. Muslim rulers (such as some of the Abbasids) who took on Persian styles of semidivine rulership were frequently murdered as blasphemers. Tensions between the universality of Islamic belief and the realities of regional particularism, ethnic hostility, and religious conflict between Sunnis and Shiites thus combined to undermine the political unity of the Islamic empire.

> Tensions between the universality of Islamic belief and the realities of regional particularism, ethnic hostility, and religious conflict between Sunnis and Shiites thus combined to undermine the political unity of the Islamic empire.

MUSLIM SOCIETY AND CULTURE, 900–1250

The political decentralization of the Muslim world did not automatically bring cultural decay, however. In fact, Islam's most creative cultural period was only beginning as the ninth century came to an end.

Islamic culture and society were extraordinarily cosmopolitan and dynamic. Islam inherited the sophistication of Byzantium and Persia; it remained centered at the crossroads of long-distance trade between the Far East and West; and the prosperous town life in most Muslim territories counterbalanced agriculture. Mu-hammad's teachings furthermore encouraged social mobility because the Qur'ān stressed the equality of all Muslims. The result was that at the courts of Baghdad and Córdoba, and later at those of the Muslim states that succeeded them, careers were open to those with talent. Since literacy was remarkably widespread—a rough esti-

mate for around the year 1000 is that 20 percent of all Muslim males could read the Arabic of the Qur'ān—many could rise through education. Offices were seldom regarded as hereditary, and "new men" could arrive at the top by enterprise and skill.

There was one major exception to this rule of Muslim egalitarianism: the treatment of women. The Qur'ān allowed a man to marry four wives, so women were at a premium, and married ones were segregated from other men. A wealthy man would also have a number of female servants and concubines, whom he kept in a part of his residence called the harem, where they were guarded by eunuchs, that is, castrated men. Although large harems could be kept only by the wealthy, the system was imitated as far as possible by all classes. Based on the principle that women were chattel property, these practices did much to debase women and to emphasize attitudes of domination in sexual life. Although male homosexual relations were tolerated in upper-class society, these relationships too were based on patterns of domination, usually of a powerful adult over an adolescent boy, much as they had been in the ancient Greek world.

Two major avenues were open to men wishing to devote themselves to Islamic religious life. One was that of the *ulama*, learned men whose job was to study and offer advice on all aspects of religion and religious law. Complementary to them were the *Sufis*, religious mystics who stressed contemplation and ecstasy as the ulama stressed religious law. Sufis were usually organized into "brotherhoods" that did much to convert outlying areas such as Africa and India. Throughout the Islamic world Sufism provided a channel for the most intense religious impulses. The ability of the ulama and the Sufis to coexist is testimony to the cultural pluralism of the Islamic world. But the absence of any avenues for religious women comparable with the convents of the Christian world is a reminder of the limits imposed by gender on that pluralism.

MUSLIM PHILOSOPHY, SCIENCE, AND MEDICINE

The two greatest influences on medieval Islamic philosophy were Aristotelianism and Neoplatonism. Muslim philosophers strove to reconcile these two quite different philosophical traditions with each

Aristotle Teaching Arab Astronomers, early thirteenth-century manuscript.
Greek philosophers, and particularly Aristotle, greatly influenced Islamic
philosophy and science.

other and with the tenets of Islamic theology. Reconciling Aristotelianism and Neoplatonism was in some ways the easier task. Reconciling Greek philosophy with Islamic theology was more difficult. Like Judaism and Christianity, Islam holds firmly to the view that a single omnipotent God created the world in time as an act of pure will, and that the world will continue to exist only for so long as God wills it to do so. Islamic theology also believes in the immortality of the individual human soul, another doctrine flatly in conflict with Aristotelian and Neoplatonic thought. There were also conflicts over predestination and free will. Although medieval Muslim theologians strongly emphasized the individual responsibility of believers to choose between good and evil, virtually all Muslims agreed that nothing good could occur unless God actively willed it. At times, such convictions could rise to a kind of fatalism wholly at odds with Greek philosophical presumptions.

Islamic philosophers took many different positions in response to these challenges. Al-Farabi (d. 950) used Aristotelian logic to support the conclusions of Muslim theology, but his Neoplatonic ideas led him into mystical positions at odds with mainstream theology. Al-Ghazzali (1058–1111), in contrast, was a much more thoroughgoing Aristotelian, who was able to resolve the conflicts between Aristotelian philosophy and Islamic theology only through a mystical conversion experience that led him finally to Sufism.

Al-Ghazzali's successor was the Spaniard Averroës (Ibn Rušd, 1126–1198). A thoroughgoing rationalist and the greatest Aristotelian scholar of his day, Averroës wrote a series of commentaries on the works of Aristotle that sought to purge them of all Neoplatonic influences. Translated from Arabic into Latin, these commentaries influenced the way all thirteenth-century Christian scholars, including Aquinas and Dante, read and understood Aristotle. Averroës was also an expert in Muslim law and theology and a physician, but he thoroughly subordinated theology to philosophy. Averroës considered both theology and philosophy to be true, but in different ways. Philosophical assertions were true in their literal meaning; theological statements, however, were often true only when interpreted allegorically or symbolically—and only philosophers were capable of determining which theological statements were literally true, because philosophers alone were the experts on literal meaning.

Such views did not sit well with the Islamic rulers of Spain. After burning several of Averroës' works, they exiled him to Morocco, where he died in 1198. His death marks a turning point in Islamic philosophy. Thereafter, philosophy tended either to blend into Sufistic mysticism, the direction taken by Al-Ghazzali, or else became too constrained by the demands of Islamic orthodoxy to lead an independent existence. But in its heyday between 900 and 1200, Islamic philosophy was far more advanced and sophisticated than anything found in Byzantium or Western Europe.

Islamic philosophers were often distinguished physicians and scientists also. Muslim observations of the heavens were so accurate, indeed, that some astronomers concluded that the earth must rotate on its axis and revolve around the sun, rather than remaining stationary with the sun and planets revolving around it. Islamic accomplishments in medicine were equally remarkable. Avicenna (Ibn Sinā, 980–1037) discovered the contagious nature of tuberculosis, described pleurisy and several varieties of nervous ail-

WHAT FORCES COMBINED TO UNDERMINE THE POLITICAL UNITY OF THE ISLAMIC EMPIRE?

THE CHANGING ISLAMIC WORLD   209

ments, and noted that diseases could spread through contaminated water and soil. His *Canon of Medicine* would remain an authoritative textbook in the Islamic world and in western Europe until the seventeenth century. Islamic scientists also made important advances in optics, chemistry, and mathematics. Islamic physicists studied the theory of magnifying lenses and the velocity, transmission, and refraction of light. Islamic mathematicians united the geometry of the Greeks with the number science of the Hindus. Utilizing what Westerners know as "Arabic numerals" (but which are in fact Hindu in origin), Muslim mathematicians developed a decimal arithmetic based on place values (the zero was critical to this). They also made fundamental advances in algebra and algorithms (both Arabic words). They also made great progress in spherical trigonometry. Muslim mathematicians thus brought together and pushed forward all the areas of mathematical knowledge that would be adopted and developed in Western Europe from the sixteenth century on.

LITERATURE AND ART

Poetry was a highly developed literary form in the Arab world even before the conversion to Islam. Thereafter, it quickly became a route to advancement at the Umayyad and Abbasid courts. The best known of these poets to Western European audiences is Umar Khayyam (d. 1123), whose *Rubiyat* was turned into a popular English poem by the Victorian Edward Fitzgerald. Although Fitzgerald's translation distorts much, the hedonism of Umar's poem ("a jug of wine, a loaf of bread—and thou") faithfully reflects a theme common to much Muslim poetry of the period.

Like Muslim philosophy and literature, Muslim art was highly eclectic. Its main influences came from Byzantium and Persia. Architecture was perhaps the most distinctive of the Islamic arts. Its characteristic elements (the dome, the column, and the arch) came initially from Byzantium, but were modified over time into a distinctive architectural style featuring bulbous domes, horseshoe arches, minarets, stone tracery, twisted columns, mosaics, and alternating strips of color. From Persia, Muslim artists drew the intricate, nonnaturalistic designs they used as decorative elements in all the arts, along with a taste (shared also by the Byzantines) for rich and sensuous color. Because Muslim theology regarded any artistic representation of Allah as idolatrous, a general prejudice developed against any portrayal of the human form in art. This

tended to inhibit the development of both painting and sculpture. Muslim artists did, however, produce gorgeous pile carpets and rugs, magnificent leather tooling, brocaded silks and tapestries, inlaid metalwork, enameled glassware, and painted pottery, all decorated with Arabic script, interlacing geometric designs, plants, fruits, flowers, and fantastic animal figures (another Persian influence). These complex designs can often seem strikingly modern, precisely because they are nonrepresentational and abstract.

TRADE AND INDUSTRY

Although the economy of seventh-century Arabia was relatively primitive, many of the territories conquered by Muhammad's followers were wealthy and highly urbanized. Syria, Egypt, and Persia in particular lay at the crossroads of the Mediterranean world, linking the major trade routes between Africa, Europe, India, and China. Conversion to Islam did not diminish their economic importance; if anything, it increased it, as their trading contacts grew in tandem with the growth of the Islamic world. By the tenth century, Muslim merchants had penetrated into southern Russia and equatorial Africa, and had become masters of the caravan routes that led eastward

Arabic Calligraphy. Muslim artists experimented with the art form of calligraphy to make complex, sometimes almost abstract designs. This ink on paper drawing of a bird from the seventh century also represents the Muslim mastery of papermaking.

to India and China. Ships from the Muslim world established new trade routes across the Indian Ocean, the Persian Gulf, and the Caspian Sea, and for a time dominated the Mediterranean world also. During the tenth and eleventh centuries, however, Western Christian merchants gradually took control over the Mediterranean sea routes; in the sixteenth century, they would extend that control into the Indian Ocean. Both these developments were serious blows to the economy of the Muslim world.

The growth of Muslim commerce in the early Middle Ages also reflects the development of a number of important industries. One product in particular deserves special mention, however, and that is paper. Muslims learned papermaking from the Chinese, but quickly became masters of the art. Paper was cheaper to produce, easier to store, and far easier to write on than papyrus or parchment. As a result, by the early eleventh century, paper had replaced papyrus even in Egypt, the heartland of papyrus production for almost four thousand years.

The ready availability of paper brought about a revolution in the Islamic world. Many of the characteristic features of Islamic civilization—bureaucratic record keeping, high levels of literacy and book production (especially copies of the Qur'ān), even the standard form of cursive Arabic script known as Kufic—would have been impossible without the widespread availability of paper. Only in the thirteenth century would Western Europeans master papermaking; when they did, however, they quickly began to undercut the market for Islamic paper. By the end of the fifteenth century, the Muslim world was importing almost all of its paper from Western Europe, despite the fact that the watermarks on European papers often contained Christian symbols offensive to Islam.

> Many of the characteristic features of Islamic civilization—bureaucratic record keeping, high levels of literacy and book production (especially copies of the Qur'ān), even the standard form of cursive Arabic script known as Kufic—would have been impossible without the widespread availability of paper.

THE IMPACT OF EARLY ISLAMIC CIVILIZATION ON EUROPE

In all the areas we have reviewed, Islamic civilization so overshadowed that of the Christian West until the twelfth century that there can be no comparison. When the West did move forward it was able to do so partly because of what it learned from Islam. In the economic sphere westerners absorbed many accomplishments of Islamic technology, such as irrigation techniques, the raising of new crops, papermaking, and the distilling of alcohol. Islamic economic influence is also reflected in the large number of common English words that were originally of Arabic or Persian origin. Among these are traffic, tariff, magazine, alcohol, muslin, orange, lemon, alfalfa, saffron, sugar, syrup, and musk. The word "admiral" also comes from Arabic—in this case deriving from the title of *emir*.

Western Europe was equally indebted to Islam in intellectual and scientific life. Here too, borrowed words tell some of the story: algebra, cipher, zero, nadir, amalgam, alembic, alchemy, alkali, soda, almanac, and names of many stars such as Aldebaran and Betelgeuse all derive from Arabic originals. Islamic civilization preserved and expanded Greek philosophical and scientific knowledge when such knowledge was almost entirely forgotten in the West. All the important Greek scientific works surviving from ancient times were translated into Arabic; during the twelfth and thirteenth centuries, most were in turn translated from Arabic into Latin through the combined efforts of Muslim, Jewish, and western Christian scholars. Above all, the preservation and interpretation of the works of Aristotle was one of Islam's most enduring accomplishments. About two-thirds of Aristotle's works were reacquired in the West by means of Latin translations from Arabic texts. Aristotle's ideas were also interpreted with Islamic help, above all that of Averroës, whose prestige was so great that he was simply called "the Commentator" by medieval Western writers. Arabic numerals, adopted from India by Muslim mathematicians, are another tremendously important intellectual legacy, as anyone will discover by trying to balance a checkbook with Roman ones.

Westerners in the high and late Middle Ages usually looked down on the Byzantine Greeks, but they respected and feared the Muslims. And they were right to do so, for Islamic civilization at its zenith (to use another Arabic word) was surely one of the world's greatest. Though loosely organized, it brought Arabs, Persians, Turks, Africans, and Indians together into a

WHAT CAUSED ECONOMIC AND SOCIAL CHANGE IN SEVENTH-CENTURY WESTERN EUROPE?

WESTERN CHRISTIAN CIVILIZATION IN THE EARLY MIDDLE AGES   211

common cultural and religious world, creating a diverse society and a splendid legacy of original discoveries and achievements.

WESTERN CHRISTIAN CIVILIZATION IN THE EARLY MIDDLE AGES

What caused economic and social change in seventh-century western Europe?

In western Europe, the seventh century marked the transition between the late antique and the early medieval worlds. At the end of the sixth century, the Frankish chronicler Gregory of Tours still saw himself as living in a discernibly Roman world of cities, trade, taxation, and local administration. Gregory was proud of his family's status as Roman senators, and took it for granted that he and his male relatives should be bishops who ruled, by right of birth and status, over their episcopal cities and the surrounding countryside. Like others of his class, Gregory still spoke and wrote Latin—a quite different Latin, to be sure, from the polished prose of Cicero six hundred years before, but a Latin that was nonetheless the same language, and that had certainly changed less since Cicero's day than English has changed since the time of Chaucer. Gregory was of course aware that the western Roman empire was now in the hands of Frankish, Visigothic, Ostrogothic, and Lombard kings. But he saw those kings as Romans nonetheless, because they ruled in accordance with Roman models and, in the case of the Franks, because they ruled with the approval of the Roman emperor in Constantinople. It was also a source of satisfaction to Gregory that in recent years, all these barbarian kings had converted to orthodox, Catholic Christianity. This too, for Gregory, reinforced their *romanitas* ("Roman-ness"), and thus lent legitimacy, both earthly and heavenly, to their rule.

Two hundred years later, however, when Charlemagne, the greatest of all the Frankish rulers, was crowned as the new Roman emperor in the West, the sense of direct continuity that Gregory of Tours had

> Charlemagne sought a *renovatio Romanorum imperii*—a renewal of the empire of the Romans—thus conceding in his very motto that he sought to revive an empire that had fallen.

had with the Roman world was gone. When Charlemagne set out to reform the cultural, religious, and political life of his empire, his goal was to revive a Roman empire from which he and his contemporaries now saw themselves as estranged. Charlemagne sought a *renovatio Romanorum imperii*—a renewal of the empire of the Romans—thus conceding in his very motto that he sought to revive an empire that had fallen. This awareness of a break with the Roman past developed during the seventh century. It marks the beginning of a new era in the history of western European civilization.

ECONOMIC DISINTEGRATION AND POLITICAL INSTABILITY

The Mediterranean world remained a reasonably well-integrated economic unit until the late sixth century. By 650, however, the economic unity of the Mediterranean world had broken down. This breakdown resulted partly from the destructiveness of Justinian's efforts to reconquer the western empire. Partly it was a consequence of ruinous Byzantine taxation of agricultural land. Piracy by Muslim raiders also played a role in undermining the economy of the seventh-century Mediterranean world—although Muslims quickly became important maritime traders, and in the long run Muslim conquests did more to reconstruct than to destroy the patterns of Mediterranean commerce.

For western Europe, however, the most important causes of these seventh-century economic changes were internal. The cities of Italy, Gaul, and Spain continued to decline. Agricultural land was passing out of cultivation, and the late Roman system of land taxes was also collapsing. The coinage systems of western Europe were also breaking down. From the 660s on, western European rulers shifted from a gold to a silver coinage. Europe would remain a silver-based economy for the next one thousand years.

During the seventh century, western Europe thus became a basically two-tier economy. Gold, silver, and luxury goods circulated among the wealthy, but the peasantry relied mainly on barter and various currency substitutes to facilitate their transactions. Lords collected rents from their peasants in foodstuffs but found it difficult to convert these payments of grain, wine, and meat into the weapons, jewelry, and silks that brought prestige in seventh-century aristocratic society. In a world in which the power of lords depended on their ability to give such high-prestige gifts to their military followers, the inability to convert peasant renders into cash was a serious handicap.

Another factor contributing to the instability of power in this world was the difficulty all the royal dynasties of the early Middle Ages experienced in trying to regulate the succession to their thrones. The kings who established themselves during the invasion period of the fifth and sixth centuries did not come from the traditional royal families of their peoples. Moreover, the barbarian armies who took over the western Roman empire during these years were rarely if ever composed of a single people anyway. They were usually made up of many different peoples, including a sizable number of disaffected Romans. Such unity as they possessed was largely the creation of the charismatic warrior-kings who led them, and this charisma was not easily passed on by inheritance.

Of all the barbarian groups that set up kingdoms in the western empire during the fifth and sixth centuries, only the Franks succeeded in establishing a single royal dynasty from which the future kings of the Franks would be drawn for the next two hundred fifty years. This dynasty was established by Clovis (d. 511), the great warrior-king of the Franks, who by converting to orthodox, Catholic Christianity also established an alliance between his dynasty and the powerful Roman bishops of Gaul. But the dynasty itself came to be known as the Merovingians, after Clovis's legendary grandfather Merovech, who was a sea dragon. We need not take this claim seriously; but it is, at the very least, a telling indication of how short was Clovis's known genealogy, that no one could be quite sure who his grandfather actually was.

Even in Gaul, however, the Merovingians were not the only noble family with a plausible claim to be kings; and in Visigothic Spain, Anglo-Saxon England, and Lombard Italy, the numbers of such rival royal families were even greater. In Visigothic Spain, the bloody succession disputes that resulted when a reigning king died so horrified the resident Roman population that they spoke of this inability to regulate the succession as a kind of a sickness: the *morbus Gothorum*, the "sickness of the Goths." In Gaul, the Franks were more successful in restricting claims to kingship to descendants of the Merovingian dynasty; but the Merovingians' custom of dividing the kingdom up into its constituent, regional parts, and installing a different king over each part, guaranteed plenty of civil strife in Merovingian Gaul also.

> During the seventh century, western Europe thus became a basically two-tier economy. Gold, silver, and luxury goods circulated among the wealthy, but the peasantry relied mainly on barter and various currency substitutes to facilitate their transactions.

MEROVINGIAN GAUL

The brutal conflicts between these rival Merovingian kings can easily obscure the real strength and sophistication of Merovingian governance. Many elements of late Roman local administration survived throughout the Merovingian period. Literacy remained an important element in Merovingian administration, providing a foundation on which the Carolingians would build. Even the cultural renaissance associated with the reign of Charlemagne really began in the late seventh century, with the production of deluxe biblical and other manuscripts at Merovingian monasteries.

Monasteries grew remarkably under the Merovingians, especially during the seventh century, reflecting the great wealth of the country. The Frankish bishoprics also prospered greatly under the Merovingians, amassing approximately three quarters of their total landed possessions by the end of the seventh century. This massive redistribution of wealth reflected a fundamental shift in the economic gravity of the Frankish kingdom. In the year 600, the wealth of Gaul was still concentrated in the south, where it had been throughout the late Roman period. By the year 750, however, the economic center of the kingdom lay north of the Loire, in the territories that extended from the Rhineland westward to the North Sea. It was here that most of the new monastic foundations of seventh-century Gaul were established.

MONASTICISM AND CONVERSION

Throughout Christian Europe, the seventh century witnessed a rapid increase in the foundation of monastic houses. Monasteries had existed in Gaul, Italy, and Spain since the fourth century, but most were located in the highly Romanized cities of southern Spain, Gaul, and northern Italy. Most of the new monastic foundations of the seventh century were deliberately located in rural areas, however, where they played an important role in the continuing struggle to Christianize the countryside. The most famous example of such monastic missionary activity is the conversion of Anglo-Saxon England. In northern England, the work of Christianization began in the late sixth century, led by missionary monks from Ireland. The decisive moment came in 597, however, when a group of forty Benedictine monks, sent by Pope Gregory I (590–604),

WHAT CAUSED ECONOMIC AND SOCIAL CHANGE IN SEVENTH-CENTURY WESTERN EUROPE?

WESTERN CHRISTIAN CIVILIZATION IN THE EARLY MIDDLE AGES   213

Book Cover. The cover of the Lindau Gospels, silver gilt encrusted with jewels.

the work of Saint Jerome, Saint Ambrose, and especially Saint Augustine of Hippo, in articulating a theology with distinctively Western elements. Among these were an emphasis on the necessity of penance for the forgiveness of sins, and the concept of purgatory as a place where the soul was purified before it was admitted into heaven. (Western belief in purgatory was thereafter to become one of the major differences in the teachings of the eastern and western churches.) Gregory emphasized the importance of pastoral care by bishops toward the laity, and popularized a powerful liturgical chant with unaccompanied vocal music that has become known as "Gregorian chant." All these innovations helped to make the Christian West religiously and culturally more independent of the Greek-speaking East than it had ever been before.

Gregory was also a statesman and ruler in the model of his Roman forebears. Within Italy he ensured the survival of the papacy against the barbarian Lombards by clever diplomacy and expert management of the papacy's estates and revenues. He maintained good relations with

brought the traditions of Roman Christianity to southeastern England. Despite some initial setbacks, by the end of the seventh century all of England had been brought firmly within the boundaries of the Roman, Christian world, and English monks had begun their own missionary campaigns in Frisia and Saxony. Frankish missionaries were also active in these areas. But it was the particular loyalty the English monks felt toward the papacy that was to have the most momentous consequences, not only for the papacy, but also for Gaul.

THE REIGN OF POPE GREGORY I

The architect of this new alliance between the Roman papacy and Benedictine monasticism was Pope Gregory I, known as Saint Gregory the Great. Until his time the Roman popes were generally subordinate to the emperors in Constantinople. Byzantine power in Italy was declining, however, and although Gregory worked hard to prevent a breach with Constantinople, he also sought to create a more autonomous, Western-oriented Latin Church. As a theologian—the fourth great "Latin Father" of the church—he built on

Pope Gregory the Great. In this tenth-century German ivory panel the pope is receiving inspiration from the Holy Spirit in the form of a dove.

Byzantium while asserting his authority as pope over the other bishops of the Western church. Above all, he patronized the order of Benedictine monks. Gregory's patronage helped the Rule of Saint Benedict become the predominant monastic rule in the West; through his encouragement, Benedictine monks emerged as the most important missionary group of the early Middle Ages. Their missionary work in Frisia and Germany brought both regions into the western Catholic Church, and laid the groundwork for an alliance between the papacy and the Frankish monarchy that would transform early medieval Europe.

THE RISE OF THE CAROLINGIANS

How did Charlemagne redefine the relationship between Christianity and kingship?

In Gaul, the weaknesses of the Merovingian dynasty were becoming steadily more apparent as the seventh century drew to a close. Tensions between noble families in the Merovingian heartland of Neustria and those in the border region of Austrasia were increasing. The Austrasian nobles had profited from their steady push into the areas east of the Rhine, acquiring wealth and

CHRONOLOGY

THE RISE OF THE CAROLINGIAN EMPIRE, 717–814

Charles Martel becomes mayor of the palace	717
The Carolingians (Charles, Pepin, and Carloman) share power with the Merovingian kings	717–751
Pepin becomes king of the Franks	751
Charlemagne succeeds Pepin	768
Charlemagne is crowned Holy Roman emperor	800
Louis the Pious becomes emperor	813
Charlemagne dies	814

military power in the process. The Merovingians, based in Neustria, had no such easy conquests at their disposal. Moreover, a considerable portion of the land they did hold had been given to the church in the course of the seventh century. A succession of short-lived Merovingian kings complicated matters further, producing a series of civil wars between Austrasians and Neustrians. Briefly, in 687, the leader of the Austrasian nobility, Pepin of Heristal, succeeded in forcing his way into office as "mayor of the palace," seeking thereby to control both Austrasia and Neustria. But not until 717, when Pepin's illegitimate son Charles Martel ("the Hammer") finally triumphed over his opponents in both territories, was Pepin's family secure in its control over the Merovingian court. Thereafter, however, the Merovingian kings were largely figureheads in a kingdom ruled by Charles Martel and his sons.

Charles Martel is sometimes considered the second founder (after Clovis) of the Frankish state. His claim to this title is twofold. First, in 733 or 734 (the traditional date of 732 is erroneous), he turned back a Muslim force from Spain at the battle of Tours (not Poitiers), some one hundred fifty miles from the Merovingian capital of Paris. Although the Muslim contingent was a raiding party rather than a full-scale army, the incursion was nonetheless the high-water mark of Umayyad progress toward northwestern Europe, and Charles's victory won him great prestige. Equally important, Charles began to develop an alliance with the English Benedictine missionaries who were attempting to convert Frisia and central Germany to Christianity. Charles's family had long been active in the drive to conquer and settle these areas, and he understood clearly how missionary work and Frankish expansion could go hand in hand. Charles assisted Saint Boniface and his followers in their conversion efforts. In return, the English Benedictines brought Martel and his descendants into contact with the papacy and assisted him in his efforts to reform (and so control) the Frankish church.

Charles Martel died in 741. Although Charles never sought to become king himself, during the last years of his life he was so clearly the effective ruler of Gaul that he did not even bother to arrange for a new king to be selected when, in 737, the reigning Merovingian king died. In 743, however, Martel's sons, Carloman and Pepin, bowed to the forces of legitimism, and a new Merovingian king took the throne. By 750, however, Pepin had decided to seize the throne for himself. To effect such a change in dynasties, Pepin needed papal approval. This did not deter Pepin. Through his family's support for Saint

HOW DID CHARLEMAGNE REDEFINE THE RELATIONSHIP BETWEEN CHRISTIANITY AND KINGSHIP?

THE RISE OF THE CAROLINGIANS   215

Boniface, Pepin was already well regarded in Rome. And the papacy, locked in a bitter fight with the Byzantine emperors over Iconoclasm and with the Lombard kings for control over central Italy, proved only too happy to cooperate in Pepin's elevation, hoping that a powerful new Frankish ruler would take over from the Byzantines the responsibility for protecting papal interests in Italy against the Lombards.

In 751 Saint Boniface, acting as papal emissary, anointed Pepin as king of the Franks. The last Merovingian king was deposed and sent to a monastery, and a new king, who had not a drop of Merovingian blood, was raised to the Frankish throne for the first time in almost three centuries. Pepin's coronation symbolized the integration of the new Frankish monarchy into the papal-Benedictine orbit. For the moment, however, Pepin had his hands full simply trying to control his new kingdom.

THE REIGN OF CHARLEMAGNE

The real consolidation of this new pattern of papal-Frankish-Benedictine relations took place during the reign of Pepin's son, Charlemagne, from whom the new dynasty takes its name of Carolingian (from "Carolus," the Latin form of "Charles"). When Charlemagne came to the throne in 768, it seemed possible that the Frankish kingdom would break up into its hostile regional parts of Austrasia, Neustria, and Aquitaine. But in an astonishing series of military campaigns, Charlemagne united the Franks by leading them on a series of conquests that annexed the Lombard kingdom of Italy, the greater part of Germany including Saxony, portions of central Europe, and Catalunya. These conquests set a seal of divine approval on the new Carolingian dynasty. They also provided the plunder, booty, and new lands that enabled Charlemagne to promote his Frankish followers to dizzying heights of wealth and grandeur.

To rule the vast empire he had conquered, Charlemagne appointed Frankish aristocrats called counts (in Latin, *comites*, meaning "followers") to supervise local administration within their territories. Among the counts' many duties were the administration of justice and the raising of armies. Charlemagne also established a network of other local administrators to supervise courts, collect tolls, administer crown lands, and extract taxation. Charlemagne also created a new coinage system, based on a division of the silver pound into two hundred forty pennies, which would last in France until the French Revolution and in Great

Pepin and Charlemagne Giving Edicts to a Clerk. Cementing the papal-Frankish–Benedictine commitment, Charlemagne's reign outshone that of his father, Pepin.

Britain until the 1970s, when it was finally replaced by a decimal-based currency.

Like Carolingian administration generally, this new monetary system depended on the regular use of written records and instructions. But Charlemagne did not rely on the written word alone to make his will felt. Periodically he sent special representatives from his court (known as *missi*) on tours through the countryside to relay his instructions personally and check up on local administrators. Charlemagne's governmental system was far from perfect. Local officials abused their positions; nobles sought to turn free peasants into unfree serfs; justice in local courts was more often denied than done. But Charlemagne's system produced nonetheless the best government Europe had seen since the Romans, and it became the model on which Western rulers would base their own administrations for the next three hundred years.

Charlemagne. A silver penny struck between 804 and 814 in Mainz (as indicated by the letter M at the bottom) showing Charlemagne in a highly stylized fashion as emperor with Roman military cloak and laurel wreath. The inscription reads KAROLVS IMP AVG (Charles, Emperor, Augustus). Charlemagne's portrait is closely modeled on the imperial portraits on Hellenistic and Roman coins.

CHRISTIANITY AND KINGSHIP

Throughout his reign, Charlemagne took seriously his responsibilities as a Christian king. As his empire expanded, however, he came to see himself not only as the ruler of the Franks, but as the leader of a unified Christian society, Christendom, which he was obliged to defend both militarily and spiritually against its enemies. The Carolingian world did not make the distinctions between the religious and the political realms that would characterize European life from the twelfth century on, any more than did Byzantium or Islam. Especially among churchmen, kingship in early medieval Europe was regarded as a sacred office created by God to protect the church, defend the Christian people, and promote their salvation. Religious reforms were therefore no less central to proper kingship than were justice and defense. In some ways, indeed, a king's responsibilities for his kingdom's religious life were even more important than his other responsibilities: for surely no kingdom could prosper if the lives of its subjects were displeasing to God.

These ideas about the spiritual responsibilities of kingship were not new in the late eighth century, but they took on a new importance as a result of the ex-

traordinary power Charlemagne wielded over his empire. Like other early medieval kings, Charlemagne appointed and deposed bishops and abbots, just as he did his counts and other officials. But he also changed the liturgy of the Frankish church, reformed rules of worship in Frankish monasteries, declared changes in basic statements of Christian belief, prohibited pagan observances, and imposed basic Christian observances, including baptism, on the conquered peoples of Saxony. To Charlemagne, such measures were clearly required if God's new Israel, the Franks, were to avoid the fate that befell biblical Israel whenever its people turned away from their obedience to God.

THE CAROLINGIAN RENAISSANCE

Similar ideals lay behind the Carolingian Renaissance, a cultural and intellectual flowering that took place around the Carolingian royal court. Like their biblical exemplars, the Hebrew kings David and Solomon, Charlemagne and Louis the Pious took seriously their role as patrons of poetry and learning. In so doing, they created an ideal of the court as an intellectual and cultural center that would profoundly influence Western European cultural life until the end of the nineteenth century. What lay behind the Carolingians' support for scholarship, however, was their conviction that classical learning was the foundation on which Christian wisdom rested, and that such wisdom was essential to the salvation of God's people. Supporting scholarship was therefore a paramount obligation for a Christian king.

To promote classical learning and Christian wisdom, Charlemagne recruited scholars from throughout Europe to his court. Carolingian scholars produced a good deal of original Latin poetry and an impressive number of theological and pastoral tracts. However, their primary efforts were devoted to collating, correcting, and recopying classical Latin texts, including the text of the Latin Bible, which had become corrupted by generations of copyists' mistakes. They also developed a new style of handwriting, with simplified letter forms and spaces inserted between words, that further reduced the likelihood that subsequent copyists would misread the corrected texts. This new style of handwriting, known as Carolingian minuscule, is the foundation for the typefaces in which almost all European books, including this one, are still printed.

HOW DID CHARLEMAGNE REDEFINE THE RELATIONSHIP BETWEEN CHRISTIANITY AND KINGSHIP?

THE RISE OF THE CAROLINGIANS 217

Carolingian Handwriting.
Even the untrained reader has little difficulty in reading this excerpt from a Carolingian manuscript. For example, the first two words in the heading read "Incipit Liber," and the two words below them "Haec Hannibal."

CHARLEMAGNE AND THE REVIVAL OF THE WESTERN ROMAN EMPIRE

The climax of Charlemagne's career came in Rome on Christmas Day 800, when he was crowned as the new Roman emperor in the West by Pope Leo III. Centuries later, popes would cite their role in this event as precedent for the political superiority they claimed over the Holy Roman emperor (a title that became common only in the twelfth century, but that can be used for convenience to designate the Western emperors from Charlemagne on). In the year 800, however, Pope Leo was entirely under Charlemagne's thumb. Although Charlemagne said later that he would never have gone to church that day had he known Leo's plans to crown him, it is highly unlikely Pope Leo would have mounted such a ceremony without Charlemagne's consent, not least because it was certain to anger the Byzantines, with whom Charlemagne already had strained relations. Nor did the imperial title add much to Charlemagne's position as king of the Franks. Why, then, did he accept it, and in 813 transfer it to his son, Louis the Pious?

Historians do not know. What is clear, however, is the symbolic significance of the action. Until 800 only the Roman emperor who ruled in Constantinople could lay claim to being the direct heir of Caesar Augustus. Although the Byzantines had lost most of their influence in the West, they continued to regard it vaguely as an outlying province of their empire. Charlemagne's assumption of the imperial title was a clear slap in the face to the Byzantines. In the West, however, it was a declaration of self-confidence and independence that was never forgotten. Whatever his specific motives may have been, Charlemagne's revival of the western Roman empire proved to be a major step in the developing self-consciousness of western European civilization.

THE COLLAPSE OF THE CAROLINGIAN EMPIRE

When Charlemagne died in 814, his empire descended intact to his only surviving son, Louis the Pious. Under Louis, however, the empire rapidly began to disintegrate. When Louis died in 843, the empire was divided between his three sons. Western Francia, which became France, went to Charles the Bald; Eastern Francia, which became Germany, went to Louis the German; and the so-called Middle Kingdom, stretching from the Rhineland to Rome, went to Lothair, along with the imperial title. When Lothair's line died out in 856, a civil war erupted between the East Franks and the West Franks for control over Lothair's former territories and

CHARLEMAGNE ON THE IMPORTANCE OF MONKS' STUDYING CLASSICAL LITERATURE

To Charlemagne and his contemporaries, a Christian king bore total responsibility for the salvation of his people. To this end, Charlemagne believed it essential to encourage the study of both classical and Christian literature within his kingdom. Copies of this letter were probably sent to most of the monasteries in the Frankish kingdom.

We, Charles, by the grace of God king of the Franks and Lombards and patrician of the Romans, to Abbot Baugulf and all your congregation. . . . Be it known to your devotion . . . that we, along with our faithful advisers, have deemed it useful that the bishoprics and monasteries, which through the favor of Christ have been entrusted to us to govern should, in addition to the way of life prescribed by their rule and their practice of holy religion, devote their efforts to the study of literature and to the teaching of it . . . so . . . that those who seek to please God by living aright may not fail to please him also by rightness in their speaking. . . . For . . . letters have often been sent to us in these last years from certain monasteries . . . and we found that in most of these writings their sentiments were sound but their speech uncouth. . . . And so . . . we began to fear that their lack of knowledge of writing might be matched by a more serious lack of wisdom in the understanding of holy scripture. We all know well that, dangerous as are the errors of words, yet much more dangerous are the errors of doctrine. Wherefore we urge you, not merely to avoid the neglect of the study of literature, but . . . to strive to learn it, so that you may be able more easily and more rightly to penetrate the mysteries of the holy scriptures. For since there are figures of speech, metaphors and the like to be found on the sacred pages, there can be no doubt that each man who reads them will understand their spiritual meaning more quickly if he is first of all given full instruction in the study of literature. . . . For we want you, as befits the soldiers of the Church, to be inwardly devout and outwardly learned, pure in good living and scholarly in speech; so that whoever comes to see you in the name of God and for the inspiration of your holy converse, just as he is strengthened by the sight of you, so he may be instructed also by your wisdom, both in reading and chanting, and return rejoicing, giving thanks to Almighty God.

H. R. Loyn and J. Percival, eds. *The Reign of Charlemagne.* Documents of Medieval History 2. (London: Edward Arnold, 1975), pp. 63–64.

HOW DID CHARLEMAGNE REDEFINE THE RELATIONSHIP BETWEEN CHRISTIANITY AND KINGSHIP?

THE RISE OF THE CAROLINGIANS   219

the imperial mantle. Lotharingia (or, in French, Alsace-Lorraine) would remain a flashpoint for hostilities between France and Germany until the end of the Second World War.

Louis was not an incompetent ruler, but he faced an almost impossible task in trying to hold together the empire his father had created. Charlemagne's empire had been built on successful conquest. By 814, however, Charlemagne had pushed the borders of his empire as far as they could reasonably go. The pressures that had driven the Frankish conquests, however—the need for booty, land, and plunder with which to reward and promote one's followers—had become even more pronounced as a result of Charlemagne's successes. Under Charlemagne, the number of counts in the Frankish empire had tripled, from approximately one hundred to three hundred. Louis the Pious could not possibly turn three hundred counts into nine hundred. The resources to do so simply did not exist.

> The increasing prosperity of the country, largely a product of the wool trade, also brought increasing power to the monarchy. By the year 1000, Anglo-Saxon England had become the most administratively sophisticated state in western Christian Europe.

Frustrated by their emperor's inability to reward them, Frankish nobles turned on each other. Civil wars erupted among Louis's quarrelsome and difficult sons; regional hostilities between Austrasians, Neustrians, and Aquitanians flared up again. As central imperial authority broke down, free peasants, a critical group in the eighth-century Carolingian world, found themselves increasingly under the thumb of powerful local nobles who treated them as if they were unfree serfs, bound to the soil and forbidden to leave it. At the same time, internal troubles in the Abbasid empire caused a breakdown in the foreign trade routes through which Viking traders brought Abbasid silver into Carolingian domains. The Vikings then turned to destructive raiding along the coasts and up the river systems. Under these combined pressures the Carolingian empire fell apart completely, and a new political map of Europe began to emerge.

THE LEGACY OF THE CAROLINGIANS

Just as the Carolingian period was crucial for marking the beginnings of a common western European civilization, so the tenth century was crucial for marking the beginnings of the major modern European political entities. England, which hitherto had been divided among smaller warring Anglo-Saxon states, became

unified in the late ninth and the tenth century owing to the work of King Alfred the Great (871–899) and his successors. Alfred and his heirs reorganized the army, infused new vigor into local government, founded new towns, and codified English laws. In addition, Alfred established a court school and fostered an interest in Anglo-Saxon writing and other elements of a national culture. In all these respects, Alfred modeled himself closely on Carolingian example. His success in defending his own West Saxon kingdom from Viking attacks, combined with the destruction of every other competing Anglo-Saxon royal dynasty by the Vikings, allowed Alfred and his successors to claim for themselves the mantle of a single, united English monarchy. The increasing prosperity of the country, largely a product of the wool trade, also brought increasing power to the monarchy. By the year 1000, Anglo-Saxon England had become the most administratively sophisticated state in western Christian Europe.

On the Continent, the most powerful monarchs of the tenth century were the dukes of Saxony, who became kings of Germany (East Francia) in 917, after the Carolingian line of kings expired. Like the West Saxon kings of England, the Saxon kings of Germany modeled their kingship closely on Carolingian example. In Germany, however, royal power in the tenth century rested much more on the profits of successful conquest than it did on trade and administration. In the eighth century, the Carolingians had built their power on successful conquests in Saxony. In the tenth century, the Ottonian kings of Germany, based in Saxony, built their authority on successful conquests into the Slavic lands that lay on their "soft" eastern frontier. They were also careful to nurture their image as Christian kings on the Carolingian model. In 955, Otto I defeated the pagan Hungarians in a decisive battle while carrying a sacred lance that had once belonged to Charlemagne. This victory established Otto as the dominant power in central Europe and as a man worthy to inherit Charlemagne's imperial throne. In 962 Otto went to Rome to be crowned western emperor by the pope, a thoroughly dissolute young man named John XII, who hoped to use Otto in his own factional squabbles in Rome. Otto, however, refused to go home when Pope John had no further use for him. Scandalized by John's behavior as

The Division of the Carolingian Empire under Charlemagne's Grandsons

TO LOUIS (WEST FRANCIA)

TO CHARLES (WEST FRANCIA)

TO LOTHAR

The empire of Charlemagne, 814
Tributary peoples
Byzantine empire

THE EMPIRE OF CHARLEMAGNE, 814

By 814, Charlemagne had created an empire that embraced most of the territory of the former western Roman empire. Could he legitimately claim to be renewing the Roman empire? How did his possession of Rome strengthen such a claim? How might it complicate his family's traditional alliance with the papacy? Note the inset in the upper left. What forces led to the division of Charlemagne's empire along these particular borders?

pope, Otto instead deposed John and selected a new pope to replace him.

By becoming emperor, Otto hoped to strengthen his control over the church in Germany and to claim a variety of dormant but potentially lucrative imperial rights in northern Italy and Burgundy, parts of the "Middle Kingdom" once held by the emperor Lothair. Protecting the papacy was, of course, Otto's responsibility as a Carolingian-style emperor, but Otto also needed papal support to achieve these other, more concrete objectives. In Italy, however, Otto quickly discovered that unless he was prepared to remain in Rome full time, he could not even control the papacy,

much less the rapidly growing and highly independent towns of northern Italy. If he remained in Italy too long, however, his authority in Saxony would break down, as local lords began to lead and profit from the continuing conquests in the Slavic east. Balancing their local concerns in Saxony with their imperial concerns in Italy presented a dilemma neither Otto I nor his son (Otto II, 973–983) nor his grandson (Otto III, 983–1002) was able to solve. The result was a gradually increasing alienation of the Saxon nobility from their emperor. This alienation accelerated dramatically after 1024, when the German throne passed to a new dynasty, the Salians, centered not in Saxony but in

HOW DID CHARLEMAGNE REDEFINE THE RELATIONSHIP BETWEEN CHRISTIANITY AND KINGSHIP?

THE RISE OF THE CAROLINGIANS   221

EUROPE IN THE ELEVENTH CENTURY

This map shows the alignment of geopolitical power that had emerged by 1050. Based on this map, which political entities would you expect to dominate the twelfth-century European world? Why? Consider the geographical position of Kievan Russia. What influences pulled it toward the West? In what respects was it isolated from the West?

Franconia. It was not until the 1070s that the Salian king Henry IV finally attempted to reassert his control over the formerly royal lands in Saxony and the Slavic east. When he did so, he touched off a civil war between himself and the Saxon nobility that was to have momentous repercussions not only for Germany, but for the entirety of western Europe. The consequences of this great Saxon war are discussed more fully in Chapter Nine.

The tenth century also witnessed a remarkable growth of towns and cities in western Europe, particularly in areas where rulers patterned themselves on Carolingian example. In Anglo-Saxon England, the West Saxon kings established new towns and encouraged existing ones. By 1066, when England fell to the invading Normans, at least 10 percent of the English population lived in towns, making it the most highly urbanized country in eleventh-century Europe. Cities also grew rapidly in the Low Countries and the Rhineland, fueled by long-distance trade (especially in wool and wool cloth) and by the discovery of silver deposits in the mountains of Saxony. In Catalunya, the growth of Barcelona was beginning to transform the political and social life of the country; while in Aquitaine, both Poitiers and Toulouse prospered from their location along the overland trade route that connected Mediterranean with Atlantic Europe.

In tenth- and eleventh-century Italy, however, urban growth occurred in the absence of an effective Carolingian-style ruler. Instead, the prosperity of tenth-century Italian cities depended on the success of the Byzantine emperors in suppressing Muslim piracy in the eastern Mediterranean. The most prosperous cities in tenth-century Italy lay in the Byzantine-controlled areas of the peninsula: Venice in the north, Amalfi, Naples, and Palermo in the south. Their prosperity rested upon their role in the trade that brought silks, spices, and other luxury goods from the Byzantine and Muslim worlds into western Europe. In the eleventh century, however, Norman invasions of southern Italy disrupted this trade, as Turkish invasions of Asia Minor turned Byzantine attentions eastward. By the end of the eleventh century, it would be the north Italian cities whose navies controlled the eastern Mediterranean, and which would profit from their role as middlemen in the lucrative traffic between Byzantium, the Muslim world, and western Europe.

On the Carolingian heartland, however, these developments had little influence. Here, Carolingian-style kingship disintegrated during the tenth century under the combined weight of Viking raids, economic collapse, and the growing power of local lords. In some areas, a few Carolingian institutions, such as public courts and a centrally minted coinage, survived in the hands of counts and dukes who utilized them in building up new, essentially autonomous territorial principalities such as Anjou, Normandy, Flanders, and Aquitaine. Elsewhere in France, even this modicum of continuity with the Carolingian world disappeared. France still had a king who continued to be recognized as the ruler of the western part of Charlemagne's former territories. After 987, however, the kings of France were no longer Carolingians. Instead, a new dynasty, the Capetians, had taken the throne, after having established their reputation as counts of Paris by defending that city against the Vikings. But it would be another century before the Capetian kings of France could reverse the trends that had destroyed their predecessors, and begin to rebuild monarchical power in France on new foundations.

Conclusion

This spectacle of Carolingian collapse may suggest that little had changed in western Europe between 750 and 1000. Any such impression would, however, be seriously misleading. It is certainly true that compared with Byzantium or the Muslim world, western Europe remained an intellectual and cultural backwater, more so perhaps by the year 1000 than it had been two centuries before. Politically, no western European ruler in the year 1000 could approach the power of the Byzantine emperor or the Umayyad caliph of Córdoba. Economically also, western Europe was a dependency of Byzantium and Islam, importing finished and luxury goods, and exporting furs, leather, and slaves. Beneath the surface, however, western European society was becoming steadily more formidable. Urbanization was proceeding rapidly on the margins of the collapsing Carolingian world. Long-distance trade was growing and Europe's borders were expanding. By the year 1000, its boundaries extended from the Baltic to the Mediterranean Sea, and from the Pyrenees to Poland. Within this vast territory, moreover, every ruler was, or would soon be, Christian. The Christian church was as yet highly localized, but the emergence of new confederations of reformed Benedictine monasteries under papal protection (to be discussed in more detail in Chapter Nine) was beginning to point the way toward a more unified and centralized Latin Christian church. Political omens were less promising. But out of the chaos of tenth-century western Europe, effective territorial principalities and kingdoms were beginning to emerge. During the early Middle Ages, Europe had become a society mobilized for war to a degree unmatched in either Byzantium or Islam. This was, to be sure, a mixed blessing. In the centuries to come, however, the militarization of western European society was to prove a decisive factor in the steadily shifting balance of power between Europe, Byzantium, and the Muslim world.

KEY TERMS

Santa Sophia	Qur'ān	Pope Gregory I
Muhammad	Shiites	Charlemagne
Mecca	Sunnis	Holy Roman empire

SELECTED READINGS

Bede. *A History of the English Church and People.* Translated by Leo Sherley-Price. Baltimore, 1955. A fascinating account by the greatest historian of eighth-century Europe.

Saint Boniface. *Letters of Saint Boniface.* Translated by Ephraim Emerton. New York, 1972.

Campbell, James, ed. *The Anglo-Saxons.* Oxford, 1982. The best and most interesting treatment of its subject, splendidly illustrated.

Collins, Roger. *Early Medieval Europe, 300–1000.* 2d ed. New York, 1999. Dry and detailed, but a useful textbook nonetheless.

Einhard and Notker the Stammerer. *Two Lives of Charlemagne.* Translated by Lewis Thorpe. Baltimore, 1969. Lively and entertaining.

Geanakoplos, Deno John, ed. *Byzantium: Church, Society and Civilization Seen through Contemporary Eyes.* Chicago, 1984. An outstanding source book, with a great deal of fresh material.

Geary, Patrick J. *Before France and Germany: The Origins and Transformation of the Merovingian World.* New York, 1988. Accessible introduction to recent scholarship, much of it otherwise unavailable in English.

Gregory of Tours. *History of the Franks.* Translated by Lewis Thorpe. Baltimore, 1974. Difficult to follow, but by far the most revealing single source on Merovingian kingship.

Herrin, Judith. *The Formation of Christendom.* Princeton, 1987. A synthetic history of the Christian civilizations of Byzantium and western Europe from 500 to 800, written by a prominent Byzantinist.

Hodges, Richard, and David Whitehouse. *Mohammed, Charlemagne and the Origins of Europe.* London, 1983. An analysis and recasting of the "Pirenne thesis," which claimed (wrongly, as this book shows) that the advent of Islam disrupted the economic unity of the Mediterranean world.

Hourani, Albert. *A History of the Arab Peoples.* New York, 1992. A sympathetic, clear, and intelligent survey written for non-specialists.

Kazhdan, Alexander P., ed. *The Oxford Dictionary of Byzantium.* 3 volumes. Oxford, 1991. An authoritative reference work.

Kennedy, Hugh. *The Early Abbasid Caliphate: A Political History.* Totowa, N.J., 1981. A standard account.

———. *The Prophet and the Age of the Caliphates.* London, 1986. A lucid introduction to the political history of Islam from the sixth through the eleventh centuries.

Leyser, Karl. *Rule and Conflict in an Early Medieval Society: Ottonian Saxony.* Oxford, 1979. A concise, challenging, brilliant account of the dynamics of rule in tenth-century Saxony, that pays special attention to the importance of royal women.

McKitterick, Rosamond. *The Frankish Kingdoms Under the Carolingians, 751–987.* New York, 1983. An authoritative account of politics and intellectual developments.

———, ed. *The Uses of Literacy in Early Medieval Europe.* New York, 1990. A superb collection of essays representing some of the freshest recent thinking on this subject.

Reuter, Timothy. *Germany in the Early Middle Ages, 800–1056.* New York, 1991. The best and most up-to-date survey in English.

Sawyer, Peter, ed. *The Oxford Illustrated History of the Vikings.* Oxford, 1997. The best one-volume account, lavishly illustrated.

Stillman, Norman A. *The Jews of Arab Lands: A History and Source Book.* Philadelphia, 1979. An essential resource.

Treadgold, Warren. *A History of the Byzantine State and Society.* Stanford, 1997. A massive, encyclopedic narrative of the political, economic, and military history of Byzantium from 284 until 1461.

Wallace-Hadrill, John Michael. *Early Germanic Kingship in England and on the Continent.* Oxford, 1971. A remarkably interesting analysis of changing ideas about the nature and responsibilities of kingship in early medieval Europe, emphasizing the links between Anglo-Saxon and Carolingian theories of kingship.

———. *The Frankish Church.* Oxford, 1983. A masterful account that links together the Merovingian and the Carolingian churches.

Watt, W. Montgomery. *Islamic Philosophy and Theology,* 2d ed. Edinburgh, 1985. The standard English account.

Whittow, Mark. *The Making of Orthodox Byzantium, 600–1025.* London, 1996. Emphasizes the centrality of orthodoxy in shaping Byzantine history. Particularly good on Byzantine relations with the peoples outside the empire.

Wood, Ian. *The Merovingian Kingdoms, 450–751.* New York, 1994. Full of the latest thinking, but detailed and difficult for beginners.

Chapter
EIGHT

THE EXPANSION OF
EUROPE: ECONOMY,
SOCIETY, AND
POLITICS IN THE
HIGH MIDDLE AGES,
1000–1300

BETWEEN 1000 AND 1300, the balance of power among western Europe, Byzantium, and the Islamic world shifted profoundly. In the year 1000, Europe remained politically fractured and militarily threatened by Viking, Hungarian, and Muslim attacks. Although towns in western Europe were beginning to grow, none could compare in size or sophistication with the ancient Mediterranean cities of Byzantium and the Islamic world. Economically, western Europe continued to depend on Byzantine and Islamic traders for its cotton, silk, spices, and gold. With respect to literature and learning, the imbalances were even greater. Europeans had access to only a small portion of the cultural and intellectual riches Byzantium and Islam had inherited from the classical world. Outside Sicily, Venice, and the Muslim-controlled areas of Spain, western Europeans knew no Arabic and virtually no Greek. Even Latin, the language of western learning for more than a thousand years, was increasingly a foreign tongue. King Alfred (871–899) complained that in his day hardly anyone in England knew enough Latin to conduct correctly the services of the Christian church. A century later, Latin learning in England and Germany was somewhat better. In France and Italy it was probably worse.

By the year 1300, however, Europe was the dominant military, economic, and political power among the three western successor civilizations to Greece and Rome. Hungary, Poland, and Bohemia were now thoroughly integrated parts of a Catholic, European world. Combining conquest with conversion, European Christians had forcefully pushed their borders eastward into Prussia, Lithuania, Livonia, and the Balkans. They had conquered Spain from the Muslims and Constantinople from the Byzantines. They had also established (and in 1300, just lost) a Latin kingdom in the Middle East, with its capital at Jerusalem. European navies controlled the Mediterranean Sea and had outposts on the Black Sea and the Caspian Sea, allowing

FOCUS QUESTIONS

• What impact did the first agricultural revolution have on the lives of Europeans?

• What were the major causes of urban growth during the High Middle Ages?

• How did the First Crusade alter the balance of power between Europe and Byzantium?

• What was the relationship between chivalry and the cult of "courtly love"?

• How did government and politics change during the High Middle Ages?

• What was the relationship between feudalism and the rise of national monarchies?

European traders to dominate the long-distance trade routes that brought eastern luxury goods into western Europe. European missionaries and traders were beginning to follow these trade routes back through Central Asia, opening up connections with Mongolia and China. To the west, Italian merchants had initiated a seaborne trade route through the Strait of Gibraltar, thus connecting the Mediterranean and the north Atlantic world.

This expansion of European commerce, both local and long distance, was accompanied by significant urbanization. By 1300, Europe could claim at least a dozen cities with populations between fifty thousand and one hundred thousand people, with hundreds of smaller towns and cities scattered across the landscape. The growth of cities mirrored the general growth in the European population which, on a rough estimate, tripled between 1000 and 1300. The economy grew even more rapidly, however, leading to increased per capita wealth and a rising standard of living. By no means, however, were these economic gains distributed equally among the entire population. Governments grew more powerful, and social stratification increased. New wealth increased the demand for luxury goods among social elites and freed up huge sums of money for investment in agriculture, commerce, and construction. It also fueled remarkable new religious, cultural, and intellectual developments that will be discussed in the next chapter.

Not all of this growth proved sustainable. By 1300, living standards for many Europeans were falling as western Europe began to approach the demographic limits of its natural resources. More powerful governments kept better internal peace, but they also claimed a larger proportion of their subjects' wealth, which they used to support bigger armies and grander campaigns of conquest and domination. In the fourteenth century, famine, war, and plague reduced the European population by at least a third, fundamentally transforming the economic, political, and social order of the High Middle Ages. Despite these setbacks, however, the predominance western Europe established over Byzantium and the Islamic world during the High Middle Ages would endure, providing the foundation on which the European world empires of the modern era would be built.

> The agricultural changes that took place in western Europe between 700 and 1300 were so sweeping, and their consequences so profound, that comparisons with the more famous agricultural revolution of the early eighteenth century seem justified.

THE FIRST AGRICULTURAL REVOLUTION

> What impact did the first agricultural revolution have on the lives of Europeans?

Like all premodern economies, the western European economy in the Middle Ages rested on agriculture. It may seem absurd to speak of agricultural changes that took place across six hundred years as constituting a "revolution." In western Europe, however, the agricultural changes that took place between 700 and 1300 were so sweeping, and their consequences so profound, that comparisons with the more famous agricultural revolution of the early eighteenth century seem justified. Technological innovations, combined with an improved climate, new crop-rotation systems, and increased investment in tools, livestock, and mills, increased the productivity of European agriculture dramatically. As agricultural productivity increased, so too did the marketing of agricultural surpluses, leading to increased specialization of production with resulting efficiencies of scale. Without these changes, western Europe could never have supported the tripling of its overall population, or the massive investments in buildings, ships, books, armies, and art that shaped the high medieval world.

TECHNOLOGICAL ADVANCES

The basic technological advances that made possible the increasing productivity of high medieval agriculture were developed in the early Middle Ages. The heavy-wheeled plow, fitted with an iron-tipped coulter and dragged by a team of oxen, could cut and turn the rich, wet soil of northern Europe to a depth impossible for the Mediterranean scratch plow to reach, thus aerating the soil and providing excellent drainage for water-logged territories. The new plow also saved labor, allowing more frequent plowing and better control of weeds.

Despite the advent of the heavy-wheeled plow, most of the work of raising crops continued to be done by individual peasant farmers using hand tools.

WHAT IMPACT DID THE FIRST AGRICULTURAL REVOLUTION HAVE ON THE LIVES OF EUROPEANS?

THE FIRST AGRICULTURAL REVOLUTION   227

The Heavy Plow. The major innovation of the heavy plow (often wheeled) was the long moldboard, which turned over the ground after the plowshare cut into it. The picture depicts a second crucial medieval invention as well—the padded horse collar, which allowed horses to throw their full weight into pulling.

As iron became more common during the High Middle Ages, the quality of these hand tools steadily improved. Iron-tipped hoes, forks, and shovels were much more effective than the wooden implements with which most eighth-century farmers had had to make do; the increasing number of iron sickles and scythes permitted speedier and more efficient harvesting of hay and grain, especially by women, whose field labor was critically important, particularly during harvesttime. Wheelbarrows were another homely but important technological innovation. Technology also had an impact on cooking techniques, and hence on nutrition. Iron pots allowed food to be boiled rather than just warmed, reducing the chances of contamination; communal ovens preserved a larger share of the nutrients in food than did boiling.

Mills represented another major technological innovation in food processing. The Romans had known about water mills but hardly used them, relying instead on human- and animal-powered wheels to grind grain into flour. Starting around 1050, however, there was a veritable craze in northern Europe for building water mills of steadily increasing efficiency. Once Europeans had mastered the complex technology of building water mills, they turned their attention to windmills, which proliferated rapidly from the 1170s on, espe-cially in flat lands such as Holland that had no swiftly flowing streams. Although the major use of mills was to grind grain, they could be adapted to drive saws, process cloth, press oil, provide power for iron forges, and crush pulp for manufacturing paper. The importance of such mills cannot be overstated. They would remain the world's only source of mechanical power for manufacturing until the eighteenth-century invention of the steam engine.

With the exception of the windmill, most of the technological innovations that lay behind the medieval agricultural revolution were already known to the Carolingians. Only from the mid-eleventh century, however, did these innovations become sufficiently widespread as to have a decisive effect on European agricultural production. Various explanations for this delay have been offered. Climatic change must have played some role; but although the warming climate benefited northern Europe by drying the soil and lengthening the growing season, it hurt Mediterranean agriculture in equal measure. Greater physical security also played a role. Viking, Hungarian, and Muslim attacks were decreasing, and more powerful governments kept better domestic peace than they had been able to do a century before. The fundamental change, however, lay in the growing confidence of entrepreneurial peasants and lords that if they invested labor and money in agricultural improvements, they would profit from the resulting surpluses.

More than anything else, it was the expanding demand for agricultural produce that encouraged peasants and landlords to make productive investments in the land. Behind the growing demand for foodstuffs lay the two fundamental economic factors that drove the high medieval economy forward: a rapidly increasing European population, and an increasingly efficient market for goods.

> Behind the growing demand for foodstuffs lay the two fundamental economic factors that drove the high medieval economy forward: a rapidly increasing European population, and an increasingly efficient market for goods.

MANORIALISM, SERFDOM, AND AGRICULTURAL PRODUCTIVITY

In England, northern France, and western Germany, increasing use of the heavy-wheeled plow between 800 and 1050 coincided with a fundamental change in patterns of peasant settlement. During the early Middle Ages, most free peasant farmers lived on individual plots of land that they farmed with their own resources, and for which they paid their landlord some kind of customary rent. Starting in the ninth century, however, many of these individual peasant holdings began to be consolidated into large, common fields that were farmed communally by peasants living in villages. The resulting complex of rents, renders, dues, fines, and fields is sometimes called a "manor."

In some areas, the impetus for these changes in settlement patterns may have come from the peasants themselves. Large fields could be farmed more efficiently than small fields. Investment costs were lower: a single plow and a dozen oxen might suffice for an entire village. Common fields also allowed the villagers to experiment with new crops and new crop-rotation systems and to support larger numbers of animals on common pastures. Peasants living together in a village might be able to support a parish church, a communal oven, a blacksmith, a mill, and a tavern. They could also converse and socialize, celebrate and mourn with their neighbors. In a difficult and demanding natural environment, these were not negligible considerations.

Despite the potential advantages the manorial system offered to peasants, lords played the dominant role in forcing its creation, and it was they who took the greatest benefits from it. It was easier for lords to control and exploit peasants living in villages than peasants living on scattered individual farms. Manorialism also allowed lords to claim a larger share of their peasants' agricultural production. On many manors, the common fields were divided into narrow strips assigned to individual peasants, for which each peasant landholder paid rent to the lord, but from which each peasant took the profits. In addition to their rents, however, most lords also claimed a third to a half of the total acreage in the common fields as their own land, from which they took all the produce for their own use. To farm this land, manorial lords imposed or increased labor services on peasant farmers, reducing many formerly free peasants to the status of serfs.

Serfs had existed in Europe for centuries, even in areas where the manorial system never took hold. There is no doubt, however, that the development of manorialism considerably increased the incidence of serfdom in northern Europe as compared with Spain, northern Italy, southern France, and central Germany. Unlike free peasants, serfs could not leave their land or their lord without his permission. Serfs worked for their lords regularly without pay, paid humiliating fines to their lord when they fornicated illicitly, married, or died, and were subject to the jurisdiction of their lord's manorial court. Like slaves, their servile status was heritable; but unlike slaves, their obligations to their lord were fixed by custom, and they were not supposed to be sold apart from the lands they held.

NEW CROP-ROTATION SYSTEMS

From the standpoint of agrarian productivity, the greatest advantage of the manorial system was the fact that it made possible the adoption of new, more efficient crop-rotation systems. For centuries, farmers had known that if they sowed the same crop on the same land year after year, they would eventually exhaust the soil. The traditional solution to this difficulty was to divide one's land, planting half in the fall to harvest in the spring, and leaving the other half to lie fallow. In the Mediterranean, this remained the most common cropping pattern throughout the Middle Ages. In the wet, fertile soils of northern Europe, however, farmers slowly discovered that a three-field crop-rotation system could produce a sustainable increase in overall

WHAT WERE THE MAJOR CAUSES OF URBAN GROWTH DURING THE HIGH MIDDLE AGES?

THE GROWTH OF TOWNS AND COMMERCE   229

Sowing Seed. When the peasant sows his seed broadcast, the crows are not far off to help themselves. Here, one is bold enough to peck at the sack while another is momentarily chased off by a dog.

agricultural production. Under this system, one third of the land would lie fallow, often being used for pasturage, so that the animals' droppings would fertilize the soil; one third would be planted with winter wheat or rye, which was sown in the fall and harvested in the early summer; and one third would be planted with another crop (usually oats, legumes, or barley) that could be sown in the spring and harvested in the fall. The fields were then rotated over a three-year cycle.

This system immediately increased the amount of land under cultivation in any given year. It also produced higher yields per acre of wheat and rye. With two separate growing seasons, the system provided some insurance against loss from natural disasters. It also produced new types of food. Oats could be consumed by both humans and horses, while legumes provided a source of protein to balance the major intake of cereal carbohydrates from bread and beer, the two main staples of the peasant diet. The new crop-rotation system also helped to spread labor more evenly over the course of the year, allowing more careful attention to weed control, liming, and fertilizing of the common fields.

SERFDOM AND THE LIMITS OF MANORIALISM

It is important to remember that, by and large, the manorial system was limited to England, northern France, and western Germany. Even in these areas, moreover, it was beginning to break down by the end of the twelfth century, as lords began to commute labor services into cash payments, to free their serfs (again in return for cash payments), and to live from rents rather than from the actual agricultural produce of their estates.

The reasons for the decline of serfdom during the thirteenth century are complex and did not affect all areas of Europe equally. As the European economy became increasingly monetarized, many lords simply found it more convenient to collect their revenues directly from their peasants in cash, rather than taking the risks associated with marketing agricultural produce directly. In England and Catalunya, by contrast, which had two of the most thoroughly commercialized agricultural economies in medieval Europe, serfdom lasted longer than almost anywhere else in western Europe. In Austria and Poland, which were far less monetized, serfdom also actually increased during the thirteenth century, as it did in northern Spain. There is thus no simple correlation between commercialization and the decline of serfdom. In most of Europe, however, the generalization holds: serfs and free peasants became increasingly indistinguishable during the thirteenth century as lords enfranchised serfs in return for cash. Even in France, however, some servile obligations would continue to exist as nagging indignities right down to the French Revolution in 1789. And in central and eastern Europe and Russia, serfdom underwent a resurgence during the later Middle Ages that would carry it into the eighteenth and nineteenth centuries.

THE GROWTH OF TOWNS AND COMMERCE

What were the major causes of urban growth during the High Middle Ages?

This agricultural revolution was the foundation on which the commercial revolution of the High Middle Ages rested. Here too, the groundwork for new developments had been laid in the ninth and tenth centuries. By the year 1000, silver from the Harz Mountains in Saxony was already fueling a triangular trade between England, Flanders, and the expanding cities of the Rhineland that brought raw wool from England to Flanders and wool cloth from Flanders to the Rhineland, whose merchants then distributed it as far away as Italy and Byzantium. Millions of silver pennies were in circulation around the North Sea, where an integrated system of exchange among English, Scandinavian, and Rhenish currencies had developed. English merchants were active in Constantinople and northern Spain, exchanging northern silver for Byzantine silks, Islamic spices, and African gold. Scandinavian merchants and warriors ranged even more widely, establishing cities in Ireland, principalities in Normandy and southern Italy, and trading outposts such as Novgorod and Kiev along the Russian trade routes that ran from the Baltic to the Black Sea (and thence to Constantinople) and to the Caspian Sea (and on into the Abbasid empire).

COMMERCE

During the eleventh and twelfth centuries, however, the greatest developments in long-distance commerce took place in the burgeoning cities of northern Italy. A series of victories by Venetian, Pisan, and Genoese naval forces gave these cities control over the carrying trade between Constantinople, Alexandria, and the West. The growing prosperity of western European nobles and churchmen created an expanding market for eastern luxury goods, while the improved domestic security of high medieval Europe made it possible for merchants to provide such goods with at least a modicum of security and safety. In the twelfth century, an organized system of fairs emerged in the central French region of Champagne, where Flemish merchants sold cloth to Italians, and Italian merchants sold Muslim spices and Byzantine silks to Flemings, French, and Germans. By 1300, however, these fairs were beginning to decline as Italian merchants succeeded in opening up a direct route by sea between Italy and the Atlantic ports of northern Europe. It now became practical to import raw wool directly from England to northern Italy, where towns like Florence could produce and finish wool cloth

themselves. As the Italian cloth industry grew, the Flemish cloth industry declined, yet another sign of the increasing extent to which Europe was becoming a unified economy.

Long-distance trade was a risky enterprise. Piracy was commonplace, and the Mediterranean Sea was notoriously dangerous to sailors and their ships. However, Italian success in opening up the new trade routes of the High Middle Ages depended on the willingness of both merchants and nobles to invest substantial sums of money in ships, cargoes, and pack animals. To facilitate such investment, Italian merchants developed new forms of commercial partnership contracts, new methods of accounting, and new credit mechanisms, some of which they borrowed from Byzantine and Muslim examples. Some of these new credit arrangements ran afoul of the western Christian church, which condemned almost all forms of moneylending as usury. But the demand for capital to fuel the new commercial economy was irresistible, and slowly attitudes began to change. From the thirteenth century on, leading churchmen also began to speak more favorably of merchants. Saint Bonaventura, a thirteenth-century Italian Franciscan, argued, for example, that in Old Testament times, God had shown special favor to shepherds such as King David; in New Testament times, he had favored fishermen such as Saint Peter; but in modern times, God's favor now went out to merchants such as Saint Francis of Assisi.

It would be misleading, however, to think of the commercial revolution or the urban revolution of the High Middle Ages as principally the result of long-distance trade. Some towns did receive great stimulus from such trade, and the growth of such major cities as Venice (about one hundred thousand people in 1300) and Genoa (eighty thousand) would have been impossible without it. But the prosperity of most towns, including such enormous cities as Paris, Florence, Milan, and London, depended primarily on the wealth of their surrounding hinterlands, from which they drew their food supplies, their raw materials, and the bulk of their population. The quickening of economic life in general was the major cause of urban growth during the High Middle Ages. Long-distance trade was but one aspect of this larger economic and commercial transformation of European life.

> To facilitate such investment, Italian merchants developed new forms of commercial partnership contracts, new methods of accounting, and new credit mechanisms, some of which they borrowed from Byzantine and Muslim examples.

WHAT WERE THE MAJOR CAUSES OF URBAN GROWTH DURING THE HIGH MIDDLE AGES?

THE GROWTH OF TOWNS AND COMMERCE   231

MEDIEVAL TRADE ROUTES

This map details the routes by which long-distance trade moved in and around Europe during the eleventh century. What was the relationship between trade routes and rivers, and why? Why was the agricultural revolution and the revival of trade crucial to the extension of major trade routes in the West? What factors led to the intense proliferation of trade routes between England, Bruges, and the Rhine Valley? What trade patterns emerged as different regions began specializing in certain goods?

TOWNS

Towns, both large and small, existed in a symbiotic relationship with the countryside around them, providing markets and manufactured goods while living off the rural food surplus and expanding through the con-stant immigration of free peasants and escaped serfs in search of a better life. Once towns started to flourish, many of them began to specialize in certain enterprises. Paris and Bologna became the homes of leading universities; Venice, Genoa, Cologne, and London became centers of long-distance trade; Milan, Florence,

View of Paris. The city looked this way at the end of the Middle Ages, around 1480. Note the prominence of the Cathedral of Nôtre Dame in the center and the large number of other church spires; note, too, how closely all the buildings are packed behind the walls.

Ghent, and Bruges specialized in manufactures. The most important urban industries were those devoted to the making and finishing of wool (and in Venice, cotton) cloth. Most urban manufacturing was done by individual artisans in small, privately owned workshops whose production was regulated by professional associations known as guilds.

Usually only master artisans, who were experts at their trade and ran their own shops, were allowed to be fully fledged, voting members of a craft guild. As a result, guilds generally promoted the interests of their richest and most successful members by trying to preserve monopolies and limit competition. To these ends, terms of employment were strictly regulated. If an apprentice or a journeyman (from the French *journée*, meaning "day," or by extension "day's work": that is, someone who had completed his apprenticeship but still worked for a master craftsman) wished to become a master, he often had to produce a "masterpiece" for judging by the masters of the guild. Craft guilds also controlled prices and wages, prohib-

ited after-hours work, and formulated detailed regulations governing methods of production and the quality of materials to be used by their members. They also served important social functions as religious associations, benevolent societies, and drinking clubs, looking after their members in times of trouble and supporting his dependents when a master craftsman died.

Merchants established guilds also, which in some towns became so powerful that membership in a merchant guild became a prerequisite for service in town government. Merchant guilds sought to maintain a monopoly of the local market for their members by restricting competition and enforcing uniform pricing. Often they also controlled admissions to citizenship in the city. By their nature, guilds were exclusionary organizations. Because they were explicitly Christian, they were almost invariably closed to Jews and Muslims. They also significantly restricted the economic opportunities available to ordinary wage earners, and especially to women. Women were not automatically excluded from most guilds, and

> Despite the important role women played as urban wage earners, however, the male-dominated guilds ensured that women would have no influence over the terms and conditions under which they worked, or the wages they would be paid for their labor.

HOW DID THE FIRST CRUSADE ALTER THE BALANCE OF POWER BETWEEN EUROPE AND BYZANTIUM?

BYZANTIUM, ISLAM, AND THE CRUSADES   233

a few craft guilds were specifically female. Despite the important role women played as urban wage earners, however, the male-dominated guilds ensured that women would have no influence over the terms and conditions under which they worked, or the wages they would be paid for their labor.

To modern eyes, most medieval towns and cities would still have seemed half rural even in 1300. Streets were often unpaved, houses had gardens for raising vegetables, and farm animals were everywhere. Sanitary conditions were poor and the air must often have reeked of excrement, both animal and human. In such a world, disease ran rampant, especially in the overcrowded neighborhoods where the poorest urban dwellers lived. At every level of urban society, however, fertility rates were low and infant mortality high. Most cities sustained their population only through continuing immigration from the countryside. Fire was an omnipresent danger, and economic tensions and family rivalries could lead to bloody riots. Yet for all this, urban folk took great pride in their new cities and ways of life. A famous paean to London, for example, written by a twelfth-century denizen of the city, boasted of its prosperity, piety, and perfect climate (!), and claimed that except for frequent fires, London's only nuisance was "the immoderate drinking of fools." His pride was echoed in scores of other European cities as their citizens increasingly asserted their distinctive local identities and their communal privileges as merchants, artisans, and self-governing corporations.

BYZANTIUM, ISLAM, AND THE CRUSADES

How did the First Crusade alter the balance of power between Europe and Byzantium?

As the power of the Abbasid caliphate declined during the ninth and tenth centuries, the Byzantine empire expanded. By 1025, Byzantium's position had been transformed. After several centuries of missionary inactivity, ninth-century Byzantine missionaries, most famously Saints Cyril and Methodius, converted the Balkan Slavs to Orthodox Christianity, devising for them a written language known as Old Church Slavonic and creating the Cyrillic alphabet, which is still used today in Bulgaria, Serbia, and Russia. Military

conquest quickly followed. By 1025, when Emperor Basil II ("the Bulgar-slayer") died, the Byzantines had firmly annexed Greece, Bulgaria, and modern-day Serbia to their empire. They had also established a military and commercial alliance with the western Rus kingdom centered around Kiev, decisively reorienting the Rus toward Constantinople and away from Islam. In 911, seven hundred Rus served with the Byzantine fleet in an attack on Muslim Crete. In 945 a commercial treaty was established. And in 989, the emperor Basil II turned to Vladimir, prince of Kiev, for the troops he needed to win a civil war against his imperial rival, Bardas Phokas, a member of the increasingly powerful nobility from the eastern borders of the empire. In return for Vladimir's help, Basil gave his sister, Anna, in marriage to Vladimir, and Vladimir, along with his people, accepted baptism into the Orthodox church. Russia has remained an Orthodox bastion until the present day.

THE BYZANTINE REVIVAL

Between the 930s and the 970s, the Byzantines also launched a series of successful campaigns along their eastern and southeastern frontiers with the Abbasids, reconquering territories that had not been in Byzantine hands since the seventh century. Although most of the peoples of the reconquered territories had remained Christian through three centuries of Islamic rule, the Armenians and the Syrians in particular had their own distinctive Christian traditions that were at odds, both doctrinally and linguistically, with the Greek-speaking church at Constantinople. For an empire that had defined itself for centuries on the basis of its orthodoxy (the word itself means "correct belief"), incorporating such "heretics" threatened the foundations on which the unity of the empire rested.

Even more important, however, the eastern conquests greatly increased the power of the local noble families who led them and profited from them, creating for the first time a center of power within the empire that lay outside the imperial capital at Constantinople. Tensions and rivalries between these eastern noble families and the imperial officials at the capital disturbed Byzantine politics for most of the tenth century. After an attempted coup by the head of one such family, the emperor Basil II (976–1025) savagely suppressed the leading eastern magnate families. But this check on the eastern magnates' ambitions proved only temporary. After Basil's death, the imperial throne passed to a series of aged and incompetent relations. In the resulting

THE BYZANTINE EMPIRE, C. 1025

What challenges faced the Byzantine empire in the eleventh century? Note the land controlled by the Muslims and the emerging power of Kievan Russia. How was the long-standing influence of the Muslims in the Near East likely to affect the character of Byzantine culture? How did the domain of Kievan Russia potentially create additional economic and military pressure on Byzantium, directly as well as indirectly?

power vacuum, noble military families came more and more to dominate the countryside; while at court, tax revenues decreased as imperial expenditures rose. To pay the bills, the emperors debased the Byzantine gold coinage, undermining Byzantine commerce precisely when Venice, Genoa, and Pisa were consolidating their

HOW DID THE FIRST CRUSADE ALTER THE BALANCE OF POWER BETWEEN EUROPE AND BYZANTIUM?

BYZANTIUM, ISLAM, AND THE CRUSADES   235

control over the eastern Mediterranean trade routes. By 1081, when the eastern magnate families triumphed by placing Alexius Comnenus on the imperial throne, the Byzantine empire had been crippled as a Mediterranean power.

THE INVASION OF THE TURKS

By the late eleventh century, Byzantium faced new threats from several quarters. Venice, Genoa, and Pisa had emerged as the dominant naval powers in the eastern Mediterranean and had to a considerable extent taken over the lucrative trade between Islamic North Africa and the west. The growing power of Fatimid Egypt was beginning to roll back Byzantine gains along the empire's southeastern frontier with Syria. But most disastrously of all, a new Sunni Muslim power, the Seljuk Turks, had emerged in central Asia and had begun to move into Asia Minor, the very heartland of the Byzantine empire. When the Turks captured Armenia, the emperor tried to eject them; but the eastern noble families refused their support, and in the decisive battle of Manzikert (1071), the imperial army was annihilated. The way now lay open for the Turks to seize all of Anatolia, the wealthiest and most productive part of the Byzantine empire. In the same year, another Turkish band captured Jerusalem from the Shiite Fatimids, restoring the Holy City to Sunni control. Within five years, almost all of Syria and Asia Minor lay in Turkish hands. In the west, a rebellion by the Balkan Slavs also erupted around this time, further reducing the already severely depleted treasury of the Byzantine empire.

By the 1090s, however, Alexius Comnenus had rebuilt the treasury, and restored Byzantine control over the Balkans, and was beginning to plan a campaign against the Turks. During the eleventh century, western knights had emerged as the most effective heavily armored cavalry troops in the world. Alexius had confronted such knights in 1085, when he repelled a Norman invasion of Greece. He was anxious to make use of them, however, against the mounted but lightly armored Turks. To recruit a force of heavy cavalry, Alexius sent a request to Pope Urban II, hoping for a contingent of a few thousand troops with which he might be able to roll back Turkish gains in Anatolia. Within a year, however, the pope had set in motion a vast crusading army of one hundred thousand Westerners to retake the Holy City of Jerusalem for Christendom.

THE FIRST CRUSADE

The reasons that Urban's summons met with such a massive response are complex. Urban himself probably saw the crusade as a means for achieving at least four ends. One was to bring the Orthodox church back into communion with the papacy. Relations between the two churches had been ruptured in 1054, when a papal emissary and the Orthodox patriarch of Constantinople had each excommunicated the other. A second motive was to embarrass Urban's greatest enemy, the German emperor Henry IV. Henry and the papacy had been at war for more than twenty years over their respective claims to supremacy within Christendom. By calling a mighty crusade to retake Jerusalem, Urban probably hoped to establish his own claims as pope to be the rightful leader of western Christian society. Third, by sending off a large contingent of fighters, Urban hoped to achieve peace at home. Earlier in the century, a number of French bishops and abbots had supported a "peace movement" that prohibited attacks on noncombatants and prohibited fighting on certain holy days. At the 1095 ecclesiastical council at Clermont where he announced the First Crusade, Urban also promulgated the first full papal approval of this peace movement. In effect, Urban told the assembled knights that if they wished to fight, they could do so justly for a Christian cause overseas. Finally, the goal of Jerusalem itself genuinely inspired Urban. Jerusalem was regarded by medieval geographers as the center of the earth as well as being the most sacred shrine of the Christian religion because it was Jesus' homeland. To the untutored knights of western Europe, as perhaps to Urban himself, it seemed only right that Christian knights should assist their Lord Christ to recover his own land from the Muslims who had seized it from him.

CHRONOLOGY

BYZANTINE EMPIRE, 900–1204

Successful campaigns against the Abbasid rulers	930–970
Russia converts to orthodoxy	911–989
Annexation of Greece, Bulgaria, and Serbia	1025
Turkish invasions (defeat of Manzikert)	1071
Reign of Alexius Comnenus	1081–1118
First Crusade	1095–1099
Fourth Crusade, capture of Constantinople	1204

The response to Urban's call exceeded all expectations. Within a year of the pope's summons, an army of a hundred thousand men, women, and children, drawn from all over western Europe, was on the march toward Constantinople, where they intended to gather before departing for Jerusalem. As with any large enterprise, the participants' motives for joining the crusade varied. Some hoped to win lands or establish principalities for themselves in the east. Others were drawn simply by the prospect of adventure. Many were dependents of greater men, accompanying their lords because it was their duty to do so. A few may have been motivated by obscure prophecies and apocalyptic fervor. Most probably had no idea how long a journey would be involved, or even what direction they would be traveling.

But the dominant motive for going on the First Crusade was religious. Except for a few of the greatest lords—and they mostly Normans from southern Italy—the prospect of winning new lands in the east was both unlikely and undesired. After fulfilling their vows, the vast majority of crusaders went home. The risks of dying on such a journey were high; the costs of embarking on it were enormous. Crusading knights needed a minimum of two years' revenues in hand to finance their journey. To raise such sums, most were forced to mortgage lands and borrow heavily from family, friends, monasteries, and merchants. They then had to find some way to pay back these loans if and when they returned home. On any rational judgment of financial advantage, the crusade was a fool's errand. But it did offer solace to the Christian soul. For centuries pilgrimages had been the most popular type of Christian penance, and the pilgrimage to Jerusalem was considered to be the most sacred and efficacious one of all. Urban II made this point explicit at Clermont, promising that crusaders would be freed from all other penances imposed by the church. Some crusade preachers went even further by promising what became known as a plenary indulgence: that crusaders would be entirely freed from otherworldly punishments in purgatory for all the sins they had committed up to that point in their lives, and that the souls of those who died on crusade would go straight to heaven.

Crusade preaching emphasized the vengeance that Christ's soldiers should exact on his enemies in the East. But to some crusaders, it seemed absurd to wait until they arrived in Jerusalem to undertake this aspect of their obligations. Muslims might hold Jesus' property at Jerusalem, but Christian theology held Jews responsible for the death of Jesus himself. During the course of the eleventh century, Jewish communities had grown up in most of the larger cities of the Rhineland and in many of the smaller towns and cities of northern France. Assaults by bands of crusaders against Jewish communities began in northern France in the spring of 1096 and quickly spread to the Rhineland as the crusaders moved east. Hundreds of Jews were killed throughout western Europe, and hundreds more were forcibly baptized as the price for escaping death at the hands of crusading knights. Despite the efforts of church authorities to prevent them, attacks on Jews would remain a regular and predictable feature of Christian crusading until the thirteenth century.

> Despite the efforts of church authorities to prevent them, attacks on Jews would remain a regular and predictable feature of Christian crusading until the thirteenth century.

Surprised by the nature and scale of the western response to his appeal, Alexius Comnenus did his best to move the crusaders quickly through Constantinople and into Asia Minor. Differences in outlook between the western crusaders and the Byzantine emperor quickly became apparent, however. From Alexius's standpoint, the crusader army was a threat, not least because it contained within it several of the Norman leaders who had attempted to conquer his empire only ten years earlier. The crusaders, however, saw themselves as on a mission from God. They did not understand the Byzantine emperor's willingness to make alliances with some Muslim rulers against other Muslim rulers, and they speedily concluded that the Byzantines were in fact working to undermine the crusading effort. Such suspicions were unfounded, but they contributed to a growing western conviction that the Byzantine empire itself was an obstacle to the successful recovery of Jerusalem for Christendom.

Against great odds the First Crusade succeeded. In 1098 the crusaders captured Antioch and with it most of Syria. At the end of 1099, they took Jerusalem, mercilessly slaughtering Muslim, Jewish, and Christian inhabitants alike. Their success stemmed mainly from the fact that the crusaders' Muslim opponents were at that moment internally divided. The Fatimids had recaptured Jerusalem from the Turks just months before the crusaders arrived, and the Turks themselves were at war with each other. But western military tactics, in particular the dominance in the open field of the heavily armored knights, also played an important role in the crusaders' success.

THE SPURIOUS LETTER OF ALEXIUS COMNENUS TO COUNT ROBERT, SEEKING HIS AID AGAINST THE TURKS

This letter to Count Robert of Flanders is a forgery from around the time of the First Crusade. It reflects the kind of propaganda that helped to spur enthusiasm for the crusade against the Turks. With its focus on the sexual sins of the Turks and the riches to be had in Constantinople, the letter offers quite different reasons for going on crusade from those advanced by Pope Urban II at Clermont. There is no evidence that any of the charges against the Turks contained in this letter were true.

O incomparable Count, great defender of the faith, it is my desire to bring to your attention the extent to which the most holy empire of the Christian Greeks is fiercely beset every day by the Patzinaks and Turks . . . and how massacres and unspeakable murders and outrages against Christians are perpetrated. . . .

For they circumcise Christian boys and youths over the baptismal fonts of Christian [churches] and spill the blood of circumcision right into the baptismal fonts and compel them to urinate over them, afterward leading them violently around the church and forcing them to blaspheme the name of the Holy Trinity. Those who are unwilling they torture in various ways and finally murder. When they capture noble women and their daughters, they abuse them sexually in turns, like animals. Some, while they are wickedly defiling the maidens, place the mothers facing, constraining them to sing evil and lewd songs while they work their evil. . . .

But what next? We pass on to worse yet. They have degraded by sodomizing them men of every age and rank—boys, adolescents, young men, old men, nobles, servants, and, what is worse and more wicked, clerics and monks, and even—alas and for shame! Something which from the beginning of time has never been spoken or heard of—bishops! They have already killed one bishop with this nefarious sin.

They have polluted and ruined the holy places in innumerable ways and threaten even worse things. In the face of all this, who would not weep— Who would not be moved? Who would not shudder? Who would not pray? Nearly the entire territory from Jerusalem to Greece, and all of Greece with its upper regions . . . have all been invaded by them, and hardly anything remains except Constantinople, which they threaten soon to take from us unless we are speedily relieved by the help of God and the faithful Latin Christians. . . .

For the sake of the name of God and the piety of all those who uphold the Christian faith, we therefore implore you to lead here to help us and all Greek Christians every faithful soldier of Christ you can obtain in your lands, great, small or middling, that they might struggle for the salvation of their souls to free the kingdom of the Greeks, just as in past years they have liberated, to some extent, Galicia and other western kingdoms from the yoke of the unbelievers. For although I am emperor, no remedy remains to me . . . and I am reduced to waiting in a single city for the imminent arrival of the Turks. And since I prefer to be subject to you, the Latins, rather than have Constantinople taken by the Turks, you should fight courageously and with all your strength so that you might receive in bliss a glorious and indescribable reward in heaven.

[The letter then goes on to describe the many Christian relics in Constantinople, and the wealth of the city, urging Robert to prevent all this from falling into the hands of the Turks.]

Act therefore while you have time, lest you lose the kingdom of the Christians and, what is worse, the sepulcher of the Lord, and so that you may earn a reward rather than a punishment hereafter. Amen.

John E. Boswell, ed. and trans. *Christianity, Social Tolerance and Homosexuality.* (Chicago: University of Chicago Press, 1980), pp. 367–369.

Equally critical was the naval support the First Crusade received from Genoa and Pisa, which hoped that a successful crusade would allow them to control the Indian spice trade that passed through the Red Sea and on to Alexandria in Egypt. In this respect, the First Crusade contributed to the further decline of Byzantine commerce, which was already suffering both from Italian competition in the Mediterranean and from the disruptive impact of the Turkish invasions on the trade routes that had previously connected Constantinople with Baghdad and the Central Asian silk route to China. All these trends were under way before the First Crusade began, but the establishment of the Latin kingdom accelerated them. To that extent, the First Crusade contributed significantly to the changing balance of power between Byzantium and the West.

THE LATER CRUSADES

The First Crusade had much less of an impact on the balance of power between Islam and the West. The crusader kingdom was never more than an underpopulated, narrow strip of colonies along the coastline of Syria and Palestine. So long as the crusaders did not control the Red Sea, the main routes of Islamic commerce with India and the Far East were unaffected by the change in Jerusalem's religious allegiance. Nor, for that matter, did the crusaders in any way wish to interfere with the overland caravan routes that led through their new territories. For the Muslims, the loss of Jerusalem was a religious affront much more than an economic one, and it was for religious reasons that they began to plan its recovery. By 1144, most of the crusader principalities in Syria had been recaptured. When Christian warriors led by the king of France and the emperor of Germany came east in the Second Crusade to recoup the losses, they were too internally divided to win any victories. Not long afterward, Syria and Egypt were united under the great Muslim leader Saladin, who finally recaptured Jerusalem in 1187. In response, the Third Crusade was launched, led by the German emperor Frederick Barbarossa, the French king Philip Augustus, and the English king Richard the Lionheart. This campaign also failed. Barbarossa drowned in Asia Minor on the way to Jerusalem, and Philip Augustus soon went home. Richard the Lionheart's heroic efforts enabled the Latin kingdom to survive for another century; but even he could not recapture Jerusalem.

The dream, however, did not die. When Innocent III became pope in 1198, his main ambition was to win back Jerusalem. He summoned the Fourth Crusade to

that end, but it proved a disaster. Civil war in Germany, combined with war between England and France, severely reduced the number of knights willing to participate; and when the Venetians, who had contracted to transport the crusader army to the Holy Land, discovered that only half the predicted crusaders would arrive and that they would therefore not be properly paid, they diverted the crusade toward a successful attack on Constantinople itself in 1204. The result was an enormous commercial windfall for Venice, but the effective destruction of the Byzantine empire, which for the next sixty years was divided into Latin-ruled and Greek-ruled provinces. In 1261 the Venetians' rivals, the Genoese, helped a new imperial claimant, Michael VIII Palaeologus, to recover the Byzantine throne and, with it, control over Constantinople. But the Byzantine empire was now reduced to little more than the city itself, leaving both Asia Minor and the Balkans open to their eventual conquest by the Ottoman Turks.

Despite the debacle of the Fourth Crusade, western efforts to recover Jerusalem continued throughout the thirteenth century. Only in 1229, however, when the western Roman emperor Frederick II negotiated a treaty with the Egyptian sultan that returned Jerusalem to Christian control for a period of ten years, did any western leader attempt to achieve this objective directly. Instead, thirteenth-century crusades were aimed mainly at Egypt (1217–1219, 1248–1254) and, in 1270, Tunis. The crusaders' strategic goal was to cut the economic lifelines that supported Muslim control

CHRONOLOGY

THE CRUSADES

First Crusade (recapture of Jerusalem)	1095–1099
Second Crusade (defeated by Seljuk Turks)	1145–1149
Third Crusade (Frederick Barbarossa and Richard "the Lionheart")	1187–1192
Fourth Crusade (sack of Constantinople)	1201-1204
Fifth Crusade (capture of Damietta)	1217–1221
Peace treaty regains Jerusalem	1228–1229
Sixth Crusade (defeat of Louis IX of France)	1248–1254
Seventh Crusade (death of Louis IX of France)	1270

HOW DID THE FIRST CRUSADE ALTER THE BALANCE OF POWER BETWEEN EUROPE AND BYZANTIUM?

BYZANTIUM, ISLAM, AND THE CRUSADES   239

THE ROUTES OF THE CRUSADERS, 1096–1204

Compare the routes followed by the first three crusades. Why were they so similar? Why was the route of the Fourth Crusade so different? Why was Genoa so much more important than Venice as an embarkation point for crusaders?

of the Holy Land. In explaining these later crusades, however, it becomes increasingly difficult to disentangle crusade-motivated calculations toward recapturing Jerusalem (which was, in any event, a shattered city with no walls and a tiny population) from the aspirations of Italian merchants to control the Far Eastern trade that ran through Egypt, and the gold trade from sub-Saharan Africa that ran through Tunis. The great mercantile city of the thirteenth century Latin kingdom was Acre, not Jerusalem. Its fall in 1291 marked the end of any further western expeditions to recover the Holy Land from Islam.

THE CONSEQUENCES OF THE CRUSADES

For Byzantium, the impact of the crusading movement was disastrous. The crusades coincided with, and to some extent caused, a decisive shift in the balance of economic and military power between western Europe and the faltering Byzantine empire. On the Islamic world, by contrast, the impact of the crusades was much more modest. Trade between Islam and the West continued despite periodic interruptions caused by crusader attacks on Syria, Egypt, and North Africa. The greatest

PREPARING TO DEPART ON CRUSADE

Before crusaders departed for the Holy Land, they were obliged to remedy all injustices they might have committed, and to put their affairs in order. This was a religious requirement for anyone setting out on a penitential pilgrimage, but it was also a practical recognition that many crusaders would die on their journey. The human emotions that accompanied such departures are clearly expressed in Jean de Joinville's account of his preparations to depart with King Louis IX of France on the Sixth Crusade (1248–1254).

At Easter, in the year of our Lord 1248, I summoned my men, and all who held fiefs from me, to Joinville. On Easter Eve, when all the people I had summoned had arrived, my son, Jean . . . was born to me by my first wife. . . . We feasted and danced the whole of that week. . . .

On the Friday I said to them: "My friends, I'm soon going overseas and I don't know whether I shall ever return. So will any of you who have a claim to make against me come forward. If I have done you any wrong I will make it good, to each of you in turn, as I have been used to do in the case of those who had any demand to make of me or my people." I dealt with each claim in the way the men on my lands considered right; and in order not to influence their decision I withdrew from the discussion, and afterwards agreed without demur to whatever they recommended.

Since I did not wish to take away with me a single penny to which I had no right, I went to Metz in Lorraine, and mortgaged the greater part of my land. I can assure you that, on the day I left our country to go to the Holy Land, I had in my possession, since my lady mother was still alive, an income of no more than a thousand *livres* from my estates. All the same I went, and took with me nine knights, and two knights-banneret besides myself. I bring these things to your notice so that you may understand that if God, who has never failed me, had not come to my help, I should scarcely have been able to hold out for so long a time as the six years that I remained in the Holy Land. . . .

On the day I left Joinville I sent for the Abbot of Cheminon, who was said to be the wisest and worthiest monk of the Cistercian Order. . . . This same abbot . . . gave me my pilgrim's staff and wallet. I left Joinville immediately after—never to enter my castle again until my return from oversea— on foot, with my legs bare, and in my shirt. Thus attired I went to Blécourt and Saint-Urbain, and to other places where there are holy relics. And all the way . . . I never once let my eyes turn back towards Joinville, for fear my heart might be filled with longing at the thought of my lovely castle and the two children I had left behind.

M. R. B. Shaw, ed. and trans. *Chronicles of the Crusades.* (Baltimore: Penguin Classics, 1963), pp. 192, 195.

WHAT WAS THE RELATIONSHIP BETWEEN CHIVALRY AND THE CULT OF "COURTLY LOVE"?

SOCIAL MOBILITY AND SOCIAL INEQUALITY IN HIGH MEDIEVAL EUROPE 241

economic gains went to the Italian maritime republics of Venice and Genoa; but Islamic merchants too came to depend increasingly on western markets for their goods. Both sides also gained in military terms: westerners learned new technques of fortification, and Muslims learned new methods of siege warfare and new respect for the uses of heavy cavalry. Finally, the crusades also helped to crystallize both Christian and Islamic doctrines of holy war against the infidel. Neither Christian holy war nor Muslim *jihad* drew much doctrinally from the other. The collision between them, however, deepened the mutual hostility that already separated the Islamic world and Christian Europe.

The impact of the crusades on western Europe is more difficult to assess. From one standpoint, the crusades were an ultimately unsuccessful chapter in a generally successful story of western expansionism during the High Middle Ages. In the Middle East, however, western Europeans overreached themselves. They could not maintain the colonies they established, and they were ultimately forced to withdraw. Nor did the crusades "open up" Europeans to a wider world of which they had previously known nothing. That wider world already existed in 1095, and Europeans were already part of it. Trade with the Islamic world did bring enormous prosperity to the Italian maritime republics, but these trading links had existed before the crusades and continued after they ended. It is arguable that crusading diminished, rather than increased, the economic and cultural exchange between western Europe and the Islamic world that might otherwise have taken place.

It would be wrong, however, to end our discussion of the crusades on such a minor note. A drive by western merchants, backed by western military force, to control the trade in spices, silks, and gold by "cutting out the Islamic middleman" is clearly visible in thirteenth-century crusading. This impulse would continue, and would eventually lead to the creation of worldwide European mercantile and colonial empires from the sixteenth century on. Nor should we ignore or diminish the lasting influence of the crusading ideal on Europeans' image of themselves. Crusading had dramatic successes in Spain, where between 1100 and 1250 the kings of Castile and Portugal and the crown of Aragon led the reconquest of the Iberian peninsula from Islam. In Iberia particularly, crusading retained its ideological significance until the end of the sixteenth century, providing an important motivation behind the Portuguese and Spanish voyages of discovery during the fifteenth century, and the conquest of the Americas during the sixteenth century. Crusading would also continue to color European relations with Islam, and especially with the Ottoman Turks, whose conquests would eventually lead them to the gates of Vienna and the borders of Italy. Even Napoleon, the last of the western Roman emperors, was not immune to the crusading ideal. He too would lead a successful, but short-lived, reconquest of Jerusalem.

SOCIAL MOBILITY AND SOCIAL INEQUALITY IN HIGH MEDIEVAL EUROPE

What was the relationship between chivalry and the cult of "courtly love"?

The increasing wealth of high medieval Europe also transformed the social structure of European society. In the tenth century, it was still possible to describe European society as being divided among "those who worked, those who prayed, and those who fought." By 1300, however, new commercial and professional elites had emerged in the burgeoning cities of western Europe. By 1300, the wealthiest members of European society were merchants and bankers, not nobles. The greatest noble families affected a disdain for commerce, but nobles too found themselves drawn increasingly into the world of trade, despite their contempt for such "calculators." Nobles still fought, of course; but so too did knights, urban crossbowmen, peasant longbowmen, citizen militias, and peasant levies. Even work had become more complex. By 1300, half the peasants in England farmed plots of land too small to support their families. They survived, and sometimes even prospered, on a shifting combination of farming, wage labor, hunting, gathering, and charity. Such lines as existed between town and countryside were easily crossed. Schools of all sorts had emerged, and the products of those schools—lawyers, doctors, estate administrators, clerks, and government officials—made up a new and growing professional class that further complicated efforts to describe European society in terms of "three orders" of workers, prayers, and fighters.

NOBLES AND KNIGHTS

New wealth brought social mobility, but it also created a more highly stratified society. We have noted already

Aristocratic Table Manners. There are knives but no forks or napkins on the table. The large stars mark these nobles as members of a chivalric order.

the hierarchies of status and wealth that characterized the guild system. With the rise of serfdom, new distinctions between free and unfree families also emerged within peasant society. Nowhere, however, is the growing stratification of European society more evident than among the nobility. In the Carolingian period, the nobility comprised a relatively small number of ancient families of approximately equal social rank who married among themselves. During the tenth and eleventh centuries, however, new families began to establish themselves as territorial lords. Some of these new families were descended from Carolingian officeholders who had taken advantage of the Carolingians' collapse to establish their independence. Others were simply freebooters whose power rested on their control over castles, knights, and manors. Until the twelfth century, the old Carolingian noble families attempted to resist the claims of these new families to noble rank and status. By the end of the thirteenth century, however, a new nobility had emerged in western Europe that included these new families of counts, castle holders, and knights, but that also made a series of careful distinctions in rank among dukes, counts, castellans (castle holders), and knights.

Knights were not necessarily nobles in the eleventh century. Knighthood was instead a social "order" consisting of men of widely varying social rank. Some eleventh-century knights were the sons of great nobles, but others were little more than peasants mounted on horseback and armed with swords. As a specialized warrior group, knights associated with the nobility. A degree of social prestige rubbed off on them from this fact. But the key developments that raised the knights

into the ranks of the nobility were directly connected with the growing wealth of medieval European society. As the costs of knightly equipment rose, the number of men who could afford the heavier horses, stronger swords, and improved armor that mid-thirteenth-century knights required declined dramatically. The style of domestic life expected of knights also became more elaborate and expensive. By 1250, a knight required a string of horses, silk clothing, and a retinue of servants, squires, and grooms. To support such an extravagant lifestyle, a knight needed either a sizable annual fee from his lord or else large estates, a minimum of twelve hundred acres.

CHIVALRY AND COURTLY LOVE

As the costs of knighthood increased, so too did its social prestige. From the mid-twelfth century on, the kings and nobles of Europe began to embrace and encourage the knightly code of values known as "chivalry," which stressed bravery, loyalty, generosity, skill with weapons, and proper manners as constituent elements in true nobility. Chivalry literally means "horsemanship," and mounted combat would for long remain the defining element in the European nobility's image of itself. First and foremost, however, chivalry was a social ideology that appealed to the knights and nobles of western Europe because it gave them a way of distinguishing themselves from all those other groups in high medieval society—merchants, lawyers, artisans, and prosperous free farmers—who were their rivals in wealth and sometimes in political influence. While chivalry began as the value system of a socially diverse knightly order, by the end of the thirteenth century it had become the ideology of a social class, functioning to demarcate those who were (or aspired to be) noble from those who were (or did) not.

Closely linked to the ideology of chivalry was the so-called cult of courtly love, which made noble women into objects of veneration for their knightly admirers. Here too, there was an important element of social class. Courtly love was "refined" love, the "courteous" love appropriate to a royal or noble court. But the exponents of courtly love distinguished sharply

WHAT WAS THE RELATIONSHIP BETWEEN CHIVALRY AND THE CULT OF "COURTLY LOVE"?

SOCIAL MOBILITY AND SOCIAL INEQUALITY IN HIGH MEDIEVAL EUROPE   243

between noble women, who alone were capable of "refined" love (and who should therefore be wooed and won through proper manners, poetry, and valiant deeds) and peasant women, on whom such "courtliness" would be wasted. Noble women were to be courted; but peasant women could be taken by force, if they would not yield willingly to the desires of a nobleman.

Although the literature of courtly love was extremely idealistic and somewhat artificial, it expressed the values of a gentler noble culture wherein upper-class women were more respected than before. Moreover, certain royal women in the twelfth and thirteenth centuries actually did rule their states on various occasions when their husbands or sons were unable to do so. From 1109 until her death in 1126, Queen Urraca ruled the combined kingdom of León-Castile in Spain. The strong-willed Blanche of Castile ruled France extremely well twice in the thirteenth century, once during the minority of her son Louis IX and again when he was off crusading. Queens are not, of course, typical women, and from a modern perspective, high medieval noblewomen were still very constrained. But from the point of view of the past, the High Middle Ages was a time of progress for the women of the upper classes. The most striking symbol of this change comes from the history of the game of chess. Before the twelfth century chess was played in the Islamic world, but there the equivalent of the queen was a male figure, the king's chief minister, who could move only diagonally, one square at a time. In twelfth-century Europe, however, this piece was turned into a queen, and sometime before the end of the Middle Ages she began to move all over the board.

POLITICS AND GOVERNMENT

How did government and politics change during the High Middle Ages?

The profound social and economic changes of the High Middle Ages also gave rise to new forms of government and political life. In the early Middle Ages, monarchy was virtually the only form of government western Europeans knew. Towns were small and usually ruled by their bishops or kings. Kingdoms too were small and were thought of as pertaining to a particular people such as the Lombards, the Visigoths, or the West Saxons. During the eighth and ninth centuries, most of these ethnic kingdoms disappeared as larger, more powerful, territorially based kingdoms emerged in England and in the Carolingian empire. In England, the West Saxon monarchy survived the ninth-century Viking invasions to become the sole rulers of a united English kingdom. In France, Catalunya, and northern Italy, however, the Carolingians' collapse came near to erasing monarchical power altogether. In the resulting power vacuum, two new structures of political authority slowly emerged in the heartland of the former Carolingian empire: feudal principalities and self-governing cities.

Images of Aristocracy. This early fifteenth-century illustration, from the *Très Riches Heures* commissioned by Jean, Duke of Berry, depicts the leisurely elegance that became such an important feature of medieval aristocratic life.

URBAN GOVERNMENT

We have spoken already of the general economic factors that led to the growth of cities during the High Middle Ages: the increasing agricultural wealth of the countryside, growing population, and developing networks of local and long-distance trade. These factors brought large numbers of immigrants into the cities. They also attracted the local nobility, many of whom became involved in the burgeoning economic and political life of the city. In northern Italy especially, nobles moved to the cities, where they lived in fortified urban towers surrounded by their knightly retainers, their servants, and their urban supporters just as they would have done in a castle in the countryside.

Considering how large the great cities of western Europe became during the twelfth and thirteenth centuries, it is astonishing to realize how informal their governmental arrangements were. Where kings or powerful feudal lords continued to rule, towns and cities often received special charters of liberty that defined their jurisdictional rights and established the basic structures of urban self-government. In northern Europe, these usually involved a mayor and a council elected from among the leading citizens of the town. Elsewhere, for example in Rome, powerful rulers such as the pope resisted all efforts to establish independent city governments. In northern Italy, however, only a few powerful lords—mostly bishops—remained to support or to resist demands for urban self-government. Urban dwellers in Italy therefore had to work out their governmental arrangements for themselves.

In the twelfth century, many north Italian cities entrusted their governments formally to "consuls," drawn from among the leading magnates of the city. Often, however, an informal association of citizens known as the "commune" undertook a wide variety of governmental functions side by side with the consuls. Even the communes, however, were distinctly oligarchical in character. As social stratification increased during the thirteenth century, many cities found themselves split between a ruling class of "magnates" and a popular party that felt itself excluded from the interlocking structures of power that controlled city government and the guilds. Others cities adopted the model of Venice and became more formally oligarchical, casting off even the pretense of being a popular republic. By 1300, however, even cities that remained republics in principle were becoming increasingly oligarchical in practice. Terms of office were getting longer; the jurisdictional claims of urban

> Where kings or powerful feudal lords continued to rule, towns and cities often received special charters of liberty that defined their jurisdictional rights and established the basic structures of urban self-government.

governments were expanding; and traditions of dynastic succession to office were beginning that would lead to the urban principalities of the later Middle Ages.

FEUDALISM AND THE EMERGENCE OF NATIONAL MONARCHIES

> What was the relationship between feudalism and the rise of national monarchies?

In theory, of course, Europe remained a continent of kingdoms even during the tenth and eleventh centuries, when monarchical power in France and Italy was at its lowest ebb. In France, the Capetian dynasty succeeded the Carolingians without interruption in 987, keeping alive the memory that all France had once owed allegiance to a single king. In northern Italy, a number of local rulers vied with each other to claim the Carolingians' fallen mantle of royalty for themselves until their claims were finally trumped, after 962, by the newly crowned Ottonian emperors of Germany. In practice, however, neither the Ottonians in Italy nor the Capetians in France were able to control the territories over which they claimed to rule. By the year 1000, effective political and military power in France lay in the hands of dukes, counts, castellans, and knights, whose power rested on their capacity to channel the increasing wealth of the countryside into their own hands. The symbol of their authority was the castle, often little more than a wooden tower set on a hill with a wooden palisade around it. From their castles, these counts, castellans, and knights constructed "lordships": self-contained territories within which they exercised not only the property rights of landlords over peasants, but also the public rights to mint money, judge legal cases, raise troops, wage war, collect taxes, and impose tolls. By the year 1000, France had thus become a patchwork kingdom composed of essentially independent territorial principalities ruled by counts or dukes, which were in turn divided into smaller lordships ruled by castellans and knights.

WHAT WAS THE RELATIONSHIP BETWEEN FEUDALISM AND THE RISE OF NATIONAL MONARCHIES?

FEUDALISM AND THE EMERGENCE OF NATIONAL MONARCHIES   245

A City on Fire. Once a fire began to spread in a medieval city, women, children, and priests were swiftly evacuated, and servants of the rich would start carrying out their masters' possessions. Here the Swiss city of Bern is shown in flames: although a "bucket brigade" tried desperately to extinguish the fire with water taken from the town moat, chronicles report that the city was leveled by flames in less than half an hour.

THE PROBLEM OF FEUDALISM

This highly decentralized political system, in which "public" powers of minting, justice, taxation and defense were vested in the hands of private lords, is conventionally referred to as *feudalism*. Feudalism took shape first and most fully in tenth- and eleventh-century France, after the Carolingian empire had disintegrated. From France, the language and customs of feudalism spread to other areas of Europe, changing as they were adapted to the particular social, economic, and political circumstances of different regions and countries. Finally, in the twelfth and thirteenth centuries, feudalism developed into an ideology justifying a hierarchical legal and political order that subordinated knights to counts and counts to kings. In this modified form, feudalism gave rise to powerful feudal monarchies and helped to lay the groundwork for the emergence of European nation-states.

What then was feudalism? At its simplest level, a "fee" or "fief" (rhymes with "reef"; in Latin, *feudum*) was a kind of contract, in which someone granted something of value—often land, but sometimes revenues from tolls or mills, or an annual grant of money—to someone else in return for service of some kind. Frequently there was a degree of inequality in such contracts, particularly if land was involved, because land was regarded as the most valuable gift one person could give to another. When a man accepted land from another in return for promises of service, a degree of subordination by the recipient toward the giver was usually implied. In some areas, the recipient of a fief might therefore become the "vassal" of the gift giver, who thereby became his "lord"; and their new relationship might be solemnized by an act of "homage," whereby the vassal became "the man" of his lord in return for his fief. It was this relationship that lay at the heart of feudalism as it emerged in the chaos of tenth-century France.

In a world in which central governmental authority had collapsed, these essentially personal relationships of service in return for land holding became an important element in ordering social and political relations between counts, castellans, and knights. At the same time, however, these relationships were entirely unsystematic. Even in France, where feudalism pervaded aristocratic life, many castellans and knights held their lands freely, owing no service whatsoever to the count or duke within whose territories their lands lay. Nor were feudal relationships necessarily hierarchical. Counts sometimes held lands from knights; knights frequently held lands from each other, and many landholders held fiefs from a number of different lords. Feudalism in the tenth and eleventh centuries created no "feudal pyramids," in which knights held from counts, and counts held from kings in an orderly, hierarchical system of land holding and loyalty. Feudalism of this sort emerged only in the twelfth and thirteenth centuries, when powerful kings began to insist that feudalism *should* be structured in such an orderly way, with kings at the apex of a political and social pyramid.

THE NORMAN CONQUEST OF ENGLAND

Feudalism first emerged as an ordered, hierarchical system of land holding and military service in England, in the peculiar circumstances resulting from the Norman Conquest of 1066. During the tenth and eleventh centuries, England was the wealthiest, most highly centralized, and administratively sophisticated kingdom in western Europe. In 1066, however, Duke William of Normandy laid claim to the English crown and crossed the Channel to conquer what he had claimed. Fortunately for him the newly installed English king, Harold, had just warded off a Viking attack in the north and thus could not offer resistance at full strength. At the battle of Hastings Harold and his English troops fought bravely, but ultimately could not withstand the onslaught of the fresher Norman troops. As the day waned Harold fell, mortally wounded by a random arrow; his forces dispersed, and the Normans took the field—and with it, the kingdom of England. Duke

William now became King William the Conqueror and set about to exploit his new prize.

William rewarded his Norman followers with extensive grants of English land. As the kingdom's conqueror, however, William could claim with some justice that all the land of England belonged ultimately to him, and therefore that all the land in England must be held from him in return for feudal service of some sort. The Norman lords were already accustomed to feudalism in Normandy. In England, however, feudalism after 1066 was much more highly centralized than it had ever been in Normandy, because in England William could draw on the administrative authority of the English state to enforce his claims to be the feudal lord of the entire country.

As king of England, William also exercised a variety of public rights that did not derive from feudalism at all. In England, only the king could coin money, and only the king's money was allowed to circulate. William and his sons also collected a national land tax, supervised justice in public courts, and had the sole authority to summon the population of England to arms. William was also able to insist that all the landholders in England owed loyalty ultimately to the king—even if they did not hold a scrap of land directly from him.

The Bayeux Tapestry. Embroidered shortly after the Battle of Hastings, the Bayeux Tapestry is a 231-foot document of the battle and the events leading up to it. Here the Saxons have sighted a shooting star (Halley's comet, actually) and, taking it for an omen, report it to King Harold.

WHAT WAS THE RELATIONSHIP BETWEEN FEUDALISM AND THE RISE OF NATIONAL MONARCHIES?

FEUDALISM AND THE EMERGENCE OF NATIONAL MONARCHIES   247

William's kingship thus represented a powerful fusion of Carolingian-style traditions of public power with the new feudal structures of power and land holding that had grown up in northern France in the tenth and eleventh centuries.

FEUDAL MONARCHY IN ENGLAND

The history of English government in the two centuries after William is primarily a story of kings tightening up the feudal system to their advantage until they superseded it altogether by creating a strong national monarchy. The first king to take steps in this direction was the Conqueror's energetic son Henry I (1100–1135). To supervise financial accounting at his court, Henry created a specialized administrative office known as the Exchequer, so called because it used an abacuslike checkered cloth to calculate receipts and expenditures. He also strengthened the Anglo-Saxon system of local administration by appointing powerful sheriffs to supervise the counties. He also instituted a system of traveling circuit judges to administer royal justice in the countryside and to act as a check on the sheriffs. Henry's overbearing style of rule was unpopular, and after his death it helped to provoke a civil war. But it also brought England many years of domestic peace and prosperity.

THE REIGN OF HENRY II

After the civil wars that marked the reign of King Stephen (1135–1154), the people of England longed for a king who would bring back the "good old days" of Henry I. They found such a king in Henry's grandson Henry II (1154–1189). Henry II was already the ruler of Normandy, Anjou, Maine, and Aquitaine when he became king of England. As a result, England quickly found itself integrated into the political and cultural world of western France. England, however, was Henry II's richest territory and his only kingdom; for both reasons, it was imperative that he repair the damage done to the country under Stephen.

Henry II restored his grandfather's administrative system with remarkable speed. In addition to reestablishing the Exchequer and the itinerant royal justices, Henry II also expanded the use of juries to determine the facts in civil cases. These innovations are the origin of our mod-

> William's kingship thus represented a powerful fusion of Carolingian-style traditions of public power with the new feudal structures of power and land holding that had grown up in northern France in the tenth and eleventh centuries.

ern system of grand and trial juries. To make it easier for plaintiffs to bring civil suits into the royal courts, Henry also developed a system of "writs," which provided a regularized, inexpensive way for common people to seek justice. These legal innovations were immensely popular because they brought many more people into the royal courts. They also strengthened people's sense of attachment to the king's government.

To improve the administration of justice, Henry II also tried to reform the operations of the church courts. In Henry I's time, criminal cases involving clerics had been tried in the county courts, where sheriffs and church officials presided jointly over them. By Henry II's day, however, a new, independent system of church courts had developed in England and elsewhere in Europe, which claimed the exclusive right to try and sentence clergy accused of committing crimes. Punishment in church courts was generally much milder than in the king's courts. This struck Henry II as unjust. In the Constitutions of Clarendon (1164), Henry tried to force the bishops of England to accept his claim that by ancient custom, clerics convicted in church courts of serious crimes should first lose their clerical status, and then be handed over to the royal court for sentencing as laymen. Archbishop Thomas Becket objected to this procedure, declaring that it amounted to "double jeopardy": punishing someone twice for the same crime. Becket and Henry had once been close friends, but Becket's stubborn insistence that Henry's real goal was to undermine the rights of the church shattered the relationship between them. Becket fled to the pope, who was then living in France under the protection of Henry II's enemy, King Louis VII of France. When Becket finally returned to England in 1170, he was murdered almost immediately in Canterbury Cathedral by four of Henry's knights after the king, in an outburst of anger, had rebuked them for doing nothing to rid him of "this meddlesome priest." Becket was immediately proclaimed a martyr and a saint; Henry was compelled to appear as a pentitent, barefoot and dressed only in a shirt, before Becket's tomb to ask the saint's forgiveness for the rash words that had provoked his murder.

In the long run, however, these dramatic events did not seriously undermine Henry II's relationship either with the papacy or with the English church. Henry was forced to surrender several of his claims, including the right to sentence criminal clerics in royal courts and to restrict appeals from English plaintiffs to the papal court. But he retained the right to nominate clerics to high church offices, and to have such elections held in his presence. As a result, the king's candidates were almost always confirmed to the offices for which he nominated them.

The most concrete proof of Henry II's success is that his government worked so well after his death. Henry's son, the swashbuckling Richard I, the "Lionheart," ruled his father's empire for ten years, from 1189 to 1199, but spent only about six months in England because he was otherwise engaged in crusading or defending his possessions on the Continent. Nonetheless, the legal system continued to develop, and the country raised two huge sums for Richard by taxation: one to pay for his crusade to the Holy Land, and the other to pay his ransom when he was captured by an enemy on his return. It also steadily supported his wars to defend the Angevin empire against King Philip Augustus of France.

THE REIGN OF JOHN AND MAGNA CARTA

Had Richard lived, the map of Europe might look very different today: had he defeated King Philip, France itself might not exist with anything like its current borders. But Richard was killed in 1199 while besieging a small castle in southern France. His successor, his brother John (1199–1216), was a much less capable military leader, who quickly lost nearly all of the Angevin lands in France to King Philip.

John devoted the rest of his reign to raising the money he would need to recover his lost French territories. To do so, he pressed his feudal rights to their limits, forcing massive fines from his nobility and imposing heavy taxes on the country. When John's 1214 military expedition to France failed, the exasperated magnates of England rebelled. In 1215 they forced John to renounce his extortionate fiscal practices in a great charter of liberties known to posterity as Magna Carta. Because John had relied so heavily on his feudal powers, most of Magna Carta's provisions dealt directly with such matters, insisting that the king must in future respect the traditional rights of his vassals. But it did also establish some important general principles: that taxation could not be raised by the crown without consent given by the nobility in a common council, and that no free man could be punished by the crown except by the judgment of his equals and by the law of the land. Above all, however, Magna Carta was important as an expression of the principle that the king is bound by the law.

In the century following Magna Carta, the progress of centralized government continued apace. In the reign of John's son, Henry III (1216–1272), the nobility vied with the king for control of the government but did so on the assumption that centralized government itself was a good thing. Throughout Henry's reign, administrators continued to perfect more efficient legal and administrative institutions, including a system of central and local courts, and a taxation system that assessed both nobles and commoners in proportion to their wealth.

The last and most famous branch of the medieval English governmental system was Parliament. This gradually emerged as a separate branch of government in the decades before and after 1300, above all owing to the wishes of Henry III's son, Edward I (1272–1307).

Martyrdom of Thomas Becket. From a thirteenth-century English psalter. One of the knights has struck Becket so mightily that he has broken his sword.

WHAT WAS THE RELATIONSHIP BETWEEN FEUDALISM AND THE RISE OF NATIONAL MONARCHIES?

FEUDALISM AND THE EMERGENCE OF NATIONAL MONARCHIES   249

CHRONOLOGY

NOTEWORTHY NORMAN AND ANGEVIN KINGS, 1066–1327

William I (the Conqueror)	1066–1087
Henry I	1100–1135
Stephen	1135–1154
Henry II	1154–1189
Richard I (the Lionheart)	1189–1199
John	1199–1216
Henry III	1216–1272
Edward I	1272–1307
Edward II	1307–1327

Although Parliament later became a check against royal absolutism, in its origins Parliament was very much a royal institution, summoned because kings found it useful to consult with their nobles, knights, and townsmen in a single assembly. Magna Carta had demanded that no taxation be imposed without the common consent of the realm. Parliament provided an efficient way to secure such consent, as well as to inform those present why such taxation was necessary. Edward also used Parliaments to take advice about pressing concerns; to hear judicial cases involving great men; and to review local administration, hear complaints from the countryside, and promulgate new laws in response to those complaints. Parliaments were thus political institutions no less than financial and judicial ones. They played an essential role in English government from the fourteenth century on.

FEUDAL MONARCHY IN FRANCE

Administrative kingship developed more slowly in France than in England, but by 1300 it had reached a comparable stage in both countries. During the tenth century, most of the Carolingian institutions of local government in France had collapsed; as a result, the new Capetian dynasty of French kings (987–1328) had to rebuild such institutions from scratch. For nearly two hundred years, it seemed unlikely they would ever be able to do so. As kings of France, the early Capetians ruled directly only a small area around Paris roughly the size of Vermont. Outside their home territory, the Capetian kings could claim only to be the feudal overlords of the independent counts and dukes who ruled the rest of France. An idea of France survived as a legacy from the Carolingian period; but in all other respects, the Capetians had to reinvent their kingdom.

In many ways the Capetians were fortunate. Quite against the biological odds, they managed to produce sons for three hundred years without interruption. They also proved surprisingly long lived: on average, each Capetian king ruled for thirty years. As a result, they avoided both succession disputes and destructive minority governments. They ruled a remarkably rich agricultural territory, which provided them with a steadily increasing source of income. They also acquired significant prestige as protectors of popes fleeing from the German emperors, and as the patrons of the University of Paris, which became the leading European center of learning during the twelfth and thirteenth centuries. Beyond all this, however, the Capetians proved to be a shrewd and wily line of kings, who carefully husbanded their strength while their more powerful enemies overreached themselves.

THE GROWTH OF ROYAL POWER IN FRANCE

The steady growth of royal power in France began under Louis VI "the Fat" (1108–1137). It was Louis who consolidated royal control and subdued the turbulent "robber barons." Once this was accomplished, agriculture and trade could prosper and the intellectual life of Paris began to flourish. Louis's son Louis VII (1137–1180) was thoroughly overshadowed by his rival, King Henry II of England. But he managed nonetheless to increase the resources and the prestige of the French monarchy. By inciting rebellions by Henry II's sons against their father, he also kept the Angevin empire in a constant state of discord.

It was Louis VII's son Philip II who finally turned the tide against the Angevins, and who marks the true beginning of administrative kingship in France. Like his father, Philip understood that he could not win a direct military confrontation with Henry II or Richard I. King John, however—known to his detractors as "soft sword"—was another matter. To facilitate his succession to his brother's throne, John agreed to do homage to Philip for all his lands in France. Philip then shrewdly took advantage of his position as John's feudal overlord to undermine John's control over these territories. When John refused to permit such incursions, Philip declared all John's lands in France to be forfeit to the French crown. A war of conquest quickly followed. By 1204, the richest part of the Angevin territories in France were in Philip's hands.

Philip now had the resources to begin building an effective system of local administration. He chose to maintain most of the administrative institutions the Angevins had created there. To supervise these territories, however, he appointed new royal officials with full judicial, administrative, and military authority. Philip also improved his central administration by adopting stricter systems of financial accounting and record keeping. The administrative pattern Philip established, of combining local diversity with centralized royal control, would continue to characterize French government for the next five hundred years. Philip's son, Louis VIII (1223–1226), would extend it to the newly conquered territories of southern France. His son, Louis IX (1226–1270), would deepen and extend it further. Even more important, however, Louis IX would legitimize it by his own extraordinary devotion to justice at home and crusading abroad. Louis IX became the epitome of thirteenth-century kingship; after his death, he would be canonized by the church as Saint Louis. His successors would draw on the prestige of "good King Louis" for centuries to come.

That prestige came close to being squandered, however, by Saint Louis's ruthless grandson Philip IV, "the Fair" (1285–1314). Philip waged aggressive wars against Flanders in the northeast and the remaining English territories in the southwest. To finance these campaigns, his administration became a voracious money-raising machine. Despite his enormous resources, Philip could not match the capacity of his enemy, Edward I, to raise cash from his subjects through voluntary taxation. Although Philip experimented with representative assemblies similar to the English Parliament, these Estates General (as they came to be called) never played a role in French government comparable to Parliament in England. There were many reasons for this, but perhaps the most fundamental one was the fact that the French nobility successfully claimed to be exempt from paying direct taxation to the crown. Ever since the Anglo-Saxon period, English monarchs had been powerful enough to ensure that their nobility must pay the taxes to which they consented. The weakness of the early Capetian kings had prevented a similar custom from taking root in France, and even Philip IV found it easier to accept this state of affairs rather than to challenge it. Noble exemptions from taxation would therefore remain a political problem for the French monarchy right on up until the French Revolution of 1789.

GERMANY

Germany in the High Middle Ages followed a very different pattern. In the year 1050, Germany appeared to be the strongest monarchy in western Europe. To rule their wide territories—which included Switzerland, eastern France, and most of the Low Countries, as well as claims to northern Italy—the emperors relied heavily on cooperation with the church. The leading royal administrators were archbishops and bishops whom the German emperors appointed and installed in their sacred offices. Even the pope was frequently an imperial appointee. Often, these leading churchmen were members of the imperial family itself, who could counterbalance the strength of the regional dukes. Germany was not so administratively sophisticated as was eleventh-century England, but there was no question about the effectiveness of monarchical authority. It simply rested on other foundations.

THE CONFLICT WITH THE PAPACY

In 1056, however, the emperor Henry III died, leaving as his heir a small boy, the future Henry IV. From this point on, the strength of the monarchy began to unravel. Henry III had installed a new group of reforming clergy at the papal court, whose policies will be discussed more fully in the next chapter. Conflicts between the regents for the boy king Henry IV and the papal reformers began almost immediately. Conflicts also erupted between the regents (who came from central and southern Germany) and the nobility of Saxony. When Henry IV began to rule on his own, the Saxon conflicts escalated. In 1073, these hostilities erupted into a disastrous and destructive civil war.

CHRONOLOGY	
NOTEWORTHY CAPETIAN KINGS, 987–1328	
Hugh Capet	987–996
Louis VI	1108–1137
Louis VII	1137–1180
Philip Augustus	1179–1223
Louis VIII	1223–1226
Louis IX	1226–1270
Philip IV	1285–1314

Legend:
- Angevin Empire under Henry II, about 1180
- French Royal Domain, 1180
- Boundary of France, 1180
- Battle sites

IRELAND

Dublin

SCOTLAND
Bannockburn • Edinburgh

Carlisle
Durham

York • Stamford Bridge

WALES

Bosworth Field
ENGLAND

Hereford

Gloucester • Ely

Oxford • Cambridge

London

Runnymede • Canterbury
Southampton • Winchester
Hastings

ATLANTIC OCEAN

English Channel

BRITTANY

Bayeux
Caen
NORMANDY
Mont-St. Michel

MAINE

Nantes

ANJOU

TOURAINE
Poitiers

POITOU

Bay of Biscay

AQUITAINE

Bordeaux • Angoulême
Périgueux

GASCONY

NAVARRE

TOULOUSE
Albi

ARAGON

CATALUNYA

Calais
Ypres • Bruges • Antwerp
FLANDERS • Lille • Brussels
Agincourt • Bouvines
Arras
Amiens

Rouen
Beauvais • VERMANDOIS
St. Denis • Rheims • Verdun
Paris

Chartres
Brétigny
ISLE DE FRANCE
CHAMPAGNE
Troyes
BURGUNDY
Bourges
Autun

Dijon

Geneva

Lyon

PROVENCE

Avignon

Montpellier
Aigues-Mortes
LANGUEDOC
Narbonne

Marseilles

MEDITERRANEAN SEA

CORSICA

HOLY ROMAN EMPIRE

LORRAINE

Rhine R.
Meuse R.
Scheldt R.
Mosel R.
Marne R.
Saône R.
Rhône R.
Seine R.
Loire R.
Garonne R.

Inset (top right): France at the Death of Philip Augustus 1223
- Royal domain
- Under English rule

ENGLAND
ATLANTIC OCEAN
Paris
FRANCE
Compostela
Bay of Biscay
AQUITAINE
LÉON

0   100   200   300 Miles
0   300 Kilometers

Inset (bottom left):
EUROPE
Area of detail
AFRICA

0   100   200 Miles
0   100   200 Kilometers

FRANCE AND ENGLAND, 1180–1223

Consider the vast geographical expanse of the Angevin empire in 1180. What were the primary requirements for holding this empire together? What advantages did the kings of France enjoy in their struggles with the Angevins? What did it mean to be "French" in such a world? Would the wars between the Angevins and the Capetians have encouraged the emergence of national identities within their kingdoms? Why or why not?

Just as the Saxon war ended, however, a new conflict broke out with the papal reformers at Rome. The newly elected pope Gregory VII (1073–1085) became convinced that to reform the spiritual life of the church, it was necessary first to free the church from the control of laymen, including the emperor. Henry refused to accept Gregory's attempts to prohibit him from selecting and installing in office his own bishops and abbots, and began to plot to remove Gregory from the papacy. Gregory, in turn, allied himself with the Saxon nobility, reigniting the civil war from which Germany had not yet recovered. The struggle between pope and emperor continued until 1122, when Henry's son Henry V finally reached a compromise with the papacy. By then, however, the German nobility had won far more practical independence from the crown than they had had before. After fifty years of nearly constant war, they had also become far more militarized and dangerous. In 1125, when Henry V died childless, they gained further authority by making good on their claims to elect a new ruler regardless of hereditary succession—a principle that would thereafter often lead them to choose the weakest successors or to embroil the country in civil war. The pope's right to crown any new Roman emperor gave him a stake in the selection process also. Although the popes valued the German emperors as counterweights to the Normans in southern Italy, they feared them in equal measure. Should the German emperors succeed in ruling northern and central Italy directly, the papacy—on whose spiritual independence the salvation of all Christians depended—risked becoming their puppet. This fear propelled the next century of papal-imperial conflict.

FREDERICK BARBAROSSA AND HENRY VI

A major attempt to stem the tide running against the German monarchy was made by Frederick I (1152–1190). Frederick, called "Barbarossa" ("red beard"), reasserted the independent dignity of the empire by calling his realm the "Holy Roman Empire," on the theory that it was a universal empire descending from Rome and blessed by God. At the same time, however, he also tried to rule in cooperation with the German princes, supporting their efforts to bring their own territorial nobles to heel, and trusting that the princes would in turn support his attempts to reassert imperial control over the wealthy but increasingly independent cities of northern Italy.

By and large, Frederick made this system work, but at the cost of a lengthy war in Italy and destructive conflict

with the papacy. Led by Milan and supported by the papacy, the north Italian cities formed an urban coalition, the Lombard League, to resist Frederick's claims to rule in Italy. Ultimately, Frederick achieved a compromise with both the Lombard League and the papacy, which guaranteed the political independence of the towns in return for large cash payments they would make to the emperor. He also secured the princes' approval for his son Henry to succeed him as king and emperor, and he arranged a marriage between Henry and the sister of the Norman king of Sicily.

Barbarossa's careful planning bore fruit in the reign of his son Henry VI. Henry succeeded to his father's throne without difficulty. He enjoyed a huge income from the north Italian towns, and when his wife's brother died suddenly without heirs, he became the king of Sicily also. This was the nightmare the papacy had always feared, for now a single, enormously powerful ruler controlled both northern and southern Italy, leaving the papal lands in central Italy surrounded on all sides. Fortunately for the papacy, however, Henry VI died in 1197 at the age of thirty-two, leaving as his heir a three-year-old son, the future Frederick II. The new pope, Innocent III (1198–1216), threw all his energy into an attempt to break the links between Germany, northern Italy, and the kingdom of Sicily. When a civil war erupted in Germany over the succession to the throne, Innocent threw his support back and forth between the two main claimants, hoping to secure some kind of promise from the successful claimant that would return Sicily to the papacy. When Otto IV, Frederick II's rival, finally appeared to have won a decisive victory, Innocent played his last card. He sent the sixteen-year-old Frederick II north with a small army, never imagining that so small a force, led by so young a man, could ever triumph. However, Otto's forces were routed at the battle of Bouvines by King Philip Augustus of France, and Frederick II wound up as the new, and undisputed, king of Germany.

FREDERICK II

Frederick II (1216–1250) was one of the most fascinating of all medieval rulers. Having grown up in Sicily, Frederick spoke Arabic as well as Latin, German, French, and Italian. He maintained a menagerie of exotic animals, a troop of Muslim archers, and a harem of veiled and secluded women, all of which traveled with him on his journeys. But despite this appearance of exoticism, he was also a very conventional medieval ruler who sought to pursue his grandfather's policies of sup-

WHAT WAS THE RELATIONSHIP BETWEEN FEUDALISM AND THE RISE OF NATIONAL MONARCHIES?

FEUDALISM AND THE EMERGENCE OF NATIONAL MONARCHIES   253

THE HOLY ROMAN EMPIRE, C. 1200

Are the borders of the Holy Roman empire defined by rivers, oceans, or mountain ranges? How would you explain this fact? Does the Kingdom of Germany have any such "natural" borders? Note the position of the Papal States in central Italy. Why would the prospect of a single heir to the Holy Roman empire and to the Kingdom of Sicily have frightened the popes? Were their fears well founded? Why or why not?

porting the territorial princes in Germany while enforcing imperial rights in Italy. Much had changed, however, since the death of the emperor Henry VI. In Germany, the princes had already become so entirely autonomous that there was little Frederick could do except to recognize their privileges. This he proceeded to do; but in exchange, he got them to elect his sons to succeed him as kings of Germany. Frederick's biggest problems lay in Italy. In northern Italy, the cities of the Lombard League had once again shaken off their obligations to pay taxes to the empire; while in Sicily, the enormously powerful and administratively sophisticated kingdom created by the Normans had fallen into chaos.

Frederick spent the next twenty-five years solidifying his relationship with the German nobility and recovering as much land as he could after twenty years of war, reestablishing his authority in Sicily and Northern Italy, and recovering Jerusalem through negotiations with the Muslim ruler of Egypt. In 1237, however, he overreached himself by asserting his rights as emperor to rule the north Italian cities directly, bypassing their own governmental structures. The result was another Lombard League, and another lengthy war, which continued until Frederick's death in 1250. With him went the last prospect for the continuation of effective monarchical rule in Germany. Emperors would continue to be elected, but in practice, monarchical authority in Germany had effectively collapsed. Power in Germany would henceforth be divided among several hundred territorial princes whose rivalries would embroil German politics until the end of the nineteenth century.

Frederick spent the next twenty-five years solidifying his relationship with the German nobility and recovering as much land as he could after twenty years of war, reestablishing his authority in Sicily and Northern Italy, and recovering Jerusalem through negotiations with the Muslim ruler of Egypt.

IBERIA

The Iberian peninsula was even more regionalized than was Germany. In contrast to Germany, however, Spain would emerge from the Middle Ages with the most powerful monarchy in Europe. The key to the strength of the Spanish monarchies of the High Middle Ages lay in their successful reconquest of the peninsula from the Muslims, and in the lands, booty, and plunder these conquests provided. During the High Middle Ages Iberia contained four major Christian kingdoms: the northern mountain state of

Navarre; Portugal in the west; the combined kingdom of Aragon and Catalunya in the southeast; and Castile in the center. Throughout the twelfth century, Christian armies steadily advanced, culminating in the year 1212 in a major victory by a combined Aragonese-Castilian army over the Muslims at Las Navas de Tolosa. By the end of the thirteenth century all that remained of earlier Muslim domination was the small state of Granada, and Granada existed mostly because it was willing to pay tribute to the Christians. Castile became by far the largest Spanish kingdom in area, but it was balanced in wealth by the more urban and trade-oriented kingdom of Aragon and Catalunya. Wars between these two rivals weakened both kingdoms during the later Middle Ages; but when the marriage of Ferdinand of Aragon and Isabella of Castile joined these two ancient enemies, a united Spanish monarchy was born. In 1492, the Catholic monarchs captured Granada, the last remaining Muslim territory in Spain. A few months later, Isabella commissioned an Italian adventurer named Christopher Columbus to sail to India by heading west across the Atlantic Ocean. Columbus failed. But his accidental encounter with the American continents made sixteenth century Spain the most powerful kingdom in Europe.

CONCLUSION

In the year 1000, Europe was the least powerful, the least prosperous, and the least intellectually sophisticated of the three Western civilizations that had emerged out of the Roman world. By 1300, its position vis-à-vis both the Byzantine and the Islamic world had been transformed. This transformation rested on economic foundations: an increasingly efficient agriculture, a growing population, and expanding trade. These changes produced a society in which individuals cast off old roles and took on new ones with bewildering speed. No less important, however, were the political and military changes Western Europe underwent during these centuries. By 1100, the heavily armored, mounted knight had emerged as the most formidable military weapon of the day. It was only during the twelfth and thirteenth centuries, however,

FREDERICK II CHANGES
THE HEIGHT OF THE HEAVENS

As a result of the propaganda war that erupted between Frederick II and the papacy during the 1240s, a series of stories began to circulate about Frederick's "exotic" intellectual and scientific interests: that he had ordered infants to be raised in isolation, to discover what language they would naturally speak; that he had had men disemboweled before him, in order to study the processes of digestion; and that he sealed a man up in a cask to die, to prove that the soul perished with the body. None of these stories has any basis in fact, but all illustrate the impact the image of Frederick had on his contemporaries.

The following story concerns Frederick's court astrologer, Michael Scot (d. 1236), an influential scholar who translated a number of Aristotelian and astronomical works and commentaries from Arabic to Latin. It is taken from the chronicle of Salimbene de Adam, a Franciscan supporter of the pope in the struggle against Frederick.

The seventh example [of Frederick's idiosyncracies] was that he once asked Michael Scot to tell him the distance of his palace from heaven. And after Michael gave the answer that seemed correct to him, the Emperor took him away for a few months as if merely on a pleasure trip, commanding his architects and stone masons in the meantime to lower that room of his palace in such a way that no one could detect it. This was done, and when the Emperor returned to his palace with the astrologer, he asked him again how far distant the palace was from heaven. And after he had completed his calcu-lations, Michael Scot answered that either the heavens had risen or the earth had sunk. Then the emperor knew that he was a true astrologer.

I have heard and know many other idiosyncrasies of Frederick, but I keep quiet for the sake of brevity, and because reporting so many of the Emperor's foolish notions is tedious to me.

Joseph Baird, Giuseppe Baglivi, and John Robert Kane, eds. and trans. *The Chronicle of Salimbene de Adam.* Medieval and Renaissance Texts and Studies, v. 4. (Binghamton, N.Y.: Medieval and Renaissance Texts and Studies, 1986), pp. 355–356.

that European governments developed the administrative and political capacity to control these knights and to direct them toward purposes larger than mere brigandage and extortion.

Until the High Middle Ages, the Western world had known two basic patterns of human government: city-states and empires. City-states were more capable of mobilizing the loyalty of their citizens, but city-states were frequently divided by internal economic and so-cial rivalries; and in the long run, they were not militarily strong enough to defend themselves against foreign conquerors. Empires, by contrast, could win battles and maintain powerful administrative bureaucracies, but they were generally too far flung and rapacious to inspire deep loyalties among their subjects.

The national monarchies of the High Middle Ages would prove to be the "golden mean" between these extremes. They were large enough to defend themselves, and wealthy enough to develop sophisticated administrative techniques. But they also commanded sufficient citizen participation and loyalty to support them in times of stress when empires would have foundered. By 1300, the kings of England, France, and the Iberian peninsula had largely succeeded in claiming the primary loyalty of their subjects, superseding the claims of locality, region, or even the church. Their victory was not yet complete, and in the later Middle Ages, France in particular would come near to collapse. But in the end, the national monarchies of the High Middle Ages would endure to become the foundations on which the nation-states of the modern era would be constructed. So important would this historical pedigree become that modern nation-states that did not have a medieval origin would often be compelled to invent one.

KEY TERMS

manorialism	First Crusade	feudalism
serfdom	chivalry	William the Conqueror
guilds	courtly love	Magna Carta

SELECTED READINGS

Abulafia, David. *Frederick II: A Medieval Emperor.* London and New York, 1988. The only reliable biography of Frederick II; it strips away much of the legend that has hitherto surrounded this monarch.

Abulafia, David, ed. *The New Cambridge Medieval History. Volume 5: c. 1198–c. 1300.* Cambridge, 1999. An up-to-date survey, with contributions by more than thirty specialists. Excellent bibliographies.

Amt, Emily, ed. *Women's Lives in Medieval Europe: A Sourcebook.* New York, 1993. An excellent source collection.

Arnold, Benjamin. *Princes and Territories in Medieval Germany.* Cambridge and New York, 1991. The best English-language survey; it correctly avoids portraying the political history of medieval Germany as a story of failure.

Baldwin, John W. *The Government of Philip Augustus.* Berkeley and Los Angeles, 1986. A landmark scholarly account, detailed but readable.

Bartlett, Robert. *The Making of Europe: Conquest, Colonization and Cultural Change, 950–1350.* Princeton, N.J., 1993. A wide-ranging examination of the economic, social, and religious expansion of Europe, full of stimulating ideas and insights.

Dunbabin, Jean. *France in the Making, 843–1180,* 2d ed. Oxford and New York, 2000. An authoritative survey of the disparate territories that came to make up the medieval French kingdom.

Dyer, Christopher. *Making a Living in the Middle Ages: The People of Britain 850–1520.* New Haven, 2002. A splendid new synthesis that combines social, economic, and archaeological evidence.

Fuhrmann, Horst. *Germany in the High Middle Ages, c. 1050–1200.* Cambridge, 1986. A useful, short account in English of the history of twelfth-century Germany.

Gillingham, John. *The Angevin Empire,* 2d ed. Oxford and New York, 2001. The best treatment by far of its subject, brief but full of ideas.

Herlihy, David, ed. *The History of Feudalism.* New York, 1970. Collects the texts on which scholarly discussion continues to focus.

Hyde, J. Kenneth. *Society and Politics in Medieval Italy.* New York, 1973. A survey that sets the political history of the Italian city-states in its social context.

Jones, P. J. *The Italian City-State: From Commune to Signoria.* Oxford and New York, 1997. A fundamental reinterpretation, with important revisions to the standard accounts of Hyde and Waley.

Jordan, William C. *Europe in the High Middle Ages: The Penguin History of Europe,* Vol. III. New York and London, 2003. An outstanding new survey, the best since Southern (see below).

Kaeuper, Richard W. *Chivalry and Violence in Medieval Europe.* Oxford and New York, 1999. A darker view of chivalry than Keen's (see below).

Keen, Maurice. *Chivalry.* New Haven, 1984. Masterful treatment of chivalry from its origins to the sixteenth century, engagingly written.

Moore, Robert I. *The First European Revolution, c. 970–1215.* Oxford and Cambridge, Mass., 2000. A remarkable description of the ways in which European society was fundamentally reshaped during the eleventh and twelfth centuries.

Otto, Bishop of Freising. *The Deeds of Frederick Barbarossa.* Translated by C. C. Mierow. New York, 1953. A contemporary chronicle interesting enough to read from start to finish.

Reilly, Bernard F. *The Medieval Spains*. New York, 1993. A succinct account that covers the entire Iberian peninsula from 500 to 1500.

Reynolds, Susan. *Fiefs and Vassals: The Medieval Evidence Reinterpreted*. Oxford and New York, 1994. A detailed revisionist account that sees feudalism as the invention of high and late medieval legal thinkers rather than as a description of tenth- and eleventh-century realities.

Southern, Richard W. *The Making of the Middle Ages*. New Haven, 1992. A classic work, first published in 1951 but still fresh and exciting.

Stow, Kenneth R. *Alienated Minority: The Jews of Medieval Latin Europe*. Cambridge, Mass., 1992. An excellent survey of a neglected topic.

Suger, Abbot of Saint Denis. *The Deeds of Louis the Fat*. Translated by R. Cusimano and J. Moorhead. Washington, D.C., 1992. A revealing picture of the challenges that faced the early twelfth-century kings of France as they fought to subdue the local nobility of the Île-de-France.

Waley, Daniel. *The Italian City-Republics*. New York, 1969. A classic introduction to the subject.

DIGITAL HISTORY

THE MARKETPLACE

All the merchants, in exposing their goods for sale there, were exposed to great inconveniences, as they had no shelter except canvas tents; for owing to the changeable gusts of wind assailing them, as is usual at that time of the year, they were cold and wet, and also suffered from hunger and thirst; their feet were soiled by the mud, and their goods rotted by the showers of rain.
—Matthew Paris, *English History*, trans. J. A. Giles (1852)

Once humankind had domesticated a number of plants and animals, it became possible for groups of people to settle in one location. Populations began to grow as did specialization and the division of labor. The marketplace was a centrally defined location where artisans, merchants, traders, retailers, and others could gather. But the marketplace was not just a site for the buying and selling of commodities. It was in the marketplace that, among other things, ideas were shared, politics discussed, and public professions of religion were made.

The marketplace served as a place to socialize and a forum for interaction among people from all walks of life. From the *agora* of ancient Athens and the *horrea* of the Roman world, through the fairs of medieval Europe and the market stalls of European vendors up to the stock and commodities exchanges, malls, and grocery stores of the present time, the marketplace has been an intense focal point of human endeavor.

At first glance, it would seem that there are many differences between the marketplaces of the past and the marketplaces of today. And while there are some significant changes in what we're buying and selling and how we're doing it, the marketplace as a place of interaction remains a constant.

When you visit the Marketplace Digital History Feature at www.wwnorton.com/wciv, consider the images of markets both past and present. Try to imagine the sorts of conversations you might hear, or the sorts of people you might meet. While you explore the primary sources, consider the following questions:

- How would you define the purpose and goal of the marketplace in western civilizations?

- In what ways has the marketplace been a focal point of human interaction?

- What are the major differences between the ancient and medieval marketplace?

THE HIGH MIDDLE AGES: RELIGIOUS AND INTELLECTUAL DEVELOPMENTS, 1000–1300

THE RELIGIOUS AND INTELLECTUAL CHANGES of the High Middle Ages altered European life profoundly. Indeed, it is not too much to say that the fundamental character of European civilization was permanently transformed by the developments that occurred during these crucial centuries. With respect to religious life, the period witnessed both the emergence of the papacy as the dominant organizational force in western Christianity and a remarkable effort on the part of the church to extend and deepen the influence of Christianity among the laity. Parish churches mushroomed across the landscape, and new monastic and religious orders developed, many of which took as their primary mission the task of ministering to the world outside the monastic cloister. For the first time since the late Roman period, preaching, confession, pilgrimages, and private prayer became central elements in the religious life of European Christians. At the same time, however, these new patterns of Christian piety emphasized the religious and social distinctions between Christians and their non-Christian neighbors. The result was a marked increase in the persecution of minority groups within European society, and the creation of what some historians have called a "persecuting society" in which the identification and oppression of heretics, Jews, gay people, lepers, and Muslims became an essential element in the growing power of both church and state.

The High Middle Ages also witnessed a remarkable revival of intellectual and cultural life. From the mid-twelfth century on, hundreds of new works of classical literature and philosophy, including the entirety of the surviving works of Aristotle, poured into western Europe from the Islamic world and, to a lesser degree, from Byzantium. Even before the stimulus of these new texts, however, European intellectuals had begun to think in new ways about fundamental problems in theology, philosophy, and law. Fueling this intellectual revolution was the emergence and rapid growth of universities, accompanied by an even more widespread expansion of primary schooling. New literary forms also began to emerge: vernacular lyric poetry, extended allegories, and above all romances. For the first time in centuries it began to be possible to speak of a European reading public.

FOCUS QUESTIONS

- How was the Latin Church reformed?
- How did the Latin Church control popular heresy?

 • How did the recovery of classical learning affect medieval intellectual life?
- What common themes unite the literature, art, and architecture of the High Middle Ages?

In education, thought, and the arts, early medieval Europe had been a backwater, especially in comparison with Byzantium and Islam. By 1300, however, Europe had become the intellectual and artistic leader among these three western civilizations. Europeans now boasted that learning and the arts had come to them from Egypt, Greece, and Rome; and that although they were pygmies who sat on the shoulders of giants, they nonetheless saw farther and more clearly than had the intellectual giants of antiquity on whose shoulders they sat. Such boasts were largely justified. In the High Middle Ages, Europeans built their intellectual and artistic accomplishments on ancient foundations, but they also began to make major contributions of their own.

THE REFORM OF THE CHURCH

How was the Latin Church reformed?

The combined effects of Carolingian collapse; Viking, Muslim, and Hungarian attacks; and the growing power of local noble families were disastrous for the religious life of ninth- and tenth-century Europe. For several centuries, church reformers had sought to improve the religious lives of the laity by strengthening the control that powerful bishops exercised over the local clergy within their dioceses. By the middle of the tenth century, however, that strategy lay in ruins. Many parish churches had been abandoned or destroyed, while those that survived were often regarded as the personal property of some powerful local family, whose responsibility for protecting these churches easily became a license to oppress them. Monasteries underwent a similar process of "privatization." Some became dumping grounds for aristocratic younger sons who might live in the monastery without ever taking monastic vows. Other monasteries had troops of knights thrust on them. Some even had lay abbots. It was all very distant from what Saint Benedict had outlined in his *Rule for Monasteries*.

In the absence of effective kingship, bishops were helpless against such entrenched local power. Nor could the papacy correct the situation. Indeed, as the bishops of Rome, the popes themselves were among the worst examples of the negative impact too much local influence could have on the spiritual standards of the clergy. Most of the tenth-century popes were incompetent or corrupt, the sons or tools of powerful Roman families who sought to control the papacy in order to rule the city of Rome itself. As the guardian of the tombs of Saints Peter and Paul and the spiritual head of western Christendom, the papacy remained a respected institution, even in its tenth-century nadir. But the popes who occupied Saint Peter's chair left a great deal to be desired as moral and spiritual leaders of Western society.

MONASTIC REFORM, 900–1050

The first stirrings of reform emerged in the monasteries of tenth-century Europe, beginning with that of Cluny in Burgundy. Founded in 910 by a pious nobleman, Cluny was a Benedictine house, but with two important constitutional innovations. One was that in order to keep it free from domination by local noble families or the local bishop, Cluny was placed directly under the protection of the papacy. The second was that it undertook the reform or foundation of a large number of "daughter" monasteries. Cluny established a network of dependent Cluniac houses across Europe, all of which remained subordinate to the mother house at Cluny. By 1049, there were sixty-seven such Cluniac priories (as the daughter monasteries were called), each one performing the same elaborate round of prayer and worship for which Cluny became famous, and each entirely free from the control of local secular or ecclesiastical powers. In the eyes of the Cluniacs, their success depended on their absolute freedom from outside interference in their religious life. When Cluny reformed a monastery, therefore, it insisted on two things: first, that the Benedictine vows be strictly enforced on all monks; and second, that the selection of new abbots and priors be accomplished by a free election of the monks, without any buying or selling of the office (a sin known as "simony.")

Cluniac influence was strongest in France and Italy, where the virtual absence of effective kingship made royally sponsored monastic reforms impossible. In Germany and England, by contrast, monastic reform emerged during the tenth and eleventh centuries as an essential responsibility of a Christian king. Following Cluniac example, these kings insisted on the strict observance of poverty, chastity, and obedience within the monastery, and instituted elaborate rounds of group liturgical prayer. In contrast to Cluny, however, it was the kings themselves who guaranteed the reformed monasteries' freedom from outside interference, and it was they who appointed the abbots, just as they also appointed the bishops of their kingdoms.

A MIRACLE OF SAINT FAITH

Although pilgrimages and relics cults had been a part of Christian religious practice for centuries, they became much more central elements in popular piety from the tenth century on. To the monasteries that housed miracle-working relics, pilgrims brought money and spiritual prestige, resulting in competition between monastic houses that sometimes led one house to steal the relics of another. But some critics worried that these newly popular pilgrimage shrines were encouraging idolatry. The author of this account, Bernard of Angers, was one such critic, but in this case he was quickly won over by the evidence of Saint Faith's miracles.

It is an ancient custom in all of Auvergne, Rodez, Toulouse and the neighboring regions that the local saint has a statue of gold, silver, or some other metal . . . [that] serves as a reliquary for the head of the saint or for a part of his body. The learned might see in this a superstition and a vestige of the cult of demons, and I myself . . . had the same impression the first time I saw the statue of Saint Gerard . . . resplendent with gold and stones, with an expression so human that the simple people . . . pretend that it winks at pilgrims whose prayers it answers. I admit to my shame that turning to my friend Bernerius and laughing I whispered to him in Latin, "What do you think of the idol? Wouldn't Jupiter or Mars be happy with it?" . . .

Three days later we arrived at St. Faith. . . . We approached [the reliquary] but the crowd was such that we could not prostrate ourselves like so many others already lying on the floor. Unhappy, I remained standing, fixing my view on the image and murmuring this prayer, "St. Faith, you whose relics rest in this sham, come to my assistance on the day of judgment." And this time I looked at my companion . . . because I found it outrageous that all of these rational beings should be praying to a mute and inanimate object. . . .

Later I greatly regretted to have acted so stupidly toward the saint of God. This was because among other miracles Don Adalgerius, at that time dean and later . . . abbot [of Conques] told me a remarkable account of a cleric named Oldaric. One day when the venerable image had to be taken to another place, . . . he restrained the crowd from bringing offerings and he insulted and belittled the image of the saint. . . . The next night, a lady of imposing severity appeared to him: "You," she said, "how dare you insult my image?" Having said this, she flogged her enemy with a staff. . . . He survived only long enough to tell the vision in the morning.

Thus there is no place left for arguing whether the effigy of St. Faith ought to be venerated since it is clear that he who reproached the holy martyr nevertheless retracted his reproach. Nor is it a spurious idol where nefarious rites of sacrifice or of divination are conducted, but rather a pious memorial of a holy virgin, before which great numbers of faithful people decently and eloquently implore her efficacious intercession for their sins.

Bernard of Angers, *The Book of the Miracles of St. Faith*, chapter 28. Slightly modified from *Readings in Medieval History*, 3d ed., edited and translated by Patrick J. Geary. (Peterborough, Ont.: Broadview Press, 2003), pp. 333–334.

As a result of these parallel movements for monastic reform, monasticism became the dominant spiritual model for tenth- and eleventh-century Latin Christianity. Monasteries also had an important influence on patterns of piety outside the cloister. For centuries, monasteries had been the repositories and guardians of the relics of departed saints, whose powers were believed to protect the monasteries that housed their earthly bodies. From the tenth century on, however, monasteries increasingly attracted the attentions of pious laypeople, who came seeking miraculous cures from the saint (or saints) whose relics were housed there. The vast majority of such pilgrimages were to local shrines. But regular long-distance pilgrimage routes also began to develop, to such places as Santiago de Compostela in Spain and the Church of Saint Faith in southern France. Traffic also increased to such traditional pilgrimage sites as Rome and Jerusalem. Pilgrimage was one of the important ways in which the new patterns of Christian piety developed in monasteries began to spread to the laity outside the monastic walls.

> Pilgrimage was one of the important ways in which the new patterns of Christian piety developed in monasteries began to spread to the laity outside the monastic walls.

THE PAPAL REFORM MOVEMENT

From the monasteries, the reform movement began to affect the bishops also. In England, kings appointed a number of reformed monks to bishoprics. In Germany, kings retained nonmonastic bishops but enforced strict requirements of personal holiness on the bishops and abbots whom they appointed to office. With royal encouragement, bishops also began to rebuild and expand their cathedral churches to make them more suitable reflections of divine majesty, in accordance with Cluniac example. The Cluniacs themselves, however, went further, and began to lobby for the reform of the entire church, including bishops, unreformed monasteries, and even the parish clergy. They centered their attacks on simony, but they also demanded that personal poverty and celibacy be enforced on all monks and priests. This last demand was in some ways the most radical. Although a series of fourth- and fifth-century church councils had declared that priests should be celibate, this requirement had been largely ignored thereafter. In the year 1000, the vast majority of the parish priests across Europe were married.

In Rome, the papacy remained resolutely unreformed until 1046, when the German emperor Henry III came to Rome, deposed all three of the local Roman nobles who claimed to be pope, and appointed in their place his own relative, a German monastic reformer who took the name Pope Leo IX (1049–1054). Leo and his supporters quickly took control of the papal court and began to promulgate decrees against simony, clerical marriage, and immorality of all sorts throughout the church. To enforce these decrees, Leo and his entourage traveled throughout Europe, disciplining and deposing clerics who had purchased their positions or who refused to give up their wives. Implicit in Leo's reforming efforts was thus a new vision of the church itself as a hierarchical organization in which priests obeyed bishops and bishops obeyed the pope not only as the spiritual and doctrinal leader of western Christendom, but as the legal and jurisdictional ruler of the entire Christian church.

Leo and the reform popes were able to enforce their decrees only in those areas of Europe where they could count on the support of secular rulers. Among these secular supporters, the most important was of course the emperor Henry III, whose protection insulated the papal reformers from the Roman noble families who would otherwise have deposed them. In 1056, however, Henry III died, leaving a young child as his heir, the future Henry IV. Without their imperial protector, the reformers were now at the mercy of the Roman political factions. When the reigning reform pope died in 1058, the Roman nobles seized their opportunity to install as pope one of their own lackeys. Briefly, it looked as if the entire reform program might be lost. But the reformers rallied outside Rome, and elected their own pope (who took the name Nicholas II). Allying themselves militarily with the Norman rulers of central and southern Italy, they drove the nonreformed pope out of Rome.

In 1059, Pope Nicholas II issued a new decree on papal elections, vesting the right to elect a pope solely with the cardinals, but "saving the rights of the Emperor." The decree is significant for two quite different reasons. First, it represents a milestone in the evolution of the College of Cardinals as a special body within the church. This decree was the first time that the cardinals' powers had been clearly recognized. Thereafter the College of Cardinals took on an increasingly well-defined identity, becoming an important force in creating continuity of papal policy, especially when there was a quick succession of pontiffs. The cardinals still elect the pope today.

The decree was also significant, however, because it opened up a breach between the reform party in Rome and the German imperial court. In the circumstances of 1059, the Electoral Decree was intended to justify the reformers' actions of the previous year and to protect future papal elections from the influence of the Roman aristocracy. But although the decree obviously drew on Cluniac ideals about free elections as an essential element in a reformed church, it was not intended to deprive the German emperor of his traditional role as papal protector. Nonetheless, the Electoral Decree greatly offended the advisors of the young king Henry IV, who saw it as a challenge to the emperors' rights to nominate new popes, and who also bitterly resented the reformers' alliance with the Normans, whose designs on imperial territories in central Italy were well known. The resulting hostility between the young king's regents and the papal court poisoned the atmosphere in which King Henry IV grew to maturity.

THE INVESTITURE CONFLICT

A new and momentous phase in the history of the reform movement began in 1073 with the election of Pope Gregory VII (1073–1085). Gregory was a Roman whose election was violently supported by a mob of Roman citizens. Gregory was already a well-known reformer with long experience at the papal court. It is likely that he would have been elected by the cardinals anyway, even without the interference of the Roman mob. But the circumstances of his election clearly violated the terms of the 1059 Electoral Decree, and this fact weakened Gregory in his first few years as pope. Henry IV was also anxious for a reconciliation with Rome, not least because between 1073 and 1075 he was involved in a major civil war with his own nobility in Saxony. Both Gregory and Henry began, therefore, by treating one another with great deference. Henry blamed the advisors of his youth for the troubles that had arisen between his own court and Rome, and promised to make amends. Gregory, in turn, spoke of pope and emperor as the two eyes of a single, Christian body, and promised to leave the church in Henry's care if he, Gregory, should lead a military expedition eastward against Islam. On the surface, it appeared that the harmonious relations between papacy and empire that had existed under Henry's father had been fully restored.

By the end of 1075, however, relations between the two men were at a breaking point. For the next half century, western Europe would be riven by conflict between the papacy and the empire—a conflict that would permanently alter the relationship between spiritual and temporal authority in western Christendom. Superficially, the issue that divided Gregory and Henry was whether Henry or any other layman could appoint a bishop or abbot and then dress him with the symbols of his spiritual office, a practice known as "lay investiture." In fact, however, the "Investiture Conflict" raised fundamental issues about the nature of Christian kingship, the relationship between political and religious authority, and the control that popes and kings should exercise over the clergy. Not all these issues were fully resolved by 1122, when a compromise known as the Concordat of Worms finally ended the Investiture Conflict. But the conflict was a turning point nonetheless, because it brought to a permanent end the old Carolingian traditions of sacred kingship and established once and for all the independent jurisdictional authority of the church versus all lay rulers.

Gregory was a devoted church reformer whose goals were the traditional ones of ending simony and clerical marriage. However, Gregory became convinced that these goals could not be achieved until the Cluniac goal of ensuring free elections to all church offices had first been fully realized. Gregory therefore proceeded to prohibit all clerics from accepting any church office from a layman. Henry IV flatly refused to accept this decree, not only because it infringed on his own traditional rights as emperor, but also because the bishops and abbots of Germany and northern Italy were critically important to his own ability to rule his kingdoms. Henry proceeded, therefore, to appoint a new archbishop in Milan in defiance of Gregory's prohibition. Gregory responded by reminding Henry that he, Gregory, occupied Saint Peter's chair, and that Henry therefore owed to Gregory the same obedience he owed to Saint Peter. To drive the point home, Gregory excommunicated a number of Henry's advisors. Henry thereupon renounced his obedience to Gregory, reminding the pope that his election had violated the terms of the 1059 Electoral Decree, and calling on him to resign. Gregory responded by excommunicating Henry.

> Superficially, the issue that divided Gregory and Henry was whether Henry or any other layman could appoint a bishop or abbot and then dress him with the symbols of his spiritual office, a practice known as "lay investiture."

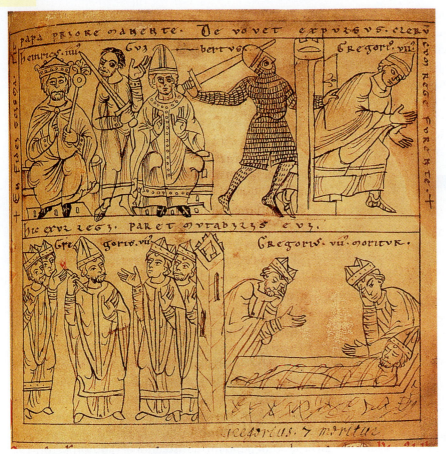

Henry IV and Gregory VII. In the top panel, King Henry appoints Wibert, Archbishop of Milan, to be the new pope, and drives Pope Gregory from Rome. In the lower panel, Pope Gregory is received by the bishops of the Norman kingdom of southern Italy, and then dies in exile. From a twelfth-century German manuscript.

In itself, the excommunication of a king was not terribly unusual. Gregory, however, went much further by declaring that since Henry was no longer a faithful son of the church, he was therefore no longer the king of Germany. Gregory now called on Henry's subjects to rebel, prompting the Saxon nobility to renew the civil war that had ended only a few months before. In January 1077, Henry was forced to make a humiliating public submission to Pope Gregory at Canossa in the Italian Alps; but when the pope absolved him of his excommunication, Henry used the opportunity to rally his forces, crush his Saxon opponents, and drive Gregory himself from Rome.

Although the ultimate solution to the Investiture Conflict was to distinguish between "church" and "state" by reserving the symbols of spiritual office to the clergy while permitting laymen to award the symbols of temporal rule, such a distinction was no part of Gregory's own world view. Indeed, it was precisely because neither Henry nor Gregory could conceive of Christendom as anything other than a thoroughly unified religious and political society that the conflict between them was so intractable. Both Henry and Gregory shared the standard Carolingian presumption that it was the responsibility of earthly rulers to lead their subjects to heaven. They disagreed only about whether the supreme ruler within this unified Christian society should be the emperor or the pope. Neither could imagine a world in which a bishop's spiritual office could be separated from the lands and military forces he controlled, or in which there could be two entirely separate systems of courts, one dealing with religious matters and controlled by the papacy, the other dealing with secular matters and controlled by kings. Without such a division between the spiritual and the temporal, however, the Investiture Conflict was irresolvable. Neither pope nor emperor was powerful enough to defeat the other; and on some level, all Europe was agreed that both spiritual and temporal authorities were necessary.

The consequences of the Investiture Conflict were thus quite different from what Pope Gregory or King Henry had imagined. On the immediate issue of lay investiture, the Concordat of Worms was a compromise. The German emperor was forbidden to invest prelates with the religious symbols of their office, but was allowed to invest them with the symbols of their rights as temporal rulers because the emperor was recognized as their temporal overlord. In practice, the German emperors, like the other kings of western Europe, thus managed to retain a great deal of influence over appointments to bishoprics and abbeys despite allowing the appearance of free elections.

The ultimate consequence of the Investiture Conflict was to create a lasting conceptual distinction between religion and politics in western Europe, and to identify the church with religious authority and the state with political authority. Both ideas had been largely absent from western Europe since the fourth century Constantinian revolution. When the Investiture Conflict began, Henry's principal supporters were his bishops. Gregory's supporters were, for the most part, the Saxon nobility and the other disaffected German princes. In no sense, therefore, did the Investiture Conflict begin as a "church-state" conflict. By 1122, however, that is what it had become. The Concordat of Worms resolved the papal-imperial conflict by distinguishing between the temporal power of kings and the spiritual power of the clergy. It also firmly identified the bishops as a part of a hierarchical clerical order headed by the pope. The boundaries between temporal and spiritual authority would continue to be subject to controversy in medieval Europe. Should kings or clerics judge clergy who committed secular crimes? Who should rule on the validity of marriages when rights to inherit property were at issue? But these were jurisdictional conflicts that sought to define the boundaries between religion and politics. These conflicts did not challenge the fundamental presumption that such a distinction existed. Therefore, these conflicts were resolvable through law—one reason that the elaboration of legal systems, both ecclesiastical and secular, became such a preoccupation for twelfth- and thirteenth-century western Europe. In this respect also, the Investiture Conflict marks a watershed in European history.

THE CONSOLIDATION OF THE PAPAL MONARCHY

The Concordat of Worms was a compromise, but the Investiture Conflict as a whole was a victory for the papacy. The conflict helped rally the western clergy behind the pope, strengthening the papacy's claim to jurisdictional supremacy over the entire clerical hierarchy. The dramatic struggle also galvanized the European populace. Pope Gregory and his successors had urged the common people of Europe to reject the authority of simoniac bishops and married priests. Thousands had responded, sometimes with violence. The result was a vastly greater popular interest in religious matters, which the church thereafter would struggle to contain within the bounds of religious orthodoxy.

> The Concordat of Worms resolved the papal-imperial conflict by distinguishing between the temporal power of kings and the spiritual power of the clergy. It also firmly identified the bishops as a part of a hierarchical clerical order headed by the pope.

Like Gregory VII, the popes of the twelfth and thirteenth century were fully committed to establishing the monarchical authority of the papacy over the church. Specially commissioned papal officials ("legates") were sent out from Rome to convey and enforce papal commands. Many of these commands arose from the hundreds of legal cases that poured into Rome from litigants seeking justice from the pope. In turn, this growing mass of litigation encouraged the development of an authoritative body of church law by which such cases could be resolved. The key step in this development was taken around 1140 in Bologna by a law teacher named Gratian, whose massive compilation and codification of the decrees of previous popes and church councils quickly became the standard collection of church law, or "canon" law.

As the power of the papacy and the prestige of the church mounted, cases in canon-law courts and appeals to Rome rapidly increased. By the mid-twelfth century legal expertise had become so important that almost all popes were trained canon lawyers, whereas previously they had usually been monks. Purists decried this development, but it was an inevitable consequence of the growing power and sophistication of the papal monarchy itself.

THE REIGN OF INNOCENT III

By common consent the most capable and successful of all the high medieval popes was Innocent III (1198–1216). Innocent, who was elected at the age of thirty-seven, was one of the youngest and most vigorous individuals ever to be raised to the papacy; more than that, he was expertly trained in theology and had also studied canon law. His major goal was to unify all Christendom under papal hegemony and thereby to bring about the "right order in the world" so fervently desired by Pope Gregory VII. Unlike Gregory, Innocent never questioned the right of kings and princes to rule directly in the secular sphere. But Innocent believed nonetheless that as pope he was obliged to discipline kings whenever they sinned.

Innocent sought to implement his goals in many different ways. In order to place papal independence on a solid territorial foundation, Innocent consoli-

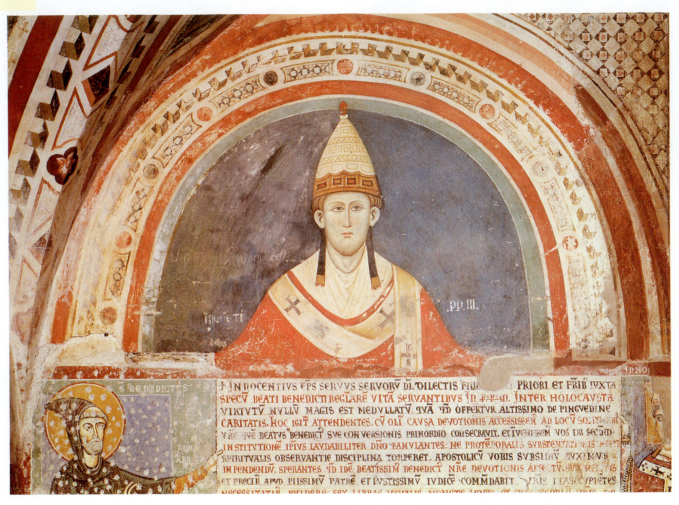

Pope Innocent III. A thirteenth-century fresco from the lower church of Sacro Speco, Subiaco, in Italy.

dated and expanded the papacy's territories in central Italy. For this reason Innocent is often regarded as the founder of the Papal States, of which Vatican City is the last surviving modern remnant. In Germany, he engineered the triumph of his own candidate for the imperial office, the emperor Frederick II—a triumph his papal successors would live to regret. He also levied the first income tax on the clergy to support a crusade to the Holy Land. The crowning achievement of Innocent's pontificate, however, was the summoning of the Fourth Lateran Council to Rome in 1215. This representative assembly of the entire western church defined central dogmas of the faith and made the leadership of the papacy within Christendom more apparent than ever.

POPES OF THE THIRTEENTH CENTURY

Innocent's reign was certainly the zenith of the papal monarchy, but it also sowed some of the seeds of future ruin. Innocent himself could administer the Papal States

and seek new sources of income without seeming to compromise the spiritual dignity of his office. But future popes who followed his policies had less of his stature and thus began to appear more like ordinary, acquisitive rulers. Moreover, because the Papal States bordered on the kingdom of Sicily, Innocent's successors quickly came into conflict with the neighboring ruler, who was none other than Innocent's protégé Frederick II. Innocent had raised up Frederick, but he could not imagine that Frederick would later become an inveterate opponent of papal power in Italy.

At first these and other problems were not fully apparent. The popes of the thirteenth century continued to enhance their powers and centralize the government of the church. They gradually asserted the right to name candidates for ecclesiastical positions, both high and low, and they asserted control over the curriculum and doctrine taught at the University of Paris. But they also became involved in a protracted political struggle that led to their own demise as temporal powers. This growth of royal power and the erosion of papal prestige. Boniface also had the misfortune to succeed a particularly pious, although inept, pope who resigned his office within a year. Since Boniface was entirely lacking in conventional piety or humility, the contrast turned many Christian observers against him. Boniface ruled assertively and presided over the first papal "jubilee" in Rome in 1300. This was an apparent, but, as events would show, hollow demonstration of papal might.

Two disputes with the kings of England and France proved to be Boniface's undoing. The first concerned the clerical taxation that had been initiated by Innocent III.

struggle began with the attempt of the popes to destroy Frederick II. To some degree they were acting in self-defense because Frederick threatened their own rule in central Italy. But in combating him they overemployed their spiritual weapons. Instead of merely excommunicating and deposing Frederick, they also called a crusade against him—the first time a crusade was called on a large scale for blatantly political purposes.

After Frederick's death in 1250 a succession of popes made a still worse mistake by renewing and maintaining their crusade against all of the emperor's heirs. By misusing the institution of the crusade and trying to raise increasingly large sums of money to support it, the popes lost much of their spiritual prestige. In 1291 the last crusader outpost in the Holy Land fell without any papal help being offered. Instead, the popes were still trying to salvage their losing crusade against Frederick's heirs. Pope Boniface VIII's papal jubilee of 1300, which offered a full crusader's indulgence to anyone who made a pilgrimage to Rome, was a tacit recognition that the Eternal City and not the Holy Land would henceforth be the central goal of Christian pilgrimage.

DECLINE OF THE PAPAL MONARCHY

The temporal might of the papal monarchy finally collapsed in the reign of Boniface VIII (1294–1303). Not all Boniface's troubles were of his own making. His greatest obstacle was that the national monarchies had gained more of their subjects' loyalties than the papacy could draw on because of the steady

Pope Boniface VIII (1294–1303) commissioned dozens of statues of himself that he distributed throughout the papal states. Despite its idealized features, this statue—from the Museo Civico in Bologna—does also suggest something of the pope's pugnacious obstinacy.

Although Innocent had levied this tax to support a crusade and had collected it himself, during the course of the thirteenth century the kings of England and France had begun to levy and collect clerical taxes on the pretext that they would use the funds to help the popes on future crusades to the Holy Land or aid in papal crusades against the Hohenstaufens. Then, at the end of the century, the kings started to levy their own war taxes on the clergy without any pretexts at all. Boniface understandably tried to prohibit this step, but quickly found that he had lost the support of the English and French clergy. Thus when the kings offered resistance, he had to back down.

Boniface's second dispute was with King Philip IV of France, who deliberately challenged the pope by preparing to try a French bishop for treason, in violation of canon-law protections for the clergy. As in the earlier struggle between Gregory VII and Henry IV of Germany, a bitter propaganda war ensued, but now hardly anyone listened to the pope. Instead, Philip pressed absurd charges of heresy against Boniface and sent his minions to arrest the pope to stand trial. At the papal residence of Anagni in 1303 Boniface, who was in his seventies, was captured and mistreated by Philip's forces. Although the pope was finally rescued by the local citizens, the shock of these events was too much for the old man's strength, and he died a month later. But still Philip pressed his advantage. He forced the new pope, Clement V, not only to justify his attack on Boniface, but to thank him publically for his zealous defence of the Catholic faith. Thereafter, any shred of papal independence in regard to the interests of the French monarchy was gone. For the next seventy years, the popes would reside not in Rome, but in Avignon, on the borders of the kingdom of France; and the papacy would come to be regarded as a virtual pawn of French diplomatic interests.

The humiliating defeat of Pope Boniface VIII at the hands of King Philip of France illustrates the enormous gap that had opened up by 1300 between the rhetoric and the reality of papal power. Although Boniface continued to lay claim to a universal spiritual and temporal authority over Christendom, declaring that kings ruled only through the "will and sufferance" of the church, in fact the papal monarchy now exercised its authority only through the will and sufferance of kings. After one hundred fifty years during which the religious nature of royal authority had been steadily undermined, the kings of the later thirteenth century were beginning to restore their sacred luster. This trend would

continue throughout the later Middle Ages. It would be shattered, finally, only in the seventeenth century, at the end of a century of religious wars brought on by the Protestant Reformation. Only then would the distinctions between religion and politics established by the Invesiture Conflict be fully and firmly established as fundamental principles of European life.

THE OUTBURST OF RELIGIOUS VITALITY

How did the Latin Church control popular heresy?

The papal reform movement spearheaded by Pope Gregory stimulated a European religious revival for two reasons. One was that the campaign to cleanse the Church actually achieved a large measure of success: the laity could now respect the clergy more, and many were inspired to join the clergy themselves. According to a reliable estimate, the number of people who joined monastic orders in England increased tenfold between 1066 and 1200, a statistic that does not include the increase in priests. The other reason that the work of Gregory VII in particular helped inspire a revival was that Gregory explicitly called on the laity to help discipline their priests. In letters of great propagandistic power he denounced the sins of "fornicating priests" and urged the laity to drive them from their pulpits or boycott their services. Not surprisingly, he touched off something close to a vigilante movement in many parts of Europe. This excitement, taken together with the fact that the papal struggle with Henry IV was really the first European event of universal interest, increased religious commitment immensely. Until about 1050, most western Europeans were Christians in name, but after the Gregorian period Christianity was becoming an ideal and a practice that really began to direct human lives.

CISTERCIANS AND CARTHUSIANS

One of the most visible manifestations of the new piety was the spread of the Cistercian movement in the twelfth century. By around 1100 no form of Benedictine monasticism seemed fully satisfactory to aspirants to holiness who sought great asceticism and, above all, intense "interiority"—unrelenting self-examination and meditative striving toward knowledge of God. The result was the founding of new orders to provide for the fullest expression of monastic idealism. One was the Carthusian order, whose monks were required to live in separate cells, abstain from meat, and fast three days each week on bread, water, and salt. The Carthusians never sought to attract great numbers and therefore remained a small group. But the same was by no means true of the Cistercians. The latter were monks who were first organized around 1100 and who sought to follow the Benedictine rule in the purest and most austere way possible. In order to avoid worldly temptations, they founded new monasteries in forests and wastelands as far away from civilization as possible. They shunned all unnecessary church decoration and ostentatious utensils, abandoned the Cluniac stress on an elaborate liturgy in favor of more contemplation and private prayer, and seriously committed themselves to hard manual labor. Under the charismatic leadership of Saint Bernard of Clairvaux (1090–1153), a spellbinding preacher, brilliant writer, and the most influential European religious personality of his age, the Cistercian order grew exponentially. There were only five houses in 1115 but no less than 343 by 1153.

At the same time that more people were entering or patronizing new monasteries, the very nature of religious belief and devotion was also changing. One of many examples was a shift away from the cult of saints to emphasis on the worship of Jesus and veneration of the Virgin Mary. In the new Cistercian order, the veneration of saints' relics was replaced by a concentration on the Eucharist, or sacrament of the Lord's Supper. Of course celebration of the Eucharist had always been an important part of the Christian faith, but only in the twelfth century was it made really central, for only then did theologians fully work out the doctrine of transubstantiation. According to this doctrine, the priest during mass cooperates with God in the performance of a miracle whereby the bread and wine on the altar are changed or "transubstantiated" into the body and blood of Christ. The new theology of the Eucharist greatly enhanced the dignity of the priest and also encouraged the faithful to meditate on the sufferings of Christ. As a result many developed an intense sense of identification with Christ and tried to imitate his life in different ways.

THE CULT OF THE VIRGIN MARY

Coming a very close second to the renewed worship of Christ in the twelfth century was veneration of the Virgin Mary. This development was more unprecedented because until then the Virgin had been only negligibly honored in the western church. Exactly why veneration of the Virgin became so pronounced in the twelfth century is not fully clear, but whatever the explanation, in the twelfth century the cult of Mary blossomed throughout all of western Europe. The Cistercians made her their patron saint, Saint Bernard constantly taught about her life and virtues, and practically all the magnificent new cathedrals of the age were dedicated to her: there was Notre Dame ("Our Lady") of Paris, and also a "Notre Dame" in

Mary and Eve. The "correct" medieval theological view of women. On the left (Latin: *sinister*) side of the naked Adam the naked Eve takes the apple of sin from the serpent and feeds it to erring mortals while a skeleton waits to carry them to hell. On Adam's right Mary counteracts Eve by feeding a different "fruit"—the Eucharistic wafer— to the devout.

Chartres, Rheims, Amiens, Rouen, Laon, and many other places. Mary's theological role was that of intercessor with her son for the salvation of human souls. Numerous stories circulated about seeming reprobates who were saved because they venerated Mary, who then spoke for them at the hour of death.

The significance of the new cult was manifold. For the first time a woman was given a central and honored place in the Christian religion. Theologians still taught that sin had entered the world through Eve, the first woman; but they now counterbalanced this by explaining how the triumph over sin had come through Mary, who gave birth to Christ, the second Adam. Artists and writers who portrayed Mary were also able to concentrate on femininity and scenes of human tenderness and family life. This contributed greatly to a general softening of artistic and literary style. But perhaps most important of all, the rise of the cult of Mary was closely associated with a general rise of hopefulness and optimism in the twelfth-century West.

HILDEGARD OF BINGEN

Not only did a woman, Mary, gain a particularly prominent role in the religious cult of the twelfth century, but a few living women gained great religious authority. By far the most famous and influential was the German nun and visionary Hildegard of Bingen (1098–1179). Hildegard's descriptions of her religious visions, dictated in freshly original Latin prose, were so compelling that contemporaries had no difficulty in believing that she was directly inspired by God. Consequently when the pope visited Germany he gave her his blessing, and religious and secular leaders sought her advice. She also composed religious songs whose beauty has been rediscovered in recent times. Visionary though she was, she probably would be surprised to see people today looking for her works in racks of compact discs, where she is often alphabetized as "Bingen" between Beethoven and Brahms.

THE CHALLENGE OF POPULAR HERESY

Sometimes the great religious enthusiasm of the twelfth century went beyond the bounds approved by the church. After Gregory VII had called on the laity to help discipline their clergy it was difficult to control lay enthusiasm. As the twelfth century progressed and the papal monarchy concentrated on strengthening its legal and financial administration, some people began to wonder whether the church, which had once been so inspiring, had not begun to lose sight of its idealistic goals. Another difficulty was that the growing emphasis on the miraculous powers of priests tended to inhibit the religious role of the laity and place it in a distinct position of spiritual inferiority. The result was that in the second half of the twelfth century large-scale movements of popular heresy swept over western Europe for the first time in its history.

The two major twelfth-century heresies were Catharism and Waldensianism. The Cathars, who were strongest in northern Italy and southern France, believed that all matter was created by an evil principle and that holiness required extreme ascetic practices. Some Cathars even argued that there were two gods, one good, the other evil; that the created world was entirely in the power of the evil god; and that spiritual people must seek to escape it. Although such teachings were at variance with Christianity, most Cathar followers believed themselves nonetheless to be Christians. Noblewomen in southern France played a particularly important role in the spread of Catharism, sheltering the sect's wandering preachers and converting their households to the new faith.

More typical of twelfth-century religious dissent was Waldensianism, a movement that originated in the French city of Lyons and spread to much of southern France, northern Italy, and Germany. Waldensians were lay folk who wished to imitate the life of Christ and the apostles to the fullest. They therefore translated and studied the Gospels and dedicated themselves to lives of poverty and preaching. Since the earliest Waldensians did not attack any Catholic doctrines, the church hierarchy did not at first interfere with them. But the papacy forbade the Waldensians to preach without authorization and condemned them for heresy when they refused to obey. At that point they became more radical and started to create an alternative church, which they maintained offered the only route to salvation.

When Innocent III became pope in 1198 he was faced with a very serious challenge from growing heresies. His two-pronged response was characteristically decisive and fateful for the future of the church. On the one hand, Innocent resolved to crush all disobedience to papal authority, but on the other, he decided to support idealistic religious groups that were willing

> On the one hand, Innocent resolved to crush all disobedience to papal authority, but on the other, he decided to support idealistic religious groups that were willing to acknowledge obedience.

to acknowledge obedience. Papal monarchy could thus be protected without frustrating all dynamic spirituality within the church.

To suppress Catharism, Innocent authorized the nobles of northern France to launch a crusade against the southern French nobles who had permitted the heresy to flourish within their territories. The crusade succeeded in destroying much of the organizational infrastructure that had supported Catharism. The papacy followed up this success by promoting inquisitorial procedures to root out the remaining heretics. Convicted heretics were sentenced to severe penalties; some were even burned at the stake. Similar procedures were also adopted against the Waldensians, but with less success. By the early fourteenth century, Catharism had been effectively destroyed, but small groups of Waldensians would survive until the seventeenth century, mainly in the mountainous regions of Switzerland and southern Germany.

> By the early fourteenth century, Catharism had been effectively destroyed, but small groups of Waldensians would survive until the seventeenth century, mainly in the mountainous regions of Switzerland and southern Germany.

Another aspect of Innocent's program was to pronounce formally new religious doctrines that would enhance the special status of priests and the ecclesiastical hierarchy. Thus at the Fourth Lateran Council of 1215 he reaffirmed the doctrine that the sacraments administered by the church were the indispensable means of procuring God's grace, and that no one could be saved without them. The decrees of the Lateran Council emphasized two sacraments: the Eucharist and penance. The doctrine of transubstantiation was formally defined. All Catholics were required—as they still are—to confess their sins to a priest and then receive the Eucharist at least once a year.

CHRONOLOGY

EUROPEAN RELIGIOUS REVIVAL, 1100–1300

Cistercian order established	1098
Cult of the Virgin Mary	c. 1100
Catharist heresy emerges	c. 1140
Waldensian heresy emerges	c. 1180
New theology of the Eucharist	c. 1150–1215
Franciscan order established	1209
Fourth Lateran Council	1215
Dominican order established	1216

FRANCISCANS AND DOMINICANS

As stated above, the other side of Innocent's policy was to support obedient, idealistic movements within the church. The most important of these were the new orders of friars—the Dominicans and the Franciscans. Friars were similar to monks in vowing to follow a rule, but they differed greatly from monks in their actual conduct. Instead of withdrawing into monasteries, they imitated the life of Jesus and his apostles, wandering through town and countryside in small groups, preaching and offering spiritual guidance. They also accepted voluntary poverty and begged for their subsistence. In these respects they resembled the Waldensian heretics, but they professed unquestioning obedience to the pope and sought to fight heresy themselves.

The Dominican order, founded by the Spaniard Saint Dominic (1170–1221) and approved by Innocent III in 1216, was particularly dedicated to the fight against heresy and also to the conversion of Jews and Muslims. At first the Dominicans hoped to achieve these ends by preaching and public debate. Hence they became intellectually oriented. Many members of the order gained teaching positions in the infant European universities and contributed much to the development of philosophy and theology. The most influential thinker of the thirteenth century, Saint Thomas Aquinas, was a Dominican who addressed one of his major theological works to converting the "gentiles" (that is, all non-Christians). The Dominicans always retained their reputation for learning, but they also came to believe that stubborn heretics were best controlled by legal procedures. Accordingly, they became the leading medieval administrators of inquisitorial trials.

In its origins the Franciscan order was quite different from the Dominican, being characterized less by a commitment to doctrine and discipline and more by a sense of emotional fervor. The founder of the Franciscans, the Italian Saint Francis of Assisi (1182–1226), was a layman who behaved at first remarkably like a social rebel and a heretic. The son of a rich merchant, he became dissatisfied with the materialistic values of his father and determined to become a servant of the poor. Giving away all his property, he threw off his clothes in public, put on the tattered garb of a beggar, and began without official approval to preach salvation

The Earliest Known Portrait of Saint Francis. Dating from the year 1228, this fresco shows the saint without the "stigmata," the wounds of Christ's crucifixion he was believed to have received miraculously toward the end of his life.

in town squares and to minister to outcasts in the darkest corners of Italian cities. He rigorously imitated the life of Christ and displayed indifference to doctrine, form, and ceremony, except for revering the sacrament of the Eucharist. But he did wish to gain the support of the pope. Some other pope might have rejected the layman Francis as a hopelessly unworldly religious anarchist. But Francis was thoroughly willing to profess obedience, and Innocent had the genius to approve Francis's rule and grant him permission to preach. With papal support, the Franciscan order spread, and though it gradually became more "civilized," conceding the importance of administrative stability and doctrinal training for all its members, it continued to specialize in revivalistic outdoor preaching and in offering a model for "apostolic living" within an orthodox framework. Thus Innocent managed to harness a vital new force that would help maintain a sense of religious enthusiasm within the Church.

The success of the Franciscans and the Dominicans in combating the appeal of heretical movements was a great victory for the church, but this success was not sufficient to make the church feel secure in its hold on the people of Europe. Quite the opposite: despite its victories over the Cathars and the Waldensians, the church's inquisitorial processes ground on, discovering heretics even where none in fact existed.

JEWS AND CHRISTIANS

The church also became more and more concerned by the threat it believed that Jews posed to the faith of Christians, despite the fact that persecution and exploitative taxation had made most Jewish communities both smaller and weaker by 1300 than they had been in 1150. Although the church never officially endorsed the wilder flights of popular anti-Semitism, it did little to combat such attitudes either. As a result, by 1300 many ordinary Christians had come to believe that the Jews who lived among them were nothing less than agents of Satan, who routinely crucified Christian children, consumed Christian blood, and profaned the body of Christ in the Eucharist. The failures of organized campaigns to convert Jews to Christianity added to the sense among Christians that there was something demonic about the continuing Jewish presence in Christian society. Fanciful stories of Jewish wealth added an economic element to the developing anti-Semitism of European society, as did the fact that across much of thirteenth-century Europe, many Jews made their living as moneylenders.

Throughout the thirteenth century, the church had cooperated with kings in imposing more and more severe restrictions on Jewish life. Starting in the late 1280s, however, kings began to expel their Jewish subjects from their kingdoms altogether: in 1288 from southern Italy, in 1290 from England, and in 1306 from France. Further expulsions followed during the fourteenth century in the Rhineland, and in 1492 from Spain. By 1500, only Italy and Poland still retained any substantial Jewish populations, where they would survive until the Nazi Holocaust during the Second World War.

HOW DID THE RECOVERY OF CLASSICAL LEARNING AFFECT MEDIEVAL INTELLECTUAL LIFE?

THE MEDIEVAL INTELLECTUAL REVIVAL   275

THE MEDIEVAL INTELLECTUAL REVIVAL

> How did the recovery of classical learning affect medieval intellectual life?

The major intellectual accomplishments of the High Middle Ages were of four related but different sorts: the expansion of primary education and lay literacy; the origin and spread of universities; the acquisition of classical and Muslim knowledge; and the development of new philosophical and theological ideas. Any one of these accomplishments would have earned the High Middle Ages a signal place in the history of Western learning. Taken together, they mark the beginning of an era in the intellectual history of Europe that would last until the scientific revolution of the seventeenth century.

Medieval Conception of Elementary Education. An illumination from a fourteenth-century manuscript depicts a master of grammar who simultaneously points to the day's lesson and keeps order with a cudgel.

THE GROWTH OF SCHOOLS

Around 800 Charlemagne ordered that primary schools be established in every bishopric and monastery in his realm. Although it is doubtful that this command was carried out to the letter, many schools were certainly founded during the Carolingian period. But their continued existence was later endangered by the Viking invasions. Primary education in some monasteries and cathedral towns managed to survive, but until around 1050 the extent and quality of basic education in the European West were meager. Thereafter, however, even contemporaries were struck by the rapidity with which schools sprang up all over Europe. The economic revival, the growth of towns, and the emergence of strong government allowed Europeans to dedicate themselves to basic education as never before.

The high medieval educational boom was more than merely a growth of schools, for the nature of the schools changed, and as time went on so did the curriculum and the clientele. The first basic mutation was that cathedral schools replaced monasteries as the main centers of European education. The papal monarchy energetically supported this development by ordering in 1179 that all cathedrals should set aside income for one schoolteacher, who could then instruct all who wished, rich or poor, without fee. The papacy believed correctly that this measure would enlarge the number of well-trained clerics and potential administrators.

At first the cathedral schools existed almost exclusively for the basic training of priests, with a curriculum designed to teach only such literacy as was necessary for performing the basic services of the church. But soon after 1100 the curriculum was broadened as the growth of both ecclesiastical and secular governments created a growing demand for trained officials who had to know more than how to read a few prayers. A thorough knowledge of Latin grammar and composition began to be inculcated, based on the study of classical Roman authors such as Cicero and Virgil. Some schools also began to focus on the study of philosophy, particularly logic, once again relying on classical authors such as Aristotle and Porphyry. This new interest in classical literary and philosophical texts has led scholars to refer to this movement as the "Renaissance of the Twelfth Century."

Until about 1200 the students in the urban schools remained predominantly clerical. Even those who hoped to become lawyers or administrators rather than priests usually found it advantageous to take church orders. But afterward more pupils who entered schools were not in the clergy and never intended to be. Customarily, these students would not go to cathedral schools but to alternate ones that were more practically oriented. Such schools grew rapidly in the course of the thirteenth century and became completely independent of ecclesiastical control. Not only were their students recruited from the laity, their teachers were usually laymen as well. As time went on instruction ceased to be in Latin, as had hitherto been the case, and was offered in the European vernacular languages instead. But the schools continued to be restricted to males. Some laywomen did become highly educated, but they were taught at home by private tutors.

The rise of lay education was an enormously important development in western European history. The growth of schools led to an enormous growth of lay literacy. By 1340 roughly 40 percent of the Florentine population could read; by the later fifteenth century about 40 percent of the total population of England was literate as well. (These figures include women, who were usually taught to read by paid tutors or by female family members at home rather than in schools.) When we consider that literacy around 1050 was almost entirely limited to the clergy and that the literate comprised less than 1 percent of the population of western Europe, we can appreciate that an astonishing revolution had taken place. Without it, many of Europe's other accomplishments would have been inconceivable.

> The growth of schools led to an enormous growth of lay literacy. By 1340 roughly 40 percent of the Florentine population could read; by the later fifteenth century about 40 percent of the total population of England was literate as well.

THE RISE OF UNIVERSITIES

The emergence of universities was part of the same high medieval educational boom. Originally, universities were institutions that offered instruction in advanced studies that could not be pursued in average cathedral schools: advanced liberal arts and the professional studies of law, medicine, and theology. The earliest Italian university was that of Bologna, an institution that took shape during the course of the twelfth century. Although liberal arts were taught at Bologna, the institution's greatest prominence from the time of its twelfth-century origins until the end of the Middle Ages was as Europe's leading center for the study of law. North of the Alps, the earliest and most prestigious university was that of Paris. The University of Paris started out as a cathedral school like many others, but in the twelfth century it began to become a recognized center of northern intellectual life.

One reason for this was that scholars there found the necessary conditions of peace and stability provided by the increasingly strong French kingship; another was that food was plentiful because the area was rich in agricultural produce; third was that the cathedral school of Paris in the first half of the twelfth century boasted the most charismatic and controversial teacher of the day, Peter Abelard (1079–1142). Abelard, whose intellectual accomplishments we will discuss later, attracted students from all over Europe in droves. As a result of his reputation, many other teachers settled in Paris and began to offer much more varied and advanced instruction than anything offered in other French cathedral schools. By 1200 the Paris school was evolving into a university that specialized in liberal arts and theology.

Every university in medieval Europe was patterned after one or the other of two different models. Throughout Italy, Spain, and southern France the standard was generally the University of Bologna, in which the students themselves constituted the corporation. They hired the teachers, paid their salaries, and fined or discharged them for neglect of duty or inefficient instruction. The universities of northern Europe were modeled after Paris, which was a guild not of students but of teachers. It included four faculties—arts, theology, law, and medicine—each headed by a dean. In the great majority of the northern universities arts and theology were the leading branches of study. Before the end of the thirteenth century separate colleges came to be established within the University of Paris. The original college was nothing more than an endowed home for poor students, but eventually the colleges became centers of instruction as well as residences. Although most of these types of colleges have disappeared from the Continent, the universities of Oxford and Cambridge still retain the pattern of federal organization copied from Paris. The colleges of which they are composed are semi-independent educational units.

Most of our modern degrees as well as our modern university organization derive from the medieval system, but actual courses of study have been greatly altered. No curriculum in the Middle Ages included history or anything like the modern social sciences. The medieval student was assumed to know Latin grammar thoroughly before entrance into a university. On admission—limited to males—he was required to spend about four years studying the basic

NORWAY

SWEDEN

■ Uppsala

DENMARK

NORTH
SEA

■ Copenhagen

■ Greifswald
■ Rostock

■ Frankfurt
■ Wittenburg
■ Leipzig

POLAND

■ Warsaw

Erfurt

HOLY ROMAN EMPIRE

■ Cracow

Prague

SCOTLAND   ■ Aberdeen
        ■ St. Andrews
    ■ Glasgow

ENGLAND
    ■ Cambridge
    ■ Oxford

ATLANTIC
OCEAN

Louvain
■ Cologne
■ Trier   ■ Mainz   ■ Würzburg
    ■ Heidelberg
    ■ Vienna
        ■ Pressburg
    Ingolstadt
Freibourg   ■ Tübingen   ■ Buda
■ Basel   AUSTRIA   HUNGARY
Besançon   SWITZERLAND
■ Dôle   ■ Fünfkirchen

Paris
■ Caen   Seine R.
■ Angers   ■ Orléans
■ Nantes   Loire R.
■ Bourges
■ Poitiers
FRANCE
■ Bordeaux   ■ Cahors
    ■ Lyons
    ■ Grenoble   ■ Turin   ■ Pavia   ■ Padua
    ■ Valence   ■ Piacenza   ■ Ferrara
    ■ Orange   Rhône R.   ■ Reggio   ■ Bologna
    ■ Avignon   ■ Florence   PAPAL
■ Toulouse   ■ Montpellier   ■ Siena   STATES   ■ Arezzo
    ■ Aix   ■ Perugia
    ■ Perpignan   ■ Rome

■ Vercelli
Treviso
VENETIAN EMPIRE
ADRIATIC SEA

PORTUGAL   ■ Palencia
    ■ Valladolid   ■ Huesca
    ■ Salamanca   ■ Lérida
■ Coimbra   ■ Saragossa   ■ Barcelona
    ■ Avila   ■ Siguenza
    ■ Toledo   SPAIN
■ Lisbon
    ■ Valencia   ■ Palma
    BALEARIC ISLANDS
■ Seville

CORSICA

SARDINIA

■ Naples
■ Salerno

KINGDOM
OF TWO
SICILIES

■ Palermo

■ Catania

MEDITERRANEAN
SEA

CENTURY UNIVERSITY
FOUNDED

■ 12th Century
■ 13th Century
■ 14th Century
■ 15th Century
— Boundaries c. 1500

0   100   200   300 Miles
0   100   200   300 Kilometers

THE RISE OF THE MEDIEVAL UNIVERSITY

This map shows the distribution and dates of origin of the major universities of medieval Europe. Why were the twelfth- and thirteenth-century universities founded primarily in France, England, and northern Italy? Notice the number and geographical distribution of universities founded in the fourteenth and fifteenth centuries. How would you explain the pattern of these later foundations?

liberal arts, which meant doing advanced work in Latin grammar and rhetoric and mastering the rules of logic. If he passed his examinations he received the preliminary degree of bachelor of arts (the prototype of our B.A.), which conferred no unusual distinction. To assure himself a place in professional life he then usually had to devote additional years to the pursuit of an advanced degree, such as master of arts (M.A.), or doctor of laws, medicine, or theology. This was accomplished by reading and commenting on standard ancient works, such as those of Euclid and especially Aristotle. The requirements for the doctor's degrees included more specialized training. Strictly speaking, doctor's degrees, including even that in medicine, conferred only the right to teach. But in practice university degrees of all grades were recognized as standards of attainment and became pathways to nonacademic careers.

Student life in medieval universities was often rowdy. Many students were very immature because it was customary to begin university studies between the ages of twelve and fifteen. Moreover, all university students believed that they constituted an independent and privileged community, apart from that of the local townspeople. Since the latter tried to reap financial profits from the students and the students were naturally boisterous, riots and sometimes pitched battles were frequent between "town" and "gown." But actual study was very intense. Because the greatest emphasis was placed on the value of authority and also because books were prohibitively expensive (they were hand written on rare parchment), there was an enormous amount of rote memorization. As students advanced in their disciplines they were also expected to develop their own skills in formal, public disputations. The most important fact pertaining to medieval university students was that, after about 1250, there were so many of them. The University of Paris in the thirteenth century numbered about seven thousand students, and Oxford somewhere around two thousand in any given year. This means that an appreciable proportion of male Europeans who were more than peasants or artisans were gaining at least some education at the higher levels.

> But suddenly an enormous burst of translating activity made almost all of ancient Greek and Arabic scientific knowledge accessible to western Europeans. This activity occurred in Spain and Sicily because Christians there lived in close proximity with Arabic speakers, or Jews who knew Latin and Arabic, either of whom could aid them in their tasks.

THE RECOVERY OF CLASSICAL LEARNING

As the numbers of those educated at all levels vastly increased during the High Middle Ages, so did the quality of learning. This was owing first and foremost to the reacquisition of Greek knowledge and to the absorption of intellectual advances made by the Muslims. Since practically no western Europeans knew Greek or Arabic, works in those languages had to be transmitted by means of Latin translations. There were very few of these before about 1140, but suddenly an enormous burst of translating activity made almost all of ancient Greek and Arabic scientific knowledge accessible to western Europeans. This activity occurred in Spain and Sicily because Christians there lived in close proximity with Arabic speakers, or Jews who knew Latin and Arabic, either of whom could aid them in their tasks. The result was that by about 1260 almost the entire Aristotelian corpus that is known today was made available in Latin. So also were basic works of such important Greek scientific thinkers as Euclid, Galen, and Ptolemy. Plato's works were still unknown in Europe, as were the works of the classical Greek poets and dramatists. For the most part, these remained the jealously guarded cultural preserve of Byzantium. But in addition to the thought of the Greeks, Western scholars also became familiar with the accomplishments of the major Islamic philosophers and scientists such as Avicenna and Averroës.

Having acquired the best of Greek and Arabic scientific and speculative thought, the West was able to build on it and make its own advances. This progress came in different ways. In natural science, westerners could build without much difficulty on this new learning, because it seldom conflicted with the principles of Christianity. One of the most advanced thirteenth-century scientists was the Englishman Robert Grosseteste (c. 1168–1253), who made very significant theoretical advances in mathematics, astronomy, and optics. He formulated a sophisticated scientific explanation of the rainbow, and he posited the use of lenses for magnification. Grosseteste's leading disciple was Roger Bacon (c. 1214–1294), who

HOW DID THE RECOVERY OF CLASSICAL LEARNING AFFECT MEDIEVAL INTELLECTUAL LIFE?

THE MEDIEVAL INTELLECTUAL REVIVAL   279

is today more famous than his teacher because he seems to have predicted automobiles and flying machines. Bacon in fact had no real interest in machinery, but he did follow up on Grosseteste's work in optics, discussing, for example, further properties of lenses, the rapid speed of light, and the nature of human vision. Grosseteste, Bacon, and some of their followers at the University of Oxford argued that natural knowledge was more certain when it was based on sensory evidence than when it rested on abstract reason. To this degree they can be seen as early forerunners of modern science. But the important qualification remains that they did not perform any real laboratory experiments.

SCHOLASTICISM

The story of the high medieval encounter between Greek and Arabic philosophy and Christian faith is basically the story of the emergence of scholasticism. This word can be, and has been, defined in many ways. In its root meaning scholasticism was simply a highly systematic method of learning and teaching that was highly respectful of authority. Yet scholasticism was not only a method of study: it was a world view. As such, it taught that there was a fundamental compatibility between the knowledge humans can obtain by experience or reason and the teachings imparted by divine revelation. Since medieval scholars believed that the Greeks were the masters of natural knowledge and that all revelation was in the Bible, scholasticism consequently was the theory and practice of reconciling classical philosophy with Christian faith.

Abelard and Heloise. Famous for his colorful personality, Abelard was popular with students but also made many enemies. After getting Heloise, one of his students, pregnant, he was castrated by her uncle and fled to a monastery. Subsequently, he wrote his most famous work, *The Story of My Calamities.*

PETER ABELARD

One of the most important thinkers who paved the way for scholasticism without yet being fully a scholastic himself was the stormy Peter Abelard, who was active in and around Paris in the first half of the twelfth century. Probably the first western European who consciously sought to forge a career as an intellectual, Abelard was so adept at logic that even as a student he easily outshone the experts of his day who had the misfortune to be his teachers. Others might have been tactful about such superiority, but Abelard gloried in openly humiliating his elders in public debate, thereby making himself many enemies. To complicate matters, in 1118 he seduced a brilliant young woman, Heloise, who had been taking private lessons with him. When Heloise became pregnant, Abelard married her (against Heloise's own wishes), but the two decided to keep the marriage secret for the sake of his career. This, however, enraged Heloise's uncle because he thought that Abelard was planning to abandon Heloise; therefore he took revenge for his family's honor by having Abelard castrated. Seeking refuge as a monk, Abelard soon witnessed his enemies engineer his first conviction for heresy. Still restless and cantankerous, he found no spiritual solace in monasticism and after quarreling and breaking with the monks of two different communities he returned to life in the world by setting himself up as a teacher in Paris from about 1132 to 1141. This was the peak of his career. But in 1141 he again was charged with heresy, now by the highly influential Saint Bernard, and condemned by a church council. Not long afterward the persecuted thinker abjured, and in 1142 he died in retirement.

Abelard told of many of these trials in a letter called *The Story of My Calamities*, one of the first autobiographical accounts written in the West since Saint Augustine's *Confessions*. Abelard's main intention was to moralize about how he had been justly punished for his "lechery" by the loss of those parts which had "offended" and for his intellectual pride by the burning of his writings after his first condemnation. Abelard's greatest contributions to the development of scholasticism were made in his *Sic et Non* ("*Yes and No*") and in a number of original theological works. In the *Sic et Non* Abelard prepared the way for the scholastic method by gathering a collection of statements from the church fathers that spoke for both sides of one hundred fifty theological questions. It was once thought that the brash Abelard did this in order to embarrass authority, but the contrary is true. What Abelard really hoped to do was begin a process of careful study whereby it could be shown that the Bible was infallible and that other authorities, despite any appearances to the contrary, really agreed with each other. Later scholastics would follow his method of studying theology by raising fundamental questions and arraying the answers that had been put forth in authoritative texts. Abelard did not propose any solutions of his own in the *Sic et Non*, but he did start to do this in his original theological writings. In these he proposed to treat theology like a science by studying it as comprehensively as possible and by applying to it the tools of logic, of which he was a master. He did not even shrink from applying logic to the mystery of the Trinity (see p. 172), one of the excesses for which he was condemned. Peter Abelard was one of the first to try to harmonize religion with rationalism and was in this capacity a herald of the scholastic outlook.

THE TRIUMPH OF SCHOLASTICISM

Immediately after Abelard's death two further developments prepared the way for mature scholasticism. One was the writing of the *Book of Sentences* between 1155 and 1157 by Abelard's student Peter Lombard. This raised all the most fundamental theological questions in rigorously consequential order, adduced answers from the Bible and Christian authorities on both sides of each question, and then proposed judgments on every case. By the thirteenth century Peter Lombard's work had become a standard text, and theologians followed its organizational procedures in their own writings. Thus the full scholastic method was born.

The other basic step in the development of scholasticism was the reacquisition of classical philosophy that occurred after about 1140. Abelard would probably have been glad to draw on the thought of the Greeks, but he could not because few Greek works were yet available in translation. Later theologians, however, could avail themselves fully of the Greeks' knowledge, above all, the works of Aristotle and his Arabic commentators. By around 1250 Aristotle's authority in purely philosophical matters became so great that he was referred to simply as "the Philosopher." Scholastics of the mid-thirteenth century accordingly adhered to Peter Lombard's organizational method, but considered Greek and Arabic philosophical authorities as well as purely Christian theological ones. In doing this they tried to construct systems of understanding that most fully harmonized the earlier separate realms of faith and natural knowledge.

THE WRITINGS OF SAINT THOMAS AQUINAS

By far the greatest accomplishments in this endeavor were made by Saint Thomas Aquinas (1225–1274), the leading scholastic theologian of the University of Paris. As a member of the Dominican order, Saint Thomas was committed to the principle that faith could be defended by reason. More important, he believed that because God created the natural world, he can be approached through its terms, even though ultimate certainty about

Saint Thomas Aquinas. Portrayed in this fourteenth century Florentine wall painting, Saint Thomas Aquinas defended studying the natural world through reason as a legitimate way of approaching Christian theology. He outlined his ideas about human reason in the *Summa Contra Gentiles* and the *Summa Theologica*.

WHAT THEMES UNITE THE LITERATURE, ART, AND ARCHITECTURE OF THE HIGH MIDDLE AGES?

THE BLOSSOMING OF LITERATURE, ART, AND MUSIC   281

the highest truths can only be obtained through the supernatural revelation of the Bible. Imbued with a deep confidence in the value of human reason and human experience, as well as in his own ability to harmonize Greek philosophy with Christian theology, Thomas was the most serene of saints. In a long career of teaching at the University of Paris and elsewhere he indulged in few controversies and worked quietly on his two great Summaries of theology: the *Summa Contra Gentiles* ("Summary against Non-Christians") and the much larger *Summa Theologica* ("Summary of Theology"). In these he hoped to set the faith on the firmest of foundations.

Saint Thomas's vast Summaries are awesome for their rigorous orderliness and intellectual penetration. Thomas relied heavily on the work of Aris-totle, but he was by no means merely "Aristotle baptized." Instead, he fully subordinated Aristotelianism to basic Christian principles and thereby created his own original philosophical and theological system. Scholars disagree about how far this system diverges from the earlier Christian thought of Saint Augustine, but there seems little doubt that Aquinas placed a higher value on human reason, on human life in this world, and on the abilities of humans to participate in their own salvation. Not long after his death Thomas was canonized, for his intellectual accomplishments seemed like miracles. His influence lives on today insofar as he helped to inspire confidence in rationalism and human experience.

THE PINNACLE OF WESTERN MEDIEVAL THOUGHT

With the achievements of Saint Thomas Aquinas in the mid-thirteenth century, western medieval thought reached its pinnacle. Not coincidentally, other aspects of medieval civilization were reaching their pinnacles at the same time. France was enjoying its ripest period of peace and prosperity under the rule of (Saint) Louis IX, the University of Paris was defining its basic organizational forms, and the greatest French Gothic cathedrals were being built. Some ardent admirers of medieval culture have fixed on these accomplishments to call the thirteenth the "greatest of centuries." Such a judgment, of course, is a matter of taste, and many might respond that life was still too harsh and requirements for religious orthodoxy too restrictive to justify this extreme celebration of the lost past. Whatever our individual judgments,

It is often thought that medieval thinkers were excessively conservative, but in fact the greatest thinkers of the High Middle Ages were astonishingly receptive to new ideas.

it seems wise to end this section by correcting some false impressions about medieval intellectual life.

It is often thought that medieval thinkers were excessively conservative, but in fact the greatest thinkers of the High Middle Ages were astonishingly receptive to new ideas. As committed Christians they could not allow doubts to be cast on the principles of their faith, but otherwise they were glad to incorporate whatever they could from the Greeks and Arabs. Considering that Aristotelian thought differed radically from anything accepted earlier in its emphasis on rationalism and the fundamental goodness and purposefulness of nature, its rapid acceptance by the scholastics was a philosophical revolution. Another false impression is that scholastic thinkers were greatly constrained by authority. Certainly they revered authority more than we do today, but such scholastics as Saint Thomas did not regard the mere citation of texts—except biblical revelation concerning the mysteries of the faith—as being sufficient to clinch an argument. Rather, the authorities were brought forth to outline the possibilities, but reason and experience then demonstrated the truth. Finally, it is often believed that scholastic thinkers were "antihumanistic," but modern scholars are coming to the opposite conclusion. Scholastics unquestionably gave primacy to the soul over the body and to otherworldly salvation over life in the here and now. But they also exalted the dignity of human nature because they viewed it as a glorious divine creation, and they believed in the possibility of a working alliance between themselves and God. Moreover, they had extraordinary faith in the powers of human reason—probably more than we do today.

THE BLOSSOMING OF LITERATURE, ART, AND MUSIC

What common themes unite the literature, art, and architecture of the High Middle Ages?

The literature of the High Middle Ages was varied, lively, and impressive. The revival of grammatical studies

A GOLIARDIC PARODY OF THE GOSPEL OF MARK, SATIRIZING THE PAPAL COURT

This selection is typical of the parodies of the liturgy and the Bible written by the freewheeling Latin poets of the twelfth century. This particular poem is written in mock biblical verse, and puns on the Christian Gospel of Mark—a mark being a sum of money equal to two thirds of a pound of silver. Like all parodies, it was meant to be humorous, but its accusations—that bribery around the papal court perverted justice—were widespread in twelfth- and thirteenth-century Europe.

Here beginneth the Holy Gospel according to the marks of silver. In those days the Holy Father said unto the Romans: "When the Son of Man shall come unto the seat of our Majesty, first say unto Him: 'Friend, why art Thou come?' but if he continue knocking and give you nothing, then cast Him forth into outer darkness."

And it came to pass that a certain poor priest came to the court of the Lord Pope and cried out, saying, "Do ye at least have pity on me, servants of the Pope, for the hand of poverty hath afflicted me. Verily I am poor and have nothing. I beseech you, therefore, have mercy upon me and pity me." They, however, hearing this were sorely wroth and said unto him, "Friend, may thy poverty go with thee to hell. Get thee behind us, Satan; thou savorest not of money. Amen, Amen we say to thee: thou shalt not enter into the blessings of thy Lord until thou hast given thy last penny."

The poor man went therefore and sold his cloak and his coat and all that he had, and gave unto the cardinals and the treasurers and the papal flunkies. But they said unto him, "And this, what is this among so many?"

And they cast him out utterly, and going forth he wept bitterly and would not be comforted.

After this there came to the court a rich priest, exceedingly wealthy, anointed with grease and great with wealth, who had committed murder for the sake of gain. He first gave unto the treasurer, then he gave unto the flunky, and then he gave unto the cardinals. But they reasoned among themselves, thinking they would receive more. Therefore when the Lord Pope heard that the cardinals and his servants had received many gifts from a priest he was sick, even unto death. But the rich man sent unto him a pallet of gold and silver, and immediately he was made whole.

The Lord Pope called unto him the cardinals and ministers and spake unto them saying: "Beware, brethren, lest any deceive you with vain words. For I have given you an example, so that as I have grasped, so should you grasp also."

Carmina Burana, 21, trans. by Helen Waddell, in *The Wandering Scholars*, 7th ed. (London: Constable, 1934), pp. 150–151, as revised by John E. Boswell.

in the cathedral schools and universities led to the production of some excellent Latin poetry. The best examples were secular lyrics, especially those written in the twelfth century by a group of poets known as the Go-

liards. Their lyrics celebrated the beauties of the changing seasons, the carefree life of the open road, the pleasures of drinking and sport, and especially the joys of love. The authors of these rollicking and satirical songs

WHAT THEMES UNITE THE LITERATURE, ART, AND ARCHITECTURE OF THE HIGH MIDDLE AGES?

THE BLOSSOMING OF LITERATURE, ART, AND MUSIC   283

were mainly wandering students, although some were men of more advanced years. The names of most are unknown. Their poetry is notable both for its robust vitality and for its clear rejection of Christian asceticism.

VERNACULAR LITERATURE

In addition to Latin, the vernacular languages of French, German, Spanish, and Italian became increasingly popular as media of literary expression. At first, most of the literature in the vernacular languages was written in the form of the heroic epic. Among the leading examples were the French *Song of Roland*, the Norse eddas and sagas, the German *Song of the Nibelungs*, and the Spanish *Poem of the Cid*. These epics portrayed a virile but unpolished warrior society. Blood flowed freely, skulls were cleaved by battle axes, and heroic warfare, honor, and loyalty were the major themes. If women were mentioned at all, they were subordinate to men. Brides were expected to die for their beloveds, but husbands were free to beat their wives. In one French epic a queen who tried to influence her husband met with a blow to the nose; even though blood flowed she replied, "Many thanks, when it pleases you, you may do it again." Although we find such passages repugnant, the best of the vernacular epics have great literary power despite their unrelentingly masculine focus.

TROUBADOUR POETRY AND COURTLY ROMANCES

In comparison to the epics, an enormous change in both subject matter and style was introduced in twelfth-century France by the troubadour poets and the writers of courtly romances. Their style was far more finely wrought and sophisticated than that of the epic poets, and the most eloquent of their lyrics, which were meant to be sung to music, originated the theme of courtly love. The troubadours idealized women as marvelous beings who could grant intense spiritual and sensual gratification. But because the women they chose to love were usually the wives of powerful lords, they wrote more often of longing than of romantic fulfillment. The literary tradition originated by the southern French troubadours was continued by the trouvères in northern France and by the

minnesingers in Germany. Thereafter many of their innovations were developed by later lyric poets in all Western languages.

An equally important twelfth-century French innovation was the composition of longer narrative poems known as romances, so called because there were written in vernacular, Romance (that is, deriving from Latin) languages. Romances told engaging stories; they often excelled in portraying character, and their subject matter was usually love and adventure. Some romances elaborated on classical Greek themes, but the most famous and best were "Arthurian." These took their material from the legendary exploits of the British hero King Arthur and his many chivalrous knights. The first great writer of Arthurian romances was the northern Frenchman Chrétien de Troyes, who was active between about 1165 and 1190. Chrétien did much to help create and shape the new form, and he also introduced innovations in subject matter and attitudes. Whereas the troubadours exalted extramarital love, Chrétien was the first to hold forth the ideal of romantic love within marriage. He also described not only the deeds but the thoughts and emotions of his characters.

> Whereas the troubadours exalted extramarital love, Chrétien was the first to hold forth the ideal of romantic love within marriage. He also described not only the deeds but the thoughts and emotions of his characters.

Not all high medieval narratives were so elevated as the romances in either form or substance. A very different new narrative form was the *fabliau*, or verse fable. Although *fabliaux* derived from the moral animal tales of Aesop, they quickly evolved into short stories that were written less to edify or instruct than to amuse. Often they were very coarse, and sometimes they dealt with sexual relations in a broadly humorous and thoroughly unromantic manner. Many were also strongly anticlerical, making monks and priests the butts of their jokes. They are significant as expressions of growing worldliness and as the first manifestations of the robust realism that was later to be perfected by Boccaccio and Chaucer.

THE DIVINE COMEDY

In a class by itself as the greatest work of medieval literature is Dante Alighieri's *Divine Comedy*. Dante (1265–1321) was active during the early part of his career in the political affairs of his native city of Florence. In 1301 he was expelled from Florence after a political upheaval and was forced to live the rest of his life in exile. The *Divine Comedy*, his major work, was

The Poet Dante Driven into Exile. On the left Dante is expelled from Florence; on the right he begins work on his great poem, the *Divine Comedy*. From a mid-fifteenth-century Florentine manuscript.

written during this final period. Dante's *Divine Comedy* is a monumental narrative in powerful rhyming Italian verse, which describes the poet's journey through hell, purgatory, and paradise. At the start Dante tells of finding himself in a "dark wood," his metaphor for a deep personal midlife crisis in which he had wandered away from his Christian faith. He is led out of this forest of despair by the Roman poet Virgil, who represents the heights of classical reason and philosophy. Virgil guides Dante on a trip through hell and purgatory; then Dante's deceased beloved, Beatrice, who symbolizes Christian wisdom and blessedness, takes over and guides him through paradise. In the course of this progress from hell to heaven Dante meets both historical personages and his own contemporaries, who explain why they met their several fates. As the poem progresses Dante grows in wisdom and understanding, until finally he returns with new confidence and certainty to his own lost Christian faith. Dante stressed the priority of salvation, but he viewed earth as existing for human benefit. He allowed humans free will to choose good and avoid evil, and accepted Greek philosophy as authoritative in its own sphere. Above all, his sense of hope and his ultimate faith in humanity— remarkable for a defeated exile—most powerfully expresses the dominant mood of the High Middle Ages

and makes Dante one of the two or three most stirringly affirmative writers who ever lived.

ART AND ARCHITECTURE

The closest architectural equivalents of the *Divine Comedy* are the great high medieval Gothic cathedrals, for they too have qualities of vast scope, balance of intricate detail with careful symmetry, soaring height, and affirmative religious grandeur. But before we approach the Gothic style, it is best to introduce it by means of its high medieval predecessor, the style of architecture known as the Romanesque. This style aimed to manifest the majesty of God in stone by rigorously subordinating all architectural details to a uniform system. The essential features of the Romanesque style were the rounded arch, massive stone walls, enormous piers (support columns), small windows, and the predominance of horizontal lines. Together, these features gave Romanesque architecture a sense of stability and permanence. Interiors were plain, but sometimes relieved by mosaics or frescoes in bright colors and—a very important innovation for Christian art—the introduction of sculptural decoration, both within and without. For the first time, full-length human figures appeared on facades. These are usually grave and elongated far beyond natural dimensions, but they have much evocative

> The essential features of the Romanesque style were the rounded arch, massive stone walls, enormous piers (support columns), small windows, and the predominance of horizontal lines.

WHAT THEMES UNITE THE LITERATURE, ART, AND ARCHITECTURE OF THE HIGH MIDDLE AGES?

THE BLOSSOMING OF LITERATURE, ART, AND MUSIC   285

power and represent the first manifestations of a revived interest in sculpting the human form.

In the course of the twelfth and thirteenth centuries the Romanesque style was supplanted throughout most of Europe by the Gothic. Although trained art historians can see how certain traits of the one style led to the development of the other, the appearance of the two styles is distinctively different. In fact, the two seem as different as the epic is different from the romance, an appropriate analogy because the Gothic style emerged in France in the mid-twelfth century exactly when the romance did, and because it was far more sophisticated, graceful, and elegant than its predecessor, in the same way that the romance compared with the epic.

Gothic architecture was one of the most intricate of building styles. Its basic elements were the pointed arch, groined and ribbed vaulting, and the flying buttress. These devices made possible a much lighter and loftier construction than could ever have been achieved with the round arch and the engaged pier of the Romanesque. In fact, the Gothic cathedral could be described as a skeletal framework of stone enclosed by enormous windows. Other features included lofty spires, rose windows, delicate tracery in stone, elaborately sculpted facades, multiple columns, and the more frequent use of gargoyles, or representations of mythical monsters, as decorative devices. Ornamentation was generally concentrated on the exterior. But the inside of the Gothic cathedral was never somber or gloomy. The stained-glass windows served not to exclude the light but to glorify it, to catch the rays of sunlight and suffuse them with a richness and

Romanesque and Gothic. Top: West front of the Church of Notre Dame la Grande, Poitiers. Constructed between 1135 and 1145, this typical example of Romanesque architecture emphasizes the repetition of rounded arches and horizontal lines. Bottom: Rheims Cathedral. Built between 1220 and 1299, this High Gothic cathedral places great stress on vertical elements. The gabled portals, pointed arches, and multitude of pinnacles all accentuate the height of this structure.

warmth of color that nature itself could hardly duplicate even in its happiest moods.

Many people still think of the Gothic cathedral as the expression of purely ascetic otherworldliness, but this estimation is highly inaccurate. Certainly all churches are dedicated to the glory of God and hope for life everlasting, but Gothic ones sometimes included stained-glass scenes of daily life that had no overt religious significance at all. Gothic sculptures of religious figures such as Jesus, the Virgin, and the saints were becoming far more naturalistic than anything hitherto created in the medieval West. Each cathedral, with its many symbolic figures, was a kind of encyclopedia of medieval knowledge carved in stone. Finally, Gothic cathedrals were manifestations of urban pride. Always located in the growing medieval cities, they were meant to be both centers of community life and expressions of a town's greatness. When a new cathedral went up the people of the entire community participated in erecting it, and rightfully regarded it as almost their own property.

DRAMA AND MUSIC

Surveys of high medieval accomplishments should not omit drama and music. Our own modern drama descends at least as much from the medieval form as from the classical one. Throughout the medieval period some Latin classical plays were known in manuscript but were never performed. Instead drama was born all over again within the church. In the early Middle Ages certain passages in the liturgy began to be acted out. Then, in the twelfth century, short religious plays in Latin began to be composed for performance inside churches. Rapidly thereafter, these Latin plays were supplemented or supplanted by ones in the vernacular so that the whole congregation could understand them. Around 1200, these started to be performed outside, in front of the church, so that they would not take time away from the services. As soon as that happened, drama entered the everyday world: nonreligious stories were introduced, character portrayal was expanded, and the way was prepared for the Elizabethans and Shakespeare.

Just as drama developed within the liturgy and then moved beyond it, so too did music. Until the High Middle Ages Western music was homophonic; that is, it developed only one melody at a time without any harmonic background. The great high medieval invention was polyphony, the playing or singing of two or more harmonious melodies together. Some experiments along these lines may have begun as early as the tenth century, but the most fundamental breakthrough was achieved at the cathedral of Paris around 1170, when the mass was first sung by two voices weaving together two different melodies in "counterpoint." Roughly concurrently, systems of musical notation were also invented. Because performers no longer had to rely on memory, music could become more complex. All the greatness of European music followed from these first steps.

CONCLUSION

For almost one hundred years, scholars have spoken of the sweeping intellectual, religious, and cultural changes of the High Middle Ages as constituting the "Renaissance of the Twelfth Century." This categorization still seems apt. Like those of the more famous Italian Renaissance of the fourteenth and fifteenth centuries, the intellectual changes of the High Middle Ages were profoundly influenced by the recovery and intensive study of classical texts. But in both periods, the use made of these classical texts was distinctive and unique. Neither of these movements were mere revivals; rather, both were creative adaptations of classical ideas to a new and distinctively Christian culture.

Even more so than the Italian Renaissance, however, the twelfth-century renaissance marks the origin of a set of distinctive attitudes and ideas that have characterized western European civilization ever since. Our modern conceptions of love and friendship; our fascination with human motivation and intention; indeed, our very interest in psychology itself, all derive from twelfth-century developments. So too does our emphasis on the essential interiority of Christian piety; our vision that "true religion" ought to be expressed in practical works of charity in the world; and our presumption that religion and politics are separable spheres of human endeavor and concern. Even our modern impulse to define and persecute minority groups has roots in twelfth- and thirteenth-century efforts to suppress Jews, heretics, and sexual minorities.

Many of the people who made such important contributions to learning, thought, literature, architecture, drama, and music must have intermingled with each other in the Paris of the High Middle Ages. Some of them no doubt prayed together in the cathedral of Notre Dame. The names of the leading scholars are remembered, but the names of most of the others are unknown. Yet taken together they did as much for the civilization of Europe, and created as many enduring monuments, as did their counterparts in ancient Athens. Their names may be forgotten, but their achievements live on still.

KEY TERMS

Cluny

Investiture Conflict

cult of the Virgin Mary

Franciscan order

Dominican order

Peter Abelard

Saint Thomas Aquinas

courtly love

Divine Comedy

Gothic style

SELECTED READINGS

Baldwin, John W. *The Scholastic Culture of the Middle Ages: 1000–1300*. Lexington, Mass., 1971. A fine introduction.

Blumenthal, Uta-Renate. *The Investiture Controversy*. Philadelphia, 1988. A clear review of a complicated subject.

Boswell, John E. *Christianity, Social Tolerance, and Homosexuality: Gay People in Western Europe from the Beginning of the Christian Era to the Fourteenth Century*. Chicago, 1980. A pioneering account, particularly good on twelfth-century poetry.

Chrétien de Troyes. *Arthurian Romances*. Translated by W. W. Kibler. New York, 1991.

Clanchy, Michael T. *Abelard: A Medieval Life*. Oxford and Cambridge, Mass., 1997. A great biography.

Cobban, Alan B. *The Medieval Universities*. London, 1975. The best short treatment in English.

Colish, Marcia. *Medieval Foundations of the Western Intellectual Tradition, 400–1400*. New Haven, 1997. An encyclopedic and exhaustive work, best used as a reference.

Dante Alighieri. *The Divine Comedy*. Translated by Mark Musa. 3 vols. Baltimore, 1984–1986.

Dronke, Peter. *Women Writers of the Middle Ages*. New York, 1984. A rich literary study.

Gottfried von Strassburg. *Tristan*. Translated by A. T. Hatto. Baltimore, 1960.

Knowles, David. *The Evolution of Medieval Thought*, 2d ed. London, 1988. An authoritative survey, thoroughly revised in the second edition.

Lambert, Malcolm. *Medieval Heresy*, 3d ed. Oxford and Cambridge, 2002. The standard synthesis; deeply learned and fully annotated.

Lawrence, Clifford Hugh. *The Friars: The Impact of the Early Mendicant Movement on Western Society*. London and New York, 1994. The best short introduction to the early history of the Franciscans and the Dominicans.

———. *Medieval Monasticism: Forms of Religious Life in Western Europe in the Middle Ages*, 3d ed. London and New York, 2000. This new edition includes material on the friars drawn from his 1994 book.

Leclerq, Jean. *Bernard of Clairvaux and the Cistercian Spirit*. Kalamazoo, Mich., 1976. An empathetic account by the greatest twentieth-century scholar of Cistercianism.

———. *The Love of Learning and the Desire for God*, 3d ed. New York, 1982. A beautiful account of twelfth-century monastic culture, seen from the perspective of Saint Bernard of Clairvaux.

The Letters of Abelard and Heloise. Translated by Betty Radice. London and New York, 1974. Includes Abelard's autobiographical *Story of My Misfortunes*.

Morris, Colin. *The Papal Monarchy: The Western Church from 1050 to 1250*. Oxford, 1989. An excellent scholarly survey; part of the Oxford History of the Christian Church series.

Newman, Barbara, ed. *Voice of the Living Light: Hildegard of Bingen and Her World*. Berkeley and Los Angeles, 1998. The best introduction to Hildegard's life and work; discusses her roles as abbess, religious thinker, prophet, correspondent, artist, medical writer, composer, dramatist, and poet.

Southern, Richard W. *Western Society and the Church in the Middle Ages*. Baltimore, 1970. An extremely insightful interpretation of the interplay between society and religion, engagingly written by one of the greatest historians of the twentieth century.

———. *Scholastic Humanism and the Unification of Europe*. Vol. 1: *Foundations*. Oxford and Cambridge, Mass., 1995. A major reinterpretation of scholasticism and humanism by the foremost historian of both traditions.

Swanson, R. N. *The Twelfth-Century Renaissance*. Manchester, Eng., 1999. The most accessible and up-to-date survey of the intellectual developments of the twelfth century.

Tierney, Brian. *The Crisis of Church and State, 1050–1300*. Toronto, 1988. An indispensable collection for both teachers and students.

Wakefield, Walter, and Austin P. Evans, eds. and trans. *Heresies of the High Middle Ages*. New York, 1969, 1991. A comprehensive collection of sources, best used in conjunction with Lambert (see above).

Wilhelm, James J., ed. and trans. *Medieval Song: An Anthology of Hymns and Lyrics*. New York, 1971. An excellent collection of sacred and secular poetry that illustrates the connections between them.

Wolfram von Eschenbach. *Parzival*. Translated by H. M. Mustard and C. E. Passage. New York, 1961.

PART IV

FROM MEDIEVAL TO MODERN

FOR MOST OF THE TWENTIETH CENTURY, historians portrayed the Italian Renaissance and the Protestant Reformation as marking a dramatic break in European history, which brought the Middle Ages to an end and ushered in the modern world. To be sure, the sixteenth and seventeenth centuries saw decisive transformations in European life. For the first time, European sailors, soldiers, and merchants forged worldwide trading networks that brought the mineral and agricultural riches of the Western Hemisphere into their Atlantic ports. The Protestant Reformation brought an end to the religious unity of Europe, and a century of religious wars served only to cement those divisions. Meanwhile, new trends in cultural and intellectual life, many of which had begun in fourteenth- and fifteenth-century Italy, began to spread widely throughout the rest of Europe.

It is increasingly clear, however, that most of the new developments of the sixteenth and seventeenth centuries had deep roots in the later Middle Ages. The voyages that took sixteenth-century Europeans around the globe began in the thirteenth century with the conquest of the "Atlantic Mediterranean." The intensive study of classical Roman and Greek literature that characterized the Italian Renaissance developed out of the classical revival in the twelfth and thirteenth centuries. Even the theological doctrines of the Protestant reformers had roots in the theological controversies of the later Middle Ages. And all these developments took place in the context of continuing cultural and economic exchange between Europe, the Islamic world, and Byzantium.

	POLITICS	SOCIETY AND CULTURE	ECONOMY	INTERNATIONAL RELATIONS
1200	Chingiz (Genghis) Khan rules over Mongol clans (1206–1227)		"Silk Road" connects Europe with India, China, and Indonesia (1200s) Polo brothers travel to China (1200s)	Mongols conquer southern Russia (1237–1240) Mongols annihilate Hungarian army at River Sajo (1241) Mongol forces withdraw from Europe (1241)
1300	Yuan dynasty in China (1279–1368) Rise of Ottoman dynasty (1300) Babylonian Captivity of the church (1305–1378)	Civic humanism begins in Italy (1300s) Francesco Petrarch (1304–1374) Giovanni Boccaccio (1313–1375) Over a tenth of Europe dies during the Great Famine (1316–1322) John Wyclif, Oxford theologian (1330–1384) Geoffrey Chaucer (1340–1400)	Development of mechanical clocks and compasses (1300) Explorers reach Azores and Cape Verde Islands (1300s) Severe flooding ruins crops, breeds pestilence (1315) Heavy cannons first employed (1330) Silver shortage begins in Europe (1340s)	Hundred Years War (1337–1453)
	Jacquerie rebellion in France (1358) Ming dynasty in China (1368–1644)	Onset of the Black Death, from which half of Europe dies (1347) Leonardo Bruni (1370–1444)		
	The Great Schism, ended by Council of Constance (1378–1417) Florentine Ciompi uprising (1378) English Peasants' Revolt (1381)	Jan van Eyck (1380–1441) University of Heidelberg founded (1385)	Medici family, originators of modern banking, flourishes (1397–1494)	Poland and Lithuania united (1386) Ottomans defeat Serbian empire at battle of Kosovo (1389)
1400	Italian territorial papacy (1417–1517)	Giovanni Aurispa returns with classical manuscripts (1423) Sandro Botticelli (1445–1510) Neoplatonism in Italy (1450–1600) Leonardo da Vinci (1452–1519)	Portugal establishes Atlantic colonies (1400–1460)	Rise of Grand Duchy of Moscow (1400s)
	Edward, duke of York dethrones Henry VI after War of the Roses (1461) Reign of Ivan III, the Great, tsar of all Russias (1462–1505)	Desiderius Erasmus (1469–1536) Niccolò Machiavelli, author of *The Prince* (1469–1527)	Invention of movable type; the Gutenberg Bible (1454)	Turks conquer Constantinople (1453) England loses Bordeaux (1453) Mehmet II conquers Constantinople (1453)
	Ferdinand of Aragon marries Isabella of Castile, forming modern Spain (1469)	Albrecht Dürer (1471–1528) Sir Thomas More (1478–1535) Raphael (1483–1520)	Explorers round the Cape of Good Hope (1487) Dias rounds southern tip of Africa (1488)	French monarchy absorbs Burgundy (1477)
		The High Renaissance begins (1490) The Catholic Reformation begins (1490)	Portugal founds slave-based plantation in St. Thomas (1490) Columbus lands in West Indies (1492) Disease kills much of Native American population (1492–1538) Vasco da Gama reaches India (1498)	Christian monarchs expel Jews (1492) and Muslims (1502) from Spain
1500	Reign of Charles V, Holy Roman emperor (1506–1556)	Roman Inquisition begins (1500) Saint Peter's Basilica erected in Rome (1500–1520) Papacy of Julius II (1503–1513) Saint Francis Xavier, missionary in Asia (1506–1552) Andrea Palladio (1508–1580) John Calvin (1509–1564) Papacy of Leo X, son of Lorenzo de Medici (1513–1521)	Grain prices in Europe increase five-fold (1500–1650)	

POLITICS	SOCIETY AND CULTURE	ECONOMY	INTERNATIONAL RELATIONS	
		Portuguese ships reach Spice Islands and China (1515)		1515
	Luther posts Ninety-five Theses (1517)		Cortes conquers Aztec empire (1519–1522)	
	Emergence of Zwinglianism, Anabaptism, and Calvinism (1520–1550)		Ottomans conquer Syria, Egypt, and the Balkans (1520–1540)	
	Edict of Worms (1521)			
	Peter Brueghel, painter of *Harvesters* and *Massacre of the Innocents* (1525–1569)		Charles V, Holy Roman emperor, sacks Rome (1527)	
	Baldassare Castiglione's *Book of the Courtier* (1528)		Francisco Pizarro topples Incas (1533)	
	Michel de Montaigne (1533–1592)			
	Henry VIII becomes head of the Church of England (1533–1534)			
	Calvin's *Institutes of the Christian Religion* (1536)			
	St. Ignatius Loyola publishes *Spiritual Exercises* (1541)	Rapid inflation marks the Price Revolution (1540s)		
	El Greco, painter of *View of Toledo* (1541–1614)	Silver found in Mexico and Bolivia (1543–1548)		
	Council of Trent (1545–1563)			
Reign of Philip II of Spain (1556–1598)	Edmund Spenser, author of *The Faerie Queen* (1552–1599)		Peace of Augsburg (1555)	
Reign of Elizabeth I of England (1558–1603)				
	First *Roman Index of Prohibited Books* established (1564)			
	William Shakespeare (1564–1616)			
	Papacy of Pius V (1566–1572)		Ottomans defeated by Habsburgs and Venetians at Lepanto (1571)	
English navy defeats the Spanish Armada (1588)	St. Bartholomew's Day massacre (1572)		Philip II annexes Portugal (1580)	
Reign of Henry IV, first of the Bourbon dynasty in France (1589–1610)		New World silver production peaks at 10 million ounces (1590s)		1600
Edict of Nantes (1598)				
Reign of James I, first of the Stuart dynasty (1603–1625)			Thirty Years' War (1618–1648)	
	John Milton (1608–1674)	Spanish economy collapses when silver imports drop (1620–1640)		
Cardinal Richelieu, first minister of France (1624–1642)	Blaise Pascal (1623–1662)			
Reign of Charles I of England (1625–1649)			Gustavus Adolphus of Sweden enters Thirty Years' War (1630)	
English Civil War (1642–1649)				
The Fronde, a series of French aristocratic revolts (1648–1653)			Peace of Westphalia (1648)	
Oliver Cromwell rules England (1649–1658)				
Louis XIV of France comes of age (1651)	Thomas Hobbes's *Leviathan* (1651)			
Charles II and the Restoration (1660–1685)				

CHAPTER TEN

THE LATER
MIDDLE AGES,
1300–1500

IF THE HIGH MIDDLE AGES were "times of feasts," then the late Middle Ages were "times of famine." From about 1300 until the middle or latter part of the fifteenth century calamities struck throughout western Europe with appalling severity and dismaying persistence. Famine first prevailed because agriculture was impeded by soil exhaustion, colder weather, and torrential rainfalls. Then, on top of those "acts of God," came the most terrible natural disaster of all: the dreadful plague known as the "Black Death," which cut broad swaths of mortality throughout western Europe. As if all that were not enough, incessant warfare continually brought hardship and desolation. Common people suffered most because they were most exposed to raping, stabbing, looting, and burning by soldiers and organized bands of freebooters. After an army passed through a region one might see miles of smoldering ruins littered with putrefying corpses; in many places the desolation was so great that wolves roamed the countryside and even entered the outskirts of the cities. In short, if the serene Virgin symbolized the High Middle Ages, the grinning death's-head symbolized the succeeding period. But despite the hardships they faced, Europeans displayed a tenacious perseverance in the face of adversity. Instead of abandoning themselves to apathy, they resolutely sought to adjust to changed circumstances. Thus civilization did not collapse, but rather a period of creativity and innovation preserved and extended the most enduring features of high medieval European life.

FOCUS QUESTIONS

• How did famine and plague transform economic life in late medieval Europe?

• What were the causes of the popular rebellions from 1300 to 1450?

• What were the main forms of late medieval popular piety?

• What caused the rise of national monarchies?

 • Why was medieval Russia so unlike any other European state?

• What trends led to the rise of vernacular literature during the later Middle Ages?

• How did technological advances affect everyday life?

ECONOMIC DEPRESSION AND THE EMERGENCE OF A NEW EQUILIBRIUM

How did famine and plague transform economic life in late medieval Europe?

By around 1300 the agricultural expansion of the High Middle Ages had reached its limits. When the Black Death struck Europe between 1347 and 1350, it provoked an economic and demographic crisis. Recurrences of the plague and protracted warfare continued to depress the European economy until deep into the fifteenth century. But between roughly 1350 and 1450 Europeans learned how to turn the new economic circumstances to their advantage. Wages rose while grain prices fell, resulting in better diets and housing among European laborers and farmers, and a gradual recovery in overall population. Although the total size of the European economy almost certainly shrank in the century after the Black Death, by 1450 Europe was wealthier per capita than it had been in 1300, and its wealth was more evenly distributed among its people. All told, therefore, Europe emerged in the later fifteenth century with a healthier economy than it had known earlier.

> Between 1316 and 1322, 10 percent to 15 percent of the entire European population perished in this "Great Famine."

CLIMATE CHANGE AND AGRICULTURAL FAILURE

The checks on agricultural expansion reached around 1300 were natural ones. There was a limit to the amount of land that could be cleared and a limit to the amount of crops that could be raised without the introduction of scientific farming. In fact, Europeans had gone further in clearing and cultivating than they should have: in the enthusiasm of the high medieval colonization movement, marginal lands had been cleared that were not rich enough to sustain intense cultivation. In addition, even the best plots were becoming overworked. To make matters worse, in the fourteenth century the climate became colder and wetter, shortening growing seasons significantly, especially in northern Europe. In-

creased rainfall also took its toll. Terrible floods deluged northern Europe in 1315, ruining crops and causing a prolonged, deadly famine that was made worse by epidemic diseases that swept through sheep flocks and cattle herds. Weakened by malnutrition, people also became more susceptible to disease. Between 1316 and 1322, 10 percent to 15 percent of the entire European population perished in this "Great Famine." Farming conditions improved after 1322, but the climate remained unsettled. With nature so recurrently capricious, economic life could only suffer.

Despite this high mortality rate, Europe in 1340 was still overpopulated relative to its food supplies. Then a disaster struck that was so horrifying that it seemed to many to presage the end of the world.

THE BLACK DEATH

The Black Death was a combined onslaught of bubonic and pneumonic plague that first swept through Europe from 1347 to 1350, returning at periodic intervals for the next three hundred years. This epidemic originated in the Gobi Desert of Mongolia. By 1346 the plague had reached the ports along the Black Sea, and from there, in 1347, Genoese galleys brought it, inadvertantly, to Sicily and northern Italy. From Italy it spread throughout western Europe along the trade routes, first striking the seaports, then moving inland.

The clinical effects of the plague were hideous. Once infected with bubonic plague by a flea bite, the diseased person would develop enormous swellings in the groin or armpits, black spots might appear on the arms and legs, diarrhea would ensue, and the victim would die between the fourth and seventh days. If the infection came in the pneumonic form (caused by inhalation) there would also be coughing of blood, and death would follow within three days. A few people recovered from the plague, and some did not catch it. But the majority of those who caught the disease died from it within a week.

The demographic effects of the plague were devastating. In England, the total population of the country declined by at least 40 percent between 1347 and 1381. The total population of eastern Normandy fell by 30 percent between 1347 and 1357, and again by 30 percent before 1380; in the rural area around Pistoia in Italy a population depletion of about 60 percent occurred between 1340 and 1404. Altogether,

HOW DID FAMINE AND PLAGUE TRANSFORM ECONOMIC LIFE IN LATE MEDIEVAL EUROPE?

ECONOMIC DEPRESSION AND THE EMERGENCE OF A NEW EQUILIBRIUM   295

Bubonic Plague. This representation from a late-fifteenth-century French painting shows a man in the throes of death from the plague. The swelling on his neck is a *bubo,* a lymphatic swelling that gave the bubonic plague its name.

the combined effects of famine, war, and plague reduced the total population of western Europe by at least one half and perhaps as much as two thirds between 1300 and 1450.

At first, the Black Death caused great hardships for most of the survivors. With large numbers of workers dead, harvests were left rotting, manufacturing was disrupted, and trade collapsed. By 1400, however, the new demographic realities began to alter the basic patterns of the European economy. The prices of staple foodstuffs (for example, grains) began to decline because production gradually returned to

normal and there were fewer mouths to feed. Since cereals were cheaper, people could afford to spend a greater percentage of their income on comparative luxuries such as dairy products, meat, and wine. Specialized regional economies resulted: parts of England were given over to sheep raising or beer production, parts of France concentrated on wine, and Sweden traded butter for cheap German grain. Most areas of Europe turned to what they could do best, and reciprocal trade of basic commodities over long distances created a prosperous new commercial equilibrium.

THE IMPACT ON TOWNS

Towns were especially sensitive barometers of the changing economic climate of the later Middle Ages. After reaching their demographic peak around 1300, many towns were already experiencing declining populations and economic crises even before the Black Death struck. The plague, however, made the existing situation infinitely worse. In some cities, mortality rates from the plague alone exceeded 60 percent. In northern Italy, southern France, and parts of Spain, warfare was even more destructive to urban life than was the plague. By 1450, however, as a century of warfare came to an end and visitations of the plague became less frequent and less devastating (presumably because Europeans were beginning to develop some resistance to the plague bacillus), urban life was well on the road to recovery. By 1500, a larger percentage of Europe's people lived in towns, and towns themselves played a larger role in the European economy, than had been the case two centuries before.

The new circumstances also helped stimulate the development of sophisticated business, accounting, and banking techniques. New forms of partnerships were created to minimize risks. Insurance contracts were also invented to take some of the risk out of shipping. Europe's most useful accounting invention, double-entry bookkeeping, was first put into use in Italy in the mid-fourteenth century and spread rapidly thereafter. This method allowed for quick discovery of computational errors and easy overview of profits and losses, credits and debits. The economic crises of the later Middle Ages also encouraged banks to alter some of their ways of doing business. Most important was the development of prudent branch-banking techniques, especially by the Florentine house of the Medici. The Medici branches, located in London, Bruges, and Avignon,

THE PROGRESS OF THE BLACK DEATH, FOURTEENTH CENTURY

Where did the Black Death come from, and where did it enter Europe, generally speaking? Why was the onslaught of the disease so devastating, and what agricultural, economic, and demographic factors helped to make Europeans around 1350 so vulnerable to the disease? Note the rapid spread of the Black Death. Would such a rapid advance have been likely during the early Middle Ages, or even in the ancient world? How did the growth of towns, trade, and travel contribute to the spread of the Black Death?

WHAT WERE THE CAUSES OF THE POPULAR REBELLIONS FROM 1300 TO 1450?

SOCIAL AND EMOTIONAL DISLOCATION   297

as well as several Italian cities, were dominated by senior partners from the Medici family who followed common policies. However, each branch was a separate, formal partnership that did not carry any other branch down with it if it collapsed.

THE NEW EQUILIBRIUM

In surveying late medieval economic history, we must emphasize both the role of nature and that of human beings. Nature intervened cruelly in human affairs, but no matter how cruel the immediate effects, the results were ultimately beneficial. By 1450 a far smaller population had a higher average standard of living than the population of 1300. In this result humans too played their part. Because people were determined to make the best of the new circumstances they managed to reorganize their economic life and place it on a sounder footing. The gross European product of about 1450 was probably lower than it was in 1300, but this is not surprising given the much smaller population. In fact, per capita output had risen with per capita income, and the European economy was ready to move on to new conquests.

SOCIAL AND EMOTIONAL DISLOCATION

> What were the causes of the popular rebellions from 1300 to 1450?

The economic crises of the later Middle Ages contributed to provoking a rash of lower-class rural and urban insurrections more numerous than Europe had ever known before. It was once thought that these were all caused by extreme deprivation, but as we will see, often that was not the case.

THE JACQUERIE

The one large-scale rural uprising that was most clearly caused by economic hardship was the northern French "Jacquerie" of 1358. This took its name from the prototypical French peasant, "Jacques Bonhomme," who had suffered more than he could endure from both plaque and war. In 1358 they rose up with astounding ferocity,

CHRONOLOGY	
FAMINE, PLAGUES, REBELLION, AND WARFARE, 1300–1450	
"Great Famine"	1315–1322
Black Death	1347–1350
"Jacquerie" rebellion	1358
Ciompi revolt	1378
English Peasants' Revolt	1381
Hundred Years' War	1337–1453
Venice, Milan, and Florence consolidate their territories	1400–1454

burning down castles, murdering lords, and raping their lords' wives. But within a month the privileged orders closed ranks, massacred the rebels, and ended the rebellion.

THE ENGLISH PEASANTS' REVOLT

The English Peasants' Revolt of 1381—the most serious lower-class rebellion in English history—is frequently bracketed with the Jacquerie, but its causes were very different. Instead of being a revolt of desperation, it arose from a combination of rising economic expectations combined with political grievances associated with English defeats in the war with France.

The spark that ignited the great revolt of 1381 was an attempt to collect a new type of national tax to pay for the failing war with France. Traditionally, English taxes had been assessed village by village in rough proportion to wealth. In 1377 and 1379, however, the government imposed a much less graduated head tax instead of the traditional income tax. These two taxes were collected without resistance, but when agents tried to collect a third, much heavier such tax in 1381, the peasants, artisans, and town dwellers of eastern England rose up to resist. First they burned local records and sacked the dwellings of those they considered their exploiters; then they marched into London, where they executed the lord chancellor and treasurer of England, whose fiscal mismanagement they blamed for recent English defeats in the French war. Recognizing the gravity of the situation, the fourteen-year-old king, Richard II,

FROISSART ON THE ENGLISH PEASANTS' REVOLT, 1381

Jean Froissart (1337?–1410?) is best known as the author of a lengthy history of the Hundred Years' War. He was not an eyewitness to the events of the Peasants' Revolt, but he had excellent English connections from whom he presumably derived his information. Froissart's perspective is entirely that of the aristocrats whom he served and with whom he associated. This fact makes his modest sympathy for the rebels of 1381 all the more interesting, particularly compared with his earlier, entirely negative portrayal of the 1358 Jacquerie rebels in France.

While these negotiations and discussions were going on, there occurred in England great disasters and uprisings of the common people, on account of which the country was almost ruined beyond recovery. Never was any land or realm in such great danger as England at that time. It was because of the abundance and prosperity in which the common people then lived that this rebellion broke out, just as in earlier days the Jack Goodmans rose in France and committed many excesses, by which the noble land of France suffered grave injury. . . .

These bad people . . . began to rebel because, they said, they were held too much in subjection, and when the world began there had been no serfs and could not be, unless they had rebelled against their Lord, as Lucifer did against God; but they were not of that stature, being neither angels nor spirits, but men formed in the image of their masters, and they were treated as animals. This was a thing they could no longer endure, wishing rather to be all one and the same; and, if they worked for their masters, they wanted to have wages for it. In these machinations they had been greatly encouraged originally by a crack-brained priest of Kent called John Ball . . . who had the habit on Sundays after mass, when everyone was coming out of church, of going to the cloisters or the graveyard, assembling the people round him and preaching thus:

"Good people, things cannot go right in England and never will, until goods are held in common and there are no more serfs and gentlefolk, but we are all one and the same. In what way are those whom we call lords greater masters than ourselves? How have they deserved it? Why do they hold us in bondage? If we all spring from a single father and mother, Adam and Eve, how can they claim or prove that they are lords more than us, except by making us produce and grow the wealth which they spend? They are clad in velvet and camlet lined with squirrel and ermine, while we go dressed in coarse cloth. They have the wines, the spices, and the good bread: we have the rye, the husks and the straw, and we drink water. They have shelter and ease in their fine manors, and we have hardship and toil, the wind and the rain in the fields. And from us must come, from our labor, the things which keep them in luxury. We are called serfs and beaten if we are slow in our service to them, yet we have no sovereign lord we can complain to, none to hear us and do us justice. Let us go to the King—he is young—and show him how we are oppressed, and tell him that we want things to be changed, or else we will change them ourselves. If we go in good earnest and all together, very many people who are called serfs and are held in subjection will follow us to get their freedom. And when the King sees and hears us, he will remedy the evil, either willingly or otherwise."

These were the kind of things which John Ball usually preached in the villages on Sundays . . . and many of the common people agreed with him.

Geoffrey Brereton, ed. and trans. *Froissart: Chronicles.* (London and New York: Penguin Books, 1968), pp. 211–213.

WHAT WERE THE CAUSES OF THE POPULAR REBELLIONS FROM 1300 TO 1450?

SOCIAL AND EMOTIONAL DISLOCATION   299

went out to meet the peasants and won their confidence by promising to abolish serfdom and keep rents low; meanwhile, during negotiations the peasant leader, Wat Tyler, was murdered in a squabble with the king's escort. Lacking leadership, the peasants, who mistakenly thought they had achieved their aims, rapidly dispersed. But once the boy king was no longer in danger of his life he kept none of his promises. Instead, the scattered peasant forces were quickly hunted down and a few alleged troublemakers were executed without any mass reprisals. The revolt itself therefore did not accomplish its objectives. Within a few decades, however, the natural play of economic forces considerably improved the lot of small- to medium-scale farmers and rural wage laborers, and within a century had brought about the effective disappearance of serfdom in England. The result was a kind of mid-fifteenth-century "golden age" for the English peasantry.

URBAN REBELLIONS

The urban revolts of the later Middle Ages are sometimes viewed as uprisings of exploited workers suffering from the changed economic circumstances of the period. But this is too great a simplification. Like the Jacquerie and the Peasants' Revolt, most urban rebellions arose from a complex combination of political, economic, and social grievances that differed from city to city. Even in Florence, where the 1378 revolt of the Ciompi (pronounced "cheeompi") did take on aspects of a proletarian rebellion, the troubles were as much political as economic. The *ciompi* were wool combers—poorly paid workers in a depressed industry, beset by high unemployment, and frequently cheated by their masters, who controlled the woolen industry and dominated the Florentine government. In 1378, however, after three years of war with the papacy, the ruling class of Florence split. When one of the factions sought to buttress its position by appealing to the lower classes, the Ciompi seized the opportunity to push through their own far more radical reform program: tax relief, fuller employment, and political representation for themselves and other workers' groups in the Florentine government. After six weeks, however, the Ciompi lost their hold on power, and a new oligarchical government revoked all their reform measures.

> Like the Jacquerie and the Peasants' Revolt, most urban rebellions arose from a complex combination of political, economic, and social grievances that differed from city to city.

Had economic grievances not existed, the urban rebellions of the later Middle Ages would probably not have occurred. But few if any of these rebellions were specifically class revolts and none succeeded in altering the fundamentally oligarchical nature of late-medieval urban life. Indeed, the usual response of the ruling classes to such rebellions was to tighten even further their grip on power within the towns.

ARISTOCRATIC INSECURITIES

Although the upper classes succeeded in overcoming popular uprisings, they were well aware of the threat these rebellions posed to their privileged social status. Late medieval aristocrats were in a precarious economic position because most of their income came from land. In times when grain prices and rents were falling and wages rising, landowners were obviously in economic trouble. Aristocrats also felt threatened by the rapid rise of merchants and financiers. The result was that they tried to set up social and cultural barriers by which to separate themselves from other classes.

Two of the most striking examples of this separation were the aristocratic emphasis on luxury and the formation of exclusive chivalric orders. The later Middle Ages were the period par excellence of aristocratic ostentation. While famine or disease raged, aristocrats entertained themselves with lavish banquets and magnificent pageants. At one feast in Flanders in 1468, a table decoration was forty-six feet high. Aristocratic clothing too was extremely ostentatious: men wore long, pointed shoes, and women ornately festooned headdresses. Throughout history rich people have always enjoyed dressing up, but the aristocrats of the later Middle Ages seem to have done so obsessively. They even imposed special sumptuary laws that defined the type of clothing that each rank in society could wear. This aristocratic insistence on maintaining a sharply defined social hierarchy also accounts for the late medieval proliferation of chivalric orders, such as those of the knights of the Garter or the Golden Fleece. By joining together in exclusive orders that prescribed special conduct and boasted special insignia of membership, aristocrats tried to set themselves off from others, in effect, by putting up a sign that read "for members only."

An Aristocratic Family Behind a Walled Garden. Wealthy aristocrats in the later Middle Ages emphasized luxury and rigid social order to combat the rising power of merchants and financiers. They threw extravagant feasts and dressed in ostentatious clothing to indicate their place in the social hierarchy.

TRIALS FOR THE CHURCH AND HUNGER FOR THE DIVINE

What were the main forms of late medieval popular piety?

The later Middle Ages were a period of deep and pervasive religiosity. The religious enthusiasm of the High Middle Ages by no means flagged after 1300; if anything, it became more intense. But religious enthusiasm took on new forms of expression because of the institutional difficulties of the church and the turmoils of the age.

THE LATE MEDIEVAL PAPACY

Following the humiliation and death of Pope Boniface VIII (1294–1303) at the hands of King Philip IV of France (see p. 270), the late medieval papacy entered upon a long period of institutional crisis. From 1305 until 1378, the papacy resided continuously at Avignon, a small papal territory on the southwestern border of France, where the popes inevitably fell under the close supervision of the French monarchy. Here they built up a vast bureaucracy, principally devoted to extracting money from the clergy of western Europe. In 1377, after a costly series of military campaigns in Italy, the pope finally succeeded in returning to Rome; but when he died soon thereafter, the resulting confusion produced first two, and ultimately three different men, each claiming to be the legitimately elected pope. This split, known as the Great Schism, would last from 1378 until 1417. But conflicts arising out of the Great Schism continued for another century, lessening the papacy's influence over the churches of western Europe and turning it more and more into an Italian territorial principality.

When the popes first settled in Avignon, they had not intended to remain there. But Avignon soon proved to have a number of advantages over Rome: it was closer to the major centers of power in fourteenth-century Europe; it was far removed from the tumultuous local politics of Rome and central Italy; and it was safe from the aggressive attentions of the German emperors. All the popes elected at Avignon were from southern France; as time went on, and the size of the papal bureaucracy grew, Avignon came increasingly to look like the new, permanent home of the bishops of Rome.

Despite Avignon's advantages, the Avignon popes never entirely abandoned the hope of returning to Rome. To do so, however, they first had to win back military control over the papal states in central Italy. This effort took decades. To finance these expensive military campaigns, the popes imposed a variety of new taxes and dues on the churches of France, England, Germany, and Spain. They also claimed the right to appoint candidates directly to vacant church offices, bypassing the rights of the local clergy to elect their own bishops and abbots. Judicial cases were another profitable exercise of papal authority, whose numbers grew enormously during the Avignon period.

By these and other measures, the Avignon popes greatly strengthened their administrative control over the church. But whatever the popes achieved in power they lost in respect and loyalty. Clergy and laity alike were alienated by the papacy's insatiable demands for money, and stories quickly spread about the unbridled luxury of the papal court. In fact, most of the Avignon popes were morally upright and personally abstemious, but one, Clement VI (1342–1352), was notoriously corrupt and immoral. Clement openly sold spiritual benefits for money, boasted that he would appoint a jackass as bishop if political circumstances warranted, and defended his incessant sexual transgressions by insisting that he fornicated on doctors' orders. His cardinals led equally luxurious lives, dining off peacocks, pheasants, grouse, and swans, and drinking from elaborately sculptured fountains that spouted the finest wines.

After one abortive attempt by Urban V in 1367, Pope Gregory XI finally returned to Rome in 1377. But when he died a year later, disaster struck. Fearful that if the new pope were a Frenchman he might return to Avignon, the Romans rioted, demanding that the cardinals (who were mainly French) elect a Roman as the new pope. Fearing for their lives, the cardinals quickly obliged, electing an Italian who took the title of Urban VI. Urban, however, immediately began quarreling with the cardinals, revealing what were probably paranoid tendencies. Fearing for their lives once again, the cardinals fled Rome, declared Urban VI's election void, and selected as the new pope a French cardinal who took the name Clement VII. Urban VI thereupon named a new, entirely Italian college of cardinals, and prepared to defend himself in Rome. Clement VII and his cardinals retreated to Avignon, and the Great Schism began.

For three decades Europe's religious allegiances were divided. Nor was there any obvious way to end this embarrassing state of affairs. Both Urban VI and Clement VII had been elected by the same group of cardinals; and thereafter, whenever a pope died, his supporters quickly elected a successor, thus prolonging the Schism. Finally, in 1409, some cardinals from both camps met at Pisa, where they deposed both popes and named a new one. But neither the Italian nor the French pope would accept the council's decision. As a result, after 1409 there were now three rival popes hurling curses at each other instead of two.

The Great Schism was finally ended in 1417 by the Council of Constance, the largest ecclesiastical gathering of the Middle Ages. This council had strong support from several European princes, including the kings of England and Germany. It also took care to depose all the other papal claimants before naming its own new pope, an Italian who took the name Martin V. The election of Pope Martin V restored the ecclesiastical unity of Europe. It did not, however, end the struggle over how the church should be governed in future. To end the schism, the Council of Constance had declared that supreme authority within the church rested not with the pope, but with itself and all future such "general councils." It also ordered that general councils should meet regularly thereafter to oversee the governance and reform of the church.

> The Great Schism was finally ended in 1417 by the Council of Constance, the largest ecclesiastical gathering of the Middle Ages.

These "conciliar" decrees were a revolutionary challenge to the traditions of papal monarchy. Not surprisingly, Martin V and his successors did all they could to undermine them. In 1423, when the next required general council met at Siena, Pope Martin immediately sent its representatives back home. Constance had specified that a council must meet, but it had not specified for how long that meeting must last! In 1431, when the next general council met at Basel, its members took steps to ensure that the pope could not dismiss it. A lengthy struggle for power quickly ensued, with the popes and the conciliarists competing for the support of Europe's princes. Finally, the Council of Basel dissolved in 1449 in abject failure, dashing the hopes of church reformers and bringing to an end this radical experiment in conciliar government.

The papacy's victory over the conciliarists was a costly one. To win the support of kings and princes against the conciliarists, the popes negotiated a series of treaties (known as "concordats") which granted these rulers extensive authority over the churches within their territories. The popes thus secured their theoretical supremacy over the church at the cost of surrendering their real power to rule it. Having given away so many of their other revenues, late-fifteenth-century popes became even more dependent on their own territories in central Italy. To build up the Papal States, however, these popes had to rule like other Italian princes: leading armies, jockeying for alliances, and undermining their opponents by every possible means. Judged in secular terms, these efforts were by no means a failure. Understandably, however, such methods did nothing to increase their reputation for piety.

THE GREAT SCHISM, 1378–1417

This map illustrates the religious divisions of Europe during the Great Schism. What common interests united the supporters of the Avignon pope? The Roman pope? Why did areas like Portugal and Austria find it so difficult to choose which side to support?

POPULAR PIETY AND POPULAR HERESY

While the papacy was enduring these vicissitudes, the local clergy throughout Europe was also losing prestige. One reason was that the pope's greater financial demands forced the clergy to demand more from the laity, but such demands were bitterly resented, especially during times of economic crisis. Then too during outbreaks of plague the clergy sometimes fled their posts just like everyone else, but in so doing they lost whatever claim they had to moral superiority.

Probably the single greatest reason for growing dissatisfaction with the clergy was the increase in lay literacy. The continued proliferation of schools and the decline in the cost of books—a subject we will treat later—made it possible for large numbers of lay people to learn how to read. Once that happened, the laity could start reading parts of the Bible, or, more frequently, popular religious primers. This reading made it clear that their local priests were not living according to the standards set by Jesus and the apostles. In the meantime, the upheavals and horrors of the age drove people to seek religious solace more than ever. Where lay people found the conventional channels of church attendance, confession, and submission to clerical authority insufficient, they sought supplementary or alternate routes to piety. These differed greatly from each other, but they all aimed to satisfy an immense hunger for the divine.

> Probably the single greatest reason for growing dissatisfaction with the clergy was the increase in lay literacy.

The most widely traveled route was to perform repeated acts of external devotion in the hope that they would gain the devotee divine favor on earth and salvation in the hereafter. People flocked to go on pilgrimages as never before and participated regularly in religious processions. Men and women also eagerly paid for thousands of masses to be said by full-time "Mass priests" for the souls of their dead relatives, and left legacies for the reading of numerous requiem masses to save their own souls after death. The most dramatic form of religious ritual in the later Middle Ages was flagellation. Flailings were not usually performed in public, but during the first onslaught of the Black Death in 1348 and 1349, bands of lay people marched through northern Europe chanting and beating each other with metal-tipped scourges in the hope of appeasing divine wrath.

MYSTICISM

An opposite route to godliness was the inward path of mysticism. Throughout the European continent, male and female mystics sought union with God by means of "detachment," contemplation, or spiritual exercises. The most original and eloquent late medieval mystical theorist was Master Eckhart (c. 1260–1327), a German Dominican who taught that there was a power or "spark" deep within every human soul that was really the dwelling place of God. By renouncing all sense of selfhood one could retreat into one's innermost recesses and there find divinity. Eckhart did not recommend ceasing attendance at church—he hardly could have because he preached in churches—but he made it clear that outward rituals were of comparatively little importance in reaching God. He also gave the impression to his lay audiences that they might attain godliness largely on their own volition. Thus ecclesiastical authorities charged him with inciting "ignorant and undisciplined people to wild and dangerous excesses." Although Eckhart pleaded his own doctrinal orthodoxy, some of his teachings were condemned by the papacy.

Most of the great teachers and practitioners of mysticism in the fourteenth century were clerics, nuns, or hermits, but in the fifteenth century a modified form of mystical belief spread among lay people. This "practical mysticism" did not aim for full ecstatic union with God, but rather for an ongoing sense of some divine presence during the conduct of daily life. The most popular manual that pointed the way to this goal was the *Imitation of Christ*, written around 1427, probably by the north German canon Thomas à Kempis. Because this book was written in a simple but forceful style and taught how to be a pious Christian while still living actively in the world, it was particularly attractive to lay readers. The *Imitation* urges its readers to participate in one religious ceremony—the sacrament of the Eucharist—but otherwise it emphasizes inward piety. According to its teachings, the individual Christian is best able to become the "partner" of Jesus Christ both by receiving communion and by engaging in biblical meditation and leading a simple, moral life.

LOLLARDS AND HUSSITES

A third distinct form of late medieval piety was outright religious protest or heresy. In England and Bohemia especially, heretical movements became serious threats to the church. The initiator of heresy in late medieval England was an Oxford theologian named John Wyclif (c. 1330–1384). Wyclif's rigorous adherence to the theology of Saint Augustine led him to believe that a certain number of humans were predestined to be saved while the rest were irrevocably damned. He thought the predestined would naturally live simply, according to the standards of the New Testament, but in fact he found most members of the church hierarchy indulging in splendid extravagances. Hence he concluded that most church officials were damned. For him the only solution was to have secular rulers appropriate ecclesiastical wealth and reform the church by replacing corrupt priests and bishops with men who would live according to apostolic standards. But toward the end of his life he moved from merely calling for reform to attacking some of the most basic institutions of the church, above all the sacrament of the Eucharist. Wyclif probably would have been formally condemned for heresy had he lived longer.

Wyclif's death brought no respite for the church, however, because he had attracted numerous lay followers—called Lollards—who zealously continued to propagate and develop his ideas. Above all, the Lollards taught that pious Christians should not entrust their salvation to the sacraments of a corrupt church, but should instead study the Bible (which Lollards speedily translated into English) and Lollard religious tracts. Lollardy gained many adherents in the last two decades of the fourteenth century, but after the introduction in England of the death penalty for heresy in 1401 and the failure of a Lollard uprising in 1414, the heretical wave receded. Nonetheless, Lollards survived until the sixteenth century, when they merged into the new religious movements set loose by the Protestant Reformation.

Much greater was the influence of Wyclifism in Bohemia. Around 1400, Czech students who had studied in Oxford brought back Wyclif's ideas to the Bohemian capital of Prague. There Wyclifism was enthusiastically adopted by an eloquent preacher named Jan Hus (c. 1373–1415), who had already been inveighing in well-attended sermons against "the world, the flesh, and the devil." In contrast to the Lollards, however, whose heretical views on the Eucharist cost them much support, Hus emphasized the centrality of the Eucharist to Christian piety by demanding that the laity too should receive not only the consecrated bread of the Mass, but also the consecrated wine, which the late medieval Church reserved solely for priests. This demand, known as Utraquism, gained broad popular support among the Bohemian laity and became a rallying symbol for the Hussite movement.

Influential aristocrats supported Hus partly out of national pride, but partly too in the hope that Hus's reforms might allow them to recover the revenues they had lost to the orthodox Catholic clergy over the previous century. Above all, however, Hus gained a mass following because of his eloquence and concern for social justice. Accordingly, most of Bohemia was behind him when Hus in 1415 agreed to travel to the Council of Constance to defend his views and try to convince the assembled prelates that only thoroughgoing reform could save the Church. But although Hus had been guaranteed his personal safety, this assurance was revoked as soon as he arrived at the Council: rather than being given a fair hearing, he was tried for heresy and burned.

Hus's supporters in Bohemia were justifiably outraged and quickly raised the banner of open revolt. The aristocracy took advantage of the situation to seize church lands, and poorer priests, artisans, and peasants rallied together in the hope of achieving Hus's goals of religious reform and social justice. Between 1420 and 1424 armies of radical Hussites known as Taborites, led by a brilliant blind general,

Title Page from the Teachings of Jan Hus. An eloquent religious reformer, Jan Hus was burned at the stake in 1415 for heresy. He accused the Catholic church of being corrupt and demanded that the church reform the Eucharist.

Jan Zizka, resoundingly defeated several invading forces of crusading knights sent against them by the papacy. These victories increased the radicalism of the Taborites, inspiring them to heights of apocalyptic fervor. Finally, in 1434 more conservative, aristocratically dominated Hussites overcame the radicals and negotiated a settlement with the Church that permitted Utraquism in the Bohemian church alongside Catholic orthodoxy. Bohemia did not return fully to the Catholic fold until the seventeenth century. The Hussite declaration of religious independence was both a foretaste of what was to come one hundred years later with Protestantism and the most successful late medieval expression of dissatisfaction with the government of the church.

POLITICAL CRISIS AND RECOVERY

What caused the rise of national monarchies?

The later Middle Ages were marked by incessant warfare. Armies became larger, military technology became deadlier, and society became more militarized. As a result, European governments (in particular, the national monarchies of Portugal, Spain, and France) were stronger and more aggressively expansionist by 1500 than they had been two centuries before. The results of this transformation would be felt around the globe, as we will see in Chapter 11. For now, however, let us examine the European conflicts that provoked this transformation.

ITALY

In southern Italy, the kingdom of Naples remained mired in endemic warfare and maladministration throughout the fourteenth and fifteenth centuries. The fourteenth century was also a time of troubles for the Papal States in central Italy. But after the end of the Great Schism in 1417 the popes consolidated their Italian territories and became the effective rulers of most of the middle part of the peninsula. Farther north some of the leading city-states—such as Florence, Venice, Siena, and Genoa—had experienced at least occasional and more often prolonged social war-

fare during the fourteenth century because of the economic pressures of the age. But sooner or later the most powerful families or interest groups overcame internal resistance. By around 1400 the three leading cities of the north—Venice, Milan, and Florence—had fixed definitively on their own different forms of government: Venice was ruled by a merchant oligarchy, Milan by a dynastic despotism, and Florence by a complex, supposedly republican system that was actually controlled by the rich. (After 1434 the Florentine republic was in practice dominated by the Medici banking family.)

Having settled their internal problems, Venice, Milan, and Florence proceeded from about 1400 to 1454 to expand territorially, conquering almost all the other northern Italian cities and towns except Genoa, which remained prosperous and independent but gained no new territory. Thus, by the middle of the fifteenth century Italy was divided into five major parts: the states of Venice, Milan, and Florence in the north; the Papal States in the middle; and the kingdom of Naples in the south. A treaty of 1454 initiated forty years of peace between these states: whenever one threatened to upset the "balance of power," the others allied against it before serious warfare could break out. In 1494, however, a French invasion began a period of renewed warfare in which the French attempt to dominate Italy was successfully countered by Spain.

GERMANY

North of the Alps political turmoil prevailed throughout the fourteenth century and lasted longer into the fifteenth. Probably the worst instability was experienced in Germany. There the virtually independent princes continually warred with the greatly weakened emperors, or else they warred with each other. Between about 1350 and 1450 near anarchy prevailed, because while the princes were warring and subdividing their inheritances into smaller states, petty powers such as free cities and knights who owned one or two castles were striving to shake off the rule of the princes. Throughout most of the German west these attempts met with enough success to fragment political authority more than ever, but in the east after about 1450 certain German princes started to create middle-sized states on the model of the larger national monarchies of England and France. The Habsburg princes of Austria and the Hohenzollern princes of

Brandenburg—a territory joined in the sixteenth century with the easternmost lands of Prussia—would be the most influential powers in Germany's future.

FRANCE

France too was torn by strife for much of the period, primarily in the form of the Hundred Years' War between France and England. The Hundred Years' War was actually a series of conflicts that lasted from 1337 to 1453 and whose roots reached back into the 1290s. Of the several different causes for this prolonged struggle, the major one was the longstanding problem of French territory held by the English kings as vassals of the French crown. But the war also involved a succession dispute over the French crown itself. In 1328, the last of King Philip IV's three sons died without leaving a son to succeed him. A new dynasty, the Valois, thereupon replaced the Capetians on the throne of France. Only by prohibiting inheritance through women, however, could the Valois kings claim to be the closest heirs to the Capetians. Otherwise, the rightful heir to the throne of France was King Edward III of England, whose mother was the daughter of Philip IV of France. In 1328, Edward was only fifteen years of age, and he did not protest the succession of his Valois cousins. In 1337, however, when hostilities erupted between France and England, Edward responded by claiming to be the rightful king of France—a claim that all subsequent English kings would uphold until the eighteenth century.

France was the richest country in Europe and outnumbered England in population by at least three to one. Nonetheless, until the 1430s the English won most of the pitched battles. One reason for this was that the English had learned superior military tactics in their earlier battles with the Welsh and the Scots, and so could use well-disciplined archers to fend off and scatter the heavily armored mounted French knights. Another reason for English success was that the war was always fought on French soil. English soldiers were eager to fight because they could look forward to rich plunder, while their own homeland suffered none of the disasters of war. Worst of all for the French was the fact that they often were badly divided. The French crown always had to fear provincial attempts to assert autonomy: during the long period of warfare, many aristocratic provincial leaders took advantage of the confusion to ally with the enemy and seek their own advantage. The most dramatic and fateful instance was the breaking away of Burgundy, whose dukes from 1419 to 1435 allied with the English, an act that called the very existence of an independent French crown into question.

It was in this dark period that the heroic figure of Joan of Arc came forth to rally the French. In 1429 Joan, an illiterate but extremely devout peasant girl, sought out the uncrowned French ruler, Charles VII, to announce that she had been divinely commissioned to drive the English out of France. Charles was persuaded to let her take command of his troops, and her piety and sincerity made such a favorable impression on the soldiers that their morale was raised immensely. Within a few months Joan inflicted several defeats on English forces in central France and had brought Charles to Rheims, where he was crowned king. But in May 1430 she was captured by the Burgundians and handed over to the English, who accused her of being a witch and tried her for heresy. Condemned in 1431 after a show trial, she was publicly burned to death in the market square at Rouen. Nonetheless, the French, fired by their initial victories, continued to move on the offensive. When Burgundy withdrew from the English alliance in 1435, and the English king Henry VI proved to be totally incompetent, an uninterrupted series of triumphs followed for the French side. In 1453 the capture of Bordeaux, the last of the English strongholds in the southwest, finally brought the long war to an end.

The Hundred Years' War resulted in greatly strengthening the powers of the French crown. The demands of war allowed the Valois kings to gather new powers, above all, the rights to collect national taxes and maintain a standing army. During the reigns of Louis XI (1461–1483) and Louis XII (1498–1515), the monarchy became ever stronger. Its greatest single achievement was the destruction of the power of Burgundy in 1477 when the Burgundian duke Charles the Bold fell in battle at the hands of the Swiss. Since Charles died without a male heir, Louis XI of France was able to march into Burgundy and reabsorb the breakaway duchy. Later, when Louis XII gained Brittany by marriage, the French kings ruled powerfully over almost all of what is today included in the borders of France.

> The French crown always had to fear provincial attempts to assert autonomy: during the long period of warfare, many aristocratic provincial leaders took advantage of the confusion to ally with the enemy and seek their own advantage.

THE CONDEMNATION OF JOAN OF ARC BY THE UNIVERSITY OF PARIS, 1431

After Joan's capture by the Burgundians, she was handed over to the English, who put her on trial for heresy. Paris was at this date in English hands, so the verdict of the Parisian masters should not be considered unbiased. On the other hand, there is no evidence that it was extracted by force. Learned theologians were not inclined to approve of peasant women who claimed to hear the voices of angels, who dressed in men's clothes, and who led aristocrats into battle. Joan was condemned for heresy and burned at the stake.

You, Joan, have said that, since the age of thirteen, you have experienced revelations and the appearance of angels, of St Catherine and St Margaret, and that you have very often seen them with your bodily eyes, and that they have spoken to you. As for the first point, the clerks of the University of Paris have considered the manner of the said revelations and appearances. . . . Having considered all . . . they have declared that all the things mentioned above are lies, falsenesses, misleading and pernicious things and that such revelations are superstitions, proceeding from wicked and diabolical spirits.

Item: You have said that your king had a sign by which he knew that you were sent by God, for St Michael, accompanied by several angels, some of which having wings, the others crowns, with St Catherine and St Margaret, came to you at the chateau of Chinon. All the company ascended through the floors of the castle until they came to the room of your king, before whom the angel bearing the crown bowed. . . . As for this matter, the clerks say that it is not in the least probable, but it is rather a presumptuous lie, misleading and pernicious, a false statement, derogatory of the dignity of the Church and of the angels. . . .

Item: you have said that, at God's command, you have continually worn men's clothes, and that you have put on a short robe, doublet, shoes attached by points; also that you have had short hair, cut around above the ears, without retaining anything on your person which shows that you are a woman; and that several times you have received the body of Our Lord dressed in this fashion, despite having been admonished to give it up several times, the which you would not do. You have said that you would rather die than abandon the said clothing, if it were not at God's command, and that if you were wearing those clothes and were with the king, and those of your party, it would be one of the greatest benefits for the kingdom of France. You have also said that not for anything would you swear an oath not to wear the said clothing and carry arms any longer. And all these things you say you have done for the good and at the command of God. As for these things, the clerics say that you blaspheme God and hold him in contempt in his sacraments; you transgress Divine Law, Holy Scripture and canon law. You err in the faith. You boast in vanity. You are suspected of idolatry and you have condemned yourself in not wishing to wear clothing suitable to your sex, but you follow the custom of Gentiles and Saracens.

Carolyne Larrington, ed. and trans. *Women and Writing in Medieval Europe.* (New York and London: Routledge, 1995), pp. 183–184.

ENGLAND

Although the Hundred Years' War was fought on French soil rather than English, the war produced great political instability in England also. When English armies in France were successful—as by and large they were during the reigns of Edward III (1327–1377) and Henry V (1413–1422)—the crown rode a crest of popularity and the country prospered from military spoils and the ransoms of captured French prisoners. When the tide of battle turned against the English, however, as it did under Richard II (1377–1399) and Henry VI (1422–1461), the exasperated taxpayers of England held their monarchs responsible for these costly and shameful military failures. Defeat abroad thus quickly undermined a king's political and fiscal support at home, making it politically impossible to withdraw from the French war despite its mounting costs. To make matters worse, an unusually large number of dangerous or incompetent kings ruled England during the later Middle Ages. Of the nine English kings who came to the throne between 1307 and 1485, no fewer than five were deposed and murdered by their subjects.

The particular propensity of the English for murdering their monarchs (a subject of comment across Europe) was a consequence of England's peculiar political system. As we have seen, England was the most tightly governed kingdom in Europe, but its political system depended on a monarch's ability to mobilize popular support for his policies through Parliament while maintaining the support of his nobility through successful wars in Wales, Scotland, and France. As a result, incompetent or tyrannical kingship was even more destabilizing and dangerous in England than it was elsewhere in Europe, because of the complexity and power of the English state itself. In France, nobles could endure the insanity of Charles VI (1380–1422) because his government was not powerful enough to threaten them. In England, however, the inanity and ultimate insanity of Henry VI (1422–1461) provoked an aristocratic rebellion against him known as the Wars of the Roses, so called (by the nineteenth-century novelist Sir Walter Scott) from the emblems of the two competing factions: the red rose of Henry's family of Lancaster, and the white rose of Henry's cousin, the rival Duke of York. In 1461, after a six-year struggle, Edward, Duke

of York finally succeeded in ousting Henry VI and ruled successfully until his death in 1483. But when Edward's brother Richard seized the throne from Edward's own young sons, political stability in England collapsed once again. In 1485, Richard III was in turn defeated and killed in the battle of Bosworth Field by the last surviving Lancastrian claimant, Henry Tudor, who resolved the feud between Lancaster and York by marrying Elizabeth of York. Henry VII systematically elimated rivals for the throne, avoided expensive foreign wars, built up a financial surplus through careful management of his estates, and reasserted royal control over the aristocracy. When he died in 1509 the new Tudor dynasty was securely established on the English throne, and English royal power was fully restored. His son Henry VIII (1509–1547) would build on the foundations his father had laid, dissolving the English monasteries and declaring his country religiously independent of Rome.

> Henry VII systematically elimated rivals for the throne, avoided expensive foreign wars, built up a financial surplus through careful management of his estates, and reasserted royal control over the aristocracy.

Despite the turmoil caused by war and rebellion, late medieval English political life had an essential stability. Local institutions continued to function; Parliament became increasingly important as a point of contact among crown, aristocracy, and local communities; and the political community itself became steadily larger as prosperity brought new social groups into prominence. Most important of all, there was never any fundamental challenge to the power of the English state itself. Even aristocratic rebels always sought to control the central government rather than destroy or break away from it. Thus when Henry VII came to the throne, he did not have to win back any English territories as Louis XI of France had to win back Burgundy. More than that, the antagonisms of the Hundred Years' War had the ultimately beneficial effect of strengthening English national identity. From the Norman Conquest until the fourteenth century, French was the preferred language of the English crown and aristocracy, but mounting anti-French sentiment contributed to the triumph of English as the national language by around 1400. The loss of lands in France was also ultimately beneficial. England became an island nation, without significant territorial interests on the European mainland. This fact gave England more diplomatic maneuverability in sixteenth-century European politics and later helped strengthen England's ability to invest its energies in overseas expansion in America and elsewhere.

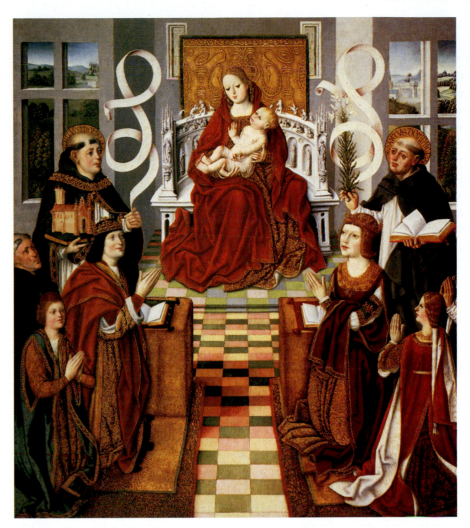

Ferdinand and Isabella Honoring the Virgin. A contemporary Spanish painting in which the royal pair are shown with two of their children in the company of saints from the Dominican order.

country was able to embark on united policies. Isabella and Ferdinand, ruling respectively until 1504 and 1516, subdued their aristocracies, and, in the same year (1492) annexed Granada, the last Muslim state in the peninsula, and expelled all of Spain's Jews. Some historians believe that the expulsion of the Jews was motivated by religious bigotry, others that it was a cruel but dispassionate act of state that aimed to keep Spanish *conversos* (Jews who had previously converted to Christianity) from backsliding. Either way, the forced Jewish exodus led Ferdinand and Isabella to suppose that they had eliminated an internal threat to cohesive nationhood and emboldened them to initiate an ambitious foreign policy: not only did they turn to overseas expansion, most famously in their support of Christopher Columbus, but they also intervened decisively in Italian politics. Enriched by the influx of American gold and silver after the conquest of Mexico and Peru, and nearly invincible on the battlefields, Spain became Europe's most powerful sixteenth-century state.

SPAIN

While Louis XI of France and Henry VII of England were reasserting royal power in their respective countries, the Spanish monarchs, Ferdinand and Isabella, were doing the same on the Iberian peninsula. Spain had also seen incessant strife in the later Middle Ages; Aragon and Castile had often fought each other, and aristocratic factions within those kingdoms had continually fought the crown. But in 1469 Ferdinand, the heir of Aragon, married Isabella, the heiress of Castile; their union laid the basis for modern Spain.

Although Aragon and Castile retained their separate institutions until 1716, warfare between the two previously independent kingdoms ended, and the new

THE TRIUMPH OF NATIONAL MONARCHIES

The later Middle Ages saw the emergence of markedly more powerful European states than had existed in 1300. But the basic patterns of high medieval political life changed remarkably little. Germany and Italy were politically divided by 1300 and remained divided in 1500, despite the emergence of a few effective, middle-sized states in both countries. England and France, the two most powerful national monarchies of the High Middle Ages, were still the most successful such states in 1500, although Spain had now emerged as a new and powerful rival to them both. Only Sicily had been fundamentally transformed. Economically exhausted by the demands of its twelfth- and thirteenth-century rulers, Sicily became in the later Middle Ages the impoverished land it has remained until the present day.

The most notable feature of later medieval politics, however, was the triumph of the national monarchies, whose superiority to rival forms of political organization is seen most clearly in Italy. Until 1494, the Italian city-states had appeared to be relatively well governed and powerful. But when France and Spain invaded the peninsula, the Italian political order collapsed like a house of cards. Germany would suffer the same fate only a few generations later. The national monarchies drew on vastly greater resources of money and troops than could the principalities of Germany or the city-states of Italy. As a result, they inherited the future of Europe.

KIEVAN RUS AND THE RISE OF MUSCOVY

Why was medieval Russia so unlike any other European state?

Just as the later fifteenth century witnessed the consolidation of the power of the western European national monarchies, so too it saw the consolidation of the state that would become the dominant power in the European east—Russia. But Russia was not at all like a Western nation-state; rather, by about 1500 Russia had taken the first decisive steps on its way to becoming Europe's leading Eastern-style empire.

THE MONGOL INVASIONS

After 1200, four epoch-making developments conspired to separate Russia from western Europe. The first was the conquest of most of the eastern Slavic states by the Mongols in the thirteenth century. Commanded by Batu, a grandson of the great Chingiz (Genghis) Khan, the Mongols cut such swaths of devastation as they advanced westward that, according to one contemporary, "no eye remained open to weep for the dead." In 1240 the Mongols overran Kiev, and two years later they created their own state on the lower Volga River—the khanate of the Golden Horde—which exerted suzerainty over almost all of Russia for the following hundred and fifty years.

THE RISE OF MUSCOVY

The native principality that finally emerged to defeat the Mongols and unify much of Russia was the grand duchy of Moscow. Moscow rose to power in the early fourteenth century as a tribute-collecting center for the Mongol khanate. Moscow's alliance with the Mongols did not necessarily protect it from Mongol attacks: the city was destroyed at the time of the Mongol invasions, and again in 1382. But despite these setbacks, Moscow was able, with Mongol support, to absorb the territory of the grand principality of Vladimir, and so gradually to become the dominant political power in northeastern Russia.

Moscow also had the advantage of being very far away from the Mongol power base on the lower Volga. This remote location made Moscow a particularly valuable ally for the Mongol khanate, while allowing the grand dukes to consolidate their strength without attracting too much attention from the khans. Despite Moscow's remote location, the grand duchy maintained some trade contacts with both the Baltic and the Black Sea regions. What really distanced Moscow from western Europe was the enormous religious hostility that existed between the eastern Orthodox churches (of which Moscow was one) and the western church headed by the papacy. The hostility between these two great branches of Christianity had deep historical roots. In the later Middle Ages, however, what particularly excited the religious animosity of Moscow toward western European Christians was the growing strength of the kingdom of Poland and the circumstances that led to the fall of Constantinople to the Ottoman Turks in 1453.

THE RIVALRY WITH POLAND

Throughout most of the Middle Ages the Kingdom of Poland had been a second-rate power, usually on the defensive against German encroachments. But in the fourteenth century that situation changed dramatically, when the marriage in 1386 of Poland's reigning queen, Jadwiga, to Jagiello, grand duke of Lithuania, more than doubled Poland's size and enabled it to become a major expansionist state. In 1410 combined Polish-Lithuanian forces inflicted a stunning defeat on the German military order of Teutonic knights who ruled neighboring Prussia. In the early fifteenth century, Poland-Lithuania extended its borders so far east that the new power

THE EXPANSION OF MUSCOVITE RUSSIA TO 1505

This map shows the expansion of the Grand Duchy of Moscow, the heart of what would soon become the Russian empire. How did the relative isolation of Moscow compared with Kiev allow for the growth of Muscovite power on the one hand, and Moscow's distinctively non-Western culture on the other? Why did the Muscovite Russians identify so closely with the Byzantines, and why did they reserve such pronounced hostility for the West and Latin Christianity? What role did the Kingdom of Poland-Lithuania play in the development of this Russian attitude? How did the natural direction of the expansion of Muscovite power until 1505 help encourage attitudes often at odds with those of western European civilization?

seemed on the verge of conquering all of Russia. Although many of the Lithuanian nobility were eastern Orthodox, Poland subscribed to Roman Catholicism, and the established church in Lithuania was also Roman Catholic. Thus when Moscow took the offensive against Poland-Lithuania in the late fifteenth century, it was able to appeal to religious as well as national sentiments. Prolonged warfare ensued, greatly exacerbating antagonisms toward Poland and toward the Latin Christian tradition it represented in the eyes of Muscovites.

MOSCOW AND BYZANTIUM

The growing alienation between Moscow and western Europe was further increased by events leading up to the fall of Constantinople to the Turks in 1453. Connections between Byzantium and the Rus went back to the tenth century, when missionaries from the Byzantine empire had converted the Kievan Slavs to Orthodox Christianity. Relations between the eastern and western churches had been tense ever since 1054, when the two churches split over papal primacy and the wording of the Nicene Creed. But embittered hatred is the only expression to describe Byzantine attitudes toward Rome after 1204 when the Fourth Crusade sacked Constantinople. Eastern Orthodox Russians sympathized with their Byzantine mentors, and felt all the more that they had a good reason to shun the "Roman infection" after the debacle of 1453. This was because in 1438 the Byzantines in Constantinople, sensing correctly that a mighty Turkish onslaught was in the offing, agreed to submit to papal authority and unite with the western church, in the hope that these promises might earn them western military support for their last stand. But despite this submission, no western help was forthcoming, and Constantinople fell to the Turks in 1453 without a single Roman Catholic knight lifting a hand.

The Orthodox hierarchy of Moscow had refused to follow Byzantium in its religious submission, regarding it as a betrayal of Christian orthodoxy. After Constantinople fell, therefore, the Muscovites concluded that the Turkish victory was a divine punishment for the Byzantines' religious perfidy. The Muscovite state thus became the center of a particularly zealous anti-Roman ideology, as Moscow began to see itself as the divinely appointed successor to Byzantium. The Russian ruler took the title of *tsar*—which means "caesar"—and Russians asserted that Moscow was both "a

second Jerusalem" and "the third Rome": "Two Romes have fallen," said a Russian spokesman, "the third is still standing, and a fourth there shall not be." This Byzantine-derived ideology underlay both the later growth of Russian imperialism and the sacred position ascribed to the rulers of the Muscovite (and later Russian) state.

THE REIGN OF IVAN THE GREAT (1462–1505)

Behind such imperial self-confidence lay the steadily growing power of the grand dukes of Moscow. Moscow itself had been effectively independent of the Mongols since the end of the fourteenth century, when a rival Mongol ruler named Timur the Lame (Tamurlane) had destroyed the Mongol khanate of the Golden Horde. But it was Ivan III, customarily known as Ivan the Great, who transformed the grand duchy of Moscow into a true imperial power. Ivan launched a series of conquests between 1468 and 1485 that annexed, one by one, all the independent Russian principalities that lay between Moscow and the Poland-Lithuania border. After two successive invasions of Lithuania in 1492 and 1501, Ivan also succeeded in bringing parts of Belarus and Ukraine under his control. By 1505, when Ivan died, he had established Muscovy as a power to be reckoned with on the European scene.

As tsar, Ivan conceived of himself as the autocratic potentate not just of Moscow but of all Russians, and even, potentially, of Belarussians and Ukrainians. In the sixteenth century, Russian expansionism was principally directed toward the south and east, against the small successor states to the Mongol Golden Horde. From the mid-seventeenth century on, however, Muscovite pressure against Ukraine would escalate, leading on to the enormous land empire Peter the Great would construct in the early eighteenth century. We cannot draw a direct line from Ivan III to Peter the Great. But Peter would appeal to the foundations Ivan laid as justification for his claims to incorporate both Russians and a wide variety of non-Russian peoples into what would become Europe's largest empire.

> The Russian ruler took the title of tsar—which means "caesar"—and Russians asserted that Moscow was both "a second Jerusalem" and "the third Rome": "Two Romes have fallen," said a Russian spokesman, "the third is still standing, and a fourth there shall not be."

WHAT TRENDS LED TO THE RISE OF VERNACULAR LITERATURE DURING THE LATER MIDDLE AGES?

THOUGHT, LITERATURE, AND ART   313

THOUGHT, LITERATURE, AND ART

What trends led to the rise of vernacular literature during the later Middle Ages?

Although the extreme hardships of the later Middle Ages in western Europe might have led to the decline or stagnation of intellectual and artistic endeavors, in fact the period was an extremely fruitful one in the realms of thought, literature, and art. In this section we will postpone treatment of certain developments most closely related to the early history of the Italian Renaissance, but will discuss some of western Europe's other important late medieval intellectual and artistic accomplishments.

THEOLOGY AND PHILOSOPHY

Theology and philosophy after about 1300 faced a crisis of doubt, not about the existence of God and his supernatural powers, but about human ability to comprehend the supernatural. Saint Thomas Aquinas and other scholastics in the High Middle Ages had serenely delimited the number of "mysteries of the faith" and believed that everything else, both in heaven and earth, could be thoroughly understood by humans. But the floods, famines, wars, and plagues of the fourteenth century helped undermine such confidence in the powers of human understanding. The result was a thoroughgoing reevaluation of the prior theological and philosophical outlook.

The leading late medieval abstract thinker was the English Franciscan William of Ockham, who was born around 1285 and died in 1349, apparently of the Black Death. Ockham denied that the existence of God and numerous other theological matters could be demonstrated apart from scriptural revelation, and he emphasized God's freedom and absolute power to do anything. In investigating earthly matters he developed the position, known as *nominalism*, that only individual things, not collectivities, are real, and that one thing therefore cannot be understood by means of another: to know a chair one has to see and touch it rather than just know what several other chairs are like. The formal logical system Ockham developed from this fundamental principle became the most influential philosophical system of the later Middle Ages.

Ockham's outlook gained widespread adherence in late medieval universities, and had an immense impact on the development of Western thought. Ockham's emphasis on God's autonomy led to a stress on divine omnipotence that became one of the basic presuppositions of sixteenth-century Protestantism. Further, Ockham's determination to find certainties in the realm of human knowledge ultimately helped make it possible to discuss human affairs and natural science without reference to supernatural explanations—one of the most important foundations of the modern scientific method. Finally, Ockham's opposition to studying collectivities and his refusal to apply logic to abstract categories helped encourage empiricism, or the belief that knowledge of the world should rest on sense experience rather than abstract reason. This too is a presupposition for scientific progress.

VERNACULAR LITERATURE

The literature of the later Middle Ages was characterized by an intense concern to describe the world as it is. Such naturalism was not new. High medieval authors such as Wolfram von Eschenbach and Dante had already established the precedents on which their late medieval successors would build. But late medieval authors went much further, especially in describing the foibles and failings of everyday human life. They also pioneered the development of new literary forms for vernacular writing, sometimes in poetry, but especially in prose. Most late medieval authors also continued to compose in Latin; but increasingly, the most innovative and ambitious literary work was being written in the vernacular languages of Europe. Behind this development lay three fundamental changes of the later Middle Ages: a growing identification between vernacular languages and nationalism; the continuing spread of lay education; and the emergence of a substantial reading public for vernacular literature. We can see these influences at work in three of the major vernacular authors of the later Middle Ages: Giovanni Boccaccio (1313–1375), Geoffrey Chaucer (c. 1340–1400), and Christine de Pisan (c.1365–c.1435).

BOCCACCIO

Boccaccio would deserve an honored place in literary history even for his lesser works, which included courtly romances, pastoral lyrics, and learned treatises. His masterpiece, however, is the *Decameron*, a collection of one hundred prose tales, mostly about love, sex, adventure, and trickery, told by a sophisticated party of seven young women and three men temporarily residing in a country villa outside Florence in order to escape the Black Death. Boccaccio borrowed the outlines of many of these tales from earlier sources, but he transformed them with his own characteristic exuberance and wit.

Boccaccio deliberately wrote in an unaffected, colloquial style, eschewing literary "elegance" in order to portray men and women exactly as they are. His women are not pallid playthings, distant goddesses, or steadfast virgins, but flesh-and-blood creatures with minds and bodies, who interact with men more comfortably and naturally than any women in Western literature had ever done before. His clerics are all too human, much more like other men than they are like angels on earth. His treatment of sexual relations is often graphic, but never demeaning. Like other natural functions, human sexual desire is insistent and controllable, but is not meant to be thwarted. For all these reasons the *Decameron* is a robust and delightful appreciation of what it means to be human.

CHAUCER

Similar in many ways to Boccaccio as a creator of naturalistic vernacular literature was the Englishman Geoffrey Chaucer (c. 1340–1400). Chaucer wrote several highly impressive works, but his masterpiece is unquestionably the *Canterbury Tales*. Like the *Decameron*, this is a collection of stories held together by a frame, in Chaucer's case the device of having a group of people tell stories while on a pilgrimage from London to Canterbury. But there are also differences between the *Decameron* and the *Canterbury Tales*. Chaucer's stories are told in sparkling verse instead of prose, and they are recounted by people of all different classes—from a chivalric knight to a dedicated university student to a thieving miller with a wart on his nose. Lively women also appear, most memorably the gap-toothed, oft-married "Wife of Bath," who knows all "the remedies of love." Each character tells a story that is particularly illustrative of his or her own occupation and outlook on the world. By this device Chaucer was able to create a highly diverse "human comedy."

His range is greater than Boccaccio's, and although he is no less witty, frank, and lusty than the Italian, he is sometimes more profound.

CHRISTINE DE PISAN

The later Middle Ages also saw the emergence of professional authors who made their living with their pens. Significantly, one of the first of these professional *litterati* was a woman, Christine de Pisan. Although she herself was born in Italy, Christine spent her adult life in France, where her husband was a member of the king's household. When he died, the widowed Christine turned to writing to support herself and her children. She wrote in a wide variety of literary genres, including treatises on chivalry and on the art of warfare that she dedicated to her patron, King Charles VI of France. But she also wrote for a larger and more popular audience. Her imaginative tract *The City of Ladies* is an extended defense of the character, nature, and capacities of women against their male detractors, written in the form of an allegory. She also took part in a vigorous pamphlet campaign that debated the misogynistic claims commonly

Christine de Pisan. A leading writer of late-medieval vernacular prose literature, Christine de Pisan (1365–c. 1430) was intent on upholding the dignity of women. She is shown here writing about a gigantic Amazon warrior who could defeat men effortlessly in armed combat.

WHAT TRENDS LED TO THE RISE OF VERNACULAR LITERATURE DURING THE LATER MIDDLE AGES?

THOUGHT, LITERATURE, AND ART   315

made against women in the literature of the period. This debate continued for several hundred years, and became so famous that it was given a name: the *querelle des femmes*, "the debate over women." Christine was by no means the first female writer of the Middle Ages, but she was the first lay woman to earn a living by her writing.

SCULPTURE AND PAINTING

As naturalism was a dominant trait of late medieval literature, so it was of late medieval art. Whereas early medieval art had emphasized abstract design, the stress was now increasingly on realism: thirteenth-century carvings of leaves and flowers must have been made from direct observation and are clearly recognizable to modern botanists as distinct species. Statues of humans also gradually became more natural and realistic in their portrayals of facial expressions and bodily proportions. By around 1290 the concern for realism had become so great that a sculptor working on a tomb portrait of the German emperor Rudolf of Habsburg allegedly made a hurried return trip to view Rudolf in person, because he had heard that a new wrinkle had appeared on the emperor's face.

In the next two centuries the trend toward naturalism continued in sculpture and was extended to manuscript illumination and painting. The latter was in certain respects a new art. The art of wall painting was common in the Middle Ages and long afterward, especially in the form of *frescoes*, paintings done on wet plaster. But in addition to frescoes, Italian artists in the thirteenth century also began painting pictures on pieces of wood or canvas. These were first done in tempera (pigments mixed with water and natural gums or egg whites), but around 1400 painting in oils was introduced in the European north. These new technical developments created new artistic opportunities. Artists were now able to paint religious scenes on altarpieces for churches and for private devotions practiced by the wealthier laity at home. Late medieval artists also painted the first Western portraits. Some of the most realistic and sensitive portraits of all time date from the fifteenth century.

The most innovative painter of the later Middle Ages was the Florentine Giotto (c. 1267–1337), who brought deep humanity to the religious images he painted on both walls and movable panels. Giotto was preeminently an imitator of nature. Not only do his human beings and animals look more lifelike than those of his predecessors, they seem to do more natural things. When Christ enters Jerusalem on Palm Sunday, boys climb trees to get a better view; when Saint Francis is laid out in death, one onlooker takes the opportunity to see whether the saint had really received Christ's wounds; and when the Virgin's parents, Joachim and Anna, meet after a long separation, they actually embrace and kiss—perhaps the first deeply tender kiss in Western art. After Giotto's death a reaction in Italian painting set in. Mid-fourteenth century artists briefly moved away from naturalism and painted stern, forbidding religious figures who seemed to float in space. But by around 1400 artists came back down to earth and started to build on Giotto's influence in ways that led to the great Italian renaissance in painting.

In the north of Europe painting did not advance impressively beyond manuscript illumination until the early fifteenth century, but then it suddenly came very much into its own. The leading northern European painters were Flemish, first and foremost Jan van Eyck (c. 1380–1441), Roger van der Weyden (c. 1400–1464), and Hans Memling (c. 1430–1494). These three were the greatest early practitioners of painting in oil, a medium that allowed them to engage in brilliant coloring and sharp-focused realism. Van Eyck and van der Weyden excelled most at two things: communicating a sense of deep religious piety and portraying minute details of familiar everyday experience. These may at first seem incompatible, but it should be remembered that contemporary manuals of practical mysticism such as the *Imitation of Christ* also sought to link deep piety with everyday existence. Thus it was by no means blasphemous when a Flemish painter portrayed behind a tender Virgin and Child a vista of contemporary life with people going about their usual business and a man even urinating against a wall. This union of the sacred and the profane tended to fall apart in the work of Memling, who excelled in either straightforward religious pictures or secular portraits, but it would return in the work of the greatest painters of the Low Countries, Brueghel and Rembrandt.

> Whereas early medieval art had emphasized abstract design, the stress was now increasingly on realism: thirteenth-century carvings of leaves and flowers must have been made from direct observation and are clearly recognizable to modern botanists as distinct species.

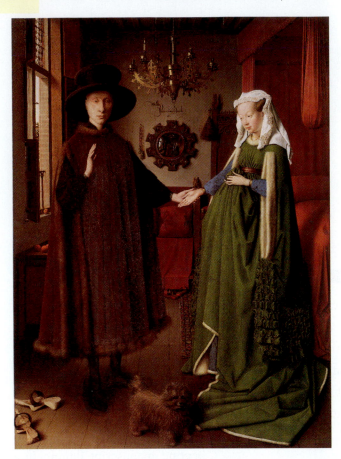

Giovanni Arnolfini and his Bride, by Jan van Eyck.
A characteristic synthesis of everyday life and religious
devotion. Scenes from Christ's Passion surround the
mirror. The artist himself appears reflected in the mirror
as if to indicate that he is a witness to the betrothal. In
addition, he wrote (above the mirror) "Johannes de eyck
fuit hic" ("Jan van Eyck was here").

ADVANCES IN TECHNOLOGY

How did technological advances affect
everyday life?

No account of enduring late medieval accomplishments would be complete without mention of certain
epoch-making technological advances. Treatment of
this subject has to begin with reference to the invention of artillery and firearms. The prevalence of warfare stimulated the development of new weaponry.
Gunpowder itself was a Chinese invention, but it was
first put to devastating military uses in the late medieval West. Heavy cannons were first employed

around 1330. The earliest cannons were primitive, but
by the middle of the fifteenth century they began to
revolutionize warfare. In 1453, heavy artillery played a
leading role in determining the outcome of two crucial
conflicts: the Ottoman Turks used German and Hungarian cannons to breach the defenses of Constantinople—hitherto the most impregnable in Europe—and
the French used heavy artillery to take the city of Bordeaux, thereby ending the Hundred Years' War. Cannons thereafter made it difficult for rebellious
aristocrats to hole up in their stone castles, and thus
they aided in the consolidation of the national monarchies. Placed aboard ships, cannons also enabled European vessels to dominate foreign waters in the
subsequent age of overseas expansion. Hand-held
firearms, also invented in the fourteenth century, were
also gradually perfected. Shortly after 1500 the most
effective new variety of gun, the musket, allowed foot
soldiers to end once and for all the military dominance
of heavily armored mounted knights. Once lance-
bearing cavalries became outmoded and fighting could
more easily be carried on by all, the monarchical states
that could turn out the largest armies completely subdued internal resistance and dominated the battlefields
of Europe.

Other late medieval technological developments
were more life enhancing. Eyeglasses, first invented in
the 1280s, were perfected in the fourteenth century.
Around 1300 the use of the magnetic compass helped
ships to sail farther away from land and venture out
into the Atlantic. Subsequent improvements in shipbuilding, map making, and navigational devices enabled Europe to start expanding overseas. In the
fourteenth century the Azores and Cape Verde Islands
were reached; then, after a long pause caused by Europe's plagues and wars, the African Cape of Good
Hope was rounded in 1488, the West Indies reached in
1492, India reached by the sea route in 1498, and
Brazil sighted in 1500. Partly as a result of technology,
the world was thus suddenly made much smaller.

Among the most familiar implements of our modern life that were invented by Europeans in the later
Middle Ages were clocks and printed books. Mechanical clocks were invented shortly before 1300 and
proliferated in the years immediately thereafter.
The earliest clocks were too expensive for private
purchase, but towns vied with each other to install
the most elaborate clocks in their prominent public
buildings. The new invention ultimately had two profound effects. One was the further stimulation of European interest in complex machinery of all sorts.

A Fifteenth-Century Siege with Cannon.

Equally if not more significant was the fact that clocks began to rationalize the course of European daily affairs. Until the advent of clocks in the later Middle Ages time was flexible. Men and women had only a rough idea of how late in the day it was and rose and retired more or less with the sun. In the fourteenth century, however, clocks first started relentlessly striking equal hours through the day and night. Thus they began to regulate work with new precision. People were expected to start and end work "on time" and many came to believe that "time is money." This emphasis on timekeeping brought new efficiencies but also new tensions: Lewis Carroll's white rabbit, who is always looking at his pocket watch and muttering "how late it's getting," is a telling caricature of time-obsessed Western humanity.

The invention of printing with movable type was equally momentous. The major stimulus for this invention was the replacement of parchment by paper as Europe's primary writing material between 1200 and 1400. Parchment, made from the skins of sheep or calves, was extremely expensive: since it was possible to get only about four good parchment leaves from one animal, it was necessary to slaughter between two to three hundred sheep or calves to gain enough parchment for a Bible! Paper, made from rags turned into pulp by mills, brought prices down dramatically. Late medieval records show that paper sold at one sixth the price of parchment. Accordingly, it became cheaper to learn how to read and write. With literacy becoming ever more widespread, there was a growing market for still cheaper books, and the invention of printing with movable type around 1450, associated most famously with the Bible produced by Johann Gutenberg in 1454, fully met this demand. By greatly saving labor, the invention made printed books about one fifth as expensive as handwritten ones within about two decades.

As books became easily accessible, literacy increased and book culture became a basic part of European life. After about 1500, Europeans could afford to read and buy books of all sorts—not just religious tracts, but instructional manuals, light entertainment, and, by the eighteenth century, newspapers. Printing ensured that ideas would spread quickly and reliably; moreover, revolutionary ideas could no longer be easily extinguished once they were set down in hundreds of copies of books. Thus the greatest religious reformer of the sixteenth century, Martin Luther, gained an immediate following throughout Germany by employing the printing press to run off pamphlets: had printing not been available to him, Luther might have died as Hus did. The spread of books also helped stimulate the growth of cultural nationalism. Before printing, regional dialects in most European countries were often so diverse that people who supposedly spoke the same language often could barely understand each other. After the invention of printing, however, each European country began to develop its own linguistic standards, which were disseminated uniformly by books. Thus communications were enhanced and governments were able to operate ever more efficiently.

CONCLUSION

Despite economic dislocation and demographic collapse, the later Middle Ages were one of the most creative and inventive periods in the history of western Europe. What lay behind the artistic, philosophical, literary, and technological developments of the period was a drive to understand, control, and replicate the workings of the natural world. This fact may help to explain the sources of these developments.

Perhaps most fundamentally, in the later Middle Ages intellectuals broke with the traditional, Neoplatonic vision of nature as a book in which one could read the mind of God. Instead, they came to see the natural world as operating according to its own laws, which were empirically verifiable but which could tell human beings nothing about the God who lay behind them. The resulting sense of the contingency and independence of the natural world was an essential step toward the emergence of a scientific world view. It also encouraged Europeans to believe that nature itself could be manipulated and directed toward human ends.

Powerful economic and political factors also encouraged the technological inventiveness of the period. Despite the disruptive impact of plague and war, the market for goods was not destroyed. Instead, labor shortages encouraged European entrepreneurs to experiment with labor-saving technologies and new crops. Incessant warfare encouraged a remarkable burst of military inventiveness. It also enabled more powerful governments to extract a larger percentage of their subjects' wealth through taxation, which they proceeded to invest in ships, cannons, muskets, and the standing armies that the new weaponry made possible. Increasing per capita wealth produced the capital necessary to invest in mills, factories, clocks, books, and compasses. It also made possible a remarkable increase in the educational level of the European population. Between 1300 and 1500 hundreds and perhaps thousands of new grammar schools were established, and scores of new universities emerged, because parents saw such schools as a reliable route to social advancement for their sons. Women were still excluded from the schools, but increasing numbers of girls were being taught at home, making women an extremely important (perhaps even the dominant) part of the "reading public" that was emerging in later medieval Europe.

Finally, it may be that dislocation itself promotes innovation, so long as it does not destroy people's confidence in the ultimate improvability of their lives. Europeans suffered enormously from war, plague, and economic crises during the later Middle Ages. But those who survived seized the opportunities their new world presented to them. The confidence they had developed in the High Middle Ages was not destroyed by the travails of the later Middle Ages. By 1500, most Europeans lived more secure lives than their ancestors had two hundred years before; and they stood on the verge of an extraordinary new period of expansion and conquest that would take European armies, merchants, and settlers around the globe.

KEY TERMS

Black Death	Master Eckhart	Ivan the Great
Jacquerie	Hundred Years' War	Boccaccio
Richard II	Joan of Arc	Canterbury Tales
Avignon	Wars of the Roses	William of Ockham

SELECTED READINGS

Allmand, Christopher T., ed. *Society at War: The Experience of England and France During the Hundred Years' War.* Edinburgh, 1973. An outstanding collection of documents.

———. *The Hundred Years' War: England and France at War, c. 1300–c. 1450.* Cambridge and New York, 1988. Still the best analytic account of the war; after a short narrative, the book is organized topically.

Boccaccio, Giovanni. *The Decameron.* Translated by Mark Musa and P. E. Bondanella. New York, 1977.

Chaucer, Geoffrey. *The Canterbury Tales.* Translated by Nevill Coghill. New York, 1951. A modern English verse translation, lightly annotated.

Cohn, Samuel K., Jr. *The Black Death Transformed: Disease and Culture in Early Renaissance Europe.* London, 2002. A stimulating revisionist account arguing that the Black Death was not bubonic plague, but some other, still-unidentified disease.

Cole, Bruce. *Giotto and Florentine Painting, 1280–1375.* New York, 1976. A clear and stimulating introduction.

Crummey, Robert O. *The Formation of Muscovy, 1304–1613.* New York, 1987. The standard account.

Dobson, R. Barrie. *The Peasants' Revolt of 1381,* 2d ed. London, 1983. A comprehensive source collection, with excellent introductions to the documents and an illuminating discussion of the revolt.

Duffy, Eamon. *The Stripping of the Altars: Traditional Religion in England, 1400–1580.* New Haven, 1992. The fullest study anywhere of the patterns of fifteenth-century piety at the parish level.

Dyer, Christopher. *Standards of Living in the Later Middle Ages: Social Change in England, c. 1200–1520.* Cambridge and New York, 1989. Detailed but highly rewarding.

Froissart, Jean. *Chronicles.* Translated by Geoffrey Brereton. Baltimore, 1968. A selection from the most famous contemporary account of the Hundred Years' War to c. 1400.

Hilton, Rodney H., and Trevor Aston, eds. *The English Rising of 1381.* Cambridge and New York, 1984. An excellent collection of articles that also includes chapters on the *Jacquerie* and the *Ciompi* rebellions.

Horrox, Rosemary, ed. *The Black Death.* New York, 1994. A fine collection of documents reflecting the impact of the Black Death, especially in England.

Huizinga, Johan. *The Waning of the Middle Ages: A Study of the Forms of Life, Thought, and Art in France and the Netherlands in the Dawn of the Renaissance,* New York, 1924. A classic picture of the "expiring" Middle Ages; a book from whose influence historians are still struggling to escape. Frequently republished, the most recent translation of this work is entitled *The Autumn of the Middle Ages.* Translated by Rodney J. Payton and Ulrich Mammitzsch. Chicago, 1996.

John Hus at the Council of Constance. Translated by M. Spinka, New York, 1965. The translation of a Czech chronicle with an expert introduction and appended documents.

Jordan, William Chester. *The Great Famine: Northern Europe in the Early Fourteenth Century.* Princeton, 1996. An outstanding social and economic study of the disastrous famines that swept northern Europe between 1315 and 1322.

Keen, Maurice, ed. *Medieval Warfare: A History.* Oxford and New York, 1999. The most attractive introduction to this crucially important subject. Lively and well illustrated.

Kempe, Margery. *The Book of Margery Kempe.* Translated by Barry Windeatt. New York, 1985. A fascinating autobiography by an early fifteenth-century Englishwoman who hoped she might be a saint.

Lerner, Robert E. *The Heresy of the Free Spirit in the Later Middle Ages,* 2d ed. Notre Dame, Ind., 1991. A revealing study of a heretical movement that terrified contemporaries, yet hardly existed at all.

Lewis, Peter S. *Later Medieval France: The Polity.* London, 1968. Still fresh and suggestive after thirty-five years. A masterwork.

Memoirs of a Renaissance Pope: The Commentaries of Pius II, abridged edition. Translated by F. A. Gragg, New York, 1959. Remarkable insights into the mind of a particularly well-educated mid-fifteenth-century pope.

Nicholas, David. *The Transformation of Europe, 1300–1600.* Oxford and New York, 1999. The best textbook presently available.

Oakley, Francis C. *The Western Church in the Later Middle Ages.* Ithaca, N.Y., 1979. The best book by far on the history of conciliarism, the late medieval papacy, Hussitism, and the efforts at institutional reform during this period. On popular piety, see Swanson (below).

Pernoud, Régine, ed. *Joan of Arc, by Herself and Her Witnesses.* New York, 1966. A collection of contemporary writings about Joan, including the transcripts of her trial.

Shirley, Janet, trans. *A Parisian Journal, 1405–1449.* Oxford, 1968. A marvelous panorama of Parisian life recorded by an eyewitness.

Swanson, R. N. *Religion and Devotion in Europe, c. 1215–c. 1515.* Cambridge and New York, 1995. An excellent study of late medieval popular piety; an excellent complement to Oakley (see above).

Sumption, Jonathan. *The Hundred Years' War.* Vol. 1, *Trial by Battle;* Vol. 2, *Trial by Fire.* Philadelphia, 1999. The first two volumes of a massive narrative history of the war take the story up to 1369.

Vaughan, Richard. *Valois Burgundy.* London, 1975. A summation of the author's four-volume study of the Burgundian dukes.

Ziegler, Philip. *The Black Death.* New York, 1969. A popular account, but reliable and engrossing.

DIGITAL HISTORY

AFTER THE BLACK DEATH

... in the illustrious city of Florence ... there made its appearance that deadly pestilence, which, whether disseminated by the influence of the celestial bodies, or sent upon us mortals by God in His just wrath by way of retribution for our iniquities, had had its origin some years before in the East, whence, after destroying an innumerable multitude of living beings, it had propagated itself without respite from place to place, and so calamitously, had spread into the West.
—Giovanni Boccaccio, *Decameron* (trans. M. Rigg)

IN OCTOBER 1347, Genoese trading ships returning from the Black Sea put into the harbor at Messina on the island of Sicily. On the ships were dead and dying sailors who had succumbed to what was soon called the Black Death. The population of Europe was cut nearly in half as the plague ravaged Europe over four years. The effects of the plague were at their worst in confined spaces like hospitals, prisons, and monasteries, and no one was immune—the Black Death destroyed at will. Whole villages simply disappeared, and according to at least one contemporary account, the city of Florence lost 96,000 people between March and October of 1348. European men and women were convinced the plague had been sent by God to afflict all sinners, and although the plague dissipated by 1351, the memories of constant and painful death remained fixed in the survivors' minds.

Other equally dramatic events took place throughout the remainder of this calamitous century. On the one hand, Europe experienced a series of peasant revolts: the French Jacquerie in 1358, the Ciompi rebellion in Florence in 1378, and the English Peasants' Revolt of 1381. Each of these rebellions was produced by the forces of profound social, political, and economic change which arose out of the Black Death. On the other hand, the medieval church faced a series of crises represented by the Babylonian Captivity (1305–78) and the Great Schism (1378–1417). The papacy was experiencing institutional decay, and it seemed the only way to prevent further deterioration was to centralize the government of the church as much as possible. So, the papacy moved to Avignon, where it could curry the favor of French kings.

The images and documents in the *After the Black Death* Digital History Feature at www.wwnorton.com/wciv explore the social and political impact of the plague that ravaged Europe in the late Middle ages. As you explore the *After the Black Death* feature, consider the following:

• Why were medieval men and women prepared to die at the hands of the plague?

• What are the similarities and differences between the French Jacquerie and the English Peasants' Revolt?

• What was wrong with the medieval papacy? Why did the institution of the church, more than thirteen centuries old, face one of its greatest challenges in the fourteenth century?

• How were the effects of the Black Death both negative and positive?

CHAPTER ELEVEN

CHAPTER CONTENTS

COMMERCE, CONQUEST, AND COLONIZATION, 1300–1600

BY 1300, the expansion of the High Middle Ages was coming to an end. In Iberia, there would be no further conquests of Muslim territory until 1492, when Granada fell to King Ferdinand and Queen Isabella. In the East, the Crusader kingdoms of Constantinople and Acre collapsed, in 1261 and 1291 respectively. Only the German drive into eastern Europe continued; but by the mid-fourteenth century, it too had been slowed by the rise of a new Baltic state in Lithuania. Internal expansion was also ending, as Europe reached the ecological limits of its resources. Thereafter, the pressure on resources was eased only by the dramatic population losses that resulted during the fourteenth century from the combined effects of famine, plague, and war.

But despite these checks, Europeans in the late Middle Ages did not turn inward. Although land-based conquests slowed, new, sea-based empires emerged in the Mediterranean world during the fourteenth and fifteenth centuries, with colonies that extended from the Black Sea to the Canary Islands. New maritime trade routes were opened up through the Strait of Gibraltar. By the late fifteenth century, Mediterranean mariners and colonists had extended their domination out into the Atlantic, from the Azores in the north to the Canary Islands in the south. Portuguese navigators were also pushing down the west coast of Africa. In 1498 one such expedition would sail all the way around the Cape of Good Hope to India.

The fifteenth-century conquest of the "Atlantic Mediterranean" was the essential preliminary to the dramatic events that began in 1492 with Columbus's attempt to reach China by sailing westward across the Atlantic Ocean and that led, by 1600, to the Spanish and Portuguese conquests of the Americas. Because these events are so familiar, we can easily underestimate their importance. For the native peoples and empires of the Americas, the results of European contact were cataclysmic. By 1600, somewhere between 50 and 90 percent of the indigenous peoples of the Americas had perished from disease, massacre, and enslavement. For Europeans, the results of their conquests were far less fatal, but no less far reaching. By 1300, Europe

FOCUS QUESTIONS

• What impact did the Mongol conquests have on Europe?

• Why were slaves so important to Ottoman society?

 • How were the Portuguese able to control Indian Ocean trade?

• What was the impact of New World silver on the European economy?

had eclipsed both Byzantium and the lands of Islam as a Mediterranean power, but outside the Mediterranean and the north Atlantic European power was negligible. By 1600, however, Europe had emerged as the first truly global power in world history, capable of pursuing its imperial ambitions and commercial interests wherever its ships could sail and its guns could reach. Europeans would not achieve full control over the interiors of the African, Asian, and American land masses until the end of the nineteenth century, and their control would last thereafter for less than a century. By 1600, however, European navies ruled the seas, and the world's resources were increasingly being channeled through European hands—patterns that have continued until the present day.

THE MONGOLS

What impact did the Mongol conquests have on Europe?

Trade between the Mediterranean world and the Far East dated back to antiquity, but it was not until the late thirteenth century that Europeans began to establish direct trading connections with India, China, and the "Spice Islands" of the Indonesian archipelago. For Europeans, these connections would prove profoundly important, although less for their economic significance than for their impact on the European imagination. For the peoples of Asia, however, the appearance of European traders on the "Silk Road" between Central Asia and China was merely a curiosity. The really consequential event was the rise of the Mongol empire that made such connections possible.

THE RISE OF THE MONGOL EMPIRE

The Mongols were a nomadic people whose homeland lay to the north of the Gobi Desert in present-day Mongolia. Like many nomadic peoples throughout history, the Mongols were highly accomplished cavalry soldiers who supplemented their own pastoralism and craft production by raiding the sedentary peoples to their south. (It was in part to control such raiding from Mongolia that, many cen-

In 1279, Chingiz's grandson Qubilai (Kublai) Khan completed the conquest of southern (Sung) China, thus reuniting China for the first time in centuries.

CHRONOLOGY

RISE OF THE MONGOL EMPIRE, 1206–1260

Temujin crowned as Chingiz Khan	1206
Mongols conquer northern China	1234
Mongols conquer southern Russia	1237–1240
Mongol forces withdraw from Europe	1241
Mamluk sultanate halts Mongol advance in Egypt	1260

turies before, the Chinese had built the famous Great Wall.) Primarily, however, China defended itself by attempting to ensure that the Mongols remained internally divided, and so turned their energies most often against each other.

In the late twelfth century, however, a Mongol chief named Temüjin began to unite the various Mongol tribes under his rule. By incorporating the army of each defeated tribe into his own army, Temüjin quickly built up a large military force. In 1206, his supremacy was formally acknowledged by all the Mongols, and he took the title Chingiz (Genghis) Khan—"the oceanic [possibly meaning universal] ruler." Chingiz now turned his enormous army against his non-Mongol neighbors. China at this time was divided into three hostile states. In 1209, Chingiz launched an attack on northwestern China; in 1211 he invaded the Chin empire in north China. At first these attacks were probably looting expeditions rather than deliberate attempts at conquest, but by the 1230s a full-scale Mongol conquest of northern and western China was under way, culminating in 1234 with the fall of the Chin. In 1279, Chingiz's grandson Qubilai (Kublai) Khan completed the conquest of southern (Sung) China, thus reuniting China for the first time in centuries.

Meanwhile, Chingiz turned his forces westward, conquering much of Central Asia and incorporating the important commercial cities of Tashkent, Samarkand, and Bukhara into his expanding empire. When Chingiz died in 1227, he was succeeded by his third son Ögedei, who completed the conquest of

EUROPE

Moscow

Kiev · · Kazan

CUMANS

KHANATE OF THE GOLDEN HORDE

· New Sarai

· Old Sarai

Lake Baikal

BLACK SEA

MEDITERRANEAN SEA

SELJUKS Trebizond

GEORGIA

CAUCASUS MTS

Tbilisi ·

CASPIAN SEA

ARAL SEA

ALTAI MTS

Karakorum ·

SEA OF JAPAN

JAPAN

Jerusalem ·

Euphrates R.

Tigris R.

· Tabriz

KHWARIZM

Oxus R.

KARA-KHITAI

Lake Balkhash

CHAGATAI EMPIRE

TIEN SHAN

GOBI

Huang He

Turfan ·

EMPIRE OF THE GREAT KHAN

Hangzhou ·

· Baghdad

· Gurgan

· Tashkent

· Bukhara

Kaifeng ·

MAMELUKS

IL-KHAN EMPIRE

Balkh

Herat

HINDU KUSH

Kabul ·

TIBET

SUNG EMPIRE (conquered 1279)

EAST CHINA SEA

RED SEA

Nile R.

Persian Gulf

· Ormuz

SULTANATE OF DELHI

Indus R.

Delhi ·

HIMALAYAS

Brahmaputra R.

Yangtze R.

Guangzhou ·

ARABIA

Ganges R.

INDIA

BURMA (MYANMAR)

ANAM

Mekong R.

CHAMPA

SOUTH CHINA SEA

ARABIAN SEA

Bay of Bengal

CEYLON

INDIAN OCEAN

to Java

Mongol campaigns post-1259

0   500   1000 Miles

0   500   1000 Kilometers

THE MONGOL SUCCESSOR STATES

Consider the breakup of Chingiz Khan's empire after 1259, and the passing similarities its fracture might possess to the disintegration of Alexander's empire, also conquered swiftly and encompassing vast swaths of Europe and Asia. Why did Chingiz Khan's empire splinter? How did the Mongol onslaught against and occupation of major sections of the Arab Muslim world possibly aid the expansion of European civilization and trade into the Mediterranean? At the same time, how did it complicate the situation for the crusader efforts in the Holy Land?

the Chin and then laid plans for a massive invasion toward the west. Between 1237 and 1240, the Mongol horde (so called from the Turkish word Ordu, meaning "tent" or "encampment") conquered southern Russia, and then launched a two-pronged assault farther west. In April 1241 the smaller Mongol force met a hastily assembled army of Germans and Poles at the battle of Liegnitz, where the two sides fought to a bloody standstill. Two days later, the larger Mongol army annihilated the Hungarian army at the River Sajo.

How much farther west the Mongol armies might have pushed will forever remain in doubt, for in December 1241 the Great Khan Ögedei died, and the

Mongol forces withdrew from eastern Europe. Mongol conquests continued in Persia, the Middle East, and China, but after 1241 the Mongols never resumed their attacks on Europe. By 1300, the period of Mongol expansion had come to an end.

But the Mongol threat did not suddenly disappear. Descendants of Chingiz Khan continued to rule this enormous land empire (the largest such empire in the history of the world) until the mid-fourteenth century. Later, under the leadership of Timur the Lame (known as Tamerlane to Europeans) it looked briefly as if the Mongol empire might be reunited. But Timur died in 1405 on his way to invade China; thereafter the various parts of the Mongol empire fell into the hands of local rulers, including (in Asia Minor) the Ottoman Turks.

The Mongols owed their success to the size, speed, and training of their mounted armies; to the intimidating savagery with which they butchered those who resisted them; and to their ability to adapt the administrative traditions of their subjects to their own purposes. Partly because the Mongols themselves put little store even in their own shamanistic religious traditions, they were also unusually tolerant of the religious beliefs of others—a distinct advantage in controlling an empire that comprised a dizzying array of Buddhist, Christian, and Muslim sects. However, little was distinctively "Mongol" about the way they governed their empire. Except in China, where the Mongol Yuan dynasty inherited and maintained a complex administrative bureaucracy, the Mongols' rule was relatively unsophisticated, being chiefly directed at securing the steady payment of tribute from their subjects.

The Head of Timur the Lame. A forensic reconstruction based on his exhumed skull.

EUROPE, THE MONGOLS, AND THE FAR EAST

Until the Mongol conquests, the "Silk Road" to China had been closed to Western merchants and travelers. But almost as soon as the Mongol empire was established, we find Europeans venturing on these routes. The most famous of these early merchants were three Venetians: Niccolo, Maffeo, and Marco Polo. Marco Polo's account of his twenty-year sojourn in China in the service of Qubilai Khan, and of his journey home through the Spice Islands, India, and Iran, is one of the most famous travel accounts of all time. Its effect on the imagination of his contemporaries was enormous. For the next two centuries, most of what Europeans knew about the Far East they learned from Marco Polo's *Travels*. Christopher Columbus's copy of this book still survives.

The "window of opportunity" that made Marco Polo's travels possible was relatively short. By the middle of the fourteenth century, hostilities between the various parts of the Mongol empire were already making travel along the Silk Road perilous. After 1368, when the Mongol (Yuan) dynasty was overthrown, Westerners were excluded from China altogether, and Mongols were restricted to cavalry service in the Ming imperial armies. The overland trade routes from China to the Black Sea continued to operate; Europeans, however, were no longer able

MARCO POLO'S DESCRIPTION OF JAVA

The Venetian merchants Niccolo and Maffeo Polo traveled overland from Constantinople to the court of Qubilai Khan between 1260 and 1269. When they returned a few years later, they brought with them Niccolo's son Marco. A gifted linguist, Marco would remain at the Mongol court until the early 1290s, when he returned to Europe after a journey through Southeast Asia, the Spice Islands, and the Indian Ocean. Marco's account of his Travels would shape European images of the Far East for centuries.

Departing from Ziamba, and steering between south and south-east, fifteen hundred miles, you reach an island of very great size, named Java. According to the reports of some well-informed navigators, it is the greatest in the world, and has a compass above three thousand miles. It is under the dominion of one king only, nor do the inhabitants pay tribute to any other power. They are worshipers of idols.

The country abounds with rich commodities. Pepper, nutmegs, spikenard, galangal, cubebs, cloves and all the other valuable spices and drugs, are the produce of the island; which occasion it to be visited by many ships laden with merchandise, that yields to the owners considerable profit.

The quantity of gold collected there exceeds all calculation and belief. From thence it is that . . . merchants . . . have imported, and to this day import, that metal to a great amount, and from thence also is obtained the greatest part of the spices that are distributed throughout the world. That the Great Khan [Qubilai] has not brought the island under subjection to him, must be attributed to the length of the voyage and the dangers of the navigation.

The Travels of Marco Polo, revised and edited by Manuel Komroff. (New York: Random House), 1926, pp. 267–268.

to travel along them. But the new, more integrated commercial world the Mongols created had a lasting impact upon Europe, despite the relatively short time during which Europeans themselves were able to participate directly in it. European memories of the Far East would be preserved, and the dream of reestablishing direct connections between Europe and China would survive to influence a new round of European commercial and imperial expansion from the late fifteenth century onward.

THE RISE OF THE OTTOMAN EMPIRE

Why were slaves so important to Ottoman society?

Like the Mongols, the Ottoman Turks were initially a nomadic people whose economy continued to depend on raiding even after they had conquered an extensive empire. The peoples who would become the Ottomans were already established in northwestern Anatolia when the Mongols arrived, and were already at least nominally Muslims. But unlike the established Muslim powers in the region, whom the Mongols destroyed, the Ottoman Turks were among the principal beneficiaries of the Mongol conquest. By toppling the Seljuk sultanate and the Abbasid caliphate of Baghdad, the Mongols eliminated the two traditional authorities that had previously kept Turkish border chieftains like the Ottomans in check. Now the Ottomans were free to raid along their soft frontiers with Byzantium unhindered. At the same time, however, they remained far enough away from the centers of Mongol authority to avoid being destroyed themselves.

THE CONQUEST OF CONSTANTINOPLE

By the end of the thirteenth century, the Ottoman dynasty had established itself as the leading family among the Anatolian border lords. By the mid-fourteenth century, it had solidified its preeminence by capturing a number of important cities. These successes brought the Ottomans to the attention of the Byzantine emperor, who in 1345 hired a contingent of Ottomans as mercenaries. Thus introduced into Europe, the Ottomans quickly made themselves at home. By 1370, they had extended their control all the way to the Danube. In 1389 Ottoman forces defeated the powerful Serbian empire at the battle of Kosovo, enabling them to consolidate their control over Greece, Bulgaria, and the Balkans.

In 1396 the Ottomans attacked Constantinople, but withdrew in order to repel a Western crusading force that had been sent against them. In 1402, they attacked Constantinople again, but once more were forced to withdraw, this time to confront a Mongolian invasion of Anatolia. Led by Timur the Lame, the Mongol army captured the Ottoman sultan and destroyed his army; for the next decade it appeared that Ottoman hegemony over Anatolia might be gone forever. By 1413, however, Timur was dead, a new sultan had emerged, and the Ottomans were able to resume their conquests. Ottoman pressure on Constantinople continued during the 1420s and 1430s, producing a steady stream of Byzantine refugees who brought with them to Italy the surviving masterworks of classical Greek literature. But it was not until 1451 that a new sultan, Mehmet II, turned his full attention to the conquest of the imperial city. In 1453, after a

brilliantly executed siege, Mehmet succeeded in breaching the city's walls. The Byzantine emperor was killed in the assault, the city itself was thoroughly plundered, and its population was sold into slavery. The Ottomans then settled down to rule their new capital in a style reminiscent of their Byzantine predecessors.

The effects of the Ottoman conquest of Constantinople on western Europe were modest. On the Ottomans themselves, however, their conquest was transformative. Vast new wealth poured into Ottoman society, which the Ottomans increased by carefully tending to the industrial and commercial interests of

Sultan Mehmet II, "The Conqueror" (1451–1481), by the Ottoman artist Siblizade Ahmed. The sultan's pose and handkerchief are Central Asian conventions in portraiture, but the subdued color and three-quarter profile show the influence of Italian Renaissance portraits. The sultan wears the white turban of a scholar, but also wears the thumb ring of an archer, neatly reflecting his combination of scholarly and military attainments.

their new capital city. Trade routes were redirected to feed the capital, and the Ottomans became a naval power in the eastern Mediterranean and the Black Sea. As a result, Constantinople's population grew from less than one hundred thousand in 1453 to more than five hundred thousand in 1600, making it the largest city in the world outside China.

WAR, SLAVERY, AND SOCIAL ADVANCEMENT

Despite the Ottomans' careful attention to commerce, their empire rested on raiding and conquest. Until the end of the sixteenth century, the Ottoman empire was therefore on an almost constant war footing. To continue its conquests, the size of the Ottoman army and administration grew exponentially. But this growth drew more and more manpower from the empire. Because the Ottoman army and administration were largely composed of slaves, the demand for more soldiers and administrators could best be met through further conquests that would capture yet more slaves. Further conquests, however, required a still larger army and an even more extensive bureaucracy; and so the cycle continued.

Slaves were the backbone of the Ottoman army and administration. But slaves were also critical to the lives of the Ottoman upper class. After 1453, new wealth permitted some Ottoman notables to maintain house-

> Because the vast majority of Ottoman slaves were household servants and administrators rather than laborers, some people willingly accepted enslavement, believing that they would be better off as slaves in Constantinople than as impoverished peasants in the countryside.

holds in which thousands of slaves attended to their masters' whims. In the sixteenth century, the sultan's household alone numbered more than twenty thousand slave attendants, not including his bodyguard and his elite infantry units, both of which were also composed of slaves.

Many of these slaves were captured in war or raids. But slaves were also recruited (some willingly, some by coercion) from rural areas of the Ottoman empire itself. Because the vast majority of Ottoman slaves were household servants and administrators rather than laborers, some people willingly accepted enslavement, believing that they would be better off as slaves in Constantinople than as impoverished peasants in the countryside. In the Balkans especially, many people were enslaved as children, handed over by their families to pay the infamous "child tax" the Ottomans imposed on rural areas too poor to pay a monetary tribute. Special academies were created at Constantinople to train the most able of these enslaved children to act as administrators and soldiers, and some rose to become powerful figures in the Ottoman empire. Slavery therefore carried relatively little social stigma. Even the sultan himself was most often the son of an enslaved woman.

Because Muslims were not permitted to enslave other Muslims, the vast majority of Ottoman slaves were from Christian families (although many converted to Islam later in life). But because so many of the elite positions within Ottoman government were held by slaves, the paradoxical result of this reliance on slave administrators was that Muslims, including Turks, were effectively excluded from the main avenues of social and political advancement in Ottoman society. Nor was Ottoman society characterized by a powerful, hereditary nobility of the sort that dominated contemporary European society. As a result, power in the fifteenth- and sixteenth-century Ottoman empire was remarkably, perhaps even uniquely, open to men of ability and talent, provided that such men were slaves and therefore not Muslims by birth. Nor was this pattern of Muslim exclusion limited to government and the army. Commerce and business also remained largely in the hands of non-Muslims, most frequently Greeks, Syrians, and Jews. Jews in particular found in the Ottoman empire a welcome refuge from the persecutions and expulsions that had characterized Jewish life in late medieval Europe. After their

CHRONOLOGY

RISE OF THE OTTOMAN EMPIRE, 1300–1571

Ottomans become leading Anatolian family	1300
Byzantine emperor hires Ottoman mercenaries	1345
Ottomans enter Europe	1350s
Ottomans defeat Serbian empire	1389
Ottomans conquer Constantinople	1453
Ottomans conquer Syria, Egypt, Balkans	1520s
Battle of Lepanto	1571

1492 expulsion from Spain, more than a hundred thousand Spanish (Sephardic) Jews ultimately immigrated into the Ottoman empire.

RELIGIOUS CONFLICTS

The Ottoman sultans were relentlessly orthodox Sunni Muslims, who lent staunch support to the religious and legal pronouncements of the Islamic scholarly schools. In 1516, the Ottomans captured the cities of Medina and Mecca, thus becoming the defenders of the holy sites. Soon after, they captured Jerusalem and Cairo,

putting an end to the Mamluk sultanate of Egypt. In 1538 the Ottoman ruler formally adopted the title of caliph, thereby declaring himself to be the legitimate successor of the Prophet Muhammad.

In keeping with Sunni traditions, the Ottomans were also religiously tolerant toward non-Muslims, especially during the fifteenth and sixteenth centuries. They organized the major religious groups of their empire into legally recognized units known as *millets*, permitting them considerable rights of religious self-government. After 1453, however, the Ottomans were particularly careful to protect and

THE GROWTH OF THE OTTOMAN EMPIRE

Consider the patterns of Ottoman expansion revealed in this map. Did the 1453 capture of Constantinople lead to immediate further conquests? Why do you suppose this was? Compare the extent of the Ottoman empire in 1566 with that of the Byzantine empire under Justinian (map, p. 184). How would you account for these similarities? Why didn't the Ottoman empire continue its rapid expansion after 1566?

promote the authority of the Greek Orthodox patriarch of Constantinople over the Orthodox Christians of their empire. As a result, the Ottomans enjoyed staunch support from their Orthodox Christian subjects during their sixteenth-century wars with the Latin Christians of western Europe. Despite the religious diversity of their empire, the Ottomans' principal religious conflicts were therefore not with their own subjects, but with the Shi'ite Muslim dynasty that ruled neighboring Persia. Time and again during the sixteenth century, Ottoman expeditions against western Europe had to be abandoned when hostilities erupted with the Persians.

THE OTTOMANS AND EUROPE

The contest between the Ottoman empire and the Western powers never really lived up to the rhetoric of "holy war" that both sides employed in their propaganda. In 1396, a Western crusader army was annihilated by the Ottomans at the battle of Nicopolis. In the sixteenth and seventeenth centuries, Ottoman armies several times besieged Vienna. But despite these dramatic moments, conflicts between the Ottomans and the rulers of western Europe were fought out mainly through pirate raids and naval battles in the Mediterranean. The main result of this contest was thus a steady escalation in the scale and cost of navies. In 1571, when a combined Habsburg and Venetian force defeated the Ottoman fleet at Lepanto, both sides deployed naval forces ten times larger than they had possessed half a century before.

After 1571 both Ottoman and Habsburg interests shifted away from their conflict with each other. The Ottomans embarked upon a long and costly war with Persia, while the Spanish Habsburgs turned their attention toward their new empire in the Atlantic. By the mid-seventeenth century, when a new round of Ottoman-European conflicts began, the strength of the Ottoman empire had been sapped by a series of indolent, pleasure-loving sultans and by the tensions that arose within the Ottoman empire itself as it ceased to expand. The Ottoman empire would last until 1918; but from the mid-seventeenth century on, it ceased to be a serious rival to the global hegemony the European powers were beginning to achieve.

MEDITERRANEAN COLONIALISM

How were the Portuguese able to control Indian Ocean trade?

During the fifteenth century, Europeans focused their colonial and commercial ambitions more and more on the western Mediterranean and the Atlantic world. Although historians have sometimes argued the contrary, this reorientation was not a result of the rising power of the Ottoman empire. Instead, this westward orientation was the product of two related developments: the growing importance to late medieval Europe of the African gold trade; and the growth of European colonial empires in the western Mediterranean Sea.

SILVER SHORTAGES AND THE SEARCH FOR AFRICAN GOLD

Europeans had been trading for African gold for centuries, mainly through Muslim middlemen who transported this precious metal in caravans from the Niger River area where it was produced to the North African ports of Algiers and Tunis. From the thirteenth century on, Catalan and Genoese merchants maintained colonies in Tunis, where they traded woolen cloth for North African grain and sub-Saharan gold.

What accelerated the late medieval demand for gold, however, was a serious silver shortage that affected the entire European economy during the fourteenth and fifteenth centuries. Silver production in Europe fell markedly during the 1340s and remained at a low level thereafter, as Europeans reached the limits of their technological capacity to extract silver ore from deep mines. This shortfall in silver production was compounded during the fifteenth century by a serious balance-of-payments problem: more European silver was flowing east in the spice trade than could be replaced using existing mining techniques on known silver deposits. Gold currencies represented an obvious alternative for large transactions, and from the

Silver production in Europe fell markedly during the 1340s and remained at a low level thereafter, as Europeans reached the limits of their technological capacity to extract silver ore from deep mines.

thirteenth century on European rulers with access to gold were minting gold coins. But Europe itself had few natural gold reserves. To maintain and expand these gold coinages, new and larger supplies of gold were needed. The most obvious source for this gold was Africa.

FROM THE MEDITERRANEAN TO THE ATLANTIC

Until the late thirteenth century, European maritime commerce had been divided between a Mediterranean and a north Atlantic world. Starting around 1270, however, Italian merchants began to sail through the Strait of Gibraltar and on to the wool-producing regions of England and the Netherlands. This was the essential first step in the extension of Mediterranean patterns of commerce and colonization into the Atlantic Ocean. The second step was the discovery (or possibly rediscovery), during the fourteenth century, of the Atlantic island chains known as the Canaries and the Azores by Genoese sailors. Efforts to colonize the Canary Islands, and to convert and enslave their inhabitants, began almost immediately. But an effective conquest of the Canary Islands did not really begin until the fifteenth century, when it was undertaken by Portugal and completed by Castile. The Canaries, in turn, became the base from which further Portuguese voyages down the west coast of Africa proceeded. They were also the "jumping-off point" from which Christopher Columbus would sail westward across the Atlantic Ocean in hopes of reaching Asia.

> Starting around 1270, however, Italian merchants began to sail through the Strait of Gibraltar and on to the wool-producing regions of England and the Netherlands. This was the essential first step in the extension of Mediterranean patterns of commerce and colonization into the Atlantic Ocean.

THE TECHNOLOGY OF SHIPS AND NAVIGATION

The European empires of the fifteenth and sixteenth centuries rested on a mastery of the oceans. The Portuguese caravel—the workhorse ship of the fifteenth-century voyages to Africa—was based on ship and sail designs that had been in use among Portuguese fishermen since the thirteenth century. Starting in the 1440s, however, Portuguese shipwrights began building larger caravels with two masts, each carrying a triangular (lateen) sail. Such ships were capable of sailing against the wind much more effectively than were the older, square-rigged vessels. By the end of the fifteenth century, even larger caravels were being constructed, with a third mast and a combination of square and lateen sails. Columbus's *Niña* was of this design, having been refitted with two square sails in the Canary Islands to enable it to sail more efficiently before the wind during the Atlantic crossing.

Europeans were also making significant advances in navigation during the fifteenth and sixteenth centuries. Quadrants, which calculated latitude in the Northern Hemisphere by the height of the North Star above the horizon, were in widespread use by the 1450s. As sailors approached the equator, however, the quadrant became less and less useful, and they were forced instead to make use of astrolabes, which reckoned latitude by the height of the sun. Like quadrants, astrolabes had been known in western Europe for centuries. But it was not until the 1480s that the astrolabe became a really useful instrument for seaborne navigation, with the preparation of standard tables sponsored by the Portuguese crown. Compasses too were also coming into more widespread use during the fifteenth century. Longitude, however, remained impossible to calculate accurately until the eighteenth century, when the invention of the marine chronometer finally made it possible to keep accurate time at sea. In the sixteenth century, Europeans sailing east or west across the oceans generally had to rely on their skill at dead reckoning to determine where they were on the globe.

European sailors also benefited from a new interest in maps and navigational charts. Especially important to Atlantic sailors were books known as *rutters* or *routiers*. These contained detailed sailing instructions and descriptions of the coastal landmarks a pilot could expect to encounter on route to a variety of destinations. Mediterranean sailors had had similar books, known as *portolani*, since at least the fourteenth century. In the fifteenth century, however, this tradition was extended to the Atlantic Ocean; by the end of the sixteenth century, rutters spanned the globe.

OVERSEAS EXPLORATION IN THE FIFTEENTH AND SIXTEENTH CENTURIES

This map shows the routes taken by major European explorers of the fifteenth and sixteenth centuries, as well as the distribution of outposts established by the Portuguese and Spanish. Why were the Portuguese and Spanish the first Europeans to underwrite and encourage such adventures? What economic and cultural factors precipitated such efforts? What were the motives for such voyages? How did the establishment of economic outposts in Africa, America, and the East Indies radically alter the balance of power in the "Old World," and why? Might the Americas have had to wait even longer for European "discovery" had da Gama found the route around Africa sooner?

PORTUGAL, AFRICA, AND THE SEA ROUTE TO INDIA

It was among the Portuguese that these dual interests—the African gold trade and Atlantic colonization—first came together. In 1415, a Portuguese expedition captured the north African port of Ceuta. During the 1420s the Portuguese colonized both the island of Madeira and the Canary Islands. During the 1430s, they extended these colonization efforts to the Azores. In 1444 Portuguese explorers first landed in the area between the Senegal and the Gambia river mouths on the African mainland, where they began to collect cargoes of gold and slaves for export back to Portugal. By the 1470s, Portuguese sailors had rounded the African "bulge" and were exploring the Gulf of Guinea. In 1483 they reached the mouth of the Congo River. In 1488 the Portuguese captain Bartholomeu Dias rounded the southern tip of Africa. Blown around it accidentally by a gale, Dias named the point "Cape of Storms," but the king of Portugal took a more optimistic view of Dias's achievement. He renamed it the Cape of Good Hope and began planning a naval expedition to India. Finally in 1497–1498, Vasco da Gama rounded the Cape, and then, with the help of a Muslim navigator named Ibn Majid, crossed the Indian Ocean to Calicutt on the southwestern coast of India, opening up for the first time a direct sea route between Europe and the Far Eastern spice trade.

Now master of the quickest route to riches in the world, the king of Portugal swiftly capitalized on da Gama's accomplishment. After 1500, Portuguese trading fleets sailed regularly to India. In 1509, the Portuguese defeated an Ottoman fleet and then blockaded the mouth of the Red Sea, attempting to cut off one of the traditional routes by which spices had traveled to Alexandria and Beirut. By 1510 Portuguese military forces had established a series of forts along the western Indian coastline, including their headquarters at Goa. In 1511 Portuguese ships seized Malacca, a center of the spice trade on the Malay peninsula. By 1515 they had reached the Spice Islands and the coast of China. So completely did the Portuguese now dominate the spice trade that by the 1520s even the Venetians were forced to buy their pepper in the Portuguese capital of Lisbon.

CHRONOLOGY

PORTUGUESE MARITIME EXPANSION, 1420s–1515

Colonization of Madeira and Canary Islands	1420s
Colonization of the Azores	1430s
Dias rounds the Cape of Good Hope	1488
Da Gama reaches India	1497–1498
Portuguese reach Malacca in Southeast Asia	1511
Portuguese reach Spice Islands	1515

ARTILLERY AND EMPIRE

Larger, more maneuverable ships and improved navigational aids made it possible for European mariners to reach Africa, Asia, and the Americas by sea. But fundamentally, these sixteenth-century European commercial empires were a military achievement. As such, they reflected what Europeans had learned in their wars against each other during the fourteenth and fifteenth centuries. Perhaps the most critical military advance of the late Middle Ages was the increasing sophistication of artillery, a development made possible not only by gunpowder, but also by improved metallurgical techniques for casting cannon barrels. By the middle of the fifteenth century, the use of artillery pieces had rendered the stone walls of medieval castles and towns obsolete, a fact brought home in 1453 by the successful French siege of Bordeaux (which brought to an end the Hundred Years' War), and by the Ottoman siege of Constantinople (which brought to an end the Byzantine empire).

One of the reasons the new ship designs (first caravels, and later the even larger galleons) were so important was that their larger size made it possible to mount more effective artillery pieces on them. Increasingly during the sixteenth century, European naval vessels were conceived as floating artillery platforms, with scores of guns mounted in fixed positions along their sides and swivel guns mounted fore and aft. These guns were vastly expensive, as were the ships that carried them; but for those rulers who could afford to possess them, such ships

> Increasingly during the sixteenth century, European naval vessels were conceived as floating artillery platforms, with scores of guns mounted in fixed positions along their sides and swivel guns mounted fore and aft.

made it possible to project military power around the world. Without this essential military component, the European maritime empires of the sixteenth century would not have existed.

PRINCE HENRY THE NAVIGATOR

Because we know that these fifteenth-century Portuguese expeditions down the African coast did ultimately open up a sea route to India and the Far East, it is tempting to presume that this was their goal from the beginning. It was not. The traditional narrative of these events, which presents exploration as their mission, India as their goal, and Prince Henry the Navigator as the guiding genius behind them, no longer commands the confidence of most historians. Only from the 1480s did India clearly become the goal toward which these voyages were directed. Prior to the 1480s, Portuguese involvement in Africa was driven instead by much more traditional goals: crusading ambitions against the Muslims of North Africa; the desire to establish direct links with the sources of African gold production south of the Sahara Desert; the desire to colonize the Atlantic islands; the burgeoning market for slaves in Europe and in the Ottoman empire; and the hope that somewhere in Africa they might find the legendary Prester John, a mythical Christian king whom Europeans believed would be their ally against the Muslims if only they could locate him. In the twelfth and thirteenth centuries, they had sought him in Asia. But from the 1340s on, he was believed to reside in Ethiopia, an expansive term that to most Europeans seems to have meant "somewhere in Africa."

Nor does Prince Henry (whose title, "the Navigator," was not assigned to him until the seventeenth century) seem so central a figure in Portuguese exploration as he was once thought to be. In fact, he directed only eight of the thirty-five Portuguese voyages to Africa between 1419 and his death in 1460; and the stories about his gathering a school of navigators and cartographers on the Atlantic coast of Portugal, about his role in designing improved ships and navigational instruments, and about his encouragement of scientific learning generally, have all been shown to be false. Henry did play an important role in organizing Portuguese colonization of Madeira, the Canary Islands and the Azores, and he also pioneered the Portuguese slave trade, first on the Canaries (whose Stone Age population was almost entirely enslaved) and then along the Sene-Gambian coast of Africa. His main goal, however, was to outflank the cross-Saharan African gold trade by intercepting

Prince Henry the Navigator, by a fifteenth-century Portuguese painter. This portrait is taken from a group portrait of the Portuguese royal family. Although thought to depict Henry, the identification is not certain.

this trade at its source. To this end, he built a series of forts along the African coastline, most famously at Arguim, to which he hoped to divert the cross-Saharan gold caravans. This was also his reason for colonizing the Canary Islands, which he saw as a staging ground for expeditions into the African interior. There is no evidence that he ever dreamed of reaching India by sailing around Africa. Indeed, quite the opposite seems to be the case. Portuguese progress toward the Cape of Good Hope proceeded much more rapidly in the years after Henry's death than it had during his lifetime. Henry himself was a crusader against Islam; a prince in search of a kingdom; a lord seeking resources to support his followers; and an aspiring merchant who hoped to make a killing in the gold trade but found his main profits in slaving. He was, in all these respects, a man of his time, which is to say, of the fifteenth century. He was not the architect, or even the visionary, of Portugal's sixteenth-century maritime empire.

ATLANTIC COLONIZATION AND THE GROWTH OF SLAVERY

The profits Prince Henry had hoped would come from the African gold trade did not materialize during his lifetime. He therefore had to make his expeditions pay by other means. One of those means was the slave trade. Although slavery in most of western Europe had effectively disappeared by the early twelfth century, slavery continued in Iberia (and to a lesser extent in Italy) throughout the high and late Middle Ages. Until the mid-fifteenth century, however, slavery on the Iberian mainland and in Italy remained very small in scale. The major Mediterranean slave markets of the fourteenth and early fifteenth centuries lay in Muslim lands, and especially in the Ottoman empire. Relatively few of the slaves who passed through these markets were Africans. Most were European Christians, predominantly Poles, Ukrainians, Greeks, and Bulgarians. Thus the patterns of slavery were not racialized in the late medieval Mediterranean world, except insofar as "primitive" peoples such as the natives of the Canary Islands or of Sardinia were more likely to be regarded as targets for enslavement.

From the mid-fifteenth century on, however, Lisbon began to emerge as a significant market for enslaved Africans. Something on the order of fifteen to twenty thousand Africans were sold in Lisbon during Prince Henry's lifetime, most of them between 1440 and 1460. In the half century after his death, the numbers grew, amounting to perhaps one hundred fifty thousand African slaves imported into Europe by 1505. For the most part, these slaves were regarded as status symbols—one reason they were so frequently depicted in paintings of the period. Even in the Atlantic colonies—Madeira, the Canaries, and the Azores—the land was worked mainly by European settlers and sharecroppers. Slave labor, if it was employed at all, was generally used only in sugar mills. But even sugar production did not lead to the widespread introduction of slavery on these islands.

A new style of slave-based sugar plantations began to emerge in Portugal's Atlantic colonies only in the 1460s, starting on the Cape Verde Islands and then extending southward into the Gulf of Guinea. These islands were not populated when the Portuguese began to settle them. They were ideally located, however, to purchase laborers from the slave traders along the nearby West African coast. No comparable system of large-scale, slave-based plantation production had been seen in Europe or Africa since the Roman period. But it was this model of sugar plantations staffed by enslaved Africans that would be exported to the Caribbean islands of the Americas by their Spanish conquerors, with incalculable consequences for Africa, the Americas, and Europe.

EUROPE ENCOUNTERS A NEW WORLD

What was the impact of New World silver on the European economy?

The decision by Spain's rulers to underwrite Columbus's famous voyage was an outgrowth of the progress of these Portuguese ventures. After 1488, when Dias successfully rounded the Cape of Good Hope, it was clear that Portugal would soon dominate the sea lanes leading eastward to Asia. The only alternative for Portugal's Spanish rivals was to finance someone bold enough to try to reach Asia by sailing west. The popular image of Christopher Columbus (1451–1506) as a visionary who struggled to convince hardened ignoramuses that the world was round does not bear up under scrutiny. In fact, the sphericity of the earth had been widely known throughout European society since at least the twelfth century. What made Columbus's scheme seem plausible to King Ferdinand and Queen Isabella was, first, the discovery and colonization of the Canary Islands and the Azores, which had reinforced a view of the Atlantic as being dotted with islands all the way to Japan; and second, the Genoese mariner's own astonishing miscalculation of the actual size of the earth, which convinced him that he could reach Japan and China in about a month's clear sailing westward from the Canary Islands. America was actually rediscovered by Europeans at the end of the fifteenth century as the result of a colossal error in reckoning. Columbus himself never realized his mistake. When he reached the Bahamas and the island of Hispaniola in 1492 after only a month's sailing, he returned to Spain to report that he had indeed reached the outer islands of Asia.

THE DISCOVERY OF A NEW WORLD

Columbus was not the first European to set foot on the American continents. Viking sailors had reached and briefly settled present-day Newfoundland, Labrador, and perhaps New England around the year 1000. But knowledge of these Viking landings had been forgot-

WHAT WAS THE IMPACT OF NEW WORLD SILVER ON THE EUROPEAN ECONOMY?

EUROPE ENCOUNTERS A NEW WORLD   337

ten or ignored throughout Europe for hundreds of years. In the fifteenth century, even the Scandinavian settlements in Greenland had been abandoned. It would be perverse, therefore, to deny Columbus credit for his accomplishments. Although Columbus himself never accepted the reality of what he had discovered, those who followed him soon did, and busily set out to exploit this new world.

Understandably, Columbus brought back no Asian spices from his voyages. He did, however, return with some small samples of gold and a few indigenous people, whose existence gave promise of entire tribes that might be "saved" (by conversion to Christianity) and enslaved by Europeans. This provided sufficient incentive for the Spanish monarchs to finance three more expeditions by Columbus and many more by others. Soon the mainland was discovered as well as further islands, and the conclusion quickly became inescapable that a new world had indeed been found. Awareness of this new world was most widely publicized by the Italian geographer Amerigo Vespucci. Though he may not have deserved this honor, the continents of the Western Hemisphere became known thereafter as "America" after Vespucci's first name.

The realization that this was indeed a new world was at first a disappointment to the Spanish, for with a major land mass lying between Europe and Asia, Spain could not hope to beat Portugal in the race for Asian spices. Any remaining doubt that not one, but two vast oceans separated Europe from Asia was completely removed in 1513, when Vasco Núñez de Balboa first viewed the Pacific Ocean from the Isthmus of Panama. Not entirely admitting defeat, Ferdinand and Isabella's grandson, the Holy Roman emperor Charles V, accepted Ferdinand Magellan's offer in 1519 to see whether a route to Asia could be found by sailing around South America. But Magellan's voyage demonstrated beyond question that the globe was simply too large for any such plan to be feasible. Of the five ships that left Spain under Magellan's command, only one returned three years later, hav-

ing been forced to circumnavigate the globe. Out of a crew of 265 sailors, only eighteen survived. Most had died from scurvy or starvation; Magellan himself had been killed in a skirmish with native peoples in the Philippines. This fiasco brought to an end all hope of discovering an easy "southwest passage" to Asia. The dream of a "northwest passage" survived, however, and continued to motivate European explorers of North America until the nineteenth century.

THE SPANISH CONQUEST OF AMERICA

Although the discovery of this new continent was initially a disappointment to the Spanish, it quickly became clear that the New World had great wealth of its own. From the start, Columbus's gold samples, in themselves rather paltry, had nurtured hopes that somewhere in America gold might lie piled in ingots, ready to enrich whatever European adventurer discovered them. Rumor fed rumor, until a few freelance Spanish soldiers really did strike it rich beyond their most avaricious imaginings. Between 1519 and 1521, the *conquistador* (Spanish for "conqueror") Hernando Cortés, with a force of six hundred Europeans but with the assistance of thousands of the Aztecs' unhappy subjects, overthrew

Spanish Conquistadors Massacring the Aztecs. Between 1519 and 1521, Cortes and a small army of conquistadors destroyed the Aztec empire in search of gold and silver.

the Aztec empire of Mexico and carried off its rulers' fabulous wealth. Then in 1533 another conquistador, Francisco Pizarro, this time with only one hundred eighty men, toppled the highly centralized South American empire of the Inkas, and carried off its great stores of gold and silver. Cortés and Pizarro had the advantage of some cannons and a few horses (both unknown to the native peoples of the Americas), but they achieved their victories primarily by sheer audacity, courage, and treachery. They were aided also by the unwillingness of the indigenous peoples whom the Aztecs and the Inkas had subjected to fight on behalf of their oppressors. Little did the Spaniards' erstwhile allies know how much worse their new conquerors would soon prove to be.

THE PROFITS OF EMPIRE IN THE NEW WORLD

Cortés and Pizarro were plunderers who captured in one fell swoop hoards of gold and silver that had been accumulated for centuries by the native civilizations of Mexico and Peru. Already, however, a search had begun for the sources of these precious metals. The first gold deposits were discovered in Hispaniola, where surface mines were speedily established utilizing native laborers who died in appalling numbers from disease, brutality, and overwork. Of the approximately one million native people who lived on Hispaniola in 1492, only one hundred thousand survived by 1510. By 1538, their numbers were down to five hundred.

With the loss of so many workers, the Hispaniola mines became uneconomical to operate, and the European colonists turned instead to cattle raising and sugar production. Modelling their sugar cane plantations on those of the Cape Verde Islands and St. Thomas in the Gulf of Guinea, they imported African slaves to labor in the new industry. Sugar production was by its nature a highly capital-intensive undertaking. The need to import slave labor added further to its costs, guaranteeing that control over the sugar industry would fall into the hands of a few extremely wealthy planters and financiers.

Despite the importance of sugar production on the Caribbean islands and of cattle ranching on the Mexican mainland, mining shaped the Spanish colonies of Central and South America most fundamentally. Gold was the lure that had initially drawn the Spanish conquerors to the New World, but silver became their most lucrative export. Between 1543 and 1548, vast silver deposits were discovered north of Mexico City and at Potosí in Bolivia. Even before the discovery of these deposits, the Spanish crown had taken steps to assume direct governmental control over its Central and South American colonies. It was therefore to the Spanish crown that the profits from these astonishingly productive mines accrued. Potosí quickly became the most important mining town in the world. By 1570, it numbered one hundred twenty thousand inhabitants, despite being located at an altitude of fifteen thousand feet where the temperature never climbs above 59 degrees Fahrenheit. As in Hispaniola, enslaved native laborers died by the tens of thousands in these mines and in the disease-infested boom towns that surrounded them.

New mining techniques (in particular, the mercury-amalgamation process, introduced into Mexico in 1555 and Potosí in 1571) made it possible to produce even greater quantities of silver, at the cost of even greater mortality among the native laborers. Between 1571 and 1586, silver production at Potosí quadrupled, reaching a peak in the 1590s, when ten million ounces of silver per year were arriving in Spain from the Americas.

This massive infusion of silver into the European economy accelerated an inflation that had begun already in the later fifteenth century. The result was what historians have termed "the Price Revolution." Although the effects of this inflation were felt throughout the European continent, Spain was affected with particular severity. Between 1500 and 1560, Spanish prices doubled; between 1560 and 1600, they doubled again. Such exceptionally high prices in turn undermined the competitiveness of Spanish industries. When the flow of New World silver to Spain slowed dramatically during the 1620s and 1630s, the Spanish economy collapsed.

After 1600, lessening quantities of New World silver entered the European economy, but prices continued

CHRONOLOGY

ENCOUNTERING THE NEW WORLD, c. 1000–1545

Vikings settle Newfoundland	c. 1000
Columbus reaches Hispaniola	1492
Balboa reaches Pacific Ocean	1513
Magellan's fleet sails around the world	1519–1522
Cortés conquers the Aztecs	1521
Pizarro conquers the Inkas	1533
Potosí silver deposits discovered	1545

ENSLAVED NATIVE LABORERS AT POTOSÍ

Since the Spanish crown received one fifth of all the revenues from mines (as well as maintaining a monopoly over the mercury used to refine the silver ore into silver), it had an important stake in ensuring the productivity of the mines. To this end, the Crown granted colonial mine owners the right to conscript native peoples to work in the mines. This account from about 1620 describes the conditions under which these forced native laborers worked. Not surprisingly, mortality rates among such laborers were horrendous.

According to His Majesty's warrant, the mine owners on this massive range [at Potosí] have a right to the conscripted labor of 13,300 Indians in the working and exploitation of the mines, both those which have been discovered, those now discovered, and those which shall be discovered. It is the duty of the *Corregidor* (municipal governor) of Potosí to have them rounded up and to see that they come in from all the provinces between Cuzco . . . and as far as the frontiers of Tarija and Tomina. . . .

The conscripted Indians go up every Monday morning to the . . . foot of the range; the *Corregidor* arrives with all the provincial captains or chiefs who have charge of the Indians assigned him for his miner or smelter; that keeps him busy till 1 P.M., by which time the Indians are already turned over to these mine and smelter owners.

After each has eaten his ration, they climb up the hill, each to his mine, and go in, staying there from that hour until Saturday evening without coming out of the mine; their wives bring them food, but they stay constantly underground, excavating and carrying out the ore from which they get the silver. They all have tallow candles, lighted day and night; that is the light they work with, for as they are underground, they have need for it all the time. . . .

These Indians have different functions in the handling of the silver ore; some break it up with bar or pick, and dig down in, following the vein in the mine; others bring it up; others up above keep separating the good and the poor in piles; others are occupied in taking it down from the range to the mills on herds of llamas; every day they bring up more than 8,000 of these native beasts of burden for this task. These teamsters who carry the metal are not conscripted, but are hired.

Antonio Vázquez de Espinosa, *Compendium and Description of the West Indies*, trans. Charles Upson Clark. (Washington, D.C.: Smithsonian Institution Press, 1968), p. 62.

to rise albeit more slowly than before. By 1650, the price of grain within Europe had risen to five or six times its level in 1500, producing social dislocation and widespread misery for many of Europe's poorest inhabitants. In England, the period between about 1590 and 1610 was probably the most desperate the country had experienced for three hundred years. Standards of living were lower in England in 1600 than they had been even in the terrible years of the early fourteenth century. It is no wonder, then, that so many Europeans found emigration to the Americas a tempting prospect. We may wonder, indeed, what might have happened in seventeenth-century Europe had the new world of the Americas not existed as an outlet for Europe's growing population.

CONCLUSION

By 1600, colonization and overseas conquest had profoundly changed both Europe and the wider world. The emergence during the sixteenth century of Portugal and Spain as Europe's leading long-distance traders permanently moved the center of gravity of European economic power away from Italy and the Mediterranean toward the Atlantic. Deprived of its role as the principal conduit for the spice trade, Venice gradually declined. The Genoese moved increasingly into the world of finance, backing the commercial ventures of others, and particularly of Spain. By contrast, the Atlantic ports of Spain and Portugal bustled with vessels and shone with wealth. By the mid-seventeenth century, however, economic predominance was passing to the north Atlantic states of England, Holland, and France. Spain and Portugal would retain their American colonies until the nineteenth century. But from the seventeenth century on, it would be the Dutch, the French, and especially the English who would establish new European empires in North America, Asia, Africa, and Australia. By and large, these new empires would last until the Second World War.

KEY TERMS

Chingiz Khan	caravels	conquistador
Marco Polo	astrolabe	New World silver
Timur the Lame	Prince Henry the Navigator	Aztecs
Canary Islands	Christopher Columbus	Inkas

SELECTED READINGS

Abu-Lughod, Janet L. *Before European Hegemony: The World System A.D. 1250–1350.* Oxford and New York, 1989. A study of the trading links between Europe, the Middle East, India, and China, with special attention to the role of the Mongol empire; extensive bibliography.

Allsen, Thomas T. *Culture and Conquest in Mongol Eurasia.* Cambridge and New York, 2001. A synthesis of the author's earlier studies, emphasizing Mongol involvement in the cultural and commercial exchanges that linked China, Central Asia, and Europe.

The Book of Prophecies, Edited by Christopher Columbus. Translated by Blair Sullivan. Edited by Roberto Rusconi. Berkeley and Los Angeles, 1996. After his third voyage, from which Columbus was returned to Spain in chains, he compiled a book of quotations from various sources, selected to emphasize the millenarian implications of his discoveries; a fascinating insight into the mind of the explorer.

Christian, David. *A History of Russia, Central Asia and Mongolia.* Volume 1: *Inner Eurasia from Prehistory to the Mongol Empire.* Oxford, 1998. The first volume of what will surely become the authoritative English-language work on the subject.

Coles, Paul. *The Ottoman Impact on Europe.* London, 1968. An excellent introductory text, still valuable despite its age.

Fernández-Armesto, Felipe. *Before Columbus: Exploration and Colonisation from the Mediterranean to the Atlantic, 1229–1492.* London, 1987. An indispensible study of the medieval background to the sixteenth-century European colonial empires.

———. *Columbus.* Oxford and New York, 1991. An excellent biography that stresses the millenarian ideas that underlay Columbus's thinking. A good book to read after the Phillips's book (see below).

Flint, Valerie I. J. *The Imaginative Landscape of Christopher Columbus.* Princeton, N.J., 1992. A short, suggestive analysis of the intellectual influences that shaped Columbus's geographical ideas.

The Four Voyages: Christopher Columbus. Translated by J. M. Cohen. New York, 1992. Columbus's own self-serving account of his four voyages to the "Indies."

Goffman, Daniel. *The Ottoman Empire and Early Modern Europe.* Cambridge and New York, 2002. A revisionist account that presents the Ottoman empire as a European state.

The History and the Life of Chinggis Khan: The Secret History of the Mongols. Translated by Urgunge Onon. Leiden, 1997. Likely to become the standard English version of this important Mongol source.

Inalcik, Halil. *The Ottoman Empire: The Classical Age, 1300-1600*. London, 1973. The standard history by the dean of Turkish historians.

Kafadar, Cemal. *Between Two Worlds: The Construction of the Ottoman State*. Berkeley and Los Angeles, 1995. An important study of Ottoman origins in the border regions between Byzantium, the Seljuk Turks, and the Mongols.

Larner, John. *Marco Polo and the Discovery of the World*. New Haven, 1999. A study of the influence of Marco Polo's *Travels* on Europeans.

Morgan, David. *The Mongols*. Oxford, 1986. An accessible introduction to Mongol history and its sources, written by a noted expert on medieval Persia.

Parker, Geoffrey. *The Military Revolution: Military Innovation and the Rise of the West (1500–1800)*, 2d ed. Cambridge and New York, 1996. A work of fundamental importance for understanding the global dominance achieved by early modern Europeans.

Phillips, J. R. S. *The Medieval Expansion of Europe*, 2d ed. Oxford, 1998. An outstanding study of the thirteenth- and fourteenth-century background to the fifteenth-century expansion of Europe. Important synthetic treatment of European relations with the Mongols, China, Africa, and North America. The second edition includes a new introduction and a bibliographical essay; the text is the same as in the first edition (1988).

Phillips, William D., Jr., and Carla R. Phillips. *The Worlds of Christopher Columbus*. Cambridge and New York, 1991. The first book to read on Columbus: accessible, engaging, and scholarly. Then read Fernández-Armesto's biography (above).

Russell, Peter. *Prince Henry "The Navigator": A Life*. New Haven, 2000. A masterly biography by a great historian who has spent a lifetime on the subject. The only book one now needs to read on Prince Henry.

Saunders, J. J. *The History of the Mongol Conquests*. London, 1971. Still the standard English-language introduction; somewhat more positive about the Mongols' accomplishments than is Morgan.

Scammell, Geoffrey V. *The First Imperial Age: European Overseas Expansion, 1400–1715*. London, 1989. A useful introductory survey, with a particular focus on English and French colonization.

The Travels of Marco Polo, trans. R. E. Latham. Baltimore, 1958. The most accessible edition of this remarkably interesting work.

Chapter Twelve

The Civilization of the Renaissance, c. 1350–1550

THE PREVALENT MODERN NOTION that a "Renaissance period" followed western Europe's Middle Ages was first expressed by numerous Italian writers who lived between 1350 and 1550. According to them, one thousand years of unrelieved darkness had intervened between the Roman era and their own times. During these "Dark Ages" the muses of art and literature had fled Europe before the onslaught of barbarism and ignorance. Almost miraculously, however, in the fourteenth century the muses suddenly returned, and Italians happily collaborated with them to bring forth a glorious "renaissance of the arts."

Ever since this periodization was advanced, historians have taken for granted the existence of some sort of "renaissance" intervening between medieval and modern times. Indeed, from the late eighteenth to the early twentieth centuries many scholars went so far as to argue that the Renaissance was not just an epoch in the history of learning and culture but that a unique "Renaissance spirit" transformed all aspects of European life—political, economic, and religious, as well as intellectual and artistic. Today, however, most experts no longer accept this characterization because they find it impossible to locate any truly distinctive "Renaissance" politics, economics, or religion. Instead, most scholars reserve the term "Renaissance" to describe certain trends in thought, literature, and the arts that emerged in Italy from roughly 1350 to 1550 and then spread to northern Europe during the first half of the sixteenth century. That is the approach that we will follow here: accordingly, when we refer to a "Renaissance" period in this chapter we mean to limit ourselves to an epoch in intellectual and cultural history.

FOCUS QUESTIONS

• How did Italian Renaissance culture differ from the culture of the High Middle Ages?

• Why did the Renaissance occur in Italy?

• What were the principal characteristics of Italian Renaissance art?

 • Why did the Renaissance decline around 1550?

• How did the northern and Italian Renaissances differ from one another?

THE RENAISSANCE AND THE MIDDLE AGES

How did Italian Renaissance culture differ from the culture of the High Middle Ages?

Since the word *renaissance* literally means "rebirth," it is sometimes thought that after about 1350 Italians initiated a rebirth of classical culture following a long period during which that culture had been essentially dead. In fact, however, the High Middle Ages witnessed no "death" of classical learning. It would be equally false to contrast an imaginary "Renaissance paganism" with a medieval "age of faith" because however much most Renaissance personalities loved the classics, none saw their classicism as superseding their Christianity. And finally, all discussions of the Renaissance must be qualified by the fact that there was no single Renaissance position on anything. Renaissance thinkers and artists were enormously diverse in their attitudes, achievements, and approaches. As we assess their accomplishments, we need to beware not to force them into too narrow a mold.

RENAISSANCE CLASSICISM

Nonetheless, in the realms of thought, literature, and the arts, we can certainly find distinguishing traits that make the concept of a "Renaissance" meaningful for intellectual and cultural history. First, regarding knowledge of the classics, there was a significant quantitative difference between the learning of the Middle Ages and that of the Renaissance. Medieval scholars knew many Roman authors, such as Virgil, Ovid, and Cicero, but during the Renaissance the works of others such as Livy, Tacitus, and Lucretius were rediscovered and made familiar. Equally if not more important was the Renaissance recovery of the literature of classical Greece from Byzantium. In the twelfth and thirteenth centuries none of the great Greek literary masterpieces and practically none of the major works of Plato were yet known. Nor could more than a handful of medieval Westerners read the Greek language. During the Renaissance, on the other hand, large numbers of Western scholars learned Greek and mastered almost the entire Greek literary heritage that is known today.

> In the twelfth and thirteenth centuries none of the great Greek literary masterpieces and practically none of the major works of Plato were yet known. Nor could more than a handful of medieval Westerners read the Greek language.

Second, Renaissance thinkers not only knew many more classical texts than their medieval counterparts, but they used them in new ways. Whereas medieval writers presumed that their ancient sources would complement and confirm their own Christian assumptions, Renaissance writers were more aware of the conceptual and chronological gap that separated their own world from that of their classical sources. At the same time, however, similarities between the ancient city-states and those of Renaissance Italy encouraged Italian thinkers to find in these ancient sources models of thought and action directly applicable to their own day. This firm determination to learn from classical antiquity was even more pronounced in the realms of architecture and art, areas in which classical models contributed most strikingly to the creation of fully distinct "Renaissance" styles.

Third, although Renaissance culture was by no means pagan, it was more worldly and overtly materialistic than was the culture of the twelfth and thirteenth centuries. Italian city-states stressed the importance of the urban political arena and of living well in this world. Such ideals helped to create a culture that was increasingly nonecclesiastical. The relative weakness of the church in Italy also contributed to the more secular culture that emerged there. Italian bishoprics were small, and for the most part poorly endowed. Italian universities were also largely independent of ecclesiastical supervision and control. Even the papacy was severely limited in its ability to intervene in the cultural life of the Italian city-states. All these factors helped to create a space within which the worldly, materialistic culture of the Renaissance could emerge effectively untrammelled by ecclesiastical opposition.

RENAISSANCE HUMANISM

One word above all comes closest to summing up Renaissance intellectual ideals, namely *humanism*. Renaissance humanism was a program of studies that aimed to replace the thirteenth- and fourteenth-century scholastic emphasis on logic and metaphysics with the study of language, literature, rhetoric, history, and ethics. Most humanists regarded vernacular literature as at best a diversion for the uneducated. Serious scholarship and literature could only be written in Latin or Greek. That Latin, moreover, had to be the Latin of Cicero and Virgil. Renaissance humanists were self-conscious elitists who condemned the living Latin of their scholastic contemporaries as a barbarous departure from ancient (and therefore correct) standards of Latin style. Despite their belief that they were thereby reviving the study of the classics, the humanists' position was thus inherently ironic. By insisting on ancient standards of Latin grammar, syntax, and word choice, the humanists of the Renaissance succeeded ultimately in turning Latin into a fossilized language that thereafter ceased to evolve. They thus contributed, quite unwittingly, to the ultimate triumph of the European vernaculars as the primary languages of intellectual and cultural life.

> By insisting on ancient standards of Latin grammar, syntax, and word choice, the humanists of the Renaissance succeeded ultimately in turning Latin into a fossilized language that thereafter ceased to evolve.

Humanists were convinced that their own educational program—which placed the study of Latin language and literature at the core of the curriculum and then encouraged students to go on to Greek—was the best way to produce virtuous citizens and able public officials. Their elitism was to this extent intensely practical, and directly connected to the political life of the city-states in which they lived. Because women were excluded from Italian political life, the education of women was therefore of little concern to most humanists, although some aristocratic women did acquire humanist training. As more and more fifteenth century city-states fell into the hands of princes, however, the humanist educational curriculum lost its immediate connection to the republican ideals of Italian political life. Nevertheless, humanists never lost their conviction that the study of the "humanities" (as the humanist curriculum came to be known) was the best way to produce leaders for European society.

THE RENAISSANCE IN ITALY

Why did the Renaissance occur in Italy?

Although the Renaissance eventually became a Europe-wide intellectual and artistic movement, it developed first and most distinctively in fourteenth- and fifteenth-

century Italy. Understanding why this was so is important not only to explaining the origins of this movement, but also to understanding its fundamental characteristics.

THE ORIGINS OF THE ITALIAN RENAISSANCE

The Renaissance originated in Italy for several reasons. The most fundamental reason was that Italy in the later Middle Ages was the most advanced urban society in all of Europe. Unlike aristocrats north of the Alps, Italian aristocrats customarily lived in urban centers rather than in rural castles and consequently became fully involved in urban public affairs. The Italian aristocracy was also less sharply set off from the class of rich merchants than in the north. In Italy so many town-dwelling aristocrats engaged in banking or mercantile enterprises and so many rich mercantile families imitated the manners of the aristocracy that by the fourteenth and fifteenth centuries the aristocracy and upper bourgeoisie were becoming virtually indistinguishable. The noted Florentine family of the Medici, for example, emerged as a family of physicians (as the name suggests), made its fortune in banking and commerce, and rose into the aristocracy in the fifteenth century. The results of these developments for the history of education are obvious: not only was there a great demand for education in the skills of reading and counting necessary to become a successful merchant, but the richest and most prominent families sought above all to find teachers who would impart to their sons the knowledge and skills necessary to argue well in the public arena. Consequently, Italy produced a large number of lay educators, many of whom not only taught students but also demonstrated their learning by producing political and ethical treatises and works of literature. Italian schools created the best-educated upper-class public in all of Europe, along with wealthy patrons ready to invest in new ideas and new forms of literary and artistic expression.

The Italian Renaissance could not have occurred without the underpinning of Italian wealth. The Italian economy as a whole was probably more prosperous in the thirteenth century than it was in the fourteenth and fifteenth. But late medieval Italy was wealthier in comparison with the rest of Europe than it had been before, a fact that meant that Italian writers and artists

THE HUMANISTS' EDUCATIONAL PROGRAM

These three selections illustrate the confidence of civic humanists such as Vergerius, Bruni, and Alberti that their elite educational program would be of supreme value to the state as well as to the individual students who pursued it. Not everyone agreed with the humanists' claims, however, and a good deal of self-promotion lies behind them..

VERGERIUS ON LITERAL STUDIES

We call those studies *liberal* which are worthy of a free man; those studies by which we attain and practice virtue and wisdom; that education which calls forth, trains, and develops those highest gifts of body and of mind which ennoble men, and which are rightly judged to rank next in dignity to virtue only. . . . It is, then, of the highest importance that even from infancy this aim, this effort, should constantly be kept alive in growing minds. For . . . we shall not have attained wisdom in our later years unless in our earliest we have sincerely entered on its search. [P. P. Vergerius (1370–1444), *"Concerning Excellent Traits"*]

ALBERTI ON THE IMPORTANCE OF LITERATURE

Letters are indeed so important that without them one would be considered nothing but a rustic, no matter how much a gentlemen [he may be by birth]. I'd much rather see a young nobleman with a book than with a falcon in his hand. . . .

Be diligent, then, you young people, in your studies. Do all you can to learn about the events of the past that are worthy of memory. Try to understand all the useful things that have been passed on to you. Feed your minds on good maxims. Learn the delights of embellishing your souls with good morals. Strive to be kind and considerate [of others] when conducting civil business. Get to know those things human and divine that have been put at your disposal in books for good reason. Nowhere [else] will you find . . . the elegance of a verse of Homer, or Virgil, or of some other excellent poet. You will find no field so delightful or flowering as in one of the orations of Demosthenes, Cicero, Livy, Xenophon, and other such pleasant and perfect orators. No effort is more fully compensated . . . as the constant reading and rereading of good things. From such reading you will rise rich in good maxims and good arguments, strong in your ability to persuade others and get them to listen to you; among the citizens you will willingly be heard, admired, praised, and loved. [Leon Battista Alberti (1404–1472), *"On the Family"*]

BRUNI ON THE HUMANIST CURRICULUM

The foundations of all true learning must be laid in the sound and thorough knowledge of Latin: which implies study marked by a broad spirit, accurate scholarship, and careful attention to details. Unless this solid basis be secured it is useless to attempt to rear an enduring edifice. Without it the great monuments of literature are unintelligible, and the art of composition impossible. To attain this essential knowledge we must never relax our careful attention to the grammar of the language, but perpetually confirm and extend our acquaintance with it until it is thoroughly our own. . . .

But the wider question now confronts us, that of the subject matter of our studies, that which I have already called the realities of fact and principle, as distinct from literary form. . . . First among such studies I place History: a subject which must not on any account be neglected by one who aspires to true cultivation. . . . For the careful study of the past enlarges our foresight in contemporary affairs and affords to citizens and to monarchs lessons . . . in the ordering of public policy. From History, also, we draw our store of examples of moral precepts. . . .

The great Orators of antiquity must by all means be included. Nowhere do we find the virtues more warmly extolled, the vices so fiercely decried. From them we may learn, also, how to express consolation, encouragement, dissuasion or advice. . . .

Familiarity with the great poets of antiquity is essential to any claim to true education. For in their writings we find deep speculations upon Nature, and upon the Causes and Origins of things, which must carry weight with us both from their antiquity and from their authorship. . . .

Proficiency in literary form, not accompanied by broad acquaintance with facts and truths, is a barren attainment; whilst information, however vast, which lacks all grace of expression would seem to be put under a bushel or partly thrown away. . . . Where, however, this double capacity exists—breadth of learning and grace of style—we allow the highest title to distinction and to abiding fame. . . . [Leonardo Bruni (1369–1444), *"Concerning the Study of Literature"*]

Vergerius and Bruni: William Harrison Woodward, ed., *Vittorino da Feltre and Other Humanist Educators*. (London: Cambridge University Press, 1897), pp. 96–110, 124–129, 132–133. Alberti: Eric Cochrane and Julius Kirshner, eds. *University of Chicago Readings in Western Civilization*, Vol. 5: *The Renaissance*. (Chicago: University of Chicago Press, 1986), pp. 81–82.

were more likely to stay at home than to seek employment abroad. During the fourteenth century, cities themselves were the primary patrons of art and learning. During the fifteenth century, however, when most Italian city-states succumbed to the hereditary rule of noble families, patronage was monopolized by the princely aristocracy. Among these great princes were the popes in Rome, who employed the greatest artists of the day and for a few decades made Rome the artistic capital of Western Europe.

THE ITALIAN RENAISSANCE: LITERATURE AND THOUGHT

In surveying the accomplishments of Italian Renaissance scholars and writers it is natural to begin with the work of Petrarch (Francesco Petrarca, 1304–1374), the "father of Renaissance humanism." Petrarch was a deeply committed Catholic who believed that scholasticism was entirely misguided because it concentrated on abstract speculation rather than on teaching people how to live virtuously and attain salvation. Petrarch thought that the Christian writer should cultivate literary eloquence so that he could inspire people to do good. For him the best models of eloquence were to be found in the classical texts of Latin literature, which were doubly valuable because they were also filled with ethical wisdom. Petrarch dedicated himself, therefore, to rediscovering such texts and to writing his own poems and moral treatises in a Latin style modeled on classical authors. But Petrarch was also a remarkable vernacular poet. The Italian sonnets—later called Petrarchan sonnets—that he wrote for his beloved Laura in the chivalrous style of the troubadours were widely imitated and admired throughout the Renaissance period, and continue to be read today.

Because he was a very traditional Christian, Petrarch's ultimate ideal for human conduct was the solitary life of contemplation and asceticism. But from about 1400 to 1450, Italian thinkers and scholars, located mainly in Florence, developed a different vision customarily called civic humanism. Civic humanists such as the Florentines Leonardo Bruni (c. 1370–1444) and Leon Battista Alberti (1404–1472) agreed with Petrarch on the need for eloquence and the value of classical literature, but they also taught that man's nature equipped him for action, for usefulness to his family and society, and for serving the state—ideally a republican city-state after the classical or contemporary Florentine model. In their view ambition and the quest for glory were noble impulses that ought to be encouraged. They refused to condemn the striving for material possessions, for they argued that the history of human progress is inseparable from our success in mastering the earth and its resources.

Perhaps the most famous of the civic humanists' writings is Alberti's *On the Family* (1443), in which he argued that the nuclear family was instituted by nature for the well-being of humanity. Within this framework, however, Alberti consigned women to purely domestic roles, asserting that "man [is] by nature more energetic and industrious," and that woman was created "to increase and continue generations, and to nourish and preserve those already born." Although such dismissals of women's intellectual abilities were fiercely resisted by a few notable women humanists, for the most part Italian Renaissance humanism was characterized by a pervasive denigration of women—a denigration expressed also in the works of classical literature that the humanists so much admired.

THE EMERGENCE OF TEXTUAL SCHOLARSHIP

The civic humanists also went far beyond Petrarch in their knowledge of classical (and especially Greek) literature and philosophy. In this they were aided by Byzantine scholars who migrated to Italy in the first half of the fifteenth century and gave instruction in the Greek language. Italian scholars also traveled to Constantinople and other Eastern cities in search of Greek masterpieces hitherto unknown in the West. By 1500, most of the Greek classics, including the writings of Plato, the dramatists, and the historians, were available to western Europe.

The greatest of these textual scholars, Lorenzo Valla (1407–1457), had no allegiance to the republican ideals of the Florentine civic humanists. Instead, he used his skills in grammar, rhetoric, and the painstaking analysis of Greek and Latin texts to show how the thorough study of language could discredit old verities. Most remarkable in this regard was Valla's brilliant demonstration that the Donation of Constantine was a medieval forgery. Whereas papal propagandists had argued that the papacy's rights to temporal rule in western Europe derived from this charter purportedly granted by the emperor Constantine in the fourth century, Valla proved that the charter was full of nonclassical Latin usages and anachronistic terms. Hence he concluded that the "Donation" was the work of a medieval forger whose "monstrous impudence" was exposed by the "stupidity of his language." Valla also applied his expert knowledge of Greek to elucidating the true meaning of Saint Paul's letters, which he

believed had been obscured by Saint Jerome's Latin Vulgate translation. This work was to prove an important link between Italian Renaissance scholarship and the subsequent Christian humanism of the north.

RENAISSANCE NEOPLATONISM

From about 1450 until about 1600 Italian thought was dominated by a school of Neoplatonists who sought to blend the thought of Plato, Plotinus, and various strands of ancient mysticism with Christianity. Foremost among these were Marsilio Ficino (1433–1499) and Giovanni Pico della Mirandola (1463–1494), both of whom were members of the Platonic Academy founded by Cosimo de' Medici in Florence. From the standpoint of posterity, Ficino's greatest achievement was his translation of Plato's works into Latin, which made them widely available to western Europeans for the first time. Ficino himself, however, regarded his *Hermetic Corpus*, a collection of passages drawn from a number of ancient mystical writings including the Hebrew Kabbalah, as his greatest contribution to learning.

Pico della Mirandola. When the young nobleman Pico arrived in Florence at age nineteen he was said to have been "of beauteous feature and shape." This contemporary portrait may have been done by the great Florentine painter Botticelli.

SOME RENAISSANCE ATTITUDES TOWARD WOMEN

Italian society in the fourteenth and fifteenth centuries was characterized by marriage patterns in which men in their late twenties or thirties customarily married women in their mid- to late teens. This demographic fact probably contributed to the widely shared belief in this period that wives were essentially children, who could not be trusted with important matters and who were best trained by being beaten. Renaissance humanism did little to change such attitudes. In some cases, it even reinforced them.

After my wife had been settled in my house a few days, and after her first pangs of longing for her mother and family had begun to fade, I took her by the hand and showed her around the whole house. I explained that the loft was the place for grain and that the stores of wine and wood were kept in the cellar. I showed her where things needed for the table were kept, and so on, through the whole house. At the end there were no household goods of which my wife had not learned both the place and the purpose. . . .

Only my books and records and those of my ancestors did I determine to keep well sealed. . . . These my wife not only could not read, she could not even lay hands on them. I kept my records at all times . . . locked up and arranged in order in my study, almost like sacred and religious objects. I never gave my wife permission to enter that place, with me or alone. . . .

[Husbands] who take counsel with their wives . . . are madmen if they think true prudence or good counsel lies in the female brain. . . . For this very reason I have always tried carefully not to let any secret of mine be known to a woman. I did not doubt that my wife was most loving, and more discreet and modest in her ways than any, but I still considered it safer to have her unable, and not merely unwilling, to harm me. . . . Furthermore, I made it a rule never to speak with her of anything but household matters or questions of conduct, or of the children.

Leon Batista Alberti, "On the Family," in *The Family in Renaissance Florence*, translated and edited by Renée N. Watkins. (Columbia: University of South Carolina Press, 1969), pp. 208–213, as abridged in *Not in God's Image: Women in History from the Greeks to the Victorians*, edited by Julia O'Faolain and Lauro Martines. (New York: Harper & Row, 1973), pp. 187–188.

It is debatable whether Ficino's own philosophy should be called humanist because he moved away from ethics to metaphysics and taught that the individual should look primarily to the hereafter. The same issue arises with respect to Ficino's disciple Giovanni Pico della Mirandola. Pico was certainly not a civic humanist, since he saw little worth in mundane public affairs. He also fully shared his teacher's penchant for extracting and combining snippets taken out of context from ancient mystical tracts. But he did also believe—and so argued in his famous *Oration on the Dignity of Man*—that there is "nothing more wonderful than man" because he believed that man is endowed with the capacity to achieve union with God if he so wills.

MACHIAVELLI

Hardly any of the Italian thinkers between Petrarch and Pico were really original: their greatness lay mostly in their manner of expression. The same, however, cannot be said of Renaissance Italy's greatest political philosopher, the Florentine Niccolò Machiavelli (1469–1527). Machiavelli's writings reflect the unstable condition of Italy in his time. Both France and Spain had invaded the peninsula and were competing for the allegiance of the Italian city-states, which were torn by internal dissension. In 1498 Machiavelli became a prominent official in the government of the Florentine republic, set up four years earlier when the French invasion had led to the expulsion of the Medici. His duties largely involved diplomatic missions to other Italian city-states. While in Rome he became fascinated with the attempt of Cesare Borgia, son of Pope Alexander VI, to create his own principality in central Italy. He noted with approval Cesare's ruthlessness and shrewdness, and his complete subordination of personal morality to political ends. In 1512 the Medici returned to overthrow the republic of Florence, and Machiavelli was deprived of his position. Disappointed and embittered, he spent the remainder of his life at his country estate, devoting his time to writing.

Machiavelli remains a controversial figure even today. Some modern scholars see him as an amoral theorist of *realpolitik*, disdainful of morality and Christian piety, caring nothing about the proper purposes of political life, but interested solely in the acquisition and exercise of power as an end in itself. Others see him as an Italian patriot, who viewed princely tyranny as the only way to liberate Italy from its foreign conquerors. Still others see him as a follower of Saint Augustine of Hippo, who understood that in a fallen world populated by sinful people, a ruler's good intentions do not guarantee that his policies will have good results. Instead, Machiavelli insisted that a prince's actions must be judged by their consequences and not by their intrinsic moral quality. Human beings, Machiavelli argued, "are ungrateful, fickle, and deceitful, eager to avoid dangers, and avid for gain." This being so, "the necessity of preserving the state will often compel a prince to take actions which are opposed to loyalty, charity, humanity, and religion. . . . So far as he is able, a prince should stick to the path of good but, if the necessity arises, he should know how to follow evil."

The puzzle is heightened by the fact that, on the surface, Machiavelli's two great works of political analysis appear to contradict each other. In his *Discourses on Livy* he praised the ancient Roman republic as a model for his own contemporaries, lauding constitutional government, equality among the citizens of a republic, political independence for city-states, and the subordination of religion to the service of the state. There is little doubt, therefore, that Machiavelli was a committed republican, who believed in the free city-state as the ideal form of human government. But Machiavelli also wrote *The Prince*, "a handbook for tyrants" in the eyes of his critics, and he dedicated this work to Lorenzo, son of Piero de' Medici, whose family had overthrown the Florentine republic that Machiavelli himself had served.

Because *The Prince* has been so much more widely read than the *Discourses*, interpretations of Machiavelli's political thought have often mistaken the admiration he expressed in *The Prince* for Cesare Borgia as an endorsement of princely tyranny for its own sake. Machiavelli's real position was quite different. In the political chaos of early sixteenth-century Italy, Machiavelli saw a ruthless prince such as Borgia as the only hope for revitalizing the spirit of independence among his contemporaries, and so making them fit, once again, for republican self-rule. However dark his vision of human nature, Machiavelli never ceased to hope that his Italian contemporaries would rise up, expel their French and Spanish conquerors, and restore their ancient traditions of republican liberty and equality. Princes such as Borgia were necessary steps toward that end, but for Machiavelli, their rule was not the ideal form of government for humankind. In Italy's sunken political situation, however, a princely state such as Borgia's was the best form of government toward which Machiavelli's downtrodden contemporaries could aspire.

> In the political chaos of early sixteenth-century Italy, Machiavelli saw a ruthless prince such as Borgia as the only hope for revitalizing the spirit of independence among his contemporaries, and so making them fit, once again, for republican self-rule.

THE IDEAL OF THE COURTIER

Far more congenial to contemporary tastes than the shocking political theories of Machiavelli were the guidelines for proper aristocratic conduct offered in *The Book of the Courtier* (1528) by the diplomat and count

CHRONOLOGY

LIVES OF ITALIAN RENAISSANCE SCHOLARS AND ARTISTS

Petrarch	1304–1374
Leon Battista Alberti	1404–1472
Giovanni Pico della Mirandola	1463–1494
Niccolò Machiavelli	1469–1527
Leonardo da Vinci	1452–1519
Titian	c. 1490–1576
Raphael	1483–1520
Michelangelo	1475–1564

Baldassare Castiglione. This cleverly written forerunner of modern handbooks of etiquette stands in sharp contrast to the earlier civic humanist treatises of Bruni and Alberti, for whereas they taught the sober "republican" virtues of strenuous service in behalf of city-state and family, Castiglione, writing in an Italy dominated by magnificent princely courts, taught how to attain the elegant and seemingly effortless qualities necessary for acting like a "true gentleman." More than anyone else, Castiglione popularized the ideal of the "Renaissance man": one who is accomplished in many different pursuits and is also brave, witty, and "courteous," meaning civilized and learned. Widely read throughout Europe for over a century after its publication, Castiglione's *Courtier* spread Italian ideals of "civility" to princely courts north of the Alps, resulting in the ever-greater patronage of art and literature by the European aristocracy.

THE ITALIAN RENAISSANCE: PAINTING, SCULPTURE, AND ARCHITECTURE

What were the principal charactersitcs of Italian Renaissance art?

Despite numerous intellectual and literary advances, the longest-lived achievements of the Italian Renaissance were made in the realm of art. Of all the arts, painting was undoubtedly supreme. We have already seen the artistic genius of Giotto around 1300, but it was not until the fifteenth century that Italian painting began to come fully of age. One reason for this was that in the early fifteenth century the laws of linear perspective were discovered and first employed to give the fullest sense of three dimensions. Fifteenth-century artists also experimented with effects of light and shade (*chiaroscuro*) and for the first time carefully studied the anatomy and proportions of the human body. By the fifteenth century, too, increasing private wealth and the growth of lay patronage had opened the domain of art to a variety of nonreligious themes and subjects. Artists sought to paint portraits that revealed the hidden mysteries of the soul. Paintings intended to appeal primarily to the intellect were paralleled by others whose main purpose was to delight the eye with gorgeous color and beauty of form. The introduction of painting in oil, probably from Flanders, also had much to do with the artistic advance of this period. Since oil does not dry as quickly as fresco pigment, the painter could now work more slowly, taking time with the more difficult parts of the picture and making corrections as he or she went along.

RENAISSANCE PAINTING IN FLORENCE

The majority of the great painters of the fifteenth century were Florentines. First among them was the precocious Masaccio (1401–1428). Masaccio's greatness as a painter is based on his success in "imitating nature," which became a primary value in Renaissance painting. To achieve this effect he employed perspective, perhaps most dramatically in his fresco of the Trinity; he also used chiaroscuro with strikingly dramatic effects.

Masaccio's best-known successor was the Florentine Sandro Botticelli (1445–1510), who depicted both classical and Christian subjects. Botticelli's work excels in linear rhythms and sensuous depiction of natural detail. He is most famous for paintings that portray figures from classical mythology without any overtly Christian frame of reference. His *Allegory of Spring* and *Birth of Venus* were once understood as the expression of "Renaissance paganism" at its fullest, a celebration of earthly delights breaking sharply with Christian asceticism. More recently, however, scholars have preferred to view them as allegories fully compatible with Christian teachings. Although Botticelli's works remain cryptic, two points remain certain: any viewer is free to

Medici ruler of the city, Lorenzo the Magnificent. But if Leonardo had any weakness, it was his slowness in working and difficulty in finishing anything. This naturally displeased Lorenzo and other Florentine patrons, who thought an artist was little more than an artisan, commissioned to produce a certain piece of work of a certain size for a certain price on a certain date. Leonardo, however, strongly objected to this view because he considered himself to be no menial craftsman but an inspired creator. Therefore in 1482 he left Florence for the Sforza court of Milan where he was given freer rein in structuring his time and work. He remained there until the French invaded Milan in 1499; after that he wandered about Italy, finally ac-

The Impact of Perspective. Masaccio's painting *The Trinity with the Virgin* illustrates the startling sense of depth made possible by the rules of perspective.

enjoy them on their naturalistic sensuous level, and Botticelli had surely not broken with Christianity, since he painted frescoes for the pope in Rome at just the same time.

LEONARDO DA VINCI

Perhaps the greatest of the Florentine artists was Leonardo da Vinci (1452–1519), one of the most versatile geniuses who ever lived. Leonardo personified the "Renaissance man": he was a painter, architect, musician, mathematician, engineer, and inventor. The illegitimate son of a notary and a peasant woman, Leonardo set up an artist's shop in Florence by the time he was twenty-five and gained the patronage of the

The Virgin of the Rocks, by Leonardo da Vinci. This painting reveals Leonardo's interest in the human face and in the atmosphere of natural settings.

The Last Supper, by Leonardo da Vinci.

cepting the patronage of the French king, Francis I, under whose auspices Leonardo lived and worked in France until his death.

The paintings of Leonardo da Vinci began what is known as the High Renaissance in Italy. Leonardo painted like a naturalist, basing his work on his own detailed observations of a blade of grass, the wing of a bird, a waterfall. Leonardo worshiped nature, and was convinced of the essential divinity in all living things. It is not surprising, therefore, that he was a vegetarian, and that he went to the marketplace to buy caged birds, which he released to their native habitat.

It is generally agreed that Leonardo's masterpieces are the *Virgin of the Rocks* (which exists in two versions), the *Last Supper,* and his portraits of the Mona Lisa and Ginevra da Benci. *The Virgin of the Rocks* typifies not only his marvelous technical skill but also his passion for science and his belief in the universe as a well-ordered place. The *Last Supper,* is a study of psychological reactions. A serene Christ, resigned to his terrible fate, has just announced to his disciples that one of them will betray him. The artist succeeds in portraying the mingled emotions of surprise, horror, and guilt in the faces of the disciples as they gradually perceive the meaning of their master's statement. The third and fourth of Leonardo's major triumphs, the *Mona Lisa* and *Ginevra da Benci,* reflect a similar interest in the varied moods of the human soul.

THE VENETIAN SCHOOL

The beginning of the High Renaissance around 1490 also witnessed the rise of the so-called Venetian school, the major members of which were Giovanni Bellini (c. 1430–1516), Giorgione (1478–1510), and Titian (c. 1490–1576). The work of all these men reflected the luxurious, pleasure-loving life of the thriving commercial city of Venice. Most Venetian painters showed little of the Florentine school's concerns with philosophical and psychological issues. Their aim was to appeal to the senses by painting idyllic landscapes and sumptuous portraits of the rich and powerful. In the subordination of form and meaning to color and elegance their paintings mirrored the grandiose tastes of the wealthy merchants for whom they were created.

PAINTING IN ROME

High Renaissance painting reached its peak in the first half of the sixteenth century. During this period, Rome became the major artistic center of the Italian peninsula, although the traditions of the Florentine school still exerted a potent influence.

RAPHAEL

Among the eminent painters of this period was Raphael (1483–1520), a native of Urbino, and perhaps the most

The School of Athens, by Raphael.

beloved artist of the entire Renaissance. The lasting appeal of his style is due primarily to his ennobling portrayals of human beings as temperate, wise, and dignified creatures. Although Raphael was influenced by Leonardo, he cultivated a much more allegorical approach to his painting. His *Disputà* illustrated the relationship between the church in heaven and the church on earth. In a worldly setting against a brilliant sky, theologians debate the meaning of the Eucharist, while in the clouds above, saints and the Trinity repose in the possession of a holy mystery. Raphael's *School of Athens* depicts the harmony between Platonism and Aristotelianism. Plato (painted as a portrait of Leonardo) is shown pointing upward to emphasize the spiritual basis of his world of Ideas, while Aristotle stretches a hand forward to exemplify his claim that the created world embodies these same principles in physical form. Raphael is noted also for his portraits and Madonnas. To the latter, especially, he gave a softness and warmth that seemed to endow them with a sweetness and piety quite different from Leonardo's enigmatic and somewhat distant Madonnas.

MICHELANGELO

The last towering figure of the High Renaissance was Michelangelo (1475–1564), a native of Florence. If Leonardo was a naturalist, Michelangelo was an idealist; where the former sought to recapture and interpret fleeting natural phenomena, Michelangelo was more concerned with expressing enduring, abstract truths. Michelangelo was a painter, sculptor, architect, and poet—and he expressed himself in all these forms with a similar power and in a similar manner. At the center of all of his paintings is the male figure, which is always powerful, colossal, magnificent. If humanity, embodied in the male body, lay at the center of Italian Renaissance culture, then Michelangelo, who depicted the male figure without cease, is the supreme Renaissance artist.

The Creation of Adam, by Michelangelo (1475–1564). One of a series of frescoes on the ceiling of the Sistine Chapel in Rome. Inquiring into the nature of humanity, it represents Renaissance affirmativeness at its height.

Michelangelo's greatest achievements in painting appear in a single location—the Sistine Chapel in Rome—yet they are products of two different periods in the artist's life and consequently exemplify two different artistic styles and outlooks on the human condition. More famous are the sublime frescoes Michelangelo painted on the ceiling of the Sistine Chapel from 1508 to 1512, depicting scenes from the book of Genesis. All the panels in this series, including *God Dividing the Light from Darkness, The Creation of Adam,* and *The Flood,* exemplify the young artist's commitment to classical Greek aesthetic principles of harmony, solidity, and dignified restraint. But a quarter of a century later, when Michelangelo returned to work in the Sistine

Chapel, both his style and mood had changed dramatically. In the enormous *Last Judgment,* a fresco done for the Sistine Chapel's altar wall in 1536, Michelangelo repudiated classical restraint and substituted a style that emphasized tension and distortion in order to communicate the older man's pessimistic conception of a humanity wracked by fear and bowed by guilt.

SCULPTURE

The Italian Renaissance took a great step forward by creating statues that were no longer carved as parts of columns or doorways on church buildings or as effigies on tombs. Instead, Italian sculptors for the first time since antiquity carved free-standing statues "in the round." By freeing sculpture from its bondage to architecture the High Renaissance re-established sculpture as a separate and potentially secular art form.

DONATELLO

The first great master of Renaissance sculpture was Donatello (c. 1386–1466). His bronze statue of David triumphant over the head of the slain Goliath imitated classical sculpture not just in the depiction of a nude body, but also in the subject's posture of resting his weight on one leg. Yet this David is clearly a lithe ado-

lescent rather than a muscular Greek athlete. Later in his career, Donatello more consciously imitated ancient statuary in his commanding portrayal of the proud warrior Gattamelata—the first monumental equestrian statue in bronze executed in the West since the time of the Romans.

MICHELANGELO

Michelangelo regarded sculpture as the most exalted of the arts because it allowed the artist to imitate God most fully in recreating human forms. But Michelangelo disdained slavish naturalism. Instead, he subordi-

David, by Donatello (c. 1386–1466). The first free-standing nude statue executed in the West since antiquity.

David, by Michelangelo. Over thirteen feet high, this serenely self-confident affirmation of the beauty of the human form was placed prominently by the Florentine government in front of Florence's city hall to proclaim the city's humanistic values.

nated naturalism to the force of his imagination and sought restlessly to express his ideals in ever more arresting forms.

Like his painting, Michelangelo's sculpture followed a course from classicism to mannerism, that is, from harmonious modeling to dramatic distortion. The sculptor's most distinguished early work, his *David*, executed in 1501, is surely his most perfect classical statue. By sculpting a serenely confident young man at the peak of physical fitness, Michelangelo celebrated the Florentine republic's own "fortitude" in resisting tyrants and upholding ideals of civic justice. The serenity seen in *David* is no longer prominent in the works of Michelangelo's middle period; rather, in a work such as his *Moses* of about 1515, the sculptor has begun to explore the use of anatomical distortion to create effects of emotional intensity—in this case, the biblical prophet's righteous rage. As Michelangelo's life drew to a close he experimented more and more with exaggerated stylistic mannerisms for the purpose of communicating moods of brooding pensiveness or outright pathos. The culmination of this trend in Michelangelo's statuary is his unfinished but intensely moving *Descent from the Cross*, a depiction of an old man resembling the sculptor himself grieving over the distorted, slumping body of the dead Christ.

ARCHITECTURE

To a much greater extent than either sculpture or painting, Renaissance architecture had its roots in the past. The new building style was a compound of elements derived from the Middle Ages and from antiquity. The great architects of the Renaissance generally adopted their building plans from Romanesque churches, some of which they believed, mistakenly, to be Roman rather than medieval. They also copied their decorative devices from the ruins of ancient Rome. The result was an architecture based on the cruciform floor plan of transept and nave, but embodying the decorative features of the column and arch, the colonnade, and frequently the dome. Renaissance architecture also emphasized geometrical proportion because Italian builders, under the influence of Neoplatonism, concluded that certain mathematical ratios reflect the harmony of the universe. A fine example of Renaissance architecture is St. Peter's Basilica in Rome, built under the patronage of popes Julius II and Leo X and designed by some of the most celebrated architects of the time, including Donato Bramante (c. 1444–1514) and Michelangelo.

THE WANING OF THE ITALIAN RENAISSANCE

Why did the Renaissance decline around 1550?

Around 1550 the Renaissance in Italy began to decline. The causes of this decline were varied. The French invasion of 1494 and the incessant warfare that ensued was one of the major factors. The French king Charles VIII viewed Italy as an attractive target for his expansive dynastic ambitions. In 1494 he led an army of thirty thousand well-trained troops across the Alps to press his claims to the Duchy of Milan and the Kingdom of Naples. An alliance among Spain, the Papal States, the Holy Roman empire, Milan, and Venice finally forced Charles to withdraw from Italy. But the respite was brief. From 1499 until 1529 warfare in Italy was virtually uninterrupted. The worst disaster came in 1527 when rampaging troops under the command of the Spanish ruler and Holy Roman emperor Charles V sacked the city of Rome, causing enormous destruction. Only in 1529 did Charles V finally manage to gain control over most of the Italian peninsula, putting an end to the fighting for a time.

To political disasters was added a waning of Italian prosperity. Italy's virtual monopoly of trade with Asia in the fifteenth century had been one of the chief economic supports for Italian Renaissance culture, but the gradual shifting of trade routes from the Mediterranean to the Atlantic region, following the overseas discoveries of around 1500, slowly but surely cost Italy its supremacy as the center of European trade. As Italian wealth diminished, there was less and less of a surplus to support artistic endeavors.

A final cause of the decline of the Italian Renaissance was the Counter-Reformation. During the sixteenth century the Roman church sought increasingly to exercise firm control over thought and art as part of a campaign to combat worldliness and the spread of Protestantism. In 1542 the Roman Inquisition was established; in 1564 the first Roman Index of Prohibited Books was published. The determination of ecclesiastical censors to enforce doctrinal uniformity could even lead to death, as in the case of the unfortunate Neoplatonic philosopher Giordano Bruno, whose insistence that there may be more than one world (in contravention of the biblical book of

EUROPE

Area of detail

AFRICA

MILAN

Milan

Padua

Venice

DUCHY OF SAVOY

Asti

Piacenza

Po R.

DUCHY OF FERRARA

Genoa

Bologna

REPUBLIC OF GENOA

Florence

REPUBLIC OF LUCCA

Pisa

REPUBLIC OF FLORENCE

Siena

PAPAL STATES

REPUBLIC OF SIENA

CORSICA (to Genoa)

Rome

SARDINIA (to Spain)

Naples

KINGDOM OF THE TWO SICILIES

ADRIATIC SEA

OTTOMAN EMPIRE

VENETIAN REPUBLIC

TYRRHENIAN SEA

Palermo

MEDITERRANEAN SEA

0   50   100 Miles
0   50   100 Kilometers

THE STATES OF ITALY DURING THE RENAISSANCE, C. 1494

This map shows the political divisions of Italy on the eve of the French invasion in 1494. Contemporary observers often described Italy as being divided among five great powers: Milan, Venice, Florence, the Papal States, and the Kingdom of Naples. Which of these powers were most interested in expanding their territory? Which neighboring territories would be most threatened by such attempts at expansion? Why did Florence and the Papal States so often find themselves in conflict with each other?

Genesis) resulted in his being burned at the stake by the Roman Inquisition in 1600.

Cultural and artistic achievement was by no means extinguished in Italy after the middle of the sixteenth century. On the contrary, impressive new artistic styles were cultivated between about 1540 and 1600 by painters who drew on traits found in the later work of Raphael and Michelangelo. In the seventeenth century

HOW DID THE NORTHERN AND ITALIAN RENAISSANCES DIFFER FROM ONE ANOTHER?

THE RENAISSANCE IN THE NORTH   359

came the dazzling Baroque style, which was born in Rome under ecclesiastical auspices. Similarly, Italian music registered enormous accomplishments virtually without interruption from the sixteenth to the twentieth century. But as Renaissance culture spread from Italy to the rest of Europe, the cultural dominance of the Italians began to wane, and the focus of European high culture shifted toward the princely courts of Spain, France, England, Germany, and Poland.

THE RENAISSANCE IN THE NORTH

How did the northern and Italian Renaissances differ from one another?

Contacts between Italy and northern Europe continued throughout the fourteenth and fifteenth centuries. Only at the end of the fifteenth century, however, did the new currents of Italian Renaissance learning begin to take firm hold in Spain and northern Europe.

A variety of explanations have been offered for this delay. Northern European intellectual life in the late Middle Ages was dominated by universities whose curricula focused on the study of philosophical logic and Christian theology. This approach left little room for the study of classical literature. In Italy, by contrast, a more secular, urban-oriented educational tradition took shape within which Renaissance humanism was able to develop. Even in the sixteenth century, northern scholars influenced by Italian Renaissance ideals usually worked outside the university system. Northern rulers were also less interested in patronizing artists and intellectuals than were the city-states and princes of Italy. Only in the sixteenth century, as northern nobles began to spend more time in residence at the royal court, did kings begin to assume a really important role as cultural leaders and patrons.

CHRISTIAN HUMANISM AND THE NORTHERN RENAISSANCE

The northern Renaissance was the product of the grafting of certain Italian Renaissance ideals onto pre-existing northern traditions. This can be seen very clearly in the case of the most prominent northern Renaissance intellectual movement, Christian humanism. Although they shared the Italian humanists' contempt for scholasticism, northern Christian humanists more often looked for ethical guidance from biblical and religious precepts rather than from Cicero or Virgil. Like their Italian counterparts, they sought wisdom from antiquity, but the antiquity they had in mind was Christian rather than classical—the antiquity, that is, of the New Testament and the early church fathers. Northern Renaissance artists were inspired by the accomplishments of Italian masters, but they depicted classical subject matter far less frequently than did the Italians, and almost never portrayed completely nude human figures.

DESIDERIUS ERASMUS

Any discussion of northern Renaissance accomplishments in the realm of thought and literary expression must begin with the career of Desiderius Erasmus (c. 1469–1536), the "prince of the Christian humanists." The illegitimate son of a priest, Erasmus was born near Rotterdam in Holland, but later, as a result of his wide travels, became in effect a citizen of all northern Europe. Forced into a monastery against his will when he was a teenager, the young Erasmus found there little religion or formal instruction of any kind but plenty of freedom to read what he liked. He devoured all the classics he could get his hands on and the writings of many of the church fathers. When he was about thirty years of age, he obtained permission to leave the monastery and enroll in the University of Paris, where he completed the requirements for the degree of bachelor of divinity. But Erasmus subsequently rebelled against what he considered the arid learning of Parisian scholasticism. Nor did he ever serve actively as a priest. Instead he made his living from teaching, writing, and the proceeds of various ecclesiastical offices that required no spiritual duties of him. By means of a voluminous correspondence that he kept up with learned friends he made wherever he went, Erasmus became the leader of a northern European humanist coterie. And through the popularity of his numerous publications, he became the arbiter of northern European cultural tastes during his lifetime.

As a Latin prose stylist, Erasmus was unequaled since the days of Cicero. Above all, Erasmus excelled in the deft use of irony, poking fun at all and sundry, including himself. But although Erasmus's urbane

Erasmus, by Hans Holbein the Younger (1497–1543). This portrait is generally regarded as the most telling visual characterization of "the prince of the Christian humanists."

examination in a more serious but still pervasively ironic tone. The most prominent treatises in his second genre are the quietly eloquent *Handbook of the Christian Knight* (1503), which urged the laity to pursue lives of inward piety, and the *Complaint of Peace* (1517), which pleaded movingly for Christian pacifism. Erasmus's pacifism was one of his most deeply held values, and he returned to it again and again in his published works.

Despite the success of his literary works, Erasmus considered his textual scholarship his greatest achievement. Revering the authority of the early Latin fathers Augustine, Jerome, and Ambrose, he brought out reliable editions of all their works. He also used his extraordinary command of Latin and Greek to produce a more accurate edition of the New Testament. After reading Lorenzo Valla's *Notes on the New Testament* in 1504, Erasmus became convinced that nothing was more imperative than divesting the New Testament of the myriad errors in transcription and translation that had piled up during the Middle Ages, for no one could be a good Christian without being certain of exactly what Christ's message really was. Hence he spent ten years studying and comparing all the best early Greek biblical manuscripts he could find in order to establish an authoritative text. When it finally appeared in 1516, Erasmus's Greek New Testament, published together with explanatory notes and his own new Latin translation, was one of the most important landmarks of biblical scholarship of all time. In the hands of Martin Luther, it would play a critical role in the early stages of the Protestant Reformation.

SIR THOMAS MORE

One of Erasmus' closest friends, and a close second to him in distinction among the ranks of the Christian humanists, was the Englishman Sir Thomas More (1478–1535). Following a successful career as a lawyer and as speaker of the House of Commons, in 1529 More was appointed lord chancellor of England. He was not long in this position, however, before he incurred the wrath of King Henry VIII. More, who was loyal to Catholic universalism, opposed the king's design to establish a national church under royal control. Finally, in 1534, when More refused to take an oath acknowledging Henry as head of the Church of England, he was thrown into the Tower of London, and a year later met his death on the scaffold as a Catholic martyr. Much

Latin style and wit earned him a wide audience for purely literary reasons, he intended everything he wrote to promote what he called the "philosophy of Christ." Erasmus believed that the entire society of his day was caught up in corruption and immorality because people had lost sight of the simple teachings of the Gospels. Accordingly, he offered to his contemporaries three different categories of publication: clever satires meant to show people the error of their ways, serious moral treatises meant to offer guidance toward proper Christian behavior, and scholarly editions of basic Christian texts.

In the first category belong the works of Erasmus that are still most widely read today—*The Praise of Folly* (1509), in which he pilloried scholastic pedantry and dogmatism as well as the ignorance and superstitious credulity of the masses; and the *Colloquies* (1518), in which he held up contemporary religious practices for

HOW DID THE NORTHERN AND ITALIAN RENAISSANCES DIFFER FROM ONE ANOTHER?

THE RENAISSANCE IN THE NORTH   361

Sir Thomas More, by Hans Holbein the Younger.

THE DECLINE OF CHRISTIAN HUMANISM

The Englishman John Colet (c. 1467–1519), the Frenchman Jacques Lefèvre d'Étaples (c. 1455–1536), and the Spaniards Cardinal Francisco Ximénez de Cisneros (1436–1517) and Juan Luís Víves (1492–1540) also made signal contributions to the collective enterprise of editing biblical and early Christian texts and expounding Gospel morality. But despite a host of achievements, the Christian humanist movement, which possessed such an extraordinary degree of international solidarity and vigor from about 1500 to 1525, was thrown into disarray by the rise of Protestantism and subsequently lost its momentum. The irony here is obvious, for the Christian humanists' emphasis on the literal truth of the Gospels and their devastating criticisms of clerical corruption and religious ceremonialism certainly helped pave the way for the Protestant Reformation initiated by Martin Luther in 1517. But, as we will see in Chapter 13, very few of the older generation of Christian humanists were willing to join Luther in rejecting the fundamental principles on which Catholicism was based, and the few who did became such ardent Protestants that they lost the sense of quiet irony that had been a hallmark of Christian humanist expression. Most Christian humanists tried to remain within the Catholic fold while still espousing their ideal of nonritualistic inward piety. But as time went on, the leaders of Catholicism grew less and less tolerant because lines were hardening in the war with Protestantism. Hence, any internal criticism of Catholic religious practices seemed like giving covert aid to the "enemy." Erasmus himself, who remained a Catholic, died early enough to escape opprobrium, but several of his less fortunate followers lived on to suffer as victims of the Inquisition.

LITERATURE, ART, AND MUSIC IN THE NORTHERN RENAISSANCE

Yet if Christian humanism faded rapidly after about 1525, the northern Renaissance continued to flourish throughout the sixteenth century in literature and art. In France, Pierre de Ronsard (c. 1524–1585) and Joachim du Bellay (c. 1522–1560) wrote elegant sonnets in the style of Petrarch, and in England the poets Sir Philip Sidney (1554–1586) and Edmund Spenser

earlier, however, in 1516, long before More had any inkling of how his life was to end, he published the one work for which he will ever be best remembered, *Utopia*. Purporting to describe an ideal community on an imaginary island, the book is really an Erasmian critique of the glaring abuses of the time— poverty undeserved and wealth unearned, drastic punishments, religious persecution, and the senseless slaughter of war. The inhabitants of Utopia hold all their goods in common, work only six hours a day so that all may have leisure for intellectual pursuits, and practice the natural virtues of wisdom, moderation, fortitude, and justice. Iron is the precious metal "because it is useful," war and monasticism do not exist, and toleration is granted to all who recognize the existence of God and the immortality of the soul. Although More advanced no explicit arguments in his *Utopia* in favor of Christianity, he clearly meant to imply that if the "Utopians" could manage their society so well without the benefit of Christian revelation, Europeans who knew the Gospels ought to be able to do even better.

(c. 1552–1599) drew impressively on Italian literary innovations. Indeed, Spenser's *Faerie Queene*, a long chivalric romance written in the manner of Ariosto's *Orlando Furioso*, communicates as well as any Italian work the gorgeous sensuousness typical of Italian Renaissance culture.

More original than any of the aforementioned poets was the French prose satirist François Rabelais (c. 1494–1553), probably the best loved of all the great European creative writers of the sixteenth century. Like Erasmus, whom he greatly admired, Rabelais satirized religious ceremonialism, ridiculed scholasticism, scoffed at superstitions, and pilloried every form of bigotry. But unlike Erasmus, who wrote in a highly cultivated classical Latin style comprehensible to only the most learned readers, Rabelais chose to address a far wider audience by writing in an extremely down-to-earth French loaded with the crudest vulgarities. Yet, aside from the critical satire in *Gargantua and Pantagruel*, there runs through all five volumes a common theme of glorifying the human and the natural. For Rabelais, every instinct of humanity was healthy, provided it was not directed toward tyranny over others. Thus in his ideal community, the utopian "abbey of Thélème," there was no repressiveness whatsoever, but only a congenial environment for the pursuit of life-affirming, natural human attainments, guided by the single rule of "love and do what thou wouldst."

Saint Jerome in His Study, by Dürer. Saint Jerome, a hero to both Dürer and Erasmus, represents inspired Christian scholarship. Note how the scene exudes contentment, even down to the sleeping lion, which seems rather like an overgrown tabby cat.

PAINTING

The most moving visual embodiments of the ideals of Christian humanism were conceived by the foremost of northern Renaissance artists, the German Albrecht Dürer (1471–1528). Dürer was the first northerner to master Italian Renaissance techniques of proportion, perspective, and modeling. Dürer also shared the contemporary Italian fascination with reproducing the manifold works of nature down to the minutest details and a penchant for displaying the human nude in various postures. But whereas Michelangelo portrayed his *David* or *Adam* entirely without covering, Dürer's nudes are seldom lacking their fig leaves, in deference to more restrained northern traditions. Dürer was inspired primarily by the more traditionally Christian ideals of Erasmus. Thus Dürer's serenely radiant engraving of Saint Jerome expresses the sense of accomplishment that Erasmus or any other contemporary Christian humanist may have had while working quietly in his study; and his *Four Apostles* intones a solemn

hymn to the dignity and penetrating insight of Dürer's favorite New Testament authors, Saints Paul, John, Peter, and Mark.

MUSIC

Music in western Europe in the fifteenth and sixteenth centuries constitutes one of the most brilliant aspects of Renaissance endeavor. The musical theory of the Renaissance was driven largely by the humanist-inspired effort to recover and imitate classical musical forms and modes. Musical practice, however, showed much more continuity with medieval musical tradition. At the same time, however, a new expressiveness emerges in Renaissance music, along with a new emphasis on coloration and emotional quality. New musical instruments were also developed, including the lute, the viol, the violin, and the harpsichord. New musical forms also emerged: madrigals, motets, and, at the end of the sixteenth century, a new Italian form, the opera. As earlier, musical leadership came from men trained in the service of the church. But the distinction between sacred and profane music was becoming less sharp, and most composers did not restrict their activities to a single field. Music was no longer regarded merely as a diversion or an adjunct to worship, but came into its own as a serious independent art.

During the fourteenth century a pre- or early Renaissance musical movement called *ars nova* ("new art") flourished in Italy and France. Its outstanding composers were Francesco Landini (c. 1325–1397) and Guillaume de Machaut (c. 1300–1377). The fifteenth century ushered in a synthesis of French, Flemish, and Italian elements in the ducal court of Burgundy. As the sixteenth century opened, Franco-Flemish composers appeared in every important court and cathedral all over Europe, gradually establishing regional-national schools, usually in attractive combinations of Flemish with German, Spanish, and Italian musical cultures. Music also flourished in sixteenth-century England, where the Tudor monarchs Henry VIII and Elizabeth I were active patrons of the arts.

CONCLUSION

The contrasts between the Italian and the northern Renaissance are real, but they must not be exaggerated. The intellectuals of Renaissance Italy were formed in a more secular, more urban educational environment than were the northerners, but they were no less fervent in their Christianity. Petrarch's criticism of scholasticism was not that it was too Christian, but

rather that it was not Christian enough. Much the same point might be made about Lorenzo Valla. His critique of the temporal claims of the papacy sprang not only from the conclusions of his textual scholarship, but also from a firm Christian piety. The Platonic Academy might honor Plato as if he were a saint of the church, but these men approached Plato's works in the same spirit with which thirteenth century scholastic theologians had approached the works of Aristotle. As committed Christians, they were convinced that the conclusions reached by the greatest philosophical minds of classical antiquity must be compatible with Christian truth. It was the task of Christian intellectuals to reveal this compatibility, and by so doing, to strengthen the one true faith.

In considering the contrasts between "civic" and "Christian" humanism, we must also keep in mind the enormous diversity of Renaissance thought. Machiavelli is no more "typical" an Italian Renaissance thinker than is Ficino, Alberti, or Bruno. In comparing Italian thinkers with northern thinkers, we must therefore be careful to compare "like" with "like." Too often, scholars overdraw the contrasts between Renaissance thought in Italy and northern Europe by choosing Machiavelli to represent all of Italian humanism and Erasmus to represent northern humanism. Two more different figures can hardly be imagined; but their differences have much more to do with their contrasting presuppositions about human nature than with their "allegiances" to Italian or northern humanism. A very different picture emerges if we compare, for example, John Colet as a representative of northern humanism with Marsilio Ficino as a representative of Italian humanism, or compare Petrarch with Sir Thomas More.

Nor should we overdraw the contrasts between the Renaissance and the High Middle Ages. Both Italian and northern humanists shared an optimistic view of human nature as improvable despite the consequences of Adam and Eve's disobedience; but none were more optimistic on this score than was Saint Thomas Aquinas. Both groups emphasized the importance of personal introspection and self-examination; but none took this injunction more seriously than did the Cistercian thinkers of the twelfth century. And finally, both groups shared a belief that the exhortations of intellectuals would lift everyone's morals and conduct them to new heights of virtue. In this regard, High Renaissance intellectual life has a kind of naïve optimism that contrasts sharply with the darker, more psychologically complex world of the Middle Ages, and with the Reformation era that was about to begin.

KEY TERMS

humanism   Baldassare Castiglione   Erasmus

Medici   Leonardo da Vinci   Utopia

Petrarch   Raphael   Rabelais

The Prince   Michelangelo

SELECTED READINGS

Alberti, Leon Battista. *The Family in Renaissance Florence (Della Famiglia)*. Translated by Renée Neu Watkins. Columbia, S.C., 1969.

Baxandall, Michael. *Painting and Experience in Fifteenth Century Italy.* Oxford, 1972. A classic study of the perceptual world of the Renaissance.

Brucker, Gene. *Florence, the Golden Age, 1138–1737.* Berkeley and Los Angeles, 1998. The standard account by a master historian.

Bruni, Leonardo. *The Humanism of Leonardo Bruni: Selected Texts.* Translated by Gordon Griffiths, James Hankins, and David Thompson. Binghamton, N.Y., 1987. Excellent translations, with introductions, to the Latin works of a key Renaissance humanist.

Burke, Peter. *The Renaissance.* New York, 1997. A brief introduction by an influential modern historian.

———. *Culture and Society in Renaissance Italy,* 2d ed. Princeton, N.J., 1999. A revision and restatement of arguments first advanced in 1972.

Burkhardt, Jacob. *The Civilization of the Renaissance in Italy.* Many editions. The nineteenth-century work that first crystallized an image of the Italian Renaissance with which scholars have been wrestling ever since.

Cassirer, Ernst, et al., eds. *The Renaissance Philosophy of Man.* Chicago, 1948. Important original works by Petrarch, Ficino, and Pico della Mirandola, among others.

Castiglione, Baldassare. *The Book of the Courtier.* Many editions. The translations by C. S. Singleton (New York, 1959) and by George Bull (New York, 1967) are both excellent.

Cellini, Benvenuto. *Autobiography.* Translated by George Bull. Baltimore, 1956. The autobiography of a Florentine goldsmith (1500–1571); the source for many of the most famous stories about the artists of the Florentine Renaissance.

Cochrane, Eric, and Julius Kirshner, eds. *The Renaissance.* Chicago, 1986. An outstanding collection, from the University of Chicago Readings in Western Civilization series.

Erasmus, Desiderius. *The Praise of Folly.* Translated by J. Wilson. Ann Arbor, Mich., 1958.

Fox, Alistair. *Thomas More: History and Providence.* Oxford, 1982. A balanced account of a man too easily idealized.

Grafton, Anthony, and Lisa Jardine. *From Humanism to the Humanities: Education and the Liberal Arts in Fifteenth- and Sixteenth-Century Europe.* London, 1986. An influential account that presents Renaissance humanism as the elitist cultural program of a self-interested group of pedagogues.

Grendler, Paul, ed. *Encyclopedia of the Renaissance.* New York, 1999. A valuable reference work.

Hale, John R. *The Civilization of Europe in the Renaissance.* New York, 1993. A synthetic volume summarizing the life's work of a major Renaissance historian.

Hankins, James. *Plato in the Italian Renaissance.* Leiden and New York, 1990. A definitive study of the reception and influence of Plato on Renaissance intellectuals.

———, ed. *Renaissance Civic Humanism: Reappraisals and Reflections.* Cambridge and New York, 2000. An excellent collection of scholarly essays reassessing republicanism in the Renaissance.

Jardine, Lisa. *Worldly Goods.* London, 1996. A revisionist account that emphasizes the acquisitive materialism of Italian Renaissance society and culture.

Kanter, Laurence, Hilliard T. Goldfarb, and James Hankins. *Botticelli's Witness: Changing Style in a Changing Florence.* Boston, 1997. This catalogue, for an exhibit of Botticelli's works at the Gardner Museum in Boston, offers an excellent introduction to the painter and his world.

King, Margaret L. *Women of the Renaissance.* Chicago, 1991. Deals with women in all walks of life and in a variety of roles.

Kristeller, Paul. O. *Renaissance Thought: The Classic, Scholastic, and Humanistic Strains.* New York, 1961. Very helpful in defining the main trends of Renaissance thought.

———. *Eight Philosophers of the Italian Renaissance.* Stanford, 1964. An admirably clear and accurate account that fully appreciates the connections between medieval and Renaissance thought.

Lane, Frederic C. *Venice: A Maritime Republic.* Baltimore, 1973. An authoritative account.

Machiavelli, Niccolò. *The Discourses* and *The Prince.* Many editions. These two books must be read together if one is to understand Machiavelli's political ideas properly.

Martines, Lauro. *Power and Imagination: City-States in Renaissance Italy*. New York, 1979. Insightful account of the connections among politics, society, culture, and art.

More, Thomas. *Utopia*. Many editions.

Murray, Linda. *High Renaissance and Mannerism*. London, 1985. The place to start for fifteenth- and sixteenth-century Italian art.

Olson, Roberta, *Italian Renaissance Sculpture*, New York, 1992. The most accessible introduction to the subject.

Perkins, Leeman L. *Music in the Age of the Renaissance*. New York, 1999. A massive new study that nonetheless needs to be read in conjunction with Reese (see below).

Rabelais, François. *Gargantua and Pantagruel*. Translated by J. M. Cohen. Baltimore, 1955. A robust modern translation.

Reese, Gustave. *Music in the Renaissance*, rev. ed. New York, 1959. A great book; still authoritative, despite the more recent work by Perkins (see above), which supplements but does not replace it.

Rice, Eugene F., Jr., and Anthony Grafton. *The Foundations of Early Modern Europe, 1460–1559*, 2d ed. New York, 1994. The best textbook account of its period.

Rowland, Ingrid D. *The Culture of the High Renaissance: Ancients and Moderns in Sixteenth-Century Rome*. Cambridge and New York, 2000. Beautifully written examination of the social, intellectual, and economic foundations of the Renaissance in Rome.

SPICES

*It is strange that we Portuguese have gone to so much trouble and expense to
have all the world's pepper in our hands. We eat so little of it! Most of it is
consumed in Germany and France.*

—Garcia de Orta, *Colloquies*

Spices have been known to give pleasure, restore health, pay ransom, provoke human greed, and ultimately lead to war. Their use in food, festivity,
and medicine is well-known. But the spice trade is an ancient one. And
although we have come to regard pepper, cinnamon, cloves, and nutmeg as
everyday seasonings, at one time spices were a valuable commodity, even
more so than gold or silver. In the book of *Genesis* we learn that Joseph was
sold to spice merchants by his brothers. The ancient Egyptians used spices
for embalming. The Greeks flavored their wine with spices, and the Romans
were heavy pepper users. And Muhammad, the founder of Islam, was perhaps fortunate to have married the wealthy widow of a spice merchant.

Spices have helped cure dyspepsia, nausea, malaria, toothaches, and
hemorrhoids. Historical sources tell us that spices have been used as
insect repellents, perfumes, cosmetics, antidotes for poisons, and aphro-
disiacs. It is well known that in the age before refrigeration spices were
used as preservatives. But in the ancient world, judges were bribed with
tribute paid in sacks of pepper. And toward the end of the Roman
empire, Alaric I demanded three thousand pounds of pepper as a substantial portion of Rome's ransom.

The Arabs controlled the spice trade along the caravan route of the Silk
Road between Europe and the Far East, where the vast majority of spices
are found. Arab caravans with as many as four thousand camels carried
their precious cargo to markets in Nineveh, Babylon, Carthage, Alexandria,
and Rome. The exclusive control of the spice trade by the Arabs ended when
the Portuguese set up trading depots in the "riche and innumerable islands
of the Mollucos and the Spiceries," now known as the Spice Islands. The
Portuguese were soon followed by French, Dutch, British, and American
merchants. By the early 19th century, European merchants dominated trade
in Sumatran pepper, with profits sometimes as high as 700 percent!

The images and documents in the *Spices* Digital History Feature at www.wwnorton.com/wciv reveal how various cultures throughout history have used spices and the lengths they would go to acquire them. As you explore the *Spices* feature, consider the following:

• Why were spices such valuable commodities?

• Why did Portuguese interests in the spice trade decline steadily throughout the seventeenth century?

• Why were American trading families so interested in dominating the pepper trade?

• What is the relationship between the spice trade and the birth of seaborne empires in the seventeenth and eighteenth centuries?

Chapter Thirteen

Reformations of Religion

After two centuries of economic, social, and political turmoil, Europe in the year 1500 was well on the road to recovery. Population was increasing, the economy was expanding, and the national monarchs of France, England, Spain, Scotland, and Poland were all securely established on their thrones. Throughout Europe, governments at every level were extending their control over their subjects' lives. Europe had also resumed its commercial and colonial expansion. Even Catholic Christianity appeared to be going from strength to strength as the sixteenth century dawned. Although the papacy remained mired in territorial wars in Italy, the church itself had weathered the storms that had beset it during the fifteenth century. The Lollards had been suppressed and the Hussites reincorporated into the church. In the struggle over conciliarism, the papacy had won the support of all the major European rulers, reducing the conciliarists to academic isolation at the University of Paris. Meanwhile, at the parish level, the devotion of ordinary Christians to their faith had probably never been higher. To be sure, there were also problems. Although the educational standards of the parish clergy were higher than they had ever been, reformers were quick to note that too many priests were still absent, ignorant, or neglectful of their spiritual duties. Monasticism, by and large, seemed to have lost its spiritual fire; among the populace, religious enthusiasm sometimes led the faithful into gross superstition and doctrinal error. But these were manageable problems. On the whole, the "prospect of Europe" had not looked brighter for several centuries.

No one in 1500 could have predicted that within fifty years Europe's religious unity would be irreparably shattered by a new and powerful Protestant reform movement—or that in the century thereafter an appallingly destructive series of religious wars would shake to their core the foundations of European political life. Yet remarkably, these extraordinary events began with a single German monk named Martin Luther (1483–1546), whose personal quest for a more certain understanding of sin, grace, and Christian salvation set off a chain reaction throughout Europe, resulting in the secession of millions of Europeans from the Roman Catholic Church and affecting the

FOCUS QUESTIONS

- What were the theological premises of Lutheranism?
- Why did Switzerland emerge as such an important center for sixteenth-century Protestantism?

 • How did notions of family and marriage change during the Reformation?
- Why did England become a Protestant country?
- How did the Catholic Reformation differ from the Counter-Reformation?

religious practices of nearly every Christian in Europe, whether Catholic or Protestant. The religious movement that Luther touched off was much larger than Luther himself; nor should Martin Luther's own spiritual journey be seen as an epitome for all of Protestantism. But that said, there is no doubt that the Reformation movement began with Martin Luther—and so must we if we are to understand the extraordinary upheaval this new religious movement brought about.

THE LUTHERAN UPHEAVAL

What were the theological premises of Lutheranism?

To explain the success of the Lutheran revolt in Germany, we must answer three central questions: (1) Why did Luther's theological ideas lead him to break with Rome? (2) Why did large numbers of Germans rally to his cause? (3) Why did so many German princes and towns impose the new religion within their territories? As we shall see, those who followed Luther found his message appealing for different reasons. Many peasants hoped the new religion would free them from the exactions of their lords; towns and princes thought it would allow them to consolidate their political independence; nationalists thought it would liberate Germany from the demands of foreign popes bent on feathering their own nest in central Italy.

What Luther's followers shared, however, was a conviction that their new, Lutheran understanding of Christianity would lead them to heaven, whereas contemporary Catholicism would not. To this degree, *reformation* is a misleading label for the movement Luther initiated. Although Luther himself did begin as a reformer seeking to cleanse contemporary Christianity from its abuses, he quickly developed into an uncompromising opponent of the basic principles of Catholic belief and practice. Many of his followers became even more radical. The religious movement that began with Martin Luther was thus no mere "reformation." It was a frontal assault on the foundations of late medieval religious life.

LUTHER'S QUEST FOR RELIGIOUS CERTAINTY

Although Martin Luther became an inspiration to millions, he was at first a terrible disappointment to his fa-

ther. The elder Luther was a Thuringian peasant who had prospered by leasing some mines. Eager to see his clever son rise still further, he sent young Martin to the University of Erfurt to study law. In 1505, however, Martin shattered his father's hopes by becoming a monk of the Augustinian order. In some sense, however, Luther always remained faithful to his father's humble roots. Throughout his life, Martin Luther always lived simply and expressed himself in the vigorous, earthy vernacular of the German peasantry.

Like many great figures in the history of religion, Luther arrived at his new understanding of religious truth by a dramatic conversion experience. As a monk, young Martin zealously pursued all the traditional means for achieving his own salvation. Yet, try as he might, Luther could find no spiritual peace because he feared that he could never perform enough good deeds to deserve so great a gift as salvation. But in 1513 he hit upon an insight that granted him relief and changed the course of his life.

Luther's guiding insight pertained to the problem of the justice of God. For years he had worried that it seemed unjust for God to issue commandments that he

Martin Luther. A portrait by Lucas Cranach.

knew human beings could not observe, and then punish them with eternal damnation for not observing them. But after becoming a professor of biblical theology at the University of Wittenberg, it suddenly struck him that God's justice had nothing to do with his power to punish, but rather with his mercy in saving sinful mortals through faith. As Luther later wrote, ". . . I felt as though I had been born again, and had gone through open gates into paradise."

After that, everything seemed to fall into place. Lecturing at Wittenberg in the years immediately following 1513, Luther pondered a passage in Saint Paul's Letter to the Romans (1:17): "[T]he just shall live by faith" until he reached his central doctrine of "justification by faith alone." Luther concluded that God's justice does not demand endless good works and religious rituals for salvation, because humans can never be saved by their own efforts. Rather, humans are saved by God's grace alone, which God offers as an utterly undeserved gift to those whom he has predestined for salvation. Because this grace comes to humans through the gift of faith, from the human perspective men and women are "justified" (i.e., made worthy of salvation) by faith alone. Those whom God has justified through faith will manifest that fact by performing works of piety and charity, but such works are not what saves them. Piety and charity are merely visible signs of each believer's invisible spiritual state, which is known to God alone.

The essence of this doctrine was not original to Luther. It harked back to around the year 400 with the predestinarianism of Saint Augustine (see Chapter 6), the patron saint of Luther's own monastic order. During the twelfth and thirteenth centuries, however, theologians developed a very different understanding of salvation, emphasizing the role that both the church itself (through its sacraments) and the individual believer (through acts of piety and charity) could play in the process of salvation. None of these theologians claimed that a human being could earn his or her way to heaven by good works alone. But the late medieval church unwittingly encouraged such misunderstandings by presenting the process of salvation in increasingly quantitative terms, declaring, for example, that by performing a specific meritorious act (such as a pilgrimage or a pious donation), a believer could reduce the penance she or he owed to God by a specific number of days. From the fourteenth century on, popes

claimed to dispense such special grace to the living from the "Treasury of Merits," a storehouse of surplus good works piled up by Christ and the saints in heaven. Most commonly, grace was withdrawn from this "Treasury" and reassigned to needy sinners through indulgences: special remissions of the penitential obligations imposed on Christians by their priests as part of the sacrament of Penance. By the end of the fifteenth century, however, indulgences were often being granted in return for monetary payments to favored papal causes. To many reformers, this looked like simony: the sin of selling grace in return for cash.

> By the end of the fifteenth century, however, indulgences were often being granted in return for monetary payments to favored papal causes. To many reformers, this looked like simony: the sin of selling grace in return for cash.

Abuses of this sort were widely criticized by early sixteenth-century church reformers such as Erasmus. But Luther's objections to indulgences and prayers for the dead had much more radical consequences, because they rested on a set of Augustinian theological presuppositions that, if taken to their logical conclusion, could only result in dismantling much of contemporary Catholic religious practice. Luther himself may not have realized this when he took the first steps that would lead to his breach with Rome. But as the implications of his ideas became clear, Luther did not withdraw from them. Instead, he pressed on, declaring to his opponents, "Here I stand; God help me, I can do no other."

THE REFORMATION BEGINS

Luther first developed his theological ideas as an academic lecturer, but in 1517 he was goaded into attacking some of the actual practices of the church by a provocation that was too much for him to bear.

A Dominican friar named Tetzel was hawking indulgences throughout much of northern Germany, deliberately giving people the impression that an indulgence was an automatic ticket to heaven for oneself or one's loved ones in purgatory. For Luther, this was doubly offensive: not only was Tetzel violating Luther's conviction that people are saved by faith, not works, he was also misleading people into thinking that if they purchased an indulgence, then they no longer needed to confess their sins to a priest. Tetzel was thus putting their very salvation at risk. So on October 31, 1517, Luther offered to his university colleagues a list of ninety-five theses objecting to Catholic indulgence doctrine, an act conventionally seen as the beginning of the Protestant Reformation.

Luther wrote his theses in Latin, not German, and meant them only for academic discussion within the University of Wittenberg. But when some unknown person translated and published Luther's theses, the hitherto obscure monk suddenly gained widespread notoriety. Tetzel and his allies demanded that Luther withdraw his theses. Rather than backing down, however, Luther became even bolder in his attacks on the church hierarchy. In 1519, in a public disputation held before throngs in Leipzig, Luther defiantly maintained that the pope and all clerics were merely fallible men and that the highest authority for an individual's conscience was the truth of Scripture. Pope Leo X responded by charging Luther with heresy; after that Luther had no alternative but to break with the Catholic Church entirely.

Luther's year of greatest creative activity came in 1520 when, in the midst of the crisis caused by his defiance, he composed a series of pamphlets setting forth his three primary theological premises: justification by faith, the primacy of Scripture, and "the priesthood of all believers." We have already examined the meaning of the first premise. By the second he simply meant that the literal meaning of Scripture took precedence over church traditions, and that beliefs (such as purgatory) or practices (such as prayers to the saints) not explicitly grounded in Scripture could be rejected as human inventions. Luther also declared all Christian believers to be spiritually equal before God. Denying that priests, monks, and nuns had any special spiritual qualities by virtue of their vocations, Luther argued instead for "the priesthood of all believers."

From these premises a host of practical consequences followed. Since works could not lead to salvation, Luther declared fasts, pilgrimages, and the veneration of relics to be spiritually valueless. He also called for the dissolution of all monasteries and convents. He also took steps to "demystify" the rites of the church, proposing the substitution of German for Latin in church services, and reducing the number of sacraments from seven to two (Baptism and the Eucharist). To further emphasize that those who presided in churches had no supernatural authority, he insisted on calling them ministers or pastors rather than priests. He also proposed to abolish the entire ecclesiastical hierarchy of popes, bishops, and archdeacons. Finally, firm in the belief that no spiritual distinction existed between clergy and laity, Luther argued that ministers could marry, and in 1525 he took a wife himself.

> Denying that priests, monks, and nuns had any special spiritual qualities by virtue of their vocations, Luther argued instead for "the priesthood of all believers."

THE BREAK WITH ROME

Luther's brilliant polemical pamphlets of 1520 electrified much of Germany, gaining him passionate popular support and touching off a national religious revolt against the papacy. As word of Luther's defiance spread, his pamphlets became a publishing sensation. Whereas the average press run of a printed book before 1520 had been one thousand copies, the first run of *To the Christian Nobility* (1520) was four thousand, which sold out in a few days. Many more thousands of copies quickly followed. Even more popular were woodcut illustrations mocking the papacy and exalting Luther. These sold in the tens of thousands, and could be readily understood even by the illiterate.

Luther's denunciations of the papacy reflected widespread public dissatisfaction with recent popes. Pope Alexander VI (1492–1503) had bribed the cardinals to gain the papacy, used the money raised from the jubilee of 1500 to support the military campaigns of his son Cesare, and was so morally corrupt that he was suspected of incest with his own daughter. Julius II (1503–1513) devoted his reign to enlarging the Papal States through war; a contemporary remarked of him that he would have gained the greatest glory if only he had been a secular prince. Leo X (1513–1521), Luther's opponent, was a member of the Medici family of Florence. Although not spectacularly corrupt or immoral, he was a self-indulgent esthete who, in the words of a modern Catholic historian, "would not have been deemed fit to be a doorkeeper in the house of the Lord had he lived in the days of the apostles."

In Germany, however, resentment of the papacy ran especially high. Because fifteenth-century Germany was so politically fractured, there were no agreements (known as concordats) between pope and emperor limiting papal authority in Germany, as there were with the rulers of Spain, France, and England. As a result, by 1500 the German princes were complaining that papal taxes were so high they were draining the country of its coin. But despite paying such large sums of money to Rome, Germans had almost no influence over papal policy. Frenchmen, Spaniards, and Italians dominated the college of cardinals and the papal bureaucracy, and the popes themselves were invariably Italian (as they would continue to be until 1978). As a result, graduates from the rapidly growing German universities almost

Pope Leo X. Raphael's highly realistic portrait shows the pope with two of his nephews.

never found employment in Rome. Instead, many joined the throngs of Luther's supporters to become leaders of the new religious movement.

THE DIET OF WORMS

Luther's personal drama was now moving swiftly toward a crisis. Late in 1520, Luther responded to Pope Leo X's bull ordering him to recant by casting not only the bull but all of church law onto a roaring bonfire in front of a huge crowd. Since in the eyes of the church Luther was now a stubborn heretic, he was formally "released" for punishment to his lay overlord, the elector Frederick the Wise of Saxony. Frederick, however, was loath to silence the pope's antagonist. Rather than burning Luther at the stake for heresy, Frederick declared that Luther had not yet received a fair hearing. Early in 1521, he therefore brought him to the city of Worms to be examined by a formal assembly (a "diet") of the princes of the Holy Roman empire.

At Worms the initiative lay with the presiding officer, the newly elected Holy Roman emperor, Charles V. Charles was not a German; indeed, it is doubtful if he had any national identity at all. As a member of the Hab-

sburg family, he had been born and bred in his ancestral holding of the Netherlands. By 1521, however, through the unpredictable workings of dynastic inheritance, marriage, election, and luck, he had become not only the ruler of the Netherlands, but also king of Germany and Holy Roman emperor, duke of Austria, duke of Milan, and ruler of Franche-Comté. As the grandson of Ferdinand and Isabella on his mother's side, he was also king of Spain; king of Naples, Sicily, and Sardinia; and ruler of all the Spanish possessions in the New World.

Governing such an extraordinary combination of territories posed enormous challenges. Charles's empire had no capital and no centralized administrative institutions; it shared no common language, no common culture, and no geographically contiguous borders. It thus stood completely apart from the growing nationalism of late medieval political life. Charles recognized the diversity of his empire, and tried wherever possible to rule it through local officials and institutions. But he could not tolerate threats to the two fundamental forces that held his empire together: the emperor himself, and Catholicism. Beyond such political calculations, however, Charles was also a faithful and committed Catholic, who was deeply disturbed by the prospect of heresy within his empire. There was therefore little doubt that the Diet of Worms would condemn Martin Luther for heresy. But when Luther refused to back down, even before the emperor himself, Frederick the Wise once more intervened, this time by arranging a "kidnapping" whereby Luther was spirited off to the elector's castle of the Wartburg and kept out of harm's way for a year.

Thereafter Luther was never again to be in danger of his life. Although the Diet of Worms proclaimed him an outlaw, this edict was never enforced. Instead, Luther went into hiding, and Charles V left Germany to conduct a war with France. In 1522 Luther returned in triumph from the Wartburg to Wittenberg to find that the changes he had called for in ecclesiastical government and worship had already been put into practice by his university supporters. Then, in rapid succession, several German princes formally converted to Lutheranism, bringing their territories with them. By 1530, a considerable part of Germany had thus been brought over to the new faith.

THE GERMAN PRINCES AND THE LUTHERAN REFORMATION

At this point, then, the last of the three major questions regarding the early history of Lutheranism arises:

THE EMPIRE OF CHARLES V, C. 1550

This map shows the lands Charles V ruled directly through inheritance and marriage; as Holy Roman Emperor, he was also the titular ruler of Germany. Which countries and rulers were most threatened by Charles's extraordinary combination of territories? Where might these threatened rulers and countries look for allies against Charles V? How did the threat posed by the Ottoman empire complicate the political and religious struggles within Christian Europe?

Why did some German princes, secure in their own powers, nonetheless heed Luther's call by establishing Lutheran religious practices within their territories? This is a crucial question, because despite Luther's popular support, his cause surely would have failed had it not been embraced by a number of powerful German princes and free cities. In 1520, Luther was more or less equally popular throughout Germany, but it was only in those territories where rulers formally established Lutheranism (mostly in the German north) that the new religion prevailed. Elsewhere, Luther's sympathizers were forced to flee, face death, or conform to Catholicism.

As early as 1520 Luther had recognized that he could never hope to institute new religious practices without the strong arm of the princes behind him, so he implicitly encouraged them to confiscate the wealth of the Catholic Church as an incentive for creating a new order. At first the princes bided their time, but when they realized that Luther had enormous public support and that Charles V would not act swiftly to defend the Catholic faith, several moved to introduce Lutheranism into their territories. Personal piety surely played a role in individual cases, but political and economic considerations were more generally decisive. By instituting Lutheranism within their territories, Protestant princes

The Seven-Headed Martin Luther. In response, a German Catholic propagandist showed Luther as Revelation's "beast." In the Catholic conception Luther's seven heads show him by turn to be a hypocrite, a fanatic, and "Barabbas"—the thief who should have been crucified instead of Jesus.

The Seven-Headed Papal Beast. Around 1530 a Lutheran cartoon was circulated in Germany that turned the papacy into the "seven-headed beast" of the Book of Revelation. The papacy's "seven heads" consist of pope, cardinals, bishops, and priests; the sign on the cross reads "for money, a sack full of indulgences"; and a devil is seen emerging from an indulgence treasure chest below.

could consolidate their authority by naming pastors, cutting off fees to Rome, and curtailing the jurisdiction of church courts. They could also guarantee that the political and religious boundaries of their territories would now coincide. No longer, therefore, would a rival ecclesiastical prince (such as a bishop or archbishop) be able to use his spiritual position to undermine a neighboring secular prince's sovereignty over his territory.

Similar considerations also moved a number of free cities (so called because they were not ruled by territorial princes) to adopt Lutheranism. By adopting the new religion, town councils and guild masters could establish themselves (rather than local aristocrats or bishops) as the supreme governing authority within their towns. Given the added fact that under Lutheranism monasteries and convents could be shut down and their lands appropriated by the newly sovereign secular authorities, the practical advantages of the new faith were overwhelming, quite apart from any considerations of religious zeal.

Once safely ensconced in Wittenberg under princely protection, Luther began to express ever more vehemently his own profound conservatism in political and social matters. In a treatise of 1523, *On Temporal Authority*, he insisted that "godly" rulers must be obeyed in all things and that even ungodly ones should never be actively resisted since tyranny "is not to be resisted but endured." Then, in 1525, when peasants throughout Germany rebelled against their landlords, Luther responded with intense hostility. In his vituperative pamphlet of 1525, *Against the Thievish, Murderous Hordes of Peasants*, he urged all who could to hunt the rebels down like mad dogs, to "strike, strangle, stab secretly or in public, and remember that nothing can be more poisonous than a man in rebellion." After the ruthless suppression of the Peasants' Revolt (which may have cost as many as one hundred thousand lives), the firm alliance of Lutheranism with state power helped to preserve and sanction the existing social order. Never again would there be a mass lower-class uprising in Germany.

As for Luther himself, he concentrated in his last years on debating with younger, more radical religious reformers and on offering spiritual counsel to all who sought it. Never tiring in his amazingly prolific literary activity, he wrote an average of one treatise every two weeks for twenty-five years. To the end Luther was unswerving in his new faith: on his deathbed in 1546 he responded to the question "Will you stand firm in Christ and the doctrine which you have preached?" with a resolute "Yes."

CHRONOLOGY

ORIGINS OF THE REFORMATION, 1450–1529

Christian humanists call for reforms	fifteenth–sixteenth centuries
Growth of German universities	1450–1517
Luther posts the Ninety-five Theses	1517
Luther charged with heresy	1519
Publication of Lutheran theological premises	1520
Diet of Worms declares Luther an outlaw	1521
Peasant Revolt defeated	1525
Luther's break with Zwingli	1529

THE SPREAD OF PROTESTANTISM

Why did Switzerland emerge as such an important center for sixteenth-century Protestantism?

Originating as a term applied to Lutherans who "protested" an action of the German Imperial Diet of 1529, the word "Protestant" was soon applied to a much wider range of European Christians in rebellion against Rome. Lutheranism itself struck lasting roots only in northern Germany and Scandinavia. Elsewhere in Europe, competing forms of Protestantism soon emerged from the seeds that Luther had sown. By the 1550s, Protestantism had become a truly international movement; in so doing, however, it also split into a number of competing traditions.

THE REFORMATION IN SWITZERLAND

In the early sixteenth century Switzerland was neither ruled by kings nor dominated by all-powerful territorial princes; instead, prosperous Swiss cities were either independent or on the verge of becoming so. Hence when the leading citizens of a Swiss municipality decided to adopt Protestant reforms no one could stop them, and Protestantism in Switzerland could usually take its own course. Although religious arrangements varied from city to city, three main forms of Protestantism emerged in Switzerland between 1520 to 1550: Zwinglianism, Anabaptism, and Calvinism.

ULRICH ZWINGLI

Zwinglianism, founded by Ulrich Zwingli (1484–1531) in Zürich, was the most theologically moderate form of the three. Although Zwingli began his career as a somewhat indifferent Catholic priest, around 1516 his humanist-inspired study of the Bible convinced him that Catholic theology and practice conflicted with the Gospels. But he did not speak out publicly until Luther set the precedent. In 1522, however, Zwingli began attacking the authority of the Catholic Church in Zürich. Soon all Zürich and much of northern Switzerland had accepted his religious leadership. Zwingli's reforms closely resembled those of the Lutherans in Germany. Zwingli

WHY WAS SWITZERLAND SUCH AN IMPORTANT CENTER FOR SIXTEENTH-CENTURY PROTESTANTISM?

THE SPREAD OF PROTESTANTISM   377

differed from Luther, however, concerning the theology of the Eucharist: whereas Luther believed in the real presence of Christ's body in the sacrament, for Zwingli the Eucharist conferred no grace at all; it was simply a reminder and communal celebration of Christ's historical sacrifice on the cross. This fundamental disagreement prevented Lutherans and Zwinglians from uniting in a common Protestant front. Fighting independently, Zwingli fell in battle against Catholic forces in 1531. Soon thereafter, his movement was absorbed by the more systematic Protestantism of John Calvin.

ANABAPTISM

Before Calvinism prevailed, however, an even more radical form of Protestantism arose in Switzerland and Germany. The first Anabaptists were members of Zwingli's circle in Zürich, but they broke with him around 1525 on the issue of infant baptism. Because Anabaptists were convinced that the sacrament of Baptism was only effective if administered to willing adults who understood its significance, they rejected infant baptism altogether, and required followers who had been baptized as infants to be baptized again as adults (the term "Anabaptism" means "rebaptism"). This doctrine reflected the Anabaptists' fundamental belief that the true church was a small community of believers gathered out of the world whose members had to make a deliberate, inspired decision to join it. No other Protestant groups were prepared to go so far in rejecting the medieval Christian view of the church as a single body to which all members of society belonged from birth. Yet in its first few years the movement did gain numerous adherents in Switzerland and Germany, above all because it appealed to sincere religious piety in calling for extreme simplicity of worship, pacifism, and strict personal morality.

Disastrously, however, an unrepresentative group of Anabaptist extremists managed to gain control of the German city of Münster in 1534. These zealots believed that God wished to institute a completely new order of justice and spirituality throughout the world, beginning with Münster, which they declared the new Jerusalem. Anabaptist religious practices were made obligatory, private property was abolished, and even polygamy was permitted on the grounds of Old Testament precedents. Such practices were deeply shocking to both Protestants and Catholics alike. Münster was besieged and captured by Catholic forces little more than a year after the Anabaptist takeover, and the Anabaptist leaders were put to death by excruciating tortures. Thereafter, Anabaptists throughout Europe were ruthlessly persecuted from all sides. Among the few who survived were

The Anabaptists' Cages, Then and Now. After the three Anabaptist leaders who had reigned in Münster for a year were executed in 1535, their corpses were prominently displayed in cages hung from a tower of the marketplace church. As can be seen from the photo on the right, the bones are now gone but the iron cages remain to this very day as a grisly reminder of the horrors of sixteenth-century religious strife.

some who banded together in the Mennonite sect, named for its founder, the Dutchman Menno Simons (c. 1496–1561). This sect, dedicated to pacifism and the simple "religion of the heart" of original Anabaptism, has continued to exist to the present day.

JOHN CALVIN'S REFORMED THEOLOGY

A year after events in Münster sealed the fate of Anabaptism, a twenty-six-year-old French Protestant named John Calvin (1509–1564), who had fled to the Swiss city of Basel to escape religious persecution, published the first version of his *Institutes of the Christian Religion*, the most influential systematic formulation of Protestant theology ever written. Born in northern France, Calvin originally had been trained for the law. But then, as he later wrote, while he was "obstinately devoted to the superstitions of Popery," a stroke of light made him feel that God was extricating him from "an abyss of filth." He thereupon became a Protestant theologian and propagandist.

Although some of these details resemble the early career of Luther, the two men were very different figures. Luther was an emotionally volatile personality and a controversialist. He responded to theological problems as they arose or as the impulse struck him, but he never attempted to write systematic theology. Calvin, however, was a coolly analytical legalist, who resolved in his *Institutes* to set forth all the principles of Protestantism comprehensively, logically, and systematically. As a result, after several revisions and enlargements (the definitive edition appeared in 1559), Calvin's *Institutes* became the most theologically authoritative statement of Protestant beliefs and the nearest Protestant equivalent to Saint Thomas Aquinas's *Summa Theologica*.

Calvin's austere theology started with the omnipotence of God and worked downward. For Calvin the entire universe is utterly dependent on the will of the Almighty, who created all things for his greater glory. Because of the original fall from grace, all human beings are sinners by nature, bound hand and foot to an evil inheritance they cannot escape. Nevertheless, the Lord for reasons of his own has predestined some for eternal salvation and damned all the rest to the torments of hell. Nothing that human beings may do can alter their fate; their souls are stamped with God's blessing or curse before they are born. Nevertheless, Christians cannot be indifferent to their conduct on earth. If they are among the elect, God will implant in them the desire to live according to his laws. Upright conduct is thus a sign, though not an infallible one, that an individual has been chosen to sit at the throne of glory. Membership in the reformed church (as Calvinist churches are often known) is another presumptive sign of election to salvation. But most of all, Calvin urged Christians to conceive of themselves as chosen instruments of God, charged to work actively to fulfill God's purposes on earth. Because sin offends God, Christians should do all they can to prevent it, not because their actions will lead to anyone's salvation (they will not), but simply because God's glory is diminished if sin is allowed to flourish unchecked by the efforts of those whom he has chosen for salvation.

Calvin always acknowledged a great theological debt to Luther, but his religious teachings differed from those of the Wittenberg reformer in several essentials. First of all, Luther's attitude toward proper Christian conduct in the world was much more passive than Calvin's. For Luther, a Christian should endure the trials of this life in suffering, whereas for Calvin the world was to be mastered in unceasing labor for God's sake. Calvin's religion was also more legalistic than Luther's. Luther, for example, insisted that his followers attend church on Sunday, but he did not demand that during the remainder of the day they refrain from all pleasure or work. Calvin, on the other hand, issued stern strictures against worldliness of any sort on the Sabbath day of rest, and forbade all sorts of minor self-indulgences even on non-Sabbath days.

The two men also differed on fundamental matters of church government and worship. Although Luther broke with the Catholic system of hierarchical church governance, Lutheran district superintendents continued to exercise some of the powers of bishops, including supervision of the parish clergy. Luther also retained many features of traditional worship, including altars, music, ritual, and vestments (special clothing for the clergy). Calvin, however, rejected everything that smacked to him of "popery." Each congregation should elect its own ministers, and assemblies of ministers and "elders" (laymen responsible for maintaining proper religious conduct among the faithful) were to govern the reformed church as a whole. Calvin also insisted on the utmost simplicity in worship, prohibiting (among much else) vestments, processions, instrumental music, and religious images of any sort, including stained-glass windows. He also dispensed with all remaining ves-

> Calvin also insisted on the utmost simplicity in worship, prohibiting (among much else) vestments, processions, instrumental music, and religious images of any sort, including stained-glass windows.

WHY WAS SWITZERLAND SUCH AN IMPORTANT CENTER FOR SIXTEENTH-CENTURY PROTESTANTISM?

THE SPREAD OF PROTESTANTISM   379

tiges of Catholic sacramental theology by making the sermon, rather than the Eucharist, the centerpiece of reformed worship. When these teachings were put into practice, Calvinist services became little more than "four bare walls and a sermon."

CALVINISM IN GENEVA

Calvin was intent on putting his religious teachings into practice. Sensing an opportunity in the French-speaking Swiss city of Geneva, he moved there late in

RELIGIOUS SITUATION IN EUROPE, C. 1560

This map shows the complicated religious boundaries of Europe around 1560, roughly forty years after Martin Luther's movement began. To what extent did the religious divisions of Europe follow its political boundaries? How would you account for the dispersed areas in which Calvinists predominated? Why did Lutheranism spread north into Scandinavia, but not south into Bavaria or west across the Rhine?

1536 and began preaching and organizing. In 1538 his activities caused him to be expelled, but in 1541 he returned and the city soon came completely under his sway. Under Calvin's guidance Geneva's government became a theocracy. Supreme authority was vested in a "Consistory" composed of twelve lay elders and between ten and twenty pastors, whose weekly meetings Calvin dominated. Aside from passing legislation proposed to it by a congregation of ministers, the Consistory's main function was to supervise morality, both public and private. To this end, Geneva was divided into districts, and a committee of the Consistory visited every household without warning to check on the behavior of its members. Dancing, card playing, attending the theater, and working or playing on the Sabbath—all were outlawed as works of the devil. Innkeepers were forbidden to allow anyone to consume food or drink without first saying grace, or to permit any patron to stay up after nine o'clock. Murder, treason, adultery, "witchcraft," blasphemy, and heresy were all capital crimes. Even penalties for lesser crimes were severe. During the first four years after Calvin gained control in Geneva, there were no fewer than fifty-eight executions out of a total population of only sixteen thousand.

As objectionable as such interference in the private sphere may seem today, in the mid-sixteenth century Calvin's Geneva was a beacon of light to thousands of Protestants throughout Europe. Calvin's disciple John Knox, who brought reformed religion to Scotland, declared Geneva under Calvin "the most perfect school of Christ that ever was on earth since the days of the Apostles." Converts such as Knox flocked to Geneva for refuge or instruction, and then returned home to become ardent proselytizers for the new religion. Geneva thus became the center of an international movement dedicated to spreading reformed religion to France and the rest of Europe through organized missionary activity and propaganda.

These missionary efforts were remarkably successful. By the end of the sixteenth century, Calvinists were a majority in Scotland (where they were known as Presbyterians), Holland (where they founded the Dutch Reformed Church), and England (where the Church of England adopted reformed theology but not reformed worship; Calvinists who sought further reforms in worship were known as Puritans). There were also substantial Calvinist minorities in France (where they were called Huguenots), Germany, Hungary, Lithuania, and Poland. God's kingdom on earth had not yet been fully realized; on his deathbed in

1564, Calvin pronounced the Genevans to be still "a perverse and unhappy nation." But an extraordinary revolution had taken place nonetheless in the religious life and practice of Europe.

THE DOMESTICATION OF THE REFORMATION, 1525–1560

How did notions of family and marriage change during the Reformation?

Protestantism had begun as a revolutionary doctrine whose radical claims for the spiritual equality of all true Christian believers had the potential to undermine the social, religious, political, and even gender hierarchies on which European society rested. Luther himself seems not to have anticipated that his ideas might have such implications, and he was genuinely shocked when the rebellious German peasants and the religious millenarianists at Münster interpreted his teachings in this way. In response to the social and political radicals, the social ideology of the Reformation movement became increasingly conservative after 1525. The Protestant reformers began to emphasize the patriarchal family as the central institution of reformed life.

PROTESTANTISM AND THE FAMILY

Protestantism brought a new emphasis on the family as a "school of godliness," in which an all-powerful father figure was expected to assume responsibility for instructing and disciplining his household according to the precepts of reformed religion. At the same time, Protestantism also introduced a new religious ideal for women. No longer was the celibate nun the exemplar of female holiness; in her place now stood the married and obedient Protestant "goodwife." As one Lutheran prince wrote in 1527: "Those who bear children please God better than all the monks and nuns singing and praying." To this extent, Protestantism resolved the tensions between piety and sexuality that had characterized late medieval Catholicism by declaring firmly in favor of the holiness of marital sexuality.

LUTHER ON CELIBACY AND WOMEN

Luther urged the dissolution of monasteries and convents on both theological and practical grounds. In theological terms, he argued that such institutions contributed nothing to the world, aside from (perhaps) the salvation of their inmates. But as the extracts below reveal, he also considered their demands for celibacy to be impossible for most men and women to meet. The result was therefore to increase, rather than decrease, sin.

Listen! In all my days I have not heard the confession of a nun, but in the light of Scripture I shall hit upon how matters fare with her and know I shall not be lying. If a girl is not sustained by great and exceptional grace, she can live without a man as little as she can without eating, drinking, sleeping, and other natural necessities. Nor, on the other hand, can a man dispense with a wife. The reason for this is that procreating children is an urge planted as deeply in human nature as eating and drinking. That is why God has given and put into the body the organs, arteries, fluxes, and everything that serves it. Therefore what is he doing who would check this process and keep nature from running its desired and intended course? He is attempting to keep nature from being nature, fire from burning, water from wetting, and a man from eating, drinking, and sleeping.

E.M. Plass, ed., *What Luther Says* (St. Louis: Concordia Publishing House, 1959), vol. II, pp. 888–889.

This did not reflect a newly elevated view of women's spiritual potential, however—quite the contrary. Luther, like his medieval predecessors, continued to regard women as more sexually driven than men and less capable of controlling their sexual desires (although, to be fair, Luther had only a slightly higher view of men's capacity for celibacy). His opposition to convents rested on his belief that, except in extraordinary circumstances, it was impossible for women to remain celibate, so convents simply made illicit sexual behavior inevitable. To control women and prevent sin, it was therefore necessary that all women should be married, preferably at a young age, and so placed under the governance of a godly husband.

PROTESTANTISM AND CONTROL OVER MARRIAGE

Protestantism also increased parents' control over their children's choice of marital partners. The medieval Catholic church defined marriage as a sacrament that did not require the involvement of a priest. The mutual free consent of the two parties, even if given without witnesses or parental approval, was enough to constitute a legally valid marriage in the eyes of the church; at the same time, however, the church would annul a marriage if either of the parties could prove that they had not freely consented to it. Opposition to this doctrine came from many quarters, but especially from parents and other relatives. Because marriage involved rights of inheritance to property, most families regarded it as far too important a matter to be left to the free choice of their children. Instead, parents wanted the power to prevent unsuitable matches, and ideally, to force their children to accept the marriage arrangements their families might negotiate on their behalf. Protestantism offered an opportunity to achieve such control. Luther had declared marriage to be a purely secular matter, not a sacrament at all, that could be regulated however the governing authorities thought best. Calvin largely followed suit, although Calvinist theocracy drew less of a distinction than did Lutheranism between the powers of church and state. Even Catholicism was eventually forced to give way. Although it never entirely abandoned its insistence that both members of the couple must freely consent to their marriage, by the end of the sixteenth century the Catholic church required formal public notice of intent to marry, and insisted on the presence of a priest at the actual wedding ceremony. Both were efforts to prevent elopements, allowing families time to intervene before an unsuitable marriage was concluded. Individual Catholic countries sometimes went even further in trying to reassert parental control over their children's choice of marital partners. In France, for example, although couples might still marry without parental consent, those who did so now forfeited all of their rights to inherit their families' property. In somewhat different ways, both Protestantism and Catholicism thus moved to strengthen the control that parents could exercise over their children—and, in the case of Protestantism, that husbands could exercise over their wives.

> Because marriage involved rights of inheritance to property, most families regarded it as far too important a matter to be left to the free choice of their children.

needed a male heir to preserve the succession of his Tudor dynasty, and since Catherine was now past childbearing age, Henry had good reasons of state to break his marriage bonds. He also had more personal motives, having become infatuated with a dark-eyed lady-in-waiting named Anne Boleyn. In order to marry Anne, Henry appealed to Rome to annul his marriage to Catherine, arguing that because Queen Catherine had previously been married to Henry's older brother Arthur (who had died shortly after the ceremony was performed), Henry's marriage to Catherine had been invalid from the beginning. As Henry's representatives pointed out, the Bible pronounced it "an unclean thing" for a man to take his brother's wife and cursed such a marriage with childlessness (Leviticus 20:31). Even a papal dispensation (which Henry and Catherine had obtained for their marriage) could not dispose of such a clear prohibition, as the marriage's childlessness proved.

HENRY VIII AND THE BREAK WITH ROME

Henry's suit put Pope Clement VII (1523–1534) in a quandary. Both Henry and Clement knew that popes in the past had granted annulments to reigning monarchs on far weaker grounds than the ones Henry was alleging. If, however, the pope granted Henry's annulment he would cast doubt on the validity of all papal dispensations. More seriously, however, he would also pro-

THE ENGLISH REFORMATION

Why did England become a Protestant country?

In England, the Reformation took a rather different course than it did in continental Europe. By 1527 the imperious King Henry VIII had been married for eighteen years to Ferdinand and Isabella's daughter Catherine of Aragon, yet all the offspring of this union had died in infancy, save only Princess Mary. Since Henry

CHRONOLOGY
SPREAD OF PROTESTANTISM, 1520–1560

Lutheranism becomes state religion in Denmark, Norway, and Sweden	1520s
England breaks with Rome	1534
Geneva adopts theocratic government based on Calvinism	1541
Calvinism spreads to Scotland, England, Netherlands, and France	1540–1560s
Elizabethan Settlement	1559

voke the wrath of the emperor Charles V, Catherine of Aragon's nephew, whose armies were in firm command of Rome and who at that moment held the pope himself in captivity. Clement was trapped; all he could do was procrastinate and hope for better days. For two years, he allowed the suit to proceed in England without ever reaching a verdict. Then, suddenly, he transferred the case to Rome, where the legal process began all over again.

Exasperated by these delays, Henry began to increase the pressure on the pope. In 1531 he compelled an assembly of English clergy to declare him "protector and only supreme head" of the church in England. In January 1533, Henry married Anne Boleyn (already pregnant) even though his marriage to Queen Catherine had still not been annulled. (The new archbishop of Canterbury, Thomas Cranmer, provided the required annulment in May.) In September, Princess Elizabeth was born; her father, disappointed again in his hopes for a son, refused to attend her christening. Nevertheless, Parliament settled the succession to the throne on the children of Henry and Anne, redirected all papal revenues from England into the king's hands, prohibited appeals to the papal court, and formally declared "the King's highness to be Supreme Head of the Church of England [having] the authority to redress all errors, heresies, and abuses." In 1536, Henry executed Thomas More for his refusal to endorse this declaration of supremacy and took the first steps toward dissolving England's monasteries. By the end of 1539, the monasteries and convents were gone, their lands and wealth confiscated by the king, who distributed them to his supporters.

These measures broke the bonds that linked the English church to Rome, but they did not make England a Protestant country. Although certain traditional practices (such as pilgrimages and relics) were prohibited, the English church remained overwhelmingly Catholic in organization, doctrine, ritual, and language. The Six Articles promulgated by Parliament in 1539 at Henry VIII's behest left no room for doubt as to official orthodoxy: oral confession to priests, masses for the dead, and clerical celibacy were all confirmed; the Latin mass continued; and Catholic Eucharistic doctrine was not only confirmed but its denial made punishable by death. To most English people, only the disappearance of the monasteries and the king's own continuing matrimonial adventures (he married six wives in all) gave certain evidence that their church was no longer part of the Roman obedience.

Henry VIII, by Hans Holbein the Younger.

EDWARD VI

For truly committed Protestants, and especially those who had visited Calvin's Geneva, the changes Henry VIII enforced on the English church did not go nearly far enough. In 1547, the accession of the nine-year-old king Edward VI (Henry's son with his third wife, Jane Seymour) gave them their opportunity to finish the task of reformation. Encouraged by the clear Protestant sympathies of the young king himself, Edward's government moved quickly to reform the creeds and ceremonies of the English church. Priests were permitted to marry; English services replaced Latin ones; the veneration of images was abolished, and the images themselves defaced or destroyed; prayers for the dead were abolished, and endowments for such prayers were confiscated; and new articles of belief were drawn up, repudiating all sacraments except Baptism and communion and affirming the Protestant doctrine of justification by faith alone. Most important, a new Prayer Book was published to define precisely how the new, English-language services of the church were to be conducted. Much remained unsettled with respect to both doctrine and worship; but by 1553, when the youthful Edward died, the English church appeared to have become a distinctly Protestant institution.

MARY TUDOR AND THE RESTORATION OF CATHOLICISM

Edward's successor, however, was his pious and deeply Catholic sister Mary (1553–1558), Henry VIII's daughter with Catherine of Aragon. Mary speedily reversed her brother's religious policies, restoring the Latin mass and requiring married priests to give up their wives. She even prevailed on Parliament to vote a return to papal allegiance. Hundreds of Protestants leaders fled abroad, many to Geneva; others, including Archbishop Thomas Cranmer, were burned at the stake for refusing to abjure their Protestantism. News of the martyrdoms spread like wildfire through Protestant Europe. In England, however, Mary's policies sparked relatively little outright resistance at the local level. After two decades of religious upheaval, most English men and women were probably hoping that Mary's reign would bring some stability to their religious lives.

This, however, Mary could not do. The executions she ordered were insufficient to wipe out religious resistance—instead, Protestant propaganda about "Bloody Mary" and the "fires of Smithfield" caused widespread disaffection, even among those who welcomed the return of traditional religious forms. Nor could she do anything to restore monasticism: too many leading families had profited from Henry VIII's dissolution of the monasteries for this to be reversed. Mary's marriage to her cousin Philip, Charles V's son and heir to the Spanish throne, was another miscalculation. Although the marriage treaty stipulated that in the event of Mary's death Philip could not succeed her, her English subjects never trusted him. When the queen allowed herself to be drawn by Philip into a war with France on Spain's behalf in which England lost Calais, its last foothold on the European continent, many English people became highly disaffected. Ultimately, however, what doomed Mary's religious counterrevolution was simply the accidents of biology. Mary was unable to conceive an heir, and when she died after only six years of rule, her throne passed to her Protestant sister Elizabeth.

THE ELIZABETHAN RELIGIOUS SETTLEMENT

The daughter of Henry VIII and Anne Boleyn, and one of the most capable and popular monarchs ever to sit on the English throne, Queen Elizabeth I (1558–1603) was predisposed in favor of Protestantism by the circumstances of her parents' marriage as well as by her upbringing. But Elizabeth was no zealot, and wisely recognized that supporting radical Protestantism in England might provoke bitter sectarian strife. Accordingly, she presided over what is customarily known as "the Elizabethan settlement." By a new Act of Supremacy (1559), Elizabeth repealed Mary's Catholic legislation, prohibiting foreign religious powers (i.e., the pope) from exercising any authority within England and declaring herself "supreme governor" of the English church—a more Protestant title than Henry VIII's "supreme head" insofar as most Protestants believed that Christ alone

Queen Elizabeth managed to mediate between the Catholic and Protestant faiths and became one of England's most popular monarchs.

HOW DID THE CATHOLIC REFORMATION DIFFER FROM THE COUNTER-REFORMATION?

CATHOLICISM TRANSFORMED   385

was the head of the church. She also adopted many of the Protestant liturgical reforms instituted by her brother Edward, including a revised version of the Edwardian Prayer Book. But she also retained vestiges of Catholic practice, including bishops, church courts, and vestments for the clergy. On most doctrinal matters, including predestination and free will, Elizabeth's Thirty-Nine Articles of Faith (approved in 1562) struck a decidedly Protestant, even Calvinist, tone. But the Prayer Book was more moderate, and on the critical issue of the Eucharist was deliberately ambiguous. By combining Catholic and Protestant interpretations ("this is my body. . . . Do this in remembrance of me") into a single declaration, the Prayer Book permitted an enormous latitude for competing interpretations of the service by priests and parishioners alike.

Despite such "latitudinarianism," religious tensions persisted in Elizabethan England, not only between Protestants and Catholics, but also between moderate and more extreme Protestants. The queen's artful "fudging" of these differences was by no means a recipe guaranteed to succeed. Rather, what preserved the Elizabethan religious settlement, and ultimately made England a Protestant country, was the extraordinary length of Queen Elizabeth's reign combined with the fact that for much of that time Protestant England was at war with Catholic Spain. Under Elizabeth, Protestantism and English nationalism gradually fused together into a potent conviction that God himself had chosen England for greatness. After 1588, when English naval forces won an improbable victory over the "invincible" Spanish Armada, Protestantism and Englishness became nearly indistinguishable to most of Queen Elizabeth's subjects. Laws against Catholic "recusants" became increasingly severe, and although an English Catholic tradition did survive, its adherents were a persecuted minority. Much more alarming was the situation in Ireland, where the vast majority of the population remained Catholic despite the government's efforts to impose Protestantism on them. By 1603, "Irishness" was as firmly identified with Catholicism as was "Englishness" with "Protestantism"; but it was the Protestants who were in the ascendant in both countries.

> In northern Europe, Christian humanists such as Erasmus and Thomas More also played a role in this Catholic reform movement, not only by criticizing abuses and editing sacred texts, but also by encouraging the laity to lead lives of simple but sincere religious piety.

CATHOLICISM TRANSFORMED

How did the Catholic Reformation differ from the Counter-Reformation?

The historical novelty of Protestantism inevitably casts the spotlight on such religious reformers as Luther and Calvin; but there was also a powerful internal reform movement within the Catholic Church during the sixteenth century. Historians differ about whether to call this movement the "Catholic Reformation" or the "Counter-Reformation." Some prefer the former term because it emphasizes that significant efforts to reform the Catholic Church began before Luther posted his theses and continued long after. Others, however, insist that from the mid-sixteenth century on, most Catholic reformers were inspired primarily by the urgent need to resist the Protestant schism. We will use both terms to refer to two complementary phases of Catholic reform: a Catholic Reformation that came before Luther, and a Counter-Reformation that followed him.

THE CATHOLIC REFORMATION

The Catholic Reformation began around 1490, and was primarily a movement for moral and institutional reform within the religious orders. Although these efforts received strong support from several secular rulers, the papacy showed little interest in them. As a result, the Catholic Reformation never became a truly international movement. In Spain, reform activities directed by Cardinal Francisco Ximenes de Cisneros (1436–1517) and supported by the monarchy led to the imposition of strict rules of behavior on Franciscan friars and the elimination of abuses prevalent among the diocesan clergy. In Italy, Reformers established several new religious orders dedicated to high ideals of piety and social service. In northern Europe, Christian humanists such as Erasmus and Thomas More also played a role in this Catholic reform movement, not only by criticizing abuses and editing sacred texts, but also by encouraging the laity to lead lives of simple but sincere religious piety.

As a response to the challenges posed by Protestantism, however, the Catholic Reformation proved entirely inadequate. Starting in the 1530s, therefore, a second, more aggressive phase of reform under a new style of vigorous papal leadership began to gather momentum. The leading Counter-Reformation popes—Paul III (1534–1549), Paul IV (1555–1559), Saint Pius V (1566–1572), and Sixtus V (1585–1590)—were collectively the most zealous reforming popes since the High Middle Ages. All led upright personal lives. Some, indeed, were so grimly ascetic that contemporaries wondered whether they were not too holy. But these Counter-Reformation popes were not merely holy men. They were also accomplished administrators who reorganized papal finances and filled ecclesiastical offices with bishops and abbots no less renowned for austerity and holiness than were the popes themselves.

These papal reform efforts intensified at the Council of Trent, a general council of the entire church convoked by Paul III in 1545 and which met at intervals thereafter until 1563. The decisions taken at Trent provided the foundations on which a new, Counter-Reformation Catholic Church would be erected. Although the council began by debating some form of compromise with Protestantism, Trent ended by reaffirming all of the Catholic doctrinal tenets challenged by Protestant critics. Good works were declared necessary for salvation, and all seven sacraments were declared indispensable means of grace, without which salvation was impossible. Transubstantiation, purgatory, the invocation of saints, and the rule of celibacy for the clergy were all confirmed as essential elements in the Catholic system. The Bible and the traditions of apostolic teaching were held to be of equal authority as sources of Christian truth. The Council of Trent even reaffirmed the doctrine of indulgences that had touched off the Lutheran revolt, although it did condemn the worst abuses connected with their sale.

The legislation of Trent was not confined to matters of doctrine. To improve pastoral care of the laity, bishops and priests were forbidden to hold more than one spiritual office. A theological seminary was to be established in every diocese. The council also decided to censor or suppress dangerous books. In 1564, a specially appointed commission published the first Index of Prohibited Books, an official list of writings that ought not to be read by faithful Catholics. All of Erasmus's works were immediately placed on the Index, even though he had been a chosen Catholic champion against Martin Luther only forty years before: a chill-

The Council of Trent. This fresco depicts the general council of the entire Catholic Church, which met from 1545 and 1563, and produced the foundation for the new Counter-Reformation church.

ing sign of the doctrinal intolerance that characterized sixteenth-century Christianity, both in its Catholic and Protestant varieties.

SAINT IGNATIUS LOYOLA AND THE SOCIETY OF JESUS

In addition to the independent activities of popes and the legislation of the Council of Trent, a third main force propelling the Counter-Reformation was the foundation of the Society of Jesus, commonly known as the Jesuit order, by Saint Ignatius Loyola (1491–1556). In the midst of a youthful career as a worldly soldier, the Spanish nobleman Loyola was wounded in battle in

OBEDIENCE AS A
JESUIT HALLMARK

The necessity of obedience in the spiritual formation of monks and nuns had been a central theme in Catholic religious thought since the Rule of Saint Benedict. By focusing its demands for obedience specifically on the papacy, however, the Society of Jesus brought a new militancy to this old ideal.

RULES FOR THINKING WITH THE CHURCH

1. Always to be ready to obey with mind and heart, setting aside all judgment of one's own, the true spouse of Jesus Christ, our holy mother, our infallible and orthodox mistress, the Catholic Church, whose authority is exercised over us by the hierarchy.
2. To commend the confession of sins to a priest as it is practised in the Church; the reception of the Holy Eucharist once a year, or better still every week, or at least every month, with the necessary preparation. . . .
4. To have a great esteem for the religious orders, and to give the preference to celibacy or virginity over the married state. . . .
6. To praise relics, the veneration and invocation of Saints: also the stations, and pious pilgrimages, indulgences, jubilees, the custom of lighting candles in the churches, and other such aids to piety and devotion. . . .
9. To uphold especially all the precepts of the Church, and not censure them in any manner; but, on the contrary, to defend them promptly, with reasons drawn from all sources, against those who criticize them.
10. To be eager to commend the decrees, mandates, traditions, rites and customs of the Fathers in the Faith or our superiors. . . .
13. That we may be altogether of the same mind and in conformity with the Church herself, if she shall have defined anything to be black which to our eyes appears to be white, we ought in like manner to pronounce it to be black. For we must undoubtingly believe, that the Spirit of our Lord Jesus Christ, and the Spirit of the Orthodox church His Spouse, by which Spirit we are governed and directed to salvation, is the same. . . .

FROM THE CONSTITUTIONS OF THE JESUIT ORDER

Let us with the utmost pains strain every nerve of our strength to exhibit this virtue of obedience, firstly to the Highest Pontiff, then to the Superiors of the Society; so that in all things . . . we may be most ready to obey his voice, just as if it issued from Christ our Lord . . . leaving any work, even a letter, that we have begun and have not yet finished; by directing to this goal all our strength and intention in the Lord, that holy obedience may be made perfect in us in every respect, in performance, in will, in intellect; by submitting to whatever may be enjoined on us with great readiness, with spiritual joy and perseverance; by persuading ourselves that all things [commanded] are just; by rejecting with a kind of blind obedience all opposing opinion or judgment of our own. . . .

Henry Bettenson, ed. *Documents of the Christian Church*, 2d ed. (Oxford: Oxford University Press, 1967), pp. 259–261.

1521 (the same year in which Luther defied Charles V at Worms). While recuperating, he decided to change his ways and become a spiritual soldier of Christ. For ten months he lived as a hermit, during which time he experienced ecstatic visions and worked out the principles of his subsequent meditational guide, the *Spiritual Exercises*. This manual, completed in 1535 and first published in 1541, offered practical advice on how to master one's will and serve God through a systematic program of meditations on sin and the life of Christ. Soon made a basic handbook for all Jesuits and widely studied by numerous Catholic laypeople as well, Loyola's *Spiritual Exercises* has had an influence second only to Calvin's *Institutes* among all the religious writings of the sixteenth century.

Originating as a small group of six disciples who gathered around Loyola in Paris in 1534, the Society of Jesus was formally constituted as an order of the Church by Pope Paul III in 1540; by the time of Loyola's death it already numbered fifteen hundred members. The Society of Jesus was by far the most militant of the religious orders fostered by the Catholic reform movements of the sixteenth century. Its organization was patterned after that of a military company, with a general as commander in chief and iron discipline enforced on all members. The Jesuit general, sometimes known as the "black pope" (from the color of the order's habit), was elected for life and was not bound to take advice offered by any other member. His sole superior was the pope, to whom all senior Jesuits took a special vow of strict obedience. As a result of this vow, all Jesuits were held to be at the pope's disposal at all times.

The activities of the Jesuits consisted primarily of missionary work and establishing schools. Early Jesuits preached to non-Christians in India, China, and Spanish America. Yet, although Loyola had not at first conceived of his society as comprising shock troops against Protestantism, that is what it primarily became as the Counter-Reformation mounted in intensity. Through preaching and diplomacy—sometimes at the risk of their lives—Jesuits in the second half of the sixteenth century fanned out across Europe in direct confrontation with Calvinists. In many places the Jesuits succeeded in keeping rulers and their subjects loyal to Catholicism, in others they met martyrdom, and in some others—notably Poland and parts of Germany and France—they succeeded in regaining territory previously lost to Protestantism. Wherever they were allowed to settle, the Jesuits set up

Early Jesuits preached to non-Christians in India, China, and Spanish America.

CHRONOLOGY

THE COUNTER-REFORMATION, 1534–1590

Counter-Reformation popes	1534–1590
Saint Ignatius Loyola founds the Jesuits	1534
Council of Trent convenes	1545–1563
Index of Prohibited Books	1564

schools and colleges, for they firmly believed that a vigorous Catholicism depended on widespread literacy and education. Their schools were so well regarded that, after the fires of religious hatred began to subside, upper-class Protestants sometimes sent their children to receive a Jesuit education.

COUNTER-REFORMATION CHRISTIANITY

The greatest achievement of these sixteenth-century Catholic reform movements was to defend and revitalize the faith. Had it not been for the determined efforts of these reformers, Catholicism would not have swept over the globe during the seventeenth and eighteenth centuries or reemerged in Europe as the vigorous spiritual force it remains today. But other results stemmed from the Counter-Reformation as well. One was the spread of literacy in Catholic countries due to the educational activities of the Jesuits. Another was the enormous importance of charitable activities to Counter-Reformation Catholicism. Spiritual leaders such as Saint Francis de Sales (1567–1622) and Saint Vincent de Paul (1581–1660) urged almsgiving in their sermons and writings, and a wave of founding of orphanages and houses for the poor swept over Catholic Europe.

The Counter-Reformation also brought a new emphasis on the importance of religious women. Counter-Reformation Catholicism did not exalt marriage as a route to holiness for women to the same degree as did Protestantism, but it did foster a distinctive role for a female religious elite—countenancing the mysticism of Saint Teresa of Avila (1515–1582) and establishing new orders of nuns such as the Ursulines and the Sisters of Charity. Both Protestants and Catholics continued to exclude women from the priesthood or ministry, but Catholic celibate women could pursue religious lives with at least some degree of independence.

The Counter-Reformation did not, however, perpetuate the tolerant Christianity of Erasmus. Instead, Christian humanists lost favor with Counter-Reformation popes. But sixteenth-century Protestantism was just as theologically intolerant as sixteenth-century Catholicism, and even more hostile to the cause of rationalism. Indeed, because Counter-Reformation theologians returned for guidance to the scholasticism of Saint Thomas Aquinas, they tended to be much more committed to the dignity of human reason than were their Protestant counterparts, who emphasized pure scriptural authority and unquestioning faith. It is not entirely coincidental, therefore, that René Descartes, one of the pioneers of seventeenth-century rationalism (and who coined the famous phrase "I think, therefore I am"), was trained as a youth by the Jesuits.

CONCLUSION

Protestantism emerged after the height of the Italian Renaissance and before the scientific revolution and the Enlightenment. It may be tempting, therefore, to think of historical events advancing in an inevitably cumulative way, from the Renaissance to the Reformation to the Enlightenment to the "Triumph of the Modern World." But history is seldom as neat as that. Although scholars continue to disagree on points of detail, most agree that the Protestant Reformation drew relatively little from the civilization of the Renaissance. Indeed, in certain basic respects Protestant principles were completely at odds with the major assumptions of most Renaissance humanists.

Certainly the Renaissance contributed something to the origins of the Protestant Reformation. Criticisms of religious abuses by Christian humanists helped prepare Germany for the Lutheran revolt. Close textual study of the Bible led to the publication of new, more reliable biblical editions used by the Protestant reformers. In this regard a direct line ran from the Italian humanist Lorenzo Valla to Erasmus to Luther. For these and related reasons, Luther addressed Erasmus in 1519 as "our ornament and our hope."

But in fact Erasmus quickly showed that he had no sympathy whatsoever with Lutheran principles. Most other Christian humanists followed suit, shunning Protestantism as soon as it became clear to them what Luther and other Protestant reformers were actually teaching. The reasons for this split are clear enough. Most humanists believed in free will, whereas Protestants believed in predestination; humanists tended to think of human nature as basically good, whereas Protestants found it unspeakably corrupt; and most humanists favored urbanity and tolerance, whereas the followers of Luther and Calvin emphasized obedience and conformity.

The Protestant Reformation did, however, contribute to certain traits characteristic of modern European historical development. Foremost among these was the increasing power of Europe's sovereign states. But we must not make any simple equation between state power and Protestantism. The power of the state was growing already by 1500, especially in such countries as France and Spain, where Catholic kings already exercised most of the same rights over the church that were forcibly seized by Lutheran German princes and Henry VIII in the course of their own reformations.

Nationalism too was already a part of this world, as we can see from the way Luther played on it in his appeals during the 1520s. But Luther also did much to foster German cultural nationalism, not least by translating the Bible into vigorous, colloquial German. Until the sixteenth century, Germans from different regions spoke such different dialects of German that they often could not understand each other. Luther's Bible, however, gained such currency that it eventually became the linguistic standard for the entire nation. Protestantism did not unite the German nation politically; instead, Germany soon divided into Protestant and Catholic camps. But elsewhere, as in Holland or parts of central Europe, where Protestants fought successfully against a foreign, Catholic overlord, Protestantism enhanced a sense of national identity. Perhaps the most familiar case of all is that of England, where a sense of nationhood existed long before the advent of Protestantism, but where the new faith lent to that nationalism a new confidence that England was indeed a nation peculiarly favored by God.

Finally, we come to the subject of Protestantism's effects on relationships between the sexes. No consensus among historians exists on this subject. What does seem clear, however, is that Protestant men as individuals could be just as ambivalent about women as their medieval Catholic predecessors had been. But if one asks how Protestantism as a belief system affected women's social roles, the answer appears to be that it enabled women to become just a shade more equal to men within a framework of continuing subjection. Because

Protestantism called on women as well as men to undertake serious study of the Bible, it encouraged primary schooling for both sexes. But Protestant male leaders still insisted that women were naturally inferior to men and should defer to men both within the family and in the larger society. As Calvin himself said, "[L]et the woman be satisfied with her state of subjection and not take it ill that she is made inferior to the more distinguished sex." Both Luther and Calvin appear to have been happily married, but that clearly meant being happily married on their own terms.

KEY TERMS

Martin Luther	Ulrich Zwingli	Mary Tudor
Lutheranism	Anabaptists	Elizabeth I
Erasmus	John Calvin	Council of Trent
Diet of Worms	Henry VIII	Society of Jesus

SELECTED READINGS

Bainton, Roland. *Here I Stand: A Life of Martin Luther*. Nashville, 1950. Although old and obviously biased in Luther's favor, this remains an absorbing and dramatic introduction to Luther's life and thought.

———. *Erasmus of Christendom*. New York, 1969. Still the best biography in English of the Dutch reformer and intellectual.

Benedict, Philip. *Christ's Churches Purely Reformed: A Social History of Calvinism*. New Haven, 2002. A wide-ranging recent survey of Calvinism in both western and eastern Europe.

Bossy, John. *Christianity in the West, 1400–1700*. Oxford and New York, 1985. A brilliant, challenging picture of the changes that took place in Christian piety and practice as a result of the sixteenth-century reformations.

Bouwsma, William J. *John Calvin: A Sixteenth-Century Portrait*. Oxford and New York, 1988. The best biography of the magisterial reformer.

Collinson, Patrick. *The Religion of Protestants: The Church in English Society, 1559–1625*. Oxford, 1982. A great book by the best contemporary historian of early English Protestantism.

Dillenberger, John, ed. *Martin Luther: Selections from His Writings*. Garden City, N.Y., 1961. The standard selection, especially good on Luther's theological ideas.

———. *John Calvin: Selections from His Writings*, Garden City, N.Y., 1971. A judicious selection, drawn mainly from Calvin's *Institutes*.

Dixon, C. Scott, ed. *The German Reformation: The Essential Readings*. Oxford, 1999. A collection of important recent articles.

Duffy, Eamon. *The Stripping of the Altars: Traditional Religion in England, c. 1400–c. 1550*. New Haven, 1992. The best study of the hesitant way in which England eventually became a Protestant country.

Hillerbrand, Hans J., ed. *The Protestant Reformation*. New York, 1967. Source selections are particularly good for illuminating the political consequences of Reformation theological ideas.

Loyola, Ignatius. *Personal Writings*. Translated by Joseph A. Munitiz and Philip Endean. London and New York, 1996. An excellent collection that includes Loyola's autobiography, his spiritual diary, and some of his letters, as well as his *Spiritual Exercises*.

Luebke, David, ed. *The Counter-Reformation: The Essential Readings*. Oxford, 1999. A collection of nine important recent essays.

MacCulloch, Diarmaid. *Reformation: Europe's House Divided, 1490–1700*. London and New York, 2003. A definitive new survey; the best single-volume history of its subject in a generation.

McGrath, Alister E. *Reformation Thought: An Introduction*. Oxford, 1993. A useful explanation, accessible to non-Christians, of the theological ideas of the major Protestant reformers.

Mullett, Michael A. *The Catholic Reformation*. London, 2000. A sympathetic survey of Catholicism from the mid-sixteenth to the eighteenth century that presents the mid-sixteenth-century Council of Trent not as a response to Protestantism, but as a continuation of reform efforts dating from the fifteenth century.

Oberman, Heiko A. *Luther: Man Between God and the Devil*. Translated by Eileen Walliser-Schwarzbart. New Haven, 1989. The best recent biography of Luther, stressing his preoccupations with sin, death, and the devil.

O'Malley, John W., *The First Jesuits*. Cambridge, Mass., 1993. A scholarly account of the origins and early years of the Society of Jesus.

———. *Trent and All That: Renaming Catholicism in the Early Modern Era*. Cambridge, Mass., 2000. Short, lively, up to date, and with a full bibliography.

Pettegree, Andrew, ed. *The Reformation World*. New York, 2000. An exhaustive multiauthor work representing the most recent thinking about the Reformation.

Pelikan, Jaroslav. *Reformation of Church and Dogma, 1300–1700.* Volume 4: *A History of Christian Dogma*. Chicago, 1984. A masterful synthesis of Reformation theology in its late medieval context.

Roper, Lyndal. *The Holy Household: Women and Morals in Reformation Augsburg*. Oxford, 1989. A pathbreaking study of how Protestantism was adopted and adapted by the town councilors of Augsburg, with special attention to its impact on attitudes toward women, the family, and marriage.

Shagan, Ethan H. *Popular Politics and the English Reformation*. Cambridge, 2002. Argues that the English Reformation reflects an ongoing process of negotiation, resistance, and response between government and people.

Tracy, James D. *Europe's Reformations, 1450–1650*. Lanham, Md., 1999. An outstanding survey, especially strong on Dutch and Swiss developments, but excellent throughout.

Williams, George H. *The Radical Reformation*, 3rd ed. Kirksville, Mo., 1992. Originally published in 1962, this is still the best book on Anabaptism and its offshoots.

Chapter FOURTEEN

Religious Wars and State Building, 1540–1660

STRANGE AS IT MAY SEEM in retrospect, Martin Luther never intended to fracture the religious unity of Europe. He sincerely believed that once the Bible was available to everyone in an accurate, vernacular translation, then everyone who read the Bible would interpret it in exactly the same way as did he himself. The result, of course, was quite different, as Luther quickly discovered in his bitter disputes with Zwingli and Calvin. Nor did Catholicism crumble in the face of reformed teachings as Luther had believed that it would. Instead, Europe's religious divisions multiplied, speedily crystallizing along political lines. By Luther's death in 1546, a clear pattern had already emerged. With only rare exceptions, Protestantism triumphed in those areas where political authorities supported the reformers. Where rulers remained Catholic, so too did their territories.

This was not the result Martin Luther had intended, but it did faithfully reflect the most basic presumptions of sixteenth-century European life. Anabaptists apart, neither Protestant nor Catholic reformers set out to challenge the standard medieval beliefs about the mutual interdependence of religion and politics—quite the contrary. Sixteenth-century Europeans continued to believe that the proper role of the state was to enforce true religion on its subjects, and sixteenth-century rulers remained convinced that religious pluralism would bring disunion and disloyalty to any state that embraced it. Ultimately, both Catholics and Protestants believed that western Europe had to return to a single religious faith enforced by properly constituted political authorities. What they could not agree on was, "Which faith?" and "Which authorities?"

The result was a brutal series of religious wars between 1540 and 1660 whose reverberations would continue to be felt until the eighteenth century. Vastly expensive and enormously destructive, these wars affected everyone in Europe, from peasants to princes. They did not arise solely from conflicts over religion. Regionalism, dynasticism, and nationalism were also potent contributors to the chaos

FOCUS QUESTIONS

- Why was the period 1540 to 1660 one of the most turbulent in European history?

- Why did religious conflicts become so deeply entwined with political conflicts during this period?

- What caused the decline of Spain in the seventeenth century?

- Why was this period such a fertile one for political philosophy?

- What was the relationship between the Baroque school and the Counter-Reformation?

into which Europe now plunged. Together, however, these forces of division and disorder brought into question the very survival of the European political order that had emerged since the thirteenth century. Faced with the prospect of political collapse, Europeans by 1660 were forced to embrace, gradually and grudgingly, a notion that in 1540 had seemed impossible to conceive: that religious toleration, however limited in scope, might be the only way to preserve the political, social, and economic order of the European world.

ECONOMIC, RELIGIOUS, AND POLITICAL TESTS

Why was the period 1540 to 1660 one of the most turbulent in European history?

The troubles that engulfed Europe between 1540 and 1660 caught contemporaries unawares. From the mid-fifteenth century on, most of Europe had enjoyed steady economic growth, and the discovery of the New World seemed the basis of greater prosperity to come. Political trends too seemed auspicious, since most western European governments were becoming ever more efficient and providing more internal peace for their subjects. By the middle of the sixteenth century, however, thunderclouds were gathering that would soon burst into terrible storms.

THE PRICE REVOLUTION

Although the causes of these storms were interrelated, we can examine each separately, starting with the great price inflation. Nothing like the upward price trend that affected western Europe in the second half of the sixteenth century had ever happened before. In Flanders the cost of wheat tripled between 1550 and 1600, grain prices in Paris quadrupled, and the overall cost of living in England more than doubled. The twentieth century would see much more dizzying inflations than this, but since the skyrocketing of prices in the later sixteenth century was a novelty, most historians agree on calling it a "price revolution."

Two developments in particular underlay the soaring prices. The first was demographic. Starting in the later fifteenth century, Europe's population began to grow

Peasants Harvesting Wheat, Sixteenth Century. The inflation that swept through Europe in the late 1500s most affected workers as the abundant labor supply dampened wages while the cost of food rose with poor harvests.

again after the plague-induced falloff: roughly estimated, Europe had about 50 million people around 1450 and 90 million around 1600. Since Europe's food supply remained more or less constant, food prices were driven sharply higher by greater demand. At the same time, wages stagnated or even declined. As a result, workers around 1600 were paying a higher percentage of their wages to buy food than ever before, even though their basic nutritional levels were declining.

Population trends explain much, but since Europe's population did not increase nearly so rapidly in the second half of the sixteenth century as did prices, other explanations for the great inflation are necessary. Foremost among these is the enormous influx of bullion from Spanish America. From 1556 to 1560 roughly 10 million ducats worth of silver passed through the Spanish entry port of Seville. Between 1576 and 1580 that figure doubled, and between 1591 and 1595 it more than quadrupled. Most of this silver was used by the Spanish crown to pay its foreign cred-

WHY DID RELIGIOUS AND POLITICAL CONFLICTS BECOME ENTWINED DURING THIS PERIOD?

A CENTURY OF RELIGIOUS WARS   395

itors and its armies abroad; as a result, this bullion quickly circulated throughout Europe, where much of it was minted into coins. This dramatic increase in the volume of money in circulation fueled the spiral of rising prices. "I learned a proverb here," said a French traveler in Spain in 1603, "everything costs much here except silver."

The price revolution also placed new pressures on the sovereign states of Europe. Since the inflation depressed the real value of money, fixed incomes from taxes and tolls yielded less and less. Thus merely to keep their incomes constant governments would have been forced to raise taxes. But to compound this problem, most states needed much more real income than previously because they were undertaking more wars, and warfare, as always, was becoming increasingly expensive. The only recourse, then, was to raise taxes precipitously, but such draconian measures aroused great resentment. Hence governments faced continuous threats of defiance and potential armed resistance.

After 1600 prices rose less rapidly, as population growth slowed and the flood of silver from America began to abate. On the whole, however, the period from 1600 to 1660 was one of economic stagnation rather than growth. The Black Death also returned, wreaking havoc in London and elsewhere during the 1660s.

> On the whole, however, the period from 1600 to 1660 was one of economic stagnation rather than growth.

RELIGIOUS CONFLICTS

It goes without saying that most people would have been far better off had there been fewer wars during this difficult century, but given prevalent attitudes, newly arisen religious rivalries made wars inevitable. Simply stated, until religious passions began to cool toward the end of the period, most Catholics and Protestants viewed each other as minions of Satan who could not be allowed to live. Worse, sovereign states attempted to enforce religious uniformity on the grounds that "crown and altar" offered each other mutual support and in the belief that governments would totter where diversity of faith prevailed. Rulers on both sides felt certain that religious minorities, if allowed to survive in their realms, would inevitably engage in sedition; nor were they far wrong, since militant Calvinists and Jesuits were indeed dedicated to subverting constituted powers in areas where their parties had not yet triumphed. Thus states tried to extirpate all potential religious resistance, but in the process

sometimes provoked civil wars in which each side tended to assume there could be no victory until the other was exterminated. And of course civil wars might become international in scope if foreign powers chose to aid their embattled religious allies elsewhere.

POLITICAL INSTABILITY

Compounding the foregoing problems were the inherent weaknesses of the major European kingdoms. Most of the major states of early modern Europe had grown during the later Middle Ages by absorbing smaller, traditionally autonomous territories, sometimes by conquest, but more often through marriage alliances or inheritance arrangements between their respective ruling families (a policy known as "dynasticism"). At first some degree of provincial autonomy was usually preserved in these newly absorbed territories. But between 1540 and 1660, when governments were making ever greater financial claims on all their subjects or trying to enforce religious uniformity, rulers often rode roughshod over the rights of these traditionally autonomous provinces. The result, once again, was civil war, in which regionalism, economic grievances, and religious animosities were compounded into a volatile and destructive mixture. Nor was that all, since most governments seeking money and/or religious uniformity tried to rule with a firmer hand than before, and thus sometimes provoked armed resistance from subjects seeking to preserve their traditional constitutional liberties. Given this bewildering variety of motives for revolt, it is not surprising that the long century between 1540 and 1660 was one of the most turbulent in all of European history.

A CENTURY OF RELIGIOUS WARS

> Why did religious conflicts become so deeply entwined with political conflicts during this period?

The greatest single cause of warfare during this period was religious conflict. The wars themselves divide into four phases: a series of German wars from the 1540s to

1555; the French wars of religion from 1562 until 1598; the Dutch wars with Spain between 1566 and 1609; and the Thirty Years' War in Germany between 1618 and 1648.

THE GERMAN WARS OF RELIGION TO 1555

Wars between Catholics and Protestants in Germany began in the 1540s when the Holy Roman emperor Charles V, a devout Catholic, tried to reestablish Catholic unity in Germany by launching a military campaign against several German princes who had instituted Lutheran worship in their territories. Despite some notable victories, Charles's efforts to defeat the Protestant princes failed. Partly this was because he was simultaneously involved in wars against France, and so could not devote his entire attention to German affairs. Primarily, however, Charles failed because the

Catholic princes of Germany feared that if Charles succeeded in defeating the Protestant princes, he might then suppress their own independence also. As a result, the Catholic princes' support for the foreign-born Charles was only lukewarm; at times, they even joined with the Protestant princes in battle against the emperor. Accordingly, religious warfare sputtered on and off until a compromise settlement was reached in the Religious Peace of Augsburg (1555). This rested on the principle of *cuius regio, eius religio* ("as the ruler, so the religion"), which meant that in those principalities where Lutheran princes ruled, Lutheranism would be the sole state religion; where Catholic princes ruled, their territories would be Catholic also. Although the Peace of Augsburg was a historical milestone inasmuch as Catholic rulers for the first time acknowledged the legality of Protestantism, it boded ill for the future in assuming that no sovereign state larger than a free city (for which it made exceptions) could tolerate religious diversity. Moreover, in excluding Calvinism entirely, it ensured that the German Calvinists would become aggressive opponents of the status quo.

THE FRENCH WARS OF RELIGION

From the 1560s on, Europe's religious wars became far more brutal, partly because the combatants had become more intransigent (Calvinists and Jesuits customarily took the lead on their respective sides), and partly because the later religious wars were aggravated by regional, political, and dynastic hostilities. Calvinist missionaries made considerable headway in France between 1541 (when Calvin took power in Geneva) and the outbreak of religious warfare in 1562. By 1562, Calvinists comprised between 10 and 20 percent of France's population, with their numbers swelling daily. Greatly assisting the Calvinist (Huguenot) cause in France was the conversion of many aristocratic French-women to Calvinism. Such women often won over their husbands, who in turn maintained large private armies. But Calvinism in France was also nourished by long-standing regional hostilities within the French kingdom, especially in southern France, where the animosities aroused by the thirteenth-century Albigensian crusade continued to fester.

Until 1562, an uneasy peace continued between the Catholic and the Calvinist forces in France. In 1562, however, the French king died unexpectedly, leaving a young child as his heir. A struggle immediately broke out between Huguenot and Catholic courtiers for control of the regency government. And since both Catholics and

***The Emperor Charles V at Muehlberg* by Titian.** Charles V's attempts to unite a Catholic Germany by military means failed, and he ultimately settled with the Religious Peace of Augsburg in 1555.

WHY DID RELIGIOUS AND POLITICAL CONFLICTS BECOME ENTWINED DURING THIS PERIOD?

A CENTURY OF RELIGIOUS WARS   397

Protestants assumed that France could have only a single *roi, foi,* and *loi* (king, faith, and law), this political struggle immediately took on a religious aspect. Soon all France was aflame. Rampaging mobs ransacked churches and settled local scores. Although the Huguenots were not strong or numerous enough to gain victory, they were too strong to be defeated, especially in their southern French stronghold. Hence, despite intermittent truces, warfare dragged on at great cost of life until 1572, when a truce was arranged by which the Protestant leader, Henry of Navarre, was to marry the Catholic sister of the reigning French king. At this point, however, the cultivated queen mother Catherine de Medici, normally a woman who favored compromise, panicked. Instead of honoring the truce, she plotted to kill the Huguenot leaders while they were assembled in Paris for her daugher's wedding to Henry of Navarre. In the early morning of St. Bartholomew's Day (August 24) most of the Huguenot chiefs were murdered in bed and two to three thousand other Protestants were slaughtered in the streets or drowned in the Seine by Catholic mobs. When word of the Parisian massacre spread to the provinces, some ten thousand more Huguenots were killed in a frenzy of blood lust that swept through France. Henry of Navarre escaped, along with his new bride; but after 1572, the conflict entered a new and even more bitter phase.

Only when the politically astute Henry of Navarre succeeded to the French throne as Henry IV (1589–1610) did the civil war finally come to an end. In 1593 Henry abjured his Protestantism in order to placate France's Catholic majority, declaring as he did so that "Paris is worth a mass." In 1598, however, he offered limited religious freedom to the Huguenots by the Edict of Nantes. Although the Edict recognized Catholicism as the official religion of the kingdom, Huguenot nobles were now allowed to hold Protestant services privately in their castles; other Huguenots were allowed to worship at specified places and to fortify some towns, especially in the south and west, for their own military defense. Huguenots were also guaranteed the right to serve in all public offices, and to enter the universities and hospitals without hindrance.

Although the Edict of Nantes did not countenance absolute freedom of worship, it nevertheless took a major stride in the direction of toleration. But despite its efforts to create one kingdom with two faiths, the effect of the Edict was to divide the French kingdom into separate religious enclaves. In southern and western France, Huguenots came to have their own law courts, staffed by their own judges. They also received substantial powers of self-government, because it was presumed on all sides that the members of one religious group could not be ruled equitably by the adherents of a competing religion. In some ways, indeed, the Huguenot areas became "a state within a state," thus raising again the perpetual fear in Paris that the kingdom of which it was the capital might once again fly apart into its constituent parts, as had happened during the Hundred Years' War. On its own terms, however, the Edict of Nantes was a success. With religious peace established, France quickly began to recover from decades of devastation, even though Henry IV himself was cut down by the dagger of a Catholic fanatic in 1610.

> In some ways, indeed, the Huguenot areas became "a state within a state," thus raising again the perpetual fear in Paris that the kingdom of which it was the capital might once again fly apart into its constituent parts, as had happened during the Hundred Years' War.

THE REVOLT OF THE NETHERLANDS

Bitter warfare also broke out between Catholics and Protestants in the Netherlands, where national resentments exacerbated the predictable religious hatreds. For almost a century the Netherlands had been ruled by the Habsburg family of Holy Roman emperors. But when Charles V retired to a monastery in 1556 (dying two years later) he ceded all his vast territories outside of the Holy Roman empire and Hungary—not only the Netherlands, but Spain, Spanish America, and half of Italy—to his son Philip II (1556–1598). Unlike Charles, Philip viewed the Netherlands primarily as a source of income necessary for pursuing Spanish affairs. Philip also tried to tighten his control over the government of the Netherlands. This aroused the resentment of the local magnates who had dominated the government under Charles V. A religious storm was also brewing. After 1559, when a long war between France and Spain ended, French Calvinists began to stream over the border into the southern Netherlands, making converts wherever they went. Soon there were more Calvinists in Antwerp than in Geneva. To Philip, an ardent supporter of Counter-Reformation Catholicism, this was intolerable. As he declared to the pope on the eve of conflict, "rather than suffer the slightest harm to the true religion and service of God, I would lose all my states and even my life a hundred times over because I am not and will not be the ruler of heretics."

Worried by the growing tensions, a group of local Catholic noblemen led by William of Orange (known as "William the Silent" because he was so successful at hiding his religious and political leanings; in fact he was quite talkative!) appealed to Philip to allow toleration for Calvinists. But before Philip could respond, radical Protestant mobs began ransacking Catholic churches throughout the country, desecrating hosts, smashing statuary, and shattering stained-glass windows. Local troops soon brought the situation under control, but Philip II nonetheless decided to dispatch an army of ten thousand Spanish troops, led by the duke of Alva, to wipe out Protestantism in the Netherlands. Alva's rule quickly became a reign of terror. Operating under martial law, his "Council of Blood" examined some twelve thousand persons on charges of heresy or sedition, of whom nine thousand were convicted and two to three thousand executed. William the Silent fled the country, and all hope for a free Netherlands seemed lost.

But the tide turned quickly for two related reasons. First, instead of giving up, William the Silent converted to Protestantism, sought help from Protestants in France, Germany, and England, and organized bands of sea rovers to harass Spanish shipping on the Netherlandish coast. And second, Alva's tyranny helped William's cause, especially when the hated Spanish governor attempted to levy a 10 percent sales tax. With internal disaffection growing, in 1572 William was able to seize the northern Netherlands even though the north until then had been predominantly Catholic. Thereafter geography played a major role in determining the outcome of the conflict. Spanish armies repeatedly attempted to win back the north, but they were stopped by a combination of impassable rivers and dikes that could be opened to flood out the invaders. Although William the Silent was assassinated by a Catholic in 1584, his son continued to lead the resistance until 1609, when the Spanish crown finally recognized the independence of the northern Dutch Republic. Meanwhile, the pressures of war and persecution had made the whole north Calvinistic, whereas the south—which remained under Spanish control—returned to uniform Catholicism.

ENGLAND AND THE DEFEAT OF THE SPANISH ARMADA

Religious strife could spark civil war, as in France, or political rebellions, as in the Netherlands. But it could also provoke warfare between sovereign states, as in the late-sixteenth-century struggle between England and Spain. A seafaring and trading people, the English in the later sixteenth century were steadily making inroads into Spanish naval and commercial domination, and were also determined to resist any Spanish attempt to block England's lucrative trade with the Low Countries. But the greatest source of antagonism lay in the Atlantic, where English privateers, with the tacit consent of Queen Elizabeth, regularly attacked Spanish treasure ships.

Because Philip II had his hands full in the Netherlands, he resolved to invade England only after the English openly allied with the Dutch rebels in 1585. Even then, Philip moved slowly and made careful plans. Finally, in 1588 he dispatched an enormous fleet, confidently called the "Invincible Armada," to invade insolent Britannia. After an initial standoff in the English Channel, however, the smaller, longer-gunned English warships outmaneuvered the Spanish fleet, while English fireships set some Spanish galleons ablaze. "Protestant gales" did the rest. After a disastrous circumnavigation of the British Isles and Ireland, the shattered flotilla limped home with almost half its ships lost.

The defeat of the Spanish Armada was one of the decisive battles of Western history. Had Spain conquered England, the Spanish might have gone on to crush Holland and perhaps even to destroy Protestantism elsewhere in Europe. But as it was, the Protestant day was saved, and not long afterward Spanish power began to decline, as English and Dutch ships seized command of the seas. In England, patriotic Protestant fervor became especially intense. Popular even before then, "Good Queen Bess" was virtually revered by her subjects until her death in 1603, and England embarked on its golden "Elizabethan Age" of literary endeavor. War with Spain dragged on inconclusively until 1604, but the fighting never brought England any serious harm and was just lively enough to keep the English people deeply committed to their queen, their country, and the Protestant religion.

> The defeat of the Spanish Armada was one of the decisive battles of Western history.

THE DESTRUCTIVENESS OF THE THIRTY YEARS' WAR

Hans Jakob Christoph von Grimmelshausen (1621–1676) lived through the horrors of the Thirty Years' War. His parents were killed, probably when he was thirteen years of age, and he himself was kidnapped the following year. By age fifteen, he was a soldier. His comic masterpiece, Simplicissimus, *from which this extract is taken, drew heavily on these wartime experiences. Although technically "fiction," it portrays with brutal accuracy the cruelty and destructiveness of this war, especially for its peasant victims.*

Although it was not my intention to take the peaceloving reader with these troopers to my dad's house and farm, seeing that matters will go ill therein, yet the course of my history demands that I should leave to kind posterity an account of what manner of cruelties were now and again practised in this our German war: yes, and moreover testify by my own example that such evils must often have been sent to us by the goodness of Almighty God for our profit. For, gentle reader, who would ever have taught me that there was a God in Heaven if these soldiers had not destroyed my dad's house, and by such a deed driven me out among folk who gave me all fitting instruction thereupon? . . .

The first thing these troopers did was, that they stabled their horses: thereafter each fell to his appointed task: which task was neither more nor less than ruin and destruction. For though some began to slaughter and to boil and to roast so that it looked as if there should be a merry banquet forward, yet others there were who did but storm through the house above and below stairs. Others stowed together great parcels of cloth and apparel and all manner of household stuff, as if they would set up a frippery market. All that they had no mind to take with them they cut in pieces. Some thrust their swords through the hay and straw as if they had not enough sheep and swine to slaughter: and some shook the feathers out of the beds and in their stead stuffed in bacon and other dried meat and provisions as if such were better and softer to sleep upon. Others broke the stove and the windows as if they had a never-ending summer to promise. Houseware of copper and tin they beat flat, and packed such vessels, all bent and spoiled, in with the rest. Bedsteads, tables, chairs, and benches they burned, though there lay many cords of dry wood in the yard. Pots and pipkins must all go to pieces, either because they would eat none but roast flesh, or because their purpose was to make there but a single meal.

Our maid was so handled in the stable that she could not come out; which is a shame to tell of. Our man they laid bound upon the ground, thrust a gag into his mouth, and poured a pailful of filthy water into his body: and by this, which they called a Swedish draught, they forced him to lead a party of them to another place where they captured men and beasts, and brought them back to our farm, in which company were my dad, my mother, and our Ursula.

And now they began: first to take the flints out of their pistols and in place of them to jam the peasants' thumbs in and so to torture the poor rogues as if they had been about the burning of witches: for one of them they had taken they thrust into the baking oven and there lit a fire under him, although he had as yet confessed no crime: as for another, they put a cord round his head and so twisted it tight with a piece of wood that the blood gushed from his mouth and nose and ears. In a word each had his own device to torture the peasants, and each peasant his several tortures.

Hans Jakob Christoph von Grimmelshausen, *Simplicissimus*. Translated by S. Goodrich (New York: Daedalus, 1995), pp. 1–3, 8–10, 32–35.

THE THIRTY YEARS' WAR

With the promulgation of the Edict of Nantes in 1598, the peace between England and Spain of 1604, and the truce between Spain and Holland of 1609, religious warfare in northwestern Europe came briefly to an end. But in 1618 a major new war broke out, this time in Germany. Since this struggle raged more or less unceasingly until 1648 it is known as the Thirty Years' War. Spain and France quickly became engaged in the conflict in Germany and eventually in war with one another. Meanwhile, domestic resentments in Spain, France, and England flared up during the 1640s into concurrent outbreaks of civil war. As an English preacher said in 1643, "these are days of shaking, and this shaking is universal."

The Thirty Years' War began as a war between Catholics and Protestants, but ended as an international struggle in which the initial religious dimension was almost entirely forgotten. Between the Peace of Augsburg in 1555 and the outbreak of war in 1618, Calvinists had replaced Lutherans in a few German territories, but the overall balance between Protestants and Catholics within the Holy Roman Empire had remained undisturbed. In 1618, however, war broke out after Ferdinand, the Catholic Habsburg prince of Poland, Austria, and Hungary, was elected king of the Protestant territory of Bohemia. The staunchly Protestant Bohemian nobility had opposed Ferdinand's election, and when Ferdinand began to suppress Protestantism in Bohemia, they rebelled. German Catholic forces ruthlessly counterattacked, first in Bohemia and then in Germany proper, led by Ferdinand, who in 1619 also became Holy Roman emperor. Within a decade, a German Catholic league seemed close to extirpating Protestantism throughout Germany.

Ferdinand's success raised once again the prospect that an overly powerful Holy Roman emperor might threaten the political autonomy of the German princes, Catholic and Protestant alike. Thus when the Lutheran king of Sweden, Gustavus Adolphus, the "Lion of the North," marched into Germany in 1630 to champion the Protestant cause, he was welcomed by several German Catholic princes who preferred to see the former religious balance restored rather than risk surrendering their sovereignty to Ferdinand II. To make matters still more ironic, Gustavus's Protestant army was secretly subsidized by Catholic France, whose policy was then dictated by a cardinal of the church, Cardinal Richelieu. This was because Habsburg Spain had been fighting in Germany on the side of Habsburg Austria, and Richelieu was determined to prevent France from being surrounded by a strong Habsburg alliance on the north, east, and south. In any event, the military genius Gustavus Adolphus started routing the Habsburgs, but after he fell in battle in 1632, French armies entered the war directly on Sweden's side. From then until 1648 the struggle was really one of France and Sweden against Austria and Spain, with Germany a helpless battleground.

Nor did the Peace of Westphalia, which finally ended the Thirty Years' War in 1648, do much to vindicate anyone's death, even though it did establish some abiding landmarks in European history. Above all, from the international perspective, the Peace of Westphalia marked the emergence of France as the predominant power on the continental European scene, replacing Spain. France

> Above all, from the international perspective, the Peace of Westphalia marked the emergence of France as the predominant power on the continental European scene, replacing Spain.

would hold this position for the next two centuries. The greatest losers in the conflict (aside, of course, from the German people themselves) were the Austrian Habsburgs, who were forced to surrender all the territory they had gained in Germany and to abandon their hopes of using the office of Holy Roman emperor to dominate central Europe. Otherwise, something very close to the German status quo of 1618 was reestablished, with Protestant principalities in the north balancing Catholic ones in the south, and Germany so hopelessly divided that it could play no united role in European history until the nineteenth century.

DIVERGENT PATHS: SPAIN, FRANCE, AND ENGLAND, 1600–1660

What caused the decline of Spain in the seventeenth century?

The long century of war between 1540 and 1660 decisively altered the balance of power among the major kingdoms of western Europe. Germany emerged from the Thirty Years' War a devastated and exhausted land.

EUROPE AT THE END OF THE THIRTY YEARS' WAR

What was at issue in the Thirty Years' War? Why did Catholic France ally with Lutheran Sweden against German and Austrian Catholics? Why did this war, which began as a religious conflict within the Holy Roman empire, turn into an international struggle? Which European powers stayed out of the war? Why did they do so?

Map labels

RUSSIA

BLACK SEA

CYPRUS (to Ottoman Empire)

OTTOMAN EMPIRE

Constantinople

AEGEAN SEA

Danube R.

Kiev

POLAND

Warsaw

Budapest

HUNGARY

CRETE (to Spain)

MEDITERRANEAN SEA

TEUTONIC ORDER

EAST PRUSSIA

Danzig

Vistula R.

Stockholm

SWEDEN

BALTIC SEA

(to Venice)

(to Venice)

Ragusa

Zara

Cattaro

ADRIATIC SEA

Vienna

AUSTRIA

Elbe R.

SAXONY

HOLY ROMAN EMPIRE

BAVARIA

VENICE

PAPAL STATES

ITALY

Rome

Naples

KINGDOM OF THE TWO SICILIES

Berlin

MECKLEN-BURG

BRANDENBURG

HANOVER

Hamburg

NORWAY

Christiana

DENMARK

Copenhagen

NETHERLANDS

Amsterdam

HESSE

WÜRTTEM-BERG

Rhine R.

LORRAINE

SPANISH NETH.

FRANCHE-COMTÉ

SWITZ.

MILAN

SAVOY

GENOA

FLORENCE

CORSICA (to Genoa)

SARDINIA (to Spain)

NORTH SEA

SCOTLAND

Edinburgh

Liverpool

ENGLAND

London

Seine R.

Paris

FRANCE

Loire R.

Bordeaux

Garonne R.

Marseilles

AVIGNON

PIEDMONT

Rhone R.

BALEARIC ISLANDS

English Channel

IRELAND

Dublin

ATLANTIC OCEAN

ARAGON

CASTILE

Madrid

Tagus R.

SPAIN

Strait of Gibraltar

PORTUGAL

Lisbon

500 Miles

500 Kilometers

250

250

0

Legend

The Church
Spain
Austria
Brandenburg–Prussia
Boundary of the Holy Roman Empire

Inset

EUROPE

Area of detail

AFRICA

But after 1600, Spain too was crippled by its unremitting military commitments and exertions. The French monarchy, by contrast, steadily increased its authority over France. By 1660 France had become the most powerful country on the European mainland, decisively eclipsing Spain. In England, meanwhile, a bloody civil war broke out between the king and his critics in Parliament; but after a short-lived experiment in republican rule, England in 1660 returned to its constitutional status as a "mixed" monarchy in which power was shared between king and Parliament.

THE DECLINE OF SPAIN

Spain's greatest underlying weakness was economic. Lacking either rich agricultural or mineral resources, Spain desperately needed to develop industries and a balanced trading pattern as its Atlantic rivals were doing. But the Spanish nobility preferred to use American silver to buy manufactured goods from other parts of Europe in order to live in splendor and dedicate itself to military exploits. As a result, few new industries were established, and when the influx of silver began to decline, the Spanish economy was left with nothing except increasing debts.

Nonetheless, the crown, dedicated to supporting the Counter-Reformation and maintaining Spain's international dominance, could not cease fighting abroad. Even in the relatively peaceful year of 1608 4 million out of a total revenue of 7 million ducats were paid for military expenditures. Thus when Spain became engaged in the Thirty Years' War it overextended itself. In 1643 French troops inflicted a stunning defeat on the famed Spanish infantry at Rocroi, the first time that a Spanish army had been overcome in battle since the reign of Ferdinand and Isabella. Worse still was the fact that by then two territories belonging to Spain's European empire were in open revolt.

In order to understand the causes of these revolts, we must recognize that in the seventeenth century the

The Battle of Rocroi. Spain's defeat at Rocroi by the French was the first time the Spanish army had lost in battle since the reign of Ferdinand and Isabella, yet another contributing factor to the decline of Spain's grand empire during the Thirty Years' War.

WHAT CAUSED THE DECLINE OF SPAIN IN THE SEVENTEENTH CENTURY?

DIVERGENT PATHS: SPAIN, FRANCE, AND ENGLAND, 1600–1660   403

governing power of Spain lay entirely in Castile. After the marriage of Isabella of Castile and Ferdinand of Aragon in 1469, Castile had emerged as the dominant partner in the Spanish union, becoming even more dominant when it took over Portugal in 1580. In the absence of any great financial hardships, semi-autonomous Catalunya (the most fiercely independent part of Aragon) endured Castilian hegemony. But in 1640, when the strains of warfare induced Castile to limit Catalan liberties in order to raise more money and men for combat, Catalunya revolted and drove out its Castilian governors. When the Portuguese learned of the Catalan uprising they revolted as well, followed by southern Italians who rose up against Castilian viceroys in Naples and Sicily in 1647. Only the momentary inability of Spain's greatest external enemies, France and England, to take advantage of its plight saved the Spanish empire from utter collapse. This gave the Castilian government time to put down the Italian revolts; by 1652 it had also brought Catalunya to heel. But Portugal retained its independence, and by the Peace of the Pyrenees, signed with France in 1659, Spain in effect abandoned its ambition of dominating Europe.

THE GROWING POWER OF FRANCE

Spain and France were of almost identical territorial extent, and both countries had been created by the same process of accretion. But when the Thirty Years' War made ruthless tax collecting urgently necessary, France weathered the storm whereas Spain did not, a result largely attributable to France's greater wealth and the greater prestige of the French crown.

In good times most French people, including those from the outlying provinces, tended to revere their king. Certainly they had excellent reason to do so during the reign of Henry IV. Having established religious peace in 1598 by the Edict of Nantes, the affable Henry, who declared that there should be a chicken in every French family's pot each Sunday, set out to restore the prosperity of a country devastated by four decades of civil war. Fortunately France had enormous economic resiliency, owing to its extremely rich and varied agricultural resources. Unlike Spain, which had to import food, France normally was able to feed itself. Henry's finance minister, the duke of Sully, financed the rebuilding or new construction of roads, bridges, and canals to facilitate the flow of goods. Henry IV also ordered the construction of royal factories to manufacture luxury goods such as crystal, glass, and tapestries, and supported the growth of silk, linen, and woolen cloth industries in many different parts of the country. Henry's patronage also allowed the explorer Samuel de Champlain to claim parts of Canada as France's first foothold in the New World. Thus Henry IV's reign certainly must be counted as one of the most benevolent in all French history.

CARDINAL RICHELIEU

Far less benevolent was Henry's de facto successor as ruler of France, Cardinal Richelieu (1585–1642). The cardinal, of course, was never the real king of France—the actual title was held from 1610 to 1643 by Henry IV's ineffectual son Louis XIII. But as first minister from 1624 to his death in 1642 Richelieu governed as he wished, enhancing centralized royal power at home and expanding French influence in Europe. Accordingly, when Huguenots rebelled against restrictions placed on them by the Edict of Nantes, Richelieu put them down with an iron fist, depriving them of their political and military rights. Richelieu also instituted a new system of local government by royal officials known as intendants, who were expressly commissioned to ride roughshod over any provincial resistance. By these and other methods Richelieu made French government more centralized than ever and managed to double the crown's income during his rule. But since he also engaged in an ambitious foreign policy directed against the Habsburgs of Austria and Spain, resulting in France's costly involvement in the Thirty Years' War, internal pressures mounted in the years after Richelieu's death.

> Having established religious peace in 1598 by the Edict of Nantes, the affable Henry, who declared that there should be a chicken in every French family's pot each Sunday, set out to restore the prosperity of a country devastated by four decades of civil war.

THE FRONDE

A reaction against French governmental centralization manifested itself in a series of revolts between 1648 and 1653 collectively known as "the slingshot tumults," or in French, the *Fronde*. By this time Louis XIII had been succeeded by his son Louis XIV, but because the latter was still a boy, France was governed by a regency consisting of Louis' mother, Anne of Austria, and her paramour Cardinal Mazarin. Both were foreigners (Anne was a Habsburg and Mazarin originally an Italian adventurer named Giulio Mazarini), and many of their subjects, including some extremely powerful nobles, hated them. Popular resentments were greater still because the costs of war, combined with several consecutive years of bad harvests, had brought France temporarily into a grave economic plight. Thus when cliques of nobles expressed their disgust with Mazarin for primarily self-interested reasons, they found much support throughout the country, and uncoordinated revolts against the regency government flared on and off for several years.

France, however, did not come close to falling apart. The French crown retained great reservoirs of prestige. Neither the aristocratic leaders of the Fronde nor the commoners who joined them in revolt claimed to be resisting the young king but only the alleged corruption and mismanagement of Mazarin. Thus when Louis XIV began to rule in his own name in 1651 and pretexts for revolt against "corrupt ministers" no longer existed, the opposition was soon silenced. Remembering the turbulence of the Fronde for the rest of his life, Louis XIV resolved never to let his aristocracy or his provinces get out of hand again and ruled as the most effective royal absolutist in all of French history.

THE ENGLISH CIVIL WAR

Of all the revolts that shook mid-seventeenth-century Europe, the most radical in its consequences was the English civil war. The causes of this conflict were similar to those that sparked rebellions in Spain and France. Only in England, however, did these conflicts lead to the deposition and execution of the king (1649), an eleven-year "interregnum" during which England was officially a republic (1649–1660), and ultimately to the restoration of the monarchy under conditions designed to safeguard Parliament's place in government and to guarantee a limited degree of religious toleration for all Protestants.

THE ORIGINS OF THE ENGLISH CIVIL WAR

The chain of events that led to war between king and Parliament in 1642 began in the last decades of Queen Elizabeth's reign (1559–1603). During the 1590s, the expenses of war with Spain, together with a rebellion in Ireland, widespread crop failures, and the inadequacies of the antiquated English taxation system drove the queen's government deeply into debt. Factional disputes around the court also became more bitter as courtiers, anticipating the aging queen's death, jockeyed for position under her presumed successor, the Scottish king

James I. "The wisest fool in Christendom."

James Stuart. Only on her deathbed, however, did the queen finally confirm that her throne should go to her Scottish cousin. As a result, neither James nor his new English subjects knew very much about one another when he took the throne at the end of 1603.

The relationship did not begin well. James's English subjects looked down on the Scots whom he brought with him to London, whom they blamed, quite unreasonably, for the crown's indebtedness. James, meanwhile, saw clearly that to resolve his debts he had to have more revenue. But rather than bargain with parliamentary representatives for increased taxation he chose to lecture them on the prerogatives of kingship. When this approach failed to produce the taxation he needed, James made peace with Spain and then took steps to raise revenues without parliamentary approval, imposing new tolls on trade and selling trading monopolies to favored courtiers. These measures aroused further resentments against the king, and so made voluntary grants of taxation from Parliament even less likely to be approved. As a result, the king's financial situation steadily worsened.

James was more adept with respect to religious policy. Scotland had been a firmly Calvinist country since the

WHAT CAUSED THE DECLINE OF SPAIN IN THE SEVENTEENTH CENTURY?

DIVERGENT PATHS: SPAIN, FRANCE, AND ENGLAND, 1600–1660   405

1560s. In England, however, the Elizabethan religious settlement had produced much less theological definition. By 1603 England was clearly a Protestant country, but a significant number of English Protestants continued to hope for a "second" or "further" reformation that would bring their church more firmly into line with Calvinist principles. Other Protestants resisted such efforts, and labeled those who supported them "Puritans." As king, James was compelled to mediate these conflicts. By and large, he did so successfully. Only in Ireland, which remained overwhelmingly Catholic, did James store up future trouble. By encouraging the "plantation" of more than eight thousand Scottish Calvinists in the northern province of Ulster, he undermined the property rights of Irish Catholics and created religious animosities that have lasted until the present day.

The delicate religious balance preserved by James I was shattered in 1625 by the accession of Charles I. Throwing his father's habitual caution to the winds, Charles immediately launched a new war with Spain, exacerbating his financial problems and alarming his Protestant subjects by proposing to raise Irish Catholic troops for military service in Germany. Protestant alarm was further increased when Charles married Henrietta Maria, the Catholic daughter of King Louis XIII of France. The situation became truly dangerous, however, when Charles openly began to favor the most anti-Calvinist elements in the English church, and then attempted to impose this religious policy on Scotland. The Scots rebelled, and in 1640 a Scottish army marched south into England to demand the withdrawal of Charles's "Catholicizing" religious reforms.

To meet the Scottish threat, Charles was forced to summon the English Parliament for the first time in eleven years. Relations between the king and his Parliament had broken down in the late 1620s, when Charles responded to Parliament's refusal to grant him additional funds by demanding forced loans from his subjects and then punishing those who refused to comply by quartering soldiers in their homes or throwing them into prison without trial. In response, in 1628 Parliament forced the king to accept the Petition of Right, which declared all taxes not voted by Parliament illegal, condemned the quartering of soldiers in private houses, and prohibited arbitrary imprisonment and martial law in time of peace. Angered rather than chastened by the Petition of Right, Charles resolved to

Charles I. This portrait by Anthony Van Dyck vividly captures the ill-fated monarch's arrogance.

rule without Parliament entirely, funding his government during the 1630s with a variety of levies and fines imposed without parliamentary consent.

It was only the Scottish invasion that forced Charles to summon a new Parliament. Once summoned, however, the parliamentarians were determined to impose a series of radical reforms on the king's government before they would even consider granting him funds to raise an army against the Scots. Charles initially cooperated with these reforms, even allowing Parliament to execute his chief minister. But it soon became clear that the parliamentary leaders had no intention of fighting the Scots. Instead, a de facto alliance emerged between them, which was reinforced by their common, Calvinist, religious outlook. By 1642, Charles had had enough. Marching his guards into the House of Commons, he tried (but failed) to arrest five of its leaders. Charles then withdrew from London to raise an army. Parliament responded by summoning its own force and voting the taxation to pay for it. By the end of 1642, open warfare had erupted between king and Parliament.

> Angered rather than chastened by the Petition of Right, Charles resolved to rule without Parliament entirely, funding his government during the 1630s with a variety of levies and fines imposed without parliamentary consent.

CIVIL WAR AND COMMONWEALTH

Arrayed on the king's side were most of England's aristocrats and largest landowners, who were loyal to the established Church of England despite their opposition to some of Charles's own religious innovations. The parliamentary forces were comprised of smaller landholders, tradesmen, and artisans, most of whom were Puritans. At first the royalists, having obvious advantages of military experience, won most of the victories. In 1644, however, the parliamentary army was reorganized, and soon afterward the fortunes of battle shifted. The royalist forces were badly beaten, and in 1646 the king was compelled to surrender. Soon thereafter, the episcopate was abolished and a Calvinist-style church was established throughout England.

The struggle might now have ended had not a quarrel developed within the parliamentary party. The majority of its members were ready to restore Charles to the throne as a limited monarch under an arrangement whereby a uniformly Calvinist faith would be imposed on both Scotland and England as the state religion. But a radical minority of Puritans, commonly known as Independents, distrusted Charles and insisted on religious toleration for themselves and all other Protestants. Their leader was Oliver Cromwell (1599–1658), who had risen to command the parliamentary army.

Taking advantage of the dissension within the ranks of his opponents, Charles renewed the war in 1648, but after a brief campaign was forced to surrender. Cromwell now resolved to end the life of "that man of blood," and, ejecting all the moderate Protestants from parliament by force of arms, obliged the "Rump" Parliament that remained to vote an end to the monarchy. On January 30, 1649 Charles I was beheaded; a short time later the hereditary House of Lords was abolished, and England became a republic.

But founding a republic was far easier than maintaining one. Officially called a Commonwealth, the new form of government did not last long. Technically the Rump Parliament continued as the legislative body, but Cromwell, with the army at his command, possessed the real power and soon became exasperated by the legislators' attempts to enrich themselves by confiscating their opponents' property. Accordingly, in 1653 he marched a detachment of troops into the Rump Parliament. Declaring "Come, I will put an end to your prating," he ordered the members to disperse. The Commonwealth thus ceased to exist and was soon replaced by the "Protectorate," a thinly disguised autocracy established under a constitution drafted by officers of the army.

Called the Instrument of Government, this text was the nearest approximation to a written constitution England has ever had. Extensive powers were given to Cromwell as "lord protector" for life, and his office was made hereditary. At first a new Parliament exercised limited authority to make laws and levy taxes, but in 1655 Cromwell abruptly dismissed its members also. Thereafter the government became a virtual dictatorship, with Cromwell wielding a sovereignty more absolute than any Stuart monarch ever dreamed of claiming.

THE RESTORATION OF THE MONARCHY

Given the choice between a Puritan military dictatorship and the old royalist regime, when the occasion arose England unhesitatingly opted for the latter. Years of unpopular Calvinist austerities had discredited the Puritans, making most people long for the milder style of the Elizabethan church. Thus not long after Cromwell's death in 1658, one of his generals seized power and called for elections to a new Parliament, which met in the spring of 1660 and proclaimed as king Charles I's exiled son, Charles II, after Charles first gave the traditional promises of good government and then promised a limited religious toleration for all Protestants.

Charles II (1660–1685) restored bishops to the Church of England, but he did not return to the provocative religious policies of his father. Declaring with characteristic good humor that he did not wish to "resume his travels," Charles agreed to respect Parliament and observe the Petition of Right. He also accepted all the legislation passed by Parliament immediately before the outbreak of civil war in 1642,

---

CHRONOLOGY

ORIGINS OF THE ENGLISH CIVIL WAR, 1603–1660

Reign of the Stuarts begins	1603
Reign of Charles I	1625–1649
Rule without Parliament	1629–1640
English civil war	1642–1649
Charles I beheaded	1649
Commonwealth	1649–1653
Protectorate	1653–1658
Restoration of the monarchy	1660

DEMOCRACY AND THE ENGLISH CIVIL WAR

The English civil war raised fundamental issues about the political rights and responsibilities of Englishmen. Many of these issues were addressed in a lengthy debate held within the General Council of Cromwell's New Model Army at Putney in October 1647. Interestingly, none of the participants in these debates seems to have recognized the implications their arguments might have for the political rights of women. Only King Charles, speaking moments before his execution in 1649, saw the radical implications of the constitutional experiment on which the Parliamentary forces had embarked—but ironically, it was his own radical assertions of monarchical authority that prompted the rebellion that overthrew him.

THE ARMY DEBATES, 1647

Colonel Rainsborough: Really, I think that the poorest man that is in England has a life to live as the greatest man; and therefore truly, sir, I think it's clear, that every man that is to live under a government ought first by his own consent to put himself under that government; and I do think that the poorest man in England is not at all bound in a strict sense to that government that he has not had a voice to put himself under . . . insomuch that I should doubt whether I was an Englishman or not, that should doubt of these things.

General Ireton: Give me leave to tell you, that if you make this the rule, I think you must fly for refuge to an absolute natural right, and you must deny all civil right; and I am sure it will come to that in the consequence. . . . For my part, I think it is no right at all. I think that no person has a right to an interest or share in the disposing of the affairs of the kingdom, and in determining or choosing those that shall determine what laws we shall be ruled by here, no person has a right to this that has not a permanent fixed interest in this kingdom, and those persons together are properly the represented of this kingdom who, taken together, and consequently are to make up the representers of this kingdom. . . .

We talk of birthright. Truly, birthright there is. . . . [M]en may justly have by birthright, by their very being born in England, that we should not seclude them out of England. That we should not refuse to give them air and place and ground, and the freedom of the highways and other things, to live amongst us, not any man that is born here, though he in birth or by his birth there come nothing at all that is part of the permanent interest of this kingdom to him. That I think is due to a man by birth. But that by a man's being born here he shall have a share in that power that shall dispose of the lands here, and of all things here, I do not think it is a sufficient ground.

Divine Right and Democracy: An Anthology of Political Writing in Stuart England, edited by David Wootton (New York: Viking Penguin, 1986), pp. 286–287 (language modernized).

CHARLES I ON THE SCAFFOLD, 1649

I think it is my duty, to God first, and to my country, for to clear myself both as an honest man, a good king, and a good Christian.

I shall begin first with my innocence. In truth I think it not very needful for me to insist long upon this, for all the world knows that I never did begin a war with the two Houses of Parliament; and I call God to witness, to whom I must shortly make an account, that I never did intend to incroach upon their privileges. . . .

As for the people—truly I desire their liberty and freedom as much as anybody whatsoever. But I must tell you that their liberty and freedom consists in having of government those laws by which their lives and goods may be most their own. It is not for having share in government. That is nothing pertaining to them. A subject and a sovereign are clean different things, and therefore, until they do that—I mean that you do put

the people in that liberty as I say—certainly they will never enjoy themselves.

Sirs, it was for this that now I am come here. If I would have given way to an arbitrary way, for to have all laws changed according to the power of the sword, I needed not to have come here. And therefore I tell you (and I pray God it be not laid to your charge) that I am the martyr of the people.

Brian Tierney, Donald Kagan, and L. Pearce Williams, eds., *Great Issues in Western Civilization* (New York: Random House, 1967), pp. 46–47.

including the requirement that Parliament be summoned at least once every three years. After one further test in the late seventeenth century, England thus emerged from its civil war as a limited monarchy, in which power was exercised by "the king in parliament."

The Problem of Doubt and the Quest for Certainty

Why was this period such a fertile one for political philosophy?

Between 1540 and 1660, Europeans were forced to confront a world in which all that they had once taken for granted was suddenly cast into doubt. An entirely new world had been discovered in the Americas, populated by millions of people whose very existence compelled Europeans to rethink some of their most basic ideas about humanity and human nature. Equally disorienting, the religious uniformity of Europe, although never absolute, had been shattered to an unprecedented extent by the Reformation and the religious wars that arose from it. In 1540, it was still possible to imagine that these religious divisions might be temporary. By 1660, it was clear they would be permanent. No longer, therefore, could Europeans regard revealed religious faith as an adequate foundation for universal philosophical conclusions, for even Christians now

disagreed about the fundamental truths of the faith. Political allegiances were similarly under threat, as intellectuals and common people alike began to assert a right to resist princes with whom they disagreed on matters of religion. Even morality and custom were beginning to seem arbitrary and detached from the natural ordering of the world.

Europeans responded to this pervasive climate of doubt in a variety of ways, ranging from radical skepticism to authoritarian assertions of religious fideism and political absolutism. What united their responses, however, was a sometimes desperate search for new foundations on which to reconstruct some measure of certainty in the face of Europe's new intellectual, religious, and political challenges.

Witchcraft Accusations and the Power of the State

Adding to the fears of Europeans was their conviction that witchcraft was a mortal and increasing threat to their world. Although most people in the Middle Ages believed that certain persons, usually women, could heal or harm through the practice of magic, it was not until the fifteenth century that learned authorities began to insist that such powers could only derive from some kind of "pact" made by the "witch" with the devil. Once this belief became accepted, judicial officers became much more active in seeking out suspected witches for prosecution. In 1484 Pope Innocent VIII ordered papal inquisitors to use all the means at their disposal to detect and eliminate witchcraft, including torture of suspected witches. Predictably, torture increased the number of accused witches who

WHY WAS THIS PERIOD SUCH A FERTILE ONE FOR POLITICAL PHILOSOPHY?

THE PROBLEM OF DOUBT AND THE QUEST FOR CERTAINTY   409

Supposed Witches Worshiping the Devil in the form of a Billy Goat. In the background other "witches" ride bareback on flying demons. This is one of the earliest visual conceptions of witchcraft, dating from around 1460.

confessed to their alleged crimes; and as more accused witches confessed, more and more witches were "discovered," accused, and executed, even in areas (such as England) where torture was not employed and where the Inquisition did not operate.

In considering the rash of witchcraft persecution that swept early modern Europe, we need to keep two facts in mind. First of all, the witchcraft trials were by no means limited to Catholic countries. Protestant reformers believed in the insidious powers of Satan just as much as Catholics did. Second, it was only when the efforts of religious authorities to detect witchcraft were backed up by the coercive powers of secular governments to execute them that the fear of "witches" became truly murderous. Between 1580 and about 1660, however, enthusiasm for catching and killing "witches" claimed tens of thousands of victims, of whom at least three quarters were women. After 1660, accusations of witchcraft gradually diminished, but isolated incidents, such as the one at Salem, Massachusetts, continued to crop up for another half century.

This witch mania reflects the fears that early modern Europeans held about the devil. But it also reflects their growing conviction that only the state, and not the church, had the power to protect them. One of the most striking features of the mania for hunting down "witches" is the extent to which these prosecutions, in both Catholic and Protestant countries, were carried out under the supervision of the state. In both Catholic and Protestant countries, the result of these witchcraft trials was thus a considerable increase in the scope of the state's powers and responsibilities to regulate the lives of its subjects.

THE SEARCH FOR AUTHORITY

The crisis of Europe's iron century (as even contemporaries sometimes called it) was fundamentally a crisis of authority. Attempts to reestablish some foundation for agreed authority took many forms. For the French nobleman Michel de Montaigne (1533–1592), who wrote during the height of the French wars of religion, the result was a searching skepticism about the possibilities of any certain knowledge whatsoever. Although the range of subjects of his *Essays* is wide, two main themes are dominant. One is a pervasive skepticism. Making his motto *Que sais-je?* ("What do I know?"), Montaigne decided that he knew very little for certain. From this Montaigne's second main principle followed—the need for moderation. Since all people think they know the perfect religion and the perfect government, yet few agree on what that perfection might be, Montaigne concluded that no religion or government is really perfect and consequently no belief is worth fighting for to the death. Instead, people should accept the teachings of religion on faith, and obey the governments constituted to rule over them, without resorting to fanaticism in either sphere.

Montaigne sought refuge from the trials of his age in skepticism, distance, and resigned dignity. His contemporary, the French lawyer Jean Bodin (1530–1596), looked instead to resolve the disorders of the day by reestablishing the powers of the state on new and more secure foundations. Like Montaigne, Bodin was particularly troubled by the upheavals caused by the religious wars in France—he had even witnessed the frightful St. Bartholomew's Day Massacre of 1572 in Paris. But instead of shrugging his shoulders about the bloodshed, he resolved to offer a political plan to make sure turbulence would cease. This he did in his monumental *Six Books of the Commonwealth* (1576), the earliest fully developed statement of absolute governmental sovereignty in Western political thought. For Bodin, sovereignty was "the most high, absolute, and perpetual power over all subjects," consisting principally in the power "to give laws to subjects without their consent." Bodin insisted that monarchs could in no way be limited, either by legislative or judicial bodies, or even by laws made by their predecessors or themselves. Even if the ruler proved a tyrant, the subject had no warrant to resist, for any resistance would open the door "to a licentious anarchy which is worse than the harshest tyranny in the world."

Like Bodin, who was moved by the events of St. Bartholomew's Day to formulate a doctrine of political absolutism, Thomas Hobbes (1588–1679) was moved by the turmoil of the English civil war to do the same in his classic of political theory, *Leviathan* (1651). Yet Hobbes differed from Bodin in several respects. For one, whereas Bodin assumed that the absolute sovereign power would be a royal monarch, Hobbes made no such assumption. Any form of government capable of protecting its subjects' lives and property might act as a sovereign (and hence all-powerful) Leviathan. Then too, whereas Bodin defined his state as "the lawful government of families" and hence did not believe that the state could abridge private property rights because families could not exist without property, Hobbes's state existed to rule over atomistic individuals and thus was licensed to trample over both liberty and property if the government's own survival was at stake.

Perhaps the most moving attempt to respond to the problem of doubt in seventeenth-century culture was offered by the French moral and religious philosopher Blaise Pascal (1623–1662). Pascal began his career as a mathematician and scientific rationalist. But at age thirty Pascal abandoned science as the result of a conversion experience and became a firm adherent of Jansenism, a puritanical faction within French Catholicism. From then until his death he worked on a highly ambitious philosophical-religious project meant to persuade doubters of the truth of Christianity by appealing simultaneously to their intellects and their emotions. Pascal's *Pensées* ("Thoughts") express the author's own terror, anguish, and awe in the face of evil and eternity, but present that awe itself as evidence for the existence of God. Pascal's hope was that on this foundation, some measure of hopefulness about humanity and its capacity for self-knowledge could be re-erected that would avoid both the dogmatism and the extreme skepticism that were so prominent in seventeenth-century society.

LITERATURE AND THE ARTS

What was the relationship between the Baroque school and the Counter-Reformation?

Doubt and the uncertainty of human knowledge were also primary themes in the literature and art produced during western Europe's iron century. The greatest writers and painters of the period were moved by a realization of the ambiguities and ironies of human existence not unlike that expressed in different ways by Montaigne and Pascal. They all were fully aware of the horrors of war and human suffering so rampant in their day, but they also sought some measure of redemption for human beings caught up in a world that treated them so cruelly. Out of this tragic balance came some of the greatest works in the entire history of European literature and art.

MIGUEL DE CERVANTES (1547–1616)

Cervantes' masterpiece, the satirical romance *Don Quixote*, recounts the adventures of a Spanish gentleman, Don Quixote of La Mancha, who becomes slightly unbalanced by his constant reading of chivalric epics. In his distorted fancy he mistakes inns for castles and serving girls for courtly ladies on fire with love. Set off in contrast to the "knight-errant" is the figure of his faithful squire, Sancho Panza. The latter represents the ideal of the practical man, with his feet on the ground and content with the modest but substantial pleasures of eating, drinking, and sleeping. Yet Cervantes clearly does not wish to say that the realism of a Sancho Panza is categorically preferable to the "quixotic" idealism of his master. Rather, the two men represent different facets of human nature. Without

WHAT WAS THE RELATIONSHIP BETWEEN THE BAROQUE SCHOOL AND THE COUNTER-REFORMATION?

LITERATURE AND THE ARTS   411

any doubt, *Don Quixote* is a devastating satire on the anachronistic chivalric mentality that was already hastening Spain's decline. But for all that, the reader's sympathies remain with the protagonist, the man from La Mancha who dares to "dream the impossible dream."

ELIZABETHAN AND JACOBEAN DRAMA

Among a bevy of great Elizabethan and Jacobean playwrights, the most outstanding were Christopher Marlowe (1564–1593), Ben Jonson (c. 1572–1637), and William Shakespeare (1564–1616). Of the three, the fiery Marlowe, whose life was cut short in a tavern brawl before he reached the age of thirty, was the most popular in his own day. In plays such as *Tamburlaine* and *Doctor Faustus* Marlowe created larger-than-life heroes who seek and come close to conquering everything in their path and feeling every possible sensation. But they meet unhappy ends because, for Marlowe, there are limits on human striving, and wretchedness as well as greatness lies in the human lot.

In contrast to the heroic tragedies of Marlowe, Ben Jonson wrote corrosive comedies that expose human vices and foibles. In the particularly bleak *Volpone* Jonson shows people behaving like deceitful and lustful animals, but in the later *Alchemist* he balances an attack on quackery and gullibility with admiration for resourceful lower-class characters who cleverly take advantage of their supposed betters.

The greatest of the Elizabethan dramatists, William Shakespeare was born into the family of a tradesman in the provincial town of Stratford-on-Avon. Little is known about his early life. He left his native village, having gained a modest education, when he was about twenty, and went to London where he found employment in the theater. How he eventually became an actor and still later a writer of plays is uncertain, but by the age of twenty-eight he had definitely acquired a reputation as an author sufficient to excite the jealousy of his rivals. Before he retired to his native Stratford about 1610 to spend the rest of his days in ease, he had written or collaborated in writing nearly forty plays, over and above one hundred fifty sonnets, and two long narrative poems.

Shakespeare's dramas fall thematically into three groups. Those written during the playwright's early years are characterized by a sense of confidence that, despite human foolishness, the world is fundamentally orderly and just. These include a number of the history plays, which recount England's struggles and glories leading up to the triumph of the Tudor dynasty; the lyrical romantic tragedy *Romeo and Juliet*; and a number of comedies including the magical *Midsummer Night's Dream*, *Twelfth Night*, *As You Like It*, and *Much Ado about Nothing*.

The plays from Shakespeare's second period are far darker in mood, being characterized by bitterness, pathos, and a troubled searching into the mysteries and meaning of human existence. The series begins with the tragedy of indecisive idealism represented by *Hamlet*, goes on to the cynicism of *Measure for Measure* and *All's Well That Ends Well*, and culminates in the searing tragedies of *Macbeth* and *King Lear*, wherein characters assert that "life's but a walking shadow . . . a tale told by an idiot, full of sound and fury signifying nothing," and that "as flies to wanton boys are we to the gods; they kill us for their sport." Despite their gloom, however, the plays of Shakespeare's second period contain some of the dramatist's greatest flights of poetic grandeur.

Shakespeare ended his dramatic career, however, with a third period characterized by a profound spirit of reconciliation and peace. Of the three plays (all idyllic romances) written during this final period, the last, *The Tempest*, is the widest ranging in its reflections on human nature and the power of art. Ancient animosities are buried and wrongs are righted by a combination of natural and supernatural means, and a wide-eyed, youthful heroine rejoices on first seeing men with the words "O brave new world, that has such people in it!" Here, then, Shakespeare seems to be saying that despite humanity's trials, life is not so bitter after all, and the divine plan of the universe is ultimately benevolent and just.

MANNERISM

The ironies and tensions inherent in human existence were also portrayed with eloquence and profundity by several immortal masters of the visual arts who flourished during this tumultuous century. The dominant goal in Italian and Spanish painting between about 1540 and 1600, was to fascinate the viewer with special effects achieved by means of two entirely different styles. (Confusingly, both styles are sometimes referred to as "Mannerism.") The first was based

> The plays from Shakespeare's second period are far darker in mood, being characterized by bitterness, pathos, and a troubled searching into the mysteries and meaning of human existence.

on the style of the Renaissance master Raphael, but moved from that painter's gracefulness to a highly self-conscious elegance bordering on the bizarre and surreal. Representatives of this approach were the Florentines Pontormo (1494–1557) and Bronzino (1503–1572). Their sharp-focused portraits are flat and cold, yet strangely riveting.

The other extreme was theatrical in a more conventional sense—highly dramatic and emotionally compelling. Painters who followed this approach were indebted to Michelangelo but went much farther than he did in emphasizing shadowy contrasts, restlessness, and distortion. Of this second group, the two most outstanding were the Venetian Tintoretto (1518–1594) and the Spaniard El Greco (c. 1541–1614). Combining aspects of Michelangelo's style with the traditionally Venetian taste for rich color, Tintoretto produced monumental canvases that still inspire awe. More emotional still is the work of Tintoretto's disciple, El Greco. Born Domenikos Theotokopoulos on the Greek island of Crete, this extraordinary artist absorbed some of the stylized elongation characteristic of Greco-Byzantine icon painting before traveling to Italy to learn color and drama from Tintoretto. Finally he settled in Spain, where he was called "El Greco"— "the Greek." El Greco's paintings were too strange to be greatly appreciated in his own age, and even now they appear so unbalanced as to seem the work of one almost deranged. Yet such a view slights El Greco's deeply mystical Catholic fervor as well as his technical achievements. Best known today is his transfigured landscape, the *View of Toledo*, with its somber but awesome light breaking where no sun shines. But equally inspiring are his stunning portraits in which gaunt, dignified Spaniards radiate a rare blend of austerity and spiritual insight.

BAROQUE ART AND ARCHITECTURE

The dominant artistic school of southern Europe from about 1600 until the early 1700s was that of the Baroque. Originating in Rome as an expression of the ideals of the Counter-Reformation papacy and the Jesuit order, Baroque architecture in particular aimed to promote a specifically Catholic world view. Similarly, Baroque painting often was done in the service of the Counter-Reformation church, which at its high tide around 1620 seemed everywhere to be on the offensive. When Baroque painters were not celebrating Counter-Reformation ideals, most of

them worked in the service of monarchs who sought their own glorification.

The most imaginative and influential figure of the Roman Baroque was the architect and sculptor Gianlorenzo Bernini (1598–1680), a frequent employee of the papacy who created a magnificent celebration of papal grandeur in the sweeping colonnades leading up to St. Peter's Basilica. Breaking with Renaissance classicism, Bernini's architecture retained such classical elements as columns and domes, but combined them in ways meant to express both aggressive restlessness and great power. Harking back to the restless motion of Hellenistic statuary—particularly the Laocoön group—and building on tendencies already present in the later sculpture of Michelangelo, Bernini's statuary emphasizes drama and incites the viewer to respond to it rather than serenely to observe.

David, by Bernini (1598–1680). Whereas the earlier conceptions of David by the Renaissance sculptors Donatello and Michelangelo were reposeful (see p. 356), the Baroque sculptor Bernini chose to portray his young hero at the peak of physical exertion.

WHAT WAS THE RELATIONSHIP BETWEEN THE BAROQUE SCHOOL AND THE COUNTER-REFORMATION?

LITERATURE AND THE ARTS   413

To view the very greatest masterpieces of southern European Baroque painting one must look to Spain and the work of Diego Velázquez (1599–1660). Velázquez was not an entirely typical exponent of the Baroque style. Certainly many of his canvases display a characteristically Baroque delight in motion, drama, and power, but Velázquez's best work is characterized by a more restrained thoughtfulness than is usually found in the Baroque. Thus his famous *Surrender of Breda* shows muscular horses and splendid Spanish grandees on the one hand, but un-Baroque sympathy for defeated, disarrayed troops on the other. Velázquez's greatest painting, *The Maids of Honor*, done around 1656 after Spain's collapse, is one of the most thoughtful and probing artistic examinations of illusion and reality ever executed.

DUTCH PAINTING IN THE GOLDEN AGE

Southern Europe's main northern rival for artistic laurels was the Netherlands, where three extremely dissimilar painters all explored the greatness and wretchedness of man to the fullest. The earliest, Peter Brueghel (c. 1525–1569), worked in a vein related to earlier Netherlandish realism. But unlike his predecessors, who favored quiet urban scenes, Brueghel exulted in portraying the life of the peasantry. Most famous in this respect are his rollicking *Peasant Wedding* and *Peasant Wedding Dance,* and his spacious *Harvesters,* in which guzzling and snoring field hands are taking a well-deserved break from their heavy labors under the noon sun. Late in his career Brueghel became appalled by the intolerance and bloodshed he witnessed in the Netherlands and expressed his criticism in an understated yet searing manner. Most powerful is Brueghel's *Massacre of the Innocents,* which from a distance looks like a snug scene of a Flemish village buried in snow. In fact, however, heartless soldiers are methodically breaking into homes and slaughtering babies, the simple peasant folk are fully at their mercy, and the artist—alluding to a Gospel forgotten by warring Catholics and Protestants alike—seems to be saying "as it happened in the time of Christ, so it happens now."

Vastly different from Brueghel was the Netherlandish Baroque painter Peter Paul Rubens (1577–1640). Since the Baroque was an international movement closely linked to the spread of the Counter-Reformation, it should offer no surprise that Baroque style was extremely well represented in just that part of the Netherlands which, after long warfare, had been retained by Spain. In

The Maids of Honor, by Diego Velázquez. The artist himself is at work on a double portrait of the king and queen of Spain (who can be seen in the rear mirror), but reality is more obvious in the foreground in the persons of the delicately impish princess, her two maids, and a misshapen dwarf. The twentieth-century Spanish artist Picasso gained great inspiration from this work.

The Massacre of the Innocents, by Brueghel (c. 1525–1569). This painting shows how effectively art can be used as a means of social commentary. Many art historians believe that Brueghel was tacitly depicting the suffering of the Netherlands at the hands of the Spanish in his own day.

fact, Rubens of Antwerp was a far more typical Baroque artist than Velázquez of Madrid, painting literally thousands of robust canvases that glorified resurgent Catholicism or exalted second-rate aristocrats by portraying them as epic heroes. Rubens reveled in the sumptuous extravagance of the Baroque manner, being perhaps most famous today his well-nourished nudes. But unlike a host of lesser Baroque artists, Rubens was not lacking in subtlety and was a man of many moods. His gentle portrait of his son Nicholas catches unaffected childhood in a moment of repose, and his late *Horrors of War* movingly portrays what he himself called "the grief of unfortunate Europe, which, for so many years now, has suffered plunder, outrage, and misery."

In some ways a blend of Brueghel and Rubens, the greatest of all Netherlandish painters, Rembrandt van Rijn (1606–1669), defies all attempts at easy characterization. Living across the border from the Spanish Netherlands in staunchly Calvinistic Holland, Rembrandt belonged to a society that was too austere to tolerate the unbuckled realism of a Brueghel or the fleshy Baroque pomposity of a Rubens. Yet Rembrandt managed to put both realistic and Baroque traits to new uses. In his early career he gained fame and fortune as a painter of biblical scenes characterized by swirling forms and stunning experiments with light. Rembrandt was also active as a portrait painter who knew how to flatter his subjects by emphasizing their Calvinistic steadfastness, to the great advantage of his purse. As personal tragedies mounted in the painter's middle and declining years, his art became more pensive and sombre, but it gained in dignity, subtle lyricism, and awesome mystery. Thus his later portraits, including several self-portraits, are imbued with introspective qualities and a suggestion that only half the story is being told. Equally moving are explicitly philosophical

WHAT WAS THE RELATIONSHIP BETWEEN THE BAROQUE SCHOOL AND THE COUNTER-REFORMATION?

LITERATURE AND THE ARTS   415

The Horrors of War, by Rubens (1577–1640). The war god Mars here casts aside his mistress Venus and threatens humanity with death and destruction. In his old age Rubens took a far more critical view of war than he did for most of his earlier career.

paintings such as *Aristotle Contemplating the Bust of Homer,* in which the philosopher seems spellbound by the radiance of the epic poet, and *The Polish Rider,* in which realistic and Baroque elements merge into a higher synthesis portraying a pensive young man setting out fearlessly into a perilous world. Like Shakespeare, Rembrandt knew that life's journey is full of perils, but his most mature paintings suggest that these can be mastered with a courageous awareness of one's human shortcomings.

Self-Portraits. Self-portraits became common during the sixteenth and seventeenth centuries, reflecting the intense introspection of the period. Left: Rembrandt painted more than sixty self-portraits; this one, dating from around 1660, captures the artist's creativity, theatricality (note the costume), and the honesty of his self-examination. Right: Judith Leyster (1609–1660) was a Dutch contemporary of Rembrandt who pursued a successful career as an artist during her early twenties, before she married. Respected in her own day, she was all but forgotten for centuries thereafter.

CONCLUSION

Between 1540 and 1660, Europe was racked by a combination of religious war, political rebellions, and economic crises that undermined confidence in traditional structures of social, religious, and political authority. The result was fear, skepticism, and a search for new, more certain foundations on which to rebuild the social, political, and religious order of Europe. For artists and intellectuals, the period proved to be one of the most creative epochs in the history of Europe. But for common people, the century was one of extraordinary suffering.

After a hundred years of destructive efforts to restore the religious unity of Europe through war, a de facto religious toleration between states was beginning to emerge by 1660 as the only way to preserve the European political order. Within states, toleration was still very limited when this terrible century ended. But in territories where religious rivalries ran too deep to be overcome, rulers were beginning to discover that loyalty to the state was a value that could override even the religious divisions among their subjects. The end result of this century of crises was thus to strengthen Europeans' confidence in the powers of the state to heal their wounds and right their wrongs, with religion relegated more and more to the private sphere of individual conscience. In the following centuries, this new confidence in the state as an autonomous moral agent that acts in accordance with its own "reasons of state," and for its own purposes, would prove a powerful challenge to the traditions of limited consensual government that had emerged out of the Middle Ages.

KEY TERMS

Peace of Augsburg

Henry of Navarre

Spanish Armada

Thirty Years' War

Cardinal Richelieu

James I

Oliver Cromwell

Michel de Montaigne

Leviathan

Don Quixote

Baroque

William Shakespeare

Rembrandt Van Rijn

SELECTED READINGS

Bonney, Richard. *The European Dynastic States, 1494–1660.* Oxford and New York, 1991. An excellent recent survey of continental Europe during the "long" sixteenth century.

Briggs, Robin. *Witches and Neighbors: The Social and Cultural Context of European Witchcraft.* New York, 1996. An influential recent account of continental witchcraft.

———. *Early Modern France, 1560–1715,* 2d ed. Oxford and New York, 1997. Updated and authoritative, with new bibliographies.

Cervantes, Miguel de. *Don Quixote.* Translated by Walter Starkie. New York, 1957.

Cochrane, Eric, Charles M. Gray, and Mark A. Kishlansky. *Early Modern Europe: Crisis of Authority.* Chicago, 1987. An outstanding source collection from the University of Chicago Readings in Western Civilization series.

Held, Julius S., and Donald Posner. *Seventeenth- and Eighteenth-Century Art: Baroque Painting, Sculpture, Architecture.* New York, 1971. The most complete and best-organized introductory review of the subject in English.

Hibbard, Howard. *Bernini.* Baltimore, 1965. The basic study in English of this central figure of Baroque artistic activity.

Hirst, Derek. *England in Conflict, 1603–1660: Kingdom, Community, Commonwealth.* Oxford and New York, 1999. A complete revision of the author's *Authority and Conflict* (1986), this is an up-to-date and balanced account of a period that has been a historical battleground over the past twenty years.

Hobbes, Thomas. *Leviathan.* Edited by Richard Tuck. 2d ed. Cambridge and New York, 1996. The most recent edition, up to date and complete.

Holt, Mack P. *The French Wars of Religion, 1562–1629.* Cambridge and New York, 1995. The most recent and best account.

Kors, Alan Charles, and Edward Peters. *Witchcraft in Europe, 400–1700: A Documentary History,* 2d ed. Philadelphia, 2000. A superb collection of documents, significantly expanded in the second edition, with up-to-date commentary.

Levack, Brian P. *The Witch-Hunt in Early Modern Europe,* 2d ed. London and New York, 1995. The best account of the persecution of suspected witches; coverage extends from Europe in 1450 to America in 1750.

Limm, Peter, ed. *The Thirty Years' War.* London, 1984. An outstanding short survey, followed by a selection of primary-source documents.

Lynch, John. *Spain, 1516–1598: From Nation-State to World Empire.* Oxford and Cambridge, Mass., 1991. The best book in English on Spain at the pinnacle of its sixteenth-century power.

MacCaffrey, Wallace. *Elizabeth I.* New York, 1993. An outstanding traditional biography by an excellent scholar.

Martin, Colin, and Geoffrey Parker. *The Spanish Armada.* London, 1988. Incorporates recent discoveries from undersea archaeology with more traditional historical sources.

Martin, John Rupert. *Baroque.* New York, 1977. A thought-provoking, thematic treatment, less a survey than an essay on the painting, sculpture, and architecture of the period.

Mattingly, Garrett. *The Armada.* Boston, 1959. A great narrative history that reads like a novel; for the latest work, however, see Martin and Parker (above).

Parker, Geoffrey. *Philip II.* Boston, 1978. A fine biography by an expert in both the Spanish and the Dutch sources.

———. *The Dutch Revolt,* 2d ed. Ithaca, N.Y., 1989. The standard survey in English on the revolt of the Netherlands.

———, ed. *The Thirty Years' War,* rev. ed. London and New York, 1987. A wide-ranging collection of essays by scholarly experts.

Pascal, Blaise. *Pensées* (French-English edition). Edited by H. F. Stewart. London, 1950.

Quint, David. *Montaigne and the Quality of Mercy: Ethical and Political Themes in the "Essais."* Princeton, N.J., 1999. A fine treatment that presents Montaigne's thought as a response to the French wars of religion.

Roberts, Michael. *Gustavus Adolphus and the Rise of Sweden.* London, 1973. Still the authoritative English-language account.

Russell, Conrad. *The Causes of the English Civil War.* Oxford, 1990. A penetrating and provocative analysis by one of the leading "revisionist" historians of the period.

PART V
EARLY MODERN EUROPE

SEVENTEENTH- AND EIGHTEENTH-CENTURY European life was shaped by the combined effects of commerce, war, and a steadily growing population. A commercial revolution spurred the development of overseas colonies and trade while opening up new markets for European industry. Agricultural productivity increased, making it possible for Europe to feed a population that had now reached unprecedented levels. Population growth in turn enabled European governments to wage more frequent wars and to employ larger and larger armies.

Although monarchs continued to meet with opposition from the various estates within their realms, they increasingly asserted their power as absolute rulers. Warfare remained the chief instrument of European foreign policy; but slowly the notion of a diplomatic and military "balance of power" began to displace the pursuit of unrestrained aggrandizement as the primary goal of European state relations.

Profound changes were also occurring in European intellectual life during these centuries. Using new instruments and applying new mathematical techniques, astronomers proved beyond question that the earth was not the center of the universe. Biologists and physicians pioneered a more sophisticated understanding of the nature and processes by which life was created and sustained, and physicists such as Sir Isaac Newton established for the first time a true science of mechanics. During the eighteenth century, these discoveries gave rise to a new confidence in the capacity of human reason alone to understand nature and so to improve human life—a confidence those who held to it declared to be a sign of Enlightenment.

	POLITICS	SOCIETY AND CULTURE	ECONOMY	INTERNATIONAL RELATIONS
1500		Copernicus's *On the Revolutions of the Heavenly Spheres* (1543) Claudio Monteverdi, father of opera (1567–1643) Johannes Kepler (1571–1630) William Harvey (1578–1657)	Enclosure movement (1500–1700s) Demand for sugar escalates in Europe (late 1500s) Widespread crop failure in France (1597–1694)	Sir Francis Drake leads attack on Spanish fleet at Cadíz (1587)
1600		Literacy increases across Europe (1600–1800) Increased urbanization (1600–1750) Smoking spreads in Europe (early 1600s) Over 80,000 leave England for the New World (1607–1650) Galileo's *Starry Messenger* (1610) Bacon's *New Instruments* (1620)	Mechanically powered saws and calico-printing from the Far East (1600s) Dutch East India Company founded (1602)	A total of 11 million Africans forcibl[y] shipped across the middle passage (1500–1800) English colonists establish Jamesto[wn] (1607)
	Jean Baptiste Colbert, French finance minister (1619–1683)	Galileo charged with heresy (1632) John Locke (1632–1704) Descartes's *Discourse on Method* (1637)		*Mayflower* lands in the New World (1620)
	Reign of Louis XIV, the Sun King (1643–1715) England promulgates Navigation Acts (1651, 1660) Restoration and return of Charles II (1660)	Plague outbreaks (1649–1665) Edmond Halley (1656–1742) Founding of the Royal Society of London and the French Academy of Sciences (1660) Daniel Defoe, author of *Robinson Crusoe* (1660–1731) The Great Fire in London (1666)	French government introduces head tax (c. 1645) Coffee consumption escalates in Europe (1650s) Bank of Sweden founded (1657)	Dutch surrender New Amsterdam [to] England (1667) Austrian Habsburgs repulse Turks' assault on Vienna (1683) Peace of Augsburg (1686)
	Louis XIV revokes the Edict of Nantes (1685)	Johann Sebastian Bach (1685–1750) George Frideric Handel (1685–1759) Newton's *Principia Mathematica* (1687)		Portugal regains independence fro[m] Spain (1688) William of Orange rules England a[nd] Holland (1688) War of the League of Augsburg (1688–1697)
	Glorious Revolution in England (1689) Reign of Peter the Great of Russia (1689–1725)	Locke's *Treatise of Civil Government* and *Essay Concerning Human Understanding* (1690)	Bank of England founded (1694)	Battle of the Boyne, English solidi[fy] control of Ireland (1690)
1700		Maize and the potato are introduced in Europe (1700s) Proliferation of salons and coffee-houses (1700s) First daily newspaper in England (1702) Rousseau's *Social Contract* (1712–1778)	Fly shuttle for weaving loom invented (early 1700s) Physiocrats promote concept of *laissez-faire* (1700s) West India replaces the Spice Islands as largest supplier of European sugar (1700s)	War of Spanish Succession (1702–1713) England and Scotland unite to for[m] Great Britain (1707)
	Reign of Charles VI, emperor of Holy Roman Empire (1711–1740) Treaty of Utrecht (1713) Reign of George I, first of Hanoverian dynasty in England (1714–1727) Louis XV (1715–1774) Robert Walpole serves as England's first prime minister (1720–1742)			

POLITICS	SOCIETY AND CULTURE	ECONOMY	INTERNATIONAL RELATIONS	
		German imperial law prohibits jour-neyman associations (1731) France establishes the Road and Bridge Corps of Engineering (1747)		1731
eign of Frederick the Great, the "enlightened despot" (1740–1786)	Voltaire's *The Philosophical Letters* (1734) Montesquieu's *Spirit of Laws* (1748) Steady increase in population begins (1750) *Encyclopedia* published by Diderot and d'Alembert (1751–1772) Wolfgang Amadeus Mozart (1756–1791) Beccaria's *On Crimes and Punishment* (1764)			
eign of George III of England 1760–1820) eign of Catherine the Great of Russia (1762–1796) aria Theresa and Joseph II of Austria rule jointly (1765–1780)		Antislavery movements emerge in Europe (1760s) James Cook explores Pacific (1768–1779) Abbe Raynal's *Philosophical History of Europeans in the Two Indies* (1770)	Seven Years' War/ French and Indian War (1756–1763) Treaty of Paris: France concedes Canada and India to England (1763) French East India Co. dissolves (1769) Russo-Turkish War (1769–1792) American Revolution (1775–1783)	
eign of Louis XVI of France 1774–1792) ench Revolution breaks out (1789)	Kant's "What Is Enlightenment?" (1784) Wollstonecraft's *Vindication of the Rights of Woman* (1792) Austen's *Pride and Prejudice* (1813–1817)	Smith's *Inquiry into the Nature and Causes of the Wealth of Nations* (1776)	Russia, Austria, and Prussia fully parti-tion Poland (1795)	1800

Chapter FIFTEEN

Absolutism and Empire, 1660–1789

The period from around 1660 (when the English monarchy was restored, and Louis XIV of France began his personal rule) to 1789 (when the French Revolution erupted) is traditionally known as the age of absolutism. *Absolutism* was a political theory that encouraged rulers to claim complete sovereignty within their territories. To seventeenth- and eighteenth-century absolutists, complete sovereignty meant that a ruler could make law, dispense justice, create and direct a bureaucracy, declare war, and levy taxation without the formal approval of any other governing authorities. Frequently, such absolutist rulers claimed to govern their territories by the same divine right that established a father's absolute authority over his household. After the chaos of Europe's "iron century," many Europeans had come to believe that it was only by exalting the sovereignty of such "patriarchal" rulers that order could be restored to European life.

The age of absolutism was also an age of empire. By 1660, the French, Spanish, Portuguese, English, and Dutch had all established important colonies in the Americas and in Asia. Rivalry among these competing colonial powers was intense and fraught with consequence. In the late seventeenth century, European wars almost always had a colonial aspect. By the midddle of the eighteenth century, however, Europe's wars were being driven by colonial considerations and imperial conflicts, as worldwide trade assumed a larger and larger role in the European economy.

Absolutism was not the only political theory according to which European governments sought to rule during this period. England, Scotland, the Dutch Republic, Switzerland, Venice, Sweden, and Poland-Lithuania were all either limited monarchies or republics; in Russia, an extreme autocracy was emerging that ascribed to the

FOCUS QUESTIONS

• What were the aims of absolutist rulers?

• Did John Locke's political principles lie behind the Glorious Revolution in England?

• How did Louis XIV strengthen his control over France?

• What changes lay behind the growing power of Prussia?

• In what ways did Russian absolutism differ from its western European counterparts?

• What factors facilitated the commercial revolution?

• How did the patterns of European colonial settlement in the Americas differ from each other?

• In what ways did eighteenth-century Europeans colonialism differ from seventeenth-century European colonialism?

tsar a degree of control over his subjects' lives and property far beyond anything imagined by western European absolutists. Even in Russia, however, absolutism was never so unlimited in practice as it was in theory. Even the most absolute monarchs of seventeenth- and eighteenth-century Europe could rule effectively only so long as their subjects (and particularly their nobility) were prepared to consent, at least tacitly, to their policies. When outright opposition erupted, even absolutists were forced to back down. And when, in 1789, an outright political revolution occurred, the entire structure of absolutism came crashing to the ground.

THE APPEAL AND JUSTIFICATION OF ABSOLUTISM

What were the aims of absolutist rulers?

Absolutist monarchs sought to gather into their own hands command of the state's armed forces, control over its legal system, and the right to collect and spend the state's financial resources at will. To achieve these goals, they also needed to create an efficient, centralized bureaucracy that owed its allegiance directly to the monarch himself. The legally privileged estates of nobility and clergy, the political authority of semi-autonomous regions, and the pretensions of independent-minded representative assemblies were all obstacles, in the eyes of absolutists, to strong, centralized monarchical government. The history of absolutism is, as much as anything, a history of attempts by aspiring absolutists to bring such institutions to heel.

In most Protestant countries, the independent power of the church had already been subordinated to the interests of the state when the age of absolutism began. In France, Spain, and Austria, however, where Roman Catholicism had remained the state religion, absolutist monarchs now devoted concerted attention to "nationalizing" the church and its clergy within their territories. Even Charles III, the devout Spanish king who ruled from 1759 to 1788, pressed successfully for a papal concordat granting him control over ecclesiastical appointments

and the right to nullify any papal bull affecting Spain of which he did not approve.

The most important potential opponents of royal absolutism were not churchmen, however, but nobles. Monarchs dealt with their threat in various ways. Louis XIV deprived the French nobility of political power in the provinces while increasing their social prestige by requiring them to reside at his own lavish court at Versailles. Peter the Great of Russia (1689–1725) forced all his nobles into lifelong government service. Later in the century, Catherine II of Russia (1762–1796) struck a bargain whereby in return for vast estates and a variety of social and economic privileges (including exemption from taxation) the Russian nobility virtually surrendered the administrative and political power of the state into the empress's hands. In Prussia the army was staffed by nobles, as was generally the case in Spain, France, and England also. But in eighteenth-century Austria, the emperor Joseph II (1765–1790) adopted a policy of confrontation rather than accommodation, denying the nobility exemption from taxation and deliberately blurring the distinctions between nobles and commoners. Rarely, however, was the path of confrontation between crown and nobility successful in the long run. The most effective absolutist monarchies of the eighteenth century established a *modus vivendi* with their nobility, in which nobles came to see their own interests as tied to those of the crown. For this reason, cooperation more often characterized the relations between kings and nobles during the eighteenth-century "old regime" (*ancien régime*) than did conflict.

ALTERNATIVES TO ABSOLUTISM

Did John Locke's political principles lie behind the Glorious Revolution in England?

Although absolutism was the dominant model for seventeenth- and eighteenth-century European monarchs, it was by no means the only system by which Europeans governed themselves. In Venice, a republican oligarchy continued to rule the city. In the Netherlands, the territories that had won their inde-

ABSOLUTISM AND PATRIARCHY

This selection shows how a political theorist justified royal absolutism by deriving it from the absolute authority of a father over his household. Bishop Jacques-Benigne Bossuet (1627–1704) was a famous French preacher who served as tutor to the son of King Louis XIV of France before becoming bishop of Meaux.

BOSSUET ON THE NATURE OF MONARCHICAL AUTHORITY

There are four characteristics or qualities essential to royal authority. First, royal authority is sacred; Secondly, it is paternal; Thirdly, it is absolute; Fourthly, it is subject to reason. . . . All power comes from God. . . . Thus princes act as ministers of God, and his lieutenants on earth. It is through them that he exercises his empire. . . . In this way . . . the royal throne is not the throne of a man, but the throne of God himself. . . .

We have seen that kings hold the place of God, who is the true Father of the human race. We have also seen that the first idea of power that there was among men, is that of paternal power; and that kings were fashioned on the model of fathers. Moreover, all the world agrees that obedience, which is due to public power, is only found . . . in the precept which obliges one to honor his parents. From all this it appears that the name "king" is a father's name, and that goodness is the most natural quality in kings. . . .

Royal authority is absolute. In order to make this term odious and insupportable, many pretend to con-fuse absolute government and arbitrary government. But nothing is more distinct, as we shall make clear when we speak of justice. . . . The prince need account to no one for what he ordains. . . . Without this absolute authority, he can neither do good nor suppress evil: his power must be such that no one can hope to escape him. . . . [T]he sole defense of individuals against the public power must be their innocence. . . .

One must, then, obey princes as if they were justice itself, without which there is neither order nor justice in affairs. They are gods, and share in some way in divine independence. . . . It follows from this that he who does not want to obey the prince . . . is condemned irremissibly to death as an enemy of public peace and of human society. . . . The prince can correct himself when he knows that he has done badly; but against his authority there can be no remedy. . . .

Jacques-Benigne Bossuet. *Politics Drawn from the Very Words of Holy Scripture,* translated by Patrick Riley (Cambridge: Cambridge University Press, 1990), pp. 46–69 and 81–83.

pendence from Spain during the early seventeenth century combined to form the United Provinces, the only truly new country to take shape in Europe during the early modern era. The Spanish wars created a deep distrust among the Dutch toward monarchs of any stripe. As a result, the House of Orange never attempted to transform the new country from a republic into a monarchy.

LIMITED MONARCHY: THE CASE OF ENGLAND

At a time when representative assemblies were being undermined across much of Europe, the English Parliament was the longest-surviving and most highly developed such body in Europe. English political theorists had for centuries seen their government as a "mixed" monarchy, composed of monarchical, noble, and non-noble elements. During the seventeenth century, however, these traditions had come under threat, first through Charles I's attempts to rule without Parliament, and then during Oliver Cromwell's dictatorial Protectorate. The restoration of the monarchy in 1660 resolved the question of whether England would in future be a republic or a monarchy; but the sort of monarchy England would become remained an open question as the reign of Charles II began.

THE REIGN OF CHARLES II

Despite the fact that he was the son of the hated Charles I, Charles II (1660–1685) was initially welcomed by most English men and women. On his accession, he declared limited religious toleration for Protestant "dissenters" (Protestants who were not members of the official Church of England). He also promised to observe Magna Carta and the Petition of Right, declaring, with characteristic good humor, that he did not wish to "resume his travels." The unbuttoned moral atmosphere of his court, with its risqué plays, dancing, and sexual licentiousness, also reflected a public desire to forget the restraints of the Puritan past.

Charles was an admirer of all things French. During the 1670s, however, he began openly to model his kingship on the absolutism of Louis XIV. As a result, the great men of England soon came to be publically divided between Charles's supporters (called by their opponents "Tories," a popular nickname for Irish Catholic bandits) and his opponents (called by their opponents "Whigs," a nickname for Scottish Presbyterian rebels). Both sides feared absolutism, just as both sides feared a return to the "bad old days" of the 1640s, when resistance to the crown had led to civil war and ultimately to republicanism. What they could not agree on was which possibility frightened them more.

Religion also remained a divisive issue. Charles was sympathetic to Roman Catholicism, even to the point of a deathbed conversion in 1685. During the 1670s, he briefly suspended civil penalties against Catholics and Protestant dissenters by asserting his right as king

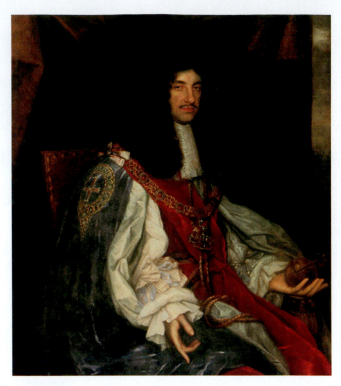

Charles II.

to ignore Parliamentary legislation. The resulting public outcry compelled him to retreat; but this controversy, together with rising opposition to Charles's ardently Catholic brother James as the heir to the throne, led to a series of Whig electoral victories between 1679 and 1681. When a group of radical Whigs attempted to exclude James by law from succeeding his brother on the throne, however, Charles stared the opposition down in the so-called Exclusion Crisis. Thereafter, Charles found that his rising revenues from customs duties, combined with a secret subsidy from Louis XIV, enabled him to govern without relying on Parliament for money. Charles further alarmed Whig politicans by executing several of them on charges of treason, and by remodeling local government to make it more amenable to royal control. Charles died in 1685 with his power enhanced, but he left behind a political and religious legacy that was to be the undoing of his less able and adroit successor.

THE REIGN OF JAMES II

James II was the very opposite of his worldly brother. A zealous Catholic convert, he alienated his Tory supporters, almost all of whom were members of the established Church of England, by suspending the laws preventing Catholics and Protestant dissenters from holding politi-

DID JOHN LOCKE'S POLITICAL PRINCIPLES LIE BEHIND THE GLORIOUS REVOLUTION IN ENGLAND?

ALTERNATIVES TO ABSOLUTISM   427

cal office. James also flaunted his own Roman Catholicism, openly declaring his wish that all his subjects might be converted, and publicly parading papal legates through the streets of London. When, in June 1688, he ordered all Church of England clergymen to read his decree of religious toleration from their pulpits, seven bishops refused and were promptly thrown in prison on charges of seditious libel. At their trial, however, they were declared not guilty, to the enormous satisfaction of the Protestant English populace.

The trial of the bishops was one event that brought matters to a head. The other was the unexpected birth of a son in 1688 to James and his second wife, Mary of Modena. This child, who was to be raised a Catholic, replaced James's much older Protestant daughter Mary Stuart as heir to the thrones of Scotland and England. So unexpected was this birth that there were widespread rumors that the child was not in fact James's son at all, but had been smuggled into the royal bedchamber in a warming pan.

With the birth of the "warming-pan baby," events moved swiftly toward a climax. A delegation of Whigs and Tories invited Mary Stuart and her Protestant husband William of Orange to cross to England with an invading army to preserve Protestantism and English liberties by summoning a new Parliament. As the leader of a Continental coalition then at war with France, William also welcomed the opportunity to make England an ally against Louis XIV's expansionist foreign policy.

Mary Stuart. Queen Mary and her husband William of Orange became Protestant joint rulers of England in a bloodless coup, taking power from her father, the Catholic James II.

THE GLORIOUS REVOLUTION

William and Mary's invasion became a bloodless coup (although James is reputed to have suffered a nosebleed at the moment of crisis). A Bill of Rights, passed by Parliament and accepted by the new king and queen in 1689, reaffirmed English civil liberties such as trial by jury and habeas corpus (a guarantee that no one could be imprisoned unless charged with a crime), and declared the monarchy subject to the law of the land. An Act of Toleration granted Protestant dissenters the right to worship freely, though not to hold political office. And in 1701, an Act of Succession ordained that every future English monarch must be a member of the Church of England. With the childless Queen Mary now dead, this meant that the throne would pass, after King William's death, first to Mary's Protestant sister Anne (1702–1714) and then, if Anne died childless, to George, elector of the German principality of Hanover and the Protestant great-grandson of James I. In 1707, a formal Act of Union between Scotland and England ensured that the Catholic heirs of King James II would in future have no more right to the throne of Scotland than they did to the throne of England.

The English soon referred to the events of 1688 and 1689 as the "Glorious Revolution": glorious because it occurred without bloodshed and also because it firmly established England as a mixed monarchy governed by the "King in Parliament." Although William and Mary and their successors continued to exercise a large measure of executive power, after 1688 no English monarch attempted to govern without Parliament, which has met annually from that time on. Parliament, and especially the House of Commons, also strengthened its control over taxation and expenditure.

Yet 1688 was not all glory. It was a revolution that consolidated the position of large property holders, whose control over local government had been threatened by Charles II and James II. It thus restored the status quo on behalf of a wealthy class of magnates that would soon become even wealthier from government patronage and the profits of war. It also brought misery to the Catholic minority in Scotland and to the Catholic majority in Ireland. After 1690, when King William won a decisive victory over James II's forces at the battle of the Boyne, power in Ireland would lie firmly in the hands of a "Protestant Ascendancy," whose dominance over Irish society would last until modern times.

JOHN LOCKE AND THE CONTRACT THEORY OF GOVERNMENT

The Glorious Revolution was the product of unique political circumstances, but it also reflected anti-absolutist theories of politics that were taking shape in the late seventeenth century. Chief among these opponents of absolutism was the Englishman John Locke (1632–1704), whose *Two Treatises of Government* were written prior to the revolution but published for the first time in 1690.

Locke maintained that humans had originally lived in a state of nature characterized by absolute freedom and equality, in which there was no government of any kind. The only law was the law of nature, by which individuals enforced for themselves their natural rights to life, liberty, and property. Soon, however, humans began to perceive that the inconveniences of the state of nature outweighed its advantages. Accordingly, they agreed first to establish a civil society based on absolute equality, and then to set up a government to arbitrate the disputes that might arise within this civil society. But they did not make government's powers absolute. Government was simply the combined power of all members of the society; as such, its authority could "be no more than those persons had in a state of nature before they entered into society, and gave it up to the community." All powers not expressly surrendered to the government were reserved to the people. If a government exceeded or abused the authority granted to it, society had the right to dissolve it and create another.

Locke condemned absolutism in every form. He denounced absolute monarchy, but he was no less critical of claims for the sovereignty of parliaments. Government, he argued, had been instituted to protect life, liberty, and property; no political authority could infringe an individual's natural rights to preserve these inviolate.

In the late eighteenth century, Locke's ideas would become an important element in the intellectual background to both the American and French revolutions.

> Locke maintained that humans had originally lived in a state of nature characterized by absolute freedom and equality, in which there was no government of any kind.

Between 1690 and 1720, however, they served a far less radical purpose. The landed magnates who replaced James II with William and Mary read Locke as a defense of their conservative revolution. Rather than protecting their liberty and property, James II had threatened both; hence the magnates were entitled to overthrow the tyranny he had established and replace it with a government that would defend their interests by preserving these natural rights. English government after 1689 would be dominated by Parliament; Parliament in turn was controlled by a landed aristocracy whose common interests far outweighed their incessant competition for office or their occasional disagreements over principle.

THE ABSOLUTISM OF LOUIS XIV

How did Louis XIV strengthen his control over France?

In Louix XIV's state portrait, it is all but impossible to discern the human being behind the façade of the absolute monarch, dressed in his coronation robes and surrounded by the symbols of his authority. That façade was artfully constructed by Louis, who recognized, perhaps more fully than any other early modern ruler, the importance of theater to effective kingship. Louis and his successors deliberately staged theatrical demonstrations of their sovereignty to enhance their position as rulers endowed with godlike powers far removed from common humanity.

PERFORMING ROYALTY AT VERSAILLES

Louis's most elaborate exhibitions of his sovereignty took place at his palace at Versailles, the town outside of Paris to which he moved his court. The palace and its grounds became a stage on which Louis mesmerized his nobles into obedience by his performance of the daily rituals and demonstrations of royalty. Noblemen vied to attend him when he arose from bed, ate his meals (usually stone cold after having traveled the distance of several city blocks from kitchen to table),

Louis XIV's State Portrait. This portrait by Hyacinthe Rigaud illustrates the degree to which absolute monarchy was defined in terms of studied performance.

strolled in his gardens (even the way the king walked was choreographed by the royal dancing master), or rode to the hunt. France's leading nobles were required to reside with him at Versailles for a portion of the year; the splendor of Louis's court was deliberately calculated to blind them to the possibility of disobedience while raising their prestige by associating them with himself.

Louis understood such theatricality as part of his duty as sovereign, a duty that he took with utmost seriousness. Though far from brilliant, he was hard working and conscientious. Whether or not he actually remarked *"L'état, c'est moi"* ("I am the State"), he clearly saw himself as serving the interests of the state. As such, he considered himself personally responsible for the well-being of his subjects. "The deference and the respect that we receive from our subjects," he wrote in a memoir he prepared for his son on the art of ruling, "are not a free gift from them but payment for the justice and the protection that they expect from us. Just as they must honor us, we must protect and defend them."

ADMINISTRATION AND CENTRALIZATION

Louis defined his responsibilities in absolutist terms: to concentrate royal power so as to produce domestic tranquillity. While coopting the nobility into his own theater of royalty, he conciliated the upper bourgeoisie by enlisting them as royal administrators. These men were not actors in the theater of Louis the Sun King; rather, they were the hard-working assistants of Louis the royal custodian of his country's welfare.

Louis's administrators devoted much of their time and energy to collecting the taxes necessary to finance the large standing army on which his aggressive and highly personal foreign policy depended. In addition to the *taille*, or land tax, which increased throughout the seventeenth century and on which a surtax was levied as well, Louis's government introduced a *capitation* (a head tax) and pressed successfully for the collection of indirect taxes on salt (the *gabelle*), wine, tobacco, and other goods. Since the nobility was exempt from the *taille*, its burden fell most heavily on the peasantry, whose local revolts Louis easily crushed.

Regional opposition was curtailed, but by no means eliminated, during Louis's reign. By removing the provincial nobility to Versailles, Louis cut them off from their local sources of power and influence. To put an end to the obstructive powers of regional parlements, Louis also decreed that members of any parlement that refused to approve and enforce his laws would be summarily exiled. He also crippled the authority of the provincial estates of Brittany, Languedoc, and Franche-Comté. The Estates-General, the national French representative assembly last summoned in 1614, did not meet at all during Louis's reign. It would not meet again until 1789.

LOUIS XIV'S RELIGIOUS POLICIES

Both for reasons of state and of personal conscience, Louis was determined to impose religious unity on France, regardless of the economic and social costs this entailed. Louis believed firmly that God would favor him in return for such fidelity.

Although the vast majority of the French population was Roman Catholic, French Catholics were divided

The Château of Versailles. Dramatically expanded by Louis XIV in the 1660s from a hunting lodge to the principal royal residence and the seat of government, the château became a monument to the international power and prestige of the Grand Monarch.

between Quietists, Jansenists, Jesuits, and Gallicans. Quietists preached personal mysticism, emphasizing a direct relationship between God and the individual human heart. Jansenism held to an Augustinian doctrine of predestination that could sound and look surprisingly like a kind of Catholic Calvinism. Louis vigorously persecuted Quietists and Jansenists. Instead, he supported the Jesuits in their efforts to create a Counter-Reformation Catholic church in France. Louis's support for the Jesuits upset the traditional Gallican Catholics of France, however, who desired a French church independent of papal, Jesuit, and Spanish influence (which they tended to equate). As a result of this dissension between Catholics, the religious aura of Louis's kingship diminished during the course of his reign.

Against the Protestant Huguenots, however, Louis waged unrelenting war. Protestant churches and schools were destroyed, and Protestants were banned from many professions. In 1685, Louis revoked the Edict of Nantes, the legal foundation of the toleration Huguenots had enjoyed since 1598. Protestant clerics were exiled; laymen were sent to the galleys as slaves; and their children were forcibly baptized as Catholics. Many families converted, but two hundred thousand Protestant refugees fled to England, Holland, Germany, and America, bringing with them their professional and artisanal skills. This was an enormous loss to France. Among many other examples, the silk industries of Berlin and London were established by Huguenots fleeing Louis XIV's persecution.

COLBERT AND ROYAL FINANCE

Louis's drive to unify and centralize France depended on a vast increase in royal revenues engineered by Jean Baptiste Colbert, the king's finance minister from 1664 until his death in 1683. Colbert tightened the process of tax collection and eliminated wherever possible the practice of tax farming (which permitted collection agents to retain for themselves a percentage of the taxes they gathered for the king). When Colbert assumed office, only about 25 percent of the taxes collected throughout the kingdom reached the treasury. By the time he died, that figure had risen to 80 percent. Colbert also tried to increase the nation's income by controlling and regulating its foreign trade. As a confirmed mercantilist (see "Mercantilism and War"), Colbert believed that France's wealth would increase if its imports were reduced and its exports increased. He therefore imposed tariffs on foreign goods imported into France, while using state money to promote the domestic manufacture of such formerly imported goods as silk, lace, tapestries, and glass. He was especially anxious to create domestic industries capable of producing all the goods France would need for war. To encourage domestic trade, he also improved France's roads, bridges, and waterways.

Despite Colbert's efforts to increase crown revenues, his policies ultimately foundered on the insatiable demands of Louis XIV's wars. Colbert himself foresaw this result when he lectured the king in 1680: "Trade is the source of public finance and public finance is the vital nerve of war . . . . I beg your Majesty to permit me only to say to him that in war as in peace he has never consulted the amount of money available in determining his expenditures." Louis, however, paid him no heed. As a result, by the end of Louis's reign, his aggressive foreign policy lay in ruins and his country's finances had been shattered by the unsustainable costs of war.

THE WARS OF LOUIS XIV TO 1697

From 1661, when Louis began his personal rule, until his death in 1715, Louis kept France on an almost constant war footing. His wars had two main objectives: to lessen the threat posed to France by the Habsburg powers that surrounded it and to promote the dynastic interests of his own family. Happily for Louis, these two objectives frequently coincided. In 1667–1668 he attacked the Spanish Netherlands, which he claimed on behalf of his wife. In 1672, Louis attacked Holland and its new leader William of Orange (1672–1702). The great-grandson of the sixteenth-century Protestant champion William the Silent, William of Orange would become the leading figure in Europe resisting Louis's wars of conquest.

The Dutch war ended in 1678–1679 with the Treaty of Nijmegen. Although Louis made little headway in the Low Countries, he did succeed in conquering and holding the eastern territory of Franche-Comté. Thus encouraged, he now turned his attentions eastward, capturing Strasbourg (1681), Luxembourg (1684), and Cologne (1688). He then pillaged and burned the middle Rhineland, which he claimed on behalf of his unhappy sister-in-law, the daughter of the territory's ruler, the Elector Palatine.

In response to these new aggressions, William of Orange organized the League of Augsburg, which eventually united Holland, England, Spain, Sweden, Bavaria, Saxony, the Rhine Palatinate, and the Austrian Habsburgs against Louis. The resulting Nine Years' War (1689–1697) was extraordinarily destructive. Most of its campaigns were fought in the Low Countries, but the conflict extended from Ireland to India to North America (where it was known as King William's War). Finally, in 1697, the Peace of Ryswick compelled Louis to return most of France's recent gains, except for Strasbourg and its surrounding territory of Alsace. This treaty also recognized William of Orange as the new king of England, thus legitimizing the Glorious Revolution of 1688 that had replaced the Catholic King James II with the Protestant monarchs William and Mary.

THE WAR OF THE SPANISH SUCCESSION

The League of Augsburg reflected the emergence of a new diplomatic goal in western and central Europe: the preservation of a "balance of power" designed to prevent any single country, such as France, from becoming so powerful as to threaten the position of the other major powers within the European state system. This goal would animate European diplomacy for the next two hundred years, until the entire balance-of-power system collapsed in 1914 with the outbreak of World War I.

A balance of power was not, however, a goal to which Louis XIV subscribed. Louis made peace in 1697 with the League of Augsburg because his country was exhausted by war and famine. But he was also looking ahead to the real prize: a French claim to succeed to the throne of Spain, and so to control the Spanish empire in the New World, Italy, the Netherlands, and the Philippines.

Louis had married, as his first wife, the elder daughter of King Philip IV of Spain (1621–1665). Philip's younger daughter had married the Holy Roman emperor, Leopold I of Austria (1658–1705). Neither daughter was expected to inherit the Spanish throne. But Philip's only

MERCANTILISM AND WAR

Jean-Baptiste Colbert (1619–1683) served as Louis XIV's finance minister from 1664 until his death. He worked assiduously to promote commerce, build up French industry, and increase exports. However much Colbert himself may have seen his economic policies as ends in themselves, to Louis they were always means to the end of waging war. Ultimately, Louis's wars undermined the prosperity that Colbert tried so hard to create. This memorandum, written to Louis in 1670, illustrates clearly the mercantlist presumptions of self-sufficiency on which Colbert operated: every item needed to build up the French navy must ultimately be produced in France, even if it could be acquired at less cost from elsewhere.

And since Your Majesty has wanted to work diligently at reestablishing his naval forces, and since afore that it has been necessary to make very great expenditures, since all merchandise, munitions and manufactured items formerly came from Holland and the countries of the North, it has been absolutely necessary to be especially concerned with finding within the realm, or with establishing in it, everything which might be necessary for this great plan.

To this end, the manufacture of tar was established in Médoc, Auvergne, Dauphiné, and Provence; iron cannons, in Burgundy, Nivernois, Saintonge and Périgord; large anchors in Dauphiné, Nivernois, Brittany, and Rochefort; sailcloth for the Levant, in Dauphiné; coarse muslin, in Auvergne; all the implements for pilots and others, at Dieppe and La Rochelle; the cutting of wood suitable for vessels, in Burgundy, Dauphiné, Brittany, Normandy, Poitou, Saintonge, Provence, Guyenne, and the Pyrenees; masts, of a sort once unknown in this realm, have been found in Provence, Languedoc, Auvergne, Dauphiné, and in the Pyrenees. Iron, which was obtained from Sweden and Biscay, is currently manufactured in the realm. Fine hemp for ropes, which came from Prussia and from Piedmont, is currently obtained in Burgundy, Mâconnais, Bresse, Dauphiné; and markets for it have since been established in Berry and in Auvergne, which always provides money in these provinces and keeps it within the realm.

In a word, everything serving for the construction of vessels is currently established in the realm, so that Your Majesty can get along without foreigners for the navy and will even, in a short time, be able to supply them and gain their money in this fashion. And it is with this same objective of having everything necessary to provide abundantly for his navy and that of his subjects that he is working at the general reform of all the forests in his realm, which, being as carefully preserved as they are at present, will abundantly produce all the wood necessary for this.

Charles W. Cole, *Colbert and a Century of French Mercantilism*, 2 vols. (New York: Columbia University Press, 1939), p. 320.

son, King Charles II of Spain (1665–1700), was a mental and physical invalid throughout his life. As it became clear during the 1690s that he would not live much longer, all the major European powers began to concern themselves with the succession to the Spanish throne. The stakes were high. If one of Leopold's sons succeeded, then France would be surrounded on all sides by a united Habsburg power. If Louis XIV's son or grandson

EUROPE AFTER THE TREATY OF UTRECHT (1713)

To what extent did the balance of power within Europe change as a result of the Treaty of Utrecht? Would this map lead you to expect the Habsburg lands to dominate eighteenth-century Europe? Why or why not?

succeeded, however, then France would become the preponderant power in Europe and the Americas.

Several schemes to resolve the crisis were floated during the 1690s. Most involved dividing the Spanish empire between the competing claimants. King Charles II's advisors, however, wanted the entire Spanish empire to pass to a single heir. To achieve this, they arranged for King Charles, in his will, to leave all his possessions to Louis XIV's younger grandson, Philip of Anjou. As soon as Charles II died, Philip V (1700–1746) was

therefore proclaimed the new king of Spain, and Louis XIV rushed French troops into the Spanish Netherlands. Louis also sent French merchants into Spanish America, and withdrew recognition from William of Orange as king of England.

The resulting war pitted England, the United Provinces, Austria, and Prussia against France, Bavaria, and Spain. The allied forces fought a series of fierce battles in the Low Countries and Germany, including an extraordinary march deep into Bavaria, where they inflicted a devastating defeat on the French and their Bavarian allies at Blenheim (1704). Soon thereafter, the English navy captured Gibraltar and the island of Minorca, thus establishing a foothold in the Mediterranean and opening a new military theater in Spain itself.

By 1709, France was on the verge of defeat. But the allies overreached themselves by demanding that Louis join their war against his own grandson in Spain. The war therefore continued, at enormous cost to both sides.

Queen Anne of England (Mary's sister and William's successor) gradually grew disillusioned with the war. English and Dutch merchants were also complaining about the damage the war was doing to trade. Meanwhile, the diplomatic situation in Europe was also changing. Leopold I of Austria had died in 1705. When his elder son and successor Joseph I died in 1711, the Austrian monarchy fell to Leopold's younger son, the archduke Charles, who had been the allies' candidate for the throne of Spain. With Charles VI (1711–1740) now the Austrian ruler and the Holy Roman emperor, the prospect of his accession to the Spanish throne threatened to upset the balance of power in Europe all over again.

THE TREATY OF UTRECHT

In 1713 the war finally came to an end with the Treaty of Utrecht. Its terms were reasonably fair to all sides. Philip V, Louis XIV's grandson, remained on the throne of Spain and retained Spain's colonial empire intact; but in return, Louis agreed that France and Spain would never be united under the same ruler. The biggest winner by far was Great Britain (as the combined kingdoms of England and Scotland were known after 1707), which kept Gibraltar and Minorca and also acquired large chunks of French territory in the New World. Even more valuable, however, Britain also extracted from Spain the right to transport and sell African slaves in Spanish America. As a result, the British were now poised to become the principal slave merchants and the dominant colonial and commercial power of the eighteenth-century world.

The Treaty of Utrecht reshaped the balance of power in western Europe. Spain's collapse was already precipitous; by 1713 it was complete. Spain would remain the "sick man of Europe" for the next two centuries. Holland's decline was more gradual, but by 1713 its greatest days were also over. The Dutch would continue to control the Spice Islands, but in the Atlantic world Britain and France were now the domi-

nant powers. They would continue to duel for another half century for control over North America, but at Utrecht the balance of colonial power shifted decisively in Britain's favor. Britain's navy, not France's army, would rule the new imperial and commercial world of the eighteenth century.

THE REMAKING OF CENTRAL AND EASTERN EUROPE

What changes lay behind the growing power of Prussia?

The decades between 1680 and 1720 were equally decisive in reshaping the balance of power in central and eastern Europe. As Ottoman power waned, the Austro-Hungarian empire of the Habsburgs emerged as the dominant power in central and southeastern Europe. To the north, Brandenburg-Prussia was also a rising power. The most dramatic changes, however, were occurring in Russia, which would emerge from a long war with Sweden as the dominant power in the Baltic Sea, and would soon become a mortal threat to the combined kingdom of Poland-Lithuania.

THE HABSBURG EMPIRE

In 1683, the Ottoman Turks launched their last assault on Vienna. Only the arrival of seventy thousand Polish troops saved the Austrian capital from capture. Thereafter, however, Ottoman power in southeastern Europe declined rapidly. By 1699, Austria had reconquered most of Hungary from the Ottomans; by 1718, it controlled all of Hungary, and also Transylvania and Serbia. In 1722, Austria also acquired the territory of Silesia from Poland. With Hungary now a "buffer state" between Austria and the Ottomans, Vienna emerged as one of the great cultural and political capitals of eighteenth-century Europe, and Austria became one of the arbiters of the European balance of power.

After 1740, the empress Maria Theresa (1740–1780) and her son Joseph II (1765–1790; from 1765 until 1780 the two were co-rulers) pioneered a new style of "enlightened absolutism" within their empire: centralizing the administration on Vienna, increasing taxation, creating a professional standing army, tightening their control over the church, creating a statewide system of primary education, relaxing censorship, and instituting a new, more liberal criminal code. But in practice, Habsburg absolutism, whether enlightened or not, was always limited by the diversity of its imperial territories and by the weakness of its local governmental institutions.

THE RISE OF BRANDENBURG-PRUSSIA

After the Ottoman collapse, the main threat to Austria came from the rising power of Brandenburg-Prussia. Like Austria, Prussia was a composite state, comprising several geographically divided territories acquired through inheritance by the Hohenzollern family. Their two main holdings, however, were Brandenburg, centered on its capital city, Berlin, and the duchy of East Prussia. Between these two territories lay Pomerania (claimed by Sweden) and an important part of the kingdom of Poland, including the port of Gdansk (Danzig). The Hohenzollerns' aim was to unite their state by acquiring these intervening territories. Over the course of more than a century of steady state building, they finally succeeded in doing so. In the process, Brandenburg-Prussia became the dominant military power of central Europe and a key player in the balance-of-power diplomacy of the mid-eighteenth century.

The foundations of Prussian greatness were laid by Frederick William, the "Great Elector" (1640–1688). By siding with Poland in a war against Sweden in the late 1650s, he obtained the Polish king's surrender of East Prussia. He also protected his western provinces from French attack by returning Pomerania, captured in a recent war, to France's Swedish ally. Behind these diplomatic triumphs, however, lay the Elector's success in building an army and mobilizing the resources to pay for it. By granting to the powerful nobles of his territories (known as *Junkers*) the right to enserf their peasants, by relying on them to staff the officer corps of his army, and by guaranteeing their immunity from taxation, Frederick William gained their support for the effective and highly autocratic taxation system he imposed on the rest of the country.

By supporting Austria in the War of the Spanish Succession, the Great Elector's son, Frederick I (1688–1713), received the right to style himself king of Prussia. (As Holy Roman emperor, the Austrian monarch had the right to create kings.) And by joining the Great Northern War on the side of Russia against

Sweden (see below), Frederick paved the way for Prussia to recover and extend its control over Pomerania. As king, however, his main attention was devoted to developing the cultural life of his new royal capital, Berlin, along the lines laid down by Louis XIV of France.

Frederick William I (1713–1740) returned to the policies of his grandfather. During his reign, the Prussian army grew from thirty thousand to eighty-three thousand men, the fourth largest army in Europe after those of France, Russia, and Austria. To support his army, Frederick William I increased taxes and streamlined their collection, while shunning the expensive luxuries of court life. For him, the "theater" of absolutism was not the palace but the office, where he personally supervised his beloved army and the offices of state that sustained it.

> To support his army, Frederick William I increased taxes and streamlined their collection, while shunning the expensive luxuries of court life.

Frederick William I made Prussia a strong state. Frederick the Great (1740–1786) raised his country to the status of a major power. As soon as he became king in 1740, Frederick mobilized the army his father had never taken into battle and occupied the Austrian province of Silesia. Emboldened by this early success, Frederick spent the rest of his reign consolidating his gains in Silesia and extending his control over the Polish territories that lay between Prussia and Brandenburg. Through relentless diplomacy and frequent war, Frederick succeeded by 1786 in transforming Prussia into a powerful, contiguous territorial kingdom.

To ensure a united domestic front against Prussia's enemies, Frederick was careful to ensure the support of the Junkers for his policies. His father had recruited civil servants according to merit rather than birth, but Frederick relied on the nobility to staff the army and his expanding administration. Remarkably, Frederick's strategy worked. His nobility remained loyal, while Frederick fashioned the most highly professional and efficient bureaucracy in Europe.

Frederick showed the same concern for Junker sensibilities in his domestic policies. Like his contemporary Joseph II of Austria, Frederick was an enlightened absolutist who supervised a series of social reforms, prohibited the judicial torture of accused criminals and the bribing of judges, and established a system of elementary schools. Although strongly anti-Semitic, he encouraged religious toleration toward Christians and even declared that he would happily build a mosque in Berlin into contact with western Europe, but his policies were decisive in making Russia a great European power.

THE EARLY YEARS OF PETER'S REIGN

Like Louis XIV of France, Peter came to the throne as a young boy, and his minority was marked by political dissension and court intrigue. In 1689, however, at the age of seventeen, he overthrew the regency of his half sister Sophia and assumed personal control of the state. Determined to make Russia into a great military power, the young tsar traveled to Holland and England during the 1690s to study shipbuilding and to recruit skilled foreign workers to help him build a navy. While he was abroad, however, his elite palace guard (the *streltsy*) rebelled, attempting to restore Sophia to the throne. Peter quickly returned home from Vienna and crushed the rebellion with striking savagery. Twelve hundred suspected conspirators were summarily executed, many of them gibbeted outside the walls of the Kremlin, where their bodies rotted for months as a graphic reminder of the fate awaiting those who dared challenge the tsar's authority.

if he could find enough Muslims to fill it. On his own royal estates he abolished capital punishment, curtailed the forced labor services of his peasantry, and granted them long leases on the land they worked. But he never attempted to extend these reforms to the estates of the nobility. To have done so would have alienated the very group on whom Frederick's rule depended.

AUTOCRACY IN RUSSIA

In what ways did Russian absolutism differ from its western European counterparts?

An even more dramatic transformation took place in Russia under the Tsar Peter I (b.1672–d.1725). Peter's accomplishments alone would have earned him his title of "Great." But his imposing height—he was six feet eight inches tall—as well as his mercurial personality—jesting one moment, raging the next—certainly added to the outsized impression he made on his contemporaries. Peter was not the first tsar to bring his country

Peter the Great. As Tsar Peter I westernized Russia with social and cultural reforms, among them the mandate that traditional nobles cut off their long beards.

IN WHAT WAYS DID RUSSIAN ABSOLUTISM DIFFER FROM ITS WESTERN EUROPEAN COUNTERPARTS?

AUTOCRACY IN RUSSIA   437

THE TRANSFORMATION OF THE TSARIST STATE

Peter is most famous as the tsar who attempted to "westernize" Russia by imposing a series of social and cultural reforms on the traditional Russian nobility: ordering noblemen to cut off their long beards and flowing sleeves; publishing a book of manners that forbade spitting on the floor and eating with one's fingers; encouraging polite conversation between the sexes; and requiring noblewomen to appear, together with men, in Western garb at weddings, banquets, and other public occasions. The children of Russian nobles were sent to western European courts for their education, and thousands of western European experts were brought to Russia to staff the new schools and academies Peter built, to design the new buildings he constructed, and to serve in the tsar's army, navy, and administration.

These measures were important, but it is misleading to see them as driven by the tsar's desire to "modernize" or "westernize" Russia. Peter's real goal was to make Russia a great military power, not to remake Russian society. His new taxation system (1724), for example, which assessed taxes on individuals rather than on households, rendered many of the traditional divisions of Russian peasant society obsolete. It was created, however, to raise more money for war. His Table of Ranks, imposed in 1722, had a similar impact on the nobility. By insisting that all nobles must work their way up from the lower (landlord) class to the (higher) administrative class and to the (highest) military class, Peter reversed the traditional hierarchy of Russian noble society, which had valued landlords by birth above administrators and soldiers who had risen by merit. But he also created a powerful new incentive to lure his nobility into service to the tsar.

As autocrat of all the Russias, Peter the Great was the absolute master of his empire to a degree unmatched elsewhere in Europe. After 1649, Russian peasants were legally the property of their landlords; by 1750, half were serfs, and the other half were state peasants who lived on lands owned by the tsar himself. State peasants could be conscripted to serve as soldiers in the tsar's army, workers in his factories (whose productive capacity increased enormously during Peter's reign), or as forced laborers in his building projects. But serfs too could be taxed by the tsar and summoned for military service, as could their lords. All Russians, of whatever rank, were thus expected to serve the tsar, and all Russia was considered in some sense to belong to him.

To further consolidate his power, Peter replaced the Duma—the nation's rudimentary national assembly—with a hand-picked senate, a group of nine administrators who supervised military and civilian affairs. In religious matters, he took direct control over the Russian Orthodox church by appointing an imperial official to manage its affairs. To cope with the demands of war, he also fashioned a new, larger, and more efficient administration, for which he recruited both nobles and non-nobles. But rank in the new bureaucracy did not depend on birth. One of his principal advisers, Alexander Menshikov, began his career as a cook and finished as a prince. This degree of social mobility would have been impossible in any contemporary western European country. Instead, noble status depended on governmental service, with all nobles expected to participate in Peter's army or administration. Peter was not entirely successful in enforcing this requirement, but the administrative machinery he devised furnished Russia with its ruling class for the next two hundred years.

> By insisting that all nobles must work their way up from the lower (landlord) class to the (higher) administrative class and to the (highest) military class, Peter reversed the traditional hierarchy of Russian noble society, which had valued landlords by birth above administrators and soldiers who had risen by merit.

PETER'S FOREIGN POLICY

The goal of Peter's foreign policy was to secure warm-water ports for Russia on the Black Sea and the Baltic Sea. In the Black Sea, his enemy was the Ottomans. Here, however, he had little success; Russia would not secure its position in the Black Sea until the end of the eighteenth century. In the north, however, Peter achieved much more. In 1700, he began what would become a twenty-one-year war with Sweden, hitherto the dominant power in the Baltic Sea. By 1703, Peter had secured a foothold on the Gulf of Finland, and immediately began to build a new capital city there, which he named St. Petersburg. After 1709, when Russian armies, supported by Prussia, decisively defeated the Swedes at the battle of Poltava, work on Peter's new capital city accelerated. An army of serfs was now conscripted to build the new city, whose centerpiece was a royal palace designed to imitate and rival Louis XIV's Versailles.

THE GROWTH OF RUSSIAN EMPIRE

How did Peter the Great expand the territory controlled by Russia? What was he trying to achieve by winning additional land? What were the costs of these expansions? How did the emergence of a bigger, more powerful Russia affect the European balance of power? What were Catherine the Great's contributions to the development of Russia as a global force?

Russia in 1584
Acquisitions, 1584–1700
Acquisitions, 1700–1772 (primarily by Peter the Great)
Acquisitions, 1772–1796 (by Catherine the Great)
Area of Pugachev rebellion, 1773–1775
Battle sites

ARCTIC OCEAN

SEA OF OKHOTSK

SEA OF JAPAN

Okhotsk 1649

Amur R.

Lena R.

Lake Baikal

SIBERIA

CHINA

Yenisei R.

Tomsk 1604

Ob R.

1000 Miles

1000 Kilometers

500

500

URAL MOUNTAINS

Archangel

ARAL SEA

Kazan

Volga R.

Ural R.

FINLAND

KARELIA

St. Petersburg

ESTONIA

Narva 1700

Pskov

LIVONIA

LITHUANIA

Smolensk

Moscow

Don R.

CASPIAN SEA

Astrakhan

Gulf of Bothnia

BALTIC SEA

POLAND

Warsaw

Minsk

Dnieper R.

Kiev

Poltava 1709

Azov

Sevastopol

Odessa

Dniester R.

CAUCASUS MTS.

BLACK SEA

Lake Balkhash

IN WHAT WAYS DID RUSSIAN ABSOLUTISM DIFFER FROM ITS WESTERN EUROPEAN COUNTERPARTS?

AUTOCRACY IN RUSSIA 439

The Great Northern War with Sweden ended in 1721 with the Peace of Nystad. This treaty marks a realignment of power in eastern Europe comparable to that effected by the Treaty of Utrecht in the west. Sweden lost its North Sea territories to Hanover and its Baltic German territories to Prussia. Its eastern territories, including the entire Gulf of Finland, Livonia, and Estonia, passed to Russia. Poland-Lithuania was a declining power also; by the end of the eighteenth century, the kingdom would disappear altogether, its territories swallowed up by its more powerful neighbors. The victors at Nystad were the Prussians and the Russians, both of whom secured their position along the Baltic coast and so positioned themselves to take advantage of the lucrative eastern European grain trade with western Europe.

Peter's victory had come at enormous cost. Direct taxation increased 500 percent during his reign, and his army in the 1720s numbered more than three hundred thousand men. Peter had made Russia a force to be reckoned with on the European scene; but in so doing, he had also aroused great resentment, especially among his nobility. Peter's only son and heir Alexis became the focus for conspiracies against the tsar, until finally Peter had him arrested and executed in 1718. As a result, when Peter died in 1725, he left no son to succeed him. A series of ineffective tsars followed, mostly creatures of the palace guard, under whom the resentful nobles reversed many of Peter the Great's reforms. In 1762, however, the crown passed to Catherine the Great, a ruler whose ambitions and determination were equal to those of her great predecessor.

CATHERINE THE GREAT AND THE PARTITION OF POLAND

Catherine was a German who came to the throne in 1762 on the death of her husband, the weak (and possibly mad) tsar Peter III, who was deposed and executed in a palace coup that Catherine herself may have helped to arrange. Although she cultivated an image of herself as an enlightened ruler (she corresponded with French philosophers, wrote plays, and began to compose a history of Russia), Catherine was determined not to lose the support of the nobility who had placed her on the throne. As a result, her efforts at social reform did not extend much beyond the founding of hospitals and orphanages and the creation of an elementary school system for the children of the provincial nobility.

Catherine's greatest achievements were gained through war and diplomacy. In 1769, she renewed Peter

the Great's push to secure a warm-water port on the Black Sea. In the resulting war with the Ottoman Turks (which ended in 1774), Russia won control over the northern coast of the Black Sea, secured the independence of Crimea (which Russia would annex in 1783), and obtained safe passage for Russian ships through the Bosporus and into the Mediterranean Sea. In the course of this campaign, Russia also won control over several Ottoman provinces along the Danube River.

Russia's gains in the Balkans alarmed Austria, however, which now found itself with the powerful Russian empire on its southern doorstep. Prussia too was threatening to become involved in the war as an ally of the Ottomans. Frederick the Great's real interests, however, lay much closer to home. To preserve the peace among Russia, Prussia, and Austria, he proposed instead a partition of Poland. Russia would abandon its Danubian conquests, and in return would acquire the grain fields of eastern Poland, along with a population of one to two million Poles. Austria would take Galicia, acquiring two and a half million Poles. Prussia, meanwhile, would take the

Dividing the Royal Spoils. A contemporary cartoon showing the monarchs of Europe at work carving up a hapless Poland.

coastal regions of Poland, including the port of Gdansk (Danzig), that separated Brandenburg and Pomerania from East Prussia. As a result of this agreement, finalized in 1772, Poland lost about 30 per cent of its territory and about half of its population.

Poland was now paying the price for its political conservatism. Alone among the major central European powers, the Polish nobility had successfully opposed any move toward monarchical centralization as a threat to its liberties, among which was the right of every individual noble to veto any measure proposed in the Polish representative assembly, the Diet. To make matters worse, Polish aristocrats were also quite prepared to accept bribes from foreign powers in return for their vote in elections for the Polish king. In 1764, Catherine the Great had intervened in this way to secure the election of one of her former lovers, Stanislaus Poniatowski, as the new king of Poland. In 1772, King Stanislaus reluctantly accepted the partition of his country because he was too weak to resist it. In 1788, however, he took advantage of a new Russo-Turkish war to try to strengthen his control over what remained of his kingdom. In May 1791 a new constitution was adopted that established a much stronger monarchy than had previously existed. But it was too late. In January 1792 the Russo-Turkish war ended, and Catherine the Great pounced. Together the Russians and Prussians took two more enormous bites out of Poland in 1793, destroying the new constitution in the process. A final swallow by Russia, Austria, and Prussia in 1795 left nothing of Poland or Lithuania at all.

COMMERCE AND CONSUMPTION

What factors facilitated the commercial revolution?

Despite the increased military power of Russia, Prussia, and Austria, the balance of power within Europe was shifting steadily toward the West during the eighteenth century. The North Atlantic economies in particular were growing more rapidly than those anywhere else in Europe. As a result, France and Britain were becoming preponderant powers both in Europe and the wider world.

ECONOMIC GROWTH IN EIGHTEENTH-CENTURY EUROPE

The reasons for this rapid economic and demographic growth in northwestern Europe are complex. In Britain and Holland, new, more intensive agricultural systems were producing more food per acre than ever before. Combined with improved transportation systems, the new farming methods resulted in fewer famines and a better-nourished population. New crops, especially maize and potatoes (both introduced to Europe from the Americas), also helped to increase the supply of food available to feed Europe's growing population. But although famines became less common and less widespread, infectious disease continued to kill half of all Europeans before they reached the age of twenty. Even here, however, some progress was being made. Plague in particular was ceasing to be a major killer, as a degree of immunity (perhaps the result of a genetic mutation) began to emerge within the European population. Together with a better diet, improved sanitation may also have played some role in reducing the infection rates from such killers as typhoid, cholera, smallpox, and measles.

> Combined with improved transportation systems, the new farming methods resulted in fewer famines and a better-nourished population.

Northwestern Europe was also becoming increasingly urbanized. Across Europe as a whole the total number of urban dwellers did not change markedly between 1600 and 1800. At both dates, approximately two hundred cities in Europe had a population of over ten thousand. What did change was, first, the fact that these cities were increasingly concentrated in northern and western Europe; and second, the extraordinary growth of the very largest cities. Amsterdam, the hub of early modern international commerce, increased from thirty thousand in 1530 to 115,000 in 1630 and 200,000 by 1800. Naples, the busy Mediterranean port, went from a population of 300,000 in 1600 to nearly half a million by the late eighteenth century. But even more spectacular population growth occurred in the administrative capitals of Europe. London grew from 674,000 in 1700 to 860,000 a century later. Paris went from 180,000 people in 1600 to more than 500,000 in 1800. Berlin grew from a population of 6,500 in 1661 to 60,000 in 1721 to 140,000 in 1783, of whom approximately 65,000 were state employees or members of their families.

Increased food supplies were needed to feed these burgeoning cities; but to the rising prosperity of northwestern Europe as a whole, developments in trade and manufacturing contributed even more than did agriculture. Spurred by improvements in transportation—better roads and bridges, and new canals—entrepreneurs began to promote the production of textiles in the countryside by distributing ("putting out") wool and flax to rural workers who would card, spin, and weave it into cloth on a piece-rate basis. The entrepreneur would then collect and sell the finished cloth in a market that now extended from local towns to international exporters. For country dwellers, this system (sometimes called "protoindustrialization") provided welcome employment during otherwise slack seasons of the agricultural year. For the merchant-entrepreneurs who administered it, the system allowed them to avoid expensive guild restrictions in the towns and to reduce their levels of capital investment, thus reducing their overall costs of production. Urban cloth workers suffered, but the system led nonetheless to markedly increased employment and to much higher levels of industrial production, not only for textiles, but also for iron, metalworking, and even toy- and clock-making.

Despite rural protoindustrialization, the role of cities as manufacturing centers continued to grow during the eighteenth century. Most urban manufacturing continued to be carried out in small shops employing anywhere from five to twenty journeymen working under the supervision of a master. But the scale of such enterprise was growing and also becoming more specialized, as workshops began to group together to form a single manufacturing district in which several thousand workers might be employed to produce the same product.

Techniques in some crafts remained much as they had been for centuries. In others, however, inventions changed the pattern of work as well as the nature of the product. Knitting frames, simple devices to speed the manufacture of textile goods, made their appearance in Britain and Holland. Wire-drawing machines and slitting mills, the latter enabling nail makers to convert iron bars into rods, spread from Germany into Britain. Techniques for printing colored designs directly on calico cloth were imported from Asia. New and more efficient printing presses appeared, first in Holland and then elsewhere. The Dutch even invented a machine called a "camel," with which the hulls of ships could be raised in the water so that they could be more easily repaired.

Workers did not readily accept innovations of this kind. Labor-saving machines threw people out of work. Often, therefore, governments would intervene to block the widespread use of machines if they threatened to increase unemployment or in some other way to create unrest. States might also intervene to protect the interests of their powerful commercial and financial backers. But the pressures for economic innovation were irresistable, because behind them lay an insatiable eighteenth-century appetite for goods.

A WORLD OF GOODS

In the eighteenth century, for the first time, a mass market for consumer goods emerged in Europe, and especially in northwestern Europe. Houses became larger, particularly in towns; but even more strikingly, the houses of relatively ordinary people were coming to be crammed with hitherto uncommon luxuries such as sugar, tobacco, tea, coffee, chocolate, newspapers, books, pictures, clocks, toys, china, glassware, pewter, and even silver plate, soap, razors, furniture (including beds with mattresses, chairs, and chests of drawers), shoes, cotton cloth, and spare clothing. Demand for such products consistently outstripped the supply, causing prices for these items to rise faster than the price of foodstuffs throughout the century. But the demand for them continued unabated. Such goods were indulgences, of course, but they were also repositories of value in which families could invest their surplus cash, knowing that they could pawn them in hard times if cash were needed.

The exploding consumer economy of the eighteenth century spurred demand for manufactured goods of all sorts. But it also encouraged the provision of services. In

> The exploding consumer economy of the eighteenth century spurred demand for manufactured goods of all sorts. But it also encouraged the provision of services.

eighteenth-century Britain, the service sector was the fastest-growing part of the economy, outstripping both agriculture and manufacturing. Almost everywhere in urban Europe, the eighteenth century was the golden age of the small shopkeeper. People bought more prepared foods and more ready-made (as opposed to personally tailored) clothing. Advertising became an important part of doing business, helping to create demand for new products and shaping popular taste for changing fashions. Even political allegiances could be expressed through consumption

***Topsy-Turvy World* by Jan Steen.** This Dutch painting depicts a household in the throes of the exploding consumer economy that hit Europe in the eighteenth century. Consumer goods ranging from silver and china to clothing and furniture cluttered the houses of ordinary people as never before.

when people purchased plates and glasses commemorating favorite rulers or causes.

The result of all these developments was a European economy vastly more complex, more specialized, more integrated, more commercialized, and more productive than anything the world had seen before.

COLONIZATION AND TRADE IN THE SEVENTEENTH CENTURY

How did the patterns of European colonial settlement in the Americas differ from each other?

Many of the new consumer goods that propelled the economy of eighteenth-century Europe, including such staples as sugar, tobacco, tea, coffee, chocolate, china, and cotton cloth, were the products of Europe's colonial empires in Asia, Africa, and the Americas. Eu-

rope's growing wealth was not simply the result of its colonial possessions, but it is impossible to imagine this prosperity without them. We need, therefore, to examine these European empires and the developing role they played in the economy of the eighteenth-century world. To do so, however, we need to begin by looking at the patterns of seventeenth-century European colonialism.

SPANISH COLONIALISM

Following the exploits of the conquistadors, the Spanish established colonial governments in Peru and in Mexico, which they controlled from Madrid. In keeping with the doctrines of mercantilism, the Spanish government allowed only Spanish merchants to trade with their American colonies, requiring all colonial exports and imports to pass through a single Spanish port where they were registered at the government-operated customs house. During the sixteenth century, this system worked reasonably well. The Spanish colonial economy was dominated by mining; the lucrative market for silver in East Asia even made it profitable to establish an outpost in Manila, where Spanish merchants exchanged Asian silk for South American bullion. But Spain also took steps to promote farming and ranching in Central and South America, and established settlements in Florida and California.

The wealth of Spain's colonial trade tempted the merchants of other countries to win a share of the treasure for themselves. Probably the boldest challengers were the English, whose leading buccaneer was the "sea dog" Sir Francis Drake. Three times Drake raided the east and west coasts of Spanish America. In 1587 he attacked the Spanish fleet at its anchorage in Cadíz harbor; and in 1588 he played a key role in defeating the Spanish Armada. His career illustrates the mixture of piracy and patriotism that characterized England's early efforts to break into the colonial trade. Until the 1650s, however, the English could only dent the lucrative Spanish trade in bullion, hides, silks, and slaves.

HOW DID EUROPEAN COLONIAL SETTLEMENTS IN THE AMERICAS DIFFER FROM EACH OTHER?

COLONIZATION AND TRADE IN THE SEVENTEENTH CENTURY   443

ENGLISH COLONIALISM

England's own American colonies had no significant mineral wealth. As a result, English colonists sought profits by establishing agricultural settlements in North America and the Caribbean basin. Their first permanent, though ultimately unsuccessful, colony was founded in 1607 at Jamestown, Virginia. Over the next forty years, eighty thousand English emigrants would sail to more than twenty autonomous settlements in the New World. Many of these early settlers were driven by religious motives. The Pilgrims who landed at Plymouth, Massachusetts, in 1620 were one of many dissident groups, both Protestant and Catholic, that sought to escape the English government's attempt to impose religious conformity by emigrating to North America.

Most of these early English settlements were privately organized. As they began to prosper, however, the governments of both Oliver Cromwell and Charles II began to intervene in their management. Mercantilist-inspired navigation acts, passed in 1651 and 1660 and rigorously enforced thereafter, decreed that all exports from English colonies to the mother country be carried in English ships and forbade the direct exporting of certain "enumerated" products directly from the colonies to Continental ports.

The most valuable of those colonial products were sugar and tobacco. Sugar, virtually unknown in Christian Europe during the Middle Ages, became a popular luxury item in the late fifteenth century, when Europeans began to produce it in their Mediterranean and African colonies. Only in the New World, however, did sugar production reach such volumes as to create a mass market for the product. By the middle of the seventeenth century, European demand for sugar had already reached enormous proportions. In the eighteenth century, the sugar England imported from its tiny West Indian colonies of Barbados and Jamaica was worth more than all of its imports from China and India combined.

Sugar, however, could only be grown in a fairly limited geographical and climatic area. Tobacco was much more adaptable. Although tobacco was first imported into Europe by the Spaniards in the mid-sixteenth century, another half century passed before Europeans took up the habit of smoking. Governments at first joined the church in condemning the use of tobacco, but by the end of the seventeenth century, having realized the profits to be made from it, they were actively encouraging its production and consumption.

> In the eighteenth century, the sugar England imported from its tiny West Indian colonies of Barbados and Jamaica was worth more than all of its imports from China and India combined.

FRENCH COLONIALISM

French colonial policy matured during the administration of Louis XIV's mercantilist finance minister, Jean Baptiste Colbert, who regarded overseas expansion as an integral part of state economic policy. To compete with the English, he encouraged the development of sugar-producing colonies in the West Indies, the largest of which was St. Domingue (present-day Haiti). France also dominated the interior of the North American continent, where French traders bought furs and missionaries preached Christianity to the Indians in a vast territory that stretched from Acadia to Quebec to Louisiana. Yet the financial returns from these lands were never commensurate with their size. Furs, fish, and tobacco were exported to European markets in large quantities but never matched the profits from the Caribbean sugar colonies or from the trading outposts the French maintained in India.

DUTCH COLONIALISM

Until the 1670s, the Dutch controlled the most prosperous commercial empire of the seventeenth century. Dutch colonialism generally followed the "fort and factory" model established by the Portuguese in Asia. In Southeast Asia, the Dutch East India Company, founded in 1602, seized control of Sumatra, Borneo, and the Moluccas (Spice Islands), driving Portuguese traders from an area they had previously dominated and establishing a Dutch monopoly within Europe over pepper, cinnamon, nutmeg, mace, and cloves. The Dutch also secured an exclusive right to trade with Japan and maintained military and trading outposts in China and India as well. In the Western Hemisphere, however, their achievements were less spectacular. Following a series of trade wars with England, in 1667 they formally surrendered their colony of New Amsterdam (subsequently renamed New York), retaining only Surinam (off the northern coast of South America) and Curaçao and Tobago (in the West Indies). Although they dominated the seventeenth-century slave trade with Africa, after 1713 the Dutch would lose this position also to the British.

THE ATLANTIC WORLD

Why were European governments so concerned with closely controlling the means by which certain products traveled from the colonies to European ports? How and why did the financial institutions of the late medieval period thrive on and encourage the economic policies of colonial powers? Why are the trade routes carrying slaves so prominently marked on this map? What does this suggest about the importance of unfree labor to the economic achievements of Europeans in the New World?

HOW DID EUROPEAN COLONIAL SETTLEMENTS IN THE AMERICAS DIFFER FROM EACH OTHER?

COLONIZATION AND TRADE IN THE SEVENTEENTH CENTURY   445

As the primary financiers of seventeenth-century Europe, the Dutch also pioneered new mechanisms for investing in colonial enterprises. One of the most important of these was the joint-stock company, of which the Dutch East India Company was among the first. Such companies raised cash by selling shares in their enterprise to investors. Even though the investors might not take any role in managing the company, they were joint owners of the business and therefore entitled to a share in its profits in proportion with the amount they had invested. Initially, the Dutch East India Company had intended to pay off its investors ten years after its founding, but the directors soon recognized the impossibility of this plan. The directors therefore urged investors anxious to realize their profits to sell their shares on the Amsterdam stock exchange to other investors, thereby ensuring the continued operation of their enterprise and, in the process, establishing a method of continuous business financing that would soon spread elsewhere in Europe.

> As the primary financiers of seventeenth-century Europe, the Dutch also pioneered new mechanisms for investing in colonial enterprises. One of the most important of these was the joint-stock company, of which the Dutch East India Company was among the first.

CONTRASTING PATTERNS OF COLONIAL SETTLEMENT

Differences in the commercial relationships European countries established with their New World colonies reflected important differences in settlement patterns among these colonies. In Central and South America, a relatively small number of Spaniards had conquered complex, highly populous Native American societies. To rule these new territories, the Spanish quickly replaced native elites with Spanish administrators and churchmen. But by and large they did not attempt to uproot or eliminate existing native cultures. Instead, Spain focused its efforts on controlling and exploiting native labor, so as to extract the maximum possible profit for the crown from the colonies' mineral resources. The native peoples of Spanish America already lived, for the most part, in large, well-organized villages and towns. Spanish colonial policy was to collect tribute from such communities and to convert them to Catholicism, but to do so without fundamentally disrupting their existing patterns of life.

The result was widespread cultural assimilation between the Spanish colonizers and the native popu-

lace, combined with a relatively high degree of intermarriage between them. Out of this reality emerged a complex and distinctive system of racial and social castes, with "pure-blooded" Spaniards at the top, peoples of mixed descent in the middle (native, Spanish, and African, in various combinations), and nontribal Indians at the bottom. In theory, these racial categories corresponded with class distinctions, but in practice race and class did not always coincide, and race itself was often a social fiction. Mixed-race individuals who prospered economically often found ways to establish their "pure" Spanish ancestry by adopting the social practices that characterized elite (i.e., Spanish) status. Spaniards, however, always remained at the top of the social hierarchy, even when they fell into poverty.

Like the Spanish colonies, the French colonies were established and administered as direct crown enterprises. French colonial settlements were conceived mainly as military outposts and trading centers; as a result, they were overwhelmingly populated by men. The elite members of French colonial society were the military officers and administrators sent out from Paris. But fishermen, fur traders, small farmers, and common soldiers constituted the bulk of the French settlers of North America. Except in the Caribbean, French colonies were dependent largely on the fur trade and on fishing; both enterprises relied in turn upon cooperative relationships with native peoples. A mutual economic interdependence therefore grew up between these French colonies and the peoples of the surrounding region. Intermarriage, especially between French fur traders and native women, was common. But most French colonies in North America remained dependent upon the wages and supplies sent to them from the mother country. Only rarely did they become truly self-sustaining economic enterprises.

The English colonies along the Atlantic seaboard followed a different model. English colonies did not begin as crown enterprises. Instead they were established either by joint-stock companies (as in Virginia and the Massachusetts Bay colony) or as private, proprietary colonies (such as Maryland and Pennsylvania). Building on their experience in Ireland, English colonists established planned settlements known as plantations, in which they attempted to replicate as many features of English life as possible. Geography also contributed to the resulting concentration of English settlement patterns. The rivers and bays of eastern North America provided the first footholds for English colonists in the New World, and the Atlantic Ocean helped to tie these separated settlements together. But aside from the Hudson, there were no great rivers to lead colonists very far inland. Instead, the English colonies clung to the seacoast, and so to each other.

Like the French colonies, the early English colonies relied on fishing and the fur trade for their exports. But primarily, English colonies were agricultural communities, populated by small- and medium-scale landholders for whom control over land was the key to wealth. Partly this was a reflection of the kinds of people whom these privately sponsored colonial enterprises could persuade to immigrate to the New World. But this focus on agriculture was also the result of the demographic catastrophe that had struck the native populations of the Atlantic seaboard during the last half of the sixteenth century. European diseases, brought by Spanish armies and by the French, English, and Portuguese fisherman who frequented the rich fishing banks off the New England coast, had already decimated the native peoples of eastern North America even before the first European colonists set foot there. By the early seventeenth century, a great deal of rich agricultural land had been abandoned simply because there were no longer enough native farmers to till it—one reason that many native groups initially welcomed the new arrivals.

Unlike the Spanish, English colonists along the Atlantic seaboard therefore had neither the need nor the opportunity to control a large native labor force. What they wanted, rather, was complete and exclusive control over native lands. To this end, the English colonists soon set out to eliminate, through expulsion and massacre, the indigenous peoples of their colonies. To be sure, there were exceptions. In the Quaker colony of Pennsylvania, colonists and Native Americans maintained friendly relations for more than half a century. In the Carolinas, by contrast, there was widespread enslavement of native people, either for sale to the West Indies or, from the 1690s, to work on the rice plantations along the coast. Elsewhere, however, attempts to enslave the native peoples of North America failed. When English planters looked for bond laborers, they therefore either recruited indentured servants from England (most of whom would be freed after a specified period of service) or else they purchased African captives (who would usually be enslaved for life).

Social relations between the English colonists and native peoples also differed from the patterns we find elsewhere in the New World. In contrast to the Spanish and French colonies, intermarriage between English colonists and natives was rare. Instead, a rigid racial division emerged that distinguished all Europeans, regardless of class, from all Native Americans and Africans. Intermarriage between natives and Africans was relatively common, but between the English and the indigenous peoples of their colonies an unbridgeable gulf soon developed.

COLONIAL RIVALRIES

The fortunes of these colonial empires changed dramatically in the course of the seventeenth and early eighteenth centuries. Spain, mired in persistent economic stagnation and embroiled in a series of expensive wars and domestic rebellions, proved unable to defend its monopoly over colonial trade. In a war with Spain in the 1650s, England captured not only the island of Jamaica but treasure ships lying off the Spanish harbor of Cadíz. Further profit was obtained by bribing Spanish customs officials on a grand scale. During the second half of the century, two thirds of the imported goods sold in Spanish colonies were smuggled in by Dutch, English, and French traders. By 1700, although Spain still possessed a colonial empire, that empire lay at the mercy of its more dynamic rivals. A brief revival of fortunes under more enlightened leadership in the mid-eighteenth century did nothing to prevent its ultimate eclipse.

Portugal, too, found it impossible to prevent foreign penetration of its colonial empire. England in particular worked diligently to win commercial advantages there. In 1703, the English signed a treaty with Portugal allowing English merchants to export woolens duty free into Portugal, and allowing Por-

> In contrast to the Spanish and French colonies, intermarriage between English colonists and natives was rare. Instead, a rigid racial division emerged that distinguished all Europeans, regardless of class, from all Native Americans and Africans.

The Defense of Cadíz Against the English by Francisco Zurbaran. The rivalry between European powers that played out over the new colonial possessions further proved the decline of Spain, which lost the island of Jamaica and ships in the harbor of Cadíz to the English in the 1650s.

of French territory in North America) and, to a lesser extent, the French, who retained Cape Breton Island, Quebec, the interior portions of North America, and their foothold in India. The eighteenth century would witness a continuing struggle between Britain and France for control over the expanding commerce that now bound the European economy to the Americas and to Asia.

THE TRIANGULAR TRADE IN SUGAR AND SLAVES

During the eighteenth century, European colonial trade came to be dominated by trans-Atlantic routes that developed in response to the lucrative West Indian sugar industry and to the demand for slaves from Africa to work

tugul to ship its wines duty free into England. Increasing English trade with Portugal also led to English trade with the Portuguese colony of Brazil, an important sugar producer and the largest of all the New World markets for African slaves. In the eighteenth century, English merchants would dominate these Brazilian trade routes.

COLONIALISM AND EMPIRE

In what ways did eighteenth-century European colonialism differ from seventeenth-century European colonialism?

The 1713 Treaty of Utrecht opened a new era in these colonial rivalries. As we have seen, the biggest losers in these negotiations were the Dutch, who gained only a guarantee of security for their own borders, and the Spanish, who were forced to concede to Britain the right to market slaves in the Spanish colonies. The winners were the British (who acquired large chunks

these Caribbean plantations. In this "triangular" trade, naval superiority gave Britain a decisive advantage over its French, Spanish, Portuguese, and Dutch rivals. Typically, a British ship might begin its voyage from New England with a consignment of rum and sail to Africa, where the rum would be exchanged for a cargo of slaves. From the west coast of Africa the ship would then cross the South Atlantic to the sugar colonies of Jamaica or Barbados, where slaves would be traded for molasses. It would then make the final leg of the journey back to New England, where the molasses would be made into rum. A variant triangle might see cheap manufactured goods move from England to Africa, where they would be traded for slaves. Those slaves would then be shipped to Virginia and exchanged for tobacco, which would be shipped to England and processed there for sale throughout Europe.

The cultivation of New World sugar and tobacco depended on slave labor. As European demand for these products increased, so too did the traffic in enslaved Africans. At the height of the Atlantic slave trade in the eighteenth century, 75,000 to 90,000 Africans were shipped across the Atlantic yearly: at

How Slaves Were Stowed Aboard Ship during the Middle Passage. Men were "housed" on the right; women on the left; children in the middle. The human cargo was jammed onto platforms six feet wide without sufficient headroom to permit an adult to sit up. This diagram is from evidence gathered by English abolitionists and depicts conditions on the Liverpool slave ship *Brookes.*

least 6 million in the eighteenth century, out of a total of over 11 million for the entire history of the trade. About 35 percent went to English and French Caribbean plantations; 5 percent (roughly 500,000) to North America; and the rest to the Portuguese colony of Brazil and to the Spanish colonies in Central and South America. By the 1780s, there were more than 500,000 slaves on the largest French plantation island, St. Domingue, and at least 200,000 on its English counterpart, Jamaica.

Although run as a monopoly by various governments in the sixteenth and early seventeenth centuries, in the eighteenth century the slave trade was open to private entrepreneurs who operated ports on the West African coast. These traders exchanged Indian cloth, metal goods, rum, and firearms with African slave merchants in return for their human cargo, who would then be packed by the hundreds into the holds of slave ships for the gruesome "middle passage" across the Atlantic (so called to distinguish it from the slave ship's

voyage from Europe to Africa, and then from the colonies back to Europe). Shackled below decks without sanitary facilities, the captive men, women, and children suffered horribly. The mortality rate, however, remained at about 10 percent, not much higher than the rate for a normal sea voyage of one hundred days or more. Since traders had to invest as much as £10 per slave in their enterprise, they were generally anxious to ensure that their consignment would reach its destination in good enough shape to be sold for a profit.

THE COMMERCIAL RIVALRY BETWEEN BRITAIN AND FRANCE

British dominance of the slave trade gave it decisive advantages in its colonial struggles with France. As one Englishman wrote in 1749, the slave trade had provided "an unexhastible fund of wealth to this nation."

But even apart from the slave trade, the value of colonial commerce was increasing dramatically during the eighteenth century. French colonial trade, valued at 25 million livres in 1716, rose to 263 million livres in 1789. In England, during roughly the same period, foreign trade increased in value from £10 million to £40 million, the latter amount more than twice that for France.

The growing value of colonial commerce tied the interests of governments and transoceanic merchants together in an increasingly tight embrace. Merchants engaged in the colonial trade depended on their governments to protect and defend their overseas investments; but governments depended in turn on merchants and their financial backers to build the ships and sustain the trade on which national power depended. In the eighteenth century, even the ability to wage war rested largely (and increasingly) on a government's ability to borrow the necessary funds from wealthy investors, and then to pay back those debts, with interest, over time. As it did in commerce, so too in finance, Britain came to enjoy a decisive advantage in this respect over France. The Bank of England, founded in the 1690s, managed the English national debt with great success, providing the funds required for war by selling shares to investors, then repaying those investors at moderate rates of interest. In contrast, chronic governmental indebtedness forced the French crown to borrow at ruinously high rates of interest, provoking a series of fiscal crises that in 1789 finally led to the collapse of the French monarchy.

War and Empire in the Eighteenth-Century World

After 1713, western Europe remained largely at peace for a generation. In 1740, however, that peace was shattered when Frederick the Great of Prussia seized the Austrian province of Silesia (see p. 435). In the resulting War of the Austrian Succession, France and Spain fought on the side of Prussia, hoping to reverse some of the losses they had suffered in the Treaty of Utrecht. As they had done since the 1690s, Britain and the Dutch Republic sided with Austria. Like those earlier wars, this war quickly spread beyond the frontiers of Europe. In India, the English East India Company lost control over the coastal area of Madras to its French rival; but in North America, British colonists from New England captured the important French

fortress of Louisbourg on Cape Breton Island, hoping to put a stop to French interference with their fishing and shipping. When the war finally ended in 1748, Britain recovered Madras and returned Louisbourg to France.

Eight years later, these colonial conflicts reignited when Prussia once again attacked Austria. This time, however, Prussia allied itself with Great Britain. Austria found support from both France and Russia. In Europe, the Seven Years' War (1756–1763) ended in stalemate. In India and North America, however, the war had decisive consequences. In India, the British East India Company joined with native allies to elimate their French competitors. In North America (where the conflict was known as the French and Indian War), British troops captured Louisbourg and Quebec and drove French forces from the Ohio River valley and the Great Lakes. In 1763, France formally surrendered both Canada and India to the British. Six years later, the French East India Company was dissolved.

The American Revolution

Along the Atlantic seaboard, however, the rapidly growing British colonies were beginning to chafe at rule from London. To recover some of the costs of the Seven Years' War and to pay for the continuing costs of protecting its colonial subjects, the British Parliament imposed a series of new taxes on its American colonies. These taxes were immediately unpopular. Colonists complained that because they had no representatives in Parliament, they were being taxed without their consent—a fundamental violation of their rights as British subjects. They also complained that British restrictions on colonial trade, particularly the requirement that certain goods pass first through British ports before being transshipped to the Continent, were strangling American livelihoods and so making it impossible to pay even the king's legitimate taxes.

The British government, led since 1760 by the young and inexperienced King George III, responded to these complaints with a badly calculated mixture of vacillation and force. Various taxes were imposed and then withdrawn in the face of colonial resistance. In 1773, however, when East India Company tea was dumped in Boston Harbor by rebellious colonials objecting to the customs duties that had been imposed on it, the British government closed the port of Boston and curtailed the colony's representative institutions.

THE SEVEN YEARS' WAR, 1756–1763

How was the Seven Years' War the first true worldwide war? What were the roles of the colonies? What were the consequences for the colonies involved in the conflict? What was the impact of naval power on the outcome of the war?

Legend:
- Spanish Empire
- Portuguese Empire
- British Empire
- Russian Empire
- Dutch Empire
- Ottoman Empire
- French Empire
- Areas of conflict

Map labels: ARCTIC OCEAN, RUSSIA, ASIA, JAPAN, PACIFIC OCEAN, PHILIPPINES, CHINA, DUTCH EAST INDIES, BENGAL, INDIA, Madras, Bombay, CEYLON, PERSIA, INDIAN OCEAN, EUROPE, SWEDEN, POLAND, AUSTRIA, HUNGARY, PRUSSIA, NETHERLANDS, GREAT BRITAIN, FRANCE, SPAIN, PORTUGAL, ICELAND, GREENLAND, AFRICA, GUINEA, ATLANTIC OCEAN, Hudson Bay, Louisbourg, Quebec, Fort Duquesne, NORTH AMERICA, FLORIDA, MEXICO, GUIANA, SOUTH AMERICA, PERU, PACIFIC OCEAN

Scale: 0 1000 2000 Miles / 0 1000 2000 Kilometers

EIGHTEENTH-CENTURY WARS

War of the Spanish Succession	1702–1713
War of the Austrian Succession	1740–1748
Seven Years' War	1756–1763
American Revolution	1775–1783
The Russo-Turkish War	1787–1792

These "Coercive Acts" galvanized the support of the other American colonies for Massachusetts. In 1774, representatives from all the American colonies met at Philadelphia to form a Continental Congress to negotiate with the crown over their grievances. In April 1775, however, local militiamen at Lexington and Concord clashed with regular British troops sent to disarm them. Soon thereafter, the Continental Congress began raising an army, and an outright rebellion erupted against the British government.

On July 4, 1776, the thirteen colonies formally declared their independence from Great Britain. During the first two years of the war, it seemed unlikely that such independence would ever become a reality. In 1778, however, France, anxious to undermine the colonial hegemony Great Britain had established since 1713, joined the war on the side of the Americans. Spain entered the war in support of France, hoping to recover Gibraltar and Florida (the latter lost in 1763 to Britain). In 1780, Britain also declared war on the Dutch Republic for continuing to trade with the rebellious colonies. Now facing a coalition of its colonial rivals, Great Britain saw the war turn against it. In 1781, combined land and sea operations by French and American troops forced the surrender of the main British army at Yorktown in Virginia. Negotiations for peace began soon after but were not concluded until September 1783. The Treaty of Paris left Great Britain in control of Canada and Gibraltar. Spain retained its possessions west of the Mississippi River and recovered Florida. The United States gained its independence; its western border was fixed on the Mississippi River, and it secured valuable fishing rights off the eastern coast of Canada. France gained only the satisfaction of defeating its colonial rival; but even that satisfaction was short lived. Six years later, the massive debts France had incurred in supporting the American Revolution helped to bring about another, very different kind of revolution in France that would permanently alter the history of Europe.

In 1781, combined land and sea operations by French and American troops forced the surrender of the main British army at Yorktown in Virginia.

CONCLUSION

Seen in this light, the American War of Independence was the final military conflict in a century-long struggle between Great Britain and France for colonial dominance. But the consequences of Britain's defeat in 1783 were far less significant than might have been expected. Even after American independence, Great Britain would remain the most important trading partner for its former American colonies, while elsewhere around the globe, the commercial dominance Britain had already established would continue to grow. The profits of slavery certainly helped to fuel the eighteenth-century British economy; by the end of the century, however, British trade and manufacturing had reached such high levels of productivity that even the abolition of the slave trade (in 1808) and of slavery itself (in 1833) did not impede its continuing growth.

The economic prosperity of late-eighteenth-century Britain was mirrored to some degree throughout northwestern Europe. Improved transportation systems, more reliable food supplies, and growing quantities of consumer goods brought improved standards of living to large numbers of Europeans, even as the overall population of Europe was rising faster after 1750 than it had ever done before. Population growth was especially rapid in the cities, where a new urban middle class was emerging whose tastes drove the market for goods and whose opinions were reshaping the world of ideas.

But the prosperity of late-eighteenth-century Europe remained very unevenly distributed. In the cities, rich and poor lived separate lives in separate neighborhoods. In the countryside, regions bypassed by the developing commercial economy of the period continued to suffer from hunger and famine, just as they had done in the sixteenth and seventeenth centuries. In eastern Europe the contrasts between rich and poor were even more extreme, as many peasants fell into a new style of serfdom that would last until the end of the nineteenth century. War too remained a fact of European life, bringing death and destruction to hundreds of thousands of people across the continent and around the world—yet another consequence of the worldwide reach of these European colonial empires.

Political change was more gradual. Throughout Europe, the powers of governments steadily increased. Administrators became more numerous, more efficient, and more demanding, partly to meet the mounting costs of war, but also because governments were starting to take on a much wider range of responsibilities for the welfare of their subjects. Despite the increasing scope of government, however, the structure and principles of government changed relatively little. Apart from Great Britain and the Dutch Republic, the great powers of eighteenth-century Europe were still governed by rulers who styled themselves as absolutist monarchs in the mold of Louis XIV. By 1789, however, the European world was a vastly different place than it had been a century before, when the Sun King had dominated European politics. The full extent of those differences was about to be revealed.

KEY TERMS

balance of power	Treaty of Utrecht	Peter the Great
Louis XIV	Versailles	Catherine the Great
William and Mary	Frederick the Great	"triangular" trade
Two Treatises on Government		

SELECTED READINGS

Blanning, T. C. W., ed. *The Eighteenth Century: Europe 1688–1815.* Oxford and New York, 2000. Chapters on political, economic, cultural, and religious developments written by leading experts.

Cameron, Euan, ed. *Early Modern Europe: An Oxford History.* Oxford and New York, 1999. A wide-ranging, stimulating, multiauthor survey, topically arranged, that spans the entire period from the Renaissance to the French Revolution.

Campbell, Peter R. *Louis XIV, 1661–1715.* London, 1993. A reliable recent biography; short, with primary source material and a good bibliography.

Collins, James B. *The State in Early Modern France.* Cambridge and New York, 1995. A challenging new account of French government and finance between 1620 and 1789.

Doyle, William. *The Old European Order, 1660–1800.* Oxford and New York, 1992. The best recent account of European society during the *ancien régime,* with chapters on population, trade, the social order, and public affairs.

Hufton, Olwen. *The Prospect Before Her: A History of Women in Western Europe, 1500–1800.* New York, 1996. A great book by a great social historian.

Hughes, Lindsey. *Russia in the Age of Peter the Great.* New Haven, 1998. A detailed, scholarly account by the leading British authority on Peter's reign.

Ingrao, Charles. *The Habsburg Monarchy, 1618–1815.* 2d ed. Cambridge and New York, 2000. A recently revised and updated edition of this standard work.

Kishlansky, Mark A. *A Monarchy Transformed: Britain, 1603–1714.* London, 1996. An excellent survey that takes seriously its claims to be a "British" rather than merely an "English" history.

Koch, H. W. *A History of Prussia.* London, 1978. Still the best account of its subject.

Locke, John. *Two Treatises of Government.* Edited by Peter Laslett. Rev. ed. Cambridge and New York, 1963. Laslett has revolutionized our understanding of the historical and ideological context of Locke's political writings.

Miller, John, ed. *Absolutism in Seventeenth-Century Europe.* London, 1990. An excellent, multiauthor survey, organized by country.

Quataert, Donald. *The Ottoman Empire, 1700–1822.* Cambridge and New York, 2000. Well balanced, up to date, and intended to be read by students.

Saint-Simon, Louis. *Historical Memoirs.* Many editions. The classic source for life at Louis XIV's Versailles.

Thomas, Hugh. *The Slave Trade: The History of the Atlantic Slave Trade, 1440–1870.* London and New York, 1997. A survey notable for its breadth and depth of coverage, and for its attractive prose style.

ASTROLOGY, ASTRONOMY, AND GALILEO

But I do not feel obliged to believe that the same God who has endowed us with senses, reason and intellect has intended us to forgo their use and by some other means to give us knowledge which we can attain by them.

—Galileo, *Letter to the Grand Duchess Christina of Tuscany*

IN THE NINETEENTH CENTURY, many westerners assumed that the ancient traditions of astrology, alchemy, and the occult were crushed by the general acceptance of Copernican heliocentricity, Kepler's laws of planetary motion, Galileo's observations of the heavens, and, ultimately, Isaac Newton's discovery of the universal laws of gravitation. Reason had seemingly triumphed over faith. Such an opinion flourished in an intellectual environment that had become increasingly secularized— what was rational was real, what was unrational needed to be abandoned since it no longer conformed to human reason.

A century after Martin Luther had divided the church, Galileo dared to suggest that the observations of the ancient and medieval authorities of Aristotle, Ptolemy, Aquinas, and Dante were incorrect. In 1633, Galileo was brought to trial by the Inquisition for demonstrating through sense observation alone that the earth was not the center of the universe and that it indeed moved. His trial highlighted a clash of cultures—Galileo was forced to abjure or recant his opinions about Copernican heliocentricity. As a result, the first wave of the revolution in science came to an end, to be followed by a second wave emanating from England, the Low Countries, and Germany.

The work of Galileo and others cannot be understood as a specific reaction to astrology, alchemy, or the occult. Instead, the occult sciences provide the general historical and psychological context in which modern science had its origins.

The images and documents in the *Astrology, Astronomy, and Galileo* Digital History Feature at www.wwnorton.com/wciv explore how the discoveries made by Galileo and other early scientists related to astrologers' and alchemists' attempts to understand the mechanics of the universe. As you explore the *Astrology, Astronomy, and Galileo* feature, consider the following:

• In what ways were astrology, alchemy, and astronomy mutually supporting sciences? Do you think modern astronomy would have developed as it did without the benefit of the occult sciences?

• Why was Copernicus so hesitant to publish his findings? Do you think scientists today are always aware of the social or psychological dimensions of their discoveries?

• What does the trial of Galileo tell us about the New Science of the sixteenth and seventeenth centuries?

• With so many in the Vatican who understood Copernican theory, why was Galileo brought to trial? What did the church stand to lose? or gain?

CHAPTER SIXTEEN

CHAPTER CONTENTS

THE SCIENTIFIC
REVOLUTION

BETWEEN THE EARLY 1500s and the late 1600s, new ideas about the physical world brought sweeping changes to European philosophy and, more broadly, to Europeans' view of their place in the world. What we call the "scientific revolution" entailed three changes: the emergence and confirmation of a heliocentric view of the universe, the development of a new physics that fit such a view, and the establishment of a method of enquiry. Thinkers associated with the new "natural philosophy," as science was called at the time, explained how the earth could, in defiance of common sense, be hurtling around the sun. In so doing, they also vindicated the role of reason, experiment, and observation in understanding the natural world. They established "science" as a new form of knowledge.

The scientific revolution was not an organized effort. Brilliant theories sometimes led to dead ends; discoveries were often accidental. Artisans grinding lenses for telescopes played as much of a role as great abstract thinkers. Most important, old and new world views often overlapped. "Science" did not necessarily undermine either religion or magic, and it did not supplant "superstition." Individual thinkers struggled to reconcile their discoveries with their faith or to make their theories (about the earth's movements, for instance) fit their everyday experiences. For all of these reasons, changes came slowly and fitfully. The new world view was, nonetheless, revolutionary, and had ramifications well beyond the small circles of scientists, theologians, and philosophers with whom it began.

FOCUS QUESTIONS

• What were the intellectual roots of the scientific revolution?

• Did scientific thinking challenge religious authority?

• What did Copernicus and Galileo contribute to the revolution in science?

 • What were the philosphical differences between Bacon and Descartes?

• What social and political changes helped disseminate scientific thinking?

THE INTELLECTUAL ROOTS OF THE SCIENTIFIC REVOLUTION

What were the intellectual roots of the scientific revolution?

Keen interest in the workings of the natural world was not new to sixteenth-century Europe. As we have seen, European artistic life had been characterized from the twelfth century on by its commitment to naturalism. Medieval sculptors carved plants and vines with such accuracy that modern botanists can still identify the species of the plants they represented. Medieval sculptors and painters poured their energies into accurately depicting the human face and form. Italian Renaissance painters took these techniques to new heights with their rediscovery of the principles of linear perspective and a preoccupation with light. During the fourteenth century, some thinkers had broadened their studies of light and begun to explore the science of optics—inventing, along the way, the first reading glasses. Astrologers too were active in the fourteenth and fifteenth centuries, charting the heavens in the firm belief that the stars controlled the fates of human beings.

Behind this high medieval fascination with nature and the natural world lay a combination of Christian Neoplatonism and Aristotelianism. By the fourteenth century, however, so-called nominalist theologians and philosophers had begun to argue that nature did not necessarily fit the stable and certain picture drawn by the Aristotelians. (See discussion on page 313 in Chapter 10.) Humans could only understand God's truths through revelation and faith. They might rationally investigate nature and record its regularities. But the laws of nature did not necessarily reveal anything about the nature of God. Thus, the nominalist challenge freed the investigation of the natural world from the constraints of theology and opened the way for the emergence of the world view we associate with modern science.

What did the scientific revolution of the sixteenth and seventeenth centuries owe to the Renaissance humanists? The educational program of the humanists placed a low value on science. None of the great scientists of the Renaissance period belonged to the humanist movement. Nonetheless, Renaissance humanists contributed to the developing interest in science. Perhaps the most important influence came from Neoplatonism, which led humanists to seek out the ideal and perfect structures that they believed lay behind the "shadows" of the everyday world.

Humanism also played some role in the growing fascination with the intricate mechanisms at work in the universe. Renaissance mechanism was stimulated by the 1543 publication of the works of the great Greek mathematician and physicist Archimedes. Archimedes taught that the universe operates on the basis of mechanical forces, like a great machine. Mechanism won some very important late Renaissance adherents, including the Italian scientist Galileo. Ultimately mechanism influenced the development of modern science because it insisted on finding observable and measurable causes and effects in the world of nature.

> Renaissance mechanism owed its greatest impetus to the publication in 1543 of the works of the great Greek mathematician and physicist Archimedes.

One other Renaissance development that contributed to the rise of modern science was the growing collaboration between artisans and intellectuals. During the High Middle Ages, well-educated clerics had theorized about the natural world, but rarely did they think of tinkering with machines—much less of dissecting corpses! On the other side, the many artisans who had developed extensive expertise in mechanical engineering had little formal education. During the fifteenth century, these two worlds began to come together. Highly respected Renaissance artists such as Leonardo da Vinci bridged both areas of endeavor. Not only were they marvelous craftsmen, but they also investigated the laws of perspective and optics, worked out geometric methods for supporting the weight of enormous architectural domes, studied the dimensions and details of the human body, and devised new and more effective weapons for war. Men and women in the leisured classes grew increasingly interested in alchemy and astrology. This vogue led some wealthy amateurs to start building laboratories and measuring the courses of the stars, assisted by telescopes made possible by the combined work of intellectuals and artisans in grinding lenses. With these developments, the modern science of astronomy was born.

WHAT DID COPERNICUS AND GALILEO CONTRIBUTE TO THE REVOLUTION IN SCIENCE?

A REVOLUTION IN ASTRONOMY   459

A REVOLUTION IN ASTRONOMY

What did Copernicus and Galileo contribute to the revolutiuon in science?

For more than three thousand years, from the age of the pharaohs until the 1500s, people believed that the sun, the stars, and the planets moved around the earth. In the Middle Ages, this idea seemed obvious and unshakable. It followed from the ancient authorities' theories and from a belief in the purposefulness of God's universe. It supported the Greeks' complex explanations of physics, which held that each fundamental element of the universe had its place, with the heaviest elements, water and earth, taking form around the center. It was confirmed by the commonsense observations of philosophers and peasants alike, who could watch the sun and the stars move from one horizon to the other each day and night.

To the astronomers of the Middle Ages, the most important classical authorities on natural philosophy were Aristotle and Ptolemy. Both had created frameworks that explained the whole universe, explanations rooted in notions of cosmic order that could be made to fit Europeans' deeper concerns about sin, transformation, and perfection. Aristotle had offered a complete explanation of the natural world, a vision grounded in the apparent orderliness of the cosmos. He suggested that each being or substance sought to reach its "natural place." On earth, the four fundamental elements were constantly trying to sort themselves out into those natural places. This ever-changing earth sat at the center of the universe, separated from the unchanging heavens that moved in perfect, regular circles. Aristotelian physics had its critics, but most of them sought to correct minor errors of logic and to improve on its basic principles, not to dismantle them.

People had long observed problems with the perfect circles that heavenly objects were supposed to describe. The planets, Mars in particular, sometimes seemed to stop and loop backward before continuing on their paths. The Greek mathematician Ptolemy had produced the most sophisticated mathematical formulas to account for these and other orbital irregularities. By the late Middle Ages, however, European astronomers were beginning to have doubts about Ptolemy's complicated formulas. During the late 1400s several European astronomers gained access to Ptolemy's texts in their original Greek. They discovered that the great astronomer's work had not been corrupted by translators, but was in fact marred by omissions and faulty mathematics.

THE COPERNICAN REVOLUTION

A crisis over the European calendar, which was based on the calculations of Ptolemy and others, made these problems immediate and practical. By the early sixteenth century the old Roman calendar was significantly out of alignment with the movement of the heavenly bodies. The major saints' days, Easter, and the other holy days were more than a week off where they should have been according to the stars. Catholic authorities spent nearly a century trying to correct this problem, summoning mathematicians and astronomers from all over Europe. One of these researchers was the Polish clergyman and university astronomer Nicholas Copernicus (1473–1543). Copernicus was a careful mathematician and a faithful Christian. He could not believe that God would create a universe as ramshackle and messy as Ptolemy's, with its mathematical trickery and circles within circles. His solution was as simple as it was radical. He concluded that the sun was not one of the planets orbiting a fixed earth. Instead, the earth itself moved through the heavens, at the third orbit out from the center. If the positions of the earth and the sun were switched, the mathematics of astronomy became simpler, the orbits of the other planets made more sense, and the calendar could be put right.

Copernicus was in many ways an extremely conservative thinker. He did not see his work as a break with either the church or the ancient authorities. He believed he had restored a pure understanding of God's design, one that had been lost over the centuries. He wanted a simple explanation of heavenly perfection that eliminated the clumsiness of Ptolemy's mathematical calculations. Yet the implications of his theory troubled him. His ideas contradicted the many biblical passages that described a fixed earth and moving heavens, and they discarded centuries of astronomical knowledge. Practical problems also presented themselves. Copernicus was not a physicist. If the earth was moving around the sun, it had to be going at a terrifying speed. Copernicus had no way to reconcile his suggestion that the earth orbited the sun with the fact that objects on earth fell to the ground or moved "normally." As he worked on the problem his astronomy became more cumbersome: he continued to assume that orbits were perfect circles, and he fell back on some of Ptolemy's devices to explain errors in those patterns.

These frustrations and complications dogged Copernicus throughout his later years. He hesitated to publish his findings until just before his death,

Nicolaus Copernicus. This anonymous portrait of Copernicus characteristically blends his devotion and his scientific achievements. His scholarly work (behind him in the form of an early planetarium) is driven by his faith (as he turns towards the image of Christ triumphant over death).

when he consented to the release of his work *On the Revolutions of the Heavenly Spheres* (*De Revolutionibus*) in 1543. To fend off scandal, his Lutheran publisher added an introduction to the book declaring that Copernicus's system was just an abstraction, another set of mathematical tools for doing astronomy—not a dangerous claim about the nature of heaven and earth. Copernicus's ideas remained politically harmless and obscure for decades, while other, less radical thinkers busied themselves with cleaning up the calendar.

TYCHO'S SYSTEM AND KEPLER'S LAWS

Copernicus's ideas were revived through the work of two astronomers who also sought a perfect explanation of the universe, but did so by observing the sky

WHAT DID COPERNICUS AND GALILEO CONTRIBUTE TO THE REVOLUTION IN SCIENCE?

A REVOLUTION IN ASTRONOMY   461

itself. Tycho Brahe (1546–1601) and Johannes Kepler (1571–1630) were each considered the greatest astronomers of their day. Tycho was a high-ranking Danish nobleman, a gifted rogue endowed with lands and wealth by his king but trained in his youth as an astronomer. He first made a name for himself by observing a completely new star. Tycho then set out to correct other flaws in ancient astronomy by observing the movement of the heavens. Before the invention of telescopes, he turned a small island that formed part of his estates into a giant laboratory, specially designed for observation. For over twenty years he spent each night carefully mapping out the motion of each significant object in the night sky, accurate to within the tiniest fraction of a degree. Before he drank himself to death, Tycho had collected the finest set of astronomical data ever seen in Europe.

Tycho did not accept Copernicus's conclusion that the earth moved around the sun. Instead he created a model in which the other planets orbited the sun, and the whole system then orbited a (stationary) earth. The "Tychonic" system proved enormously successful. It allowed accurate astronomical and astrological predictions to be made more easily than in the old Ptolemaic system, and it avoided the upsetting theological implications of the Copernican system.

In his old age, Tycho moved to Prague. One of his assistants, Johannes Kepler, combined Copernicus's system with his own interest in mysticism, astrology, and the religious power of mathematics. Kepler's work offered the first credible physical explanation of a moving earth and the astronomy that went with it.

Kepler believed that everything in creation, from human souls to the orbits of the planets, had been created according to mathematical laws. Understanding those laws would thus allow human beings to share God's wisdom and the inner secrets of the universe. Kepler was driven by spiritual goals, but he also respected empirical data. Relying on Tycho's astronomical tables, Kepler was able to recognize that two of Copernicus's assumptions about planetary motion simply did not fit with the observable facts. Specifically, Kepler replaced Copernicus's view that planetary orbits were circular with his own "First Law" that the earth and the other planets travel in elliptical paths around the sun. Further, he argued that magnetic attractions between the sun and the planets kept the planets in orbital motion. That approach was rejected by most seventeenth-century mechanistic scientists as being far too magical, but in fact it paved the way for the law of universal gravitation formulated by Isaac Newton at the end of the seventeenth century.

> Kepler believed that everything in creation, from human souls to the orbits of the planets, had been created according to mathematical laws.

NEW HEAVENS, NEW EARTH, AND WORLDLY POLITICS: GALILEO GALILEI (1564–1642)

Galileo transformed Copernicanism from a theory about astronomy into a larger debate about the role of natural philosophy in understanding the world. He offered evidence that the earth moved, discovered a variety of new celestial bodies, and was able to form some idea of the enormous distances between the stars. But he also made a case for a new relationship between religion and science, a proposal that challenged some of the most powerful churchmen of his day. His firm belief in his new ideas and his penchant for controversy made him the best-known natural philosopher of his day, but ultimately brought him into conflict with the authority of the Catholic Church.

By the early 1600s, Galileo was already a successful mathematician at the prestigious university at Padua, in northern Italy. He did not make his name by mathematical skill, however. Fame and scientific opportunity came his way through his innovative use of the telescope, and through his skill as a participant in Italy's networks of courtly patronage. In 1610, after hearing of the newly invented telescope from a Flemish friend, Galileo procured one, and rather than training it on earthly sights he pointed it at the night sky. The results changed his career. He observed sunspots, which he sketched and documented as real irregularities on the surface of the sun. Jupiter yielded the greatest prize: evidence of orbiting moons around the great planet, providing solid proof that the earth was not the only body with objects in orbit around it. Galileo published these astonishing results in his book *The Starry Messenger* (1610). This book gained him entry into Italy's centers of power and patronage. By naming Jupiter's moons the "Medicean stars," and through his great skill in debating such controversial subjects, he gained the favor of the Medici rulers of Florence.

With a court appointment and Medici support, Galileo was able to pursue his work on astronomy and his conviction that Copernicus's heliocentric (sun-centered) model of the universe was correct.

Before long, both of Galileo's goals—promoting Copernicanism and challenging Aristotelianism—brought him into conflict with powerful opponents. The great Jesuit astronomers of the day argued that Galileo's telescopic discoveries fitted perfectly well with Tycho's system, and so did not require displacing the earth from its position at the center of the universe. The most important of these critics was Cardinal Robert Bellarmine (1542–1621). Perhaps the most influential Jesuit of his day, Bellarmine was a skilled mathematician who had helped repair the calendar when he was a young man. In the decades since, he had become the Catholic Church's champion in theological debates with Protestant critics. Bellarmine argued that Copernicanism was wrong in practice, for all the reasons that had worried Coper-

nicus himself. Other churchmen however, considered Copernicanism a direct threat to church doctrine. Bellarmine was asked to caution Galileo about pursuing those ideas too far. Galileo had been expecting such a warning, and responded at once. In his *Letter to the Grand Duchess Christina di Medici* (1615), Galileo launched his first and most famous reply to his critics, and his clearest defense of Copernican science.

Galileo was a sincere Catholic and a sincere Copernican. He believed that if the church refused to acknowledge the "new science" and its explanation of the natural world, the authority of the church would suffer. What Galileo wanted was a new and more equal partnership between natural philosophy and the church in finding and proving truth. The church's senior clergy did the vital work of saving souls, but that did not mean that the church, or the university philosophers in whom it had placed too much trust, had any power to explain the physical world. The natural philosopher, who created solid mathematical explanations of the visible world, was

Galileo Galilei before the Inquisition by Francois Richard Fleury. A romanticized view of the Scientific Revolution. This nineteenth-century painting portrays the myth that Galileo openly defied the Inquisition to the last. According to the story, Galileo renounced his convictions before the Inquisition, but then stamped his foot saying "and still it moves!" In reality Galileo submitted—in order to keep working under house arrest and publish again, secretly, in the Netherlands.

GALILEO ON NATURE, SCRIPTURE, AND TRUTH

One of the clearest statements of Galileo's convictions about religion and science comes from his 1615 letter to the Grand Duchess Christina. The grand duchess was the mother of Galileo's patron, Cosimo de Medici, and a powerful figure in her own right. Galileo knew that others had raised objections to his work. He had been warned that Copernicanism was not just inaccurate but impious; it could be disproved scientifically and it contradicted the authority of those who interpreted the Bible. Thoroughly dependent on the Medicis for support, he wrote to the grand duchess to explain his position.

In this section of the letter, Galileo reflects on the problems of interpreting both the Bible and nature. He sets out his understanding of the parallel but distinct roles of the church and natural philosophers. He walks a fine line between acknowledging the authority of the church and standing firm in his convictions.

They know that . . . I hold the sun to be situated motionless in the center of the revolution of the celestial orbs while the earth rotates on its axis and revolves about the sun. They know also that I support this position not only by refuting the arguments of Ptolemy and Aristotle, but by producing many counterarguments; in particular, some which relate to physical effects whose causes can perhaps be assigned in no other way. In addition there are astronomical arguments derived from many things in my new celestial discoveries that plainly confute the Ptolemaic system while admirably agreeing with and confirming the contrary hypothesis. Possibly because they are disturbed by the known truth of other propositions of mine which differ from those commonly held, and therefore mistrusting their defense so long as they confine themselves to the field of philosophy, these men have resolved to fabricate a shield for their fallacies out of the mantle of pretended religion and the authority of the Bible. . . .

Copernicus never discusses matters of religion or faith, nor does he use arguments that depend in any way upon the authority of sacred writings which he might have interpreted erroneously. He stands always upon physical conclusions pertaining to the celestial motions, and deals with them by astronomical and geometrical demonstrations, founded primarily upon sense experiences and very exact observations. He did not ignore the Bible, but he knew very well that if his doctrine were proved, then it could not contradict the Scriptures when they were rightly understood. . . .

I think that in discussions of physical problems we ought to begin not from the authority of scriptural passages, but from sense-experiences and necessary demonstrations; for the holy Bible and the phenomena of nature proceed alike from the divine Word, the former as the dictate of the Holy Ghost and the latter as the observant executrix of God's commands. It is necessary for the Bible, in order to be accommodated to the understanding of every man, to speak many things which appear to differ from the absolute truth so far as the bare meaning of the words is concerned. But Nature, on the other hand, is inexorable and immutable; she never transgresses the laws imposed upon her, or cares a whit whether her abstruse reasons and methods of operation are understandable to men. For that reason it appears that nothing physical which sense-experience sets before our eyes, or which necessary demonstrations prove to us, ought to be called in questions (much less condemned) upon the testimony of biblical passages which may have some different meaning beneath their words. For the Bible is not chained in every expression to conditions as strict as those which govern all physical effects; nor is God any less excellently revealed in Nature's actions than in the sacred statements of the Bible. . . .

Galileo, "Letter to the Grand Duchess Christina," in Stillman Drake, ed., *The Discoveries and Opinions of Galileo Galilei* (Garden City, N.Y.: Doubleday, 1957), pp. 177–183.

much better qualified to offer those explanations. Any conflict between what natural philosophers revealed and a literal interpretation of the Bible was a false problem. The Bible was a notoriously difficult book, and the church's theologians, Galileo argued, would be able to reconcile the complex language of the Bible with the new conclusions of natural philosophy. Natural philosophers and theologians were therefore partners in a search for truth, but they had very different roles to play. Galileo quoted one of Bellarmine's fellow cardinals against him: the church's role was to "tell us how to go to Heaven, and not how heaven goes."

In response to the Reformation, the church had given senior clergy the right of final appeal in matters of theology. Galileo's protests notwithstanding, the church believed his work challenged its authority. In 1616, it placed Copernicus's work on the Index of Prohibited Books. Galileo's friends and critics alike now suggested that he leave Copernican ideas alone and put limits on his great ambitions.

For nearly a decade after the debate with Bellarmine, Galileo did as he was asked. During the 1620s, however, the political and philosophical climate seemed to be changing. Several of Galileo's most formidable critics, including Bellarmine, died, and Galileo's old friend Barberini became Pope Urban VIII. Seizing his chance, Galileo drafted a "dialogue," a debate between supporters of the old and new sciences. He took great care in publishing the new work. He showed this Copernican tract—for that was just what it was—to the church authorities, who edited for content, suggested the bland title *A Dialogue Between the Two Great World Systems*, and allowed its publication in 1632. In the book, Galileo's opponents won the mock debate, but along the way Galileo made a thorough case for Copernicanism, with great detail and biting wit. The book was an international success, but it created a scandal within Italy's networks of sacred and worldly patronage. Barberini was offended by Galileo's portrait; he also needed the support of church conservatives during a difficult stretch of the Thirty Years' War. His anger at Galileo's disregard for political judgment broke their relationship. Galileo was cast to his critics and charged with heresy.

The trial that followed shocked Europe. Galileo was the most famous natural philosopher of his day, the pride of one of the great intellectual centers of the continent. The church's legal arm, the Inquisition in Rome, backed its weak case against the philosopher with threats of death and excommunication. The elderly Galileo bent rather than let himself be broken. He recanted his belief in Copernicus's ideas; he was banned from working on or even discussing those ideas, and placed under house arrest for life. Yet he continued to refine his ideas about the problems of motion. His physics for a moving earth, compiled under the title *The Two New Sciences* (1638), was smuggled out of Italy and published in Protestant Holland.

Galileo left two great legacies. He combined abstract mathematics and practical experiments to produce a new physics, one that explained how objects behaved "normally" on a moving earth. Galileo's second legacy, however, was exactly the disaster he had hoped to avoid. Galileo hoped that Copernicanism could coexist peacefully with the religious wisdom of the Catholic Church. His trial made such coexistence impossible. The trial silenced Copernican voices in southern Europe, and the church's leadership retreated into conservative reaction. It was therefore in northwest Europe that the "new philosophy" Galileo had championed would ultimately flourish.

> The elderly Galileo bent rather than let himself be broken. He recanted his belief in Copernicus's ideas; he was banned from working on or even discussing those ideas, and placed under house arrest for life.

METHODS FOR A NEW PHILOSOPHY: BACON AND DESCARTES

What were the philosophical differences between Bacon and Descartes?

By the early 1600s the increasingly "Copernican" sciences of mathematics and astronomy were changing quickly. At first those changes were haphazard and very loosely related. As the practice of the new sciences became concentrated in Protestant northwestern Europe, however, several important thinkers began to produce not only new discoveries, but new principles of and goals for science, or natural philosophy. In the process, natural philosophers spelled out standards of practice, new ideas about what proved a theory correct, fresh judgments about what answers to questions about the natural world were most complete and satisfying, and what methods served best to reach those answers.

BACON AND DESCARTES

The new methods were refined by two men in particular: the Englishman Sir Francis Bacon and the Frenchman René Descartes. Both men believed they lived in a new age of profound change and great opportunities for discovery. Both also believed that the bedrock of natural philosophy, the ideas of Aristotle, no longer met the needs of the times, and that a fresh approach would take European "moderns" well beyond the knowledge of the ancients. The methods they created were very different, but between them they shaped the practice of natural philosophy in the later seventeenth century and left a deep mark on the evolution of modern science.

Sir Francis Bacon (1561–1626), a leading judge who became lord chancellor of England, was an extremely influential theorist of the new philosophy. Bacon's view, best expressed in his *Novum Organum* (*New Instrument*) of 1620, was that natural science could not advance unless it cast off the inherited errors of the past. The knowledge of ancient authorities was no longer the best guide to truth. To put it more cautiously, too much reverence for accepted doctrines could block discovery and full understanding. The worth of knowledge could be proven only through "progressive stages of certainty," or what philosophers would term an empirical approach. For Bacon this meant gaining knowledge of nature through the senses. Using the "inductive method," philosophers would combine evidence from a huge number of particular observations to draw general conclusions. Bacon sought "useful knowledge," practical forms of understanding grounded in the detailed study of each part of the natural world.

Bacon's contemporary, the French philosopher René Descartes (1596–1650), agreed with him on the importance of questioning established knowledge. Yet Descartes offered a completely different method for reaching useful knowledge. Unlike Bacon, Descartes was a rationalist and a champion of pure logic and mathematics. In his *Discourse on Method* (1637), Descartes explained how, during a period of solitude, he submitted all knowledge and ideas to a process of systematic doubt. His first rule was "never to receive anything as a truth which [he] did not clearly know to be such," and he found himself doubting everything until he accepted that the process of thought proved

his own existence. Reckoning back from this famous position—*cogito ergo sum* ("I think, therefore I am")—Descartes made rationality the point of departure for his entire philosophical enterprise.

THE POWER OF METHOD AND THE FORCE OF CURIOSITY: SEVENTEENTH-CENTURY EXPERIMENTERS

What social and political changes helped disseminate scientific thinking?

For nearly a century after Bacon and Descartes, most of England's natural philosophers were Baconian, while most of their colleagues in France and northern Europe were Cartesian (the name given to followers of Descartes). The Cartesians turned instead toward mathematics and philosophical theory. Descartes himself pioneered analytical geometry. Blaise Pascal (1623–1662) worked on probability theory and invented a calculating machine before applying his mathematical skills to theology.

CHRONOLOGY

THE EXPERIMENTERS OF THE SCIENTIFIC REVOLUTION

Nicholas Copernicus	1473–1543
Tycho Brahe	1546–1601
Francis Bacon	1561–1626
Galileo Galilei	1564–1642
Johannes Kepler	1571–1630
William Harvey	1578–1657
René Descartes	1596–1650
Blaise Pascal	1623–1662
Robert Boyle	1627–1691
Christian Huygens	1629–1695
Baruch Spinoza	1632–1677
Robert Hooke	1635–1703
Isaac Newton	1642–1727

TWO REACTIONS TO THE "NEW PHILOSOPHY"

In his poem, "An Anatomie of the World" (1609), the English poet John Donne (1572–1631) summed up the sense of loss and confusion created by new work in natural philsophy. "The element of fire" refers to Aristotle's physics. The second selection below is an excerpt from Francis Bacon's Novum Organum *(1620), a "new" Organon. The Organon was Aristotle's treatise on the elements of philosophy, one of the basic texts of a university education. Bacon's work constituted a bold summing up of the new learning and its implications. Bacon, like Donne, was English; his world view, however, was very different, and he tried to spell out the real possibilities of human knowledge. Educated English people would have had both books on their shelves.*

"AN ANATOMIE OF THE WORLD"

And new Philosophy calls all in doubt,
The element of fire is quite put out;
   The sun is lost, and th' earth,
And no man's wit
Can well direct him where to look for it.
'Tis all in pieces, all coherence gone,
Prince, subject,
Father, son,
All just supply,
And all relation. . . .

APHORISMS FROM *NOVUM ORGANUM*

XXXI

It is idle to expect any great advancement in science from the superinducing and engrafting of new things upon old. We must begin anew from the very foundations, unless we would revolve forever in a circle with mean and contemptible progress. . . .

XXXVI

One method of delivery alone remains to us which is simply this: we must lead men to the particulars themselves, and their series and order; while men on their side must force themselves for a while to lay their notions by and begin to familiarize themselves with facts. . . .

XLV

The human understanding is of its own nature prone to suppose the existence of more order and regularity in the world than it finds. And though there be many things in nature which are singular and unmatched, yet it devises for them parallels and conjugates and relatives which do not exist. Hence the fiction that all celestial bodies move in perfect circles. . . . Hence too the element of fire with its orb is brought in, to make up the square with the other three which the sense perceives. . . . And so on of other dreams. And these fancies affect not dogmas only, but simple notions also. . . .

English followers of Bacon pursued the same goal by very different means. They sought a different kind of conclusion to their research: empirical laws, which were general conclusions based on evidence rather than absolute statements about how the universe worked. Among the many English laboratory scientists of the era were the physician William Harvey (1578–1657), the chemist Robert Boyle (1627–1691), and the biologist Robert Hooke (1635–1703). Harvey's research continued the work of Vesalius. Unlike his predecessor however, Harvey was willing to dissect living animals and therefore was able to observe and describe the circulation of blood through the arteries and back to the heart through the veins. The English experimenter Robert Hooke also helped to add the microscope to the natural philosopher's toolkit. Like the telescope, the microscope seemed to unlock a boundless new dimension of material phenomena. Examining even the most ordinary objects revealed detailed structures of perfectly connected smaller parts and persuaded many that with improved instruments they would uncover even more of the world's intricacies. The microscope also provided new, convincing evidence of God's existence. The way that each minute structure of every living organism when viewed under a microscope corresponded harmoniously with its adaptive purpose testified not only to God's existence, but to God's magnificence as well.

Robert Hooke's *Micrographia*. Hooke's diagram of a fly's eye as seen through a microscope seemed to reveal just the sort of intricate universe the mechanists predicted.

SCIENCE, SOCIETIES, AND THE STATE

Boyle and Hooke shared a long working relationship and harbored great ambitions for the power of experiments. In 1660, when England's monarchy was restored after years of civil war and religious division, the two men helped establish a formal society of natural philosophers. The group caught the eye of the newly crowned King Charles II, who voiced his approval and granted the dignified name of the Royal Society. Its founders, Boyle in particular, believed the Royal Society could play a vital role in the much larger task of restoring order and consensus to English society. Boyle hoped the Society would combine Bacon's goal of collective research and discovery with the task of offering scientific support for the restoration of royal power and the authority of the Church of England. Members of the Society would conduct formal experiments, record the results, and exchange them with other researchers, who could study, reproduce, and criticize the outcome. This would give England's natural philosophers a common sense of purpose and a system of reasoned, gentlemanly agreement on "matters of fact." The society reached out to professional scholars and experimenters in England, Scotland, and continental Europe. Similar societies appeared across Europe soon after, and together these groups of gentleman philosophers provided a new model for scientific organization and new standards of success. Information and theories could be exchanged easily across national and philosophical boundaries, and the modern scientific custom of crediting discoveries to those who were first to publish their results emerged. During the 1690s however, this philosophy was suddenly overturned by the work of one man: Isaac Newton.

"AND ALL WAS LIGHT": ISAAC NEWTON

Sir Isaac Newton (1642–1727), an English experimenter, empiricist, and university mathematician, is considered one of the greatest scientific minds of all time. That genius was masked by an unattractive personality—Newton was secretive, obsessive, vindictive, and petty. The son of a small landholding family, Newton received a working scholarship to Cambridge, and by dint of his skills in mathematics, received a minor chair in the university's Trinity College. He had few close friends and tended to work alone. Newton was nearly as good with his hands as he was with mathematics, putting those skills to use in his study of alchemy and optics. He was also a secret Antitrinitarian (a dissident Protestant sect) and produced several books that combined his interests in alchemy and theology. To the end of his life he considered these his most important achievement.

Newton shared the Cartesians' belief in the power of mathematics to describe nature, but he disliked their dry logic. He did not share their indifference to studying the behavior of objects in nature. His respect for observation was fueled by his obsessive personality. Once he became involved with a problem—the nature of light, for example—it consumed his efforts for months or years at a time. He dismantled the larger question into its component parts and studied them to exhaustion. If he lacked the tools to do his experiments properly, Newton built his own. He im-

Isaac Newton. Newton, apparently during the period in which he was at work on gravitation. Newton rarely posed for paintings; he was a difficult loner, with few close friends and a distrustful attitude toward the public eye.

proved ordinary prisms in order to understand the nature of light and color. When he became interested in the problem of orbits, Newton lacked the mathematics to describe heavenly objects moving in curves. He created the first form of calculus to do the job.

The work on optics brought Newton out of his sheltered obscurity at Cambridge. He presented his results to the Royal Society in 1672. These results made his name immediately and provoked the first in a series of arguments with the society's president, Robert Hooke. Several of the arguments were quite bitter, for each man believed he was the brightest natural philosopher of his generation and was determined to prove himself right. Hooke challenged Newton's theories of orbital motion on the same grounds: they described but did not explain. Stung by these exchanges, Newton withdrew to his college and continued his work in alchemy and theology. Two of his few close friends—the astronomer and architect Sir Cristopher Wren (1632–1723), and the physicist and astronomer Edmond Halley (1656–1742)—brought him back to his work on orbits, however, which led him to even greater fame. Halley, skeptical of Hooke's mechanical explanation of orbits, asked Newton for his thoughts on the subject. Newton claimed to have done some research on the problem, but to have mislaid the papers. The lost work launched him into a fresh, five-year obsession, and brought him back to the fundamental problems of motion.

Newton had already done work on forces of attraction, refining Galileo's theory of inertia and suggesting that equal and opposite "forces" of motion were at work when any two objects came into contact. What Newton wanted was a descriptive answer to the problem of motion, one that not only explained how objects fell toward a moving earth, but also why the earth and other bodies moved in such a regular way. Newton wanted a single, clear, mathematical description of forces at work. To achieve this he took individual examples of falling objects on a moving earth and bodies in orbit, and managed to reach a formula that covered all cases. The formula described universal gravitation, and Newton explained it with the clarity of mathematics. It was a descriptive law, and it offered a single system for understanding motion in the heavens and on the earth.

The result, Newton's *Principia Mathematica* (*Mathematical Principles of Natural Philosophy*), went to press in 1687. Newton did not win the argument all at once. Yet Newton's geometry was backed by powerful evidence from observation and experience. This evidence did not just prove his theories—it showed that his conclusions could be applied to the everyday world.

What were the practical consequences of this majestic intellectual synthesis? Newton's laws of motion helped engineers design new kinds of working parts for machinery. The push and pull of gravitation showed geographers that the earth was not a perfect sphere, a finding that altered the nature of map making. The mathematics of gravity could be used to predict the ebb and flow of tides, even in waters where European ships had never sailed, a gigantic leap in an age of seaborne empires and maritime trade. His comprehensive explanation of motion not only provided an orderly and comprehensible picture of the heavens and earth, it also gave humanity greater power over its environment.

Modern historians of science still consider Newton's law of universal gravitation to be the greatest contribution to physics ever made by a single person. The praise was just as great in Newton's own time. He became an English national hero. Newton's countryman, the poet Alexander Pope, expressed the awe that Newton inspired in a famous eulogy: "Nature and nature's law lay hid in night; / God said, 'Let Newton be!' and all was light."

Newton was more cautious about his own achievements. Near the end of his life, in his *General Scholium* (1714), Newton explained the crucial difference between his own work and that of the mechanists. He enforced it sternly during his presidency of the Royal Society. It was spelled out in Latin: *hypotheses non fingo*, "I frame no hypotheses." Newton believed it vain and scientifically improper to seek out an underlying explanation for what he still saw as God's handiwork. Trying to understand why the universe was as it was would lead to futile speculation. What could be understood, with mathematical certainty, was how the universe operated as it did.

Newton and Satire. The English artist and satirist William Hogarth mocking both philosophy and "Newton worship" in 1763. The philosophers' heads are being weighed on a scale that runs from "absolute gravity" to "absolute levity" or "stark fool."

Establishment of the Academy of Sciences and Foundation of the Observatory, 1667. The 1666 founding of the Academy of Sciences was a measure of the new prestige of science and the potential value of research. Louis XIV sits at the center, surrounded by the religious and scholarly figures who offer the fruits of their knowledge to the French state.

The great scientific minds of the seventeenth century were driven by goals and priorities that were not radically different than those of their medieval predecessors. Natural philosophy did not break with religion. Many mechanists, far from being atheists, argued that such an intricate universe was "evidence of design" by God. Classical arguments collapsed in the face of new discoveries, but natural philosophers seldom gave up on the project of restoring a picture of an orderly universe, with explanations that strove toward perfection.

What, then, had changed? Seventeenth-century natural philosophers produced different answers to fundamental questions about the physical world. Scientific work took new forms. During the seventeenth century the most innovative scientific work moved out of the universities. Natural philosophers began talking and working with each other in organizations that developed standards of research. England's Royal Society spawned imitators across Europe, in Florence, Berlin, and later in Russia. The French Royal Academy of Sciences had a particularly direct relationship with the monarchy and the French state. France's

statesmen wanted some control over these societies, and wanted to share in the rewards of any discoveries they made.

New, too, were beliefs about the purpose and practice of science. The practice of breaking a complex problem down into parts that could be understood, abstracted, and explained in the clear language of mathematics made it possible to tackle more and different questions in the physical sciences. Mathematical language and solutions assumed more central role in the "new science." Finally, rather than simply proving established truths, the new methods could explore the unknown, and predict what might be found next.

CONCLUSION

The pioneering natural philosophers remained circumspect about their abilities. They also believed their science to be fully compatible with their faith. Some natural philosophers sought to lay bare the inner mechanisms of nature, to show how the whole system worked. Others believed humans could only catalogue and order the regularities observed in nature, but never truly understand them. Newton, for instance, worked toward explanations that would reveal the logic of creation laid out in mathematics. Yet in the end he set those goals aside, and was content to have solid theories explaining actions and substances that could be observed.

The eighteenth-century heirs to Newton's success were often much more daring. Laboratory science and the work of the scientific societies largely stayed true to the experimenters' rules and limitations. But as we will see, the natural philosophers who began investigating the "human sciences" cast aside some of their predecessors' caution. Society, technology, government, religion, even the individual human mind seemed to be mechanisms or parts of a larger nature waiting for study. If they could be explained in terms of laws, like gravity, humanity itself could be perfected. The revolution in science changed Europeans' understanding of the world; it also inspired thinkers much more interested in revolutions in society.

KEY TERMS

Nicholas Copernicus

Galileo Galilei

Novum Organum

Johannes Kepler

Discourse on Method

Isaac Newton

SELECTED READINGS

Biagioli, Mario. *Galileo, Courtier*. Chicago, 1993. Emphasizes the importance of patronage and court politics in Galileo's science and career.

Cohen, I. B. *The Birth of a New Physics*. New York, 1985. Emphasizes the mathematical nature of the revolution; unmatched at making the mathematics understandable.

Drake, Stillman. *Discoveries and Opinions of Galileo*. Garden City, N.Y., 1957. The classic translation of Galileo's most important papers by his most admiring modern biographer.

Gaukroger, Stephen. *Descartes: An Intellectual Biography*. Oxford, 1995. Detailed and sympathetic study of the philosopher.

Gooding, David, Trevor Pinch, et al. *The Uses of Experiment: Studies in the Natural Sciences*. Cambridge, 1989. An important reconsideration of the motives driving seventeenth-century research.

Hall, A. R. *The Scientific Revolution, 1500–1800: The Formation of the Modern Scientific Attitude*. London, 1954. The classic formulation of the concept of a "scientific revolution"; basic and readable.

Jones, Richard Foster. *Ancients and Moderns: A Study of the Rise of the Scientific Movement in Early Modern England*. Berkeley, 1961. Still a persuasive study of the scientific revolutionaries' attempts to situate their work in relation to that of the Greeks.

Kuhn, Thomas. *The Structure of Scientific Revolutions*. Chicago, 1962. A classic and much-debated study of how scientific thought changes.

Porter, Roy, and M. Teich, eds. *The Scientific Revolution in National Context*. Cambridge, 1992. A crucial set of articles questioning the focus on northern Europe's role in the scientific revolution.

Ruestow, Edward G. *The Microscope in the Dutch Republic: The Shaping of Discovery*. Cambridge, 1996.

Scheibinger, Londa. *The Mind Has No Sex? Women in the Origins of Modern Science*. Cambridge, Mass., 1989. A lively and important recovery of the lost role played by women mathematicians and experimenters.

Shapin, Steven. *The Scientific Revolution*. Chicago, 1996. The best recent survey.

Shapin, Steven, and Simon Schaffer. *Leviathan and the Air Pump*. Princeton, 1985. A modern classic, on one of the most famous philosophical conflicts in seventeenth-century science.

Stephenson, Bruce. *The Music of the Heavens: Kepler's Harmonic Astrology*. Princeton, N.J., 1994. An engaging and important explanation of Kepler's otherworldly perspective.

Thoren, Victor. *The Lord of Uraniborg: A Biography of Tycho Brahe*. Cambridge, 1990. A vivid reconstruction of the scientific revolution's most flamboyant astronomer and his path-breaking scientific center.

Westfall, Richard. *The Construction of Modern Science*. Cambridge, 1977.

———. *Never at Rest: A Biography of Isaac Newton*. Cambridge, 1980. The standard work.

Wilson, Catherine. *The Invisible World: Early Modern Philosophy and the Invention of the Microscope*. Princeton, 1995. An important study of how the "microcosmic" world revealed by technology reshaped scientific philosophy and practice.

CHAPTER
SEVENTEEN

THE
ENLIGHTENMENT

I N 1762, THE *PARLEMENT* (law court) of Toulouse, in France, convicted Jean
Calas of murdering his son. Calas was Protestant, and Catholic-Protestant tensions ran high in the region. Witnesses called before the court claimed that the
young Calas had wanted to break with his family and convert to Catholicism, and
they convinced the magistrates that Calas had killed his son rather than let him fall
from the Protestant faith. French law stipulated the punishment. Calas was tortured
twice: first in an attempt to get him to confess, and next, as a formal part of certain
death sentences, to force him to name his alleged accomplices. His arms and legs
were slowly pulled apart, gallons of water were poured down his throat, and his
body was publicly broken on the wheel, which meant that each of his limbs was
smashed with an iron bar. Then the executioner cut off his head. Throughout the
trial, torture, and execution, Calas maintained his innocence. Two years later, the
Parlement reversed its verdict, declared Calas not guilty, and offered the family a payment in compensation.

François Marie Arouet, also known as Voltaire, was one of those appalled by the
verdict and punishment. At the time of the case, Voltaire was the most famous Enlightenment thinker in Europe. Well connected and a prolific writer, Voltaire took
up his pen to clear Calas' name; he contacted friends, hired lawyers for the family,
and wrote briefs, letters, and essays to bring the case to the public eye. Calas' case
exemplified nearly everything Voltaire opposed in his culture. Intolerance, ignorance, and what Voltaire throughout his life called religious "fanaticism" and
"infamy" had made a travesty of justice. "Shout everywhere, I beg you, for Calas and
against fanaticism, for it is *l'infame* that has caused their misery," he wrote to his
friend Jean Le Rond d'Alembert, a fellow Enlightenment thinker. Using torture to
uncover truth demonstrated the power of unquestioned and centuries-old practices.
Legal procedures that included secret interrogations, trials behind closed doors,
summary judgment (Calas was executed the day after being convicted, with no
review by a higher court), and barbaric punishments defied reason, morality, and

human dignity. Any criminal, however wretched, "is a man," wrote Voltaire, "and you are accountable for his blood."

Voltaire's comments on the Calas case illustrate the classic concerns of the Enlightenment: the dangers of arbitrary and unchecked authority, the value of religious toleration, and the overriding importance of law, reason, and human dignity in all affairs. He borrowed most of his arguments from others—from his predecessor the baron de Montesquieu and from the Italian writer Cesare Beccaria, whose *On Crimes and Punishments* appeared in 1764. Voltaire's reputation did not rest on his originality as a philosopher. It came from his effectiveness as a writer and advocate, his desire and ability to reach a wide audience. In this, too, he was representative of the Enlightenment project.

THE FOUNDATIONS OF THE ENLIGHTENMENT

What were the basic characteristics of Enlightenment writings?

The Enlightenment was an eighteenth-century phenomenon, lasting for close to the entire century. Not every important thinker who lived and worked in the eighteenth century rallied to the Enlightenment banner. Some, such as the Italian philosopher of history G. B. Vico (1668–1744), opposed almost everything the Enlightenment stood for, and others, most notably Jean-Jacques Rousseau, accepted certain Enlightenment values but sharply rejected others. Patterns of Enlightenment thought varied from country to country, and they changed in each country over the course of the century. Many eighteenth-century thinkers nonetheless shared the sense of living in an exciting new intellectual environment in which the "party of humanity" would prevail over customary practices and traditional thought.

Enlightenment writings shared several basic characteristics. They were marked, first, by a confidence in the powers of human reason. This self-assurance stemmed from the accomplishments of the scientific revolution (see Chapter 16). Even when the details of Newton's physics were poorly understood, his methods provided a model for scientific inquiry into other phenomena. Nature operated according to laws that could be grasped by study, observation, and thought. Understanding and the exercise of human reason, however, required freedom from old authorities and traditions. "Dare to know!" the German philosopher Immanuel Kant challenged his contemporaries in his classic 1784 essay "What is Enlightenment?" For Kant, the Enlightenment represented a declaration of intellectual independence. Coming of age meant the "determination and courage to think without the guidance of someone else," as an individual. Reason needed autonomy and freedom.

Despite their declarations of independence from the past, Enlightenment thinkers recognized a great debt to their immediate predecessors. Voltaire called Bacon, Newton, and John Locke his "Holy Trinity." Indeed, much of the eighteenth-century Enlightenment consisted of translating, republishing, and thinking through the implications of the great works of the seventeenth century. Enlightenment thinkers drew heavily on Locke's studies of human knowledge, especially his *Essay Concerning Human Understanding* (1690), which was even more influential than his political philosophy. Locke's theories of knowledge gave education and environment a critical role in shaping human character. All knowledge, he argued, originates from sense perception. The human mind at birth is a "blank tablet" (in Latin, *tabula rasa*). Only when an infant begins to experience things, to perceive the external world with its senses, does anything register in its mind. Locke's starting point, which became a central premise for those who followed, was the goodness and perfectibility of humanity. Building on Locke, eighteenth-century thinkers made education central to their project, for education promised individual moral improvement and social progress.

Third, Enlightenment thinkers were extraordinarily ambitious and wide ranging. They sought nothing less than the organization of all knowledge. The "scientific method," by which they meant the empirical observation of particular phenomena in order to arrive at general laws, offered a way to pursue research in all areas—to study human affairs as well as natural ones. They took up a strikingly wide array of subjects in this systematic manner: knowledge and the mind, natural history, economics, government, religious beliefs, customs of indigenous peoples in the New World, human nature, and sexual (or what we would call gender) and racial differences.

Historians have called the Enlightenment a "cultural project," emphasizing Enlightenment thinkers' interest in practical, applied knowledge, and their determination to spread knowledge and to promote free public discussion. They intended, as Denis Diderot wrote, "to change the common way of thinking," and to advance the cause of "enlightenment" and humanity. While they shared many of their predecessors' theoretical concerns, they wrote in a very different style and for a much larger au-

HOW DID THE FRENCH *PHILOSOPHES* DIFFER IN THEIR THEMES AND STYLES?

THE WORLD OF THE *PHILOSOPHES* 475

dience. Hobbes and Locke had published treatises for small groups of learned seventeenth-century readers. Voltaire, in contrast, wrote plays, essays, and letters; Rousseau composed music, published his *Confessions*, and wrote novels that moved his readers to tears; David Hume, one of the giants of the Scottish Enlightenment, wrote history for a wide audience. A British aristocrat or a governor in the North American colonies would have read Locke. But a middle-class woman might have read Rousseau's fiction, and shopkeepers and artisans could become familiar with popular, Enlightenment-inspired pamphlets. More broadly, the intellectual achievements and goals of the Enlightenment followed from cultural developments in the eighteenth century. Those developments included the expansion of literacy and growing markets for books, new networks of readers, new forms of intellectual exchange, and the emergence of what some historians call the first "public sphere."

In sum, Enlightenment thinkers confronted their culture, exposing time-worn practices, beliefs, and authority to the shining "light" of reason. That often meant criticism and satire. They combined an irreverence for custom and tradition with a belief in human perfectibility and progress, a confidence in their ability to understand the world with a passionate interest in the relationship between "nature" and culture, or environment, history, and human character and society. Their program of reform had immediate political implications. In a remarkably short time it changed the premises of government and society throughout the Atlantic world.

> Historians have called the Enlightenment a "cultural project," emphasizing Enlightenment thinkers' interest in practical, applied knowledge, and their determination to spread knowledge and to promote free public discussion.

of where they lived, are often called by the French word *philosophes*. Yet hardly any of the *philosophes*—with the exceptions of David Hume and Immanuel Kant—were philosophers in the sense of being highly original abstract thinkers. Especially in France, Enlightenment thinkers shunned forms of expression that might seem incomprehensible, priding themselves instead on their clarity and style. *Philosophe*, in French, simply meant a free thinker, a person whose reflections were unhampered by the constraints of religion or dogma in any form.

VOLTAIRE

At the time, the best known of the *philosophes* was Voltaire, born François Marie Arouet (1694–1778). Voltaire virtually personified the Enlightenment,

THE WORLD OF THE PHILOSOPHES

How did the French *philosophes* differ in their themes and styles?

Enlightenment thought was European in a broad sense, including southern and eastern Europe as well as Europe's colonies in the New World. France, however, provided the stage for some of the most widely read Enlightenment books and the most closely watched battles. For this reason, Enlightenment thinkers, regardless

Voltaire, the brilliant and sharp tongued writer who helped establish the international reputation of the French philosophes. Portrait by Jean Antoine Houdon.

commenting on an enormous range of subjects in a wide variety of literary forms. Educated by the Jesuits, he emerged quite young as a gifted and sharp-tongued writer. His gusto for provocation landed him in the Bastille (a notorious prison in Paris) for libel, and soon afterward in temporary exile in England. In his three years there, Voltaire became an admirer of British political institutions, British culture, and British science; above all, he became an extremely persuasive convert to the ideas of Newton, Bacon, and Locke. His single greatest accomplishment may have been popularizing Newton's work in France and more generally championing the cause of British empiricism and the scientific method against the more Cartesian French.

Voltaire's famous battlecry, "Écrasez l'infâme," translates as "crush infamy," and by "infamy" he meant all forms of repression, fanaticism, and bigotry. He wrote the following to an opponent, and it is a statement often cited as the first principle of civil liberty: "I do not agree with a word you say, but I will defend to the death your right to say it." Of all forms of intolerance Voltaire opposed religious bigotry most, and with real passion he denounced religious "fraud," faith in miracles, and superstition. He did not oppose religion per se; rather he sought to rescue morality, which he believed to come from God, from dogma—elaborate ritual, dietary laws, formulaic prayers—and from a powerful church bureaucracy. He argued for common sense and simplicity, persuaded that these would bring out the goodness in humanity and establish stable authority.

> Voltaire's famous battlecry, "Écrasez l'infâme," translates as "crush infamy," and by "infamy" he meant all forms of repression, fanaticism, and bigotry.

Voltaire relished his position as a critic, and it never stopped him from being successful. He was regularly exiled from France and other countries, his books banned and burned. As long as his plays attracted large audiences, however, the French king felt he had to tolerate their author. Voltaire had an attentive international public, including Frederick of Prussia, who invited him to his court at Berlin, and Catherine of Russia, with whom he corresponded about reforms she might introduce in Russia. Voltaire described himself as "contraband," but that seemed only to enhance his value. When he died in 1778, a few months after a triumphant return to Paris, he was possibly the best-known writer in Europe.

MONTESQUIEU

The Baron de Montesquieu (1689–1755) was a very different kind of Enlightenment figure. Montesquieu was born to a noble family. He inherited both an estate and, since state offices were property that passed from father to son, a position as magistrate in the *Parlement*, or law court, of Bordeaux. He was not a stylist or a provocateur like Voltaire, but a relatively cautious jurist.

Montesquieu's serious treatise *The Spirit of Laws* (1748) may have been the most influential work of the Enlightenment. It was a groundbreaking study in what we would call comparative historical sociology, and very Newtonian in its careful, empirical approach. Montesquieu asked about the structures that shaped law. How had different environments, histories, and religious traditions combined to create such a variety of governmental institutions? What were the different forms of government: what "spirit" characterized each, and what were their respective virtues and shortcomings? Montesquieu proposed a threefold classification of states. A republic was governed by the many—in his view either an elite aristocracy or the people. In the second type, monarchy, a single authority ruled in accordance with the law. "Despotism," Montesquieu's most important negative example, allowed a single ruler to govern unchecked by law or other powers, sowing corruption and capriciousness. The soul or spirit of a republic was virtue; of monarchy, honor; of despotism, where no citizen could feel secure and punishment took the place of education, fear. Lest this seem abstract, Montesquieu devoted two chapters to the French monarchy, in which he spelled out what he saw as a dangerous drift toward despotism in his own land. Like other Enlightenment thinkers, Montesquieu admired the British system and its separate and balanced powers—executive, legislative, and judicial—which guaranteed liberty in the sense of freedom from the absolute power of any single governing individual or group. His idealization of "checks and balances" had formative influence on Enlightenment political theorists and members of the governing elites, particularly those who wrote the United States Constitution in 1787.

Montesquieu. The French baron's *Spirit of the Laws* (1748) was probably the most influential single text of the high Enlightenment.

DIDEROT AND THE *ENCYCLOPEDIA*

Voltaire's and Montesquieu's writings represent the themes and style of the French Enlightenment. But the most remarkable French publication of the century was a collective venture: the *Encyclopedia*. The *Encyclopedia* intended to summarize and disseminate all the most advanced contemporary philosophical, scientific, and technical knowledge. In terms of sheer scope, this was the grandest statement of the *philosophes'* goals. It demonstrated how scientific analysis could be applied in nearly all realms of thought. It aimed to reconsider an enormous range of traditions and institutions, and to put reason to the task of bringing happiness and progress to humanity. The guiding spirit behind the ven-ture was Denis Diderot. Diderot was helped by the Newtonian mathematician Jean Le Rond d'Alembert (1717–1783), and other leading "men of letters," including Voltaire and Montesquieu. The *Encyclopedia* was published, in installments, between 1751 and 1772; by the time it was completed, it ran to seventeen large volumes of text and eleven more of illustrations. A collaborative project, it helped create the *philosophes'* image as the "party of humanity."

The *Encyclopedia* sought to "change the general way of thinking." Diderot commissioned articles that explained recent achievements in science and technology, showing how machines worked and illustrating new industrial processes. The point was to demonstrate how the everyday applications of science could promote progress and alleviate all forms of human misery. Diderot turned the same methods to matters of religion, politics, and the foundations of the social order, including articles on economics, taxes, and the slave trade. The French government revoked permission for the *Encyclopedia* to be published, declaring in 1759 that the Encyclopedists were trying to "propagate materialism," which meant atheism, "to destroy Religion, to inspire a spirit of independence, and to nourish the corruption of morals." The volumes sold remarkably well despite such bans and their hefty price. Purchasers belonged to the elite: aristocrats, government officials, prosperous merchants, and a scattering of members of the higher clergy. That elite stretched across Europe, including its overseas colonies.

INTERNATIONALIZATION OF ENLIGHTENMENT THEMES

How did the Enlightenment themes influence life around Europe?

The "party of humanity" was international. French became the lingua franca of much Enlightenment discussion, but "French" books were often published in Switzerland, Germany, and Russia. As we have seen, Enlightenment thinkers admired British institutions and British scholarship, and they used both as points of reference. Great Britain also produced among the most important Enlightenment thinkers: the historian Edward Gibbon and the Scottish philosophers David Hume and Adam Smith. The *philosophes* considered Thomas Jefferson and Benjamin Franklin part of their group. Despite stiffer resistance from religious authorities, stricter state censors, and smaller networks of educated elites to discuss and support progressive thought, the Enlightenment flourished across central and southern Europe. Frederick II of Prussia housed Voltaire during one of his exiles from France, though the *philosophe* quickly wore out his welcome. Frederick also patronized a small but unusually productive group of Enlightenment thinkers. Enlightenment thinkers across Europe raised similar themes: humanitarianism, or the dignity and worth of all individuals, religious toleration, and liberty.

ENLIGHTENMENT THEMES: HUMANITARIANISM AND TOLERATION

Among the most influential writers of the entire Enlightenment was the Italian (Milanese) jurist Cesare Beccaria (1738–1794). Beccaria's *On Crimes and Punishments* (1764) sounded the same general themes as did the French *philosophes*—arbitrary power, reason, and human dignity—and it provided Voltaire with most of his arguments in the Calas case. Beccaria also proposed concrete legal reforms. He attacked the prevalent view that punishments should represent society's vengeance on the criminal. The only legitimate rationale for punishment was to maintain social order, and to prevent other crimes. Beccaria argued for the greatest possible leniency compatible with deterrence; respect for individual dignity and humanity dictated that humans should punish other humans no more than is absolutely necessary. Above all, Beccaria's book eloquently opposed torture and the death penalty. The spectacle of public execution, which sought to dramatize the power of the state and the

horrors of hell, in fact dehumanized victim, judge, and spectators. *On Crimes and Punishments* was quickly translated into a dozen languages. Owing primarily to its influence, most European countries by around 1800 abolished torture, branding, whipping, and various forms of mutilation, and reserved the death penalty for capital crimes.

Humanitarianism and reason also counseled religious toleration. Enlightenment thinkers spoke almost as one on the need to end religious warfare and the persecution of "heretics" and religious minorities. It is important, though, to differentiate between the church as an institution and dogma, against which many Enlightenment thinkers rebelled, and religious belief, which most accepted. Many (Voltaire, for instance) were deists, holding a religious outlook that saw God as a "divine clockmaker" who, at the beginning of time, constructed a perfect timepiece and then left it to run with predictable regularity. Enlightenment inquiry proved compatible with very different stances on religion.

"Toleration" was limited. Although Enlightenment thinkers deplored persecution, they commonly viewed Judaism and Islam as backward religions mired in superstition and obscurantist ritual. One of the few Enlightenment figures to treat Jews sympathetically was the German *philosophe* Gotthold Lessing (1729–1781). Lessing's extraordinary play *Nathan the Wise* (1779)

Instruments of Torture. A man being stretched on the rack (left) and a thumbscrew (right), both from an official Austrian government handbook. By 1800, Beccaria's influence had helped phase out the use of such instruments.

takes place in Jerusalem during the Fourth Crusade and begins with a pogrom, or violent, orchestrated attack, in which the wife and children of Nathan, a Jewish merchant, are murdered. Nathan survives to become a sympathetic and wise father figure. He adopts a Christian-born daughter and raises her with three religions: Christianity, Islam, and Judaism. At several points, authorities ask him to choose the single true religion. Nathan shows none exists. The three great monotheistic religions are three versions of the truth. Religion is authentic, or true, only insofar as it makes the believer virtuous.

Lessing modeled his hero on his friend Moses Mendelssohn (1729–1786), a self-educated rabbi and bookkeeper (and the grandfather of the composer Felix Mendelssohn). In a series of writings, the best-known of which is *On the Religious Authority of Judaism* (1783), Mendelssohn defended Jewish communities against anti-Semitic policies and Jewish religion against Enlightenment criticism. At the same time, he promoted reform within the Jewish community, arguing that his community had special reason to embrace

the broad Enlightenment project: religious faith should be voluntary, states should promote tolerance, humanitarianism would bring progress to all.

ECONOMICS, GOVERNMENT, AND ADMINISTRATION

Enlightenment ideas defended reason and knowledge for humanitarian reasons. But they also promised to make nations stronger, more efficient, and more prosperous. In other words, the Enlightenment spoke to individuals, but also to states. The *philosophes* addressed issues of liberty and rights, but also took up matters of administration, tax collection, and economic policy.

The rising fiscal demands of eighteenth-century states and empires made these issues newly urgent. Which economic resources were most valuable to states? How could governments tap them? Enlightenment economic thinkers such as the physiocrats argued that long-standing mercantilist policies were misguided. By the eighteenth century, mercantilism had become a term for a very wide range of policies that shared a belief in government regulation of trade in manufactured goods and precious metals. The physiocrats, most of them French, held that real wealth came from the land and agricultural production. More important, they advocated simplifying the tax system and following a policy of *laissez-faire*, which comes from the French expression *laissez faire la nature* ("let nature take its course"), letting wealth and goods circulate without government interference.

The now-classic expression of laissez faire economics, however, came from the Scottish economist Adam Smith (1723–1790), and especially from Smith's landmark treatise *Inquiry into the Nature and Causes of the Wealth of Nations* (1776). Smith disagreed with the physiocrats on the value of agriculture, but he shared their opposition to mercantilism. For Smith, the central issues were the productivity of labor and how labor was used in different sectors of the economy. Mercantile restrictions—such as high taxes on imported goods, which was one of the grievances of the colonists throughout the American empires—did not encourage the productive deployment of labor and thus did not create real economic health. For Smith, general prosperity could best be obtained by allowing the famous "invisible hand" to guide economic activity. Individuals, in other words, should pursue their own interests without competition from state-chartered monopolies or legal restraints.

The German philosopher **Gotthold Lessing** visiting his friend **Moses Mendelssohn,** one of the major Jewish figures of the Enlightenment.

The Wealth of Nations' perspective owed much to Newton and to the Enlightenment's idealization of both nature and human nature. Smith wanted to follow what he called, in classic Enlightenment terms, the "obvious and simple system of natural liberty." Smith thought of himself as the champion of justice against state-sponsored economic privilege and monopolies. He was a theorist of human feelings as well as market forces. Smith emerged as the most influential of the new eighteenth-century economic thinkers. In the following century, ironically, his work and his followers became the target of reformers and critics of the new economic world.

EMPIRE AND ENLIGHTENMENT

How did the *philosophes* view the New World?

Smith's *Wealth of Nations* formed part of a debate about the economics of empire: *philosophes* and statesmen alike asked how the colonies could be profitable, and to whom. The colonial world loomed large in Enlightenment thinking in several other ways. The "new" world across the Atlantic offered a foil to the "old" civilization of Europe, in other words, an often idealized portrait of natural humanity and simplicity, by comparison with which Europe looked decadent or corrupt. Second, Europeans' colonial activities—especially, by the eighteenth century, the slave trade—could not help but raise pressing issues about humanitarianism, individual rights, and natural law. The effects of colonialism on Europe were a central Enlightenment theme.

Adam Smith wrote in *The Wealth of Nations* that the "discovery of America, and that of a passage to the East Indies by the cape of Good Hope are two greatest and most important events recorded in the history of mankind. What benefits, or what misfortunes to mankind may herafter result form those great events," he continued, "no human wisdom can foresee." Smith's language was nearly identical to that of a Frenchman, the Abbé Guillaume Thomas François Raynal. Raynal's massive *Philosophical History . . . of Europeans in the Two Indies* (1770), a co-authored work like the *Encyclopedia*, was one of the most widely read works of the Enlightenment.

> The "new" world across the Atlantic offered a foil to the "old" civilization of Europe, in other words, an often idealized portrait of natural humanity and simplicity, by comparison with which Europe looked decadent or corrupt.

Raynal drew his inspiration from the *Encyclopedia* and aimed at nothing less than a total history of colonization: customs and civilizations of indigenous peoples, natural history, exploration, and commerce in the Atlantic world and India. He also tried to draw up a balance sheet, asking as did Smith, if colonization had made humanity happier, more peaceful, or better. The question was fully in the spirit of the Enlightenment. So was the answer. Raynal believed that industry and trade brought improvement and progress. Like other Enlightenment writers, however, he and his co-authors considered natural simplicity an antidote to the corruptions of their culture. They condemned the tactics of the Spanish in Mexico and Peru, of the Portuguese in Brazil, and of the British in North America. They echoed Montesquieu's theme that good government required checks and balances against arbitrary authority. In the New World, they argued, Europeans found themselves with virtually unlimited power, which encouraged them to be arrogant, cruel, and despotic. Eighteenth-century radicals repeatedly warned that overextended empires sowed seeds of decadence and corruption at home.

SLAVERY AND THE ATLANTIC WORLD

Discussing Europe's colonies and economies inevitably raised the issue of slavery. The sugar islands of the Caribbean were among the most valued possessions of the colonial world, and the sugar trade one of the leading sectors of the Western economy. The Atlantic slave trade reached its peak in the eighteenth century. European slave traders sent at least 1 million Africans into New World slavery in the late seventeenth century, and at least 6 million in the eighteenth century. On this topic, however, even thinkers as radical as Raynal and Diderot hesitated, and their hesitations are revealing about the tensions in Enlightenment thought. Enlightenment thinking began with the premise that individuals could reason and govern themselves. Individual moral freedom lay at the heart of what the Enlightment considered to be a just, stable, and harmonious society. Slavery defied natural law and natural freedom. Nearly all Enlightenment thinkers condemned "slavery" in the metaphorical sense. That the "mind should break free of its chains," or that "despotism enslaved the king's subjects" were phrases that echoed through much eighteenth-century writ-

THE IMPACT OF THE NEW WORLD ON ENLIGHTENMENT THINKERS

The Abbé Guillaume Thomas François Raynal (1713–1796) was a clergyman and intellectual who moved in the inner circles of the Enlightenment. As a senior cleric he had access to the royal court; as a writer and intellectual he worked with the Encyclopedists and other authors who criticized France's institutions, including the Catholic church of which Raynal himself was a part. Here he tries to offer a perspective on the profound effects of discovering the Americas, and ends by asking a typical Enlightenment question: will particular historical developments and institutions lead to the betterment of society, or not?

There has never been any event which has had more impact on the human race in general and for Europeans in particular, as that of the discovery of the New World, and the passage to the Indies around the Cape of Good Hope. It was then that a commercial revolution began, a revolution in the balance of power, and in the customs, the industries and the government of every nation. It was through this event that men in the most distant lands were linked by new relationships and new needs. The produce of equatorial regions were consumed in polar climes. The industrial products of the north were transported to the south; the textiles of the Orient became the luxuries of Westerners; and everywhere men mutually exchanged their opinions, their laws, their customs, their illnesses, and their medicines, their virtues and their vices. Everything changed, and will go on changing. But will the changes of the past and those that are to come, be useful to humanity? Will they give man one day more peace, more happiness, or more pleasure? Will his condition be better, or will it be simply one of constant change?

Abbé Guillaume Thomas François Raynal, *Philosophical and Political History of European Establishments and Commerce in the Two Indies* (1770), as cited in Dourinda Outram, *The Enlightenment* (Cambridge: Cambridge University Press, 1995), p. 73.

ing. Writers dealt more gingerly, however, with the actual enslavement and slave labor of Africans.

Some Enlightenment thinkers skirted the issue of slavery. Others reconciled principle and practice in different ways.

The *Encyclopedia's* article on the slave trade did condemn the slave trade in the clearest possible terms, as a violation of self-government. Humanitarian antislavery movements, which emerged in the 1760s, advanced similar arguments. From deploring slavery to imagining freedom for enslaved people, however, proved a very long step, and one that few were willing to take. In the end, the Enlightenment's environmental determinism—the belief that environment shaped character—provided a common way of postponing the entire issue. Slavery corrupted its victims, destroyed their natural virtue, and crushed their natural love of liberty. Enslaved people, by this logic, were not ready

SLAVERY AND THE ENLIGHTENMENT

The Encyclopedists made an exhaustive and deliberate effort to comment on every institution, trade, and custom in Western culture. The project was conceived as an effort to catalogue, analyze, and improve each facet of society. Writing in an age of burgeoning maritime trade and expanding overseas empires they could not, and did not wish to, avoid the subject of slavery. These were their thoughts on plantation slavery, the African slaves who bore its brunt, and broader questions of law and liberty posed by the whole system.

Thus there is not a single one of these hapless souls—who, we maintain, are but slaves—who does not have the right to be declared free, since he has never lost his freedom; since it was impossible for him to lose it; and since neither his ruler nor his father nor anyone else had the right to dispose of his freedom; consequently, the sale of his person is null and void in and of itself: this Negro does not divest himself, indeed cannot under any condition divest himself of his natural rights; he carries them everywhere with him, and he has the right to demand that others allow him to enjoy those rights. Therefore, it is a clear case of inhumanity on the part of the judges in those free countries to which the slave is shipped, not to free the slave instantly by legal declaration, since he is their brother, having a soul like theirs.

From *Encyclopédie*, Vol. 16. Neuchâtel, 1765, p. 532 as cited in David Brion Davis, *The Problem of Slavery in Western Culture* (Ithaca, N.Y.: Cornell University Press, 1966), p. 416.

for freedom. Only a very few advocated abolishing slavery, and they insisted that emancipation be gradual. Slavery proved one of several realms where different currents in Enlightenment thought ran toward very different conclusions.

EXPLORATION AND THE PACIFIC WORLD

The Pacific world also figured prominently in Enlightenment thinking. Systematically mapping new sections of the Pacific was among the crucial developments of the age, and one with tremendous impact on the public imagination. These explorations were also scientific missions, sponsored as part of the Enlightenment project of expanding scientific knowledge. In 1767 the French government sent Louis-Anne de Bougainville (1729–1811) to the South Pacific in search of a new route to China, new lands suitable for colonization, and new spices for the ever lucrative trade. They sent along scientists and artists to record his findings. Like many other explorers, Bougainville found none of what he sought, but his travel accounts—above all his lush descriptions of the earthly paradise of Tahiti—captured the attention and imaginations of many at home. The British captain James Cook (1728–1779) made two trips into the South Pacific (1768–1771 and 1772–1775), with impressive results. The artists and scientists who accompanied Cook as well as Bougainville vastly expanded the boundaries of European botany, zoology, and geology.

Maoris in War Canoe near Lookout Point. This engraving copies an illustration by Sidney Parkinson from James Cook's explorations of the Pacific. Artists accompanied explorers in the name of Enlightenment knowledge, and depictions of the "exotic" Pacific world captured the public's imagination.

THE IMPACT OF THE SCIENTIFIC MISSIONS

Back in Europe, Enlightenment thinkers drew freely on reports of scientific missions. Since they were already committed to understanding human nature and the origins of society, and to studying the effects of the environment on character and culture, stories of new peoples and cultures were immediately fascinating. In 1772 Diderot, one of many eager readers of Bougainville's accounts, published his own reflections on the cultural significance of those accounts, the *Supplément au Voyage de Bougainville.* For Diderot, the Tahitians were the original human beings, and unlike the inhabitants of the New World, virtually free of European influence. They represented humanity in its natural state, Diderot believed, uninhibited about sexuality and free of religious dogma. Their simplicity exposed the hypocrisy and rigidity of overcivilized Europeans. Enlightenment thinkers found it impossible to see other peoples as anything other than "primitive" versions of Europeans. Even these views, however, marked a change from former times. In earlier periods Europeans had understood the world as divided between Christendom and heathen "others." In sum, during the eighteenth century a religious understanding of Western identity was giving way to more secular conceptions.

Europeans who looked outward did so for a variety of reasons and reached very different conclusions. For some Enlightenment thinkers and rulers, scientific reports from overseas fitted into a broad inquiry about "civilization" and "human nature." That inquiry sometimes encouraged self-criticism, and at others simply shored up Europeans' sense of their superiority. The late-eighteenth-century revolutions brought this Enlightenment discussion to a close. Yet these themes reemerged during the nineteenth century, when new empires were built and West's place in the world reassessed.

NATURE, GENDER, AND ENLIGHTENMENT RADICALISM: ROUSSEAU AND WOLLSTONECRAFT

Was the Enlightenment "revolutionary"?

How "revolutionary" was the Enlightment? Enlightenment thought did undermine central tenets of eighteenth-century culture and politics. It did have a wide resonance, well beyond a small group of intellectuals. Yet Enlightenment thinkers did not hold to any single political position. Even the most radical among them disagreed on the implications of their thought. Jean-Jacques Rousseau and Mary Wollstonecraft provide good examples of such radical thinkers.

THE WORLD OF ROUSSEAU

Jean-Jacques Rousseau (1712–1778) was an "outsider" who quarreled with the other *philosophes* and contradicted many of their assumptions. He shared the *philosophes'* search for intellectual and political freedom, attacked inherited privilege, and believed in the good of humanity and the possibility of creating a just society. Yet he introduced other strains into Enlightenment thought, especially morality and what was then called "sensibility," or the cult of feeling. He was also considerably more radical than his counterparts, one of the first to talk about popular sovereignty and democracy. He was surely the most utopian, which made his work popular at the time and has opened it to different interpretations since. In the late eighteenth century he was the most influential and most often cited of the *philosophes*, the thinker who brought the Enlightenment to a larger audience.

Rousseau's milestone and difficult treatise on politics, *The Social Contract*, began with a now famous paradox. "Man was born free, and everywhere he is in chains." How had humans freely forged these chains? To ask this was to reformulate the key questions of seventeenth- and eighteenth-century thought. What were the origins of government? Was government's authority legitimate? If not, Rousseau asked, how could it become so? Rousseau argued that in the state of nature, all men had been equal. (On women, men, and nature, see below.) Social inequality, anchored in private property, profoundly corrupted "the social contract," or the formation of government. Under conditions of inequality, governments and laws represented only the rich and privileged. They became instruments of repression and enslavement. Legitimate governments could be formed, Rousseau argued. "The problem is to find a form of association . . . in which each, while uniting himself with all, may still obey himself alone, and remain as free as before." Freedom did not mean the absence of restraint, it meant that equal citizens obeyed laws they had made themselves.

Rousseau believed that legitimate authority arose from the people alone. His argument has three parts. First, sovereignty should not be divided among different branches of government (as suggested by Montesquieu), and it emphatically could not be "usurped" by a king. In the late seventeenth century, Locke had spelled out the people's right to rebel against a tyrannical king. Rousseau argued that a king never became sovereign to begin with. Instead, the people themselves acted together as legislators, executives, and judges. Second, exercising sovereignty transformed the nation. Rousseau argued that when individual citizens formed a "body politic," that body became more than just the sum of its parts. He offered what was to many an appealing image of a regenerated and more powerful nation, in which citizens were bound by mutual obligation rather than coercive laws and united in equality rather than divided and weakened by privilege. Third, the national community would be united by what Rousseau called the "general will." This term is notoriously difficult. Rousseau proposed it as a way to understand the common interest, which rose above particular individual demands. The general will favored equality; that made it general, and in principle at least equality guaranteed that citizens' common interests would be represented in the whole.

Rousseau was better known for his writing on education and moral virtue. His widely read novel *Emile* (1762) tells the story of a young man who learns virtue and moral autonomy—and in the school of nature rather than in the academy. Rousseau disagreed with other *philosophes'* emphasis on reason, insisting instead that "the first impulses of nature are always right."

> Rousseau's milestone and difficult treatise on politics, *The Social Contract*, began with a now famous paradox. "Man was born free, and everywhere he is in chains."

Enlightenment Education as illustrated in *Emile*. These colored engravings from Rousseau's influential novel depict Emile's studies in the great outdoors as opposed to the classroom.

Children should not be forced to reason early in life. Books, which "teach us only to talk about things we do not know," should not be central to learning until adolescence. Emile's tutor thus walked him through the woods, studying nature and its simple precepts, cultivating his conscience and, above all, his sense of independence. "Nourished in the most absolute liberty, the greatest evil he can imagine is servitude."

Such an education aimed to give men moral autonomy and make them good citizens. Rousseau argued that women should have very different educations. "All education of women must be relative to men, pleasing them, being useful to them, raising them when they are young and caring for them when they are old, advising them, consoling them, making their lives pleasant and agreeable, these have been the duties of women since time began." Women were to be useful socially as mothers and wives. At times, Rousseau seemed convinced that women "naturally" sought out such a role: "Dependence is a natural state for women, girls feel themselves made to obey." At other moments he insisted that girls needed to be disciplined, and weaned from their "natural" vices.

How did Rousseau's ideas fit into Enlightenment views on gender? As we have seen, Enlightenment thinkers considered education key to human progress. Many lamented the poor education of women, espe-

cially since, as mothers, governesses, and teachers, many women were charged with raising and teaching children. What kind of education, however, should girls receive? Here, again, Enlightenment thinkers sought to follow the guidance of nature, and they produced scores of essays and books in philosophy, history, literature, and medicine, discussing the "nature" or "character" of the sexes. Were men and women different? Were those differences natural, or had they been created by custom and tradition? To speculate on the subject, as Rousseau did, was a common Enlightenment exercise.

Some disagreed with his conclusions. Diderot, Voltaire, and the German thinker Theodor Von Hippel among many others deplored legal restrictions on women. Rousseau's prescriptions for women's education drew especially sharp criticism. The English writer and historian Catherine Macaulay set out to refute his points. The marquis de Condorcet argued on the eve of the French Revolution that the Enlightenment promise of progress could not be fulfilled unless women were educated— and Condorcet was virtually alone in asserting that women should be granted political rights.

THE WORLD OF WOLLSTONECRAFT

Rousseau's sharpest critic was the British writer Mary Wollstonecraft (1759–1797). Wollstonecraft published her best known work, *A Vindication of the Rights of Woman*, in 1792. Her argument was anchored in Enlightenment debates. Wollstonecraft shared Rousseau's political views and admired his writing and influence. Like Rousseau and her countryman Thomas Paine, a British writer who supported the American and French revolutionaries, Wollstonecraft was a republican. She spoke even more forcefully than Rousseau against inequality and the artificial distinctions of rank, birth, or wealth. She contended that society should seek "the perfection of our nature and capability of happiness." She argued more forcefully than any other Enlightenment thinker that: (1) women had the same innate capacity for reason and self-government as men; (2) "virtue" should mean the same thing for men and women; and (3) relations between the sexes should be based on equality.

Mary Wollstonecraft.

CHRONOLOGY

LIVES OF ENLIGHTENMENT THINKERS	
Baron de Montesquieu	1689–1755
Voltaire	1694–1778
David Hume	1711–1776
Jean-Jacques Rousseau	1712–1778
Guillaume Thomas François Raynal	1713–1796
Denis Diderot	1717–1783
Adam Smith	1723–1790
Mary Wollstonecraft	1759–1797

Wollstonecraft did what few of her contemporaries even imagined. She applied the radical Enlightenment critique of monarchy and inequality to the family. The legal inequalities of marriage law, which among other things deprived married women of property rights, gave husbands "despotic" power over their wives. Just as kings cultivated their subjects' deference, so culture, she argued, cultivated women's weakness. Middle-class girls learned manners, grace, and seductiveness in order to win a husband; they were trained to be dependent creatures. "My own sex, I hope, will excuse me, if I treat them like rational creatures instead of flattering their *fascinating* graces, and viewing them as if they were in a state of perpetual childhood, unable to stand alone. I earnestly wish to point out in what true dignity and human happi-ness consists—I wish to persuade women to endeavor to acquire strength, both of mind and body. . . ." A culture that encouraged feminine weakness produced women who were childish, cunning, cruel—and vulnerable. To Rousseau's specific prescriptions for female education, which included teaching women timidity, chasteness, and modesty, Wollstonecraft replied that Rousseau wanted women to use their reason to "burnish their chains rather than to snap them." Instead, education for women had to promote liberty and self-reliance.

The Enlightenment as a whole left a mixed legacy on gender, one that closely paralleled that on slavery. Enlightenment writers developed and popularized arguments about natural rights. They also elevated natural differences to a higher plane by suggesting that nature should dictate different, and quite possibly unequal, social roles. Mary Wollstonecraft and Jean-Jacques Rousseau shared a radical opposition to despotism and slavery, a moralist's vision of a corrupt society, and a concern with virtue and community. Their divergence on gender is characteristic of Enlightenment disagreements about "nature" and its imperatives, and a good example of different directions in which the logic of Enlightenment thinking could lead.

THE ENLIGHTENMENT AND EIGHTEENTH-CENTURY CULTURE

How did the "public sphere" expand during the eighteenth century?

THE BOOK TRADE

What about the social structures that produced these debates and received these ideas? To begin with, the Enlightenment was bound up in a much larger expansion of printing and print culture. From the early eighteenth century on, book publishing and selling flourished,

ROUSSEAU AND HIS READERS

Jean-Jacques Rousseau's writings provoked very different responses from eighteenth-century readers—women as well as men. Many women readers loved his fiction and found his views about women's character and prescriptions for their education inspiring. Other women disagreed vehemently with his conclusions. In the first excerpt below, from Rousseau's novel Emile *(1762), the author sets out his views on a woman's education. He argues that her education should fit with what he considers her intellectual capacity and her social role. It should also complement the education and role of a man. The second selection is an admiring response to* Emile *from Anne-Louise-Gennaine Necker, or Madame de Staël (1766–1817), a well known French woman writer and literary critic. While she acknowledged that Rousseau sought to keep women from participating in political discussion, she also thought that he had granted women a new role in matters of emotion and domesticity. The third excerpt is from Mary Wollstonecraft, who shared many of Rousseau's philosophical principles but sharply disagreed with his assertion that women and men should have different virtues and values. She believed that women like Madame de Staël were misguided in embracing Rousseau's ideas.*

ROUSSEAU'S *EMILE*

Researches into abstract and speculative truths, the principles and axioms of sciences—in short, everything which tends to generalize our ideas—is not the proper province of women; their studies should be relative to points of practice; it belongs to them to apply those principles which men have discovered. . . . All the ideas of women, which have not the immediate tendency to points of duty, should be directed to the study of men, and to the attainment of those agreeable accomplishments which have taste for their object; for as to works of genius, they are beyond their capacity; neither have they sufficient precision or power of attention to succeed in sciences which require accuracy; and as to physical knowledge, it belongs to those only who are most active, most inquisitive, who comprehend the greatest variety of objects. . . .

She must have the skill to incline us to do everything which her sex will not enable her to do herself, and which is necessary or agreeable to her; therefore she ought to study the mind of man thoroughly, not the mind of man in general, abstractedly, but the dispositions of those men to whom she is subject either by the laws of her country or by the force of opinion. She should learn to penetrate into the real sentiments from their conversation, their actions, their looks and gestures. She should also have the art, by her own conversation, actions, looks, and gestures, to communicate those sentiments which are agreeable to them without seeming to intend it. Men will argue more philosophically about the human heart; but women will read the heart of men better than they. . . . Women have most wit, men have most genius; women observe, men reason. From the concurrence of both we derive the clearest light and the most perfect knowledge which the human mind is of itself capable of attaining.

MADAME DE STAËL

Though Rousseau has endeavoured to prevent women from interfering in public affairs, and acting a brilliant part in the theatre of politics; yet in speaking of them, how much has he done it to their satisfaction! If he wished to deprive them of some rights foreign to their sex, how has he for ever restored to them all those to which it has a claim! And in attempting to diminish their influence over the deliberations of men, how sa-credly has he established the empire they have over their happiness! In aiding them to descend from an usurped throne, he has firmly seated them upon that to which they were destined by nature; and though he be full of indignation against them when they endeavour to resemble men, yet when they come before him with all the *charms*, *weaknesses*, *virtues*, and *errors* of their sex, his respect for their *persons* amounts almost to adoration.

MARY WOLLSTONECRAFT

Rousseau declares that a woman should never, for a moment, feel herself independent, that she should be governed by fear to exercise her *natural* cunning, and made a coquettish slave in order to render her a more alluring object of desire, a *sweeter* companion to man, whenever he chooses to relax himself. He carries the arguments, which he pretends to draw from the indications of nature, still further, and insinuates that truth and fortitude, the corner stones of all human virtue, should be cultivated with certain restrictions, because, with respect to the female character, obedience is the grand lesson which ought to be impressed with unrelenting rigour.

What nonsense! when will a great man arise with sufficient strength of mind to puff away the fumes which pride and sensuality have thus spread over the subject! If women are by nature inferior to men, their virtues must be the same in quality, if not in degree, or virtue is a relative idea; consequently, their conduct should be founded on the same principles, and have the same aim.

Jean-Jacques Rousseau, *Emile* (1762), and Madame de Staël as cited in Mary Wollstonecraft, *A Vindication of the Rights of Woman* (New York and London: Penguin Books, 1992), pp. 124–25, 203–4. Mary Wollstonecraft as cited in Susan Bell and Karen Offen, eds. *Women, the Family, and Freedom: The Debate in Documents*, Vol. 1, *1750–1880*. (Stanford: Stanford University Press, 1983). p. 58.

especially in Britain, France, the Netherlands, and Switzerland. National borders, though, mattered very little. Much of the book trade was both international and clandestine. Readers bought books from stores, by subscription, and by special mail order from book distributors abroad. Cheaper printing and better distribution also helped to multiply the numbers of journals, some specializing in literary or scientific topics and others quite general. They helped bring daily newspapers, which first appeared in London in 1702, to Moscow, Rome, and cities and towns throughout Europe. By 1780, Britons could read one hundred fifty different magazines, and thirty-seven English towns had local newspapers. These changes have been called a "revolution in communication," and they form a crucial part of the larger picture of the Enlightenment.

Governments did little to check this revolutionary transformation. Some regimes granted more permissions than others. The French government, for instance, alternately banned and tolerated different volumes of the *Encyclopedia*, depending on the subjects covered in the volume, the political climate in the capital, and economic considerations. Russian, Prussian, and Austrian censors tolerated much less dissent, but those governments also sought to stimulate publishing and, to a certain degree, they permitted public discussion. In the smaller states of Germany and Italy, governed by many local princes, it was easier to find progressive local patrons, and English and French works also circulated widely through those regions. That governments were patrons as well as censors of new scholarship illustrates the complex relationship between the age of absolutism and the Enlightenment.

As one historian puts it, censorship only made banned books expensive, keeping them out of the hands of the poor. Clandestine booksellers, most near the French border in Switzerland and the Rhineland, smuggled thousands of books across the border to bookstores, distributors, and private customers. What did readers want, and what does this tell us about the

HOW DID THE "PUBLIC SPHERE" EXPAND DURING THE EIGHTEENTH CENTURY?

THE ENLIGHTENMENT AND EIGHTEENTH-CENTURY CULTURE   489

reception of the Enlightenment? Many clandestine dealers specialized in what they called "philosophical books," which meant subversive literature of all kinds: stories of languishing in prison, gossipy memoirs of life at the court, pornographic fantasies (often about religious and political figures), and tales of crime and criminals. Much of this flourishing eighteenth-century "literary underground," as the historian Robert Darnton calls it, echoed the radical Enlightenment's themes, especially the corruption of the aristocracy and the monarchy's degeneration into despotism. Less explicitly political writings, however, such as Raynal's *History*, Rousseau's novels, travel accounts, biographies, or futuristic fantasies proved equally popular. Even expensive volumes like the *Encyclopedia* sold remarkably well. It is worth underscoring that Enlightenment work circulated in popular form, and that Rousseau's novels sold as well as his political theory.

HIGH CULTURE, NEW ELITES, AND THE "PUBLIC SPHERE"

The "Enlightenment" was not simply embodied in books; it was produced in networks of readers and new forms of sociability and discussion. Eighteenth-century elite or "high" culture was small in scale but cosmopolitan and very literate, and it took discussion seriously. A new elite joined together members of the nobility and wealthy people from the middle

classes. Among the institutions that produced this new elite were "learned societies". Such groups organized intellectual life outside of the universities, and they provided libraries, meeting places for discussion, and journals that published members' papers or organized debates on issues from literature and history to economics and ethics. Elites also met in "academies," financed by governments to advance knowledge, whether through research into the natural sciences (the Royal Society of London, the French Academy of Science, both founded in 1660), promoting the national language (the Académie Française, or French Academy of Literature), or safeguarding traditions in the arts (the various academies of painting). The Berlin Royal Academy, for instance, was founded in 1701 to demonstrate the Prussian state's commitment to learning. Works such as Rousseau's *Discourse on the Origins of Inequality* were entered in academy-sponsored essay contests. Learned societies and academies both brought together different social groups (most from the elite) and in so doing, they fostered a sense of common purpose and seriousness.

"Salons" did the same, but operated informally. Usually they were organized by well-connected and learned aristocratic women. The prominent role of women distinguished the salons from the academies and universities. Salons brought together men and women of letters with members of the aristocracy for conversation, debate, drink, and food. Salons in London, Vienna, Rome, and Berlin, like academies, promoted among their participants a sense of belonging to an active, learned elite.

Scores of similar societies emerged in the eighteenth century. Masonic lodges, organizations with elaborate secret rituals whose members pledged themselves to the regeneration of society, attracted a remarkable array of aristocrats and middle-class men, such as Mozart, Frederick II, and Montesquieu. Other networks of sociability were less exclusive. Coffeehouses multiplied with the colonial trade in sugar, coffee, and tea, and they occupied a central spot in the circulation of ideas.

The eighteenth century gave birth to the very idea of "public opinion." A French observer described the changes this way: "In the last thirty years alone, a great and important revolution has occurred in our ideas. Today, public opinion has a preponderant force in Europe that cannot be resisted." Few thought the "public" involved more than the elite. Yet by the late eighteenth century, European governments recognized the existence of a civic-minded group that

CHRONOLOGY

MAJOR PUBLICATIONS OF THE ENLIGHTENMENT, 1734–1792

Voltaire, *Philosophical Letters*	1734
Montesquieu, *The Spirit of Laws*	1748
The *Encyclopedia*	1751–1772
Beccaria, *On Crime and Punishments*	1764
Smith, *Inquiry into Nature and Causes of the Wealth of Nations*	1776
Raynal, *Philosophical History*	1770
Rousseau, *The Social Contract*	1762
Rousseau, *Emile*	1762
Wollstonecraft, *A Vindication of the Rights of Woman*	1792

A Coffeehouse in London, 1798. Coffeehouses served as centers of social networks and hubs of opinion, contributing to a public consciousness that was new to the Enlightenment. This coffeehouse scene illustrates a mixing of classes, lively debate, and the bourgeoning reading culture.

stretched from salons to coffeehouses, academies, and circles of government, and to which they needed, in some measure, to respond.

MIDDLE-CLASS CULTURE AND READING

Enlightenment fare constituted only part of the new cultural interests of the eighteenth-century middle classes. Lower down on the social scale, shopkeepers, small merchants, lawyers, and professionals read more and more different kinds of books. Instead of owning one well-thumbed Bible to read aloud, a middle-class family would buy and borrow books to read casually, pass on, and discuss. This literature including much more science, history, biography, travel literature, and

fiction. A great deal of it was aimed at middle-class women, among the fastest-growing groups of readers in the eighteenth century. Etiquette books sold very well; so did how-to manuals for the household. Scores of books about the manners, morals, and education of daughters, popular versions of Enlightenment treatises on education and the mind, illustrate close parallels between the intellectual life of the high Enlightenment and everyday middle-class reading matter.

The rise of a middle-class reading public, much of it female, helps to account for the soaring popularity and production of novels, especially in Britain. Novels were the single most popular new form of literature in the eighteenth century. The novel's more recognizable, nonaristocratic characters seemed more relevant to common middle-class experience. Moreover, examining emotion and inner feeling also linked novel

HOW DID THE "PUBLIC SPHERE" EXPAND DURING THE EIGHTEENTH CENTURY?

THE ENLIGHTENMENT AND EIGHTEENTH-CENTURY CULTURE 491

writing with a larger eighteenth-century concern with personhood and humanity.

Many historians have noted that women figured prominently among fiction writers. The works of Jane Austen (1775–1817), especially *Pride and Prejudice* and *Emma*, are to many readers the height of a novelist's craft. Women writers, however, were not the only ones to write novels, nor were they alone in paying close attention to the domestic or private sphere. Their work took up central eighteenth-century themes of human nature, morality, virtue, and reputation. Their novels, like much of the nonfiction of the period, explored those themes in domestic as in public settings.

POPULAR CULTURE: URBAN AND RURAL

How much did books and print culture touch the lives of the common people? Literacy rates varied dramatically by gender, social class, and region, but were generally higher in northern than in southern and eastern Europe. Not surprisingly, literacy ran highest in cities and towns— higher, in fact, than we might expect. In early eighteenth-century Paris, 85 percent of men and 60 percent of women could read. Well over half the residents of poorer Parisian neighborhoods, especially small shopkeepers, domestic servants and valets, and artisans, could read and sign their names. Even the illiterate, however, lived in a culture of print. They saw one-page newspapers and broadsides or flysheets posted on streets and tavern walls, and regularly heard them read aloud. Moreover, visual material—inexpensive woodcuts especially, but also prints, drawings, satirical cartoons—figured as prominently as text in much popular reading material.

To be sure, poorer households had few books on their shelves, and those tended to be religious texts. But popular reading was boosted by the increasing availability of new materials. From the late seventeenth century on, a French firm published a series of inexpensive small paperbacks, the so-called blue books, which itinerant peddlers carried from cities to villages in the countryside for a growing popular market. The blue library included traditional popular literature. That meant short catechisms, quasireligious tales of

> In early eighteenth-century Paris, 85 percent of men and 60 percent of women could read. Well over half the residents of poorer Parisian neighborhoods, especially small shopkeepers, domestic servants and valets, and artisans, could read and sign their names.

miracles, and stories of the lives of the saints, which the church hoped would provide religious instruction. It also included almanacs, books on astrology, and manuals of medical cures for people or farm animals. In the eighteenth century, book peddlers began to carry abridged and simple novels, and to sell books on themes popular in the middle classes, such as travel and history. Books provided an incentive to read.

Like its middle-class counterpart, popular culture rested on networks of sociability. Guild organizations offered discussion and companionship. Street theater and singers mocking local political figures offered culture to people from different social classes. The difficulties of deciphering popular culture are considerable. Most testimony comes to us from outsiders who regarded the common people as hopelessly superstitious and ignorant. Still, popular culture did not exist in isolation. Particularly in the countryside, market days and village festivals brought social classes together, and popular entertainments reached a wide social audience.

It remains true that the countryside, especially in less economically developed regions, was desperately poor. Life there was far more isolated than in towns. A yawning chasm separated peasants from the world of the high Enlightenment. The *philosophes*, well established in the summits of European society, looked at popular culture with distrust and ignorance. They saw the common people of Europe much as they did indigenous peoples of other continents. They were humanitarians, critical thinkers, and reformers; they were not democrats. The Enlightenment, while well entrenched in eighteenth-century elite culture, nonetheless involved changes that reached well beyond elite society.

EIGHTEENTH-CENTURY MUSIC

European elites sustained other forms of high culture. English gentlemen who read scientific papers aloud in clubs also commissioned architects to design classical revival country houses for the weekends. Royal courts underwrote the academies of painting, which upheld aristocratic taste and aesthetics; Austrian salons that hosted discussions of Voltaire also staged performances of Mozart. We have already noted that the *philosophes'* work crossed genres, from political theory to fiction. Rousseau not only wrote discourses and novels, he composed music and wrote an opera. A flourishing musical culture was one of the most important features of the eighteenth century.

BACH AND HANDEL

The early eighteenth century brought the last phase of Baroque music and two of the greatest composers of all time: Johann Sebastian Bach (1685–1750) and George Frideric Handel (1685–1759). Bach was an intensely pious man who remained in the backwaters of provincial Germany all his life. As a church musician in Leipzig for most of his adult career, Bach had to supply music for nearly all Sunday and holiday services, and he combined imagination and brilliance with steely self-discipline and an ability to produce music on demand. He was an ardent Protestant, entirely unaffected by the secularism of the Enlightenment: each one of his church pieces is full of such fervor that the salvation of the world appears to hang on every note. He was also prolific, writing across the entire gamut of contemporary forms (excluding opera), from unaccompanied instrumental pieces to large-scale works for vocal soloists, chorus, and orchestra. Much of his work consists of religious cantatas (over two hundred surviving), motets, and Passions, but he also wrote concertos and suites for orchestra, and composed the purest of "pure" music—subtle and complex fugues for keyboard.

Handel, by contrast, was a public-pleasing cosmopolitan, who sought out large, secular audiences. After spending his early years mastering Baroque compositional techniques in Italy, Handel established himself in London. He tried to make a living by composing Italian operas, but after initial success opera sounded foreign and flowery to British ears. Handel eventually found a more marketable genre, the oratorio: a musical drama to be performed in concert, in English, without staging. Handel's oratorios were usually set to biblical stories but featured very worldly music, replete with ornate instrumentation and frequent flourishes of drums and trumpets. These heroic works succeeded in packing London's halls full of prosperous Britons, who interpreted the victories of the ancient Hebrews in such oratorios as *Israel in Egypt* and *Judas Maccabaeus* as implicit celebrations of Britain's own burgeoning national greatness.

> As a church musician in Leipzig for most of his adult career, Bach had to supply music for nearly all Sunday and holiday services, and he combined imagination and brilliance with steely self-discipline and an ability to produce music on demand.

HAYDN AND MOZART

Bach and Handel were among the last and certainly the greatest composers of Baroque music; the Austrians Joseph Haydn (1732–1809) and Wolfgang Amadeus Mozart (1756–1791) were the leading representatives of the "Classical" style, which swept Europe in the second half of the eighteenth century. Classicism here had nothing to do with imitating music written in classical antiquity. It sought to imitate classical principles of order, clarity, and symmetry—in other words, to sound as a Greek temple looked. Composers of the Classical school created music that adhered rigorously to certain structural principles. For example, nearly all Classical symphonies have four movements, and nearly all symphonies open with a first movement in sonata form, characterized by the successive presentation of themes, development, and recapitulation.

Mozart's short and famously difficult life captures the problems that even prodigiously talented eighteenth-century artists faced. Wolfgang began composing at four, became known as a keyboard virtuoso at six, and wrote his first symphony at nine. Wolfgang's father promoted his son, touring him as a child prodigy (with his very gifted sister) through the courts of Europe. Wolfgang gathered awards and honors from the pope and the Austrian empress Maria Theresa, attracted attention across Europe, and became a moneymaker for his family. But once he was no longer a child prodigy, like nearly all eighteenth-century artists and writers he had to rely on patronage. Mozart, a difficult person himself, suffered in the service of the cantankerous archbishop of Salzburg, a town he hated. He tried to support himself as a freelance composer and keyboard performer in Vienna. Despite his immense productivity and well-known genius, he could barely make ends meet. He lived hand to mouth, borrowing money from his fellow Masons in the Lodge of Beneficence. He was only thirty-five when he died of rheumatic fever. It is not true that he was buried, unrecognized, in a pauper's grave. His funeral was simple and cheap, in keeping with his poverty, but also with his Masonic principles and Enlightenment opposition to Catholic ritual. His fellow composer Joseph Haydn rued that "we have lost the greatest among us."

The career of Joseph Haydn (1732–1809) provides a revealing contrast. Knowing much better how to take

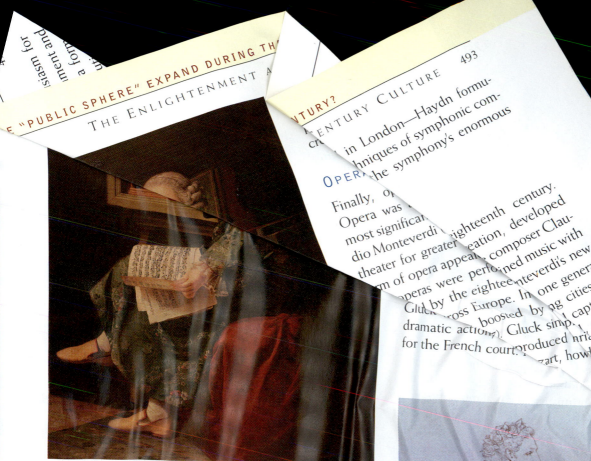

Young Mozart at the Piano, 1767. The child prodigy who was known throughout Europe for his musical master-pieces, died at 35.

in London—Haydn formu-
hniques of symphonic com-
he symphony's enormous

OPERA

Finally, o
Opera was
most significa eighteenth century.
dio Monteverdi eation, developed
theater for greate composer Clau-
peras were performed music with
Gluck by the eighteenteverdi's new
ross Europe. In one genera-
boosted by ng cities of
dramatic action). Gluck sim captured
for the French court.produced nria d von
zart, howl en sized
as the ent
est

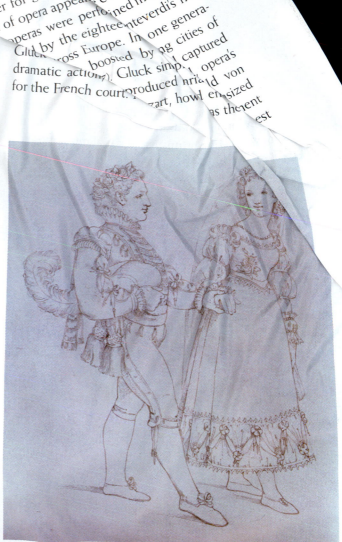

Figaro and Susanna from *The Marriage of Figaro*. Mozart's opera fused social commentary, satire, and extravagant staging and costumes in the story of two servants who are the target of their noble masters vengeful and amorous intentions.

care of himself, he spent most of his life employed by an extremely wealthy Austro-Hungarian aristocratic family that maintained its own private orchestra. Only toward the end of his life, in 1791, did Haydn, then famous, strike out on his own by traveling to London, where for five years (excluding a brief interval) he supported himself handsomely by writing for a paying public rather than for private patrons. Eighteenth-century London was one of the rare places with a commercial market for culture. In this regard London was the wave of the future, for in the nineteenth century serious music would leave the aristocratic salon for urban concert halls all over Europe. In deeply aristocratic Austria Haydn had been obliged to wear servants' livery; in London he was greeted as a creative genius, one of the earliest composers to be regarded as such. Although not the first writer of symphonies, Haydn is often termed the "father of the symphony." In over one hundred works in the symphonic form—especially his last twelve sympho-

operatic compose[r]...
garo, Don Giovann[i] ...ed by changing
best-loved opere[...] ...ward secularism,

Eighteenth-c[...] ...rt for much every-
writers, found[...]aydn's in London is
structures of [...]ed by the market. Ar[...]
the church [...]wever, remained th[...]es:
day music[...]g. And musician[...]
one—comm[...] ambivalent rel[...]
tocratic as[...]e. The British w[...] be
lars of [...]olent wretches."[...]w
Enlight[...] [a]rchbishop of Salz[...] not know
with th[...] important, ensur[...]
Johns[...]nted his positi[...]st popular op-
on t[...] One of Moza[...] French play—cir-
sio[...] [a]*Figaro*, base[...]ations between masters
the[...]ese theme[...]...privilege and the presumptu-
[...]rou[...] abuses [...]...nobility. Satire, self-criticism, the
[serv][...] [E]uropea[...]...optimism and social mobility, and a
ou[...]nes[...]erarchy[...] supported by what was in many
[cos]m...[...]ditional society—all of these are key to under-
wa[...]ng eighteenth-century culture as well as the En-
sta[...]
l[...]enment.

...ature, belief,
science cre[...] ...authority, reason
new form[...] ...religion, economics,
the sci[...] ...well-known *philosophes* or
know[...]contemporaries, and even them-
re[...]...able. Ideas circulated in popular forms
[...]s and operas to journalism. Intellectual
...went hand in hand with social and cultural
...footing, the emergence of a new elite, and the expan-
...government efforts to put their states on a new
sion of the public sphere.

The Atlantic revolutions (the American Revolution of 1776, the French Revolution of 1789, and the
Latin American upheavals of the 1830s) were steeped
in the language of the Enlightenment. The constitutions of the new nations formed by these revolutions
followed the basic ideas of Enlightenment liberalism:
neither religion nor the state could impede individual freedom of conscience; government authority
could not be arbitrary; equality and freedom were
natural; humans sought happiness, prosperity, and
the expansion of their potential. These arguments
had been made, tentatively, earlier. But when the
North American colonists declared their independence from Britain in 1776, they called these ideas
"self-evident truths." That bold declaration marked
both the distance traveled since the late seventeenth
century and the self-confidence that was the Enlightenment's hallmark.

CONCLUSION

The Enlightenment arose from the scientific revolution, from the new sense of power and possibility that

salons
Wolfgang Amadeus Mozart

KEY TERMS

Voltaire
The Encyclopedia
Adam Smith

Jean-Jacques Rousseau
A Vindication of the Rights of
Women

SELECTED READINGS

Baker, Keith. *Condorcet: From Natural Philosophy to Social Mathematics.* Chicago, 1975. An important reinterpretation of
Condorcet as a social scientist.

Bell, Susan and Karen Offen, eds. *Women, the Family, and Freedom:
The Debate in Documents.* Vol. 1, 1750–1880. Stanford, 1983.
An excellent introduction to Enlightenment debates about
gender and women.

Blum, Carol. *Rousseau and the Republic of Virtue: The Language of
Politics in the French Revolution.* Ithaca and London, 1986. Fas-

HOW DID THE "PUBLIC SPHERE" EXPAND DURING THE EIGHTEENTH CENTURY?

THE ENLIGHTENMENT AND EIGHTEENTH-CENTURY CULTURE   493

Young Mozart at the Piano, 1767. The child prodigy who was known throughout Europe for his musical master-pieces, died at 35.

nies, which he composed in London—Haydn formulated the most enduring techniques of symphonic composition and demonstrated the symphony's enormous creative potential.

OPERA

Finally, opera flourished in the eighteenth century. Opera was a seventeenth-century creation, developed most significantly by the Italian Baroque composer Claudio Monteverdi (1567–1643), who combined music with theater for greater dramatic intensity. Monteverdi's new form of opera appealed immediately: within one generation operas were performed in all the leading cities of Italy, and by the eighteenth century they had captured attention across Europe. In the Classical period, opera's popularity was boosted by Christoph Willibald von Gluck (1714–1787). Gluck simplified arias, emphasized dramatic action, and produced high-end entertainment for the French court. Mozart, however, was the greatest

care of himself, he spent most of his life employed by an extremely wealthy Austro-Hungarian aristocratic family that maintained its own private orchestra. Only toward the end of his life, in 1791, did Haydn, then famous, strike out on his own by traveling to London, where for five years (excluding a brief interval) he supported himself handsomely by writing for a paying public rather than for private patrons. Eighteenth-century London was one of the rare places with a commercial market for culture. In this regard London was the wave of the future, for in the nineteenth century serious music would leave the aristocratic salon for urban concert halls all over Europe. In deeply aristocratic Austria Haydn had been obliged to wear servants' livery; in London he was greeted as a creative genius, one of the earliest composers to be regarded as such. Although not the first writer of symphonies, Haydn is often termed the "father of the symphony." In over one hundred works in the symphonic form—especially his last twelve sympho-

Figaro and Susanna from *The Marriage of Figaro.* Mozart's opera fused social commentary, satire, and extravagant staging and costumes in the story of two servants who are the target of their noble masters vengeful and amorous intentions.

operatic composer of the Classical era. *The Marriage of Figaro, Don Giovanni,* and *The Magic Flute* remain among the best-loved operas of all time.

Eighteenth-century musicians, like eighteenth-century writers, found their careers and art shaped by changing structures of culture. Despite a trend toward secularism, the church continued to provide support for much everyday music. In a very few cases—Haydn's in London is one—composers could be supported by the market. Aristocratic and court patronage, however, remained the pillars of support for musicians. And musicians, like Enlightenment writers, had an ambivalent relationship with their patrons and culture. The British writer Samuel Johnson called patrons "insolent wretches." Mozart relied on the overbearing archbishop of Salzburg to commission work and, just as important, ensure that it would be performed, but he resented his position: "I did not know that I was a valet." One of Mozart's most popular operas—*The Marriage of Figaro,* based on a French play—circled around just these themes: relations between masters and servants, the abuses of privilege, and the presumptuousness of the European nobility. Satire, self-criticism, the criticism of hierarchy, optimism and social mobility, and a cosmopolitan outlook supported by what was in many ways a traditional society—all of these are key to understanding eighteenth-century culture as well as the Enlightenment.

CONCLUSION

The Enlightenment arose from the scientific revolution, from the new sense of power and possibility that science created, and from the rush of enthusiasm for new forms of inquiry. Together, the Enlightenment and the scientific revolution created science as a form of knowledge. Eighteenth-century thinkers scrutinized a remarkably wide range of topics: human nature, reason and the processes of understanding, religion, belief, law, the origins of government authority, economics, and social practices. Whether well-known *philosophes* or underground journalists, they raised problems that made regimes, their contemporaries, and even themselves uncomfortable. Ideas circulated in popular forms from plays and operas to journalism. Intellectual changes went hand in hand with social and cultural ones: government efforts to put their states on a new footing, the emergence of a new elite, and the expansion of the public sphere.

The Atlantic revolutions (the American Revolution of 1776, the French Revolution of 1789, and the Latin American upheavals of the 1830s) were steeped in the language of the Enlightenment. The constitutions of the new nations formed by these revolutions followed the basic ideas of Enlightenment liberalism: neither religion nor the state could impede individual freedom of conscience; government authority could not be arbitrary; equality and freedom were natural; humans sought happiness, prosperity, and the expansion of their potential. These arguments had been made, tentatively, earlier. But when the North American colonists declared their independence from Britain in 1776, they called these ideas "self-evident truths." That bold declaration marked both the distance traveled since the late seventeenth century and the self-confidence that was the Enlightenment's hallmark.

KEY TERMS

Voltaire

The Encyclopedia

Adam Smith

Jean-Jacques Rousseau

A Vindication of the Rights of
   Women

salons

Wolfgang Amadeus Mozart

SELECTED READINGS

Baker, Keith. *Condorcet: From Natural Philosophy to Social Mathematics.* Chicago, 1975. An important reinterpretation of Condorcet as a social scientist.

Bell, Susan and Karen Offen, eds. *Women, the Family, and Freedom: The Debate in Documents.* Vol. 1, *1750–1880.* Stanford, 1983. An excellent introduction to Enlightenment debates about gender and women.

Blum, Carol. *Rousseau and the Republic of Virtue: The Language of Politics in the French Revolution.* Ithaca and London, 1986. Fascinating account of how eighteenth-century readers interpreted Rousseau.

Calhoun, Craig, ed. *Habermas and the Public Sphere*. Cambridge, Mass., 1992. Calhoun's introduction is a good starting point for Habermas's argument.

Cassirer, E. *The Philosophy of the Enlightenment*. Princeton, 1951.

Chartier, Roger. *The Cultural Origins of the French Revolution*. Durham, N.C., 1991. Looks at topics from religion to violence in everyday life and culture.

Darnton, Robert. *The Business of Enlightenment: A Publishing History of the* Encyclopédie, *1775–1800*. Cambridge, Mass., 1979. Darnton's work on the Enlightenment offers a fascinating blend of intellectual, social, and economic history. See his other books as well: *The Literary Underground of the Old Regime* (Cambridge, Mass., 1982); *The Great Cat Massacre and Other Episodes in French Cultural History* (New York, 1984); and *The Forbidden Best Sellers of Revolutionary France* (New York and London, 1996).

Davis, David Brion. *The Problem of Slavery in Western Culture*. New York, 1988. A Pulitzer-Prize-winning examination of a central issue as well as a brilliant analysis of different strands of Enlightenment thought.

Gay, Peter. *The Enlightenment: An Interpretation*. Vol. 1, *The Rise of Modern Paganism*. Vol. 2, *The Science of Freedom*. New York, 1966–1969. Combines an overview with an interpretation. Emphasizes the *philosophes'* sense of identification with the classical world and takes a generally positive view of their accomplishments. Includes extensive annotated bibliographies.

———. *Mozart*. New York, 1999.

Goodman, Dena. *The Republic of Letters: A Cultural History of the French Enlightenment*. Ithaca, N.Y., 1994. Important in its attention to the role of literary women.

Hazard, Paul. *The European Mind: The Critical Years (1680–1715)*. New Haven, 1953. A basic and indispensable account of the changing climate of opinion that preceded the Enlightenment.

Hildesheimer, Wolfgang. *Mozart*. New York, 1982. An exceptionally literate and thought-provoking biography.

Israel, Jonathan Irvine. *Radical Enlightenment: Philosophy and the Making of Modernity, 1650–1750*. New York, 2001.

Munck, Thomas. *The Enlightenment: A Comparative Social History 1721–1794*. London, 2000. An excellent recent survey, especially good on social history.

Porter, Roy. *The Creation of the Modern World: The Untold Story of the British Enlightenment*. New York, 2000.

Outram, Dorinda. *The Enlightenment*. Cambridge, 1995. An excellent short introduction and a good example of new historical approaches.

Rendall, Jane. *The Origins of Modern Feminism: Women in Britain, France and the United States, 1780–1860*. New York, 1984.

Sapiro, Virginia. *A Vindication of Political Virtue: The Political Theory of Mary Wollstonecraft*. Chicago, 1992. A subtle and intelligent analysis for more advanced readers.

Shklar, Judith. *Men and Citizens: A Study of Rousseau's Social Theory*. London, 1969.

———. *Montesquieu*. Oxford, 1987.

Taylor, Barbara. *Mary Wollstonecraft and the Feminist Imagination*. Cambridge and New York, 2003.

Venturi, Franco. *The End of the Old Regime in Europe, 1768–1776: The First Crisis*. Translated by R. Burr Litchfield. Princeton, 1989.

———. *The End of the Old Regime in Europe, 1776–1789*. Princeton, 1991. Both detailed and wide-ranging, particularly important on international developments.

Watt, Ian P. *The Rise of the Novel*. London, 1957. The basic work on the innovative qualities of the novel in eighteenth-century England.

PART VI
THE FRENCH AND INDUSTRIAL REVOLUTIONS AND THEIR CONSEQUENCES

FEW EVENTS more profoundly altered the shape of Western culture than the French and Industrial revolutions. The major developments of the nineteenth and early twentieth centuries—the decline of landed aristocracies and the rise of new social groups, the emergence of dramatically new forms of politics, changes in political and social thought, economic expansion, and Europe's expanding hegemony in the world—all had their roots in these two revolutions.

The French and Industrial revolutions took place at about the same time and affected many of the same people, though in different ways and to varying degrees. Together they brought about the collapse of absolutism, mercantilism, and what was left of feudalism. Together they produced the theory and practice of economic individualism and political liberalism. And together, the wrenching changes they wrought polarized Europe for several generations. What historians call the "age of revolution" lasted from the 1770s through at least half the nineteenth century.

Each revolution, of course, produced results peculiarly its own. The French Revolution helped make such terms as *citizen, nation,* and *liberty* central to the political vocabulary of modern times. It encouraged the growth of nationalism—in both liberal and authoritarian forms. The Industrial Revolution changed the economic and cultural landscape of Europe, with ramifications for the private worlds of men and women as well as the economic organization of the world. Despite their unique contributions, the two revolutions must be studied together, for the effects of each magnified the importance of the other.

	POLITICS	SOCIETY AND CULTURE	ECONOMY	INTERNATIONAL RELATIONS
1750		Johann Wolfgang von Goethe (1749–1852)	British export production increases 80 percent (1750–1770)	
		William Blake (1757–1827)	British Parliament increases enclosures (1750–1860)	
	Reign of Catherine the Great of Russia (1762–1796)		Spinning jenny, water frame, and spinning mule invented (1764–1799)	Poland partitioned by Russia, Austria, and Prussia (1772, 1793, 1795)
	American Revolution (1774–1782)	William Wordsworth (1770–1850)	James Watt patents improved steam engine (1769)	
		Goethe's *Faust* (1790)		
			Industrial Revolution (1780–1880)	
	Louis XVI calls Assembly of Notables (1788)			
	The French Revolution breaks out (1789)	Jeremy Bentham's *Introduction to the Principles of Morals and Legislation* (1789)		
	Great Fear in the French countryside (1789)			
	Declaration of the Rights of Man and of the Citizen (1789)			
	French National Assembly abolishes feudal rights and privileges (1789)			
1790	Slave revolt in St. Domingue (1791)	Edmund Burke's *Reflections on the Revolution in France* (1790)		Slave rebellion in St. Domingue sparks British and Spanish invasion (1791)
	Louis XVI of France overthrown and French Republic declared (1792)	Thomas Paine's *Rights of Man* (1791)		France declares war on Austria and Prussia (1792)
	Reign of Terror (1793–1794)	French Convention abolishes slavery and primogeniture (1793–1794)	Eli Whitney invents cotton gin (1793)	England enters war against France (1793)
	Maximilien Robespierre executed (1794)			Revolutionary France occupies Low Countries, Rhineland, and parts of Spain and Italy (1794–1796)
		Heinrich Heine, German poet (1797–1856)		
		Wordsworth's and Coleridge's *Lyrical Ballads* (1798)		
		Thomas Malthus's *Essay on the Principle of Population* (1798)		
		Eugène Delacroix, French painter (1799–1837)		
	Napoleon Bonaparte is declared temporary consul (1799)	Honoré de Balzac, French novelist (1799–1850)		
1800	President Thomas Jefferson (1800–1808)	Emergence of Romanticism (early 1800s)	Women make up 50 percent of British textile work force (c. 1800)	Peace of Amiens temporarily halts war between Britain and France (1801)
	Bonaparte's Concordat with the pope (1801)	Continental population doubles (1800–1850)		Napoleon unsuccessfully tries to restore slavery in St. Domingue (1801–1803)
	Bonaparte elected Consul for Life by plebiscite (1802)			Louisiana Purchase (1803)
	Bonaparte crowns himself Emperor Napoleon I (1804)	Napoleonic Code (1804)		Independent state of Haiti (formerly St. Domingue) (1804)
		George Sand, novelist (1804–1876)		Nelson's victory at Trafalgar breaks French naval power (1805)
				Napoleon defeats Austria and Russia at battle of Austerlitz (1805)
			Napoleon's Continental System imposed (1806)	
			Serfdom abolished in Prussia (1807)	
1808	Prussian reform era begins (1808)	Johann Gottlieb Fichte's *Addresses to the German Nation* (1808)		Napoleon invades Spain (1808)

POLITICS	SOCIETY AND CULTURE	ECONOMY	INTERNATIONAL RELATIONS	
			Napoleon marries Mary Louise of the Habsburgs (1809)	1809
	Grimm's Fairy Tales by the Brothers Grimm (1813)		Napoleon's Russian campaign (1812)	
Bourbon monarchy restored in France (1815)			Napoleon exiled to Elba (1814) Congress of Vienna (1814–1815) Napoleon defeated at Waterloo (1815) German Confederation created by Congress of Vienna (1815)	
	Gustav Courbet, French painter (1819–1877)	Prussian Zollverein (customs union) founded (1818)	Quintuple Alliance formed (1818) Greek war of independence (1821–1827) Monroe Doctrine (1823)	
Decembrist Revolt in Russia (1825)			Serbia emerges from within Ottoman empire (1828)	
Revolution in France, Belgium (1830) Mazzini founds Young Italy society (1831) Electoral Reform Act in England (1832)		First railway to carry passengers (1830)		
Poor Laws Reform in England (1834) Reign of Queen Victoria (1837–1901) British Chartist movement (1838–1848)	Alexis de Tocqueville's *Democracy in America* (1835–1840) *The Economist* is founded (1838) Emergence of Realism in art and literature (1840s)	Rail transport spreads across Continent (1840s) Zollverein expands to include nearly all German states (1840s) Poor harvests contribute to economic crisis across Europe (1845)		
Repression of revolutionary movements in central and eastern Europe (1848–1850)	Great Famine in Ireland (1845–1849)	Great Irish Famine (1845–1849) California gold rush (1849)	Treaty of Guadalupe Hidalgo ends war between United States and Mexico (1848) United States buys western territory, including California, for $15 million (1848)	
	Seneca Falls Convention (1848) Florence Nightingale's medical reforms (1850s)	Serfdom abolished in southern and eastern Europe (1850)		1850
Louis Napoleon Bonaparte overthrows Second Republic (1851)	Great Exhibit of the Works of Industry in All Nations, London (1851)	Great Exhibition of the Works of Industry in All Nations, London (1851) Britain exports half of world's iron (1852) Cotton accounts for 40 percent of domestic exports from Britain (1852)		
	Charles Darwin's *On the Origin of Species* (1859) John Stuart Mill's *On Liberty* (1859)	Agricultural laborers still largest work force in Britain (1860) Britain and France sign free-trade agreement (1860)	Crimean War (1854–1856) Sardinia takes Lombardy, Papal States, and various duchies (1859)	
Reign of Kaiser Wilhelm I (1861–1888) Civil War in the United States (1861–1865) Otto von Bismarck appointed Prime Minister of Germany (1862)	Victor Hugo's *Les Misérables* (1862)	Emancipation of serfs in Russia (1861)	Victor Emmanuel II claims title of king of Italy (1861–1878)	
	Fyodor Dostoyevsky's *Crime and Punishment* (1866)	Slavery abolished in United States (1865)	Seven Week's War; Prussia takes Schleswig-Holstein (1866) Canada gains independence (1867)	
Reform Bill of 1867 in England (1867)	Mill's *Subjection of Women* (1869)	Railroad connects Mississippi valley with Pacific coast (1869)		
			Franco-Prussian War (1870–1871) Italians take Rome from Napoleon III's protection (1870) German empire proclaimed (1871)	1870

Chapter
EIGHTEEN

THE FRENCH
REVOLUTION

IN 1789, ONE EUROPEAN out of every five lived in France. Many Europeans considered France the center of European culture. It followed that a revolution in France would immediately command the attention of Europe and assume international significance. Yet the French Revolution attracted and disturbed men and women for much more important reasons. Both its philosophical ideals and its political realities mirrored attitudes, concerns, and conflicts that had occupied the minds of educated Europeans for several decades. When the revolutionaries pronounced in favor of liberty, they spoke not only with the voice of the eighteenth-century *philosophes*, but with that of the English aristocracy in 1688 and the North American revolutionaries of 1776.

They also raised issues that resonated across Europe. Aristocrats throughout Europe and the colonies resented monarchical inroads on their ancient freedoms. Members of the middle class, many of whom were very successful, chafed under a system of official privilege that they increasingly considered outmoded. Peasants fiercely resented what seemed to them the never-ceasing demands of central government on their limited resources. Nor were resentments focused exclusively on absolutist monarchs. Tensions existed as well between country and city dwellers, between rich and poor, overprivileged and underprivileged, slave and free. The French Revolution marked part of a crisis that shook all of late eighteenth-century Europe and its colonies, bringing revolutionary movements to the British Empire, to Belgium and the Netherlands, and to South America. The age of revolution restructured the nations of the West.

The opening of the age of revolution came in the North American colonies. The American Revolution of 1776 was one of the last in a series of conflicts over colonial control of the New World, conflicts that had wracked England and France throughout the eighteenth century. It also became one of the first crises of the old regime at home. Among "enlightened" Europeans, the success with which citizens of the new nation had thrown off British rule and formed a republic based on Enlightenment

FOCUS QUESTIONS

- What were the causes of the French Revolution?
- How did popular uprisings shape the first stage of the French Revolution?

- Why did the French Revolution become more radical?
- Why did the Directory fail?
- How did Napoleon centralize his authority?
- What led to Napoleon's downfall?

principles was the source of tremendous optimism. Change would come. Reform was possible. The costs would be modest.

If the American Revolution first dramatized Europeans' "fears and aspirations," the events in France deepened them. The French Revolution proved a more radical project, though it did not necessarily begin that way. It became immeasurably more costly—protracted, complex, and violent. It aroused much greater hopes and consequently, in many cases, bitter disillusionment. It raised issues that would not be settled for half a century.

THE FRENCH REVOLUTION: AN OVERVIEW

The "French Revolution" is a shorthand for a complex series of events between 1789 and 1799. (Napoleon ruled from 1799 to 1814–1815.) To simplify, those events can be divided into three stages. In the first stage, from 1788 to 1792, the struggle was constitutional and relatively peaceful. An increasingly bold elite articulated its grievances against the king. Like the American revolutionaries, elites refused taxation without representation, attacked "despotism," or arbitrary authority, and offered an Enlightenment-inspired program to rejuvenate the nation. Reforms, many of them breathtakingly wide ranging, were instituted—some accepted or even offered by the king, and others passed over his protests. The peaceful, constitutional phase did not last. Reforms met with resistance, dividing the country. The threat of change in France created international tensions. In 1792, these tensions exploded into war and the monarchy fell, to be replaced with a republic. The second stage of the Revolution, which lasted from 1792 to 1794, was one of crisis. A ruthlessly centralized government mobilized all the country's resources to fight the foreign enemy as well as counterrevolutionaries at home, to destroy traitors and the vestiges of the Old Regime. The Terror, as this policy was called, did save the republic, but it exhausted itself in factions and recriminations. In the third phase, from 1794 to 1799, the government, still at war with Europe, drifted into corruption and almost inevitably into military rule under Napoleon. Napoleon continued the war until his final defeat in 1815.

THE COMING OF THE REVOLUTION

What were the causes of the French Revolution?

The central causes of the revolution in France lie in eighteenth-century French society. That society was increasingly dominated by a new elite or social group that brought together aristocrats, officeholders, professionals, and, to a lesser degree, merchants and businessmen. To understand the Revolution, we need to understand tensions within this group and its conflict with the government of Louis XVI.

French society was divided into three Estates. (An individual's "estate" marked his standing, or status, and it determined legal rights, taxes, and so on.) The First Estate included all the clergy; the Second Estate, the nobility. The Third Estate, by far the largest, included everyone else, from wealthy lawyers and businessmen to urban laborers and poor peasants. Within the political and social elite of the country, a small but powerful group, these legal distinctions often seemed artificial. In the very upper reaches of society, the social boundaries between nobles and wealthy commoners were ill defined. Noble title was accessible to those who could afford to buy an ennobling office. For example, close to fifty thousand new nobles were created between 1700 and 1789. The order depended for its vigor on a constant infusion of talent and economic power from the wealthy social groups of the Third Estate.

Wealth did not take predictable forms. Most noble wealth was "proprietary," that is, tied to land, urban properties, purchased offices, and the like. Yet noble families did not disdain trade or commerce, as historians long thought. In fact, noblemen financed most industry, and they also invested heavily in banking and such enterprises as ship owning, the slave trade, mining, and metallurgy. Moreover, the very wealthy members of the Third Estate also preferred to invest in secure, proprietary holdings. Thus throughout the century, much "bourgeois" wealth was transformed into "noble" wealth, and a significant number of rich "bourgeois" became noblemen. This economically important bourgeois group saw itself as different from and often opposed to the common people, who worked with their hands. For all of these reasons, wealthy and well-educated members of the Third Estate believed that they belonged in the elite and that the king needed to hear their voice on issues of government and policy.

Many French people, from the middle classes to the common people, considered social, political, and legal hierarchies increasingly difficult to justify. "Privilege," mainly in the form of noble exemption from nearly all taxes and labor requirements, special hunting rights, guild restrictions, or trade monopolies, was under attack. Although ideas did not "cause" the Revolution, the Enlightenment played a central role in undermining traditional assumptions and articulating the discontents felt by many. Voltaire was popular because of his attacks on noble privilege and arrogance, and Montesquieu provided the language for criticizing "despotism."

The campaign for change was also fueled by proponents of economic reform. The "physiocrats," as they were called in France, urged the government to simplify the tax system and free the economy from mercantilist regulations. They urged the government to lift its controls on the price of grain, for example, which had been imposed to keep the cost of bread low but, they argued, had interfered with the natural workings of the market.

Whether or not the public accepted the physiocrats' prescriptions, it agreed that the French economy was ailing. A general price rise during much of the eighteenth century, which permitted the French economy to expand by providing capital for investment, created hardship for the peasantry and for urban tradesmen and laborers. At the end of the 1780s, when poor harvests sent bread prices sharply higher. In 1788 families found themselves spending more than 50 percent of their income on bread, which made up the bulk of their diet. The following year the figure rose to as much as 80 percent. Poor harvests reduced demand for manufactured goods, and contracting markets in turn created unemployment. Many peasants left the countryside for the cities, hoping to find work there, only to discover that urban unemployment was far worse than that in rural areas.

Peasants on the land were caught in a web of obligations to landlords, church, and state. They paid a tithe, or levy on farm produce owed to the church, fees for the use of a landlord's mill or wine press, fees to the landlord as well when land changed hands. In addition, peasants paid a disproportionate share of both direct and indirect taxes—the most onerous of which was the salt tax—levied by the government. Further grievances stemmed from the requirement to maintain public roads (the corvée) and from the hunting privileges that nobles for centuries had regarded as the distinctive badge of their order.

An inefficient tax system further weakened the country's financial position. Not only was taxation tied to differing social standings, it varied as well from region to region—some areas, for example, were subject to a

Prerevolutionary Propaganda, 1788–1789. This print supports the popular view that the third estate (commoners) was carrying the burden of national taxation on its shoulders while doing the productive work of the nation. The privileged orders enjoyed the fruits of the peasants' labors, tax free.

CHRONOLOGY

ORIGINS OF THE FRENCH REVOLUTION, 1788–1789

Failure of fiscal reform	1787–1788
Louis XVI summons the Estates General	May 1788
Bread riots across France	Spring 1789
Estates General convenes in Paris	May 1789
Third Estate declares itself the National Assembly	May 1789
Oath of the Tennis Court	June 1789
Fall of the Bastille	July 14, 1789

much higher rate than others. The financial system, already burdened by debts incurred under Louis XIV, all but broke down completely under the increased expenses brought on by French participation in the American Revolution.

THE DESTRUCTION OF THE OLD REGIME

How did popular uprisings shape the first stage of the French Revolution?

The fiscal crisis precipitated the Revolution. In 1787 and 1788 the king's principal ministers attempted to institute a series of reforms to stave off bankruptcy. To meet the mounting deficit, they proposed new taxes, notably a stamp duty and a direct tax on the annual produce of the land.

Hoping to persuade the nobility to agree to these reforms, the king summoned an Assembly of Notables from among the aristocracy. This group used the financial emergency to attempt major constitutional reforms. Most important, they insisted that any new tax scheme must have the approval of the Estates General, the representative body of the three estates of the realm. In what seemed the only solution to France's deepening problems, Louis XVI summoned the Estates General (which had not met since 1614) to meet in 1789. His action appeared to many as the only solution to France's deepening problems. Long-term grievances and short-

term hardships had produced bread riots across the country in the spring of 1789.

By tradition, each estate met and voted as a body. In the past, this had generally meant that the First Estate (the clergy) had combined with the Second (the nobility) to defeat the Third. Now the Third Estate made it clear it would not tolerate such an arrangement. The leaders of the Third Estate agreed that the three orders should sit together and vote as individuals. More important, they insisted that the Third Estate should have twice as many members as the First and Second.

The king's unwillingness to take a strong stand on voting procedures cost him support. Shortly after the Estates General opened at Versailles in May 1789, the Third Estate, angered by the king's attitude, took the revolutionary step of leaving the body and declaring itself the National Assembly. Locked out of the Estates General meeting hall on June 20, the Third Estate and a handful of sympathetic nobles and clergymen moved to a nearby indoor tennis court, where they bound themselves by a solemn oath not to separate until they had drafted a constitution for France. This Oath of the Tennis Court, sworn on June 20, 1789, can be seen as the beginning of the French Revolution. By claiming the authority to remake the government in the name of the people, the National Assembly was not merely protesting against the rule of Louis XVI but asserting its right to act as the highest sovereign power in the nation. On June 27 the king virtually conceded this right by ordering all the delegates to join the National Assembly.

FIRST STAGES OF THE FRENCH REVOLUTION

The first stage of the French Revolution extended from June 1789 to August 1792. In the main, this stage was moderate, its actions dominated by the leadership of liberal nobles and men of the Third Estate. Yet three events in the summer and fall of 1789 furnished evidence that the Revolution was to penetrate to the very heart of French society.

POPULAR REVOLTS

The political crisis captured public attention. The economic crisis heightened anger and fear. Many believed that the aristocracy and the king were conspiring to punish the Third Estate by encouraging scarcity and high prices. Rumors circulated in Paris during June 1789 that the king was about to attack the National

HOW DID POPULAR UPRISINGS SHAPE THE FIRST STAGE OF THE FRENCH REVOLUTION?

THE DESTRUCTION OF THE OLD REGIME   505

Assembly. Workshop masters, artisans, and shopkeepers formed a provisional municipal government and organized a militia of volunteers to maintain order. Determined to obtain arms, they made their way on July 14 to the Bastille, an ancient fortress where guns and ammunition were stored. Built in the Middle Ages, the Bastille had served as a prison for many years but was no longer much used. Nevertheless, it symbolized hated royal authority. When crowds demanded arms from its governor, he opened fire, killing ninety-eight of the attackers. The crowd took revenge, capturing the fortress (which held only seven prisoners—five common criminals and two persons confined for mental incapacity) and decapitating the governor. The fall of the Bastille was the first instance of the people's role in revolutionary change.

The second popular revolt occurred in the countryside. Peasants, too, anticipated and feared a monarchical and aristocratic counterrevolution. Rumors flew that the king's armies were on their way, that Austrians, Prussians, or "brigands" were invading. Frightened and uncertain, peasants and villagers organized militias; others attacked and burned manor houses, sometimes to look for grain, but usually to find and destroy records of tax. This "Great Fear," as historians have labeled it, compounded the confusion abroad in rural areas. The news, when it reached Paris, convinced deputies at Versailles that the administration had simply collapsed.

The third instance of popular uprising, the "October Days" of 1789, was brought on by economic crisis. This time Parisian women from the market district, angered by the soaring price of bread and fired by rumors of the king's continuing unwillingness to cooperate with the Assembly, marched to Versailles on October 5 and demanded to be heard. On the afternoon of the following day the king yielded. The National Guard, sympathetic to the agitators, led the crowd back to Paris, the procession headed by a soldier holding aloft a loaf of bread on his bayonet.

The Tennis Court Oath, by Jacques Louis David (1748–1825). In June 1789, in the hall where royalty played a game known as *jeu de paume* (similar to tennis) leaders of the Revolution swore to draft a constitution. In the center of this painting, standing on the table, is Jean Bailly, president of the National Assembly. Seated at the table below him is Abbé Sieyès. Mirabeau stands in the right foreground with a hat in his left hand.

Women of Paris Leaving for Versailles, October 1789. A crowd of women, accompanied by Lafayette and the National Guard, marched to Versailles to confront the king about shortages and rising prices in Paris.

These popular uprisings had an immediate effect on the political events at Versailles. The storming of the Bastille persuaded the king and nobles to agree to the creation of the National Assembly. The "Great Fear" compelled the most sweeping changes of the entire revolutionary period. In an effort to quell rural disorder, on the night of August 4 the Assembly took a giant step toward abolishing all forms of privilege. It eliminated the church tithe, the labor requirement known as the corvée, the nobility's hunting privileges, and a wide variety of tax exemptions and monopolies. In effect, these reforms obliterated the remnants of feudalism. One week later, the Assembly abolished the sale of offices, thereby sweeping away one of the fundamental institutions of the Old Regime. Last, the king's return to Paris after the October Days undercut his ability to resist further changes.

THE NATIONAL ASSEMBLY AND THE LIBERAL REVOLUTION

The Assembly issued its charter of liberties, the Declaration of the Rights of Man and of the Citizen, in September 1789. It declared property to be a natural right, along with liberty, security, and "resistance to oppression." It declared freedom of speech, religious toleration, and liberty of the press inviolable. All citizens were to be treated equally before the law. No one was to be imprisoned or otherwise punished except in accordance with due process of law. Sovereignty was affirmed to reside in the people, and officers of the government were made subject to deposition if they abused the powers conferred on them. These were not new ideas; they represented the outcome of Enlightenment discussions and revolutionary debates and deliberations. The Declaration became the preamble to the new constitution, which the Assembly finished in 1791.

Whom did the Declaration mean by "man and the citizen"? Which men could be trusted to participate in politics and on what terms was a hotly contested issue. So, to a certain extent, were the rights of religious minorities. The revolution gave full civil rights to Protestants, though in areas long divided by religious conflict those rights were challenged by Catholics. The revolution did, hesitantly, give civil rights to Jews, a measure that sparked protest in areas of eastern France. Religious toleration, a central theme of the Enlightenment, meant ending persecution; it did not mean that the regime was prepared to accommodate religious differ-

DECLARATION OF THE RIGHTS OF MAN AND OF THE CITIZEN

One of the first important pronouncements of the National Assembly after the Tennis Court Oath was the Declaration of the Rights of Man and of the Citizen. The authors drew inspiration from the American Declaration of Independence, but the language is even more heavily influenced by the ideals of French Enlightenment philosophers, particularly Rousseau. Following are the Declaration's preamble and some of its most important principles.

The representatives of the French people, constituted as the National Assembly, considering that ignorance, disregard, or contempt for the rights of man are the sole causes of public misfortunes and the corruption of governments, have resolved to set forth, in a solemn declaration, the natural, inalienable, and sacred rights of man, so that the constant presence of this declaration may ceaselessly remind all members of the social body of their rights and duties; so that the acts of legislative power and those of the executive power may be more respected . . . and so that the demands of the citizens, grounded henceforth on simple and incontestable principles, may always be directed to the maintenance of the constitution and to the welfare of all. . . .

Article 1. Men are born and remain free and equal in rights. Social distinctions can be based only on public utility.

Article 2. The aim of every political association is the preservation of the natural and imprescriptible rights of man. These rights are liberty, property, security, and resistance to oppression.

Article 3. The source of all sovereignty resides essentially in the nation. No body, no individual can exercise authority that does not explicitly proceed from it.

Article 4. Liberty consists in being able to do anything that does not injure another; thus the only limits upon each man's exercise of his natural laws are those that guarantee enjoyment of these same rights to the other members of society.

Article 5. The law has the right to forbid only actions harmful to society. No action may be prevented that is not forbidden by law, and no one may be constrained to do what the law does not order.

Article 6. The law is the expression of the general will. All citizens have the right to participate personally, or through representatives, in its formation. It must be the same for all, whether it protects or punishes. All citizens, being equal in its eyes, are equally admissable to all public dignities, positions, and employments, according to their ability, and on the basis of no other distinction than that of their virtues and talents. . . .

Article 16. A society in which the guarantee of rights is not secured, or the separation of powers is not clearly established, has no constitution.

Declaration of the Rights of Man and of the Citizen, as cited in K. M. Baker, ed. *The Old Regime and the French Revolution* (Chicago: University of Chicago Press, 1987), pp. 238–239.

OLYMPE DE GOUGES, DECLARATION OF THE RIGHTS OF WOMAN AND OF THE CITIZEN

Opposition to the Declaration of the Rights of Man and of the Citizen did not come from conservatives alone. Some radicals did not think the Declaration went nearly far enough. In this pamphlet from 1791 Olympe de Gouges, a literate butcher's daughter and political radical, chastised the Declaration's authors for their arrogance in presuming to speak for the rights and best interests of a large part of the Third Estate—its women. Note her satirical attack on the revolutionaries' fascination with "natural laws," a legacy of Enlightenment thought.

Man, are you capable of being just? It is a woman who asks you this question; at least you will not deny her this right. Tell me! Who has given you the sovereign authority to oppress my sex? Your strength? Your talents? Observe the creator in his wisdom; regard nature in all her grandeur, with which you seem to want to compare yourself; and give me, if you dare, an example of this tyrannical empire. Go back to the animals, consult the elements, study the plants, then glance over the modifications of organized matter, and cede to the evidence when I offer you the means. Seek, search, and distinguish, if you can, the sexes in the administration of nature. Everywhere you will find them mingled, everywhere they cooperate in harmony with this immortal masterpiece.

Only man has fashioned himself a principle out of this exception. Bizarre, blind, bloated by science and degenerate, in this century of enlightenment and wisdom, he, in grossest ignorance, wishes to exercise the command of a despot over a sex that has received every intellectual faculty; he claims to rejoice in the Revolution and claims his rights to equality, at the very least.

"The Declaration of the Rights of Woman and of the Citizen," as cited in Susan Bell and Karen Offen, eds. *Women, the Family and Freedom: The Debate in Documents*, Vol. 1, *1750–1880* (Stanford: Stanford University Press, 1983), pp. 104–106.

ence. The Assembly abolished serfdom and banned slavery in continental France. It remained silent on colonial slavery. Events in the Caribbean, as we will see, later forced the issue.

The rights and roles of women became the focus of sharp debate. The Englishwoman Mary Wollstonecraft's milestone book *A Vindication of the Rights of Woman* (see Chapter 12) was penned during the revolutionary debate over national education. Women's political rights found a colorful proponent in Marie Gouze, also known as Olympe de Gouges, the self-educated daughter of a butcher who had become an intellectual and playwright. Gouges composed her own manifesto, the Declaration of the Rights of Woman and the Citizen (1791).

Beginning with the proposition that "social distinctions can only be based on the common utility," she declared that women had the same rights as men, including resistance to authority, participation in government, and naming the fathers of illegitimate children—a revealing glimpse of issues of economic distress, shame, and isolation as experienced by women of the era. Women participated in the everyday activities of the revolution, joining clubs, demonstrations, and debates; women artisans' organizations had a well-established role in municipal life; market women were familiar public figures, often central to the circulation of news and spontaneous popular demonstrations. The regime celebrated the support of women "citizens," and female figures were allegories for liberty. Those conceptions, however, were increasingly tied to an image of women as supportive mothers, educators, and tenders of the private sphere, not to be involved in public.

In this early period of the revolution, the most divisive issue involved religion. In November 1789, the National Assembly resolved to confiscate the lands of the church and to use them as collateral for the issue of assignats, interest-bearing notes that eventually circulated as paper money. In 1790, the Civil Constitution of the Clergy made bishops and priests subject to the authority of the state. Their salaries were to be paid out of the public treasury, and they were required to swear allegiance to the new state, making it clear they served France rather than Rome. The Assembly's aim was to make the Catholic Church of France a truly national and civil institution.

Reforming the church polarized large sections of France. Many resented the church's wealth and privilege. The local priest, however, not only baptized, married, and buried people, he helped with any written documents. The church provided poor relief and other services. In many areas peasants relied on and respected their priests. The dramatic changes devised by the Assembly thus encountered considerable resistance, driving many local people in the deeply Catholic areas of western France into counterrevolution.

A New Stage: Popular Revolution

Why did the French Revolution become more radical?

In the summer of 1792, the Revolution entered a second stage. The moderate leaders were toppled and replaced by much more radical "republicans" claiming to rule on behalf of the common people. Why this abrupt and drastic change? Was the Revolution "blown off course"? These are among the most difficult questions about the French Revolution. Answers need to take account of three factors: changes in popular politics, a crisis of leadership, and international polarization.

First, the revolution produced a remarkable politicization of the common people, especially in cities. Newspapers filled with political and social commentary multiplied, freed from restrictions on printing. From 1789 forward, a wide variety of political clubs became part of daily political life. Some were formal, almost like political parties, gathering members of the elite to debate issues facing the country and influence decisions in the assembly. Other clubs opened their doors to those excluded from formal politics, and they read aloud from newspapers and discussed the options facing the country, from the provisions of the constitution to the trustworthiness of the king and his ministers. This political awareness was heightened by the crisis of nearly constant shortages and fluctuating prices. Club leaders also articulated the frustrations of a mass of men and women who felt cheated by the constitution.

A second major reason for the change of course was a lack of effective national leadership. Louis XVI remained a weak, vacillating monarch. He was compelled to support measures personally distasteful to

CHRONOLOGY

THE FIRST FRENCH REVOLUTION, 1789–1792

Fall of the Bastille	July 14, 1789
The "Great Fear"	Summer of 1789
Declaration of the Rights of Man and of the Citizen	August 1789
The "October Days"	1789
National Assembly enacts the Civil Constitution of the Clergy	July 1790
Royal family tries to escape Paris	June 1791
National Assembly declares war on Austria and Prussia	April 1792

him. He was thus sympathetic to the plottings of the queen, who was in contact with her brother Leopold II of Austria. Urged on by Marie Antoinette, Louis agreed to attempt an escape from France in June 1791, hoping to rally foreign support for counterrevolution. The members of the royal family managed to slip past their palace guards in Paris, but they were apprehended near the border at Varennes and brought back to the capital. Louis was now little more than a prisoner of the Assembly.

The third major reason for the dramatic turn of affairs was war. From the outset of the Revolution, men and women across Europe had been compelled, by the very intensity of events in France, to take sides in the conflict. Political societies in Britain proclaimed their allegiance to the principles of the new revolution. In the Low Countries, a "patriot" group organized strikes and plotted a revolution of its own. Revolutionaries in western Germany and Italy thought a French invasion would bring radical change within their own countries.

Others opposed the Revolution from the start. Nobles, who had fled France for sympathetic royal courts in Germany and elsewhere, did all they could to stir up counterrevolutionary sentiment. In Britain the conservative cause was strengthened by the publication in 1790 of Edmund Burke's *Reflections on the Revolution in France.* A Whig politician who had sympathized with the American revolutionaries, Burke nevertheless attacked the Revolution in France as a monstrous crime against the social order. The French failure to pay proper respect to tradition and custom had destroyed the fabric of French civilization, woven by centuries of national history.

Burke's famous pamphlet helped arouse sympathy for the counterrevolutionary cause. That sympathy did not turn to active opposition until France became a threat to international stability and the individual ambitions of the great powers. It was that threat which led to war in 1792, and which kept the Continent in arms for a generation.

WAR

The first European states to express public concern about events in revolutionary France were Austria and Prussia. In August 1791, they declared that restoring order and the rights of the monarch of France was a matter of "common interest to all sovereigns of Europe." The leaders of the French government pronounced the declaration an affront to national sovereignty, hoping that enthusiasm for a war would unite the French people and strengthen the revolution. On April 20, 1792, the Assembly declared war against Austria and Prussia.

Almost all of the various political factions in France welcomed the war. Counterrevolutionaries hoped the intervention of Austria and Prussia would undo the Revolution. Radicals, suspicious of aristocratic leaders and the king, believed that war would expose "traitors" who harbored misgivings about the Revolution. As the radicals expected, the French army met serious reverses. By August 1792 the allied armies of Austria and Prussia had crossed the frontier and were threatening to capture Paris. Many, including soldiers, believed that the military disasters were evidence of the king's treason. On August 10, Parisian crowds, organized by their radical leadership, attacked the royal palace. The king was imprisoned and a second and far more radical revolution began.

> On August 10, Parisian crowds, organized by their radical leadership, attacked the royal palace. The king was imprisoned and a second and far more radical revolution began.

THE JACOBINS

In September 1792, a national Convention, elected by free white men, became the effective governing body of the country. The Convention was far more radical than its predecessor, and its leadership was determined to end the monarchy. On September 21, the Convention declared France a republic. In December it placed the king on trial, and in January he was condemned to death by a narrow margin. The heir to the grand tradition of French absolutism met his end bravely as "Citizen Louis Capet," beheaded by the guillotine, the frightful mechanical headsman that had become the symbol of revolutionary fervor.

Meanwhile, the Convention turned its attention to further domestic reforms. Among its most significant accomplishments over the next three years were the abolition of slavery in French colonies and the repeal of primogeniture, so that property would not be inherited exclusively by the oldest son but would be divided in substantially equal portions among all immediate heirs. Some large estates were broken up and offered for sale to poorer citizens on relatively easy terms. It abruptly canceled the policy of compensating nobles for their lost privileges. To curb ris-

The Execution of Louis XVI. A revolutionary displays the king's head moments after it is severed by the guillotine in January 1793.

ing prices, the government set maximum prices for grain and other necessities. In an effort to root out Christianity from everyday life, the Convention adopted a new calendar. The calendar year began with the birth of the republic (September 22, 1792), and divided months in such a way as to eliminate the Catholic Sunday.

The Convention also accomplished an astonishingly successful reorganization of its armies. In August 1793, the revolutionary government mustered all men capable of bearing arms. Fourteen hastily drafted armies were flung into battle under the leadership of young and inexperienced officers. What they lacked in training and discipline they made up for in organization, mobility, flexibility, courage, and morale. In 1793–1794, the French armies preserved their homeland. In 1794–1795, they occupied the Low Countries, the Rhineland, and parts of Spain, Switzerland, and Savoy. In 1796, they invaded and occupied key parts of Italy and broke the coalition that had arrayed itself against them.

THE REIGN OF TERROR

These achievements exacted a heavy price. To ensure their accomplishment, the rulers of France resorted to a bloody authoritarianism that has come to be known as the Terror. The Convention prolonged its own life year after year, and increasingly delegated its responsibilities to a group of twelve leaders, or the Committee of Public Safety.

Foremost among the political leadership were Jean Paul Marat, Georges Jacques Danton, and Maximilien Robespierre, the latter two members of the Committee of Public Safety. Jean Paul Marat opposed nearly all of his moderate colleagues' assumptions, including their admiration for Great Britain, which Marat considered corrupt and despotic. He edited the popular news sheet, *The Friend of the People*. Exposure to infection left him with a chronic skin disease, from which he could find relief only through frequent bathing. In the summer of 1793, at the height of the crisis of the revolution, he was stabbed in his bath by Charlotte

The Death of Marat. This painting by the French artist David immortalized Marat. The note in the slain leader's hand is from Charlotte Corday, his assassin.

in the Jacobin Club. Later he became president of the National Convention and a member of the Committee of Public Safety. Though he had little to do with starting the Terror, he was nevertheless responsible for enlarging its scope. He came to justify ruthlessness as necessary to revolutionary progress.

The two years of the Terror brought dictatorship and repression. Pressed by foreign enemies from without, the Committee faced opposition from both the political right and left at home. The government's attempts to conscript troops into its armies fanned long-smoldering resentments into open rebellion. By 1793, peasant counterrevolutionaries in the west posed a serious threat to the Convention. Determined to stabilize France, whatever the cost, the Committee dispatched commissioners into the countryside to suppress the enemies of the state.

During the period of the Terror, from September 1793 to July 1794, the most reliable estimates place the number of executions as high as twenty-five to thirty thousand in France as a whole, fewer than twenty thousand of whom were condemned by the courts. In addition, approxi-

Corday, a young royalist, and became a revolutionary martyr.

Georges Jacques Danton, like Marat, was a popular political leader, well known in the more plebian clubs of Paris. Elected a member of the Committee of Public Safety in 1793, he had much to do with organizing the Terror. As time went on, however, he wearied of ruthlessness and displayed a tendency to compromise that gave his opponents in the Convention their opportunity. In April 1794 Danton was sent to the guillotine.

The most famous of the radical leaders was Maximilien Robespierre. Born of a family reputed to be of Irish descent, Robespierre was trained for the law and speedily achieved modest success as a lawyer. His eloquence, and his consistent, or ruthless, insistence that leaders respect the "will of the people" eventually won him a following

CHRONOLOGY

THE SECOND FRENCH REVOLUTION, 1792–1794

First Republic established	Summer 1792
National Convention elected	September 1792
Execution of the king	January 1793
War between Britain, Holland, Spain, and France	February 1793
"Reign of Terror"	September 1793–July 1794
Purge of the Jacobins	July 27, 1794
Execution of Robespierre	July 28, 1794

FRANCE AND ITS SISTER REPUBLICS

The French revolutionaries, fighting against the conservative monarchs of Europe, conquered and annexed large sections of Italy, the Austrian Netherlands, and Switzerland. Napoleon did not begin these wars, though he continued and greatly expanded them.

Map legend:
- French Republic, 1792
- Annexed to France, 1792–1795
- Sister republics

CHRONOLOGY

REIGN OF NAPOLEON, 1799–1815

Napoleon becomes First Consul	1799
Concordat with the pope	1801
Napoleon becomes consul for life	1802
Napoleon abolishes the republic and crowns himself emperor	1804
Napoleonic Code	1804
The Continental System	1806
Napoleon invades Spain	1808
Invasion of Russia	1812
Abdication of Napoleon	1814
Return and final exile of Napoleon	1815

Sieyès was asked what he had done to distinguish himself during the Terror, he responded dryly, "I lived."

FROM THE TERROR TO BONAPARTE: THE DIRECTORY

Why did the Directory fail?

The Committee of Public Safety, though able to save France, could not save itself. Inflation became catastrophic. The long string of military victories convinced growing numbers that the Terror was no longer justified. On July 27 (9 Thermidor), Robespierre was shouted down by his enemies while attempting to speak on the floor of the Convention. The following day, along with twenty-one other conspirators, he met his death by guillotine as an enemy of the state.

In 1795 the National Convention adopted a new and more conservative constitution. It granted suffrage to all adult male citizens who could read and write. Yet it set up indirect elections: citizens voted for electors, who in turn chose the legislative body. Wealthy citizens thus held authority. Eager to avoid

mately five hundred thousand were incarcerated between March 1793 and August 1794. Few victims of the Terror were aristocrats. Many more were peasants or laborers accused of hoarding, treason, or counterrevolutionary activity. Anyone who appeared to threaten the republic, no matter what his or her social or economic position, was at risk. When some time later the Abbé personal dictatorship, it vested executive authority in a board of five men known as the Directory, chosen by the legislative body.

Although the Directory lasted longer than its revolutionary predecessor, it could not stabilize the government. Its members faced discontent on both the radical left and the conservative right. After four years of unrest, the Directory was overthrown by the brilliant young general Napoleon Bonaparte.

Bonaparte's first military victory in 1793, the recapture of Toulon from royalist and British forces, had earned him promotion from captain to brigadier general at the age of twenty-four. He had registered a remarkable series of victories in Italy, forcing Austria to withdrawal (temporarily) from the war. Most recently, he had attempted to defeat Britain by staging an attack on British forces in Egypt and the Near East. That campaign had gone well on land, but when the French fleet was defeated by Admiral Horatio Nelson (Abukir Bay, 1798), Bonaparte found himself trapped by the British. A year of further fighting had not brought him nearer to decisive victory.

In 1799, Bonaparte slipped away from Egypt and appeared in Paris, already having agreed to participate in a coup d'état. On November 9, 1799 (18 Brumaire), Bonaparte was declared a "temporary consul." He was the answer to the prayers of the Directory: a strong, popular leader who was not a king. Sieyès declared that Bonaparte would provide "Confidence from below, authority from above." With those words Sieyès pronounced the end of the revolutionary period.

> On November 9, 1799 (18 Brumaire), Bonaparte was declared a "temporary consul." He was the answer to the prayers of the Directory: a strong, popular leader who was not a king.

THE HAITIAN REVOLUTION

Throughout all of these events, the French colonies across the Atlantic were reshaping the revolution and its legacy. The Caribbean islands of Guadeloupe, Martinique, and St. Domingue occupied a central role in the French economy because of the sugar trade. Their planter elites had powerful influence in Paris. The French National Assembly (like its American counterpart) declined to discuss the matter of slavery in the colonies, unwilling to encroach on the property rights of slave owners and fearful of losing the lucrative sugar islands to their British or Spanish rivals. More difficult, from the point of view of the

French men in the Assembly, was the question of rights for free men of color, a group that included a significant number of wealthy owners of property (and slaves).

St. Domingue had about forty thousand whites of different social classes, thirty thousand free people of color, and five hundred thousand slaves, most of them recently enslaved in West Africa. In 1790, free people of color from St. Domingue sent a delegation to Paris, asking to be seated by the Assembly, underscoring that they were men of property and, in many cases, of European ancestry. The Assembly refused to seat them.

In August 1791 the largest slave rebellion in history broke out in St. Domingue. The British and the Spanish invaded St. Domingue, confident they could crush the rebellion and take the island. In 1792, the French government, scrambling to win allies in St. Domingue, made free men of color citizens and dispatched commissioners to St. Domingue with troops to hold the island. Those commissioners promised freedom to slaves who would join them.

The new situation brought new leaders to the fore, chief among them a former slave, Toussaint Bréda, later Toussaint L'Ouverture, meaning "the one who opened the way." Over the course of the next five years, Toussaint and his soldiers, now allied with the French army, emerged victorious over the French planters, the British (in 1798), and the Spanish (in 1801). Toussaint also broke the power of his rival generals in both the mulatto and former slave armies, becoming the statesman of the revolution. In 1801, Toussaint set up a constitution, swearing allegiance to France but denying France any right to interfere in St. Domingue affairs.

Toussaint's accomplishments, however, put him on a collision course with another French general whose career was remarkably like his own: Napoleon Bonaparte. St. Domingue stood at the center of Bonaparte's ambitions for the New World, and in January 1802, he dispatched twenty thousand troops to bring the island under control. Toussaint, captured when he arrived for discussions with the French, was shipped under heavy guard to a prison in the mountains of eastern France where he died in 1803. Fighting continued in St. Domingue, however, with fires now fueled by Bonaparte's determination to restore slavery. The war

NAPOLEON AND IMPERIAL FRANCE

How did Napoleon centralize his authority?

Few figures in Western history have compelled the attention of the world as Napoleon Bonaparte did during the fifteen years of his rule in France. Few men lived on with such persistence as myth, not just in their own countries, but across the West. For the great majority of ordinary Europeans, memories of the French Revolution were dominated by those of the Napoleonic wars, which devastated Europe, convulsed its politics, and traumatized its peoples for a generation. What had begun as political revolution and popular revolt ended in war and efforts to create a new kind of European empire. To many observers, that transformation seemed embodied in the career of one man. From the onset of war in 1792, France's revolutionaries had turned to the armies of France for defense and survival. It seemed all too natural that the future of the Revolution should be bound up with the successes of its greatest general, Napoleon Bonaparte.

Bonaparte's relationship to the Revolution, however, was not simple. His regime consolidated some of the revolution's political and social changes but sharply repudiated others. He presented himself as the son of the revolution, but he also borrowed freely from very different regimes, fashioning himself as the heir to Charlemagne, or to the Roman empire. His regime remade revolutionary politics and the French state, transformed the nature of European warfare, and left a legacy of conflict and legends of French glory that lingered in the dreams, or nightmares, of Europe's statesmen and citizens for more than a century.

Toussaint L'Ouverture. A portrait of L'Ouverture, leader of what would become the Haitian revolution, as a general.

turned into a nightmare for the French and in January 1804, Jean-Jacques Dessalines, a general in the army of former slaves, declared the independent state of Haiti.

The Haitian revolution was the only successful slave revolution in history, and by far the most radical of the revolutions that occurred in this age. It suggested that the emancipatory ideas of the revolution and Enlightenment might apply to non-Europeans and enslaved peoples. Combined with later rebellions in the British colonies, it contributed to the British decision to end slavery in 1838. And it cast a long shadow over nineteenth-century slave societies from the southern United States to Brazil.

> The Haitian revolution was the only successful slave revolution in history, and by far the most radical of the revolutions that occurred in this age.

CONSOLIDATING AUTHORITY: 1799–1804

The son of a provincial Corsican nobleman, Bonaparte attended the Ecole Militaire in Paris. In pre-Revolutionary

France, he would have been unable to rise beyond the rank of major, which required buying a regimental command. The Revolution, however, had abolished the purchase of military office, and Bonaparte quickly became a general. His character seemed suited to the age, at least to his early admirers, who noted his wide range of talents and intellectual interests. He pursued serious interests in history, law, and mathematics. His particular strengths as a leader lay in his ability to create financial, legal, or military plans and then to master their every detail; in his capacity for inspiring others, even those initially opposed to him; and in his belief that he was the destined savior of France. That last conviction eventually led to Napoleon's undoing.

> The Napoleonic Code cleared through the thicket of different legal traditions, creating one uniform law.

In the first five years of his reign, Bonaparte quickly consolidated personal power. When he overthrew the government in 1799, he governed in the name of the Republic. A new constitution established universal white male suffrage and set up two legislative bodies. Elections, however, were indirect, and the power of the legislative bodies sharply curbed. "The government?" said one observer. "There is Bonaparte." Throughout, his regime retained the appearance of consulting with the people, but its most important feature was the centralization of authority.

That authority came from reorganizing the state. Bonaparte's regime confirmed the abolition of privilege, thereby promising "careers open to talent." Through centralization of the administrative departments, he established what no recent French regime had yet achieved: an orderly and generally fair system of taxation. As we have seen, the revolutionaries began the work of reorganizing the administration, abolishing the ancient fiefdoms with their separate governments, and setting up a uniform system of departments. Bonaparte continued that work, but with an accent on centralization. He replaced elected officials and local self-government with centrally appointed "prefects" and "subprefects" whose administrative duties were defined in Paris, where local government policy was made as well. Napoleon's state was a point midway between absolutism and the modern state.

LAW, EDUCATION, AND A NEW ELITE

Napoleon's most significant accomplishment, and one exported to the areas he conquered, was the completion of the legal reforms begun during the revolutionary period and the promulgation of a new legal code in 1804.

The Napoleonic Code cleared through the thicket of different legal traditions, creating one uniform law. It confirmed the abolition of feudal privileges of all kinds: not only noble and clerical privileges but the special rights of craft guilds, municipalities, and so on. It set the conditions for exercising property rights: the drafting of contracts, leases, and stock companies. The code's provisions on the family, which Napoleon developed personally, insisted on the importance of paternal authority and the subordination of women and children.

Bonaparte also rationalized the educational system. He ordered the establishment of *lycées* (high schools) in every major town to train civil servants and army officers and a school in Paris to train teachers. To sup-

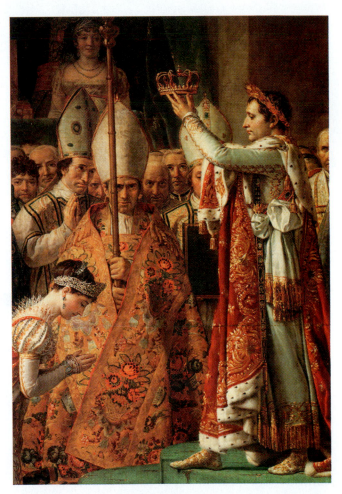

Coronation of Napoleon and Josephine. Napoleon crowned himself, but Jaques Louis David diplomatically painted the moment when he bestowed a crown on his wife, Josephine.

plement these changes, Napoleon brought the military and technical schools under state control and founded a national university to supervise the entire system. Napoleon also embraced the burgeoning social and physical sciences of the Enlightenment. He sponsored the Académie Française and retained several of the revolutionaries' more practical attempts to rationalize society and commerce, such as the metric system.

Who benefited from these changes? Like Bonaparte's other new institutions, the new schools helped confirm the power of a new elite. The new elite included businessmen, bankers, and merchants, but was still composed primarily of powerful landowners. Finally, like most of Bonaparte's reforms, changes in education aimed to strengthen the power of the state: "My object in establishing a teaching corps is to have a means of directing political and moral opinion," Napoleon said bluntly. Another act to court the new elite came in 1801, with Bonaparte's concordat with the pope, an agreement that put an end to more than a decade of hostility between the

NAPOLEON'S EMPIRE AT ITS HEIGHT

EUROPE IN 1812
- French territory
- French dependencies
- Allied with Napoleon
- Independent states

NAPOLEON'S INVASION OF RUSSIA, 1812
- → Advance
- ◄-- Retreat
- ✶ Battle sites

What did Napoleon want from the rest of Europe? Where was he successful; where did he fail, and why? Where did his rule leave the most lasting impact? Could he have maintained his empire?

TWO LETTERS FROM NAPOLEON

Napoleon placed his brothers on the thrones of different vassal states in conquered territories throughout Europe. The first excerpt below is from a letter to his brother Eugène, head of one of the new Italian states, in which Napoleon explains how Italy's lucrative silk trade was to be diverted in order to damage English commercial interests and bolster the French empire. It provides a revealing glimpse of Napoleon's vision of a united Europe, with the other countries' futures tied to France's.

On March 1, 1815, Napoleon landed in the south of France, having escaped from his exile on the island of Elba. The restored Bourbon king abdicated, and Napoleon ruled for one hundred more days, until his defeat at the battle of Waterloo in June. The second selection below is excerpted from a proclamation, addressed to the sovereigns of Europe, explaining the emperor's return. It is an excellent illustration of Napoleon's self-image, his rhetoric, and his belief that he represented the force of history itself.

LETTER TO PRINCE EUGÈNE, 23 AUGUST 1810

I have received your letter of August 14. All the raw silk from the Kingdom of Italy goes to England, for there are no silk factories in Germany. It is therefore quite natural that I should wish to divert it from this route to the advantage of my French manufacturers: otherwise my silk factories, one of the chief supports of French commerce, would suffer substantial losses. I cannot agree with your observations. My principle is *France first*. You must never lose sight of the fact that, if English commerce is supreme on the high seas, it is due to her sea power: it is therefore to be expected that, as France is the strongest land power, she should claim commercial supremacy on the continent: it is indeed our only hope. And isn't it better for Italy to come to the help of France, in such an important matter as this, than to be covered with Customs Houses? For it would be short-sighted not to recognise that Italy owes her independence to France; that it was won by French blood and French victories; that it must not be misused; and that nothing could be more unreasonable than to start calculating what commercial advantages France gets out of it.

Piedmont and Parma produce silk too; and there also I have prohibited its export to any country except France. It is no use for Italy to make plans that leave French prosperity out of account; she must face the fact that the interests of the two countries hang together. Above all, she must be careful not to give France any reason for annexing her; for if it paid France to do this, who could stop her? So make this your motto too—*France first*.

CIRCULAR LETTER TO THE SOVEREIGNS OF EUROPE, 4 APRIL 1815

Monsieur, My Brother,

You will have learnt, during the course of last month, of my landing again in France, of my entry into Paris, and of the departure of the Bourbon family. Your Majesty must by now be aware of the real nature of these events. They are the work of an irresistable power, of the unanimous will of a great nation conscious of its duties and of its rights. A dynasty forcibly reimposed upon the French people was no longer suitable for it: the Bourbons refused to associate themselves with the natural feelings or the national customs; and France was forced to abandon them. The popular voice called for a liberator. The expectation which had decided me to make the supreme sacrifice was in vain. I returned; and from the place where my foot first touched the shore I was carried by the affection of my subjects into the bosom of my capital.

My first and heartfelt anxiety is to repay so much affection by the maintenance of an honourable peace.

The re-establishment of the Imperial throne was necessary for the happiness of Frenchmen: my dearest hope is that it may also secure repose for the whole of Europe. Each national flag in turn has had its gleam of glory: often enough, by some turn of fortune, great victories have been followed by great defeats. . . . I have provided the world in the past with a programme of great contests; it will please me better in future to acknowledge no rivalry but that of the advocates of peace, and no combat but a crusade for the felicity of mankind. It is France's pleasure to make a frank avowal of this noble ideal. Jealous of her independence, she will always base her policy upon an unqualified respect for the independence of other peoples. . . .

Monsieur my Brother,
Your good Brother,
Napoléon.

K. M. Baker, ed. *The Old Regime and the French Revolution* (Chicago: University of Chicago Press, 1987), pp. 419–20, 426–27.

French state and the Catholic Church. Although it shocked anticlerical revolutionaries, Napoleon, ever the pragmatist, believed that reconciliation would create domestic harmony and international solidarity.

Such political balancing acts increased Bonparte's general popularity. Combined with early military successes (peace with Austria in 1801 and with Britain in 1802), they muffled any opposition to his personal ambitions. He had married Josephine de Beauharnais, a Creole from Martinique and an influential mistress of the Revolutionary period. Neither Bonaparte nor his ambitious wife were content to be first among equals, however, and in December of 1804, he finally cast aside any traces of republicanism. In a ceremony that evoked the splendor of medieval kingship and Bourbon absolutism, he crowned himself Emperor Napoleon I in the Cathedral of Notre Dame in Paris.

IN EUROPE AS IN FRANCE: NAPOLEON'S WARS OF EXPANSION

The nations of Europe had looked on—some in admiration, others in horror, all in astonishment—at the phenomenon that was Napoleon. A coalition of European powers led by Austria, Prussia, and Britain had fought France from 1792 until 1795, in hopes of maintaining European stability. This first coalition collapsed in disarray, defeated by the French armies and by financial exhaustion. The coalition was revived in 1798, at Britain's behest, but in the end it fared no better than the first effort. Despite Napoleon's debacle in Egypt, French victories in Europe split the alliance. Russia and Austria withdrew from the fray in 1801, and even the intransigent British were forced to make peace the following year.

Out of these victories Napoleon created his new empire and affiliated states. These included a series of small republics carved from Austria's empire and the old German kingdoms. These were presented as France's revolutionary gift of independence to patriots elsewhere in Europe, but in practice they were a military buffer and a system of client states for a new French empire.

Napoleon's reign accelerated developments already underway in the territories of central Europe. The Napoleonic program of reform applied to the empire principles that had already transformed France. It eliminated manorial and church courts. It joined previously separate provinces into an enormous bureaucratic network that reached directly back to Paris. It codified laws and modernized tax systems, and freed individuals to work at whatever trade they chose. These new freedoms of law, property, and profession, however, did not extend to politics. Governmental direction emanated from Napoleon.

The effect of these changes on the men and women who experienced them was profound. In those small principalities previously ruled by princes—the patchwork states of Germany, for example, or the repressive kingdom of Naples—reforms that provided for more efficient, less corrupt administration, a workable tax structure, and an end to customary privilege were welcomed by most of the local population. Yet the Napoleonic presence proved a mixed blessing. The French levied taxes, drafted men, and required states to support occupying armies. From the point of view of the common people, the local lord and priest had been replaced by the French tax collector and army recruiting board. This arrogance slowly but irretriev-

ably cost Napoleon the support of revolutionaries, former Enlightenment thinkers, and liberals across the Continent.

THE RETURN TO WAR AND NAPOLEON'S DEFEAT: 1806–1815

What led to Napoleon's downfall?

Britain had bitterly opposed each of France's revolutionary regimes since the death of Louis XVI; now it tried to rally Europe against Napoleon with promises of generous financial loans and trade. The Continen-

Napoleon on the Battlefield of Eylau. Amidst bitter cold and snow, Napoleon engaged with the Russian army in February of 1807. Although technically a victory for the French, it was only barely that, with the French losing at least 10,000 men, and the Russians twice as many. This painting, characteristic of Bonaparte propaganda, emphasizes not the losses but the Emperor's saint-like clemency—even enemy soldiers reach up toward him.

tal System, established by Napoleon in 1806, sought to choke Britain's trade and force its surrender. The system failed for several reasons. Britain retained control of the seas. The British naval blockade of the Continent, begun in 1807, effectively countered Napoleon's system. The system hurt the Continent more than Britain. Stagnant trade in Europe's ports and unemployment in its manufacturing centers eroded public faith in Napoleon's dream of a working European empire.

The Continental System was Napoleon's first serious mistake. A second cause of his decline was his unmasterable ambition. Napoleon's goal was to remake Europe as a new Roman empire, ruled from Paris. The symbols of his empire—reflected in painting, architecture, and the design of furniture and clothing—were deliberately Roman in origin. This was not a novelty; the early revolutionaries, Jacobins in particular, harked back to the Roman republic as their model for political virtue, drawing on its imagery in art and political rhetoric. But the triumphal columns and arches Napoleon had erected to commemorate his victories recalled the ostentatious monuments of the Roman emperors. Even Napoleon's admirers began to wonder if his empire would reflect simply a larger, more efficient, and ultimately more dangerous absolutism than the monarchies of the eighteenth century.

War had broken out again in 1805, with the Russians, Prussians, Austrians, and Swedes joining the British in an attempt to contain France. Their efforts were to no avail. Napoleon's military superiority led to defeats, in turn, of all three Continental allies. Napoleon was a master of well-timed, well-directed shock attacks on the battlefield. He led an army that had transformed European warfare: first raised as a revolutionary militia, it was now a trained, conscript army of native Frenchmen, loyal, well supplied by a nation whose economy was committed to serving the war effort, and led by generals promoted largely on the basis of talent. This new kind of army, directed with Napoleon's lethal flair, inflicted crushing defeats on his enemies. The battle of Austerlitz, in December 1805, was a mighty triumph for the French against the combined forces of Austria and Russia and became a symbol of the emperor's apparent invincibility. His subsequent victory against the Russians at Friedland in 1807 only added to his reputation.

> The battle of Austerlitz, in December 1805, was a mighty triumph for the French against the combined forces of Austria and Russia and became a symbol of the emperor's apparent invincibility.

Yet the myth of Napoleon's invincibility worked against him as well, as he took ever greater risks with France's military and national fortunes. Russian numbers and Austrian artillery inflicted horrendous losses on the French at Wagram in 1809, although these difficulties were forgotten in the glow of victory. Napoleon's allies and supporters shrugged off the British admiral Horatio Nelson's victory at Trafalgar in 1805 as no more than a temporary check to the emperor's ambitions. But Trafalgar broke French naval power in the Mediterranean and helped lead to a rift with Spain, which had been France's equal partner in the battle and suffered equally in the defeat. In the Americas, too, Napoleon was forced to cut growing losses, giving up on St. Domingue in the face of disaster and selling France's territories along the Mississippi to the United States for badly needed cash.

A crucial moment in Napoleon's undoing came with his invasion of Spain in 1808. The invasion aimed, eventually, toward the conquest of Portugal, which had remained a stalwart ally of the British. Napoleon overthrew the Spanish king, installed his own brother on the throne, and then imposed a series of reforms similar to those he had instituted elsewhere in Europe. But he reckoned without two factors that led to the ultimate failure of his Spanish mission: the presence of British forces under Sir Arthur Wellesley (later the duke of Wellington), and the determined resistance of the Spanish people. The peninsular wars, as the Spanish conflicts were called, were long and bitter. Terrible atrocities were committed by both sides; the French military's torture and execution of Spanish guerrillas and civilians was immortalized by the Spanish artist Francisco Goya (1746–1828) with sickening accuracy in his prints and paintings. The Spanish campaign was the first indication that Napoleon could be beaten, and it encouraged resistance elsewhere.

The second, and most dramatic stage in Napoleon's downfall began with the disruption of his alliance with Russia. As an agricultural country, Russia had suffered a severe economic crisis when it was no longer able to trade its surplus grain for British manufactures. The consequence was that Tsar Alexander I began to wink at trade with Britain and to ignore or evade the protests from Paris. By 1811 Napoleon decided that he could endure this flouting of their agreement no

Execution of the Rebels on 3 May 1808, by Francisco Goya. This painting of the execution of Spanish rebels by Napoleon's army as it marched through Spain is one of the most memorable depictions of a nation's martyrdom.

longer. Accordingly, he collected an army of six hundred thousand and set out for Russia in the spring of 1812. Only a third of the soldiers in this "Grande Armée" were French: nearly as many were Polish or German, joined by soldiers and adventurers from the rest of France's client states. It was the grandest of Napoleon's imperial expeditions, an army raised from across Europe and sent to punish the autocratic tsar. It ended in disaster. The Russians drew the French farther and farther into the heart of their country. Just before Napoleon reached the ancient Russian capital of Moscow, the Russian army drew the French forces into a bloody, seemingly pointless battle in the narrow streets of a town called Borodino, where both sides suffered terrible losses of men and supplies, harder on the French who were now so far from home. After the battle, the Russians permitted Napoleon to occupy Moscow. But on the night of his entry, Russian parti-

sans put the city to the torch, leaving little but the blackened walls of the Kremlin palaces to shelter the invading troops.

Hoping that the tsar would eventually surrender, Napoleon lingered amid the ruins for more than a month. On October 19 he finally ordered the homeward march. The delay was a fatal blunder. Long before he had reached the border, the terrible Russian winter was on his troops. Frozen streams, mountainous drifts of snow, and bottomless mud slowed the retreat almost to a halt. To add to the miseries of frostbite, disease, and starvation, mounted Cossacks rode out of the blizzard to harry the exhausted army. Each morning the miserable remnant that pushed on left behind circles of corpses around the campfires of the night before. On December 13 a few thousand broken soldiers crossed the frontier into Germany—a fragment of the once proud Grande Armée. Nearly three hundred thousand of its soldiers and untold thousands of Russians lost their lives in Napoleon's Russian adventure.

Following the retreat from Russia, the anti-Napoleonic forces took renewed hope. United by a belief that they might finally succeed in defeating the emperor, Prussia, Russia, Austria, Sweden, and Britain renewed their attack. Citizens of many German states in particular saw this as a war of liberation, and indeed most of the fighting took place in Germany. By the beginning of 1814, they had crossed the Rhine into France. Left with an inexperienced army of raw youths, Napoleon retreated to Paris, urging the French people to further resistance despite constant setbacks at the hands of the larger invading armies. On March 31, Tsar Alexander I of Russia and King Frederick William III of Prussia made their triumphant entry into Paris. Napoleon was forced to abdicate unconditionally and was sent into exile on the island of Elba, off the Italian coast.

Napoleon was back on French soil in less than a year. In the interim the allies had restored the Bourbon dynasty to the throne, in the person of Louis XVIII, brother of Louis XVI. Despite his administrative abilities, Louis could not fill the void left by Napoleon's abdication. It was no surprise that, when the former emperor staged his escape from Elba, his fellow countrymen once more rallied to his side. The allies, meeting in Vienna to conclude peace treaties with the French, were stunned by the news of Napoleon's return. They dispatched a hastily organized army to meet the emperor's typically bold offensive push into the Low Countries. At the battle of Waterloo, fought over three bloody days from June 15 to 18, 1815, Napoleon was stopped by the forces of his two most persistent enemies, Britain and Prussia, and suffered his final defeat. This time the allies took no chances and shipped their prisoner off to the bleak island of St. Helena in the South Atlantic. The once-mighty emperor, now the exile Bonaparte, lived out a dreary existence writing self-serving memoirs until his death in 1821.

CONCLUSION

The tumultuous events in France formed part of a broad pattern of late eighteenth-century democratic upheaval. The French Revolution was the most violent, protracted, and contentious of the revolutions of the era, but the dynamics of revolution were much the same everywhere. One of the most important developments of the French Revolution was the emergence of a popular movement, which included political clubs representing people previously excluded from politics, newspapers read by and to the common people, and political leaders who spoke for the people. In the French Revolution as in other revolutions, the popular movement challenged the early and moderate revolutionary leadership, pressing for more radical and democratic measures. And as in other revolutions, the popular movement in France was defeated, and authority was reestablished by a quasi-military figure. Likewise, the revolutionary ideas of liberty, equality, and fraternity were not specifically French; their roots lay in the social structures of the eighteenth century and in the culture of the Enlightenment. Yet French armies brought them, literally, to the doorsteps of many Europeans.

What was the larger impact of the Revolution and the Napoleonic era? Its legacy can be summed up in three key concepts: liberty, equality, and nation. Liberty meant individual rights and responsibilities, and more specifically freedom from arbitrary rule. By equality, as we have seen, the revolutionaries meant the abolition of legal distinctions of rank among European men. Though their concept of equality was limited, it became a powerful mobilizing force in the nineteenth century. The most important legacy of the revolution may have been the new term *nation*. Nationhood was a political concept. A "nation" was formed of citizens, not a king's subjects. A nation was ruled by law and treated citizens as equal before the law. Sovereignty did not lie in dynasties or historic fiefdoms, but in the nation of citizens. By the Napoleonic period, this new political body of freely associated citizens was most powerfully embodied in a centralized state, its army, its greatest general turned Emperor of the French, and a kind of citizenship defined by individual commitment to the needs of "the nation" at war.

The revolutionary concept of nationhood spread throughout Europe in response to French aggression. The French did not hesitate to champion their revolutionary principles abroad. France's enemies responded with a growing sense of their own commonality. In the German and Italian principalities the domination of an alien emperor and his unwelcome agents helped forge opposition and a national identity of their own.

When the revolutionary period closed, the three concepts of liberty, equality, and nationality were no longer merely ideas. They had taken shape in new communities and institutions. They had created new alliances between countries. They also polarized Europe and much of the world, giving rise to debates, grievances, and conflict that would shape the nineteenth century.

KEY TERMS

Louis XVI

Third Estate

Declaration of the Rights of Man
 and of the Citizen

Olympe de Gouges

Jacobins

Committee of Public Safety

St. Domingue

Napoleon Bonaparte

lycées

SELECTED READINGS

Applewhite, Harriet B., and Darline G. Levy, eds. *Women and Politics in the Age of the Democratic Revolution*. Ann Arbor, 1990. Essays cover women's activities in France, Britain, the Netherlands, and the United States.

Bergeron, Louis. *France under Napoleon*. Princeton, 1981. Concentrates on the social history of the Napoleonic period.

Best, Geoffrey. *War and Society in Revolutionary Europe, 1770–1870*. Leicester, 1982.

Blackburn, Robin. *The Overthrow of Colonial Slavery*. London and New York, 1988.

Blum, Carol. *Rousseau and the Republic of Virtue: The Language of Politics in the French Revolution*. Ithaca, N.Y., 1986. Excellent on how Rousseau was read by the revolutionaries.

Bruun, Geoffrey. *Europe and the French Imperium, 1799–1814*. Westport, Conn., 1983. Describes the impact of Napoleon on Europe.

Cobb, Richard. *The People's Armies*. New Haven, 1987. Brilliant and detailed analysis of the sans-culottes.

Cobban, Alfred. *The Social Interpretation of the French Revolution*. Cambridge, 1964. A penetrating critique of the radical interpretation of the Revolution, more important for its questions than for its conclusions.

Doyle, William. *Oxford History of the French Revolution*. New York, 1989.

———. *Origins of the French Revolution*. 2d ed. New York, 1988. A revisionist historian surveys recent research on the political and social origins of the Revolution and identifies a new consensus.

Forrest, Alan. *The French Revolution and the Poor*. New York, 1981. An account that argues the poor fared little better under revolutionary governments than under the Old Regime.

Furet, Francois. *Revolutionary France, 1770–1880*. Translated by Antonia Nerill. Cambridge, Mass., 1992.

Geyl, Pieter. *Napoleon: For and Against*. Rev. ed. New Haven, 1964. The ways in which Napoleon was interpreted by French historians and political figures.

Hesse, Carla. *Publishing and Cultural Politics in Revolutionary Paris 1789–1810*. Berkeley, 1991.

Hunt, Lynn. *Politics, Culture, and Class in the French Revolution*. Berkeley, 1984. An analysis of the interaction between political events and sociocultural phenomena out of which grew a new culture of democracy and republicanism.

———. *The French Revolution and Human Rights*. Boston, 1996.

Landes, Joan B. *Women and the Public Sphere in the Age of the French Revolution*. Ithaca, N.Y., 1988. Discusses the revolutionaries' exclusionary policy toward women.

Lefebvre, Georges. *The Coming of the French Revolution*. Princeton, 1947. An excellent study of the causes and early events of the Revolution.

———. *The French Revolution*. 2 vols. New York, 1962–1964. An impressive synthesis by the greatest modern scholar of the Revolution.

———. *The Great Fear of 1789*. New York, 1973. The best account of the rural disturbances.

Lewis, G., and C. Lucas. *Beyond the Terror: Essays in French Regional and Social History, 1794–1815*. New York, 1983.

O'Brien, Connor Cruise. *The Great Melody: A Thematic Biography of Edmund Burke*. Chicago, 1992.

Palmer, R. R. *The Age of the Democratic Revolution: A Political History of Europe and America, 1760–1800*. 2 vols. Princeton, 1964. Impressive for its scope; places the French Revolution in the larger context of a worldwide revolutionary movement.

———. *Twelve Who Ruled: The Year of the Terror in the French Revolution*. Princeton, 1958. Excellent biographical studies of the members of the Committee of Public Safety.

Rudé, George. *The Crowd in the French Revolution*. Westport, Conn., 1986. An important monograph that analyzes the composition of the crowds that participated in the great uprisings of the Revolution.

Schama, Simon. *Citizens: A Chronicle of the French Revolution*. New York, 1989. Particularly good on art and politics.

Soboul, Albert. *The Sans-Culottes: The Popular Movement and Revolutionary Government, 1793–1794*. Garden City, N.Y., 1972. A classic study of the pressures on the Convention in the year of the Terror.

Sutherland, D. M. G. *France, 1789–1815: Revolution and Counter-revolution*. Oxford, 1986. An important synthesis of work on the revolution, especially in social history.

Thompson, J. M. *Robespierre and the French Revolution*. London, 1953. An excellent short biography.

Tilly, Charles. *The Vendée: A Sociological Analysis of the Counter-Revolution of 1793*. Cambridge, Mass., 1964. An important economic and social analysis of the factors that led to the reaction in the Vendée.

Tocqueville, Alexis de. *The Old Regime and the French Revolution*. Garden City, N.Y., 1955. Originally written in 1856, this remains a classic analysis of the causes of the French Revolution.

Trouillot, Michel Rolph. *Silencing the Past*. Boston, 1995.

Woloch, Isser. *The New Regime: Transformations of the French Civic Order, 1789–1820*. New York, 1994. The fate of revolutionary civic reform.

Woolf, Stuart. *Napoleon's Integration of Europe*. New York, 1991.

DIGITAL HISTORY

REVOLUTIONARY PARIS

Frenchmen, it is for you to give to the world the example which Paris has given to France; prepare yourselves by order and by confidence in your destiny for the firm institutions which you are about to be called upon to establish.
— *Proclamation of the Provisional Government,* Paris, February 24, 1848

THE FRENCH REVOLUTION of 1789 has long stood as a watershed in the history of modern Europe. Although the revolution began with the rather moderate aim of creating a constitution, it developed into a struggle between the forces of republicanism and the *ancien regime.* The city of Paris played a formative role in the revolutionary spirit of late-eighteenth-century France. However, Paris was again visited by revolutions in 1830, 1848, 1871, and 1968. How is it possible that one European city should serve as the heart of so much revolutionary activity?

Although each revolution was precipitated by different forces, there is little doubt that the intellectuals, professionals, artisans, commoners, and students of Paris were the engines of social, political, and economic change. In each instance, there were specific grievances that needed to be addressed by the government. In 1789, near financial collapse led Louis XVI to convoke the Estates General. Ten years later, the *ancien regime* had been destroyed. In 1830, the Bourbons were overthrown and replaced by the more liberal regime of Louis-Philippe. 1848 was a revolutionary year throughout Europe. The euphoria that brought Louis-Philippe to the throne was short-lived, and those students and workers who had fought on the barricades in 1830 remained unrepresented. On March 18, 1871, the revolutionary workers of Paris barricaded the streets and established the Commune. The French government fled to Versailles and declared war on Paris. Almost a century later, in May 1968, students at the Sorbonne fought against the "system," and the people of Paris sided with the students. In the end, 12 million workers went on strike and more than 120 factories were occupied.

The images and documents in the *Revolutionary Paris* Digital History Feature at www.wwnorton.com/wciv highlight the similarities between the French Revolution of 1789 and the subsequent revolutions up to the student protests of 1968. As you explore the *Revolutionary Paris* feature, consider the following:

• In what ways did the "language" of revolution change between 1789 and 1968?

• What social, political, economic, and intellectual forces made Paris such a focus of revolutionary activity?

• Is there any continuity between these various revolutions, or were they all the result of specific historical circumstances?

• How did the student revolt at the Sorbonne in 1968 serve as a rallying point for the workers of Paris?

CHAPTER NINETEEN

THE INDUSTRIAL
REVOLUTION AND
NINETEENTH-
CENTURY SOCIETY

THE FRENCH REVOLUTION TRANSFORMED the political and diplomatic landscape of Europe suddenly and dramatically. The transformation of industry came more gradually. By the 1830s or 1840s, however, writers and social thinkers were increasingly aware of unexpected and extraordinary changes in their economic world. They spoke of an "industrial revolution," one that seemed to parallel the ongoing revolution in politics. The term has stayed with us. The Industrial Revolution spanned the hundred years after 1780. It represented the first breakthrough from an agricultural, artisanal, and overwhelmingly rural economy to one characterized by larger-scale manufacturing, more capital-intensive enterprises, and urbanization. It involved new sources of energy and power, faster transportation, mechanization, higher productivity, and new ways of organizing human labor. It triggered social changes with revolutionary consequences for the West and its relationship with the world.

Of all the changes, perhaps the most revolutionary came at the very root of human endeavor: new forms of energy. Over the space of two or three generations, a society and an economy that had drawn on water, wind, and wood for most of its energy needs came to depend on steam engines and coal. In 1800, the world produced 10 million tons of coal. In 1900, it produced 1 billion: one hundred times more. The Industrial Revolution brought the beginning of the "fossil fuel age." It shattered the constraints of previous times, it opened an era of unprecedented economic growth, and it began to alter irrevocably the balance of humanity and the environment. Within a few more generations, by the end of the nineteenth century, the new energy regime would include oil and electricity—but historians refer to that period as the second Industrial Revolution.

Machines gripped contemporaries' imaginations, dazzling some observers and disquieting others. Mechanization made possible enormous gains in productivity in some sectors. In so doing it shifted the basis of the economy, creating entirely new livelihoods and industrial regions while rendering others obsolete. Yet the "revolution" did not lie in machines themselves. Instead, it lay in the mushrooming growth of new economic system based on mobilizing capital and labor on a much larger scale. Its sweeping effects redistributed wealth, influence, and power. It created new social classes and produced new social tensions.

It also prompted deep-seated cultural shifts. The English cultural critic Raymond Williams has pointed out that in the eighteenth century, "industry" referred to a human

FOCUS QUESTIONS

• Why did the Industrial Revolution first take hold in Britain?

• How was the Industrial Revolution different on the Continent?

 • What were the consequences of industrialization?

• How did working- and middle-class lives differ?

quality: a hard-working woman was "industrious;" an ambitious clerk showed "industry." By the middle of the nineteenth century, "industry" had come to mean an economic system, one that followed its own inner logic and worked on its own—seemingly independent of humans. This is our modern understanding of the term, and it was born during the early nineteenth century. As the Industrial Revolution altered the foundations of the economy, it also changed the very assumptions with which people approached economics and the ways in which they regarded the role of human beings in the economy. These new assumptions could foster a sense of power—but also anxieties about powerlessness.

> The "revolution" did not lie in machines themselves. Instead, it lay in the mushrooming growth of new economic system based on mobilizing capital and labor on a much larger scale.

Living as we do in the early twenty-first century, an age of economic and technological transformations, we may identify with the 1840s' sense of extraordinary, far-reaching, and little-understood change. We feel the economic and social world shifting but are unable to grasp the effects, and the changes are simultaneously exhilarating and unsettling. The cascading effects of new technologies, new forms of communication, and new economic imperatives make it difficult to differentiate results from causes. Are new technologies the driving force of change, or are they the effects of other structural transformations? What sectors of the economy and which kinds of employment will expand and which become obsolete? Will dizzying rises in productivity benefit workers? Will all social groups share in economic growth? These questions and others that haunt us today arose during the first Industrial Revolution. Only in retrospect can we piece together the answers.

THE INDUSTRIAL REVOLUTION IN BRITAIN, 1760–1850

> Why did the Industrial Revolution first take hold in Britain?

Great Britain in the eighteenth century had a fortunate combination of natural, economic, and cultural resources. It was a small and secure island nation with a robust empire and control over crucial lanes across the oceans. It had ample supplies of coal, rivers, and a well-developed network of canals—all of which proved important at different stages of early industrialization.

Industrialization's roots lay in agriculture. By the middle of the eighteenth century, agriculture in Britain was more thoroughly commercialized than it was elsewhere. British agriculture had been transformed by a combination of new techniques, new crops, and changes in patterns of property holding, especially the "enclosure" of fields and pastures, which turned small holdings, and in many cases commonly held lands, into large fenced tracts that were privately owned and individually managed by commercial landlords. The British Parliament encouraged enclosure with a series of bills in the second half of the eighteenth century. Commercialized agriculture was more productive, and yielded more food for a growing and increasingly urban population. Last, commercialized agriculture produced higher profits and more wealth for a class of landed investors, wealth that would be invested in industry.

A key precondition for industrialization was Britain's growing supply of available capital, in the forms of private wealth and well-developed banking and credit institutions. London had become the leading center for international trade, and the city was a headquarters for the transfer of raw material, capital, and manufactured products throughout the world. This made capital more readily available to underwrite new economic enterprises, and eased the transfer of money and goods—importing, for instance, silks from points east or Egyptian and North American cottons.

Social and cultural conditions also encouraged investment in enterprises. In Britain far more than on the Continent, the pursuit of wealth was perceived to be a worthy goal. Since the Renaissance the nobility of Europe had cultivated the notion of "gentlemanly" conduct, in part to hold the line against those moving up from below. British aristocrats, whose ancient privileges were meager when compared with those of Continental nobles, respected commoners with a talent for making money and did not hesitate to invest themselves. Growing domestic and international markets also made eighteenth-century Britain prosperous. The British were voracious consumers. The court elite followed and bought up yearly fashions, and so did most of Britain's landed and professional society. "Nature may be satis-

WHY DID THE INDUSTRIAL REVOLUTION FIRST TAKE HOLD IN BRITAIN?

THE INDUSTRIAL REVOLUTION IN BRITAIN, 1760–1850   531

fied with little," one London entrepreneur declared. "But it is the wants of fashion and the desire of novelties that causes trade." The country's small size and the fact that it was an island encouraged the development of a well-integrated domestic market.

Foreign markets promised even greater returns than domestic ones, though with greater risks. British foreign policy responded to its commercial needs. At the end of every major eighteenth-century war, Britain wrested overseas territories from its enemies. At the same time, Britain was penetrating hitherto unexploited territories, such as India and South America, in search of further potential markets and resources. Production for export rose by 80 percent between 1750 and 1770; production for domestic consumption gained just 7 percent over the same period. The British possessed a merchant marine capable of transporting goods around the world, and a navy practiced in the art of protecting its commercial fleets. By the 1780s, Britain's markets, together with its fleet and its established position at the center of world commerce, gave its entrepreneurs unrivaled opportunities for trade and profit.

> By the 1780s, Britain's markets, together with its fleet and its established position at the center of world commerce, gave its entrepreneurs unrivaled opportunities for trade and profit.

INNOVATION IN THE TEXTILE INDUSTRIES

The Industrial Revolution began with dramatic technological leaps in a few well-placed industries, the first of which was cotton textiles. The industry was already well established. Tariffs prohibiting imports of East Indian cottons, which Parliament had imposed to protect British woolen goods, had spurred the manufacture of British cotton. British textile manufacturers imported raw materials from India and the American South, and borrowed patterns from Indian spinners and weavers. What, then, were the "revolutionary" breakthroughs?

In 1733, John Kay's invention of the flying shuttle speeded the process of weaving. The task of spinning thread, however, had not kept up. A series of comparatively simple mechanical devices eliminated this spinning-to-weaving bottleneck. The most important device was the spinning jenny, invented by James Hargreaves, a carpenter and hand-loom weaver, in 1764 (patented 1770). The spinning jenny, named after the inventor's wife, was a compound spinning wheel, capable of producing sixteen threads at once—though the threads were not strong enough to be used for the longitudinal fibers, or warp, of cotton cloth. The invention of the water frame by Richard Arkwright, a barber, in 1769, made it possible to produce both warp and woof (latitudinal fibers) in great quantity. In 1799 Samuel Compton invented the spinning mule, which combined the features of both the jenny and the frame. All of these important technological changes were accomplished by the end of the eighteenth century.

The water frame and the spinning mule had enormous advantages over the spinning wheel. A jenny could spin from six to twenty-four times more yarn than a hand spinner. By the end of the eighteenth century, a mule could produce two to three hundred times more. Just as important, the new machines made better-quality—stronger and finer—thread. These machines revolutionized production across the textile industry. Last, the cotton gin, invented by the American Eli Whitney in 1793, mechanized the process of separating cotton seeds from the fiber, thereby speeding up the production of cotton and reducing its price. The supply of cotton fibers could now expand to keep pace with rising demand from cotton cloth manufacturers. This cotton gin had many effects, including, paradoxically, changing the economics of slavery in the United States. The cotton-producing slave plantations in the American south became significantly more profitable, their labor now enmeshed in the very brisk and lucrative trade with merchant exporters of raw cotton and manufacturers who produced cotton textiles in the northern United States and England. From 1780 on, British cotton textiles flooded the world market.

The explosive growth of textiles prompted a debate about the benefits and "tyranny" of the new industries. The British Romantic poet William Blake famously wrote in biblical terms of the textile mills' blight on the English countryside.

> And did the Countenance Divine
> Shine forth upon our clouded hills?
> And was Jerusalem builded here
> Among these dark Satanic mills?

POPULATION DENSITY, 1801
- 390–800 people per square mile
- 260–389 people per square mile
- 150–259 people per square mile
- Under 150 people per square mile
- ◉ Major town
- ⚓ Major port
- Principal canal, 1801
- Principal railway, 1851
- Coalfield
- I Iron ore mining
- C Copper mining
- L Lead mining
- T Tin mining

Area of detail
EUROPE
AFRICA

THE FIRST INDUSTRIAL NATION

The Industrial Revolution first took hold in Great Britain. How did its size and status as an island effect industrialization? Why did Great Britain build its first railroad between Durham and Darlington? Why did the railroad system expand more quickly in Great Britain than on the continent?

By the 1830s, the British House of Commons was holding hearings on employment and working conditions in factories, recording testimony about working days that stretched from 3:00 A.M. to 10:00 P.M., the employment of very small children, and workers who lost hair and fingers in the mills' machinery. Women and children counted for roughly two thirds of the labor force in textiles. The principle of regulating any labor (and emphatically that of adult men), however, was controversial. Only gradually did a series of "factory acts" prohibit hiring children under nine and limit the labor of persons under eighteen to ten hours a day.

COAL AND IRON

Meanwhile, decisive changes were transforming the production of iron. As in the textile industry, many important technological changes came during the eighteenth century. A series of innovations (coke smelting, rolling, and puddling) enabled the British to substitute coal, which they had in abundance, for wood, which was scarce and inefficient, to heat molten metal and make iron. The new "pig iron" was higher quality and could be used in building an enormous variety of iron products: machines, engines, railway tracks, agricul-

WHY DID THE INDUSTRIAL REVOLUTION FIRST TAKE HOLD IN BRITAIN?

THE INDUSTRIAL REVOLUTION IN BRITAIN, 1760–1850   533

Cotton Mill in Lancashire, 1834. Women and girls prepare the cotton by carding, drawing, and roving the fibers.

tural implements, and hardware. Those iron products became, literally, the infrastructure of industrialization. Britain found itself able to export both coal and iron to rapidly expanding markets around the industrializing regions of the world. Between 1814 and 1852, exports of British iron doubled, rising to over 1 million tons of iron, over half of the world's total production.

Rising demand for coal required mining deeper veins. In 1711, Thomas Newcomen had devised a steam engine for pumping water from mines. Though it was immensely valuable to the coal industry, its usefulness in other industries was limited by the amount of fuel it consumed. In 1763, James Watt, who made scientific instruments at the University of Glasgow, was asked to repair a model of the Newcomen engine. While tinkering with the machine, he hit on a way to improve it: adding a separate chamber to condense the steam eliminated the need to cool the cylinder. Watt patented his first engine incorporating this device in 1769. The steam engine decisively transformed the nineteenth century world with one application: the steam-driven locomotive. Railroads revolutionized industry, markets, public and private financing, and ordinary people's conceptions of space and time.

> British engineers, industrialists, and investors were quick to realize the global opportunities available in constructing railways overseas; a large part of Britain's industrial success in the later nineteenth century came through building other nations' infrastructures.

THE COMING OF RAILWAYS

Building railways became a massive enterprise and a risky but potentially profitable opportunity for investment. No sooner did the first combined passenger and goods service open in 1830, operating between Liverpool and Manchester, England, than plans were formulated and money pledged to extend rail systems throughout Europe, the Americas, and beyond. In 1830, there were no more than a few dozen miles of railway in the world. By 1840, there were over 4,500 miles; by 1850, over 23,000. British engineers, industrialists, and investors were quick to realize the global opportunities available in constructing railways overseas; a large part of Britain's industrial success in the later nineteenth century came

THE FACTORY SYSTEM, SCIENCE, AND MORALITY: TWO VIEWS

Reactions to the Industrial Revolution and the factory system it produced ranged from celebration to horror. Dr. Andrew Ure, a Scottish professor of chemistry, was fascinated with these nineteenth-century applications of Enlightenment science. He believed that the new machinery and its products would create a new society of wealth, abundance, and, ultimately, stability through the useful regimentation of production.

Friedrich Engels (1820–1895) was one of the many socialists to criticize Dr. Ure as shortsighted and complacent in his outlook. Engels was himself part of a factory-owning family and so was able to examine the new industrial cities at close range. He provides a classic nineteenth-century analysis of industrialization. The Condition of the Working Class in England *is compellingly written, angry, and revealing about middle-class concerns of the time, including female labor.*

DR. ANDREW URE

This island [Britain] is preeminent among civilized nations for the prodigious development of its factory wealth, and has been therefore long viewed with a jealous admiration by foreign powers. This very pre-eminence, however, has been contemplated in a very different light by many influential members of our own community, and has even been denounced by them as the certain origin of innumerable evils to the people, and of revolutionary convulsions to the state. . . .

The blessings which physico-mechanical science has bestowed on society, and the means it has still in store for ameliorating the lot of mankind, has been too little dwelt upon; while, on the other hand, it has been accused of lending itself to the rich capitalists as an instrument for harassing the poor, and of exacting from the operative an accelerated rate of work. It has been said, for example, that the steam-engine now drives the power-looms with such velocity as to urge on their attendant weavers at the same rapid pace; but that the hand-weaver, not being subjected to this restless agent, can throw his shuttle and move his treddles at his convenience. There is, however, this difference in the two cases, that in the factory, every member of the loom is so adjusted, that the driving force leaves the attendant nearly nothing at all to do, certainly no muscular fatigue to sustain, while it produces for him good, unfailing wages, besides a healthy workshop *gratis*: whereas the non-factory weaver, having everything to execute by muscular exertion, finds the labour irksome, makes in consequence innumerable short pauses, separately of little account, but great when added together; earns therefore proportionally low wages, while he loses his health by poor diet and the dampness of his hovel.

Andrew Ure. *The Philosophy of Manufacturers: or, An Exposition of the Scientific, Moral and Commercial Economy of the Factory System of Great Britain, 1835,* as cited in J. T. Ward, *The Factory System,* v. 1. (New York: Barnes and Noble, 1970), pp. 140–41.

FRIEDRICH ENGELS

Histories of the modern development of the cotton industry, such as those of Ure, Baines, and others, tell on every page of technical innovations. . . . In a well-ordered society such improvements would indeed be welcome, but social war rages unchecked and the benefits derived from these improvements are ruthlessly monopolized by a few persons. . . . Every improvement in machinery leads to unemployment, and the greater the technical improvement the greater the unemployment. Every improvement in machinery affects a number of workers in the same way as a commercial crisis and leads to want, distress, and crime. . . .

Let us examine a little more closely the process whereby machine- continually supesedes hand-labour. When spinning or weaving machinery is installed practically all that is left to be done by the hand is the piecing together of broken threads, and the machine does the rest. This task calls for nimble fingers rather than muscular strength. The labour of grown men is not merely unnecessary but actually unsuitable. . . . The greater the degree to which physical labour is displaced by the introduction of machines worked by water- or steam-power, the fewer grown men need be employed. In any case women and children will work for lower wages than men and, as has already been observed, they are more skillful at piecing than grown men. Consequently it is women and children who are employed to do this work. . . . When women work in factories, the most important result is the dissolution of family ties. If a woman works for twelve or thirteen hours a day in a factory and her husband is employed either in the same establishment or in some other works, what is the fate of the children? They lack parental care and control. . . . It is not difficult to imagine that they are left to run wild.

Friedrich Engels, *The Condition of the Working Class in England in 1844*, trans. and eds. W. O. Henderson and W. H. Chaloner (New York: Macmillan, 1958), pp. 150–51, 158, 160.

---

through building other nations' infrastructures. The English contractor Thomas Brassey, for instance, built railways in Italy, Canada, Argentina, India, and Australia.

Throughout the world, a veritable army of construction workers built the railways. In Britain, they were called "navvies," derived from "navigator," a term first used for the construction workers on Britain's eighteenth-century canals. Navvies were a rough lot, living with a few women in temporary encampments as they migrated across the countryside. Often they were immigrant workers and faced local hostility. A sign posted by local residents outside a mine in Scotland in 1845 warned the Irish navvies to get "off the ground and out of the country" in a week, or else be driven out "by the strength of our armes and a good pick shaft." Later in the century railway building projects in Africa and the Americas were lined with camps of immigrant Indian and Chinese laborers, who also became targets of nativist (a term that means opposed to foreigners) anger.

Steam engines, textile machines, new ways of making iron, and railways—all these were interconnected. Changes in one area endorsed changes in another. Pumps run by steam engines made it possible to mine deeper veins of coal; steam-powered railways made it possible to transport coal. Mechanization fueled the production of iron for machines and the mining of coal to run steam engines. The railway boom multiplied the demand for iron products: rails, locomotives, carriages, signals, switches, and the iron to make all of these. Building railroads called for engineering expertise: scaling mountains, designing bridges and tunnels. Railway construction, which required capital investment beyond the capacity of any single individual, forged new kinds of public and private financing. The scale of production expanded and the tempo of economic activity quickened, spurring the search for more coal, the production

CHRONOLOGY

THE INDUSTRIAL REVOLUTION IN GREAT BRITAIN, 1733–1825

Invention of the fly shuttle	1733
Invention of the spinning jenny	1764
Invention of the water frame	1769
Invention of the steam engine	1769
Invention of the spinning mule	1779
Invention of the cotton gin	1793
First railroad built	1825

Navvies and Steam Excavation Machine. Despite help from new construction technology, much of the work on mid-18th century railways was manual labor done by navvies, many of whom were immigrant workers.

of more iron, the mobilization of more capital, and the recruitment of more labor. Steam and speed were becoming the foundation of the economy and of a new way of life.

The Industrial Revolution on the Continent

How was the Industrial Revolution different on the Continent?

Continental Europe, with its different natural, economic, and political resources, followed a different path. For a variety of reasons, changes along the lines seen in Britain did not occur until the 1830s. Britain's transportation system was highly developed; those of

France and Germany were not. Much of Central Europe was divided into small principalities, each with its own set of tolls and tariffs, which complicated the transportation of raw materials or manufactured goods over any considerable distance. The Continent had fewer raw materials, coal in particular, than Britain. Capital, too, was less readily available. Early British industrialization was underwritten by private wealth; this was less feasible elsewhere. Different patterns of landholding formed obstacles to the commercialization of agriculture. In the east, serfdom was a powerful disincentive to labor-saving innovations. In the west, especially in France, the large number of small peasants, or farmers, stayed put on the land.

The wars of the French Revolution and Napoleon did hasten legal changes and the consolidation of state power, but they disrupted economies. During the eighteenth century, the population had grown and mechanization had begun in a few key industries. The ensuing political upheaval, the financial strains of warfare, and the thundering hooves of armies, however, did virtually nothing to help economic development. The ban on

British-shipped cotton stalled the growth of cotton textiles for decades, though the armies' greater demand for woolen cloth kept that sector of textiles humming. Iron processing increased to satisfy the military's rising needs, but techniques for making iron remained largely unchanged. Probably the revolutionary change most beneficial to industrial advance in Europe was the removal of previous restraints on the movement of capital and labor—for example, the abolition of craft guilds and the reduction of tariff barriers across the Continent.

After 1815, a number of factors combined to change the economic climate. In those regions with a well-established commercial and industrial base—the northeast of France, Belgium, and swaths of territory across the Rhineland, Saxony, Silesa and northern Bohemia (see map on p. 547)—population growth further boosted economic development. Rising population did not by itself produce industrialization, however: in Ireland, where other necessary factors were absent, more people meant less food.

Transportation improved. The Austrian empire added over 30,000 miles of roads between 1830 and 1847; France built not only new roads but 2,000 miles of canals. These improvements, combined with the construction of railroads in the 1830s and 1840s, opened up new markets and encouraged new methods of manufacturing. It is nonetheless the case that in many of the Continent's manufacturing regions, industrialists could long continue to tap large pools of skilled but inexpensive labor. Thus older methods of putting out industry and handwork persisted alongside new-model factories.

In what other ways was the Continental model of industrialization different? Governments played a considerably more direct role in industrialization. France and Prussia, for instance, granted considerable subsidies to private companies that built railroads. After 1849, the Prussian state took on the task itself, as did Belgium and, later, Russia—an undertaking that required importing material and expertise but that often yielded

Silk Weavers of Lyons, 1850. The first significant working-class uprisings in nineteenth-century France occurred in Lyons in 1831 and 1834. Note the domestic character of the working conditions.

significant profits. In Prussia, the state also operated a large proportion of that country's mines. Governments on the Continent provided incentives for and laws favorable to industrialization. Limited-liability laws, to take the most important example, allowed investors to own shares in a corporation or company without becoming liable for the company's debts—and it enabled enterprises to recruit many small investors to put together the capital for massive investments in railroads, other forms of industry, and commerce. Finally, Continental Europeans also actively promoted invention and technological development. They were willing for the state to establish educational systems whose aim, among others, was to produce a well-trained elite capable of assisting in the development of industrial technology. In sum, what Britain had produced almost by chance, the Europeans began to reproduce by design.

> It is nonetheless the case that in many of the Continent's manufacturing regions, industrialists could long continue to tap large pools of skilled but inexpensive labor. Thus older methods of putting out industry and handwork persisted alongside new-model factories.

INDUSTRIALIZATION AFTER 1850

Until 1850 Britain remained the preeminent industrial power. Between 1850 and 1870, however, France, Germany, Belgium, and the United States emerged as challengers to the power and place of British manufacturers. The British iron industry remained the largest in the

THE INDUSTRIAL REVOLUTION

Why were the effects of the Industrial Revolution more rapidly apparent in Great Britain and in north central Europe? How did the presence of an extensive railroad system help to accelerate industrialization? What effects did the Industrial Revolution have on urban population densities?

Map labels

RUSSIAN EMPIRE

Moscow

St. Petersburg

NORWAY

SWEDEN

Upsala
Stockholm

DENMARK

Copenhagen

BALTIC SEA

NORTH SEA

Warsaw
Posen
Lodz
SILESIA
Breslau
Cracow
Lemberg

GERMAN EMPIRE

Hamburg
Bremen
Berlin
Dresden
Leipzig
Kassel
Cologne
RUHR
Eisenach
Zwickau
Chemnitz
Prague
Pilsen
Frankfurt
Nuremberg
SAAR
Karlsruhe
Stuttgart
Strasbourg
Mulhouse

AUSTRIAN EMPIRE

Budapest
Vienna
Steyr
Munich
SWITZ.
Zurich
Basel

BLACK SEA

OTTOMAN EMPIRE

NETHERLANDS

Amsterdam

BELGIUM

Brussels
Liège

FRANCE

Le Havre
Paris
Amiens
Orleans
Tours
Limoges
Nantes

Lyons
Avignon
Marseilles

ITALY

Turin
Milan
Florence
Livorno
Rome
Naples

MEDITERRANEAN SEA

Barcelona

Gijon
Santander
Bilbao
Oviedo

Madrid
Granada
Seville
Jerez

Lisbon

ATLANTIC OCEAN

UNITED KINGDOM

Glasgow
Darlington
Leeds
Sheffield
Liverpool
Manchester
Birmingham
Cardiff
London
Dublin

Scale

300 Miles
0   100   200   300
0   100   200   300 Kilometers

Inset map

Area of detail

EUROPE

AFRICA

Legend

PERCENT OF POPULATION LIVING IN CITIES OF 100,000 OR MORE

- 5 percent or less
- 6 to 10 percent
- 20 percent or more

— Railroads in 1850
□ Centers of industry
● Iron ore deposits
● Coal and lignite deposits

world (in 1870 Britain still produced half the world's pig iron), but it grew more slowly than did its counterparts in France or Germany. The first phase of the "industrial revolution," one economic historian reminds us, had been confined to a narrow set of industries, and can be summed up rather simply: "cheaper and better clothes (mainly made of cotton), cheaper and better metals (pig iron, wrought iron, and steel) and faster travel (mainly by rail)." The second half of the century brought changes farther afield, and in areas where the Great Britain's early advantages were no longer decisive. Transatlantic cable (starting in 1865) and the telephone (invented in 1876) laid the ground for a revolution in communications. New chemical processes, dyestuffs, and pharmaceuticals emerged. So did new sources of energy: electricity, in which the United States and Germany led both invention and commercial development; and oil, which was being refined in the 1850s and widely used by 1900. Among the early exploiters of Russian oil discoveries were the Swedish Nobel brothers and the French Rothschilds.

In eastern Europe, the nineteenth century brought different patterns of economic development. Spurred by the ever-growing demand for food and grain, large sections of eastern Europe developed into concentrated, commercialized agriculture regions which played the specific role of exporting food to the West. Many of those large agricultural enterprises were based on serfdom and remained so, in the face of increasing pressure for reform, until 1850.

Although industry continued to take a back seat to agriculture, eastern Europe had several important manufacturing regions. By the 1880s, the number of men and women employed in the cotton industry in the Austrian province of Bohemia exceeded that in the German state of Saxony. In the Czech region, textile industries, developed in the eighteenth century, continued to thrive. By the 1830s, there were machine-powered Czech cotton mills and iron works. In Russia, a factory industry producing coarse textiles—mostly linens—had grown up around Moscow. Many who labored in Russian industry actually remained serfs until the 1860s—about 40 percent of them employed in mines. Of the over eight hundred thousand Russians engaged in manufacturing by 1860, however, most were employed in small workshops of about forty persons.

By 1870, then, the core industrial nations of Europe included Great Britain, France, Germany, Italy, the Netherlands, and Switzerland. Austria stood at the margins. Russia, Spain, Bulgaria, Greece Hungary, Romania, and Serbia formed the industrial periphery—and some regions of these nations seemed virtually untouched by the advance of industry. What was more, even in Great Britain, the most fully industrialized nation, agricultural laborers still constituted the single largest occupational category in 1860 (although they formed only 9 percent of the overall population). In Russia, the number was 80 percent. "Industrial," moreover, did not mean automation or machine production, which long remained confined to a few sectors of the economy. As machines were introduced in some sectors to do specific tasks, they usually intensified the tempo of hand work in other sectors. Thus even in the industrialized regions, much work was still accomplished in tiny workshops—or at home.

> As machines were introduced in some sectors to do specific tasks, they usually intensified the tempo of handwork in other sectors. Thus even in the industrialized regions, much work was still accomplished in tiny workshops—or at home.

INDUSTRY AND EMPIRE

From an international perspective, nineteenth-century Europe was the most industrial region of the world. Europeans, particularly the British, jealously guarded their international advantages. They preferred to do so through financial leverage. Britain, France, and other European nations gained control of the national debts of China, the Ottoman empire, Egypt, Brazil, Argentina, and other non-European powers. They also supplied large loans to other states, which bound those nations to their European investors. If the debtor nations expressed discontent, as Egypt did in the 1830s when it attempted to establish its own cotton textile industry, they confronted financial pressure and shows of force. Coercion, however, was not always necessary or even one sided. Social change in other empires—China, Persia, and the Mughal empire of India, for example—made those empires newly vulnerable and created new opportunities for the European powers and their local partners. Ambitious local elites often reached agreements with Western governments or groups such as the British East India Company. These trade agreements transformed regional economies on terms that sent the greatest profits to Europe after a substantial gratuity to the Europeans' local partners. Where agreements could not be made, force prevailed, and Europe took territory and trade by conquest.

Industrialization tightened global links between Europe and the rest of the world, creating new networks of trade and interdependence. To a certain extent, the world

British Clipper Ships in Calcutta Harbor, 1860. Calcutta, a long-established city on the eastern coast of India, was one of the hubs of the British empire—a center for trade in cotton, jute, opium, and tea. The dazzling new clipper ships, first built in the 1830s and 1840s, were very fast and were central to the global economy of the nineteenth century.

economy divided between the producers of manufactured goods—Europe itself—and suppliers of the necessary raw materials and buyers of finished goods—everyone else. In 1811 Britain imported 3 percent of the wheat it consumed. By 1891, that portion had rise to 79 percent. Those simple percentages, in other words, dramatize the new interdependence of the nineteenth century; they illustrate as well as any statistics can how ordinary Britons' lives—like their counterparts' in other nations—were embedded in an increasingly global economy.

THE SOCIAL CONSEQUENCES OF INDUSTRIALIZATION

What were the consequences of industrialization?

Population growth was one important factor in industrial development. By any measure, the nineteenth century constituted a turning point in European demo-

graphic history. In 1800 the population of Europe as a whole was estimated roughly at 205 million. By 1850, it had risen to 274 million; by 1900, 414 million; on the eve of World War I it was 480 million. (Over the same span of time, world population went from about 900 million to 1.6 billion.) Britain, with its comparatively high standard of living, saw its population rise from 16 million to 27 million. Increases, however, came in the largely rural regions as well. In Russia, the population rose from 39 to 60 million during the same period.

POPULATION

How do historians explain this population explosion? Some speculate that the cyclical potency of microbes made certain fatal diseases less virulent. From 1796 on, Edward Jenner's technique of vaccinating for smallpox gradually gained acceptance and made the disease less fatal. Improved sanitation helped to curb cholera, though not until much later in the nineteenth century. Governments were better able and more determined to monitor and improve the lives of their people. Less expensive foods of high nutritional value—most notably the potato—and the ability to transport foodstuffs cheaply by railroad meant that many European populations were better nourished and so less susceptible to debilitating illness. But real changes in mortality and life expectancy only came late in the nineteenth or the beginning of the twentieth century. In 1880, the average male life expectancy in the city of Berlin was no more than 30 years, and in rural districts nearby it was 43. Historians now attribute the population growth of the nineteenth century to rising fertility rather than to falling mortality. Men and women married earlier, which raised fertility (the number of births per woman) and family size. The spread of rural manufacturing allowed couples in the countryside to marry and set up households—even before they inherited any land. And population growth has its own dynamic, increasing the number of young and fertile people, thus raising significantly increasing the ratio of births to total population.

LIFE ON THE LAND: THE PEASANTRY

Even as the West grew more industrial, the majority of people continued to live on the land. Conditions in the countryside were harsh. Peasants—as farmers of humble origin were called in Europe—still did most of their sowing and harvesting by hand. Millions of tiny farms produced, at most, a bare subsistence living, and families wove, spun, made knives, and sold butter to make ends meet. The average daily diet for an entire family in a "good" year might

> By many measures, living conditions for rural inhabitants of many areas in Europe grew worse in the first half of the nineteenth century.

amount to no more than two or three pounds of bread—a total of about 3,000 calories daily. By many measures, living conditions for rural inhabitants of many areas in Europe grew worse in the first half of the nineteenth century. Rising population put more pressure on the land. Over the course of the century some 37 million people—most of them peasants—left Europe, eloquent testimony to the bleakness of rural life. They settled where land was plentiful and inexpensive: the vast majority in the United States and others in places from South America to Australia.

The most tragic combination of famine, poverty, and population in the nineteenth century came to Ireland in the Great Famine of 1845–1849. Potatoes, which had come to Europe from the New World, transformed the diets of European peasants, providing much more nutrition for less money than corn and grain. They also grew more densely, an enormous advantage for peasants scraping a living from small plots of land. Nowhere did they become more important than in Ireland, where the

climate and soil made growing grain difficult, and both overpopulation and poverty were rising. When a fungus hit the potato crop, first in 1845 and again, fatally, in 1846 and 1847, no alternate foods were at hand. At least one million Irish died of starvation, of dysentery from spoiled foods, or of fever, which spread through villages and the overcrowded poorhouses. Before the famine, tens of thousands of Irish were already crossing the Atlantic to North America; they accounted for one third of all voluntary migration to the New World. In the ten years after 1845, 1.5 people million left Ireland for good. The potato blight also struck in Germany, Scotland, and the Netherlands, but with less catastrophic results. Europe had known deadly famines for centuries. The Irish famine, however, came at a time when many thought that starvation was receding into the past, and it illustrated just how vulnerable the nineteenth-century countryside remained to bad harvests and shortages.

Changes in the land depended on politics and law. States that were more sympathetic to commercialized agriculture passed legislation making it simpler to transfer and reorganize land, encouraging the elimination of small farms and the creation of larger, more efficient units of production. European serfdom, which bound hundreds of thousands of men, women, and children to particular estates for generations, made it difficult to buy and sell land freely, and created an obstacle to the commercialization and consolidation of agriculture. Yet the opposite was also so the case. In France, peasant landholders who had benefited from the the French Revolution's sale of lands and laws on inheritance stayed in the countryside, continuing to work their small farms. Although French peasants were poor, they could sustain themselves on the land. This had important consequences. France suffered less agricultural distress, even in the 1840s, than did other European countries; migration from country to city was slower than in the other nations; far fewer peasants left France for other countries.

Industrialization changed the countryside in other forms. Improved communication networks not only gave rural populations a keener sense of events and opportunities elsewhere, but also made it possible for governments to intrude into the lives of these men and women to a degree previously impossible. Central bureaucracies now found it easier to collect taxes from the peasantry and to conscript sons of peasant families into armies. Rural cottage industries faced competition from

THE IRISH FAMINE:
INTERPRETATIONS AND RESPONSES

When the potato blight appeared for the second year in a row in 1846, famine came to Ireland. The first letter excerpted below is from Father Theopold Mathew, a local priest, to Charles Edward Trevelyan, the English official in charge of Irish relief. While Father Mathew attributes the potato blight to "divine providence," he also worries that businessmen opposed to government intervention in a free market will let the Irish starve.

The second and third excerpts are from letters that Trevelyan wrote to other British officials concerned with the crisis. Trevelyan makes clear that while he does not want the government to bear responsibility for starving its people, he believes that the famine will work to correct "social evils" in Ireland, by which he means everything from families having too many children to farmers failing to plant the right crops. In the nineteenth century, reactions to food crises were reshaped by the rise of new economic doctrines, changing social assumptions, and the shifting relationship between religion and government. These letters provide a good example of those changes and how they affected government officials.

REV. THEOBALD MATHEW TO TREVELYAN

Cork, 7 August 1846.

Divine providence, in its inscrutable ways, has again poured out upon us the viol [sic] of its wrath. A blot more destructive than the simoom of the desert has passed over the land, and the hopes of the poor potato-cultivators are totally blighted, and the food of a whole nation has perished. On the 27th of last month I passed from Cork to Dublin, and this doomed plant bloomed in all the luxuriance of an abundant harvest. Returning on the 3rd instant, I beheld, with sorrow, one wide waste of putrefying vegetation. In many places the wretched people were seated on the fences of their decaying gardens, wringing their hands and wailing bitterly the destruction that had left them foodless.

It is not to harrow your benevolent feelings, dear Mr. Trevelyan, I tell this tale of woe. No, but to excite your sympathy in behalf of our miserable peasantry. It is rumoured that the capitalists in the corn and flour trade are endeavoring to induce government not to protect the people from famine, but to leave them at their mercy. I consider this a cruel and unjustifiable interference.

TREVELYAN TO ROUTH

Treasury, 3 February 1846.

That indirect permanent advantages will accrue to Ireland from the scarcity and the measures taken for its relief, I entertain no doubt; but if we were to pursue these incidental objects to the neglect of any of the precautions immediately required to save the people from actual starvation, our responsibility would be fearful indeed. Besides, the greatest improvement of all which could take place in Ireland would be to teach the people to depend upon themselves for developing the resources of their country, instead of having recourse to the assistance of the government on every occasion. Much has been done of late years to put this important matter on its proper footing; but if a firm stand is not made against the prevailing disposition to take advantage of this crisis to break down all barriers, the true permanent interest of the country will, I am convinced, suffer in a manner which will be irreparable in our time.

TREVELYAN TO LORD MONTEAGLE

To the Right Hon. Lord Monteagle.

My Dear Lord,

I need not remind your lordship that the ability even of the most powerful government is extremely limited in dealing with a social evil of this description. It forms no part of the functions of government to provide supplies of food or to increase the productive powers of the land. In the great institution of the business of society, it falls to the share of government to protect the merchant and the agriculturist in the free exercise of their respective employments; but not itself to carry on those employments; and the condition of a community depends upon the result of the efforts which each member of it makes in his private and individual capacity. . . .

I must give expression to my feelings by saying that I think I see a bright light shining in the distance through the dark cloud which at present hangs over Ireland. A remedy has been already applied to that portion of the maladies of Ireland which was traceable to political causes, and the morbid habits which still to a certain extent survive are gradually giving way to a more healthy action. The deep and inveterate root of social evil remains, and I hope I am not guilty of irreverence in thinking that, this being altogether beyond the power of man, the cure has been applied by the direct stroke of an all-wise providence in a manner as unexpected and unthought of as it is likely to be effectual. God grant that we may rightly perform our part and not turn into a curse what was intended for a blessing. The ministers of religion and especially the pastors of the Roman Catholic Church, who possess the largest share of influence over the people of Ireland, have well performed their part; and although few indications appear from any proceedings which have yet come before the public that the landed proprietors have even taken the first step of preparing for the conversion of the land now laid down to potatoes to grain cultivation, I do not despair of seeing this class in society still taking the lead which their position requires of them, and preventing the social revolution from being so extensive as it otherwise must become.

Believe me, my dear lord, yours very sincerely,

C. E. Trevelyan. Treasury, 9 October 1846.

Noel Kissane. *The Irish Famine: A Documentary History* (Dublin: National Library of Ireland, 1995), pp. 17, 47, 50–51.

---

factory-produced goods, which meant less work or lower rates and falling incomes for families. Changes in the market could usher in prosperity, or they could bring entire regions to the verge of starvation.

Vulnerability often led to political violence. Rural rebellions were common in the early nineteenth century. In southern England in the late 1820s, small farmers and day laborers joined forces to burn barns and haystacks protesting the introduction of threshing machines, a symbol of the new agricultural capitalism. In the southwest of France, peasants, at night and in disguise, attacked local authorities who had barred them from collecting wood in the forests. Similar rural disturbances broke out across Europe in the 1830s and 1840s: insurrections against landlords, against "tithes," or taxes to the church, against laws curtailing customary rights, against unresponsive governments. Peasants were land poor, deep in debt, and precariously dependent on markets. More important, however, a government's inability to contend with rural misery made it look autocratic, indifferent, or inept—all political failings.

THE URBAN LANDSCAPE

The growth of cities was one of the most important facts in nineteenth-century social history, and one with significant cultural reverberations. Over the course of the nineteenth century, as we have seen, the overall population of Europe doubled. Urban populations rose sixfold. Like industrialization, urbanization generally moved from the northwest of Europe to the southeast, but it also followed very specific demands for resources, labor, and transportation. In mining and manufacturing areas, or along newly built railway lines, it sometimes seemed that cities (like Manchester, Birmingham, or Essen) sprang up from nowhere. Industrialization swelled the size of port cities such as

Danzig (modern Gdansk), Le Havre, and Rotterdam. Most striking to contemporaries was the very rapid expansion of Europe's old cities. Sometimes the rates of growth were dizzying. Between 1750 and 1850, London (Europe's largest city) grew from 676,000 to 2.3 million. The population of Paris went from 560,000 to 1.3 million, adding 120,000 new residents between 1841 and 1846 alone!

Almost all nineteenth-century cities were overcrowded and unhealthy, their largely medieval infrastructures strained by the burden of new population and the demands of industry. Construction lagged far behind population growth, especially in the working-class districts of the city. In many of the larger cities, old and new, working men and women who had left families behind in the country lived in temporary lodging houses. The poorest workers dwelt in wretched basement or attic rooms, often without any light or drainage. Governments gradually adopted measures in an attempt to cure the worst of these ills, if only to prevent the spread of catastrophic epidemics. Legislation was designed to rid cities of their worst slums by tearing them down, and to improve sanitary conditions by supplying both water and drainage. Yet by 1850, these projects had only just begun. Paris, perhaps better supplied with water than any other European city, had enough for no more than two baths per person per year; in London, human waste remained uncollected in two hundred fifty thousand domestic cesspools; in Manchester, fewer than a third of the dwellings were equipped with toilets of any sort.

INDUSTRY AND ENVIRONMENT IN THE NINETEENTH CENTURY

The Industrial Revolution began many of the environmental changes of the modern period. Nowhere were those changes more visible than in the burgeoning cities. Dickens' description of the choking air and polluted water of "Coketown," the fictional city in *Hard Times* is deservedly well known:

> It was a town of red brick, or of brick that would have been red if the smoke and ashes had allowed it. . . . It was a town of machines and tall chimneys, out of which interminable serpents of smoke trailed themselves forever and ever, and never got uncoiled. It had a black canal in it, and a river that ran purple with ill-smelling dye, and vast piles of building full of windows where there was a rattling and a trembling all day long . . .

Wood-fired manufacturing and heating for home had long spewed smoke across the skies, but the new concentration of industrial activity and the transition to coal made the air measurably worse. In London especially, where even homes switched to coal early, smoke from factories, railroads, and domestic chimneys hung heavily over the city, and the last third of the century brought the most intense pollution in its history. Over all of England, air pollution took an enormous toll in health, contributing to the bronchitis and tuberculosis that accounted for 25 percent of British deaths.

Toxic water—produced by industrial pollution and human waste—posed the second critical environmental hazard in urban areas. London and Paris led the way in building municipal sewage systems, though those emptied into the Thames and the Seine. Cholera, typhus, and tuberculosis were natural predators in areas without adequate sewage facilities or fresh water. The Rhine river, which flowed through central Europe's industrial heartland and intersected with the Ruhr, was thick with detritus from coal mining, iron-processing, and

Agricultural Disturbances. Violence erupted in southern England in 1830 in protest against the introduction of threshing machines.

Nineteenth Century Working-Class Housing. As cities grew, medieval neighborhoods with tiny narrow streets were cleared to make way for new, improved buildings such as the ones below.

the chemical industry. Spurred by several epidemics of cholera, in the late nineteenth century the major cities began to purify their water supplies, but conditions in the air, rivers, and land continued to worsen until at least the mid-twentieth century.

SOCIAL CHANGE: THE MIDDLE CLASSES

How did working- and middle-class lives differ?

The best windows onto the social world of the nineteenth century are the novels of the period, works such as Jane Austen's *Pride and Prejudice*, Victor Hugo's *Les Misérables*, Charles Dickens's *Hard Times* and *Oliver Twist*, or any of the scores of works by Honoré de Balzac—to mention just a few. These are sweeping panoramas of a society in transition, peopled with characters from the middle and working classes whose lives captured something distinctly new about the period. These writers were fascinated by social

The middle class was not one homogeneous unit, in terms of occupation or income. Movement within middle-class ranks was often possible in the course of one or two generations.

mobility, youthful ambition, and strategies for getting ahead in the changing social world. They traced shifts in the ways that society measured status, showing how the French and industrial revolutions had eroded hierarchies based on rank and privilege and given rise to new distinctions based on wealth or social class. They set out to capture (and often to caricature) new social values. Dickens's middle class characters (like Balzac's) are often heartless, rigid, obtuse, and materialistic. The French artist Honoré Daumier's famous caricatures of nineteenth-century lawyers are veritable portraits of power and arrogance. What can historians add to these artistic studies of middle and working-class life?

Who were the middle classes? (Another common term for this social group, the *bourgeoisie*, originally meant city (*bourg*) dweller.) The middle class was not one homogeneous unit, in terms of occupation or income. Movement within middle-class ranks was often possible in the course of one or two generations. Very few, however, moved from the working class into the middle class. Upward mobility was almost impossible without education, and education was a rare, though not unattainable, luxury for working-class children. Careers open to talents, that goal achieved by the

View of London with Saint Paul's Cathedral in the Distance by **William Henry Crome.** Despite the smog-filled skies and intense pollution, many entrepreneurs and politicians celebrated the new prosperity of the industrial revolution. As W.P. Rend, a Chicago businessman, wrote in 1892, "Smoke is the incense burning on the altars of industry. It is beautiful to me. It shows that men are changing the merely potential forces of nature into articles of comfort for humanity."

French Revolution, frequently meant opening jobs to middle-class young men who could pass exams. The examination system was an important path upward within government bureaucracies.

The journey from from middle class to aristocratic, landed society was equally difficult. In Britain, mobility of this sort was easier to achieve than on the Continent. William Gladstone, son of a Liverpool merchant, attended the exclusive educational preserves of Eton (a private boarding school) and Oxford University, married into the aristocratic Grenville family, and became prime minister of England. Yet Gladstone was an exception to the rule, even in Britain, and most upward mobility was much less spectacular.

Nevertheless, the European middle class helped sustain itself with the belief that it was possible to get ahead by means of intelligence, pluck, and serious devotion to work. The middle classes' claim to political power and cultural influence rested on arguments that they constituted a new and deserving social elite, superior to the common people yet sharply different from the older aristocracy. "Respectability" was key to the middle class outlook. It stood for many values. It meant financial independence, providing responsibly for one's family, avoiding gambling and debt. It suggested merit and character as opposed to aristocratic privilege, and hard work as opposed to living off noble estates. "Respectable" middle-class gentlemen might be wealthy, but they should live modestly and soberly, avoiding conspicuous consumption, lavish dress, womanizing and other forms of "dandyish" behavior associated with the aristocracy. We need to emphasize that these were aspirations, not

A Lawyer, by Honoré Daumier. Lawyers with their theatrical poses, dramatic robes, and displays of power, were among Daumier's favorite subjects, and he drew countless caricatures of the courtroom.

social realities. They nonetheless remained crucial to the middle-class sense of self and understanding of the world.

PRIVATE LIFE AND MIDDLE-CLASS IDENTITY

Family and home played a central role in forming middle-class identity. Few themes were more common in nineteenth-century fiction than men and women pursuing mobility and status by or through marriage. Families served intensely practical purposes: sons, nephews, and cousins were expected to assume responsibility in family firms when it came their turn, wives managed accounts, and parents-in-law provided business connections, credit, inheritance, and so on. The family's role in middle-class thought, however, did not arise only from these practical considerations; family was part of a larger world view. A well-governed household offered a counterpoint to the business and confusion of the world, and families offered continuity and tradition in a time of rapid change.

GENDER AND THE CULT OF DOMESTICITY

Wives and mothers were supposed to occupy a "separate sphere" of life, in which they lived in subordination to their spouses. "Man for the field and woman for the hearth; man for the sword and for the needle she. . . . All else confusion," wrote the British poet Alfred Lord Tennyson in 1847. These prescriptions were directly applied to young people. Boys were educated in secondary schools; girls at home. Throughout Europe, laws subjected women to their husbands' authority. The Napoleonic Code, a model for other countries after 1815, classified women, children, and the mentally ill together as legally incompetent. In Britain, a woman transferred all her property rights to her husband on marriage.

The idea or doctrine of "separate spheres", however, was meant to underscore that men's and women's spheres complemented each other. Thus, for instance middle-class writings were full of references to spiritual equality between men and women, and middle-class people wrote, proudly, of marriages in which the wife was a "companion" and "helpmate." It was understood that being a good wife and mother was a demanding task, requiring an elevated character. This belief, sometimes called the "cult of domesticity, was central to middle-class Victorian thinking about women. Home life, and by extension the woman's role in that life, were infused with new meaning.

As a housewife, a middle-class woman had the task of keeping the household functioning smoothly and harmoniously. She maintained the accounts and directed the activities of the servants. Having at least one servant was a mark of middle-class status, and in wealthier families governesses and nannies cared for children, idealized views of motherhood notwithstanding. The work of running and maintaining a home, however, was enormous. Linens and clothes had to be made and mended. Only the wealthy had the luxury of running water, and others had to carry and heat water for cooking, laundry, and cleaning. Heating with coal and lighting with kerosene involved hours of cleaning, and so on. If the "angel in the house" was a cultural ideal, it was partly because she had real economic value.

Outside the home, women had very few respectable options for earning a living. Unmarried women might act as companions or governesses—the British novelist Charlotte Brontë's heroine Jane Eyre did so and led a generally miserable life until "rescued" by marriage to her difficult employer. But nineteenth-century convictions about women's moral nature, combined as they were with middle-class aspirations to political leadership, encouraged middle-class wives to undertake voluntary charitable work or to campaign for social reform. Throughout Europe, a wide range of movements to improve conditions for the poor in schools and hospitals, for temperance, against prostitution, or for legislation on factory hours were often run by women. Florence Nightingale, who went to the Crimean Peninsula in Russia to nurse British soldiers fighting there in the 1850s, remains the most famous of those women, whose determination to right social wrongs compelled them to defy conventional notions of woman's "proper" sphere. Equally famous—or infamous, at the time—was the French female novelist George Sand (1804–1876), whose real name was Amandine Aurore Dupin Dudevant. Sand dressed like a man and smoked cigars, and her novels often told the tales of independent women thwarted by convention and unhappy marriage.

"PASSIONLESSNESS": GENDER AND SEXUALITY

"Victorian" ideas about sexuality are among the most remarked-on features of nineteenth-century culture. They have become virtually synonymous with anxiety, prudishness, and ignorance. An English mother counseling her daughter about her wedding night is said to have told her to "lie back and think of the Empire." Etiquette apparently required that piano legs be covered. Historians have tried to disentangle the teachings of etiquette books and marriage manuals from the actual beliefs of men and women. Equally important, they have sought to understand each on its own terms. Beliefs about sexuality followed from convictions, described above, concerning "separate spheres." Science reinforced the certainty that specific characteristics were inherent to each sex. Men and women had different social roles, and those differences were rooted in their bodies. Women were unsuited for higher education because their brains were smaller, or because their bodies were fragile. "Fifteen or 20 days of 28 (we may say nearly always) a woman is not only an invalid, but a wounded one. She ceaselessly suffers from love's eternal wound," wrote the well-known French author Jules Michelet about menstruation.

Scientists and doctors considered women's alleged moral superiority to be literally embodied in an absence of sexual feeling, or "passionlessness." By contrast, male sexual desire was natural—an unruly force that had to be channeled. Many governments legalized and regulated prostitution—which included the compulsory examination of women for venereal disease—precisely because it provided an outlet for male sexual desire.

Convictions like these reveal a great deal about Victorian science and medicine, but they did not necessarily dictate people's intimate lives. The absence of any reliable contraception mattered more in people's experiences and feelings than scientists'. Abstinence and withdrawal were the only common techniques for preventing pregnancy. Their effectiveness was limited, since until the 1880s doctors continued to believe that a woman was most fertile during and around her menstrual period. Midwives and prostitutes knew of other forms of contraception and abortifacients (all of them dangerous and most ineffective), and surely some middle-class women did as well, but such information was not respectable middle-class fare. Concretely, then, sexual intercourse was directly related to the very real dangers of frequent pregnancies. In England, one in one hundred childbirths ended in the death of the mother. At a time when a woman might become pregnant eight or nine times in her life, childbirth was a sobering prospect. Those dangers varied with social class, but even among wealthy and better-cared-for women, they took a real toll. Not surprisingly, middle-class women's diaries and letters are full of their anticipations of childbirth, both joyful and anxious.

MARRIAGE, SEXUALITY, AND THE FACTS OF LIFE

In the nineteenth century sexuality became the subject of much anxious debate, largely because it raised other issues: the roles of men and women, morality, and social respectability. Doctors threw themselves into the discussion, offering their expert opinions on the health (including the sexual lives) of the population. Yet doctors did not dictate people's private lives. Nineteenth-century men and women responded to what they experienced as the facts of life more than to expert advice. The first document provides an example of medical knowledge and opinion. The second offers a glimpse of the daily realities of family life.

A French Doctor Denounces Contraception

One of the most powerful instincts nature has placed in the heart of man is that which has for its object the perpetuation of the human race. But this instinct, this inclination, so active, which attracts one sex towards the other, is liable to be perverted, to deviate from the path nature has laid out. From this arises a number of fatal aberrations which exercise a deplorable influence upon the individual, upon the family and upon society. . . .

We hear constantly that marriages are less fruitful, that the increase of population does not follow its former ratio. I believe that this is mainly attributable to genesiac frauds. It might naturally be supposed that these odious calculations of egotism, these shameful refinements of debauchery, are met with almost entirely in large cities, and among the luxurious classes, and that small towns and country places yet preserve that simplicity of manners attributed to primitive society, when the *pater familias* was proud of exhibiting his numerous offspring. Such, however, is not the case, and I shall show that those who have an unlimited confidence in the patriarchal habits of our country people are deeply in error. At the present time frauds are practiced by all classes. . . .

The laboring classes are generally satisfied with the practice of Onan [withdrawal]. . . . They are seldom familiar with the sheath invented by Dr. Condom, and bearing his name.

Among the wealthy, on the other hand, the use of this preservative is generally known. It favors frauds by rendering them easier; but it does not afford complete security. . . .

Case X.—This couple belongs to two respectable families of vintners. They are both pale, emaciated, downcast, sickly. . . .

They have been married for ten years; they first had two children, one immediately after the other, but in order to avoid an increase of family, they have had recourse to conjugal frauds. Being both very amorous, they have found this practice very convenient to satisfy their inclinations. They have employed it to such an extent, that up to a few months ago, when their health began to fail, the husband had intercourse with his wife habitually two and three times in twenty-four hours.

The following is the condition of the woman: She complains of continual pains in the lower part of the abdomen and kidneys. These pains disturb the functions of the stomach and render her nervous. . . . By the touch we find a very intense heat, great sensibility to pressure, and all the signs of a chronic metritis. The patient attributes positively her present state to the too frequent approaches of her husband.

The husband does not attempt to exculpate himself, as he also is in a state of extreme suffering. It is not in the genital organs, however, that we find his disorder, but in the whole general nervous system; his history will find its place in the part of this work relative to general disturbances. . . .

DEATH IN CHILDBIRTH

Mrs. Ann B. Pettigrew was taken in Labour after returning from a walk in the garden, at 7 o'clock in the evening of June 30, 1830. At 40 minutes after 11 o'clock, she was delivered of a daughter. A short time after, I was informed that the Placenta was not removed, and, at 10 minutes after 12 was asked into the room. I advanced to my dear wife, and kissing her, asked her how she was, to which she replied, I feel very badly. I went out of the room, and sent for Dr. Warren.

I then returned, and inquired if there was much hemorrhage, and was answered that there was. I then asked the midwife (Mrs. Brickhouse) if she ever used manual exertion to remove the placenta. She said she had more than fifty times. I then, fearing the consequences of hemorrhage, observed, Do, my dear sweet wife, permit Mrs. Brickhouse to remove it: To which she assented. . . . After the second unsuccessful attempt, I desired the midwife to desist. In these two efforts, my dear Nancy suffered exceedingly and frequently exclaimed: "O Mrs Brickhouse you will kill me," and to me, "O I shall die, send for the Doctor." To which I replied, "I have sent."

After this, my feelings were so agonizing that I had to retire from the room and lay down, or fall. Shortly after which, the midwife came to me and, falling upon her knees, prayed most fervently to God and to me to forgive her for saying that she could do what she could not. . . .

The placenta did not come away, and the hemorrhage continued with unabated violence until five o'clock in the morning, when the dear woman breathed her last 20 minutes before the Doctor arrived.

So agonizing a scene as that from one o'clock, I have no words to describe. O My God, My God! have mercy on me. I am undone forever . . .

Cited in Erna Olafson Hellerstein, Leslie Parker Hume, and Karen M. Offen, eds. *Victorian Women: A Documentary Account of Women's Lives in Nineteenth-Century England, France, and the United States.* (Stanford: Stanford University Press, 1981) pp. 193–94, 219–20.

MIDDLE-CLASS LIFE IN PUBLIC

The public life of middle-class families literally, reshaped the nineteenth-century landscape. Houses and their furnishings were powerful symbols of material security. Solidly built, heavily decorated, they proclaimed the financial worth and social respectability of those who dwelt within. In provincial cities they were often freestanding "villas." In London, Paris, Berlin, or Vienna, they might be in rows of five- or six-story townhouses, or large apartments. Whatever particular shape they took, they were built to last a long time. The rooms were certain to be crowded with furniture, art objects, carpets, and wall hangings. The size of the rooms, the elegance of the furniture, the number of servants—all depended, of course, on the extent of one's income. A bank clerk did not live as elegantly as a bank director. Yet they shared many standards and aspirations, and those common values helped bind them to the same class, despite the differences in their material way of life.

As cities grew, they became increasingly segregated. Middle-class people lived far from the unpleasant sights and smells of industrialization. Their residential areas, usually built to the west of the cities, out of the path of the prevailing breeze and therefore of industrial pollution, were havens from congestion. The public buildings in the center, many constructed during the nineteenth century, were celebrated as signs of development and prosperity. The middle classes increasingly managed their cities' affairs, although members of the aristocracy retained considerable power, especially in Central Europe. And it was these new middle-class civic leaders who provided new industrial cities with many of their architectural landmarks: city halls, stock exchanges, museums, opera houses, outdoor concert halls, and department stores. One historian has called these buildings the new cathedrals of the industrial age. Projects intended to express the community's values and represent public culture, they were monuments to social change.

Apartment Living in Paris. This print shows that on the Continent rich and poor often lived in the same buildings, the rich on the lower floors, the poor at the top. This sort of residential mixing was unknown in Britain.

WORKING-CLASS LIFE

Like the middle class, the working class was divided into various subgroups and categories, determined in this case by skill, wages, gender, and workplace. Workers' experiences varied, depending on where they worked, where they lived, and, above all, how much they earned. A skilled textile worker lived a life far different from that of a ditch digger, the former able to afford the food, shelter, and clothing necessary for a decent existence, the latter barely able to scrape by.

Working-class housing was unhealthy and unregulated. In older cities single-family dwellings were broken up into apartments, often of no more than one room per family. In new manufacturing centers, rows of tiny houses, located close by smoking factories, were built back to back, thereby eliminating any cross-ventilation or space for gardens. Crowding was commonplace. A newspaper account from the 1840s noted that in Leeds, a textile center in northern Britain, an "ordinary" worker's house contained no more than 150 square feet, and that in most cases those houses were "crammed almost to suffocation with human beings both day and night."

Household routines, demanding in the middle classes, were grinding for the poor. The family remained a survival network, in which everyone played a crucial role. In addition to working for wages, wives were expected to house, feed, and clothe the family on the very little money different members of the family earned. A "good wife" was able to make ends meet even in bad times. Working women's daily lives involved constant rounds of carrying and boiling water, cleaning, cooking, and doing laundry—in one- and two-room crowded, unventilated, poorly lit apartments. Families could not rely on their own gardens to help supply them with food. City markets catered to their needs for cheap goods, but these were regularly stale, nearly rotten, or dangerously adulterated. Formaldehyde was added to milk to prevent spoilage. Pounded rice was mixed into sugar. Fine brown earth was introduced into cocoa.

WORKING WOMEN IN THE INDUSTRIAL LANDSCAPE

Few figures raised more public anxiety and outcry in the nineteenth century than the working woman. Contemporaries worried out loud about the "promiscuous mixing of the sexes" in crowded and humid workshops. Nineteenth-century writers chronicled what they considered to be the economic and moral horrors of female labor: unattended children running in the streets, small children caught in accidents at the mills or the mines, pregnant women hauling coal, or women laboring alongside men in shops.

Women's work was not new. Industrialization made it more visible. Women and children formed nearly half the labor force in some of the most "modern" industries, such as textiles. Most began to work at the age of ten or eleven. Once they had children, they either put their children out to wet nurses, brought them to the mills, or continued to earn wages doing piecework (paid by the piece rather than by the hour) at home.

Still, most women did not work in factories and the gender division of labor remained remarkably unchanged. Most women labored at home or in small workshops—"sweatshops," as they came to be called—for notoriously low wages, paid not by the hour but by the piece for each shirt stitched or each matchbox glued. By far the greatest number of un-married working-class women worked, less visibly, in domestic service, a job that brought low wages and, to judge by a great many women's testimony, coer-cive sexual relationships with male employers or their sons. Domestic service, how-ever, provided room and board, necessities for a single woman.

> Most women labored at home or in small workshops—"sweatshops," as they came to be called—for notoriously low wages, paid not by the hour but by the piece for each shirt stitched or each matchbox glued.

Poverty and the vulnerabilities of working-class women made working-class sexuality very different from its middle-class counterpart. Illegitimacy rose dramatically between 1750 and 1850. In Frankfurt, Germany, for example, where the illegitimacy rate had been a mere 2 percent in the early 1700s, it reached 25 percent in 1850. In Bordeaux, France, in 1840, one third of the recorded births were illegitimate. Eco-nomic hardship drove many single women into tempo-rary relationships that produced children and a continuing cycle of poverty and abandonment. Historians have shown, however, that in the city as in the country-side, many of these temporary relationships became enduring ones; the parents of illegitimate children would marry later.

Working-class families trans-mitted expectations about gender roles and sexual be-havior: girls should expect to work, daughters were responsible for caring for their younger siblings as well as for earning wages, sexuality was a fact of life, midwives could help desperate pregnant girls, mar-riage was an avenue to respectability, and so on. The gulf that separated these expectations and codes from those of middle-class women was one of the most im-

"Capital and Labour." In its earliest years, the British magazine *Punch,* though primarily a humorous weekly, manifested a strong social conscience. This 1843 cartoon shows the capitalists reveling in the re-wards of their investments while the workers shiver in cold and hunger.

portant factors in the development of nineteenth-century class identity.

A LIFE APART: "CLASS" CONSCIOUSNESS

The new demands of factory life also created common experiences and difficulties. The factory system, emphasizing as it did standard rather than individual work patterns, denied skilled laborers the pride in craft they had previously enjoyed. Many workers found themselves stripped of the protections of guilds and formal apprenticeships that had bound their predecessors to a particular trade or place, and that were outlawed or sharply curtailed by legislation in France, Germany, and Britain in the first half of the nineteenth century. Factory hours were long; before 1850 workdays were usually twelve to fourteen hours long. Textile mills remained unventilated, so that minute particles of material lodged in workers' lungs. Machines were unfenced and posed a particular danger to child workers, often hired, because of their supposed agility, to clean under and around the moving parts.

Factories also imposed new routines and disciplines. Artisans in earlier times worked very long hours for very little pay. But at least to some degree, they could set their own hours and structure their own activities, moving from their home workshops to their small garden plots and back again as they wished. In a factory, all "hands" learned the discipline of the whistle. To function efficiently, a factory demanded that all employees begin and end work at the same time. Most workers could not tell time; fewer possessed clocks. None was accustomed to the relentless pace of the machine. In order to increase production, the factory system encouraged the breaking down of the manufacturing process into specialized steps, each with its own assigned time, an innovation that upset workers accustomed to completing a task at their own pace. Workers began to see machinery itself as the tyrant that had changed their lives and bound them to a kind of industrial slavery.

Perhaps the defining feature of working-class life was vulnerability—to unemployment, sickness, accidents in dangerous jobs, family problems, and spikes in the prices of food. Seasonal unemployment, high in almost all trades, made it impossible to collect regular wages. Markets for manufactured goods were small and unstable, producing cyclical economic depressions; when those came, thousands of workers found themselves laid off with no system of unemployment insurance to sustain them. The early decades of industrialization were also marked by several severe agricultural depressions and economic crises. The chronic insecurity of working-class life helped fuel the creation of workers' self-help societies, fraternal associations, and early socialist organizations. It also meant that economic crises could have explosive consequences.

CONCLUSION

Between 1800 and 1900, the population of Europe doubled. Over that same period, Europe's gross national product more than doubled. Yet even startling statistics on growth only begin to suggest how profoundly Europe's economics, politics, and culture were transformed. The Industrial Revolution was one of the turning points in the history of the world. It did not happen overnight and it did not happen evenly. In 1900 agriculture was still the largest single sector of employment. Villages and farms in vast stretches of Europe could seem virtually untouched by industry. Landowners still exercised enormous political and social clout, even when they had to share power with new elites. Yet the changes were by any measure extraordinary; they reached across the globe and into the private lives of ordinary people. Family structures changed. Industry changed the European landscape and, even more fundamentally, humanity's relationship to the environment. As we will see in later chapters, the revolutionary transformations in communication, transportation, and economics had among their many effects the expansion of national states and bureaucracies. Europe's economic surge forward also decisively altered the global balance of power, tilting the scales toward an increasingly industrialized West. Economic development became a new yardstick of value, technology a measure of progress. Increasingly, the "West" came to be associated with—or even defined as—those nations with advanced industrial economies.

Industrialization created new forms of wealth alongside new kinds of poverty. It also fostered an acute awareness of the disparity between social groups. In the eighteenth century, that disparity would have been described in terms of birth, rank, or privilege. In the nineteenth century, it was increasingly seen in terms of class. Champions and critics of the new order alike spoke of a "class society," and new class identities were another key feature of the period. They were embodied in the growing and overcrowded working-class districts of the new cities, in the daily experiences of work, in new conceptions of "respectability," and in middle-class homes. Those new identities would be sharpened in the political events to which we now turn.

KEY TERMS

enclosure

spinning jenny

James Watt

"navvies"

Irish Potato Famine

Charles Dickens

Human Comedy

"cult of domesticity"

Queen Victoria

sweatshops

SELECTED READINGS

Berg, Maxine. *The Age of Manufactures: Industry, Innovation, and Work in Britain, 1700–1820.* Oxford, 1985. Good on new scholarship and on women.

Bridenthal, Renate, Claudia Koonz, and Susan Stuard, eds. *Becoming Visible: Women in European History*, 2d ed. Boston, 1987. Excellent, wide-ranging introduction.

Briggs, Asa. *Victorian Cities.* New York, 1963. A survey of British cities, stressing middle-class attitudes toward the new urban environment.

Cameron, R. E. *France and the Industrial Development of Europe.* Princeton, 1968. Valuable material on the Industrial Revolution outside Britain.

Chevalier, Louis. *Laboring Classes and Dangerous Classes during the First Half of the Nineteenth Century.* New York, 1973. An important, though controversial, account of crime, class, and middle-class perceptions of life in Paris.

Cipolla, Carlo M., ed. *The Industrial Revolution, 1700–1914.* New York, 1976. A collection of essays that emphasizes the wide range of industrializing experiences in Europe.

Cott, Nancy. *The Bonds of Womanhood: "Woman's Sphere" in New England, 1780–1935.* New Haven and London, 1977. One of the most influential studies of the paradoxes of domesticity.

Davidoff, Leonore, and Catherine Hall. *Family Fortunes: Men and Women of the English Middle Class, 1780–1850.* Chicago, 1985. A brilliant and detailed study of the lives and ambitions of several English families.

Ferguson, Niall. "The European Economy, 1815–1914." In *The Nineteenth Century,* edited by T.C.W. Blanning. Oxford and New York, 2000. See, by the same author, *The Cash Nexus: Money and Power in the Modern World, 1700–2000* (New York, 2001) for a very stimulating and fresh overview of the period.

Gay, Peter. *The Bourgeois Experience: Victoria to Freud.* New York, 1984. A multivolume, path-breaking study of middle-class life in all its dimensions. See also Gay's synthesis of some of those arguments in *Schnitzler's Century: The Making of Middle-Class Culture, 1815–1914.* New York and London, 2002.

Hellerstein, Erna, Leslie Hume, and Karen Offen, eds. *Victorian Women: A Documentary Account.* Stanford, 1981. Good collection of documents, with excellent introductory essays.

Hobsbawm, Eric J. *The Age of Revolution, 1789–1848.* London, 1962.

———. *The Age of Capital, 1848–1875.* London, 1975. Among the best introductions.

Hobsbawm, Eric, and George Rudé. *Captain Swing: A Social History of the Great English Agricultural Uprising of 1830.* New York, 1975. Analyzes rural protest and politics.

Kemp, Tom. *Industrialization in Nineteenth-Century Europe.* London, 1985.

Kindelberger, Charles. *A Financial History of Western Europe.* London, 1984.

Landes, David S. *The Unbound Prometheus: Technological Change and Industrial Development in Western Europe from 1750 to the Present.* London, 1969. Excellent and thorough on technological change and its social and economic context.

Langer, William L. *Political and Social Upheaval, 1832–1852.* New York, 1969. Comprehensive and detailed survey.

McNeill, J.R. *Something New Under the Sun: An Environmental History of the Twentieth-Century World.* New York and London, 2000.

O'Gráda, Cormac. *The Great Irish Famine.* Cambridge, 1989. A fascinating and recent assessment of scholarship on the famine.

———. *Black '47 and Beyond: The Great Irish Famine.* Princeton, 1999.

Rose, Sonya O. *Limited Livelihoods: Gender and Class in Nineteenth-Century England.* Berkeley, 1992.

Sabean, David Warren. *Property, Production, and Family Neckarhausen, 1700–1870.* New York, 1990. Brilliant and very detailed study of gender roles and family.

Sabel, Charles, and Jonathan Zeitlin. "Historical Alternatives to Mass Production." *Past and Present* 108 (August 1985): 133–76.

Schivelbusch, Wolfgang. *The Railway Journey*. Berkeley, 1986.

Thompson, E. P. *The Making of the English Working Class*. London, 1963. Shows how the French and Industrial Revolutions fostered the growth of working-class consciousness. A brilliant and important work.

Tilly, Louise, and Joan Scott. *Women, Work and the Family*. New York, 1978. Now the classic study.

Valenze, Deborah. *The First Industrial Woman*. New York, 1995. Excellent and readable on industrialization and economic change in general.

Williams, Raymond. *Keywords: a vocabulary of culture and society*. New York. 1976

Zeldin, Theodore. France, 1848–1945, 2 vols. Oxford, 1973–1977.

Chapter TWENTY

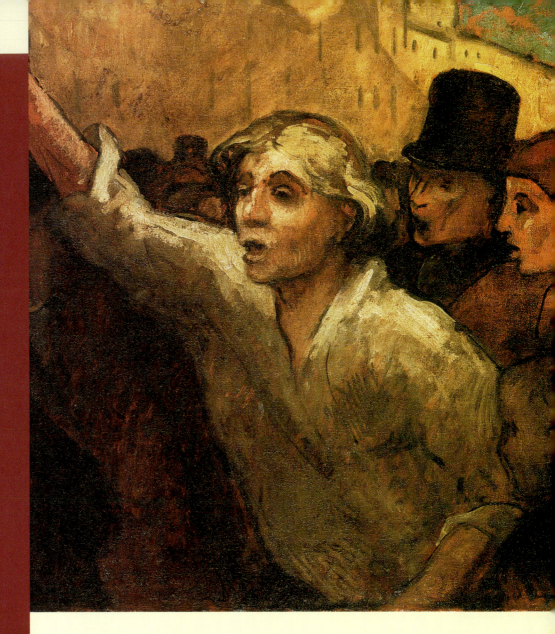

FROM RESTORATION TO REVOLUTION, 1815–1848

When Napoleon left the field of battle at Waterloo on June 18, 1815, his victorious opponents hoped the age of revolution had ended. The Austrian foreign minister Klemens von Metternich, perhaps the most influential conservative diplomat of the early nineteenth century, called revolution a "sickness," "plague," and "cancer," and with his allies set out to inoculate Europe against any further outbreaks. As Metternich and others saw it, revolution produced war. Peace, therefore, rested on avoiding political turmoil and keeping a firm grip on domestic affairs in all the countries of Europe.

Within Metternich's lifetime, however, waves of revolution would again sweep across Europe—in the 1820s, 1830s, and again in 1848. Conservative efforts to restore the old order only succeeded in part. Why? To begin with, the developments of the eighteenth century proved impossible to reverse. The expansion of an informed reading public, a development that went back to the Enlightenment, continued. The word *citizen*, and the political rights that it implied, were controversial in the tumultuous aftermath of the French Revolution, but it was difficult to banish the term from the West's vocabulary. More people thought about and participated in politics. New political ideologies, new political groups and allegiances made the early nineteenth century very different from the world that conservatives sought to retrieve. Second, industrialization and the far-reaching changes we surveyed in the last chapter eroded the foundations of the conservative order. Steam presses transformed printing; railroads changed the speed at which newspapers traveled. Cities became centers of political activity. Above all, social changes created new antagonisms and conflicts.

This is not to say that the revolutionaries carried the day. Many of the revolutions failed or were repressed. And although the old order was not restored, conservatism, renovated and adapted, gained a new foothold. This period offers a fascinating case study in sudden changes, vaulting hopes, partial successes, unintended consequences, and political adaptation—for revolutionaries and conservatives alike.

FOCUS QUESTIONS

• What principles guided the Congress of Vienna?

• What were the new political ideologies of the nineteenth century?

 • What were the key themes of Romanticism?

• How did the events of 1830 bring the restoration to an end?

In culture as well as in politics, imagination and a sense of possibility were among the defining characteristics of the first half of the century. Romanticism broke with what many artists considered the cold Classicism and formality of eighteenth-century art. The Enlightenment had championed reason; the Romantics prized subjectivity, feeling, and spontaneity. Their revolt against eighteenth-century conventions had ramifications far beyond literature and painting. The Romantics had no single political creed: some were fervent revolutionaries and others fervent traditionalists who looked to the past, to religion or history for inspiration. Their sensibility, however, infused politics and culture. And to look ahead, their collective search for new means of expression sent nineteenth-century art off in a new direction.

BACK TO THE FUTURE: RESTORING ORDER, 1815–1830

What principles guided the Congress of Vienna?

In 1814 the victorious European powers met at the Congress of Vienna. The peace settlement aimed high, seeking to satisfy the great powers' territorial ambitions and guarantee international tranquillity. The Congress became a long affair and produced two peace treaties: one in 1814 and another in 1815, after Napoleon's startling escape from exile and his final defeat at Waterloo.

THE CONGRESS OF VIENNA AND THE RESTORATION

The central cast at the Congress were the major powers, with Tsar Alexander I (1801–1825) and the Austrian diplomat Klemens von Metternich (1773–1859) in dominant roles. In the wake of Napoleon's fall Russia had emerged as the most powerful Continental state. The Russian Tsar Alexander, raised in the court of Catherine the Great, had learned Enlightenment doctrines from his French tutor and belief in absolutist authority from his autocratic father. In 1801 he succeeded his assassinated father and during the Napoleonic wars he presented himself as the "liberator" of Europe. Many

feared that he would substitute an all-powerful Russia for an all-powerful France.

Klemens von Metternich, the architect of the peace, grew up the son of an Austrian diplomat in the unstable patchwork of the small German states. As a student at the University of Strasbourg the young Metternich witnessed popular violence connected with the French Revolution and to this he attributed his lifelong hatred of political change. At the Congress of Vienna, he attempted at every turn to arrange international affairs with equal neatness to suit his own diplomatic designs. His central concerns were checking Russian expansionism and preventing political and social change. He feared that Tsar Alexander might provoke revolution in order to establish Russian supremacy in Europe. For this reason he favored treating the defeated French with moderation. Metternich was an archconservative who readily resorted to harsh repressive tactics, including secret police and spying. Yet the peace he crafted was enormously significant and helped to prevent a major European war until 1914.

The Congress sought to restore order and "legitimate" authority. It recognized Louis XVIII as the legitimate sovereign of France and confirmed the restoration of Bourbon rulers in Spain and the two Sicilies. The peace built strong barriers against any renewed French expansions. Here the guiding principle was the balance of power, according to which no country should be powerful enough to destabilize international relations. The Dutch Republic was restored as the kingdom of the Netherlands to discourage any future French expansion. For the same reason, the allies ceded the German left bank of the Rhine to Prussia. Austria expanded its empire in northern Italy, regaining the territories lost to Napoleon.

The peace of 1815 had especially important consequences for Germany and Poland. Napoleon had reorganized the German states into the Confederation of the Rhine. At Vienna the great powers reduced the number of German states and principalities and linked them with Prussia into a loose German Confederation under the honorary presidency of Austria. This Confederation would later become the basis for German unification, but such was not the intent of the peacemakers. Poland, which had been partitioned out of existence by Russia, Austria, and Prussia in the 1790s, became an object of the great powers' territorial ambitions. In the end, the parties compromised. They created a nominally independent kingdom of Poland but gave control over it to Tsar Alexander. Other sections of Poland also went to Prussia and Austria. Like the

THE CONGRESS OF VIENNA

Note how the borders of European nations were established after the final defeat of Napoleon. How had Napoleon's conquests irrevocably changed the political geography of Europe. Did the delegates at Vienna build on some of Napoleon's ideas for organizing his own empire? Was the settlement reached at Vienna a success? What were the major social and political concerns of the diplomats, and how did they try to address them?

other victorious powers, Britain demanded compensation for long years at war and received territories that had been under French dominion in South Africa and South America, as well as the island of Ceylon. Britain's military successes in the Napoleonic wars helped secure her growing commercial empire (see Chapter 19).

The Congress of Vienna also called for a "Concert of Europe" to secure the peace and create permanent stabil-ity. Britain, Austria, Prussia, and Russia formed the Quadruple Alliance (renamed the Quintuple Alliance when France was admitted in 1818). Its members pledged to meet regularly and to cooperate in the suppression of any disturbances—either attempts to overthrow legitimate governments or to change international boundaries. Tsar Alexander I persuaded the allies to join him in the declaration of a "Holy Alliance" dedicated to establishing justice, Christian charity, and peace. Yet this second alliance only made Europe's leaders suspicious of Alexander's intentions. Many of the aristocratic states-men gathered at Vienna were steeped in the values of the Enlightenment and wary of crusading. Many shared the British foreign minister's belief that the Holy Alliance was "a piece of sublime mysticism and nonsense." In any event, they attempted to forge a different conception of authority, centered on "legitimacy." What made a ruler "legitimate" and reinforced his power was not divine right but international treaties, support, and a series of guarantees.

REVOLT AGAINST RESTORATION

From the beginning, the restoration met opposition. Much of the early resistance was clandestine, centered in secret organizations driven underground by repres-sive tactics. In Metternich's own backyard, for instance, the Italian Carbonari vowed to oppose the government in Vienna and its conservative allies, whose power ex-tended down into the Italian peninsula. The Carbonari's influence spread through southern Europe and France during the 1820s. Some Carbonari called for constitu-tions, political representation, and other liberal reforms. Others sang the praises of Bonaparte. The former em-peror, indeed, became more popular in exile—where he became a mythologized alternative to the restored Bour-bons—than he had been during his war-torn reign.

In Spain, and in Naples and Piedmont on the Italian peninsula, opposition to the restoration turned to revolt. In both cases, restored monarchs who had pledged to re-spect constitutional reforms abandoned their promises, attempting to squelch elections and reinstate privileges. Metternich felt he had diplomatic permission to sup-press the uprisings in Italy, forcing the rebels into prison or exile. The French took on the Spanish revolution. They sent two hundred thousand troops to the Iberian Peninsula in 1823. This force crushed the Spanish revo-lutionaries and restored the beleaguered King Ferdi-nand's authority. Ferdinand tortured and publicly executed hundreds of rebels.

REVOLUTION IN LATIN AMERICA

Ferdinand's empire in Latin America, however, would not be restored. Napoleon's earlier conquest of Spain (1807) had shaken the foundations of colonial rule. Elites in the Spanish colonies had long chafed under imperial control, resenting taxes, restrictive trade poli-cies, and privileges granted to *peninsulares* (persons born

Secret meeting of the Carbonari. Not all resistance took the form of open protest. An Italian organization named for the charcoal that obscured the faces of its members, the Carbonari were an underground expression of opposi-tion to the Restoration.

in Spain). From 1810 on, independence movements gathered momentum, beginning in Río de la Plata (now Argentina), which declared its independence in 1816. The general of the Río de la Plata forces, José de San Martín (1778–1850), led an extraordinary march across the Andes to confront royalist forces and liber-ate Chile and Peru. The other key military and politi-cal figure of the South American revolutions, Simón Bolívar (1783–1830), led a series of uprisings from Venezuela across to Bolivia, eventually joining forces with San Martín.

These revolutions, which brought sweeping changes to the entire continent, arguably marked the end of an age that had opened in 1492. They also dramatized the global significance of the French revolution of 1789, which reached well beyond the core states of Europe and remade states across a significant portion of the world.

RUSSIA: THE DECEMBRISTS

Revolt also broke out in Russia, the heart of the conser-vative alliance. In 1825, Tsar Alexander died, and un-certainty about his heir sparked an uprising among a group of army officers. Many of the Decembrists, as they were called, came from noble families and were members of elite regiments. Many of them had served in the tsarist armies that drove Napoleon back to France and had been posted there during the years while the peace was being settled. Young and idealistic, they took seriously Tsar Alexander's claim that Russia was the "liberator" of Europe. If Russia was to assume that kind of "moral greatness," though, it needed to reform. Serfdom contradicted the promise of liberation, and so did the autocratic tsar's monopoly on political power. Not only were Russian peasants enslaved, they argued, but Russian nobles were "slaves to the tsar."

The Decembrists hoped to persuade Alexander's liberal-minded brother, Constantine, to assume the throne and guarantee a constitution. The attempt failed. The new tsar, Nicholas I (1825–1855), ruthlessly interrogated hundreds of mutinous soldiers, sentencing many to hard labor and exile. The leaders of the revolt were hanged at dawn inside the walls of the Peter and Paul Fortress in St. Petersburg and buried in secret graves, so that neither their funerals nor their gravesites could provide occasions for unrest.

Nicholas went on to become perhaps Europe's most uncompromising conservative. Still, Russia showed signs of change. Bureaucracy became more centralized and more efficient, and less dependent on the nobility for political support and everyday operation. The government systematically codified laws in 1832. Rising demand for Russian grain encouraged large landowners to reorganize their estates for more effective production and the state to build railways to transport grain to western markets. Other opponents of the regime, like Alexander Herzen, who admired the Decembrists, would carry on the Decembrists' unresolved political legacy.

SOUTHEASTERN EUROPE: GREECE AND SERBIA

The conservative European powers were more open to rebellion when it was directed against rival empires. Such was the case in Greece and Serbia, both provinces in the Balkan region of the sprawling and once powerful Ottoman empire, where local movements began to demand autonomy and to ask the Europeans to sponsor their struggles.

Of all the revolts of the early nineteenth century, none captured more attention and sympathy than the Greek war for independence (1821–1827). Why was this con-

The Massacre at Chios, by Eugène Delacroix (1798–1863). Delacroix was a Romantic painter of dramatic and emotional scenes. Here he put his brush to work for the cause of liberty, eulogizing the more than twenty thousand Greeks slain by the Turks during the Greek war of independence in 1822. The painting is another example of the manner in which the emotionalism of Romanticism came to the aid of reformist nationalism.

flict significant? The answer has little to do with realities in the Balkans; it lies instead in conceptions of European identity. "We are all Greeks," wrote Percy Shelley, the Romantic poet. "Our laws, our literature, our religion, our arts have their roots in Greece. But for Greece . . . we might still have been savages and idolators." Celebrating the Greeks went hand in hand with demonizing the Turks and reviving the theme of "Turkish despotism," which had figured prominently in the Enlightenment. A British official remarked, "Almost the whole extent of European Turkey presents a dreadful picture of anarchy, rebellion, and barbarism." Europeans of different political persuasions sought to identify themselves with a Greek heritage which they contrasted with images of "eastern" or "Islamic" tyranny. Europeans, in short, saw the struggle through their own lens.

On the ground in Greece, both sides were ruthless. On several occasions Greek forces besieged Turkish towns and killed the inhabitants. In March of 1822,

CHRONOLOGY

CONCERT OF EUROPE, 1815–1830

Congress of Vienna	1814–1815
Quintuple Alliance	1818
France restores King Ferdinand in Spain	1823
South American revolutions	1810–1825
Decembrist revolt in Russia	1825
Greek war of independence	1821–1827
Serbian independence	1828

Greeks invaded and proclaimed the independence of the island of Chios. When Ottoman troops arrived to retake the island, the Greek invaders killed their Turkish prisoners and fled. The Turks took their revenge by slaughtering thousands of Greeks and selling forty thousand more into slavery. Delacroix's *Massacre at Chios*, characteristically, depicted only Turkish brutality.

Ultimately, Greek independence depended on great power politics. In 1827, British, French, and Russian troops went in against the Turks. Two London Protocols, in 1829 and 1830, established Greek independence from the Ottoman Empire.

The struggle between the European powers and the Ottomans also helped to create the independent nation of Serbia in 1828. With Russian encouragement and aid Serbia became semi-independent: an Orthodox Christian principality (with significant minority populations) under Ottoman rule. Serbia went on to press for more territory, claiming territories held by another power in the region, the Austrian empire, a struggle that would escalate at the end of the nineteenth century.

TAKING SIDES: NEW IDEOLOGIES IN POLITICS

What were the new political ideologies of the nineteenth century?

These rebellions made it clear that issues raised by the French Revolution were very much alive. Early nineteenth-century politics did not have parties as we know them today. But more clearly defined groupings and competing doctrines, or ideologies, took shape during this time. An ideology may be defined as a coherent system of thought regarding the social and political order, one that consciously competes with other views of how the world is or should be. The major political ideologies of modern times—conservatism, liberalism, socialism, and nationalism—were first articulated in this period. Their roots lay in earlier times, but ongoing political battles brought them to the fore. The Industrial Revolution (see Chapter 19) and the social changes that accompanied it proved a tremendous spur to political and social thought. Would the advance of industry yield progress or misery? What were the "rights of man," and who would enjoy them? Did equality necessarily go hand in hand with liberty? This exceptionally fertile period cast up several different responses to these questions. A brief survey of the political horizon will show how these alternatives were taking shape, and dramatize how the ground had shifted since the eighteenth century.

PRINCIPLES OF CONSERVATISM

What was the basis of early nineteenth-century conservatism? At the Congress of Vienna and in the Restoration generally, the most important guiding concept was "legitimacy." Legitimacy might be best understood as a code word for a new political order. Conservatives aimed to make legitimate—and thus to solidify—both the monarchy's authority and a hierarchical social order. The most thoughtful conservatives of the period did not believe that the old order would survive completely intact. They did believe, however, that the monarchy guaranteed political stability, that the nobility were the rightful leaders of the nation, and that both needed to play active and effective roles in public life. Conservatives believed that change had to be slow, incremental, and managed in order to strengthen the structures of authority. Conserving the past and cultivating tradition would ensure an orderly future.

Edmund Burke's writings, especially *Reflections on the Revolution in France* became a point of reference for nineteenth-century conservatives. Burke did not oppose all change; he had argued, for instance, that the British should let the North American colonies go. But he opposed talk of natural rights, which he considered dangerous abstractions. He believed enthusiasm for constitutions to be misguided and the Enlightenment's emphasis on what he called the "conquering power of reason" to be dangerous. Instead, Burke coun-

WHAT WERE THE NEW POLITICAL IDEOLOGIES OF THE NINETEENTH CENTURY?

TAKING SIDES: NEW IDEOLOGIES IN POLITICS   563

seled deference to experience, tradition, and history. Other conservatives such as the French writers Joseph de Maistre (1753–1821) and Louis-Gabriel-Ambroise Bonald (1754–1840) penned carefully elaborated defenses of absolute monarchy and its main pillar of support, the Catholic Church. As conservatives saw it, monarchy, aristocracy, and the church were the mainstays of the social and political order. Those institutions needed to stand together in face of the challenges of the new century.

LIBERALISM

Liberalism's core was a commitment to individual liberties, or rights. Liberals believed that the most important function of government was to protect liberties, and that doing so would benefit all, promoting justice, knowledge, progress, and prosperity. Liberalism had three components. First, liberalism called for equality before the law, which meant ending traditional privileges and the restrictive power of rank and hereditary authority. Second, liberalism held that government needed to be based on political rights and the consent of the governed. Third, in economics, liberalism meant a belief in the benefits of unfettered economic activity, or economic individualism.

The roots of legal and political liberalism lay in the late seventeenth century, in the work of John Locke, who had defended the English Parliament's rebellion against absolutism, and the "inalienable" rights of the British people (see Chapter 15). Freedom from arbitrary authority, imprisonment, or censorship; freedom of the press, the right to assemble and deliberate: these principles were the starting points for nineteenth-century liberalism. Liberals believed that individual rights were inalienable, and that they should be guaranteed in written constitutions. (Conservatives, as we saw above, considered constitutions abstract and dangerous.) Most liberals called for constitutional as opposed to hereditary monarchy; all agreed that a monarch who abused power could legitimately be overthrown.

Liberals advocated direct representation in government—at least for those who had the property and public standing to be trusted with the responsibilities of power. Liberalism by no means required democracy. To the contrary, deciding who should have the right to vote was a hotly debated issue. Nineteenth-century liberals, with fresh memories of the French Revolution of 1789, were torn between their belief in rights and their fears of political turmoil. They considered property and education essential prerequisites for participation in politics.

Economic liberalism was newer. Its founding text was Adam Smith's *Wealth of Nations* (1776), which attacked mercantilism (the government practice of regulating manufacturing and trade in order to raise revenues) in the name of free markets. Smith's argument that the economy should be based on a "system of natural liberty" was reinforced by a second generation of economists. The economists (or political economists, as they were called) sought to identify basic economic laws: the law of supply and demand, the balance of trade, the law of diminishing returns, and so on. They believed that economic activity should be unregulated. Labor should be contracted freely, unhampered by guilds or unions.

Adam Smith Pointing to his Book *The Wealth of Nations* (1776). Smith was an Enlightenment thinker whose work was popularized in the nineteenth century. Adam Smith is credited with founding economic liberalism with his 1776 book challenging mercantilism in favor of free markets.

Property should be unencumbered by feudal restrictions. Goods should circulate freely, which meant, concretely, an end to government-granted monopolies and traditional practices of regulating markets, especially in valuable commodities such as grain, flour, or corn. Government's role was to preserve order and protect property, but not to interfere with the natural play of economic forces, a doctrine known as *laissez-faire*, which translates, roughly, as "leave things to go on their own". This strict opposition to government intervention makes nineteenth-century liberalism significantly different from liberalism as we know it today.

RADICALISM, REPUBLICANISM, AND EARLY SOCIALISM

The liberals were flanked on their left by a two radical groups: republicans and socialists. Whereas liberals advocated a constitutional monarchy, republicans, as their name implies, pressed further, demanding a government by the people, an expanded franchise, and democratic participation in politics. Where liberals called for or individualism and laissez-faire, socialists put the accent on equality. To put it in the terms that were used at the time, socialists raised the "social question." How could growing social inequality and the miseries of working people be remedied?

> To put it in the terms that were used at the time, socialists raised the "social question." How could growing social inequality and the miseries of working people be remedied?

Socialism was a nineteenth-century system of thought and a response in large measure to the visible problems ushered in by industrialization: the intensification of labor, the poverty of working-class neighborhoods in industrial cities, and the widespread perception that a hierarchy based on rank and privilege had been abolished only to be replaced by one based on social class. For the socialists, the problems of industrial society were not incidental; they arose from the core principles of competition, individualism, and private property. The socialists did not oppose industry and economic development. They took from the Enlightenment a

Quadrille Dancing at Lanark. Robert Owen created a utopian town in New Lanark, Scotland organized around the principle of cooperation in social life as well as labor.

WHAT WERE THE NEW POLITICAL IDEOLOGIES OF THE NINETEENTH CENTURY?

TAKING SIDES: NEW IDEOLOGIES IN POLITICS   565

commitment to human progress, and believed society could be both industrial and humane.

Robert Owen, a wealthy industrialist turned reformer, bought a large cotton factory in Scotland and proceeded to organize the mill and the surrounding town according to the principles of cooperation rather than those of profitability. New Lanark organized good housing and sanitation, good working conditions, child care, free schooling, and a system of social security for the factory's workers. Some radical thinkers were utopian; others were practical. Other socialists proposed simpler, practical reforms. Louis Blanc, a French politician and journalist, campaigned for universal male suffrage with an eye to giving working-class men control of the state. Instead of protecting private property and the manufacturing class, the transformed state would extend credit to those who needed it, and establish "associations of production," or workshops governed by laborers that would guarantee jobs and security for all. Pierre-Joseph Proudhon (1809–1865) also proposed establishing producers' cooperatives that would sell goods at a price workers could afford, working-class credit unions, and so on. Proudhon's "What is Property?"—to which the famous answer was "property is theft"—became one of the most widely read socialist pamphlets, familiar to artisans, laborers, and middle-class intellectuals, including Karl Marx.

KARL MARX'S SOCIALISM

The father of modern socialism, Karl Marx (1818–1883), was barely known in the early nineteenth century. His reputation rose later, after 1848, when a wave of revolutions and violent confrontation seemed to confirm his distinctive theory of history and to make earlier socialists' emphasis on cooperation, setting up experimental communities, and peaceful reorganization of industrial society seem naive.

Marx grew up in Trier, in the western section of Germany, in a region and a family keenly interested in the political debates and movements of the revolutionary era. His family was Jewish, but his father had converted to Protestantism in order to be able to work as a lawyer. Marx studied law briefly at the University of Berlin before turning to journalism. From 1842 to 1843 he edited the *Rhineland Gazette* (*Rheinische Zeitung*). The paper's criticism of legal privilege and political repression put it on a collision course with the Prussian government, which closed it down and sent Marx into exile—first in Paris, then Brussels, and eventually London.

Karl Marx (1818–1883). The young Marx created a theory of history and philosophy of socialism that combined European thought and politics in the 1840s. The *Communist Manifesto* published on the eve of the revolutions of 1848, became much more influential in their aftermath.

While in Paris Marx studied early socialist theory, economics, and the history of the French Revolution. He also began a lifelong intellectual and political partnership with Friedrich Engels (1820–1895). Marx and Engels joined a small international group of radical artisans renamed the Communist League. The League asked Marx to draft a statement of its principles, published in 1848 as the *Communist Manifesto*.

The *Communist Manifesto* laid out Marx's theory of history in short form. World history had passed through three major stages, each characterized by conflict between social groups: master and slave in ancient slavery, lord and serf in feudalism, and bourgeois and proletariat in capitalism. According to Marx's theory, the stage of feudal or aristocratic property relations had ended in 1789, when the French Revolution overthrew the old order, ushering in bourgeois political power and industrial capitalism. In the *Communist Manifesto*, Marx and Engels admired the revolutionary accomplishments of capitalism, saying that the bourgeoisie had "created more impressive and more colossal productive forces than had all preceding generations together." But, they argued, the revolutionary character of capitalism would also undermine the bourgeois economic order. As capital became more concentrated in the hand of the few, a growing army of wage workers would become increasingly aware of its economic and political disenfranchisement; struggle between these classes was central to industrial capitalism itself. Eventually, the *Communist Manifesto* predicted, recurring economic crises, caused by capitalism's unending need for new markets and the cyclical instability of overproduction, would bring capitalism to collapse. Workers would seize the state, reorganize the means of production, abolish private property, and eventually create a communist society.

Marx synthesized international cross-currents of European thought and politics in the 1840s. His focus on the relationship between economics and politics was characteristic of his time. Like other radicals, he addressed the gap between liberal demands for freedom and liberal silence on social equality. He was only one of many socialists, however, and before the revolutions of 1848 one of the least well known. Those revolutions erupted the same year the *Communist Manifesto* was published, but well before it had any effect. Only in the second half of the century would Marxism become the leading socialist doctrine.

CITIZENSHIP AND COMMUNITY: NATIONALISM

Of all the political ideologies of the early nineteenth century, nationalism is most difficult to grasp. Its premises are elusive. What, exactly, counted as a nation? Who demanded a nation, and what did their demand mean? In the early nineteenth century, nationalism was usually aligned with liberalism. As the century progressed, however, it became increasingly clear that nationalism could be molded to fit any doctrine.

The meaning of nation has changed over time. The term comes from the Latin verb *nasci*, "to be born" and suggests "common birth." In sixteenth-century England, the "nation" designated the aristocracy, or those who shared noble birthright. The French nobility also referred to itself as the "nation." Those earlier and unfamiliar usages are important. They highlight the most significant development of the late eighteenth and early nineteenth centuries: the French Revolution redefined "nation" to mean the people, or the sovereign people. The revolutionaries of 1789 boldly claimed that the nation, and no longer the king, was the sovereign power. "Vive la nation," or "long live the nation," celebrated a new political community, not a territory or an ethnicity. In the aftermath of the French Revolution of 1789, the "nation" became what one historian calls "the collective image of modern citizenry."

In the early nineteenth century, then, "nation" symbolized legal equality, constitutional government, and unity, or an end to feudal privileges and divisions. Nationalism became an important rallying cry for liberals across Europe in the early nineteenth century precisely because it was associated with political transformation.

> Nationalism became an important rallying cry for liberals across Europe in the early nineteenth century precisely because it was associated with political transformation.

Nationalism also went hand in hand with liberal demands for economic modernity. Economists, such as the influential German economist Friedrich List (1789–1846), sought to develop national economies and national infrastructures: larger, stronger, better integrated, and more effective systems of banking, trade, transportation, production, and distribution. List linked ending the territorial fragmentation of the German states and the development of manufacturing to "culture, prosperity, and liberty."

Nationalism, however, could easily undermine other liberal values. When liberals insisted on the value and importance of individual liberties, those committed to building nations replied that their vital task might require the sacrifice of some measure of each citizen's freedom. The Napoleonic army, a particularly powerful symbol of nationhood, appealed to conservative proponents of military strength and authority as well as to liberals who wanted an army of citizens.

Political leaders associated the nation with specific causes. Nineteenth-century governments sought to develop national feeling, to link their peoples more closely to their states. State-supported educational sys-

WHAT WERE THE NEW POLITICAL IDEOLOGIES OF THE NINETEENTH CENTURY?

TAKING SIDES: NEW IDEOLOGIES IN POLITICS   567

EUROPEAN LANGUAGE GROUPS, C. 1850

Examine the distribution of language groups throughout Europe. What is the relationship between language and nationalism? How did states encourage the development of a national identity? Why would the divisions between language groups have created problems for the European empires?

tems taught a "national" language, fighting the centrifugal forces of traditional dialects. Textbooks and self-consciously nationalist theater, poetry, and painting helped to elaborate and sometimes "invent" a national heritage. The different meanings of "nationhood," the various political beliefs it evoked, and the powerful emotions it tapped made nationalism exceptionally unpredictable.

These were the principal political ideologies of the early nineteenth century. They were rooted in the eighteenth century but were brought to the forefront by the political turmoil of early nineteenth century. All of these ideologies could incite loyalty and passion. All could be reinterpreted. All became increasingly common points of reference as the century unfolded.

CULTURAL REVOLT: ROMANTICISM

What were the key themes of Romanticism?

Romanticism, the most significant cultural movement of the early nineteenth century, also took form in the polarized aftermath of Enlightenment and revolution. An exceptionally diverse intellectual movement, it touched all the arts and permeated politics as well. Put most simply, it marked a reaction against the Classicism of the eighteenth century and against many of the values of the Enlightenment. Eighteenth-century Classical art had aspired to reason, discipline, and harmony. Romanticism, in contrast, stressed emotion, freedom, and imagination. Romantic artists prized the individual, individuality, and subjective experience; many were personally rebellious and sought out intense experiences. In contrast to Enlightenment thinkers, they considered intuition, emotion, and feelings better guides to truth—and to human happiness—than reason and logic.

BRITISH ROMANTIC POETRY

Romanticism developed earliest in England and Germany, where it arose as part of a reaction against the Enlightenment and French classicism; it came later to France. Like any intellectual or artistic movement, Romanticism did not completely break with its predecessors. Indeed, the early Romantics developed themes first raised by Jean-Jacques Rousseau (see Chapter 17). Rousseau's key themes—nature, simplicity, and feeling—ran through the very influential *Lyrical Ballads* (1798) of William Wordsworth (1770–1850) and Samuel Taylor Coleridge (1772–1834). Wordsworth considered emotions, or soul, the core of humanity; for him, poetry was "the spontaneous overflow of powerful feelings." Like Rousseau, Wordsworth also emphasized the ties of compassion and feeling that bind all of humankind, regardless of social class. "We have all of us one human

heart," he wrote; "men who do not wear fine clothes can feel deeply." Like Rousseau, Wordsworth considered nature to be humanity's most trustworthy teacher, and he considered the experience of nature the source of true feeling. Poetic insights could be inspired by landscapes and the memories those evoked—in Wordsworth's case the wild hills and tumbledown cottages of England's Lake District. At the head of his poem "The Ruined Cottage," Wordsworth quoted from the Scottish romantic poet Robert Burns:

> Give me a spark of Nature's fire,
> 'Tis the best learning I desire…
> My muse, though homely in attire,
> May touch the heart.

The Lake Poets, as Wordsworth and Coleridge were sometimes called, offered one key theme of nineteenth-century Romanticism: a view of nature that rejected the abstract mechanism of eighteenth-century thought.

Lord Byron. One of the great English romantic poets, Byron's liberal politics also helped make him a romantic hero. He went to Greece to fight in the independence movement against the Ottoman Turks, but ended up dying there of tuberculosis.

Mary Shelley's *Frankenstein*. Perhaps the best-known work of Romantic fiction, *Frankenstein* joined the Romantic critique of Enlightenment reason with early nineteenth-century ambivalence about science to create a striking horror story. Mary Shelley (pictured at right at 19, around the time she published *Frankenstein*) was the daughter of the philosopher William Godwin and the feminist Mary Wollstonecraft, and married the poet Percy Shelley.

Nature was not a system whose operations were to be observed with a critical eye. Instead, humanity was immersed in nature; the human soul needed to be opened to nature's sublime (literally, inspiring wonder and awe) power.

English Romanticism reached its height with the next generation of English romantic poets—George Gordon, Lord Byron (1788–1824), Percy Bysshe Shelley (1792–1822), and John Keats (1795–1821). Some of these poets' lives and loves appealed as much as their writing for their adventures seemed to personify their poetic themes. Lord Byron's countless love affairs helped create the association between Romanticism and rebellion against conformity and inhibition. Byron also rebelled against political convention. He assailed British political leaders as corrupt, narrow minded, and repressive, defended working-class movements in the name of liberty, and sailed off to fight in the Greek movement for independence from the Ottoman Turks. When he died in Greece (of tuberculosis, not in battle)

he seemed to epitomize the liberal Romantic hero. Byron's close friend Percy Shelley continued to take Romantic poetry and politics to new heights. The subject of Shelley's *Prometheus Unbound* (1820) virtually defines romantic heroism and its cult of individual audacity. Prometheus, defying Zeus, had stolen fire for humanity and as punishment found himself chained to a rock while an eagle tore out his heart.

WOMEN WRITERS, GENDER, AND ROMANTICISM

Perhaps the best-known work of Romantic fiction, however, is Mary Godwin Shelley's *Frankenstein* (1818). Mary was the daughter of two radical literary "celebrities": the philosopher William Godwin and the feminist Mary Wollstonecraft (see Chapter 17), who died as her daughter was born. Mary Godwin met Shelley at sixteen, had three children by him before they married, and published *Frankenstein* when she was twenty. The novel captures especially well the Romantic critique of Enlightenment reason and early nineteenth-century ambivalence about science. The story turns around a madly ambitious and eccentric Swiss scientist determined to find the secret of human life. Dr. Frankenstein finally does produce life, in the form of a freakish monster. Though the monster is artificially made, he has human feelings, and when he finds himself spurned by his horrified creator, he becomes consumed by loneliness, longing, and murderous self-hatred, wreaking havoc on all. Shelley cast the novel in characteristically Romantic fashion, as a twisted creation myth, a story of individual genius gone wrong, and a study of agonizingly powerful feeling. For all these reasons, the novel became a

point of reference in Western culture. Dr. Frankenstein, forced to acknowledge that he "had been the author of unalterable evils," became one of the most memorable characterizations of the limits of reason and the impossibility of controlling nature.

First, then, Romanticism stressed the limits of reason and the power of emotion. Second, it insisted on the uniqueness and subjectivity of individual experience. The mind was not a "blank tablet" on which one's senses imprinted knowledge, which was John Locke's image, and central to most Enlightenment philosophy. Instead Romantics regarded the mind as a source of imagination. Romanticism stimulated new thinking about gender. In the eighteenth and nineteenth centuries it was common to assert that men were rational and women emotional, or intuitive. Ro-

Weymouth Bay, by John Constable. "It is the soul that sees," wrote Constable. Like other romantic artists, Constable explored new forms of feeling and perception.

manticism, though, valued the emotional and intuitive as creative. And claiming the role of artist-genius became a way for some women to subvert social norms. Romanticism also suggested that men could be emotional, and that men and women shared a common human nature.

ROMANTIC PAINTING

Painters of the early nineteenth century carried the Romantic interest in imagination onto their canvases. In Great Britain, romantic painting was best represented by John Constable (1776–1837) and J. M. W. Turner (1775–1851). Both British painters tried to develop more emotional and poetic approaches to nature. "It is the soul that sees," wrote Constable, echoing Wordsworth. Constable pored over Isaac Newton's prisms, studying the properties of light, but with an eye to capturing the "poetry" of a rainbow. His landscapes emphasized the artist's individual technique and way of seeing. Turner's intensely subjective, personal, and imaginative paintings were even more unconventional. Turner experimented with brush strokes and color to produce some of the most remarkable paintings of his time. Critics assailed the paintings, saying they were too abstract, incomprehensible. "I did not paint it to be understood," Turner retorted on one occasion.

In France the leading Romantic painters were Théodore Géricault (1791–1824) and Eugène Delacroix (1799–1863). The poet Charles Baudelaire, who represents the last stages of French Romanticism, credited Delacroix with showing him new ways to see: "The whole visible universe is but a storehouse of images and signs. . . . All the faculties of the human soul must be subordinated to the imagination." Romanticism opened new ways visualizing the world and pointed the way toward experiments, later in the century, that launched modernism.

> The twenty-three-volume, lavishly illustrated *Description of Egypt,* published in French between 1809 and 1828, became an intellectual event in Europe, heightening the soaring interest in Eastern languages and history.

ROMANTIC POLITICS: LIBERTY, HISTORY, AND NATION

Romanticism had many dimensions, and Romantic artists championed contradictory causes. "Romanticism, so often ill-defined, is only . . . liberalism in literature. Liberty in Art, liberty in Society, behold the double

banner that rallies the intelligence." So wrote Victor Hugo (1802–1885) whose poetry, plays, and immensely influential historical novels focused sympathetically on the experience of the common people. *Nôtre Dame de Paris* (1831) and *Les Misérables* (1862) are the most famous. Delacroix's *Liberty Leading the People* represented revolutionary Romanticism (see page 575). So did the poetry of Shelley and Byron.

Yet Romantics could be ardently conservative. The French conservative François Chateaubriand's *Genius of Christianity* (1802) argued that the religious experiences of the national past were woven into the present, and could not be unraveled without destroying the fabric of culture. In characteristically Romantic terms, Chateaubriand put the accent on religious emotion, feeling, and subjectivity. Artistic and literary interest in religion had much wider resonance, and the period witnessed a broad and popular religious revival. It also renewed interest in medieval literature, art, and architecture. Romanticism cut across political lines, providing imagery for both conservatives and liberals.

ORIENTALISM

The early nineteenth century also created a wave of interest in the "Orient." Napoleon had invaded Egypt in 1798, seeking military advantage against the British, but also and perhaps more important in the long run, knowledge, cultural splendor, and imperial glory. The dozens of scholars who accompanied Napoleon's Army of the Orient established the Egyptian Institute, charged with systematically collecting facts about Egyptian natural history, culture, and industry. Other discoveries during the same period opened a new world of knowledge. Among the many artifacts the French took from Egypt was the soon to be famous Rosetta Stone, a block with what scholars discovered to be versions of the same text in three different languages and scripts: hieroglyphic writing (pictorial script), demotic (a version of early alphabetic script), and Greek, which, since it was familiar, enabled scholars to begin deciphering the first two. Egyptian obelisks, with their now readable hieroglyphic inscriptions, yielded more clues about ancient Egypt. The twenty-three-volume, lavishly illustrated *Description of Egypt*, published in French between 1809 and 1828, became an intellectual event in Europe, heightening the soaring interest in Eastern languages and history. Great-power rivalries in Egypt, the British incursions into India, the Greek civil war, the French invasion of Algeria in 1830: all these developments raised Europeans' interests in the region and were the political accompaniment to the "Oriental renaissance."

Nineteenth-century Europeans cast the "Orient" in a specific political and cultural role. In the words of one scholar, "[T]he Orient has helped to define Europe (or the West) as its contrasting image, idea, personality, experience." We saw above that during the 1820s Greek rebellion against the Ottoman Turks, Europeans sought to identify themselves with a Greek heritage and against what they called "Oriental" or "Islamic" despotism. Rebelling against the rules of eighteenth-century Classicism, social conventions, and Enlightenment rationalism, European artists and intellectuals were quick to classify the East as the land of bold color, sensuality, mystery, and irrationality. The "Oriental renaissance" supplied a rich imagery for nineteenth-century Western painting, literature, and scholarship. It also helped create what would become well-established habits of mind. Europeans built up oversimplified images of the differences between "the west" and "the orient."

Women of Algiers, by Eugène Delacroix. This is one of many paintings done during Delacroix's trips through North Africa and a good example of the Romantics' "Orientalism."

GOETHE AND BEETHOVEN

Many artists of the turn of the century are hard to classify. Johann Wolfgang von Goethe (1749–1832) had an enormous influence on the Romantic movement and on German writers trying to cast off the French style and develop their own language and voice. His early novel *The Sorrows of Young Werther* (1774), a story of a young man's yearnings and restless love, captivated readers all over Europe. Yet Goethe backed away from what he came to consider the excessiveness of Romanticism: its cult of feeling over restraint and order, which Goethe

considered self-indulgent and "morbid." In 1790 Goethe published the first part of his masterpiece, *Faust*, a drama in verse, which he finished one year before he died in 1832. The play retold the German legend of the man who sold his soul to the devil in return for eternal youth and universal knowledge. It was more classical in its tone than other works of the Romantic era, though it still reflected a Romantic concern with spiritual freedom and humanity's daring.

The composer Ludwig van Beethoven (1770–1827) considered himself a Classicist and was steeped in the principles of the eighteenth century. The glorification of nature and Romantic individuality ring clearly through his work, and his insistence that instrumental music (without vocal accompaniment) could become more poetic and expressive of emotion made him the key figure for later Romantic composers. Beethoven's life and politics also became part of his legacy. Like many of his contemporaries he was caught up in a burst of enthusiasm for the French Revolution of 1789. Disillusionment set in when Napoleon, whom he had admired as a revolutionary and for whom he had originally named the *Eroica* Symphony, crowned himself emperor and repudiated his principles, and Beethoven's disappointment continued through the Napoleonic wars. At the same time, by the age of thirty-two, Beethoven knew that he was losing his hearing. He hoped the problem could be cured, but it slowly put an end to his career as a virtuoso pianist, and by 1819 he was completely deaf. As his condition worsened and his disenchantment deepened, he withdrew into composing, his solitude a powerful symbol of alienation and extraordinary creativity.

REFORM AND REVOLUTION

How did the events of 1830 bring the restoration to an end?

The most decisive blow against the conservative restoration came in 1830 in France. There, the Congress of Vienna had returned a Bourbon monarch, Louis XVIII, to the throne. Louis claimed absolute power, but in the name of reconciliation he granted a "charter," and conceded some important rights: legal equality, careers open to talent, and a two-chamber parliamentary government. Voting rights excluded most citizens from government. This narrowly based rule, combined with the sting of military defeat, nostalgia for a glorious Napoleonic past and, for some, memories of the revolution, undermined the restoration in France.

THE REVOLUTIONS OF 1830

Louis XVIII's far less conciliatory brother Charles X (1824–1830), was determined to reverse the legacies of the revolutionary and Napoleonic eras. His policies provoked widespread discontent. The rising tide of liberal public opinion was also swollen by economic hard times. In Paris and the provinces, worried police reports flagged the extent of unemployment, hunger, and anger. Confronted with alarming evidence of the regime's unpopularity, Charles and his ministers called new elections, and when those went against them, the king tried, essentially, to overthrow the parliamentary regime.

In return, Charles got revolution. Parisians—especially workers, artisans, students, and writers—took to the streets. Aware that his support had evaporated, Charles abdicated. Many of the revolutionaries on the barricades wanted a republic. But other leaders of the movement wanted to avoid the domestic and international turmoil of the revolution of 1789. They ushered in the duke of Orléans as King Louis Philippe (1830–1848), promoting him as a constitutional monarch accountable to the people: king of the French, not king of France. The new regime, called the July Monarchy, doubled the number of eligible voters. Yet voting was still a privilege, not a right, and was still based on steep requirements of property ownership. The major beneficiaries of the revolution were the propertied classes.

For opponents of the restoration across Europe, 1830 assumed enormous importance. It suggested that history was moving in a new direction and that the political landscape had changed, opening up new possibilities.

In 1815, the Congress of Vienna had agreed to join Belgium (then called the Austrian Netherlands) to Holland, forming one large state as a buffer against France. The union had never been popular in Belgium, and news of the July revolution in France catalyzed Belgian opposition. The city of Brussels rebelled; the Dutch king sent in troops; faced with barricades and intense street fighting, the troops withdrew. The great powers, preoccupied with other matters and unwilling to allow one of the group intervene, agreed to guarantee Belgian neutrality—a provision that remained in force in 1914.

Revolt also spread to Poland, where it faced the far more formidable forces of the Russian empire. Poland was not an independent state; by the provisions of the Congress of Vienna it was under Russian governance. News of the French revolution of 1830 tipped the country into revolt. The revolutionaries—an initially well-organized coalition of Polish aristocrats defending their autonomy and students, military officers, and middle-class people demanding political reforms—drove the Russians out. Within less than a year, however, the fiercely conservative tsar Nicholas crushed the Polish revolt with the same heavy hand that he had just used on the Decembrists at home and put Poland under military rule.

POPULAR UNREST IN PARIS, 1828

Throughout Europe the police regularly reported on the mood of the common people. This police report, filed in Paris in 1828, captured the rising anger of citizens in the capital. Poor grain harvests in the years before had helped to drive up prices. In the working-class districts of Paris, the economic crisis fueled criticism of the regime. The document also reflects the anxieties of the police, who were not persuaded they could enforce order.

A handwritten placard has been put up at the corner of the rue Saint-Nicolas in the quartier des Quinze-Vingts: "Long live Napoleon! War to the death against Charles X and the priests who are starving us to death!" Several workers cheered, saying that "they would make an end of it, if die they must, since there was no work for them. . . ." Similar leaflets have been distributed in the rue de Charenton and the rue de Charonne in the faubourg Saint-Marceau and the faubourg Saint-Martin. . . . People are saying in the wine shops and workshops that the people must assemble and march on the Tuileries to demand work and bread and that they do not fear the soldiery, since many of them have been won over. This exasperation on the part of the workers has been noted ever since the recent rise in prices, and professional agitators (there are plenty of them in the faubourgs) are trying to exploit it to incite the workers to indulge in excesses. Circumstances are favorable. A great many workers have been suffering for a long time and the price of bread is driving them to utter despair. . . . I have begged the Prefect of Police to get some digging and similar work started from which they can earn at least a pittance.

From Louis Chevalier, *Laboring Classes and Dangerous Classes in Paris during the First Half of the Nineteenth Century.* (Princeton: Princeton University Press, 1973), p. 266.

REFORM IN GREAT BRITAIN

Why was there no revolution in England? One answer is that there almost was. After an era of political conservatism that paralleled that on the Continent, British politics took a different direction, and Britain became one of the most liberal nations in Europe.

The end of the Napoleonic wars brought with it a major agricultural depression in Britain, and the combination of low wages, unemployment, and bad harvests provoked regular social unrest. In the new industrial towns of the north, where economic conditions were especially bad, radical members of the middle class joined with workers to demand increased representation in Parliament. For centuries Parliament had represented the interests of the major propertied class. About two thirds of the members of the House of Commons were either directly nominated by or indirectly owed their election to the patronage of the richest titled landowners in the country. Many of the parliamentary electoral districts, or boroughs, which returned members to the House of Commons, were controlled by landowners who used their power to return candidates sympathetic to their interests. De-

Among the best-known images of the revolutions of 1830 is **"Liberty Leading the People"** by Eugene Delacroix, the same artist who had mourned the extinction of liberty in his painting of the "Massacre of Chios" in Greece (see page 561). The allegorical female figure of liberty leads representatives of the united people: a middle-class man (identified by his top hat), a worker, and a boy of the streets wielding a pistol. Neither middle class people nor children fought on the barricades, and the image of revolutionary unity was romanticized. But optimistic images of what the French called the "Three Glorious Days" of July 1830 were widespread.

fending the system, the Tories argued that Parliament looked after the interests of the nation at large, which they perceived to coincide with the interests of landed property. Liberals in the opposing Whig party, the new industrial middle class, and radical artisans argued passionately for reform. Liberals in particular were by no means proponents of democracy; they wanted to enfranchise "responsible" citizens. Yet they made common cause with well-organized middle- and working-class radicals to intensify the push for re-

form. Middle-class shopkeepers announced they would withhold taxes and, if necessary, form a national guard. Also plagued by an outbreak of cholera, the country appeared to be on the verge of serious general disorder, if not outright revolution. Lord Grey, head of the Whig party, seized the opportunity to press through reform.

The Reform Bill of 1832 reallocated 143 parliamentary seats, most of them from the rural south, to the industrial north. It expanded the franchise, but with

CHRONOLOGY

REFORM IN GREAT BRITAIN, 1832–1867

Electoral Reform Bill	1832
Slavery abolished in British West Indies	1838
Chartist Movement	1840s
Corn Laws repealed	1846
Great Reform Bill	1867
Woman Suffrage movement grows	1860s

property qualifications only one in six men could vote. Produced by nearly revolutionary conditions, the bill ended as a relatively modest measure. It reduced but did not destroy the political strength of landed aristocratic interests. It admitted British liberals, including some of the industrial middle classes, into a junior partnership with the landed elite that had ruled Britain for centuries and was to rule it for at least one more generation.

BRITISH RADICALISM AND THE CHARTIST MOVEMENT

Disappointment with the narrow gains of the 1832 reform focused attention on farther reaching political change, in the form of what was called the "People's Charter." This document, circulated across the country by committees of Chartists, as they were known, and signed by millions, contained six demands: universal white male suffrage, institution of the secret ballot, abolition of property qualifications for membership in the House of Commons, annual parliamentary elections, payment of salaries to members of the House of Commons, and equal electoral districts.

Democracy was a very radical demand in the 1840s. Not surprisingly, Chartists faced fierce opposition. They persisted. Committees presented massive petitions for the Charter to Parliament in 1839 and 1842; on both occasions they were summarily rejected. In the north of England, political demands took shape against a backdrop of strikes, trade-union demonstrations, and attacks on factories and manufacturers who imposed low wages and long hours, or who harassed unionists. The movement peaked in April of 1848. Partly inspired by revolution in continental Europe, Chartist leaders planned a major demonstration and show of force in London. A procession of twenty-five thousand workers assembled, and carried to Parliament a petition containing 6 million signatures demanding the six points. Special constables and contingents of the regular army were marshaled under the now aged duke of Wellington, hero of the battle of Waterloo, to resist this threat to order. In the end, only a small delegation of leaders presented the petition to Parliament. Rain, poor management, and unwillingness on the part of many to do battle with the well-armed constabulary put an end to the Chartists' campaign.

THE HUNGRY FORTIES

The economic and political conditions that sowed unrest in England produced revolution on the Continent. Poor harvests began in the early 1840s. In 1845–1846, the crisis became acute. For two years in a row, the grain harvest failed completely. The potato

The Revolution of 1848 in France. A contemporary engraving celebrating the renewal of revolutionary feeling. Note the themes borrowed from Delacroix's painting of 1830 (see p. 575).

TWO VIEWS OF THE JUNE DAYS, FRANCE, 1848

These two passages make for an interesting comparison. The socialist Karl Marx reported on the events of 1848 in France as a journalist for a German newspaper. For Marx, the bloodshed of the June days shattered the "fraternal illusions" of February 1848, when the king had been overthrown and the provisional government established. That bloodshed also symbolized a new stage in history: one of acute class conflict.

The French liberal politician Alexis de Tocqueville also wrote about his impressions of the revolution. (Tocqueville's account, however, is retrospective, for he wrote his memoirs well after 1848.) For Marx, a socialist observer, the June Days represented a turning point: "the working class was knocking on the gates of history." For Tocqueville, a member of the government, the actions of the crowd sparked fear and conservative reaction. Unlike Marx, Tocqueville was not sympathetic to the revolutionaries of June. Yet he, too, underscored the historical significance of the events.

KARL MARX'S JOURNALISM

The last official remnant of the February Revolution, the Executive Commission, has melted away, like an apparition, before the seriousness of events. The fireworks of Lamartine [French Romantic poet and member of the provisional government] have turned into the war rockets of Cavaignac [French general, in charge of putting down the workers' insurrection]. *Fraternité*, the fraternity of antagonistic classes of which one exploits the other, this *fraternité*, proclaimed in February, on every prison, on every barracks—its true, unadulterated, its prosaic expression is civil war, civil war in its most fearful form, the war of labor and capital. This fraternity flamed in front of all the windows of Paris on the evening of June 25, when the Paris of the bourgeoisie was illuminated, whilst the Paris of the proletariat [Marxist term for the working people] burnt, bled, moaned. . . . The February Revolution was the beautiful revolution, the revolution of universal sympathy, because the antagonisms, which had flared up in it against the monarchy, slumbered peacefully side by side, still undeveloped, because the social struggle which formed its background had won only a joyous existence, an existence of phrases, of words. The June revolution is the ugly revolution, the repulsive revolution, because things have taken the place of phrases, because the republic uncovered the head of the monster itself, by striking off the crown that shielded and concealed it.— Order! was the battle cry of Guizot . . . Order! shouts Cavaignac, the brutal echo of the French National Assembly and of the republican bourgeoisie. Order! thundered his grape-shot, as it ripped up the body of the proletariat. None of the numerous revolutions of the French bourgeoisie since 1789 was an attack on order; for they allowed the rule of the class, they allowed the slavery of the workers, they allowed the bourgeois order to endure, however often the political form of this rule and of this slavery changed. June has attacked this order. Woe to June!"

Neue Rheinische Zeitung (New Rhineland Gazette), June 29, 1848; from Karl Marx, *The Class Struggles in France*. (New York: International Publishers, 1964), pp. 57–58.

ALEXIS DE TOCQUEVILLE REMEMBERS THE JUNE DAYS

Now at last I have come to that insurrection in June which was the greatest and the strangest that had ever taken place in our history, or perhaps in that of any other nation: the greatest because for four days more than a hundred thousand men took part in it, and there were five generals killed; the strangest, because the insurgents were fighting without a battle cry, leaders, or flag, and yet they showed wonderful powers of coordination and a military expertise that astonished the most experienced officers.

Another point that distinguished it from all other events of the same type during the last sixty years was that its object was not to change the form of government, but to alter the organization of society. In truth it was not a political struggle (in the sense in which we have used the word "political" up to now), but a class struggle, a sort of "Servile War." . . . One should not see it only as a brutal and a blind, but as a powerful effort of the workers to escape from the necessities of their condition, which had been depicted to them as an illegitimate depression, and by the sword to open up a road towards that imaginary well-being that had been shown to them in the distance as a right. It was this mixture of greedy desires and false theories that engendered the insurrection and made it so formidable. These poor people had been assured that the goods of the wealthy were in some way the result of a theft committed against themselves. They had been assured that inequalities of fortune were as much opposed to morality and the interests of society as to nature. This obscure and mistaken conception of right, combined with brute force, imparted to it an energy, tenacity and strength it would never have had on its own.

From Alexis de Tocqueville, *Recollections: The French Revolution of 1848.* Edited by J. P. Mayer and A. P. Kerr, translated by George Lawrence. (New Brunswick, N.J.: Transaction Books, 1987), pp. 436–437.

---

blight struck, bringing starvation to Ireland (see page 541) and hunger to Germany, another potato-growing region. By 1846–1847, food prices had, on average, doubled. Bread riots broke out across Europe; city and village dwellers attacked carts carrying grain, refusing to let merchants take it to other markets; or they simply took the grain and sold it at what they considered a fair price. Starving peasants and unemployed laborers swamped public-relief organizations. The years 1846 and 1847 were "probably the worst of the entire century in terms of want and human suffering," and the decade has earned the name of "the Hungry Forties."

Hunger itself did not cause revolution. It did, however, test governments' abilities and their legitimacy. When the inadequate public relief systems in France foundered, when troops moved to repress potato riots in Berlin, or when regimes armed middle-class citizens to protect themselves against the poor, governments looked both authoritarian and inept. Under those circumstances, states lost the confidence of their supporters, starting a wave of revolution that swept across Europe, breaking first in France.

> Defying the king's threats, the opposition called a final, giant banquet for February 22, 1848. When the government banned the meeting, revolution broke out.

THE FRENCH REVOLUTION OF 1848

The French monarchy installed after the July revolution of 1830 seemed to differ little from its predecessor. The new king, Louis Philippe, gathered around him representatives of the banking and industrial elite. The regime often gave the impression of complacency, and disappointed the high hopes that it had inspired. By 1847, its opponents had organized a campaign for electoral reform throughout France. Since political meetings were outlawed, the opposition organized political "banquets," where opponents of the regime drank toasts to reform—though not to outright revolution. Defying the king's threats, the opposition called a final, giant banquet for February 22, 1848. When the government banned the meeting, revolution broke out. In a surprisingly short time, Louis Philippe abdicated the throne.

The provisional government of the new republic was a remarkable group, consisting of a combination of liberals, republicans and, for the first time, socialists. It set about making a new constitution, with elections based on universal male suffrage. For working men and women, by far the most widely supported demand involved the "right to work," which meant the ability to earn a living wage, to be able to support oneself. The provisional government cautiously supported this demand, creating what were called National Workshops, a program of public works in and around Paris. Initial plans called for the employment of no more than ten or twelve thousand persons. But with unemployment running as high as 65 percent in the construction trades and 51 percent in textiles and clothing, workers streamed in, as many as sixty-six thousand by April, and one hundred twenty thousand by June 1848.

By late spring 1848, a majority of the French assembly believed that the workshop system had become a financial drain and, worse, a serious threat to social order. At the end of May, the government closed the workshops to new enrollment, excluded anyone who had resided in Paris for less than six months, and sent all members between the ages of eighteen and twenty-five to the army. On June 21, the government simply ended the program, repudiating any responsibility for the social question. The reaction brought some of the bloodiest conflict of the period. For four days, June 23–26, laborers, journeymen, socialists, and some republican leaders defended themselves in an ultimately hopeless military battle against armed forces recruited, in part, from willing provincials eager enough to assist in the repression of the urban working class. The repression itself was ferocious, shocking many observers.

In the aftermath of the "June Days," the French government moved quickly to bring order to the country. Assembly members hoped a strong leader would bring dissidents to heel. Four candidates ran for president of the republic: Alphonse de Lamartine, the moderate republican; General Louis Eugène Cavaignac, who had commanded the troops in June; Alexandre August Ledru-Rollin, a socialist; and Louis Napoleon Bonaparte, nephew of the former emperor, who polled more than twice as many votes as the other three candidates combined.

"All facts and personages of great importance in world history occur twice . . . the first time as tragedy, the second as farce." This was how Karl Marx (no admirer of Napoleon I) summarized the relationship of Louis Napoleon to his uncle. Louis Napoleon's name gave him a wide and suitably vague appeal. Conservatives believed he would protect property and order. "Napoleon" evoked glory and greatness. Louis Napoleon's role as an "an all purpose personage" helped secure his electoral victory. As one old peasant expressed it, "How could I

The Barricade, by Ernest Meissonier (1815–1891). A very different view of 1848, one that foreshadows the defeat of revolutionary hopes.

help voting for this gentleman—I whose nose was frozen at Moscow?"

Not surprisingly, Louis Napoleon used his position to consolidate his power. He enlisted the support of the Catholics by permitting them to regain control over the schools and by sending an expedition to Rome in 1849 to rescue the pope from revolutionaries. In 1851 he invited the people to grant him the power to draw up a new constitution. A plebiscite shortly thereafter authorized his actions. After one year Louis Napoleon Bonaparte ordered another plebiscite and, with the approval of over 95 percent of the voters, established the Second Empire and assumed the title of Napoleon III (1852–1870), emperor of the French.

Why was the French Revolution of 1848 significant? First, its dynamics would be repeated elsewhere. The middle classes played a pivotal political role. Louis Philippe's regime had been proudly "bourgeois" but ended up alienating many of its supporters. Denied a direct political voice, key groups of the middle class swung to the opposition, allying themselves with radicals who never would have toppled the regime alone. Yet demands for reform soon ran up against fears of disorder and desire for a strong state. This familiar dynamic led to the collapse of the republic and to the rule of Louis Napoleon Bonaparte. Second, many contemporaries saw the June Days as simply naked class struggle. The violence of the June Days shattered many of the liberal aspirations of the earlier period. The romantic image of revolutionary unity captured in Delacroix's *Liberty Leading the People* now seemed naïve. In the aftermath of 1848, the interests and politics of middle- and working-class people were more sharply differentiated and more directly at odds. Socialism would come into its own as an independent political force.

Conclusion

The French revolution of 1789 had polarized Europe; in its aftermath new political identities formed and new political ideologies were spelled out. The Congress of Vienna, or peace settlement of 1815, had aimed to establish a new international system and to inoculate Europe against revolution. It succeeded in the first aim, but only partially in the second. The combination of new politics with industrialization and rapid social change undermined the conservative order. From the 1820s through the 1840s, a combination of social grievances and political disappointments created powerful movements for change, first in Latin America and the Balkans, then in western Europe and Great Britain.

The French revolution of 1848 (the second since the defeat of Napoleon) became the opening act of a much larger drama. In Southern and Central Europe, as we will see in Chapter 21, the issues were framed differently. Still, the dynamics of revolution in France foreshadowed the turn of events in other lands: exhilarating revolutionary successes were followed by the unraveling of revolutionary alliances and the emergence of new forms of conservative government. Throughout the West, the mid-century crisis of 1848 became a turning point. In its aftermath, the kinds of broad revolutionary alliances that had produced revolution were vanquished by class politics, and utopian socialism gave way to Marxism. In culture as in politics Romanticism faded, its expansive sense of possibility replaced by the more biting viewpoint of realism. Economies and states changed. Conservatism, liberalism, and socialism adapted to new political conditions. How this happened, and the explosive role of nationalism in the process, are the subjects of the next chapter.

Key Terms

Congress of Vienna
Simón Bolívar
Nicholas I
Greek Civil War
conservatism

liberalism
The Wealth of Nations
socialism
The Communist Manifesto
nationalism

Romanticism
Chartist Movement
French Revolution of 1848

Selected Readings

Agulhon, Maurice. *The Republican Experiment, 1848–1852.* New York, 1983. A full treatment of the revolution in France.

Anderson, Benedict. *Imagined Communities: Reflections on the Origin and Spread of Nationalism.* London, 1983. The most influential recent study of the subject, highly recommended for further reading.

Briggs, Asa. *The Age of Improvement, 1783–1867.* New York, 1979. A survey of England from 1780 to 1870, particularly strong on Victorian attitudes.

Colley, Linda. *Britons: Forging the Nation, 1707–1837.* New Haven, 1992. An important analysis of Britain's emerging national consciousness in the eighteenth and early nineteenth centuries.

Furet, François. *Revolutionary France, 1770–1880.* New York, 1970. An excellent and fresh overview by one of the preeminent historians of the revolution of 1789.

Gilbert, Sandra M., and Susan Gubar. *The Madwoman in the Attic: The Woman Writer and the Nineteenth-Century Literary Imagination.* New Haven and London, 1970. An examination of history of women writers and women writers as historians of their time.

Hobsbawm, Eric. *The Age of Revolution: Europe 1789 to 1848*. New York, 1970. A classic, and still very useful, account of the period.

Kramer, Lloyd. *Nationalism: Political Cultures in Europe and America, 1775–1865*. London, 1998. Excellent recent overview.

Langer, William. *Political and Social Upheaval, 1832–1851*. New York, 1969. Long the standard, and still the most comprehensive survey.

Laven, David and Lucy Riall. *Napoleon's Legacy: Problems of Government in Restoration Europe*. London, 2002. A new collection of essays.

Levinger, Matthew. *Enlightened Nationalism: The Transformation of Prussian Political Culture 1806–1848*. New York, 2000. A new and nuanced study of Prussian conservatism, with implications for the rest of Europe.

Macfie, A. L. *Orientalism*. London, 2002. Introductory but very clear.

Merriman, John M., ed. *1830 in France*. New York, 1975. Emphasizes the nature of revolution and examines events outside Paris.

Pinkney, David. *The French Revolution of 1830*. Princeton, N.J., 1972. A reinterpretation, now the best history of the revolution.

Porter, Roy, and Mikulas Teich, eds. *Romanticism in National Context*. Cambridge, 1988.

Raeff, Marc. *The Decembrist Movement*. New York, 1966. A study of the Russian uprising with documents.

Sahlins, Peter. *Forest Rites: The War of the Demoiselles in Nineteenth-Century France*. Cambridge, Mass., 1994. A fascinating study of relations among peasant communities, the forests, and the state.

Said, Edward W. *Orientalism*. New York, 1979. A brilliant and biting study of the imaginative hold of the "Orient" on European intellectuals.

Saville, John. *1848: The British State and the Chartist Movement*. New York, 1987. A detailed account of the movement's limited successes and ultimate failure.

Schroeder, Paul. *The Transformation of European Politics, 1763–1848*. Oxford and New York, 1994. For those interested in international relations and diplomacy; massively researched and a fresh look at the period. Especially good on the Congress of Vienna.

Sewell, William H. *Work and Revolution in France: The Language of Labor from the Old Regime to 1848*. Cambridge, 1980. A very influential study of French radicalism and its larger implications.

Smith, Bonnie. *The Gender of History: Men, Women, and Historical Practice*. Cambridge, Mass., 1998. On Romanticism and the historical imagination.

Wordsworth, Jonathan, Michael C. Jaye, and Robert Woof. *William Wordsworth and the Age of English Romanticism*. New Brunswick, 1987. Wide ranging and beautifully illustrated, a good picture of the age.

DIGITAL HISTORY

NATIONALISM AND MUSIC

I think our reputation as a musical nation is fairly old and well-known, and to preserve this, to infuse new spirit into it and to enhance it more and more is the task of every artist who is at the same time inspired by true patriotism. As for me, I am merely making the beginning.

—Smetana, Bedřich, and František Bartoš. Bedřich Smetana, Letters and Reminiscences. Prague: Artia, 1955. p. 70

Toward the end of the eighteenth century, a vast cultural movement began to sweep across Europe. The movement, known as Romanticism, called into question many of the principles of the eighteenth-century Enlightenment—human reason, the uniformity of human nature, and the life of the mind. The Romantics were a mixed bag of philosophers, historians, painters, poets, and musicians who believed that the excessive rationality of the eighteenth-century *philosophe* had actually done more harm than good. Because they emphasized the diversity of humanity, and the importance of spontaneity, creativity, emotion, and passion, the Romantics appeared to be an antidote or corrective to many aspects of European cultural and intellectual life.

Within the Romantic movement, a group of composers were inspired by new ideas about national identity and the revolutions occurring throughout Europe. They merged the political ideology of nationalism, its celebration of the nation in all its simplicity and history, with Romantic music to create a new movement called Musical Nationalism. In Eastern Europe and Russia, composers began to tap into folk heroes, tales, songs, and dances in order to establish a new identity, a nationalist one. Musical nationalism in Germany, Hungary, Czechoslovakia, Russia, and elsewhere helped create a new soul of the nation, one that celebrated the people and their traditions. In operas and symphonic poems, the nineteenth-century musical nationalists exposed the distant and exotic for all to see. In this way, the ideals of the Enlightenment were challenged at the same time that many nations began to develop distinct cultural identities.

The primary sources in the Nationalism and Music Digital History Feature at www.wwnorton.com/wciv reveal how composers expressed the new national fervor felt by millions of people throughout Central, Southern, and Eastern Europe. While reading some of the writings of the musical nationalists and listening to their music, think about the following questions:

• Why did musical nationalism appear in the nineteenth century and not earlier? What forces were largely responsible for its development?

• Why did musical nationalism appear in Eastern Europe and Russia first?

• Is there American nationalist music?

• Do you think that musical nationalism helped create new national identities?

Chapter
TWENTY-ONE

WHAT IS A NATION?
TERRITORIES, STATES,
AND CITIZENS,
1848–1871

Eighteen forty-eight was a tumultuous year. From Berlin to Budapest to Rome, insurgents rushed to hastily built barricades and forced kings and princes to beat an equally hasty—though only temporary—retreat. Across the Atlantic, the treaty of Guadalupe Hidalgo ended the war between Mexico and the United States with a massive territorial transaction: for a sum of $15 million, the United States acquired half a million square miles of western territory, including California. The exchange nearly completed the United States' continental expansion, but it also ushered in conflicts that led to the American Civil War. In July of 1848, the Seneca Falls Convention marked the emergence of an organized movement for woman suffrage in the United States, which was paralleled in Europe. The New York *Herald* detected a disturbing connection among the year's events and commented nervously that "To whatever part of the world the attention is directed, the political and social fabric is crumbling. . . . [T]he work of revolution is no longer confined to the Old World, nor to the masculine gender." It was in 1848, too, that miners struck gold in California, launching an event with transatlantic resonance, the gold rush. When news of California gold reached Paris in the fall of 1848 after a summer of bitter social conflict, Karl Marx acidly remarked that "golden dreams were to supplant the socialist dreams of the Paris workers."

The social and political upheavals of 1848 marked the high point of the "age of revolution" and their failure signaled the end of that age. Yet the mid-century crisis was an equally important turning point in the history of nationalism and nation building. Nationalism, as defined in the last chapter, is the sense of belonging to a community that shares historical, geographic, cultural, or political traditions. As historians point out, this sense is both powerful and diffuse. It could be—and was—cultivated by intellectuals, revolutionaries, and governments for different purposes. Nationalism could serve liberal or conservative politics and goals. During the first part of the nineteenth century, nationalism was usually linked to liberal goals; by the end of the century it had been given a conservative meaning. 1848 was an important moment in this larger sea change.

FOCUS QUESTIONS

• What different forms did nationalism take and why?

• Why did the efforts to unify Italy and Germany succeed during the 1860s?

• What were the similarities between slavery and serfdom?

• How did journalists' depictions of the Crimean War reflect cultural trends?

Nation building refers to the process of creating new states and reconstructing older ones, a process in which the nineteenth century marked a crucial stage. Territorial changes, such as the treaty of Guadalupe Hidalgo, which dramatically transformed the boundaries of the United States, were significant. But so were political reforms and new state structures that changed how governments worked and how they related to their citizens. The American Civil War, and the unification of Italy and of Germany involved wrenching political change as well as territory, and all three had far-reaching ramifications for the international order. France, Britain, Russia, and Austria were also rebuilt during this period—their bureaucracies overhauled and their electorates expanded, relations between ethnic groups reorganized, Russian serfdom, like American slavery, abolished. Changing relations between states and those they governed lay at the heart of nation building. And these changes were hastened by reactions against the revolutionary upheavals of 1848.

NATIONALISM AND REVOLUTION IN 1848

What different forms did nationalism take and why?

In central and eastern Europe, the spring of 1848 brought a dizzying sequence of revolution and repression. The roots of revolution lay in social antagonisms, economic crisis, and political grievances. But these conflicts were also shaped decisively by nationalism. Reformers and revolutionaries had liberal goals: representative government, an end to privilege, economic development, and so on. But they also sought some form of national unity. Indeed, reformers in Germany, Italy, Poland, and the Austrian empire believed that their liberal goals might only be realized in a vigorous, "modern" nation-state. The fate of the 1848 revolutions in these regions demonstrated nationalism's power to mobilize opponents of the regime, but also its potential to splinter revolutionary alliances and to override other allegiances and values entirely.

WHO MAKES A NATION? GERMANY IN 1848

In 1815, there was no "Germany." The Congress of Vienna had created a "German Confederation," a loose organization of thirty-eight states, including Austria and Prussia but not their non-German territories in sections of Poland and Hungary. As a practical matter, Prussia was, with Austria, the great power in the area, and would play a central role in German politics.

Prussia aimed to establish itself as the leading German state and a counter to Austrian power in the region. Prussian's most significant victory in this respect came with the Zollverein, or customs union, in 1834, which established free trade among the German states and a uniform tariff against the rest of the world—an openly protectionist policy advocated by the economist Friedrich List. By the 1840s, the union included almost all of the German states except German Austria and offered manufacturers a market of almost 34 million people. The spread of the railways after 1835 accelerated exchange within this expanded internal market.

During the 1840s, in both Prussia and the smaller German states, political clubs of students and other radicals joined with middle-class groups of lawyers, doctors, and businessmen to press new demands for representative government and reform. Newspapers multiplied, defying censorship. Liberal reformers resented both Prussian domination of the German Confederation and the conservatism of the Habsburgs who ruled the Austrian empire. They attacked the combination of autocracy and bureaucratic authority that stifled political life in Prussia and Austria. German nationhood, they reasoned, would break Austrian or Prussian domination and end the sectional fragmentation that made reform so difficult.

When Frederick William IV (1840–1861) succeeded to the Prussian throne in 1840, hopes ran high. The new king did gesture toward liberalizing reforms. However, the king also opposed constitutionalism, and any representative participation in issues of legislation and budgets. As in France, liberals and radicals in Prussia and the German states continued their reform campaigns. And when revolution came to France in the spring of 1848, unrest spread across the Rhine. In the smaller German states, kings and princes yielded surprisingly quickly to revolutionary movements. The governments promised freedom of the

GERMAN CONFEDERATION, 1815

What helped to bring the various states of the German Confederation together? What was their relationship with German-speaking Prussia? What factors prevented a more formally unified German state at this time?

press, elections, expanded suffrage, jury trials, and other liberal reforms. In Prussia, Frederick William IV, shaken by unrest in the countryside and stunned by a showdown in Berlin between the army and revolutionaries in which two hundred and fifty were killed, finally capitulated.

THE FRANKFURT ASSEMBLY AND GERMAN NATIONHOOD

The second and most idealistic stage of the revolution began with the election of delegates to an all-German assembly in Frankfurt, where representatives from

Prussia, Austria, and the small German states met to discuss the unification of a single German nation. Most of the delegates came from the professional classes—lawyers, professors, administrators—and most were moderate liberals. Many had assumed that the Frankfurt Assembly would draft a constitution for a liberal, unified Germany, much as an assembly of Frenchmen had done for their country in 1789. Yet, the Frankfurt Assembly had no resources, no sovereign power no single legal code. It did not even have a suitable meeting place: for eleven months the delegates worked in a single public room in an old church with terrible acoustics—no place to debate and decide on legislation. Although the Assembly benefited from the energy, idealism, and devotion of the delegates, it faced enormous obstacles, and at times it teetered on the brink of chaos.

On the Assembly floor, questions of nationality proved contentious and destructive. Which Germans would be in the new state? A majority of the Assembly's delegates argued that Germans were all those who, by language, culture, or geography, felt themselves bound to the enterprise of unification. They believed the German nation should include as many Germans as possible—a position encouraged by the spectacle of disintegration in the Habsburg empire. This was the "Great German" position. It was countered by a minority who called for a "Small Germany," one that left out all lands of the Habsburg empire, including German Austria. The Assembly retreated to the "Small German" solution and in April of 1849 offered the crown of the new German nation to Frederick William IV.

Frederick William refused the offer. The Assembly's proposed constitution, he argued, was too liberal, and to owe his crown to a parliament would be demeaning. He called it the "crown from the gutter." The Prussian monarch wanted both the crown and a larger German state, but on his own terms. After a brief protest, summarily suppressed by the military, the delegates went home, disillusioned by their experience, with many convinced that their liberal and nationalist goals were incompatible.

Beyond the walls of the church in Frankfurt, popular revolution took its own course. Peasants ransacked tax offices and burned castles; workers smashed machines. In towns and cities, a groundswell of political activity produced citizen militias, new daily newspapers, pamphleteering, and political clubs. For the first time, many of these clubs admitted women, although they denied them the right to speak. In Berlin and other German cities newly founded women's clubs sought to participate in an expanded political world. Such popular politics made moderate reformers uneasy, however; full male suffrage alone was a deeply disturbing prospect. Peasant and worker protests had forced the king to make concessions in the early spring of 1848; now moderate reformers found popular influence threatening.

National unification increasingly appealed to moderates as a way to maintain order. In that context, nationhood stood for a new constitution and political community, but also for a sternly enforced rule of law.

PEOPLES AGAINST EMPIRE: THE HABSBURG LANDS

In the sprawling Austrian empire, nationalism played a different, centrifugal role. The empire included a wide array of ethnic and language groups: Germans, Czechs, Magyars, Poles, Slovaks, Serbs, and Italians, to name only the most prominent. In some areas of the empire, these groups lived in relative separation and isolation. Elsewhere they co-existed, though not always harmoniously. The Habsburgs found it increasingly difficult to hold their empire together as these groups' varying national demands escalated after 1815.

One grave threat to the empire came from the Hungarian region. There, national claims were advanced by the relatively small Magyar aristocracy, led by the gifted and influential Lajos (Louis) Kossuth. A member of the lower nobility, Kossuth was by turns a lawyer, publicist, newspaper editor, and political leader. To protest the closed-door policy of the empire's barely representative Diet (Parliament) Kossuth published transcripts of parliamentary debates and distributed them to a broader public. He campaigned for independence and a separate Hungarian parliament, but he

CHRONOLOGY

NATION BUILDING IN GERMANY, 1800–1850

Napoleon defeats Prussia	1806
Edict abolishing serfdom	1807
Municipal Ordinance of 1808	
Creation of the Zollverein	1834
Liberal protests	1820s–1840s
Revolution of 1848	
Frankfurt Assembly meets	1848
Frederick Willam grants Prussian constitution	1850

FREDERICK WILLIAM IV REFUSES THE "THRONE FROM THE GUTTER"

In March 1849, after months of deliberation and constitution making, the Frankfurt Assembly offered the throne of its proposed German state to the Prussian monarch Frederick William IV, who quickly turned it down. He had already reflected on the matter. In an earlier (December, 1848) letter to one of his advisors, the diplomat Christian von Bunsen, he had set out his reasoning as follows.

I want the princes' approval of neither *this* election nor *this* crown. Do you understand the words emphasized here? For you I want to shed light on this as briefly and brightly as possible. First, *this* crown is no crown. The crown which a Hohenzoller [the Prussian royal house] could accept, *if* circumstances *permitted*, is not one *made* by an assembly sprung from a revolutionary seed in the genre of the crown of cobble stones of Louis Philippe—even if this assembly was established with the sanction of princes . . . but one which bears the stamp of God, one which makes [the individual] on whom it [the crown] is placed, after his anointment, a "divine right" monarch—just as it has elevated more than 34 princes to Kings of the Germans by divine right and just as it bonds the last of these to his predecessors. The crown worn by Ottonians, Staufens [earlier German royal houses], Habsburgs can of course also be worn by a Hohenzoller; it honors him overwhelmingly with the luster of a thousand years. But *this* one, to which you regrettably refer, overwhelmingly dishonors [its bearer] with its smell of the gunpowder of the 1848 revolution—the silliest, dumbest, worst, though—thank God!—not the most evil of this century. Such an imaginary headband, baked out of dirt and the letters of the alphabet, is supposed to be welcome to a legitimate divine right king: to put it more precisely, to the King of Prussia who is blessed with a crown which may not be the oldest but, of all those which have never been stolen, is the most noble? . . . I will tell you outright: if the thousand-year-old crown of the German nation . . . should be bestowed again, it will be *I* and my equals who will bestow it. And woe to those who assume [powers] to which they have no title.

Ralph Menning, *The Art of the Possible: Documents on Great Power Diplomacy, 1814–1914* (New York: McGraw-Hill, 1996), p. 82.

also wanted to bring politics to the people. The Hungarian political leader combined aristocratic style with rabble-rousing politics: a delicate balancing act but one that, when it worked, catapulted him to the center of Habsburg politics. He was as well known in the Habsburg capital of Vienna as he was in Pressburg and Budapest.

The other major nationalist movement that plagued the Habsburg emperor was pan-Slavism. Slavs included Russians, Poles, Ukrainians, Czechs, Slovaks, Slovenes, Croats, Serbs, Macedonians, and Bulgarians. Before 1848 pan-Slavism was primarily a cultural movement. It was internally divided, however, by the competing claims of different Slavic languages and traditions.

Tsar Nicholas of Russia sought to use pan-Slavism to his advantage, making arguments about "Slavic" uniqueness part of a program of "autocracy, orthodoxy, nationality" after 1825. The tsar's pan-Slavism alienated

Western-oriented Slavs who resented Russian rule. Pan-Slavism was a volatile and unpredictable political force in the regions of Eastern Europe where Austrian and Russia vied for power and influence.

1848 IN AUSTRIA AND HUNGARY: SPRINGTIME OF PEOPLES AND THE AUTUMN OF EMPIRE

1848 brought the empire's combustive combination of political, social, and ethnic tensions to the point of explosion. The Habsburgs faced multiple challenges to their authority. The opening salvo came from the Hungarians. Emboldened by uprisings in France and Germany, Kossuth stepped up his reform campaigns, demanding representative institutions throughout the empire and autonomy for the Hungarian "Magyar" nation. In Vienna, the seat of Habsburg power, a popular movement of students and artisans demanding political and social reforms built barricades and attacked the imperial palace. The government conceded to radical demands for male suffrage and a single house of representatives, and agreed to begin dismantling serfdom. The government also yielded to Czech demands in Bohemia, granting that kingdom its own constitution. To the south, Italian liberals and nationalists attacked the empire's territories. As what would be called "the springtime of peoples" unfolded, Habsburg control of its various provinces seemed to be coming apart.

Yet the explosion of national sentiment that shook the empire later allowed it to recoup its fortunes. The paradox of nationalism in central Europe was that no cultural or ethnic majority could declare independence in a given region without prompting rebellion from other minority groups that inhabited the same area.

The Austrians were able to divide and conquer. In May 1848, during a Slav congress, an insurrection broke out in Prague. Austrian troops entered the city to restore order, sent the Slav congress packing, and reasserted control in Bohemia. The regime also sent troops to regain control in the Italian provinces of Lombardy and Venetia, and quarrels among the Italians helped the Austrians succeed.

Nationalism and counternationalism in Hungary set the stage for the final act of the drama. To prevent a peasant insurrection, the Hungarian parliament also abolished serfdom and ended noble privilege. It established freedom of the press and of religion, and changed the suffrage requirements, enfranchising small property holders. Many of these measures (called the March laws) were hailed by Hungarian peasants, Jewish communities, and liberals. But other provisions, particularly the extension of Magyar control, provoked opposition from the Croats, Serbs, and Romanians within Hungary. The Austrian government took advantage of these divisions. It appointed the anti-Magyar Josip Jelacic as governor of the breakaway province of Croatia. Encouraged by the Austrians, Jelacic attacked. Kossuth rallied the Hungarian forces and turned the tide in their favor. On April 14, 1848, Kossuth upped the ante, severing all ties between Hungary and Austria. The new Austrian emperor, Franz Josef, now played his last card: he asked for military support from Nicholas I of Russia. The Habsburgs were unable to win their "holy struggle against anarchy," but the Russian army of over three hundred thousand found it an easier task. By mid-August 1849, the Hungarian revolt was crushed.

In the city of Vienna itself, the revolutionary movement had lost ground. When economic crisis and unemployment helped spark a second popular uprising, the emperor's forces, with Russian support, descended on the capital. On October 31, the liberal government

Hungarian revolutionary Lajos Kossuth, 1851. A leader of the Hungarian nationalist movement who combined aristocratic style with rabble-rousing politics, Kossuth almost succeeded in an attempt to separate Hungary from Austria in 1849.

WHY DID THE EFFORTS TO UNIFY ITALY AND GERMANY SUCCEED DURING THE 1860s?

BUILDING THE NATION-STATE   591

capitulated. The regime reestablished censorship, disbanded the National Guard and student organizations, and put twenty-five revolutionary leaders to death in front of a firing squad. Kossuth went into hiding in Turkey, and lived the rest of his life in exile.

1848 AND THE EARLY STAGES OF ITALIAN UNIFICATION

The Italian penninsula had not been united since the Roman empire. At the beginning of the nineteenth century it was a patchwork of small states. Austria occupied the northernmost states of Lombardy and Venetia, which were also the most urban and industrial. Habsburg dependents also ruled Tuscany, Parma, and Modena, extending Austria's influence over the north of the penninsula. The independent Italian states included the southern kingdom of the Two Sicilies, governed by members of the Bourbon family; the Papal States, ruled by Pope Gregory XVI (1831–1846); and most important, Piedmont-Sardinia, ruled by the reform-minded monarch Charles Albert (1831–1849) of the House of Savoy. Charles Albert had no particular commitment to creating an Italian national state, but by virtue of Piedmont-Sardinia's economic power, geographical location, and long tradition of opposition to the Habsburgs, Charles Albert's state played a central role in nationalist and anti-Austrian politics.

The leading Italian nationalist in this period was Giuseppe Mazzini (1805–1872) from the city of Genoa, in Piedmont. In 1831 Mazzini founded Young Italy, which was an anti-Austrian movement in favor of constitutional reforms and Italian unification. Under his charismatic leadership Young Italy clubs multiplied. Yet the organization's favored tactics, plotting mutinies and armed rebellions, proved ineffective. In 1834, Mazzini launched an invasion of the kingdom of Sardinia. Without sufficient support, it fizzled, driving Mazzini into exile in England.

The turmoil that swept across Europe in 1848 raised hopes for political and social change and put Italian unification on the agenda. In the north, the provinces of Venetia and Lombardy rebelled against the Austrian occupation. Charles Albert of Piedmont-Sardinia provided them with military support and took up the banner of Italian nationalism, although many charged that he was primarily interested in expanding his own power. In

> The turmoil that swept across Europe in 1848 raised hopes for political and social change and put Italian unification on the agenda.

Rome, a popular uprising challenged the power of the pope and established a republic, with Mazzini as its head. These movements were neither coordinated nor ultimately successful. Within a year, the Austrians had regained the upper hand in the north. French forces under Louis Napoleon intervened in the Papal States, and although they met fierce resistance from the Roman republicans joined by Giuseppe Garibaldi (see below), they nonetheless restored the pope's power. Like most of the radical movements of 1848, these uprisings failed. Still, they lifted the spirits of nationalists who spoke of a *risorgimento*, or Italian resurgence, that would restore the nation to the position of leadership it had held in Roman times and during the Renaissance.

BUILDING THE NATION-STATE

> Why did the efforts to unify Italy and Germany succeed during the 1860s?

In the wake of the revolutions of 1848, new nation-states were built—often, ironically, by former critics of nationalism. Since the French Revolution of 1789, conservative politicians had associated "nationhood" with liberalism: constitutions, reforms, new political communities. Nationalism evoked memories of popular movements clashing with authoritarian governments. During the second half of the century, however, the political ground shifted dramatically. States and governments took the national initiative. Alarmed by revolutionary ferment, they promoted economic development, pressed social and political reforms, and sought to shore up their base of support. Rather than allow popular nationalist movements to emerge from below, statesmen consolidated their governments' powers and built nations from above.

FRANCE UNDER NAPOLEON III

Napoleon III, like his uncle, believed in personal rule and the development of a centralized state. His constitution, modeled on that of the first French empire, gave control of finance, the army, and foreign affairs exclusively to the emperor. The assembly, elected by universal male suffrage, held virtually no power and could only approve legislation drafted at the emperor's direction by a Council of State. Through bureaucratic expansion, the regime aimed to put the countryside under the political and administrative thumb of the modern state, undermining traditional elites and cultivating a new relationship with the people. "The confidence of our rough peasants can be won by an energetic authority," as one of the regime's representatives put it.

Napoleon III and his government also took steps to develop the economy, harboring a near utopian faith in the ability of industrial expansion to bring prosperity, political support, and national glory. The government thus encouraged a variety of progressive economic developments, including credit and other new forms of financing. It passed new limited-liability laws to spur

growth and signed a free-trade treaty with Britain in 1860. The government also supported the founding of the Crédit Mobilier, an investment banking institution that sold shares publicly and financed such enterprises as railroads, insurance and gas companies, the coal and construction industries, and the building of the Suez Canal (see Chapter 22). In a different vein, Napoleon III also reluctantly permitted the existence of trade unions and the legalization of strikes. By appealing to both workers and the middle class, he sought to symbolize his country's reemergence as a leading world power.

Perhaps the best illustration of the Second Empire's policies was the transformation of the nation's capital. In Paris, as in other nineteenth-century cities, the medieval infrastructure was buckling under the weight of industrial development. Cholera epidemics had killed twenty thousand in 1832 and

Paris rebuilt. Much of the medieval infrastructure of Paris was razed by Baron Haussman and replaced with new streets and buildings. This photograph shows the new design for the area surrounding the Arc de Triomphe in an "etoile" (star) pattern, with the wide boulevards named after Napoleon I's famous generals.

WHY DID THE EFFORTS TO UNIFY ITALY AND GERMANY SUCCEED DURING THE 1860s?

BUILDING THE NATION-STATE   593

nineteen thousand in 1849. In 1850, only one house in five had running water. Economic and public-health incentives to rebuild were multiplied by political concerns, for such "unhealthy conditions" bred not only disease but also crime—and revolution. The massive rebuilding, financed by the Crédit Mobilier among other investment institutions, razed much of the medieval center of the city and erected thirty-four thousand new buildings, including elegant new hotels with the first elevators. Wide new boulevards, many named for Napoleon I's most famous generals, radiated outward from the Arc de Triomphe. This wholesale renovation did not benefit everyone. Although the regime built model worker residences, demolitions and rising rents drove working people out of the city center into the increasingly segregated suburbs. Baron Haussmann, who presided over the project, considered the city a monument to "cleanliness and order"; but others called him an "artist of demolition." For centuries monarchs had taken on massive building projects, but this was different, an unprecedented and conscious state effort to change what contemporaries conceived of as the "mechanics" or "system" of modern urban life.

MILL'S LOGIC, OR FRANCHISE FOR FEMALES
"Pray clear the way, there, for these—ah—persons."

John Stuart Mill and Suffragettes. Cartoon published in 1860, by which time Mill had established a reputation as a liberal political philosopher and supporter of woman suffrage. The famous political thinker Mill argued that women's enfranchisement was essential to personal liberty and to social progress.

VICTORIAN BRITAIN AND THE SECOND REFORM BILL (1867)

Less disturbed by the revolutionary wave of 1848, Great Britain was more willing and able to chart a course of significant social and political reform, continuing a process that had begun in 1832 with the First Reform Bill. The government faced mounting demands to extend the franchise beyond the middle classes. Industrial expansion sustained a growing stratum of highly skilled and relatively well-paid workers (almost exclusively male). These workers, concentrated for the most part within the building, engineering, and textile industries, turned away from the tradition of militant radicalism that had characterized the "Hungry Forties."

Instead they favored collective self-help through cooperative societies or trade unions, whose major role was to accumulate funds for insurance against old age and unemployment. They saw education as a tool for advancement, and patronized the mechanics' institutes and similar institutions founded by them or on their behalf. These prosperous workers created real pressure for electoral reform.

Working-class leaders and middle-class dissidents joined in a countrywide campaign for a new reform bill and a House of Commons responsive to their interests. They were backed by some shrewd Conservatives, such as Benjamin Disraeli (1804–1881), who argued that political life would be improved, not disrupted, by including the "aristocrats of labor." In actuality, Disraeli was betting that the newly enfranchised demographic would vote Conservative, and in 1867, he steered through Parliament a bill that reached farther than anything proposed by his political opponents. The 1867 Reform Bill doubled the franchise by extending the vote to any men who paid poor rates or rent of ten pounds or more a year in urban areas (this meant, in general, skilled workers), and to rural tenants paying rent of twelve pounds or more. As in 1832, the bill redistributed seats, with large northern cities gaining representation at the expense of the rural south. The "responsible" working class had been deemed worthy to participate in the affairs of state.

The reform bill was silent on women; but an important minority insisted that liberalism should include women's enfranchisement. Their cause found a passionate supporter in John Stuart Mill, perhaps the century's most brilliant, committed, and influential defender of personal liberty. In 1859, Mill wrote *On Liberty*, which many consider the classic defense of individual freedom in the face of the state and the "tyranny of the majority." During the same period he coauthored—with his lover and eventual wife, Harriet Taylor—essays on women's political rights, the law of marriage, and divorce. His *The Subjection of Women* (1869), published after Harriet died, argued what few could even contemplate: that women had to be considered individuals on the same plane as men, and that women's freedom was a measure of social progress. *Subjection* was an international success, and with *On Liberty* became one of the defining texts of Western liberalism. Mill's arguments, however, did not carry the day. Only militant suffrage movements and the crisis of World War I brought women the vote.

The decade or so following the passage of the Reform Bill of 1867 marked the high point of British liberalism. By opening the doors of political participation, liberalism had accomplished a peaceful restructuring of political institutions and social life. It did so under considerable pressure from below, however, and in Britain as elsewhere, liberal leaders made it clear that these doors were unquestionably not open to everyone. Casting a ballot was a specific privilege granted to specific social groups in return for their contributions to and interests in society. Men of property might champion the rule of law and representative government, but they balked at the prospect of a truly democratic politics and did not shy from heavy-handed, law-and-order politics.

ITALIAN UNIFICATION: CAVOUR AND GARIBALDI

The failed efforts to unify Italy in 1848 left behind two different visions of Italian statehood. The first was most closely associated with Mazzini who, as we have seen, believed in a republican Italy, built by the people.

Mazzini's cause was taken up by the colorful figure Giuseppe Garibaldi. No political theorist, Garibaldi was a guerilla fighter who had been exiled twice: first in Latin America, where he fought along with independence movements, and again in the United States. Like Mazzini, Garibaldi was committed to achieving national unification through a popular movement.

> No political theorist, Garibaldi was a guerilla fighter who had been exiled twice: first in Latin America, where he fought along with independence movements, and again in the United States.

More moderate nationalists, sought economic and political reforms but intended to steer clear of democracy and the forces it might unleash. Rather than arousing popular movements, these moderates pinned their hopes on the kingdom of Piedmont-Sardinia. Victor Emmanuel II (1849–1861), the king, brought a man into his government who would embody the conservative vision of nationhood: the shrewd Sardinian nobleman Count Camillo Benso di Cavour (1810–1861). Cavour pursued ambitious but pragmatic reforms guided by the state. First as minister of commerce and agriculture and then as prime minister, he promoted economic expansion, encouraged the construction of a modern transportation infrastructure, reformed the currency, and sought to raise Piedmont-Sardinia's profile in international relations. Garibaldi and Cavour thus represented two different routes to Italian unification: Garibaldi stood for unification from below, Cavour for unification guided from above.

Cavour's plan depended on diplomacy. Since Piedmont-Sardinia did not have the military capacity to counter the Austrians in northern Italy, Cavour skillfully cultivated an alliance with one of Austria's traditional rivals: Napoleonic France. France and Italy went to war with Austria in 1859, but Napoleon III suddenly withdrew, making it impossible to expel the Austrians from Venetia. Yet the campaign made extensive gains, and by 1860, Piedmont-Sardinia had grown to more than twice its original size and was by far the most powerful state in Italy.

As Cavour consolidated the northern and central states, events in the southern states seemed to put those areas up for grabs as well. A fast-spreading peasant revolt rekindled the hopes of earlier insurrections of the 1820s and 1840 in Sicily. That revolt got a much needed boost from Garibaldi, who landed in Sicily in May of 1860. "The Thousand," as Garibaldi's volunteer fighters called themselves, embodied the widespread support for Italian unification: they came from the north as well as the

WHY DID THE EFFORTS TO UNIFY ITALY AND GERMANY SUCCEED DURING THE 1860s?

BUILDING THE NATION-STATE   595

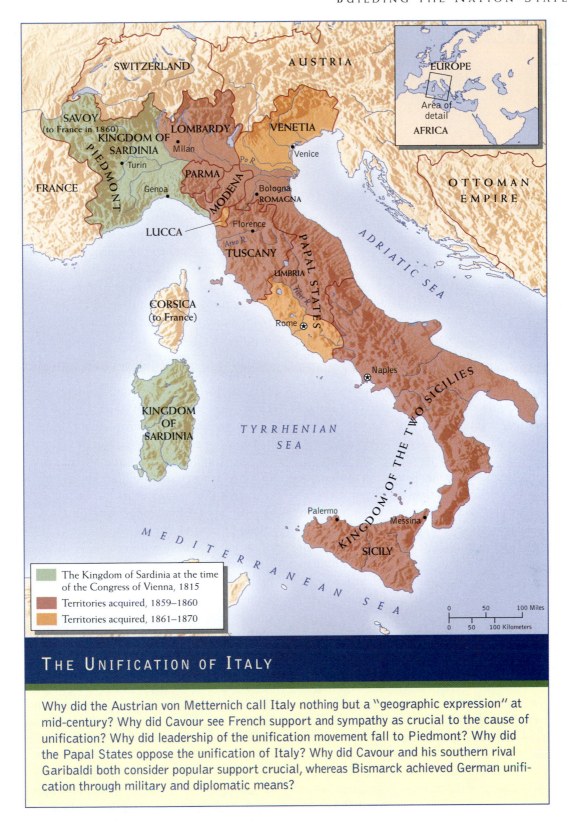

THE UNIFICATION OF ITALY

Why did the Austrian von Metternich call Italy nothing but a "geographic expression" at mid-century? Why did Cavour see French support and sympathy as crucial to the cause of unification? Why did leadership of the unification movement fall to Piedmont? Why did the Papal States oppose the unification of Italy? Why did Cavour and his southern rival Garibaldi both consider popular support crucial, whereas Bismarck achieved German unification through military and diplomatic means?

south, and counted among them members of the middle class, as well as workers and artisans. Garibaldi's troops took Sicily in the name of Victor Emmanuel. By November 1860, Garibaldi's forces, alongside local insurgents,

had taken Naples. Emboldened by success, Garibaldi looked to Rome.

Garibaldi's rising popularity put him on a collision course with Cavour. Cavour worried that Garibaldi's

CHRONOLOGY

UNIFICATION OF ITALY, 1848–1870

Revolutions of 1848	
Italian war with Austria	1859
Conquest of the kingdom of Two Sicilies	1860
Austria cedes Venetia	1866
Occupation of Rome	1870
Law of Papal Guaranties enacted	1870

forces would bring French or Austrian intervention, with unknown consequences. Above all Cavour preferred that Italian unification happen quickly, under Piedmont-Sardinia's stewardship, without domestic turmoil or messy, unpredictable negotiations with other Italian states. Flush with success, Victor Emmanuel ordered Garibaldi to cede him military authority, and Garibaldi obeyed. Most of the peninsula was united under a single rule, and Victor Emmanuel assumed the title of king of Italy (1861–1878). Cavour's vision of Italian nationhood had won the day.

The final steps of Italy's territorial nation building came indirectly. Venetia remained in the hands of the Austrians until 1866, when Austria was defeated by Prussia and forced to relinquish their last Italian stronghold. Rome had resisted conquest largely because of French military protection. But in 1870 the outbreak of the Franco-Prussian War compelled Napoleon to withdraw his troops. That September, Italian soldiers occupied Rome, and in July 1871, Rome became capital of the united Italian kingdom.

What of the pope's authority? The Italian parliament passed a Law of Papal Guaranties to define and limit the pope's status—an act promptly defied by the reigning pontiff, Pius IX, who refused to have anything to do with a disrespectful secular government. His successors continued to close themselves off in the Vatican until 1929, when a series of agreements between the Italian government and Pius XI settled the dispute.

In 1871 Italy was a state but nation building was hardly over. A minority of the "Italian" population in fact spoke Italian; the rest used local and regional dialects so diverse that schoolteachers sent from Rome to Sicily were mistaken for foreigners. The gap between an increasingly industrialized north and a poor and rural south remained wide. Cavour and those who succeeded him as prime minister had to contend with those economic and social inequalities, with rising tensions between landlords and agricultural workers in rural regions, and with lingering resentments of the centralized, northern-oriented state. Regional differences and social tensions, then, made building the Italian nation an ongoing process.

THE UNIFICATION OF GERMANY: REALPOLITIK

In 1853, the former revolutionary August Ludwig von Rochau wrote a short book with a long title: *The Principles of* Realpolitik *Applied to the Conditions of Germany.* He wrote, "Practical politics has to do with the simple fact that it is power alone than can rule." In Rochau's view, power would not accrue to those with a "just" cause—those who supported constitutions and Enlightenment conceptions of rights. Instead power came indirectly, through diverse forms such as the expansion of the economy and social institutions. "Realpolitik" became the watchword of the 1850s and 1860s and was most closely associated with the deeply conservative and pragmatic Otto von Bismarck, whose skillful diplomacy and power politics played such an important role in German unification. Yet the German nation was not built by one statesman's efforts. It was the product of the growth of national feeling, recalculations of middle-class interests, diplomacy, war, and struggles between the regime and its opponents.

Despite its decisive defeat in 1848, German liberalism had revived within a decade, in the face of considerable odds. The staunchly antirevolutionary King Frederick William had granted a Prussian constitution that established a bicameral (two-house) parliament, with the lower house elected by universal male suffrage. A series of edicts, however, modified the electoral system to reinforce hierarchies of wealth and power. The relatively few wealthy voters who together paid one third of the country's taxes elected one third of the legislators, meaning a large landowner or industrialist exercised nearly a hundred times the voting power of a common workingman. In 1858 William I, who had led troops against the revolutionaries of 1848 in his youth, became prince regent of Prussia. (William became king in 1861 and ruled until 1888.) Although a notoriously conservative state, Prussia was not a monolith. A decade of industrial growth had expanded the size and confidence of the middle class. By the late 1850s, Prussia had an active liberal intelligensia, a thoughtful and engaged press, and a liberal civil service dedicated to

WHY DID THE EFFORTS TO UNIFY ITALY AND GERMANY SUCCEED DURING THE 1860S?

BUILDING THE NATION-STATE   597

TOWARD THE UNIFICATION OF GERMANY

This map outlines the stages leading to the unification of the German state. How did the German state of Prussia expand at the expense of Poland and the Austrian empire? How did the nineteenth-century wars with France strengthen the emergent Prussian state? Examine closely the fragmented states of the region. What challenges did Bismarck face in building a unified Germany? What cultural and historical factors could he use to his advantage?

political and economic modernization. These changes helped to forge a liberal political movement that won a majority in elections to the lower house and could confidently confront the king.

The particular bone of contention (though hardly the only issue) between liberals and the king was military spending. William wanted to expand the standing army, reduce the role of reserve forces (a more middle-class group), and, above all, ensure that military matters were not subject to parliamentary control. Faced with a crisis, in 1862 William named Otto von Bismarck minister-president of Prussia. (A prime minister answers to Parliament; Bismarck did not.) This crucial moment in Prussian domestic politics became a decisive turning point in the history of German nationhood.

Born into the Junker class of conservative, land-owning aristocrats, Bismarck not only supported the monarchy during the revolutionary period of 1848–1849, he had fiercely opposed the liberal movement. He was not a nationalist. He was before all else a Prussian. He did not institute domestic reforms because he favored the "rights" of a particular group, but because he thought that these policies would unify and strengthen Prussia. When he maneuvered to bring other German states under Prussian domination, he did so not in pursuit of a grand German design, but because he believed that union in some form was inevitable and that Prussia had to seize the initiative. Bismarck happily acknowledged that he admired power and that he considered himself destined for greatness. Whatever his post, he intended to command and to turn opportunities to his advantage. "I want to play the tune the way it sounds good to me or not at all," he declared. He had a reputation for cynicism, arrogance, and uninhibited frankness in expressing his views. Yet the Latin phrase he fondly quoted distills his more careful assessment of politics, and of the relationship between even masterful individuals and history: "Man cannot create or control the tide of time, he can only move in the same direction and try to direct it."

In Prussia, Bismarck defied parliamentary opposition. When the liberal majority refused to levy taxes, he dissolved Parliament and collected them anyway, claiming that the constitution, whatever its purposes, had not been designed to subvert the state. His most decisive actions, however, were in foreign policy. Once opposed to nationalism, Bismarck skillfully played the national card to preempt his liberal opponents at home and to make German nation building an accomplishment— and an extension—of Prussian authority.

The other "German" power was Austria, which wielded considerable influence within the German Confederation and especially over the largely Catholic regions in the south. Bismarck saw a stark contrast between Austrian and Prussian interests; he believed that the Confederation had outlived its usefulness and skillfully exploited Austria's disadvantages. He inflamed a long-smoldering dispute with Denmark over Schleswig and Holstein, two provinces peopled by Germans and Danes and claimed by both the German Confederation

Bismarck Sweeping Away the Stubborn Germans.
Bismarck helped provoke the Franco-Prussian War of 1870–71 by cultivating the perception that France was a threat to Germany. This caricature reads "Here is Bismarck, still with his big broom, who scolds and picks up all of the recalcitrant Germans. Let's go! Go or die! Faster than that! Or the French will eat your sauerkraut!"

and Denmark. In 1864, he persuaded Austria to join Prussia in a war against Denmark. The war was short, and it forced the Danish ruler to cede the two provinces to Austria and Prussia. As Bismarck hoped, the victorious alliance promptly fell apart. This time casting Prussia as the defender of larger German interests, in 1866 he declared war on Austria. The conflict, known as the Seven Weeks' War, ended in Prussian victory. Austria agreed to dissolve the German Confederation. In its place Bismarck created the North German Confederation, a union of all the German states north of the Main River.

The final step in the completion of German unity was the Franco-Prussian War of 1870–1871. Bismarck hoped that a conflict with France would play to German nationalism in Bavaria, Württemberg, and other

WHY DID THE EFFORTS TO UNIFY ITALY AND GERMANY SUCCEED DURING THE 1860s?

BUILDING THE NATION-STATE   599

CHRONOLOGY

UNIFICATION OF GERMANY, 1854–1871

Crimean War	1854–1856
Bismarck becomes prime minister	1862
Danish War	1864
Seven Weeks' War	1866
Franco-Prussian War	1870–1871

southern states still outside the Confederation and overcome their historic wariness of Prussia. A diplomatic tempest concerning the right of the Hohenzollerns (Prussia's ruling family) to occupy the Spanish throne created an opportunity to foment a Franco-German misunderstanding. Although King William initially acquiesced in French demands, the French blundered and Bismarck exploited their mistakes, editing a telegram from the king to make it less conciliatory and accusing the French of scheming to seize the Rhineland, all of which aroused public opinion on both countries.

As soon as war was declared, the south German states rallied to Prussia's side. The conflict was quickly over. No European powers come to France's aid. Austria, the most likely candidate, remained weakened by its recent war with Prussia. In the battlefield, France could not match Prussia's professionally trained and superbly equipped forces. The war began in July and ended in September with the defeat of the French and the capture of Napoleon III at Sedan in France. Insurrectionary forces in Paris continued to hold out against the Germans through the winter of 1870–1871, but the French imperial government collapsed.

On January 18, 1871, in the Hall of Mirrors at Versailles, symbol of the powerful past of French absolutism, the German empire was proclaimed. All the German states that had not already been absorbed into the Prussian fold, except Austria, declared their allegiance to William I, henceforth emperor or kaiser. Four months later, at Frankfurt, a treaty between the French and Germans ceded the border region of Alsace to the new German empire, and forced the French to pay an indemnity of 5 billion francs. Prus-

> On January 18, 1871, in the Hall of Mirrors at Versailles, symbol of the powerful past of French absolutism, the German empire was proclaimed.

sia accounted for 60 percent of the new state's territory and population. The Prussian kaiser, prime minister, army, and most of the bureaucracy remained intact, now reconfigured as the German nation-state. This was not the new nation for which Prussian liberals had hoped. It marked a "revolution from above" rather than from below. Still, the more optimistic believed that the German empire would evolve in a different political direction, that they could eventually "extend freedom through unity."

THE STATE AND NATIONALITY: CENTRIFUGAL FORCES IN THE AUSTRIAN EMPIRE

Germany emerged from the 1860s a stronger, unified nation. The Austrian empire faced a very different situation, with different resources, and emerged a weakened, precariously balanced, multiethnic Dual Monarchy, also called Austria-Hungary.

As we have seen, ethnic nationalism was a powerful force in the Habsburg monarchy in 1848. Yet the Habsburg state, with a combination of military repression and tactics that divided its enemies, had proved more powerful. It abolished serfdom but made few other concessions to its opponents. The Hungarians, who had nearly won independence in the spring of 1848, were essentially reconquered. The empire nominally accommodated representatives of the nationalities. Administrative reforms created a new and more uniform legal system, rationalized taxation, and imposed a single-language policy that favored German. The issue of managing ethnic relations, however, only grew more difficult. The Czechs in Bohemia, for instance, grew increasingly alienated by policies that favored the German minority of the province and increasingly insistent on their Slavic identity. The Hungarians, or Magyars, the most powerful of the subject nationalities, sought to reclaim the autonomy they had glimpsed in 1848.

In this context, Austria's international weakness became especially significant. The 1866 defeat at the hands of Prussia forced the emperor Francis Joseph to renegotiate the very structure of the empire. In order to stave off a revolution by the Hungarians, Francis Joseph agreed to a new federal structure in the form of the Dual Monarchy. Austria-Hungary had a common system of taxation, a common army, and made foreign and military policy together. Francis Joseph was emperor of Austria and king of Hungary. But internal and constitutional affairs were separated. The Hungarians established their own constitution, their own legislature, and their own capital, combining the cities of Buda and Pest.

What of the other nationalities? The official policy of the Dual Monarchy stated that they were not to be discriminated against, and that they could use their own languages. Official policy was only loosely enforced. On the Austrian side of the Dual Monarchy, minority nationalities such as the Poles, Czechs, and Slovenes resented their second-class status. The Hungarians attemped to make the state, the civil service, and the schools more thoroughly Hungarian—an effort that did not sit well with Serbs and Croats. The Habsburgs tried instead to build a state and administrative structure strong enough to keep the pieces from spinning off, playing different minorities against each other, and conceding autonomy only when essential. As the nineteenth century unfolded, subject nationalities would appeal to other powers—Serbia, Russia, the Ottomans—and this balancing act would become more difficult.

NATION AND STATE BUILDING IN RUSSIA, THE UNITED STATES, AND CANADA

What were the similarities between slavery and serfdom?

The challenges of nationalism and nation building also occupied Russia, the United States, and Canada. In all three countries, nation building entailed territorial and economic expansion, the incorporation of new peoples, and, in Russia and the United States, contending with the enormous problems of slavery and serfdom.

TERRITORY, THE STATE, AND SERFDOM: RUSSIA

Serfdom in Russia, which had been legally formalized in 1649, had begun to draw significant protest from the in-

telligentsia under the reign of Catherine the Great (1762–1796). After 1789, and especially after 1848, the abolition of serfdom elsewhere in Europe made the issue more urgent. Abolishing serfdom became part of the larger project of building Russia as a modern nation. The Russian nobility, however, tenaciously opposed emancipation. Tangled debates about how lords would be indemnified for the loss of "their" serfs, and how emancipated serfs would survive without full-scale land redistribution, also checked progress on the issue. The Crimean War (see below) broke the impasse. In its aftermath, Alexander II (1855–1881) forced the issue. Worried that the persistence of serfdom had sapped Russian strength and contributed to its defeat in the war, and persuaded that serfdom would only continue to prompt violent conflict, he ended serfdom by decree in 1861.

The emancipation decree of 1861 was a reform of massive scope, but it produced limited change. It granted legal rights to some 22 million serfs and authorized their title to a portion of the land they had worked. It also required the state to compensate landowners for the properties they relinquished. Large-scale landowners vastly inflated their compensation claims, however, and managed to retain much of the most profitable acreage for themselves. As a result, the land granted to peasants was often of poor quality and insufficient to sustain themselves and their families. Moreover, the newly liberated serfs had to pay in installments for their land, which was not in fact granted to them individually, but rather to a village commune that collected their payments. As a result, the pattern of rural life in Russia did not change drastically. The system of payment kept peasants in the villages—not as free-standing farmers, but as agricultural laborers for their former masters.

While the Russian state undertook reforms, it also expanded its territory. After mid-century, the Russians pressed east and south. They invaded and conquered several independent Islamic kingdoms along the old "Silk Road" and expanded into Siberia in search of natural resources. Russian diplomacy wrung various commercial concessions from the Chinese that led to the founding of the Siberian city of Vladivostok in 1860. Racial, ethnic, and religious differences made governing a daunting task. When the state sporadically made efforts to impose Russian culture, the results were disastrous. Whether power was wielded by the nineteenth-century tsars or, later, by the Soviet Union, powerful centrifugal forces pulled against genuine unification. Expansion helped Russia create a vast empire that was geographically of one piece, but by no means one nation.

THE ABOLITION OF SERFDOM IN RUSSIA

TSAR ALEXANDER II'S DECREE EMANCIPATING THE SERFS, 1861

The abolition of serfdom was central to Tsar Alexander II's program of modernization and reform after the Crimean War. Emancipated serfs were now allowed to own their land, ending centuries of peasant bondage. The decree, however, emphasized the tsar's benevolence and the nobility's generosity—not peasant rights. The government did not want emancipation to bring revolution to the countryside; it sought to reinforce the state's authority, the landowners' power, and the peasants' obligations. After spelling out the detailed provisions for emancipation, the decree added:

And We place Our hope in the good sense of Our people.

When word of the Government's plan to abolish the law of bondage [serfdom] reached peasants unprepared for it, there arose a partial misunderstanding. Some [peasants] thought about freedom and forgot about obligations. But the general good sense [of the people] was not disturbed in the conviction that anyone freely enjoying the goods of society correspondingly owes it to the common good to fulfill certain obligations, [a conviction held] both by natural reason and by Christian law, according to which "every soul must be subject to the governing authorities." . . .

Rights legally acquired by the landlords cannot be taken from them without a decent return or [their] voluntary concession; and that it would be contrary to all justice to make use of the lords' land without bearing the corresponding obligation.

And now We hopefully expect that the bonded people, as a new future opens before them, will understand and accept with gratitude the important sacrifice made by the Well-born Nobility for the improvement of their lives.

James Cracraft, ed., *Major Problems in the History of Imperial Russia* (Lexington, Mass.: D. C. Heath, 1994), pp. 340–344.

EMANCIPATION: THE VIEW FROM BELOW

Emancipation did not solve problems in the Russian countryside. On the contrary, it unleashed a torrent of protest, including complaints from peasants that nobles were undermining attempts to reform. These petitions detail the struggles that came in the wake of emancipation in two villages.

PETITION FROM PEASANTS IN PODOSINOVKA (VORONEZH PROVINCE) TO ALEXANDER II, MAY 1863

The most merciful manifesto of Your Imperial Majesty from 19 February 1861, with the published rules, put a limit to the enslavement of the people in blessed Russia. But some former serfowners—who desire not to improve the peasants' life, but to oppress and ruin them—apportion land contrary to the laws, choose the best land from all the fields for themselves, and give the poor peasants . . . the worst and least usable lands.

To this group of squires must be counted our own, Anna Mikhailovna Raevskaia. . . . Of our fields and resources, she chose the best places from amidst our strips, and, like a cooking ring in a hearth, carved off 300 dessiatines [measures of land] for herself. . . . But our community refused to accept so ruinous an allotment and requested that we be given an allotment in accordance with the local Statute. . . . The peace arbitrator . . . and the police chief . . . slandered us before the governor, alleging that we were rioting and that it is impossible for them to enter our village.

The provincial governor believed this lie and sent 1,200 soldiers of the penal command to our village. . . . Without any cause, our village priest Father Peter—rather than give an uplifting pastoral exhortation to stop the spilling of innocent blood—joined these reptiles, with the unanimous incitement of the authorities. . . . They summoned nine township heads and their aides from other townships. . . . In their presence, the provincial governor—without making any investigation and without interrogating a single person—ordered that the birch rods be brought and that the punishment commence, which was carried out with cruelty and mercilessness. They punished up to 200 men and women; 80 people were at four levels (with 500, 400, 300 and 200 blows); some received lesser punishment . . . and when the inhuman punishment of these innocent people had ended, the provincial governor said: "If you find the land unsuitable, I do not forbid you to file petitions wherever you please," and then left. . . .

We dare to implore you, Orthodox emperor and our merciful father, not to reject the petition of a community with 600 souls, including wives and children. Order with your tsarist word that our community be allotted land . . . as the law dictates without selecting the best sections of fields and meadows, but in straight lines. . . . [Order that] the meadows and haylands along the river Elan be left to our community without any restriction; these will enable us to feed our cattle and smaller livestock, which are necessary for our existence.

Gregory L. Freeze, ed., *From Supplication to Revolution: A Documentary Social History of Imperial Russia* (New York: Oxford University Press, 1988), pp. 170–173.

PETITION FROM PEASANTS IN BALASHOV DISTRICT TO GRAND DUKE CONSTANTIN NIKOLAEVICH, JANUARY 25, 1862

Your Imperial Excellency! Most gracious sire! Grand Duke Konstantin Nikolaevich! . . .

After being informed of the Imperial manifesto on the emancipation of peasants from serfdom on 1861 . . . we received this [news] with jubilation. . . . But from this moment, our squire ordered that the land be cut off from the entire township. But this is absolutely intolerable for us: it not only denies us profit, but threatens us with a catastrophic future. He began to hold repeated meetings and [tried to] force us to sign that we agreed to accept the above land allotment. But, upon seeing so unexpected a change, and bearing in mind the gracious manifesto, we refused. . . . After assembling the entire township, they tried to force us into making illegal signatures accepting the land cut-offs. But when they saw that this did not succeed, they had a company of soldiers sent in. . . . Then [Colonel] Globbe came from their midst, threatened us with exile to Siberia, and ordered the soldiers to strip the peasants and to punish seven people by flogging in the most inhuman manner. They still have not regained consciousness.

Gregory L. Freeze, ed., *From Supplication to Revolution: A Documentary Social History of Imperial Russia* (New York: Oxford University Press, 1988), pp. 170–173.

TERRITORY, THE NATION-STATE, AND SLAVERY: THE UNITED STATES

The American Revolution had bequeathed to the United States a loose union of slave and free states, tied together in part by a commitment to territorial expansion. The so-called Jeffersonian Revolution combined democratic aspirations with a drive to expand the nation's boundaries. Expansion brought complications. While it did provide land for many yeomen farmers in the North and South, it also added millions of acres of prime cotton land, thus extending the empire of slavery.

HOW DID JOURNALISTS' DEPICTIONS OF THE CRIMEAN WAR REFLECT CULTURAL TRENDS?

EASTERN QUESTIONS AND INTERNATIONAL RELATIONS   603

The purchase of the port of New Orleans made lands in the South well worth developing, but led the American republic forcibly to remove Native Americans from the Old South west of the Mississippi River. This process of expansion and expropriation stretched from Jefferson's administration through the age of Jackson, or the 1840s.

Territorial expansion made it impossible for the United States government to avoid the question of slavery. The Haitian revolution (see page 514) had begun the long and uneven process of dismantling slavery. Great Britain ended the transatlantic slave trade in 1807, as did the United States; Britain abolished slavery in 1838. Spanish America abolished slavery in the first decades of the nineteenth century; France during the revolution of 1848. In the face of growing antislavery sentiment, southern planters, like Russian serf owners, continued to insist that without the slave system they would go bankrupt. Like the Russian nobility, they responded to abolitionists with arguments based on theories of inherited inferiority and warnings of the chaos they believed abolition would bring. As the country expanded west, North and South engaged in a protracted tug of war about whether new states were to be "free" or "slave." The failure of a series of elaborate compromises led to the outbreak of the Civil War in 1861.

The protracted and costly struggle—a first experience of the horrors of modern war—decisively transformed the nation. First, it abolished slavery. Second, it established the preeminence of the national government over states' rights. The Fourteenth Amendment to the Constitution stated specifically that all Americans were citizens of the United States, and not of an individual state or territory. In declaring that no citizen was to be deprived of life, liberty, or property without due process of law, it established that "due process" was to be defined by the national, not the state or territorial, government. Third, in the aftermath of the Civil War, the United States' economy expanded with stunning rapidity. Industrial and agricultural production rose, putting the United States in a position to compete with Great Britain. As we will see later on, American industrialists, bankers, and retailers introduced innovations in assembly-line manufacturing, corporate organization, and advertising that startled their European counterparts and gave the United States new power in world politics. In these ways, the Civil War laid the foundations for the modern American nation-state.

> In the face of growing antislavery sentiment, southern planters, like Russian serf owners, continued to insist that without the slave system they would go bankrupt.

TERRITORIAL EXPANSION: CANADA

The expansion of the United States also had an important effect on its neighbor to the north. In 1763, the Treaty of Paris had passed the territories of New France to Britain. Throughout the nineteenth century, westward expansion dispossessed native populations and forced their resettlement in separate territories. The drive westward, which made available vast wheat lands and timber resources in the Canadian prairies and forests, fueled demands for greater autonomy. The fear of falling prey to the United States' expansionist drive, however, made English-speaking Canadians less eager to break completely with British rule. In 1867, an Act of Parliament gave Canada independence, but the country remained a "dominion" within the British Commonwealth. With dominion status in place, the Canadian government, like its American counterpart, pursued a policy of economic expansion and settlement. It annexed territories, offered attractive homestead grants to lure European immigrants, policed settler-Indian relations, and built vast railroads. The government encouraged economic developments that connected Canadian cities, forging networks independent of the United States.

EASTERN QUESTIONS AND INTERNATIONAL RELATIONS

How did journalists' depictions of the Crimean War reflect cultural trends?

During the nineteenth century, questions of national identity and international power were inextricable from contests over territory. War and diplomacy drew and redrew boundaries as European nations groped toward a tenable balance of power. The rise of new powers, principally the German empire, posed one set of challenges to Continental order. The waning power of older regimes proved equally destabilizing. The Crimean War, which lasted from 1854 to 1856, was a particularly gruesome attempt to cope with the most serious such collapse. As the Ottoman

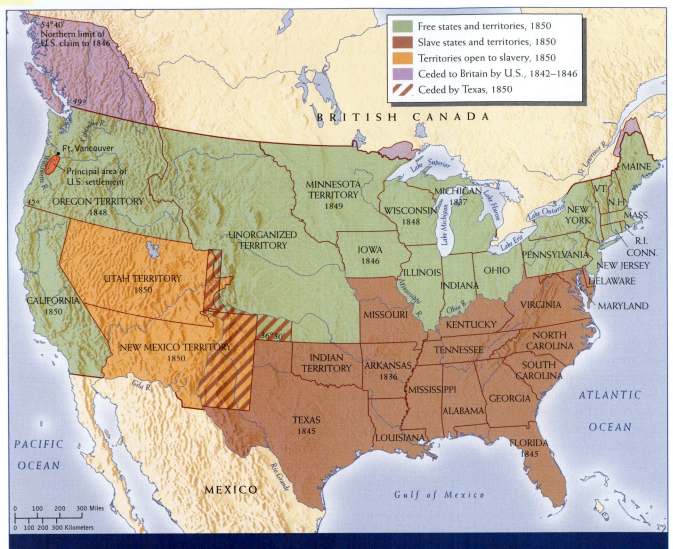

Legend:
- Free states and territories, 1850
- Slave states and territories, 1850
- Territories open to slavery, 1850
- Ceded to Britain by U.S., 1842–1846
- Ceded by Texas, 1850

AMERICAN EXPANSION IN THE LATE NINETEENTH CENTURY

Note the stages by which American settlement progressed across the North American continent, and the organization of newly acquired territory by the American government. How was American expansion different from European colonialism? How was it similar? What considerations informed the compromises made by the American government in establishing less ambitious northern borders? Why were the Utah and New Mexico territories opened to slavery even though the West and Southwest had previously been considered free? What role did California statehood play in such considerations?

empire lost its grip on its provinces in southeastern Europe, the "Eastern Question" of who would benefit from Ottoman weakness drew Europe into war. Though this war occurred before the unification of the German and Italian states, it structured the system of Great Power politics that guided Europe until (and indeed toward) the First World War.

THE CRIMEAN WAR, 1853–1856

The root causes of the war lay in the "Eastern Question." The crisis that provoked it, however, involved religion, namely French and Russion claims to protect religious minorities and the Holy Places of Jerusalem within the Muslim Ottoman Empire. In 1853 a three

HOW DID JOURNALISTS' DEPICTIONS OF THE CRIMEAN WAR REFLECT CULTURAL TRENDS?

EASTERN QUESTIONS AND INTERNATIONAL RELATIONS   605

0   100   200 Miles
0   100   200 Kilometers

RUSSIA

AUSTRIAN EMPIRE

DANUBIAN PRINCIPALTIES, INCLUDING MOLDAVIA AND WALACHIA

CRIMEA

Sevastopol   Balaklava

Ceded to Danubian Principalties by Russia, 1856

MONTENEGRO

Danube R

BLACK SEA

Sinope

OTTOMAN

Constantinople

Dardanelles

AEGEAN SEA

GREECE

IONIAN SEA

EMPIRE

EUROPE

Area of detail

AFRICA

MEDITERRANEAN SEA

★ Battle
← Russian attack
← Allied attack

THE CRIMEAN WAR

This map depicts the theater of operations and the major assaults of the Crimean War. Why did the Crimean War erupt? Who fought whom and why? In what ways was the Crimean War the first "modern" war? In what ways did the Allies achieve their objectives?

way quarrel between France (on behalf of Roman Catholics), Russia (representing Eastern Orthodox Christians) and Turkey devolved into a Russion confrontation with the Turkish sultan. Confident that Turkey would be unable to resist, concerned that other powers might take advantage of Turkish weakness, and persuaded (mistakenly) that they had British support, the Russians moved troops into the Ottoman governed territories of Moldavia and Walachia. (These territories lie north and west of the point where the Danube river meets the Black Sea.) In October, 1853, also persuaded they would be supported by the British, Turkey declared war on Russia. The war became a disaster for the Turks, who lost their fleet at the battle of Sinope in November. But Russia's success alarmed the British and the French, who considered Russian expansion a threat to their interests in the Balkans, the eastern Mediterranean, and, for the British, the route to India. Determined to check that expansion, France and Britain each declared war on Russia in March, 1854. In September, they landed on the Russian peninsula of Crimea, headed for the Russian naval base at Sevastopol, to which they laid siege. France, Britain, and the Ottomans were joined in 1855 by the small but ambitious Italian state of Piedmont-Sardinia, all fighting against the Russians. This was the closest Europe had come to a general war since 1815.

The war was relatively short, but its conduct was devastating. Conditions on the Crimean Peninsula were dire, and the disastrous mismanagement of supplies and hygiene by the British and French led to epidemics among the troops. At least as many soldiers died from typhus or cholera as in combat. The fighting was bitter, marked by such notoriously inept strategies as the British "charge of the Light Brigade," in which a British cavalry unit was slaughtered by massed Russian artillery. Vast battles pitted tens of thousands of British and French troops against Russian formations, combat that was often settled with bayonets. Despite the disciplined toughness of the British and French troops, and despite their nations' dominance of the seas around Crimea, the Russians denied them a clear victory. Sevastopol, under siege for nearly a year, did not fall until September, 1855. The bitter, unsatisfying conflict was ended by treaty in 1856.

For the French and Sardinians, the bravery of their soldiers bolstered positive national sentiments at home; for the British and Russians, however, the poorly managed war provoked waves of intense criticism. As far as international relations were concerned, the peace settle-

The Stone Breakers by Gustave Courbet, 1849. Courbet was a French Realist painter who depicted everyday men and women in an honest and unromantic manner. Considered one of his most important works, this painting of two ordinary peasants building a road was destroyed in Dresden during World War II.

ment was a severe setback for Russia, whose influence in the Balkans was drastically curbed. The Crimean War embarrassed France and left Russia and Austria considerably weaker, opening an advantage for Bismarck in the 1860s, as we saw above.

The Crimean War was important in other ways as well. Though fought largely with the same methods and mentalities employed in the Napoleonic Wars forty years earlier, the war brought a handful of innovations that forecast the direction of modern warfare. It saw the first significant use of rifled muskets, underwater mines, and trench warfare, as well as the first tactical use of railroads and telegraphs. In addition, the war was covered by the first modern war correspondents and photojournalists, making it the most "public" war to date. Reports from the theater of war were sent "live" by telegraph to Britain and France with objective and sobering detail. The British government and commercial publishers both sent photographers to document the war's progress, and perhaps also to counter charges that troops were undersupplied and malnourished. Roger Fenton, the most prominent and prolific of these war photographers, employed the new medium to capture the grim realities of camp life, though technological limitations and political considerations kept him from photographing the more gruesome carnage of the battlefield. Nonetheless, Fenton's photographs lacked the elegant distortions of paintings and engravings and thus introduced a new level of realism and immediacy to the public's conception of war.

REALISM: "DEMOCRACY IN ART"

The journalistic reporting from the Crimean War was in part remarkable because it avoided the heroic and jingoistic language to which nineteenth-century readers were accustomed. In this way, it reflected a dominant cultural trend of the mid-nineteenth century: the rise of the artistic movement known as realism. In both painting and literature, realism signaled a strict rejection of artistic "conventions" and ready-made formulas in favor of what artists saw as more honest, objective, and authentic representations of the world. Whereas Romanticism had sought higher truths, with an emphasis on emotion and imagination, realism trained its gaze on empirical reality. As the French painter Gustave Courbet (1819–1877) claimed, "[T]he art of painting can only consist of the representation of objects which are visible and tangible for the artist."

Realism's focus on the material world owed much to the ideals of nineteenth-century science, which seemed

to cut through traditional moral and philosophical concerns in pursuit of empirical facts. The French novelist Émile Zola (1840–1902), who along with Honoré de Balzac and Gustave Flaubert was among the most prominent realist writers, aimed for an exact, scientific presentation of society. Like many realists, Zola was also motivated by a powerful sympathy for common people and a desire for social justice. His novels confronted the many social problems of working-class industrial life—alcoholism, poverty, hunger, strikes. Realist painters also shared this sympathy for commonplace men and women, and they shocked refined sensibilities by making beggars, miners, laundry women, railroad workers, prostitutes, and peasants the subjects of their work.

In Russia, writers felt similarly compelled to take on social and political issues such as poverty, crime, and gender roles, but they joined those topics to larger philosophical themes, creating a distinctive hybrid of realism and Romanticism. Ivan Turgenev, who spent much of his life in France, was the first Russian novelist to become well known to western Europe. His brooding novel *Fathers and Sons* (1861), which condemned the existing social order, provided inspiration to a group of young Russian intellectuals who sought to reform society by abandoning their parents' emphasis on status, wealth, and leisure, turning instead to serve "the people." Feodor Dostoevsky (1821–1811), whose novels mirrored his harrowing personal life, explored the psychology of anguished minds with broad sympathy and morbid intensity. The third outstanding novelist of the late nineteenth century, Leo Tolstoy, examined Russian society in such epic novels as *War and Peace* (1862–1869) which focused on the fate of individuals caught up in powerful movements of history.

CONCLUSION

The twenty years between 1850 and 1870 were a time of intense nation building in the Western world. The unification of Germany and Italy changed the map of Europe, with important consequences for the balance of power. The emergence of the United States as a major power also had international ramifications. For old as well as new nation-states, economic development and political transformation—often on a very large scale—were important means of increasing and securing the state's power. Yet demands for more representative government, the abolition of privilege, and land reform had to be reckoned with, as did the systems of slavery and serfdom. Trailing the banner of nationhood was an explosive set of questions about how to balance the power and interests of minorities and majorities, of the wealthy and poor, of the powerful and the dispossessed. In short, nation building forced a transformation of relations between states and their citizens.

Yet these transformations were anything but predictable. Nationalism showed itself to be a volatile, erratic, and malleable force during the mid-nineteenth century. It provided much of the fuel for revolutionary movements in 1848, but it also helped to tear these movements apart, undermining liberal gains. Those who had linked their democratic goals to the rise of new nation-states were sorely disappointed. In the aftermath of the defeated revolutions, most nation building took a conservative tack. Nationalism came to serve the needs of statesmen and bureaucrats who did not seek an "awakening of peoples," and who had serious reservations about popular sovereignty. For them, nations simply represented modern, organized, and stronger states. The upshot of this fit of nation building was a period of remarkable stability on the Continent, which ushered in an era of unprecedented capitalist and imperial expansion. The antagonisms unleashed by German unification and the crumbling of the Ottoman empire would reemerge, however, in the Great Power politics that precipitated the First World War.

KEY TERMS

Frankfurt Assembly

pan-Slavism

Giuseppe Mazzini

John Stuart Mill

Giuseppe Garibaldi

Camillo Benso di Cavour

Realpolitik

Otto von Bismarck

Crimean War

realism

SELECTED READINGS

Beales, Derek. *The Risorgimento and the Unification of Italy.* New York, 1971. Objective, concise survey of Italian unification.

Blackbourn, David. *The Long Nineteenth Century: A History of Germany, 1780–1918.* New York, 1998.

Blackburn, Robin. *The Overthrow of Colonial Slavery.* London, 1988. Brilliant and detailed overview of the social history of slavery and antislavery movements.

Brophy, James M. *Capitalism, Politics, and Railroads in Prussia, 1830–1870.* Columbus, 1998. Important, clear, and helpful.

Coppa, Frank. *The Origins of the Italian Wars of Independence.* London, 1992.

Craig, Gordon. *Germany, 1866–1945.* New York, 1978. An excellent and thorough synthesis.

Deak, Istvan. *The Lawful Revolution: Louis Kossuth and the Hungarians, 1848–1849.* New York, 1979.

Eyck, Erich. *Bismarck and the German Empire.* 3d ed. London, 1968. The best one-volume study of Bismarck.

Hamerow, Theodore S. *The Social Foundations of German Unification, 1858–1871.* 2 vols. Princeton, N.J., 1969–1972. Concentrates on economic factors that determined the solution to the unification question. An impressive synthesis.

———. *The Birth of a New Europe: State and Society in the Nineteenth Century.* Chapel Hill, N.C., 1983. A discussion of political and social change, and their relationship to industrialization and the increase in state power.

Higonnet, Patrice. *Paris: Capital of the World.* London, England, 2002. Brilliant and imaginative study of Paris as "capital of the nineteenth century."

Hobsbawm, Eric J. *Nations and Nationalism since 1870: Programme, Myth, Reality.* 2d ed. Cambridge, 1992. A clear, concise analysis of the historical and cultural manifestations of nationalism.

Howard, Michael. *The Franco-Prussian War.* New York, 1981. The war's effect on society.

Hutchinson, John, and Anthony Smith, eds. *Nationalism.* New York, 1994. A recent collection of articles, not particularly historical, but with the merit of discussing non-European nationalisms.

Johnson, Susan. *Roaring Camp.* New York, 2000. A fascinating story of one mining camp in California, and a micro-history of the larger forces changing the West and the world.

Kolchin, Peter. *Unfree Labor: American Slavery and Russian Serfdom.* Cambridge, Mass., 1987. Pioneering comparative study.

Mack Smith, Denis. *Cavour and Garibaldi.* New York, 1968.

———. *The Making of Italy, 1796–1870.* New York, 1968. A narrative with documents.

Nochlin, Linda. *Realism.* New York, 1971.

Pflanze, Otto. *Bismarck and the Development of Germany.* 2d ed. 3 vols. Princeton, N.J., 1990. Extremely detailed analysis of Bismarck's aims and policies.

Pinkney, David. *Napoleon III and the Rebuilding of Paris.* Princeton, N.J., 1972. An interesting account of the creation of modern Paris during the Second Empire.

Robertson, Priscilla. *Revolutions of 1848: A Social History.* Princeton, N.J., 1952. Old-fashioned narrative, but very readable.

Sammons, Jeffrey L. *Heinrich Heine: A Modern Biography.* Princeton, N.J., 1979. An excellent historical biography, as well as a study of culture and politics.

Sheehan, James J. *German Liberalism in the Nineteenth Century.* Chicago, 1978. Fresh and important synthesis.

Sperber, Jonathan. *Rhineland Radicals: The Democratic Movement and the Revolution of 1848–1849.* Princeton, N.J., 1993. A detailed study of Germany, by the author of the most recent overview of the revolutions of 1848.

———. *The European Revolutions, 1848–1851.* New York, 1994. Now the best single volume on the period, with new bibliography.

Stearns, Peter N. *1848: The Revolutionary Tide in Europe.* New York, 1974. Stresses the social background of the revolutions.

Zeldin, Theodore. *The Political System of Napoleon III.* Compact and readable, by one of the major scholars of the period.

PART VII

THE WEST AT THE WORLD'S CENTER

THE YEARS BETWEEN 1870 and 1945 have been called the "European era." Three developments run through this period. The first is the rapid and dramatic expansion of European empires. The industrial development of western Europe and the United States gave those nations unprecedented power in the world arena. The West's trade, its wars, and its methods of wielding political power were global. That newfound, worldwide power produced both confidence and crisis. Although the economic might of the Western nations enabled them to dominate the less-developed quarters of the globe, it also created new and dangerous competition among them. The old system of the "balance of power," designed to preserve peace by ensuring that no one country could dominate others, was strained to the breaking point by rivalries that grew swiftly and stretched around the world. The second development, slower and more uneven, was the emergence of "mass" politics and culture: the expansion of suffrage and of liberal and parliamentary democracy, new techniques for mobilizing (or manipulating) citizens, and modern cultural forms ranging from mass-market newspapers and advertising to radio and movies. The third theme to consider involves the wrenching transformations brought by war. Twice during the period, in 1914 and 1939, international and domestic pressures exploded. Twice during the period, war proved shockingly different from what citizens, soldiers, or political leaders expected. And twice during the period, in 1918 and 1945, Europeans awoke to a world they barely recognized. The two world wars had far reaching consequences, among them the fracturing of the European empires and the transformation of Europe's place in the world.

POLITICS	SOCIETY AND CULTURE	ECONOMY	INTERNATIONAL RELATIONS
			British expand foothold in India (1797–1818)
		Britain monopolizes opium trade in China (1830s)	Opium Wars (1839–1842)
			Treaty of Nanjing (1842)
	Karl Marx and Friedrich Engels publish *Communist Manifesto* (1848)	Production of steel alloys revolutionized (1850–1870s)	
Reign of Alexander II (1855–1881)	Gustave Flaubert's *Madame Bovary* (1856)		
Sepoy Rebellion in India (1857–1858)			
1860	Darwin's *On the Origin of Species* (1859)		
American Civil War (1861–1864)	Leo Tolstoy's *War and Peace* (1862–1869)		
Emancipation of serfs in Russia (1861)			
Otto von Bismarck unifies Germany (1862–1871)	Fyodor Dostoyevsky's *Crime and Punishment* (1866)		
Reform Bill of 1867 in England (1867)			
Pope Pius IX's pronouncement of papal infallibility (1869)			
Bismarck's Kulturkampf (1871–1878)	First Impressionist salon with Claude Monet and others (1874)	Limited liability laws change investment strategies (1870)	Franco-Prussian War (1870–1871)
Paris Commune repressed (1871)		Birth of vertical and horizontal monopolies (1870)	European scramble for Africa (1870–1900)
Third French Republic (1875)			Britain gains control of Suez Canal (1875)
		Electricity demand rises (1880s)	Congress of Berlin redraws Balkan states (1878)
1880		Rockefeller's Standard Oil Company controls over 90 percent of U.S. oil (1880s)	
The progressive movement in the United States (1880–1914)			
Alexander III and the Counter Reforms (1881–1894)		Russia launches industrialization program (1880–1890s)	British occupation of Egypt begins (1882)
Bismarck's health and social legislation (1883–1884)	Friedrich Nietzsche's *Thus Spoke Zarathustra* (1883)	Sherman Anti-Trust Act in the United States (1890)	France moves into Vietnam, Laos, and Cambodia (1883–1893)
Reform Bill expands male suffrage in Britain (1884)	Émile Zola's *Germinal* (1885)		Berlin West Africa Conference (1884–85)
Kaiser Wilhelm II ascends throne (1888)	Completion of the Eiffel Tower (1889)		
	Anti-Semitic League founded in Paris (1889)		
	Vincent Van Gogh's *The Starry Night* (1889)	Birth of the department store (1890s)	Sino-Japanese War (1894–1905)
Bismarck resigns (1890)			Italian forces defeated by Ethiopians (1896)
			Fashoda Crisis (1898)
			Boer War (1898–1901)
The Dreyfus Affair (1894–1899)			Spanish-American War (1898)
			United States annexes Puerto Rico and makes Cuba a Protectorate (1898)
1900	Sigmund Freud publishes *The Interpretation of Dreams* (1899)	Discovery of oil fields in Russia, Borneo, Persia, and Texas (1900)	London Pan-African Conference (1900)
Boxer Rebellion in China (1900)			
Sinn Fein party forms in Ireland (1900)			
French laws separate church and state (1901–1905)			
Labour party established in Britain (1901)			
Vladimir Lenin's "What Is to Be Done?" (1902)			
Russian Marxists split into Bolsheviks and Mensheviks (1903)			United States occupies Panama (1903)
British House of Lords loses veto power (1911)			First and Second Balkan Wars (1912–1913)
			First World War (1914–1918)
			Battle of the Marne (1914)
	Albert Einstein proposes theory of relativity (1915)		*Lusitania* sunk by German U-boat (1915)
			Battles of Verdun and the Somme (1916)
Russian Revolution in February and October (1917)		Bread riots and strikes against wartime shortages in Britain (1917)	United States enters World War I (1917)

POLITICS	SOCIETY AND CULTURE	ECONOMY	INTERNATIONAL RELATIONS	
		Vladimir Lenin's *Imperialism: The Highest Stage of Capitalism* (1917)	Treaty of Brest-Litovsk (1918)	1917
Russian Civil War (1918–1920) Britain extends vote to men and women over age thirty (1918) German (Weimar) Republic declared (1918) Nineteenth Amendment gives American women vote (1919) Separate parliaments for north and south Ireland (1920) Mussolini's fascists march on Rome (1922)	Dadaist and Surrealist artistic movements flourish (1920–1940) Marie Stopes opens birth control clinic in London (1921) T. S. Eliot's *The Waste Land* (1922) Hitler writes *Mein Kampf* in prison (1924)	Hyperinflation in Weimar Republic (1920–1924) Beginning of New Economic Policy in U.S.S.R. (1921)	Treaty of Versailles (1919–1920)	
Joseph Stalin's Revolution from Above (1927–1928)		Joseph Stalin's First Five-Year Plan for modernization of Russian economy (1928–1932) American stock market crash (1929) Great Depression (1929–1933)	Kellogg-Briand Pact (1928)	
Hitler appointed chancellor of Germany, proclaims the Third Reich (1933) Concentration camp for political prisoners opens at Dachau (1933) Popular Front government formed by Leon Blum (1936) Spanish Civil War (1936–1939) Great Terror of Stalin (1937–1938) Nazis begin deporting Jews in occupied territories to ghettos (1939)	James Chadwick discovers the neutron (1932) German laws exclude Jews from public office (1933) Leni Riefenstahl's *Triumph of the Will* (1934) Otto Hahn and Fritz Strassman split the atom (1939)	Britain abandons gold standard (1931) United States abandons gold standard (1933) One third of American workers unemployed (1933) President Franklin Roosevelt announces the New Deal (1933)	Japan invades Manchuria (1931) Italy conquers Ethiopia (1935–1936) Germany and Italy form Axis (1935) Germany annexes Austria (1938) Hitler invades Czechoslovakia (1939) Soviet Union signs nonaggression pact with Germany (1939) Soviets and Germans invade Poland (1939) Britain and France declare war on Germany (1939)	1930
Winston Churchill becomes prime minister of England (1940)	Charlie Chaplin's *The Great Dictator* (1940) Enrico Fermi stages first controlled nuclear chain reaction (1942)	Winston Churchill brokers Lend-Lease program with Franklin Roosevelt (1940)	France surrenders to Germany (1940) Battle of Britain (1940–1941) Germany invades the Soviet Union (1941) Japan strikes Pearl Harbor; United States enters World War II (1941) Japan invades Philippines (1941) American island-hopping campaigns in the Pacific (1942) Rommel and the Afrika Korps defeated in Tunisia (1942) Warsaw ghetto uprising (1943) D-Day: Allies land at Normandy (1944) Germany surrenders (1945) United States detonates nuclear bombs over Hiroshima and Nagasaki in August (1945) Conferences at Potsdam and Yalta (1945) Nuremberg trials (1945) United Nations founded (1945)	1940 1945

CHAPTER TWENTY-TWO

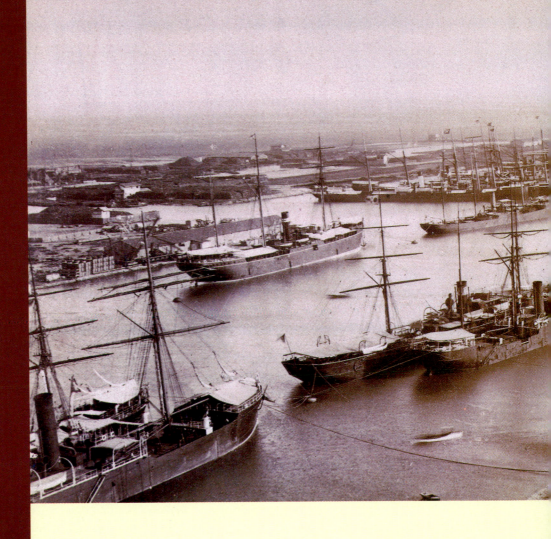

IMPERIALISM AND COLONIALISM, 1870–1914

IN 1869, THE SUEZ CANAL opened with a grandiose celebration. The imperial yacht *Eagle*, Empress Eugénie of France on board, entered the canal on November 17, followed by sixty-eight steamships carrying the rest of the party—the emperor of Austria, the crown prince of Prussia, the grand duke of Russia, and scores of other dignitaries. Flowery speeches flowed freely, as did the champagne. The ceremony cost a staggering £1.3 million. Even so, the size of the celebration paled in comparison to the canal itself. The largest project of its kind, and a masterful feat of engineering, the canal sliced through one hundred miles of Egyptian desert to link the Mediterranean and Red seas, which cut the trip from London to Bombay in half. As a fast, cheap, and efficient route to the East, the canal had instant strategic importance. Moreover, the canal dramatically showcased—and to many Europeans, justified—the abilities of Western power and technology to transform the globe.

The building of the canal was the result of half a century of France and Britain's increasingly pervasive commercial, financial, and political involvement in Egypt. French troops under Napoleon led the way, but Britain's bankers soon followed. European financial interests developed a close relationship with those who governed Egypt as a semi-independent state inside the Ottoman empire. By 1875 the canal itself had come under the control of Britain, which had purchased 44 percent of the shares in the canal from the khedive (viceroy) of Egypt when he was threatened with bankruptcy. By the late 1870s, these economic and political relationships had produced debt and instability in Egypt, and consternation among European investors who wanted returns on their loans. In a bid to produce both an independent state and an Egyptian nation—not so different from the European model—free of foreign "interference," a group of Egyptian army officers (led by 'Urabi Pasha) took control of Egypt's government in 1882.

After much debate, the British government decided to intervene. They did not believe Suez to be at risk, but they were determined to protect their investments by controlling the budget and enforcing a debt settlement. The Royal Navy shelled Egyptian forts along the canal into rubble. A special task force of troops led by Britain's most successful colonial general, "Garnet" Wolseley, landed along the shore of the

FOCUS QUESTIONS

- What were the causes of the "new imperialism"?
- How was the Indian empire reorganized after the Mutiny of 1857?
- How did Western countries "open" China?
- What was the "civilizing mission"?
- What events set off the "scramble for Africa"?
- How did empire affect European identity?
- Why was the Boer War unique?

canal near 'Urabi Pasha's central base. Wolseley planned his attack down to the last detail—the order of maneuvers looked very much like a railway timetable—and overwhelmed the Egyptian lines just before dawn, at bayonet point. This striking success rallied immediate popular support at home, but the political consequences ran much deeper and lasted for more than seventy years. Britain took over effective control of the province of Egypt. Britain put conditions on the repayment of loans owed by the former Egyptian government, and regulated the trade in Egyptian cotton that helped supply Britain's textile mills. Most important, intervention secured the route to India and the markets of the East.

The convergence of technology, money, and politics involved in the Suez Canal epitomizes the interplay of economics and empire in late-nineteenth-century Europe. The years 1870 to 1914 brought both rapid industrialization throughout the West and the stunningly rapid expansion of Western power abroad. The "new imperialism" of the late nineteenth century was distinguished by its scope, intensity, and long-range consequences. It transformed cultures, economies, and states. Projects such as the Suez Canal changed—literally—the landscape and map of the world. They not only brought together newly made money and fresh desires for power, they also represented an ideology: the belief in technology and in Western superiority.

The new imperialism, however, was not a one-way street, nor did it allow the West simply to conquer vast territories and dictate its terms to the rest of the world. The new political and economic relationships between colonies and dependent states on the one hand and the "metropole" (the colonizing power) on the other ran both ways, bringing changes to both parties. Fierce competition among nations upset the balance of power. The new imperialism was an expression of European strength, but it was also profoundly destabilizing.

> The new imperialism, however, was not a one-way street, nor did it allow the West simply to conquer vast territories and dictate its terms to the rest of the world.

IMPERIALISM

What were the causes of the "new imperialism"?

"Imperialism" is the process of extending one state's control over another—a process that takes many forms. Historians begin by distinguishing between for-

mal and informal imperialism. "Formal imperialism," or colonialism, was sometimes exercised by direct rule: the colonizing nations annexed territories outright and established new governments to subjugate and administer other states and peoples. Sometimes colonialism worked through indirect rule: the conquering Europeans reached agreements with indigenous leaders and governed them. There was no single technique of colonial management; as we will see, resistance forced colonial powers to shift strategies frequently. "Informal imperialism" refers to a more subtle and less visible exercise of power, in which the stronger state allowed the weaker state to maintain its independence while reducing its sovereignty. Informal imperialism took the form of carving out zones of European sovereignty and privilege, such as treaty ports, within other states. It could mean using European economic, political, and cultural power to get advantageous treaties or terms of trade. Informal imperialism was not only common, it played an even more fundamental role in shaping global power relations.

Both formal and informal imperialism expanded dramatically in the nineteenth century. The "scramble for Africa" was the most sudden and startling case of formal imperialism: from 1875 to 1902 Europeans seized up to 90 percent of the continent. The overall picture is no less remarkable: between 1870 and 1900, a small group of Western states (France, Britain, Germany, the Netherlands, Russia, and the United States) colonized about one quarter of the world's land surface. In addition to these activities, Western states extended informal empire in sections of China and Turkey, across South and East Asia, and into Central and South America. So striking was this expansion of European power and sovereignty that by the late nineteenth century contemporaries were speaking of the "new imperialism."

Imperialism was not new. It is more helpful to think of nineteenth-century developments as a new stage of European empire building. The "second European empires" took hold after the first empires, especially those in the New World, had by and large collapsed. The British empire in North America was shattered in 1776 by the American Revolution. French imperial ambitions across the Atlantic were toppled along with Napoleon. Spanish and Portuguese domination of Central and South America ended with the Latin American revolutions of the early nineteenth century. In what ways were the second, nineteenth-century European empires different?

The nineteenth-century empires developed against the backdrop of developments we have considered in the preceding chapters: industrialization, liberal revolutions, and the rise of nation-states. These developments changed Europe, and they changed European imperialism. First, industrialization created new economic needs for raw materials. Second, industrialization, liberalism, and science forged a new view of the world, history, and the future. A distinguishing feature of nineteenth-century imperialism lay in Europeans' conviction that economic development and technological advances would inevitably bring progress to the rest of the world. Third, especially in the case of Britain and France, the nineteenth-century imperial powers were also in principle democratic nations, where government authority rested on consent and on the equality of most citizens. This made conquest and subjugation more difficult to justify and raised increasingly thorny questions about the status of colonized peoples. Nineteenth-century imperialists sought to distance themselves from earlier histories of conquest. They spoke not of winning souls for the Church or subjects for the king, but rather of building railroads and harbors, encouraging social reform and fulfilling Europe's secular mission to bring civilization to the world.

The "new" aspects of nineteenth-century imperialism, however, resulted equally from changes and events outside Europe. Resistance, rebellion, and recognition of colonial failures obliged Europeans to develop new strategies of rule. The Haitian revolution of 1804, echoed by slave rebellions in the early nineteenth century, compelled the British and French, slowly, to end the slave trade and slavery in their colonies in the 1830s and 1840s, although new systems of forced labor cropped up to take their places. The example of the American Revolution encouraged the British to grant self-government to white settler states in Canada (1867), Australia (1901), and New Zealand (1912). In India, as we will see, the British responded to rebellion by taking the area away from the East India Company and putting it under control of the crown, by requiring civil servants to undergo more training, and by much more careful policing of indigenous peoples. Almost everywhere, nineteenth-century empires established carefully codified racial hierarchies to organize relationships between Europeans and different indigenous groups. (Apartheid in South Africa is but one

The Inauguration of the Suez Canal. This allegory illustrates the union of the Mediterranean and Red Seas attended by Ismail Pasha, the Khedive of Egypt, Abdul Aziz, Sultan of the Ottoman empire, Ferdinand de Lesseps, President of the Suez Canal Company, Empress Eugenie of France, and several mermaids. It also represents the nineteenth-century vision of imperialism as a bearer of global progress, promoting technological advance and breaking down barriers between the "Orient" and the West.

example.) In general, nineteenth-century imperialism involved less independent "entrepreneurial" activity by merchants and traders (such as the East India Company) and more "settlement and discipline." This meant that empire became a vast project, involving legions of administrators, schoolteachers, and engineers. Nineteenth-century imperialism, then, arose from new motives. It produced new forms of government and management in the colonies. Last, it created new kinds of interactions between Europeans and indigenous peoples.

THE NEW IMPERIALISM AND ITS CAUSES

Historians now would agree that economic pressures were one, though only one, important cause of imperialism. In the case of Great Britain, roughly half its total of £4 billion in foreign investments was at work within its empire. Late-nineteenth-century London was rapidly becoming the banker of the world. In all western European countries, demand for raw materials made colonies seem a necessary investment and helped persuade governments that imperialism was a worthwhile policy. Rubber, tin, and minerals from the colonies supplied European industries, and foods, coffee, sugar, tea, wool, and grain supplied European consumers. Yet the economic explanation has limits. Colonial markets were generally too poor to meet the needs of European manufacturers. Africa, the continent over which Europeans frantically "scrambled," was the poorest and least profitable to investors. Many nineteenth-century Europeans, however, expected the colonies to produce profits. French newspapers, for instance, reported that the Congo was "rich, vigorous, and fertile virgin territory," with "fabulous quantities" of gold, copper, ivory, and rubber. Such hopes certainly contributed to expansionism, even if the profits of empire did not match Europeans' expectations.

A second interpretation of imperialism emphasizes strategic and nationalist motives more than economic interests. International rivalries reinforced the belief that vital national interests were at stake, and made European powers more determined to control both the governments and economies of less-developed nations and territories. French politicians supported imperialism as a means of restoring national prestige and honor, lost in the humiliating defeat by the Prussians in 1870–1871. The Germans, recently unified in a modern nation, viewed overseas empire as a "national" birthright possession and as a way of entering the "club" of Great Powers.

This second, noneconomic, interpretation stresses the new links between imperialism and nineteenth-century

CHRONOLOGY	
MAJOR IMPERIAL CONFLICTS, 1857–1905	
First Opium War, China	1839–1842
Great Mutiny, India	1857–1858
Siege of Khartoum, Sudan	1884–1885
Italian invasion of Ethiopa	1896
Crisis of Fashoda, Sudan	1898
Boer War, South Africa	1899–1902
Spanish-American War	1898
Boxer Rebellion, China	1900
Russo-Japanese War	1904–1905

state and nation building. That nations should be empires was not always self-evident. Otto von Bismarck, the architect of German unification, long considered colonialism overseas a distraction from far more serious issues on the continent of Europe. By the last decades of the century, however, Germany had joined France and England in what seemed an urgent race for territories. Advocates of colonialism—from businessmen and explorers to writers (such as Rudyard Kipling) and political theorists—spelled out why empire was important to a new nation. Colonies did more than demonstrate military power; they showed the vigor of a nation's economy, the strength of its convictions, the will of its citizenry, the force of its laws, and the power of its culture. A strong national community could assimilate others, bring progress to new lands and new peoples.

Third, imperialism had important cultural dimensions. A French diplomat once described the British imperial adventurer Cecil Rhodes as "a force cast in an idea"; the same might be said of imperialism itself. Imperialism as an idea excited such explorers as the Scottish missionary David Livingston, who believed that the British conquest of Africa would put an end to the East African slave trade, and "introduce the Negro family into the body of corporate nations." Rudyard Kipling, the British poet and novelist, wrote of the "white man's burden" (see p. 634), a notorious phrase that referred to the European mission to "civilize" what Kipling and others considered the "barbaric" and "heathen" quarters of the globe. These convictions did not cause imperialism, but they illustrate how central empire building became to the West's self-image.

In short, it is difficult to disentangle economic, political, and strategic "causes" for imperialism. Strategic interests often persuaded policy makers that economic issues

HOW WAS THE INDIAN EMPIRE REORGANIZED AFTER THE MUTINY OF 1857?

IMPERIALISM IN SOUTH ASIA   619

were at stake. Different constituencies—the military, international financiers, missionaries, colonial lobby groups at home—held different and often clashing visions of the purpose and benefits of imperialism. "Imperial policy" was less a matter of long-range planning than of a series of quick responses, often improvised, to particular situations. International rivalries led policy makers to redefine their ambitions. So did individual explorers, entrepreneurs, or groups of settlers who established claims to hitherto unknown territories that home governments then felt compelled to recognize and defend. Finally, Europeans were not the only players on the stage. Their goals and practices were shaped by social changes in the countries in which they became involved, by the independent interests of local peoples, and by resistance, which, as often as not, they found themselves unable to understand and powerless to stop.

IMPERIALISM IN SOUTH ASIA

How was the Indian empire reorganized after the Mutiny of 1857?

India was the center of the British empire, the jewel of the British crown. It was also an inheritance from eighteenth-century empire building, secured well before the period of the "new imperialism." The conquest of most of the subcontinent began in the 1750s and quickened during the age of revolution. Conquering India helped compensate for "losing" North America. General Cornwallis, defeated at Yorktown, went on to a brilliant career in India. By the mid-nineteenth century, India had become the focal point of Britain's newly expanded global power, which reached from southern Africa across South Asia and to Australia. Keeping this region involved changing tactics and forms of rule.

Until the mid-nineteenth century, British territories in the subcontinent were under the control of the British East India Company. The company had its own military, divided into European and (far larger) Indian divisions. The company held the right to collect taxes on land from Indian peasants. Until the early nineteenth century, the company had legal monopolies over trade in all goods, including indigo, textiles, salt, minerals, and, most lucrative of all, opium. The British government had granted trade monopolies in its northern American colonies. Unlike North America, however, India never became a settler state. In the 1830s Europeans were a tiny minority, numbering forty-five thousand in an Indian population of 150 million. The company's government was military and repressive. Soldiers collected taxes; civil servants wore military uniforms; British troops brashly commandeered peasants' oxen and carts for their own purposes. Typically, though, the company could not enforce its rule uniformly. It governed some areas directly, others through making alliances with local leaders, and others still by simply controlling goods and money. Indirect rule, here as in other empires, meant finding indigenous collaborators and maintaining their good will.

FROM MUTINY TO REBELLION

The Company's rule often met resistance and protest. In 1857–1858, it was particularly badly shaken by what the British called the "Sepoy [soldiers'] Rebellion," now known in India as the Great Rebellion of 1857. The uprising began near Delhi, when the military disciplined a regiment of sepoys (the traditional term for Indian soldiers employed by the British) for refusing to use rifle cartridges greased

British Executing Leaders of Indian Rebellion of 1857. The British were determined to make an example of the rebel Indian soldiers of the Sepoy Mutiny. This engraving shows executions in which the condemned were blown apart by cannons.

with pork fat—unacceptable to either Hindus or Muslims. Yet as the British prime minister Disraeli later observed, "The decline and fall of empires are not affairs of greased cartridges." The causes of the mutiny were much deeper and involved social, economic, and political grievances. Indian peasants attacked law courts and burned tax rolls, protesting debt and corruption. In areas such as Oudh, which had recently been annexed, rebels defended their traditional leaders, who had been summarily ousted by the British. Religious leaders, both Hindu and Muslim, seized the occasion to denounce Christian missionaries sent in by the British and their assault on local traditions and practices.

At first the British were faced with a desperate situation, with areas under British control cut off from one another and pro-British cities under siege. Loyal Indian troops were brought south from the frontiers, and troops were shipped directly from Britain to suppress the rebellion. The fighting lasted more than a year, and the British matched the rebels' early massacres and vandalism with a systematic campaign of repression. At a political level, British leaders were stunned by how close the revolt had brought them to disaster and were determined never to repeat the same mistakes.

> At a political level, British leaders were stunned by how close the revolt had brought them to disaster and were determined never to repeat the same mistakes.

After "the mutiny," the British were compelled to reorganize their Indian empire, developing new strategies of rule. The East India Company was abolished, replaced by the British crown. The British raj (or rule) was governed directly, though the British also sought out collaborators and cooperative interest groups. The British also reorganized the military, and tried to change relations among soldiers. Indigenous troops were separated from each other, in order to avoid the kind of "fraternization" that proved subversive. As one British officer put it, "If one regiment mutinies I should like to have the next so alien that it would fire into it." Even more than before, the British sought to rule through the Indian upper classes rather than in opposition to them. Civil-service reform opened up new positions to members of the Indian upper classes. The British had to reconsider their relationship to Indian cultures. Missionary activity was subdued, and the British channeled their reforming impulses into the more secular projects of economic development, railways, roads, irrigation, and so on. Still, consensus on effective colonial strategies was elusive. Some administrators counseled more reform and change; others sought to give the princes more support; the British tried both, in fits and starts, until the end of British rule in 1947.

How did the British raj shape Indian society? The British practice of indirect rule sought to create an Indian elite that would serve British interests, a group "who may be the interpreters between us and the millions whom we govern—a class of persons Indian in colour and blood, but English in tastes, in opinion, in morals, and in intellect," as one British writer put it. Eventually, this practice created a large social group of British-educated Indian civil servants and businessmen, well trained for government and skeptical about British claims that they brought progress to the subcontinent. This group provided the leadership for the nationalist movement that challenged British rule in India. At the same time, this group became increasingly distant from the rest of the nation. The overwhelming majority of Indians remained desperately poor peasants, many of them unable to pay taxes and thus in debt to British landlords, all struggling to subsist on diminishing plots of land, villagers working in the textile trade beaten down by imports of cheap manufactured goods from England, all residents of what would become the most populous nation in the world.

IMPERIALISM IN CHINA

How did Western countries "open" China?

In China, too, European imperialism escalated early, well before the period of the "new imperialism." Yet there it took a different form. Europeans did not conquer and annex whole regions. Instead, they forced favorable trade agreements at gunpoint, set up treaty ports where Europeans lived and worked under their own jurisdiction, and established outposts of European missionary activity—all with such dispatch that the Chinese spoke of their country as being "carved up like a melon."

Since the seventeenth century European trade with China—in coveted luxuries such as silk, porcelain, art objects, and tea—had run up against resistance from the Chinese government, which was determined to

An Opium Factory in Patna, India, c. 1851. Balls of opium dry in a huge warehouse before being shipped to Calcutta for export to China and elsewhere.

keep foreign traders, and foreign influence in general, at bay. By the early nineteenth century, however, Britain's global ambitions and rising power were setting the stage for a confrontation. Freed from the task of fighting Napoleon, the British set their sights on improving the terms of the China trade, demanding the rights to come into open harbors and to have special trading privileges. By the 1830s, these diplomatic conflicts had been heightened by the opium trade.

THE OPIUM TRADE

Opium provided a direct link among Britain, British India, and China. In fact, opium (derived from the poppy plant) was one of the very few commodities that Europeans could sell in China, and for this reason it became crucial to the balance of East-West trade.

From India, the East India Company sold the opium to "country traders"—small fleets of British,

Dutch, and Chinese shippers who carried the drug to southeast Asia and China. Silver paid for the opium came back to the East India company, which used it, in turn, to buy Chinese goods for the European market. The trade, therefore, was not only profitable, it was key to a triangular European-Indian-Chinese economic relationship. In the 1830s the Chinese government began a full-scale campaign to purge the drug from China. That campaign set the Chinese emperor on a collision course with British opium traders. In one confrontation the Chinese drug commissioner Lin confiscated 3 million pounds of raw opium from the British and washed it out to sea. In another the Chinese authorities blockaded British ships in port, and local citizens demonstrated angrily in front of British residences.

In 1839, these simmering conflicts broke into what was called the first "Opium War." Drugs were not the core of the matter. They highlighted larger issues of

AFGHANISTAN

NORTH-WEST FRONTIER PROVINCE

KASHMIR
• Srinagar

BRITISH
BALUCHISTAN

PUNJAB
• Amritsar
• Lahore

TIBET

SIKKIM

NEPAL

BHUTAN

BALUCHISTAN
AGENCY

RAJPUTANA
AGENCY

• Delhi

UNITED PROVINCES

EAST BENGAL
AND ASSAM

SIND

B O M B A Y

GWALIOR

CENTRAL INDIA AGENCY

BENGAL

• Dacca

UPPER
BURMA

• Ahmadabad
• Baroda

CENTRAL
PROVINCES

Calcutta •

P R E S I D E N C Y

ORISSA

LOWER
BURMA

Bombay •
• Poona

HYDERABAD

A R A B I A N

M A D R A S   P R E S I D E N C Y

B a y   o f

B e n g a l

GOA

S E A

MYSORE

Madras •

ANDAMAN AND
NICOBAR IS.

TRAVANCORE

CEYLON

Native states and territories

British India

International boundary

Provincial boundary

0   200   400 Miles

0   200   400 Kilometers

ASIA

Area of
detail

INDIA: POLITICAL DIVISIONS AND MUTINY

How and why did the British become involved in India, and why did India soon become central to the foreign policy and economic interests of Great Britain? Why did the British decide to annex directly the various parts of India, and what political conditions made the advance of British control easier? Why did formal, direct British rule—with the appointment of a viceroy—only come in 1861?

sovereignty and economic status: the Europeans' "rights" to trade with whomever they pleased, by-passing Chinese monopolies; to set up zones of European residence in defiance of Chinese sovereignty; and to proselytize and open schools.

WAR AND REBELLION

War flared up several times over the course of the century. After the first war of 1839–1842, in which British steam vessels and guns overpowered the Chinese fleet, the Treaty of Nanking (1842) compelled the Chinese to give the British trading privileges, the right to reside in five cities, and the port of Hong Kong "in perpetuity." After a second war, the British secured yet more treaty ports and privileges, including the right to send in missionaries. In the aftermath of those agreements between the Chinese and British, other countries demanded similar rights and economic opportunities.

Surrendering privileges to Europeans and the Japanese seriously undermined the authority of the Chinese Qing (Ching) emperor at home, and only heightened popular hostility to foreign intruders. Authority at the imperial center had been eroding for more than a century by 1900, hastened by the Opium Wars and by the vast Taiping Rebellion (1852–1864), an enormous bitter, and deadly conflict in which radical Christian rebels in south-central China challenged the authority of the emperors themselves. On the defensive against the rebels, the dynasty hired foreign generals, including the British commander Charles Gordon to lead its forces. The war devastated China's agricultural heartland, and the death toll, never confirmed, may have reached 20 million. This ruinous disorder, and the increasing inability of the emperor to keep order and collect the taxes necessary to stabilize trade and repay foreign loans, led European countries to take more and more direct control of their side of "the China trade."

THE BOXER REBELLION

From a Western perspective, the most important of the nineteenth-century rebellions against the corruptions of foreign rule was the Boxer Rebellion of 1900. The Boxers were a secret society of young men trained in Chinese martial arts and believed to have spiritual powers. Antiforeign and antimissionary, they provided the spark for a loosely organized but widespread uprising in northern China. Bands of Boxers attacked foreign engineers, tore up railway lines, and in the spring of 1900 marched on Beijing. They laid siege to the foreign legations in the city, home to several thousand Western diplomats and merchants and their families. The rebellion, and particularly the siege at Beijing, mobilized a global response. Twenty thousand troops—combining the forces of Britain, France, the United States, Germany, Italy, Japan, and Russia—ferociously repressed the Boxer movement. The outside powers then demanded indemnities, new trading concessions, and reassurances from the Chinese government.

The Boxer Rebellion illustrated the vulnerability of Europeans' imperial power. It dramatized the resources Europeans would have to devote to maintaining their far-flung influence. In the process of repression, the Europeans became committed to propping up corrupt and fragile governments in order to protect their agreements and interests, and they were drawn into putting down popular uprisings against local inequalities and foreign rule.

RUSSIAN IMPERIALISM

Russia was a persistently imperialist power throughout the nineteenth century. Its rulers championed a policy of annexation—by conquest, treaty, or both—of lands bordering on the existing Russian state. Beginning in 1801, with the acquisition of Georgia following a war with Persia, the tsars continued to pursue their expansionist dream. Bessarabia and Turkestan (taken from the Turks) and Armenia (from the Persians) vastly increased the empire's size. This southward colonization brought the Russians close to war with the British twice: first in 1881, when Russian troops occupied territories in the trans-Caspian region, and again in 1884–1887, when the tsar's forces advanced to the frontier of Afghanistan. In both cases the British feared incursions into areas they deemed within their sphere of influence in the Middle East. They were concerned, as well, about a possible threat to India. The maneuvering, spying, and support of friendly puppet governments by Russia and Britain became known as

> The maneuvering, spying, and support of friendly puppet governments by Russia and Britain became known as the "Great Game," and foreshadowed Western countries' jockeying for the region's oil resources in the twentieth century.

SOUTH AND EAST ASIA, c. 1914

Why were European powers (and to some extent, the United States) anxious to establish treaty ports and spheres of influence in China? Why was control of Chinese markets particularly crucial to British economic interests? What was the relationship among colonial powers, capitalist investors, and the Chinese government? How did the Boxer Rebellion and the effects of the Open Door Policy encourage more intensive exploitation in other parts of Southeast Asia?

the "Great Game," and foreshadowed Western countries' jockeying for the region's oil resources in the twentieth century.

Russian expansion also moved east. In 1875, the Japanese traded the southern half of Sakhalin Island for the previously Russian Kurile Islands. The tsars' eastward advance was finally halted in 1904. Russian expansion in Mongolia and Manchuria came up against Japanese expansion, and the two powers went to war. Russia's huge imperial army more than met its match in a savage, bloody conflict. Russia's navy was sent halfway round the world to reinforce the beleaguered Russian troops, but was ambushed and sunk by the better-trained and equipped Japanese fleet. This national humiliation helped provoke a revolt in Russia and led to an American-brokered peace treaty in 1905 (see Chapter 23). The defeat shook the already unsteady regime of the tsar, and proved that European nations were not the only ones who could play the imperial game successfully.

THE FRENCH EMPIRE AND THE CIVILIZING MISSION

What was the "civilizing mission"?

Like British expansion into India, French colonialism in Northern Africa began before the so-called new imperialism of the late nineteenth century. By the 1830s, the French had created a general government of their possessions in Algeria. From the outset the Algerian conquest was different from most other colonial ventures: Algeria became a settler state, one of the few apart from South Africa. The settlers were by no means all French; they included Italian, Spanish, and Maltese merchants and shopkeepers of modest means, laborers, and peasants. With the French military's help, the settlers appropriated land, and French business concerns took cork forests and established mining in copper, lead, and iron. Economic activity was for European benefit. The first railroads, for instance, did not even carry passengers; they took iron ore to the coast for export to France, where it would be smelted and sold.

Before the 1870s, colonial activities aroused relatively little interest among the French at home. But after the humiliating defeat in the Franco-Prussian war (1870–1871) and the establishment of the Third Re-

public, colonial lobby groups and, gradually, the government, became increasingly adamant about the benefits of colonialism. These benefits were not simply economic. Taking on the "civilizing mission" would reinforce the purpose of the French republic and the prestige of the French people. It was France's duty "to contribute to this work of civilization." Jules Ferry, a republican political leader, successfully argued for expanding the French presence in Indochina. In what Ferry ironically considered an attack on the racism of his contemporaries, he argued that "the superior races have a right vis-à-vis the inferior races . . . they have a right to civilize them."

Under Ferry, the French acquired Tunisia (1881), northern and central Vietnam (Tonkin and Annam; 1883), and Laos and Cambodia (1893). They also carried this "civilizing mission" into their colonies in West Africa. European and Atlantic trade with the west coast of Africa, in slaves, gold, and ivory, had been well established for centuries. In the late nineteenth century, trade gave way to formal administration. The year 1895 saw the establishment of a Federation of French West Africa, a loosely organized administration to govern an area nine times the size of France, including Guinea, Senegal, and the Ivory Coast. Even with reforms and centralization in 1902, French control remained uneven. Despite military campaigns of pacification, resistance remained, and the French dealt gingerly with tribal leaders, at some times deferring to their authority and at others trying to break their power. The federation embarked on an ambitious program of public works. Engineers rebuilt the huge harbor at Dakar, the most important on the coast, to accommodate rising exports. With some utopian zeal they redesigned older cities, tried to improve sanitation and health, improved water systems, and so on. The French republic was justifiably proud of the Pasteur Institute for bacteriological research, which opened in France in 1888; overseas institutes became part of the colonial enterprise.

Such programs plainly served French interests. "Officially this process is called civilizing, and after all, the term is apt, since the undertaking serves to increase the degree of prosperity of our civilization," remarked one Frenchman who opposed the colonial enterprise. None of these measures aimed to give indigenous peoples political rights. As one historian puts it, "the French Government General was in the business not of making citizens, but of civilizing its subjects." More telling, however, the French project was not often successful. The French government did

Slaves in Chains, 1896. In Africa, native labor was exploited by Europeans and by other natives, as here.

powers conquered and colonized, asserting formal control was astonishing. The effects were profound. In 1875, 11 percent of the continent was in European hands. By 1902, the figure was 90 percent. European powers mastered logical problems of transport and communication; they learned how to keep diseases at bay. They also had new weapons. The Maxim gun, adopted by the British army in 1889 and first used by British colonial troops, pelted out as many as five hundred rounds a minute; it turned encounters with indigenous forces into bloodbaths and made armed resistance virtually impossible.

THE CONGO FREE STATE

In the 1870s, the British had formed new imperial relationships along the costs of south and east Africa, in the north and west. A new phase of European involvement struck right at the heart of the continent. Until the latter part of the nineteenth century this territory had been out of bounds for Europeans. The rapids downstream on such strategic rivers as the Congo and the Zambezi made it difficult to move inland, and tropical diseases against which Europeans had little or no resistance were lethal to most explorers. But during the 1870s, a new drive into central Africa produced results. The target was the fertile valleys around the river Congo, and the European colonizers were a privately financed group of Belgians paid by their king, Leopold II (1865–1909). They followed in the footsteps of Henry Morton Stanley, an American newspaperman and explorer who later became a British subject and a knight of the realm. Stanley hacked his way through thick canopy jungle and territory where no European had previously set foot. His "scientific" journeys inspired the creation of a society of researchers and students of African culture in Brussels, in reality a front organization for the commercial company set up by Leopold. The ambitiously named International Association for the Exploration and Civilization of the Congo was set up in 1876, and proceeded to sign treaties with local elites that opened the whole Congo River basin to commercial exploitation. The vast resources of palm oil and natural rubber, and the promise of minerals (including diamonds) were now within Europeans' reach.

not have the resources to carry out its plans, which proved much more expensive and complicated than anyone imagined. Transportation costs ran very high. Labor posed the largest problems. Here as elsewhere, Europeans faced massive resistance from the African peasants, whom they wanted to do everything from building railroads to working mines and carrying rubber. The Europeans resorted to forced labor, signing agreements with local tribal leaders to deliver workers, and they turned a blind eye to the continuing use of slave labor in the interior. For all of these reasons, the colonial project did not produce the profits some expected. In important respects, however, the French investment in colonialism was cultural. Railroads, schools, and projects such as the Dakar harbor were, like the Eiffel Tower (1889), symbols of the French nation's modernity, power, and world leadership.

THE "SCRAMBLE FOR AFRICA" AND THE CONGO

What events set off the "scramble for Africa"?

French expansion into West Africa was but one instance of Europe's voracity on the African continent. The scope and speed with which the major European

In reality the "Congo Free State" Leopold established was run by Leopold's private company, and the

ATROCITIES IN THE CONGO

George Washington Williams (1849–1891), an African American pastor, journalist, and historian, was among a hand-ful of international observers who went to the Congo in the 1890s to explore and report back on conditions. He wrote sev-eral reports: one for the United States government, another that he presented at an international antislavery conference, several newspaper columns, and an open letter to King Léopold, from which the following is excerpted.

Good and Great Friend,

I have the honour to submit for your Majesty's consideration some reflections respecting the Independent State of Congo, based upon a careful study and inspection of the country and character of the personal Government you have established upon the African Continent. . . .

I was led to regard your enterprise as the rising of the Star of Hope for the Dark Conti-nent, so long the habitation of cruelties. . . . When I arrived in the Congo, I naturally sought for the results of the brilliant programme:—"fostering care," "benevolent enterprise," an "honest and practical effort" to increase the knowledge of the natives "and secure their welfare." . . .

I was doomed to bitter disappointment. Instead of the natives of the Congo "adopting the fostering care" of your Majesty's Government, they everywhere com-plain that their land has been taken from them by force; that the Government is cruel and arbitrary, and declare that they neither love nor respect the Govern-ment and its flag. Your Majesty's Government has se-questered their land, burned their towns, stolen their property, enslaved their women and children, and committed other crimes too numerous to mention in detail. It is natural that they everywhere shrink from "the fostering care" your Majesty's Government so eagerly proffers them.

There has been, to my absolute knowledge, no "hon-est and practical effort made to increase their knowledge and secure their welfare." Your Majesty's Government has never spent one franc for educational purposes, nor instituted any practical sys-tem of industrialism. Indeed the most un-practical measures have been adopted *against* the natives in nearly every respect; and in the capital of your Majesty's Govern-ment at Boma there is not a native employed. The labour system is radically unpractical. . . .

[R]ecruits are transported under circumstances more cruel than cattle in European countries. They eat their rice twice a day by the use of their fingers; they often thirst for water when the season is dry; they are exposed to the heat and rain, and sleep upon the damp and filthy decks of the vessels often so closely crowded as to lie in human ordure. And, of course, many die. . . .

All the crimes perpetrated in the Congo have been done in *your* name, and *you* must answer at the bar if Public Sentiment for the misgovernment of a people, whose lives and fortunes were entrusted to you by the august Conference of Berlin, 1884–1885. . . .

George Washington Williams, "An Open Letter to His serene Majesty Leopold II, King of the Belgians, and Sovereign of the Independent State of Congo, July 1890" in John Hope Franklin, *George Washington Williams: A Biography* (Chicago: University of Chicago Press, 1985), pp. 243–254.

region was opened up to unrestricted exploitation by a series of large European corporations. The older slave trade was suppressed, but the European companies took the "free" African labor guaranteed in Berlin and placed workers in equally bad conditions. Huge tracts of land, larger than whole European countries, became diamond mines or plantations for the extraction of palm oil, rubber, or cocoa. African workers labored in appalling conditions, with no real medicine or sanitation, too little food, and according to production schedules that made European factory labor look mild by comparison. Hundreds of thousands of African workers died from disease and overwork. Because European managers did not respect the different cycle of seasons in central Africa, whole crop years were lost, leading to famines. Laborers working in the heat of the dry season often carried individual loads on their backs that would have been handled by heavy machinery in a European factory. Thousands of Africans were pressed into work harvesting goods Europe wanted. They did so for little or no pay, under the threat of beatings and ritual mutilation for dozens of petty offenses against the plantation companies, who made the laws of the "Free State." Eventually the scandal of the Congo became too great to go on unquestioned. A whole generation of authors and journalists, most famously Joseph Conrad in his *Heart of Darkness*, publicized the arbitrary brutality and the vast scale of suffering. In 1908, Belgium was forced to take direct control of the Congo, turning it into a Belgian colony. A few restrictions at least were imposed on the activities of the great plantation companies that had brought a vast new store of raw materials to European industry by using slavery in all but name.

> Eventually the scandal of the Congo became too great to go on unquestioned. A whole generation of authors and journalists, most famously Joseph Conrad in his *Heart of Darkness,* publicized the arbitrary brutality and the vast scale of suffering.

THE PARTITION OF AFRICA

The occupation of Congo, and its promise of great material wealth, pressured other colonial powers into expanding their holdings. By the 1880s, the "scramble for Africa" was well underway, hastened by stories of rubber forests or diamond mines in other parts of central and southern Africa. The guarantees made at the 1884 Berlin conference allowed the Europeans to take further steps. The French and Portugese increased their holdings. Italy moved into territories along the Red Sea, beside British-held land and the independent kingdom of Ethiopia.

Germany came relatively late to empire overseas. Bismarck was reluctant to engage in an enterprise that he believed would do little to profit the empire either politically or economically. Yet he did not want either Britain or France to dominate Africa, and Germany seized colonies in strategic locations. The German colonies in Cameroon and most of modern Tanzania separated the territories of older, more established powers. Though the Germans were not the most enthusiastic colonialists, they were still fascinated by the imperial adventure, and jealous of their territories. When the Herero people of German Southwest Africa (now Namibia) rebelled in the early 1900s, the Germans responded with a vicious campaign of village burning and ethnic killing that nearly annihilated the Herero.

Great Britain and France had their own ambitions. The French aimed to move west to east across the continent, an important reason for the French expedition to Fashoda (in the Sudan) in 1898 (see page 636). Britain's part in the "scramble" took place largely in southern and eastern Africa, and was encapsulated in the dreams and career of one man: the diamond tycoon, colonial politician, and imperial visionary Cecil Rhodes. Rhodes made a fortune from the South African diamond mines in the 1870s and 1880s. (He left part of this fortune for the creation of the Rhodes scholarships to educate future leaders of the empire at Oxford.) Rhodes's personal goal was to build a southern African empire that was founded on diamonds. "Rhodesia" would fly the

C H R O N O L O G Y	
THE "SCRAMBLE FOR AFRICA," 1870–1908	
European drive into Central Africa	1870s
French acquire Tunisia	1881
Berlin Congress	1884
Germany colonizes Cameroon and Tanzania	1884
Federation of French West Africa	1895
Congo becomes a Belgian colony	1908

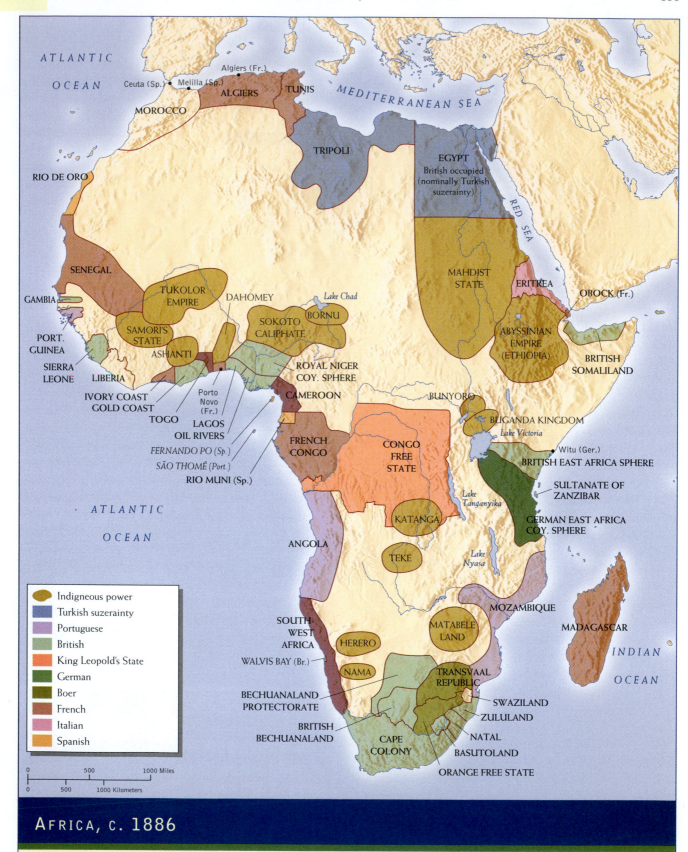

ATLANTIC
OCEAN

Algiers (Fr.)
Ceuta (Sp.) Melilla (Sp.)
MEDITERRANEAN SEA
MOROCCO
ALGIERS
TUNIS

TRIPOLI

EGYPT
British occupied
(nominally Turkish
suzerainty)

RED SEA

RIO DE ORO

SENEGAL

GAMBIA

MAHDIST
STATE

ERITREA

OBOCK (Fr.)

TUKOLOR
EMPIRE

DAHOMEY

Lake Chad

BORNU

PORT.
GUINEA

SAMORI'S
STATE

SOKOTO
CALIPHATE

ABYSSINIAN
EMPIRE
(ETHIOPIA)

SIERRA
LEONE

LIBERIA

ASHANTI

ROYAL NIGER
COY. SPHERE

BRITISH
SOMALILAND

IVORY COAST
GOLD COAST

Porto
Novo
(Fr.)

CAMEROON

BUNYORO

TOGO
LAGOS
OIL RIVERS

FERNANDO PO (Sp.)

SÃO THOMÉ (Port.)

RIO MUNI (Sp.)

FRENCH
CONGO

CONGO
FREE
STATE

BUGANDA KINGDOM

Lake Victoria

Witu (Ger.)

BRITISH EAST AFRICA SPHERE

SULTANATE OF
ZANZIBAR

Lake
Tanganyika

GERMAN EAST AFRICA
COY. SPHERE

ATLANTIC

OCEAN

ANGOLA

KATANGA

TEKE

Lake
Nyasa

MOZAMBIQUE

MADAGASCAR

INDIAN

OCEAN

SOUTH-
WEST
AFRICA

HERERO

MATABELE
LAND

WALVIS BAY (Br.)

NAMA

TRANSVAAL
REPUBLIC

BECHUANALAND
PROTECTORATE

SWAZILAND

ZULULAND

BRITISH
BECHUANALAND

NATAL

CAPE
COLONY

BASUTOLAND

ORANGE FREE STATE

Indigenous power
Turkish suzerainty
Portuguese
British
King Leopold's State
German
Boer
French
Italian
Spanish

0   500   1000 Miles
0   500   1000 Kilometers

AFRICA, c. 1886

Before World War I, who were the "winners" and "losers" in the scramble for Africa? Although the French claim was the largest, why were the British imperial gains more impressive? Given their late arrival as a unified nation and colonial power, how did Germany fare in the race for colonial possessions? Why did Italy, despite an advan-

ATLANTIC OCEAN

SPANISH MOROCCO

MOROCCO

IFNI (Sp.)

RIO DE ORO

MEDITERRANEAN SEA

TUNISIA

ALGERIA

TRIPOLITANIA

LIBYA

CYRENAICA

EGYPT (British occupation)

MAURITANIA

UPPER SENEGAL AND NIGER

FRENCH WEST AFRICA

CHAD

RED SEA

SENEGAL

GAMBIA (Br.)

PORT. GUINEA

FRENCH GUINEA

SIERRA LEONE

LIBERIA

UPPER VOLTA

IVORY COAST

GOLD COAST

DAHOMEY

NORTHERN

NIGERIA

SOUTHERN

TOGOLAND

CAMEROON

Lake Chad

ANGLO-EGYPTIAN SUDAN

FRENCH EQUATORIAL AFRICA

UBANGI SHARI CHAD

ERITREA

FRENCH SOMALILAND

BRITISH SOMALILAND

EMPIRE OF ETHIOPIA

ITALIAN SOMALILAND

FERNANDO PO (Sp.)
SPANISH GUINEA
SÃO THOMÉ (Port.)

GABON COLONY

MIDDLE CONGO

CABINDA

BELGIAN CONGO

Lake Victoria

UGANDA

BRITISH EAST AFRICA

Lake Tanganyika

GERMAN EAST AFRICA

ZANZIBAR (Br.)

INDIAN OCEAN

ATLANTIC OCEAN

ANGOLA

NORTHERN RHODESIA

Lake Nyasa

NYASALAND

MOZAMBIQUE

SOUTHERN RHODESIA

MADAGASCAR

SOUTH-WEST AFRICA

WALVIS BAY (Br.)

BECHUANA-LAND

SWAZILAND (British Protectorate)

UNION OF SOUTH AFRICA

BASUTOLAND (British Protectorate)

Legend:
- British
- French
- Belgian
- Spanish
- Portuguese
- German
- Italian
- Independent state

0   500   1000 Miles
0   500   1000 Kilometers

AFRICA, C. 1914

tageous geographical relationship to Africa, fare so poorly in carving out an African empire? What does the ultimate result of the prewar scramble for Africa suggest to us about the ways in which European powers regarded each other, and why they felt maintaining economic and material resources was so important?

Union Jack out of pride but send its profits into Rhodes' own companies. He helped carve out territories occupying the modern nations of Zambia, Zimbabwe, Malawi, and Botswana—most of the savannah of southern Africa. Rhodes had a broader imperial vision of a British presence along the whole of eastern Africa, symbolized by the goal of a "Cape-to-Cairo" railway. He also believed that the empire should make Britain self-sufficient, with British industry able to run on the goods and raw materials shipped in from its colonies, then exporting many finished products back to those lands.

> Empire, however, was not simply background; it played an important part in establishing European identity.

As each European power sought its "place in the sun," in the famous phrase of the German kaiser William II, they brought more and more of Africa under direct colonial control. African peoples faced a combination of direct European control and "indirect rule" which allowed local elites friendly to European interests literally to lord over those who resisted. The partition of Africa was the most striking instance of the new imperialism, with international and domestic repercussions.

IMPERIAL CULTURE

How did empire affect European identity?

The relationship between the metropole and the colonies was not carried on at a distance. Imperialism was thoroughly anchored in late nineteenth-century Western culture. Images of empire were not just in the propagandist literature distributed by the proponents of colonial expansion, but on tins of tea and boxes of cocoa. Museums and world's fairs displayed the products of empire and introduced spectators to "exotic peoples" who were now benefiting from European "education." Music halls rang to the sound of imperialist songs. Empire was almost always present in novels of the period, sometimes appearing as a faraway setting for fantasy, adventure, or stories of self-discovery. Sometimes imperial themes and peoples were presented as a subtly menacing presence at home. As a realm of fantasy, overseas empires and "exotic" cultures became part of the century's sexual culture. Photos and postcards of North African harems or "unveiled" Arab women were common in European pornography, as were colonial memoirs that chronicled the sexual adventures of their authors.

Empire, however, was not simply background; it played an important part in establishing European identity. In the case of France, the "civilizing mission" demonstrated to French citizens the grandeur of their nation. Building railroads and "bringing progress to other lands" illustrated the vigor of the French republic. Many British writers spoke in similar tones. One called the British empire "the greatest secular agency for good known to the world." Another, using more religious language, argued, "The British race may safely be called a missionary race. The command to go and teach all nations is one that the British people have, whether rightly or wrongly, regarded as specially laid upon themselves." The sense of high moral purpose was not restricted to male writers or authority figures. In England, the United States, Germany, and France, the speeches and projects of women's reform movements were full of references to empire and the civilizing mission. Britain's woman suffrage movement, for instance, was fiercely critical of the British government but often equally nationalist and imperialist. Asking that women be brought into British politics seemed to involve calling on them to take on imperial, as well as civic, responsibilities. British women reformers wrote about the oppression of Indian women by child marriage and sati, and saw themselves taking up the "white woman's burden" of reform.

Imperial culture also gave new prominence to theories of race. In the 1850s, Count Arthur de Gobineau (1816–1882) had written a massive tome on *The Inequality of the Races*, but the book sparked little interest until the period of the new imperialism, when it was translated into English and widely discussed. For Gobineau, race offered the "master key" to understanding problems in the modern world. Unlike his Enlightenment predecessors, however, Gobineau did not believe that environment had any effect on politics, culture, or morals. Race was all. He argued that a people degenerated when it no longer had "the same blood in its veins, continual adulteration having gradually affected the quality of that blood." Enlightenment thinkers often argued that slavery made its victims unable to understand liberty. Gobineau, by contrast, asserted that slavery proved its victims' racial inferiority.

Houston Stewart Chamberlain (1855–1927), the son of a British admiral, tried to make Gobineau's theories more "scientific," tying them to the new scientific writing about evolution, Charles Darwin's natural science, and Herbert Spencer's views about social evolution. (On Darwin and Spencer, see Chapter 23.) Chamberlain's books proved extremely popular, selling tens of thousands of copies in England and Germany. Francis Galton (1822–1911), a British scientist who studied evolution, explored how hereditary traits were communicated from generation to generation. In 1883, Galton first used the term "eugenics" to refer to the science of improving the "racial qualities" of humanity through selective breeding of "superior types."

These theories did not, by themselves, produce an imperialist mindset, and they were closely linked with other developments in European culture, particularly renewed antagonism about social class and a fresh wave of European anti-Semitism (see Chapter 23). Yet the increasingly scientific racism of late-nineteenth-century Europe made it easier for many to reconcile the rhetoric of progress with contempt for other peoples. It also provided a rationale for imperial conquest and a justification for the bloodshed that imperialism brought, for instance, in Africa.

Still, Europeans did not speak with one voice. Politicians and writers who championed imperialism, or offered racial justifications for it, met with opposition. Writers such as Joseph Conrad, who shared many of their contemporaries' racism, nevertheless believed that imperialism signaled deeply rooted pathologies in European culture. One result of imperialism was serious debate on its effects and causes.

Many of the anti-imperialists were men and women from the colonies themselves, who brought their case to the metropole. Perhaps the most defiant

Imperialism gave new prominence to dramatically different theories of race. British scientist Francis Galton (left) originated the term "eugenics" and helped to develop the scientific racism that justified imperial conquest. African American intellectual W.E.B. Dubois (right) attended the Pan-African conference of 1900, and was one of those whose anti-imperialism sprung from his work with the antislavery movement.

RUDYARD KIPLING AND HIS CRITICS

Rudyard Kipling (1865–1936) remains one of the most famous propagandists of empire. His novels, short stories, and poetry about the British imperial experience in India were defining texts for the cause in which he believed. Kipling's poem, "The White Man's Burden," reprinted below, was published in 1899 during the Spanish-American War and the struggle for the Philippines. The poem called on the United States to shoulder the burden of empire. It became an instant classic and, as the response on the follwing page shows, it soon became part of the turn-of-the-century debate about imperialism.

Take up the White Man's burden—
   Send forth the best ye breed—
Go, bind your sons to exile
   To serve your captives' need;
To wait, in heavy harness,
   On fluttered folk and wild—
Your new-caught sullen peoples,
   Half devil and half child.

Take up the White Man's burden—
   In patience to abide,
To veil the threat of terror
   And check the show of pride;
By open speech and simple,
   An hundred times made plain,
To seek another's profit
   And work another's gain.

Take up the White Man's burden—
   The savage wars of peace—
Fill full the mouth of Famine,
   And bid the sickness cease;
And when your goal is nearest
   (The end for others sought)
Watch sloth and heathen folly
   Bring all your hope to nought.

Take up the White Man's burden—
   No iron rule of kings,
But toil of serf and sweeper—
   The tale of common things.
The ports ye shall not enter,
   The roads ye shall not tread,

Go, make them with your living
   And mark them with your dead.

Take up the White Man's burden,
   And reap his old reward—
The blame of those ye better
   The hate of those ye guard—
The cry of hosts ye humour
   (Ah, slowly!) toward the light:—
"Why brought ye us from bondage,
   Our loved Egyptian night?"

Take up the White Man's burden—
   Ye dare not stoop to less—
Nor call too loud on Freedom
   To cloak your weariness.
By all ye will or whisper,
   By all ye leave or do,
The silent sullen peoples
   Shall weigh your God and you.

Take up the White Man's burden!
   Have done with childish days—
The lightly-proffered laurel,
   The easy ungrudged praise:
Comes now, to search your manhood
   Through all the thankless years,
Cold, edged with dear-bought wisdom,
   The judgment of your peers.

Rudyard Kipling, "The White Man's Burden," *McClure's Magazine* 12 (Feb. 1899).

Sir: The cable informs us that "Kipling's stirring verses, the 'Call to America,' have created a . . . profound impression" on your side. What that impression may be, we can only conjecture. There is something almost sickening in this "imperial" talk of assuming and bearing burdens for the good of others. They are never assumed or held where they are not found to be of material advantage or ministering to honor or glory. Wherever empire (I speak of the United Kingdom) is extended, and the climate suits the white man, the aborigines are, for the benefit of the white man, cleared off or held in degradation for his benefit. . . .

Taking India as a test, no one moves a foot in her government that is not well paid and pensioned at her cost. No appointments are more eagerly contended for than those in the Indian service. A young man is made for life when he secures one. The tone of that service is by no means one "bound to exile," "to serve . . . captives' need," "to wait in heavy harness," or in any degree as expressed in Mr. Kipling's highfalutin lines. It is entirely the contrary: "You are requested not to beat the servants" is a not uncommon notice in Indian hotels. . . . So anxious are we, where good pay is concerned, to save Indians the heavy burden of enjoying them, that, while our sons can study and pass at home for Indian appointments, her sons must study and pass in England; and even in India itself whites are afforded chances closed to natives. . . .

There never was a fostered trade and revenue in more disastrous consequences to humanity than the opium trade and revenue. There never was a more grinding and debilitating tax than that on salt. . . .

Alfred Webb, "Mr. Kipling's Call to America," *The Nation* 68 (Feb. 23, 1899).

---

of anti-imperialist actions was the London Pan-African conference of 1900, staged at the height of the "scramble for Africa" and during the Boer War (see below). The conference grew out of an international tradition of African American, British, and American antislavery movements, and out of groups like the African Association (founded in 1897), which turned the arguments used earlier to abolish slavery against European imperialism. They protested forced labor in the mining compounds of South Africa as akin to slavery, and asked in very moderate tones for some autonomy and representation for native African peoples. The Pan-African Conference of 1900 was small, but it drew delegates from the Caribbean, West Africa, and North America, including the thirty-two-year-old Harvard Ph.D. and leading African American intellectual W. E. B. Dubois (1868–1963). The conference issued a proclamation "To the Nations of the World," with a famous introduction written by DuBois. "The Problem of the twentieth century is the problem of the color line. . . . In the metropolis of the modern world, in this the closing year of the nineteenth century," the proclamation read, "there has been assembled a congress of men and women of African blood, to deliberate solemnly the present situation and outlook of the darker races of mankind." The British government ignored the conference completely. Yet Pan-Africanism, like Indian nationalism, grew by sudden (and, for imperialists, disturbing) leaps after World War I.

COLONIAL CULTURE

In recent years historians have become increasingly interested in colonial cultures, or the results of the imperial encounter across the world. The variety of national experiences makes generalization very difficult, but we can underscore a few points. First, colonialism created new, hybrid cultures. Both European and indigenous institutions and practices, especially religion, were transformed by their contact with each other. Second, although Europeans often considered the areas they annexed "laboratories" for creating well-disciplined and orderly societies, the social changes Europeans brought in their wake confounded such plans. In both western and southern Africa, European demands for labor brought men out of their villages, leaving their families behind, and crowded them by the thousands into the shantytowns bordering sprawling new cities. Enterprising locals set up all manner of illegal businesses catering to transitory male workers, disconcerting European authorities in the process. Hopes that European rule would create a well-disciplined labor force and well-patrolled cities were quickly dashed.

Third, authorities on both side of the colonial encounter worried enormously about preserving national traditions and identity in the face of an inevitably hybrid and constantly changing colonial culture. Especially in China and India, debates about whether education should be "westernized" or continue on traditional lines set off fierce debates. Chinese elites, already divided over such customs as foot binding and concubinage (the legal practice of maintaining formal sexual partners for men outside their marriage), found their dilemmas heightened as imperialism became a more powerful force. Uncertain whether such practices should be repudiated or defended, they wrestled with great anguish over the ways in which their own culture had been changed by the corruption of colonialism. For their part, British, French, and Dutch colonial authorities fretted that too much familiarity between colonized and colonizer would weaken European traditions and undermine European power. In Phnom Penh, Cambodia (then part of French Indochina), where French citizens lived in neighborhoods separated from the rest of the city by a moat, colonial authorities nonetheless required "dressing appropriately and keeping a distance from the natives."

Not surprisingly, sexual relations provoked the most anxiety and also the most contradictory responses. "In this hot climate, passions run higher" wrote a French administrator in Algeria. "The French soldiers seek out Arab women due to their strangeness and newness." "It was common practice for unmarried Englishmen resident in China to keep a Chinese girl, and I did as others did," reported a British man stationed in Shanghai. European administrators fitfully tried to prohibit liaisons between European men and indigenous women, labeling such affairs as "corrupting" and "nearly always disastrous." They grew increasingly hostile to the children of such unions. But such prohibitions only drove relations underground, increasing the gap between the public façade of colonial rule and the private reality of colonial lives. In this and other spheres, colonial culture forced a series of compromises about "acceptability," and created changing, sometimes subtle, ethnic hierarchies.

CRISES OF EMPIRE AT THE TURN OF THE TWENTIETH CENTURY

Why was the Boer War unique?

The turn of the twentieth century brought a series of crises to the Western empires. Those crises created sharp tensions between Western nations. They also drove imperial nations to expand their economic and military commitments in territories overseas. They shook Western confidence. In all of these ways, they became central to Western culture in the years before World War I.

FASHODA

The first crisis, in the fall of 1898, pitted Britain against France at Fashoda, in the Egyptian Sudan. Britain's establishment of a "protectorate" in Egypt after the 1880s had encouraged British activity in the region. In the name of protecting the new, pro-British ruler, Britain intervened in an Islamic uprising in the Sudan up the Nile, south of Egypt. An Anglo-Egyptian force was sent to the Sudanese capital, Khartoum, led by the most flamboyant—and perhaps least sensible—of Britain's colonial generals, Charles "Chinese" Gordon, well known for his role in suppressing the Taiping Rebellion. The Sudanese rebels, led by a Mahdi (a religious leader who claimed to be the successor to the prophet Muhammad), besieged Gordon. British forces were ill prepared to move south on the Nile in strength; Gordon ended up dying a "hero's death" as the rebels stormed Khartoum. Avenging Gordon occupied officials in Egypt and the British popular imagination for more than a decade. In 1898, a second large-scale rebellion provided the opportunity. An Anglo-Egyptian army commanded by a methodi-

> Britain's establishment of a "protectorate" in Egypt after the 1880s had encouraged British activity in the region.

Boer Commandos under Louis Botha. Botha became the first prime minister of the Union of South Africa following the Boer War.

cal and ambitious engineer, General Horatio Kitchener, sailed south up the Nile and attacked Khartoum. Using modern rifles, artillery, and machine guns, they massacred the Mahdi's army at the town of Omdurman and retook Khartoum. Gordon's body was disinterred and reburied with pomp and circumstance as the British public celebrated a famous and easy victory.

That victory, however, brought complications. France, which held territories in central Africa next door to the Sudan, saw the British presence along the eastern side of Africa as a prelude to Britain's dominance of the whole continent. A French expedition was sent to the Sudanese town of Fashoda to challenge British claims to the southernmost part of the territory. The French faced off against troops from Kitchener's army. For a few weeks in September 1898 the situation teetered on the brink of war. The matter was resolved when Britain not only called France's bluff but also provided guarantees against further expansion by cementing borders for the new "Anglo-Egyptian Sudan," an even greater extension of the political control that had begun with the Suez Canal.

SOUTH AFRICA: THE BOER WAR

In southern Africa vaulting ambitions led to a difficult kind of conflict: Europeans fighting European settlers. Afrikaner settlers, also called Boers (an appropriation of the Dutch word for "farmer"), had arrived in South Africa with the Dutch East India Company in the early

1800s. Over the course of the nineteenth century the Afrikaners trekked inland from the Cape, setting up two independent republics away from the influence of Britain: the Transvaal and the Orange Free State. In the mid 1880s, gold reserves were discovered in the Transvaal. The British diamond magnate Cecil Rhodes had actually tried to provoke war between Britain and the Boers in hopes of adding the Afrikaners' prosperous diamond mines and pastureland to his own territory of "Rhodesia." In 1899, Britain did go to war with the Afrikaners. The British army was woefully unprepared for the war: supplies, communications, and medicine for the army in South Africa were a shambles. These initial problems were followed by several humiliating defeats as British columns were shot to pieces by Afrikaner forces who knew the terrain. British garrisons at the towns of Ladysmith and Mafeking were besieged. The British government refused any compromise. When British forces steamrolled the Boers, relieved the besieged British garrisons, and took the Afrikaner capital at Pretoria, there were celebrations in London.

The Afrikaners, however, were determined never to surrender. Supplied by other European nations, particularly Germany and the Netherlands, they took to the wilderness in "commandos" (small raiding parties) and fought a guerrilla war that lasted three years. Black Africans suffered the effects of famine and disease as the war destroyed valuable farmland. The British also instituted "concentration camps"—the first use of the term—where Afrikaner civilians were rounded up and forced to live in appalling conditions so that they would be unable to lend aid to the guerrillas. Nearly twenty thousand civilians died due to disease and poor sanitation over the course of two years. These measures provoked an international backlash. The concentration camps bred opposition in Britain itself where protesters, labeled "pro-Boers" by the conservative press, campaigned against these violations of white Europeans' rights while saying very little about the fate of native Africans in the conflict. In the end, the Afrikaners acquiesced. Afrikaner politicians signed their old republics over to a new, British "Union of South Africa" that gave them a share of political power.

U.S. IMPERIALISM

Another imperial power began to emerge in the 1890s: the United States. During the late nineteenth century, American governments and private interests that supported imperial expansion played a double game. The United States acted as the champion of the underdeveloped countries in the Western Hemisphere when they were threatened from Europe. Yet America was willing, whenever it suited, to prey on its neighbors either "informally" or formally. This ultimately brought conflict with another, fragile Western empire. Spain's feeble hold on its Caribbean and Pacific colonies was plagued by rebellion in the 1880s and 1890s. The American popular press talked up the cause of the rebels, and when an American battleship accidentally exploded in port at Havana, Cuba, American imperialists and the press clamored for a war of revenge. The administration of President William McKinley was extremely wary of going to war, but McKinley also understood political necessity. The United States stepped in to protect its investments, to guarantee the maritime security of trade routes in the Americas and the Pacific, and to demonstrate the power of the newly built-up American navy. It declared war on Spain in 1898 on trumped-up grounds and swiftly won. In Spain, the Spanish-American War provoked an entire generation of writers, politicians, and intellectuals to national soul searching.

In the same year that the United States won its "splendid little war" against Spain, it also annexed Puerto Rico, established a "protectorate" over Cuba, and fought a short but brutal war against Philippine rebels who liked American colonialism no better than the Spanish kind. In the Americas, the United States continued its interventions. When the Colombian province of Panama threatened to rebel in 1903, the

An English Concentration Camp during the Boer War.
In an attempt to block support to guerrilla fighters, the English restricted Afrikaner civilians to camps where appalling conditions led to the death of nearly 20,000 people over 2 years. This illustration appeared in *Le Petit Journal* in 1901.

Americans quickly backed the rebels, recognized Panama as a republic, and then proceeded to grant it protection while Americans built the Panama Canal on land leased from the new government. The Panama Canal (which opened officially in 1914), like Britain's canal at Suez, cemented American dominance of the seas in the Americas and the eastern Pacific. Interventions in Hawaii and later Santo Domingo were further proof that the United States was no less an imperial power than the nations of Europe.

CONCLUSION

In the last quarter of the nineteenth century, the long-standing relationship between European nations and the rest of the world entered a new stage. That stage was distinguished by the stunningly rapid extension of formal European control and by new patterns of discipline and settlement. It was driven by the rising economic needs of the industrial West, by territorial conflict, and by nationalism, which by the late nineteenth century linked nationhood to empire. Among its immediate results was the creation of a "self-consciously imperial" culture in the West. At the same time, however, it plainly created unease in Europe, and contributed powerfully to the sense of crisis that swept through the late-nineteenth-century West.

For all its force, this European expansion was never unchallenged. Imperialism provoked resistance and required constantly changing strategies of rule. During World War I, mobilizing the resources of empire would become crucial to victory. In the aftermath, reimposing the conditions of the late nineteenth century would become nearly impossible. And over the longer term, the political structures, economic developments, and patterns of race relations established in this period would be contested throughout the twentieth century.

KEY TERMS

New imperialism	Leopold II	Boer War
Indian Rebellion of 1857	Arthur de Gobineau	Spanish-American War
Opium Wars	Eugenics	
Boxer Rebellion	Pan-African Conference	

SELECTED READINGS

Adas, Michael. *Machines as the Measure of Man: Science, Technology, and Ideologies of Western Dominance.* Ithaca and London, 1989.

Bayly, C. A. *Indian Society and the Making of the British Empire.* Cambridge, 1988. A good introduction, and one that bridges eighteenth- and nineteenth-century imperialisms.

Burton, Antoinette. *Burdens of History: British Feminists, Indian Women, and Imperial Culture, 1865–1915.* Chapel Hill, 1994.

Cain, P. J. and A. G. Hopkins. *British Imperialism, 1688–2000.* London, 2002. A new edition of one of the most influential studies. Excellent overview and exceptionally good on economics.

Clancy Smith, Julia, and Frances Gouda. *Domesticating the Empire: Race, Gender, and Family life in French and Dutch Colonialism.* Charlottesville and London, 1998. A particularly good collection of essays that both breaks new historical ground and is accessible to nonspecialists. Essays cover daily life and private life in new colonial cultures.

Conklin, Alice. *A Mission to Civilize: The Republican idea of Empire in France and West Africa, 1895–1930.* Stanford, 1997.

Cooper, Frederick, and Ann Laura Stoler. *Tensions of Empire: Colonial Cultures in a Bourgeois World.* Berkeley, 1997. New approaches, combining anthropology and history, with an excellent bibliography.

Headrick, Daniel R. *The Tools of Empire: Technology and European Imperialism in the Nineteenth Century.* Oxford, 1981. A study of the relationship between technological innovation and imperialism.

Hobsbawm, Eric. *The Age of Empire, 1875–1914.* New York, 1987. Surveys the European scene at a time of apparent stability and real decline.

Hochschild, Adam. *King Leopold's Ghost.*

Lorcin, Patricia. *Imperial Identities: Stereotyping, Prejudice and Race in Colonial Algeria.* New York, 1999.

Louis, William Roger. *The Oxford History of the British Empire.* 5 vols. Oxford, 1998. Excellent and wide-ranging collection of the latest research.

Metcalf, Thomas. *Ideologies of the Raj.* Cambridge, 1995.

Pakenham, Thomas. *The Scramble for Africa, 1876–1912.* London, 1991. A well-written narrative of the European scramble for Africa in the late nineteenth century.

Prochaska, David. *Making Algeria French: Colonialism in Bône, 1870–1920.* Cambridge, 1990.

Robinson, Ronald, and J. Gallagher. *Africa and the Victorians: The Official Mind of Imperialism.* London, 1961.

Said, Edward. *Culture and Imperialism.* New York, 1993.

Sangari, Kumkum, and Sudesh Vaid. *Recasting Women: Essays in Colonial History.* New Delhi, 1989.

Schneer, Jonathan. *London 1900: The Imperial Metropolis.* New Haven, 1999. Excellent recent study of the empire—and opposition to empire—in the metropole.

Spence, Jonathan. *The Search for Modern China.* New York, 1990.

Chapter
Twenty-three

Modern Industry and Mass Politics, 1870–1914

"We are on the extreme promontory of ages!" decreed the Italian poet and literary editor F. T. Marinetti in 1909. In a bombastic manifesto—a self-described "inflammatory declaration" printed on the front page of a Paris newspaper—Marinetti introduced Europe to an aggressive art movement called futurism. Revolting against what he considered a tired and impotent Italian culture, Marinetti called for a radical renewal of civilization through "courage, audacity, and revolt." Enamored with the raw power of modern machinery, with the dynamic bustle of urban life, he trumpeted "a new form of beauty, the beauty of speed." Most notably, Marinetti celebrated the heroic violence of warfare and disparaged the moral and cultural traditions of nineteenth-century liberalism.

At the time Marinetti issued his manifesto, five years before the First World War, people across Europe indeed felt themselves to be living in a radically new world. In the years since 1870, a series of explosive developments had unfolded across Europe. A second industrial revolution spurred enormous growth in the scope and scale of industry. Mass consumption became a fact of life, as did mass politics. New blocs of voters brought new demands to the political arena, and national governments struggled to maintain order and legitimacy. Socialists mobilized growing numbers of industrial workers, while suffragists demanded the franchise for women. In the arts and sciences, new theories challenged age-old notions of nature, society, truth, and beauty. These changes, however, did not simply ride roughshod over nineteenth-century traditions. Few Europeans embraced the modern era with the unflinching abandon of the futurists. As we will see, the great dynamism and signifacnce of this period arose from the ambivalent, uneven way that groups, individuals, and governments responded to the challenge of a changing world.

FOCUS QUESTIONS

• What developments sparked the second industrial revolution?

• Why did working-class movements grow so dramatically during this period?

• What rights did women claim, and why were they so controversial?

 • How did nation-states respond to the rise of mass politics?

• What impact did new scientific theories have on culture?

NEW TECHNOLOGIES AND GLOBAL TRANSFORMATIONS

What developments sparked the second industrial revolution?

In the last third of the nineteenth century, new technologies transformed the face of manufacturing in Europe, leading to new levels of economic growth and complex realignments among industry, labor, and national governments. Like Europe's first industrial revolution, which began in the late eighteenth century centered on coal, steam, and iron, this "second" industrial revolution relied on innovations in three key areas: steel, electricity, and chemicals.

Harder, stronger, and more malleable than iron, steel had long been prized as a construction material. But until the mid-nineteenth century, producing steel cheaply and in large quantities was impossible. That changed between the 1850s and 1870s, as new processes for refining and mass-producing alloy steel revolutionized the metallurgical industry. Although iron did not disappear overnight, it was soon eclipsed by soaring steel production. Britain's shipbuilders made a quick and profitable switch to steel construction, and thus kept their lead in the industry. Germany and America, however, dominated the rest of the steel industry. By 1901 Germany was producing almost half again as much steel as Britain, allowing Germany to build a massive national and industrial infrastructure.

Like steel, electricity had been discovered earlier, and its advantages were similarly well known. Easily transmitted over long distances to be converted into heat, light, and other types of energy, electricity was finally made available for commercial and domestic use by another set of nineteenth-century innovations. By the 1880s, engineers and technicians had developed alternators and transformers capable of producing high-voltage alternating current. By century's end, large power stations, which often utilized cheap water power, could send electric current over vast distances. In 1879 Thomas Edison and his associates invented the incandescent-filament lamp and changed electricity into light. The demand for electricity skyrocketed, and soon entire metropolitan areas were electrified. As a leading sector in the new economy, electrification powered subways, tramways, and, eventually, long-distance railroads; it made possible new techniques in the chemical and metallurgical industries; and gradually, it dramatically altered living habits in ordinary households.

The chemical industry was a third sector of important new technologies. The efficient production of alkali and sulfuric acid transformed the manufacture of such consumer goods as paper, soaps, textiles, and fertilizer. Britain and particularly Germany became leaders in the field. The British led the way in the production of hand soap and household cleaners. Heightened concerns for household hygiene and new techniques in mass marketing enabled the British entrepreneur Harold Lever to market his soaps and cleansers around the world. German production, on the other hand, focused on industrial use, such as developing synthetic dyes and methods for refining petroleum, and came to control roughly 90 percent of the world's chemical market.

Other innovations contributed to the second industrial revolution. For instance, the growing demand for efficient power spurred the invention of the liquid-fuel internal combustion engine. By 1914 most navies had converted from coal to oil, as had domestic steamship companies. The new engines' dependence on crude petroleum and distilled gasoline at first threatened their general application, but the discovery of oil fields in Russia, Borneo, Persia, and Texas around 1900 allayed fears. Protecting these oil reserves thus became a vital state prerogative. The adoption of oil-powered machinery had another important consequence: industrialists who had previously depended on nearby rivers or coal mines for power were free to take their enterprises to regions bereft of natural resources. The potential for worldwide industrialization was in place.

Annual Output of Steel (in millions of metric tons)

Year	Britain	Germany	France	Russia
1875–1879	0.90	—	0.26	0.08
1880–1884	1.82	0.99	0.46	0.25
1885–1889	2.86	1.65	0.54	0.23
1890–1894	3.19	2.89	0.77	0.54
1895–1899	4.33	5.08	1.26	1.32
1900–1904	5.04	7.71	1.70	2.35
1905–1909	6.09	11.30	2.65	2.63
1910–1913	6.93	16.24	4.09	4.20

Source: Carlo Cipolla, *The Fontana Economic History of Europe*, vol. 3(2) (London: Collins/Fontana Books, 1976), p. 775.

A German electrical engineering works illustrates the scale of production during the second industrial revolution.

CHANGES IN SCOPE AND SCALE

Technologies were both causes and consequences of the Western race toward a bigger, faster, cheaper, and more efficient world. At the end of the nineteenth century, size mattered. The rise of heavy industry and mass marketing had factories and cities growing hand in hand, while advances in media and mobility advanced the creation of national mass cultures. For the first time, ordinary people followed the news on national and global levels. They watched as European powers divided the globe, enlarging their empires with prodigious feats of engineering mastery; railroads, dams, canals, and harbors grew to monumental proportions. Such projects generated enormous income for builders, investors, bankers, entrepreneurs, and, of course, makers of steel and concrete.

Yet industrialization also brought profound, if less spectacular, changes in Europe. The population grew constantly, particularly in central and eastern Europe. Thanks to improvements in both crop yields and shipping, food shortages declined, which rendered entire populations less susceptible to illness and high infant mortality. Advances in medicine, nutrition, and personal hygiene diminished the prevalence of dangerous diseases such as cholera and typhus, and improved conditions in housing and public sanitation transformed the urban environment.

Population Growth in Major States between 1871 and 1911 (population in millions)

	c. 1871	c. 1911	% increase
German Empire	41.1	64.9	57.8
France	36.1	39.6	9.7
Austria-Hungary*	35.8	49.5	38.3
Great Britain	31.8	45.4	42.8
Italy	26.8	34.7	29.5
Spain	16.0	19.2	20.0

*Not including Bosnia-Herzegovina.
Source: Colin Dyer, *Population and Society in Twentieth Century France* (New York: Holmes and Meier, 1978), p. 5.

Changes in scope and scale not only transformed production, they also altered consumption. Department stores that offering both practical and luxury goods to the middle class were one mark of the times—of urbanization, economic expansion, and the new importance attached to merchandising. Advertising took off as well. The lavishly illustrated posters of the late nineteenth century advertising concert halls, soaps, bicycles, and sewing machines were only one sign of underlying economic changes. Even more significant, by the 1880s new stores sought to attract working-class people by introducing the all-important innovation of credit payment. In earlier times, working-class families pawned watches, mattresses, or furniture to borrow money, now they began to buy on credit; a change that would eventually have seismic effects on both households and national economies. These new, late nineteenth-century patterns of consumption were largely urban. In the countryside peasants continued to save money under mattresses; pass down a few pieces of furniture for generations; make, launder, and mend their own clothes and linens; and offer a kilo of sugar as a generous household gift. Only slowly did retailers whittle away at these traditional habits. Mass consumption remained difficult to imagine in what was still a deeply stratified society.

THE RISE OF THE CORPORATION

Economic growth and the demands of mass consumption spurred reorganization, consolidation, and regulation of capitalist institutions. Although capitalist enterprises had been financed by individual investors through the joint-stock principle at least since the sixteenth century, it was during the late nineteenth century that the modern corporation came into its own. To mobilize the enormous funds needed for large-scale enterprises, entrepreneurs needed to offer better guarantees on investors' money. To provide such protection, most European countries enacted or improved their limited- liability laws, which ensured that stockholders could lose only the value of their shares in the event of bankruptcy. Insured in this way, many thousands of middle-class men and women now considered corporate investment a promising venture.

Equally important, the second industrial revolution created a strong demand for technical expertise, which undercut traditional forms of family management. University degrees in engineering and chemistry became more valuable than on-the-job apprenticeships. The emergence of a white-collar class, middle-level salaried managers who were neither owners nor laborers, marked a significant change in work life and for society's evolving class structure.

The drive toward larger business enterprises was spurred by a desire for increased profits. It was also encouraged by a belief that consolidation protected society against the hazards of boom-and-bust economic fluctuations and against the wasteful inefficiencies of unbridled, "ruinous" competition. Some industries combined vertically, attempting to control every step of production from the acquisition of raw materials to the distribution of finished products. A second form of corporate self-protection was horizontal alignment. Organizing into cartels, companies in the same industry would band together to fix prices and control competition, if not eliminate it outright. Coal, oil, and steel companies were especially suited to the organization of cartels, since only a few major players could front the huge expense of building, equipping, and running mines, refineries, and

Poster for *Motocycles Comiot,* 1899. The rise in consumer consumption created a new emphasis on advertising, leading to lavish portrayals of merchandise aimed at the middle class.

WHY DID WORKING-CLASS MOVEMENTS GROW SO DRAMATICALLY DURING THIS PERIOD?

LABOR POLITICS, MASS MOVEMENTS   645

foundries. Cartels were particularly strong in Germany and America but less so in Britain, where dedication to free-trade policies made price fixing difficult, and in France, where family firms and laborers both opposed cartels, and where there was also less heavy industry.

Though governments sometimes tried to stem the burgeoning power of cartels (in the United States, for instance, where the "trust-buster" president Theodore Roosevelt put teeth into earlier antitrust laws) the dominant trend of this period was increased cooperation between governments and industry. Contrary to the laissez-faire mentality of early capitalism, corporations developed close relationships with states in the West, most noticeably in colonial industrial projects, such as the construction of railroads, harbors, and seafaring steamships. Such interdependence was underscored by the appearance of businessmen and financiers as officers of state. The German banker Bernhard Dernburg was the German secretary of state for colonies. And in France, Charles Jonnart, president of the Suez Canal Company and the Saint-Étienne steel works, was later governor general of Algeria. Tied to imperial interests, the rise of modern corporations had an impact around the globe.

INTERNATIONAL ECONOMICS

From the 1870s on, the rapid spread of industrialization heightened competition among nations. The search for markets, goods, and influence often put countries at odds with each other. Trade barriers arose to protect home markets. All nations except Britain raised tariffs, arguing that the needs of the nation-state trumped laissez-faire doctrine. Despite protectionism, a worldwide system of manufacturing, trade, and finance continued to grow. For example, the near universal adoption of the gold standard in currency exchange greatly facilitated world trade. Pegging the value of currencies, the value of gold meant that currencies could be readily exchanged. The common standard also allowed nations to use a third country to mediate trade and exchange to mitigate trade imbalances—a common problem for the industrializing West. Almost all European countries, dependent on vast supplies of raw materials to sustain their rate of industrial production, imported more than they exported. To avoid the mounting deficits that would otherwise have resulted from this practice, they relied on "invisible" exports: shipping, insurance, and banking

services. The extent of Britain's exports in these areas was far greater than that of any other country and London was the money market of the world. Britain also used its invisible trade to secure relationships with food-producing nations, becoming the major overseas buyer for the wheat of the United States and Canada, the beef of Argentina, and the mutton of Australia. These goods, shipped cheaply aboard refrigerated vessels, kept down food prices for working-class families and eased the demand for increased wages.

Coal, oil, and steel companies were especially suited to the organization of cartels, since only a few major players could front the huge expense of building, equipping, and running mines, refineries, and foundries.

LABOR POLITICS, MASS MOVEMENTS

Why did working-class movements grow so dramatically during this period?

The rapid capitalist expansion of the late nineteenth century brought a parallel growth in the size, cohesion, and activism of Europe's working classes. Corporations had devised new methods of protecting and promoting their interests, and workers did the same. Labor unions, which were traditionally limited to skilled male workers in small-scale enterprises, evolved during the late nineteenth century into mass, centralized, nationwide organizations. This "new unionism" stressed organization across entire industries, and for the first time, brought unskilled workers into the ranks. The new unions' broad scope gave labor increased power to negotiate wages and job conditions. More important, though, the creation of national unions provided a framework for a new type of political movement: the socialist mass party.

This shift to popular mass politics, and the accompanying success of labor movements, owed as much to an upsurge in activism by intellectuals as it did to the efforts of workers and unions. Chief among these intellectuals was Karl Marx, whose early career was discussed in Chapter 20. Since the 1840s Marx and his collaborator Fredrick Engels had been intellectuals and activists, writing pamphlets and participating in the organization of fledgling socialist movements. Then, in 1867, Marx published the first of three volumes of *Capital*, a work he believed was his greatest contribution to the struggle for human emancipation. It provided historical materialism with a theoretical foundation, and it also attacked capitalism on the battlefield of economics. In the spirit of nineteenth-century science, Marx claimed to offer a systematic analysis of how capitalism forced workers to exchange their labor for subsistence wages while enabling owners of the means of production to amass both wealth and power. Splicing together the scholarly study of economics with calls for revolutionary politics, the book became the preeminent socialist critique of capitalism.

Throughout Europe, though particularly in the western nations, Marxist socialism provided a crucial foundation for building a democratic mass politics. Few other groups pushed so strongly to secure civil liberties, expand conceptions of citizenship, or build a welfare state. As a theoretical matter, Marxism also made powerful claims for gender equality, though in practice woman suffrage took a backseat to class politics. Marxist utopianism was a crucial element, too, for its powerful promise of a better and attainable future for laborers rallied large numbers of workers to the cause.

> Throughout Europe, though particularly in the western nations, Marxist socialism provided a crucial foundation for building a democratic mass politics.

Not all working-class movements, however, were Marxist. Differences between the philosophies, objectives, and methods of varying left-wing groups remained strong. The most divisive issues were the role of violence and whether socialists should cooperate with liberal, or "bourgeois" governments—and if so, to what end. Some "gradualists," particularly in Britain, were willing to work with liberals for piecemeal reform, while more radical socialists sought parliamentary power as a way to hasten the overthrow of capitalism. Anarchists and syndicalists rejected parliamentary politics altogether.

THE SPREAD OF SOCIALIST PARTIES— AND ALTERNATIVES

From the 1870s on organized labor politics developed rapidly. Marxism spread through a number of socialist and social democratic parties founded between 1875 and 1905. These parties were disciplined, politicized workers' organizations aimed at seizing control of the state for revolutionary change: the model among them was the SPD, the German Social Democratic party. Formed in 1875, the SPD first aimed for political change within Germany's parliamentary political system. Later, it adopted an explicitly Marxist platform—preparing a politically conscious working class for the imminent collapse of capitalism. By the outbreak of the First World War, the Social Democrats were the largest, best organized workers' party in the world. Several key factors made Germany particularly receptive to social democracy: rapid and extensive industrialization, a large urban working class, a national government hostile to organized labor, and no tradition of liberal reform.

The importance of this last factor is most evident when we consider the case of Britain, which was the world's first—and most—industrialized country, yet had a much smaller and more moderate socialist presence than other European nations. Through the end of the nineteenth century, much of the progressive socialist agenda was advanced by radical Liberals in Britain, which forestalled the growth of an independent socialist party. Even when a separate Labour party was formed in 1901, it remained distinctively moderate, committed to incremental reform of the capitalist system rather than its overthrow. For the range of political activists who belonged to the Labour party, and for Britain's many trade unions as well, Parliament remained a legitimate vehicle for effecting social change, limiting the appeal of revolutionary Marxism.

If parliamentary reform provided one popular alternative to the Marxist program, the doctrine of anarchism provided another. Opposed to centrally organized economies and politics, and to the very existence of state authority, anarchists advocated individual sovereignty and small-scale, localized democracy. Renouncing parties, unions, or any form of modern mass organization, anarchists fell back on the tradition of conspiratorial vanguard violence, which Marx had so forcefully opposed. Consequently, one of anarchism's defining characteristics was its reliance on terrorism, or what the Italian anarchists called "propaganda by the deed." Though not all adopted such methods, anarchists infamously assassinated Tsar Alexander II in 1881, and five other heads of state in the following years. Revealing the vulnerability of powerful political leaders, they thought, would create chaos and embolden the people. Though anarchism (perhaps inherently) made no sub-

WHAT RIGHTS DID WOMEN CLAIM, AND WHY WERE THEY SO CONTROVERSIAL?

DEMANDING EQUALITY: SUFFRAGE AND THE WOMEN'S MOVEMENT   647

Socialist Party Pamphlet, c. 1895. Socialism emerged as a powerful political force throughout Europe in the late nineteenth century although in different forms depending on the region. This German pamphlet quotes from the Communist Manifesto of 1848, calling for workers of the world to unite.

stantial gains as a movement, it kept alive a radical, violent alternative to Marxism's emphasis on parliamentary politics.

Another type of socialist movement, known as syndicalism, gained popularity around the turn of the century, particularly among agricultural laborers in France, Italy, and Spain. Following socialist principles, syndicalism demanded that workers share ownership and control of the means of production, and that the capitalist state be overthrown and replaced by workers' syndicates, or trade associations. Although often elided with anarchism (as in the term *anarcho-syndicalism*), syndicalism was a distinct doctrine that did not call for terror, but rather for mass forms of direct action, including strikes and sabotage.

THE LIMITS OF SUCCESS

By the turn of the century, popular socialist movements had made impressive gains all across Europe: in 1895, seven socialist parties captured between a quarter and a third of the votes in their countries. But just as socialists gained a permanent foothold in national politics, they were also straining under limitations and internal conflicts that had hindered their parties from the outset. Working-class movements, in fact, had never gained anywhere near full worker support. Although some workers remained loyal to older parties, many others were excluded from socialist politics by its narrow definition of who constituted the working class—that is, only male industrial workers. In terms of elections at least, socialist parties were running up against a wall that they themselves had constructed.

Conflicts over strategy peaked just before the First World War, as moderates, reformists, and orthodox Marxists debated about how to respond to the threat of international conflict. Yet these divisions did not diminish the strength and appeal of turn-of-the-century socialism. Indeed, on the eve of the war, governments discreetly consulted with labor leaders about rank-and-file workers' willingness to enlist and fight. Having built impressive organizational and political strength since the 1870s, working-class parties now affected the ability of nation-states to wage war. In short, they had come of age.

DEMANDING EQUALITY: SUFFRAGE AND THE WOMEN'S MOVEMENT

What rights did women claim, and why were they so controversial?

Since the 1860s, the combination of working-class activism and liberal constitutionalism had expanded male suffrage rights across Europe: by 1884, Germany, France, and Britain had enfranchised most men. But nowhere did women have the right to vote. Nineteenth-century political ideology relegated women to the status of second-class citizens, and even egalitarian-minded socialists seldom challenged this entrenched hierarchy. Excluded

Anarchism and Syndicalism. Anarchists with their reliance on violence stood at the radical end of the socialist spectrum. Anarchists committed several high-profile political assassinations such as the assassination of French president Marie Francois Carnot in 1894 (left). Syndicalists also on the radical side of the socialist spectrum favored massive movements of direct action, such as the general strike depicted in this poster (right).

from the workings of parliamentary and mass party politics, women pressed their interests through independent organizations and through forms of direct action. The new women's movement won some crucial legal reforms during this period, and after the turn of the century, its militant campaign for suffrage fed the growing sense of political crisis, most notably in Britain.

Women's organizations pressed first for educational and legal reforms: the establishment of women's colleges and women's right to control their own property. (Previously women surrendered their property, including wages, to their husbands.) Divorce became legal. After these important changes in women's status, suffrage crystallized as the next logical goal. Indeed, votes became *the* symbol for women's ability to attain full personhood. As the suffragists saw it, enfranchisement meant not merely political progress but economic, spiritual, and moral advancement as well.

By the last third of the century, middle-class women throughout western Europe had founded clubs, pub-

> The new women's movement won some crucial legal reforms during this period, and after the turn of the century, its militant campaign for suffrage fed the growing sense of political crisis, most notably in Britain.

lished journals, organized petitions, sponsored assemblies, and initiated other public activities to press for the vote. To the left of middle-class movements were flanked by organizations of feminist socialists, women such as Clara Zetkin and Lily Braun who believed that only a socialist revolution would free women from economic as well as political exploitation.

In Britain, woman suffrage campaigns exploded in violence. Moderate suffragists became increasingly exasperated by their inability to win over either the Liberal or Conservative party, each of which feared that female suffrage would benefit the other. For this reason Emmeline Pankhurst founded the Women's Social and Political Union in 1903, which adopted tactics of militancy and civil disobedience. The government countered violence with repression. When arrested women went on hunger strikes in prisons, wardens fed them by force—tying them down, holding their mouths open with wooden and metal clamps, and running tubes down their throats. In 1910 the suffrag-

WHAT RIGHTS DID WOMEN CLAIM, AND WHY WERE THEY SO CONTROVERSIAL?

DEMANDING EQUALITY: SUFFRAGE AND THE WOMEN'S MOVEMENT   649

ists' attempt to enter the House of Commons set off a six-hour riot with policemen and bystanders, shocking and outraging a nation unaccustomed to such kinds of violence from women. The intensity of suffragists' moral claims was dramatically embodied by the 1913 martyrdom of Emily Wilding Davison who, wearing a "Votes for Women" sash, threw herself in front of the king's horse on Derby Day and was trampled to death.

REDEFINING WOMANHOOD

The campaign for woman suffrage was the most controversial aspect of a larger cultural shift, in which traditional Victorian gender roles were redefined. In the last third of the nineteenth century, economic, political, and social changes were undermining the view that men and women should occupy distinctly different spheres. Women became increasingly visible in the work force as growing numbers of them took up a greater variety of jobs. Some working-class women joined the new factories and workshops in an effort to stave off their families' poverty, the expansion of government and corporate bureaucracies, coupled with a scarcity of male labor in the face of industrial growth, brought middle-class women to the work force as social workers and clerks. The increase in hospital services and the advent of national compulsory education required more nurses and teachers. Thus women, who had campaigned vigorously for access to education, began to see doors opening to them. In Prussia, for instance, 14,600 full-time women teachers were staffing schools by 1896. These changes in women's employment began to deflate the myth of female domesticity.

In addition, some women began to work in the political arena—an area previously termed off limits. First with charity work in religious associations and later with hundreds of secular associations, women directed their energies toward poor relief, prison reform, Sunday school, temperance, ending slavery and prostitution, and expanding educational opportunities for women. And while some women in reform groups supported political emancipation, many others were drawn into reform politics by appeals to the belief that women had a special moral mission. Nineteenth-century reform movements had opened up the world beyond the home, particularly

for the middle classes, and widened the scope of possibilities for later generations.

These changes in women's roles were paralleled by the emergence of a new social type, dubbed the "new woman." A "new" woman demanded education and a job; she refused to be escorted by chaperones when she went out; she rejected the restrictive corsets of mid-century fashion. In other words, she claimed the right to a physically and intellectually active life and refused to conform to the norms that defined nineteenth-century womanhood. The new woman was an image—in part the creation of artists and journalists, who filled newspapers, magazines, and advertising billboards with pictures of women riding bicycles in bloomers (voluminous trousers with a short skirt); smoking cigarettes; and enjoying the cafés, dance halls, tonic waters, soaps, and other emblems of consumption. Very few women actually fitted this image: among other things, most were too poor. Still, middle- and working-class women demanded more social freedom and redefined gender norms in the process.

Opposition to these changes was intense, sometimes violent, and not exclusively male. Conservatives such as Mrs. Humphrey Ward maintained that bringing women into the political arena would sap the virility of the English empire. Christian commentators criticized suffragists for bringing moral decay through selfish individualism. Still others believed feminism would dissolve the family, a theme that fed into a larger discussion on the decline of the West amid a growing sense of cultural crisis. Indeed, the struggle for women's rights provided a flashpoint for an array

Militant Martyrdom for Woman Suffrage. Emily Davison throwing herself under the king's horse at the Derby in 1913.

Organized anti-feminism. Male students demonstrate against opening some universities to women.

of European anxieties over labor, politics, gender, and biology—all of which suggested that an orderly political consensus, so ardently desired by middle-class society, seemed increasingly elusive.

LIBERALISM AND ITS DISCONTENTS: NATIONAL POLITICS AT THE TURN OF THE CENTURY

How did nation-states respond to the rise of mass politics?

Before 1870 political power had rested on a balance between middle-class interests and traditional elites. The landed aristocracy shared power with industrial magnates; monarchical rule coexisted with constitutional freedoms. But during the late nineteenth century, the rise of mass politics upset this balance. An expanding franchise and rising expectations brought newcomers to the political stage. Governments responded in turn, with a jarring mix of conciliatory and repressive measures. As the twentieth century approached, political struggles became increasingly fierce. For both the left and the right, for both insiders and outsiders, negotiating this unfamiliar terrain required the creation of new and distinctly modern forms of mass politics.

FRANCE: THE EMBATTLED REPUBLIC

The Franco-Prussian War of 1870, which completed the unification of the victorious Germany, was a bruising defeat for France. The government of the Second Empire folded. The new Third Republic signaled a triumph of democratic and parliamentary principles. Establishing democracy, however, was a volatile process, and the Third Republic faced class conflicts, scandals and the rise of new forms of right-wing politics that would poison politics for decades to come.

No sooner had France surrendered to Prussia than it faced a crisis that pitted the nation's representatives against the radical city of Paris. During the war, the city had appointed its own municipal government, the Commune. Paris not only refused to surrender to the Germans, it proclaimed itself the true government of France. The city had been besieged by the Germans for four months; most people who could afford to flee had done so and the rest, hungry and radicalized, defied the French government sitting in Versailles and negotiating the terms of an armistice with the Germans. The armistice signed, the French government turned its attention to the city. After long and fruitless negotiations, in March 1871 the government sent troops to disarm the capital. Since the Commune's strongest support came from the workers of Paris, the conflict became a class war. For a week, the "communards" battled against the government's troops. The French government's repression was brutal. At least twenty-five thousand Parisians were executed, killed in fighting, or consumed in the fires that raged through the city; thousands more were deported to the penal colony of New Caledonia in the South Pacific. The Paris Commune was a brief episode, but it cast a long shadow and reopened old political wounds. For Marx, who wrote about the Commune, and for other socialists, it illustrated the futility of an older insurrectionary tradition on the left and the need for more mass-based democratic politics.

THE DREYFUS AFFAIR AND ANTI-SEMITISM AS POLITICS

On the other side of the French political spectrum, new forms of radical right-wing politics emerged that would foreshadow developments elsewhere. Stung by the defeat of 1870 and critical of the republic, the new right was nationalist, antiparliamentary, and antiliberal. During the first half of the nineteenth century, nationalism had been associated with the left (see Chapter 20). Now it was more often invoked by the right, and linked to xenophobia (fear of foreigners) in general and anti-Semitism in particular.

Édouard Drumont's career provides a case in point. Drumont was an extraordinarily successful anti-Semitic journalist, who attributed all of late-nineteenth-century France's problems to the baneful influence of an international Jewish conspiracy and labeled all of the right wing's enemies "Jewish." "Jews in the army" subverted the national interest, financial scandals came from "international conspiracies"; mass culture, the women's movement, dance halls, and all the developments that were supposedly corrupting French culture simply demonstrated the strength of "cosmopolitan and international Jewish interests." Drumont pounded at these themes in his newspaper, *La Libre Parole* ("Free Speech") founded in 1892, through his Anti-Semitic League, and in his massive, five-hundred-page best-seller, *Jewish France* (1886), which sold one hundred thousand copies in the first two months.

This politicized anti-Semitism exploded with the Dreyfus Affair, a pivotal political moment in the life of the French Republic. In 1894 a group of monarchist officers in the French army accused Alfred Dreyfus, a Jewish captain on the French general staff, of selling military secrets to Germany. Tried by court-martial, Dreyfus was convicted, stripped of his rank, and deported for life to Devil's Island, a ghastly prison in the Atlantic Ocean. In 1896 Colonel Georges Picquart, a new head of the Intelligence Division, questioned the verdict and, after an initial probe, announced that the trial documents were forgeries.

When the War Department denied Dreyfus a new trial, the "case" became an "affair," polarizing the country. Republicans, socialists, liberals, and such figures as the writer Émile Zola backed Dreyfus. As the Drey-

> Despite Jewish emancipation, or the granting of civil rights, Herzl came to believe Jewish people might never be assimilated into Western culture, and that staking the Jewish community's hopes on acceptance and tolerance was dangerous folly.

fusards, as they were called, saw it, they stood for progress and justice against reaction and prejudice, and the survival of the republic lay in the balance. Zola, for instance, blasted the French establishment in a provocative newspaper essay "J'accuse!" that accused the government, the courts, and the military of falsifying documents, covering up treason, and blatantly ignoring basic issues of justice. On the other side, the anti-Dreyfusards included other socialists who considered the affair a distraction from more important economic issues monarchists, militarists, and some clergy. One Catholic newspaper insisted that the question was not whether Dreyfus was guilty or innocent but whether Jews and unbelievers were not the "secret masters of France."

After six years of bitter controversy, an executive order in 1899 set Dreyfus free. In 1906, the Supreme Court cleared him of all guilt. Among the Affair's many consequences was the separation of church and state in France. Republicans were convinced that the church and the army were hostile to the republic. Laws passed between 1901 and 1905 prohibited religious orders in France not authorized by the state, forbade clerics to teach in schools, and, finally, dissolved the union of the Catholic church and state.

ZIONISM

Among the many people to watch with alarm as the Dreyfus Affair unfolded was Theodor Herzl (1860–1904), a Hungarian-born journalist working in Paris. The rise of virulent anti-Semitism in the land of the French Revolution troubled Herzl deeply. He considered the Dreyfus Affair "only the dramatic expression of a much more fundamental malaise." Despite Jewish emancipation, or the granting of civil rights, Herzl came to believe Jewish people might never be assimilated into Western culture, and that staking the Jewish community's hopes on acceptance and tolerance was dangerous folly. Herzl endorsed a different strategy of Zionism, or building a separate Jewish homeland outside of Europe (though not necessarily in Palestine). A small movement of Jewish settlers, mainly refugees from Russia, had already begun to establish settlements outside of Europe. Herzl was not the first to

ANTI-SEMITISM IN LATE-NINETEENTH-CENTURY FRANCE

Over the course of the nineteenth century, European (though not Russian) Jewish people slowly gained more legal and political rights: access to occupations from which they had been barred, the right to vote and hold political office, the right to marry non-Jews, and so on. France, the land of the revolution of 1789, appeared to many European Jews the beacon of liberty. But in the late nineteenth century, France also proved the birthplace of new forms of anti-Semitism. This excerpt from Édouard Drumont's best-selling Jewish France *(1885) illustrates some themes of that ideology: the effort to displace economic grievances, conservative hatred of the republic, parliamentary government, and the legacy of 1789, and conservative nationalism.*

The only one who has benefitted from the Revolution [of 1789] is the Jew. Everything comes from the Jew; everything returns to the Jew.

We have here a veritable conquest, an entire nation returned to serfdom by a minute but cohesive minority, just as the Saxons were forced into serfdom by William the Conqueror's 60,000 Normans.

The methods are different, the result is the same. One can recognize all the characteristics of a conquest: an entire population working for another population, which appropriates, through a vast system of financial exploitation, all of the profits of the other. Immense Jewish fortunes, castles, Jewish townhouses, are not the fruit of any actual labor, of any production: they are the booty taken from an enslaved race by a dominant race.

It is certain, for example, that the Rothchild family, whose French branch alone possesses a declared fortune of three billion [francs], did not have that money when it arrived in France; it has invented nothing, it has discovered no mine, it has tilled no ground. It has therefore appropriated these three billion francs from the French without giving them anything in exchange. . . .

Thanks to the Jews' cunning exploitation of the principles of '89, France was collapsing into dissolution. Jews had monopolized all of the public wealth, had invaded everything, except the army. The representatives of the old [French] families, whether noble or bourgeois . . . gave themselves up to pleasure, and were corrupted by the Jewish prostitutes they had taken as mistresses or were ruined by the horse-sellers and money-lenders, also Jews, who aided the prostitutes. . . .

The fatherland, in the sense that we attach to that word, has no meaning for the Semite. The Jew . . . is characterized by an *inexorable universalism.*

I can see no reason for reproaching the Jews for thinking this way. What does the word "Fatherland" mean? Land of the fathers. One's feelings for the Fatherland are engraved in one's heart in the same way that a name carved in a tree is driven deeper into the bark with each passing year, so that the tree and the name eventually become one. You can't become a patriot through improvization; you are a patriot in your blood, in your marrow.

Can the Semite, a perpetual nomad, ever experience such enduring impressions? . . .

Édouard Drumont, *La France juive. Essai d'histoire contemporaine* (Paris: C. Marpon and E. Flammarion, 1885), excerpt translated by Cat Nilan, 1997.

voice these goals, but he was the most effective advocate of political Zionism. He argued that Zionism should be recognized as a modern nationalist movement, capable of negotiating with other states. In 1896 Herzl published *The State of the Jews* (1896); a year later he convened the first Zionist Congress in Switzerland. Throughout he was involved in high politics, meeting with British and Ottoman heads of state. Herzl's vision of a Jewish homeland had strong utopian elements, for he believed that building a new state had to be based on a new and transformed society, eliminating inequality and establishing rights. Although Herzl's writings met with much skepticism, they received an enthusiastic reception in areas of Eastern Europe where anti-Semitism was especially violent. During the turmoil of World War I, specific wartime needs prompted the British to become involved in the issue, embroiling Zionism in international diplomacy (see Chapter 24).

GERMANY'S SEARCH FOR IMPERIAL UNITY

Through deft foreign policy, three short wars, and a groundswell of national sentiment, Otto von Bismarck united Germany under the banner of Prussian conservatism during the years 1864 to 1871. In constructing a federal political system, Bismarck sought to create the centralizing institutions of a modern nation-state while safeguarding the privileges of Germany's traditional elites, including a dominant role for Prussia. Bismarck's constitution assigned administrative, educational, and juridical roles to local state governments and established a bicameral parliament to oversee Germany's national interests. In the executive branch, power rested solely with Wilhelm I, the Prussian king and German kaiser (emperor), who wielded full control of foreign and military affairs. Unlike in France or Britain, Germany's cabinet ministers had no responsibility to the parliament but answered only to kaiser.

Under a government that was neither genuinely federal nor democratic, building a nation with a sense of common purpose was no easy task. The German government successfully created imperial agencies for banking, coinage, federal courts, and railroads, all of which fostered administrative and economic union. But the question of political unity remained. Three

fault lines in Germany's political landscape especially threatened to crack the national framework: the divide between Catholics and Protestants; a growing Social Democratic party; and the potentially divisive economic interests of agriculture and industry.

Between 1866 and 1876, Bismarck governed principally with liberal factions interested in promoting free trade and economic growth. To strengthen ties with these liberal coalitions, Bismarck unleashed an anti-Catholic campaign in Prussia. The campaign backfired, however, and public sympathy for the persecuted clergy helped the Catholic Center party to win fully one quarter of the seats in the Reichstag in 1874. Recognizing that he needed Catholic support for new economic legislation, Bismarck negotiated an alliance of convenience with the Catholic Center party in 1878.

An economic downturn had undercut support for free trade policies in the late 1870s, prompting Bismarck to fashion a new coalition that included agricultural and industrial interests, as well as socially conservative Catholics. This new alliance passed protectionist legislation (grain tariffs, duties on iron and steel) that riled both laissez-faire liberals and the German working class, which was represented by the Social Democratic party. In 1878, after two separate attempts on the life of the emperor, Bismarck declared a national crisis to push through a series of antisocialist laws that forbade Social Democrats to assemble or distribute their literature. In effect, these laws obliged the Social Democratic party (known as the SPD) to become a clandestine organization, fostering a subculture of workers who increasingly viewed socialism as the sole answer to their political needs.

Having made the stick to beat down organized-labor politics, Bismarck now offered a carrot to German workers with an array of social reforms. Workers were guaranteed sickness and accident insurance, rigorous factory inspection, limited working hours for women and children, a maximum workday for men, public employment agencies, and old-age pensions. However the laws failed to achieve Bismarck's short-term political goal of winning workers' loyalty. In spite of all legal hindrances, votes for the Social Democratic party more than quadrupled between 1881 and 1890, the year that Bismarck resigned.

The embittered atmosphere created by Bismarck's domestic politics prompted the new kaiser, Wilhelm II, to move in a new direction; he dramatically suspended

> Having made the stick to beat down organized-labor politics, Bismarck now offered a carrot to German workers with an array of social reforms.

the antisocialist legislation in 1890, legalizing the SPD. By 1912, the Social Democrats polled a third of the votes cast and elected the largest single bloc to the Reichstag; yet the kaiser refused to allow any meaningful political participation beyond a tight-knit circle of elites. Meanwhile, commercial, industrial, and agriculture interests deadlocked over tariffs. German politics were fast approaching a stalemate, but any conclusion to this volatile standoff was preempted by the outbreak of World War I.

BRITAIN: FROM MODERATION TO MILITANCE

During the half century before 1914, the British prided themselves on what they believed to be an orderly and workable system of government. Following the passage of the Second Reform Bill in 1867, which extended suffrage to more than a third of the nation's adult males.

Two central figures, the Conservative Benjamin Disraeli and the Liberal William Gladstone, dominated the new parliamentary politics. Disraeli, a converted Jew and best-selling novelist, was eminently pragmatic, while Gladstone, a devout Anglican and moral reformer, viewed politics as "morality writ large." Despite their opposing sensibilities and bitter parliamentary clashes, the two men led parties that, in retrospect, seem to share largely similar outlooks. Managed by cabinet ministers drawn from the upper middle class and the landed gentry, both Liberals and Conservatives offered moderate programs that appealed to the widening electorate. Cabinet ministers prepared legislation but acknowledged the ultimate authority of the House of Commons, which could remove a governing cabinet with a vote of no

confidence. Steered by men whose similar education and outlooks promised middling solutions, the British political system was stable and "reasonable."

After 1900, however, Britain's liberal parliamentary framework—which had so successfully channeled the rising demands of mass society since the 1860s—began to buckle, as an array of groups rejected legislative activity in favor of radical action. Industrial militants launched enormous labor protests. Woman suffragists adopted violent forms of direct action Irish nationalists began to favor armed revolution as the solution to the parliamentary wrangling over of Irish home rule, or self-government.

Ireland had been put under the direct government of the British Parliament in 1800, and various political and military efforts to regain Irish sovereignty over the course of the nineteenth century had failed. By the 1880s, a modern nationalist party (the Irish Parliamentary party) had begun to make substantial political gains through the legislative process, but as with other reform-minded groups (such as women's suffrage), its agenda was increasingly eclipsed toward the turn of the century by more radical organizers. These proponents of "new nationalism" disdained the party's representatives as ineffectual and out of touch. New groups revived interest in Irish history and culture and provided organizational support to the radical movement, as did such militant political organizations as Sinn Féin and the Irish Republican Brotherhood. In 1913, as a Liberal plan to grant home rule was once again on the table (prompting panic in Ulster, the Protestant-majority counties of northern Ireland, which feared Catholic rule) Irish nationalists called a number of paramilitary groups into action. Already awash in domestic crises, Britain now seemed on the verge of a civil war—a prospect delayed only by the outbreak of the World War in Europe.

RUSSIA: THE ROAD TO REVOLUTION

The industrial and social changes that swept Europe proved especially unsettling in Russia. An autocratic political system was ill equipped to handle conflict and the pressures of modern society. Western industrialization challenged Russia's military might. Western political doctrines—liberalism, democracy, socialism—threatened its internal political stability. Like other nations, tsarist Russia negotiated these challenges with a combination of repression and reform.

In the 1880s and 1890s Russia launched a program of industrialization that made it the world's fifth largest

CHRONOLOGY

GERMANY'S QUEST FOR POLITICAL UNITY, 1871–1890

Bismarck's Kulturkampf	1871–1878
Conciliation with the Vatican	1878
Bismarck's antisocialist legislation	1878–1884
Bismarck launches social legislation	1883–1890
Bismarck resigns	1890

JEWISH MIGRATION IN THE LATE NINETEENTH CENTURY

What drove Jewish people to flee from eastern Europe in the late nineteenth century? Why did certain cities have larger Jewish populations than others? Why did many Jewish people migrate to the United States or to Palestine?

economy by the early twentieth century. The state largely directed this industrial development. In fact, the Russian state financed more domestic industrial development than any other major European government during the nineteenth century.

Real legal reform, however, would threaten the regime's stability. Alexander II (1855–1881), the "Tsar Liberator" (emancipator of the serfs), had grown wary of change. In 1864, his regime had set up a system of provincial and county assemblies, or zemstvos, elected

CHRONOLOGY

THE RUSSIAN ROAD TO REVOLUTION, 1861–1905

Emancipation of the serfs	1861
State-directed industrialization begins	1880s–1890s
Alexander II assassinated	1881
Alexander III launches counterreforms	1881–1894
Nicholas II continues "Russification" policies	1894–1905
Russo-Japanese War	1904–1905
The first Russian revolution: "Bloody Sunday" and October Manifesto	1905

by all social classes (though dominated by the nobility); now it curtailed their rights and ability to discuss politics. When the tsar was assassinated in 1881, his successor, Alexander III (1881–1894), steered the country sharply to the right. Russia had nothing in common with western Europe, Alexander III claimed; his people had been nurtured on mystical piety for centuries and would be utterly lost without a strong autocratic system. The regime further reined in the zemstvos, increased the authority of the secret police, and subjected villages to the governmental authority of nobles appointed by the state.

Nicholas II (1894–1917) continued in the same direction. Like his father, he ardently advocated Russification, or government programs to extend the language, religion, and culture of Greater Russia over the empire's non-Russian subjects. Russification amounted to coercion, expropriation, and physical oppression: Finns lost their constitution, Poles studied their own literature in Russian translation, and Jewish communities were attacked. Other groups whose repression by the state led to long-lasting undercurrents of anti-Russian nationalism included the Georgians, Armenians, and Azerbaijanis of the Caucasus Mountains.

The most important radical political group in late-nineteenth-century Russia who called themselves populists. Populists believed that Russia needed to modernize on its own terms, not the West's. They envisioned an egalitarian Russia based on the ancient institution of the village commune (mir). They formed secret bands, plotting the overthrow of tsarism through anarchy and insur-

rection. Populism's historical importance lies not so much in what it accomplished, which was little, but in what it promised for the future. It acted as a seedbed of organized agitation in Russia, which would in time produce general revolution.

The emergence of industrial capitalism and a new, desperately poor working class created Russian Marxism. Organized as the Social Democratic party, Russian Marxists concentrated their efforts on behalf of urban workers and saw themselves as part of the international working-class movement. They made little headway in a peasant-dominated Russia before the First World War, but they provided disaffected urban factory workers and intellectuals alike with a powerful ideology that stressed the necessity of overthrowing the tsarist regime and the inevitability of a better future.

In 1903 the leadership of the Social Democratic party split over an important disagreement on revolutionary strategy. One group, temporarily in the majority and quick to name itself the Bolsheviks ("majority group"), believed that the Russian situation called for a strongly centralized party of active revolutionaries. The Bolsheviks also insisted that the rapid industrialization of Russia meant that they did not have to follow Marx's model for the West. Instead of working for liberal capitalist reforms, Russian revolutionaries could skip a stage, and immediately begin to build a socialist state. The Mensheviks ("minority group") were more cautious or "gradualist," seeking slow changes and reluctant to depart from Marxist orthodoxy. When the Mensheviks regained control of the Social Democratic party, the Bolsheviks formed a splinter party under the leadership of the young, dedicated revolutionary Vladimir Ilyich Ulanov, who lived in political exile in western Europe between 1900 and 1917. He wrote under the pseudonym of Lenin from the Lena river in Siberia where he was exiled.

From exile Lenin preached unrelenting class struggle, the need for a coordinated revolutionary socialist movement throughout Europe, and, most important, the belief that Russia was passing into an economic stage that made it ripe for revolution. It was the Bolsheviks' responsibility to organize a revolutionary party on behalf of workers, for without the party's discipline, workers could not effect change. Lenin considered revolution the only answer to Russia's problems, and he argued that organizing for revolution needed to be done, soon, by "vanguard" agents of the party acting in the name of the working class.

Execution of the conspirators against Alexander II. Known as the liberator of the serfs, Tsar Alexander II grew increasingly restrictive and unpopular late in his reign, and was assassinated in 1881 by radicals. Six were ultimately hanged for the crime, although the execution of the woman at the center was delayed due to her pregnant state.

THE FIRST RUSSIAN REVOLUTION

The revolution that came in 1905, however, took all of these radical movements by surprise. Its unexpected occurrence resulted from Russia's resounding defeat in the Russo-Japanese War of 1904–1905. But the revolution had deeper roots. Rapid industrialization had transformed Russia unevenly; certain regions were heavily industrial, while others were less integrated into the market economy. The economic boom of the 1880s and 1890s turned to bust in the early 1900s, high levels of unemployment. Low grain prices resulted in a series of peasant uprisings, which, combined with students' energetic radical organizing, became overtly political.

As newspapers reported the defeats of the tsar's army and navy, the Russian people grasped the full extent of the regime's inefficiency. Previously apolitical middle-class subjects clamored for change, and radical workers organized strikes and held demonstrations in every important city. Trust in the benevolence of the tsar was severely shaken on January 22, 1905—"Bloody Sunday"—when a group of two hundred thousand workers and their families, led by a priest,

Father Gapon, went to demonstrate their grievances at the tsar's winter palace in St. Petersburg. When guard troops killed 130 demonstrators and wounded several hundred, the government seemed not only ineffective, but arbitrary and brutal.

Over the course of 1905 general protest grew. The autocracy lost control of entire rural towns and regions as local authorities were ejected and often killed by enraged peasants. Forced to yield, Tsar Nicholas II issued the October Manifesto, pledging guarantees of individual liberties, an expanded franchise and a more powerful Duma. Between 1905 and 1907, however, Nicholas revoked most of the promises made in the October Manifesto. Above all, he deprived the Duma of its principal powers and decreed that it be elected indirectly on a class basis, which ensured a legislative body of obedient followers. Russian agriculture remained suspended between an emerging capitalist system and the traditional peasant commune; Russian industry, though powerful enough to allow Russia to maintain its status as a world power, had hardly created a modern, industrial society capable of withstanding the enormous strains that Russia would face during the First World War.

Bloody Sunday. Demonstrating workers who sought to bring their grievances to the attention of the tsar were met and gunned down by government troops, January 1905.

established the independent kingdom of Bulgaria. In 1908 Austria simply annexed the provinces of Bosnia and Herzegovina. Since 1878, and in 1911–1912 Italy entered into war. The power vacuum in the Orient significantly strained Europe's imperial balance of power.

A nationalist movement also emerged in Turkey itself. Invoking a Western liberal variant of nationalism, these reformers called themselves "Young Turks" and in 1908 successfully forced the sultan to establish a constitutional government. The following year, they deposed Sultan Abdul Hamid II and placed on the throne his brother, Mohammed V (1909–1918). Ministers were now responsible to an elected parliament. The new representative government did not, however, extend liberties to the empire's non-Turkish inhabitants. On the contrary, the Young Turks launched a vigorous effort to "Ottomanize" all their imperial subjects, trying to bring both Christian and Muslim communities under more centralized control and to spread Turkish culture. That effort, intended to compensate for the loss of territories in Europe, undercut the popularity of the new regime.

NATIONALISM AND IMPERIAL POLITICS: THE BALKANS

In southeastern Europe rising nationalism continued to divide the disintegrating Ottoman empire. Before 1829 the entire Balkan peninsula was controlled by the Turks. Over the course of the next eighty-five years, however, the Turkish empire ceded territories to rival European powers, especially Russia and Austria, as well as to nationalist revolts by the empire's Christian subjects. In 1829, a war between Russia and Turkey, 1875–1876 brought uprisings in Bosnia, Herzegovina, and Bulgaria, which the sultan suppressed with effective ferocity. A war between Turkey and Russia (1877–1878) forced the sultan to surrender nearly all of his territory in Europe, except for a remnant around Constantinople. Alarmed at Russia's expansion the Great Powers intervened. Austria and Great Britain were especially opposed to granting Russia jurisdiction over so large a portion of the Near East. In 1878 a congress of the Great Powers, meeting in Berlin, transferred Bessarabia to Russia, Thessaly to Greece, and Bosnia and Herzegovina to the control of Austria. Montenegro, Serbia, and Romania also became independent states, thus launching the modern era of Balkan nationalism. Seven years later the Bulgars, who had been granted some degree of autonomy by the Congress of Berlin, seized territory from Turkey. In 1908 they

THE SCIENCE AND SOUL OF THE MODERN AGE

What impact did new scientific theories have on culture?

The decades before the First World War brought a profound shift in society's relationship to both science and art. Ninteenth-century liberals had confidence in science. Not only did Science deliver technological and material progress, it also confirmed liberals' faith in the power of human reason to uncover and command the laws of nature. Toward the end of the century, however, scientific developments defied these expectations. Evolutionary theory, psychology, and social science all introduced visions of humanity that were sharply at odds with conventional wisdom. Artists and intellectuals revolted against nineteenth-century conventions. These upheavals in the world of ideas unsettled older conceptions of individuality, culture, and consciousness. The modern individual no longer seemed the free and rational agent of Enlightenment thought, but rather the product of irrational inner drives and uncontrollable external circumstances.

EUROPE AFTER THE CONGRESS OF BERLIN, 1878

What events precipitated the Congress of Berlin? What issues did the delegates hope to resolve? How did the Congress strengthen the German position within Europe, and why? What national groups won sovereignty and independence, and at whose expense? How did the settlement complicate matters for supranational empires, such as Austria-Hungary?

DARWIN'S REVOLUTIONARY THEORY

If Marx changed conceptions of society, Charles Darwin did him one better, perhaps, for his theory of organic evolution by natural selection transformed conceptions of nature itself. As both a scientific explanation and an imaginative metaphor for political and social change, Darwin's theory of evolution introduced an unsettling new picture of human biology, behavior and society.

Theories of evolution did not originate with Darwin but none had gained widespread scientific or popular currency. One important attempt at an answer was proposed in the early nineteenth century by the French biologist Jean Lamarck, who argued that behavioral changes could alter an animal's physical characteristics within a single generation, and that these new traits would be passed on to offspring.

A more convincing hypothesis of organic evolution appeared in 1859, however, with the publication of the *Origin of Species* by British naturalist Charles Darwin. The son of a small-town physician, Darwin had spent five years in the 1830s as an unpaid naturalist aboard the H.M.S. *Beagle*, a ship that had been chartered for scientific exploration on a trip around the world. The voyage gave Darwin an unparalleled opportunity to observe firsthand the manifold variations of animal life. He contrasted island-dwelling species with related animals on nearby continents and compared the traits of living creatures with those of fossilized remains. From a familiarity with pigeon breeding, Darwin knew that particular traits could be artificially selected by means of controlled mating. Was a similar process of "selection" at work in nature?

Darwin's revolutionary answer was *yes*. He theorized that variations within a population (such as longer beaks or protective coloring) made certain individual organisms better equipped for survival, increasing their chances of breeding and thus passing their advantageous traits to the next generation. To reach this conclusion, Darwin drew on the ideas of the economist and demographer Thomas Malthus, who earlier argued that in nature many more individuals are born than can survive, and that consequently, the weaker ones must perish in the struggle for food. In Darwin's explanation, this Malthusian competition led to adaptation and, if adaptation was successful, to survival. The environment, he argued, "selects" those variants among offspring that are best able to survive and reproduce while eliminating other, less "fit" biological traits.

Darwin used this theory of variation and natural selection to explain the origin of new species. He believed that individual plants and animals with favorable characteristics would transmit their inherited qualities to their descendants over generations, and that successive eliminations of the least fit would eventually produce a new species. Darwin applied his concept of evolution not only to plant and animal species but also to humans. In his view, the human race had evolved from an apelike ancestor, long since extinct, but proba-

> The son of a small-town physician, Darwin had spent five years in the 1830s as an unpaid naturalist aboard the H.M.S. *Beagle*, a ship that had been chartered for scientific exploration on a trip around the world.

bly a common precursor of the existing anthropoid apes and humans. Darwin introduced this unsettling idea in his second great work, *The Descent of Man* (1871).

DARWINIAN THEORY AND RELIGION

The implications of Darwin's writings went far beyond the domain of the evolutionary sciences. Most notably, they challenged the basis of deeply held religious beliefs, sparking a public discussion on the existence and knowability of God. Although popular critics denounced Darwin for contradicting literal interpretations of the Bible, those contradictions were not what made religious middle-class readers uncomfortable. What religious readers in the nineteenth century found difficult to accept was Darwin's challenge to their belief in a benevolent God and a morally guided universe. By Darwin's account, the world was governed not by order, harmony, and divine will, but by random chance and constant, undirected struggle. Moreover, the Darwinian worldview seemed to redefine notions of good and bad only in terms of an ability to survive, thus robbing humanity of critical moral certainties.

SOCIAL DARWINISM

The theory of natural selection also influenced the social sciences, which were just developing at the end of the nineteenth century. New disciplines such as sociology, psychology, anthropology, and economics aimed to apply scientific methods to the analysis of society, and introduced new ways of quantifying, measuring, and interpreting human experience. Under the authoritative banner of "science," these disciplines exerted a powerful influence on society, oftentimes to improve the health and well-being of European men and women. But, as we will see with the impact of "Social Darwinism," the social sciences could also provide justification for forms of economic, imperial, and racial dominance.

The so-called Social Darwinists, whose most famous proponent was the English philosopher Herbert Spencer (1820–1903), adapted Darwinian thought in a way that would have shocked Darwin himself, by applying his concept of individual competition and survival to relationships among classes, races, and nations.

DARWIN AND HIS READERS

Charles Darwin's Origin of Species *(1859) and his theory of natural selection transformed Western knowledge of natural history. The impact of Darwin's work, however, extended well beyond scientific circles. It assumed a cultural importance that exceeded even Darwin's scholarly contribution. How Darwinism was popularized is a complex question, for writers and readers could mold Darwin's ideas to fit a variety of political and cultural purposes. The first excerpt below comes from the conclusion to* The Origin of Species *itself, and it sets out the different laws that Darwin thought governed the natural world. The second excerpt, on the next page, comes from the autobiography of Nicholas Osterroth (1875–1933), a clay miner from western Germany. Osterroth was ambitious and self-educated. The passage recounts his reaction to hearing about Darwin and conveys his enthusiasm for late-nineteenth-century science.*

The natural system is a genealogical arrangement, in which we have to discover the lines of descent by the most permanent characters, however slight their vital importance may be.

The framework of bones being the same in the hand of a man, wing of a bat, fin of the porpoise, and leg of the horse,—the same number of vertebrae forming the neck of the giraffe and of the elephant,—and innumerable other such facts, at once explain themselves on the theory of descent with slow and slight successive modifications. The similarity of pattern in the wing and leg of a bat, though used for such different purposes,—in the jaws and legs of a crab,—in the petals, stamens, and pistils of a flower, is likewise intelligible on the view of the gradual modification of parts or organs, which were alike in the early progenitor of each class. . . .

It is interesting to contemplate an entangled bank, clothed with many plants of many kinds, with birds singing on the bushes, with various insects flitting about, and with worms crawling through the damp earth, and to reflect that these elaborately constructed forms, so different from each other, and dependent on each other in so complex a manner, have all been produced by laws acting around us. These laws, taken in the largest sense, being Growth with Reproduction; Inheritance which is almost implied by reproduction; Variability from the indirect and direct action of the external conditions of life, and from use and disuse; a Ratio of Increase so high as to lead to a Struggle for Life, and as a consequence to Natural Selection, entailing Divergence of Character and the Extinction of less-improved forms. Thus, from the war of nature, from famine and death, the most exalted object which we are capable of conceiving, namely, the production of the higher animals, directly follows. There is grandeur in this view of life, with its several powers, having been originally breathed into a few forms or into one; and that, whilst this planet has gone cycling on according to the fixed law of gravity, from so simple a beginning endless forms most beautiful and most wonderful have been, and are being, evolved.

Charles Darwin, *The Origin of Species* (Harmondsworth: Penguin, 1968), pp. 450–51, 458–60.

The book was called *Moses or Darwin?* . . . Written in a very popular style, it compared the Mosaic story of creation with the natural evolutionary history, illuminated the contradictions of the biblical story, and gave a concise description of the evolution of organic and inorganic nature, interwoven with plenty of striking proofs.

What particularly impressed me was a fact that now became clear to me: that evolutionary natural history was monopolized by the institutions of higher learning; that Newton, Laplace, Kant, Darwin, and Haeckel brought enlightenment only to the students of the upper social classes; and that for the common people in the grammar school the old Moses with his six-day creation of the world still was the authoritative world view. For the upper classes there was evolution, for us creation; for them productive liberating knowledge, for us rigid faith; bread for those favored by fate, stones for those who hungered for truth!

Why do the people need science? Why do they need a so-called Weltanschauung [world view]? The people must keep Moses, must keep religion; religion is the poor man's philosophy. Where would we end up if every miner and every farmhand had the opportunity to stick his nose into astronomy, geology, biology, and anatomy? Does it serve any purpose for the divine world order of the possessing and privileged classes to tell the worker that the Ptolemaic heavens have long since collapsed; that out there in the universe there is an eternal process of creation and destruction; that in the universe at large, as on our tiny earth, everything is in the grip of eternal evolution; that this evolution takes place according to inalterable natural laws that defy even the omnipotence of the old Mosaic Jehovah; . . . Why tell the dumb people that Copernicus and his followers have overturned the old Mosaic creator, and that Darwin and modern science have dug the very ground out from under his feet of clay?

That would be suicide! Yes, the old religion is so convenient for the divine world order of the ruling class! As long as the worker hopes faithfully for the beyond, he won't think of plucking the blooming roses in this world. . . .

The possessing classes of all civilized nations need servants to make possible their godlike existence. So they cannot allow the servant to eat from the tree of knowledge.

Alfred Kelly, ed., *The German Worker: Working-Class Autobiographies from the Age of Industrialization* (Berkeley: University of California Press, 1987), pp. 185–86.

Spencer, who coined the phrase "survival of the fittest," used evolutionary theory to expound the virtues of free competition and attack state welfare programs. As a champion of individualism, Spencer condemned all forms of collectivism as primitive and counterproductive, relics of an earlier stage of social evolution.

Unlike the science of biological evolution, the popularized notion of Social Darwinism was easy to comprehend, and its concepts (centering on a struggle for survival) were soon integrated into the political vocabulary of the day. Proponents of laissez-faire capitalism and opponents of socialism used Darwinist rhetoric to justify marketplace competition and the "natural order" of rich and poor. Nationalists embraced Social Darwinism to rationalize imperialist expansion and warfare. Spencer's doctrine also became closely tied to theories of racial hierarchy and white superiority, which claimed that the white race had reached the height of evolutionary development and had thus earned the right to dominate and rule other races (see Chapter 22). Despite its unsettling potential, Darwinism was used to advance a range of political objectives and to shore up an array of ingrained prejudices.

EARLY PSYCHOLOGY: PAVLOV AND FREUD

Although the new social scientists self-consciously relied on the use of rational, scientific principles, their findings often stressed the opposite: the irrational, even animalistic nature of human experience. Physiological experiments, which could establish connections between body and mind, promised an entirely new way to comprehend the mental makeup of humans. For instance, the work of the Russian physician Ivan Pavlov (1849–1936) explained a type of behavior called "classical conditioning," in which a random stimulus can be made to produce a (sometimes unintended) physical reflex reaction. Pavlov's famous experiment showed that if dogs were fed following the ringing of a bell, the animals would eventually salivate

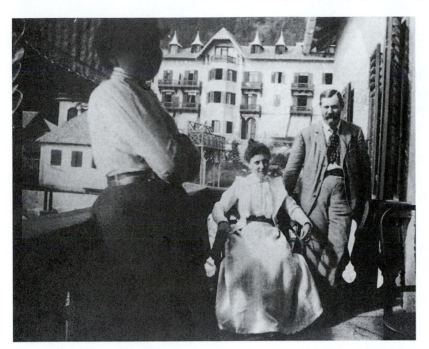

Sigmund Freud and his Family.

understanding of seemingly "irrational" behavior. Indeed, Freud's search for an all-encompassing theory of the mind was deeply grounded in the tenets of nineteenth-century science. By stressing the irrational, however, Freud's theories fed a growing anxiety about the value and limits of human reason. Likewise, they brought to fore a powerful critique of the constraints imposed by the moral and social codes of Western civilization.

NIETZSCHE'S ATTACK ON TRADITION

No one provided a more sweeping or more influential assault on Western values than the German philosopher Friedrich Nietzsche (1844–1900). With an exuberant embrace of emotion, instinct, and irrationality, Nietzsche skewered the moral certainties of the nineteenth century. Like Freud, Nietzsche had observed a middle-class culture dominated by illusions and self-deceptions, and he sought to unmask them. In a series of works that rejected rational argumentation in favor of an elliptical, suggestive prose style, Nietzsche presented his critque of Western culture. Essentially, he argued that bourgeois faith in such concepts as science, progress, democracy, and religion represented a futile, and thus reprehensible, search for security and truth. Nietzsche categorically denied the possibility of knowing "truth" or "reality," since all knowlege comes filtered through linguistic, scientific, or artistic systems of representation. He also famously ridiculed Judeo-Christian morality for instilling a repressive conformity that drained civilization of its vitality. Though Nietzsche's philosophy did not offer any concrete political or social objectives, it resounded with themes of personal liberation, especially from the stranglehold of history and tradition. Indeed, Nietzsche's ideal individual, or "superman," was one who abandoned the burdens of cultural conformity and

at the sound of the bell alone, exactly as if they smelled and saw food. Moreover, Pavlov insisted that such conditioning constituted a significant part of human behavior as well. Known as "behaviorism," this type of physiological psychology eschewed vague concepts such as mind and consciousness, concentrating instead on the reaction of muscles, nerves, glands, and visceral organs.

Like behavorism, a second major school of psychology also suggested that human behavior was largely motivated by unconcious and irrational forces. Founded by the Austrian physician Sigmund Freud (1856–1939), the discipline of psychoanalysis posited a new, dynamic, and unsettling theory of the mind, in which a variety of unconscious drives and desires conflict with a rational and moral conscience. Freud believed that most cases of mental disorder result from an irreconcilable tension between natural drives and cultural restraints, which leave innate impulses buried in

> Though Nietzsche's philosophy did not offer any concrete political or social objectives, it resounded with themes of personal liberation, especially from the stranglehold of history and tradition.

the subconscious. Freud believed that by studying such disorders, as well as dreams and slips of the tongue, scientists could glimpse the submerged areas of consciousness, and thus formulate an objective created an independent set of values based on artistic vision and strength of character. Only through individual struggle against the chaotic universe did Nietzsche forecast salvation for Western civilization.

NEW READERS AND THE POPULAR PRESS

The effect of various scientific and philosophical challenges on the men and women who lived at the end of the nineteenth century cannot be measured precisely. Millions went about the business of life untroubled by the implications of evolutionary theory. Certainly, for most members of the middle class, the challenge of socialism was more concrete than the challenges of science and philosophy. Yet the changes we have been discussing eventually had a profound impact. Darwin's theory could be popularized. If educated men and women had neither the time nor inclination to read the *Origin of Species*, they read magazines and newspapers that summarized (not always correctly) its implications. They encountered some of its central concepts in other places, from political speeches to novels and crime reports.

In those countries where literacy rates were highest, commercial publishers such as Alfred Harmsworth in Britain and William Randolph Hearst in the United States hastened to serve the new reading public. Middle-class readers had for some time been well supplied with newspapers catering to their interests and point of view. By 1900, however, other newspapers were appealing to the newly literate, and doing so by means of sensational journalism and spicy, easy-to-read serials. Advertisements drastically lowered the costs of the mass-market newspapers, enabling even workers to purchase one or two newspapers a day. The "yellow" journalism of the penny presses merged entertainment and sensationalism with the news, aiming to increase circulation and thus secure more lucrative advertising sales. Publishers and marketing men weren't the only ones eager to reach this emerging mass market, however. As the new century progressed, artists, activists, politicians—and above all, governments—would become increasingly preoccupied with communicating their messages to the masses.

THE FIRST MODERNS: INNOVATIONS IN ART

In the crucible of late-nineteenth-century Europe—bubbling with scientific, technological, and social transformations—new generations of painters, poets, writers, and composers began to question the moral and cultural values of liberal, middle-class society. Some did so with grave hesitation, others with heedless abandon. The pioneers of what would later be termed "modernism" developed the artistic forms and aesthetic values that came to dominate much of the

The New Power of the Press. With the spread of literacy, newspapers adapted to the needs and desires of the new mass audience. Here British railway passengers scramble for the latest edition.

twentieth century. Like all such terms, *modernism* is notoriously difficult to define: it encompassed a diverse and often contradictory set of theories and practices than spanned the entire range of cultural production—from painting, sculpture, literature, and architecture to theater, dance, and musical composition. Despite such diversity, however, modernist movements did share certain key characteristics: first, a self-conscious sense of rupture from history and tradition; second, a rejection of established values and assumptions; and third, a radical insistence on expressive and experimental freedom.

Early modernism was distinguished by a new understanding of the relationship between art and society. The abstract painter Wassily Kandinsky (1866–1944),

for instance, who was a devotee of occult mysticism (especially popular around the turn of the century), believed that visionary artists would carry society from "the soulless-material life of the nineteenth century" toward "the psychic-spiritual life of the twentieth century." Notions that contemporary society was materialistic and morally bankrupt figured prominently in modernist critiques of European culture. And while artists like Kandinsky pointed to salvation in a utopian future, others used their art to examine the present unflinchingly, probing the psychological and social pathologies of urban industrial society. In the political arena, modernist hostility toward conventional values sometimes translated into support for antiliberal movements at the political peripheries—radical anarchism

Iris Beside a Pond by Claude Monet (1840–1926). Monet called some of his paintings impressions, and the name soon came to designate a school.

on the left and proto-fascism on the right. This push toward the ideological edges mirrored the modernists' aesthetic tendencies.

THE REVOLT ON CANVAS

Like most artistic movements, modernism defined itself in opposition to a set of earlier principles. Since the Renaissance, Western art had sought to accurately depict three-dimensional visual reality; paintings were considered to be "mirrors," or "windows" on the world. But during the late nineteenth century, artists turned their backs to the visual world, focusing instead on subjec-

tive, psychologically oriented, intensely emotional forms of self-expression. As the Norwegian painter Edvard Munch claimed: "Art is the opposite of nature. A work of art can come only from the interior of man."

Though challenges to the tradition of representational art occurred earlier in the nineteenth century, the first significant breaks emerged with the French impressionists, who came to prominence as young artists in the 1870s. Instead of painting objects themselves, they captured the transitory play of light on surfaces, giving their works a sketchy, ephemeral quality that differed sharply from realist art. And though subsequent artists revolted against what they deemed the sterile objectivity of this

Mont Sainte-Victoire by Paul Cézanne (1839–1906). Cézanne's reduction of the exterior world to forms and planes of color provided an important bridge between impressionism and cubism.

scientific approach, the impressionist painters, most famously Claude Monet (1840–1926) and Pierre-Auguste Renoir (1841–1919), left two important legacies to the European avant-garde. First, by developing new techniques without reference to past styles, the impressionists paved the way for younger artists to experiment more freely. Second, because the official salons rejected their work, the impressionists organized their own independent exhibitions from 1874 to 1886. These shows effectively undermined the French Academy's centuries-old monopoly on artistic display and aesthetic standards, and they established a tradition of autonomous outsider exhibits, which figures prominently in the history of modernism.

In the wake of impressionism, a handful of innovative artists working at the end of the nineteenth century laid the groundwork for an explosion of creative experimentation after 1900. Chief among them was the Frenchman Paul Cézanne (1839–1906), whose efforts to "make of Impressionism something solid and durable" entailed a reduction of natural forms to their geometric equivalents, a rejection of traditional perspective, and (most important) an emphasis on the subjective arrangement of color and form. Perhaps more so than anyone, Cézanne shattered the window of representational art. The Dutchman Vincent van Gogh also explored art's expressive potential, with greater emotion and subjectivity. For Van Gogh, painting was a labor of faith, a way to channel his vio-

lent passions. For Paul Gauguin, who fled to the Pacific islands in 1891, art promised a utopian refuge from the corruption of Europe. Gauguin in particular was influenced by the symbolist movement around the turn of the century. The symbolists were a group of artists and writers who were deeply suspicious of material reality, and who sought transcendental truth though imagination, personal feelings, and psychological perceptions.

After the turn of the century, a diverse crop of avant-garde movements flowered across Europe. In bohemian Paris, the Frenchman Henri Matisse (1869–1954) and Pablo Picasso (1881–1973), a Catalan Spaniard, pursued their groundbreaking aesthetic experiments in relative quiet. The cubists in Paris, vorticists in Britain, and futurists in Italy all embraced a hard, angular aesthetic of the machine age. While other modernists sought an antidote to fin-de-siècle malaise by looking "backward" to so-called primitive cultures, these new movements embraced the future in all its uncertainty—often with the kind of aggressive, hypermasculine language that later emerged as a hallmark of fascism.

The breadth and diversity of modern art defy simple categories and explanations. The profound changes that swept the visual arts were paralleled across the cultural spectrum (developments discussed in Chapter 28). And though they remained the province of a small group of artists and intellectuals before 1914, these radical revisions of artistic values entered the cultural mainstream soon after the First World War.

CONCLUSION

Many Europeans who had grown up in the period from 1870 to 1914, but lived through the hardship of the First World War, looked back on the prewar period as a golden age of European civilization. In one sense this retrospective view is apt. After all, the Continental powers had successfully avoided major wars, enabling a second phase of industrialization to provide better living standards for the growing populations of mass society. An overall spirit of confidence and purpose pervaded Europe's perceived mission to exercise political, economic, and cultural dominion in the far reaches of the world. Yet European politics and culture also registered the presence of powerful—and destabilizing—forces of change. Industrial expansion, relative abundance, and rising literacy produced a political climate of rising expectations. As the age of mass politics arrived, democrats, socialists, and feminists clamored for access to political life, threatening violence, strikes, and revolution. Marxist socialism especially changed radical politics, redefining the terms of debate for the next century. Western science, literature, and the arts explored new perspectives on the individual, undermining some of the cherished beliefs of nineteenth-century liberals. The competition and violence central to Darwin's theory of evolution, the subconscious urges that Freud found in human behavior, and the rebellion against representation in the arts all pointed in new and baffling directions. These experiments, hypotheses, and nagging questions accompanied Europe into the Great War of 1914. They would help to shape Europeans' responses to the enormity of mass death and destruction that devastated the continent. After the war, the political changes and cultural unease of the period from 1870 to 1914 would reemerge in the form of mass movements and artistic developments that would define the twentieth century.

KEY TERMS

second industrial revolution	Dreyfus Affair	Charles Darwin
Capital	Irish home rule	Sigmund Freud
anarchism	"Bloody Sunday"	Friedrich Nietzsche
woman suffrage	"Young Turks"	modernism

SELECTED READINGS

Berlanstein, Lenard. *The Working People of Paris, 1871–1914.* Baltimore, 1984. A social history of the workplace and its impact on working men and women.

Berlin, Isaiah. *Karl Marx: His Life and Environment.* 4th ed. New York, 1996. An excellent short account.

Blackbourn, David. *The Long Nineteenth Century: A History of Germany, 1780–1918.* New York, 1998. The best current survey of German society and politics.

Bredin, Jean-Denis. *The Affair: The Case of Alfred Dreyfus.* New York, 1986. Detailed, up to date, and readable.

Burns, Michael. *Dreyfus: A Family Affair.* New York, 1992. Follows the story Dreyfus through the next generations.

Chipp, Herschel B. *Theories of Modern Art: A Source Book by Artists and Critics.* Berkeley, 1968.

Clark, T. J. *The Painting of Modern Life: Paris in the Art of Manet and His Followers.* New York, 1985. Argues for seeing impressionism as a critique of French society.

Eley, Geoff. *Forging Democracy.* Oxford, 2002. Wide-ranging and multinational account of European radicalism from 1848 to the present.

Gay, Peter. *The Bourgeois Experience: Victoria to Freud,* 5 vols. New York, 1984–2000. Imaginative and brilliant study of private life and middle class culture.

———. *Freud: A Life of Our Time.* New York, 1988. Beautifully written and lucid about difficult concepts; now the best biography.

Herbert, Robert L. *Impressionism: Art, Leisure, and Parisian Society.* New Haven, 1988. An accessible and important study of the impressionists and the world they painted.

Hughes, H. Stuart. *Consciousness and Society.* New York, 1958. A classic study on late-nineteenth-century European thought.

Jelavich, Peter. *Munich and Theatrical Modernism: Politics, Playwriting, and Performance, 1890–1914.* Cambridge, Mass., 1985.

Jones, Gareth Stedman. *Outcast London.* Oxford, 1971. Studies the breakdown in class relationships during the second half of the nineteenth century.

Joyce, Patrick. *Visions of the People: Industrial England and the Question of Class, 1848–1914.* New York, 1991. A social history of the workplace.

Kelly, Alfred. *The German Worker: Autobiographies from the Age of Industrialization.* Berkeley, 1987. Excerpts from workers' autobiographies provide fresh perspective on labor history.

Kern, Stephen. *The Culture of Time and Space.* Cambridge, Mass., 1983. A cultural history of the late nineteenth century.

Landes, David. *The Unbound Prometheus: Technological Change and Industrial Development in Western Europe from 1750 to the Present.* New York, 1969. Includes a first-rate analysis of the second industrial revolution.

Lidtke, Vernon. *The Alternative Culture: Socialist Labor in Imperial Germany.* New York, 1985. A probing study of working-class culture.

Marrus, Michael Robert. *The Politics of Assimilation: A Study of the French Jewish Community at the Time of the Dreyfus Affair.* Oxford, 1971.

Micale, Mark S. *Approaching Hysteria: Disease and Its Interpretations.* Princeton, N.J., 1995. Important study of the history of psychiatry before Freud.

Rupp, Leila J. *Worlds of Women: The Making of an International Women's Movement.* Princeton, N.J., 1997.

Silverman, Deborah L. *Art Nouveau in Fin-de-Siècle France: Politics, Psychology, and Style.* Berkeley, 1989. A study of the relationship between psychological and artistic change.

Smith, Bonnie. *Changing Lives: Women in European History since 1700.* New York, 1988. A useful overview of European women's history.

Tickner, Lisa. *The Spectacle of Women: Imagery of the Suffrage Campaign, 1907–14.* Chicago, 1988. A very engaging study of British suffragism.

Verner, Andrew. *The Crisis of Russian Autocracy: Nicholas II and the 1905 Revolution.* Princeton, N.J., 1990. A detailed study of this important event.

Vital, David. *A People Apart: A Political History of the Jews in Europe, 1789-1939.* Oxford and New York, 1999. Comprehensive and extremely helpful.

Weber, Eugen. *Peasants into Frenchmen: The Modernization of Rural France, 1870–1914.* Stanford, 1976. A study of how France's peasantry was assimilated into the Third Republic.

Wynn, Charters. *Workers, Strikes, and Pogroms: The Donbass-Dnepr Bend in Late Imperial Russia, 1870–1905.* Princeton, N.J., 1992. Excellent on Russian industrialization and Russian workers' politics.

DIGITAL HISTORY

THE OLYMPICS PAST AND PRESENT

The goal of Olympism is to place everywhere sport at the service of the harmonious development of man, with a view to encouraging the establishment of a peaceful society concerned with the preservation of human dignity. To this effect, the Olympic Movement engages, alone or in cooperation with other organizations and within the limits of its means, in actions to promote peace.
—The Olympic Charter (July 4, 2003)

The first recorded Olympic Games took place in the Valley of Olympia in 776 B.C.E. and were held at four-year intervals ("Olympiads") until 394 C.E., when they were abolished by the Roman emperor Theodosius I. Begun as a religious festival, the first Olympics contained only one event, the foot race, but over time boxing, wrestling, the javelin throw, and chariot racing were added. Winners received a simple olive tree branch, which the Greeks believed would bring the victor the vitality of the sacred tree. The winning athlete gave thanks to Zeus, and his city-state was considered to be in favor with the gods.

In 1894, Pierre de Coubertin created the institutional structure of Olympism, and the modern Olympic Games were born. Hoping to revive the flagging French educational system, Coubertin saw sport as a vehicle for social and moral change. In 1896, the International Olympic Committee (IOC) oversaw the first modern Olympics at Athens—245 athletes (all men) from fourteen nations competed in the ancient Panathenaic stadium before huge crowds.

The modern Olympic movement is now more than a century old. Technology has changed the training and execution of all sport, and digital records are made of every event. Media coverage can make or break a young star's career. Commercial endorsements are numerous, and the lines between amateur and professional athletes are more blurred than ever. Meanwhile, cities around the globe vie for the honor of hosting the Olympic Games.

There is, however, one constant—athletic competition—with which the modern Olympic movement continues to inspire all who participate in and view its games.

The images and documents in the "The Olympics Past and Present" Digital History Feature at www.wwnorton.com/wciv, reveal how the significance of international athletic competition has changed from the ancient world until the present. As you explore this feature, consider the following:

• What role did athletic competition play in the ancient Greek world?

• How have the lines between professional and amateur been blurred by modern sport?

• To what extent are the modern Olympic Games driven by economics and politics?

• Do you think the goals of modern Olympism as stated by the IOC are still valid?

Chapter
Twenty-four

Chapter Contents

The First
World War

In several crucial respects, the twentieth century began in August 1914, with the outbreak of the First World War—a four-year conflict that spurred the collapse of nineteenth-century ideals and institutions. Soldiers marched into battle with the confidence and ambition bred by imperial successes. The leading nations of Europe were at the height of their power. Europe was the center of the world economy and commanded far-flung empires. Many Europeans entered the war with faith in modernity, and in its ability to deliver not only prosperity but all the advantages of "civilization," especially peace and progress.

Despite those expectations, many people harbored fears about the future. The war justified that quiet dread. The "Great War" introduced the ugly face of industrial warfare and the grim capacities of the modern world. It caught Europeans unprepared not only militarily, but economically and politically. In a catastrophic combination of old mentalities and new technologies, the war left 9 million dead soldiers in its wake. Yet soldiers were not the only casualties. World War I was waged against entire nations and had profound economic and political ramifications for the people of Europe. Four years of fighting destroyed many of the institutions and assumptions of the previous century, from monarchies and empires to European economic hegemony. The war strained relations between classes and generations. It disillusioned many, even citizens of the victorious nations. As the British writer Virginia Woolf put it, "It was a shock—to see the faces of our rulers in the light of shell-fire." The war banished older forms of authoritarianism and ushered in new ones that bore the distinctive mark of the twentieth century. Finally, the war proved nearly impossible to settle; antagonisms bred in battle only intensified in the war's aftermath, and would eventually lead to the Second World War. Postwar Europe faced more problems than peace could manage.

FOCUS QUESTIONS

- What were the causes of World War I?
- Why did the Schlieffen Plan fail?
- Why did the war become a stalemate?
- Why did the Allies persist with an offensive strategy?

 • What was the role of empire in World War I?
- How did the war change women's lives?
- How did the Bolsheviks seize power?
- How did the Allies win the war?

THE JULY CRISIS

What were the causes of World War I?

In 1914 Europe had built a seemingly stable peace. Through the complex negotiations of Great Power geopolitics, Europe had settled into two systems of alliance: the Triple Entente (later the Allied Powers) of Britain, France, and Russia rivaled the Triple Alliance (later the Central Powers) of Germany, Austria-Hungary, and Italy. Within this balance of power, the nations of Europe challenged one another for economic, military, and imperial advantage. The scramble for colonies abroad accompanied a fierce arms race at home, where military leaders assumed that superior technology and larger armies would result in a quick victory in a European war. Indeed, in the prevailing atmosphere of international suspicion, such a war seemed likely to many of Europe's political and military elites. Yet none of the diplomats, spies, military planners, or cabinet ministers of Europe—nor any of their critics—predicted the war they eventually got. Nor did many expect that the Balkan crisis of July 1914 would touch off that conflict, engulfing all of Europe in just over a month's time.

The Balkans lay between two empires, the Austro-Hungarian and the Ottoman. Balkan politics were a -traditional focus for Russian intervention in European affairs, and also for German and British diplomacy. The Great Powers tried to avoid direct intervention in the region seeking instead to bring the new Balkan states into the web of alliances. In 1912 the independent states of Serbia, Greece, Bulgaria, and Montenegro launched the First Balkan War against the Ottomans; in 1913, the Second Balkan War was fought over the spoils of the first. Through reasonable diplomacy these wars remained localized. When diplomacy failed, as it did in the summer of 1914, the Great Powers' system of alliances would actually hasten the outbreak of a wider war.

Tensions in the Balkans heightened the problems of the Austro-Hungarian empire, which was struggling to survive amid increasing nationalist ambitions. Czechs and Slovenes protested their second-class status in the German half of the empire; Poles, Croats, and ethnic Romanians chafed at Hungarian rule. The province of Bosnia was particularly volatile, home to several Slavic ethnic groups and formerly part of the Ottoman empire. Bosnian Serbs, in particular, had hoped to secede and join the independent kingdom of Serbia. But now the Austrians blocked their plans. So with the support of Serbia, the Bosnian Serbs began an underground war against the empire to achieve their goals. Bosnia would be the crucible of European conflict.

On June 28, 1914, Franz Ferdinand (1889–1914), archduke of Austria and heir to the Austro-Hungarian Empire, paraded through Sarajevo, the capital of Bosnia. As a hotbed of Serb resistance, Sarajevo was an admittedly dangerous place for the head of the hated empire to parade in public. The archduke had escaped an assassination attempt earlier in the day, with a bomb barely missing his automobile; but when his car made a wrong turn and stopped to back up, a nineteen-year-old Bosnian student named Gavrilo Princip shot Ferdinand and his wife at point-blank range. Princip saw his violent act as a part of a struggle for his people's independence—we see it as the start of World War I.

Shocked by Ferdinand's death, the Austrians saw the assassination as a direct attack by the Serbian government. Eager for retribution, Austria issued an ultimatum to Serbia three weeks later, demanding that the Serbian government denounce the aims and activities of the Bosnian Serbs, prohibit further propaganda and subversion, and allow Austro-Hungarian officials to prosecute and punish Serbian officials who the Austrians believed were involved in the assassination. The demands were deliberately unreasonable. Austria wanted war, a punitive campaign to restore order in Bosnia and crush Serbia. The Serbs recognized the provocation and mobilized their army three hours before sending a reply, which agreed to all but the most important Austrian demands. Austria responded with its own mobilization and declared war three days later, on July 28, 1914.

For a brief moment, it seemed possible to avoid a wider war. At first diplomats and politicians hoped to write the confrontation off as another crisis in the Balkans. Austria's steady escalation, coupled with Russia's traditional ties to Serbia, ultimately made that impossible. (Many historians also argue that Germany might have coaxed Austria back from the brink.) For Austria, the conflict was a matter of prestige and power politics—a chance to reassert the fraying empire's authority. For Russia, too, the emerging conflict was an opportunity to regain some of the tsar's authority by standing up for the rights of "brother Slavs." By July 30, Russia mobilized fully—its troops were readied to fight both Austria and Germany.

The crisis spread. Sitting in the most precarious geographic position, Germany had the most detailed plans for fighting a war of necessity. As Russia began to mo-

EUROPEAN ALLIANCES ON THE EVE OF WORLD WAR I

Study the pattern of alliances shown in this map. How had the alliance system emerged to protect the varied interests and the integrity of the balance of power in Europe? Why were Germany and the Austro-Hungarian empire allied? Why would the Ottoman empire join such an alliance? Why would the Russian empire gravitate toward Great Britain and France? Did colonial rivalries inform this pattern at all? How did such a system of alliances contribute to global conflict?

bilize, Kaiser William II (1888–1918) sent an ultimatum to St. Petersburg demanding that Russian mobilization cease within twelve hours. The Russians refused. Meanwhile, the German ministers demanded to know France's intentions. Premier René Viviani (1914–1915) replied that France would act "in accordance with her interests"—which meant an immediate mobilization against Germany. Finally facing the dual threat it had long anticipated, Germany mobilized on August 1 and declared war on Russia—two days later,

on France. The next day, the German army invaded Belgium on its way to take Paris.

The invasion of neutral Belgium provided a rallying cry for the British generals and diplomats who wanted Britain to join the nascent continental conflict. Despite Britain's secret pacts with France and despite its public guarantee of Belgium's neutrality, British entry into the Great War was not a foregone conclusion. Proponents of war, however, could resort to an irrefutable tenet of British foreign policy: that to maintain the balance of

THE BALKANS, 1878 AND 1914

How did the decline of the Ottoman empire affect the Balkans? Why did the European empires get involved in the affairs of southeast Europe? What were the most important changes in the region between 1878 and 1914? Why was Bosnia-Herzegovina particularly volatile?

power, no single nation should be allowed to dominate the Continent. Thus, on August 4, Britain entered the war against Germany.

The diplomatic maneuvers during the five weeks that followed the assassination at Sarajevo have been characterized as "a tragedy of miscalculation." Diplomats' hands were tied, however, by the strategic thinking and rigid timetables set by military leaders. Speed was of prime importance to generals. To them, once war seemed certain, time spent on diplomacy was time lost on the battlefield. A number of other factors also contributed to the outbreak of war when it came. For instance, while Austria negotiated about its ultimatum for three weeks, during the delay both Russia and Germany felt obliged to make shows of strength. Reasoned debate about the problem never occurred. During the crisis government officials had little contact with each other, and even less with the diplomats

TOWARD WORLD WAR I: DIPLOMACY IN THE SUMMER OF 1914

The assassination of Franz Ferdinand in Sarajevo on June 28, 1914 set off an increasingly desperate round of diplomatic negotiations. As the following exchanges show, diplomats and political leaders on both sides swung from trying to provoke war to attempting to avert or, at least, contain it.

EMPEROR FRANZ JOSEPH OF AUSTRIA-HUNGARY TO KAISER WILLIAM II OF GERMANY, JULY 5, 1914

A week after his nephew, the heir to the throne, was shot, Franz Joseph set out his interpretation of the long-standing conflict with Serbia and its larger implications.

The plot against my poor nephew was the direct result of an agitation carried on by the Russian and Serb Pan-Slavs, an agitation whose sole object is the weakening of the Triple Alliance and the destruction of my realm.

So far, all investigations have shown that the Sarajevo murder was not perpetrated by one individual, but grew out of a well-organized conspiracy, the threads of which can be traced to Belgrade. Even though it will probably be impossible to prove the complicity of the Serb government, there can be no doubt that its policy, aiming as it does at the unification of all Southern Slavs under the Serb banner, en-

courages such crimes, and that the continuation of such conditions constitutes a permanent threat to my dynasty and my lands. . . .

This will only be possible if Serbia, which is at present the pivot of Pan-Slav policies, is put out of action as a factor of political power in the Balkans.

You too are [surely] convinced after the recent frightful occurrence in Bosnia that it is no longer possible to contemplate a reconciliation of the antagonism between us and Serbia and that the [efforts] of all European monarchs to pursue policies that preserve the peace will be threatened if the nest of criminal activity in Belgrade remains unpunished.

AUSTRO-HUNGARIAN DISAGREEMENTS OVER STRATEGY

The following comes from an account of a meeting of the Council of Ministers of the Austro-Hungarian empire on July 7, 1914. The ministers disagreed sharply about diplomatic strategies and about how crucial decisions should be made.

[Count Leopold Berchtold, foreign minister of Austria-Hungary] . . . both Emperor Wilhelm and [chancellor] Bethmann Hollweg had assured us emphatically of Germany's unconditional support in the event of military complications with Serbia. . . . It was clear to him

that a military conflict with Serbia might bring about war with Russia. . . .

[Count Istvan Tisza, prime minister of Hungary] . . . We should decide what our demands on Serbia will be [but] should only present an ultimatum if Serbia rejected them. These demands must be hard but not so that they cannot be complied with. If Serbia accepted them, we could register a noteworthy diplomatic success and our prestige in the Balkans would be enhanced. If Serbia rejected our demands, then he too would favor military action. But he would already now go on record that we could aim at the down-sizing but not the complete annihilation of Serbia because, first, this would provoke Russia to fight to the death and, second, he—as Hungarian premier—could never consent to the monarchy's annexation of a part of Serbia. Whether or not we ought to go to war with Serbia was not a matter for Germany to decide. . . .

[Count Berchtold] remarked that the history of the past years showed that diplomatic successes against Serbia might enhance the prestige of the monarchy temporarily, but that in reality the tension in our relations with Serbia had only increased.

[Count Karl Stürgkh, prime minister of Austria] . . . agreed with the Royal Hungarian Prime Minister that we and not the German government had to determine whether a war was necessary or not . . . [but] Count Tisza should take into account that in pursuing a hesitant and weak policy, we run the risk of not being so sure of Germany's unconditional support. . . .

[Leo von Bilinsky, Austro-Hungarian finance minister] . . . The Serb understands only force; a diplomatic success would make no impression at all in Bosnia and would be harmful rather than beneficial. . . .

Austro-Hungary's Ultimatum to Serbia

The British foreign secretary Sir Edward Grey, for one, was shocked by Austria's demands, especially its insistence that Austrian officials would participate in Serbian judicial proceedings. The Serbian government's response was more conciliatory than most diplomats expected, but diplomatic efforts to avert war still failed. The Austrians' ultimatum to Serbia included the following demands:

The Royal Serb Government will publish the following declaration on the first page of its official *journal* of 26/13 July:

"The Royal Serb Government condemns the propaganda directed against Austria-Hungary, and regrets sincerely the horrible consequences of these criminal ambitions.

"The Royal Serb Government regrets that Serb officers and officials have taken part in the propaganda above-mentioned and thereby imperiled friendly and neighbourly relations.

"The Royal Government . . . considers it a duty to warn officers, officials and indeed all the inhabitants of the kingdom [of Serbia], that it will in future use great severity against such persons who may be guilty of similar doings.

The Royal Serb Government will moreover pledge itself to the following:

1. to suppress every publication likely to inspire hatred and contempt against the Monarchy;

2. to begin immediately dissolving the society called *Narodna Odbrana**; to seize all its means of propaganda and to act in the same way against all the societies and associations in Serbia, which are busy with the propaganda against Austria-Hungary.

3. to eliminate without delay from public instruction everything that serves or might serve the propaganda against Austria-Hungary, both where teachers or books are concerned;

4. to remove from military service and from the administration all officers and officials who are guilty of having taken part in the propaganda against Austria-Hungary, whose names and proof of whose guilt the I. and R. Government [Imperial and Royal, that is, the Austro-Hungarian empire] will communicate to the Royal Government;

5. to consent to the cooperation of I. and R. officials in Serbia in suppressing the subversive movement directed against the territorial integrity of the Monarchy;

6. to open a judicial inquest [*enquête judiciaire*] against all those who took part in the plot of 28 June, if they are to be found on Serbian territory; the I. and R. Government will delegate officials who will take an active part in these and associated inquiries;

The I. and R. Government expects the answer of the Royal government to reach it not later than Saturday, the 25th, at six in the afternoon. . . .

*Narodna Odbrana, or National Defense, was pro-Serbian and anti-Austrian, but nonviolent. The Society of the Black Hand, to which Franz Ferdinand's assassin belonged, considered Narodna Odbrana too moderate.

Ralph Menning, *The Art of the Possible: Documents on Great Power Diplomacy, 1814–1914* (New York: McGraw Hill, 1996), pp. 400, 402–403, and 414–415 (source for all three document excerpts).

and ambassadors of other countries. Several heads of state, including the kaiser and the president of France, along with many of their ministers, spent most of July on vacation; they returned to find their generals holding orders for mobilization, waiting for signature. Austria's mismanagement of the crisis and Russia's inability to find a way to intervene without mobilizing its army contributed greatly to the spiraling confrontation. Powerful German officials insisted that Germany should fight before Russia recovered from its 1905 loss to Japan, and before the French army could benefit from its new three-year conscription law, which would put more men in uniform. The same sense of urgency characterized the strategies of all combatant countries. The lure of a bold, successful strike against one's enemies, and the fear that too much was at stake to risk losing the advantage, created a rolling tide of military mobilization that carried Europe into battle.

THE MARNE AND ITS CONSEQUENCES

Why did the Schlieffen Plan fail?

Declarations of war were met with a mix of public fanfare and private concern. Though saber-rattling romantics envisioned a war of national glory and spiritual renewal, plenty of Europeans recognized that a continental war put decades of progress and prosperity at risk. Bankers and financiers correctly predicted that a major war would create financial chaos. Many young men, however, enlisted with excitement. On the continent, volunteer soldiers added to the strength of conscript armies, while in Britain over seven hundred thousand men volunteered for the army in the first eight weeks alone. Like many a war enthusiast, these men expected the war to be over by Christmas.

Military planners foresaw a short, limited, and decisive war—a tool to be used where diplomacy failed. They thought that a modern economy simply could not function amid a sustained war effort, and that modern weaponry made protracted war impossible. They placed their bets on size and speed: bigger armies, more powerful weapons, and faster offensives would win the war. But for all of their planning, they were unable to respond to the uncertainty and confusion of the battlefield. In the Great War, one historian has noted,

CHRONOLOGY

WORLD WAR I BEGINS

Assassination of Archduke Franz Ferdinand of Austria	June 28, 1914
Austria and Russia mobilize for war	July 28, 1914
Germany declares war on Russia and France	August 1–3, 1914
Britain enters war against Germany	August 4, 1914

military success was achieved "through improvisation, not planning."

The Germans based their offensive on the plans of Count Alfred von Schlieffen. The Schlieffen Plan was designed to suit Germany's efficient, well-equipped, but outnumbered army. It called for attacking France first to secure a quick victory that would neutralize the Western Front, and free the German army to fight Russia in the east. For over a month, the German army advanced swiftly. Yet the plan overestimated the army's physical and logistical capabilities. The speed of the operation—advancing twenty to twenty-five miles a day—was simply too much for soldiers and supply lines to keep up with. They were also slowed by the resistance of the poorly armed but determined Belgian army and by the intervention of Britain's small but highly professional field army. There were also changes of plan. First fearing the Russians would move faster than expected, German commanders altered Schlieffen's plan by dispatching some troops to the east instead of committing them all to the assault on France. Second, they chose to attack Paris from the northeast instead of completely circling to the southwest.

Nevertheless, German plans seemed to be working during August. French attacks into Alsace-Lorraine were a chaotic failure, and casualties mounted as the French lines retreated toward Paris. Yet German successes began to erode. The Belgian and British defense collapsed the German front into a single major thrust towards Paris. In September, with the Germans just thirty miles outside of the capital, Britain and France launched a successful counteroffensive at the battle of the Marne. The German line retreated to the Aisne

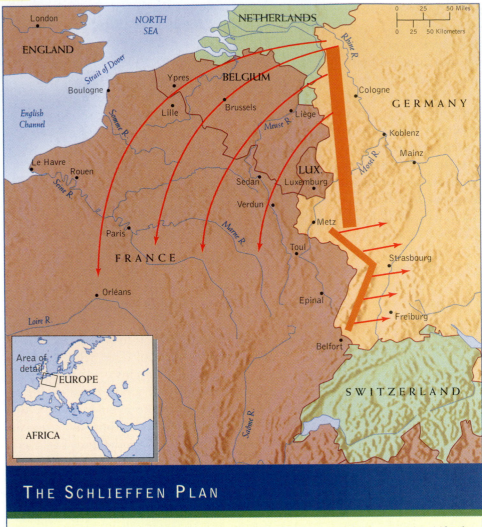

THE SCHLIEFFEN PLAN

This map details the plan developed by the Prussian general and strategist Alfred von Schlieffen in the 1890s. Schlieffen outlined the plan as part of what he believed was inevitable conflict with Russia. Why did Schlieffen seek to send German military resources to France in the event of a war with Russia? Why would he wish to defeat France first? What does the willingness of the German high command to commit to the violation of neutral territory (in this case Belgium) suggest about the breakdown of the diplomatic system carved out over the previous two generations?

river, and the Schlieffen Plan was dead. After the Marne, unable to advance, the armies tried to outflank one another to the north, creating a race to the sea that neither side won. After four months of swift charges across open ground, Germany set up a fortified, defensive position that the Allies could not break. Along an immovable front, stretching over four hundred miles from the northern border of Switzerland to the English Channel, the Great Powers dug fortifications for a protracted battle. By Christmas, trench warfare was born, and the war had just begun.

STALEMATE, 1915

Why did the war become a stalemate?

In the search for new points of attack, both the Allies and the Central Powers added new partners. The Ottoman empire (Turkey) joined Germany and Austria at the end of 1914. In May 1915, Italy joined the Allies, persuaded by the popular support of its citizens and by the lure of land and money. The entry of these new belligerents expanded the geography of the war and introduced the possibility of breaking the stalemate in the west by waging offensives on other fronts.

GALLIPOLI AND NAVAL WARFARE

Turkey's involvement, in particular, altered the dynamics of the war, for it threatened Russia's supply lines and endangered Britain's control of the Suez Canal. To defeat Turkey quickly—and in hopes of bypassing the western stalemate—the British First Lord of the Admiralty, Winston Churchill (1911–1915), argued for a naval offensive in the Dardanelles, the narrow strait separating Europe and Asia Minor. Under particularly incompetent leadership, however, the Royal Navy lacked adequate planning, supply lines, and maps to mount a successful campaign. The Allies attempted a land invasion of the Gallipoli peninsula, beginning on April 25, 1915. The combined force of French, British, Australian, and New Zealand troops made little headway, however. The Turks defended the narrow coast from positions high on fortified cliffs, and the shores were covered with nearly impenetrable barbed wire. The battle became entrenched on the beaches at Gallipoli, and the casualties mounted for seven months before the Allied commanders admitted defeat and ordered a withdrawal in December. The Gallipoli campaign—the first large-scale amphibious attack in history—was a major defeat for the Allies. It brought death into London's neighborhoods and the cities of Britain's industrial north. Casualties were particularly devastating in the "white dominions"—practically every town and hamlet in Australia, New Zealand, and Canada lost young men, sometimes all the sons of a single family.

By 1915 both sides realized that fighting this prolonged and costly "modern" war would require countries to mobilize all of their resources. The Allies started to wage war on the economic front. Germany was vulnerable, dependent as it was on imports for at least one third of its food supply. The Allies' naval blockade against all of central Europe aimed to slowly drain their opponents of food and raw materials. Germany responded with a submarine blockade, threatening to attack any vessel in the seas around Great Britain.

Lusitania, drawing by Claus Bergen, 1915. The sinking of the passenger liner *Lusitania* by a German submarine provoked outrage from the Allied countries, as well as the United States.

The Lines of Battle on the Western Front. A British reconnaissance photo showing three lines of German trenches (right), No Man's Land (the black strip in the center), and the British trenches (partially visible to the left). The upper right hand quadrant of the photo shows communications trenches linking the front to the safe area.

On May 7, 1915, the German submarine *U-20*, without warning, torpedoed the passenger liner *Lusitania*, which was secretly carrying war supplies. The attack killed 1,198 people, including 128 Americans. The attack provoked the animosity of the United States, and Germany was forced to promise that it would no longer fire without warning. (This promise proved only temporary: in 1917 Germany would again declare unrestricted submarine warfare, drawing America into the war.) Although the German blockade against Britain destroyed more tonnage, the blockade against Germany was more devastating in the long run, as the continued war effort placed increasing demands on the national economy.

TRENCH WARFARE

While the war escalated economically and politically, life in the trenches remained largely the same: a cramped and miserable existence of daily routines and continual killing. Some twenty-five thousand miles of trenches snaked along the Western Front, normally in three lines on each side of "No Man's Land." The front line was the

attack trench, lying anywhere from fifty yards to a mile away from the enemy. Behind the front was the second line, a support trench; and behind that, a third trench for reserves. But despite the similar layouts, the two sides' trenches were remarkably different. The Germans saw their position as permanent, and they built elaborate bunkers—fully enclosed rooms with electric light, running water, and overstuffed furniture. Some even had kitchens, wallpaper, curtains, and doorbells. These comforts contrasted sharply with the ramshackle constructions of the French and British, who refused to abandon their offensive strategy, and so saw little value in fortifying a defensive position. The British trenches were wet, cold, and filthy. Rain turned the dusty corridors into squalid mud pits and flooded the floors up to waist level.

As the war progressed, new weapons added to the frightening dimensions of daily warfare. Besides artillery, machine guns, and barbed wire, the instruments of war now included exploding bullets, liquid fire, and poison gas. Gas, in particular, brought visible change to the battlefront. First used effectively by the Germans in April 1915 at the second battle of Ypres, poison gas was not only physically devastating—especially in its later forms—but also psychologically disturbing. The deadly cloud frequently hung over the trenches, although the quick appearance of gas masks limited its effectiveness. Like other new weapons, poison gas solidified the lines and took more lives, but could not end the stalemate. Soldiers grew accustomed to the stalemate, while their leaders plotted ways to end it.

SLAUGHTER IN THE TRENCHES: THE GREAT BATTLES, 1916–1917

Why did the Allies persist with an offensive strategy?

The bloodiest battles of all—those that epitomize the First World War—occurred in 1916–1917. These battles encapsulated the military tragedy of the war: a strategy of soldiers in cloth uniforms marching against machine guns. The result, of course, was carnage. The common response to these staggering losses was to replace the generals in charge. But though commanders changed, commands did not. Military planners continued to believe that their original strategies were the right ones, and that their plans had simply been frustrated by bad luck and German determination. The "cult of the offensive" insisted that a breakthrough was possible with enough troops and enough weapons.

But the manpower needed could not be moved efficiently or protected adequately. Railroad networks made it possible to bring large numbers of troops to the front, but mobility ended there. Heavy mud, labyrinthine trenches, and tangles of barbed wire made movement arduous, if not impossible. More important, the new technologies of killing made movement deadly. Unprotected soldiers armed with rifles, grenades, and bayonets were simply no match for machine guns and deep trenches. Another major problem of military strategy—and another explanation for the continued slaughter—was the lack of effective communication between the front lines and general headquarters. If something went wrong at the front (which happened frequently) it was impossible for the leaders to know in time to make meaningful corrections. As the great battles of the Great War illustrate, firepower had outpaced mobility, and the Allied generals simply did not know how to respond.

VERDUN

The first of these major battles was the German attack on the French stronghold of Verdun, near France's eastern border, in February 1916. Germany's goal was not necessarily to take the city, but rather to break French morale—France's "remarkable devotion"—at a moment of critical weakness. One million shells were fired on the first day of battle, inaugurating a ten-month struggle of back-and-forth fighting, offensives and counteroffensives of intense ferocity, at enormous cost and zero gain. Neither side could gain a real advantage—one small village on the front changed hands thirteen times in one month alone—but both sides incurred devastating losses of life. By the end of June, over four hundred thousand French and German soldiers were dead. In the end, however, the advantage fell to the French. They simply survived, and bled the Germans as badly as they suffered themselves.

THE SOMME

Meanwhile, the British opened their own offensive against Germany farther west, beginning the battle of the Somme on June 24, 1916. The Allied attack began with a fierce five-day bombardment, blasting the German lines with a massive amount of artillery. The blasts could be heard all the way across the English Channel. The British assumed that this preliminary attack would break the mesh of German wire, destroy Germany's trenches, and clear the way for Allied troops to advance forward and upright, virtually unprotected. They were tragically wrong. The shells the British used were designed for surface combat, not to penetrate the deep, reinforced trenches dug by the Germans. When the British soldiers were ordered "over the top" toward enemy lines, they found themselves snared in wire and facing fully operational German machine guns. A few British commanders who had disobeyed orders and brought their men forward before the shelling ended were able to break through German lines. Elsewhere it was hardly a battle; whole British divisions were simply mowed down. Those who made it to the enemy trenches faced bitter hand-to-hand combat with pistols, grenades, knives, bayonets, and bare hands. On the first day of battle alone, a stunning twenty thousand British soldiers died, and another forty thousand were wounded. The carnage continued from July until mid-November, resulting in massive casualties on both sides: five hundred thousand German, four hundred thousand British, and two hundred thousand French. The losses were unimaginable, and the outcome was equally hard to fathom: for all their sacrifices, neither side made any real gains.

Off the Western Front, fighting produced further stalemate. The Austrians continued to fend off attacks in Italy and Macedonia, while the Russians mounted a successful offensive against them on the Eastern Front. The initial Russian success brought Romania into the war on Russia's side, but the Central Powers quickly retaliated and knocked the Romanians out of the war within a few months. The war at sea was equally indecisive, with neither side willing to risk the loss of enormously expensive battleships. The British and German navies fought only one major naval battle early in 1916, which ended in stalemate. Afterward they used their fleets primarily in the economic war of blockades.

As a year of great bloodshed and growing disillusionment, 1916 showed that not even the superbly organized Germans had the mobility or fast-paced communications to win the western ground war. Increasingly, warfare would be turned against entire nations, including civilian populations on the "home front" and in the far reaches of the European empires.

> By the end of June, over four hundred thousand French and German soldiers were dead.

Verdun, 1916. French soldiers look out from their trenches during a round of shelling. A dead body lies at the right.

WAR OF EMPIRES

What was the role of empire in World War I?

Coming as it did at the height of European imperialism, the Great War quickly became a war of empires, with far-reaching repercussions. As the demands of warfare rose, Europe's colonies provided soldiers and material support. Britain brought in soldiers from Canada, Australia, New Zealand, India, and South Africa. These colonial troops fought with the Allies on the Western Front, as well as in Mesopotamia and Persia against the Turks and in East Africa against Germany. They suffered eight hundred thousand casualties, with one fourth fatalities—losses double those of the United States. Colonial recruits were also employed in industry. In France, the international labor force numbered over two hundred fifty thousand—including workers from China, Vietnam, Egypt, India, the West Indies, and South Africa.

With the stalemate in Europe, colonial areas also became strategically important theaters for armed engage-

ment. Although the campaign against Turkey began poorly for Britain with the debacle at Gallipoli, beginning in 1916 Allied forces won a series of battles, pushing the Turks out of Egypt and eventually capturing Baghdad, Jerusalem, Beirut, and other cities throughout the Middle East. The British commander in Egypt and Palestine was Edmund Allenby (1919–1925), who led a multinational army against the well-drilled Turks. Allenby was a shrewd general and an excellent manager of men and supplies in desert conditions, but in his campaigns the support of different Arab peoples seeking independence from the Turks proved crucial. Allenby allied himself to the successful Bedouin revolts that split the Ottoman empire; the British officer T. E. Lawrence (1914–1918) popularized the Arabs' guerrilla actions. When one of the senior Bedouin aristocrats, the emir Abdullah, captured the strategic port of Aqaba in July 1917, Lawrence took credit and entered popular mythology as "Lawrence of Arabia."

Britain encouraged Arab nationalism for its own strategic purposes, offering a qualified acknowledgment of Arab political aspirations. At the same time, for similar but conflicting strategic reasons, the British declared their support of "the establishment in Palestine of a national home for the Jewish people." Britain's foreign secretary, Arthur Balfour, made the pledge. European Zionists, seeking a Jewish homeland, took the Balfour Declaration very seriously. The conflicting pledges to Bedouin leaders and Zionists sowed the seeds of future Arab-Israeli conflict. The war drew Europe more deeply into the Middle East, where conflicting dependencies and commitments created numerous postwar problems.

IRISH REVOLT

Britain's own empire was also vulnerable, and the demands of war strained precarious bonds to the breaking point. Before the war, long-standing tensions between Irish Catholics and the Protestant British government had reached fever pitch, and civil war was likely. The Sinn Fein ("Ourselves Alone") party had formed in 1900 to fight for Irish independence, and a home rule bill had passed Parliament in 1912. But with the outbreak of war in 1914, national interests took precedence over domestic politics: the "Irish question" was tabled, and two hundred thousand Irishmen volunteered for the British army. The problem festered,

however, and on Easter Sunday, 1916, a group of nationalists revolted in Dublin. The British army arrived with artillery and machine guns; they shelled parts of Dublin and crushed the uprising within a week.

The revolt was a military disaster, but it was a striking political success. Britain shocked the Irish public by executing the rebel leaders. Even the British prime minister David Lloyd George (1916–1922) thought the military governor in Dublin exceeded his authority with these executions. The martyrdom of the "Easter Rebels" seriously damaged Britain's relationship with its Irish Catholic subjects. The deaths galvanized the cause of Irish nationalism and touched off guerrilla violence that kept Ireland in turmoil for years. Finally, a new home rule bill was enacted in 1920, establishing separate parliaments for the Catholic south of Ireland and for Ulster, the northeastern counties where the majority population was Protestant. The leaders of the so-called Dáil Éireann (Irish Assembly), which had proclaimed an Irish Republic in 1918 and therefore been outlawed by Britain, rejected the bill, but accepted a treaty that granted dominion status to Catholic Ireland in 1921. Dominion was followed almost immediately by civil war between those who

Easter Rebellion, Dublin, 1916. British troops line up behind a moveable barricade made up of household furniture during their repression of the brief, ill-fated Irish revolt.

abided by the treaty and those who wanted to absorb Ulster, but the conflict ended in an uneasy compromise. The Irish Free State was established, and British sovereignty was partially abolished in 1937. Full status as a republic came, with some American pressure and Britain's exhausted indifference, in 1945.

The Home Front

How did the war change women's lives?

When the war of attrition began in 1915, the belligerent governments were unprepared for the strains of sustained warfare. The costs of war—in both money and manpower—were staggering. In 1914 the war cost Germany 36 million marks per day (five times the cost of the war of 1870), and by 1918 the cost had skyrocketed to 146 million marks per day. Great Britain had estimated it would need one hundred thousand soldiers but ended up mobilizing 3 million. The enormous task of feeding, clothing, and equipping the army became as much of a challenge as breaking through enemy lines. Bureaucrats and industrialists led the effort to mobilize the "home front," focusing all parts of society on the single goal of military victory. The term *total war* was introduced to describe this intense mobilization of society. Goverment propagandists insisted that civilians were as important to the war effort as soldiers, and in many ways they were. As workers, taxpayers, and consumers, civilians were vital parts of the war economy. They produced munitions, purchased war bonds, and shouldered the burden of tax hikes, inflation, and material privations.

Women in the War

As Europe's adult men left farms and factories to become soldiers, the composition of the work force changed: thousands of women were recruited into fields that had previously excluded them. Young people, foreigners, and unskilled workers were also pressed into newly important tasks; in the case of colonial workers, their experiences had equally critical repercussions. But because they were more visible, it was women who became symbolic of many of the changes brought by the Great War. In Germany, one third of the labor force in heavy industry was female by the end of the war, and in France, 684,000 women worked in the munitions industry alone. In the villages of France, England, and Germany, women became mayors, school principals, and mail carriers. Hundreds of thousands of women worked with the army as nurses and ambulance drivers, jobs that brought them very close to the front lines.

In some cases, war offered new opportunities. Middle-class women often said that the war broke down the restrictions on their lives; those in nursing learned to drive and acquired rudimentary medical knowledge. At home they could now ride the train, walk the street, or go out to dinner without an older woman present to chaperone them. In terms of gender roles, an enormous gulf sometimes seemed to separate the wartime world from nineteenth-century Victorian society. In one of the most famous autobiographies of the war, Vera Brittain's *Testament of Youth*, Brittain (1896–1970) recorded the dramatic new social norms that she and others forged during the rapid changes of wartime. "As a generation of women we were now sophisticated to an extent which was revolutionary when compared with the romantic ignorance of 1914. Where we had once spoken with polite evasion of 'a certain condition,' or 'a certain profession,' we now unblushingly used the words 'pregnancy' and 'prostitution.'"

How long lasting were these changes? In the aftermath of the war, governments and employers scurried to send women workers home, in part to give jobs to veterans, in part to deal with male workers' complaints that women were undercutting their wages. Efforts to demobilize women faced real barriers. Many women wage earners—widowed, charged with caring for relatives, or faced with inflation and soaring costs—needed their earnings more than ever. It was also difficult to persuade women workers who had grown accustomed to the relatively higher wages in heavy industry to return to their poorly paid traditional sectors of employment: the textile and garment industries and domestic service. Governments passed "natalist" policies to encourage women to go home, marry, and most important, have children. These policies did make maternity benefits—time off, medical care, and some allowances for the poor—available to women for the first time. Nonetheless, birth rates had been falling across Europe by the early twentieth century, and they continued to do so after the war. One upshot of the war was the increased availability of birth control—Marie Stopes (1880–1958) opened a birth-control clinic in London in 1921—and a combination of economic hardship, increased knowledge, and the demand for freedom made men and women more likely to use it. Universal suffrage, and the vote for all adult men and women, and for women in particular, had been one of the most controversial issues in European politics before the war. At the end of the fighting it came in a legislative rush. Britain was first off the mark, granting the vote to all men and women over thirty with the Representation of the People Act in 1918; the United States gave women the vote with the Nineteenth Amendment the following year. Germany's new republic and the Soviet Union did likewise. France was much slower to offer woman suffrage (1945), but did provide rewards and incentives for the national effort.

MOBILIZING RESOURCES

Along with mobilizing the labor front, the wartime governments had to mobilize men and money. All the belligerent countries had conscription laws before the war, except for Great Britain. Military service. The French began the war with about 4.5 million trained soldiers, but by the end of 1914—just four months into the war—three hundred thousand were dead and six hundred thousand injured. Conscripting citizens and mustering colonial troops became increasingly important. Eventually, France called up 8 million citizens: almost two thirds of Frenchmen aged 18 to 40. In 1916, the British finally introduced conscription, dealing a serious blow to civilian morale; by the summer of 1918, half its army was under nineteen.

Financing the war was another heavy obstacle. Governments had to borrow money or print more of it.

> In 1916, the British finally introduced conscription, dealing a serious blow to civilian morale; by the summer of 1918, half its army was under nineteen.

The Allied nations borrowed heavily from the British, who borrowed even more from the United States. And though economic aid from the United States was a decisive factor in the Allies' victory, it left Britain with a $4.2 billion debt and hobbled the United Kingdom as a financial power after the war. The situation was far worse for Germany, which faced a total blockade of money and goods. In an effort to get around this predicament, and lacking an outside source of cash, the German government funded its war effort largely by increasing the money supply. The amount of paper money in circulation increased by over 1,000 percent during the war, triggering a dramatic rise in inflation. For middle-class people living on pensions or fixed incomes, these price hikes were a push into poverty.

THE STRAINS OF WAR, 1917

The demands of total war worsened as the conflict dragged into 1917. On the front lines, morale fell as war-weary soldiers began to see the futility of their commanders' strategies.

The war's toll also mounted for civilians, who often suffered from the same shortages of basic supplies that afflicted the men on the front. In 1916–1917, the lack of clothing, food, and fuel was aggravated in central Europe by abnormally and unbearably cold and wet weather. These strains provoked rising discontent on the home front. In urban areas, where undernourishment was worst, people stood in lines for hours to

Women at Work. The all-out war effort combined with a manpower shortage at home brought women into factories across Europe in unparalleled numbers. In this photo men and women work side by side in a British shell factory.

ONE WOMAN'S WAR

Vera Brittain (1893–1970) was talented, ambitious, and privileged. She was among the few women to attend Oxford University the year before the war. When war broke out, her fiancé enlisted in the British army. Brittain later joined the Voluntary Aid Detachment and served as a nurse in Europe and in the Mediterranean. In the following excerpt from her memoir, Testament of Youth, *Brittain writes home to her family from France in 1917, worrying about morale on the home front. She also reflects on women's different and often conflicting duties, and on what the war meant to her as a sheltered girl from a well-to-do family.*

"Conditions . . . certainly seem very bad," I wrote to my family on January 10th [1917] . . . "But do if you can," I implored, "try to carry on without being too despondent and make other people do the same . . . for the great fear in the Army and all its appurtenances out here is not that it will ever give up itself, but that the civil population at home will fail us by losing heart—and so of course morale—just at the most critical time. . . .

This despondency at home was certainly making many of us in France quite alarmed: because we were women we feared perpetually that, just as our work was reaching its climax, our families would need our youth and vitality for their own support. One of my cousins, the daughter of an aunt, had already been summoned home from her canteen work in Boulogne; she was only one of many, for as the War continued to wear out strength and spirits, the middle-aged generation, having irrevocably yielded up its sons, began to lean with increasing weight upon its daughters. . . .

What exhausts women in wartime is not the strenuous and unfamiliar tasks that fall upon them, nor even the hourly dread of death for husbands or lovers or brothers or sons; it is the incessant conflict between personal and national claims which wears out their energy and breaks their spirit. . . .

When I was a girl . . . I imagined that life was individual, one's own affair; that the events happening in the world outside were important enough in their own way, but were personally quite irrelevant. Now, like the rest of my generation, I have had to learn again and again . . . about the invasion of personal preoccupations by the larger destinies of mankind, and at last to recognise that no life is really private, or isolated, or self-sufficient. People's lives were entirely their own, perhaps . . . when the world seemed enormous, and all its comings and goings were slow and deliberate. But this is so no longer, and never will be again, since man's inventions have eliminated so much of distance and time; for better, for worse, we are now each of us part of the surge and swell of great economic and political movements, and whatever we do, as individuals or as nations, deeply affects everyone else.

Vera Brittain, *Testament of Youth: An Autobiographical Study of the Years 1900–1925* (London, New York: Penguin Books, 1989), pp. 401, 422–423, 471–472.

get food and fuel rations that scarcely met their most basic needs. Consumers worried aloud that speculators were hoarding supplies and creating artificial shortages, selling tainted goods, and profiting from others' miseries. They decried the government's "reckless inattention" to families. Governments, however, were concentrated on the war effort and faced difficult decisions about who needed supplies the most—soldiers at the front, workers in the munitions industry, or hungry and cold families.

Hunger continued despite mass bureaucratic control. Governments regulated not only food but also working hours and wages, and unhappy workers directed their anger at the state, adding a political dimension to labor disputes and household needs. The

bread lines, filled mainly by women, were flash points of political dissent, petty violence, even large-scale riots. Likewise, the class conflicts of prewar Europe had been briefly muffled by the outbreak of war and mobilization along patriotic lines, but as the war ground on, political tensions reemerged with new intensity. Thousands of strikes erupted throughout Europe, involving millions of frustrated workers. In April of 1917, three hundred thousand in Berlin went on strike to protest ration cuts. In May, a strike of Parisian seamstresses touched off a massive work stoppage that included even white-collar employees and munitions workers. Shipbuilders and steelworkers in Glasgow went on strike as well, and the British government replied by sending armored cars to "Red Glasgow." Stagnation had given way to crisis on both sides. The strains of total war and the resulting social upheavals threatened political regimes throughout Europe. Governments were pushed to their limits. The Russian Revolution, which resulted in the overthrow of the tsar and the rise of Bolshevism, was only the most dramatic response to widespread social problems.

THE RUSSIAN REVOLUTION

How did the Bolsheviks seize power?

The first country to break under the strain of total war was tsarist Russia. The outbreak of war temporarily united Russian society against a common enemy, but Russia's military effort quickly turned sour. All levels of Russian society became disillusioned with Tsar Nicholas II who was unable to provide leadership, but nonetheless unwilling to open government to those who could. The political and social strains of war brought two revolutions in 1917. The first, in February, overthrew the tsar and established a transitional government. The second, in October, was a communist revolution that marked the emergence of the Soviet Union.

British Propaganda Poster, World War I. The mad beast, meant to represent Germany, with "militarism" on his helmet, threatens British civilization with a club of "Kultur" (culture). All the warring countries produced similar propaganda.

WORLD WAR I AND THE FEBRUARY REVOLUTION

Like the other participants in World War I, Russia entered the war with the assumption that it would be over quickly. Autocratic Russia, plagued by internal difficulties before 1914 (see Chapter 22), could not sustain the political strains of extended warfare. In all the warring countries success depended on leaders' ability not only to command, but also to maintain social and political cooperation. Tsar Nicholas II's political authority had been shaky for many years, undermined by his unpopular actions following the October Revolution of 1905 and his efforts to erode the minimal political power he had grudgingly granted to the Duma, Russia's parliament.

In 1914 the Russians advanced against the Austrians into Galicia in the south, but during 1915 Russia suffered terrible defeats. All of Poland and substantial territory in the Baltics fell to the Germans at the cost of a million Russian casualties. Although the Russian army was the largest in Europe, it was poorly trained and, at the beginning of the war, undersupplied and inadequately equipped. By 1915, to the surprise of many, Russia was producing enough food, clothing, and ammunition, but political problems blocked the supply effort. Demoralized and poorly supplied, the hastily trained peasants in the Russian armies found their will to fight disappearing fast. When word came that the government was requisitioning grain from the countryside to feed the cities, peasants began to desert en masse, returning to their farms to guard their families' holdings. By the end of 1916, a combination of political ineptitude and military defeat brought the Russian state to the verge of collapse.

The same problems that hampered the Russian war effort also crippled the tsar's ability to override domestic discontent and resistance. As the war dragged on, the government faced not only liberal opposition in the Duma, soldiers unwilling to fight, and an increasingly militant labor movement, but also a rebellious urban population. City dwellers were impatient with inflation and shortages of food and fuel. In February 1917, these forces came together in Petrograd (now St. Petersburg). The revolt began on International Women's Day, February 23, an occasion for a loosely organized march of women—workers, mothers, wives, and consumers—demanding food, fuel, and political reform. Within a few days the unrest spiraled into a mass strike of three hundred thousand people. Nicholas II sent in police and military forces to quell the disorder. When nearly sixty thousand troops in Petrograd mutinied and joined the revolt, what was left of the tsar's power evaporated.

> By 1915, to the surprise of many, Russia was producing enough food, clothing, and ammunition, but political problems blocked the supply effort.

Nicholas II abdicated the throne on March 2. This abrupt decision brought a century-long struggle over Russian autocracy to a sudden end.

After the collapse of the monarchy, two parallel centers of power emerged. Each had its own objectives and policies. The first was the provisional government, organized by leaders in the Duma and composed mainly of middle-class liberals. The new government hoped to establish a democratic system under constitutional rule. It acted to grant and secure civil liberties, release political prisoners, and redirect power into the hands of local officials. The other center of power lay with the *soviets*, a Russian term for local councils elected by workers and soldiers. Since 1905, socialists had been active in organizing these councils, which claimed to be the true democratic representatives of the people. The increasingly powerful soviets pressed for social reform, the redistribution of land, and a negotiated settlement with Germany and Austria. Yet the provisional government refused to concede military defeat. Continuing the war effort made domestic reform impossible and cost valuable popular support. More fighting during 1917 was just as disastrous as before, and this time the provisional government paid the price. By autumn desertion in the army was rampant, administering the country was nearly impossible, and Russian politics teetered on the edge of chaos.

THE BOLSHEVIKS AND THE OCTOBER REVOLUTION

The Bolsheviks, a branch of the Russian social democratic movement, had little to do with the events of February 1917. Over the course of the next seven months, however, they became enough of a force to overthrow the provisional government. In 1903 the leadership of the Russian Social Democrats split over revolutionary strategy and the steps to socialism. One group, which won a temporary majority (and chose to call itself the Bolsheviks, or "members of the majority"), favored a centralized party of active revolutionaries. They believed that revolution alone would lead directly to a socialist regime. The Mensheviks ("members of the minority"), like most European socialists, wanted to move toward socialism gradually, supporting "bourgeois" or liberal revolution in the short term. Since peas-

Russian soldiers join the Bolsheviks in front of the Winter Palace, fall 1917.

nounce to a stunned meeting of Soviet representatives that "all power had passed to the Soviets." The head of the provisional government fled to rally support at the front lines, and the Bolsheviks took over the Winter Palace, the seat of the provisional government. The initial stage of the revolution was quick and relatively bloodless. In fact, many observers believed they had seen nothing more than a coup d'état, one that might quickly be reversed.

The Bolsheviks took the opportunity to rapidly consolidate their position. First, they moved against all political competition, beginning with the Soviets. They immediately expelled parties that disagreed with their actions, creating a new government in the soviets comprised entirely of Bolsheviks. Lenin's Bolsheviks ruled socialist Russia, and later the Soviet Union, as a one-party dictatorship.

ants constituted 80–85% of the population, the Mensheviks also reasoned that a proletarian revolution was premature and that Russia needed to complete its capitalist development first. The Mensheviks regained control of the party, but the Bolshevik splinter party survived under the leadership of the young, dedicated revolutionary Vladimir Ilyich Ulyanov, who adopted the pseudonym Lenin.

Lenin believed that the development of Russian capitalism made socialist revolution possible. To bring revolution, he argued, the Bolsheviks needed to organize on behalf of the new class of industrial workers. Without the party's disciplined leadership, Russia's factory workers could not accomplish change on the necessary scale. The Bolshevik's dedication to the singular goal of revolution and their tight, almost conspiratorial organization gave them tactical advantages over larger and more loosely organized opposition parties.

Throughout 1917 the Bolsheviks consistently demanded an end to the war, improvement in working and living conditions for workers, and redistribution of aristocratic land to the peasantry. While the provisional government struggled to hold together the Russian war effort, Lenin led the Bolsheviks on a bolder course, shunning any collaboration with the "bourgeois" government and condemning its imperialist war policies.

In October 1917, Lenin convinced his party to act. On October 25, Lenin appeared from hiding to an-

In the countryside, the new Bolshevik regime did little more than ratify a revolution that had been going on since the summer of 1917. When peasant soldiers on the front heard that a revolution had occurred, they streamed home to take land they had worked for generations and believed was rightfully theirs. The Bolsheviks simply approved the spontaneous redistribution of Russian nobles' land to peasants without compensation to former owners. They nationalized banks and gave workers control of factories.

Most important, the new government sought to take Russia out of the war. It eventually negotiated a separate treaty with Germany, signed at Brest-Litovsk in March 1918. The Bolsheviks surrendered vast Russian territories: the rich agricultural region of Ukraine, Georgia, Finland, Russia's Polish territories, the Baltic states, and more. However humiliating, the treaty ended Russia's role in the fighting and saved the fledgling communist regime from almost certain military defeat at the hands of the Germans. The treaty enraged Lenin's political enemies, both moderates and reactionaries, who were still a force to be reckoned with—and who were prepared to wage a civil war rather than accept the revolution. Withdrawing from Europe's war only plunged the country into a vicious civil conflict (see Chapter 28).

John Reed, an American journalist covering the Russian Revolution, called the events of October "ten days that shook the world." What had been shaken? First, the

Lenin Speaking to Crowds in Moscow. To the right of the platform, in uniform, is Trotsky.

With striking results, Germany shifted its offensive strategy to infiltration by small groups under flexible command. On March 21, Germany initiated a major assault on the west and quickly broke through the Allied lines. The British were hit hardest. Some units, surrounded, fought to the death with bayonets and grenades, but most recognized their plight and surrendered. The British were in retreat everywhere.

When it came in July and August, the Allied counterattack was devastating and quickly gathered steam. New offensive techniques had finally materialized. The Allies improved their use of tanks and the "creeping barrage," in which infantry marched close behind a rolling wall of shells to overwhelm their targets. In another of the war's ironies these new tactics were pioneered by the conservative British, who launched a crushing counterattack in July. The French made use of the burgeoning numbers of American troops, whose generals attacked the Germans with the same harrowing indifference to casualties shown in 1914. When combined with more experienced French and Australian forces, they punched several large holes through German lines, crossing into the "lost provinces" of Alsace and Lorraine by October. At the beginning of November, the sweeping British offensive had joined up with the small Belgian army and was pressing toward Brussels.

The Allies finally brought their material advantage to bear on the Germans, who were suffering acutely by the spring of 1918. This was not only because of the continued effectiveness of the Allied blockade, but also because of growing domestic conflict over war aims. On the front lines, German soldiers were exhausted. Following the lead of their distraught generals, the troops let morale sink, and many surrendered. Popular discontent mounted, and the government, which was now largely in the hands of the military, seemed unable either to win the war or to meet basic household needs.

Germany's network of allies was also coming undone. By the end of September, the Central Powers were headed for defeat. In the Middle East, Allenby's army, which combined Bedouin guerrillas, Indian sepoys, Scottish highlanders, and Australian light cavalry, decisively defeated Ottoman forces in Syria and Iraq. In the Balkans, France's capable battlefield commander, Louis Franchet d'Esperey (1914–1921), completely reorganized the Allied war effort. He transformed the Allied

Allies, for the revolution allowed the Germans to win the war on the Eastern Front. Second, conservative governments, which in the aftermath of the war worried about a wave of revolution sweeping away other regimes. Third, the expectations of many socialists, startled to see a socialist regime gain and hold power in what many considered a backward country. Over the long run, 1917 was to the twentieth century what the French Revolution had been to the nineteenth century. It was a political transformation, it set the agenda for future revolutionary struggles, and it created the frames of mind on the right and the left for the century that followed.

THE ROAD TO GERMAN DEFEAT, 1918

How did the Allies win the war?

Russia's withdrawal dealt an immediate strategic and psychological blow to the Allies. Germany could soothe domestic discontent by claiming victory on the Eastern Front, and it could now concentrate its entire army in the west. The Allies feared that Germany would win the war before the United States, which entered the conflict in April 1917, could make a difference. It almost happened.

expedition that had been sent to Greece and with the help of sympathetic Greek politicians drew that country into the war. The results were remarkable. In September, a three-week offensive by the Greek and Allied forces knocked Bulgaria out of the war. Austria-Hungary faced disaster on all sides, collapsing in Italy as well as the Balkans. Czech and Polish representatives in the Austrian government began pressing for self-government. Croat and Serb politicians proposed a "kingdom of Southern Slavs" (soon known as Yugoslavia). When Hungary joined the chorus for independence the emperor, Karl I, accepted reality and sued for peace. The empire that had started the conflict surrendered on November 3, 1918, and disintegrated soon after.

Germany was now left with the impossible task of carrying on the struggle alone. By the fall of 1918, the country was starving and on the verge of civil war. German forces in Belgium stemmed the British attack short of Brussels but were still reeling from French and American attacks to the south. Revolutionary tremors swelled into an earthquake. On November 8, a republic was proclaimed in Bavaria, and the next day nearly all of Germany was in the throes of revolution. The kaiser's abdication was announced in Berlin on November 9; he fled to Holland early the next morning. His successors immediately took steps to negotiate an armistice. The Germans could do nothing but accept the Allies' terms, so at five o'clock in the morning of November 11, 1918, two German delegates met with the Allied army commander and signed papers officially ending the war. Six hours later the order "cease fire" was given across the Western Front. That night thousands of people danced through the streets of London, Paris, and Rome, engulfed in a different delirium from that four years before, a joyous burst of exhausted relief.

THE UNITED STATES AS A WORLD POWER

The final turning point of the war had been the entry of the United States in April 1917. Although America had supported the Allies financially throughout the war, its official intervention undeniably tipped the scales. The United States created a fast and efficient wartime bureaucracy, instituting conscription in May 1917. Ten million men were registered, and by the next year, three hundred thousand soldiers a month were being shipped "over there." Large amounts of food and supplies also crossed the Atlantic, under the armed protection of the U.S. Navy. This system of convoys effectively neutralized the

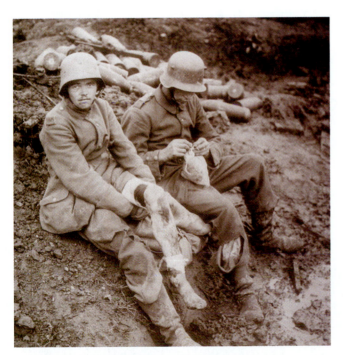

Wounded German Soldiers, 1917. Toward the end of the war, morale among German soldiers plummeted in the face of domestic conflict and the Allied blockade.

CHRONOLOGY

MAJOR EVENTS OF WORLD WAR I AND ITS AFTERMATH, 1914–1920

Battle of the Marne	September 1914
Gallipoli campaign	April–December 1915
Sinking of the *Lusitania*	May 1915
Battle of Verdun	February–July 1916
Battle of the Somme	July–November 1916
Russian Revolution:	
Tsar Nicholas II overthrown	February 1917
Communist Revolution	October 1917
Treaty of Brest-Litovsk	March 1918
Russian Civil War	1918–1920
United States enters the war	April 1917
Final offensives	March–November 1918
Germany surrenders	November 11, 1918
Paris negotiations	1919–1920

TERRITORIAL CHANGES IN EUROPE AND THE NEAR EAST AFTER WORLD WAR I

Note the changes in geography as a result of World War I. What areas were most affected by the changes within Europe, and why? Can you see any obvious difficulties created by the redrawing of the map of Europe? What historical circumstances and/or new threats guided the victors to create such geopolitical anomalies?

threat of German submarines to Allied merchant ships: the number of ships sunk fell from 25 to 4 percent. America's entry—though not immediately decisive—gave a quick, colossal boost to British and French morale, while severely undermining Germany's.

Wilson vowed that America would fight to "make the world safe for democracy," to banish autocracy and militarism, and to establish a league or society of nations in place of the old diplomatic maneuvering. The Americans' primary interest was maintaining the international balance of power. For years, U.S. diplomats and military leaders believed that American security depended on the equilibrium of strength in Europe. American involvement restored the balance in 1918, but the monumental task of establishing peace still lay ahead.

THE PEACE SETTLEMENT

Making peace was a tenuous process, complicated by the conflicting ambitions and interests of the victor nations. Negotiations were held in Paris in 1919 and 1920. In all, five separate treaties were signed, one with each of the defeated nations: Germany, Austria, Hungary, Turkey, and Bulgaria. (The settlement with Germany was called the Treaty of Versailles, after the town in which it was signed.) The peace conference involved representatives from many nations, including small, newly formed states and even non-European ones.

The peace progress began in a spirit of idealism, expressed in Wilson's widely publicized Fourteen Points, which he had promoted as the foundation of a permanent peace. It also called for the "self-determination of peoples" and for the establishment of a League of Nations to settle international conflicts. Thousands of copies of the Fourteen Points had been scattered by Allied planes over the German trenches and behind the lines in an attempt to convince both soldiers and civilians that the Allied nations were striving for a just and durable peace.

The negotiations, however, followed other dictates. Throughout the war, Allied propaganda led soldiers and civilians to believe that their sacrifices to the war effort would be compensated by payments extracted from the enemy; total war demanded total victory. The devastation of the war, and the fiction that Germany could be made to pay for it, made compromise impossible. The settlement with Germany reflected this desire for punishment.

The Versailles treaty required Germany to surrender the "lost provinces" of Alsace and Lorraine to France, and to give up territories in the north to Denmark and a large part of Prussia to the new state of Poland. The treaty gave Germany's coal mines in the Saar basin to France for fifteen years, at which point the German government could buy them back. Germany's province of East Prussia was cut off from the rest of its territory. Germany was also disarmed. It was forbidden to build an air force, while its navy was reduced to a token force to match an army capped at the strength of one hundred thousand volunteers. To protect France and Belgium, all German soldiers and fortifications were to be removed from the Rhine valley.

The most important part of the Versailles treaty, and the part most at odds with Wilson's original plan, was the "war-guilt" provision in Article 231. Versailles held Germany and its allies responsible for the loss and damage suffered by the Allied governments and their citizens "as a consequence of the war imposed upon them by the aggression of Germany and her allies." Germany would be forced to pay reparations on a crippling scale. The exact amount was left to a Reparations Commission, which set the total at $33 billion in 1921. The Germans deeply resented these harsh demands, but others outside Germany also warned of the dangers of punitive reparations. In *The Economic Consequences of the Peace*, the noted British economist John Maynard Keynes (1883–1946) argued that reparations would doom Europe's most important task: repairing the world economy.

The treaties signed by the other Central Powers were based partly on the Allies' strategic interests, but also on the principle of national self-determination. The experience of the prewar years convinced leaders that they should draw nations' boundaries to conform to the ethnic, linguistic, and historical traditions of the people they were to contain. This combined with Wilson's idealism about freedom and equal representation, and seemed sensible to most factions at Versailles. It was more difficult to accomplish in practice. National boundaries did not follow ethnic divisions; they were created according to political dictates of the moment. The frustrated expectations of eastern and central European nationalists, combined with other factors, would produce dangerous challenges to European stability during the 1930s.

The treaties also reflected European ambitions to shore up, or even expand, their overseas empires. The

> Germany would be forced to pay reparations on a crippling scale. The exact amount was left to a Reparations Commission, which set the total at $33 billion in 1921.

settlement with Turkey marked the end of the Ottoman empire. It also created an opportunity for Allied leaders to haggle over the spoils of the dismantled state. It did not, however, create the truly independent kingdoms that Bedouin leaders had hoped for during the war. Choice pieces of land were divided up as "mandates" held by Britain and France. The peoples of the Allies' existing colonies were less fortunate. Well-organized deputations from French West Africa and the Congress Party of India, which favored dominion status in return for the wartime efforts of millions of sepoys who had fought for the British Empire, were also snubbed. Although the European powers spoke about reforming colonial rule, little was done. Many nationalists in the colonies who had favored moderate, legislative change decided that active struggle might be the only answer to the injustices of colonialism.

> Although the European powers spoke about reforming colonial rule, little was done. Many nationalists in the colonies who had favored moderate, legislative change decided that active struggle might be the only answer to the injustices of colonialism.

Incorporated in each of the five peace treaties was the Covenant of the League of Nations, an organization envisioned as the arbiter of world peace but that never achieved the idealistic aims of its founders. The League was handicapped from the start by a number of changes to its original design. The arms-reduction requirement was watered down, and the League's power to enforce it was rendered almost nonexistent. The League received an even more debilitating blow when the United States Congress, citing the long-standing national preference for isolation, refused to approve U.S. membership of the League. Hobbled from the start, the international organization had little potential to avert conflicts. Indeed, the League of Nations' failures originated in, and reflected, the larger problems of power politics that emerged after the war.

CONCLUSION

Europe fought the First World War on every front possible—military, political, social, and economic. Consequently, the war's effects extended far beyond the devastated landscapes of the Western Front. Statistics can only hint at the enormous loss of human life: of the 70 million men who were mobilized, nearly 9 million were killed. Russia, Germany, France, and Hungary recorded the highest number of deaths, but the smaller countries of southeast Europe had the highest percentages of soldiers killed. Almost 40 percent of Serbia's soldiers died in battle. With the addition of war-related deaths cause by privation and disease, Serbia lost 15 percent of its population. In comparison, Britain, France, and Germany lost only 2 to 3 percent of their populations. But the percentages are much more telling if we focus on the young men of the war generation. Germany lost one third of men aged nineteen to twenty-two in 1914. France and Britain sustained similar losses, with mortality among young men reaching eight to ten times the normal rate. This was the "lost generation."

The war planted seeds of political and social discontent around the globe. Relations between Russia and western Europe grew sour and suspicious. The Allied nations feared that Russia would dominate the new states of eastern Europe, building a "Red Bridge" across the continent. Elsewhere, the conflicting demands of colonialism and nationalism struck only a temporary balance, while the redrawn maps left ethnic and linguistic minorities in every country. The fires of discontent raged most fiercely in Germany, where the Treaty of Versailles was decried as outrageously unjust. Nearly all national governments agreed that it would eventually have to be revised. Neither war nor peace had ended the rivalries that caused the First World War.

The war also had powerful and permanent economic consequences. Beset by inflation, debt, and the difficult task of industrial rebuilding, Europe found itself displaced from the center of the world economy. The war had accelerated the decentralization of money and markets. Many Asian, African, and South American nations benefited financially as their economies became less dependent on Europe, and they were better able to profit from Europe's needs for their natural resources. The United States and Japan reaped the biggest gains and emerged leaders in the new world economy.

Socially, the war's most potent legacy was the death and disfigurement of millions. Its most powerful cultural legacy was disillusionment. In the postwar period many younger men and women mistrusted the "old men" who had dragged the world into the war. These feelings of loss and alienation were voiced in the vastly popular genre of "war literature," memoirs and fiction that commemorated the experience of soldiers on the front lines. The German writer and ex-soldier Erich Maria Remarque captured the disillusion of a generation in his novel *All Quiet on the Western Front*: "Through the years our business has been killing;—it was our first calling in life. Our knowledge of life is limited to death. What will happen afterwards? And what shall come out of us?"

That was the main question facing postwar Europe. The struggle to define this new world would increasingly be conceived in terms of rival ideologies—democracy, communism, and fascism—competing for the future of Europe. The eastern autocracies had fallen with the war, but liberal democracy was soon on the decline as well. While militarism and nationalism remained strong, calls for major social reforms gained force during worldwide depression. Entire populations had been mobilized during the war, and they would remain so afterward—active participants in the age of mass politics. Europe was about to embark on two turbulent decades of rejecting and reinventing its old social and political institutions. As Tomas Masaryk, the first president of newly formed Czechoslovakia, described it, postwar Europe was "a laboratory atop a graveyard."

KEY TERMS

Allied Powers	trench warfare	Tsar Nicholas II
Central Powers	Lusitania	Vladimir Lenin
Franz Ferdinand	Sinn Fein	Treaty of Versailles
Schlieffen Plan	Testament of Youth	

SELECTED READINGS

Chickering, Roger. *Imperial Germany and the Great War, 1914–1918.* New York, 1998. An excellent new synthesis.

Eksteins, Modris. *Rites of Spring: The Great War and the Birth of the Modern Age.* New York, 1989. Fascinating, though impressionistic, on war, art, and culture.

Ferro, Marc. *The Great War, 1914–1918.* London, 1973. Very concise overview.

Figes, Orlando. *A People's Tragedy: A History of the Russian Revolution.* New York, 1997. Excellent, detailed narrative.

Fischer, Fritz. *War of Illusions.* New York, 1975. Deals with Germany within the context of internal social and economic trends.

Fitzpatrick, Sheila. *The Russian Revolution, 1917–1932.* New York and Oxford, 1982. Concise overview.

Ferguson, Niall. *The Pity of War.* London, 1998. A fresh look at the war, including strategic issues, international relations, and economics.

Fussell, Paul. *The Great War and Modern Memory.* New York, 1975. A brilliant examination of British intellectuals' attitudes toward the war.

Higonnet, Margaret Randolph, et al., eds. *Behind the Lines: Gender and the Two World Wars.* New Haven, 1987.

Hynes, Samuel. *A War Imagined: The First World War and English Culture.* New York, 1991. The war as perceived on the home front.

Jelavich, Barbara. *History of the Balkans: Twentieth Century.* New York, 1983. Useful for an understanding of the continuing conflict in Eastern Europe.

Joll, James. *The Origins of the First World War.* London, 1984. Comprehensive and very useful.

Keegan, John. *The First World War.* London, 1998. The best overall military history.

Mazower, Mark. *Dark Continent: Europe's Twentieth Century.* New York, 1999. An excellent new survey, attentive to the Balkans and Eastern Europe.

Rabinowitch, Alexander. *The Bolsheviks Come to Power.* New York, 1976. A well-researched and carefully documented account.

Roberts, Mary Louise. *Civilization without Sexes: Reconstructing Gender in Postwar France, 1917–1927.* Chicago, 1994. A prize-winning study of the issues raised by the "new woman."

Smith, Leonard. *Between Mutiny and Obedience: The Case of the French Fifth Infantry Division during World War I.* Princeton, N.J., 1994. An account of mutiny and the reasons behind it.

Stites, Richard. *Revolutionary Dreams: Utopian Visions and Experimental Life in the Russian Revolution.* New York, 1989. The influence of utopian thinking on the revolution.

Williams, John. *The Home Fronts: Britain, France and Germany, 1914–1918.* London, 1972. A survey of life away from the battlefield and the impact of the war on domestic life.

Winter, J. M. *The Experience of World War I.* New York, 1989. Comprehensive illustrated history viewing the war from different perspectives.

CHAPTER TWENTY-FIVE

TURMOIL BETWEEN THE WARS

THE GREAT WAR TOPPLED four empires and left 9 million dead in its wake. Death reached across borders, ideologies, classes, and generations; it touched ancient mansions, industrial cities, towns, and farmsteads across Europe and its overseas dominions. It destroyed lives and futures, shook cherished standards and pillars of stability, and produced haunting revelations of brutality. Coming to terms with the war's incalculable losses produced a wide range of reactions, from dogged efforts to return to prewar "normalcy," to cultural experimentation, repudiation of the past, or the splintering of older political regimes and arrangements. From the perspective of the late 1930s, the most striking development of the interwar period was the near collapse of democracy. At that time, few Western democracies remained. Even in those that did, most notably Great Britain, France, and the United States, regimes were frayed by the same pressures and strains that in other countries wrecked democracy entirely.

The reasons for the decline of democracy varied according to particular national circumstances. We can, however, identify some general causes. The foremost was a series of continuing disruptions in the world economy. These were brought about by dislocations that came in the wake of the First World War and the Versailles reparations settlements, and, later, with the Great Depression of 1929–1933. A second source of the crisis of democracy lay in increased social conflict. Across the West, the strains of war deepened long-standing social rifts, and the disappointments of the postwar period created serious polarization. Many expected the peace to bring change. After the sacrifices of the war years, most citizens had been rewarded with the vote. It was far from clear, however, that their votes counted, or that the traditional elites who dominated the economy and seemed to hold the reins of politics had lost any of their power. Broad swaths of the electorate became increasingly attracted to political parties, many of them extremist, that promised to represent their interests. Finally, nationalism, sharpened by the war, provided a key source of discontent in its aftermath. In Italy and Germany frustrated nationalist sentiment turned against governments. In new countries such as Czechoslovakia, and across

FOCUS QUESTIONS

• How did the Soviet Union industrialize during the 1930s?

• What were the components of Italian fascism?

• Why did German democracy fail?

 • How did the Nazis come to power?

• How did the Western democracies deal with the Great Depression?

• How did the mass media change everyday life?

eastern and southern Europe, friction among national minorities posed enormous problems for relatively fragile democratic regimes.

The most dramatic instance of democracy's decline came with the rise of new authoritarian dictatorships, especially in the Soviet Union, Italy, and Germany. As we shall see, the experiences of those three countries differed significantly as a result of varying historical circumstances and personalities. Yet in each case, many citizens allowed themselves to be persuaded that only drastic measures could bring order from chaos. Those measures, including the elimination of parliamentary government, strict restrictions on political freedom, and increasingly virulent repression of the "enemies" of the state were implemented with a combination of violence, intimidation, and propaganda. That so many citizens seemed willing to sacrifice their freedoms was a measure of their alienation, impatience, or desperation.

THE SOVIET UNION UNDER LENIN AND STALIN

How did the Soviet Union industrialize during the 1930s?

THE RUSSIAN CIVIL WAR

The Bolshevik takeover in October of 1917 was only the beginning of revolutionary events in Russia. After signing a separate peace with Germany in March of 1918, the Bolsheviks, under Lenin's leadership, moved to consolidate their internal political power (see pp. 712–714). But the Bolshevik seizure of power and withdrawal from the war polarized Russian society and ignited a civil war that was far more costly than conflict with Germany. The peace treaty galvanized the enemies of the Bolsheviks, especially those associated with the ousted tsarist regime, who began to attack the new government from the periphery of the old empire. Known collectively as "Whites," the Bolsheviks' opponents were a varied lot, only loosely bound by their common goal of removing the "Reds" from power. Their military force came mainly from supporters of the old regime. The Whites were joined by groups as diverse as liberal supporters of the provisional government, Mensheviks, Social Revolutionaries, and anarchist peasant bands known as "Greens"

who opposed all central state power. The Bolsheviks also faced insurrections from strong nationalist movements in some parts of the former Russian empire, including Ukraine, Georgia, and the north Caucasus regions. Finally, several foreign powers, including the United States, Great Britain, and Japan, launched small but threatening interventions on the periphery of the old empire. Their intervention solidified Bolshevik mistrust of the capitalist world powers, which would, in the Marxist view, naturally oppose the existence of the world's first "socialist" state.

The Bolsheviks eventually won the civil war because they gained greater support—or at least tacit acceptance—from the majority of the population, and because they were better organized for the war effort itself. The Bolsheviks quickly mobilized to fight, foregoing many of their radical concerns about egalitarianism and political self-control in favor of strong bureaucratic and military structures. Leon Trotsky, the revolutionary hero of 1905 and 1917, became the new commissar of war and created a hierarchical, disciplined military machine that grew to some 5 million men by 1920. Trotsky's Red Army triumphed over the White armies by the end of 1920, although fighting continued into 1922. The Bolsheviks also invaded Poland, and nearly reached Warsaw before being thrown back.

When the conflict was over, the country had suffered some one million combat casualties, several million deaths from hunger and disease caused by the war, and one hundred thousand to three hundred thousand executions of noncombatants as part of Red and White terror. The barbarism of the war engendered permanent hatreds within the emerging Soviet nation, especially among ethnic minorities, and it brutalized the fledgling society that came into existence under the new Bolshevik regime.

The civil war also shaped the Bolsheviks' approach to economic aspects of "socialism." On taking power in 1917, Lenin expected to create, for the short term at least, a state-capitalist system that resembled the successful European wartime economies. The civil war pushed the new government toward a more radical economic stance known as "war communism." The Bolsheviks began to requisition grain from the peasantry, outlawed private trade in consumer goods as "speculation," militarized production facilities, and abolished money. Some radical Bolsheviks hoped that war communism would replace the capitalist system that had collapsed in 1917.

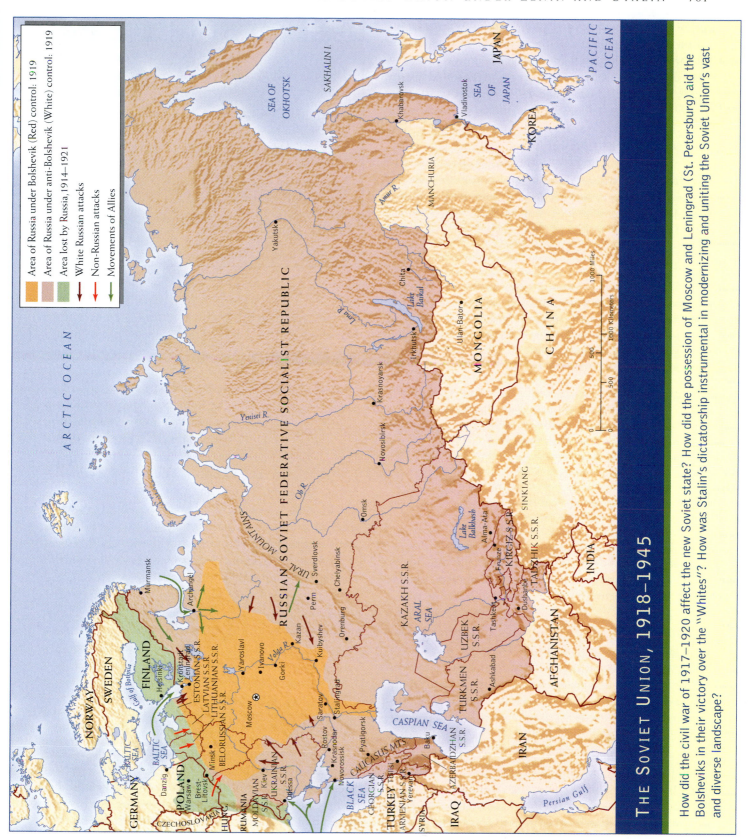

THE SOVIET UNION, 1918–1945

How did the civil war of 1917–1920 affect the new Soviet state? How did the possession of Moscow and Leningrad (St. Petersburg) aid the Bolsheviks in their victory over the "Whites"? How was Stalin's dictatorship instrumental in modernizing and uniting the Soviet Union's vast and diverse landscape?

Such hopes were largely unfounded. War communism, though it sustained the civil war effort, further disrupted the already war-ravaged economy. The civil war devastated Russian industry and emptied major cities. Industrial output had fallen by 1920–1921 to only 20 percent of prewar levels. Most devastating were the effects of war communism on agriculture. On the one hand, the civil war had solved the "land question" to the benefit of peasants, who spontaneously seized and redistributed noble lands. Nonetheless, the agricultural system was severely disrupted by the civil war, by the grain requisitioning of war communism, and by the outlawing of all private trade in grain. Large-scale famine resulted in 1921 and claimed some 5 million lives.

As the civil war came to a close, urban workers and soldiers became increasingly impatient with the Bolshevik regime, which had promised socialism and workers' control but had delivered something more akin to a military dictatorship. Large-scale strikes and protests broke out in late 1920, but the Bolsheviks moved swiftly and effectively to subdue the "popular revolts." In crushing dissent, the Bolshevik regime that emerged from the civil war had made a clear statement that internal competition would not be tolerated.

> In crushing dissent, the Bolshevik regime that emerged from the civil war had made a clear statement that internal competition would not be tolerated.

THE NEP PERIOD

In response to these political and economic difficulties, the Bolsheviks abandoned war communism and in March 1921 embarked on a radically different course known as the New Economic Policy (NEP). The NEP reverted to the state capitalism that had been tried immediately after the Revolution. The state was to continue to own all major industry and monetary concerns, while individuals were to be allowed to own private property, trade freely within limits, and most important, farm their land for their own benefit. Peasants were encouraged to "enrich themselves" so that their taxes could support urban industrialization and the working class. Lenin himself described the NEP as "one step backward in order to take two steps forward."

The NEP was undeniably successful in allowing Soviet agriculture to recover from the civil war; by 1924 agricultural harvests had returned to prewar levels. It was a prosperous time for peasants—what one historian describes as the "golden age of the Russian peasantry." Peasants were largely left alone to do as they pleased,

CHRONOLOGY

THE EARLY SOVIET UNION, 1917–1929

Bolsheviks seize power	October 1917
Treaty of Brest-Litovsk	March 1918
Russian civil war	1918–1920
Bolsheviks suppress nationalist rebellions	1920–1921
Launch of the NEP	1921
Lenin dies	1924
Stalin, Trotsky, Bukharin vie for power	1924–1928
Stalin seizes full power	1928–1929

and they responded by redividing noble lands among themselves to level wealth discrepancies between rich and poor, by reinforcing traditional social structures in the countryside (especially the peasant commune), and by producing enough grain to feed the country, though they continued to use very primitive farming methods to do so. The NEP was less successful, however, in encouraging peasants to participate in markets to benefit urban areas. The result was a series of shortages in grain deliveries to cities, a situation that prompted many Bolsheviks to call for revival of the radical economic practices of war communism. The fate of these radical proposals, however, was tied to the fate of the man who would, contrary to all expectations, replace Lenin as the leader of the USSR and become one of the most notorious dictators of all time: Joseph Stalin.

STALIN AND THE "REVOLUTION FROM ABOVE"

Stalin's rise was swift and unpredicted. His political success was rooted in intraparty conflicts in the 1920s, but it was also closely tied to the abrupt end of the NEP period in the late 1920s and to the beginning of a massive program of social and economic modernization.

Stalin (1879–1953) was a Bolshevik from the Caucasus nation of Georgia; his real name was Iosep Jughashvili. He was an important member of the Bolshevik party before and during the Russian Revolution. Yet

Lenin and Stalin. Under Stalin this picture was used to show his close relationship with Lenin. In fact, the photograph has been doctored.

Stalin was not one of the central figures of the early Bolshevik party, and he was certainly not a front runner for party leadership. The question of Lenin's successor arose with the leader's poor health after 1922 and his death in 1924, but the civil war hero Leon Trotsky was widely assumed to be the best candidate for Lenin's position.

Though not a brilliant orator like Trotsky, Stalin was nonetheless a master political strategist, and he played the game of internal party politics almost without fault after Lenin's death. Trotsky was the first to go, driven out of top party circles by a coalition of Stalin and others who, ironically, feared Trotsky's desire to take control of the party himself. Stalin then turned on his former allies and removed them in turn.

Stalin's campaign against his former allies was not just political. It was also connected to Stalin's desire to discard the NEP system and to launch an all-out industrialization drive. Stalin began to push for an increase in the tempo of industrialization as early as 1927, prompted by fears of "falling behind" the West and by the perceived threat of

> Between 1929 and 1933, some 1.5 million peasants were uprooted, dispossessed of their property, and resettled from their farmlands to either inhospitable reaches of the Soviet east and north or to poor farmland closer to their original homes.

another world war. Almost all of the top-level Bolshevik leaders supported Stalin's plan to step up the tempo of industrialization. But hardly anybody supported what happened next: an abrupt turn toward forced industrialization and collectivization of agriculture.

In 1927 a poor harvest caused yet another crisis in the grain-collection system. In early 1928 Stalin ordered local officials in the distant Urals and Siberian areas, which were alleged to have bumper crops but to be behind in tax payments, to begin requisitioning grain. He soon applied this revival of war communism to the entire country. In 1929, the upper echelons of the party abruptly reversed the course set by NEP, and embarked on the complete collectivization of agriculture, beginning in the major grain-growing areas. Peasants there were to be convinced, by force if necessary, to give up private farmlands. They would either join collective farms, pooling resources and giving a set portion of the harvest to the state, or work on state farms, where they were paid as laborers.

COLLECTIVIZATION

Collectivization was initially expected to be a gradual process, but in late 1929 Stalin embarked on collectivization of agriculture by force. Within a few months, the Politburo began to issue orders to use force against peasants who resisted collectivization, though those orders were at first shrouded in secrecy. Local party and police officials forced peasants to give up their private land, farming implements, and livestock and to join collective farms. Peasants resisted, often violently. There were some sixteen hundred large-scale rebellions in the USSR between 1929 and 1933; some involved several thousand people, and quelling them required military intervention, including the use of artillery. Stalin deftly called the process to a temporary halt in early 1930, but soon thereafter ordered the process to proceed more gradually, and by 1935 collectivization of agriculture was complete in most areas of the USSR.

To facilitate collectivization, Stalin also launched an all-out attack on peasants designated as "kulaks" (a derogatory term for well-to-do farmers, literally meaning "tight-fisted ones"). Most kulaks, though, were not any better off than their neighbors, and the word became one of many terms for peasants hostile to collectivization. Between 1929 and 1933, some 1.5 million peasants were uprooted, dispossessed of their property, and resettled

STALIN'S INDUSTRIALIZATION OF THE SOVIET UNION

"THE TASKS OF BUSINESS EXECUTIVES"

*Stalin gave the following speech at a Conference of Managers of Socialist Industry in 1931. In his usual style, he invoked
fears of Soviet backwardness and Russian nationalism while summoning all to take up the task of industrial production.*

It is sometimes asked whether it is not possible to slow down the tempo somewhat, to put a check on the movement. No, comrades, it is not possible! The tempo must not be reduced! On the contrary, we must increase it as much as is within our powers and possibilities. This is dictated to us by our obligations to the workers and peasants of the USSR. This is dictated to us by our obligations to the working class of the whole world.

To slacken the tempo would mean falling behind. And those who fall behind get beaten. But we do not want to be beaten. No, we refuse to be beaten! One feature of the history of old Russia was the continual beatings she suffered because of her backwardness. She was beaten by the Mongol khans. She was beaten by the Turkish beys. . . . She was beaten by the British and French capitalists. She was beaten by the Japanese barons. All beat her—for her backwardness: for military backwardness, for cultural backwardness, for political backwardness, for industrial backwardness, for agricultural backwardness. . . .

We are fifty or a hundred years behind the advanced countries. We must make good this distance in ten years. Either we do it, or we shall be crushed. . . .

In ten years at most we must make good the distance which separates us from the advanced capitalist countries. We have all the 'objective' possibilities for this. The only thing lacking is the ability to take proper advantage of these possibilities. And that depends on us. *Only* on us! . . . It is time to put an end to the rotten policy of non-interference in production. It is time to adopt a new policy, a policy adapted to the present times—the policy of interfering in everything. If you are a factory manager, then interfere in all the affairs of the factory, look into everything, let nothing escape you, learn and learn again. Bolsheviks must master technique. It is time Bolsheviks themselves became experts . . . .

There are no fortresses which Bolsheviks cannot capture. We have assumed power. We have built up a huge socialist industry. We have swung the middle peasants to the path of socialism. . . . What remains to be done is not so much: to study technique, to master science. And when we have done that we will develop a tempo of which we dare not even dream at present.

"The Tasks of Business Executives," speech at the First All-Union Conference of Managers of Socialist Industry, February 4, 1931, in Joseph Stalin, *Problems of Leninism* (New York: International Publishers, c. 1934), pp. 350, 354–5, 357–8. As found in Richard Sakwa, *The Rise and Fall of the Soviet Union, 1917–1991* (New York and London: Routledge, 1999), pp. 187–188.

STALIN'S INDUSTRIAL DEVELOPMENT: THE VIEW FROM BELOW

How did the Soviet people experience Stalin's industrialization drive? New archives have helped historians glimpse what the common people lived through and how they responded. The following letters come from several hundred that workers and peasants sent to Soviet newspapers and authorities recounting their experiences and offering their opinions. Both were sent to the Soviet paper Pravda.

It should not be forgotten that many millions of workers are participating in the building of socialism. A horse with its own strength can drag seventy-five poods,* but its owner has loaded it with a hundred poods, and in addition he's fed it poorly. No matter how much he uses the whip, it still won't be able to move the cart.

This is also true for the working class. They've loaded it with socialist competition, shock work, overfulfilling the industrial and financial plan, and so forth. A worker toils seven hours, not ever leaving his post, and this is not all he does. Afterward he sits in meetings or else attends classes for an hour and a half or two in order to increase his skill level, and if he doesn't do these things, then he's doing things at home. And what does he live on? One hundred fifty grams of salted mutton, he will make soup without any of the usual additives, neither carrots, beets, flour, nor salt pork. What kind of soup do you get from this? Mere "dishwater."

—B.N. Kniazev, Tula, Sept. 1930.

Comrade Editor, Please give me an answer. Do the local authorities have the right to forcibly take away the only cow of industrial and office workers? What is more, they demand a receipt showing that the cow was handed over voluntarily and they threaten you by saying if you don't do this, they will put you in prison for failure to fulfill the meat procurement. How can you live when the cooperative distributes only black bread, and at the market goods have the prices of 1919 and 1920? Lice have eaten us to death, and soap is given only to railroad workers. From hunger and filth we have a massive outbreak of spotted fever.

—Anonymous, from Aktybinsk, Kazakhstan

*A pood is a Russian unit of weight, equal to 36.11 pounds.

Lewis Siegelbaum and Andrei Sokolov, *Stalinism as a Way of Life: A Narrative in Documents* (New Haven and London: Yale University Press, 2000), pp. 39–41.

---

from their farmlands to either inhospitable reaches of the Soviet east and north or to poor farmland closer to their original homes. The land and possessions of these unfortunate peasants were distributed to collective farms or, just as often, to the local officials and peasants participating in the liquidation process. Peasants who were forced into collective farms had little incentive to produce extra food, and exiling many of the most productive peasants not surprisingly weakened the agricultural system. In 1932–1933, famine spread across the southern region of the Soviet Union. This was the most productive agricultural area in the country, and the famine that struck there was thus particularly senseless. The 1933 famine cost some 3 to 5 million lives. During the famine, the Bolsheviks maintained substantial grain reserves in other parts of the country, enough to save many hundreds of thousands of lives at a minimum, but they refused to send this grain to the affected areas, preferring instead to seal off famine-stricken regions and allow people to starve. Grain reserves were instead sold overseas for hard currency and

stockpiled in case of war. Yet resistance had forced the state to cede small private plots of land to peasant families; this land provided as much as 50 percent of the nation's produce from a tiny fraction of the land.

THE FIVE-YEAR PLANS

In Stalin's view, collectivization provided the resources for the other major aspect of his "revolution from above": a rapid campaign of forced industrialization. The roadmap for this industrialization process was the first Five-Year Plan (1928–1932), an ambitious set of goals that Stalin and his cohorts drew up in 1927 and continued to revise upward. Its results rank as one of the most stunning periods of economic growth the modern world has ever seen. The industrial output of the USSR increased by 50 percent in five years; the annual rate of growth during the first Five-Year Plan was between 15 and 22 percent. This rate of growth seemed even more impressive in the context of the economic

"The Five-Year Plan in Four Years." Stalin faces down capitalist enemies in this Soviet propaganda poster of the 1930s. The caption translates: "Under the banner of Lenin, we triumphed in the battles of the October Revolution. Under the banner of Lenin, we achieved decisive successes in the battle for the victory of socialist construction. Under this banner, we will triumph in the proletarian revolution in all the world."

duction levels entirely planned in advance in Moscow, never functioned in a rational way. Heavy industry was always favored over light industry, and the emphasis on quantity made quality practically meaningless. A factory that was charged with producing a certain number of pairs of shoes, for example, could cut costs by producing all one style and size. The consumer would be left with useless goods, but the producer would fulfill the plan. Stalin's industrialization drive did transform the USSR from an agrarian nation to a world industrial power in the space of a few short years, but in the longer run, the system would become an economic disaster.

At the same time, Stalin promoted a sharply conservative shift in all areas of culture and society. Early Bolshevik activists had promoted a utopian attempt to rebuild one of the basic structures of pre-Revolutionary society—the family—and to create a genuinely new proletarian social structure. Stalin abandoned these ideas of communist familial relations in favor of efforts to strengthen traditional family ties: divorce became more difficult, abortion was outlawed in 1936 except in cases that threatened the life of the mother, and homosexuality was declared a criminal offense. State subsidies and support for mothers, which were progressive for the time, could not change the reality that Soviet women were increasingly forced to carry the double burden of familial and wage labor to support Stalin's version of Soviet society. All areas of Soviet cultural and social policy experienced similar reversals.

THE GREAT TERROR

The apogee of Stalinist repression came with the "Great Terror" of 1937–1938, which left nearly a million people dead and as many as a million and a half more in labor camps. As Stalin consolidated his personal dictatorship over the country, he eliminated enemies—real and imagined—along with individuals and groups he considered superfluous to the new Soviet society. As we have seen, repression was central to the Stalinist system from the early 1930s, yet the years 1937–1938 brought a qualitative and quantitative

depression that was shaking the foundations of Western economies in the late 1920s and early 1930s. The Bolsheviks built entirely new industries in entirely new cities. Cities such as Moscow and Leningrad doubled in size in the early 1930s, while new cities sprang up across the USSR. In 1926, only one fifth of the population lived in towns. Fifteen years later, in 1939, roughly a third did. The USSR was well on its way to becoming an urban, industrial society.

This rapid industrialization, however, came at enormous human cost. Many large-scale projects were carried out with prison labor, especially in the timber and mining industries. The labor camp system, known as the *gulag*, became a central part of the Stalinist economic system. People were arrested and sent to camps on a bewildering array of charges, ranging from petty criminal infractions to contact with foreigners to having the ill fortune to be born of bourgeois or kulak parents. The camp system spread throughout the USSR in the 1930s: by the end of the decade, roughly 3.6 million people were incarcerated by the regime.

The economic system created during this "revolution from above" was also fraught with structural problems that would plague the USSR for its entire history. The command economy, with each year's prochange—a whirlwind of mass repression unprecedented in scale.

The Terror was aimed at various categories of internal "enemies," from the top to the very bottom of Soviet society. Former and current political elites were perhaps the most visible victims. The top level of the Bolshevik party itself was purged almost completely; some one hundred thousand party members were removed, most facing prison sentences or execution. Between 1937 and 1938, Stalin purged the military of people he deemed potential threats, arresting some forty thousand officers and shooting at least ten thousand. These purges disrupted the government and the economy but allowed Stalin to promote a new, young cadre of officials who had no experience in the pre-Stalinist era and who owed their careers, if not their lives, to Stalin personally. Whole ethnic groups were viewed with suspicion, including Poles, Ukrainians, Lithuanians, Latvians, Koreans, and others with supposed cross-border ties that, in Stalin's mind, represented a national security threat. From the "bottom," some two hundred to three hundred thousand "dekulakized" peasants, petty criminals, and other social misfits were arrested, and many shot.

The results of the Stalin revolution were profound. No other regime in the history of western Europe had ever attempted to reorder completely the politics, economy, and society of a major nation. The Soviets had done so in a mere ten years. By 1939 private manufacturing and trade had been almost entirely abolished. Factories, mines, railroads, and public utilities were exclusively owned by the state. Stores were either government enterprises or cooperatives in which consumers owned shares. Agriculture had been almost completely socialized. The decade was not entirely grim, however. There were advances, especially in the area of social reform. Illiteracy was reduced from nearly 50 percent to about 20 percent, and higher education was made available to increasingly large numbers. Government assistance for working mothers and free hospitalization did a great deal to raise the national standard of health. The society that emerged from this terrible decade was industrial, more urban than rural, and more modern than traditional. But it was a society badly pummeled in the process, one in which many of the most productive peasants, gifted intellectuals, and experienced economic and social elites were purged from society in the name of total dictatorial power. The USSR that emerged from this tumultuous period would barely be able to withstand the immense strains placed on it when the Germans struck less than three years after the end of the Terror.

THE EMERGENCE OF FASCISM IN ITALY

What were the components of Italian fascism?

Like many European nations, Italy emerged from the First World War as a democracy in distress. Italy was on the winning side and had been among the Big Four nations (with France, Great Britain, and the United States) that put together the postwar settlement. Yet the war had cost Italy nearly seven hundred thousand lives and over $15 billion. These sacrifices were no greater than those of France or Britain but were hard to bear for a much poorer nation. Moreover, Italy had received secret promises of specific territorial gains during the war, only to find those promises withdrawn when they conflicted with principles of self-determination. Italy received most of the Austrian territories it demanded, but many maintained that these were inadequate rewards for their sacrifices. At first Italian nationalists blamed the "mutilated victory" on President Wilson, but after a short time they turned on their own rulers and what they considered the weaknesses of parliamentary democracy.

Italy had long-standing problems that were made worse by the war. Since unification, the Italian nation had been rent by an unhealthy economic split—divided into a prosperous industrialized north and a

CHRONOLOGY	
THE STALINIST REVOLUTION, 1927–1938	
Launch of collectivization	1927
Launch of the first Five-Year Plan	1928
Stalin breaks with the NEP	1929
Stalin pauses collectivization	1930
Liquidation of the kulaks	1929–1933
The Great Terror	1937–1938

EUROPE IN 1923

Which countries lost the most territory after World War I? How did those losses affect each nation? What problems were solved by the new national boundaries? What difficulties might the new borders have created?

poor agrarian south. Social conflict over land, wages, and local power caused friction in the countryside as well as in urban centers. Governments were often seen as corrupt, indecisive, and defeatist. This was the background for the more immediate problems that Italy faced after the war.

Inflation and unemployment were perhaps the most destructive effects of the war. Inflation pro-

duced high prices, speculation, and profiteering. And though normally wages would have risen also, the postwar labor market was glutted by returning soldiers. The parliamentary government that was set up after the war failed to ease these dire conditions, and Italians wanted radical reforms. For the working class, this meant socialism. In the countryside, most peasants were land poor, and many had no land at all, but instead worked for wages as rural laborers on large estates. Demands for land reform grew more militant. In some rural areas, so-called Red Leagues tried to break up large estates and force landlords to reduce their rents. In all these actions, the model of the Russian revolution, although it was only vaguely understood, encouraged the development of local radicalism. In large numbers, voters abandoned the poorly organized parties of the center and the moderate left. They supported two more radical groups: the Socialists and the Catholic People's party (newly formed with the pope's blessing) which appealed to the common people, especially in the countryside. Neither party preached revolution, yet both urged wide-ranging social and economic reforms.

The rising radical tide, especially seen against the backdrop of the Bolshevik revolution, worried other social groups. Industrialists and landowners feared for their property. Small shopkeepers and white-collar workers—social groups that did not think the working-class movement supported their interests—found themselves alienated by business elites on the one hand and by apparently revolutionary radicals on the other. The threat from the left provoked a strong surge to the right. Fascism appeared in the form of vigilante groups breaking up strikes, fighting with workers in the streets, or ousting the Red Leagues from lands occupied in the countryside.

> Members of the *fasci* were young idealists, fanatical nationalists. After the war, these groups formed the base of Mussolini's fascist movement.

THE RISE OF MUSSOLINI

"I am fascism," said Benito Mussolini, and indeed, the success of the Italian fascist movement depended heavily on his leadership. Mussolini (1883–1945) was the son of a socialist blacksmith. Expelled from the country for fomenting strikes, he returned to Italy, where he became a journalist and eventually the editor of *Avanti*, the leading socialist daily. When war broke out in August 1914, Mussolini insisted that Italy should remain neutral. He had scarcely adopted this position when he began urging participation on the Allied side. Deprived of his position as the editor of *Avanti*, he founded a new paper, *Il Popolo d'Italia*, and dedicated its columns to arousing enthusiasm for war.

As early as October 1914, Mussolini had organized groups, called *fasci*, to help drum up support for the war. Members of the *fasci* were young idealists, fanatical nationalists. After the war, these groups formed the base of Mussolini's fascist movement. (The word *fascism* derives from the Latin *fasces*: an ax surrounded by a bundle of sticks that represented the authority of the Roman state. The Italian *fascio* means "group" or "band.") In 1919 Mussolini drafted the original platform of the Fascist party.

The fascists gained the respect of the middle class and landowners, and intimidated many others, by forcefully repressing radical movements of industrial workers and peasants. They attacked socialists, often physically, and succeeded in taking over some local governments. As the national regime weakened, Mussolini's coercive politics made him look like a solution to the absence of leadership. In September 1922, he began to negotiate with other parties and the king for fascist participation in government. On October 28 an army of about fifty thousand fascist militia, in black-shirted uniforms, marched into Rome and occupied the capital. The premier

Mussolini Reviews a Fascist Youth Parade. Mobilizing youth was central to fascism and Nazism; it demonstrated the vigor of the movements.

resigned, and the following day the king, Victor Emmanuel III, reluctantly invited Mussolini to form a cabinet. Without firing a shot the Black Shirts had gained control of the Italian government. The explanation of their success is to be found less in the strength of the fascist movement itself than in the Italian disappointments after the war and the weakness of the older governing classes.

The doctrines of Italian fascism had three components. The first was statism. The state was declared to incorporate every interest and every loyalty of its members. There was to be "nothing above the state, nothing outside the state, nothing against the state." The second was nationalism. Nationhood was the highest form of society, with a life and a soul of its own apart from the lives and souls of the individuals who composed it. The third was militarism. Nations that did not expand would eventually wither and die. War ennobled man and regenerated sluggish and decadent peoples.

Mussolini began to rebuild Italy in accordance with these principles. The first step was to change electoral laws so they granted his party solid parliamentary majorities and to intimidate the opposition; he then moved to close down parliamentary government and other parties entirely. He abolished the cabinet system and all but extinguished the powers of the Parliament. He made the Fascist party an integral part of the Italian constitution. Mussolini assumed the dual position of prime minister and party leader (*duce*), and he used the party's militia to eliminate his enemies by violent means. Mussolini's government also controlled the police, muzzled the press, and censored academic activity.

The Italian dictator boasted that fascism had pulled the country back from economic chaos. Like other European economies, the Italian economy did improve in the late 1920s. The regime did a great deal to create the appearance of efficiency, and Mussolini's admirers famously claimed that he had at last "made the trains run on time." Fascism, however, did little to lessen Italy's plight during the worldwide depression of the 1930s.

Like Nazism later, fascism had contradictory elements. It sought to restore traditional authority and, at the same time, mobilize all of Italian society for economic and nationalist purposes. It created new authoritarian organizations and activities that furthered these goals such as exercise programs to make the young fit and mobilized, youth camps, awards to mothers of large families, political rallies, and parades in small towns in the countryside. Activities like these offered people a feeling of political involvement though they no longer enjoyed any political rights. This mobilized but essentially passive citizenship was a hallmark of fascism.

WEIMAR GERMANY

Why did German democracy fail?

On November 9, 1918—two days before the armistice ending the First World War—thousands of Germans swarmed the streets of Berlin in a nearly bloodless overthrow of the imperial government. A massive and largely unexpected uprising, the demonstration converged on the Reichstag in the city center, where a member of the Social Democratic Party (SPD) announced the birth of the new German republic. The kaiser had abdicated only hours before, turning the government over to the Social Democratic leader Friedrich Ebert. The majority of socialists steered a cautious, democratic course: they wanted reforms, but were willing to leave much of the existing imperial bureaucracy intact. Above all, they wanted a popularly elected national assembly to draft a constitution for the new republic.

Two months passed, however, before elections could be held—a period of crisis that verged on civil war. Once in control, the Social Democratic leadership made order its top priority. The revolutionary movement that had brought the SPD to power now threatened it. Independent socialists and a nascent Communist party wanted radical reforms, and in December 1918 and January 1919, they staged armed uprisings in the streets of Berlin. Fearful of a Bolshevik-style revolution, the Social Democratic government turned against its former allies and sent militant bands of workers and volunteers to crush the uprisings. Violence continued into 1920, creating a lasting bitterness among groups on the left.

The politics of the Freikorps were fiercely right wing. Anti-Marxist, anti-Semitic, and antiliberal, they had scant affection for the new German republic or its parliamentary democracy.

More important, the revolutionary aftermath of the war gave rise to bands of militant counterrevolutionaries. Veterans and other young nationalists joined so-called *Freikorps* (free corps). Such groups developed throughout the

The German Election of 1919. Here German women line up to vote for the first time.

country, drawing as many as several hundred thousand members. Former army officers who led these militias continued their war experience by fighting against "Bolsheviks," Poles, and communists. The politics of the Freikorps were fiercely right wing. Anti-Marxist, anti-Semitic, and antiliberal, they had scant affection for the new German republic or its parliamentary democracy. Many of the early Nazi leaders had fought in World War I and participated in Freikorps units.

Germany's new government—known as the Weimar Republic for the city where its constitution was drafted—rested on a coalition of socialists, Catholic centrists, and liberal democrats, a necessary compromise since no single party won a majority of the votes in the January 1919 election. The Weimar constitution was based on the values of parliamentary liberalism, and set up an open, pluralistic framework for German democracy. Through a series of compromises, the constitution established universal suffrage (for both women and men) and a bill of rights that guaranteed not only civil liberties but also a range of social entitlements. On paper, at least, the revolutionary movement had succeeded.

Yet the Weimar government lasted just over a decade. Many of Weimar's problems were born from Germany's defeat in the First World War, which was not only devastating but also humiliating. The ignominious loss to the Allies shocked many Germans, who

soon latched onto rumors that the army hadn't actually been defeated in battle, but instead had been "stabbed in the back" by socialists and Jewish leaders in the German government. Army officers cultivated this story even before the war was over, and though untrue, it helped to salve the wounded pride of German patriots. What was needed, many critics argued, was authoritative leadership to guide the nation and regain the world's respect.

The Treaty of Versailles magnified Germany's sense of dishonor. Germany was forced to cede a tenth of its territory, accept responsibility for the war, and slash the size of its army to a mere one hundred thousand men. Most important, the treaty saddled Germany with crippling reparations. Negotiating the $33 billion debt created problems for the government and provoked nothing but anger from the public.

Major economic crises also played a central role in Weimar's collapse. The first period of emergency occurred in the early twenties. Still reeling from wartime inflation, the government was hard pressed for revenues. Funding postwar demobilization programs, social welfare, and reparations forced the government to continue to print money. Inflation became nearly unstoppable. A pound of potatoes cost about nine marks in January, 40 million marks by October. Beef went for almost 2 trillion marks per pound. The government finally took drastic measures to stabilize the currency in 1924, but millions of Germans had already been ruined. For those on fixed incomes, such as pensioners and stockholders, savings and security had vanished. Middle-class employees, farmers, and workers were all hard hit by the economic crisis, and many of them abandoned the traditional political parties in protest. In their eyes, the parties that claimed to represent the middle classes had created the problems and proved incapable of fixing them.

The Great Depression pushed Weimar's political system to the breaking point. In 1929, there were 2 million unemployed; in 1932, 6 million. In those three years production dropped by 44 percent. Artisans and small shopkeepers lost both status and income. Farmers fared even worse, having never recovered from the crisis of the early twenties. Peasants staged mass demonstrations against the government's agricultural policies even before the depression hit. For white-collar and civil service employees, the depression meant lower salaries, poor working conditions, and a constant threat of unemployment. Finally, the crisis created an opportunity for Weimar's opponents. Many leading industrialists supported a return to authoritarian government, and they were allied with equally conservative landowners, united by a desire for protective economic policies to stimulate the sale of domestic goods and foodstuffs. Those conservative forces wielded considerable power in Germany, beyond the control of the government. So too did the army and the civil service, which were staffed with opponents of the republic—men who rejected the principles of parliamentary democracy and international cooperation that Weimar represented.

> The Great Depression pushed Weimar's political system to the breaking point. In 1929, there were 2 million unemployed; in 1932, 6 million. In those three years production dropped by 44 percent.

Ambitious and outspoken, Hitler quickly moved up the rather short ladder of party leadership as a talented stump orator. By 1921 he was the *Führer*—the leader—to his followers in Bavaria. The wider public saw him as a "vulgar demagogue"—if they noticed him at all. In November of 1923, during the worst days of the inflation crisis, the Nazis made a failed attempt at overthrowing the state government of Bavaria. Hitler spent the next seven months in prison, where he wrote his autobiography and political manifesto *Mein Kampf* ("My Struggle") in 1924. Combining anti-Semitism with anticommunism, the book set out at great length the popular theory that Germany had been betrayed by its enemies and that the country needed strong leadership to regain international prominence. Released from prison in 1924, Hitler resumed leadership of the party. In the next five years, he consolidated his power over a growing membership of ardent supporters. Actively cultivating the image of the

HITLER AND THE NATIONAL SOCIALISTS

How did the Nazis come to power?

Adolf Hitler was born in 1889 in Austria, not Germany. The son of a petty customs official in the Austrian civil service, Hitler dropped out of school and went to Vienna in 1909 to become an artist. Rejected from the academy and temporarily homeless, he eked out a dismal existence doing manual labor and painting cheap watercolors in Vienna. Meanwhile he developed the violent political prejudices that would become the guiding principles of the Nazi regime. He ardently admired the Austrian politicians preaching anti-Semitism, anti-Marxism, and Pan-Germanism. When war broke out in 1914, Hitler was among the jubilant crowds in the streets of Munich; and though he was an Austrian citizen, he enlisted in the German army, where he claimed to have finally found meaning in his life. After the war, he joined the newly formed German Workers' Party, whose name changed in 1920 to the National Socialist Workers' Party (abbreviated in popular usage to Nazi). The Nazis were but one among many small, militant groups of disaffected Germans devoted to racial nationalism and to the overthrow of the Weimar Republic.

Nazism and the Rural Myth. To stress the rural roots of Aryan Germany, Hitler appeared in lederhosen in the 1920s.

Nazi movement as a crusade against (Jewish) Marxism and capitalism, he portrayed himself as the heroic savior of the German people.

The 1928 election was a pivotal moment for both Weimar and for the Nazis for two reasons. First, from this point on, politics became polarized between right and left, making it virtually impossible to put together a coalition that would support the continuation of Weimar democracy. Second, it was apparent that alienated voters, especially peasants, were deserting their traditional political parties and voting for other interest-group organizations that would voice their grievances and push their demands. The Nazis quickly learned how to benefit from this splintering of the electorate. Guided by its chief propagandist, Joseph Goebbels, the party stepped up its efforts to attract members of the urban and rural middle classes. The answers to Germany's problems, the Nazis argued, could only be found by breaking with Weimar. Presenting itself as young and dynamic, the party built a national profile as an alternative to the parties of middle-class conservatives. In 1930, bolstered by the economic crisis, the Nazis were better funded and better organized than ever, and they won 18.3 percent of the vote.

Who voted for the Nazis? Recent analysis of election results and campaign materials suggests that different groups supported the Nazis at varying times and for varying reasons. The Nazis polled highly with small property holders and the rural middle class long before the depression. The Nazis offered these voters economic protection and renewed social status. Other segments of the middle class—notably pensioners, the elderly, and war widows—came to support the Nazis during the economic crisis, when they feared reduction of insurance or pension benefits. The Nazis also courted the traditionally elitist civil service. And though they failed to win votes from industrial workers, the Nazis found some of their strongest support among workers in handicrafts and small-scale manufacturing.

In 1930, the Nazi party won 107 of 577 seats in the Reichstag, second only to the Social Democrats, who controlled 143. No party could gain a majority. No governing coalition was possible without Nazi support. And the Nazis refused to join any cabinet that was not headed by Hitler. In 1932, Hitler ran for president and narrowly lost, although he staged an unprecedented campaign by airplane, visiting twenty-one cities in six days. When another parliamentary election was called in July 1932, the Nazis won 37.4 percent of the vote, which, though not a majority, was a significant plurality. The Nazis could claim that they were the party able to draw support across class, geographic, and generational lines. They benefited from their position as outsiders, untainted by involvement in unpopular parliamentary coalitions. Indeed, the failure of the traditional parties was key to the success of the Nazis.

Despite its electoral success in 1932, the Nazi party had not won a majority; Hitler was not in power. He was appointed chancellor in January 1933 by President Hindenburg, who hoped to create a conservative coalition government by bringing the Nazis into line with the less radical parties. But Hindenburg and others in the government had underestimated the Nazis' power and popularity. Legally installed in office, Hitler immediately made the most of it. When a Dutch anarchist with links to the communist party set fire to the Reichstag on the night of February 27, Hitler seized the opportunity to suspend civil rights "as a defensive measure against communist acts of violence." He convinced Hindenburg to dissolve the Reichstag and to order a new election on March 5, 1933. Under Hitler's sway, the new parliament legally granted him unlimited powers for the next four years. Hitler proclaimed his new government the Third Reich. (The first Reich was the German empire of the Middle Ages; the second was that of the kaisers.)

> Other segments of the middle class—notably pensioners, the elderly, and war widows—came to support the Nazis during the economic crisis, when they feared reduction of insurance or pension benefits.

NAZI GERMANY

By the fall of 1933, Germany had become a one-party state. The socialist and communist left was crushed by the new regime. Almost all non-Nazi organizations had been either abolished or forced to become part of the Nazi system. Party propaganda sought to impress citizens with the regime's "monolithic efficiency." But in fact, the Nazi government was a tangled bureaucratic maze, with both agencies and individuals vying fiercely for Hitler's favor.

Ironically, at the end of the party's first year in power, the most serious challenges to Hitler came from within the party. Hitler's paramilitary Nazi storm troopers (the SA) had been formed to maintain discipline within the party and impose order in society.

Such radicalism was alarming to the more traditional conservative groups that had helped make Hitler chancellor. If Hitler was to maintain power, then, he needed to tame the SA. On the night of June 30, 1934, more than a thousand high-ranking SA officials, including several of Hitler's oldest associates, were executed in a bloody purge known as the Night of Long Knives. The purge cleared the way for a second paramilitary organization, the *Schutzstaffel* (bodyguard), or SS. Headed by the fanatical Heinrich Himmler, the SS became the most dreaded arm of Nazi terror. As Himmler saw it, the mission of the SS was to fight political and racial enemies of the regime, which included building the system of concentration camps. The first camp, at Dachau, opened in March 1933. The secret state police, known as the Gestapo, were responsible for the arrest, incarceration in camps, and murder of thousands of Germans. But the police force was generally understaffed and deluged with paperwork—as one historian has shown, anything but "omniscient, omnipotent, and omnipresent." In fact, the majority of arrests was based on voluntary denunciations made by ordinary citizens against each other, often as petty personal attacks. It was not lost on the Gestapo leadership that these denunciations created a level of control that the Gestapo itself could never achieve.

Despite—or perhaps because of—these efforts to quash opposition, Hitler and the Nazis enjoyed a sizable amount of popular support. Many Germans approved of Hitler's use of violence against the left. The Nazis could play on deep-seated fears of communism, and they spoke a language of intense national pride and unity that had broad appeal. Many Germans saw Hitler as a symbol of a strong, revitalized Germany. Propagandists fostered a Führer cult, depicting Hitler as a charismatic leader with the magnetic energy to bring people to their knees. Hitler's appeal also rested on his ability to give the German people what they wanted: jobs for workers, a productive economy for industrialists, a bulwark against communism for those who feared the wave of revolution. Finally, he promised to lead Germany back to national greatness and to "overthrow" the Versailles settlement, and through the 1930s he seemed to be doing so with a series of bloodless diplomatic triumphs.

Hitler's plans for national recovery called for full-scale rearmament and economic self-sufficiency. With policies similar to those of other Western nations, the Nazis made massive public investments, set strict market controls to stop inflation and stabilize the currency, and sealed Germany off from the world economy. Late in the decade, as the Nazis rebuilt the entire German military complex, unemployment dropped from over 6 million to under two hundred thousand. The German economy looked better than any other in Europe: Hitler claimed this as his "economic miracle." Such improvements were significant, especially in the eyes of Germans who had lived through the continual turmoil of war, inflation, political instability, and economic crisis.

Like Mussolini, Hitler moved to abolish class conflict by stripping working-class institutions of their power. He outlawed trade unions and strikes, froze wages, and organized workers and employers into a National Labor Front. Popular organizations cut across class lines, especially among the youth. The Hitler Youth, a club modeled on the Boy Scouts, was highly successful at teaching children the values of Hitler's Reich; the National Labor Service drafted students for a term to work on state-sponsored building and reclamation projects. Government policy encouraged women to withdraw from the labor force, both to ease unemployment and to conform to Nazi notions of a woman's proper role.

NAZI RACISM

At the core of Nazi ideology lay a particularly virulent racism. Much of this racism was not new. Hitler and the Nazis drew on a revived and especially violent form of nineteenth-century social Darwinism, according to which nations and people struggled for survival, with the superior peoples strengthening themselves in the process. By the early twentieth century, the rise of the social sciences had taken nineteenth-century prejudices and racial thinking into new terrain. Across the West, scientists and intellectuals worked to purify the body

---

CHRONOLOGY

THE RISE OF NAZISM, 1920–1934

National Socialist Workers' Party founded	1920
Beer Hall Putsch in Munich	1923
Hitler writes *Mein Kampf* in prison	1924
Hitler consolidates power	1924–1929
Hitler loses presidential election	1932
Hitler appointed chancellor of Germany	1933
Nazi party rules Germany	1933
Night of Long Knives	1934

NAZI PROPAGANDA

Joseph Goebbels, "Why Are We Enemies of the Jews?"

The Nazis promised many things to many people. As the following document shows, anti-Semitism allowed them to blend their racial nationalism, vaguely defined (and anti-Marxist) socialism, and disgust with the state of German culture and politics. Joseph Goebbels, one of the early members of the party, became director of propaganda for the party in 1928. Later Hitler appointed him head of the National Ministry for Public Enlightenment and Propaganda.

We are NATIONALISTS because we see in the NATION the only possibility for the protection and the furtherance of our existence.

The NATION is the organic bond of a people for the protection and defense of their lives. He is nationally minded who understands this IN WORD AND IN DEED. . . .

Young nationalism has its unconditional demands, BELIEF IN THE NATION is a matter of all the people, not for individuals of rank, a class, or an industrial clique. The eternal must be separated from the contemporary. The maintenance of a rotten industrial system has nothing to do with nationalism. I can love Germany and hate capitalism; not only CAN I do it, I also MUST do it. The germ of the rebirth of our people LIES ONLY IN THE DESTRUCTION OF THE SYSTEM OF PLUNDERING THE HEALTHY POWER OF THE PEOPLE.

WE ARE NATIONALISTS BECAUSE WE, AS GERMANS, LOVE GERMANY. And because we love Germany, we demand the protection of its national spirit and we battle against its destroyers.

WHY ARE WE SOCIALISTS?

We are SOCIALISTS because we see in SOCIALISM the only possibility for maintaining our racial existence and through it the reconquest of our political freedom and the rebirth of the German state. SOCIALISM has its peculiar form first of all through its comradeship in arms with the forward-driving energy of a newly awakened nationalism. Without nationalism it is nothing, a phantom, a theory, a vision of air, a book. With it, it is everything, THE FUTURE, FREEDOM, FATHERLAND! . . .

WHY DO WE OPPOSE THE JEWS?

We are ENEMIES OF THE JEWS, because we are fighters for the freedom of the German people. THE JEW IS THE CAUSE AND THE BENEFICIARY OF OUR MISERY. He has used the social difficulties of the broad masses of our people to deepen the unholy split between Right and Left among our people. He has made two halves of Germany. He is the real cause for our loss of the Great War.

The Jew has no interest in the solution of Germany's fateful problems. He CANNOT have any. FOR HE LIVES ON THE FACT THAT THERE HAS BEEN NO SOLUTION. If we would make the German people a unified community and give them freedom before the world, then the Jew can have no place among us. He has the best trumps in his hands when a people lives in inner and outer slavery. THE JEW IS RESPONSIBLE FOR OUR MISERY AND HE LIVES ON IT.

That is the reason why we, AS NATIONALISTS and AS SOCIALISTS, oppose the Jew. HE HAS CORRUPTED OUR RACE, FOULED OUR MORALS, UNDERMINED OUR CUSTOMS, AND BROKEN OUR POWER. . . .

National Socialist Campaign Pamphlet, 1932

The Nazis worked hard to win the rural vote, as evidenced by the Nazi campaign pamphlet reprinted below. The Nazis tried to appeal to farmers' economic grievances, their fears of socialism on the one hand and big business on the other, and their more general hostility to urban life and culture.

German Farmer You Belong To Hitler! Why?

The German farmer stands between two great dangers today:

The one danger is the American economic system—Big capitalism!

   it means "world economic crisis"
   it means "eternal interest slavery" . . .
   it means that the world is nothing more than a bag of booty for Jewish finance in Wall Street, New York, and Paris
   it enslaves man under the slogans of progress, technology, rationalization, standardization, etc.
   it knows only profit and dividends
   it wants to make the world into a giant trust
   it puts the machine over man
   it annihilates the independent, earth-rooted farmer, and its final aim is the world dictatorship of Jewry [. . .]
   it achieves this in the political sphere through parliament and the swindle of democracy. In the economic sphere, through the control of credit, the mortgaging of land, the stock exchange and the market principle [. . .]
The farmer's leagues, the Landvolk and the Bavarian Farmers' League all pay homage to this system.

The other danger is the Marxist economic system of bolshevism:

   it knows only the state economy
   it knows only one class, the proletariat
   it brings in the controlled economy
   it doesn't just annihilate the self-sufficient farmer economically—it roots him out [. . .]
   it brings the rule of the tractor
   it nationalizes the land and creates mammoth factory-farms
   it uproots and destroys man's soul, making him the powerless tool of the communist idea—or kills him
   it destroys the family, belief, and customs [. . .]
   it is anti-Christ, it desecrates the churches [. . .]
   its final aim is the world dictatorship of the proletariat, that means ultimately the world dictatorship of Jewry, for the Jew controls this powerless proletariat and uses it for his dark plans
Big capitalism and bolshevism work hand in hand; they are born of Jewish thought and serve the master plan of world Jewry.

Who alone can rescue the farmer from these dangers?

NATIONAL SOCIALISM!

Anton Kaes, Matin Jay, and Edward Dimendberg, *The Weimar Republic Sourcebook* (Los Angeles: University of California Press, 1994), pp. 137–38, 142. (Source for both documents.)

---

politic, improve the human race, and eliminate the "unfit." Even progressive-minded individuals sometimes subscribed to eugenics, a program of racial engineering to improve either personal or public fitness. Eugenic policies in the Third Reich began with a 1933 law for the compulsory sterilization of "innumerable inferior and hereditarily tainted" people. This "social-hygienic racism" later became the systematic murder of mentally and physically ill patients. Social policy was governed by a basic division between those who possessed "value" and those who did not, with the aim of creating a racial utopia.

The centerpiece of Nazi racism was anti-Semitism. This centuries-old phenomenon was part of Christian society from the Middle Ages on. By the nineteenth century, traditional Christian anti-Semitism was joined by a current of nationalist anti-Jewish theory. At the end of the nineteenth century, during the Dreyfus affair in France (see Chapter 23), French and European anti-Semites launched a barrage of propaganda against

HOW DID THE WESTERN DEMOCRACIES DEAL WITH THE GREAT DEPRESSION?

THE GREAT DEPRESSION IN THE DEMOCRACIES   717

Anti-Nazi Poster, 1932, reads "The worker in the Reich of the Swastika" at top, and "Vote Social Democratic" at bottom.

Jews—scores of books, pamphlets, and magazines blamed Jews for all the troubles of modernity, from socialism to international banks and mass culture. The late nineteenth century also brought a wave of pogroms—violent assaults on Jewish communities—especially in Russia. Racial anti-Semitism drew the line between Jews and non-Jews on the basis of erroneous biology. Religious conversion, which traditional Christian anti-Semites encouraged, would not change biology. Nor would assimilation, which was counseled by more secular nationalist thinkers.

To what extent was the Nazis' virulent anti-Semitism shared? Although the "Jewish Question" was clearly Hitler's primary obsession during the early 1920s, he made the theme less central in campaign appearances as the Nazi movement entered mainstream politics, shifting instead to attacks on Marxism and the Weimar democracy. Moreover, anti-Semitic beliefs would not have distinguished the Nazi from any other party on the

political right; it was likely of only secondary importance to people's opinions of the Nazis. Soon after Hitler came to power, though, German Jews faced discrimination, exclusion from rights as citizens, and violence. Racial laws excluded Jews from public office as early as April 1933. The Nazis encouraged a boycott of Jewish merchants, while the SA created a constant threat of random violence. In 1935, the Nuremberg Decrees deprived Jews (defined by bloodline) of their German citizenship and prohibited marriage between Jews and other Germans. Violence escalated. In November 1938, the SA attacked some seventy-five hundred Jewish stores, burned nearly two hundred synagogues, killed ninety-one Jews, and beat up thousands more in a campaign of terror known as *Kristallnacht*, the Night of Broken Glass. Violence like this did raise some opposition from ordinary Germans. Legal persecution, however, met only silent acquiescence. And from the perspective of Jewish people, *Kristallnacht* made it plain that there was no safe place for them in Germany. Unfortunately, only one year remained before the outbreak of war made it impossible for Jews to escape.

What did national socialism and fascism have in common? Both arose in the interwar period as responses to World War I and the Russian Revolution. Both were violently antisocialist and anticommunist, determined to "rescue" their nations from the threat of Bolshevism. Both were intensely nationalistic; they believed that national solidarity came before all other allegiances and superseded all other rights. Both opposed parliamentary government and democracy as cumbersome and divisive. Both found their power in mass-based authoritarian politics. Similar movements existed in all the countries of the West, but only in a few cases did they actually form regimes. Nazism, however, distinguished itself by making a racially pure state central to its vision, a vision that would lead to global struggle and mass murder.

THE GREAT DEPRESSION IN THE DEMOCRACIES

How did the Western democracies deal with the Great Depression?

The histories of the three major Western democracies—Great Britain, France, and the United States—run roughly parallel during the years after the First World

War. In all three countries governments put their trust in prewar policies and assumptions until the Great Depression forced them to make major social reforms, laying the foundations of the modern welfare state. These nations weathered the upheavals of the interwar years, but they did not do so easily.

France continued to fear Germany and took every opportunity to keep the Germans as weak as possible. Under the leadership of the moderate conservative Raymond Poincaré during the 1920s, France tried to keep the price of manufactured goods low by restraining wages. This policy of deflation kept businessmen happy but put a heavy burden on the working class. Meanwhile, class conflict simmered just below the surface. As industries prospered, employers refused to bargain with labor unions. A period of major strikes immediately after the war was followed by a sharp decline in union activity. And even though the government passed a modified social insurance program in 1930—insuring against sickness, old age, and death—workers remained dissatisfied.

Social conflict flared in Britain as well. Anxious to regain its position as the major industrial and financial power in the world, Britain also pursued a policy of deflation, hoping to make its manufactured goods cheaper and more attractive on the world market. The result was a reduction in wages that undermined the standard of living of many British workers. Their resentment helped to elect the first Labour party government in 1924, and a second in 1929. The Labour party accomplished little, however, because of its minority position in Parliament. The Conservative government returned to power in 1925 under Stanley Baldwin and refused to abandon its deflationary policy, which continued to drive down wages. British trade unions grew increasingly militant in response, and in 1926, the unions staged a nationwide general strike. The strike's only appreciable effect was to heighten middle-class antipathy toward workers.

The United States was the bastion of conservatism among the democracies. The presidents elected in the 1920s—Warren G. Harding, Calvin Coolidge, and Herbert Hoover—upheld a social philosophy formulated by the barons of big business in the nineteenth century. The Supreme Court used its power of judicial review to nullify progressive legislation enacted by state governments and occasionally by Congress.

> Black Thursday was followed by Black Monday and then Black Tuesday: falling prices, combined with an enormously high number of trades, made for the worst day in the history of the stock exchange to that point.

The conservative economic and social policies of the prewar period were dealt their deathblow by the Great Depression of 1929. This worldwide depression peaked during the years 1929–1933, but its effects lasted a decade. For those who went through it, the depression was perhaps the formative experience of their lives and the decisive crisis of the interwar period. It was an important factor in the rise of Nazism, but in fact, it forced every country to forge new economic policies, and to deal with unprecedented economic turmoil.

THE ORIGINS OF THE GREAT DEPRESSION

What caused the Great Depression? Its deepest roots lay in the instability of national currencies, and in the interdependence of national economies. Throughout the 1920s, Europeans had seen a sluggish growth rate. A major drop in world agricultural prices hurt the countries of southern and eastern Europe, where agriculture was small in scale and high in cost. Unable to make a profit on the international market, these agricultural countries bought fewer manufactured goods from the more industrial sectors of northern Europe, causing a widespread drop in industrial productivity. Restrictions on free trade crippled the economy even more. Although debtor nations needed open markets to sell their goods, most nations were raising high trade barriers to protect domestic manufacturers from foreign competition.

Then in October of 1929, prices on the New York Stock Exchange collapsed. On October 24, "Black Thursday," 12 million shares were traded amid unprecedented chaos. Even more surprising, the market kept falling. Black Thursday was followed by Black Monday and then Black Tuesday: falling prices, combined with an enormously high number of trades, made for the worst day in the history of the stock exchange to that point. The rise of the United States as an international creditor during the Great War meant that the crash had immediate, disastrous consequences in Europe. When the value of stocks dropped, banks found themselves short of capital and then, when not rescued by the government, forced to close. International investors called in their debts. A series of banking houses shut their doors.

HOW DID THE WESTERN DEMOCRACIES DEAL WITH THE GREAT DEPRESSION?

THE GREAT DEPRESSION IN THE DEMOCRACIES   719

U.S. Farmers on Their Way West in the 1930s. Forced from their land by depression, debts, and drought, thousands of farmers and their families headed to California, Oregon, and Washington in search of employment.

followed suit in 1933. By no longer pegging their currencies to the price of gold, these countries hoped to make money cheaper, and thus more available for economic recovery programs. In another important move, Great Britain abandoned its time-honored policy of free trade in 1932, raising protective tariffs as high as 100 percent. But monetary policy alone could not end the hardships of ordinary families. Governments were increasingly forced to address their concerns with a wide range of social reforms.

Britain was the most cautious in its relief efforts. A national government composed of Conservative, Liberal, and Labour party members came to power in 1931. To underwrite effective programs of public assistance, however, the government would have to spend beyond its income—something it was reluctant to do. France, on the other hand, adopted the most advanced set of policies to combat the effects of the depression. In 1936, responding to a threat from ultraconservatives to overthrow the republic, a Popular Front government was formed by the Radical, Radical Socialist, and Communist parties, and lasted for two years. The Popular Front nationalized the munitions industry and reorganized the Bank of France to break the largest stockholders' monopolistic control over credit. The government also decreed a forty-hour week for all urban workers and initiated a program of public works. For the benefit of the farmers it established a wheat office to fix the price and regulate the distribution of grain.

The most dramatic response to the depression came in the United States for two reasons. First, the United States had clung longest to nineteenth-century economic philosophy. Second, the depression was more severe in the United States than in the European democracies. America had survived the First World War unscathed—and indeed, had benefited enormously—but now its economy was ravaged even more than Europe's. In 1933, Franklin D. Roosevelt succeeded Herbert Hoover as president and announced the New Deal, a program of reform and reconstruction to rescue the country.

Workers did not simply lose their jobs, manufacturers laid off virtually entire work forces. In 1930, 4 million Americans were unemployed, in 1933, 13 million—nearly a third of the workforce. By then, per capita income in the United States had fallen 48 percent. In Germany, too, the drop was brutal. In 1929, 2 million were unemployed; in 1932, 6 million. Production dropped 44 percent in Germany, 47 percent in the United States. The stock-market collapse led to widespread bank failure and brought the economy virtually to a standstill.

The governments of the West initially responded to the depression with monetary measures. In 1931 Great Britain abandoned the gold standard; the United States

The New Deal aimed to get the country back on its feet without destroying the capitalist system. The government would manage the economy, sponsor relief programs, and fund public-works projects to increase mass purchasing power. These policies were shaped by the theories of the British economist John Maynard Keynes, who had already proved influential during the 1919 treaty meetings at Paris. Keynes argued that capitalism could create a just and efficient society if governments played a part in its management. First, Keynes abandoned the sacred cow of balanced budgets. Without advocating continuous deficit financing, he would have the government deliberately operate in the red whenever private investments weren't enough. Keynes also favored the creation of large amounts of venture capital—money for high-risk, high-reward investments—which he saw as the only socially productive form of capital. Finally, he recommended monetary control to promote prosperity and full employment.

Through Social Security and other programs, the New Deal helped both individuals and the country to recover, but it left the crucial problem of unemployment unsolved. In 1939, after six years of the New Deal, the United States still had more than 9 million jobless workers—a figure that exceeded the combined unemployment of the rest of the world. Only with the outbreak of a new world war—which required millions of soldiers and armament workers—did the United States reach the full recovery that the New Deal had failed to deliver.

INTERWAR CULTURE: ARTISTS AND INTELLECTUALS

How did the mass media change everyday life?

We have seen how governments and their citizens responded to social, political, and economic crises. The interwar period brought equally dramatic upheavals in the arts and sciences. Revolutionary artistic forms that were pioneered at the turn of the century moved from the margins to the mainstream. Artists, writers, architects, and composers rejected traditional aesthetic values and experimented with new forms of expression. Further affronts to tradition came from scientists and psychologists, whose work challenged deeply held beliefs about the universe and about human nature. Finally, mass culture, in the form of radio, movies, and advertising, sharpened many anxieties, and stood as a stark example of the promise and peril of modern times.

INTERWAR INTELLECTUALS

Like many other people, novelists, poets, and dramatists were disillusioned by the brute facts of world war and by the failure of victory to fulfill its promises. Much of the literature of the interwar period reflected themes of frustration, cynicism, and disenchantment; but many writers were also fascinated by revolutionary developments in science, including the probing of psychoanalysts into the hidden secrets of the mind. The works of several writers came to represent the mood of the era: the early novels of the American Ernest Hemingway, for example, along with the poetry of the Anglo-American T. S. Eliot and the plays of the German Bertolt Brecht. In *The Sun Also Rises* (1926), Hemingway gave the public a powerful description of the so-called lost generation, a pattern followed by other writers, such as the American F. Scott Fitzgerald. In his monumental poem *The Waste Land* (1922), Eliot presented a philosophy that was close to despair: life is a living death, to be endured as boredom and frustration. Other writers focused their attention on consciousness and inner life, often experimenting with new forms of prose. The Irish writer James Joyce was much renowned for his experiments with language and literacy forms—especially with the "stream of consciousness" technique, which he perfected in *Ulysses* (1922). The same was true, though to a lesser extent, of the novels of the Englishwoman Virginia Woolf (1882–1941). Woolf's essays and novels, among them *Mrs. Dalloway* (1925), *To the Lighthouse* (1927), and *A Room of One's Own* (1929), offered an eloquent and biting critique of Britain's elite institutions, from the universities that isolated women in separate, underfunded colleges to the suffocating decorum of middle-class families and relationships.

The depression of the 1930s forced many writers to reexamine the style and purpose of their work. Authors

> In his monumental poem *The Waste Land* (1922), Eliot presented a philosophy that was close to despair: life is a living death, to be endured as boredom and frustration.

felt themselves called to indict injustice and cruelty, and to point the way to a better society. Moreover, they no longer directed their work to fellow intellectuals alone, but to ordinary men and women as well. In *The Grapes of Wrath* (1939), for example, the American writer John Steinbeck depicted the plight of impoverished farmers fleeing from the Dust Bowl to California only to find that all the land had been monopolized by companies that exploited their workers. Young British writers such as W. H. Auden, Stephen Spender, and Christopher Isherwood were communist sympathizers who believed that it was their duty as artists to politicize their work to support the revolution. They rejected the pessimism of their immediate literary forebears in favor of optimistic commitment to their cause.

The First International Dada-Fair, Berlin, 1920. This gathering of artists features Otto Burchard (standing second from left), George Grosz (standing second from right), Hannah Höch (seated left) and a decor of bizarre juxtapositions that was a trademark of the dada school.

INTERWAR ARTISTS

Trends in art tended to parallel those in literature. Visual art responded to the rapid transformations of twentieth-century society—changes brought about by new technologies, scientific discoveries, the abandonment of traditional beliefs, and the influence of non-Western cultures. Like writers of the period, visual artists pushed the boundaries of aesthetics, moving far from the conventional tastes of average men and women.

Pablo Picasso followed his particular genius as it led him further into cubist variations and inventions. Another group, known as expressionists, argued that color and line express inherent psychological qualities all by themselves, and so a painting need not have a "subject" at all.

Another school rebelled against the very idea of aesthetic principle. Principles were based on reason, their argument went, and the world had proved beyond all doubt—by fighting itself to death—that reason did not exist. Calling themselves dadaists (allegedly after a

name picked at random from the dictionary), these artists were led by the Frenchman Marcel Duchamp, the German Max Ernst, and the Alsatian Jean (Hans) Arp. Rejecting all formal artistic conventions, dadaists concocted haphazard "fabrications" from cutouts and juxtapositions of wood, glass, and metal, and gave them bizarre names, for example, *The Bride Stripped Bare by her Bachelors, Even* (Duchamp). The artists claimed their works were meaningless and playful, but critics thought otherwise, seeing them instead as expressions of the subconscious. Dadaism also took on political undertones, especially in Germany, by offering a nihilistic social critique that bordered on anarchism. Extending their attacks on rationalism to theater and print, these artists challenged the very basis of national culture.

Some artists responded to the sense of international crisis much as writers did. During the thirties, their paintings expressed pain and outrage directly to a mass audience. The most important members of this new movement were the Mexican muralists Diego Rivera and José Clemente Orozco, and the Americans Thomas Hart

Architectural Style in Germany between the Wars. The Bauhaus, by Walter Gropius (1883–1969). This school in Dessau, Germany, is a starkly functional prototype of the interwar "international style."

Benton and Reginald Marsh. These men sought to depict the social conditions of the modern world, presenting in graphic detail the hopes and struggles of ordinary people. Though they broke with the conventions of the past, there was nothing unintelligible about their work. It was art intended for everyone. Much of it bore the sting of social satire.

Architects, too, rejected sentimentality and tradition. Between 1880 and 1890 designers in Europe and America announced that the prevailing architectural styles were out of harmony with the needs of modern civilization. Modern architects pioneered a style known as "functionalism". The basic principle of functionalism was that the appearance of a building should proclaim its actual use and purpose. Ornamentation was designed to reflect an age of science and machines. A leading European practitioner of functionalism was the German Walter Gropius, who in 1919 established a school—the Bauhaus—in Dessau to serve as a center for the theory and practice of modern architecture. Gropius and his followers declared that their style of design, which in time came to be called "international," was the only one that permitted an honest application of new materials—chromium, glass, steel, and concrete.

INTERWAR SCIENTIFIC DEVELOPMENTS

One powerful influence on the artists and intellectuals of the day was neither social nor political, but scientific. The pioneering work of the German physicist Albert Einstein revolutionized not only the entire structure of physical science, it also challenged ordinary people's most basic beliefs about the universe. Quickly recognized as one of the greatest intellects of all time, Einstein began to question the very foundations of traditional physics early in the twentieth century. By 1915, he had proposed entirely new ways of thinking about space, matter, time, and gravity. His most famous theory, the principle of relativity, states that space and motion are relative to each other instead of being absolute. To the familiar three dimensions, Einstein added a fourth—time—and represented all four as fused in the space-time continuum. This meant that mass depends on motion, so that bodies in motion (especially at very high velocities) have a different shape and mass than they would at rest.

Einstein's theories paved the way for another revolutionary development in physics—the splitting of the atom. As early as 1905 Einstein became convinced of the equivalence of mass and energy and worked out a formula for the conversion of one into the other. Expressed as $E = mc^2$, the equation states that the amount of energy locked within the atom is equal to the mass multiplied by the square of the velocity of light. The formula had no practical application for years. Then in 1932, when the Englishman Sir James Chadwick discovered the neutron, which carries no electric charge, scientists had an ideal weapon for bombarding the atom—that is, a way to split it. In 1939 two German physicists, Otto Hahn and Fritz Strassman, successfully split atoms of uranium by bombarding them with neutrons. The initial reaction produced a chain of reactions: each atom that was split shot off more neutrons, which split even more atoms. Scientists in Germany, Great Britain, and the United States were spurred on by governments anxious to turn these discoveries into weapons during the Second World War. American scientists soon prepared an atomic bomb, the most destructive weapon ever created. The legacy was ironic for Einstein, a man who devoted much of his life to promoting pacifism, liberalism, and social justice.

Another important contribution to physics that quickly entered popular culture was the "uncertainty principle" posited by the German physicist Werner Heisenberg in 1927. Heisenberg, who was strongly influenced by Einstein, showed that it is impossible—even in theory—to measure both the position and the speed of an object at the same time. The theory was of consequence only when dealing with atoms or subatomic particles, because of the interconnected nature of waves and particles on such a small scale. Though the public had little to no understanding of these ground-breaking scientific concepts, metaphorical invocations of "relativity" and the "uncertainty principle" fitted the ambiguities of the modern world. For many people, nothing was definite, everything was changing—and science seemed to be proving it.

MASS CULTURE AND ITS POSSIBILITIES

Cultural change, however, extended far beyond circles of artistic and intellectual elites. The explosive rise of mass media in the interwar years transformed popular culture and the lives of ordinary people. New mass media—especially radio and films—reached audiences of unprecedented size. Political life incorporated many of these new media, setting off worries that the common people, increasingly referred to as the "masses," could be manipulated by demagogues and propaganda. In 1918, mass politics was rapidly becoming a fact of life: that meant nearly universal suffrage (varying by country), well-organized political parties reaching out to voters, and in general, more participation in political life.

The expansion of mass culture rested on widespread applications of existing technologies. Wireless communication, for instance, was invented before the turn of the century, and saw limited use in the First World War. With major financial investment in the 1920s, though, the radio industry boomed. Three out of four British families had a radio by the end of the 1930s, and in Germany, the ratio was even higher. In every European country, broadcasting rights were controlled by the government; in the United States, radio was managed by corporations. The radio broadcast soon became the national soapbox for politicians, and it played no small role in creating new kinds of political language. President Franklin Roosevelt's reassuring "fireside chats" took advantage of the way that radio bridged the public world of politics with the private world of the home. Hitler cultivated a different kind of radio personality, barking his fierce invectives; he made some fifty addresses in 1933 alone. In Germany, Nazi propagandists beamed their messages into homes or blared them through loudspeakers in town squares, constant and repetitive. Broadcasting created new rituals of political life—and new means of communication and persuasion.

The most dramatic changes came on movie screens. The technology of moving pictures came earlier; the 1890s were the era of nickelodeons and short action pictures. And in that period, France and Italy had strong film industries. Further popularized by news shorts during the war, film boomed in the war's aftermath. When sound was added to movies in 1927, costs soared, competition intensified, and audiences grew rapidly. By the 1930s, an estimated 40 percent of British adults went to the movies once a week, a strikingly high figure. Many went more often than that. The United States' film industry gained a competitive edge in Europe, buoyed by the size of its home market, by huge investments in equipment and distribution, by aggressive marketing, and by Hollywood's star system of long-term contracts with well-known actors who, in a sense, standardized the product and guaranteed a film's success.

Germany, too, was home to a particularly talented group of directors, writers, and actors, and to a major production company, UFA (Universum Film AG), which ran the largest and best-equipped studios in Europe. UFA's history paralleled the country's: it was run by the government during World War I, devastated by the economic crisis of the early twenties, rescued by wealthy German nationalists in the late twenties, and finally taken over by the Nazis. Though production continued unabated during the Third Reich, many of the industry's most talented members fled from the oppressive regime, ending the golden age of German cinema.

Many found the new mass culture disturbing. As they perceived it, the threat came straight from the United States, which deluged Europe with cultural exports after the war. Hollywood westerns, cheap dime novels, and jazz music—which became increasingly popular in the 1920s—introduced Europe to new ways of life. Advertising, comedies, and romances disseminated new and

Scene from *Metropolis,* 1926. In German expressionist-director Fritz Lang's science fiction film, the worker girl Maria attempts to calm the workers of a modernistic city, but a mad scientist creates an evil robot of her to stir up revolt.

often disconcerting images of femininity. With bobbed haircuts and short dresses, "new women" seemed assertive, flirtatious, capricious, and materialistic. Conservative critics abhorred the fact that "the parson's wife sat nearby his maid at Sunday matinees, equally rapt in the gaze of Hollywood stars." American critics expressed many of the same concerns. Yet the United States enjoyed more social and political stability than Europe. War and revolution had shaken Europe's economies and cultures, and in that context "Americanization" seemed a handy shorthand for economic as well as cultural change.

Authoritarian governments, in particular, decried these developments as decadent threats to national culture. Fascist, communist, and Nazi governments tried to control not only popular culture, but also high culture and modernism, which were typically out of line with the designs of the dictators. Stalin much preferred "socialist realism" to the new Soviet avant garde. Mussolini had a penchant for classical kitsch, though he was far more accepting of modern art than Hitler, who despised its "decadence." Nazism had its own cultural aesthetic, promoting "Aryan" art and architecture and rejecting the modern, "international" style they associated with the "international Jewish conspiracy."

The Nazis, like other authoritarian governments, used mass media as efficient means of indoctrination and control. Movies became part of the Nazis' pioneering use of "spectacular politics." Media campaigns, mass rallies, parades and ceremonies: all were designed to display the strength and glory of the Reich, and to impress and intimidate spectators. In 1934 Hitler commissioned the filmmaker Leni Riefenstahl to record a political rally staged in Nuremberg. The film, entitled *Triumph of the Will,* was a visual hymn to the Nordic race and the Nazi regime. Everything in the film was on a huge scale: masses of bodies stood in parade formation, flags rose and fell in unison; the film invited viewers to surrender to the power of grand ritual and symbolism. The comedian Charlie Chaplin riposted in his celebrated lampoon *The Great Dictator* (1940), an enormously successful parody of Nazi pomposities.

The Nazis also tried to eliminate the influences of American popular culture, which even before 1933 had been decried as an example of biological and cultural degeneracy. With culture, however, the Nazis were forced to strike a balance between party propaganda and popular entertainment. The regime allowed many cultural imports, including Hollywood films, to continue, while consciously cultivating German alternatives to American cinema, music, fashions, and even dances. During the Third Reich, the German film industry turned out comedies, escapist fantasies, and sentimental romances. It developed its own star system and tried to keep audiences happy; meanwhile it became a major competitor internationally. For domestic consumption, the industry also produced vicious anti-Semitic films, such as *The Eternal Jew* (1940) and *Jew Suss* (1940), a fictional tale of a Jewish moneylender who brings the city of Württemberg to ruin in the eighteenth century. In the final scene of the film, the town expels the entire Jewish community from its midst, asking that "posterity honor this law." Goebbels reported that the entire Reich cabinet had viewed the film and considered it "an incredible success."

ONCLUSION

The strains of World War I created a world that few recognized—transformed by revolution, mass mobilization, and loss. In retrospect, it is hard not to see the period that followed as a succession of failures. Capitalism foundered in the Great Depression, democracies collapsed in the face of authoritarianism, and the Treaty of Versailles proved hollow. Yet we better understand the experiences and outlooks of ordinary people if we do not treat the failures of the interwar period as inevitable. By the late 1920s, many were cautiously optimistic that the Great War's legacy could be overcome and that problems were being solved. The Great Depression (1929–1933) wrecked these hopes, bringing economic chaos and political paralysis. Paralysis and chaos, in turn, created new audiences for political leaders who offered authoritarian solutions and more voters for their political parties. Finally, economic troubles and political turmoil made contending with rising international tensions, to which we now turn, vastly more difficult. By the 1930s, even cautious optimism about international relations had given way to apprehension and dread.

KEY TERMS

Bolsheviks

Joseph Stalin

collectivization

"Great Terror"

Benito Mussolini

Weimar Republic

Nazi party

Adolf Hitler

Kristallnacht

Great Depression

New Deal

Albert Einstein

UFA

SELECTED READINGS

Carr, E. H. *The Bolshevik Revolution, 1917–1923.* London and New York, 1950–1953. One of the classics.

Cohen, Stephen F. *Bukharin and the Bolshevik Revolution: A Political Biography, 1888–1938.* New York, 1973.

Conquest, Robert. *The Great Terror: A Reassessment.* New York, 1990.

Crew, David F. *Nazism and German Society, 1933–1945.* New York, 1994. An excellent and accessible collection of essays.

Figes, Orlando. *Peasant Russia, Civil War: The Volga Countryside in Revolution, 1917–1921.* Oxford, 1989.

Friedlander, Saul. *Nazi Germany and the Jews.* New York, 1998. Excellent; the first of a projected two-volume study.

Gay, Peter. *Weimar Culture.* New York, 1968. Concise and elegant overview.

Getty, J. Arch and Oleg V. Naumov. *The Road to Terror: Stalin and the Self-Destruction of the Bolsheviks, 1932–1939.* New Haven, 1999. Combines analysis with many newly discovered documents.

Gilbert, Felix and David C. Large, *The End of the European Era, 1890 to the Present.* New York, 2001.

Goldman, Wendy Z. *Women, the State, and Revolution: Soviet Family Policy and Social Life, 1917–1936.* New York, 1993.

Kershaw, Ian. *The Hitler Myth: Image and Reality in the Third Reich.* New York, 1987.

———. *Hitler.* 2 vols: *1889–1936, Hubris,* New York, 1999; *1936–1945, Nemesis,* New York, 2001.

Klemperer, Victor. *I Will Bear Witness: A Diary of the Nazi Years, 1933–1941.* New York, 1999. *I Will Bear Witness: A Diary of the Nazi Years, 1942–1945.* New York, 2001. Certain to be a classic.

Lewin, Moshe. *The Making of the Soviet System: Essays in the Social History of Interwar Russia.* New York, 1985. One of the best to offer a view from below.

Rentschler, Eric. *The Ministry of Illusion: Nazi Cinema and Its Afterlife.* Cambridge, Mass., 1996. For the more advanced student.

Suny, Ronald Grigor. *The Revenge of the Past: Nationalism, Revolution, and the Collapse of the Soviet Union.* Stanford, Calif., 1993.

Tucker, Robert C. *Stalin as Revolutionary, 1879–1929.* New York, 1973.

———. *Stalin in Power: The Revolution from Above, 1928–1941.* New York, 1990.

Chapter
TWENTY-SIX

THE SECOND
WORLD WAR

IN SEPTEMBER 1939, Europe was consumed by another world war. The Second World War was not simply a continuation of the First. Both were triggered by threats to the European balance of power. Yet even more than the Great War, the Second World War was a conflict among nations, whole peoples, and fiercely opposing ideals. The methods of warfare in the Second World War had little in common with those of the First. In 1914 military firepower had outmatched mobility, resulting in four years of static, mud-sodden slaughter. In 1939, mobility was joined to firepower on a massive scale. The results were terrifying. On the battlefield, the tactics of high-speed armored warfare (*Blitzkrieg*), aircraft carriers sinking ships far below the horizon, and submarines used in vast numbers to dominate shipping lanes changed the scope and the pace of fighting. This was not a war of trenches and barbed wire but a war of motion, dramatic conquests, and terrible destructive power. The devastation of 1914–1918 paled in comparison to this new, global conflict.

The other great change involved not of tactics, but of targets. Much of the unprecedented killing power now available was aimed directly at civilians. Cities were laid waste by artillery and aerial bombing. Whole regions were put to the torch, while towns and villages were systematically cordoned off and leveled. Whole populations were targeted as well, in ways that continue to appall. The Nazi regime's systematic murder of gypsies, homosexuals, and other "deviants," along with the effort to exterminate the Jewish people completely, made the Second World War a horrifyingly unique event. So did the United States' use of a weapon whose existence would dominate politics and society for the next fifty years: the atomic bomb. The naive enthusiasm that had marked the outbreak of the Great War was absent from the start. Terrible memories of the first conflict lingered. Yet those who fought against the Axis Powers (and many of those who fought for them) found

FOCUS QUESTIONS

- What were the long-term causes of World War II?
- What was the policy of "appeasement"?
- What accounts for the early German successes in World War II?
- What made World War II a global war?

- How were the Nazis able to rule over a continental empire?
- In what ways was World War II a "racial war"?
- How did the war transform the home fronts?
- How did the Soviets defeat the Germans?

that their determination to fight and win grew as the war went on. Unlike the seemingly meaningless killing of the Great War, the Second World War was cast as a war of absolutes, of good and evil, of national and global survival. Nevertheless the scale of destruction brought with it a profound weariness. It also provoked deep-seated questions about the value of Western "civilization" and the terms on which it, and the rest of the world, might live peaceably in the future.

THE CAUSES OF THE WAR: UNSETTLED QUARRELS, ECONOMIC FALLOUT, AND NATIONALISM

What were the long-term causes of World War II?

The causes of the Second World War were rooted in the peace settlement of 1919–1920. The peace had created as many problems as it had solved. The senior Allied heads of state yielded to demands that involved annexing German territory and creating satellite states out of the eastern European empires. In doing so, the peacemakers created fresh bitterness and conflict. The Versailles treaty and its champions, such as President Woodrow Wilson, proclaimed the principle of self-determination for the peoples of eastern and southern Europe. Yet the new states created by the treaty crossed ethnic boundaries, involved political compromises, and frustrated many of the expectations they had raised. The Allied powers also kept up the naval blockade against Germany after the end of the fighting. This forced the new German government to accept harsh terms that deprived Germany of its political power in Europe, and saddled the German economy with the bill for the conflict in a "war guilt" clause. The blockade and its consequences created grievances that many angry, humiliated Germans considered legitimate.

A second cause of World War II was the failure to create lasting, binding standards for peace and security. Diplomats spent the ten years after Versailles trying to restore such standards. Some put their faith in the legal and moral authority of the League. Others saw disarmament as the most promising means of guaranteeing

peace. Throughout the 1920s, a number of important European statesmen tried to reach a set of agreements that would stabilize the peace and prevent rearmament. Despite the good faith of many of the statesmen involved, none of these pacts carried any real weight. Each nation tried to include special provisions and exceptions for "vital interests" and these efforts compromised the treaties from the start. Had the League of Nations been better organized, it might have relieved some of the tensions or at least prevented clashes between nations. But the League was never a league of all nations. Essential members were absent, since Germany and the Soviet Union were excluded for most of the interwar period, and the United States never joined. The depression of the 1930s contributed to the coming of the war in several ways. It intensified economic nationalism. Baffled by problems of unemployment and business stagnation, governments imposed high tariffs in an effort to preserve the home market for their own producers.

These inward-looking policies among the Allies left the door open to more aggressive tactics elsewhere. In Germany, the depression was the last blow to the Weimar Republic. In 1933 power passed to the Nazis, who promised a total program of national renewal. In the fascist states (and, exceptionally, the United States) public works projects of one kind or another were prescribed as an answer to mass unemployment. This produced highways, bridges, and railroads; it also produced a new arms race.

Despite the misgivings of many inside the governments of Britain and France, Germany was allowed to ignore the terms of the peace treaties and rearm. Armaments expansion on a large scale first began in Germany in 1935, with the result that unemployment was reduced and the effects of the depression eased. Other nations followed the German example, not simply as a way to boost their economies but in response to growing Nazi military power. In the Pacific, the decline of Japanese exports meant that the nation did not have enough foreign currency to pay for vital raw materials from overseas. This played into the hands of Japan's military regime. Japanese national ambitions, and Japanese leaders' perception of the political and cultural inferiority of the Chinese, led Japan to fresh imperial adventures in the name of establishing economic stability in East Asia. They began in 1931 with the invasion of Manchuria, and moved from there to create a "Greater Pacific Co-Prosperity Sphere" that involved seizing other territories as Japanese colonies. Raw materials could then be bought with Japanese money, and more of Asia would serve the needs of Japan's empire.

The tremendous economic hardship of the depression, a contested peace treaty, and political weakness underminded international stability. But the decisive factor in the crises of the 1930s, and the trigger for another world war, lay in a blend of violent nationalism and modern ideologies that glorified the nation and national destiny. This blend, particularly in the forms of fascism and militarism, appeared around the world in many countries. By the middle of the 1930s, recognizing common interests, fascist Italy and Nazi Germany formed an "Axis," an alliance binding their goals of national glory and international power. They were later joined by Japan's military regime. In Spain, the ultranationalist forces that tried to overthrow the Spanish Republic, setting off the Spanish Civil War (see below), believed they were reviving the stability, authority, and morality of the nation. Fascist or semifascist regimes spread in Eastern Europe, in Yugoslavia, Hungary, and Romania.

THE 1930S: CHALLENGES TO THE PEACE, APPEASEMENT, AND THE "DISHONEST DECADE"

What was the policy of "appeasement"?

The 1930s brought the tensions and failures caused by the treaties of 1919–1920 to a head. Fascist and nationalist governments flouted the League of Nations by launching new conquests and efforts at national expansion. Each new conflict seemed to warn that another, much wider war would follow unless it could somehow be averted. Ordinary people, particularly in Britain, France, and the United States, were divided. Some saw the actions of the aggressors as a direct challenge to civilization, one that had to be met with force if necessary. Others hoped to avoid premature or unnecessary conflict. Their governments tried instead at several points to negotiate with the fascists and keep a tenuous peace. The 1930s were not just a time of renewed warfare and global crisis; many saw the period as a series of missed opportunities to prevent the larger war to come. In 1939, on the first day of the Second World War, the British poet and leftist W. H. Auden condemned the behavior of Western governments, calling the 1930s "a low, dishonest decade."

The object of Auden's venom was the policy of "appeasement" pursued by Western governments in the face of German, Italian, and Japanese aggression. Appeasement was neither simple power politics nor pure cowardice. It was grounded in three deeply held assumptions. The first assumption was that the outbreak of another war was unthinkable. Second, many in Britain and the United States argued that Germany had been mistreated by the Versailles treaty and harbored legitimate grievances that should be acknowledged and resolved. Finally, many appeasers were staunch anticommunists. They believed that the fascist states in Germany and Italy were an essential bulwark against the advance of Soviet communism. Yet this last point divided the appeasers. All were concerned with maintaining Europe's balance of power. One group, however, believed that the Soviets posed the greater threat, and that accommodating Hitler might create a common interest against a common enemy. The other faction believed that Nazi Germany presented the true threat to European stability; nevertheless, they believed, Hitler would have to be placated until Britain and France finished rearming. At that point, they hoped, their greater military power would deter Hitler or Mussolini from risking a general European war. It took most of the 1930s for the debate between appeasers to come to a head. In the meanwhile, the League of Nations faced more immediate and pressing challenges.

The 1930s brought three crucial tests for the League: the crises in China, Ethiopia, and Spain. In China, the Japanese invasion of Manchuria in 1931 turned into an invasion of the whole country. In 1937, the Japanese laid siege to the strategic city of Nanjing. Their orders on taking the city were simple: "kill all, burn all, destroy all." More than two hundred thousand Chinese citizens were slaughtered in what came to be known as the "Rape of Nanjing." The League voiced shock and disapproval but did nothing. In 1935 Mussolini began his efforts to make the Mediterranean an Italian empire by returning to Ethiopia to avenge the defeat of 1896. This time the Italians came with tanks, bombers, and poison gas. The Ethiopians fought bravely but hopelessly, and this imperial massacre aroused world opinion. The League attempted to impose sanctions on Italy and condemned Japan. But for two reasons, no enforcement followed. The first was British and French fear of communism, and their hope that Italy and Japan would act as counterweights to the

Soviets. The second reason was practical. Enforcing sanctions would involve challenging Japan's powerful fleet or Mussolini's newly built battleships. Britain and France were unwilling, and dangerously close to unable, to use their navies to those ends.

THE SPANISH CIVIL WAR

The third challenge came closer to home. In 1936 civil war broke out in Spain. A series of weak republican governments, committed to large-scale social reforms, could not overcome opposition to those measures and political polarization. War broke out as extreme right-wing military officers rebelled. Although Hitler and Mussolini had signed a pact of nonintervention with the other Western powers, both leaders sent troops and equipment to assist the rebel commander, Francisco Franco (1939–1975). The Soviet Union countered with aid to communist

troops serving under the banner of the Spanish Republic. Again, Britain and France failed to act decisively. Thousands of volunteers from England, France, and the United States, including many working-class socialists and writers, took up arms as private soldiers for the Republican government. They saw the war as a test of the West's determination to resist fascism and military dictatorships. Their governments were much more hesitant. In Spain, despite some heroic fighting, the Republican camp degenerated into a hornet's nest of competing factions: republican, socialist, communist, and anarchist.

The Spanish Civil War was brutal. Both the German and Soviet "advisors" saw Spain as a "dress rehearsal" for a later war between the two powers. They each brought in their newest weapons and practiced their skills in destroying civilian targets from the air. In April 1937, a raid by German dive bombers utterly destroyed the town of Guernica in northern Spain, in an effort to cut off Republican supply lines and terrorize civilians. It shocked public opinion, and was commemorated by Pablo Picasso in one of the most famous paintings of the twentieth century. Both sides committed atrocities. The Spanish Civil War lasted three years, ending with a complete victory for Franco in 1939. Franco sent one million of his Republican enemies to prison or concentration camps. Hitler in particular drew lessons from Spain. The first was that if Britain, France, and the Soviet Union ever tried to contain fascism, they would have a hard time coordinating their efforts. The second was that Britain and France were deeply averse to fighting another European war. This meant that the Nazis could use every means short of war to achieve their goals.

Main Nationalist attacks	Nationalist, October 1937
Main Republican attacks	Nationalist, July 1938
"International Brigade" bases	Nationalist, February 1939
Nationalist, July 1936	Republican, February 1939

THE SPANISH CIVIL WAR

Why did thousands of foreign fighters join the war? How did the strategies and weapons used in the war anticipate those used in World War II? What were the consequences of Franco's victory?

GERMAN REARMAMENT AND THE POLITICS OF APPEASEMENT

Hitler took advantage of this combination of international tolerance and war weariness to advance his ambitions. As Germany rearmed, Hitler played on Germans' sense of shame and betrayal, proclaiming their right to regain their former power in the world. Hitler's stated goals were the restoration of Germany's power and dignity inside Europe, and the unification of all ethnic Germans inside his "Third German Reich." As the first step in this process, Germany reoccupied the Rhineland in 1936. It was a risky move, chancing war with the much more powerful French army. But France and Britain did not mount a military response. In retrospect, this was an important turning point; the balance of power tipped in Germany's favor.

Guernica (1937), by Pablo Picasso. One of Picasso's most influential paintings, *Guernica* was painted as a mural for the Spanish republican government as it fought for survival in the Spanish Civil War. The Basque town of Guernica had been bombed by German fighters just a few months earlier, in April 1937. Near the center a horse writhes in agony; to the left a distraught woman holds her dead child.

In March of 1938, Hitler annexed Austria, reaffirming his intention to bring all Germans into his Reich. Once more, no official reaction came from the West. The Nazis' next target was the Sudetenland in Czechoslovakia, which had a large ethnic German population. Hitler declared that the Sudetenland was a natural part of the Reich and that he intended to occupy it. The Czechs did not want to give way. Hitler's generals were wary of this gamble. Czechoslovakia had a strong, well-equipped army and a line of fortifications along the border. Many in the French and Polish governments were willing to come to the Czechs' aid. According to plans already being laid for a wider European war, Germany would not be ready for another three to four years. But Hitler did gamble, and the British prime minister, Neville Chamberlain, obliged him. Chamberlain's logic was that this dispute was about the balance of power in Europe. If Hitler were allowed to unify all Germans in one state, he reasoned, then German ambitions would be satisfied. Chamberlain also believed that his country could not commit to a sustained war. Finally, defending eastern European boundaries against Germany ranked low on Great Britain's list of priorities, at least in comparison to ensuring free trade in western Europe and protecting the strategic centers of the British empire.

On September 29, 1938, Hitler met with Chamberlain, Premier Édouard Daladier (1938–1940) of France, and Mussolini in a four-power conference in Munich.

The four negotiators bargained away a major slice of Czechoslovakia, while Czech representatives were left to await their fate outside the conference room. Chamberlain returned to London proclaiming "peace in our time." Hitler soon proved that boast hollow. In March 1939 Germany invaded what was left of Czechoslovakia and established a puppet regime in its capital, Prague. This was Germany's first conquest of non-German territory, and it sent shock waves across Europe. It convinced public and political opinion outside Germany of the futility of appeasement. Chamberlain was forced to shift his policies completely. British and French rearmament sped up dramatically. Together with France, Britain guaranteed the sovereignty of the two states now directly in Hitler's path, Poland and Romania.

Meanwhile, the politics of appeasement had fueled Stalin's fears that the Western democracies might strike a deal with Germany at Soviet expense, thus diverting Nazi expansion eastward. The Soviet Union had not been invited to the Munich conference, and, suspicious that Britain and France were unreliable allies, Stalin became convinced that he should look elsewhere for security. In a cynical reversal of their anti-Nazi proclamations, the Soviets signed a nonaggression pact with the Nazis in August 1939. By going to Munich, Britain and France had put their interests first; the Soviet Union would now look after its own.

CHRONOLOGY

THE ROAD TO WORLD WAR II, 1931–1940

Japanese invasion of Manchuria	1931
Germany leaves the League of Nations	1933
Germany begins remilitarization	March, 1935
Spanish Civil War	April, 1936–April, 1939
Germany reoccupies the Rhineland	March, 1936
Germany annexes Austria	March, 1938
Munich Conference	September, 1938
Nazi-Soviet Pact	August, 1939
Germany invades Poland	September, 1939
Germany invades the Low Countries and France	May, 1940

THE OUTBREAK OF HOSTILITIES AND THE FALL OF FRANCE

What accounts for the early German successes in World War II?

After his success in Czechoslovakia, Hitler demanded the abolition of the Polish Corridor. This was a narrow strip of land connecting Poland with the Baltic Sea. The corridor also divided East Prussia from the rest of Germany, separating yet another large German population from union with the Reich. With the Soviets now in his camp, he expected that Poland would consent and the Western allies would back down again. When Poland stood firm instead, Hitler attacked. On September 1, 1939, German troops crossed the Polish border. Britain and France sent a joint warning to Germany to withdraw. There was no reply. On September 3, Britain and France declared war.

The conquest of Poland was shockingly quick. It demanded great resources—Germany committed nearly all of its combat troops and planes to the invasion—but the results were remarkable. Well-coordinated attacks by German panzers (tanks) and armored vehicles, supported by devastating air power, cut the large but slow-moving Polish army to pieces. German infantry still moved on foot or via horse-drawn transport, but their disciplined advance followed the devastating work of the panzers. The Poles fought doggedly, but were so stunned and disorganized that they had little hope of mounting an effective defense. The "lightning war" (*Blitzkrieg*) for which the German officer corps had trained so long was a complete success. Poland, a large country with a large army, was dismembered in four weeks.

To the west, after the fall of Poland the conflict became an ominous "phony war" or "sitzkrieg," as it was sometimes called. The fighting in Poland was followed by a winter of anxious nonactivity with occasional headlines about naval skirmishes. In the spring of 1940 that calm was broken by a terrible storm. The Germans struck first in Scandinavia, taking Denmark in a day and invading Norway. Britain and France tried to aid the Norwegian defense and sank a large number of German ships, but the Allied expedition failed. Then the real blow was struck. On May 10, German forces swarmed through Belgium and the Netherlands on their way to France. The two nations were conquered in short order.

The large French army was carved up by the *Blitzkrieg*. Its divisions were isolated, outflanked, and overwhelmed by German aircraft and armored columns working according to an exacting plan. French units either fought fierce battles until they were hopelessly surrounded, or simply collapsed. French armor and artillery, much of it better built than the German equivalents, were poorly organized and rendered useless in the face of rapid German maneuvers. The defeat turned quickly into a rout. The disorganized British made a desperate retreat to the port of Dunkirk on the English Channel. Despite heavy German air attacks, Britain's Royal Navy evacuated more than three hundred thousand British and French troops, with the help of commercial and pleasure boats that had been pressed into emergency service.

After Dunkirk, the conflict was bitter but the outcome inevitable. The Germans swept through the northwest and the heart of the country, reaching Paris in mid-June. The political will of France's government collapsed along with its armies. Rather than withdrawing to Britain or French colonies in North Africa, the French surrendered on June 22. The armistice cut France in two. The Germans occupied all of northern France, including Paris and the Channel ports. The south, and French territories in North Africa, lay under the jurisdiction of a deeply conservative government formed at the spa town of Vichy under the leadership of an elderly First World War hero, Marshal Henri Philippe Pétain. France had

WHAT ACCOUNTS FOR THE EARLY GERMAN SUCCESSES IN WORLD WAR II?

THE OUTBREAK OF HOSTILITIES AND THE FALL OF FRANCE   733

Legend:
- Germany
- German advances
  - Reoccupied Rhineland, March 1936
  - Annexed Austria, March 1938
  - Annexed Sudetenland, October 1938
  - Annexed Bohemia and Moravia, March 1939
  - Annexed Memel, March 1939
- Italy
  - Annexed Albania, April 1939
- Poland and Hungary
  - Annexed Czech territory, 1938 and 1939
- ( ) Former independent nations: Albania, Austria, and Czechoslovakia

GERMAN EXPANSION, 1936–1939

What were Hitler's first steps to unify all the ethnic Germans in Europe? How did he use these initial gains to annex territory from the Czechs? What were the official reactions from Britain, France, and the Soviet Union? After winning Czechoslovakia, why did Hitler choose to invade Poland? How were the Germans able to conquer Poland and France so quickly?

London during the Battle of Britain. German air raids that lasted from August 1940 to June 1941 wrought destruction but did not achieve Hitler's goal of breaking the British. The Holland House Library in London lost its roof, but managed to engage in business as usual.

fallen. One of Germany's historic enemies, the victor of the previous war, an imperial power and nation of almost 60 million citizens, was reduced to chaos and enemy occupation in forty days.

NOT ALONE: THE BATTLE OF BRITAIN AND THE BEGINNINGS OF A GLOBAL WAR

What made World War II a global war?

Before launching an invasion across the Channel, the Nazis attempted to establish superiority in the air. From July 1940 to June 1941, in the Battle of Britain, thousands of planes dropped millions of tons of bombs on British targets: first aircraft and airfields and then, as the focus shifted to breaking Britain's will, civilian targets such as London. More than forty thousand British civilians died. Yet the British stood firm. This was possible in part

because of a German mistake. After a daring British bombing raid on Berlin, Hitler angrily told his generals to concentrate on civilian targets. This spared the Royal Air Force, whose bases had been steadily devastated up to that point. Given the chance to keep fighting, the R.A.F. forced a costly stalemate in the air. Hitler scrapped the invasion plans, turning his attention east toward Russia.

Another important reason for the determined British resistance was a change of political leadership. In May 1940, Chamberlain's catalogue of failures finished his career. He was toppled by a coalition government that brought together Conservative, Liberal, and Labour politicians for the sake of national unity. It was led by the most unlikely of the choices offered to replace him: Winston Churchill (1940–1945, 1951–1955). Churchill was a political maverick who had changed parties more than once. As prime minister he was not much of an administrator, constantly proposing wild schemes, but he had two genuine gifts. The first was language. Churchill spoke extraordinary words of courage and defiance just when the British public wanted and needed to hear them. He was utterly committed to winning the war. The second was personal diplomacy. He convinced the American president Franklin Roosevelt (1933–1945), who supported the Allies, to break with American neutrality and send massive amounts of aid and weapons to Britain

WORLD WAR II IN EUROPE

This map shows the alliance systems and major offensives of the European Theatre in World War II. What explains the rapid expansion of Axis control May 1941? In what ways did geography both aid and potentially hinder the Axis effort to conquer Europe? How did Adolf Hitler hope to neutralize either the Soviet Union or Great Britain early in the war? How did the sieges at Leningrad and Stalingrad prove instrumental in sustaining the Allied effort?

free of charge, under a program called Lend-Lease. Churchill also allowed the new government coalition to work to best effect. The ablest Conservative ministers stayed, but Labour politicians were also allowed to take positions of genuine power. Most of the Labour representatives turned out to be excellent administrators and were directly in touch with Britain's huge working class, which now felt fully included in the war effort.

With Britain's survival, the European war quickly became a global war in four ways. The first was Germany's submarine campaign to starve out the British. The second came with fighting in North Africa, which threatened the Suez Canal and the Allies' access to Middle Eastern oil. The third came with Japan's successful attack on the Allies in the Pacific. The fourth was the great conflict Hitler had always imagined, a war of annihilation against Soviet Russia and Europe's Jewish population.

The first of these, the battle of the Atlantic, was a dire threat to the Allies. Learning from World War I, the Germans sent hundreds of submarines (U-boats) out in "wolf packs" to stalk the major sea lanes to Britain. German submarines sank millions of tons of merchant shipping, as far away as the coasts of Brazil and Florida. Britain's supplies of weapons, raw materials, and food hung in the balance. The British devoted a huge naval effort and great technical resourcefulness to saving their convoys. Despite continued losses, these efforts kept supplies coming. When the United States entered the war, the British supplied experience and technology, the Americans the numbers and firepower to sink many more U-boats. By late 1942 the threat receded.

The war in North Africa began because Britain had to protect the Suez Canal, but Britain was soon drawn into a larger conflict. A small, well-led British army in Egypt humiliated a much larger Italian invasion force. The British nearly captured Italy's colony of Libya, and this forced Germany to intervene. An elite armored force called the Afrika Korps, led by Germany's most daring tank commander, Erwin Rommel, drove the British back in the Spring of 1941 and started a grudging two-year war in the desert. When Rommel tried to invade Egypt, his forces were stopped and badly defeated near the town of El Alamein in the autumn of 1942, then driven back toward Tunisia. The United States intervened in November 1942, landing in the French territories of Algeria and Morocco. Rommel still defended Tunisia against the Allies for four months but a joint offensive broke the German lines in March 1943, ending the fighting.

The war became truly global when Japan struck the American naval base at Pearl Harbor, Hawaii, on the morning of December 7, 1941. In order to win and to establish a Japanese empire throughout Asia, they would have to destroy America's Pacific fleet and seize the colonies of the British, Dutch, and French empires.

Like Germany, Japan began with lightning blows. The attack on Pearl Harbor was a brilliant act of surprise that devastated the American fleet and shocked the American public. It was not, however, the success that the Japanese wanted. Eight U.S. battleships were sunk and more than two thousand lives lost, but much of the American fleet, including its aircraft carriers, submarines, and many smaller ships, were safely at sea on the day of the strike. The unprovoked attack galvanized American public opinion in a way the war in Europe had not. When Germany rashly declared war on the United States as well, America declared itself ready to take on all comers and joined the Allies.

Despite the mixed results at Pearl Harbor the Japanese enjoyed stunning successes elsewhere. For the European colonial powers, Japan's entry into the war was a catastrophe. Japanese troops swept through the British protectorate of Malaya in weeks. Britain's fortified island port at Singapore, the keystone of British defenses in the Pacific, fell at the end of December 1941. The Japanese also invaded the Philippines in December 1941, and while American soldiers and marines held out on the island of Corregidor for some time, they too were forced to surrender. Some took to the hills to fight as guerrillas; the rest were forced on a "Death March" to Japanese labor camps.

> The war became truly global when Japan struck the American naval base at Pearl Harbor, Hawaii, on the morning of December 7, 1941.

Reeling from Japan's blows, the Allies finally reorganized during 1942. In New Guinea, Australian troops fresh from North Africa were first to defeat the Japanese on land in bitter hand-to-hand fighting, and staged a counterattack through the high mountain jungles. At sea, America's navy benefited from a rapidly increased production schedule that turned out new ships and planes to outnumber the Japanese, and two gifted admirals, Chester Nimitz and William Halsey, who outfought them. In 1942 the United States won crucial victories in the Coral Sea and at Midway, a battle fought at sea but won and lost by aircraft flown from each side's carriers. American marines landed on the island of Guadalcanal in early 1942 and captured this strategic Japanese base after months of bitter fighting. Their success began a campaign of "island hopping" as the marines destroyed Japan's network of island bases throughout the Pacific. By 1943, the Japanese victories had been halted, the Japanese navy had lost most of its capital ships, and the Allies began a slow march to Singapore and the Philippines.

"A Date that will live in Infamy," December 7, 1941. The USS West Virginia was one of eight battleships sunk during the Japanese surprise attack targeting "Battleship Row" at the American naval base at Pearl Harbor. Two thousand people were killed but most of the American fleet, en route to or from other locations in the Pacific, was spared.

THE RISE AND RUIN OF NATIONS: GERMANY'S WAR IN THE EAST AND THE OCCUPATION OF EUROPE

How were the Nazis able to rule over a continental empire?

While battles ebbed and flowed in the Atlantic and the North African desert, Germany moved south-east into the Balkans. In 1941 Germany took over Yugoslavia almost without a fight. The Germans split Yugoslavia's ethnic patchwork by establishing a Croatian puppet state, pitting Croats against their Serb neighbors who

were ruled directly by the Nazis. Romania, Hungary, and Bulgaria joined the Nazis' cause as allies. The Greeks, who had dealt a crushing defeat to an Italian invasion, were suddenly confronted with a massive German force that overran the country. These victories, and the economy of plunder that enriched Germany with forced labor and other nations' money, won Hitler considerable popularity at home. But these were only the first steps in a larger plan.

Hitler's ultimate goals, and his conception of Germany's national destiny, lay to the east. Hitler had always seen the nonaggression pact with the Soviet Union as an act of convenience to last only until Germany was ready for this final conflict. By the summer of 1941, it seemed Germany was ready. On June 22, 1941, Hitler began Operation Barbarossa, the invasion of the Soviet Union. The elite of the German army led the way, defeating all the forces the Russians could put in front of them. Stalin's purges of the 1930s had exiled or executed many of his most capable army officers, and the effects showed in Russian disorganization and disaffection in the face of the panzers. Like Napoleon, the Germans led a multinational army that included Italians, Hungarians, most of the Romanian army, and freelance soldiers from the Baltics and the Ukraine who bore grudges against Stalin's authoritarian regime. During the fall of 1941, the Nazis destroyed much of the Red Army's fighting strength and vigorously pursued their two goals: the destruction of communism and racial purification.

The war against the Soviets was a war of ideologies and of racial hatred. The advancing Nazi forces left burning fields and towns in their wake and methodically wiped the occupied territories clean of "undesirable elements." By the end of 1941 it was clear that the war in the East was a war of destruction, and that both sides believed that only one side would be allowed to survive. In 1941, it seemed the victors would be German. Their forces were on the march towards the capital at Moscow. On orders from Berlin, however, German forces pushing toward Moscow were diverted south to attack Russia's industrial heartland in an effort to destroy the Soviets' ability to resist before the Russian winter set in. This left the Soviet capital free, and the Russian population, its leaders, and its armies, began to organize a much more determined resistance.

Hitler nonetheless managed to piece together an empire that stretched across the entire continent of Europe. Occupied countries paid inflated "occupation costs" in taxes, food, industrial production, and manpower. More than 2 million foreign workers were brought into Germany in 1942–1943 from France, Belgium, Holland, and the Soviet Union.

The demands of enemy occupation, and the political and moral questions of "collaboration" and resistance, were issues across occupied Europe. The Nazis set up puppet regimes in a number of occupied territories. Both Norway and the Netherlands were deeply divided by the occupation. In each country a relatively small but dedicated party of Nazis governed in the name of the Germans, while at the same time well-organized and determined resistance movements gathered information for the Allies and carried out acts of sabotage. In Denmark, the population was much more united against their German occupiers, engaging in regular acts of passive resistance that infuriated German administrators. They also banded together as private citizens to smuggle most of the country's Jewish population to safety in neutral Sweden.

Elsewhere the relationship between collaboration, resistance, and self-interested indifference was more complex. Collaboration ranged from simple survival tactics under occupation to active support for Nazi ideals and goals. The worst example of this was the Vichy regime's active anti-Semitism and the aid given by French authorities in isolating, criminalizing, and deporting French Jews to the concentration camps. Living with the Germany conquerers forced citizens in France (and elsewhere) to make choices. Many chose to protect their own interests by sacrificing those of others, particularly such "undesirables" as Jews and communists. At the same time, communist activists, some members of the military, and ordinary citizens, such as the people of France's central mountains, who had a long tradition of smuggling and resisting government, became active guerrillas (*maquis*) and saboteurs. They established links with the Free French movement in London, led by the charismatic, stiff-necked general Charles de Gaulle, and supplied important intelligence to the Allies. In eastern Europe, resistance movements provoked both open warfare against the fascists and civil war within their own countries. The Germans' system of occupation in Yugoslavia pitted a fascist Croat regime against most Serbs. Ironically, a Croat, Josip Broz (Tito), emerged as the leader of the most powerful Yugoslavian resistance movement—militarily the most significant resistance in the war. They fought Germans, Italians, and

French Man reacting as Germans march the fallen national flag through the streets of Marseilles, 1941. Split between a German occupation and a pro-German government, French people confronted the choice between collaboration and resistance.

Croat fascists, and they gained support and supplies from the Allies.

Perhaps the most important moral issue facing citizens of occupied Europe was not their national allegiance, but rather their personal attitude to the fate of the Nazis' sworn enemies: Jews, communists, gypsies, homosexuals, and political "undesirables." Some French Jews along the Riviera found Italian Catholic army officers who occupied the area more willing to save them from deportation than their fellow Frenchmen. This deeply personal dilemma—whether to risk family, friends, and careers to aid the deportees, or simply look the other way and allow mass murder—was one of the most powerful of the war.

RACIAL WAR, ETHNIC CLEANSING, AND THE HOLOCAUST

In what ways was World War II a "racial war"?

From the beginning, the Nazis had seen the conflict as a racial war. Thus as soon as the war broke out, the Nazis began to implement ambitious plans for redrawing the racial map of the Reich, or what is now called ethnic cleansing. In the fall of 1939, with Poland conquered, Heinrich Himmler directed the SS to begin massive population transfers. Over two hundred thousand ethnic Germans from the Baltic states were resettled in Western Prussia. Welcoming these ethnic Germans went hand in hand with a brutal campaign of terror against the Poles, especially Polish Jews. The Nazis sought to rootout all sources of potential resistance to allow SS troops to occupy the asylums' barracks. The Nazis began to transport Jews by the thousands to the region of Lublin, south of Warsaw. Special death squads also began to shoot Jews in the streets and in front of synagogues. These Polish campaigns took one hundred thousand Jewish lives in 1940.

The elimination of European Jewry stood at the center of the Nazis' *Rassenkampf*, or "racial struggle." We have seen the role of anti-Semitism in Hitler's rise to power and the escalating campaign of terror against the Jewish community inside Germany in the 1930s, including the Night of the Broken Glass (see Chapter 25).

The war radicalized that campaign. The invasion of the Soviet Union in June 1941 marked a turning point in the deadly path to the Holocaust. Operation Barbarossa, as the invasion was called, brought several changes. First, it was animated by the Nazis' intense ideological and racial hatreds, directed against Slavs, Jews, and Marxists. The invasion of Poland had been vicious. The invasion of the USSR was openly a "war of extermination." Second, the invading German army succeeded more quickly than it expected. The huge gains created euphoria in the Nazi hierarchy; Hitler seemed very close to realizing his dreams of an eastern empire. But success also bred fear, or worry at the prospect of controlling the millions of Soviet prisoners, Soviet civilians, and Soviet Jews who had now fallen into Nazi hands. The combination of elation and anxiety was deadly. It led, quickly, from systematic brutality to atrocities, and then to murder on a scale few could have imagined.

As the Nazi army swept into the Soviet Union in 1941, captured communist officials, political agitators, and any hostile civilians were imprisoned, tortured, or shot. Five and one half million military prisoners were taken and marched to camps. Over half of them died of starvation or were executed. Poles from regions that had been under Soviet rule, Jews, and Russians were deported to Germany to work as slave labor in German factories. On the heels of the army came special battalions of *Einsatzgruppen*, or death squads. Joined by eleven thousand extra SS troops, they stormed through Jewish villages and towns with Russian or Polish populations identified as "difficult." The men of the villages were shot; the women and children either deported to labor camps or massacred along with the men. By September 1941, the *Einsatzgruppen* reported that in their efforts at "pacification" they had killed eighty-five thousand persons, most of them Jews. By April 1942, the number was five hundred thousand. This killing began before the gas chambers had gone into operation and continued through the campaigns on the eastern front. As of 1943, the death squads had killed roughly 2.2 million Jews.

As Operation Barbarossa progressed, German administrations of occupied areas herded local Jewish populations even more tightly into the "ghettos" some Jewish communities had occupied for centuries: Warsaw and Lodz in Poland were the largest. There, administrators, accusing Jewish people in the ghettos with hoarding supplies, refused to allow food to go in. The ghettos became centers of starvation and disease. Those who left the ghetto were shot rather than returned.

THE HOLOCAUST: MASSACRES IN UKRAINE

The following account of a mass shooting in the Ukraine comes from a German engineer testifying at the Nuremberg trials in 1946. Events like these happened so often that his is but one of many such descriptions. Note that the SS allowed him to witness these events.

From September 1941 until January 1944, I was the manager and chief engineer of a branch of the construction firm, Josef Jung of Solingen with its headquarters in Sdolbunow, Ukraine. In this capacity I had to visit the firm's building sites. The firm was contracted by an Army construction office to build grain silos on the former air field near Dubno in the Ukraine.

When I visited the site office on 5 October 1942 my foreman, Hubert Moennikes of Hamburg–Harburg, Aussenmühlenweg 21, told me that Jews from Dubno had been shot near the site in three large ditches which were about thirty metres long and three metres deep. Approximately 1,500 people a day had been killed. All of the approximately 5,000 Jews who had been living in Dubno up to the action were going to be killed. Since the shootings had taken place in his presence he was still very upset.

Whereupon I accompanied Moennikes to the building site and near it saw large mounds of earth about thirty metres long and two metres high. A few lorries were parked in front of the mounds from which people were being driven by armed Ukrainian militia under the supervision of an SS man. The militia provided the guards on the lorries and drove them to and from the ditch. All these people wore the prescribed yellow patches on the front and back of their clothing so that they were identifiable as Jews.

Moennikes and I went straight to the ditches. We were not prevented from doing so. I could now hear a series of rifle shots from behind the mounds. The peo-ple who had got off the lorries—men, women, and children of all ages—had to undress on the orders of an SS man who was carrying a riding or dog whip in his hand. They had to place their clothing on separate piles for shoes, clothing and underwear. I saw a pile of shoes containing approximately 800–1,000 pairs, and great heaps of underwear and clothing.

Without weeping or crying out these people undressed and stood together in family groups, embracing each other and saying good-bye while waiting for a sign from an-other SS man who stood on the edge of the ditch and also had a whip. During the quar-ter of an hour in which I stood near the ditch, I did not hear a single complaint or a plea for mercy. . . .

I walked round the mound and stood in front of the huge grave. The bodies were lying so tightly packed together that only their heads showed, from al-most all of which blood ran down over their shoulders. Some were still moving. Others raised their hands and turned their heads to show they were still alive. The ditch was already three quarters full. I estimate that it already held about a thousand bodies. I turned my eyes towards the man doing the shooting. He was an SS man; he sat, legs swinging, on the edge of the ditch. He had an automatic rifle resting on his knees and was smoking a cigarette. The people, completely naked, climbed down steps which had been cut into the clay wall of the ditch, stumbled over the heads of those lying there and stopped at the spot indicated by the SS man. They lay down on top of the dead or wounded; some stroked those still living and spoke quietly to them. Then I heard a series of rifle shots. I looked into the ditch and saw the bodies contorting or, the heads already inert, sinking on the corpses beneath. Blood flowed from the nape of their necks. I was surprised not to be ordered away, but I noticed three postmen in uniform standing nearby. Then the next batch came up, climbed down into the ditch, laid themselves next to the previous victims and were shot.

On the way back, as I rounded the mound, I saw another lorry load of people which had just arrived. This one included the sick and infirm. An old and very emaciated woman with frightfully thin legs was being undressed by others, already naked. She was being supported by two people and seemed paralysed. The naked people carried the woman round the mound. I left the place with Moennikes and went back to Dubno by car. . . .

I am making the above statement in Wiesbaden, Germany on 10 November 1945. I swear to God that it is the whole truth.

Fred. Gräbe

J. Noakes and G. Pridham, *Nazism: A History in Document and Eyewitness Accounts, 1919–1945*, Vol. 2 (New York: Schocken, 1988), pp. 1100–1101.

Through the late summer and fall of 1941, Nazi officials discussed and put together plans for mass killings in death camps. The ghettos had already been sealed; now orders came down that no Jews were to leave any occupied areas. That summer the Nazis had experimented with vans equipped with poison gas, which could kill thirty to fifty people at a time. Those experiments and the gas chambers were designed with the help of scientists from the T-4 euthanasia program, which had already killed eighty thousand racially, mentally, or physically "unfit" persons in Germany. By October 1941, the SS was building camps with gas chambers and deporting people to them. Auschwitz-Birkenau, which had been built to hold Polish prisoners, was built up to be the largest of the camps. Auschwitz eventually held many different types of prisoners—"undesirables" like Jehovah's Witnesses and homosexuals, Poles, Russians, and even some British POWs, but Jews and gypsies were the ones systematically annihilated there. Between the spring of 1942 and the fall of 1944 over a million people were killed at Auschwitz-Birkenau alone. The opening of the death camps set off the greatest wave of slaughter from 1942 to 1943. Freight cars hauled people to the camps, first from the ghettos of Poland, then from France, Holland, Belgium, Austria, the Balkans, and later from Hungary and Greece. Bodies were buried in pits dug by prisoners or burned in crematoria.

The death camps have come to symbolize the horrors of Nazism as a system of modern mass murder. Yet it is worth emphasizing that much of the slaughter was not anonymous, industrialized, or routine, and that it took place in face-to-face encounters outside the camps. Jews and other victims were not simply killed. They were tortured, beaten, and executed publicly while soldiers and other onlookers recorded the executions with cameras—and sent photos home to their families. During the last phases of the war, inmates still in the concentration camps were taken on "death marches" whose sole purpose was suffering and death.

How many knew of the extent of the Holocaust? No operation of this scale could be carried out without the cooperation or knowledge of many: the Nazi hierarchy; architects who helped build the camps; engineers who designed the gas chambers and crematoria; municipal officials of cities from which people were deported; train drivers; residents of villages near the camps, who reported the smell of bodies burning; and so on. Not surprisingly, most who suspected the worst were terrified and powerless. Not surprisingly, many people did not want to know, and did their best to ignore evidence and carry on with their lives. Many who continued to support the Nazis did so for other reasons, out of personal opportunism, or because they opposed communism and wanted order restored. Yet mere popular indifference does not provide a satisfactory explanation for the Nazis' ability to accomplish the murder of so many people. Many Europeans—German, French, Dutch, Polish, Swiss, and Russian—had come to believe that there was a "Jewish problem" that had to be "solved." The Nazis tried to conceal the death camps. Yet they knew they could count on vocal support for requiring Jews to be specially identified, for restrictions on marriage and property ownership and for other kinds of discrimination. For reasons that had to do with both traditional Christian anti-Semitism and modern, racialized nationalism, most Europeans had come to see Jewish people as "foreign," no longer members of their national communities.

What of other governments? Their level of cooperation with the Nazis' plans varied. The French Vichy regime, on its own initiative, passed laws that required Jews to wear identifying stars and strictly limited their movements and activities. When the German government demanded roundups and deportations of Jews, Vichy cooperated. On the other hand, the Hungarian government, also fascist and allied with the Nazis, persecuted Jews but dragged its heels about deportations. Thus the Hungarian Jewish community survived—until March 1944, when Germans, disgusted with their Hungarian collaborators, took direct control and immediately began mass deportations. So determined were the Nazis to carry out their "final solution" that they killed up to twelve thousand Hungarian Jews a day at Auschwitz in May of 1944, contributing to a total death toll of six hundred thousand.

In the face of this determination, little resistance was possible. The concentration camps were designed to numb and incapacitate their inmates, making them acquiesce in their own slow deaths even if they were not killed right away. A few rebellions in Auschwitz and Treblinka were repressed with savage efficiency. In the villages, people rounded up to be deported or shot had to make split-second decisions in order to escape. Saving oneself nearly always meant abandoning one's children or parents, which very few could do. The countryside offered no shelter; local populations were usually either hostile or too terrified to help. Reprisals horrified all. Families of Jews and gypsies were ordinary people whose lives could not have prepared them for the kind of violence that rolled over them. The largest Jewish resistance came in the Warsaw ghetto, in the spring of 1943. The previous summer, the Nazis had deported 80 percent of the ghetto's residents to the camps, making it clear that those left behind had little hope of survival. These people had virtually no resources, yet, when deportations started again, a small Jewish underground movement—a thousand fighters, perhaps, in a community of seventy thousand—took on the Nazis with a tiny arsenal of gasoline bombs, pistols, and ten rifles. The Nazis responded by burning the ghetto to the ground and executing and deporting to the camps nearly everyone who was left. "The Warsaw Ghetto is no more," reported the SS commander at the end; some fifty-six thousand Jews died. Word of the rising did

spread, but the repression made it clear that the targets of Nazi extermination could choose only between death in the streets or death in the camps. Sustained resistance, as one person remarked, would have required "the prospect of victory."

The Holocaust claimed between 4.1 and 5.7 million Jewish lives. Even those numbers do not register the nearly total destruction of some cultures. In the Baltic states (Latvia and Lithuania), Germany, Czechoslovakia, Yugoslavia, and Poland, well over 80 percent of the long-established Jewish communities were annihilated. Elsewhere, the figures were closer to 50 percent. The Holocaust was unique. It occurred, however, in a period of racial war and the liquidation of undesirables, and within an even longer period of ethnically motivated mass murder. Through both world wars and afterward ethnic and religious groups—Armenians, Poles, Serbian Orthodox, ethnic Germans—were hunted, massacred, and legally deported en masse. Hitler's government had planned to build a "new Europe," safe for ethnic Germans and their allies and secure against communism, on the graveyards of whole cultures.

> In the Baltic states (Latvia and Lithuania), Germany, Czechoslovakia, Yugoslavia, and Poland, well over 80 percent of the long-established Jewish communities were annihilated.

TOTAL WAR: HOME FRONTS, THE WAR OF PRODUCTION, BOMBING, AND "THE BOMB"

How did the war transform the home fronts?

The Second World War was a "total war." Even more than World War I, it involved whole populations. Larger armed forces were moving much more swiftly across territory, locked in constant battle with equally well-armed opponents. This demanded massive resources and national commitment to industry, drawing in the whole economies of the combatants. Standards of living changed around the world. In the United States, Detroit produced no new models of car or truck between 1940 and 1945. Work schedules were grueling. Women and the elderly, pressed back into wage

THE HOLOCAUST: TWO PERSPECTIVES FROM THE SS

THE DEATH CAMPS

An SS officer charged with inspecting the death camps wrote this account of his visit to Belzec, a camp in occupied Poland, near the former Russian border. He opposed the regime. Shortly after leaving this description, in 1945, he committed suicide.

Next morning, shortly before seven, I was told: 'the first transport will arrive in ten minutes'. And, in fact, after a few minutes, the first train arrived from the direction of Lemberg (Lvov). 45 wagons with 6,700 people, of whom 1,450 were already dead on arrival. Behind the barred hatches stared the horribly pale and frightened faces of children, their eyes full of the fear of death. Men and women were there too. . . .

The chambers fill up. 'Pack them in'— that is what Captain Wirth has ordered. People are treading on each others' toes. 700–800 in an area of twenty-five square metres, in forty-five cubic metres! The SS push them in as far as possible. The doors shut; in the meantime, the others are waiting outside in the open, naked. 'It is the same in winter', I was told. 'But they could catch their death of cold', I say. 'But that's just what they are there for', replied an SS man in dialect. Now at last I understood why the whole apparatus is called the Heckenholt Foundation. Heckenholt is the driver of the diesel engine, a little technician who constructed the installation. The people are going to be killed by the diesel exhaust gases. But the diesel engine won't start! Captain Wirth arrives. He is clearly embarrassed that this should happen just on the day when I am here. Yes indeed, I can see the whole thing. And I wait. My stop watch faithfully records it all. Fifty minutes, 70 seconds [*sic!*]. Still the diesel won't start. The people wait in their gas chambers. In vain. One can hear them crying, sobbing. . . . Captain Wirth hits the Ukrainian who is responsible for helping *Unterscharführer* Heckenholt with the diesel engine twelve or thirteen times in the face with his riding whip. After two hours forty-nine minutes—the stop watch has recorded it all—the engine starts. Up to this moment, the people have been living in these four chambers, four times 750 people in four times forty-five cubic metres. A further twenty-five minutes pass. That's right, many are now dead. One can see through the little peepholes when the electric light illuminates the chambers for a moment. After twenty-eight minutes, only a few are still alive. At last, after thirty-two minutes, they are all dead. . . .

HIMMLER'S INSTRUCTIONS TO THE SS

Heinrich Himmler (1900–1945), one of the founding members of the Nazi party and head of the SS, became one of the most powerful members of the Nazi government. He directed the purge of the rebellious SA in 1934, expanded the SS, supervised the network of death camps, and by 1943, when this speech was given, had become minister of the interior for the administration of the Reich. Few represent better the combination of ambition, ideology, and ruthlessness that characterized Nazi leaders. Himmler committed suicide when captured by Allied troops in 1945.

I also want to talk to you quite frankly about a very grave matter. We can talk about it quite frankly among ourselves and yet we will never speak of it publicly. Just as we did not hesitate on 30 June 1934 to do our duty as we were bidden, and to stand comrades who had lapsed up against the wall and shoot them, so we have never spoken about it and will never speak of it. It appalled everyone, and yet everyone was certain that he would do it the next time if such orders should be issued and it should be necessary.

I am referring to the Jewish evacuation programme, the extermination of the Jewish people. It is one of those things which are easy to talk about. 'The Jewish people will be exterminated', says every party comrade, 'It's clear, it's in our programme. Elimination of the Jews, extermination and we'll do it.' And then they come along, the worthy eighty million Germans, and each one of them produces his decent Jew. It's clear the others are swine, but this one is a fine Jew. Not one of those who talk like that has watched it happening, not one of them has been through it. Most of you will know what it means when a hundred corpses are lying side by side, or five hundred or a thousand are lying

there. To have stuck it out and—apart from a few exceptions due to human weakness—to have remained decent, that is what has made us tough. This is a glorious page in our history and one that has never been written and can never be written. For we know how difficult we would have made it for ourselves if, on top of the bombing raids, the burdens and the deprivations of war, we still had Jews today in every town as secret saboteurs, agitators and troublemakers. We would now probably have reached the 1916–17 stage when the Jews were still part of the body of the German nation.

We have taken from them what wealth they had. I have issued a strict order, which SS *Obergruppenführer* Pohl has carried out, that this wealth should, as a matter of course, be handed over to the Reich without reserve. We have taken none of it for ourselves. . . . All in all, we can say that we have fulfilled this most difficult duty for the love of our people. And our spirit, our soul, our character has not suffered injury from it. . . .

J. Noakes and G. Pridham, *Nazism: A History in Document and Eyewitness Accounts, 1919–1945*, Vol. 2 (New York: Schocken, 1988), pp. 1151–1152, 1199–1200.

---

work or working for the first time, put in long shifts before returning home to cook, clean, and care for families and neighbors. Diets changed. Though Germany lived comfortably off the farmlands of Europe for several years, and the United States could lean on its huge agricultural base, food, gasoline, and basic household goods were still rationed. In occupied Europe and the Soviet Union rations were just above starvation level, and sometimes fell below in areas near the fighting. Britain, dependent on its empire and other overseas sources for food and raw materials, ran a comprehensive rationing system that kept up production and ensured a drab but consistent diet on the table.

Production—the industrial ability to churn out more tanks, tents, planes, bombs, and uniforms than the

other side—was essential to winning the war. Britain, the Soviet Union, and America each launched comprehensive, well-designed propaganda campaigns that encouraged the production of war equipment on an unmatched scale. Appeals to patriotism, to communal interests, and to a common stake in winning the war struck a chord. The Allied societies proved willing to regulate themselves and commit to the effort. Despite strikes and disputes with government officials, the three great Allied powers devoted more of their economies to war production, more efficiently, than any nations in history. Not only did they build tanks, ships, and planes capable of competing with advanced German and Japanese designs, they built them by the tens of thousands, swamping the enemy with constant

HITLER'S "FINAL SOLUTION": JEWS MARKED FOR DEATH

On January 20, 1942, German officials met at Wannsee (just outside Berlin) to discuss the "final solution" to the "Jewish problem." They also discussed what they believed to be the remaining number of Jewish people in territories they controlled or soon hoped to control. Examine these figures closely. How many millions of innocent people did the Nazis propose to slaughter?

reinforcements and superior firepower. Japan nearly reached comparable levels of production but then slowly declined, as Allied advances on land and American submarines cut off overseas sources of vital supplies. Germany, despite its reputation for efficiency and its access to vast supplies of slave labor, was less efficient in its use of workers and materials than the Allied nations.

Since industry was essential to winning the war, centers of industry became vital military targets. The Allies began bombing German ports and factories almost as soon as the Germans started their own campaigns. Over time, American and British planners became equally ruthless on an even larger scale. Both of these Allied nations made a major commit-ment to "strategic bombing," developing new planes and technology that allowed them to put thousands of bombers in the air both night and day over occupied Europe. As the war wore on and Germany kept fighting, the Allies expanded their campaign. They moved from pinpoint bombing of the military and industry in Germany to striking such targets across all of occupied Europe, and bombing Germany's civilian population in earnest. After the Allied invasion of Europe, bombing expanded well beyond targets of military value. The German city of Dresden, a center of culture and education that lacked heavy industry, was firebombed with a horrifying death toll. This gave Allied generals and politicians pause, but strategic bombing continued. German industry was slowly degraded, but the German will to keep fighting, like that of Britain's or the Soviet Union's, remained intact.

THE RACE TO BUILD THE BOMB

While the Allies carried out their bombing campaigns over Germany and Japan, Allied scientists in America were at work on the most powerful bomb ever designed. British physicists—who led the field along with German scientists—believed that it would be possible to split the structure of an atom. The process, called fission, would split the subatomic particles apart in a huge burst of energy. This would produce an explosion of extraordinary scope and power.

The governments of the United States and Germany were both racing toward a military application of fission. The Germans were hampered in their efforts from the start. Many of their best specialists were Jewish or anti-Nazi refugees now working for the Americans. The Germans also lacked crucial bits of technical information and had fewer resources. When specially trained Norwegian commandos destroyed the Germans' "heavy water" facility (used to separate out the uranium needed for the bomb) at Telemark, Norway, the German project went with it. Yet American officials feared that it had not been destroyed, and they also sensed the enormous power of the new weapon. A government project, code-named "Manhattan," had already been set up to manage an all-out effort at building an American atomic bomb. The project went on under the tightest security of the war; most of President Roosevelt's cabinet, and the United States Congress, did not know the real purpose of "Manhattan."

"Just a Good Afternoon's Work!" A British poster mobilizing women for part-time factory work.

In 1943 a laboratory was established at Los Alamos, New Mexico, bringing together the most capable nuclear physicists in the country, citizens and immigrants, old and young, to come up with a working design for a bomb. The physicist J. Robert Oppenheimer was placed in charge of the project, along with a U.S. Army Air Corps supervisor. After nearly two years they came up with a working design whose prototype would be dropped by plane and detonated in midair above the target, for maximum effect. The first test of the device was held on July 16, 1945, near Los Alamos. The wave of heat and the roar of the explosion were indescribable. The test tower was vaporized. The ball of fire that rose in a mushroom shape overhead was the physical expression of a blast equal to twenty thousand tons of dynamite. "Manhattan" was a success. America now possessed the most destructive weapon ever devised. After watching the blast, Oppenheimer was moved to recite a phrase from an ancient Hindu text, a bitter commentary on his own work: "I am become Death, and the destroyer of worlds."

THE ALLIED COUNTERATTACK AND THE DROPPING OF THE ATOMIC BOMB

How did the Soviets defeat the Germans?

Hitler had invaded the Soviet Union in June 1941. Within two years the war in the East had become his undoing; within four years it brought about his destruction.

The early successes of the German-led invasion were crippling. Nearly 90 percent of the Soviets' tanks, most of their aircraft, and huge stores of supplies were destroyed or captured. Nazi forces penetrated deep into European Russia. The Soviets fought regardless. By late 1941 German and Finnish forces had cut off and besieged Leningrad (St. Petersburg). Yet the city held out for 844 days—through three winters, massive destruction by artillery and aircraft, and periods of starvation—until a large relief force broke the siege. Russian partisans stepped up their campaigns of ambush and terrorism, and many of the Germans' former allies in the Ukraine and elsewhere turned against them in reaction to Nazi "pacification" efforts.

THE EASTERN FRONT

Most important, the character of the war on the Eastern Front changed. What had begun as a struggle between Nazi invaders and Stalin's regime became a war to save the *rodina*, the Russian motherland, as Russians fought for their own homes and families. Stalin, a shrewd politician, understood this; the message of Soviet propaganda changed to include a healthy dose of praise for Mother Russia. After surviving the winter of 1941–1942, the Russian public became convinced that they could indeed survive the war and became committed to driving the Germans from their homeland, whatever the cost. The second change in the war was a Russian victory won by what Stalin called "General Winter." Successive winters, followed by hot, muddy summers, took a steady toll in Nazi lives and supplies, sapping German morale. The third change was the astonishing recovery of Soviet industry. Whole industries were rebuilt behind the safety of the Ural Mountains, and entire populations of cities were displaced to work in them, turning out tanks, fighter planes, machine guns, and ammunition. The fourth change in the war had more to do with the Germans, who became victims of their own success. The *Blitzkrieg*, at first a brilliantly inventive way of fighting a war, became a predictable set of maneuvers run according to a checklist. The Russians learned each stage of the

CHRONOLOGY	
THE EASTERN FRONT	
Germans invade Soviet Union	June 1941
Siege of Leningrad	Sept. 1941–Jan. 1944
Battle of Stalingrad	Sept. 1942–Jan. 1943
Battle of Kursk	July, 1943
Soviet forces reach Berlin	April 1945
Germany surrenders	May 1945

process well, exploited its weaknesses, and became particularly good at lulling the Germans into a false sense of success before overwhelming them from unexpected angles.

The crucial year on the Russian Front came in 1943, as German efforts to break the back of Soviet industry resulted in the largest, most destructive battles the world has ever seen. The first of these began in 1942, with a massive German-led offensive in the Volga River valley, aimed at the city of Stalingrad. The Germans hoped to split Soviet forces and destroy valuable factories. The outnumbered Soviet forces fought beyond the "last cartridge," using rocks and knives when they had to. Germany's panzers were rendered useless with grenades and firebombs in the narrow streets. The city was reduced to rubble, which only gave the Russians cover to surprise German and Romanian units. Russian forces were pushed back to the Volga River as winter came on, but the Nazis' supplies began to run low.

> The crucial year on the Russian Front came in 1943, as German efforts to break the back of Soviet industry resulted in the largest, most destructive battles the world has ever seen.

Infuriated, Hitler demanded that his commanders relieve the embattled troops. Every attempt to break through was defeated, and at the end of January 1943 the German commander in Stalingrad defied orders and surrendered the haggard survivors of his army. More than a quarter of a million German, Romanian, and Italian bodies were dragged from the wrecked city. Two times that many German troops died in the whole course of the battle. The Russians suffered up to a million casualties, including 100,000 civilians. Despite the unparalleled casualties—the battle dwarfed even Verdun in the Great War, or the fighting between China and Japan—the Russians had won a crucial victory. After Stalingrad Hitler appeared less and less often in public, and his worst tendencies to gloom and paranoia grew as the Russian front turned against his dreams.

Following Stalingrad, the Soviets mounted a series of offensives that turned German forces back from the heart of Russia. The Russians, led by their commander at Stalingrad and the shrewdest opponent of the *Blitzkrieg*, Grigorii Zhukov, then launched a major offensive into Ukraine. By the spring of 1944 Ukraine was back in Soviet hands. Romania was knocked out of the war during 1944, and Soviet armies poured into the Balkans, eventually meeting up with Tito's victorious partisans in Yugoslavia. Zhukov, who had taken charge of most of the Soviet armies, ground down German resistance in Poland during the winter of 1944. Several German armies collapsed, and Soviet forces, joined by communist partisans from the eastern European countries, retook large parts of Czechoslovakia. It was these battles, along with the fighting in Italy and Yugoslavia, that destroyed the German army. Hitler's most ambitious goal had brought the downfall of the Nazi regime and death to a generation of German soldiers.

THE WESTERN FRONT

During the campaigns in the East, Stalin continually pressured his allies to open a second front in the West. The American-led attack on Italy was a response to that pressure. Allied forces first invaded Sicily and then the Italian mainland. Italy's government deposed Mussolini and surrendered in the summer of 1943. A civil war ensued, for most Italians, especially communist partisans, sided with the Allies, while dedicated fascists continued to fight for their exiled leader. Italy was invaded by both sides; large Allied armies and more than a dozen elite German divisions occupied the country. The result was eighteen months of bitter fighting on Italy's muddy hillsides, consuming vast resources and tens of thousands of lives on each side. Nevertheless, the fighting in Italy cost Germany much more than it did the Allies,

CHRONOLOGY

THE WESTERN FRONT

Germany invades the Low Countries	May 1940
French surrender	June 1940
Battle of Britain	July 1940–June 1941
D-Day invasion	June 1944
Liberation of Paris	August 1944
Battle of the Bulge	December 1944
Allies invade Germany	April 1945
Germany surrenders	May 1945

D-Day. Cargo ships are seen pouring supplies ashore during the invasion of France on June 6, 1944. Barrage balloons float overhead to protect the ships from low-flying enemy planes.

who liberated all the major Italian cities and entered Austria by the spring of 1945.

The major "second front" was opened on June 6, 1944, with the massive Allied landings in Normandy. The Germans fiercely defended the dense hedgerows of Normandy, but Allied air superiority and a vast buildup of men and matériel led to a breakthrough. An American landing on the Riviera in August had much more immediate success, aided by the French resistance. In late July and August the Allies swept through France, liberating Paris on August 14 and pushing into Belgium. The Germans mounted their own devastating attack in December 1944, under cover of winter storms, in the Battle of the Bulge. It was a last effort with their best men and equipment; they captured thousands of prisoners and nearly broke through Allied lines. Nevertheless, several elite American units beat off much larger German

> The major "second front" was opened on June 6, 1944, with the massive Allied landings in Normandy.

forces at key points until the snow cleared and the Allies mounted a crushing counterattack. In April 1945, the Allies crossed the Rhine—in one of the war's ironies, French troops were the first to do so. The Germans collapsed. American tanks swept south, British and Canadian forces north. This genuine military success was helped by the fact that most Germans preferred to surrender to Americans or Britons than face the Russians to the east.

At the same time, those Soviet troops were approaching fast. On April 21, 1945, Zhukov's forces hammered their way into the suburbs of Berlin. During the next ten days a savage battle raged amid the ruins and heaps of rubble. More than a hundred thousand Russians and Germans died. Adolf Hitler killed himself in a bomb-proof shelter beneath the Chancellery on April 30. On May 2 the heart of the city was captured, and the Soviets' red banner flew from the Brandenburg Gate. On May 7 the German high command signed a document of unconditional surrender. By the next day the war in Europe was over.

THE WAR IN THE PACIFIC

The war in the Pacific came to an end four months later. The Japanese were rolled back on all fronts. The United States Navy had won one of its greatest victories the previous fall, when William Halsey's task force destroyed most of Japan's surviving surface ships in the gulfs of the Philippine islands. American forces landed and within weeks the Philippine capital of Manila fell, taken house by house in bloody fighting. The remaining battles, amphibious assaults on a series of islands running toward the Japanese mainland, were just as brutal. Japanese pilots, hopelessly outnumbered in the air, mounted suicide attacks on

American ships, while American marines and Japanese soldiers fought over every inch of the shell-blasted rocks in the middle of the Pacific. In June 1945, the Japanese island of Okinawa fell to American forces after eighty-two days of desperate fighting. Chinese forces, Nationalist and communist alike, combined to force the Japanese back on Hong Kong. The Soviets chose this moment to enter the fray. Their forces marched rapidly through Manchuria and into the colonial territory of Korea.

On July 26 the heads of the United States, British, and Chinese governments issued a joint proclamation calling on Japan to surrender or be destroyed. The United States had already begun that process of destruction by using its most advanced bomber, the B-29, which could fly above Japanese efforts to shoot it down, in the systematic bombing of Japanese cities. Many of the wooden Japanese cities were hit with firebombs, which created storms of flame

View of Hiroshima after the First Atom Bomb Was Dropped, August 6, 1945. This photo, taken one month later, shows the utter devastation of the city. Only a few steel and concrete buildings remained intact.

CHRONOLOGY

THE WAR IN THE PACIFIC

Japanese bomb Pearl Harbor	December 1941
Singapore falls to Japan	December 1941
Battles of Midway, Coral Sea, and Guadalcanal	1942
Invasion of the Philippines	Fall 1944
Battle of Okinawa	June 1945
Soviets invade Manchuria and Korea	June–July 1945
Atomic bombs dropped on Hiroshima and Nagasaki	August 6 and 9, 1945
Japan surrenders	August 14, 1945

and killed hundreds of thousands of civilians. Yet the Japanese refused to surrender. In the absence of that surrender the United States chose to use the atomic bomb.

Many senior military and naval officers argued that use of the bomb was not necessary, on the assumption that Japan was already beaten. Some of the scientists involved, who had done their part hoping to counter the Nazis, believed that using the bomb for political ends would set a deadly precedent. Harry Truman, who had succeeded Roosevelt following the latter's death in April 1945, decided otherwise. On August 6, a single atomic bomb was dropped on Hiroshima, obliterating about 60 percent of the city. Three days later a second bomb was dropped on Nagasaki. President Truman warned that the United States would use as many atom bombs as necessary to bring Japan to its knees. On August 14, Japan surrendered unconditionally.

The decision to drop the bomb, and its consequences, were extraordinary. It did not greatly alter the scope or the plans for the American destruction of Japan. Many more Japanese died in the earlier fire bombings than in the two atomic blasts. Yet the bomb was an entirely new kind of weapon, built with untried technology; some of its designers feared that the test blast might split *every* atom in the universe. It was one of the most terrifying results of the new relationship between science and political power. The nature of the bomb mattered as well. The instant, total devastation of the blasts, along with the cancerous radiation that lingered for years and claimed victims decades later, was something terribly new. The world now had a weapon that could destroy not just cities and peoples, but humanity itself.

CONCLUSION

After World War I, many Europeans awoke to find a world they no longer recognized. In 1945 many Europeans came out from shelters or began the long trips back to their homes, faced with a world that hardly existed at all. The products of industry—tanks, submarines, strategic bombing—had destroyed the structures of industrial society—factories, ports, and railroads. The tools of mass culture—fascist and communist appeals, patriotism proclaimed via radios and movie screens, mobilization of mass armies and industry—had been put to full use. In the aftermath, much of Europe lay destroyed and, as we will see, vulnerable to the rivalry of the postwar superpowers: the United States and the Soviet Union.

The two world wars profoundly affected Western empires. Nineteenth-century imperialism had made twentieth-century war a global matter. In both conflicts the warring nations had used the resources of empire to their fullest. Key campaigns, in North Africa, Burma, Ethiopia, the Pacific, were fought in and over colonial territories. Hundreds of thousands of colonial troops—sepoys and Gurkhas from India and Nepal, Britain's King's African Rifles, French from Algeria and West Africa, served in armies on both sides of the conflict. After two massive mobilizations, many anticolonial leaders found renewed confidence in their own peoples' courage and resourcefulness, and they seized the opportunity of European weakness to press for independence. In many areas that had been under European or Japanese imperial control—sections of China to Korea, Indochina, Indonesia and Palestine—the end of World War II only paved the way for a new round of conflict. This time, the issue was when imperial control would be ended, and by whom.

The Second World War also carried on the Great War's legacy of massive killing. Historians estimate that nearly 50 million people died. The killing fields of the East took the highest tolls: perhaps 25 million

Soviet lives. Of those, 8.5 million were in the military, and the rest civilians; 20 percent of the Polish population and nearly 90 percent of the Polish Jewish community; 1 million Yugoslavs, including militias of all sides; 4 million German soldiers and five hundred thousand German civilians, not including the hundreds of thousands of ethnic Germans who died while being deported west at the end of the war, in one of the many acts of ethnic cleansing that ran through the period. Even the United States, shielded from the full horrors of total war by two vast oceans, lost 292,000 soldiers in battle and more to accidents or disease.

Why was the war so murderous? The advanced technology of modern industrial war and the openly genocidal ambitions of the Nazis offer part of the answer. The global reach of the conflict offers another. Finally World War II overlapped with, and eventually devolved into, a series of smaller, no less bitter conflicts: a civil war in Greece; conflicts between Orthodox, Catholics, and Muslims in Yugoslavia; and political battles for control of the French resistance. Even when those struggles claimed fewer lives, they left deep political scars. So did memories of the war. Hitler's empire could not have lasted as long as it did without active collaboration or passive acquiescence from many, a fact that produced bitterness and recrimination for years.

In this and many other ways, the war haunted the second half of the century. Fifty years after the battle of Stalingrad, the journalist, Timothy Rybeck discovered that hundreds of skeletons still lay, in the open, on the fields outside the city. Many bodies had never been buried. Others had been left in shallow, mass graves. As wind and water eroded the soil, farmers plowed the fields, and teenagers dug for medals and helmets to sell as curiosities, more bones kept rising to the surface. One of the supervisors charged with finding permanent graves and building memorials responded to the task by voicing more than simple weariness. "This job of reburying the dead," he said, "will never be done."

KEY TERMS

Blitzkreig	Winston Churchill	Auschwitz-Birkenau
appeasement	Pearl Harbor	Manhattan Project
Guernica	Operation Barbarossa	Hiroshima
Dunkirk		

SELECTED READINGS

Bartov, Omer. *Hitler's Army: Soldiers, Nazis, and War in the Third Reich.* New York, 1991.

Burrin, Philippe. *France under the Germans: Collaboration and Compromise.* New York, 1996.

Browning, Christopher R. *The Path to Genocide: Essays on Launching the Final Solution.* Cambridge, 1992.

Carr, Raymond. *The Spanish Tragedy: The Civil War in Perspective.* London, 1977. A thoughtful introduction to the Spanish Civil War and the evolution of Franco's Spain.

Dawidowicz, Lucy S. *The War against the Jews, 1933–1945.* New York, 1975. A full account of the Holocaust.

Divine, Robert A. *Roosevelt and World War II.* Baltimore, 1969. A diplomatic history.

Gilbert, Martin. *The Appeasers.* Boston, 1963. Excellent study of British pro-German sentiment in the 1930s.

———. *The Second World War: A Complete History.* Rev. ed. New York, 1991. An up-to-date general account.

Hilberg, Raul. *The Destruction of the European Jews,* 2d ed. 3 vols. New York, 1985. Another excellent treatment of the Holocaust, its origins, and its consequences.

Kedward, Roderick. *In Search of the Maquis: Rural Resistance in Southern France, 1942–1944.* Oxford, 1993.

Keegan, John. *The Second World War.* New York, 1990. A classic.

Marrus, Michael R. *The Holocaust in History.* Hanover, N.H., 1987. Thoughtful analysis of central issues.

Michel, Henri. *The Shadow War: The European Resistance, 1939–1945.* New York, 1972. Compelling reading.

Milward, Alan S. *War, Economy, and Society, 1939–1945.* Berkeley, 1977. Analyzes the impact of the war on the world economy and the ways in which the economic resources of the belligerents determined strategies.

Noakes, Jeremy, and Geoffrey Pridham. *Nazism: A History in Documents and Eyewitness Accounts, 1919–1945.* New York, 1975. An excellent combination of analysis and documentation.

Overy, Richard. *Russia's War.* New York, 1998.

Paxton, Robert O. *Vichy France: Old Guard and New Order, 1940–1944.* New York, 1982.

Stoff, Michael B. *The Manhattan Project: A Documentary Introduction to the Atomic Age.* New York, 1991.

Weinberg, Gerhard L. *A Global History of World War II.* New York, 1995. Now the most comprehensive history.

Wilkinson, James D. *The Intellectual Resistance in Europe.* Cambridge, Mass., 1981. A comparative study of the movement throughout Europe.

Wright, Gordon. *The Ordeal of Total War, 1939–1945.* New York, 1968. Particularly good on the domestic response to war and the mobilization of the resources of the modern state.

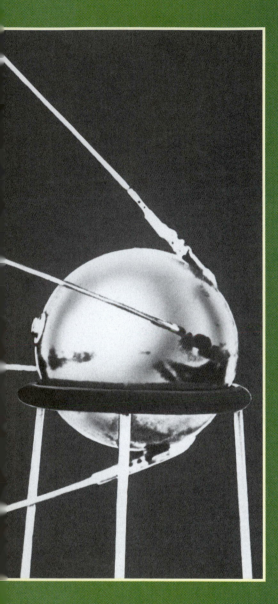

COLD WAR

It is quite clear from Soviet theory and practice that the Kremlin seeks to bring the free world under its dominion by the methods of the cold war. The preferred technique is to subvert by infiltration and intimidation. Every institution of our society is an instrument which it is sought to stultify and turn against our purposes. Those that touch most closely our material and moral strength are obviously the prime targets, labor unions, civic enterprises, schools, churches, and all media for influencing opinion.

NSC 68: United States Objectives and Programs for National Security

Although the United States and Soviet Union became allies during World War II, there seemed to be little doubt that their opposing ideologies would ultimately produce a cold war. And overshadowing such a war was the atomic bomb. Before the war had even ended, the Soviets were convinced that Eastern European buffer states had to be created to protect the Soviet Union from future invasion. The United States saw these same nations as buffer states against the Soviet Union. The Truman Doctrine, Marshall Plan, and NATO were all intended to keep Russian ideology within its own borders. This notion of containment was first voiced by George Kennan's "Long Telegram" of 1946. Throughout the 1950s and into the 1960s and 1970s, the United States clung to this policy—indeed, containment conditioned our cold war.

The cold war was a global phenomenon and was clearly conditioned by the political, economic, and social aspirations of the two superpowers. Between 1945 and 1989 Europe became a testing ground for the cold war itself. The 1956 uprising in Hungary and the Prague Spring of 1968 are two examples of the form in which these battles would be fought. Ultimately the cold war came to an end following the collapse of the Berlin Wall in November 1989. Soviet-style communism was considered a spent force in Eastern Europe, and on October 3, 1990, East and West Germany were reunited.

The images and documents in the "Cold War" Digital History Feature at www.wwnorton.com/wciv reveal how the new Soviet and American superpowers shaped foreign policy, politics, and everyday life after 1945. As you explore the feature on the *Western Civilizations* Web site, consider the following:

• What events led to the control of the world by two heavily armed nations, each with the capability of initiating a nuclear holocaust?

• Why did the Soviet Union find it essential to intervene in Hungary in 1956 and in Czechoslovakia in 1968?

• What is the significance of the cold war? How have historians shaped the way that the cold war is understood?

• In any war there are winners and losers. What does it mean to have won or lost the cold war?

PART VIII

THE WEST AND THE WORLD

THE SECOND WORLD WAR was perhaps the great watershed of the twentieth century. Its legacies were many and pervasive. The "hot war" between the Allies and the Axis was superseded by a rivalry between the most powerful of the Allies: the United States and the Soviet Union. The superpowers possessed nuclear weapons, global reach, and networks of alliances that gave them the authority of empires. The "cold war" between these powers dominated the recovery from the world war, and global politics in general, for four decades. The rise and fall of cold-war politics is a fundamental theme in twentieth-century history; it is one of the two historical trends followed here.

While the cold war seemed to centralize the political, cultural, and economic life of the world around the twin poles of the superpowers, the other key theme of the later twentieth century involves the decentralizing effects of globalization. This began with the breaking apart of Europe's old colonial empires and the emergence of new nations. New forms of politics and protest emerged as well, based on social movements of women, ethnic "minorities," and peoples denied a political voice in the age of imperialism. The Western European empires were not the only ones to collapse. With the end of the cold war, the unofficial empire of the Soviet Union collapsed as well, producing new nations and new hopes. These events seemed to leave the United States as the world's leading power, yet the rest of the world would not simply become an American empire by default or consent to being "Americanized" on the United States' terms. As the twentieth century came to an end, it was clear that the west operated in a much tighter network of world civilizations. The circumstances in which this "globalized" world emerged are the focus of this last section.

	POLITICS	SOCIETY AND CULTURE	ECONOMY	INTERNATIONAL RELATIONS
				Mohandas Gandhi (1869–1948)
	Malcolm X (1925–1965) Martin Luther King Jr. (1929–1968)	Alexander Fleming discovers first antibiotic, penicillin (1928)		
1940		Albert Camus, *The Stranger* (1942)		Gandhi leads independence movement in India (1940s) Soviet Union draws "Iron Curtain" over eastern Europe (1945–1948) Chinese Communist Revolution (1945–1949) India gains independence; formation of Pakistan (1947) Truman Doctrine (1947) Vietnam War, French phase (1947–1954)
	Germany divided; Berlin airlift (1948–1949)		Marshall Plan (1948)	Civil war in Greece (1948) Josip Tito declares Yugoslavia independent of Soviet Union (1948) State of Israel formed (1948) Formation of NATO (1949)
1950	Konrad Adenauer, chancellor of West Germany (1949–1963) Mao Zedong's Great Leap Forward (1950s)	George Orwell, *1984* (1949) Simone de Beauvoir, *The Second Sex* (1949)	European Coal and Steel Community created (1951)	Korean War (1950–1953) Abdel Nasser becomes president of Egypt (1952) United States and Soviet Union test hydrogen bombs (1953)
	Joseph Stalin dies (1953) Khrushchev's regime (1953–1964)	Samuel Beckett, *Waiting for Godot* (1953) Francis Crick and James Watson discover structure of DNA (1953) Jonas Salk develops polio vaccine (1953)		Algerian war ends with Algerian independence (1954–1962) Formation of Warsaw Pact (1955) Vietnam War, U.S. phase (1955–1975)
	Nikita Khrushchev begins de-Stalinization (1956) Charles de Gaulle forms Fifth Republic in France (1958)	Boris Pasternak, *Dr. Zhivago* (1957)	European Economic Community (EEC, Common Market) formed (1958)	Suez Crisis (1956) Hungarian rebellion repressed by Soviets (1956)
1960	Cultural Revolution in China (1960s) John F. Kennedy, president (1961–1963) Berlin Wall built (1961) Martin Luther King Jr. leads March on Washington (1963) Leonid Brezhnev leads Soviet Union (1964–1982)	Günter Grass, *The Tin Drum* (1959) Joseph Heller, *Catch-22* (1961) Frantz Fanon, *The Wretched of the Earth* (1961) Rachel Carson, *Silent Spring* (1962) Betty Friedan, *The Feminine Mystique* (1963) Herbert Marcuse, *One-Dimensional Man* (1964) The Beatles play in New York (1964) Birth control pill becomes available (mid-1960s)	Inflation rates rise across western Europe (late 1960s–1970s)	Castro to power in Cuba (1959) Cuban Missile Crisis (1962) Vietnam War (1963–1975)
	Student protests and worker strikes in Paris (1968) Czech revolt; Prague Spring (1968)			Six-Day War between Israel and Arab nations (1967)

POLITICS	SOCIETY AND CULTURE	ECONOMY	INTERNATIONAL RELATIONS	
Willy Brandt, chancellor of West Germany (1970–1974)			SALT treaties (1970s and early 1980s)	**1970**
			Gradual détente between Soviet Union and Western powers (1970s)	
Watergate scandal (1972–1974); President Richard Nixon resigns		Western European citizens elect representatives to EEC parliament (1972)	Nixon visits China (1972)	
		Oil prices rise steadily, worsening widespread recession (1973–1980s)	OPEC embargo against Western powers (1973)	
			Arab-Israeli War (1973)	
			Camp David Accords (1978)	
Margaret Thatcher prime minister of England (1979–1990)			Soviet military intervention in Afghanistan (1979–1989)	
Polish Solidarity workers movement organizes strikes (1980)		Computer revolution begins (1980s)		**1980**
Ronald Reagan, president (1980–1988)				
Helmut Kohl becomes chancellor of West Germany (1982)				
Mikhail Gorbachev, leader of Communist party (1985–1991)	Asian population reaches 3 billion (1986)			
Renewed Solidarity strikes in Poland, demonstrations across Eastern bloc (1988)	Nuclear reactor accident at Chernobyl (1986)			
Break-up of Soviet power in eastern Europe (1989)				
Berlin Wall falls (1989)				
Tiananmen Square massacre (1989)				
Germany reunifies (1990)		Eastern European economies in crisis (1990s)	Persian Gulf War (1991)	**1990**
Boris Yeltsin elected president of Russian Federation (1990)		Internet revolution begins (1990s)	Yugoslavian civil wars (1991–1992, 1992–1995)	
Soviet Union dissolved (1992)				
		NAFTA signed by Canada, Mexico, and United States (1993)	Genocide in Rwanda (1994)	
Nelson Mandela elected president of South Africa; end of apartheid (1994)			Russia's war with Chechnya begins (1994)	
			Pakistan and India test nuclear weapons (late 1990s)	
	Scientists in Scotland clone a sheep (1997)		War in Kosovo (1999)	
	Global population exceeds 6 billion (2001)		United States declares war on terrorism (2001)	**2001**

CHAPTER TWENTY-SEVEN

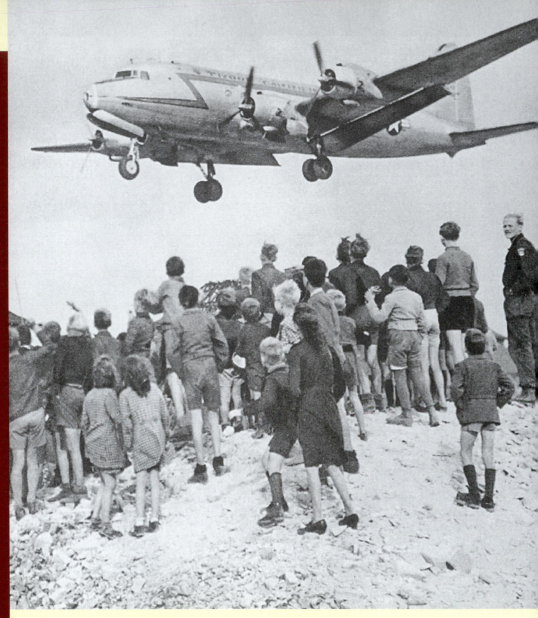

THE COLD WAR WORLD: GLOBAL POLITICS, ECONOMIC RECOVERY, AND CULTURAL CHANGE

The war ended the way a passage through a tunnel ends," wrote Heda Kovály, a Czech woman who survived the concentration camps. "From far away you could see the light ahead, a gleam that kept growing, and its brilliance seemed ever more dazzling to you huddled there in the dark the longer it took to reach it. But when at last the train burst out into the glorious sunshine, all you saw was a wasteland." The war left Europe a land of wreckage and confusion. Millions of refugees trekked hundreds or thousands of miles on foot to return to their homes while others were forcibly displaced from their lands. In some areas housing was practically nonexistent, with no available means to build anew. Food remained in dangerously short supply; a year after the war, roughly 100 million people in Europe still lived on less than 1,500 calories per day. Families scraped vegetables from their gardens or traded smuggled goods on the black market. Governments continued to ration food, and without rationing a large portion of the Continent's population would have starved. During the winter of 1945–1946, many regions had little or no fuel for heat. What coal there was—less than half the prewar supply— could not be transported to the areas that needed it most. The brutality of international war, civil war, and occupation had divided countries against themselves, shredding relations among ethnic groups and fellow citizens. Ordinary people's intense relief at liberation often went hand in hand with recriminations over their neighbors' wartime betrayal, collaboration, or simple opportunism.

How does a nation, a region, or a civilization recover from a catastrophe on the scale of World War II? Nations had to do much more than deliver food and rebuild economic infrastructures. They had to restore—or create—government authority, functioning bureaucracies, and legitimate legal systems. They had to rebuild bonds of trust and civility between citizens, steering a course between demands for justice on the one hand and the overwhelming desire to bury memories of the past on the other. Rebuilding entailed a commitment to renewing democracy—to creating democratic institutions that could withstand threats such as those the West had experienced in the 1930s. Some aspects of this process were extraordinarily successful, more so than even the most optimistic forecaster might have thought possible in 1945. Others failed or were deferred until later in the century.

FOCUS QUESTIONS

- What were the causes of the cold war?
- How did Western Europe recover from World War II?
- What were the links between decolonization, World War II, and the cold war?
- What themes defined postwar culture?

Berlin, 1945.

The war's devastating effects brought two dramatic changes in the international balance of power. The first change was the emergence of the so-called superpowers, the United States and the Soviet Union, and the swift development of a "cold war" between them. The cold war divided Europe, with Eastern Europe occupied by Soviet troops, and Western Europe dominated by the military and economic presence of the United States. The second great change came with the dismantling of the European empires that had once stretched worldwide. The collapse of empires and the creation of newly emancipated nations raised the stakes in the cold war and brought superpower rivalry to far-flung sections of the globe. Those events, which shaped the postwar recovery and necessarily created a new understanding of what "the West" meant, are the subject of this chapter.

THE COLD WAR AND A DIVIDED CONTINENT

What were the causes of the cold war?

No peace treaty ended World War II. Instead, as the war drew to a close, relations between the Allied powers began to fray over issues of power and influence in Central and Eastern Europe. After the war, they de-

scended from mistrust to open conflict. The United States and Soviet Union rapidly formed the centers of two imperial blocs. Their rivalry, which came to be known as the cold war, pitted against each other two military powers, two sets of state interests, and two ideologies: capitalism and communism. The cold war's manifold repercussions reached well beyond Europe, for anticolonial movements, sensing the weakness of European colonial powers, turned to the Soviets for help in their struggles for independence. The cold war thus structured the peace, shaped international relations for four decades, and affected governments and peoples across the globe who depended on either of the superpowers.

THE IRON CURTAIN

The Soviet Union had insisted during the wartime negotiations at Teheran (1943) and Yalta (1945) that it had a legitimate claim to control Eastern Europe, a claim that some Western leaders accepted as the price of defeating Hitler and others ignored so as to avoid a dangerous confrontation. The country's catastrophic losses made the Soviets determined to maintain political, economic, and military control of the lands they had liberated from Nazi rule. For the Soviets, Eastern Europe served as both "a sphere and a shield." When their former allies resisted their demands, the Soviets became suspicious, defensive, and aggressive.

In Eastern Europe, the Soviet Union used a combination of diplomatic pressure, political infiltration, and military power to create "people's republics" sympathetic to Moscow. In country after country, the same process unfolded: first, states set up coalition governments that excluded only former Nazi sympathizers; next came coalitions dominated by communists; finally, one party took hold of all the key positions of power. This was the process that prompted Winston Churchill, speaking at a college graduation in Fulton, Missouri, in 1946, to say that "an Iron Curtain" had "descended across Europe." By 1948, governments dependent on Moscow had also been established in Poland, Hungary, Romania, and

Legend

- Allied occupation of Germany and Austria, 1945–1955
- Territory lost by Germany
- Territory gained by Soviet Union
- Postwar national boundaries, to 1989
- "Iron Curtain" to 1989
- **1945** Year Communist control of government was gained

NORWAY
Oslo

SWEDEN
Stockholm

FINLAND
Helsinki
From Finland, 1940–1956
Leningrad

NORTH SEA

DENMARK
Copenhagen

BALTIC SEA

ESTONIA
To U.S.S.R. 1940

LATVIA
To U.S.S.R., 1940

LITHUANIA
To U.S.S.R. 1940

NETHERLANDS
Amsterdam

U.S. Zone
British Zone
Bremen
Soviet Zone
Berlin

BELGIUM
Brussels

Bonn

EAST GERMANY (1949)

Incorporated into U.S.S.R., 1945
Gdansk (Danzig)

Incorporated into Poland, 1945

Warsaw

POLAND (1947)

Brest

WHITE RUSSIA

From Poland, 1940–1947

UKRAINE

SOVIET UNION (1917)

French Zone
WEST GERMANY
Rhine R.
U.S. Zone

LUXEMBOURG

Elbe R.
Oder R.

Prague

CZECHOSLOVAKIA (1948)

From Czechoslovakia, 1945–1947

From Romania, 1940–1947

SWITZERLAND
Bern

Munich

U.S. Zone
Vienna
Soviet Zone
French Zone
AUSTRIA
British Zone

Budapest

HUNGARY (1949)

ROMANIA (1947)

Bucharest

BESSARABIA

CRIMEA
Yalta

Milan
Po R.

From Italy, 1945

YUGOSLAVIA (1945)

Danube R.

From Romania, 1940–1947

BLACK SEA

CORSICA (Fr.)

ITALY
Rome

ADRIATIC SEA

BULGARIA (1946)
Sofia

Istanbul

SARDINIA (It.)

Tirane

ALBANIA (1944)

TURKEY

GREECE

Athens

SICILY (It.)

CRETE

CYPRUS

MEDITERRANEAN SEA

0   200   400 Miles
0   200   400 Kilometers

Berlin detail

EAST GERMANY

French Sector
WEST BERLIN
British Sector
EAST
Soviet Sector
U.S. Sector
BERLIN

Potsdam

— Berlin Wall (1961–1989)

0   10 Miles
0   10 Kilometers

Area of detail inset

EUROPE
AFRICA
Area of detail

TERRITORIAL CHANGES AFTER WORLD WAR II

At the end of World War II, the Soviet Union annexed territory in Eastern Europe to create a buffer between it and Western Europe. At the same time, the United States established a series of military alliances in Western Europe to stifle the spread of communism in Europe. How did these new territorial boundaries aggravate tensions between Soviet Union and the United States?

Bulgaria. Together these states were referred to as the Eastern bloc. Determined to reassert control elsewhere, the Soviets demanded purges in the parties and administrations of various satellite governments. These began in the Balkans and extended through Czechoslovakia, East Germany, and Poland. The purges succeeded by playing on fears and festering hatreds; in several areas those purging the governments attacked their opponents as Jewish. Anti-Semitism, far from being crushed, remained a potent political force—as Heda Kovály explained, it became common to blame Jews for bringing the horrors of war.

The end of war did not mean peace. In Greece, as in Yugoslavia and through much of the Balkans, war's end brought a local communist-led resistance to the verge of seizing power. The British and the United States, however, were determined to keep Greece in their sphere of influence, as per informal agreements with the Soviets. Only large infusions of aid to the anticommunist monarchy allowed them to do so. The bloody civil war that lasted until 1949 took a higher toll than the wartime occupation. Greece's bloodletting became one of the first crises of the cold war and a touchstone for the United States' escalating fear of communist expansion. "Like apples in a barrel infected by the corruption of one rotten one, the corruption of Greece would infect Iran and all to the East . . . Africa . . . Italy and France," warned Dean Acheson in 1947, then deputy head of America's State Department. "[N]ot since Rome and Carthage had there been such a polarization of power on this earth."

Defeated Germany lay at the heart of these two polarizing power blocs and soon became the front line of their conflict. The Allies had divided Germany into four zones of occupation. Although the city of Berlin was deep in Soviet territory, it too was divided. The occupation zones were intended to be temporary, pending an official peace settlement. But the Soviets and the French, British, and Americans quarreled over reparations and policies for the economic development of Germany. Administrative conflicts among the Western powers were almost as intense as their disagreements with the Soviets; Britain and the United States nearly had a serious falling out over food supply and trade in their zones. Yet the quickening cold war put those arguments on hold, and in 1948 the three Western allies began to create a single government for their territories. The Soviets retaliated by cutting all road, train, and river access from the western zone to West Berlin. The Western allies refused to cede control over

the capital. For eleven months they airlifted supplies over Soviet territory to the besieged western zone of Berlin, a total of 12,000 tons of supplies carried by hundreds of flights every day. The Berlin blockade lasted nearly a year, from June 1948 to May 1949. It ended with the creation of two Germanies, the Federal

GERMANY DIVIDED AND THE BERLIN AIRLIFT

In the summer of 1948, the Soviet Union blocked routes through the German Democratic Republic to the Western Allies zone of Berlin. The blockade exacerbated tensions between the Soviet Union and the United States and forced the Allies to airlift supplies to West Berlin. At one point, planes landed in Berlin every three minutes.

Republic in the West and the German Democratic Republic in former Soviet zone. Within a few short years both countries looked strikingly like armed camps.

THE MARSHALL PLAN

The United States countered the expansion of Soviet power and locally based communist movements with massive programs of economic and military aid to Western Europe. In a 1947 speech to Congress arguing for military assistance to anticommunists in Greece, President Harry Truman set out what would come to be called the Truman Doctrine, a pledge to support the resistance of "free peoples" to communism. The Truman Doctrine, however, also tied the contest for political power to economics. A few months later, Secretary of State George Marshall outlined an ambitious plan of economic aid to Europe including, initially, the Eastern European states: the European Recovery Program. The Marshall Plan provided $13 billion of aid over four years (beginning in 1948), targeted to industrial redevelopment. Unlike a relief plan, however, the Marshall Plan encouraged the participating states to diagnose their own economic problems and to develop their own solutions. The American program, however, required measures such as decontrol of prices, restraints on wages, and balanced budgets. The Americans encouraged opposition to left-leaning politicians and movements that might be sympathetic to communism.

The United States also hastened to shore up military defenses. In April 1949, Canada, the United States, and representatives of Western European states signed an agreement establishing the North Atlantic Treaty Organization (NATO). Greece, Turkey, and West Germany were later added as members. An armed attack against any one of the NATO members would now be regarded as an attack against all and bring a united military response. West German rearmament had been the subject of agonizing debate, particularly in Britain and France, but American pressure and a sense of strategic necessity led to its acceptance within Western Europe. Among the most striking aspects of World War II's aftermath was how rapidly Germany was reintegrated into Europe. In the new cold war world, "the West" quickly came to mean anticommunism. Potentially reliable allies, whatever their past, were not to be punished or excluded.

> In the new cold war world, "the West" quickly came to mean anticommunism. Potentially reliable allies, whatever their past, were not to be punished or excluded.

TWO WORLDS AND THE RACE FOR THE BOMB

The Soviets viewed NATO, the Marshall Plan, and especially the United States' surprising involvement in Europe's affairs with mounting alarm. They responded to NATO with the establishment of their own military alliances, confirmed by the Warsaw Pact of 1955. This agreement set up a joint command among the states of Albania, Bulgaria, Czechoslovakia, Hungary, Poland, Romania, and East Germany, and guaranteed the continued presence of Soviet troops in all those countries. These conflicts were darkened by the shadow of the nuclear arms race. In 1949, the USSR surprised American intelligence by testing its first atom bomb. In 1953 both superpowers demonstrated a new weapon, the hydrogen or "super" bomb, which was one thousand times more powerful than the bomb dropped on Hiroshima. The "nuclearization of warfare" fed into the polarizing effect of the cold war, for countries without nuclear arms found it difficult to avoid joining either the Soviet or American pact. Over the long term, it encouraged a disparity between two groups of nations: on the one hand, the superpowers, with enormous military budgets, and on the other, nations that came to rely on agreements and international law. It changed the nature of face-to-face warfare as well, encouraging "proxy wars" between clients of the superpowers and raising fears that local conflicts might trigger general war. The bomb became the single most compelling symbol of the age. It seemed to confirm both humanity's power and its vulnerability. The leaps in knowledge that it represented boosted contemporaries' confidence in science and progress. At the same time, weapons of mass destruction and humanity's emerging power to obliterate itself raised gnawing questions about whether that confidence was misplaced.

A new international balance of power quickly produced new international policies. In 1946 George Kennan argued that the United States needed to make containing the Soviet threat a priority. Containment became the point of reference of U.S. foreign policy for the next forty years.

At its height, the cold war had a chilling effect on domestic politics in both countries. In the Soviet Union writers and artists were attacked for deviation from the party line. The party disciplined economists for suggesting that Western European industry might recover from

The Cold War: A Soviet View. "Nyet!" or "No!" and an arm raised in protest and fear.

the damage it had sustained. The radio blared news that Czech or Hungarian leaders had been exposed as traitors. In the United States, congressional committees launched campaigns to root out "communists" everywhere. On both sides of the Iron Curtain, the cold war intensified everyday anxiety, bringing air-raid drills, spy trials, a belief that a way of life was at stake, and appeals to defend family and home against the menacing "other".

KHRUSHCHEV AND THE "THAW"

Stalin died in 1953. Nikita Khrushchev's slow accession to power, not secure until 1956, signaled a change of

direction. Khrushchev possessed a kind of earthy directness that, despite his hostility to the West, helped for a time to ease tensions. Stalin had secluded himself in the Kremlin; Khrushchev traveled throughout the world. Showing his desire to reduce international conflict, Khrushchev soon agreed to a summit meeting with the leaders of Britain, France, and the United States. This summit led to a series of understandings that eased the frictions in heavily armed Europe and produced a ban on testing nuclear weapons above ground in the early 1960s.

Khrushchev's other change of direction came with his famous "secret speech" of 1956, in which he acknowledged (behind the closed doors of the Twentieth Party Congress) the "excesses" of Stalin's era. Though the speech was secret, Krushchev's accusations were widely discussed. The harshness of Stalin's regime had generated popular discontent and demands for a shift from the production of heavy machinery and armaments to the manufacture of consumer goods, for a measure of freedom in the arts, for an end to police repression. Soviet citizens besieged the regime with requests to rehabilitate relatives who had been executed or imprisoned under Stalin, partly to make themselves again eligible for certain privileges of citizenship, such as housing. In the new cultural climate, private life—family issues, the shortage of men after the war, and the problem of orphans—became a legitimate subject of concern and discussion.

The thaw provided a brief window of opportunity for some of the Soviet Union's most important writers. In 1957, Boris Pasternak's novel *Doctor Zhivago* could not be published in the Soviet Union, and Pasternak was barred from receiving his Nobel Prize. That Aleksandr Solzhenitsyn's first novel, *One Day in the Life of Ivan Denisovich*, could be published in 1962 marked the relative cultural freedom of the thaw. *Ivan Denisovich* was based on Solzhenitsyn's own experiences in the camps, where he had spent eight years for criticizing Stalin in a letter, and was a powerful literary testimony to the repression Khrushchev had acknowledged. By 1964, however, Khrushchev had fallen and the thaw ended, driving criticism and writers such as Solzhenitsyn underground. Solzhenitsyn kept working on what would become *The Gulag Archipelago*, the first massive historical and literary study of the Stalinist camps (gulags). He secretly collected memoirs and personal testimony from prisoners, kept notes on cigarette rolling papers, and buried drafts of chapters behind his house. *The Gulag Archipelago* was published nonetheless in 1973 in Paris, but one year later the regime arrested Solzhenitsyn on charges of treason and sent him into exile. The most

THE COLD WAR: SOVIET AND AMERICAN VIEWS

The excerpt below is from a speech titled "The Sinews of Peace" that was delivered by Winston Churchill at Westminster College in Fulton, Missouri in early 1946. In it, he coined the phrase "Iron Curtain," warning of the rising power of the Soviet Union in Eastern Europe.

The next excerpt is from an address by Nikita Khrushchev, who became first secretary of the Communist party in 1953. Three years later, his power secure, he began publicly to repudiate the crimes of Joseph Stalin. Khrushchev presided over a short-lived thaw in Soviet-American relations. Yet, as can be seen in his address, Khrushchev shared Winston Churchill's conception of the world divided into two mutually antagonistic camps.

WINSTON CHURCHILL'S "IRON CURTAIN" SPEECH

A shadow has fallen upon the scenes so lately lighted by the Allied victory. Nobody knows what Soviet Russia and its Communist international organization intend to do in the immediate future, or what are the limits, if any, to their expansive and proselytizing tendencies. I have a strong admiration and regard for the valiant Russian people and for my wartime comrade, Marshal Stalin. There is deep sympathy and goodwill in Britain . . . towards the people of all the Russias and a resolve to persevere through many differences and rebuffs in establishing lasting friendships. We understand the Russian need to be secure on her western frontiers by the removal of all possibility of German aggression. We welcome Russia to her rightful place among the leading nations of the world. We welcome her flag upon the seas. Above all, we welcome constant, frequent and growing contacts between the Russian people and our own people on both sides of the Atlantic. It is my duty however . . . to place before you certain facts about the present position in Europe.

From Stettin in the Baltic to Trieste in the Adriatic, an iron curtain has descended across the Continent. Behind that line lie all the capitals of the ancient states of Central and Eastern Europe. Warsaw, Berlin, Prague, Vienna, Budapest, Belgrade, Bucharest and Sofia, all these famous cities and the populations around them lie in what I must call the Soviet sphere, and all are subject in one form or another, not only to Soviet influence but to a very high and, in many cases, increasing measure of control from Moscow. . . .

From what I have seen of our Russian friends and Allies during the war, I am convinced that there is nothing they admire so much as strength, and there is nothing for which they have less respect than for weakness, especially military weakness. For that reason the old doctrine of a balance of power is unsound. We cannot afford, if we can help it, to work on narrow margins, offering temptations to a triad of strength. If the Western Democracies stand together in strict adherence to the principles of the United Nations Charter, their influences for furthering those principles will be immense and no one is likely to molest them. If however they become divided or falter in their duty and if these all-important years are allowed to slip away then indeed catastrophe may overwhelm us all.

Winston Churchill, *Winston S. Churchill: His Complete Speeches, 1897–1963,* vol. 7, 1943–1949, edited by Robert Rhodes James (New York: Chelsea House Publishers, 1983), pp. 7290–7291.

Nikita Khrushchev, "Report to the Communist Party Congress (1961)"

Comrades! The competition of the two world social systems, the socialist and the capitalist, has been the chief content of the period since the 20th party Congress. It has become the pivot, the foundation of world development at the present historical stage. Two lines, two historical trends, have manifested themselves more and more clearly in social development. One is the line of social progress, peace and constructive activity. The other is the line of reaction, oppression and war.

In the course of the peaceful competition of the two systems capitalism has suffered a profound moral defeat in the eyes of all peoples. The common people are daily convinced that capitalism is incapable of solving a single one of the urgent problems confronting mankind. It becomes more and more obvious that only on the paths to socialism can a solution to these problems be found. Faith in the capitalist system and the capitalist path of development is dwindling. Monopoly capital, losing its influence, resorts more and more to intimidating and suppressing the masses of the people, to methods of open dictatorship in carrying out its domestic policy and to aggressive acts against other countries. But the masses of the people offer increasing resistance to reaction's acts.

It is no secret to anyone that the methods of intimidation and threat are not a sign of strength but evidence of the weakening of capitalism, the deepening of its general crisis. As the saying goes, if you can't hang on by the mane, you won't hang on by the tail! Reaction is still capable of dissolving parliaments in some countries in violation of their constitutions, of casting the best representatives of the people into prison, of sending cruisers and marines to subdue the "unruly." All this can put off for a time the approach of the fatal hour for the rule of capitalism. The imperialists are sawing away at the branch on which they sit. There is no force in the world capable of stopping man's advance along the road of progress.

Current Soviet Policies IV, edited by Charlotte Saikowski and Leo Gruliow, from the translations of the Current Digest of the Soviet Press. Joint Committee on Slavic Studies, 1962, pp. 42–45.

---

celebrated Soviet dissident was neither a democrat nor pro-Western. He was an idealist and a moralist, with roots among nineteenth-century Russian authors and philosophers. From exile Solzhenitsyn attacked the corruptions of American commercialism as well as Soviet repressiveness.

REPRESSION IN EASTERN EUROPE

In 1956, emboldened by Khrushchev's de-Stalinization, Poland and Hungary rebelled, demanding more independence in the management of their domestic affairs. Striking workers led the opposition in Poland. The government wavered, responding first with military repression and then with a promise of liberalization. Eventually Poland won Soviet permission for his country to pursue its own "ways of Socialist development" by pledging Poland's loyalty to the terms of the Warsaw Pact.

Events in Hungary turned out very differently. The charismatic leader of Hungary's communist government, Imre Nagy, was as much a Hungarian nationalist as a communist. Under his government, protests against Moscow's policies developed into a much broader anticommunist struggle and, even more important, attempted secession from the Warsaw Pact. Khrushchev might contemplate looser ties

CHRONOLOGY	
THE EARLY COLD WAR IN EUROPE, 1946–1968	
Churchill's "Iron Curtain" speech	1946
Truman Doctrine	1947
Soviets launch Cominform and COMECON	1947
Eastern bloc established	1948
Marshall Plan	1948
Berlin blockade	1948–1949
Formation of NATO	1949
Stalin dies	1953
Revolts in East Germany, Poland, and Hungary	1953–1956
Formation of the Warsaw Pact	1955
Khrushchev visits the United States	1959
Building of the Berlin wall	1961

between Eastern Europe and Moscow, but he would not tolerate an end to the pact. On November 4, 1956, Soviet troops occupied Budapest, arresting and executing leaders of the Hungarian rebellion. The Hungarians took up arms, and street fighting continued for several weeks. Soviet forces installed a new government under the staunchly communist Janos Kadar, the repression continued, and tens of thousands of Hungarian refugees fled for the West. Khrushchev's efforts at presenting a gentler, more conciliatory Soviet Union to the West had been shattered by revolt and repression.

Khrushchev's policy of "peaceful coexistence" with the West did not reduce his determination to stave off any military threat to Eastern Europe. By the mid-1950s, NATO's policy of putting battlefield nuclear weapons in West Germany seemed evidence of just such a threat. What was more, East Germans continued to flee the country via West Berlin. Between 1949 and 1961, 2.7 million East Germans left, blunt evidence of the unpopularity of the regime. Attempting to stem the tide, Khrushchev demanded that the West recognize the permanent division of Germany with a free city in Berlin. When that demand was refused, in 1961 the East German government built a ten-foot wall separating the two sectors of the city. The newly elected

American president, John F. Kennedy, marked Berlin's contested status with a visit when he proclaimed that "all free men" were fellow citizens of noncommunist West Berlin. For almost thirty years, until 1989, the Berlin wall remained a monument to how the "hot" war had gone "cold," and mirrored, darkly, the division of Germany and Europe as a whole.

ECONOMIC RENAISSANCE

How did Western Europe recover from World War II?

Despite the ongoing tensions of a global superpower rivalry, the postwar period brought a remarkable recovery in Western Europe: the economic "miracle." Economists still debate its causes. Some factors resulted directly from the war, which encouraged a variety of technological innovations that could be applied in peacetime: improved communications the development of synthetic materials, the increasing use of aluminum and alloy steels, and advances in the techniques of prefabrication. Wartime manufacturing had added significantly to nations' productive capacity. The Marshall Plan seems to have been less central than many claimed at the time, but it solved immediate problems having to do with the balance of payments and a shortage of American dollars to buy American goods. This boom was fueled by a third set of factors: high consumer demand and, consequently, very high levels of employment throughout the 1950s and 1960s. Brisk domestic and foreign consumption encouraged expansion, continued capital investment, and technological innovation. Rising demand for Europe's goods hastened agreements that encouraged the free flow of international trade and currencies (see next page).

It was now assumed that states would do much more economic management—directing investment, making decisions about what to modernize, coordinating policies between industries and countries. This, too, was a legacy of wartime. The result was a

The Berlin Wall, 1961. Thirteen years after the blockade, the East German government built a wall between East and West Berlin to stop the flow of escapees to the West. This manifestation of the "Iron Curtain" was dismantled in 1989.

series of "mixed" economies combining public and private ownership. These government policies and programs contributed to astonishing growth rates. Not only did the economies recover from the war, they reversed prewar economic patterns of slack demand, overproduction, and insufficient investment.

West Germany's recovery was particularly spectacular, and particularly important to the rest of Europe. Production increased sixfold between 1948 and 1964. Unemployment fell to record lows, reaching 0.4 percent in 1965, when there were six jobs for every unemployed person. The contrast with the catastrophic unemployment of the Great Depression heightened the impression of a "miracle." Prices rose but then leveled off, and many citizens could plunge into a domestic buying spree that caused production to soar. German cars, specialized mechanical goods, optics, and chemicals returned to their former role leading world markets. West German women were included in the process: during the 1950s, German politicians encouraged women to take up a role as "citizen consumers," as active but prudent buyers of goods that would keep the German economy humming.

> Not only did the economies recover from the war, they reversed prewar economic patterns of slack demand, overproduction, and insufficient investment.

Under the direction of a minister for planning, Jean Monnet, the French government played a direct role in industrial reform, contributing not only capital but expert advice, and facilitating shifts in the national labor pool to place workers where they were most needed. The plan gave priority to basic industries; the production of electricity doubled, the steel industry was thoroughly modernized, and the French railway system became the fastest and most efficient on the Continent. Italy's industrial "miracle" came later but was even more impressive. Stimulated by infusions of capital from the government and from the Marshall Plan, Italian companies soon began to compete with other European international giants. Electric power production doubled between 1938 and 1953. By 1954 real wages were 50 percent higher than they had been in 1938.

European nations with little in common in terms of political traditions or industrial patterns all shared in the general prosperity. However, Britain remained a special case. British growth was respectable when compared with past performance. Yet the British economy remained sluggish. The country was burdened with obsolete factories and methods, the legacy of its early industrialization, and by an unwillingness to adopt new techniques in old industries or invest in more successful new ones. It was plagued as well by a series of balance-of-payments crises precipitated by an inability to sell more goods abroad than it imported.

EUROPEAN ECONOMIC INTEGRATION

The Western European renaissance was a collective effort. From the Marshall Plan on, a series of international economic organizations began to bind the Western European countries together. The first of these was the European Coal and Steel Community, founded in 1951 to coordinate trade in and the management of Europe's most crucial resources. In 1957, the Treaty of Rome transformed France, West Germany, Italy, Belgium, Holland, and Luxembourg into the European Economic Community (EEC), or Common Market. The EEC aimed to abolish trade barriers among its members. Moreover, the organization pledged itself to common external tariffs, the free movement of labor and capital among the member nations, and to building uniform wage structures and social security systems in order to create similar working conditions throughout the Common Market. A commission headquartered in Brussels administered the program; by 1962, Brussels had more than three thousand "Eurocrats."

Despite several political rough patches, notably over whether Great Britain would join or not, the European Economic Community was a remarkable success. By 1963, it had become the world's largest importer. Its steel production was second only to that of the United States, and total industrial production was over 70 percent higher than it had been in 1950. Last, it established a new long-term political trend: individual countries sought to "Europeanize" solutions to their problems.

Likewise, crucial agreements reached in Bretton Woods, New Hampshire, in July 1944 aimed to coordinate the movements of the global economy and to "internationalize" solutions to economic crises, avoiding catastrophes such as those that plagued the 1930s. Bretton Woods created the International Monetary Fund and the World Bank, both designed to establish predictable and stable exchange rates, prevent speculation, and enable currencies—and consequently trade—to move freely. All other currencies were pegged to the

Heating Fuel Shortage in Great Britain. This scene of British householders lining up for coal during the bitterly cold winter of 1948 shows that "winners" as well as "losers" suffered in the immediate aftermath of the Second World War.

dollar, which both reflected and enhanced the United States' role as the foremost financial power. The new international system was formed with the American-European sphere in mind, but these organizations soon began to play a role in economic development in what came to be known as the Third World. The postwar period, then, quickened global economic integration, largely on American terms.

ECONOMIC DEVELOPMENT IN THE EAST

Although economic development in Eastern Europe was not nearly so dramatic as that in the West, significant advances occurred there as well. National incomes rose and output increased. Poland and Hungary,

in particular, strengthened their economic connections with the West, primarily with France and West Germany. Nevertheless, the Soviet Union required its satellites to design their economic policies to serve more than their own national interests. Regulations governing COMECON, the Eastern European equivalent of the Common Market, ensured that the Soviet Union could sell its exports at prices well above the world level and compelled other members to trade with the Soviet Union to their disadvantage. However, political tension in countries such as Hungary and Poland forced the Soviets eventually to moderate their policies so as to permit the manufacture of more consumer goods and the development of a modest trade with the West.

THE WELFARE STATE

Economic growth became one of the watchwords of the postwar era. Social welfare was another. Clement Atlee, a socialist and the leader of the British Labour party, coined the term "welfare state"; his government, in power until 1951, led the way in enacting legislation that provided free medical care to all through the National Health Service, assistance to families, and guaranteed secondary education of some kind. The welfare state also rested on the assumption that governments could and should try to support popular purchasing power, generate demand, and provide either employment or unemployment insurance, assumptions spelled out earlier by John Maynard Keynes (*General Theory*, 1936) or William Beveridge's important 1943 report on full employment. Although the British Labour party and continental socialist parties pressed these measures, welfare was a consensus issue, backed by the moderate coalitions that governed most postwar Western European states.

Understood in this way, welfare was not poor relief, but an entitlement. Thus it marked a break with centuries-old ways of thinking about poverty and citizenship.

EUROPEAN POLITICS

Postwar political leaders were overwhelmingly pragmatic. Konrad Adenauer, the West German chancellor from 1949 to 1963, despised German militarism and blamed that tradition for Hitler's rise to power. Still, he was apprehensive about German parliamentary democracy and governed in a paternalistic, sometimes

EUROPE DURING THE COLD WAR

Examine the membership of NATO and the Warsaw Pacts, respectively. What type of government characterized the member states of each? Why did the membership of each alliance stay relatively stable for nearly half a century? Why did certain socialist governments (Sweden, France) and federal democracies (Switzerland) remain neutral rather than join either pact? Why did Yugoslavia, under a communist government, not join the Warsaw Pact?

WHAT WERE THE LINKS AMONG DECOLONIZATION, WORLD WAR II, AND THE COLD WAR?

REVOLUTION, ANTICOLONIALISM, AND THE COLD WAR   773

authoritarian, manner. Alcide De Gasperi, the Italian premier from 1948 to 1953, was also centrist. Among postwar French leaders, the most colorful was the Resistance hero General Charles de Gaulle. De Gaulle had retired from politics in 1946 when French voters refused to accept his proposals for strengthening the executive branch of the government. In 1958, faced with civil turmoil caused by the Algerian war (see below) and an abortive coup attempt by a group of right-wing army officers, France's government collapsed and de Gaulle was invited to return. De Gaulle accepted, but insisted on a new constitution that increased the power of the president. Resisting U.S. influence in Europe, he pulled French forces out of NATO in 1966. He also cultivated better relations with the Soviet Union and with West Germany. Finally, he accelerated French economic and industrial expansion by building a modern military establishment, complete with atomic weapons. Like his counterparts, de Gaulle was not, by nature, a democrat. He steered a centrist course, working hard to produce "practical" solutions to political problems and thereby undermine radicalism of any form. Most other Western European did the same.

REVOLUTION, ANTICOLONIALISM, AND THE COLD WAR

What were the links among decolonization, World War II, and the cold war?

In the colonial world as in Europe, the end of war unleashed new conflicts. Those conflicts became closely bound up with Europe's political and economic recovery, they had an enormous if delayed effect on Western culture, and they complicated the cold war. The cold war, as we have seen, created two powerful centers of gravity for world politics. But the wave of anticolonial independence movements that swept through postwar Asia and Africa created a new group of nations that would attempt to avoid aligning with one or the other bloc, and would call itself the "Third World."

THE CHINESE REVOLUTION

The first in this wave of movements was also the single most radical change in the developing world after World War II: the Chinese Revolution. A civil war had raged in China since 1926, when Nationalist forces under Jiang Jeishi (Chiang Kai-shek, 1887–1975) had fought first in the south, then in the north, against communist insurgents under the leadership of Mao Zedong (1893–1976). A truce in 1937 brought the warring sides together to face the Japanese. When Japan was defeated and the occupation ended, the communists, still led by Mao, refused to surrender the northern provinces they controlled. Civil war broke out again. The United States intervened, first to mediate and then with massive military support for the Nationalists. But the Nationalists, corrupt and unrepresentative, were defeated in the field and surrendered in 1949.

Even more than the Russian Revolution, the Chinese Revolution was the act of a nation of peasants. With a program that emphasized radical reform in the countryside (reducing rents, providing health care and education, and reforming marriage) peasant mobilization, and autonomy from Western colonial powers, Mao adapted Marxism to conditions very different from those imagined by its founders. And as in Russia, communism in China provided a model—not necessarily successful—for economic development.

As a successful peasant revolt, the Chinese Revolution stood as a model to anticolonial activists the world over. To colonial powers, it represented a dangerous possible outcome of decolonization. The "loss of China" provoked fear and consternation in the West, particularly in the United States. Although Mao and Stalin distrusted each other, and relations between the two largest communist countries were extremely difficult, the United States considered these two nations a "communist bloc" until the early 1970s. In its immediate aftermath, the Chinese Revolution seemed to tip the balance in a standoff between communism and capitalism and it intensified Western military and diplomatic anxiety about governments throughout Asia.

> As a successful peasant revolt, the Chinese Revolution stood as a model to anticolonial activists the world over.

A Red Guard Demonstration. Middle-school students display their solidarity with Mao Zedong's revolution by waving copies of a book of his quotations. The slogan proclaims, "Not only are we able to destroy the old world, we are able to build a new world instead—Mao Zedong."

THE KOREAN WAR

This anxiety helped make Korea into one of the "hot spots" of the cold war. Effectively a Japanese colony since the 1890s, Korea suffered as its Japanese occupiers subjected the country to horrendous violence and exploited its resources for generations. At the end of World War II the Soviet Union's eastern offensive forced the Japanese out; Korea was then divided between those Russian troops in the north and their American counterparts in the south. As in Germany two new states were established, communist North Korea, run by the Soviet client Kim Jong II, and South Korea, run by the anticommunist autocrat Syngman Rhee. North Korea's government soon decided this arrangement should not last. In June 1950, communist North Korean troops attacked across the border, crushing resistance in the south and forcing noncommunist forces and a small American garrison to retreat to the far end of the peninsula. The United States took advantage of a temporary Russian boycott of the United Nations and brought the invasion before the Security Council. The council passed a resolution permitting an American-led "police action" to defend South Korea and counter the communists.

That action fell to General Douglas MacArthur, a hero of the Second World War and the military governor of occupied Japan. He mounted an audacious amphibious attack behind North Korean lines and cut northern forces to pieces. MacArthur drove the Korean communists to the Chinese border and pressed for the authority to attack them as they retreated into China, hoping to punish China and help reverse the Chinese Revolution. President Harry S. Truman (1945–1953) denied this rash request and relieved MacArthur of command for exceeding his authority. The price had already been paid, however; more than a million Chinese troops flooded across the border in support of the North Koreans. The international troops aiding South Korea were forced into a bloody, headlong retreat in the dead of winter. During that difficult winter the able and patient American general Matthew Ridgeway took over from MacArthur and stemmed the retreat. The war, however, became a stalemate. Chinese and North Korean troops dug in against the United Nations force, com-

WHAT WERE THE LINKS AMONG DECOLONIZATION, WORLD WAR II, AND THE COLD WAR?

REVOLUTION, ANTICOLONIALISM, AND THE COLD WAR   775

posed largely of American and South Korean troops but drawn from around the world—small contingents from Britain, Australia, Ethiopia, the Netherlands, and Turkey distinguished themselves in the fighting. The conflict dragged on for two years as peace talks began. The end, decreed in June of 1953, was inconclusive. Korea remained divided roughly along the original line drawn in 1945, no longer at war but not at peace. With fifty-three thousand Americans and over a million Koreans and Chinese dead, South Korea had not been "lost," but neither had China or the United States won a decisive victory. As in Germany, the inability of major powers to achieve their ultimate goals resulted in a divisive settlement and a divided nation.

DECOLONIZATION

The Chinese Revolution proved the start of a larger wave. Between 1947 and 1960 the sprawling European empires built during the nineteenth century disintegrated. Imperialism had always provoked resistance. Opposition to colonial rule had stiffened after World War I, forcing war-weakened European states to renegotiate the terms of empire. After World War II, older forms of empire quickly became untenable. In some regions, European states simply sought to cut their losses and withdraw, their financial, political, and human resources depleted. In others, well-organized and tenacious nationalist movements successfully demanded new constitutional arrangements and independence. In a third set of cases, European powers were drawn into complicated, multifaceted, and extremely violent struggles between different movements of indigenous peo-

ples and European settler communities—conflicts the European states had helped create.

THE BRITISH EMPIRE UNRAVELS

India was the first and largest of the colonies to win self-government following the war. During the early stages of the Second World War, the Indian National Congress (founded 1885), the umbrella party for the independence movement, called on Britain to "quit India." The extraordinary Indian nationalist Mohandas K. (Mahatma) Gandhi (1869–1948) had been at work in India since the 1920s, and had pioneered anticolonial ideas and tactics that echoed the world over. In the face of colonial domination, Gandhi advocated not violence but *swaraj*, or self-rule, urging Indians individually and collectively to develop their own resources and to withdraw from the imperial economy. By 1947 Gandhi and his fellow nationalist Jawaharlal Nehru (1889–1964, prime minister 1947–1964), the leader of the proindependence Congress party, had gained such widespread support that the British found it impossible to continue in power.

While talks after 1945 established the procedures for independence, however, India was torn by ethnic and religious conflict. A Muslim League, led by Mohammed Ali Jinnah (1876–1948), wanted autonomy in largely Muslim areas and feared the predominantly Hindu Congress party's authority in a single united state. Cycles of rioting broke out between the two religious communities. In June 1947, British India was "partitioned" into the nations of India (majority Hindu) and Pakistan (majority Muslim). The process of partition brought brutal religious and ethnic warfare. More than a million Hindus and Muslims died, and an estimated 12 million became refugees, evicted from their lands or fleeing the fighting. Conflict continued between the independent states of India and Pakistan. Nehru, who became first prime minister of India, embarked on a program of industrialization and modernization—not at all what Gandhi would have counseled. Nehru proved particularly adept at maneuvering in the cold war world, steering a course of nonalignment with either of the blocs, getting aid for industry from the USSR and food imports from the United States.

PALESTINE

The year 1948 brought more crises for the British empire, including an end to the British mandate in Palestine. During WWI, British diplomats had encouraged

CHRONOLOGY

MAJOR DEVELOPMENTS IN ASIA, 1947–PRESENT

India gains independence	1947
Chinese Communist Revolution	1949
Korean War	1950–1953
Vietnamese defeat the French	1954
Chinese Cultural Revolution	1960s
Vietnam war (U.S.)	1964–1975
United States recognizes Communist China	1972
Tiananmen Square	1989

Leaders of Indian Nationalism—Nehru and Gandhi. Mohandas Gandhi was assassinated in 1948. Jawaharlal Nehru served as prime minister of India from 1947 to his death in 1964.

Arab nationalist revolts against the Ottoman empire. With the 1917 Balfour Declaration, they had also promised a "Jewish homeland" in Palestine for European Zionists. Contradictory promises and the flight of European Jews from Nazi Germany contributed to rising conflict between Jewish settlers and Arabs in Palestine during the 1930s and provoked an Arab revolt bloodily suppressed by the British. At the same time, the newly important oil concessions in the Middle East were multiplying Britain's strategic interests in the Suez Canal, Egypt, and the Arab nations generally. In 1939, in the name of regional stability the British strictly limited further Jewish immigration. They tried to maintain that limit after the war, but now they faced pressure from tens of thousands of Jewish refugees from Europe. The conflict quickly became a three-way war: among Palestinian Arabs fighting for what they considered their land and their independence, Jewish settlers and Zionist militants determined to defy British restrictions, and British administrators with divided sympathies, embarrassed and shocked by the plight of Jewish refugees and committed to maintaining good Anglo-Arab relations. The British responded militarily. By 1947, there was one British soldier for every eighteen inhabitants of the Mandate. The years of fighting, however, with terrorist tactics on all sides, persuaded the British to leave. The United Nations voted (by a narrow margin) to partition the territory into two states. Neither Jewish settlers nor

Palestinian Arabs found the partition satisfactory and both began to fight for territory even before British troops withdrew. No sooner did Israel declare its independence in May 1948 than five neighboring states invaded. The new but well-organized Israeli nation survived the war and extended its boundaries. On the losing side a million Palestinian Arabs who fled or were expelled found themselves clustered in refugee camps in the Gaza strip and on the West Bank of the Jordan river, which the armistice granted to an enlarged state of Jordan. The new nation marked a permanent change to the culture and balance of power in the region.

AFRICA

A number of West African colonies established assertive independence movements before and during the 1950s, and the British government moved hesitantly to meet their demands. By the middle of the 1950s, Britain agreed to a variety of terms for independence in these territories, leaving them with written constitutions and a British legal system, but little else in terms of modern infrastructure or economic support. Belgium and France also withdrew from their holdings. By 1965 virtually all of the former African colonies had become independent, and virtually none of them possessed the means to redress losses from colonialism to make that independence work.

The process of decolonization was relatively peaceful—except where large populations of European settlers complicated European withdrawal. In the north, settler resistance made the French exit from Algeria wrenching and complex (see page 779). In southern Africa, the exceptionally large and wealthy population of European settlers controlled huge tracts of fertile farmland along with some of the most lucrative gold and diamond mines on earth. This was especially true in South Africa. There, during the late 1940s, Britain's Labour government set aside its deep dislike of Afrikaner racism in a fateful political bargain. In return for guarantees that South African gold would be used carefully to support Britain's global financial power, Britain tolerated the introduction of apartheid in South Africa. Even by other standards of segregation, apartheid was especially harsh. Under its terms, Africans, Indians, and

MOHANDAS GANDHI AND NONVIOLENT ANTICOLONIALISM

After leading a campaign for Indian rights in South Africa between 1894 and 1914, Mohandas K. Gandhi (1869–1948), known as Mahatma ("great-souled") Gandhi, became a leader in the long battle for home rule in India. This battle was finally won in 1947 and brought with it the partition of India and the creation of Pakistan. Gandhi's insistence on the power of nonviolent noncooperation brought him to the forefront of Indian politics and provided a model for many later liberation struggles, including the American civil rights movement. Gandhi argued that only nonviolent resistance, which dramatized the injustice of colonial rule and colonial law, had the spiritual force to unite a community and end colonialism.

Passive resistance is a method of securing rights by personal suffering; it is the reverse of resistance by arms. When I refuse to do a thing that is repugnant to my conscience, I use soul-force. For instance, the Government of the day has passed a law which is applicable to me. I do not like it. If by using violence I force the Government to repeal the law, I am employing what may be termed body-force. If I do not obey the law and accept the penalty for its breach, I use soul-force. It involves sacrifice of self.

Everybody admits that sacrifice of self is infinitely superior to sacrifice of others. Moreover, if this kind of force is used in a cause that is unjust, only the person using it suffers. He does not make others suffer for his mistakes. Men have before now done many things which were subsequently found to have been wrong. . . . It is therefore meet that he should not do that which he knows to be wrong, and suffer the consequence whatever it may be. This is the key to the use of soul-force. . . .

It is contrary to our manhood if we obey laws repugnant to our conscience. Such teaching is opposed to religion and means slavery. If the Government were to ask us to go about without any clothing, should we do so? If I were a passive resister, I would say to them that I would have nothing to do with their law. But we have so forgotten ourselves and become so compliant that we do not mind any degrading law.

A man who has realized his manhood, who fears only God, will fear no one else. Man-made laws are not necessarily binding on him. Even the Government does not expect any such thing from us. They do not say: "You must do such and such a thing." But they say: "If you do not do it, we will punish you." We are sunk so low that we fancy that it is our duty and our religion to do what the law lays down. If man will only realize that it is unmanly to obey laws that are unjust, no man's tyranny will enslave him. This is the key to self-rule or home-rule.

M. K. Gandhi, "Indian Home Rule (1909)," in *The Gandhi Reader: A Source Book of His Life and Writings*, edited by Homer A. Jack (Bloomington: Indiana University Press, 1956), pp. 104–121.

colored persons of mixed descent lost all political rights. All the institutions of social life, including marriage and schools, were segregated. What was more, the government tried to block the dramatic social consequences of the expansion of mining and industrialization in general, especially African migration to cities and a new wave of labor militancy in the mines. Apartheid required Africans to live in designated "homelands," forbade them to travel without specific permits, and created elaborate government bureaus to manage the labor essential to the economy. The government also banned any political protest. These measures made Western powers uncomfortable with the segregationist regime, but white South Africans held on to American support by presenting themselves as a bulwark against communism.

CRISIS IN SUEZ AND THE END OF AN ERA

For postwar Britain, empire was not only politically complicated, it cost too much. Britain began to withdraw from naval and air bases around the world because they had become too expensive to maintain.

In Egypt, however, the British refused to yield a traditional point of imperial pride. In 1951 nationalists compelled the British to agree to withdraw their troops from Egyptian territory within three years. In 1952 a group of nationalist army officers deposed Egypt's King Farouk, who had close ties to Britain, and proclaimed a republic. Shortly after the final British withdrawal an Egyptian colonel, Gamal Abdel Nasser (1918–1970), became president of the country (1956–1970). His first major public act as president was to nationalize the Suez Canal Company. So doing would help finance the construction of the Aswan Dam on the Nile, and both the dam and nationalizing the canal represented economic independence and Egyptian national pride. Nasser also helped to develop the anticolonial ideology of pan-Arabism, proposing that Arab nationalists throughout the Islamic world should create an alliance of modern nations, no longer beholden to the West. Finally, Nasser was also willing to take aid and support from the Soviets in order to achieve that goal, which made the canal into a cold war issue.

Three nations found Nasser and his pan-Arab ideals threatening. Israel, surrounded on all sides by unfriendly neighbors, was looking for an opportunity to seize the strategic Sinai Peninsula and create a buffer against Egypt. France, already fighting a war against Algerian nationalists, hoped to destroy what it considered the Egyptian source of Arab nationalism. Britain depended on the canal as a route to its strategic bases and was stung by this blow to imperial dignity. In the autumn of 1956, the three nations colluded in an attack on Egypt. Israel occupied the Sinai while British and French jets destroyed Egypt's air force on the ground. The former colonial powers landed troops at the mouth of the canal but lacked the resources to push on in strength toward Cairo. As a result the war left Nasser in power and made him a hero to the Egyptian public for holding the imperialists at bay. The attack was condemned around the world. The United States angrily called its allies' bluff, inflicting severe financial penalties on Britain and France. Both countries were forced to withdraw their expeditions. For policy makers in Great Britain and France, the failure at Suez marked the end of an era.

FRENCH DECOLONIZATION

In two particular cases, France's experience of decolonization was bloodier, more difficult, and more damaging to French prestige and domestic politics than any in Britain's experience, with the possible exception of Northern Ireland. The first was Indochina, where French efforts to restore imperial authority after losing it in World War II only resulted in military defeat and further humiliation. The second case, Algeria, became not only a violent colonial war but also a struggle with serious political ramifications at home.

CHRONOLOGY

MAJOR DEVELOPMENTS IN AFRICA, 1952–PRESENT

Egypt gains independence	1952
Congo gains independence	1960
Ethnic and tribal conflicts throughout Africa	1960s–present
Algeria gains independence	1962
Rhodesia gains independence	1965
Massive economic decline	1970s–1990s
Apartheid ends in South Africa	1992–1994

WHAT WERE THE LINKS AMONG DECOLONIZATION, WORLD WAR II, AND THE COLD WAR?

REVOLUTION, ANTICOLONIALISM, AND THE COLD WAR   779

THE FIRST VIETNAM WAR, 1946–1954

Indochina was one of France's last major imperial acquisitions in the nineteenth century. Here, as elsewhere, the two world wars had helped galvanize first nationalist and then, also, communist independence movements. In Indochina, the communist resistance became particularly effective under the leadership of Ho Chi Minh. Ho was French educated and, his expectations raised by the Wilsonian principles of self-determination, had hoped his country might win independence at Versailles in 1919. He read Marx and Lenin, and absorbed the Chinese communists' lessons about organizing peasants around social and agrarian as well as national issues. During World War II, Ho's movement fought first the Vichy government of the colony and later Japanese occupiers, and provided intelligence reports for the Allies. In 1945, however, the United States and Britain repudiated their relationship with Ho's independence movement and allowed the French to reclaim their colonies throughout Southeast Asia. The Vietnamese communists, who were fierce nationalists as well as Marxists, renewed their guerrilla war against the French.

The fighting was protracted and bloody; France saw in it a chance to redeem its national pride. After one of France's most capable generals, Jean de Lattre de Tassigny, finally achieved a military advantage against the rebels in 1951, the French government might have decolonized on favorable terms. Instead, it decided to press on for total victory, sending troops deep into Vietnamese territory to root out the rebels. One major base was established in a valley bordering modern Laos, at a hamlet called Dien Bien Phu. Ringed by high mountains, this vulnerable spot became a base for thousands of elite French paratroopers and colonial soldiers from Algeria and West Africa—the best of France's troops. The rebels besieged the base. Tens of thousands of Vietnamese nationalist fighters hauled heavy artillery by hand up the mountainsides and bombarded the network of forts set up by the French. The siege lasted for months, becoming a protracted national crisis in France.

When Dien Bien Phu fell in May 1954, the French government began peace talks in Geneva. The Geneva Accords, drawn up by the French, Vietnamese politicians including the communists, the British, and the Americans, divided Indochina into three countries: Laos, Cambodia, and Vietnam, partitioned into two states. North Vietnam was taken over by Ho Chi Minh's party; South Vietnam by a succession of Western-supported politi-

"Dien-Bien-Phu: . . . they sacrificed themselves for liberty." The sentiments expressed in this poster, which was intended to commemorate the French soldiers who died at Dien-Bien-Phu in May 1954, helped to deepen French commitments to colonial control in Algeria.

cians. Corruption, repression, and instability in the south, coupled with Ho Chi Minh's nationalist desire to unite Vietnam, guaranteed that the war would continue.

ALGERIA

Still reeling from the humiliation of Dien Bien Phu, France faced a complex colonial problem closer to home, in Algeria. Since the 1830s, the colony had evolved into a settler society of three social groups. First, in addition to a small class of French soldiers and administrators, there were also one million European settlers. All of them were citizens of the three administrative districts of Algeria, which were legally part of France. In the small towns and villages of Algeria lived a second group of (largely Muslim) Berbers, whose long history of service in the French army entitled them to certain formal and informal privileges within the colony. Finally, there were millions of Muslim Arabs, some living in the desert south but most crowded into impoverished neighborhoods in the cities. The Arabs were the largest and most deprived group in Algerian society.

At the end of the Second World War, Algerian nationalists called on the Allies to recognize Algeria's independence in return for good service during the war. Public demonstrations became frequent, and in several cases turned into attacks on settler-landowners. In one rural town, Setif, celebrations of the defeat of Germany flared into violence against settlers. French repression was harsh and immediate: security forces killed several thousand Arabs. After the war the French government approved a provincial assembly for all of Algeria, elected by two pools of voters, one made up of settlers and mostly Berber Muslims, the other of Arabs. This very limited enfranchisement gave Arab Algerians no political power. The more important changes were economic. Algeria suffered in the difficulties after the war. Many Arab Algerians felt they had to emigrate; several hundred thousand went to work in France. By the middle of the 1950s, a younger generation of Arab activists, unhappy with the leadership of the moderates, had taken charge of a movement dedicated to independence by force. The National Liberation Front (FLN) was organized, which leaned toward socialism and demanded equal citizenship for all.

The war in Algeria became a war on three fronts. The first was a guerrilla war between the regular French Army and the FLN, fought in the mountains and deserts of the country. This war continued for years, a clear military defeat for the FLN but never a clear-cut victory for the French. The second war, fought out in Algeria's cities, began with an FLN campaign of bombing and terrorism. European civilians were killed, and the French administration retaliated with its own campaign. French paratroopers hunted down and destroyed the networks of FLN bombers. The information that allowed the French to break the FLN network was extracted through systematic torture conducted by French security forces. The torture became an international scandal, bringing waves of protest in France. This third front of the Algerian war divided France, brought down the government, and ushered de Gaulle back into power.

De Gaulle visited Algiers to wild cheering from settlers and declared that Algeria would always be French. After another year of violence, he and his advisors had changed their minds. By 1962 talks had produced a formula for independence: a referendum would be held, voted on by the whole population of Algeria. On July 1, 1962, the referendum passed by a landslide vote. Arab political groups and guerrillas from the FLN entered Algiers in triumph. Settlers and Berbers who had fought for the French army fled Algeria for France by the hundreds of thousands. Later, these refugees were joined in France by another influx of Arab economic migrants.

Algeria illustrated the dramatic domestic impact of decolonization. The war cut deep divides through French society, largely because the very identity of France seemed at stake. Withdrawing from Algeria meant reorienting French views of what it meant to be a modern power. In France and other imperial powers, the conclusions seemed clear. Traditional forms of colonial rule could not withstand the demands of postwar politics and culture; the leading European nations, once distinguished by their empires, would have to look for new forms of influence.

POSTWAR CULTURE AND THOUGHT

What themes defined postwar culture?

The postwar period brought a remarkable burst of cultural production. Writers and artists did not hesitate to take up big issues: freedom, civilization, or what many called the human condition. The search for democratic renewal gave this literature urgency; the moral dilemmas of war, occupation, and resistance gave it resonance and popular appeal. The process of decolonization, too, forced the issues of race, culture, and colonialism to center stage in Western debates.

THE BLACK PRESENCE

The journal *Présence Africaine* ("African Presence"), founded in Paris in 1947, was only one in a chorus of new cultural voices. *Présence Africaine* published such writers as Aimé Césaire (b. 1913), the surrealist poet from Martinique, and Léopold Senghor of Senegal (1906–2001). Césaire and Senghor were brilliant students, educated in the most elite French universities, and elected to the French National Assembly. Both men, in important respects models of Frenchness, became the most influential exponents of

ANTICOLONIALISM AND VIOLENCE

Born in the French Caribbean colony of Martinique, Frantz Fanon (1925–1961) studied psychiatry in France before moving on to work in Algeria in the early 1950s. Fanon became a member of the Algerian revolutionary National Liberation Front (FLN) and an ardent advocate of decolonization. Black Skin, White Masks, published in 1952 with a preface by Jean Paul Sartre, was a study of the psychological effects of colonialism and racism on black culture and individuals. The Wretched of the Earth (1961) was a revolutionary manifesto, one of the most influential of the period. Unlike Gandhi, Fanon believed that violence lay at the heart of both the colonial relationship and anticolonial movements. Fanon attacked nationalist leaders for their ambition and corruption. He believed that revolutionary change could come only from poor peasants, those who "have found no bone to gnaw in the colonial system." Diagnosed with leukemia, Fanon sought treatment in the Soviet Union and then in Washington, D.C., where he died.

In decolonization, there is therefore the need of a complete calling in question of the colonial situation. If we wish to describe it precisely, we might find it in the well-known words: "The last shall be first and the first last." Decolonization is the putting into practice of this sentence. . . .

The naked truth of decolonization evokes for us the searing bullets and blood-stained knives which emanate from it. For if the last shall be first, this will only come to pass after a murderous and decisive struggle between the two protagonists. That affirmed intention to place the last at the head of things, and to make them climb at a pace (too quickly, some say) the well-known steps which characterize an organized society, can only triumph if we use all means to turn the scale, including, of course, that of violence.

You do not turn any society, however primitive it may be, upside down with such a program if you have not decided from the very beginning, that is to say from the actual formation of that program, to overcome all the obstacles that you will come across in so doing. The native who decides to put the program into practice, and to become its moving force, is ready for violence at all time.

From birth it is clear to him that this narrow world, strewn with prohibitions, can only be called in question by absolute violence.

Frantz Fanon, *The Wretched of the Earth,* translated by Constance Farrington (New York: Grove Press, 1963), pp. 35–37.

Négritude, which could be translated as "black consciousness" or "black pride."

Césaire's early work took its lead from surrealism and the exploration of consciousness. Later, his work became more political. *Discourse on Colonialism* (1950) was a powerful indictment of the material and spiritual squalor of colonialism, which, he argued, not only dehumanized colonial subjects, but degraded the colonizers themselves.

Césaire's student Frantz Fanon (1925–1961), also from Martinique, went further. He argued that withdrawing into an insular black culture was not an effective response to racism. People of color, he believed, needed a theory of radical social change. More than

Simone de Beauvoir.

Césaire, and bluntly rejecting Gandhi's theories and practice, Fanon argued that violence was rooted in colonialism and, therefore, in anticolonial movements. But he also believed that many anticolonial leaders would be corrupted by their ambition and by collaboration with former colonial powers. Revolutionary change, he believed, could only come from poor peasants, or those who "have found no bone to gnaw in the colonial system."

How did these writers fit into postwar culture? Western intellectuals sought to revive humanism and democratic values after the atrocities of World War II. Fanon and others pointed out that the struggles over colonialism made that project more difficult; the violent repression of anticolonial movements in places such as Algeria seemed to be a relapse into brutality. They pointed to the ironies of Europe's "civilizing mission" and demanded a reevaluation of blackness as a central concept in Western culture. The West's postwar recovery would entail eventually facing this challenge to the universal claims of its culture.

EXISTENTIALISM

The French existentialist writers, most prominently Jean-Paul Sartre (1905–1980) and Albert Camus

(1913–1960), put the themes of individuality, commitment, and choice at center stage. Their starting point was that "existence precedes essence." In other words, meaning in life is not given, but created. Thus individuals were "condemned to be free," and to give their lives meaning by making choices and accepting responsibility. War, collaboration and resistance, genocide, and the development of weapons of mass destruction all provided specific points of reference and gave these abstractions new meaning. The existentialists' writing was also clear and accessible, which contributed to their enormous popularity. Although Sartre wrote philosophical treatises, he also published plays and short stories. Camus's own experience in the resistance gave him tremendous moral authority—he became the symbol of a new generation. His novels—including *The Stranger* (1942), *The Plague* (1947), and *The Fall* (1956)—often revolved around metaphors for the war, showing that people were responsible for their own dilemmas and, through a series of antiheroes, exploring the limited ability of men and women to help each other.

Existentialist insights opened other doors. The existentialist approach to race, for instance, emphasized that no meaning inhered in skin color; instead race derived meaning from a lived experience or situation. The same approach could be applied to gender. In her famous introduction to *The Second Sex* (1949), Simone de Beauvoir (1908–1986) argued that "One is not born a woman, one becomes one." Women, like men, were condemned to be free. Beauvoir went on to ask why women seemed to accept their secondary status or why, in her words, they "dreamed the dreams of men." Beauvoir had little to do with feminism, however, until the late 1960s. When *The Second Sex* was published, it was associated with existentialism; only later would it become a key text of the women's movement (see Chapter 28).

MEMORY AND AMNESIA: THE AFTERMATH OF WAR

Questions of terror and dictatorship haunted social and political thought of the postwar era, and especially the work of émigrés from Europe. Representatives of the "Frankfurt school" of German Marxism, by wartime refugees in the United States, sought to understand how fascism and Nazism had taken root in Western culture and politics. Theodor Adorno joined Max Horkheimer in a series of essays, *Dialectic of Enlightenment* (1947), the best known of which indicted the "culture industry" for depoliticizing the masses and crippling democracy. Hannah Arendt (1906–1975), a Jewish refugee from Germany, was the first to propose that both Nazism and Stalinism should be understood as forms of a novel, twentieth-century form of government: totalitarianism (*The Origins of Totalitarianism*, 1951). Unlike earlier forms of tyranny or despotism, totalitarianism worked by mobilizing mass support. It used terror to crush resistance, break down political and social institutions, and atomize the public. Totalitarianism, Arendt argued, also forged new ideologies. Totalitarian regimes did not concern themselves with whether killing was justified by law; they justified camps and extermination by pointing to the objective laws of history or racial struggle. By unleashing destruction and eliminating entire populations, totalitarian politics made collective resistance virtually impossible.

Discussions of the war and its legacy, however, were limited. Of all the memoirs about the war, *The Diary of a Young Girl* by Anne Frank, published in 1947, was undoubtedly the most widely read. Yet the main current in postwar culture ran in a different direction, toward repressing painful issues and bad memories. Postwar governments could not or would not purge all those implicated in war crimes. In France, the courts sentenced 2,640 to death and executed 791; in Austria 13,000 were convicted of war crimes and 30 executed. For ten years French television considered *The Sorrow and the Pity* (1969), Marcel Ophüls's brilliant and unsparing documentary on a French town under Vichy, too "controversial" for broadcast. Most Jewish survivors, wherever they lived, found that few editors were interested in publishing their stories. In 1947, only a small publishing house would take on the Italian survivor Primo Levi's *Survival in Auschwitz*; the book and Levi's other writings did not find a wide audience until later.

The cold war was an important factor in burying and distorting memories. West of the Iron Curtain, the eagerness to embrace West Germany as an ally, the single-minded emphasis on economic development, and ardent anticommunism blurred views of the past. In the Eastern bloc, regimes declared fascism to be a thing of the past, and did not scrutinizing the past or seek out the many who collaborated with the Nazis. Thus, reckoning with history was postponed until the fall of the Soviet Union. On both sides of the Iron Curtain, the vast majority of people turned inward, cherishing their domestic lives, relieved to have privacy.

> Questions of terror and dictatorship haunted social and political thought of the postwar era, and especially the work of émigrés from Europe.

CONCLUSION

One of the last serious and most dramatic confrontations of the cold war came in 1962, in Cuba. A revolution in 1958 had brought the charismatic communist Fidel Castro to power. Immediately after, the United States began to work with exiled Cubans, supporting among other ventures a bungled attempt to invade via the Bay of Pigs in 1961. Castro not only aligned himself with the Soviets, he invited them to base nuclear missiles on Cuban soil, only a few minutes' flying time from Florida. When American spy planes identified the missiles and related military equipment in 1962, Kennedy confronted Khrushchev. After three nerve-wracking weeks, the Soviets agreed to withdraw and to remove the bombers and missiles already on Cuban soil. But citizens of both countries had spent many anxious hours in their bomb shelters, and onlookers the world over wrestled with their rising fears that a nuclear Armageddon was upon them.

The Cuban missile crisis provided one inspiration for Stanley Kubrick's classic *Dr. Strangelove* (1964), a devastating and dark comedy with many cold war themes. The story concerns an "accidental" nuclear attack and the demented characters responsible for it. It also concerns the repression of memory and the sudden reversals of alliances brought by the cold war. The wildly eccentric German scientist Dr. Strangelove shuttles between his present life working for the Americans and his barely repressed past as an enthusiastic follower of Hitler. The Cuban missile crisis brought the plot so close to home that when the film came out Columbia Pictures felt compelled to issue a disclaimer: "It is the stated position of the United States Air Force that their safeguards would prevent the occurrence of such events as are depicted in this film."

In sum, the cold war dominated postwar culture and politics. It decisively shaped the development of both the Soviet and American states. In his farewell address, President Eisenhower warned that a "military-industrial complex" had taken shape and that its "total influence—economic, political, even spiritual—is felt in every city, every statehouse, every office of the federal government." Yet other, equally important developments marked the period. The nation-state expanded in nonmilitary realms, taking on new roles in economic planning and management, in educating citizens, and in ensuring social welfare. Those changes were driven by a search for democracy and stability. Former colonies became nations. In the long run the formation of the Third World mattered as much, if not more, than the bipolar divisions established by the cold war. Global and regional economic integration quickened.

Economic growth helped all the Western nations (in different measures) recover from the devastation of war, though whether Europe would regain its former global power was doubtful. Finally, economic growth had unintended consequences. By the 1960s, social and cultural changes were beginning to undermine the cold war settlement.

KEY TERMS

Marshall Plan

NATO

Khrushchev

Aleksandr Solzhenitsyn

Mao Zedong

Mohandas K. (Mahatma) Gandhi

Ho Chi Minh

Algerian War

existentialism

Berlin Wall

Berlin blockade

ECSC

social democracy

SELECTED READINGS

Aron, Raymond. *The Imperial Republic: The United States and the World, 1945–1973.* Lanham, Md., 1974. An early analysis by a leading French political theorist.

Carter, Erica. *How German Is She? Postwar West German Reconstruction and the Consuming Woman.* Ann Arbor, 1997. A thoughtful examination of gender and the reconstruction of the family in West Germany during the 1950s.

Clayton, Anthony. *The Wars of French Decolonization.* London, 1994. Good survey.

Connelly, Matthew. *A Diplomatic Revolution: Algeria's Fight for Independence and the Origins of the Post–Cold War Era.* New York and Oxford, 2003. An international history.

Cooper, Frederick, and Ann Laura Stoler, eds. *Tensions of Empire: Colonial Cultures in a Bourgeois World.* Berkeley, 1997. Collection of new essays, among the best.

Darwin, John. *Britain and Decolonization: The Retreat from Empire in the Postwar World.* New York, 1988. Best overall survey.

Deák, István, Jan T. Gross, and Tony Judt, eds. *The Politics of Retribution in Europe: World War II and Its Aftermath.* Princeton, N.J., 2000. Collection focusing on the attempt to come to terms with the Second World War in Eastern and Western Europe.

Farmer, Sarah. *Martyred Village: Commemorating the 1944 Massacre at Oradour-sur-Glane.* Berkeley, 1999. Gripping story of French attempts to come to terms with collaboration and complicity in atrocities.

Fulbrook, Mary, ed. *Europe Since 1945.* Oxford, 2001. A recent and excellent collection of essays.

Gilbert, Felix, and David Clay Large. *The End of the European Era, 1890 to the Present.* 5th ed. New York, 2002. Comprehensive overview of political developments.

Herf, Jeffrey. *Divided Memory: The Nazi Past in the Two Germanys.* Cambridge, Mass., 1997.

Holland, R. F. *European Decolonization 1918–1981: An Introductory Survey.* New York, 1985. Sprightly narrative and analysis.

Jarausch, Konrad Hugo, ed. *Dictatorship as Experience: Towards a Socio-Cultural History of the GDR.* Translated by Eve Duffy. New York, 1999. Surveys recent research on the former East Germany.

Judt, Tony. *Past Imperfect: French Intellectuals, 1944–1956.* Berkeley, 1992. Very readable, on French intellectuals, who loomed large during this period.

———. *A Grand Illusion? An Essay on Europe.* New York, 1996. Short and brilliant.

———. *The Burden of Responsibility: Blum, Camus, and the French Twentieth Century.* Chicago and London, 1998. Also on French intellectuals.

Kolko, Gabriel. *The Politics of War: The World and United States Foreign Policy, 1943–1945.* New York, 1990. Argues that the blame for the cold war rests with the Western Allies.

Koven, Seth, and Sonya Michel. *Mothers of a New World: Maternalist Politics and the Origins of Welfare States.* New York, 1993. Excellent essays on the long history of welfare politics.

LaFeber, Walter. *America, Russia, and The Cold War.* New York, 1967. A classic, now in its ninth edition.

Laqueur, Walter. *Europe In Our Time: A History, 1945–1992.* New York, 1992. A useful, thorough survey.

Large, David Clay. *Berlin.* New York, 2000.

Leffler, Melvyn P. *A Preponderance of Power: National Security, the Truman Administration, and the Cold War.* Stanford, 1992.

Macey, David. *Frantz Fanon.* New York, 2000. Comprehensive recent biography.

Medvedev, Roy. *Khrushchev.* New York, 1983. A perceptive biography of the Soviet leader by a Soviet historian.

Milward, Alan S. *The Reconstruction of Western Europe, 1945–1951.* Berkeley, 1984. A good discussion of the "economic miracle."

Moeller, Robert G. *Protecting Motherhood: Women and the Family in the Politics of Postwar West Germany.* Berkeley, 1993.

———. *War Stories: The Search for a Usable Past in the Federal Republic of Germany.* Berkeley, 2001. Revealing analyses of postwar culture and politics.

Reynolds, David. *One World Divisible: A Global History Since 1945.* New York, 2000. Fresh approach, comprehensive, and very readable survey.

Rousso, Henri. *The Vichy Syndrome: History and Memory in France since 1944.* Cambridge, Mass., 1991. First in a series of books by one of the preeminent French historians.

Schissler, Hanna, ed. *The Miracle Years: A Cultural History of West Germany, 1949–1968.* Princeton, N.J., 2001. The cultural effects of the "economic miracle."

Schneider, Peter. *The Wall Jumper: A Berlin Story.* Chicago, 1998. A fascinating novel about life in divided Berlin.

Trachtenberg, Mark. *A Constructed Peace: The Making of the European Settlement, 1945–1963.* Princeton, N.J., 1999.

Yergin, Daniel. *Shattered Peace: The Origins of the Cold War.* New York, 1977.

Young, Marilyn B. *The Vietnam Wars, 1945–1990.* New York, 1991. Excellent account of the different stages of the war and its repercussions.

CHAPTER
TWENTY-EIGHT

RED FLAGS AND
VELVET
REVOLUTIONS: THE
END OF THE COLD
WAR, 1960–1990

The year 1960 seemed golden and full of promise. Despite nearly constant international tension, everyday life in Europe and North America seemed to be improving. Economies recovered, many standards of living rose, and new forms of culture flourished. The economic horizon looked bright. By 1990, most of that familiar landscape had been dramatically transformed. Western Europeans could no longer be certain of their prosperity or of their leaders' ability to provide the sort of life they took for granted. Societies had fragmented in unexpected ways. The startlingly sudden dissolution of the Soviet bloc brought down the foundation of the cold war world, which raised both hopes for peace and fears of conflict from unexpected quarters.

How can we explain this transformation? By the middle of the 1960s, social and economic tensions were undermining the consensus that postwar prosperity and created in the West. The economic expansion after 1945 ushered in dramatic changes: new industries, new economic values, new social classes, and a newly acute sense of generational difference. Governments faced demands from new social groups and were frequently baffled in their efforts to respond. Tensions exploded in the late 1960s. In 1968 uprisings and strikes broke out across the West, from Czechoslovakia to Germany, France, the United States, and Mexico. Problems were compounded after 1975 by a continuing economic crisis that threatened the security a generation had labored so hard to achieve. As the economy stalled, social protest continued in Europe and the United States for at least a decade after "the Sixties" technically ended.

The challenges of these decades proved even more fundamental in the Soviet sphere. Economic decay combined with political and social stagnation to produce another wave of revolt. The year 1989 marked the beginning of an extraordinarily rapid and surprising series of events. Communist rule collapsed in Eastern Europe, and the Soviet Union itself disintegrated. The cold war no longer seemed to matter. What these changes meant for the future of democracy, and the political stability of a vast region stretching from the borders of China in the east to the borders of Poland in the west, remained an open question.

FOCUS QUESTIONS

- How was daily life transformed during this period?

- What spurred the social movements of the 1960s?

 • What caused the economic stagnation of the 1970s and 1980s?

- What caused the collapse of communism?

SOCIETY AND CLASS, 1945–1968

How was daily life transformed during this period?

The "boom" of the 1950s, made especially striking by contrast with the bleak years immediately after World War II, had profound and far-reaching effects on social life. To begin with, the population expanded, though unevenly. It shifted across the Continent. Both West Germany and France found it necessary to import workers in order to sustain their production booms. By the mid-1960s, there were 1.3 million foreign workers in West Germany and 1.8 million in France as wages rose and unemployment fell. Most came from the south, particularly from the agrarian areas of southern Italy, where unemployment remained high. Workers from former colonies emigrated to Britain, often to take low-paid, menial jobs and encounter pervasive discrimination at work and in the community. Migrations of this sort, in addition to the vast movement of political and ethnic refugees that occurred during and immediately after the war, contributed to the breakdown of national barriers that was accelerated by the creation of the Common Market.

Change also came in the workplace, eroding traditional social distinctions. Many commentators noted the striking growth in the number of middle-class, white-collar employees—the result, in part, of the dramatic bureaucratic expansion of the state. By 1964, the total number of men and women employed in government service in most European states exceeded 40 percent of the labor force, significantly higher than the number in the 1920s and 1930s. In business and industry, the number of "middle-management" employees grew as well. In industry, even within the factory work force, salaried employees—supervisors, inspectors, technicians, and drafters—multiplied. Industrial labor meant something far different from what it had in the nineteenth century. Skills were more specialized, based on technological expertise rather than custom and routine. More women entered the work force, meeting less resistance than they had in

> By 1964, the total number of men and women employed in government service in most European states exceeded 40 percent of the labor force, significantly higher than the number in the 1920s and 1930s.

the past, and their jobs were less starkly differentiated from men's.

Nineteenth-century society had been marked by clearly defined class cultures. The working class lived "a life apart," with easily identifiable patterns of consumption, dress, leisure, notions of respectability, gender relations, and so on (see Chapter 19). Economic changes after 1950 chipped away at those distinctive cultures. Trade unions remained powerful institutions, and Communist parties had powerful electoral clout. But new social movements also grew. Workers still identified themselves as such, but class had a less rigidly defined meaning.

The expansion of education helped shift social hierarchies. All Western nations passed laws providing for the extension of compulsory secondary education—up to the age of sixteen in France, West Germany, and Britain. New legislation combined with rising birthrates to boost school populations dramatically. Education did not automatically produce social mobility, but when combined with economic prosperity, new structures of labor, and the consumerist boom, it began to lay the foundation for what would be called "postindustrial" society.

How did patterns differ in the Eastern bloc? Soviet workers were not noted for their specialized skills—in fact, a major factor in the slowdown of the Soviet economy was its failure to innovate. Workers in the "workers' state" commonly enjoyed higher wages than people in middle-class positions (with the exception of managers), but they had far less status. Their relatively high wages owed little to trade unions, which had been weakened under Stalin; they were the product of persistent labor shortages and the accompanying fear of labor unrest. Educational reforms instituted by Nikita Khrushchev in 1958 encouraged bright children to pursue a course of study leading eventually to managerial positions. Soviet education also aimed to unify a nation that remained culturally heterogeneous. Turkish Muslims, for instance, constituted a sizable minority in the Soviet Union. Concern lest the pull of ethnic "nationality" tear at the none-too-solid fabric of the Soviet "union" increased the government's desire to impose one unifying culture by means of education, not always with success.

Morning Calisthenics at Russian Factory, 1961. The growing number of industrial workers and women in the workforce in the latter half of the twentieth century was reflected in this Soviet factory. The "worker state" still bestowed little status on its workers, however, a factor that contributed to the weakened Russian economy.

In Eastern Europe and the Soviet Union, consumption was organized differently. Governments rather than markets determined how consumer goods would be distributed. Economic policy channeled resources into heavy industry at the expense of consumer durables. This resulted in general scarcity, erratic shortages of even basic necessities, and often poor-quality goods. As one historian puts it, the failure of policies on consumption was "one of the major dead ends of communism," and it contributed to the downfall of Communist regimes.

MASS CONSUMPTION

Rising employment, higher earnings, and lower agricultural prices combined to give households and individuals more purchasing power. They had more to spend on newspapers, cigarettes, tickets to sporting events, movies, and health and hygiene (which registered the largest increase). Household appliances and cars were the most striking emblems of what was virtually a new world of everyday objects. In 1956, 8 percent of British households had refrigerators. By 1979 that figure had skyrocketed to 69 percent. In 1948, 5 million Western Europeans had cars; in 1965, 40 million. Cars captured imaginations throughout the world; in magazines, advertisements, and countless films, the car symbolized romance, movement, freedom, and vacation.

These changes marked a new culture of mass consumption. They were boosted by new industries devoted to marketing, advertising, and credit payment. They also entailed shifts in values. In the nineteenth century, a responsible middle-class family did not go into debt; discipline and thrift were hallmarks of "respectability." By the second half of the twentieth century, banks and retailers, in the name of mass consumption and economic growth, were persuading middle- and working-class people alike not to be ashamed of debt. Abundance, credit, consumer spending, and standards of living—all these terms became part of the vocabulary of everyday economic life.

MASS CULTURE

New patterns of consumption spurred wide-ranging changes in mass culture. The social transformations of the 1950s, which we have traced above, meant that families had both more spending money and more leisure time. The combination created a golden opportunity for the growing culture industry. The postwar desire to break with the past created further impetus for change. The result can fairly be called a cultural revolution: a transformation of culture, of its role in the lives of ordinary men and women, and of the power wielded by the media.

MUSIC AND YOUTH CULTURE

Much of the new "mass culture" of the 1960s depended on the spending habits and desires of the new generation. Young people had more distance from their parents and the work force and more time to be with each other. From the late 1950s on, music became *the* cultural expression of this new generation. The transistor radio came out at the time of the Berlin airlift; by the mid-1950s these portable radios began to sell in the United States and Europe. Radio sets gave birth to new radio programs and, later, to magazines reporting on popular singers and movie stars. All of these helped create new communities of interest. Social changes also affected the content of music: its themes and lyrics aimed to reach the young. Technological changes made records more than twice as long as the old 78s, and less expensive. The price of record players fell,

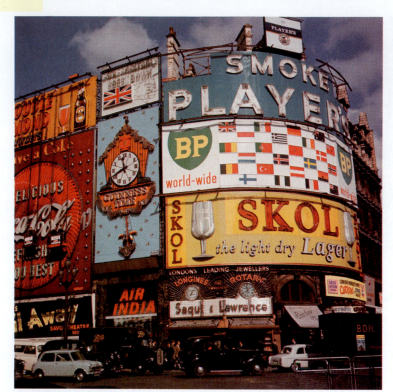

Piccadilly Square, London. In the 1960s and 1970s, a growing consumer culture encountered an influx of automobiles and the expansion of the marketing and advertising industries.

successful artists and bands, collectively referred to as the "British invasion." By the time of Woodstock (1969), rock became the sound of worldwide youth culture. It provided a bridge across the cold war divide: despite Eastern bloc limits on importing "capitalist" music, pirated songs circulated—sometimes on X-ray plates salvaged from hospitals. Recording studios latched on to the earning potential of the music, and became corporations as powerful as car manufacturers or steel companies.

ART AND PAINTING

Painting and art, too, were changed by the rise of mass and consumer culture. The art market boomed. The power of the dollar was one factor in the rise of New York as a center of modern art, one of the most striking developments of the period. Immigration was another: a slow stream of immigrants from Europe nourished "American" art as well as social and political thought (see Chapter 27) and New York proved hospitable to European artists. The creative work of the school of abstract expressionism sealed New York's postwar reputation. Abstract Expressionists emphasized the physical aspects of paint and the act of painting. Jackson Pollock is a good example. He poured and even threw paint on the canvas, creating powerful images of personal and physical expressiveness. His huge-scale canvases, which defied conventional artistic structures, gained immediate attention. Mark Rothko created a series of remote yet extraordinarily compelling abstractions with glowing or somber rectangles of color imposed on other rectangles, saying they represented "no associations, only sensation."

But abstract expressionism also produced its opposite, sometimes called pop art. Pop artists took their distance from the moody and elusive meditations of abstract expressionism. They refused to distinguish between "avant garde" and "popular" art, or between the "artistic" and the "commercial." They lavished attention on commonplace, instantly recognizable, often commercial images; they borrowed techniques from graphic design; they were interested in the immediacy of everyday art and ordinary people's visual experience. Jasper Johns's paintings of the American flag formed part of this trend. So did the work of Andy Warhol and Roy Lichtenstein, who took objects such as soup cans and images of comic-strip heroes as their subjects. Treating popular culture with this tongue-in-

multiplying the number of potential buyers. Combined, these developments changed how music was produced, distributed, and consumed. It was no longer confined to the concert hall or café but instead reverberated through people's homes or cars and teenagers' rooms—providing a soundtrack for everyday life.

Postwar youth culture owed much to the hybrid musical style known as rock and roll. During the 1930s and 1940s, the synthesis of music produced by whites and African Americans in the American South found its way into northern cities. After World War II, black rhythm and blues musicians and white Southern "rockabilly" performers found much wider audiences through the use of new technology—electric guitars, better equipment for studio recording, and wide-band radio stations in large cities. The blend of styles and sounds and the cultural daring of white teenagers who listened to what recording studios at the time called "race music" came together to create rock and roll. The music was exciting, sometimes aggressive, and full of energy—all qualities that galvanized young listeners.

In Europe, rock and roll found its way into working-class neighborhoods, particularly in Britain and Ireland. There, local youths took American sounds, echoed the inflections of poverty and defiance, and added touches of music-hall showmanship to produce

Abstract Expressionism. *Sea Change,* by Jackson Pollock (1912–1956). Pollock, one of the new American "moderns," improvised with new techniques to express gesture, movement, and feeling.

cheek seriousness became one of the central themes of 1960s art.

FILM

Mass culture made its most powerful impact in the visual world, especially through film. Film flourished after World War II, developing along several different lines. The Italian neorealists of the late 1940s and 1950s set out to capture authenticity, or "life as it was lived," by which they usually meant working-class existence. They dealt with the same themes that marked the literature of the period: loneliness, war, and corruption. They shot on location, using natural light and little-known actors, deliberately steering away from the artifice and high production values they associated with the tainted cinema of fascist and wartime Europe. Federico Fellini's break-out film *La Dolce Vita* (1959) (starring Marcello Mastroianni) took Italian film to screens throughout Europe and the United States, and it established Fellini's signature surrealist and carnivalesque style, developed in 8½ (1963).

The French directors of the "new wave" continued to develop this unsentimental, naturalistic, and enigmatic social vision. New wave directors worked closely with each other, casting each other (and their wives and lovers) in their films, encouraged improvisation, and experimented with disjointed narrative. François Truffaut's (1932–1984) *400 Blows* (1959) and *The Wild Child* (1969) and Jean-Luc Godard's (1930–) *Breathless* (1959) and *Contempt* (1963, with Brigitte Bardot) are leading examples. The new wave raised the status of the director, insisting that the film's camera work and vision (rather than the writing) constituted the real art—part, again, of the new value accorded to the visual. Yet France made other contributions to international film by sponsoring the Cannes Film Festival.

HOLLYWOOD AND THE AMERICANIZATION OF CULTURE

The American film industry, however, had considerable advantages, and the devastating aftereffects of World War II in Europe allowed Hollywood to consolidate its earlier gains (see Chapter 25). The United States' huge domestic market gave Hollywood its biggest advantage. In 1946 an estimated 100 million Americans went to the movies every week. By the 1950s Hollywood was making five hundred films a year and counted for between 40 and 75 percent of films shown in Europe. The same period brought important innovations in filmmaking: the conversion to color and new optical formats, including widescreen. As far as their themes were concerned, some American directors moved in the same direction as the European neorealists. As one critic put it, they tried to "base fictional pictures on fact and, more importantly, to shoot them not in painted studio sets but in actual places."

> Mass culture made its most powerful impact in the visual world, especially through film.

Hollywood's expanding influence was but one instance of the "Americanization" of Western culture. Europeans had worried about United States as a model since at least the 1920s; the U.S. seemed to be the center for the "production and organization of mass civilization." American films in the 1950s multiplied these worries. So did television, which by 1965 had found its way into 62 million homes in the United States, 13 million in Britain, 10 million in West Germany, and 5 million each in France and Italy and had an even more important impact on everyday life and sociability. The issues were not simply cultural; they included the power of American corporations, American business techniques, aggressive marketing, and American domination of global trade networks. Many concerns were raised, and sometimes they contradicted each other. Some observers believed that the United States and its cultural exports were materialistic, conformist, and complacent. Others considered "Americans" to be rebellious, lonely, and sexually unhappy. *Rebel without a Cause* (1955), for instance, with James Dean as an alienated teenager in a dysfunctional family and its scenes of knife fights and car races provoked cries of outrage from German critics who deplored the permissiveness of American parents and expressed shock that middle-class children behaved like "hoodlums."

James Dean in *Rebel Without a Cause.* While some argued that American movies exported notions of juvenile delinquency, films from the 1950s and 1960s did contribute to the romanticization of automobiles, sexuality, and youthful rebellion.

Is it helpful, though, to speak of the "Americanization" of culture? To begin with, the term refers to many different processes. United States industrialists openly sought greater economic influence and economic integration: opening markets to American goods, industry to American production techniques, and so on. The United States government also aimed to export American political values, above all anticommunism, via organizations such as Radio Free Europe. Yet the farthest-reaching American influences were conveyed, unintentionally, by music and film. These images could not be completely controlled, and they had no single effect. Movies about young Americans might represent the romance of American power; they might represent a rebellion against that power. Second, American goods were put to different use in local cultures. Third, journalists, critics, and ordinary men and women tended to use "American" as an all-purpose label for various "modern" or "mass culture" developments that were more properly global, such as inexpensive electronics from Asia. As one historian puts it, "America" was less of a reality than an idea—and a contradictory one at that.

GENDER ROLES AND SEXUAL REVOLUTION

What some called the "sexual revolution" of the 1960s had several aspects. The first was less censorship, which we have already seen in film, and fewer taboos regarding discussion of sexuality in public. In the United States, the notorious "Kinsey reports" on male and female sexuality (in 1948 and 1953 respectively) made morality and sexual behavior front-page news. Alfred Kinsey was a zoologist turned social scientist, and the way in which he applied science and statistics to sex attracted considerable attention. An enthusiastic journalist in Europe reported that the massive numbers Kinsey compiled would, finally, reveal the "truth of sex." The truth, though, was elusive for moral codes and private behaviors did not line up neatly. For instance, 80 to 90 percent of the women Kinsey interviewed disapproved of premarital sex, but 50 percent of the women he interviewed had had it.

A second aspect of the "revolution" was the centrality of sex and eroticism to mass consumer culture. Magazines, which flourished in this period, offered advice on how to succeed in love and be attractive. Advertising, advice columns, TV, and film blurred boundaries between buying consumer goods, seeking personal fulfillment, and sexual desire. There was nothing new about

THE "WOMAN QUESTION" ON BOTH SIDES OF THE ATLANTIC

How did Western culture define "femininity" and did women internalize those definitions? These questions were central to postwar feminist thought, and they were sharply posed in two classic texts: Simone de Beauvoir's The Second Sex *(1949) and Betty Friedan's* The Feminine Mystique *(1963). Beauvoir (1908–1986) started from the existentialist premise that humans were "condemned to be free" and to give their own lives meaning. Why, then, did women accept the limitations imposed on them and, in Beauvoir's words, "dream the dreams of men?" Although dense and philosophical,* The Second Sex *sent shock waves through Catholic France and was published throughout the world. Betty Friedan's equally influential bestseller took up much the same issue, trying to find the origins of the "feminine mystique," Friedan's term for the model of femininity promoted by experts, advertised in women's magazines, and seemingly accepted by middle-class housewives in the postwar United States. As Friedan points out in the excerpt below, the new postwar "mystique" was in many ways more conservative than prewar ideals had been, despite continuing social change, a greater range of careers opening up to women, the expansion of women's education, and so on. Friedan (1921–) co-founded the National Organization for Women in 1966 and served as its president until 1970.*

SIMONE DE BEAUVOIR, *THE SECOND SEX*

But first we must ask: what is a woman? . . .

All agree in recognizing the fact that females exist in the human species; today as always they make up about one half of humanity. And yet we are told that femininity is in danger; we are exhorted to be women, remain women, become women. . . . Although some women try zealously to incarnate this essence, it is hardly penetrable. It is frequently described in vague and dazzling terms that seem to have been borrowed from the vocabulary of the seers. . . .

If her functioning as a female is not enough to define woman, if we decline also to explain her through "the eternal feminine," and if nevertheless we admit, provisionally, that women do exist, then we must face the question: what is a woman?

To state the question is, to me, to suggest, at once, a preliminary answer. The fact that I ask it is in itself significant. A man would never get the notion of writing a book on the peculiar situation of the human male. But if I wish to define myself, I must first of all say: "I am a woman"; on this truth must be based all further discus-sion. A man never begins by presenting himself as an individual of a certain sex; it goes without saying that he is a man. The terms *masculine* and *feminine* are used symmetrically only as a matter of form, as on legal papers. In actuality the relation of the two sexes is not quite like that of two electrical poles, for man represents both the positive and the neutral . . . whereas woman represents only the negative, defined by limiting criteria, without reciprocity. . . .

A man is in the right in being a man; it is the woman who is in the wrong. Woman has ovaries, a uterus; these peculiarities imprison her in her subjectivity, circumscribe her within the limits of her own nature. . . .

For him she is sex—absolute sex, no less. She is defined and differentiated with reference to man and not he with reference to her; she is the incidental, the inessential as opposed to the essential. He is the subject, he is the Absolute—she is the Other.

Simone de Beauvoir, *The Second Sex*, translated and edited by H. M. Parshley (New York: Random House, 1974), p. xix.

BETTY FRIEDAN, *THE FEMININE MYSTIQUE*

In 1939, the heroines of women's magazine stories were not always young, but in a certain sense they were younger than their fictional counterparts today. They were young in the same way that the American hero has always been young: they were New Women, creating with a gay determined spirit a new identity for women—a life of their own. There was an aura about them of becoming, of moving into a future that was going to be different from the past. . . .

These stories may not have been great literature. But the identity of their heroines seemed to say something about the housewives who, then as now, read the women's magazines. These magazines were not written for career women. The New Woman heroines were the ideal of yesterday's housewives; they reflected the dreams, mirrored the yearning for identity and the sense of possibility that existed for women then. . . .

In 1949 . . . the feminine mystique began to spread through the land. . . .

The feminine mystique says that the highest value and the only commitment for women is the fulfillment of their own femininity. It says that the great mistake of Western culture, through most of its history, has been the undervaluation of this femininity. . . . The mistake, says the mystique, the root of women's troubles in the past, is that women envied men, women

tried to be like men, instead of accepting their own nature, which can find fulfillment only in sexual passivity, male domination, and nurturing maternal love.

But the new image this mystique gives to American women is the old image: "Occupation: housewife." The new mystique makes the housewife-mothers, who never had a chance to be anything else, the model for all women; it presupposes that history has reached a final and glorious end in the here and now, as far as women are concerned. . . .

It is more than a strange paradox that as all professions are finally open to women in America, "career woman" has become a dirty word; that as higher education becomes available to any woman with the capacity for it, education for women has become so suspect that more and more drop out of high school and college to marry and have babies; that as so many roles in modern society become theirs for the taking, women so insistently confine themselves to one role. Why . . . should she accept this new image which insists she is not a person but a "woman," by definition barred from the freedom of human existence and a voice in human destiny?

Betty Friedan, *The Feminine Mystique* (New York: W. W. Norton & Company, Inc., 2001), pp. 38, 40, 42–43, 67–68.

appeals to eroticism. But the fact that sexuality was now widely considered a form of self-expression—perhaps even the core of oneself —was new to the twentieth century. These developments helped to propel change, and they also made the "sexual revolution" prominent in the politics of the time.

The third aspect of the "revolution" came with legal and medical or scientific changes in contraception. Oral contraceptives, first approved for development in 1959, became mainstream in the next decade. By 1975, two thirds of British women between fifteen and forty-four said they were taking the pill. By and large, Western countries legalized contraception in the 1960s and abortion in the 1970s. In 1965, for instance, the U.S. Supreme Court struck down laws banning the use of contraception, though selling contraceptives remained illegal in Massachusetts until 1972. The Soviet Union legalized abortion in 1950, after banning it during Stalin's regime.

Since World War II the assumption that middle-class women belonged in the home had been challenged by the steadily rising demand for workers, especially in education and the service sector. Thus many more married women and many more mothers were part of the labor force. Moreover, across the West young middle-class women, like men, were part of the rising number of university students. But in the United States, to take just one example, only 37 percent of women who enrolled in college in the 1950s finished their degrees, believing they should marry instead. Women found it difficult to get nonsecretarial jobs, received less pay for the same work, and, even when employed, had to rely on their husbands to establish credit.

The tension between rising expectations that stemmed from abundance, growth, and the emphasis on self-expression on the one hand and the reality of narrow horizons on the other created quiet waves of discontent.

Betty Friedan's *Feminine Mystique* (1963) brought much of this discontent into the open, contrasting the cultural myths of the fulfilled and happy housewife with the realities of economic inequality, hard work, and unequal opportunity. In 1949, Simone de Beauvoir had asked how Western culture (myth, literature, and psychology) had created an image of woman as the second, and lesser sex; Friedan, using a more journalistic style and writing at a time when social change had made readers more receptive to her ideas, showed how the media, the social sciences, and advertising at once exalted femininity and lowered women's expectations and possibilities. For this generation of feminists, reproductive freedom was both a private matter and a basic right—a key to women's control over their lives. Outlawing contraception and abortion made women alone bear responsibility for the consequences of sweeping changes in Western sexual life.

In sum, the legal changes followed from political demands, and those in turn reflected a quiet or subterranean rebellion of many women (and men)—one with longer-term causes. Mass consumption, mass culture, and startlingly rapid transformations in public and private life were all intimately related.

Martin Luther King, Jr., 1964. The African American civil rights leader is welcomed in Oslo, Norway, on a trip to accept the Nobel Peace Prize. He would be assassinated four years later.

and America. Black and Asian immigration into those nations produced tension and frequent violence. In the West, particularly in the United States, people of color identified with these social and economic grievances.

SOCIAL MOVEMENTS DURING THE 1960S

What spurred the social movements of the 1960s?

The social unrest of the sixties was international. Its roots lay in the political struggles and social transformations of the postwar period. Of these, the most important were anticolonial and civil rights movements. The successful anticolonial movements (see Chapter 27) reflected a growing racial consciousness and also helped to encourage that consciousness. Newly independent African and Caribbean nations remained wary about revivals of colonialism and the continuing economic hegemony of Western Europe

THE CIVIL RIGHTS MOVEMENT

The emergence of new black nations in Africa and the Caribbean was paralleled by growing African American insurgency. World War II increased African American migration from the American South to northern cities, intensifying a drive for rights, dignity, and independence began in the prewar era. The preeminent figure in the civil rights movement in the United States during the 1960s was Martin Luther King, Jr. (1929–1968). A Baptist minister, King embraced the philosophy of nonviolence promoted by the Indian social and political activist Mohandas K. Gandhi. King's personal participation in countless demonstrations, his willingness to go to jail for a cause that he believed to be just, and his ability as an orator to arouse both blacks and whites with his message led to his position as the most highly regarded—and most widely feared—defender of black rights. His inspiring career was tragically ended by assassination in 1968.

Other charismatic and important black leaders believed that integration would leave African Americans without the spiritual or material resources necessary for a community's pride, dignity, and autonomy. The most influential of the black nationalists was Malcolm X (1925–1965), he was also assassinated, in 1965 while addressing a rally in Harlem.

These problems were not confined to the United States. West Indian, Indian, and Pakistani immigrants in Britain met with discrimination in jobs, housing, and everyday interaction with the authorities—producing frequent racial disturbances in major British cities. France witnessed hostility toward Algerian immigration, Germany toward the importation of Turkish labor. In Western Europe, as in the United States, struggles for racial and ethnic integration became central to the postcolonial world.

THE ANTIWAR MOVEMENT

The United States' escalating war in Vietnam became a lightning rod for discontent. In 1961, President John F. Kennedy (1917–1963) promised to "bear any burden" necessary to fight communism and to ensure the victory of American models of representative government and free-market economics in the developing nations. Kennnedy's plan provided the impetus for humanitarian institutions such as the Peace Corps, intended to improve local conditions. Bearing burdens, however, also meant fighting guerrillas who turned to the Soviets for aid. This involved covert interventions in Latin America, the Congo, and, most important, Vietnam.

By the time of Kennedy's death in 1963, nearly fifteen thousand American "advisors" were on the ground alongside South Vietnamese troops. Kennedy's successor, Lyndon B. Johnson, began the strategic bombing of North Vietnam and rapidly drew hundreds of thousands of American troops into combat in South Vietnam. The rebels in the South, known as the Viet Cong, were solidly entrenched, highly experienced guerrilla fighters, and were backed by the professional, well-equipped North Vietnamese army under Ho Chi Minh. The South Vietnamese government resisted efforts at reform, losing popular support. Massive efforts by the United States produced only stalemate, mounting American casualties, and rising discontent.

Vietnam did much to cause the political turmoil of the 1960s in the United States. As Martin Luther King, Jr., pointed out, the war—which relied on disproportionate number of black soldiers to conduct a war against a small nation of color—echoed and magnified racial inequality at home. Exasperated by troubles in the field, American planners continued to escalate military comittments, with no effect. Peace talks in Paris stalled while the death toll on all sides increased. The involuntary draft of young American men expanded and polarized the public. In 1968 criticism forced President Johnson to abandon his plans to run for a second term. Johnson's successor, Richard M. Nixon, who won a narrow victory on the basis of promises to end the war, expanded it instead. Student protests against the war frequently ended in violence. From other countries' points of view, the Vietnam War became a spectacle: one in which the most powerful, wealthiest nation of the world seemed intent on destroying a land of poor peasants in the name of anticommunism, democracy, and freedom. The tarnished image of Western values stood at the center of 1960s protest movements in the United States and Western Europe.

THE STUDENT MOVEMENT

The student movement itself can be seen as a consequence of postwar developments: a growing cohort of young people with more time and wealth than in the past, generational consciousness heightened, in part, by the marketing of mass youth culture, and educational institutions unable to deal with rising numbers or expectations. Universities, which had been created to educate a small elite, found both their teaching staffs and their facilities overwhelmed: lecture halls were packed, university bureaucracies did not respond to requests, and thousands of students took exams at the same time. More philosophically, students raised questions about the role and meaning of elite education in a democratic society, and about the relationships between the university as a "knowledge factory," consumer culture, and neocolonial ventures such as the Vietnam War and, for the French, the Algerian wars. In addition, student demands for fewer restrictions on personal life—for instance, permission to have a member of the opposite sex in a dormitory room—provoked au-

> The student movement itself can be seen as a consequence of postwar developments: a growing cohort of young people with more time and wealth than in the past, generational consciousness heightened, in part, by the marketing of mass youth culture, and educational institutions unable to deal with rising numbers or expectations.

thoritarian reactions from university representatives. Waves of student protest were not confined to the United States and Western Europe. They swept across Poland and Czechoslovakia where students protested one-party bureaucratic rule, stifling intellectual life, and authoritarianism. By the mid 1960s, simmering anger in Eastern Europe had once again reached a dangerous point.

1968

Nineteen sixty-eight was an extraordinary year, quite similar to 1848 with its wave of revolution (see Chapter 20). It was even more intensely international, a reflection of tightening global ties. The wave of unrest shook both the Eastern and Western blocs. Protest movements assailed bureaucracy and the human costs of the cold war: on the Soviet side, bureaucracy, authoritarianism, and indifference to civilians; on the Western side, bias and monopolies in the news media, the "military-industrial complex," and American imperialism. The Soviet regime, as we have seen, responded with repression. In the United States and Western Europe, traditional political parties had little idea what to make of these new movements and those who participated in them. In both cases, events rapidly overwhelmed political systems.

PARIS

The most serious outbreak of student unrest in Europe came in Paris in the spring of 1968. The French Republic had been shaken by conflicts over the Algerian war in the early 1960s. Even more important, the economic boom had undermined the foundations of the regime and de Gaulle's traditional style of rule. French students at the University of Paris demanded reforms that would modernize their university. In the face of growing disorder, the University of Paris shut down—sending students into the streets. The police reacted with repression and violence, which startled onlookers and television audiences and backfired on the regime. Sympathy with the students' cause expanded rapidly, bringing in other opponents of President de Gaulle's regime. Workers in the automobile industry, technical workers, and public-sector employees—from gas and electricity utilities, the mail system, to radio and television—went on strike. By mid-May, an astonishing 10 million French workers had walked off their jobs. At one point, it looked as if the government would fall. The regime, however, was able to satisfy the strikers with wage increases and to appeal to public demand for order. The student movements, isolated, gradually petered out and agreed to resume university life. The regime did recover, but the events of 1968 helped weaken de Gaulle's position as president and contributed to his retirement from office the following year.

There had been protest and rebelliousness in the 1950s, but the scale of events in 1968 was astonishing. Paris was not the only city to explode in 1968. Student protest broke out in West Berlin, targeting the government's close ties to the autocratic shah of Iran and the power of media corporations. Clashes with the police turned violent. The London School of Economics was nearly shut down by protest. In Vietnam, the Viet Cong defied American claims to have turned the tide by launching a new offensive. The Tet offensive, named for the Vietnamese new year, brought the highest casualty rates to date in the Vietnam War and an explosion of protest: intense antiwar demonstrations and student rebellions across the country. 1968 also saw damage and trauma for the country's political future, because of the assassinations of Martin Luther King, Jr. (April 4, 1968) and presidential candidate Robert F. Kennedy (June 5, 1968). King's assassination was followed by a wave of rioting in more than fifty cities across the United States, followed in late summer by street battles between police and student protesters at the Democratic National Convention in Chicago. Some saw the flowering of protest as another "springtime of peoples." Others saw it as a long nightmare.

PRAGUE

The student movement in the United States and Western Europe also took inspiration from one of the most significant challenges to Soviet authority since the Hungarian revolt of 1956 (see Chapter 27): the "Prague spring" of 1968. The events began with the emergence of a liberal communist government in Czechoslovakia, led by the Slovak Alexander Dubček. Dubček had outmaneuvered the more traditional, authoritarian party leaders. He advocated "socialism with a human face"; he encouraged debate within the party, academic and artistic freedom, and less censorship. The reformers also gained support from outside the party, from student organizations, the press, and networks of dissidents. As in Western Europe and the United States, the protest movement overflowed traditional party politics.

> The most serious outbreak of student unrest in Europe came in Paris in the spring of 1968.

LUDVÍK VACULÍK,
"TWO THOUSAND WORDS"

During the Prague spring of 1968, a group of Czech intellectuals published a document titled "Two Thousand Words that Belong to Workers, Farmers, Officials, Scientists, Artists, and Everybody" that has become known simply as the "Two Thousand Words." This manifesto called for further reform, including increased freedom of the press. Seen as a direct affront by Moscow, the manifesto heightened Soviet-Czech tensions. In August 1968, Warsaw Pact tanks rolled into Prague, overthrowing the reformist government of Alexander Dubček.

Most of the nation welcomed the socialist program with high hopes. But it fell into the hands of the wrong people. It would not have mattered so much that they lacked adequate experience in affairs of state, factual knowledge, or philosophical education, if only they had enough common prudence and decency to listen to the opinion of others and agree to being gradually replaced by more able people. . . .

The chief sin and deception of these rulers was to have explained their own whims as the "will of the workers." Were we to accept this pretense, we would have to blame the workers today for the decline of our economy, for crimes committed against the innocent, and for the introduction of censorship to prevent anyone writing about these things. The workers would be to blame for misconceived investments, for losses suffered in foreign trade, and for the housing shortage. Obviously no sensible person will hold the working class responsible for such things. We all know, and every worker knows especially, that they had virtually no say in deciding anything. . . .

Since the beginning of this year we have been experiencing a regenerative process of democratization. . . .

Let us demand the departure of people who abused their power, damaged public property, and acted dishonorably or brutally. Ways must be found to compel them to resign. To mention a few: public criticism, resolutions, demonstrations, demonstrative work brigades, collections to buy presents for them on their retirement, strikes, and picketing at their front doors. But we should reject any illegal, indecent, or boorish methods. . . .

Let us convert the district and local newspapers, which have mostly degenerated to the level of official mouthpieces, into a platform for all the forward-looking elements in politics; let us demand that editorial boards be formed of National Front representatives, or else let us start new papers. Let us form committees for the defense of free speech. . . .

There has been great alarm recently over the possibility that foreign forces will intervene in our development. Whatever superior forces may face us, all we can do is stick to our own positions, behave decently, and initiate nothing ourselves. We can show our government that we will stand by it, with weapons if need be, if it will do what we give it a mandate to do. . . .

The spring is over and will never return. By winter we will know all.

Originally published as "Dva Tisice Slov," *Literarny Listy* (Prague) June 27, 1968. Translated by Mark Kramer, Joy Moss, and Ruth Tosek. From Jaromir Navratil, *The Prague Spring 1968* (Budapest: Central European Press, 1998), pp. 177–181.

In the Soviet Union, Khrushchev had fallen in 1964, and the reins of Soviet power passed to Leonid Brezhnev as secretary of the Communist party. Brezhnev was more conservative than Khrushchev, less inclined to bargain with the West, and prone to defensive actions to safeguard the Soviet sphere of influence. Initially, the Soviets tolerated Dubček as a political eccentric. The events of 1968 raised their fears. When Dubček attempted to democratize the Communist party and did not attend a meeting of members of the Warsaw Pact, the Soviets sent tanks and troops into Prague in August of 1968. Again the world watched as streams of Czech refugees left the country and a repressive government, picked by Soviet security forces, took charge. Dubček and his allies were subjected to imprisonment or "internal exile." After the destruction of the "Prague spring," Soviet diplomats consolidated their position according to the new "Brezhnev doctrine." The doctrine stated that no socialist state could adopt policies endangering the interests of international socialism, and that the Soviet Union could intervene in the domestic affairs of any Soviet-bloc nation if communist rule was threatened.

When Dubček attempted to democratize the Communist party and did not attend a meeting of members of the Warsaw Pact, the Soviets sent tanks and troops into Prague in August of 1968.

What were the effects of 1968? De Gaulle's government recovered. The Republican Richard M. Nixon won the U.S. election of 1968. From 1972 to 1975 the United States withdrew from Vietnam; in the wake of that war came a refugee crisis and a new series of horrific regional conflicts. In Prague, Warsaw Pact tanks put down the uprising, and in the Brezhnev Doctrine the Soviet regime reasserted its right to control its satellites. Over the long term, however, the protesters' and dissidents' demands proved more difficult to contain. In Eastern Europe and the Soviet Union, dissent was defeated but not eliminated. In Czechoslovakia the events of 1968 prefigured the collapse of Soviet control in 1989. In Western Europe and the United States, the student movement subsided but its issues and the kinds of politics that it pioneered proved more enduring. Feminism (or, more accurately, second-wave feminism) really came into its own after 1968, its numbers expanded by women a generation younger than Simone de Beauvoir and Betty Friedan. The antiwar movement took up the issue of nuclear weapons—a particularly volatile issue in Europe. Finally, the environmental movement took hold—concerned not only with pollution and the world's dwindling resources, but also a protest against mushrooming urbanization and the kind of unrestrained economic growth that had given rise to the 1960s.

ECONOMIC STAGNATION: THE PRICE OF SUCCESS

What caused the economic stagnation of the 1970s and 1980s?

Economic as well as social problems plagued Europe during the 1970s and 1980s, but these problems had begun earlier. By the middle of the 1960s, for example, the West German growth rate had slowed. Demand for manufactured goods fell, and in 1966 the country suffered its first postwar recession. Though new industries continued to prosper, the basic industries—coal, steel, and railways—began to run up deficits. Unemployment was rising in tandem with prices.

Oil prices spiked for the first time in the early 1970s, compounding these difficulties. In 1973, the Arab-dominated Organization of Petroleum Exporting Countries (OPEC) instituted an oil embargo against the Western powers. In 1973, a barrel of oil cost $1.73; by the early 1980s, the price had risen to over $30. This increase produced an inflationary spiral. Interest rates rose and with them the price of almost everything else Western consumers were used to buying. European manufacturers encountered serious competition from the increasingly active economies of Asia and Africa.

Western governments struggled for effective reactions to the abrupt change in their economic circumstances. The new, radically conservative leader of the British Conservative party, Margaret Thatcher, was elected prime minister in 1979 on a program of curbing trade-union power, cutting taxes to stimulate the economy, and privatizing publicly owned enterprises. The economy remained weak, with close to 15 percent of the work force unemployed by 1986. In West Germany, a series of Social Democratic governments attempted to combat economic recession with job-training programs and tax incentives, both financed by higher taxes. These programs did little to assist economic recovery, and the country shifted to the right.

Unemployment Demonstration, 1974. A crowd of workers in Rome, Italy, gathered to protest inflation and unemployment, in a strike that lasted 24 hours.

The fact that governments of right and left were unable to recreate Europe's unprecedented postwar prosperity suggests the degree to which economic forces remain outside the control of individual states. The continuing economic malaise renewed efforts to "Europeanize" common problems. By the end of the 1980s, the EEC embarked on an ambitious program of integration. Long-term goals, agreed on when the EU (European Union) was formed in 1991, included a monetary union, with a central European bank and a single currency, and unified social policies to reduce poverty and unemployment. As the twenty-first century opened, the European member states had begun to institute several of these steps. It remained unclear whether that new European "federal" state would overcome its members' claims of national sovereignty or whether it would develop the economic and political strength to counter the global domination of the United States.

SOLIDARITY IN POLAND

The economies in the Soviet bloc also stalled. The expansion of heavy industry had helped recovery in the postwar period, but by the 1970s, those sectors no longer provided growth or innovation. The Soviet Communist party proclaimed in 1961 that by 1970 the USSR would exceed the United States in per capita production. By the

end of the 1970s, however, Soviet per capita production was not much higher than in the less industrialized countries of southern Europe. The Soviets were also overcommitted to military defense industries that had become inefficient, though lucrative for the party members who ran them. Although there was virtually no unemployment in Eastern Europe, men and women were by no means happy with their economic situation. Working hours were longer than in Western Europe, and goods and services, even in prosperous times, were scarce.

In 1980, unrest again peaked in the Eastern Europe, this time with the Polish labor movement Solidarity. Polish workers organized strikes that brought the government of the country to a standstill. The workers formulated several key demands. First, they objected to working conditions imposed by the government to combat a severe economic crisis. Second, they protested high prices and, especially shortages, both of which had roots in government policy and priorities. Above all, though, the Polish workers in Solidarity demanded truly independent labor unions instead of labor organizations sponsored by the government. Their belief that society had the right to organize itself and, by implication, create its own government, stood at the core of the movement. Again, however, the Soviets assisted a military regime in reimposing authoritarian rule. The Polish president, General Wojciech Jaruzel-

CHRONOLOGY

DEVELOPMENT OF THE EUROPEAN ECONOMIC COMMUNITY

European coal and steel community founded	1951
Rome treaty forms EEC	1957
European community expanded	1985
Treaty of Maastricht creates European union	1991

ski, had learned from Hungary and Czechoslovakia and played a delicate game of diplomacy to maintain the Polish government's freedom of action while repressing Solidarity itself. But the implied Soviet threat remained.

EUROPE RECAST: THE COLLAPSE OF COMMUNISM AND THE END OF THE SOVIET UNION

What caused the collapse of communism?

One of history's fascinations is its unpredictability. There has been no more telling example of this in recent times than the sudden collapse of the Eastern European communist regimes in 1989, the dramatic end to the cold war, and the subsequent disintegration of the once-powerful Soviet Union.

GORBACHEV AND SOVIET REFORM

This sudden collapse flowed, unintended, from a new wave of reform begun in the mid-1980s. In 1985 a new generation of officials began taking charge of the Soviet Communist party, a change heralded by Mikhail Gorbachev's appointment to the party leadership. Gorbachev was frankly critical of the repressive aspects of communist society as well as its sluggish economy, and he did not hesitate to voice those criticisms openly. His twin policies of *glasnost* (intellectual openness) and *perestroika* (economic restructuring) held out hope for a freer, more prosperous Soviet Union.

The policies of perestroika took aim at the privileges of the political elite and the immobility of the state bureaucracy by instituting competitive elections to official positions and limiting terms of office. Gorbachev's program of perestroika called for a shift from the centrally planned economy instituted by Stalin to a mixed economy combining planning with the operation of market forces. Even these dramatic reforms, however, were too little too late. Ethnic unrest, a legacy of Russia's nineteenth-century imperialism, threatened to split the Soviet Union apart, while secession movements gathered steam in the Baltic republics and elsewhere.

Gorbachev encouraged open discussion—glasnost—not only in his own country but also in the satellite nations. He revoked the Brezhnev Doctrine's insistence on single-party socialist governments and made frequent and inspiring trips to the capitals of neighboring satellites.

Glasnost rekindled the flame of opposition in Poland, where Solidarity had been defeated but not destroyed. In 1988 the union launched a new series of strikes. These disturbances culminated in an agreement between the government and Solidarity that legalized the union and promised open elections. The results, in June 1989, astonished the world: virtually all of the government's candidates lost; the Citizen's Committee, affiliated with Solidarity, won a sizable majority in the Polish parliament.

In Hungary and Czechoslovakia, events followed a similar course. Janos Kadar, the Hungarian leader since

Gorbachev and the Old Guard. Gorbachev is pictured here at the height of his power in 1986, with KGB chief Victor Chebrikov, President Andrei Gromyko, and Premier Nikolai Rzyhkov. Perestroika aimed at the privileges of the political elite and would eventually lead to the fall from power of all these men.

the Soviet crackdown of 1956, resigned in the face of continuing demonstrations in May 1988 and was replaced by the reformist government of the Hungarian Socialist Workers' party. By the spring of 1989 the Hungarian regime had been purged of Communist party supporters. The government also began to dismantle its security fences along the Austrian border.

The Czechs, too, staged demonstrations against Soviet domination in late 1988. Brutal beatings of student demonstrators by the police in 1989 radicalized the nations' workers and provoked mass demonstrations. Civic Forum, an opposition coalition, called for the installation of a coalition government to include non-communists, for free elections, and for the resignation of the country's communist leadership. It reinforced its demands with continuing mass demonstrations and threats of a general strike that resulted in the toppling of the old regime and the election of the playwright and Civic Forum leader Václav Havel as president.

FALL OF THE BERLIN WALL

The most significant political change in Eastern Europe during the late 1980s was the collapse of communism in East Germany and the unification of East and West Germany. Although long considered the most prosperous of the Soviet satellite countries, East Germany suffered from severe economic stagnation and environmental degradation. Waves of East Germans registered their discontent with worsening conditions by massive illegal emigration to the West. This exodus combined with evidence of widespread official corruption to force the resignation of East Germany's long-time, hard-line premier, Erich Honecker. On November 4, 1989, the government, in a move that acknowledged its powerlessness to hold its citizens captive, opened its border with Czechoslovakia. This move effectively freed East Germans to travel to the West. In a matter of days, the Berlin wall—the embodiment of the cold war, the Iron Curtain, and the division of East from West—was demolished by groups of ordinary citizens. Jubilant throngs from both sides walked through the gaping holes that now permitted men, women, and children to take the few steps that symbolized the return to freedom and a chance for national unity. With heavy emigration continuing, reunification talks with West Germany quickly culminated in the formal proclamation of a united Germany on October 3, 1990.

The public mood, in Eastern Europe and perhaps worldwide, was swept up with the jubilation of these

The Fall of the Berlin Wall, 1989. When East German officials announced that citizens could leave the country through any border crossing, rendering the Berlin Wall obsolete, people gathered at the wall to celebrate and to tear it down with picks, axes, and small hammers.

peaceful "velvet revolutions" during the autumn of 1989. Yet the end of one-party rule in Eastern Europe was not accomplished without violence. The single most repressive government in the old Eastern bloc, Nicolae Ceaucescu's outright dictatorship in Romania, came apart with much more bloodshed. By December, faced with the wave of popular revolts in surrounding countries and riots by the ethnic Hungarian minority in Transylvania, a number of party officials and army officers in Romania tried to hold on to their own positions by deposing Ceaucescu. His extensive secret police, however, organized resistance to the coup; the result was nearly two weeks of bloody street fighting in the capital Bucharest. Ceaucescu himself and his wife were seized by populist army units and executed; images of their bloodstained bodies flashed worldwide by satellite television.

Meanwhile, in the Soviet Union itself, inspired by events in Eastern Europe, the Balkan republics of Lithuania and Latvia strained to free themselves from Soviet rule. In 1990 they unilaterally proclaimed their independence from the Soviet Union, throwing into sharp relief the tension between "union" and "republics." Gorbachev reacted with an uncertain mixture of armed intervention and promises of greater local autonomy. In the fall of 1991 Lithuania and Latvia, along with the third Baltic state of Estonia, won international recognition as independent republics.

THE COLLAPSE OF THE SOVIET UNION

While Soviet influence eroded in Eastern Europe, at home the unproductive Soviet economy continued to fuel widespread ire. With the failure of perestroika—largely the result of a lack of resources and an inability to increase production—came the rise of a powerful political rival to Gorbachev, his erstwhile ally Boris Yeltsin. The reforming mayor of Moscow, Yeltsin was elected president of the Russian Federation—the largest Soviet republic—on an anti-Gorbachev platform in 1990. Pressure from the Yeltsin camp weakened Gorbachev's ability to maneuver independent of reactionary factions in the Politburo and the military, undermining his reform program and his ability to remain in power.

The Soviet Union's increasingly severe domestic problems led to mounting protests in 1991, when Gorbachev's policies failed to improve—indeed diminished—the living standard of the Soviet people. Sensing their political lives to be in jeopardy, a group of highly placed hard-line Communist party officials staged an abortive coup in August 1991. The Soviet citizenry, espe-

cially in large cities like Moscow and Leningrad, defied their self-proclaimed saviors. Led by Boris Yeltsin, who at one point mounted a tank in a Moscow street to rally the people, they gained support among the Soviet republics and the military, and successfully called the plotters' bluff. Within two weeks, Gorbachev was back in power and the coup leaders were in prison.

Ironically, this people's counterrevolution returned Gorbachev to office while destroying the power of the Soviet state he led. Throughout the fall of 1991, as Gorbachev struggled to hold the Union together, Yeltsin joined the presidents of the other large republics to capitalize on the discontent. On December 8, 1991, the presidents of the republics of Russia, Ukraine, and Byelorussia (now called Belarus) declared that the Soviet Union was no more. The once-mighty Soviet Union, founded seventy-five years before in a burst of revolutionary fervor and violence, had evaporated nearly overnight, leaving in its wake a collection of eleven far from powerful nations loosely joined together as the Commonwealth of Independent States.

> Throughout the fall of 1991, as Gorbachev struggled to hold the Union together, Yeltsin joined the presidents of the other large republics to capitalize on the discontent.

Boris Yeltsin Faces Down the Coup, August 1991. Russian president Boris Yeltsin stood his ground at the Russian parliament building against the hardliners who attempted to overthrow Mikhail Gorbachev. Here Yeltsin is encouraging the people to fight the takeover of the central government.

On December 25, 1991, Gorbachev resigned and left political life, not pushed from office in the usual way but made irrelevant as other actors dismantled the state.

The mighty fall left mighty problems in its wake. Food shortages worsened during the winter of 1992. The value of the ruble plummeted. The republics could not agree on common military policies or resolve difficult and dangerous questions concerning the control of nuclear warheads. Yeltsin's pleas for economic assistance from the West resulted in massive infusions of private and public capital, which nevertheless failed to prevent serious economic hardship and dislocation. Free enterprise brought with it unemployment and encouraged profiteering through crime. Yeltsin's determination to press ahead with his economic program met with stiff resistance from a parliament and citizenry alarmed by the ruthlessness and rapidity of the change they were experiencing. When the parliament balked at Yeltsin's proposals in September 1993, he dissolved it. This helped provoke an attempted coup two months later, staged by conservative politicians and army officers. Officials loyal to Yeltsin put the revolt down with far more force than the 1991 coup attempt—television viewers worldwide watched artillery shells slam into the rebel-occupied parliament building in Moscow during a bloody shootout.

Meanwhile, ethnic and religious conflict plagued the republics. The most serious conflict arose in the predominantly Muslim area of Chechnya, bordering Georgia in the Caucasus, which had declared its independence from Russia in late 1991. The Chechen rebels were heirs to a tradition of banditry and separatism against Russian authority that stretched into the nineteenth century. In 1994 the Russian government, weary of this continuing challenge to its authority, launched a concerted effort to quash resistance. As Russian forces moved into the Chechen capital, Grozny, they were ambushed with firepower largely stolen from disused Russian armories. The result was a massacre of the invading Russians, followed by a long and bloody siege to take the city. This in turn fueled a long and particularly bloody guerrilla war between Russian and Chechen forces, marked by repeated atrocities on both sides. After brief pauses in 1995 and 1997, this Chechen war dragged on into the new century, echoing Russia's conflict in Afghanistan (see Chapter 29) on a scale that was both bloodier and closer to home.

POSTREVOLUTIONARY TROUBLES: EASTERN EUROPE AFTER 1989

The "velvet revolutions" of central and Eastern Europe raised high hopes: local hopes that an end to authoritarian government would produce economic prosperity and cultural pluralism, and Western hopes that these countries would join them as capitalist partners in an enlarged European Community. The reality was slower and harder than the optimists of 1989 foresaw. For instance, although there has been great progress in integrating elections and the bureaucracies of the two German states, economic and cultural unity has been much harder to come by.

Eastern Europe in attempts to create free-market economies have brought inflation, unemployment, and—in their wake—anticapitalist demonstrations. Czechoslovakia's "velvet revolution" collapsed into a "velvet divorce," as Slovakia declared itself independent from the Czechs, forcing Havel's resignation and slowing down the promising cultural and economic reforms begun in 1989. Eastern Europe's economic difficulties have been accompanied by revived ethnic tensions formerly suppressed by centralized communist governments.

> Eastern Europe's economic difficulties have been accompanied by revived ethnic tensions formerly suppressed by centralized communist governments.

The most extreme example of these conflicts came with the implosion of the state of Yugoslavia. The 1960s and 1970s brought uneven economic growth, benefiting the capital, Belgrade, and the provinces of Croatia and Slovenia the most, but heavy industrial areas in Serbia, Bosnia-Hercegovina, and the tiny district of Kosovo began to lag far behind. During the 1980s, a number of Serb politicians, most notably Slobodan Milosevic, began to redirect Serbs' frustration with economic hardship toward subjects of national pride and sovereignty.

Nationalism, particularly Serb and Croat nationalism, had long dogged Yugoslavia's firmly federal political system. Milosevic and the Serb nationalists who gathered around him ignited those political flashpoints in ways that caught the fears and frustrations of his times. More important for Milosevic, it catapulted him into crucial positions of authority. In those posts, he alienated representatives from the non-Serb republics. Inspired by the peaceful transformations of 1989, representatives of the small province of Slovenia declared they had been denied them adequate representation and economic support inside the republic. In 1991, on a

EASTERN EUROPE IN 1989

What political changes in the Soviet Union allowed for the spread of demonstrations throughout the Eastern Europe? Why did the first political upheavals of 1989 occur in Poland and East Germany?

tide of nationalism and reform, the Slovenes seceded from Yugoslavia. After a brief attempt to hold the union together by force, the Yugoslav government relented and let Slovenia claim its independence.

The large republic of Croatia, once part of the Habsburg empire and briefly an independent state allied with the Nazis during World War II, cited injustices by Serb officials in the Yugoslav government and declared independence as a free, capitalist state. War broke out between federal Yugoslav forces and the well-armed militias of independent Croatia, a conflict that ended in arbitration by the United Nations. The religious nature of the conflict—between Catholic Croats and Orthodox Serbs—and the legacies of fighting in the Second World War produced violence on both sides. Towns and villages where Serbs and Croats had lived together since the 1940s were torn apart as each ethnic group rounded up and massacred members of the other.

The next conflict came in the same place that in 1914 had sparked a much larger war: the province of Bosnia-Hercegovina. Bosnia was the most ethnically diverse republic in Yugoslavia. Its capital, Sarajevo, was home to several major ethnic groups and had often been praised as an example of peaceful coexistence. When Bosnia joined the round of secessions from Yugoslavia in 1992, ethnic coexistence came apart. Bosnia began the war with no formal army: armed bands equipped by the governments of Serbian Yugoslavia, Croatia, and Bosnia battled each other throughout the new country. The Serbs and Croats, both of whom disliked the Muslim Bosnians, were especially well equipped and organized. They rained shells and bullets on towns and villages, burned houses with families inside, rounded up Muslim men in detention camps and starved them to death, and raped thousands of Bosnian women. All sides committed atrocities. The Serbs, however, orchestrated and carried out the worst crimes. These included what came to be called "ethnic cleansing." This involved sending irregular troops on campaigns of murder and terror through Muslim or Croat territories in order to encourage much larger populations to flee the area. During the first eighteen months of the fighting as many as one hundred thousand people were killed, including eighty thousand civilians, mostly Bosnian Muslims. Although the campaigns appalled Western governments, those countries considered the Balkan conflict a civil war more complex than that in Spain during the 1930s. They worried that intervention would only result in another Vietnam or

> When Bosnia joined the round of secessions from Yugoslavia in 1992, ethnic coexistence came apart.

Afghanistan (see Chapter 29) with no clear resolution of the horrific ethnic slaughter itself.

The crisis came to a head in the autumn of 1995. Sarajevo had been under siege for three years, but a series of mortar attacks on public marketplaces in Sarajevo produced fresh Western outrage and moved the United States to act. Already Croat forces and the Bosnian army had turned the war on the ground against the Serb militias, and now they were supported by a rolling wave of American air strikes. The American bombing, combined with a Croat-Bosnian offensive, forced the Bosnian Serbs to negotiate. The agreement divided Bosnia, with the majority of land in the hands of Muslims and Croats, and a small, autonomous "Serb Republic" in areas that included land "ethnically cleansed" in 1992. Stability was restored, but three years of war had killed over two hundred thousand people.

The legacy of Bosnia flared into conflict again over Kosovo, the medieval homeland of the Orthodox Christian Serbs, now occupied by a largely Albanian, Muslim population. Milosevic accused the Albanians of plotting secession and of challenging the Serb presence in Kosovo. In the name of a "greater Serbia," Serb soldiers fought Albanian separatists rallying under the banner of "greater Albania," with both sides using terrorist tactics. Western nations were anxious lest the conflict might spread to the strategic, ethnically divided country of Macedonia and touch off a general Balkan conflict. Western political opinion was outraged, however, as Serbian forces used many of the same murderous tactics in Kosovo as they employed earlier in Bosnia. Talks between Milosevic's government and the Albanian rebels were sponsored by the NATO powers but fell apart in early 1999. That failure was followed by a fresh wave of American-led bombing against Serbia itself, as well as against Serbian forces in Kosovo. A new round of ethnic cleansing drove hundreds of thousands of Albanians from their homes. The Russian government, bothered by this unilateral attack on fellow Slavs, nonetheless played an important part in brokering a cease-fire. Milosevic was forced to withdraw from Kosovo, leaving it in the hands of another force of armed NATO peacekeepers. Finally, Serb-dominated Yugoslavia, worn by ten years of war and economic sanctions, turned against Milosevic's regime. Wars and corruption had destroyed Milosevic's credentials as a nationalist and populist. After he attempted to reject the results of a democratic election in 2000, his government fell to popular protests.

Soviet Union to 1991

Soviet-dominated Eastern Europe to 1989

German Democratic Republic (GDR)
united with Federal Republic of
Germany 1990

Czechoslovakia to December 1992

Yugoslavia to 1991

Other communist states before 1991

1990 Date of first free election

KAZAKHSTAN
1991: President Nazarbayev
runs in election unopposed
1995: Nationwide referendum
extends his term to 2000

KYRGYZSTAN

TAJIKISTAN

AFGHANISTAN

UZBEKISTAN

TURKMENISTAN

ARAL
SEA

IRAN

CASPIAN SEA

RUSSIAN
FEDERATION
1993

AZERBAIJAN
1995

to AZERBAIJAN

GEORGIA
1991

ARMENIA
1995

1992: Tensions between Russia
and Ukraine over whether Black
Sea Fleet is part of strategic
forces controlled by CIS

1993: Joins the CIS to
secure Russian military
support against ousted
President Gamsakhurdia

TURKEY

BLACK
SEA

UKRAINE

MOLDAVIA
1994

FINLAND

ESTONIA
1992

LATVIA
1993

LITHUANIA
1990

BELORUSSIA
1995

RUSS. FED.

ROMANIA
1990

BULGARIA
1990

MACEDONIA
1990

GREECE

SWEDEN

NORWAY

BALTIC SEA

POLAND
1991

SLOVAKIA
1992

HUNGARY
1990

YUGOSLAVIA
1991

ALBANIA
1991

DENMARK

EAST
GERMANY
1990

CZECH
REPUBLIC
1992

AUSTRIA

SLOVENIA
1992

BOSNIA
AND
HERZEGOVINA
1992

ADRIATIC
SEA

NORTH
SEA

GERMANY

SWITZ.

CROATIA
1992

ITALY

Area of
detail

EUROPE

AFRICA

500 Miles

500 Kilometers

250

250

0

THE POST–COLD WAR WEST

How did the collapse of the Soviet Union and the end of the cold war allow for the reemergence of certain forces in the political landscape of Europe? Examine closely the geography of southeastern and central Europe. What happened here in terms of the reorganization of political boundaries?

Mass Funeral in Kosovo, 1999. Ethnic Albanians bury victims of a Serbian massacre toward the end of Yugoslavia's ten years of fighting.

As we gain perspective on the twentieth century, it is clear that the Yugoslavian wars of the 1990s were not an isolated instance of "Balkan" violence. The issues are thoroughly Western. The Balkans form one of the West's borderlands, where cultures influenced by Roman Catholicism, Eastern Orthodoxy, and Islam meet, overlap, and contend for political domination and influence. Since the nineteenth century, this region of enormous religious, cultural, and ethnic diversity has struggled with the implications of nationalism. We have seen how conflicts over the creation of new national states drawn mostly on ethnic lines were worked out in central Europe, with many instances of tragic violence. The Yugoslav wars fit into some of the same patterns.

Conclusion

The Eastern European revolutions of 1989 and the subsequent collapse of the Soviet Union were a revolutionary turning point. Like the French Revolution of 1789, they brought down not only a regime, but an empire. Like the French Revolution, they gave way to violence. And again like the French Revolution, they had sweeping international consequences. These revolutions and the fall of the Soviet Union marked the end of the cold war, which had structured international politics and shaped the everyday lives of millions of people since the end of World War II. In the last chapter of this book, we consider how the cold war itself has given way to more complex global relations.

Key Terms

abstract expressionism	NAACP	"velvet revolutions"
French "new wave"	Prague spring	Slobodan Milosevic
The Feminine Mystique	perestroika	Boris Yeltsin

SELECTED READINGS

Bailey, Beth. *From Front Porch to Back Seat: Courtship in Twentieth-Century America.* Baltimore, 1988. Good historical perspective on the "sexual revolution."

Beschloss, Michael, and Strobe Talbott. *At the Highest Levels: The Inside Story of the End of the Cold War.* Boston, 1993. An analysis of the relationship between presidents Gorbachev and Bush, and their determination to ignore hard-liners.

Brown, Archie. *The Gorbachev Factor.* Oxford and New York, 1996.

Caute, David. *The Year of the Barricades: A Journey through 1968.* New York, 1988. A well-written global history of 1968.

Charney, Leo, and Vanessa R. Schwartz, eds. *Cinema and the Invention of Modern Life.* Berkeley, 1995. Collection of essays.

Dallin, Alexander, and Gail Lapidus. *The Soviet System: From Crisis to Collapse.* Boulder, 1995.

Echols, Alice. *Daring to be Bad: Radical Feminism in America, 1967–1975.* Minneapolis, 1989. Good narrative and analysis.

Eley, Geoff. *Forging Democracy: The History of the Left in Europe, 1850–2000.* Oxford and New York, 2002. Among its other qualities, one of the best historical perspectives on the 1960s.

Fink, Carole, Phillipp Gassert, and Detlef Junker, eds. *1968: The World Transformed.* Cambridge, 1998. A transatlantic history of 1968.

Fulbrook, Mary, ed., *Europe Since 1945.* Oxford, 2001. Particularly good articles on economics and political economy. Structural analysis.

Garton Ash, Timothy. *In Europe's Name: Germany and the Divided Continent.* New York, 1993. An analysis of the effect of German reunification on the future of Europe.

Glenny, Misha. *The Balkans, 1804–1999: Nationalism, War and the Great Powers.* London, 1999. Good account by a journalist who covered the fighting.

Horowitz, Daniel. *Betty Friedan and the Making of the Feminine Mystique: The American Left, the Cold War, and Modern Feminism.* Amherst, 1998. An excellent new account.

Hosking, Geoffrey. *The Awakening of the Soviet Union.* Cambridge, Mass., 1990. The factors that led to the end of the Soviet era.

Hughes, H. Stuart. *Sophisticated Rebels: The Political Culture of European Dissent, 1968–1987.* Cambridge, Mass., 1990. The nature of dissent on both sides of the disintegrating Iron Curtain in the years 1988–1989.

Hulsberg, Werner. *The German Greens: A Social and Political Profile.* New York, 1988. The origins, politics, and impact of environmental politics.

Jarausch, Konrad. *The Rush to German Unity.* New York, 1994. The problems of reunification analyzed.

Judah, Tim. *The Serbs: History, Myth, and the Destruction of Yugoslavia.* New Haven, 1997.

Kaplan, Robert D. *Balkan Ghosts: A Journey through History.* New York, 1993.

Kotkin, Stephen. *Armageddon Averted: The Soviet Collapse, 1970–2000.* Oxford, 2001.

Lewin, Moshe. *The Gorbachev Phenomenon,* expanded ed., Berkeley, 1991. Written as a firsthand account, tracing the roots of Gorbachev's successes and failures.

Lieven, Anatol. *Chechnya, Tomb of Russia Power.* New Haven and London, 1998.

Maier, Charles S. *Dissolution: The Crisis of Communism and the End of East Germany.* Princeton, N.J., 1997.

Marwick, Arthur. *The Sixties.* Oxford and New York, 1998.

Pells, Richard. *Not Like Us: How Europeans Have Loved, Hated, and Transformed American Culture since World War II.* New York, 1997.

Poiger, Uta G. *Jazz, Rock, and Rebels: Cold War Politics and American Culture in a Divided Germany.* Berkeley, 2000. Pioneering cultural history.

Sheehan, Neil. *A Bright Shining Lie: John Paul Vann and America in Vietnam.* New York, 1988.

Strayer, Robert. *Why Did the Soviet Union Collapse? Understanding Historical Change.* Armonk, N.Y., and London, 1998. A good introduction, with bibliography.

Wright, Patrick. *On Living in an Old Country: The National Past in Contemporary Britain.* New York, 1986. The culture of Britain in the 1980s.

DIGITAL HISTORY

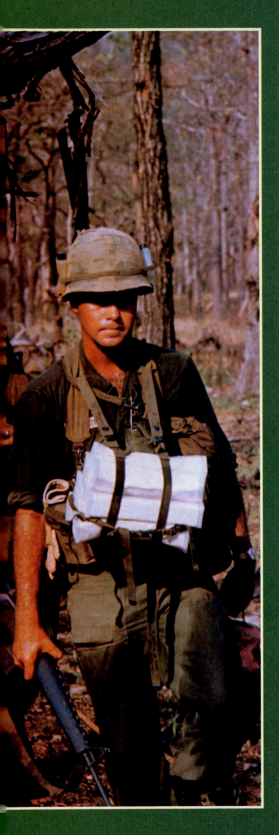

WAR AND TECHNOLOGY

No mockeries now for them; no prayers nor bells;
Nor any voice of mourning save the choirs, —
The shrill, demented choirs of wailing shells;
And bugles calling for them from sad shires.
What candles may be held to speed them all?
Not in the hands of boys but in their eyes
Shall shine the holy glimmers of goodbyes.

—Wilfred Owen, *Anthem for a Dammed Youth* (1917)

The four battles covered in this Digital History Feature all serve as "snapshots of a cultural tradition of war making."

In the battle at Rorke's Drift in 1879, the supply station manned by 139 British soldiers with Martini-Henry rifles, was attacked by four thousand Zulus. When the battle ended, 15 British soldiers had been killed and the bodies of 600 Zulu warriors lay scattered over the terrain.

Although Hitler and the Soviets had signed a nonaggression pact, by 1941 Hitler had invaded the Soviet Union. Late in 1942, Hitler diverted his forces to Stalingrad in order to slow Soviet war production and destroy Stalin's city. The German 6th Army seemed to have the upper hand until the end of 1943, when Soviet sniper fire combined with a will to fight led to the defeat of the German army.

In mid-November 1965, Lt. Col. Hal Moore took 400 men of the 7th Cavalry into the Ia Drang Valley near the Cambodian border of South Vietnam. Completely outnumbered by PAVN (People's Army of Vietnam) forces, Moore's men fought for four days and nights until finally subduing the PAVN army. Both sides claimed victory at Ia Drang, the first major battle between the American army and the PAVN.

On March 19, 2003, the United States and coalition forces began military operations to disarm Iraq and bring down President Saddam Hussein. With the invasion of Iraq, the United States moved away from policies of deterrence and containment and toward the idea of the preemptive strike. The invasion, named "Operation Iraqi Freedom," was swift, and the Iraqi government and military collapsed in about three weeks. On December 13, 2003, Saddam Hussein was captured in a "spider hole"; however, the future of Iraq still hangs in the balance.

The images and documents in the War and Technology Digital History Feature at www.wwnorton.com/wciv show how new tactics and technologies determined the outcomes of four landmark battles. As you explore this feature on the *Western Civilizations* Web site, consider the following:

• What lessons might have been learned from each of these battles?

• Does technology—spears, shields, arrows, guns, tanks, aircraft, and bombs, among other things—always determine the outcome of a battle?

• Why is the "Bush Doctrine," as outlined by President George W. Bush in 2002, such a radical departure from previous American foreign policy initiatives?

• How has the face of war changed over the past century?

CHAPTER
TWENTY-NINE

A WORLD
WITHOUT WALLS:
GLOBALIZATION
AND THE WEST

In the twenty-first century, the world has reentered a period in which basic assumptions about the role of nation-states, the roots of prosperity, and the boundaries of cultures are changing fast. We say "reentered" because, as we have seen, a disconcerting sense of seismic and little-understood change has been central to Western culture during several different historical periods. The Industrial Revolution of the nineteenth century is an example, and just as "industrial revolution," a term coined in the early nineteenth century, seemed to capture contemporaries' perceptions of changes in their own time, so "globalization" seems to capture ours.

We know, intuitively, what globalization means: the Internet, protests against the WTO, outsourcing of jobs and services, Wal-Mart in Mexico, the dismantling of the Berlin wall. All of these are powerful images of larger, enormously significant developments. The Internet represents the stunning transformation of global communication, the media, and forms of knowledge. The Berlin wall once stood for a divided cold war world; its fall marked a dramatic reconfiguration of international relations, an end to the ideological battle over communism, the creation of new alliances, markets, and communities. The bombing of the World Trade Centers in 2001 gave the term "globalization" a new and frightening meaning as well. It shattered many Americans' sense of relative isolation and security. "Globalization," then, conjures up new possibilities and new vulnerabilities.

What, precisely, does the term mean? What causes or drives globalization, and what are its effects? Is it new? To begin simply, globalization means integration. It is the process of creating a rising number of networks—political, social, economic, and cultural—that span the globe. New technologies, new economic imperatives, and changing laws have combined to make global exchange faster and, by the same token, to intensify economic, social, and cultural relationships. Information, ideas, goods, and people now move rapidly and easily across national boundaries.

FOCUS QUESTIONS

• What is globalization?

• Why did postcolonial development unfold differently in different regions?

 • How did the global demand for oil reshape politics, religion, and society in the Middle East?

• How has globalization changed the politics of terrorism?

Globalization has radically altered the distribution of industry and patterns of trade around the world, as Asian nations in particular emerge as industrial giants and Western powers become increasingly dependent on energy resources drawn from former colonies. Globalization has forced the reorganization of economic enterprises from banking and commerce to manufacturing. Supranational economic institutions such as the International Monetary Fund are examples of globalization and also work to quicken its pace. New, rapid, and surprisingly intimate forms of mass communication (Web logs, Internet-based political campaigns, and so on) have spawned new forms of politics whose long-term effects are hard to predict. International human-rights campaigns, for instance, owe an enormous debt to global communications and the communities they create. Perhaps most interesting, the sovereignty of nation-states and the clear boundaries of national communities seem to be eroded by many globalizing trends.

Although globalization means integration, it does not necessarily produce peace, equality, or homogeneity. The term *globalization* can be misleading, for it suggests a uniform, leveling process, one that operates similarly everywhere. Globalization has very different and disparate effects, effects shaped by vast asymmetries of power and wealth between nations or regions, and in the last several decades, worldwide inequality has increased. Globalization has hastened new kinds of cultural blending and new forms of sociability, but it has also produced a backlash against that blending. Finally, globalization is not new. It is at a new stage. As we have seen, empires, religion, and commerce have all had globalizing impulses and effects. The East India Company, to take one example, was certainly a global enterprise; how it differs from Microsoft is a fascinating question. Historians are only beginning to write that story.

In this chapter, then, we explore three subjects crucial to our early efforts to understand globalization, especially as it relates to the post–cold war world of the twenty-first century. The first subject is the set of global changes that have accelerated the free flow of money, people, products, and ideas. The second subject is what we have come to call "postcolonial" politics—the varied trajectories that mark the contemporary experience of former colonies. Finally, we will consider in greater depth the complex and important role of Middle Eastern politics in contemporary global affairs. Throughout, we hope to suggest ways in which recent developments relate to familiar historical issues we have already examined in other contexts.

LIQUID MODERNITY? THE FLOW OF MONEY, IDEAS, AND PEOPLES

What is globalization?

A key feature of globalization has been the transformation of the world economy, highlighted by the rapid integration of markets since 1970. In a series of historic changes, the international agreements that had regulated the movement of people, goods, and money since the Second World War were overturned. To begin with, the postwar economic arrangements sealed at Bretton Woods (see Chapter 27) steadily eroded in the late 1960s, as Western industrial nations faced a double burden of inflation and economic stagnation. A crucial shift in monetary policy occurred in 1971, when the United States abandoned the postwar gold standard and allowed the dollar—the keystone of the system—to range freely. As a result, formal regulations on currencies, international banking, and lending among states faded away. They were replaced with an informal network of arrangements managed autonomously by large private lenders, their political friends in leading Western states, and independent financial agencies such as the International Monetary Fund and the World Bank. The economists and administrators who dominated these new networks steered away from the interventionist policies that shaped postwar planning and recovery. Instead they relied on a broad range of market-driven models dubbed "neoliberalism." In a variation on classic liberal economics, neoliberal economists stressed the value of free markets, profit incentives, and sharp restraints on both budget deficits and social welfare programs, whether run by governments or corporations. The new systems of lending they backed had mixed re-

> The new systems of lending they backed had mixed results, creating jarring juxtapositions of development and deterioration across entire continents even within single cities—a phenomenon described as a "checkerboard of poverty and affluence."

sults, creating jarring juxtapositions of development and deterioration across entire continents even within single cities—a phenomenon described as a "checkerboard of poverty and affluence."

At the same time, the world's local, national, and regional economies became far more connected and interdependent. Export trade flourished and, with the technological advances of the 1960s and 1980s, came to include an increasing proportion of high-technology goods. The boom in export commerce was tied to important changes in the division of labor worldwide. More industrial jobs emerged in the postcolonial world, not just among the Asian "tigers" but also in India, Latin America, and elsewhere. Although such steady, skilled manual employment started to disappear in Western nations—often replaced by lower-paying menial work—financial and service sector employment leaped ahead. The exchange and use of goods became much more complex. Goods were designed by companies in one country, manufactured in another, and tied into a broader interchange of cultures. Taken together, these global economic changes had deep political effects, forcing painful debates over the nature of citizenship and entitlement inside national borders, about the power and accountability of transnational corporations, and about the human and environmental costs of global capitalism.

Another crucial change involved not only the widespread flow of information but also the new commercial and cultural importance attached to information itself. By the early 1990s increasingly sophisticated computers brought people into instant communication with each other across continents, not only by new means, but also in new cultural and political settings. The Internet revolution shared features of earlier print revolutions: entrepreneurs with utopian ambitions; a fascination with culturally illicit and politically scandalous materials published easily and informally; the new social settings made available to specific groups, and the eager efforts of large, established corporate interests to cash in on new channels of culture and business.

However common their use seems, the Internet and similar technologies have had wide-ranging effects on

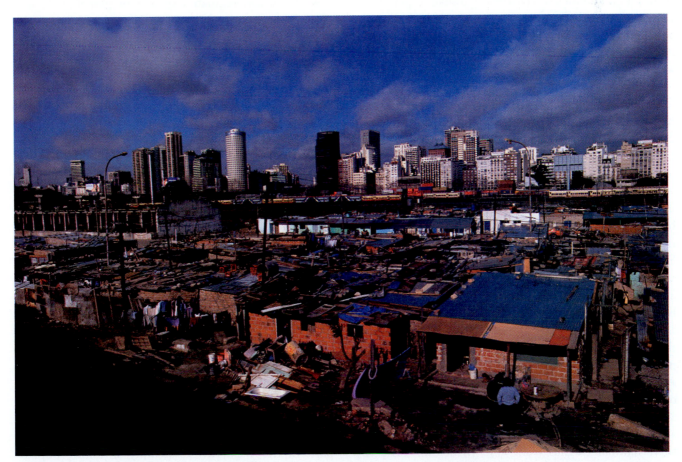

"Checkerboard of poverty and affluence." Scenes of slums confronting towering skylines, such as this one from Argentina in 2000, were visible around the world as one of the side effects of development and deterioration.

political struggles around the globe. Embattled ethnic minorities have found worldwide audiences through on-line campaign sites. Satellite television arguably sped the sequence of popular revolts in Eastern Europe in 1989. That same year, fax machines brought Chinese demonstrators at Tiananmen Square news of international support for their efforts. Meanwhile, leaps forward in electronic technologies provided new worldwide platforms for commercial interests. Companies such as Sony, RCA, and others produced entertainment content, including music, motion pictures, and television shows, as well as the electronic equipment to play that content. Bill Gates's Microsoft emerged as the world's major producer of computer software—with a corporate profit margin that surpassed Spain's gross domestic product. At the level of production, marketing, and management, information industries are global, spread widely across the United States, India, Western Europe, and parts of the developing world. Their corporate headquarters, however, typically remain in the West and support neoliberal politics. The international media, news, and entertainment conglomerates run by the Australian Rupert Murdoch or by AOL/TimeWarner, for example, are firmly allied to Western institutions and world views, edging aside state-run companies and providing local venues with a particular version of the free market.

Like the fluid movement of money, goods, and ideas, the free flow of labor has become a central aspect of globalization. Since 1945, the widespread migration of peoples, particularly between former colonies and imperial powers, has changed everyday life around the world. Groups of immigrant workers have filled the lower rungs of thriving economies not only in Europe but also in oil-rich Arab states that attracted South Asian and Filipino laborers, and in the United States, where both permanent and seasonal migrations from Mexico and other Latin American nations have spread across the continent. This fusion of peoples and cultures has produced novel multicultural encounters, including striking new blends of music, food, language, and other forms of popular culture and sociability. It has also raised tensions over the definition of citizenship and the boundaries of political and cultural communities—familiar themes from modern history. As a result, cycles of violent xenophobic backlash, bigotry, and political extremism have appeared in host countries and regions, but so too have new conceptions of civil rights and cultural belonging.

> Since 1945, the widespread migration of peoples, particularly between former colonies and imperial powers, has changed everyday life around the world.

Sharp divides exist between the most successful global players and the poorer, disadvantaged, sometimes embattled states and cultures. In one particular area of manufacture, however, poorer postcolonial regions have been able to respond to a steady and immensely profitable market in the West. The production of illegal drugs such as opium, heroin, and cocaine is a thriving industry in countries such as Colombia, Myanmar (formerly Burma), and Malaysia. Though the trade in such substances is banned, the fragile economies of the countries where they are produced have encouraged public and private powers to turn a blind eye to their production—or even to intervene for their own profit. The organizations behind these criminal trades grew out of the political violence and economic breakdown of failing postcolonial states, or from the human and commercial traffic between these parts of the world and leading Western economic powers. They have exploited cracks, loopholes, and unsupervised opportunities in the less regulated system of global trade and carved out centers of power not directly subject to the laws of any single state.

DEMOGRAPHICS AND GLOBAL HEALTH

The developments of globalization are tied in complex ways to the evolving size and health of the world's population. Between 1800 and the middle of the twentieth century, the worldwide population roughly tripled, rising from 1 to 3 billion. Between 1960 and 2000, however, population doubled again, to 6 billion or more. Haphazard but huge improvements in basic standards of health, particularly for young children and childbearing women, contributed to the increase—as did localized efforts to improve the urban-industrial environment in postcolonial regions. Such growth has placed tremendous strains on underdeveloped social services, public-health facilities, and urban infrastructures—increasing the potential for epidemic disease, as well as for cycles of ethnic and ideological violence nursed by poverty and dislocation.

A different type of demographic crisis confronts parts of the West, where steadily shrinking populations erode social welfare systems. While such nations

An Afghan girl weeds a poppy field, 2004. Though Afghanistan was historically a center for the silk trade, opium is its most important cash crop today.

the 1970s the acceleration of airplane travel led to fears that an epidemic would leapfrog the globe much faster than the pandemics of the Middle Ages. Such fears were confirmed by the worldwide spread of human immunodeficiency virus disease (HIV), whose final stage is acquired immune deficiency syndrome (AIDS), which first appeared at the end of the 1970s. As HIV-AIDS became a global health crisis—particularly in Africa, where the disease spread catastrophically—international organizations recognized the need for an early, swift, and comprehensive response to future outbreaks of disease, as evidenced by the successful global containment of severe acute respiratory syndrome (SARS) in 2003.

Meanwhile, the work of multinational medical research firms continued to extend the ability to prevent and treat disease. One of the most powerful tools in this endeavor was the development of genetic engineering, which stemmed from the monumental discovery of DNA in the 1950s. By the 1990s, several laboratories were engaged in the most ambitious medical research ever attempted: the mapping of the human genome—that is, the entire architecture of chromosomes and genes contained in basic human DNA. By 1997 British researchers succeeded in producing a clone (an exact genetic copy) of a sheep. Genome research also broadened and deepened medical understanding of biological "defects" and diversions from the genetic norms of human development. As a new form of knowledge in an age of global interconnection, genetic engineering leaped across the legal and moral boundaries of human societies. The question of who would govern these advances—nations, international bodies, or local cultural and religious communities—was open to passionate debate. So were fresh arguments about where to draw lines between lifesaving intervention and cultural preference, between individual agency and biological determinism. Like past scientific investigations directed at humankind, genetics raised fundamental questions about ethics, citizenship, and the measure of humanity.

as the United States and Great Britain have kept stable populations or seen mild growth thanks to immigration, other locales such as Italy and Scandinavia have faced sharp declines in the birth rate, leading to actual, absolute population decline. During the 1990s Russia also took a sudden and potentially disastrous lurch in this direction, spurred by post-Soviet poverty, emigration, and dislocation. Declining birth rates have been accompanied by growing populations of older adults, whose health and vitality resulted from decades of improved medical standards and state-run entitlement programs. Maintaining the long-term solvency of such programs poses difficult choices for European countries in particular, as they struggle to balance guarantees of social well-being with fiscal and political realities.

Globalization has also changed the arena of public health and medicine, creating dangerous new threats as well as promising new treatments. Better and more comprehensive health care has generally accompanied other kinds of prosperity, and has thus been more accessible in the West. In Africa, Latin America, and elsewhere, political chaos, imbalances of trade, and the practices of some large pharmaceutical companies have often resulted in shortages of medicine and a rickety medical infrastructure, making it difficult to combat deadly new waves of disease. Indeed, the worldwide risk of exposure to epidemic diseases is a new reality of globalization. By

AFTER EMPIRE: POSTCOLONIAL POLITICS IN THE GLOBAL ERA

Why did postcolonial development unfold differently in different regions?

Even after the superpower rivalry of the cold war collapsed, another legacy of the postwar era continued to shape international relations into the twenty-first century. The so-called postcolonial relationships between former colonies and Western powers emerged from the decolonization struggles detailed in Chapter 27. Former colonies, as well as other nations that had fallen under the political and economic sway of imperial powers, gained formal independence at the least, along with new kinds of cultural and political authority. In other respects, however, very little changed for people in the former colonies. The very term *postcolonial* underlines the fact that colonialism's legacies endured even after independence. Within these regions, political communities new and old handled the legacies of empire and the postcolonial future in a variety of ways. In some cases the former colonizers or their local allies retained so much power that formal independence actually meant very little. In others, bloody independence struggles poisoned the political culture. The emergence of new states and new kinds of politics was sometimes propelled by economic goals, sometimes by the revival of cultural identities that preceded colonization, and in other cases by ethnic conflict. During the cold war, these postcolonial regions were often the turf on which the superpower struggle was waged. They benefited from superpower patronage, but also became the staging ground for proxy wars funded by the West in the fight against communism. Their various trajectories point to the complex legacy of the imperial past in the post–cold war world of globalization.

The emergence of new states and new kinds of politics was sometimes propelled by economic goals, sometimes by the revival of cultural identities that preceded colonization, and in other cases by ethnic conflict.

EMANCIPATION AND ETHNIC CONFLICT IN AFRICA

The legacies of colonialism weighed heavily on sub-Saharan Africa. Most of the continent's former colonies came into their independence after World War II with their basic infrastructure deteriorating after decades of imperial negligence. The cold war decades brought scant improvement, as governments across the continent were plagued by both homegrown and externally imposed corruption, poverty, and civil war. In sub-Saharan Africa, two very different trends began to emerge around 1989, each shaped by a combination of the end of the cold war and volatile local conditions.

The first trend can be seen in South Africa, where politics had revolved for decades around the brutal racial policies of apartheid, sponsored by the white minority government. The most prominent opponent of apartheid, Nelson Mandela, who led the African National Congress (ANC), had been imprisoned since 1962. Intense repression and violent conflict continued into the 1980s and reached a dangerous impasse by the end of the decade. Then the South African government chose a daring new tack: in early 1990 it released Mandela from prison. He resumed leadership of the ANC and turned the party toward a combination of renewed public demonstrations and plans for negotiation. Politics changed within the Afrikaner-dominated white regime as well when F. W. de Klerk succeeded the reactionary P. W. Botha as prime minister. A pragmatist who feared civil war and national collapse over apartheid, De Klerk was well matched to Mandela. In March 1992 the two men began direct talks to establish majority rule. Legal and constitutional reforms followed, and in May 1994, during elections in which all South Africans took part, Nelson Mandela was chosen the country's first black president. Although many of his government's efforts to reforms foundered, Mandela defused the climate of organized racial violence. He also gained and kept tremendous personal popularity among black and white South Africans alike as a living symbol of a new political culture. Mandela's popularity extended abroad, within sub-Saharan Africa and worldwide.

The other major trend ran in a different, less encouraging direction. Some former autocracies gave way to calls for pluralism, but other states across the continent collapsed into ruthless ethnic conflict. In Rwanda, a former Belgian colony, conflicts between the Hutu and Tutsi populations erupted into a highly organized campaign of genocide against the Tutsi after the country's president was assassinated. Carried out by ordinary Hutus of all backgrounds, the ethnic slaughter left over

DECOLONIZATION IN AFRICA TO 1980

How do the modern borders of African nations still bear the stamp of European colonization? What effect do you suspect this has had on ethnic tensions within these nations?

eight hundred thousand Tutsi dead in a matter of weeks. International pressure eventually turned local Rwandan politics against the perpetrators. Many of them fled to neighboring Zaire and became hired mercenaries in the many-sided civil war that followed the collapse of Mobutu Sese Seko, the country's long-time dictator, infamous for diverting billions of dollars in foreign aid into his personal bank accounts. A number of ambitious, neighboring countries intervened in Zaire, hoping not only to secure its valuable resources but also to settle conflicts with their own ethnic minorities that spilled over the border. Fighting continued through the late 1990s into the new century, dubbed "Africa's world war" by many observers. Public services, normal trade, even basic health and safety inside Zaire—renamed the Democratic Republic of Congo by an ineffective government in Kinshasa—collapsed. With a death toll that reached into the millions from combat, massacre, and disease, the fighting remained unresolved in the next decade.

ECONOMIC POWER ON THE PACIFIC RIM

By the end of the twentieth century, East Asia had become a center of industrial and manufacturing production. China, whose communist government began to establish commercial ties with the West in the 1970s, was the world's leading heavy industrial producer by the year 2000. Its state-owned companies acquired contracts from Western firms to produce products cheaply and in bulk, for sale back to home markets in the United States and Europe.

Other Asian nations emerged as global commercial powers as well. Industry flourished in a string of countries, starting with Japan and extending along Asia's Pacific coastline into Southeast Asia and Oceania, during the decades after World War II. By the 1980s their robust industrial expansion and their apparent staying power earned them the collective nickname of "the tigers," taken from the ambitious, forward-looking tiger in Chinese mythology. These "Pacific rim" states collectively formed the most important industrial region in the world outside the United States and Europe. Among them, Japan not only led the way but also became the most influential model of success. Japanese firms concentrated on the efficiency and technical reliability of their products. Japanese diplomacy and large state subsidies supported the success of Japanese firms, while a well-funded program of technical education

hastened research and development of new goods. Japanese firms also appeared to benefit from collective loyalty among civil servants and corporate managers, attitudes that were encouraged by Japan's long experience of trade guilds and feudal politics.

The Pacific rim's boom, however, also contained the makings of a first "bust." During the 1990s a confluence of factors resulted in an enormous slowdown of growth and the near collapse of several currencies. Japan fell prey to rising production costs, overvalued stocks, rampant speculation on its high-priced real estate market, and the customary kickbacks that rewarded staunch corporate loyalty. In Southeast Asia, states such as Indonesia found they had to pay the difference on overvalued industrial capital to Western lenders who set rigid debt repayment schedules. Responses to the economic downturn varied widely. Japan launched programs of monetary austerity to cope with its first serious spike in unemployment in two generations. In Indonesia, inflation and unemployment reignited sharp ethnic conflicts that prosperity and violent state repression had dampened in earlier times. This predominantly Muslim country, with a long tradition of tolerance and pluralism inside the faith, also saw outbursts of violent religious fundamentalism popularly associated with another region—the Middle East.

A NEW CENTER OF GRAVITY: ISRAEL, OIL, AND POLITICAL ISLAM IN THE MIDDLE EAST

How did the global demand for oil reshape politics, religion, and society in the Middle East?

Perhaps no other region has drawn more attention from the West in the age of globalization than the Middle East, where a volatile combination of Western military, political, and economic interests converged with deep-seated regional conflicts and transnational Islamic politics. The results of this ongoing confrontation promise to shape the twenty-first century. Here we consider three of the most important aspects of recent history in

HOW DID THE GLOBAL DEMAND FOR OIL RESHAPE POLITICS, RELIGION, AND SOCIETY IN THE MIDDLE EAST?

ISRAEL, OIL, AND POLITICAL ISLAM IN THE MIDDLE EAST   821

THE ARAB-ISRAELI WARS OF 1967 AND 1973

This map shows the changes in the political geography in the Middle East as a result of the Arab-Israeli conflicts of 1967 and 1973. What factors led to the Arab attacks on Israel in these two wars? Why did the Israelis wish to occupy the Sinai and West Bank regions at the end of the 1967 war? What problems did this create, and how might it have led to the conflict in 1973? Study the distribution of Israeli-occupied and Egyptian-occupied territory at the end of the 1973 war. Why was the resolution of the Sinai problem considered a top priority by many political figures in the West?

the region. First is the unfolding of the Arab-Israeli conflict. Second is the region's vital development as the global center of oil production. The third was the development of a specific, modern brand of Islamic radicalism that challenged the legacies of imperialism and promised revolutionary and sometimes apocalyptic change in postcolonial nations, and whose most violent elements generated a cycle of fear, anger, and ultimately direct conflict with Western governments.

THE ARAB-ISRAELI CONFLICT

As we saw in Chapter 27, Israel's existence was a battleground from the start. The national aspirations of Jewish immigrants from Europe, determined to survive and transcend the Holocaust and violent postwar anti-Semitism, clashed directly with the motives of pan-Arabists—secular, anticolonial nationalists who urged Arab pride and self-reliance against European domination. By the late 1970s, in the aftermath of two Arab-Israeli wars, it appeared that a generation of fighting might come to an end. American mediators began sponsoring talks to prevent further, sudden outbursts of conflict, while Soviet leaders remained neutral but supportive of peace efforts. Most notably, the Egyptian president Anwar Sadat, who authorized and directed the 1973 war against Israel, decided that coexistence rather than the destruction of Israel was the long-term answer to regional conflict. Aided by the American president Jimmy Carter, Sadat brokered a peace between Egypt and Israel's staunchly conservative leader, Menachem Begin, in 1978.

But hopes for a lasting peace were soon dashed. Hostilities escalated between Israel and the Palestinian Arabs displaced by Arab-Israeli warfare. On each side of the Israeli-Palestinian conflict, a potent blend of ethnic and religious nationalism began to control both debate and action. Conservatives in Israel played to a public sentiment that put security ahead of other priorities. On the other side, younger Palestinians, angered by their elders' failures to provoke revolution, turned against the secular radicalism of the Palestinian Liberation Organization and toward radical Islam.

In this combustible political environment, the desperately overcrowded Palestinians living on the West Bank and in the Gaza Strip revolted in an outburst of street rioting in 1987. This rebellion—called the *intifada* (literally, a "throwing off" or uprising)—continued for years in daily battles between stone-throwing Palestinian youths and armed Israeli security forces. The street fights escalated into cycles of Palestinian terrorism, particularly suicide bombings of civilian targets, and reprisals from the Israeli military. International efforts to broker a peace produced some results, including the official autonomy of a Palestinian "authority" led by the PLO chief, Yasser Arafat. Yet the peace was always fragile at best—suffering perhaps fatal damage from the assassination of Israel's reformist prime minister Yitzhak Rabin in 1995 by a reactionary Israeli and from continued attacks by Islamist terrorists. By the turn of the twenty-first century the cycle of violence flared again, with a "second *intifada*" launched by Palestinians in late 2000. Thus continued the war of riots and bombings fought by next-door neighbors.

> With the pan-Arab nationalists fading from the scene, the rising revolutionary force gathered instead around modern readings of Islamic fundamentalism, now tied to postcolonial politics.

OIL, POWER, AND ECONOMICS

The struggles that still surround the state of Israel and its Arab neighbors have been important in their own right. Yet one of the most compelling reasons that this conflict mattered to outside powers was material—oil. The global demand for oil skyrocketed during the postwar era and has accelerated since. The need for oil and the desires for profit and power that went with it, drew Western corporations and governments steadily toward the oil-rich states of the Middle East, whose vast reserves were discovered in the 1930s and 1940s. Large corporations conducted joint diplomacy with Arab states and their own home governments to design concessions for drilling, refining, and shipping the oil. Pipelines were laid by contractors based around the world, from California to Rome to Russia.

The long-term economic value of the Arab oil reserves made oil a tool in new struggles over political power. Many producer states sought to turn their resources into leverage with the West's former imperial powers. In 1960, the leading Arab, African, and Latin American producers formed the Organization of Petroleum Exporting Countries (OPEC) to regulate the production and pricing of crude oil. During the 1970s, OPEC played a leading role in the global economy. After the 1973 Arab-Israeli war, an embargo inspired by the hard-liners sparked spiraling inflation and economic troubles in Western nations, triggering a cycle of dangerous recession that lasted nearly a decade.

In response, Western governments treated the Middle Eastern oil regions as a vital strategic center of gravity, the subject of constant Great Power diplomacy. If conflict directly threatened the stability of oil production or friendly governments, Western powers were prepared to intervene by force, as the 1991 gulf war demonstrated. By the 1990s another new front of competition and potential conflict emerged as the energy demands of postcolonial nations also grew. In particular, the new industrial giants China and India eyed the Middle Eastern oil reserves with the same nervousness as the West. The oil boom also generated violent conflict inside Middle Eastern producer states. Oil, however, offered a uneven form of economic development. The huge gaps between or inside Middle Eastern societies that divided oil's "haves" and "have-nots" produced deep resentments, continued official corruption, and

HOW DID THE GLOBAL DEMAND FOR OIL RESHAPE POLITICS, RELIGION, AND SOCIETY IN THE MIDDLE EAST?

ISRAEL, OIL, AND POLITICAL ISLAM IN THE MIDDLE EAST   823

spurred a new wave of radical politics. With the pan-Arab nationalists fading from the scene, the rising revolutionary force gathered instead around modern readings of Islamic fundamentalism, now tied to post-colonial politics.

THE RISE OF POLITICAL ISLAM

In North Africa and the Middle East, processes of modernization and globalization produced tremendous discontents. Disappointment with the new nations that emerged from decolonization ran deep, perhaps nowhere more so than in the seat of pan-Arabism, Nasser's Egypt. During the 1960s, Egyptian academics and cultural critics leveled charges against Nasser's regime that became the core of a powerful new political movement. Their critique offered modern interpretations of certain legal and political currents in Islamic thought, ideas linked loosely across centuries by their association with revolt against foreign interference and official corruption. They denounced Egypt's nationalist government as greedy, brutal, and corrupt.

There was a twist to their claims, however: that the roots of the Arab world's moral failure lay in centuries of colonial contact with the West. The most influential of these Islamist critics, Sayyid Qutb (1906–1966), presented these ideas in a series of essays for which he was arrested several times by Egyptian authorities and ultimately executed. He argued that the nation's elites were morally bankrupt—their lives defied codes of morality, self-discipline, and communal responsibility rooted in Islamic faith. To maintain power, the elites lived in the pockets of Western imperial and corporate powers, which caused cultural impurity, and eroded authentic Muslim faith. This dire judgment of Arab societies—that they were poisoned from without and within—required an equally drastic solution. Arab societies should reject not only oppressive postcolonial governments but also all the political and cultural ideas that traveled with them, especially those that could be

Gamal Abdel Nasser and Aleksey Kosygin, 1966. As the most prominent spokesman for secular pan-Arabism, Nassar became a target for Islamist critics, such as Sayyid Qutb and the Muslim Brotherhood, angered by the Western-influenced policies of his regime.

labeled "Western." After popular revolts, the Arab autocracies would be replaced by an idealized form of conservative Islamic government—a system in which a rigid form of Islam would link law, government, and culture.

This brand of Islamist politics combined popular anger, intellectual opposition to "foreign" influences, and a highly idealized vision of the past. Beginning in the 1970s, Qutb's ideas were put into practice by Egypt's Muslim Brotherhood, a secretive but widespread society rooted in anticolonial politics, local charity, and violently fundamentalist Islam. Radical Islam emerged as a driving force in criticism and defiance of autocratic Arab regimes. Secular critics and more liberal Islamists, who called for elections and a free press, were more fragmented and thus easier to silence, whereas the new wave of fundamentalists were allowed to preach and publish so long as they did not launch actual revolts. Despite the movement's steady rise, the most dramatic turn still managed to surprise observers. Like Protestantism's emergence in the fractious German states, for example, or communism's successful revolution in Russia, radical Islam's defining moment as a political force came in an unexpected place: Iran.

IRAN'S ISLAMIC REVOLUTION

Iran offered one of the most dramatic examples of "modernization" gone sour in the Middle East. Despite tremendous economic growth during the 1960s and 1970s, Iranians labored with legacies of foreign intervention and corrupt rule at the hands of the shah, Reza Pahlavi, a Western-friendly leader installed during a 1953 military coup supported by Britain and the United States. In return for the shah's role as a friend to the West during the cold war and for providing a steady source of reasonably priced oil, the Iranian government received vast sums in oil contracts, weapons, and development aid. Thousands of Westerners, especially Americans, also came to Iran, introducing foreign influences that not only challenged traditional local values but also offered new economic and political alternatives. The shah, however, kept these alternatives out of reach, consistently denying democratic representation to "westernizing" middle-class Iranian workers and deeply religious university students alike. He governed through a small aristocracy divided by constant infighting. His army and secret police conducted regular and brutal campaigns of repression. De-

spite this, and the public protests it spurred in the West, governments such as the conservative Nixon administration embraced the shah as a strategically vital ally: an important cold war ally, a key to anti-Soviet alliances, and a safe source of oil.

Twenty-five years after the coup of 1953, the shah's autocratic route to an industrial state came to an end. After a lengthy economic downturn, public unrest, and personal illness, the shah realized he could not continue in power. He simply retired from public life under popular pressure in February 1979. Eight months of uncertainty followed, most Westerners fled the country, and the provisional government appointed by the shah collapsed. The strongest political coalition among Iran's revolutionaries surged into the vacuum—a broad Islamic movement centered on the ayatollah Ruhollah Khomeini (1902–1989), Iran's senior cleric and theologian, returned from exile in France. Other senior clerics and the country's large population of unemployed, deeply religious university students provided the movement's energy. Disenfranchised secular protesters joined the radical Islamists in condemning decades of Western indifference and the shah's oppression. Under the new regime, some limited economic and political populism combined with strict constructions of Islamic law, restrictions on women's public life, and the prohibition of many ideas or activities linked to Western influence.

CHRONOLOGY

MAJOR DEVELOPMENTS IN THE MIDDLE EAST, 1948–PRESENT

Israeli state formed	1948
First Arab-Israeli War	1948–1949
Egypt gains independence	1952
Israeli-Egyptian War	1956
Formation of OPEC	1960
Six-Day War; Israel occupies West Bank	1967
Second Arab-Israeli War	1973
Camp David peace accords	1978
Iran-Iraq War	1980–1990
Persian Gulf war	1991
Palestinians granted self-rule	1995
Israeli-Palestinian conflict continues	present

HOW DID THE GLOBAL DEMAND FOR OIL RESHAPE POLITICS, RELIGION, AND SOCIETY IN THE MIDDLE EAST?

ISRAEL, OIL, AND POLITICAL ISLAM IN THE MIDDLE EAST   825

The new Iranian government also defined itself against its enemies: against the Sunni religious establishment of neighboring Arab states, against "atheistic" Soviet communism, but especially against Israel and the United States. Iranians feared the United States would try to overthrow Khomeini as it had other leaders. Violence in the streets of Tehran reached a peak when militant students stormed the American embassy in November 1979 and seized fifty-two hostages. The act quickly became an international crisis that heralded a new kind of confrontation between Western powers and postcolonial Islamic radicals. President Jimmy Carter's administration ultimately gained the hostages' release, but not before the catalog of earlier failures led to the election of the conservative Ronald Reagan.

IRAN, IRAQ, AND UNINTENDED CONSEQUENCES OF THE COLD WAR

Iran's victory in the hostage crisis was fleeting. During the later part of 1980, Iran's Arab neighbor and tradi- tional rival Iraq invaded, hoping to seize Iran's south- ern oil fields during the revolutionary confusion. Iran counterattacked. The result was a murderous eight- year conflict marked by the use of chemical weapons and human waves of young Iranian radicals fighting the Soviet-armed Iraqis. The war ended with Iran's de- feat, but not the collapse of its theocratic regime. The strongest threats to the Iranian regime ultimately came from within, from a new generation of young students and disenfranchised service workers who found their prospects for prosperity and active citizenship had not changed much since the days of the shah.

The Iran-Iraq conflict created another problem for Western interests and the governments of leading OPEC states: Iraq. Various governments—including an unlikely alliance of France, Saudi Arabia, the So- viet Union, and the United States—supported Iraq during the war in an effort to bring down Iran's cler- ics. Their patronage went to one of the most violent governments in the region, Saddam Hussein's dicta- torship. Iraq exhausted itself in the war, politically and economically. In order to shore up his regime

The Iraqi Threat to Stability in the Middle East: The Case of Jordan. Left: In the wake of the Iraqi invasion and occu- pation of Kuwait, thousands of refugees fled from Kuwait to Jordan, where they were stranded in tent cities. Added to the existing Palestinian refugee problem, this latest wave of displaced people placed an enormous burden on Jordan's fragile economy. Right: Large numbers of Jordanians and Palestinians rallied to Saddam Hussein's call for a "holy war" to free Arab soil of Western imperialists and their agents. Caught between Iraq and an international force led by a U.S. army of over four hundred thousand men and women, the government of King Hussein of Jordan faced the specter of revolution.

and restore Iraq's influence, Hussein looked elsewhere in the region. In 1990 Iraq invaded its small, oil-rich neighbor Kuwait. With the cold war on the wane, Iraq's Soviet supporters would not condone Iraqi aggression. A number of Western nations led by the United States reacted more forcefully. Within months Iraq faced the full weight of the United States military—trained intensively since Vietnam to rout much more capable Soviet-armed forces than Iraq's—along with forces from several OPEC states, French troops, and armored divisions from Britain, Egypt, and Syria. This coalition pummeled Iraqi troops from the air for six weeks, then routed them and retook Kuwait in a brief, well-executed ground campaign. This changed the tenor of relations between the United States and Arab oil producers, encouraging not only closeness between governments but also anti-American radicals angry at a new Western presence. It was also the beginning rather than the end of a Western confrontation with Iraq, centered on Hussein's efforts to develop nuclear and biological weapons.

Elsewhere in the region, the proxy conflicts of the cold war snared both superpowers in the new and growing networks of Islamic radicalism. In 1979 the socialist government of Afghanistan turned against its Soviet patrons. Fearing a result like Iran, with a spread of fundamentalism into the Muslim region of Soviet Central Asia, Moscow responded by overthrowing the Afghan president and installing a pro-Soviet faction. The new government, backed by more than one hundred thousand Soviet troops, found itself immediately at war with fighters who combined local conservatism with militant Islam, and who attracted volunteers from radical Islamic movements in Egypt, Lebanon, Saudi Arabia, and elsewhere. These fighters, who called themselves *mujahidin*, viewed the conflict as a holy war. The *mujahidin* benefited from advanced weapons and training, given by Western powers led by the United States. Those who provided the aid saw the conflict in cold war terms, as a chance to sap Soviet resources in a fruitless imperial war. On those terms the aid worked; the war dragged on for nearly ten years, taking thousands of Russian lives and damaging the Soviet government's credibility at home. Soviet troops withdrew in 1989. After five years of clan warfare, hard-line Islamic factions tied to the foreign elements in the *mujahidin* took over the country. Their experiment in theocracy made Iran's seem mild by comparison.

VIOLENCE BEYOND BOUNDS: WAR AND TERRORISM IN THE TWENTY-FIRST CENTURY

How has globalization changed the politics of terrorism?

The global networks of communication, finance, and mobility discussed at the beginning of this chapter gave radical political violence a disturbing new character at the end of the twentieth century. By the 1980s and increasingly during the 1990s, a new brand of terrorist organization emerged, one that ranged freely across territory and local legal systems. These newer, apocalyptic terrorist groups called for decisive, world-ending conflict to eliminate their enemies and grant themselves martyrdom. Some such groups emerged from the social dislocations of the postwar boom, others were linked directly to brands of radical religion. They often divorced themselves from the local crises that first spurred their anger, roamed widely among countries in search for recruits to their cause.

A leading example of such groups, and soon the most famous, was the radical Islamist umbrella organization al Qaeda. It was created by leaders of the foreign *mujahidin* who had fought in the war against the Soviet Union in Afghanistan. Its official leader and financial supporter was the Saudi-born multimillionaire Osama bin Laden. Among its operational chiefs was the famous Egyptian radical Ayman al-Zawahiri, whose political career linked him directly to Sayyid Qutb and other founding thinkers in modern revolutionary Islam. These leaders organized broad networks of largely self-contained terrorist cells around the world, from the Islamic regions of Southeast Asia to Europe, East Africa, and the United States. Their organization defied borders, and so did their goals. They did not seek to negotiate for territory, or to change the government of a specific state. Instead, they spoke of the destruction of the state of Israel and American, European, and other non-Islamic systems of government worldwide, and called for a united, apocalyptic revolt by fundamentalist Muslims to create an Islamic community bounded only by faith.

New York's World Trade Center towers, September 11, 2001.

At the beginning of the twenty-first century, al Qaeda's organizers struck again at their most obvious political enemy, the symbolic seat of "globalization": the United States. Small teams of suicidal radicals, aided by al Qaeda's banner organization, planned to hijack airliners and use them as flying bombs to strike the most strategically important symbols of America's global power. On September 11, 2001, they carried through this mission in the deadliest series of terrorist attacks ever to occur on American soil. In the space of an hour, hijacked planes struck the Pentagon—the headquarters of the U.S. military—and the commercial hub of the World Trade Center in New York City. A fourth plane, possibly aimed at the U.S. Capitol, crashed in open farmland, its attack compromised when the passengers fought back against their captors. The World Trade Center towers, among the tallest buildings in the world, crumbled into ash and wreckage in front of hundreds of millions of viewers on satellite television and the Internet. In these several simultaneous attacks roughly three thousand people died.

The bombing was at once a new brand of terror, deeply indebted to globalization in both its outlook and method, and something older: the extreme, opportunistic violence of marginal groups against national cultures during a period of general dislocation and uncertainty. The immediate American response was action against al Qaeda's central haven in Afghanistan, a state in total collapse after the warfare of the previous thirty years (see above). The United States quickly routed al Qaeda's Taliban sponsors and scattered the terrorists themselves. That effort, however, failed to pinpoint and eliminate the hidden networks of leadership, finance, and information that propel apocalyptic terrorism. The rebuilding and rehabilitation of Afghanistan, a necessary consequence of American and European action, began from almost nothing in terms of administration and infrastructure; pressing crises elsewhere and the changeable nature of Western popular concerns made a recovery difficult.

One reason for the persistent fears about such groups has to do with the increasing power and availability of weapons they might use: chemical substances, biological agents that could kill millions, even portable nuclear weapons. With the end of the cold war, methods and technologies that the superpowers employed to maintain their nuclear "balance of terror" became more available on the margins to displaced groups with the financial or political leverage to seek them out. Anxiety that states such as Iraq might transfer such weapons to apocalyptic terrorists, a fear given new life after the attacks on New York and Washington, provided the rationale for an American-led invasion of Iraq in the spring of 2003. The campaign, which used a remarkably small force both on the ground and in the air, quickly took Iraq over and deposed Hussein. No immediate evidence of recent, active weapons development programs were found, however, and in the process the United States inherited the complex reconstruction of a broken state, punctuated by guerilla violence and anti-Western terrorism.

A similar threat remained present in North Korea. After the loss of Soviet patronage in 1991, the isolated North Korean state careened from one economic disaster to another, with verified reports of local starvation in some regions of the country and a breakdown of government into military and political fiefdoms. The North Korean government pursued the development of a nuclear arsenal as a bargaining chip against the other major states of northeast Asia and the United States. Those neighbors each understood the grim chance that North Korea might break the last and perhaps most crucial nuclear threshold, providing nuclear weapons not to hard-pressed states but instead to stateless organizations. By the early twenty-first century, warfare and the terrifying killing power of modern technology, threatened to elude the control of national states and clearly defined political communities.

CONCLUSION

In such a complex world, the loss of familiar moorings makes fundamental questions about human behavior and political community difficult to answer. History offers no quick solutions. Historians are loath to offer what historian Peter Novick calls "pithy lessons that fit on a bumper sticker." As Novick puts it:

> If there is, to use a pretentious word, any wisdom to be acquired from contemplating an historical event, I would think it would derive from confronting it in all its complexity and its contradictions; the ways in which it resembles other events to which it might be compared as well as the way it differs from them. . . . If there are lessons to be extracted from encountering the past, that encounter has to be with the past in all its messiness; they're not likely to come from an encounter with a past that's been shaped so that inspiring lessons will emerge.

The untidy and contradictory evidence that historians discover in the archives rarely yields unblemished heroes or unvarnished villains. Instead, good history reveals to us the complex processes and dynamics of change over time. It does help us understand the many layers of the past that have formed and constrain us in our present world. At the same time, it shows again and again that these constraints do not preordain what happens next or how we can make the history of the future.

KEY TERMS

globalization

AIDS

DNA

Nelson Mandela

Rwanda

intifada

OPEC

Sayyid Qutb

Saddam Hussein

al Qaeda

SELECTED READINGS

Achebe, Chinua. *Things Fall Apart.* Expanded edition with notes. Portsmouth, N.H., 1996. An annotated edition of the now classic novel about postcolonial Africa.

Bates, Robert H. *Essays on the Political Economy of Rural Africa.* Cambridge, 1983. Still an important study of debt, food production, and postcolonial Africa, written at the leading edge of the sub-Saharan debt crisis.

Coetzee, J.M. *Waiting for the Barbarians.* London, 1980. A searing critique of apartheid-era South Africa by a leading Afrikaner novelist.

Cooper, Frederick. *Colonialism in Question: Theory, Knowledge, History.* Los Angeles and Berkeley, 2005.

———— "What is the Concept of Globalization Good For? An African Historian's Perspective." *African Affairs* (2001). Helpful critical analysis, and a useful antidote to loose use of the term.

Geyer, Michael, and Charles Bright. "World History in a Global Age." *American Historical Review* (October 1995). An excellent short discussion.

Held, David, et al. *Global Transformations: Politics, Economics, and Culture.* Stanford, 1999. Major survey of the globalization of culture, finance, criminality, and politics.

Hopkins, A. G., ed. *Globalization in World History.* New York, 2002. Written by one of the first historians to engage social scientific debates on globalization. Excellent introduction and articles on different stages of globalization.

Keddie, Nikki. *Modern Iran: Roots and Results of Revolution.* New Haven, 2003. A revised edition of her major study of Iran's 1979 revolution, with added perspective on Iran's Islamic government.

Lacqueur, Walter. *The Age of Terrorism.* Boston, 1987. An important study of the first wave of post-1960s terrorism.

Landes, David. *The Wealth and Poverty of Nations: Why Some Are So Rich and Some So Poor.* New York, 1998. Leading economic historian's account of globalization's effects on the international economy.

Lewis, Bernard. *The Crisis of Islam: Holy War and Unholy Terror.* New York, 2003. Conservative scholar of the Arab world discussing the political crises that fueled terrorism.

McNeill, J. R. *Something New Under the Sun: An Environmental History of the Twentieth-Century World.* New York and London, 2000. Fascinating new approach to environmental history.

Ngugi wa Thiong'o. *Petals of Blood.* New York, 1977. A scathing critique of neocolonialism in Kenya by Africa's best-known novelist.

Novick, Peter. *The Holocaust in American Life.* Boston, 1999.

Power, Samantha. *The Problem from Hell: America in the Age of Genocide.* A prize-winning survey of the entire twentieth century, its genocides, and the different human rights movements that responded to them.

Reynolds, David. *One World Divisible: A Global History since 1945.* New York and London, 2000. Excellent study of the different dimensions of globalization.

Shlaim, Avi. *The Iron Wall: Israel and the Arab World.* New York, 2000. Leading Israeli historian on the evolution of Israel's defensive foreign policy.

Stiglitz, Joseph E. *Globalization and Its Discontents.* New York, 2002. A recent and important consideration of contemporary globalization's character and the conflicts it creates, particularly over commerce and culture.

Shilts, Randy. *And the Band Played On: Politics, People, and the AIDS Epidemic.* New York, 1987. An impassioned attack on the individuals and governments that failed to come to grips with the early spread of the disease.

Turkle, Sherry. *Life on the Screen: Identity in the Age of the Internet.* New York, 1995. An important early study of "Web culture" and the fluid possibilities of electronic communication.

RULERS OF PRINCIPAL STATES

THE CAROLINGIAN DYNASTY

Pepin of Heristal, Mayor of the Palace, 687–714
Charles Martel, Mayor of the Palace, 715–741
Pepin III, Mayor of the Palace, 741–751; King, 751–768
Charlemagne, King, 768–814; Emperor, 800–814
Louis the Pious, Emperor, 814–840

MIDDLE KINGDOMS
Lothair, Emperor, 840–855
Louis (Italy), Emperor, 855–875
Charles (Provence), King, 855–863
Lothair II (Lorraine), King, 855–869

WEST FRANCIA
Charles the Bald, King, 840–877; Emperor, 875–877
Louis II, King, 877–879
Louis III, King, 879–882
Carloman, King, 879–884

EAST FRANCIA
Ludwig, King, 840–876
Carloman, King, 876–880
Ludwig, King, 876–882
Charles the Fat, Emperor, 876–887

HOLY ROMAN EMPERORS

SAXON DYNASTY
Otto I, 962–973
Otto II, 973–983
Otto III, 983–1002
Henry II, 1002–1024

FRANCONIAN DYNASTY
Conrad II, 1024–1039
Henry III, 1039–1056
Henry IV, 1056–1106
Henry V, 1106–1125
Lothair II (Saxony), 1125–1137

HOHENSTAUFEN DYNASTY
Conrad III, 1138–1152
Frederick I (Barbarossa), 1152–1190
Henry VI, 1190–1197
Philip of Swabia, 1198–1208 } Rivals
Otto IV (Welf), 1198–1215
Frederick II, 1220–1250
Conrad IV, 1250–1254

INTERREGNUM, 1254–1273

EMPERORS FROM VARIOUS DYNASTIES
Rudolf I (Habsburg), 1273–1291
Adolf (Nassau), 1292–1298
Albert I (Habsburg), 1298–1308
Henry VII (Luxemburg), 1308–1313
Ludwig IV (Wittelsbach), 1314–1347
Charles IV (Luxemburg), 1347–1378
Wenceslas (Luxemburg), 1378–1400
Rupert (Wittelsbach), 1400–1410
Sigismund (Luxemburg), 1410–1437

HABSBURG DYNASTY
Albert II, 1438–1439
Frederick III, 1440–1493
Maximilian I, 1493–1519
Charles V, 1519–1556
Ferdinand I, 1556–1564
Maximilian II, 1564–1576
Rudolf II, 1576–1612

Matthias, 1612–1619
Ferdinand II, 1619–1637
Ferdinand III, 1637–1657
Leopold I, 1658–1705
Joseph I, 1705–1711
Charles VI, 1711–1740

Charles VII (not a Habsburg), 1742–1745
Francis I, 1745–1765
Joseph II, 1765–1790
Leopold II, 1790–1792
Francis II, 1792–1806

RULERS OF FRANCE FROM HUGH CAPET

CAPETIAN DYNASTY
Hugh Capet, 987–996
Robert II, 996–1031
Henry I, 1031–1060
Philip I, 1060–1108
Louis VI, 1108–1137
Louis VII, 1137–1180
Philip II (Augustus), 1180–1223
Louis VIII, 1223–1226
Louis IX (St. Louis), 1226–1270
Philip III, 1270–1285
Philip IV, 1285–1314
Louis X, 1314–1316
Philip V, 1316–1322
Charles IV, 1322–1328

VALOIS DYNASTY
Philip VI, 1328–1350
John, 1350–1364
Charles V, 1364–1380
Charles VI, 1380–1422
Charles VII, 1422–1461
Louis XI, 1461–1483
Charles VIII, 1483–1498
Louis XII, 1498–1515
Francis I, 1515–1547

Henry II, 1547–1559
Francis II, 1559–1560
Charles IX, 1560–1574
Henry III, 1574–1589

BOURBON DYNASTY
Henry IV, 1589–1610
Louis XIII, 1610–1643
Louis XIV, 1643–1715
Louis XV, 1715–1774
Louis XVI, 1774–1792

AFTER 1792
First Republic, 1792–1799
Napoleon Bonaparte, First Consul, 1799–1804
Napoleon I, Emperor, 1804–1814
Louis XVIII (Bourbon dynasty), 1814–1824
Charles X (Bourbon dynasty), 1824–1830
Louis Philippe, 1830–1848
Second Republic, 1848–1852
Napoleon III, Emperor, 1852–1870
Third Republic, 1870–1940
Péain regime, 1940–1944
Provisional government, 1944–1946
Fourth Republic, 1946–1958
Fifth Republic, 1958–

RULERS OF ENGLAND

ANGLO-SAXON DYNASTY
Alfred the Great, 871–899
Edward the Elder, 899–924
Ethelstan, 924–939
Edmund I, 939–946
Edred, 946–955
Edwy, 955–959
Edgar, 959–975
Edward the Martyr, 975–978
Ethelred the Unready, 978–1016

Canute, 1016–1035 (Danish Nationality)
Harold I, 1035–1040
Hardicanute, 1040–1042
Edward the Confessor, 1042–1066
Harold II, 1066

HOUSE OF NORMANDY
William I (the Conqueror), 1066–1087
William II, 1087–1100

Henry I, 1100–1135
Stephen, 1135–1154

HOUSE OF PLANTAGENET
Henry II, 1154–1189
Richard I, 1189–1199
John, 1199–1216
Henry III, 1216–1272
Edward I, 1272–1307
Edward II, 1307–1327
Edward III, 1327–1377
Richard II, 1377–1399

HOUSE OF LANCASTER
Henry IV, 1399–1413
HenryV, 1413–1422
Henry VI, 1422–1461

HOUSE OF YORK
Edward IV, 1461–1483
Edward V, 1483
Richard III, 1483–1485

HOUSE OF TUDOR
Henry VII, 1485–1509
Henry VIII, 1509–1547
Edward VI, 1547–1553
Mary, 1553–1558
Elizabeth I, 1558–1603

HOUSE OF STUART
James I, 1603–1625
Charles I, 1625–1649

COMMONWEALTH AND PROTECTORATE, 1649–1659

HOUSE OF STUART RESTORED
Charles II, 1660–1685
James II, 1685–1688
William III and Mary II, 1689–1694
William III alone, 1694–1702
Anne, 1702–1714

HOUSE OF HANOVER
George I, 1714–1727
George II, 1727–1760
George III, 1760–1820
George IV, 1820–1830
William IV, 1830–1837
Victoria, 1837–1901

HOUSE OF SAXE-COBURG-GOTHA
Edward VII, 1901–1910
GeorgeV, 1910–1917

HOUSE OF WINDSOR
George V, 1917–1936
Edward VIII, 1936
George VI, 1936–1952
Elizabeth II, 1952–

RULERS OF AUSTRIA AND AUSTRIA-HUNGARY

*Maximilian I (Archduke), 1493–1519
*Charles V, 1519–1556
*Ferdinand I, 1556–1564
*Maximilian II, 1564–1576
*Rudolf II, 1576–1612
*Matthias, 1612–1619
*Ferdinand II, 1619–1637
*Ferdinand III, 1637–1657
*Leopold I, 1658–1705
*Joseph I, 1705–1711
*Charles VI, 1711–1740
Maria Theresa, 1740–1780

*also bore title of Holy Roman Emperor

*Joseph II, 1780–1790
*Leopold II, 1790–1792
*Francis II, 1792–1835 (Emperor of Austria as Francis I after 1804)
Ferdinand I, 1835–1848
Francis Joseph, 1848–1916 (after 1867 Emperor of Austria and King of Hungary)
Charles I, 1916–1918 (Emperor of Austria and King of Hungary)
Republic of Austria, 1918–1938 (dictatorship after 1934)
Republic restored, under Allied occupation, 1945–1956
Free Republic, 1956–
*Frederick I, 1701–1713
*Frederick William I, 1713–1740
*Frederick II (the Great), 1740–1786

RULERS OF PRUSSIA AND GERMANY

*Frederick William II, 1786–1797
*Frederick William III,1797–1840
*Frederick William IV, 1840–1861
*William I, 1861–1888 (German Emperor after 1871)
Frederick III, 1888
*William II, 1888–1918
Weimar Republic, 1918–1933
Third Reich (Nazi Dictatorship), 1933–1945

*Kings of Prussia

Allied occupation, 1945–1952
Division into Federal Republic of Germany in west and
    German Democratic Republic in east, 1949–1991
Federal Republic of Germany (united), 1991–

RULERS OF RUSSIA

Ivan III, 1462–1505
Vasily III, 1505–1533
Ivan IV, 1533–1584
Theodore I, 1534–1598
Boris Godunov, 1598–1605
Theodore II,1605
Vasily IV, 1606–1610
Michael, 1613–1645
Alexius, 1645–1676
Theodore III, 1676–1682
Ivan V and Peter I, 1682–1689
Peter I (the Great), 1689–1725
Catherine I, 1725–1727
Peter II, 1727–1730

Anna, 1730–1740
Ivan VI, 1740–1741
Ellzabeth, 1741–1762
Peter III, 1762
Catherine II (the Great), 1762–1796
Paul, 1796–1801
Alexander I,1801–1825
Nicholas I, 1825–1855
Alexander II,1855–1881
Alexander III, 1881–1894
Nicholas II, 1894–1917
Soviet Republic, 1917–1991
Russian Federation, 1991–

RULERS OF SPAIN

Ferdinand { and Isabella, 1479–1504
          { and Philip I, 1504–1506
          { and Charles I, 1506–1516
Charles I (Holy Roman Emperor Charles V), 1516–1556
Philip II, 1556–1598
Philip III, 1598–1621
Philip IV, 1621–1665
Charles II, 1665–1700
Philip V, 1700–1746
Ferdinand VI, 1746–1759
Charles III, 1759–1788
Charles IV, 1788–1808

Ferdinand VII, 1808
Joseph Bonaparte, 1808–1813
Ferdinand VII (restored), 1814–1833
Isabella II, 1833–1868
Republic, 1868–1870
Amadeo, 1870–1873
Republic, 1873–1874
Alfonso XII, 1874–1885
Alfonso XIII, 1886–1931
Republic, 1931–1939
Fascist Dictatorship, 1939–1975
Juan Carlos I, 1975–

RULERS OF ITALY

Victor Emmanuel II, 1861–1878
Humbert I, 1878–1900
Victor Emmanuel III, 1900–1946

Fascist Dictatorship, 1922-1943 (maintained in northern Italy until 1945)
Humbert II, May 9–June 13, 1946
Republic, 1946–

PROMINENT POPES

Silvester I, 314–335
Leo I, 440–461
Gelasius I, 492–496
Gregory I, 590–604
Nicholas I, 858–867
Silvester II, 999–1003
Leo IX, 1049–1054
Nicholas II, 1058–1061
Gregory VII, 1073–1085
Urban II, 1088–1099
Paschal II, 1099–1118
Alexander III, 1159–1181
Innocent III, 1198–1216
Gregory IX, 1227–1241
Innocent IV, 1243–1254
Boniface VIII, 1294–1303
John XXII, 1316–1334
Nicholas V, 1447–1455
Pius II, 1458–1464

Alexander VI, 1492–1503
Julius II, 1503–1513
Leo X, 1513–1521
Paul III, 1534–1549
Paul IV, 1555–1559
Sixtus V, 1585–1590
Urban VIII, 1623–1644
Gregory XVI, 1831–1846
Pius IX, 1846–1878
Leo XIII, 1878–1903
Pius X, 1903–1914
Benedict XV, 1914–1922
Pius XI, 1922–1939
Pius XII, 1939–1958
John XXIII, 1958–1963
Paul VI, 1963–1978
John Paul I, 1978
John Paul II, 1978–

GLOSSARY

Peter Abelard (1079–1142) Famed French theologian, logician, and university lecturer.

Absolutism Form of government in which one body, usually the monarch, controls the right to make war, tax, judge, and coin money. The term was often used to refer to the state monarchies in seventeenth- and eighteenth-century Europe.

Abstract Expressionism The mid-twentieth-century school of art based in New York that included Jackson Pollock, Willem de Kooning, and Franz Kline. It emphasized form, color, gesture, and feeling instead of figurative subjects.

acid rain Precipitation laced with heavy doses of sulfur, mainly from coal-fired plants.

African National Congress (ANC) Multiracial organization founded in 1912 whose goal was to end racial discrimination in South Africa.

Afrikaners Descendants of the original Dutch settlers of South Africa; formerly referred to as Boers.

AIDS Acquired immune deficiency syndrome. AIDS first appeared in the 1970s and has developed into a global health catastrophe; it is spreading most quickly in developing nations in Africa and Asia.

Akhenaten The fourteenth-century B.C.E. pharaoh who developed a sun-oriented religion and ultimately damaged Egypt's position in the ancient world.

Alexander (356–323 B.C.E.) The Macedonian general who conquered northwest Asia Minor, and Persia, and built an empire that stretched as far east as the Indus River.

Allied Powers The World War I coalition of Great Britain, Ireland, Belgium, France, Italy, Russia, Portugal, Greece, Serbia, Montenegro, Albania, and Romania.

al-Qaeda The radical Islamic organization founded in the late 1980s by former *mujahedin* who had fought against the Soviet Union in Afghanistan. Al-Qaeda carried out the 9/11 terrorist attacks and is responsible as well for attacks in Africa, Southeast Asia, Europe, and the Middle East.

Amnesty International Nongovernmental organization formed in 1961 to defend "prisoners of conscience"—those detained for their beliefs, color, sex, ethnic origin, language, or religion.

Anabaptists Swiss Protestant movement that began in 1521 and insisted that only adults could be baptized Christians. The movement's first generation, who had been baptized as infants according to Catholic practice, was "re-baptized," hence the name.

Anarchism The social and political movement that began in the mid-nineteenth century and advocated the destruction of the state through violence and terrorism.

Apartheid The racial segregation policy of the Afrikaner-dominated South African government. Legislated in 1948 by the Afrikaner National Party, it existed in South Africa for many years.

aqueducts Engineering system that brought water from the mountains down to Roman cities.

Saint Thomas Aquinas (1225–1274) Italian Dominican monk and theologian whose intellectual style encouraged the study of ancient philosophers and science as complementary to theology.

Arians The fourth-century followers of a priest named Arius, who rejected the idea that Christ could be equal with God.

Asiatic Society A cultural organization founded in 1784 by British Orientalists who lauded native culture but believed in colonial rule.

Assyrians A Semitic-speaking people that emerged around 2400 B.C.E. in northern Mesopotamia. Their highly militarized empire dominated Near-Eastern politics for close to two thousands years.

astrolabe An ancient navigational instrument, thought to have been invented in 150 B.C.E., that was used to find latitude while at sea.

Atlantic system A system of trade and expansion that linked Europe, Africa, and the Americas. It emerged in the sixteenth century in the wake of European voyages across the Atlantic Ocean.

Saint Augustine (c. 354–397) One of the most influential Christian theologians of all time, Saint Augustine described his conversion in his autobiographical *Confessions* and formulated new aspects of Christian theology in *On the City of God*.

Augustus (63 B.C.E.–14 C.E.) The grandnephew and adopted son of Julius Caesar and first emperor of the Roman empire.

Auschwitz-Birkenau The Nazi concentration camp in Poland that was designed to systematically murder Jews and gypsies. Between 1942 and 1944 over one million people were killed in Auschwitz-Birkenau.

Austro-Hungarian empire   The dual monarchy established by the Habsburg family in 1867; it collapsed at the end of World War I.

authoritarianism   A centralized and dictatorial form of government, proclaimed by its adherents to be superior to parliamentary democracy and especially effective at mobilizing the masses. Authoritarianism was prominent in the 1930s.

Avignon   City on the southeastern border of France. Between 305 and 378 it was the seat of the papacy.

Aztecs   Native American people of central Mexico; their empire was conquered by the Spanish in the sixteenth century.

baby boom (1950s)   The post–World War II upswing in U.S. birth rates; it reversed a century of decline.

Baghdad Pact (1955)   The Middle Eastern military alliance among countries friendly with America who were also willing to align themselves with the Western countries against the Soviet Union.

Balfour Declaration   A letter dated November 2, 1917, by Lord Arthur J. Balfour, British Foreign Secretary, that promised a homeland for the Jews in Palestine.

Baroque   An ornate style of art and music associated with the Counter Reformation (from the French word for "irregularly shaped pearl").

Bay of Pigs (1961)   The unsuccessful invasion of Cuba by Cuban exiles, supported by the U.S. government. The rebels intended to incite an insurrection in Cuba and overthrow the Communist regime of Fidel Castro.

Beer Hall Putsch (1923)   The Nazi invasion of a meeting of Bavarian leaders and supporters in a Munich beer hall; Adolf Hitler was imprisoned for a year after the incident.

Saint Benedict of Nursia (c. 480–c. 547)   Considered the father of western monasticism, Saint Benedict created the Benedictine rule that became the guide for nearly all western monks. Monks were required to follow the rules laid down by Saint Benedict: poverty, sexual chastity, obedience, labor, and religious devotion.

Berlin Airlift (1948)   The supply of vital necessities to West Berlin by air transport primarily under U.S. auspices. It was initiated in response to a blockade of the city that had been instituted by the Soviet Union to force the Allies to abandon West Berlin.

Berlin Wall   The wall built in 1961 by East German Communists to prevent citizens of East Germany from fleeing to West Germany; it was torn down in 1989.

Bill of Rights   The first ten amendments to the U.S. Constitution; it was ratified in 1791.

Otto von Bismarck (1815–1890)   The prime minister of Prussia and later the first chancellor of Germany, Bismarck helped consolidate the German people's economic and military power.

Black Death   The epidemic of bubonic plague that ravaged Europe, East Asia, and North Africa in the fourteenth century, killing one-third of the European population.

Black Jacobins   A nickname for the rebels in Saint Domingue, including Toussaint L'Ouverture, a former slave who in 1791 led the slaves of this French colony in the largest and most successful slave insurrection.

Black Panthers   A radical African American group that came together in the 1960s; the Black Panthers advocated black separatism and pan-Africanism.

Blackshirts   The troops of Mussolini's fascist regime; the squads received money from Italian landowners to attack socialist leaders.

Black Tuesday (October 24, 1929)   The day on which the U.S. stock market crashed, plunging the U.S. and international trading systems into crisis and leading the world into the "Great Depression."

Blitzkreig   The German "lightning war" strategy used during World War II; the Germans invaded Poland, France, Russia, and other countries with fast-moving well-coordinated attacks using aircraft, tanks and other armored vehicles, followed by infantry.

Bloody Sunday   On Sunday, January 22, 1905, the Russian tsar's guards killed 130 demonstrators who were protesting the tsar's mistreatment of workers and the middle class.

Giovanni Boccaccio (1313–1375)   Italian prose writer famed for his *Decameron*, one hundred short stories about the human condition, mostly from a comic or cynical point of view.

Boer War   Conflict between British and ethnically European Afrikaners in South Africa, 1898–1902, with terrible casualties on both sides.

Simon de Bolivar (1783–1830)   Venezuelan-born general called "The Liberator" for his assistance in helping Bolivia, Panama, Colombia, Ecuador, Peru, and Venezuela win independence from Spain.

Bolsheviks   Former members of the Russian Social Democratic Party who advocated the destruction of capitalist political and economic institutions and started the Russian Revolution. In 1918 the Bolsheviks changed their name to the Russian Communist Party.

Napoleon Bonaparte (1769–1821)   Corsican-born French general who seized power and ruled as dictator 1799–1814. After successful conquest of much of Europe, he was defeated by Russian and Prussian forces and died in exile.

Bourgeoisie   The French term for the middle class, which emerged in Europe during the Middle Ages. The Bourgeoisie sought to be recognized not by birth or title, but by capital and property.

Boxer Uprising (1899–1900)   Chinese peasant movement that opposed foreign influence, especially that of Christian missionaries; it was finally put down after the Boxers were defeated by a foreign army comprised mostly of Japanese, Russian, British, French, and American soldiers.

British Commonwealth of Nations   Formed in 1926, the Commonwealth conferred "dominion status" on Britain's white settler colonies in Canada, Australia, and New Zealand.

Brownshirts   Troops of young German men who dedicated themselves to the Nazi cause in the early 1930s by holding street marches, mass rallies, and confrontations. They engaged in beatings of Jews and anyone who opposed the Nazis.

bubonic plague   An acute infectious disease caused by a bacterium that is transmitted to humans by fleas from infected rats. It ravaged Europe and parts of Asia in the fourteenth century. Sometimes referred to as the "black death."

Julius Caesar (100–44 B.C.E.) The Roman general who conquered the Gauls, invaded Britain, and expanded Rome's territory in Asia Minor. He became the dictator of Rome in 46 B.C.E. and was murdered by Brutus and Cassius, which led to the rise of Augustus and the end of the Roman republic.

caliphs Rulers of the Islamic community who claimed descent from Muhammad.

John Calvin (1509–1564) French-born Protestant theologian who stressed the predestination of all human beings according to God's will.

Canary Islands Islands off the western coast of Africa conquered by Portugal and Spain in the mid-1400s. Used to supply expeditions around the African coast and across the Atlantic.

Canterbury Tales Middle English verse stories by Geoffrey Chaucer (c.1340–1400) that reflect different classes and experiences in late medieval England.

caravans Companies of men who transported and traded goods along overland routes in North Africa and central Asia; large caravans consisted of 600 to 1,000 camels and as many as 400 men.

caravel Sailing vessel suited for nosing in and out of estuaries and navigating in waters with unpredictable currents and winds.

Carthage A great maritime empire that rivaled Rome; at its height, it stretched across the northern coast of Africa from modern-day Tunisia to the Strait of Gibraltar. Carthage fought against Rome in the Punic Wars that began in 264 B.C.E. The wars ended with the destruction of Carthage in 146 B.C.E.

Cassiodorus (490–583) Author of the *Institutes*, which instructed medieval readers on the essential works of literature a monk should know before moving on to more intensive study of theology and the Bible.

caste system A hierarchical system of organizing people and distributing labor, often based on heredity or regional origin.

Baldassare Castiglione (1478–1529) Author of *The Book of the Courtier*, a popular treatise on upper-class social graces.

Catherine the Great (1729–1796) German-born empress of Russia who maintained an absolutist feudal system but encouraged Enlightenment philosophy and the arts at court.

Catholicism Branch of Christianity headed by the pope.

Camillo Benso di Cavour (1810–1861) Anti-papist Italian leader who led the initial stages of revolution against the Habsburgs.

Central Powers The World War I alliance between Germany, Austro-Hungary, Bulgaria, and Turkey.

Charlemagne (742–814) Frankish ruler 767–813 who consolidated much of western Europe by adding Lombardy and Saxony to the Frankish kingdoms. With a strong sense of divine purpose, he forced the Christian conversion of pagan peoples and sponsored arts and learning at court. In 800 he became the first Roman emperor in the west since the 5th century.

Chartism (1834–1848) Mass democratic movement to pass the Peoples' Charter in Britain, granting male suffrage, secret ballot, equal electoral districts, and annual Parliaments, and absolving the requirement of property ownership for members of Parliament.

Chernobyl (1986) Site of the world's worst nuclear power accident; in Ukraine, formerly part of the Soviet Union.

chivalry From the word for "horsemanship"; an aristocratic ideology originating with the knights of eleventh-century Europe that encouraged military prowess and social graces.

Winston Churchill (1874–1965) The British prime minister who led the country during World War II. He also coined the phrase "Iron Curtain" in a speech at Westminster College in 1946.

Church of England Founded by Henry VIII in the 1530s after his excommunication from the Catholic Church by Pope Clement VII, it is the established form of Christianity in England.

Cicero (106–43 B.C.E.) The most famous Stoic philosopher and orator of Rome.

Civil Rights Act (1964) U.S. legislation that banned segregation in public facilities, outlawed racial discrimination in employment, and marked an important step in correcting legal inequality.

Civil War (1861–1865) Conflict between the northern and southern states of America that cost over 600,000 lives; this struggle led to the abolition of slavery in the United States.

Cluny A Benedictine monastery, founded in 910, whose reform ideology tried to separate its network of religious houses from control by lay people.

Cold War (1945–1990) Ideological conflict in which the U.S.S.R. and Eastern Europe opposed the United States and Western Europe.

collectivization The process under Stalin in the 1920s and 1930s where peasants were forced to give up private farmland and join collective farms, which were supported by the state.

Colons French settler population in Algeria that ran the colonial government between 1830 and 1962.

Committee of Public Safety Political body during the French Revolution that was controlled by the Jacobins, who enforced party rule by executing thousands during the Reign of Terror, September 1793–July 1794.

***The Communist Manifesto* (1818–1883)** Radical pamphlet by Karl Marx that predicted the downfall of the capitalist system and its replacement by a system that operated in the interests of the working class (proletariat).

Compromise of 1867 Agreement between the Habsburgs and the peoples living in Hungarian parts of the empire that the Habsburg state would be officially known as the Austro-Hungarian Empire.

concession areas Territories, usually ports, established by the 1842 Treaty of Nanjing, where Chinese emperors allowed European merchants to trade and European people to settle.

Congo Independent State Large colonial state in Africa created by Leopold II, king of Belgium, during the 1880s, and ruled by him alone. After reports of mass slaughter and enslavement, the Belgian parliament took the land and formed a Belgian colony.

Congress of Vienna (1814–1815) International conference to reorganize Europe after the downfall of Napoleon. European monarchies agreed to respect each other's borders and to cooperate in guarding against future revolutions and war.

Conquistador Spanish term for "conqueror," applied to European leaders of campaigns against indigenous peoples in central and southern America.

conservativism   Reactionary mode of thinking that held that tradition, including hereditary monarchy, would dispel the divisive ideas of the Enlightenment.

Constantinople   Former capital of the Byzantine empire, eventually renamed Istanbul after its conquest by the Ottomans in 1453.

Constitutional Convention (1787)   Meeting to formulate the Constitution of the United States of America.

Nicholas Copernicus (1473–1543)   Polish astronomer who advanced the radical idea that the earth moved around the sun in *De Revolutionibus*.

Corn Laws   Laws that imposed tariffs on grain imported to Great Britain, intended to protect British farming interests. The Corn Laws were abolished in 1846 as part of a British movement in favor of free trade.

Council of Trent   Intermittent meeting of Catholic leaders (1545–1563) that reaffirmed Catholic doctrine against Protestant criticisms while also reforming the church.

Counter Reformation Movement   To counter the spread of the Reformation, the Counter Reformation was initiated by the Catholic Church at the Council of Trent in 1545.

coup d'état   Overthrow of established state by a group of conspirators, usually from the military.

courtly love   Codes of refined romantic behavior between men and women of high station.

courtly romances   Long narrative poems written in vernacular languages based on myths and legends but expressing ideals of medieval aristocratic conduct.

creoles   Persons of European descent who were born in the West Indies or Spanish America.

Crimean War (1854–1856)   War waged by Russia against Great Britain and France. Spurred by Russia's encroachment on Ottoman territories, the conflict revealed Russia's military weakness when Russian forces fell to British and French troops.

Oliver Cromwell (1599–1658)   Puritan leader of the Parliamentary army that defeated the royalist forces in the English Civil War. After the 1649 execution of King Charles I and dispersion of Parliament, Cromwell ruled as self-styled Lord Protector from 1653 until his death.

Crusades (1096 to 1291)   Series of wars undertaken to free Jerusalem and the Holy Lands from Muslim control.

Cuban Missile Crisis (1962)   Diplomatic standoff between the United States and the Soviet Union that was provoked by the Soviet Union's attempt to base nuclear missiles in Cuba; it brought the world closer to nuclear war than ever before or since.

"Cult of domesticity"   Concept associated with Victorian England that idealized women as nurturing wives and mothers.

Cult of the Virgin Mary   A surge in veneration of the mother of Jesus beginning in the twelfth century that seemed to portend a change in how women were regarded as religious and moral beings.

cuneiform   One of the earliest writing systems, beginning around 3500 B.C.E., it was the Mesopotamian form of writing on clay tablets using a stylus.

Cyrus (c.585–529 B.C.E.)   The ruler of the Persians from circa 559 B.C.E. until 529 B.C.E.

Charles Darwin (1809–1882)   British naturalist who wrote *Origin of the Species* and developed the theory of natural selection to explain the evolution of organisms.

David   King of the Hebrews from around 1000 B.C.E. to 973 B.C.E. David united Israel and made Jerusalem his capital.

Leonardo da Vinci (1452–1519)   Florentine painter, architect, musician, and inventor whose breadth of interests typifies Renaissance ideals.

D-Day (June 6, 1944)   Date of the Allied invasion of Normandy under General Dwight Eisenhower to liberate Western Europe from German occupation.

Decembrists   Russian army officers who were influenced by events in France and formed secret societies that espoused liberal governance. They were put down by Nicholas I in December 1825.

Declaration of Independence   Historic U.S. document stating the principles of government on which America was founded.

Declaration of the Rights of Man and Citizen (1789)   French charter of liberties formulated by the National Assembly that marked the end of dynastic and aristocratic rule. The seventeen articles later became the preamble to the new constitution, which the Assembly finished in 1791.

Olympe de Gouges (1745–1793)   French political radical and feminist whose *Declaration of the Rights of Women* demanded an equal place for women in the new French republic.

Dhimmis   "Peoples of the Book"; i.e., Jews and Christians, who were given a protected but subordinate place in Muslim society.

Charles Dickens (1812–1870)   Hugely popular English novelist whose fiction exposed urban crime, poverty, and injustice but maintained Victorian domestic ideals.

Dien Bien Phu (1954)   Defining battle in the war between French colonialists and the Viet Minh that secured North Vietnam for Ho Chi Minh and his army and left the south to form its own government to be supported by France and the United States.

The Diet of Worms   Examination of Luther by a church council in 1521. The council condemned him, and Luther was rescued by Frederick of Saxony.

Directory   Temporary military committee that took over the affairs of the state of France in 1795 from the radicals and held control until the coup of Napoleon Bonaparte.

Discourse on Method   Philosophical treatise by René Descartes (1596–1650) proposing that the path to knowledge was through logical speculation, beginning with one's own self: "I think, therefore I am."

Divine Comedy   Italian verse narrative by Dante Alighieri (1265–1321); its complex themes exemplify the concerns of medieval learning.

DNA (deoxyribonucleic acid)   Discovered by James Watson and Francis Crick in 1953, DNA contains an organism's genetic information and hereditary characteristics.

Dominion in the British Commonwealth   Canadian promise to keep up their fealty to the British crown, even after their independence in 1867. Later applied to Australia and New Zealand.

Don Quixote   Comical adventure by Spanish writer Miguel de Cervantes (1547–1616) that mocks chivalric ideas.

Dreyfus Affair   The 1894 French scandal surrounding accusations that a Jewish captain, Alfred Dreyfus, sold military secrets to the Germans. Convicted, Dreyfus was sentenced to life in prison. However, after public outcry, it was revealed that the trial documents were forgeries and Dreyfus was released.

Il Duce   Term designating the fascist Italian leader Benito Mussolini.

Duma   The Russian parliament.

Dunkirk   The French port on the English Channel where the British and French forces retreated after sustaining heavy losses against the German military. Between May 27 and June 4, 1940, the Royal Navy evacuated over three hundred thousand troops using commercial and pleasure boats.

Earth Summit (1992)   Meeting in Rio de Janeiro between many of the world's governments in an effort to address international environmental problems.

Eastern Front   Battlefront between Berlin and Moscow during World War I and World War II.

East India Company (1600–1858)   British charter company created to outperform Portuguese and Spanish traders in the Far East; in the eighteenth century the company became, in effect, the ruler of a large part of India. There was also a Dutch East India Company.

Edict of Nantes (1598)   Edict issued by Henry IV to end the French Wars of Religion. The edict declared France a Catholic country, but tolerated some Protestant worship.

Eiffel Tower   Named after its creator, Gustave Eiffel, the tower was completed in 1889 for the Paris Exposition. This steel monument was twice the height of any other building at the time.

Albert Einstein (1879–1955)   German physicist who developed the theory of relativity, which states that space and motion are relative to each other instead of being absolute.

Elizabeth I (1533–1603)   Protestant daughter of Henry VIII, Queen of England 1558–1603. During her long reign, the doctrines and services of the Church of England were defined and the Spanish Armada was defeated.

Enabling Act (1933)   Emergency act passed by the *Reichstag* (German parliament) that helped transform Hitler from Germany's chancellor, or prime minister, into a dictator, following the suspicious burning of the *Reichstag* building and a suspension of civil liberties.

enclosure   Long process of privatizing what had been public agricultural land in the eighteenth century that changed the nature of economic activity in England.

The Encyclopedia   Joint venture of French *philosophe* writers, helmed by Denis Diderot (1713–1784), which proposed to summarize all modern knowledge.

Endeavor   Ship of Captain James Cook, whose widely celebrated voyages to the South Pacific at the end of the eighteenth century supplied Europe with information about the plants, birds, landscapes, and people of this uncharted territory.

Friedrich Engels (1820–1895)   German social and political philosopher who collaborated with Karl Marx on many publications.

English Navigation Act of 1651   Act stipulating that only English ships could carry goods between the mother country and its colonies.

Enlightenment   Intellectual movement stressing natural laws and classifications in nature, in eighteenth-century Europe.

Epicureanism   Greek philosophy that emphasized the individual, denied the existence of spiritual forces, and proposed that the highest good is pleasure.

Desiderius Erasmus (c. 1469–1536)   Dutch-born scholar and social commentator who proclaimed his humanist views in lively treatises like *In Praise of Folly* and the *Colloquies*.

Estates-General   French quasi-parliamentary body called in 1789 to deal with the financial problems that afflicted France at the time. It had not met since 1614.

Etruscans   Non-Indo-European-speaking settlers of the Italian peninsula who dominated the region from the late Bronze Age until the rise of the Romans in the sixth century B.C.E.

Euclid   Hellenistic mathematician whose book *Elements of Geometry* was the basis of modern geometry.

eugenics   Term, meaning "good birth," referring to the project of "breeding" a superior human race. It was popularly championed by scientists, politicians, and social critics in the late nineteenth and early twentieth centuries.

Eurasia   The combined area of Europe and Asia.

European Union (EU)   An international political body that was organized after World War II to reconcile Germany and the rest of Europe as well as to forge closer industrial cooperation. Over time, member states of the EU have relinquished some of their sovereignty, and cooperation has evolved into a community with a single currency, the euro, and a common European parliament.

Exclusion Act of 1882   U.S. congressional act prohibiting nearly all immigration from China to the United States; fueled by animosity toward Chinese workers in the American West.

Existentialism   The philosophy that arose out of World War II and emphasized the human condition. Led by Jean Paul Sartre and Albert Camus, existentialists encouraged humans to take responsibility for their own decisions and dilemmas.

Fascists   Radical right-wing group of the disaffected that formed around Mussolini in 1919 and a few years later came to power in Italy.

February Revolution (1917)   The first of two uprisings of the Russian Revolution, which led to the end of the Romanov dynasty.

Federal Deposit Insurance Corporation (FDIC)   Created in 1933 to guarantee all bank deposits up to $2,000 as part of the New Deal in the United States.

Federalists   Supporters of the ratification of the U.S. Constitution, which was written to replace the Articles of Confederation.

Federal Republic of Germany (1949–1990)   Country formed of the areas occupied by the Allies after World War II. Also known as West Germany, this country experienced rapid demilitarization, democratization, and integration into the world economy.

Federal Reserve Act (1913)   U.S. legislation that created a series of boards to monitor the supply and demand of the nation's money.

Feminine Mystique   Groundbreaking book by feminist Betty Friedan (b. 1921), which tried to define "femininity" and explored how women internalized those definitions.

Fertile Crescent   An area of fertile land in what is now Syria, Israel, Turkey, eastern Iraq, and western Iran that was able to sustain settlements due to its wetter climate and abundant natural food resources. Some of the earliest known civilizations emerged there between 9000 and 4500 B.C.E.

feudalism   A loose term reflecting the political and economic situation in eleventh- and twelfth-century Europe. In this system, lords were owed agricultural labor and military service by their serfs, and in turn owed allegiance to more powerful lords and kings.

First Crusade (1095–1099)   Forces were sent by Pope Urban II to assist Byzantine emperor Alexius Comnenus in fighting Turkish forces in Anatolia. The struggle to recapture Jerusalem for western Christianity was eventually successful. This crusade prompted attacks against Jews throughout Europe and resulted in six subsequent military campaigns to the Holy Land.

First World War   A total war from August 1914 to November 1918, involving the armies of Britain, France, and Russia (the Allies) against Germany, Austria-Hungary, and the Ottoman empire (the Central Powers). Italy joined the Allies in 1915, and the United States joined them in 1917, helping to tip the balance in favor of the Allies, who also drew upon the populations and material of their colonial possessions. Also known as the Great War.

Five-Year Plan   Soviet effort launched under Stalin in 1928 to replace the market with a state-owned and state-managed economy in order to promote rapid economic development over a five-year period and thereby "catch and overtake" the leading capitalist countries. The First Five-Year Plan was followed by the Second Five-Year Plan (1933–1937), and so on, until the collapse of the Soviet Union in 1991.

Flagellants   European social group that came into existence during the bubonic plague in the fourteenth century; they believed that the plague was caused by the wrath of God and chose to beat and mutilate themselves as a form of religious penance.

Franciscan order   Order of monks established in 1209 by Saint Francis of Assisi (1182–1226); its members strove to imitate the life and example of Jesus.

Frankfurt Assembly   An 1848 gathering of delegates from all German states that attempted to unify them into one nation. The liberal agenda and squabbling over whose plan for the nation was best led to the failure of the gathering.

Franz Ferdinand (1863–1914)   Archduke of Austria and heir to the Austro-Hungarian empire; his assassination led to the beginning of World War I.

Frederick the Great (1740–1786)   Prussian ruler who engaged the nobility in maintaining a strong military and bureaucracy, and led Prussian armies to notable military victories. He also encouraged Enlightenment rationalism and artistic endeavors.

French New Wave   A group of filmmakers in the 1950s and 1960s that emphasized naturalistic and unsentimental portrayals of ordinary life. Famous New Wave directors included Francois Truffaut (1932–1984), Jean-Luc Godard (b. 1930), and Eric Rohmer (b. 1920).

French Revolution of 1848   Brief uprising caused by economic grievances; it was violently quelled by the government.

Sigmund Freud (1865–1939)   The Austrian physician who founded the discipline of psychoanalysis and suggested that human behavior was largely motivated by unconscious and irrational forces.

Front de Libération Nationale **(FLN)/Algerian Revolutionary National Liberation Front**   An anti-colonial, nationalist party that waged an eight-year war, beginning in 1954, against French troops for Algerian independence; the war forced nearly all of the 1 million French colonists to leave.

Galileo Galilei (1564–1642)   Italian physicist and inventor. The implications of his ideas raised the ire of the Catholic Church, and he was forced to retract most of his findings.

Mohandas K. (Mahatma) Gandhi (1869–1948)   The Indian leader who advocated nonviolent noncooperation and helped win home rule for India in 1947.

Giuseppe Garibaldi (1807–1882)   Italian revolutionary leader who led the fight to free Sicily and Naples from the Habsburg empire; the lands were then peaceably annexed by Sardinia.

garrisons   Military bases inside cities that were often used for political purposes, such as protecting the rulers and putting down domestic revolt or enforcing colonial rule.

Gaul   The region of the Roman empire that is modern Belgium, Germany west of the Rhine, and France.

Gdansk shipyard   Site of mass strikes in Poland that led to the formation in 1980 of the first independent trade union, Solidarity, in the Communist bloc.

Geneva Peace Conference (1954)   International conference to restore peace in Korea and Indochina. The chief participants were the United States, the Soviet Union, Great Britain, France, the People's Republic of China, North Korea, South Korea, Vietnam, the Viet Minh party, Laos, and Cambodia. The conference resulted in the division of North and South Vietnam.

German Democratic Republic   Nation founded from the Soviet zone of occupation of Germany after World War II; also known as East Germany.

German Social Democratic Party   Founded in 1875, it was the most powerful Socialist party in Europe before 1917.

Gilgamesh   The hero of the Sumerian epic, which was recorded in written form around 2000 B.C.E. Gilgamesh was a powerful ruler who, along with his friend Enkidu, battled monsters and gods and searched for immortality.

Girondins   Liberal revolutionary group that supported the creation of a constitutional monarchy during the early stages of the French Revolution.

globalization   The term used to describe political, social, and economic networks that span the globe. These global exchanges are not limited by nation states and often rely on new technologies, international laws, and economic imperatives.

Arthur de Gobineau (1816–1882)   French writer whose pseudoscientific, racist ideology provided a rationale for European imperialism.

Gold Coast Name that European mariners and merchants gave to that part of West Equatorial Africa from which gold and slaves were exported. Originally controlled by the Portuguese, this area later became the British colony of the Gold Coast.

Gothic style Period of graceful architecture emerging after the Romanesque style in twelfth- and thirteenth-century France. The style is characterized by pointed arches, delicate decoration, and large windows.

Great Depression Period following the U.S. stock market crash on October 29, 1929, and ending in 1941 with America's entry into World War II.

great divide Refers to the division between economically developed nations and less developed nations.

Great East Asia Co-Prosperity Sphere Term used by the Japanese during the 1930s and 1940s to refer to Hong Kong, Singapore, Malaya, Burma, and other states that they seized during their run for expansion.

The "Great Terror" The systematic murder of nearly a million people and the deportation of another million and a half to labor camps by Stalin's regime during 1937 in an attempt to consolidate power and remove perceived enemies.

The Great War (1914–1918) World War I.

Greek Civil War (1821–1827) Conflict between Greek Christians and Muslim Ottomans.

Pope Gregory I (540?–604) Roman Catholic Pope 590–604. Used his political influence and theological teachings to separate the western Latin from the eastern Greek church. He also encouraged the Benedictine monastic movement and missionary expeditions.

Guerillas Portuguese and Spanish peasant bands who resisted the revolutionary and expansion efforts of Napoléon; after the French word for war, *guerre*.

Guernica The Basque town bombed by German planes in April 1937 during the Spanish Civil War. It is also the subject of Pablo Picasso's famous painting from the same year.

guest workers Migrants looking for temporary employment.

guilds Professional organizations in commercial towns that regulated the business conditions and privileges of those practicing a particular craft.

gulag The vast system of forced labor camps under the Soviet regime; it originated in 1919 in a small monastery near the Arctic Circle and spread throughout the Soviet Union and to other Soviet-style socialist countries. Penal labor was required of both ordinary criminals and those accused of political crimes (counterrevolution, anti-Soviet agitation).

Gulf War (1991) Armed conflict between Iraq and a coalition of thirty-two nations, including the United States, Britain, Egypt, France, and Saudi Arabia. The seeds of the war were planted with Iraq's invasion of Kuwait on August 2, 1990.

Habsburg empire Ruling house of Austria, which once ruled the Netherlands, Spain, and Central Europe but came to settle in lands along the Danube River. It played a prominent role in European affairs for many centuries. In 1867, the Habsburg empire was reorga-

nized into the Austro-Hungarian Dual Monarchy, and in 1918 it collapsed.

Hadith Sayings attributed to the Prophet Muhammad and his early converts. Used to guide the behavior of Muslim peoples.

Hagia Sophia The largest house of worship in all of Christendom, located in Constantinople and built by the emperor Justinian. When Constantinople fell to Ottoman forces in 1453, it was turned into a mosque.

Hajj The pilgrimage to Mecca; an obligation for Muslims.

Hammurabi The ruler of Babylon from 1792 to 1750 B.C.E. Hammurabi issued a collection of laws that were greatly influential in the Near East for centuries.

harem Secluded women's quarters in Muslim households.

Harlem Renaissance Cultural movement in the 1920s that was based in Harlem, a part of New York City where a large African American population resided. The movement gave voice to black novelists, poets, painters, and musicians, many of whom used their art to protest racial subordination; also referred to as the "New Negro Movement."

Henry VIII (1491–1547) Oft-married English monarch who broke with the Roman Catholic church when the pope refused to grant him an annulment. The resulting modified version of Christianity became the Church of England, or Anglicanism.

Henry of Navarre (1553–1610) Crowned King Henry IV of France, he renounced his Protestantism but granted limited toleration to Huguenots (French Protestants) with the 1598 Edict of Nantes.

Prince Henry the Navigator (1394–1460) Portuguese noble who encouraged conquest of western Africa and trade in gold and slaves.

hero cults Important ancient Greek families would claim that an impressive Mycenean tomb was that of their own famous ancestor and would practice sacrifices and other observances to strengthen their claim. This devotion could extend to their followers, and eventually whole communities would identify with such local heroes.

Hiroshima Japanese port devastated by an atomic bomb on August 6, 1945.

Adolf Hitler (1889–1945) The author of *Mein Kampf* and leader of the Nazis. Hitler and his Nazi regime started World War II and orchestrated the systematic murder of over five million Jews.

Hittites An Indo-European-speaking people that migrated into Anatolia (now Turkey) around the beginning of the second millennium B.C.E.

Ho Chi Minh (1890–1969) The Vietnamese communist resistance leader who drove the French out of Vietnam and controlled North Vietnam after the Geneva Accords divided the region into four countries.

Holy Roman Empire The collection of lands in central and western Europe ruled over by the kings of Germany (and later Austria) from the twelfth century until 1806.

Holy Russia Name applied to Muscovy, and then to the Russian empire, by Slavic Eastern Orthodox clerics who were appalled by the Muslim conquest in 1453 of Constantinople (the capital of

Byzantium and of Eastern Christianity), and who were hopeful that Russia would become the new protector of the faith.

home charges   Fees India was forced to pay to Britain as its colonial master; these fees included interest on railroad loans, salaries to colonial officers, and the maintenance of imperial troops outside India.

Homo sapiens   Term defined by Linnaeus in 1737 and commonly used to refer to fully modern human beings.

hoplite   A Greek foot soldier armed with a spear or short sword and protected by a large round shield (a hopla). In battle, hoplites stood shoulder to shoulder in a close formation called a phalanx.

Huguenots   French Protestants who endured severe persecution in the sixteenth and seventeenth centuries.

Human Comedy   Masterpiece of French novelist Honoré de Balzac (1799–1850) that criticized materialist values.

humanism   Medieval program of study built around the seven liberal arts: grammer, logic, rhetoric, arithmetic, music, geometry, and astronomy.

Hundred Years' War (1337–1453)   Long conflict, fought mostly on French soil, between England and France, centering on English claims to the throne of France.

Saddam Hussein (b. 1937)   The former dictator of Iraq who invaded Iran in 1980 and started the eight-year-long Iran-Iraq War; invaded Kuwait in 1990, which caused the Gulf War of 1991; and was overthrown when the United States invaded Iraq in 2003. Involved in Iraqi politics since the mid-1960s, Hussein became the official head of state in 1979.

Il-khanate   Mongol-founded dynasty in thirteenth-century Persia.

Imam   Muslim religious leader and also a politico-religious descendant of Ali; believed by some to have a special relationship with Allah.

Imhotep   The chief adviser to the Pharaoh Djoser, who ruled in the 27th century B.C.E. Often considered to be the first architect, Imhotep designed tombs and other structures to express the power of the Egyptian pharaohs.

Indian National Congress   Formed in 1885, this political party was deeply committed to constitutional methods, industrialization, and cultural nationalism.

Indo-Europeans   A group of people that spoke variations of the same language and moved into the Near East and Mediterranean shortly after 2000 B.C.E.

indulgences   Remissions of the penances owed by Catholics as part of the process by which their sins are forgiven.

Inquisition   Tribunal of the Roman Catholic Church that aimed to enforce religious orthodoxy and conformity.

International Monetary Fund (IMF)   Established in 1945 to promote the health of the world economy, the IMF is a specialized agency of the United Nations.

Intifada   Uprising in the Palestinian occupied territories from 1987 to 1993, in protest against the Israeli occupation and politics. The Oslo Agreement (1993) helped to reduce the tension between the two sides and the Intifada all but ceased by the end of 1993. In early 2000, the Intifada resumed.

Investiture Conflict   A disagreement between Pope Gregory VII and Emperor Henry IV of Germany that tested the power of kings over church matters. After years of diplomatic and military hostility, it was settled by the Concordat of Worms in 1122.

invisible hand   Described in Adam Smith's *The Wealth of Nations*, the idea that the operations of a free market would produce economic efficiency and economic benefits for all.

Irish Home Rule   The late-nineteenth- and early-twentieth-century movement, led by Sinn Fein (established 1905), for Irish self-government.

Irish potato famine   Period of agricultural blight from 1845 to 1849 whose devastating results prompted a mass emigration to America.

Iron Curtain   Term coined by Winston Churchill in 1946 to refer to the division of Western Europe, under American influence, from Eastern Europe, under the domination of the Soviet Union.

Ivan the Great (1440–1505)   Emperor of Russia who annexed neighboring territories and began Russia's career as a European power.

Jacobins   Radical French political group that came into existence during the French Revolution, executed the French king, and sought to remake French culture.

Jacquerie   Violent 1358 peasant uprising in northern France, incited by disease, war, and taxes.

James I (1566–1625)   Monarch of Scotland and England from 1603 to 1625. He oversaw the English vernacular translation of the Bible known by his name.

Janissaries   Corps of enslaved soldiers recruited as children from the Christian provinces of the Ottoman empire and brought up with intense loyalty to the Ottoman state and its sultan. The sultan used these forces to curb local autonomy and to serve as his personal bodyguards.

Jesuits   Religious order founded in 1540 by Ignatius Loyola to counter the inroads of the Protestant Reformation; the Jesuits were active in politics, education, and missionary work.

Jihad   A struggle and, if need be, a holy war toward the advancement of the cause of Islam.

Joan of Arc (c. 1412–1431)   French teenager, supposedly divinely inspired, who led forces against the English during the Hundred Years' War. Burned at the stake for heresy by the English and later made a Catholic saint.

Justinian (527–565)   Emperor of eastern Rome. Justinian codified Roman law in the Corpus Juris Civilis and tried to reunify the eastern and western halves of the old Roman empire.

***Das Kapital* (Capital)**   The 1867 book by Karl Marx that outlined the theory behind historical materialism and attacked the socioeconomic inequities of capitalism. Mixing economic theory and revolutionary politics, the book became the preeminent socialist critique of capitalism.

Johannes Kepler (1571–1601)   Mathematician and astronomer who elaborated on and corrected Copernicus's theory and is chiefly remembered for his discovery of the three laws of planetary motion that bear his name.

Keynesian Revolution Post-Depression economic ideas developed by the British economist John Maynard Keynes, wherein the state took a greater role in managing the economy, stimulating it by increasing the money supply and creating jobs.

KGB Soviet political police and spy agency, first formed as the Cheka not long after the Bolshevik coup in October 1917. It grew to more than 750,000 operatives with military rank by the 1980s.

Chingiz Khan (c. 1167–1227) Title taken by Mongol chief Temujin meaning "The Oceanic Ruler." Began dynasty that conquered much of southern Asia.

Khanate Major political unit of the vast Mongol empire. There were four Khanates, including the Yuan empire in China, forged by Chingiz Khan's grandson Kubilai in the 13th century.

Nikita Khrushchev (1894–1971) Leader of the Soviet Union during the Cuban Missile Crisis, Khrushchev had quickly reached power soon after Stalin's death in 1953. His reforms and criticisms of the excesses of the Stalin regime led to his fall from power in 1964.

Kremlin Once synonymous with the Soviet government, it refers to Moscow's walled city center.

Kristallnacht The Nazi destruction of seventy-five hundred Jewish stores and two hundred synagogues on November 9, 1938.

kulaks Originally a pejorative term used to designate better-off peasants, it was used in the late 1920s and early 1930s to refer to any peasant, rich or poor, perceived as an opponent of the Soviet regime. Russian for "fist."

Labour Party Founded in Britain in 1900, this party represented workers and was based on socialist principles.

League of Nations International organization founded after World War I to solve international disputes through arbitration; it was dissolved in 1946 and transferred its assets to the United Nations.

Nikolai Lenin (1870–1924) Leader of the Bolshevik Revolution in Russia (1917) and the first leader of the Soviet Union.

Leopold II (1835–1909) Belgian king who sponsored colonizing expeditions into Africa.

Leviathan A book by Thomas Hobbes (1588–1679) that recommended a ruler have unrestricted power.

liberalism Political and social theory that advocates representative government, free trade, and freedom of speech and religion.

lithograph Art form that involves putting writing or design on stone and producing printed impressions.

Long March (1934–1935) Trek of over 10,000 kilometers by Mao Zedong and his Communist followers to establish a new base of operations.

lord Privileged landowner who exercised authority over the people who lived on his land.

lost generation Refers to the 17 million former members of the Red Guard and other Chinese youth who were denied education from the late 1960s to the mid-1970s as part of the Chinese government's attempt to forestall political disruptions.

Louis XIV (1638–1715) The "Sun King," known for his opulent court and absolutist political style.

Louis XVI (1754–1793) Well-meaning but ineffectual king of France, finally deposed and executed with his family by revolutionaries.

Luftwaffe Literally "air weapon," this is the name of the German air force, which was founded during World War I, disbanded in 1945, and reestablished when West Germany joined NATO in 1950.

Lusitania The passenger liner that was secretly carrying war supplies and was sunk by a German U-boat (submarine) on May 7, 1915.

Lutheranism Branch of Protestantism that followed Martin Luther's (1483–1546) rejection of the Roman Catholic "doctrine of works."

lycées System of high schools instituted by Napoleon as part of his domestic reform campaign.

madrassas Muslim schools devoted to the study of the Quran and Islam.

Magna Carta "Great Charter" of 1215 signed by King John of England, which limited the king's fiscal powers and is seen as a landmark in the political evolution of the West.

Moses Maimonides (1135–1204) Spanish-born Jewish scholar, physician, and scriptural commentator.

Nelson Mandela (b. 1918) The South African opponent of *apartheid* who led the African National Congress and was imprisoned from 1962 until 1990. After his release from prison, he worked with Prime Minister Frederik Willem De Klerk to establish majority rule. Mandela became the first black president of South Africa in 1994.

Manhattan Project The secret U.S. government research project in Los Alamos, New Mexico, to develop the first nuclear bomb. The first test of a nuclear bomb was near Los Alamos on July 16, 1945.

manorialism System common to England, northern France, and Germany in the Middle Ages of communal peasant farming under the protection of a landholding lord.

Mao Zedong (1893–1976) The leader of the Chinese Revolution who defeated the Nationalists in 1949 and established the Communist regime in China.

Marshall Plan Economic aid package given to Europe after World War II in hopes of a rapid period of reconstruction and economic gain and to secure the countries from a Communist takeover.

Master Eckhart (c. 1260–1327) Dominican monk who preached an introspective and charismatic version of Christian piety.

Karl Marx (1818–1883) German philosopher and economist who believed that a revolution of the working classes would overthrow the capitalist order and create a classless society. Author of *Das Kapital* and *The Communist Manifesto*.

Maxim gun Invented in 1885 by an American, Hiram Maxim, the Maxim gun was the first portable machine gun. Quickly adopted by the majority of European armies and capable of firing 500 rounds per minute, it played a major role in the imperial conquests of the African continent.

Mayans Native American peoples whose culturally and politically sophisticated empire encompassed lands in present-day Mexico and Guatemala.

Giuseppe Mazzini (1805–1872) Founder of Young Italy and an ideological leader of the Italian Nationalist movement.

Mecca Major commercial city of the Arabian peninsula in the sixth century C.E., at which time the founder of Islam, Muhammad, was born and achieved prominence. From the earliest days of the spread of Islam, the city was the destination of the chief religious pilgrimage for Muslims, and it is now considered the holiest site in the Islamic world.

Medici Dynasty of Florentine bankers and politicians known for their patronage of the arts.

Meiji empire Empire created under the leadership of Mutsuhito, emperor of Japan from 1868 until 1912. During the Meiji period Japan became a world industrial and naval power.

Menander (342 B.C.E.?–292 B.C.E.) Ancient Greek dramatist who wrote over 100 plays, many of which were standards of Western literature for hundreds of years. Only one complete surviving play is known, *The Grouch*, which was rediscovered in 1957.

mercantilism A popular Western belief between 1600 and 1800 that a country's wealth and power was based on a favorable balance of trade (more exports and fewer imports) and the accumulation of precious metals.

Michelangelo (1475–1564) Virtuoso artist, best known for the Sistine Chapel ceiling in Rome and his sculptures *David* and *Pieta*.

John Stuart Mill (1806–1873) English radical philosopher whose writings advocated aspects of socialism and civil liberties.

Slobodan Milosevic (b. 1941) The Serbian nationalist politician who took control of the Serb government and orchestrated the genocide of thousands of Croatians, Bosnian Muslims, Albanians, and Kosovars. After ten years of war, he was ousted by a popular revolt in 2000.

Minoans A sea empire that flourished on Crete and in the Aegean Basin from 1900 B.C.E. until the middle of the second millennium B.C.E.

Modernism The series of artistic movements, manifestos, innovations, and experiments that redefined art in the first half of the twentieth century. Modernism rejected history and tradition in favor of expressive and experimental freedom.

Michel de Montaigne (1533–1592) French philosopher known for his *Essays*.

mosque Place of worship for the people of Islam.

Wolfgang Amadeus Mozart (1756–1791) Austrian child prodigy and composer of instrumental music and operas.

Muhammad (570–632 C.E.) The founder of Islam, he claimed to be the prophet whom God (Allah) had chosen for his final revelation to mankind.

Mullahs Iranian religious leaders who led the opposition movement against the shah and denounced the depravity of late-twentieth-century American materialism and secularism.

multinational corporations Corporations based in many different countries that have global investment, trading, and distribution goals.

Muslim Brotherhood Egyptian organization founded in 1938 by Hassan al-Banna. It attacked liberal democracy as a façade for middle-class, business, and landowning interests and fought for a return to a purified form of Islam.

Muslim League National Muslim party of India.

Benito Mussolini (1883–1945) The Italian founder of the Fascist party who came to power in Italy in 1922 and allied himself with Hitler and the Nazis during World War II.

Mutiny of 1857 Uprising of Indian soldiers against the ruling British, sometimes called the Sepoy Rebellion.

Mycenaens The ancient Greek civilization that settled in Greece during the second millennium B.C.E. and organized around powerful citadels.

Nagasaki Second Japanese city on which the United States dropped an atomic bomb. The attack took place on August 9, 1945; the Japanese surrendered shortly thereafter, ending World War II.

Napoleonic Code Legal code drafted by Napoleon in 1804; it distilled different legal traditions to create one uniform law. The code confirmed the abolition of feudal privileges of all kinds and set the conditions for exercising property rights.

National Assembly of France Governing body of France that succeeded the Estates-General in 1789 during the French Revolution. It was composed of, and defined by, the delegates of the Third Estate.

National Association for the Advancement of Colored People (NAACP) Founded in 1910, this U.S. civil rights organization was dedicated to ending inequality and segregation for black Americans.

Nationalism Movement to unify a country based on a people's common history and social traditions.

NATO The North Atlantic Treaty Organization, which was a 1949 agreement between the United States, Canada, Great Britain, and 8 European countries that declared that an armed attack against any one of the members would be regarded as an attack against all. Other European countries have since joined.

"navvies" Slang for laborers who built railroads and canals.

Nazi Party Founded in the early 1920s, the National Socialist German Workers' Party (NDSAP) gained control over Germany under the leadership of Adolf Hitler in 1933 and continued in power until Germany was defeated in 1945.

Nefertiti The wife of Akhenaten, the fourteenth-century B.C.E. Egyptian pharaoh.

Neolithic The "New" Stone Age, which began around 11,000 B.C.E., saw new technological and social developments, including managed food production, the beginnings of semipermanent and permanent settlements, and the rapid intensification of trade.

New Deal President Franklin Delano Roosevelt's package of government reforms that were enacted during the 1930s to provide jobs for the unemployed, social welfare programs for the poor, and security to the financial markets.

new imperialism Expansion of colonial power by Western European nations, especially in Asia, in the last three decades of the nineteenth century.

Isaac Newton (1642–1727) One of the foremost scientists of all time, Newton was an English mathematician and physicist; he is noted for his development of calculus, work on the properties of light, and theory of gravitation.

Nicholas I (1796–1855) Russian tsar who executed the leaders of the 1825 December Revolution and pursued an absolutist reign.

Tsar Nicholas II (1868–1918) The last Russian tsar, who abdicated the throne in 1917. He and his family were executed by the Bolsheviks on July 17, 1918.

Nicomachean Ethics The treatise on moral philosophy by Aristotle, which teaches that the highest good consists of the harmonious functioning of the individual human mind and body.

Friedrich Nietzsche (1844–1900) The German philosopher who denied the possibility of knowing absolute "truth" or "reality," since all knowledge comes filtered through linguistic, scientific, or artistic systems of representation. He also criticized Judeo-Christian morality for instilling a repressive conformity that drained civilization of its vitality.

Non-governmental organizations (NGOs) Private organizations like the Red Cross that play a large role in international affairs.

North American Free Trade Agreement (NAFTA) Treaty negotiated in the early 1990s to promote free trade among Canada, the United States, and Mexico.

Novum Organum Work by English statesman and scientist Francis Bacon (1561–1626) that advanced a philosophy of study through observation.

OPEC (Organization of Petroleum Exporting Countries) Organization created in 1960 by oil-producing countries in the Middle East, South America, and Africa to regulate the production and pricing of crude oil.

Operation Barbarossa The codename for Hitler's invasion of the Soviet Union.

Opium War (1839–1842) War fought between the British and Qing China to protect British trade in opium; resulted in the ceding of Hong Kong to the British.

Oracle at Delphi Dating to 1400 B.C.E., the oracle was the most important shrine in ancient Greece. A priestess of Apollo who attended the shrine was believed to be able to predict the future. The shrine ceased to function in the fourth century C.E.

Ottoman slavery Social system of using slave labor for domestic, administrative, and military work that permitted social advancement and religious diversity within the Muslim empire.

Pan-African Conference 1900 assembly in London which sought to draw attention to the sovereignty of African people and their mistreatment by colonial powers.

Pan-Slavism Cultural movement that sought to unite native Slavic peoples within the Russian and Habsburg empires.

papal Of, relating to, or issued by a pope.

Patria Latin, meaning "fatherland."

patricians The uppermost elite class of ancient Rome.

Paul One of the twelve apostles of Jesus, Paul spread Christianity throughout the Near East and Greece.

Pearl Harbor The American Navy base in Hawaii that was bombed by the Japanese on December 7, 1941, which brought the United States into World War II.

Peloponnesian War The ancient Greek war between Sparta and Athens that began in 431 B.C.E. and ended with the destruction of the Athenian fleet in 404 B.C.E.

People's Charter An action of the Chartist Movement (1839–1848); between 1839 and 1842 over 3 million British signed this document calling for universal suffrage for adult males, the secret ballot, electoral districts, and annual parliamentary elections.

Perestroika Introduced by Soviet leader Mikhail Gorbachev in June 1987, *Perestroika* was the name given to economic and political reforms begun earlier in his tenure. It restructured the state bureaucracy, reduced the privileges of the political elite, and instituted a shift from the centrally planned economy to a mixed economy, combining planning with the operation of market forces.

Pericles The fifth-century B.C.E. Athenian leader who served as strategos for thirty years and pushed through reforms to make Athens more democratic by giving every citizen the right to propose and amend legislation and making it easier for citizens to participate in the assembly and the great appeals court of Athens by paying an average day's wage for attendance.

Peterloo Massacre (1819) The killing of 11 and wounding of 460 following a peaceful demonstration for political reform by workers in Manchester, England.

Peter the Great (1672–1725) Energetic tsar who transformed Russia into a leading European country by centralizing government, modernizing the army, creating a navy, and reforming education and the economy.

Francesco Petrarch (1304–1374) Italian scholar and writer who revived interest in classical writing styles and was famed for his love sonnets.

Pharisees A group of Jewish teachers and preachers that emerged in the third century B.C.E. and insisted that all of Yahweh's (God's) commandments were binding on all Jews.

Philip II (382–336 B.C.E.) The Macedonian king who consolidated the southern Balkans and the Greek city-states; he was the father of Alexander.

Phoenicians The semitic-speaking residents of present-day Lebanon from around 1200 to 800 B.C.E. The Phoenician cities were centers for trade throughout the Mediterranean.

Plato's *Republic* The first systematic treatment of political philosophy ever written, it argued for an elitist state in which most people would be governed by intellectually superior "philosopher-kings."

plebians The citizen population of ancient Rome that included farmers, merchants, and the urban poor; plebians comprised the majority of the population.

Plotinus (204–270 C.E.) The neo-Platonist philosopher who taught that everything that exists proceeds from the divine and that the highest goal of life should be the mystic reunion of the soul with the divine, which can be achieved through contemplation and asceticism.

Polis One of the major political innovations of the ancient Greeks was the Polis, or city-state. They were independent social and political structures, organized around an urban center, containing markets, meeting places, and a temple; they controlled a limited amount of the surrounding territory.

Marco Polo (1254–1324)   Venetian merchant who traveled through Asia for twenty years and published his observations in a widely read memoir, *Travels*.

Populists   Members of a political movement that supported U.S. farmers in late nineteenth-century America. The term is often used generically to refer to political groups who appeal to the mass of the population.

potato famine (1845–1850)   Severe famine in Ireland that led to the migration of large numbers of Irish to the United States.

Prague Spring   A period of political liberalization in Czechoslovakia between January and August 1968 that was initiated by Alexander Dubĉek, the Czech leader. This period of expanding freedom and openness in this Eastern bloc nation ended on August 20, when the USSR and Warsaw Pact countries invaded with 200,000 troops and 5,000 tanks.

The Praise of Folly   1511 satire by Erasmus that attacked the corruption of the papacy.

Pre-Socratics   A group of philosophers on the Greek island of Miletus, including Thales, Anaximander, and Anaximenes, who raised questions about the relationship between the natural world, the gods, and humans, and formulated rational theories to explain the physical universe they observed.

Primitivism   Movement in Western art forms in the late nineteenth and early twentieth centuries that used the so-called primitive art forms of Africa, Oceania, and pre-Columbian America to inspire a break with the established art world.

The Prince   Influential treatise by Niccolo Machiavelli (1469–1527) that attempts to lay out methods to secure and maintain political power.

Protestantism   Division of Christianity that emerged in sixteenth-century western Europe at the time of the Reformation. It focused on individual spiritual needs and rejected the social authority of the papacy and the Catholic clergy.

Ptolemy (c. 85–165 C.E.)   One of the most influential ancient Greeks; he was a leading astronomer, mathematician, and geographer who lived his entire life in Alexandria and helped to transform that city into a center of scientific study and scholarship.

puppet states   Governments that have little power in the international arena and follow the dictates of their more powerful neighbors or patrons.

Puritans   Seventeenth-century reform group of the Church of England; also known as dissenters or nonconformists.

Quran (often Koran)   Islam's holy book, comprised of Allah's revelations.

Sayyid Qutb (1906–1966)   The Egyptian critic who became one of the most important intellectual leaders of the Muslim Brotherhood and whose writings are often cited as philosophical inspiration for Osama bin Laden and other Islamic radicals.

François Rabelais (c. 1494?–1553)   French humanist satirist best known for his crudely comic *Gargantua and Pantagruel*, in which he

espouses the "eat, drink, and be merry" lifestyle. Originally a novice in the Franciscan order, later a Benedictine monk who left the order to study medicine, Rabelais spent time in hiding for fear of being labeled a heretic, and some of his books were banned.

radicals   Widely used term in nineteenth-century Europe that referred to those individuals and political organizations that favored the total reconfiguration of Europe's old state system.

Raj   Term referring to the British crown's administration of India following the end of the East India Company's rule after the Indian Mutiny of 1857.

Ramadan   Ninth month of the Muslim year, during which all Muslims must fast during daylight hours.

Raphael (1483–1520)   Italian painter noted for his warmly human treatment of religious subjects, particularly his Madonnas and large-figure compositions in the Vatican in Rome.

Realism   Artistic and literary style which sought to portray common situations as they would appear in reality.

Realpolitik   Political strategy advancing power for its own sake.

Rebellion of 1857   Indian rebellion against the English East India Company to bring religious purification, an egalitarian society, and local and communal solidarity without the interference of British rule.

Reds   The Bolsheviks.

Reformation   Religious and political movement in sixteenth-century Europe that led to the breakaway of Protestant groups from the Catholic Church; notable figures include Martin Luther and John Calvin.

Reich   A term for the German state. The first Reich corresponded to the Holy Roman Empire (9th century to 1806), the second Reich was from 1871 to 1919, and the third Reich lasted from 1933 through May 1945.

Reign of Terror   Campaign at the height of the French Revolution (1793–1794) in which violence, including systematic executions of opponents of the Revolution, was used to purge France of its "enemies" and to extend the Revolution beyond its borders; radicals executed as many as 40,000 persons who were judged enemies of the state.

Religious Peace of Augsburg   1555 settlement between factions within the Holy Roman Empire that stated a territory would follow the religion of its ruler, whether Catholic or Protestant.

Renaissance   Term meaning "rebirth" that historians use to refer to the expanded cultural production of European nations between 1300 and 1600.

Restoration period (1815–1848)   European movement after the defeat of Napoleon to restore Europe to its pre-French revolutionary status and to prevent radical movements from arising.

Richard II (1367–1400)   King of England (r. 1377–1399), chiefly remembered for his successful resolution of the Peasants' Rebellion (1381) and as a vacillating, yet tyrannical monarch. He was deposed by his cousin Henry Bolingbroke (Henry IV) and assassinated.

Cardinal Richelieu (1585–1642)   First minister to French King Louis XIII, who centralized political power and deprived the Huguenots of many rights.

Romanticism Beginning in Germany and England in the late 18th century and continuing up to the end of the 19th century, a movement in art, music, and literature that countered the rationalism of the Enlightenment by stressing a highly emotional response to nature.

Jean-Jacques Rousseau (1718–1778) Philosopher and radical political theorist whose *Social Contract* attacked privilege and inequality. One of the primary principles of Rousseau's political philosophy is that politics and morality should not be separated.

Russification Programs designed to assimilate people of over 146 dialects into the Russian empire by the tsars in the late 19th century.

Rwanda A former Belgian colony in central Africa that has been torn by ethnic violence between the Hutus and the Tutsis since before the country's independence in 1962.

Saint Bartholomew's Day Massacre Massacre of French Protestants (Huguenots) by Catholic crowds that began in Paris on August 24, 1572, spreading to other parts of France and continuing into October of that year. More than 70,000 were killed.

St. Domingue Former French Caribbean colony and site of a slave rebellion in 1791, which embroiled English and French forces until 1804, when St. Domingue was declared the independent nation of Haiti.

salons Informal gatherings of intellectuals and aristocrats that allowed discourse about Enlightenment ideas.

Santa Sophia The Byzantine church in Constantinople, constructed by emperor Justinian I in the sixth century, and famous for its dome, which rested on the keystones of four great arches.

Sappho (c. 620–c. 550 B.C.E.) One of the most famous Greek lyric poets, she wrote beautiful poetry about romantic longing and sexual lust, sometimes about men, but more often about women.

Sargon (r. 2334–2279 B.C.E.) The Akkadian leader who unified Mesopotamia.

Schlieffen Plan Devised by Count Alfred von Schlieffen in 1905 and put into operation on August 2, 1914, the Schlieffen Plan required France to be attacked first through Belgium and a quick victory to be secured so that the German army could fight Russia on the Eastern Front.

Scramble for Africa European rush to colonize parts of Africa at the end of the nineteenth century.

Second Industrial Revolution The technological developments in the last third of the nineteenth century, which that included new techniques for refining and producing steel; increased availability of electricity for industrial, commercial, and domestic use; advances in chemical manufacturing; and the creation of the internal combustion engine.

Second World Term invented during the cold war to refer to the Communist countries, as opposed to the West (or First World) and the former colonies (or Third World).

Second World War Worldwide war that began in September 1939 in Europe, and even earlier in Asia (1930s), and that pitted Britain, the United States, and especially the Soviet Union (the Allies) against Nazi Germany, Italy, and Japan (the Axis).

Seleucus (d. 280 B.C.E.) The Macedonian general who ruled the Asian territory of Alexander the Great's empire and founded Greek colonies such as Antioch and Selsucia.

Semitic The Semitic language family has the longest recorded history of any linguistic group and is the root language for most of the languages of the Middle and Near East. Ancient Semitic languages include the language of the ancient Babylonians and Assyrians, Phoenician, the classical form of Hebrew, early dialects of Aramaic, and the classical Arabic of the *Quran*.

sepoys Hindu and Muslim recruits of the East India Company's military force.

serfdom Slavery-like system of customs and laws whereby peasants were kept poor and stationary by their manor lords; it had spread throughout the West by the 10th century and its peak was the Middle Ages.

Seven Years War (1756–1763) Worldwide war that ended when Prussia defeated Austria, establishing itself as a European power, and when Britain gained control of India and many of France's colonies through the Treaty of Paris. It is known as the French and Indian War in the United States.

Shah Traditional title of Persian rulers.

Shiism One of the two main branches of Islam. Shiites recognize Ali, the fourth caliph, and his descendants as rightful rulers of the Islamic world; practiced in the Safavid empire.

Shiites An often-persecuted minority religious party within Islam that insists only descendants of Ali can have any authority over the Muslim community. Today, Shiites rule Iran and are numerous in Iraq but make up only 10 percent of the worldwide population of Islam.

Silicon Valley Valley between California's San Francisco and San Jose, known for its innovative computer and high-technology industry.

Sinn Fein The Irish revolutionary organization that formed in 1900 to fight for Irish independence.

Sino-Japanese War (1894–1895) Conflict over the control of Korea in which China was forced to cede the province of Taiwan to Japan.

Adam Smith (1723–1790) Scottish economist and philosopher who proposed that individual self-interest naturally promoted a healthy national economy. He became famous for his influential book, *The Wealth of Nations* (1776).

Social Darwinism Belief that Charles Darwin's theory of natural selection (evolution) was applicable to human societies and justified the right of the ruling classes or countries to dominate the weak.

socialism Political ideology that calls for a classless society with collective ownership of all property.

Social Security Act (1935) New Deal act that instituted old-age pensions and insurance for the unemployed in the United States.

Society of Jesus Also called the Jesuit order, a group of priests influenced by military discipline. The society was founded by Saint Ignatius of Loyola (1491–1556) and is still very active in the field of education.

Socrates (469–399 B.C.E.) The ancient Greek philosopher who emphasized the reexamination of all inherited assumptions and tried to base his philosophical speculations on sound definitions of words. He also wished to advance to a new system of truth by examining ethics rather than by studying the physical world.

Solidarity   The communist bloc's first independent trade union; it was established in Poland at the Gdansk shipyard in 1980.

Solon (d. 559 B.C.E.)   Elected archon in 594 B.C.E., this ancient Greek aristocrat enacted a series of political and economic reforms that made Athenian democracy possible.

Aleksandr Solzhenitsyn (b. 1918)   This Soviet novelist was a critic of the Soviet regime and wrote *The Gulag Archipelago*, which was published in 1974.

Sophists   Ancient Greek professional teachers who taught that sense perception was the source of all knowledge and that only particular truths could be valid for the individual knower.

South African War (1899–1902)   Often called the Boer War, this conflict between the British and Dutch colonists of South Africa resulted in bringing two Afrikaner republics under the control of the British.

Soviet bloc   International alliance that included the East European countries of the Warsaw Pact as well as the Soviet Union, but also came to include Cuba.

Spanish-American War (1898)   War between the United States and Spain in Cuba, Puerto Rico, and the Philippines. It ended with a treaty in which the United States took over the Philippines, Guam, and Puerto Rico; Cuba won partial independence.

Spanish Armada   Supposedly invincible fleet of warships sent against England by Philip II of Spain in 1588, but routed by the English and bad weather in the English Channel.

Spartiate   A full citizen of Sparta who was a professional soldier of the hoplite phalanx.

spinning jenny   Invention of James Hargreaves (c. 1720–1774) that revolutionized the British textile industry.

S.S. (*Schutzstaffel*)   Formed in 1925 to serve as Hitler's personal security force and to guard Nazi party (NDSAP) meetings, the SS were notorious for their participation in carrying out Nazi policies.

Joseph Stalin (1879–1953)   The Bolshevik leader who succeeded Lenin as the leader of the Soviet Union in 1924 and ruled until his death.

Strategic Defense Initiative (Stars Wars)   Master plan initiated by President Ronald Reagan that envisioned the deployment of satellites and space missiles to insulate the United States from nuclear bombs missiles.

Stoicism   The ancient Greek and Roman philosophy that held that the cosmos is an ordered whole in which all contradictions are resolved for ultimate good. Everything that happens is rigidly determined in accordance with rational purpose, and no individual is master of his or her fate. Founded in the fourth century B.C.E. and still popular well into the fifth century C.E.

Suez Canal   Built in 1869 across the Isthmus of Suez to connect the Mediterranean Sea with the Red Sea and to lower the costs of international trade.

Sufism   Emotional and mystical form of Islam that appealed to the common people.

sultan   An Islamic political leader. In the Ottoman empire, the sultan combined a warrior ethos with an unwavering devotion to Islam.

Sumerians   The civilization and people that arose in southern Mesopotamia (modern Iraq and Kuwait) around 4000 B.C.E. and developed one of the first written languages.

Sunnism   Orthodox Islam, as opposed to Shiite Islam.

supranational organizations   International organizations such as NGOs, the World Bank, and the IMF.

survival of the fittest   A main concept of Charles Darwin's theory of natural selection (evolution), which holds that as animal populations grow and resources become scarce, a struggle for existence arises, the outcome of which is that only the "fittest" survive.

sweatshops   Textile factories with poor pay and work conditions.

Syndicalism   Late-nineteenth-century organization of workplace associations that included unskilled labor.

tabula rasa   Term used by John Locke (1632–1704) to describe man's mind before he acquired ideas as a result of experience; Latin for "clean slate."

Testament of Youth   The memoir by Vera Brittain about the home front and the changing social norms during World War I.

Tetrarchy   Diocletian's political reform, which divided the Roman empire into two halves ruled by two rulers and two lieutenants.

Third Estate   Delegates from the common class to the Estates General, the French legislature, whose refusal to capitulate to the nobility and clergy in 1789 led to the Revolution.

Third Reich   The German state from 1933 to 1945 under Adolf Hitler and the Nazi party.

Third World   Nations—mostly in Asia, Latin America, and Africa—that are not highly industrialized and developed.

Thirty Years' War (1618–1648)   Beginning as a conflict between Protestants and Catholics in Germany, it escalated into a general European war fought in Germany by Sweden, France, and the Holy Roman Empire.

Tiananmen Square   Largest public square in the world, located in Beijing, the site of the Chinese pro-democracy movement in 1989 that resulted in the killing of as many as 1,000 protesters by the Chinese army.

Timur the Lame (1336–1405)   Mongol ruler who was the last leader of the Khans' south Asian empire. Also known as Tamerlane.

total war   All-out war involving civilian populations as well as military forces, often used in reference to World War II.

Treaty of Brest-Litovsk (1918)   Separate peace between imperial Germany and the new Bolshevik regime in Russia. The treaty acknowledged the German victory on the Eastern Front and withdrew Russia from the war.

Treaty of Nanjing (1842)   Treaty between China and Britain following the Opium War; it called for indemnities, the opening of new ports, and the cession of Hong Kong to the British.

Treaty of Utrecht (1713)   Resolution to the War of Spanish Succession that redistributed territory among the warring nations of Europe and encouraged England's colonial conquests.

Treaty of Versailles   Signed on June 28, 1919, this peace settlement ended World War I and required Germany to surrender a large part of its most valuable territories and to pay huge reparations to the Allies.

trench warfare   The twenty-five thousand miles of holes and ditches that stretched across the Western Front during World War I and where most of the fighting took place.

"triangular" trade   The eighteenth-century commercial Atlantic shipping pattern that took rum from New England to Africa, traded it for slaves taken to the West Indies, and brought sugar back to New England to be processed into rum.

Tripartite Pact (1940)   A pact that stated that the countries of Germany, Italy, and Japan would act together in all future military ventures.

Triple Entente   Alliance developed before World War I that eventually included Britain, France, and Russia.

Truman Doctrine (1947)   Declaration promising U.S. economic and military intervention, whenever and wherever needed, for the sake of preventing further communist expansion.

Truth and Reconciliation Commission   Quasi-judicial body established after the overthrow of the apartheid system in South Africa and the election of Nelson Mandela as the country's first black president in 1994. The commission was to take evidence about the crimes committed during the apartheid years. Those who showed remorse could appeal for clemency. The South African leaders believed that an airing of the grievances from this period would promote racial harmony and reconciliation.

tsar   Russian translation, similar to the German *kaiser*, of the Roman title "caesar" (emperor), a title claimed by the rulers of medieval Muscovy and then the Russian empire.

Mary Tudor (1516–1558)   Catholic daughter of Henry VIII who reinstituted Catholicism in England when she acceded to the throne; she was called "Bloody Mary" for her violent suppression of Protestants during her five-year reign.

Two Treatises on Government   Published in 1690, this work by John Locke (1632–1704) defended humans' right to freedom against absolutist ideas and served as one of the underpinnings of the U.S. Constitution.

Ubaid   This cultured flourished in Mesopotamia between 5500 and 4000 B.C.E., characterized by large village settlements and the first temples built in that area. A precursor to the Sumerians and the development of "urban" civilizations.

UFA   The German film company that produced films by expressionist directors like F. W. Murnau and Fritz Lang during the 1920s. Under Hitler, it was controlled by the state and began turning out Nazi propaganda.

Universal Declaration of Human Rights (1948)   United Nations declaration that laid out the rights to which all human beings were entitled.

Utopia   Humanist social critique by English statesman Thomas More (1478–1535).

utopian socialism   The most visionary of all Restoration-era movements, Utopian socialists, like Charles Fourier, dreamt of transforming states, workplaces, and human relations, and proposed actual plans to do so.

"velvet revolutions"   The peaceful political revolutions throughout Eastern Europe in 1989.

Versailles   Splendid palace outside Paris where Louis XIV and his nobles resided.

Versailles Conference (1919)   Peace conference between the victors of World War I; resulted in the Treaty of Versailles, which forced Germany to pay reparations and to give up its colonies to the victors.

Queen Victoria (1819–1901)   Influential monarch who reigned from 1837 to her death; she presided over the expansion of the British empire as well as the evolution of English politics and social and economic reforms.

Viet Cong   Vietnamese communist group formed in 1954; committed to overthrowing the government of South Vietnam and re-unifying North and South Vietnam.

A Vindication of the Rights of Woman   Noted work of Mary Wollstonecraft (1759–1797), English republican who applied Enlightenment political ideas to issues of gender.

Virgil (70–19 B.C.E.)   One of the most influential Roman authors, his surviving works include the Eclogues and the Roman epic poem, the *Aeneid*.

Visigoths   The German "barbarians" who sacked Rome in 410.

Voltaire   Pseudonym of French philosopher and satirist Francois Marie Arouet (1694–1797), who championed the cause of human dignity against state and church oppression. Noted Deist and author of *Candide*.

Voting Rights Act (1965)   Law that granted universal suffrage in the United States.

War of the Roses   Fifteenth-century conflict between the English dynastic houses of Lancaster and York (each symbolized in heraldry by the rose), ultimately won by Lancastrian Henry VII.

Warsaw Pact (1955–1991)   Military alliance between the U.S.S.R. and other Communist states that was established as a response to the creation of the NATO alliance.

James Watt (1736–1819)   Scottish inventor and scientist who developed the steam engine.

Wealth of Nations   1776 treatise by Adam Smith, whose *laissez-faire* ideas predicted the economic boom of the Industrial Revolution.

Weimar Republic   The government of Germany between 1919 and the rise of Hitler and the Nazi party.

Western Front   Military front that stretched from the English Channel through Belgium and France to the Alps during World War I.

Whites   Refers to the "counterrevolutionaries" of the Bolshevik Revolution (1918–1921) who fought the Bolsheviks (the "Reds"); included former supporters of the tsar, Social Democrats, and large independent peasant armies.

William and Mary (1650–1702 and 1662–1694)   Dutch noble couple who supplanted the deposed Catholic King James II in 1688 as monarchs of England.

William the Conqueror (1027–1087)   Duke of French Normandy who crossed the English Channel and defeated Harold for the English throne in 1066. Imposed a centralized feudal system on England and introduced French as the official language.

women's suffrage   The movement to win legal and political rights, including the right to vote for all women.

Works Progress Administration (WPA)   New Deal program instituted in 1935 that put nearly 3 million people to work building roads, bridges, airports, and post offices.

World Bank   International agency established in 1944 to provide economic assistance to war-torn and poor countries. Its formal title is the International Bank for Reconstruction and Development.

Yalta Accords   Meeting between President Franklin D. Roosevelt, Prime Minister Winston Churchill, and Premier Josef Stalin that occurred in the Crimea in 1945 to to prepare for the postwar order.

yellow press   Newspapers that sought increased circulation by featuring sensationalist reporting that appealed to the masses.

"Young Turks"   The 1908 Turkish nationalist movement to depose Sultan Abdul Hamid II.

Zionism   Formally founded in 1897, a political movement holding that the Jewish people constitute a nation and are entitled to a national homeland, originally advocating the reestablishment of a Jewish homeland in Palestine

Zoroastrians   Founded by Zoroaster around 600 B.C.E., this Persian religion urged people to be truthful, to help each other, and to practice hospitality. Those who did would be rewarded in an afterlife after a "judgment day."

Zulus   African tribe that, under Shaka, created a ruthless warrior state in southern Africa in the early 1800s.

TEXT CREDITS

Chapter 1: 15: from *The Epic of Gilgamesh*. Copyright 1997, Bolchazy-Carducci Publishers; **16:** from the Revised Standard Version of the Bible, copyright © 1946, 1952, and 1971 by the Division of Christian Education of the National Council of the Churches of Christ in the USA. All rights reserved. Used by permission; **24:** from *Law: A Treasury of Art and Literature*, Hugh Lauter Levin Assoc./Beaux Arts Editions, Copyright 1990; **34:** from *Readings in Ancient History: Thought and Experience from Gilgamesh to St. Augustine*. Copyright 1995, Houghton Mifflin. **Digital History, 38:** from "Hymn to the Nile" in *The Library of Original Sources*, vol. 1. Copyright 1907, University Research Extension Co.

Chapter 2: 50 (top): Pritchard, James B. (ed.); *Ancient Near Eastern Texts Relating to the Bible*, 3rd rev. ed. with supplement. Copyright © 1969 by Princeton University Press. Reprinted by permission of Princeton University Press; **50 (bottom):** from the Revised Standard Version of the Bible, copyright © 1946, 1952, and 1971 by the Division of Christian Education of the National Council of the Churches of Christ in the USA. All rights reserved. Used by permission; **65:** from *Ancient Records of Assyria and Babylonia*. Copyright 1926–1927, University of Chicago Press.

Chapter 3: 88: from Herodotus, v. 92, translated by David Greene. Copyright 1987, University of Chicago Press; **103:** from *The Clouds*. Copyright 1973, Penguin Books; **104:** from *The Landmark Thucydides*. Copyright 1995, Landmark Press.

Chapter 4: 115 (top): from *Isocrates*. Copyright 1995, Harvard University Press; **(bottom):** from *Demosthenes*. Copyright 1930, Harvard University Press; **120:** from the Revised Standard Version of the Bible, copyright © 1946, 1952, and 1971 by the Division of Christian Education of the National Council of the Churches of Christ in the USA. All rights reserved. Used by permission. **Digital History, 130:** from *The Ancient Mysteries: A Sourcebook of Sacred Texts*. Copyright 1987, HarperCollins Publishers.

Chapter 5: 142: from *Life of Lucullus*. Copyright 1992, Modern Library; **152:** from *Juvenal: The Sixteen Satires*. Copyright 1974, Penguin Books.

Chapter 6: 170–171: from *Western Societies: A Documentary History*. Copyright 1984, Knopf; **177–178:** from *Sidonius, Poems and Letters*. Copyright 1980, Harvard University Press. **Digital History, 188 (top):** Hesiod's *Works and Days*, ll. 582–596. Hugh G. Evelyn-White, trans. (1914); **188 (bottom):** Pliny the Elder, *Natural History*, Book xiv. Sect. 141. Reprinted in *Familiar Quotations*, 10th ed. John Bartlett, ed. (1919).

Chapter 7: 199: from *Byzantium: Church, Society, and Civilization Seen through Contemporary Eyes*. Copyright 1984, University of Chicago Press; **204:** Reprinted from *The Jews of Arab Lands: A History and Source Book*. Copyright © 1979, by The Jewish Publication Society. Used by permission; **218:** from *The Reign of Charlemagne*. Copyright 1975, Edward Arnold.

Chapter 8: 237: from *Christianity, Social Tolerance, and Homosexuality*. Copyright 1980, University of Chicago Press; **240:** from *Chronicles of the Crusades*. Copyright 1963, Penguin Books; **255:** from *The Chronicle of Salimbene de Adam*. Copyright 1986, Medieval and Renaissance Texts and Studies. **Digital History, 258:** from *English History*, vol. II, J. A. Giles, trans. (London, 1852). Reprinted in *A Source Book for Medieval Economic History*. Copyright 1965, Biblo & Tannen.

Chapter 9: 263: from *Readings in Medieval History*. Copyright 1997, Broadview Press; **282:** Extract from *The Wandering Scholars*, copyright 1934, by kind permission of Constable & Robinson Ltd., London.

Chapter 10: 289: from *Froissart: Chronicles*. Copyright 1968, Penguin Books; **307:** from *Women and Writing in Medieval Europe*. Copyright 1995, Routledge. **Digital History, 320:** from Boccaccio's *Decameron*, vol. 1, J. M. Rigg, trans. Copyright 1921, David Campbell.

Chapter 11: 327: from *The Travels of Marco Polo*. Copyright 1926, Random House; **339:** from *The Compendium and Description of the West Indies*. Copyright 1968, Smithsonian Institution Press.

Chapter 12: 346 (top): from *Vittorino da Feltre and Other Humanist Educators*. Copyright 1897, Cambridge University Press; **(middle):** from *University of Chicago Readings in Western Civilizations*. Copyright 1986, University of Chicago Press; **(bottom):** from *University of Chicago Readings in Western Civilizations*. Copyright 1986, University of Chicago Press; **349:** from *The Family in Renaissance Florence*. Copyright 1969, University of South Carolina Press. **Digital History, 366:** from *Dangerous Tastes: The Story of Spices*. Copyright 2000, British Museum Press.

Chapter 13: 381: from *What Luther Says*. Copyright 1959, Concordia Publishing House; **387:** from *Documents of the Christian Church*. Copyright 1967, Oxford University Press.

Chapter 14: 399: from *Simplicissimus*. Copyright 1995, Daedalus; **407 (top):** from *Divine Right and Democracy: An Anthology of Political Writing in Stuart England*. Copyright 1986, Viking Penguin; **(bottom):** from *Great Issues in Western Civilization*. Copyright 1967, Random House.

ILLUSTRATION CREDITS

Illustration Credits: National Geographic Society Image Collection 00–00

Part I

2–3: King Tutankhamen Fighting the Nubians (Giraudon/Art Resource, NY)

Chapter 1: 6: An Egyptian Scribe (The Louvre, Paris. Photo: Giraudon/Art Resource, NY); 9: Courtesy Dept. of Library Services, American Museum of Natural History; 10 (top): © Richard Nowitz Photos; 10 (bottom): Hirmer Fotoarchiv; 15, 24, 34: A Sumerian Banquet (Bettmann/Corbis); 17: Hirmer Fotoarchiv; 18: From *The Origins of War*, by Arthur Ferrill, published by Thames and Hudson, Inc., New York; 20 (top left): Iraq Museum, Baghdad, Iraq. Photo: Scala/Art Resource, NY; 20 (top right): University of Pennsylvania Museum; 22: The Nelson-Atkins Museum of Art, Kansas City, Missouri (Purchase: Nelson Trust); 23: Hirmer Fotoarchiv; 27: Copyright Jurgen Liepe, Berlin; 28: Bettmann/Corbis; 29 (top): Roger Wood/Corbis; 29 (bottom): Charles & Josette Lenars/Corbis; 32: Excavations of the Metropolitan Museum of Art, 1929; Rogers Fund, 1930. (30.3.31) Photograph © 1978 The Metropolitan Museum of Art; 35: The Nelson Gallery Foundation, The Nelson-Atkins Museum of Art. **Digital History, 38**: Erich Lessing/Art Resource, NY; 39 (top): Erich Lessing/Art Resource, NY; 39 (bottom): Erich Lessing/Art Resource, NY.

Chapter 2: 40: Egyptian Slaves at Work (Egyptian expedition of The Metropolitan Museum of Art, Rogers Fund, 1930 (30.4.77); 45: British Museum, London, Great Britain,: Erich Lessing/Art Resource, NY; 46: Erich Lessing/Art Resource, NY; 48 (top): Courtesy, Museum of Fine Arts, Boston; 50, 65: King Tutankhamen Fighting Nubians (Giraudon/Art Resource, NY); 51: Wolfgang Kaehler/Corbis; 53 (top): Martin A. Ryerson Collection, 1922.4914. Photograph © 1997, The Art Institute of Chicago. All rights reserved; 53 (bottom): Alison Frantz; 58: Ancient Civilizations, 2/E by Scarre/Fagan, © 2003. Reprinted by permission of Pearson Education, Inc., Upper Saddle River, NJ; 63: Assyrian Winged Human-Headed Bull (Courtesy of The Oriental Institute of The University of Chicago); 64: Assurbanipal Feasting with His Wife in a Garden (Courtesy of The Oriental Institute of The University of Chicago); 66: Staatliche Museen zu Berlin—Preußischer Kulturbesitz, Vorderasiatisches Museum; 67: American Numismatic Society; 70: The Metropolitan Museum of Art, Fletcher Fund, 1954. (54.3.3) Photograph © 1982 The Metropolitan Museum of Art.

Part II

76–77: Battle of Issus (© Scala/Art Resource, NY)

Chapter 3: 80: © Alinari/Art Resource, NY; 82: Art Resource, NY; 85, 88, 103: Greek Infantry Advancing into Combat (Hirmer Fotoarchiv); 86: Réunion des Musées Nationaux/Art Resource, NY; 89: Naples National Museum, Photo: Gianni Dagli Orti/Corbis; 95: Scala/Art Resource, NY; 96 (top): George Brockway/Warder Collection, NY; 96 (bottom): Vanni/Art Resource, NY; 98 (left): Hartwig Koppermann; 98 (center): © Photo RMN, Paris; 98 (right): Nimatallah/Art Resource, NY; 99: Museo Nazionale Romano; 101: Photo: Paul Lipke/Trireme Trust, Montague, MA; 102: Erich Lessing/Art Resource, NY.

Chapter 4: 108, 115, 120: Scala/Art Resource, NY; 111 (left): The Metropolitan Museum of Art, Rogers Fund, 1923. (23.160.20) Photograph © by The Metropolitan Museum of Art; 111 (right): The Metropolitan Museum of Art, H. O. Havemeyer Collection, Bequest of Mrs. H. O. Havemeyer, 1929. (29.100.377) Photograph © by The Metropolitan Museum of Art; 113: Gianni Dagli Orti/Corbis; 116: Erich Lessing/Art Resource, NY; 124 (left): University Prints; 124 (right): The Metropolitan Museum of Art, Rogers Fund, 1909. (09.39) Photograph © 1977 The Metropolitan Museum of Art; 125: (left): Giraudon/Art Resource, NY; 125 (right): Laocoön (Nimatallah/Art Resource, NY). **Digital History, 130**: © Alinari/Art Resource, NY; 131 (top): Scala/Art Resource, NY; 131 (bottom) © Gilles Mermet/Art Resource, NY.

Chapter 5: 132: Portrait of Pasquio Proculo and his wife © Alinari/Art Resource, NY; 135: Musei Capitolini, Rome, Italy; Photo: Scala/Art Resource, NY; 138: Scala/Art Resource, NY; 139: American Numismatic Society; 142, 152: Rehearsal for a Satyr Play (© Archive Iconografico, S.A./Corbis); 144: Scala/Art Resource, NY; 146: Scala/Art Resource, NY; 147: Scala/Art Resource, NY; 150: Scala/Art Resource, NY; 151: Scala/Art Resource, NY; 153: Scala/Art Resource, NY; 155: Scala/Art Resource, NY.

Chapter 6: 160: Alinari/Art Resource, NY; 162: The Warder Collection, NY; 164: Scala/Art Resource, NY; 166: Scala/Art Resource, NY; 169: Scala/Art Resource, NY; 170, 177: Mosaic of Justinian (Scala/Art Resource, NY); 180: Scala/Art Resource, NY; 181: Biblioteca Medicea Laurenziana, Florence; 183 (top): Scala/Art Resource, NY; 183: (bottom) Scala/Art Resource, NY. **Digital History, 188**: Erich Lessing/Art Resource, NY; 189 (top): © Werner Forman/Art Resource, NY; 189 (bottom): © Scala/Art Resource, NY.

Part III

190–191: Anonymous, 15th century. The death of Charlemagne. Vincent de Beauvais, Le Miroir Historial. Ms. 722/1196, fol. 113 v. French, 15th c. (Photo: Giraudon/Art Resource, NY)

Chapter 7: 194: Muslim Pilgrims on Their Way to Mecca (Bibliothèque Nationale de France, Paris); 197: Werner Forman/Art Resource, NY; 199, 204, 218: Book cover (Scala/Art Resource, NY); 200: The Art Archive/Dagli Orti; 201: The Art Archive/HarperCollins Publishers; 205: cliché Bibliothèque Nationale de France, Paris; 208: Giraudon/Art Resource, NY; 209: Bildarchiv Preussischer Kulturbesitz/Art Resource, NY; 213 (top): The Pierpont Morgan Library/Art Resource, NY; 213 (bottom): Kunsthistorisches Museum, Vienna; 215: The Art Archive/Biblioteca del Duomo Modena/Dagli Orti (A); 216: cliché Bibliothèque Nationale de France, Paris; 217: Vatican Library: MS. Reg. Ret. 762, fol. 82r, written at Tours 800 A.D. (detail).

Chapter 8: 224: Limbourg Brothers (15th C.E.). June. Tres Riches Heures du Duc de Berry, (Palace and Ste. Chapelle in background). Giraudon/Art Resource, NY; 227: Biblioteca Riccardiana, Florence, Manuscript Ricc. 492 c. 18, with the permission of the Ministero per I Beni Culturali e Ambientali; 229: By permission of the British Library; 232, 237, 240, 255: View of Paris (cliché Bibliothèque Nationale de France, Paris); 242: cliché Bibliothèque Nationale de France, Paris; 243: Art Resource, NY; 245: Diebold Schilling, Official Bernese Chronicle, vol. 1, Burgerbibliothek, Berne, Ms.h.h.I.1, 289; 246: Giraudon/Art Resource, NY; 248: The Walters Art Gallery, Baltimore. Digital History, 258 (left): Tate Gallery, London/Art Resource, NY; 258 (right): Vanni/Art Resource, NY; 259 (top): Peter Beck/CORBIS; 259 (bottom): Historical Picture Archive/CORBIS.

Chapter 9: 260: A Lecture Class in a Medieval University (The Bettmann Archive); 263, 282: Scala/Art Resource, NY; 266: Thüringer Universität–Und Landesbibliothek, Jena; 268: The Bettmann Archive; 269: Bettmann/Corbis; 271: Bayerische Staatsbibliothek, München; 274: Scala/Art Resource, NY; 275: cliché Bibliothèque Nationale de France, Paris; 279: Giraudon/Art Resource, NY; 280: © Alinari Archives/Corbis; 284: cliché Bibliothèque Nationale de France, Paris; 285 (top): Richard List/Corbis; 285 (bottom): Richard List/Corbis.

Part IV

288–289: A Portuguese galleon (National Maritime Museum, London)

Chapter 10: 292: Erich Lessing/Art Resource, NY; 295: The Walters Art Gallery, Baltimore; 298, 307: A Party of Late Medieval Aristocrats (cliché Bibliothèque Nationale de France, Paris); 300: The Art Archive/Stadelisches Kunstinstitut Frankfurt; 304: The Art Archive/British Library; 309: Museo del Prado, Madrid; 314: By permission of the British Library; 316: Reproduced by courtesy of the Trustees, The National Gallery, London. Photograph © The National Gallery, London; 317: Bibliothèque Royale Albert I, Brussels. Digital History, 320: "Reponse a Charles VI. et lamentation au roi sur son etat" by Pierre

Salmon; Paris, Bibliotheque Nationale; photo: akg-images, London; 321 (top): © Werner Forman/Art Resource, NY, 321 (bottom): © Snark/Art Resource, NY.

Chapter 11: 322: The Art Archive/Topkapi Museum Istanbul/Dagli Orti; 326: John Massey Stewart Picture Library; 327, 339: The Battle of Lepanto, by Vicentino (Leabharlann Chester Beatty Library); 328: Mehmet II (Werner Forman Archive/ Topkapi Palace Library, Istanbul/Art Resource, NY); 335: José Pessoa, Arquivo Nacional de Fotografia, Instituto Português de Museus; 337: The Art Archive/Biblioteca Nacional de Madrid/Dagli Orti.

Chapter 12: 342, 354: The School of Athens, by Raphael (Scala/Art Resource, NY); 346, 349, 355: The Creation of Adam, by Michelangelo (Scala/Art Resource, NY); 348: © Photo RMN, Paris; 352 (top): Erich Lessing/Art Resource, NY; 352 (bottom): © Photo RMN, Paris; 353 (bottom): Scala/Art Resource, NY; 356 (left): Nimatallah/Art Resource, NY; 356 (right): Scala/Art Resource, NY; 360: © The Frick Collection, New York; 361: © Photo RMN, Paris; 362: Bildarchiv Preussischer Kulturbesitz/Art Resource, NY. Digital History, 366: London/Art Resource, NY; 367 (top): Victoria & Albert Museum, London/Art Resource, NY; 367 (bottom): Erich Lessing/Art Resource, NY.

Chapter 13: 368: The Art Archive/Nationalmuseet Copenhagen Denmark/Dagli Orti (A); 370: Martin Luther, portrait by Louis Cranach (Scala/Art Resource, NY); 373: Alinari/Art Resource, NY; 375 (left): Staatliche Museen zu Berlin—Preußischer Kulturbesitz, Kupferstichkabinett; 375 (right): By permission of the British Library; 377: The Warder Collection, NY; 381, 387: Henry VIII with Jane Seymour and children (The Royal Collection © Her Majesty Queen Elizabeth II); 383: National Trust/Art Resource, NY; 384; Scala/Art Resource, NY; 386: Scala/Art Resource, NY.

Chapter 14: 392: The Metropolitan Museum of Art, H. O. Havemeyer Collection, Bequest of Mrs. H. O. Havemeyer, 1929. (29.100.6) Photograph © 1992 The Metropolitan Museum of Art; 394: Bettmann/Corbis; 396: Gianni Dagli Orti/Corbis; 399, 407: detail from View of Toledo, by El Greco (The Metropolitan Museum of Art, H. O. Havemeyer Collection, Bequest of Mrs. H. O. Havemeyer, 1929 (29.100.6). Photograph © 1992 by the Metropolitan Museum of Art); 402: Archivo Iconografico, S.A./Corbis; 404: Courtesy of the National Portrait Gallery, London; 405: Photo Bulloz, Coll. Privée; 409: Bibliothèque Royale, Brussels; 412: Scala/Art Resource, NY; 413: Museo del Prado, Madrid; 414: Erich Lessing/Art Resource, NY; 415 (top): Nimatallah/Art Resource, NY; 415 (bottom left): © English Heritage Photo Library; 415 (bottom right): Gift of Mr. and Mrs. Robert Woods Bliss, © 1997 Board of Trustees, National Gallery of Art, Washington, DC.

Part V

418–419: Last Naval Battle in the Dutch-English War, August 11, 1637. Backhuyzen Ludolf (1631-1708) (Erich Lessing/Art Resource, NY)

Chapter 15: 422: © National Gallery Collection; By kind permission of the Trustees of the National Gallery, London/CORBIS; 425, 432: A fountain at Versailles (Giraudon/Art Resource, NY);

426: Courtesy of The National Portrait Gallery, London; 427: NGS68415 Mary II (1662–94), wife of William III (1650–1702) by William Wissing or Wissmig (1656–87), Scottish National Portrait Gallery, Edinburgh, Scotland/Bridgeman Art Library; 429: Louis XIV (Erich Lessing/Art Resource, NY); 430: Giraudon/Art Resource, NY; 436: The Art Archive/Russian Historical Museum Moscow/Dagli Orti (A); 439: Giraudon/Art Resource, NY; 442: Ali Meyer/CORBIS; 447: Gianni Dagli Orti/Corbis; 448: The Warder Collection, NY. **Digital History, 454:** © Scala/Art Resource, NY; 455 (top): Erich Lessing/Art Resource, NY; 455 (bottom) © Snark/Art Resource, NY.

Chapter 16: 456: *The Comet of December 1680*, by Lieve Verschuier (Courtesy of Historisch Museum, Rotterdam); 460: Erich Lessing/Art Resource, NY; 462: Erich Lessing/Art Resource, NY; 463, 466: Erich Lessing/Art Resource, NY; 467: Bodleian Library; 468: Giraudon/Art Resource, NY; 469: Bodleian Library; 470: Giraudon/Art Resource, NY.

Chapter 17: 472: *A Literary Salon in the 18th Century* (pen and sepia wash on paper), Dandre-Bardon, Michel Francois (1700–83) / Louvre (Cabinet de dessins), Paris, France, (Archives Charmet / www.bridgeman.co.uk); 475: Voltaire, by Jean Antoin Houdon (Giraudon/Art Resource, NY); 477: Giraudon/Art Resource, NY; 478: Historisches Museum der Stadt Wien; 479: Moritz Daniel Oppenheim, "Lavater and Lessing Visit Moses Mendelssohn." In the permanent collections, Judah L. Magnes Museum. Photo: Ben Ailes; 481, 482, 487: *The Salon of Madame Geoffrin* (Giraudon/Art Resource, NY); 483: © Stapletib Collection/Corbis; 485: Bibliotheque Nationale, Paris, France/Bridgeman Art Library, Flammarion; 486: Tate Gallery, London/Art Resource, NY; 490: Bettmann/Corbis; 493 (bottom): Costume designs for Figaro and Susanna from the opera 'The Marriage of Figaro' by Wolfgang Amadeus Mozart (1756-91) (engraving), Austrian School, (18th century)/Mozart Museum, Vienna, Austria,/www.bridgeman.co.uk; 493 (top): Erich Lessing/Art Resource, NY.

Part V

496–497: *The Fall of the Bastille, July 14, 1789* (Giraudon/Art Resource, NY)

Chapter 18: 500, 512: *The Death of Marat*, by Jacques Louis David (Giraudon/Art Resource, NY); 503: Bibliothèque Nationale de France, Paris; 505: Giraudon/Art Resource, NY; 506: Giraudon/Art Resource, NY; 507, 508, 518: Gianni Dagli Orti/Corbis; 511: Giraudon/Art Resource, NY; 515: Gianni Dagli Orti/Corbis; 516: Erich Lessing/Art Resource, NY; 520: Erich Lessing/Art Resource, NY; 522: Museo del Prado, Madrid. **Digital History, 526:** Erich Lessing/Art Resource, NY; 527 (top): Bettmann/CORBIS; 527 (bottom): Bettmann/CORBIS.

Chapter 19: 528: *The Gare St. Lazare* by Claude Monet © National Gallery Collection; by kind permission of the Trustees of the National Gallery, London/Corbis; 533: A cotton mill in Lancashire, 1834 (The Granger Collection, New York); 534: *The Steam Hammer* (The Hulton Deutsch Collection); 536: Mary Evans Picture Library; 537: City Archives of Lyons; 540: Hulton Deutsch Collection/Corbis; 542, 549: A soup kitchen in Manchester, England

(The Warder Collection, NY); 544: The Hulton Deutsch Collection; 545: Giraudon/Art Resource, NY, 546: Geoffrey Clements/Corbis; 547: Roger-Viollet; 551: cliché Bibliothèque Nationale de France, Paris; 552: The Granger Collection, New York.

Chapter 20: 556: The Uprising (1848), by Honoré Daumier. (The Phillips Collection), 560: CHT214192 Meeting of the Carbonari, c.1815–30 (colour litho) by French School (19th century), Private Collection/Bridgeman Art Library, Archives Charmet; 561: © Photo RMN, Paris; 563: Bettmann/Corbis; 564: STC75993 Mr Owen's Institution, New Lanark (Quadrille Dancing), engraved by George Hunt, pub. 1825 by English School (19th century), Private Collection/Bridgeman Art Library, The Stapleton Collection; 565: Hulton-Deutsch Collection/Corbis; 568: Portrait of George Byron (1788–1824), English School, (19th century) / The Fine Art Society, London, UK, / www.bridgeman.co.uk; 569 (left): JF105430 Illustration from 'Frankenstein' by Mary Shelley (1797–1851) (engraving) (b/w photo) by English School (19th century), Private Collection/Bridgeman Art Library; 569 (right): RUS90774 Portrait of Mary Shelley (1797–1851) at the Age of Nineteen, c.1816 (litho) by English School (19th century), Russell-Cotes Art Gallery and Museum, Bournemouth, UK/Bridgeman Art Library; 570: Victoria & Albert Museum, London. Photo: Victoria & Albert Museum/Art Resource, NY; 572: Archivo Iconografico, S.A./Corbis; 574, 577: The July Revolution of 1830, in Paris (Giraudon/Art Resource, NY); 575: © Photo RMN, Paris; 576: Reproduced by the Gracious Permission of Her Majesty the Queen; 579: Giraudon/Art Resource, NY. **Digital History, 582:** Archivo Iconografico, S.A./CORBIS; 583 (top): Archivo Iconografico, S.A./CORBIS; 583 (bottom): Bettmann/CORBIS.

Chapter 21: 584, 589, 601: *The March Days* (Erich Lessing/Art Resource, NY); 590: Corbis; 592: Charles E. Rotkin/Corbis; 593: Hulton-Deustch Collection/Corbis; 598: Gianni Dagli Orti/Corbis; 606: Foto Marburg/Art Resource, NY.

Part VII: 610-611: *The Funeral Procession*, by George Grosz (VAGA/Art Resource, NY)

Chapter 22: 614: Sean Sexton Collection/Corbis; 617: Archives Charmet/www.bridgeman.co.uk; 619: Bettmann/Corbis; 621: An opium factory in Patna, India, c. 1851 (The British Library); 627: The Hulton Deutsch Collection; 628, 634: Construction of the Suez Canal (The Warder Collection, NY); 633 (left): Photo by Hulton Archive/Getty Images; 633 (right): Corbis; 637: The New York Public Library: Astor, Lenox, and Tilden Foundations; 638: Private collection/The Bridgeman Art Library International.

Chapter 23: 640: © The Museum of Modern Art, licensed by Scala/Art Resource, NY; 643: AKG London; 644: Bildarchiv Preussischer Kulturbesitz/Art Resource, NY; 647: Austrian Archives/Corbis; 648 (left): Hulton Archive/Getty; 648 (right): Poster proclaiming a general strike (Archives de la Préfecture de Police de la Ville de Paris); 649: The Hulton Deutsch Collection/Corbis; 650: The Hulton Deutsch Collection/Corbis; 652, 661, 664: Newspapers for sale in a British railway station (The Warder Collection, NY); 657: Schefler Collection/Corbis; 658: Staatliche Museen zu Berlin—Preußisher Kulturbesitz; 663: Library of Congress/Corbis; 665: © The Art Institute of Chicago;

666: The Metropolitan Museum of Art, H. O. Havemeyer Collection, Bequest of Mrs. H. O. Havemeyer, 1929. (29.100.64) Photograph © 1984 The Metropolitan Museum of Art. **Digital History, 670:** Hulton-Deutsch Collection/CORBIS; **671 (top):** Leonard de Selva/CORBIS; **671 (bottom):** Reuters NewMedia Inc./CORBIS.

Chapter 24: 672: The Art Archive/Imperial War Museum; **677, 688:** French soldiers (Imperial War Museum); **681:** Bettmann/CORBIS; **682:** Trustees of the Imperial War Museum, London; **684:** Getty Images, Inc; **685:** Bettmann/CORBIS; **687:** The Imperial War Museum, London; **689:** Hoover Institution Archives, Stanford University; **691:** The Warder Collection, NY; **692:** The Warder Collection, NY; **693:** Bettmann/CORBIS.

Chapter 25: 698: *The Funeral Procession*, by George Grosz (VAGA/Art Resource, NY); **703:** Staatliche Museen zu Berlin—Preußischer Kulturbesitz; **704, 715:** *Detroit Industry*, by Diego Rivera (Gift of Edsel B. Ford. © 1998 Institute Nacional de Bellas Artes, Mexico City. Photograph © The Detroit Institute of Arts); **706:** The Fotomas Index, London/The Warder Collection, NY; **709:** Brown Brothers; **711:** Stefan Lorant/The Warder Collection, NY; **712:** Stefan Lorant/The Warder Collection, NY; **717:** The New York Public Library: Astor, Lenox, and Tilden Foundations; **719:** © Arthur Rothstein/CORBIS; **721:** © Bildarchiv Preussischer Kulturbesitz/Art Resource, NY; **722:** The Museum of Modern Art, New York. Photograph Courtesy The Museum of Modern Art, New York; **724:** Bettmann/Corbis.

Chapter 26: 726: Winston Churchill, Franklin Roosevelt, and Joseph Stalin at the Yalta Conference, 1945 (Snark/Art Resource, NY); **731, 740, 743:** *Guernica*, by Pablo Picasso (Giraudon/Art Resource, NY. © 2005 Estate of Pablo Picasso/Artists Rights Society (ARS), New York); **734:** Hulton Deutsch Collection/Corbis; **737:** Corbis; **738:** Bettmann/Corbis; **746:** Public Record Office Image Library; **749:** The National Archives/Corbis; **750:** Hulton Deutsch

Collection/Corbis. **Digital History, 754:** Bettmann/CORBIS; **754 (top):** Bettmann/CORBIS; **755 (bottom):** Bettmann/CORBIS.

Part VIII

756–757: A scene from the fall of the Berlin Wall (David and Peter Tumley/Corbis)

Chapter 27: 760: The Berlin airlift (UPI/Corbis-Bettmann); **762:** UPI/Corbis-Bettmann; **766:** Yerevan, Armgosizdat, 1958; **767, 777, 781:** A scene from the Soviet occupation of Czechoslovakia (Hulton Deutsch Collection/Corbis); **769:** German Information Center/The Warder Collection, NY; **771:** AP/Wide World Photos; **774:** Sovfoto/Eastfoto; **776:** The Warder Collection, NY; **779:** Corbis; **782:** Hulton Deutsch Collection/Corbis.

Chapter 28: 786: Bettmann/Corbis; **789:** Bettmann/Corbis; **790:** Paul Almasy/Corbis; **791:** Seattle Art Museum/Corbis. © 2005 Pollock-Krasner Foundation/Artists Rights Society (ARS), New York; **792:** Bettmann/Corbis; **793, 798:** A scene from the student uprisings in Paris, May, 1968. (Bettmann/Corbis); **795:** Associated Press; **800:** Bettmann/Corbis; **801:** AP/World Wide Photos; **802:** © Alexandra Avakian/Woodfin Camp; **803:** AP/Wide World Photos; **808:** Patrick Robert/Corbis Sygma. **Digital History, 810:** Tim Page/CORBIS; **811 (top):** Olivier Coret/In Visu/CORBIS; **811 (bottom):** Olivier Coret/In Visu/CORBIS.

Chapter 29: 812: Antoine Serra/In Visu/Corbis; **815:** Michale Brennan/Corbis; **817:** Shaul Schwaz/Corbis; **823:** Bettmann/Corbis; **825 (left):** Reuters/Corbis-Bettmann; **825 (right):** Reuters/Corbis-Bettmann; **827:** Reuters/Corbis.

Every effort has been made to contact the copyright holders of the selections. Any corrections should be forwarded to W. W. Norton & Company, Inc., 500 Fifth Avenue, New York, NY 10110.

INDEX

WORLD · POLITICAL

NATIONAL BOUNDARIES

Winkel Tripel Projection

NORTH POLAR REGION

ARCTIC OCEAN

NORTH PACIFIC OCEAN

NORTH ATLANTIC OCEAN

NORTH AMERICA

SOUTH AMERICA

SOUTH PACIFIC OCEAN

SOUTH ATLANTIC OCEAN

ANTARCTICA

EQUATOR

TROPIC OF CANCER

TROPIC OF CAPRICORN

ARCTIC CIRCLE

ANTARCTIC CIRCLE

GLOBAL SATELLITE MOSAIC

The beauty and complexity of Earth's landscapes—above and below the oceans—is revealed with the Global Satellite Mosaic. The mosaic was produced for the National Geographic Society by NASA's Jet Propulsion Laboratory using more than 500 images from the National Oceanic and Atmospheric Administration. The cloud-free images show Earth in its natural colors as it appears seen from space. One can easily identify the world's major glaciers, deserts, mountain ranges, and rain forests. For example, follow the green ribbon of lush vegetation along the Nile into the stark, dry Sahara. The mountain ranges seem to rise off the map thanks to digital elevation databases from the Department of Defense. The deepest areas of the ocean realm are colored dark blue in contrast to the light blue areas highlighting continental shelves, submarine ridges, and underwater mountains.

BIOSPHERE

Thousands of satellite images were combined to show a picture of biological productivity in the oceans and on land. Red, yellow, and green indicate high-potential plant productivity, turquoise and green areas show high-potential plant productivity, turquoise and green areas show high-potential plant productivity, but blue areas suffer from productivity limitations due to aridity and temperature.

THE
SAT

SOUTH POLAR
REGION

ANTARCTICA

THE NEED FOR SATELLITES

SURFACE
TEMPERATURE

RLD
AP